Farrar's Company Law

Farrar's Company Law

Fourth edition

John H Farrar

Professor of Law, Bond University, Queensland and Professorial Associate, University of Melbourne

Brenda Hannigan MA, LLM

Solicitor, Ireland
Reader in Corporate Law, University of Southampton

With contributions by

Nigel E Furey LLM

Solicitor of the Supreme Court
Professor of Law, University of Bristol

and

Philip Wylie LLB, FCA, FTII

Senior Lecturer in Law, Cardiff Law School

Butterworths
London Edinburgh and Dublin
1998

Members of the LexisNexis Group worldwide

United Kingdom	LexisNexis Butterworths Tolley, a Division of Reed Elsevier (UK) Ltd, Halsbury House, 35 Chancery Lane, LONDON, WC2A 1EL, and 4 Hill Street, EDINBURGH EH2 3JZ
Argentina	LexisNexis Argentina, BUENOS AIRES
Australia	LexisNexis Butterworths, CHATSWOOD, New South Wales
Austria	LexisNexis Verlag ARD Orac GmbH & Co KG, VIENNA
Canada	LexisNexis Butterworths, MARKHAM, Ontario
Chile	LexisNexis Chile Ltda, SANTIAGO DE CHILE
Czech Republic	Nakladatelství Orac sro, PRAGUE
France	Editions du Juris-Classeur SA, PARIS
Hong Kong	LexisNexis Butterworths, HONG KONG
Hungary	HVG-Orac, BUDAPEST
India	LexisNexis Butterworths, NEW DELHI
Ireland	Butterworths (Ireland) Ltd, DUBLIN
Italy	Giuffrè Editore, MILAN
Malaysia	Malayan Law Journal Sdn Bhd, KUALA LUMPUR
New Zealand	Butterworths of New Zealand, WELLINGTON
Poland	Wydawnictwo Prawnicze LexisNexis, WARSAW
Singapore	LexisNexis Butterworths, SINGAPORE
South Africa	Butterworths SA, DURBAN
Switzerland	Stämpfli Verlag AG, BERNE
USA	LexisNexis, DAYTON, Ohio

© Reed Elsevier (UK) Ltd 1998

Reprinted 2000
Reprinted 2002

A CIP Catalogue record for this book is available from the British Library.

First edition 1985
Second edition 1988
Third edition 1991

ISBN 0 406 04800 2

Printed and bound in Great Britain by The Bath Press, Bath.

Visit Butterworths LexisNexis *direct* at www.butterworths.com

Preface

Writing about English Company Law is like shooting at a moving target. It is necessary to accommodate the large number of reported cases now available and to take into account the endless stream of consultation papers and reports from bodies such as the Department of Trade and Industry and now the Law Commission which is increasingly concerned with company law matters. The European Union continues to be a source of complexity as well as inspiration for UK company lawyers with its all-pervasive influence evident in matters such as the on-going debate on the draft 13th Directive on Takeovers, the question of the redenomination of share capital into euros and the possibility of a European company statute. At the same time the Government has proposed radical reform of the Byzantine system of legal and self-regulation of financial services.

Just as this edition was going to print, the Department of Trade and Industry issued a consultation document entitled *Modern Company Law for a Competitive Economy* which sets out the Department's plans for a comprehensive review of company law over the period of the next three years. This will be the most extensive review of company law since that which led to the Jenkins Committee Report in 1962.

Broadly speaking, the task of the review, as indicated by the consultation document, will be to develop a legal framework, based on the principles reflected in the Companies Act, which covers the requirements for the birth, existence, and death of companies. It will examine the rights and responsibilities of the entity and its participants and identify in which areas there should be mandatory rules to protect the interests of shareholders, creditors, employees, and other participants; and it will also address questions of sanctions and enforcement, including the balance between civil and criminal sanctions. The review will be conducted by various working groups, the first one of which will devise the overall strategic framework while subsequent working groups might cover areas such as finance and external relations; corporate governance; administration (including the role of Companies House); disclosure and financial reporting; and the impact of information technology.

The Department has outlined a broad indicative timetable which envisages the working groups consulting on their draft proposals around the end of 1999 with their final reports being completed by mid-2000. The final report will be published in March 2001 in conjunction with a White Paper with the resulting legislation being brought forward in the next Parliament.

This review is long overdue and is to be welcomed although it is to be hoped that this already lengthy timescale will not be prolonged beyond 2001 and that there will be a commitment by the Government of the day to implement such recommendations as are made. A common problem with any reform proposals (see, for example, the Insolvency Service's proposals for an improved company voluntary arrangement procedure made in 1995) is that, however worthwhile they are, they simply fail to progress through a lack of Parliamentary time. The same fate must not befall the Company Law review.

As we completed the work on this edition we heard of the death of 'Jim' Gower which together with the recent deaths of H.L.A. Hart, Glanville Williams and John Fleming marks the end of an era. To Jim we acknowledge a great debt for showing us the way to master and transcend the 'black letter' rules of English Company Law and making it fun.

The logistics of co-operation from a distance have been difficult for the authors and to this can be added the fact that John Farrar was involved in a complex exercise in corporate governance as Acting Vice Chancellor and a Director of Australia's first private university which was the subject of hostile bids by three public universities. We wish to thank Professor Eddy Wymeersch of the University of Ghent for help with European Union matters. We also wish to thank Ben Shepherd and Alex Merritt who helped John Farrar with some areas of research. We are particularly grateful to the editorial staff at Butterworths for their patience and perseverance.

We have attempted to state the law as it stood at the end of 1997 but it has been possible to note some subsequent developments. The division of responsibility for chapters in this edition was:

John Farrar	Chapters 1-14, 20, 22, 31-33, 35, 37, 38, 42-44
	Appendix, Glossary of Terms
Brenda Hannigan	Chapters 15-19, 24-28, 30, 34, 36, 39-41
Nigel Furey	Chapters 23, 29
Philip Wylie	Chapter 21

John Farrar

May 1998

Contents

PART I

Incorporation and its consequences

Chapter 1

The company as a business medium   3

Chapter 2

A brief general history of English company law   15

Chapter 3

Harmonisation of company law in the EU   26

PART II

The corporate constitution

Chapter 10

The memorandum of association and the question of corporate capacity 97

Chapter 11

Articles of association 116

Chapter 12

Supplementing the statutory constitution 135

Chapter 13

Constitutions and the company as a legal actor in contract, criminal law and tort 143

PART III

Financial structure and membership

Chapter 14

The concept of capital and the financing of companies 155

Chapter 20

Debt capital—debentures, debenture stock and new developments   253

Chapter 21

The taxation of companies   262

Part IV

Corporate power and its regulation

Chapter 22

Corporate governance: the distribution and regulation of power in a company   301

Chapter 23

Company general meetings   308

Chapter 29

Public regulation by disclosure of information concerning companies   463

Chapter 30

Investigations and inspections   497

PART V

Structural problems and change

Chapter 31

Structural problems and change—the issues   515

Chapter 32

Small incorporated firms   518

Chapter 38

Company charges and other security interests **631**

Chapter 39

Receivers and administrative receivers **663**

Chapter 40

Administration orders and voluntary arrangements **685**

Chapter 41

Winding up **705**

PART VII

The international dimension

Chapter 42

International dimensions of company law **747**

Chapter 43

Transnational enterprise and cross-frontier mergers 752

Chapter 44

Multinational and transnational companies 769

Appendix

Derivatives 779

Glossary of terms

Administration   Administration is a procedure introduced by the Insolvency Act 1985 to provide an alternative to receivership and winding up in the case of a company experiencing financial problems. The aim of the procedure is the rehabilitation of the company or its business. The present provisions are contained in Pt II of the Insolvency Act 1986.

Agency theories of the firm   The theory of the firm is that part of economics which seeks to explain the theory of production. Firms are not real firms but theoretical constructs. The agency theories of the firm explain the firm by reference to a nexus of agency contracts.

Allotment   In relation to shares the process by which a person acquires the unconditional right to be included in the company's register of members in respect of those shares: Companies Act 1985, s 738.

Alternative Investment Market (AIM)   This replaced the Unlisted Securities Market (USM) in 1995 and is a regulated lower-tier market for young companies which do not have the track record for admission to the Official List.

Amalgamation   A merger of at least two companies usually characterised by the formation of a third company to act as holding company.

Annual general meeting   A meeting of members of the company held once a year in pursuance of the statutory obligation under Companies Act 1985, s 366(1).

Annual return   A return to be made by a company to the Registrar of Companies every year giving prescribed details: Companies Act 1985, s 363(1).

Arbitrage   To take advantage of differences in price or rate between one market and another. This concept was developed in respect of foreign exchange but is also used in the futures and stock markets.

Articles of Association   The internal regulations of the company.

Audit committee   A committee usually of at least three members of the board of directors, two of whom are non-executive directors. The functions of the committee are to review with the external auditors and company financiers the accounting policies of the group and external control of the group's assets.

Auditor   A person who audits the accounts of a company.

Bear   A bear is an investor who sells a security short in the belief that the market will fall. See *Short selling*.

Bearer bond   A bond transferable by delivery.

Big Bang   The term refers to the day when minimum commissions on the London Stock Exchange were abolished. However, it has eventually become a shorthand expression for a whole range of developments on world financial markets and in the City of London in particular. These include the increased use of technology and the development of global trading in securities.

Board of Directors   The directors of a company as a collective body.

Bona vacantia   Property belonging to no one. On the dissolution of a company all property vested in it is deemed to be *bona vacantia* and belongs to the Crown, the Duchy of Lancaster or the Duke of Cornwall: Companies Act 1985, s 658(1).

Bond   A type of debenture usually characterised by a certificate giving a right to receive a specified sum on maturity and interest in the meantime. In the USA debentures are usually called bonds.

Bonus share   A share given by the company to a member usually proportionate to his or her existing holding and requiring no fresh consideration to be provided by him or her. Such shares usually result from a capitalisation of net profits.

Bull   A bull is someone who trades on the expectation of a price rise.

Call   A demand made on a member by the company to pay up the amount remaining or part of the amount remaining unpaid on his or her shares.

Capital redemption reserve   A reserve constituted by a transfer of a notional amount on the redemption or purchase by a company of its own shares: Companies Act 1985, s 170.

Certificate of incorporation   A document issued by the Registrar of Companies evidencing the formation of the company.

Charge   An encumbrance on property which is either fixed or floating. A fixed legal charge is a statutory creation, a fixed equitable charge a creation of equity. A floating charge is a species of equitable charge which does not attach to specific assets until crystallisation. See *Floating charge*.

Churning   Trading for trading's sake or to push up prices.

Class   In company law usually a reference to an issue of company shares characterised by certain class rights.

Class rights   Rights expressly described in the memorandum, articles or terms of issue as rights attaching to a class of shares or rights which relate to dividends, return of capital or voting. To this concept has been added rights which although not attached to any particular shares are conferred on the beneficiary in the capacity of member or shareholder of the company: *Cumbrian Newspapers Group Ltd v Cumberland & Westmorland Herald Newspaper & Printing Co Ltd* [1987] Ch 1.

Commencement of winding up   The date when a winding up is deemed to have started.

Commercial paper A US term which is catching on in the UK referring to short-term unsecured debt or loan capital.

Committee of inspection A committee consisting of creditors and members appointed to assist a liquidator in winding up.

Company limited by guarantee A company, the liability of whose members is limited by guarantee.

Company limited by shares A company, the liability of whose members is limited to the amount, if any, unpaid on their shares.

Compulsory winding up A winding up by the court.

Contributory A person liable to contribute to the assets of a company in the event of its being wound up. It usually refers to a shareholder.

Control contract means a contract in writing conferring such a right of control authorised by the memorandum or articles of the undertaking in question and permitted by the law under which that undertaking is established (Companies Act 1985, Sch 10A, para 4(2)). Such contracts are common in relation to groups in Germany and although mentioned in the Seventh EU Directive and Companies Act 1989 are rare in the UK.

Convertible Usually a debenture or debenture stock which can be converted at a later date into shares in an issuing company. The actual mechanics of this involve using the money to subscribe for shares at an agreed price.

Debenture A written acknowledgement of indebtedness by a company.

Debenture stock That part of the debt or loan capital of a company consolidated into stock and constituted by a debenture stock trust deed.

Derivatives Instruments whose value stems from that of some underlying asset such as equities or interest rates on debt capital. See Appendix.

Directive An EU source of law directed to the government of a member state to implement.

Director A person who is a member of the board of directors having in that capacity overall direction of the company's business or affairs. See also *Executive* and *Non-executive director*.

Dissolution of a company The corporate equivalent of death. It usually follows winding up.

Dividend A distribution out of the profits of a company to a shareholder in proportion to his/her shares and in accordance with his or her rights. Once declared a dividend constitutes a debt.

Dominant influence means a right to give directions with respect to the operating and financial policies of another undertaking which the directors of that undertaking are obliged to comply with whether or not they are for the benefit of that undertaking (Companies Act 1985, Sch 10A, para 4(1)). This is to establish whether there is a group relationship for the purpose of consolidated accounts.

Equity In investment language it usually refers to ordinary shares of a company which are the residual claimants to the profits of the company. Hence an analogy with equity of redemption.

Eurodollar   A US dollar held by a non-resident of the US outside the US. These have become a type of international currency and the dealings in them have contributed to the international financial revolution.

Executive director   A director who is full-time or under an obligation to devote a substantial amount of his or her time to the management of his or her company. Not all executives are directors and not all directors are executive directors. Some directors are non-executive directors. See *Non-executive director*.

Extraordinary general meeting   A general meeting other than an annual general meeting.

Extraordinary resolution   A resolution passed by a majority of not less than three-fourths of the members voting in person or by proxy at a general meeting of which the appropriate notice has been given: Companies Act 1985, s 378(1).

Firm   In ordinary language a business organisation. In economic theory something more abstract and in its true nature only capable of comprehension by a few economists.

Flotation   The process by which the shares or debentures of a company are offered to the public for subscription or purchase. The term refers to new issues not to the secondary market in those shares or debentures. The secondary market is a market by individual shareholders or debenture holders rather than the company itself or an issuing house.

Floating charge   A species of equitable charge created by a company which only becomes a fixed equitable charge on crystallisation.

Futures contract   A contract to buy or sell at a future date.

Gearing   The relationship of debt to equity in a company's capital structure. The more long term debt there is the higher the gearing. Shareholders benefit to the extent that the return on the borrowed money exceeds the interest costs. Also known as leverage in the USA.

General meeting   A meeting of the members of the company entitled to attend and vote thereat. The articles may permit proxies to attend and vote in their stead. The general meeting and board of directors are the two principal decision-making organs of the company.

Hedging   Taking steps to reduce risk.

Holding company   A company which controls a subsidiary company. A parent company of a group of companies.

Insider dealing or trading   Improper use of price sensitive information in respect of listed securities by a person for private gain.

Issue at a discount   An issue of shares or debentures at an amount less than their par value.

Issue at a premium   An issue of shares or debentures at a price above their par value.

Issued share capital   That part of a company's share capital which has been issued.

Leverage   See *Gearing*.

Liquidation   See *Winding up.*

Loan capital   The debt capital of a company as opposed to its share capital. Whereas share capital is normally permanent capital loan capital is usually not permanent capital although it is technically possible to have irredeemable debentures.

Liquidator   A statutory officer charged with the responsibility of winding up the company.

Listed securities   Securities which are listed on a recognised stock exchange.

Management buyout (MBO)   A situation where existing management buy out outside shareholders to gain control of a company. They usually do so by borrowing. Hence the company will usually have a higher gearing or leverage as a result of the transaction.

Managing Director   A director of the company appointed to deal with the day-to-day management of the company.

Member   Usually another name for a registered shareholder or stockholder.

Memorandum of association   One of the two constitutional documents of a company, the other being the articles of association. A memorandum states the name of the company, the country in which its registered office is situated, its objects, the basis of limitation of liability of the members and its initial share capital.

Merger   An ambiguous term which refers in English law to a reconstruction, amalgamation or takeover.

Minority shareholders   Shareholders who are not in the majority. The meaning of minority is determined by what constitutes the majority for the matter in hand. The Companies Act requires different majorities for different purposes.

Negative pledge   An undertaking given by a company to a creditor that it will not create any security. This is often accompanied by a provision for equal participation if any security is to be created. The term is sometimes used to describe a restrictive clause in a floating charge to similar effect.

Netting   Set off of payables against receivables.

Nominal capital   The legal measure of the share capital with which the company is initially formed or as subsequently increased and up to which the company can issue shares.

Nominee shareholder   A shareholder who holds his or her shares as nominee for another person.

Non-executive director   A term of variable meaning which usually refers to a director who is not under an obligation to devote the whole or substantially the whole of his or her time to the affairs of the company. The two main roles of non-executive directors are to act as a check on management and to give an external perspective. Non-executive directors are often directors of a number of companies. Some of them are put on boards because of a connection with a financial institution.

Officer   A broad generic term which includes a director, manager or secretary: Companies Act 1985, s 744.

Official notification   A formal procedure involving proof by the Registrar of Companies of receipt of certain documents.

Official receiver A civil servant attached to the court for bankruptcy purposes. He or she also deals with winding up of companies.

Options A contract giving the purchaser the right to buy (a call option) or sell (a put option) a given security within or at a specified time.

Ordinary resolution A resolution passed by a simple majority of members present at a general meeting.

Ordinary share A share entitling its holder to any dividend which is declared after dividends have been paid on preference shares. Sometimes called an equity share.

Par value The authorised or nominal value of a share.

Parent company See *Holding company.*

Poll A method of voting whereby each member can vote for or against a resolution according to the number of shares which he or she holds.

Pre-emption A right given to shareholders to purchase the shares of any member wishing to sell his or her shares. The term is also used to refer to the right of certain shareholders to subscribe for further shares on a new issue.

Preference shares A share giving its holder preferential rights in respect of dividends, and/or return of capital on a solvent winding up. Such shares usually have limited voting rights.

Preferential debts Certain unsecured debts which on the grounds of public policy are given preferential status on the insolvent winding up of a company.

Pre-incorporation contract A contract entered into before a company has been incorporated.

Private company A company which is not a public company.

Privatisation A loose term used to refer to the process by which a nationalised industry is sold off to the public through the medium of shares. It is to be contrasted with corporatisation whereby the particular enterprise continues under public ownership but is run on corporate lines.

Promoter A person who takes steps to form a company or set it in motion. The term can also extend to someone involved in its subsequent flotation.

Prospectus An invitation to the public to subscribe for shares or debentures of the company.

Proxy A person appointed by a shareholder to vote for him or her at a meeting.

Public company A company limited by shares or limited by guarantee and having a share capital which states in its memorandum that it is to be a public company and in respect of which the formalities laid down by the Companies Act for public companies have been complied with.

Quorum The minimum number of persons necessary to constitute a valid meeting.

Receiver A person appointed by a debenture holder or debenture stock trustee to take over the whole or part of the property of a company on default by the company. In the former case the receiver will be an administrative receiver.

Reconstruction Where one company transfers the whole of its undertaking and property to a new company in consideration of the issue of shares by the new company to the shareholders in the old company.

Redeemable shares Shares of a company which can be redeemed by the company.

Reduction of capital The diminution or extinguishment of the share capital of a company. Normally this requires the consent of the court.

Register of charges This refers to either a register of charges created by the company kept by the company itself or the register kept by the Registrar of Companies.

Register of members A register kept by the company of membership of the company.

Registrar of Companies A public official recognised by the Companies Act whose responsibility is primarily to register certain documents under the Companies Act 1985. He or she also is the person responsible for official notification under s 711 of the Companies Act 1985. This is the public notice by him or her in the *Gazette* of receipt and issue of a sub-class of registrable documents.

Regulation An EU source of law which is immediately binding in member states.

Regulations A term sometimes used to describe the articles.

Resolution A formal decision by a majority of the members of the company or the board of directors.

Rights issue A right given to a shareholder to subscribe for further shares usually at an advantageous price.

Scheme of arrangement A compromise or arrangement between the company and its creditors or between the company and its members.

Securitisation Conversion of a loan into a security which is then a marketable commodity.

Share A unit in the share capital of a company.

Share capital That part of the permanent part of the capital of a company which is constituted into shares. It is usual to think of the share capital as a fund.

Share premium account A notional account to which is credited in the books of the company a sum equal to the amount of any premiums on the issue of shares.

Short selling Sale of a security not actually held without the cover of an actual purchase in the hope of a decline in price.

Special resolution A resolution passed by a majority of not less than three-fourths of members voting at a general meeting of the company of which not less than 21 days' notice has been given: Companies Act 1985, s 378(2).

Stag Someone who buys on a new issue with the intention of selling immediately at a profit.

Stock In the strict sense the aggregate of fully paid shares which have been consolidated. In practice such consolidation is rare. In the USA stock is the usual term used for a share. Stock can also refer to debenture stock.

Stock exchange An exchange which provides a primary and secondary market for securities.

Subscriber of memorandum A person who signs the memorandum of association. As such this person is one of the original members of the company.

Subsidiary company A company controlled by another company. For the definition of control see Companies Act 1985, s 736(1).

Table A   A model set of articles of association originally contained in the Companies Act but now contained in a statutory instrument.

Takeover   A loose term used to describe the situation whereby one company ('the bidder') makes an offer to the shareholders of another company ('the target'). A takeover bid can be made over the heads of existing management. In the USA this is described as a tender offer.

Transfer   This normally refers to a form of transfer of shares or debentures or debenture stock. For listed securities a simple form is prescribed.

Transmission   The vesting of a member's shares in another person by operation of law.

Ultra vires   An act in excess of powers. Normally it refers to something not authorised expressly or impliedly by the objects clause of a company. Sometimes the phrase is used to describe an act by directors which is in excess of authority. Since the Companies Act 1989 reforms its significance is largely in respect of the latter.

Undertaking   means a body corporate or partnership, or an unincorporated association carrying on a trade or business with or without a view to profit (Companies Act 1985, s 259(1)). Undertakings may be members of a group in which case they are either a parent undertaking or a subsidiary undertaking for the purpose of group accounts.

Underwriting   An arrangement under which a person promises to take up shares on a public issue which are not taken up by the public.

Unlisted Securities Market   A regulated lower-tier market for young companies replaced in 1995 by the Alternative Investment Market (AIM).

Voluntary arrangement   An arrangement with creditors which does not take the form of a scheme of arrangement sanctioned by the court: see Pt I of the Insolvency Act 1986.

Winding up   The process of liquidation of a company. This can either be compulsory, ie winding up by the court, or voluntary. Voluntary winding up can either be a members' voluntary winding up in case of solvency, or a creditors' winding up in case of insolvency.

Table of statutes

References in this Table to *Statutes* are to Halsbury's Statutes of England (Fourth Edition) showing the volume and page at which the annotated text of the Act will be found.

Page references printed in **bold** type indicate where the section of an Act is set out in part or in full.

Table of cases

C

PAGE

E

H

Incorporation and its consequences

CHAPTER 1

The company as a business medium

THE NATURE AND PURPOSE OF BUSINESS ENTERPRISE

This book is about the law relating to companies and, unless otherwise stated, references are to the Companies Act 1985 (abbreviated as CA 1985). 'Company' is an ambiguous term with no strictly technical meaning[1]. It can refer loosely to a group of persons associated together for a common purpose such as a partnership of businessmen or it can refer to a species of business corporation. We are concerned here with the latter but it will be useful at the outset to discuss the nature and history of business enterprise in general and the place of the business corporation as a distinct form of organisation within it. Business enterprise is a wide term which connotes a unit of ownership in pursuit of profits[2]. Economists usually prefer to use the general term 'firm' while lawyers refer to the particular legal species.

Firms in Western societies are creatures of a market economy. In such an economy, the price system is the final arbiter of production and consumption[3]. Instead of central planning by the state[4], the vital questions of who produces what goods in which quantities and in which places are answered by countless decisions by numerous people acting without knowledge or with limited knowledge of the others. The co-ordinating mechanism is the 'invisible hand'[5] of the price system of the market. This is the theory at any rate. It is a characteristic of the modern economy that production is typically carried out by firms, not by individuals. This is not a logically necessary consequence of the price system[6]. It is theoretically possible that all production could be carried out by individuals who specialised in producing particular goods or services. This is true of simple societies, but as society and technology grow more complex, the problems

1   *Re Stanley* [1906] 1 Ch 131 at 134.
2   See N S Buchanan *The Economics of Corporate Enterprise* (1940), p 15.
3   *Buchanan*, ibid, pp 10–15.
4   Cf the old Eastern Bloc countries. Today the Russian system is in a state of flux. Central planning and inefficient management resulted in increasing difficulties. There are experiments with democratisation and increasing recognition of private property but Russia lags behind Hungary and Poland in its concept of business enterprise and its development of efficient markets.
5   Adam Smith *An Inquiry into the Nature and Causes of the Wealth of Nations* (New York: Modern Library, 1937), p 423.
6   *Buchanan*, op cit, p 13.

of co-ordination by the price system become increasingly difficult and costly. The firm represents to some extent an alternative to the price system for the various factors involved in production[7]. One eminent writer, Professor Alfred Chandler Jr of Harvard Business School, has defined the modern industrial firm as 'a collection of operating units, each with its own specific facilities and personnel, whose combined resources and activities are coordinated, monitored and allocated by a hierarchy of middle and top managers'[8]. Instead of a host of market transactions and the time and cost involved in negotiating them, the firm purchases some agents of production and hires others. The defining characteristic of the firm is in 'a *team* use of inputs and a centralised position of some party in the contractual arrangements of *all* other inputs'[9]. In a sense it is a specialised surrogate market[10]. As Ronald Coase, an economist at Chicago Law School, once wrote: 'Within the firm, these market transactions are eliminated and in place of the complicated market structure with exchange transactions is substituted the entrepreneur-coordinator who directs production'[11]. This produces economies in transaction costs.

Business decisions are frequently taken in conditions of uncertainty and risk. Risk averseness[12] as well as lack of capital probably accounts for particular people becoming employees rather than individual owners and, as we shall see, it enters into the decision to spread one's investment over a number of firms. It does not, however, necessarily account for the existence and organisation of the classical firm which is more due to economies in transaction costs although it helps to explain the evolution of the form of the modern limited liability company which restricts the liability of investors.

A basic issue in the theory of the firm is the nature of profit and its allocation. Profit is another ambiguous term. In economics it usually refers to the excess of total revenue over total cost including what are called the opportunity costs of equity or risk capital[13]. Opportunity costs mean the return necessary to attract that kind of capital from alternative uses. Accountants and lawyers treat the opportunity costs as part of profit. Profit in economics serves to attract and allocate additional investment, entrepreneurial skills and other scarce resources[14].

The next question is who shares in the profit and in what proportions? Is it to go to management as quasi-entrepreneurs, to shareholders, or to other stakeholders of the firm, and on what basis? This requires decision-making hierarchies and monitoring procedures.

7   Ronald H Coase (1937) 4 Economica (NS) 386, *The Firm, the Market and the Law* (1988); H Demsetz *The Economics of Business* (1995).
8   *Scale and Scope: The Dynamics of Industrial Capitalism* (1990), p 13.
9   A Alchian and H Demsetz (1972) 62 Am Econ Rev 777.
10   See note 7.
11   Coase, op cit. For a discussion of this and neoclassical and managerialist theories of the firm see John Coffee Jr (1987) 85 Mich L Rev 1.
12   For a useful recent discussion of risk see Coffee, op cit, pp 16–24.
13   R A Posner and K E Scott *Economics of Corporation Law and Securities Regulation* (1980), p 2.
14   Ibid.

TYPES OF BUSINESS ENTERPRISE

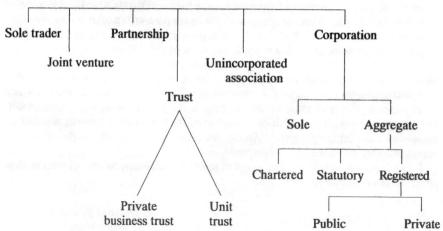

The sole trader

The simplest economic and legal unit is the sole trader—that is, an individual carrying on business either entirely alone or employing others. As an economic unit, he or she is very vulnerable since he or she can be made personally bankrupt for his or her business debts. Until 1861[15], this was an advantage in the sense that only traders could be made bankrupt and escape perpetual harassment from their creditors and the risk of the Debtors' Prison. Since 1861, bankruptcy applies to non-traders as well. Today, English law does not distinguish between traders and non-traders except in some areas of consumer protection. Most Continental European systems perpetuate the basic distinction.

Partnership

Partnership is a relationship of two or more persons carrying on a business in common with a view to profit. Partnership is a species of contract involving principles of commercial agency. The utilitarian reform philosophy of the nineteenth century combining with commercial self-interest culminated in the codification of the law in the Partnership Act 1890. This Act, while comprehensive, is not a complete code, since the administration of partnership assets on death or bankruptcy and the question of goodwill are not dealt with[16], and the existing rules of common law and equity prevail unless they are inconsistent with the Act. The Act, unlike Scots and Continental systems, does not confer legal personality on the partnership. Partners are collectively called a 'firm' in s 4 of the Act but the firm is not a body corporate. The firm is the aggregate of partners who share profits, have individual authority to bind the firm for transactions in the course of business and are ultimately liable to the extent of their personal fortunes for the debts of the partnership. To overcome the risks and administrative disadvantages, partners often incorporate their business and in the case of partnerships of more than 20, incorporation is mandatory. Section 716(1) of CA 1985 provides inter alia:

15   Until 1861, bankruptcy in England and Wales only applied to traders. Non-traders could not be made, nor could they make themselves, bankrupt.
16   See *Lindley and Banks on the Law of Partnership* (17th edn, 1995), para 1–04. For insolvent partnerships see now Insolvent Partnerships Order 1994 (SI 1994 No 2421).

No company, association or partnership consisting of more than 20 persons shall be formed for the purpose of carrying on any business that has for its object the acquisition of gain by the company, association, or partnership or by its individual members, unless it is registered as a company under this Act or is formed in pursuance of some other Act of Parliament, or of letters patent.

However, certain professions are prevented by the rules of their professional bodies from incorporating and statutory recognition of this is given by s 716(2) and (3) which relax the rule of a maximum of 20 partners in the case of solicitors, accountants, stockbrokers and other partnerships exempted by the Secretary of State by regulations made under the latter subsection. Architects, chartered engineers, estate agents and surveyors inter alia have been exempted.

Linked with partnership is the concept of joint venture. Many but not all joint venture agreements constitute partnerships.

Unincorporated associations

Section 716(1) refers not only to 'company' and 'partnership' but also to 'association'. This is a reference to unincorporated associations. Most of these do not in fact have as their object the acquisition of profit but exist for the mutual benefit and often the recreation of their members and thus escape the compulsion to incorporate in s 716(1). Unlike some other systems, English law does not recognise that association predicates corporateness[17] and treats such bodies in a rather complicated way. The mechanism of the trust has proved useful for the holding of property by such associations but difficult questions have arisen over the extent of personal liability of the executive and members[18]. For these reasons some of these associations voluntarily incorporate as companies.

Trusts

Quite apart from unincorporated associations, some business is conducted through private trust, often for tax purposes and the unit trust is a common mode of pooling investments with a separate trustee and manager.

Corporations

Sir Edward Coke in *The Case of Sutton's Hospital* in 1612[19] described a corporation as 'invisible, immortal', and existing 'only in intendment and consideration of the Law'. *Kyd on Corporations*[20] defined a corporation as 'a collection of many individuals, united into one body, under a special denomination, having perpetual succession under an artificial form, and vested, by the policy of the law, with the capacity of acting, in several respects, as an individual ...'. Some jurists have seized upon such statements as support for the proposition that a corporation is essentially a legal fiction[1]. However,

---

17 See F W Maitland *Selected Essays* (1936) ed H D Hazeltine et al, p 209.
18 See Harold A J Ford *Unincorporated Non-Profit Associations* (1959) and S Stoljar *Group and Entities* (1973) passim.
19 (1612) 10 Co Rep 1a at 32b.
20 Vol 1, p 13.
1   Pope Innocent IV, Savigny and Salmond. For a discussion of the other theories such as the 'purpose', 'enterprise', 'bracket' and 'concession' theories, see R W M Dias *Jurisprudence* (5th edn, 1985), ch 12.

all that Coke and Kyd were putting forward was a theory of law, a statement of how a corporation is to be treated legally. In law all persons recognised by law are legal persons and hence, in a sense, legal fictions. The theory thus rests on a tautology[2]. The most rational approach to the concept of legal corporateness lies in a concentration on the ways in which the legal requirements for corporations have been worked out by analogy with the legal relations between individuals and the reasons why this has taken place[3]. Perhaps too much emphasis in the past has been put on the separate legal personality of corporations. This has created metaphysical problems which have had to be solved before the courts could get down to the practical issues, and has obscured the fact that corporations are distinct and developing methods of owning and holding property and organising production by individuals or groups which in their turn determine certain relationships of control, agency and monitoring of agency performance.

Corporation is a genus with two traditional species—sole and aggregate. Corporations sole confer corporate status on the single holder of an office, eg the Archbishop of Canterbury. Corporations aggregate confer corporate status on a group of persons. There is a criss-crossing classification into charitable and civil corporations which can be either sole or aggregate. The type of company with which we are principally concerned—the company limited by shares—is a sub-species of civil corporation.

Economists look upon the company as a way of organising capital by a firm which has acquired distinctive legal attributes. We have seen how the firm represents an alternative arrangement to the market by the various factors in production represented by the company. This tells us why much economic activity takes place in firms but not why many of those firms are companies. The answer is, as Richard Posner[4] has pointed out, that the company is primarily a method of solving problems encountered in raising substantial amounts of capital. As such it is a kind of standard form contract. Capital is raised by many risk-averse investors contributing to a common fund. The capital raised enables a potentially elaborate organisation to be set up with professional management. Instead of a series of separate investment contracts and contracts with the various factors in production, there is substituted the master contract constituted by the company. This produces economies in transaction costs on both fronts. Most companies have limited liability for their members but not of course themselves. This transfers the ultimate risks of business failure to their creditors but in practice this only means trade and involuntary creditors since financial creditors take guarantees from the principal shareholders and directors in private companies[5]. On the other hand the use of the corporate form involves the cost of monitoring the performance of management and employees to prevent shirking and manipulation of corporate assets for personal advantage. Here one has to balance these agency costs against the benefits derived[6]. The shareholders retain the authority to change the membership of the management and over major decisions affecting the structure of the company. Economic theories of transaction costs, information and monitoring provide insights not only into incorporation but also the financing, management and growth of companies. They also help to explain why some companies merge and why some

2   See *Max Weber on Law in Economy and Society* (1954) ed Max Rheinstein, p 156.
3   See H L A Hart (1954) 70 LQR 37.
4   R Posner *Economic Analysis of Law* (3rd edn, 1986), p 368; see also P Halpern, M Trebilcock and S Turnbull (1980) 30 U of TLJ 959. Cf Coffee, op cit, p 16 et seq.
5   *Posner*, op cit, p 370; Coffee, op cit, p 67 et seq.
6   See N Wolfson (1980) 34 Miami LR 959; M Jensen and W Meckling (1976) 3 J Financial Econ 305; Coffee, op cit, p 31 et seq.

companies fail. We shall consequently refer to them from time to time where this is helpful.

The concept of the enterprise and undertaking

German law recognises the concept of the enterprise as such but has problems in giving a clear definition to the concept and marking the relationship with firm. It seems to be a broader concept than firm taking into account sociological as well as legal and economic phenomena[7]. The concept is occasionally used in English company law as a basis for piercing the corporate veil in the case of related companies. The reality of the economic enterprise is then looked at. Recently, the Companies Act 1989, implementing the Seventh EC Directive on Harmonisation of Company Laws, has used the term 'undertaking' which conveys some of the same looseness as 'enterprise'. It is broader than company and corporate group. There it is used in a modest sense in connection with accounts of associated business entities.

MAJOR ECONOMIC THEMES IN THE DEVELOPMENT OF MODERN COMPANY LAW

There are eight major economic themes which characterise the development of modern company law. The first is a growth of larger business units. The history of limited liability companies is one of increasing concentration. This is the logic of the system. The mechanism of this species of corporation enabled capital to be accumulated from a number of small investors and the natural tendency is towards monopoly. As Berle and Means stated in their classic study, *The Modern Corporation and Private Property*[8]: 'The corporate system has done more than evolve a norm by which business is carried on. Within it exists a centripetal attraction which draws wealth together into aggregations of constantly increasing size, at the same time throwing control into the hands of fewer and fewer men.' This was one of the central theses of their book and one of their conclusions was that such organisations had passed beyond the realm of private enterprise and had become 'nearly social institutions'. Later, they wrote: 'The law of corporations ... might well be considered as a potential law for the new economic state, while business prestige is increasingly assuming the aspect of economic statesmanship.' This undoubtedly overstated the case. The relationship of such companies to the market is one of the more controversial areas of economics. Are they the creature or the controller of the particular market? In the UK there has been an increasing degree of concentration, especially in the last 30 years. Like Germany and France, it has experienced a substantial upward trend in average manufacturing industry concentration levels. Thus a survey by Professor K George of 157 product lines in the UK revealed a 10% point average increase in five firms' sales concentrating ratios between 1958 and 1968[9]. The weight of evidence from a number of surveys indicates

---

7   See G Teubner 'Enterprise Corporatism: New Industrial Policy and the Essence of the Legal Person' 36 Am J of Comp L 130 (1988). See also T Reiser 'The Theory of Enterprise Law in the FDR' ibid 111. See also P Blumberg *The Multinational Challenge to Corporation Law—The Search for a New Corporate Personality* (1993) and Sally Wheeler *A Reader on the Law of the Business Enterprise* (1994).

8   Revised edition, 1968, p 18.

9   K D George (1975) 85 Economic Journal 124; S Prais *The Evolution of Giant Firms in Britain* (1976), p 16.

that UK industries are on average more concentrated than US industries[10]. Government policy has at times been somewhat mixed in its attitudes. Sometimes it has favoured concentration and has actively fostered it, as in the setting up of the Industrial Reorganisation Corporation by the first Wilson Government. Sometimes it has sought to curb restrictive trade practices and monopolies. The principal instrument for the latter has been not company law but separate legislation originating with the Monopolies and Restrictive Practices (Inquiry and Control) Act 1948 and now contained in the Fair Trading Act 1973 and the EU Council Regulation No 4064/89. A similar attitude characterises the EU's attitude to concentration. Company law measures, such as the draft convention on transnational mergers and the European company project favour concentration, but there are strong provisions in the Treaty of Rome on concentration and the abuse of a dominant position[11].

A second theme is the development of increasingly elaborate structures. The simplest corporate structure is a single company whose constitutional organs are the board of directors and general meeting of shareholders. Their precise relationship to each other is partly a matter of law, partly a matter of contract constituted by the memorandum and articles of association[12]. Sometimes this is supplemented by an extrinsic agreement and some managerial systems are sometimes superimposed on the legal framework. In a large company there will often be an elaborate vertical chain of command extending from the Board through middle management to the workforce. In this century, the group of companies developed as an extension of the corporate concept[13]. This originally arose as a method of expansion and pooling of resources which extended the surrogate market. When the private company was introduced, the use of subsidiary private companies enabled a public company to devolve parts of its business to subsidiaries and escape the disclosure requirements imposed on public companies. Later, this was curtailed by changes in the disclosure requirements. The group enterprise has created problems for the law which have not yet been solved. The group enabled not only vertical integration but also horizontal integration. As a result of the latter, there have developed large groups known as conglomerates with subsidiaries in a number of different industries. The American Federal Trade Commission in its statistical analyses in fact breaks these down into five separate categories: horizontal extension, where the firms are actual competitors in some relevant market; vertical extension, where the firms occupy adjacent stages in some vertical chain of production and distribution; product extension, where the firms, although not in actual competition, sell products functionally related in terms of manufacture or distribution; market extension, where the firms sell in geographically distinct markets; and pure conglomerates, where the firms are in essentially unrelated fields[14].

The third theme is a shift from ownership to control of the firm[15]. The early entrepreneurs both owned and managed their businesses. With the growth of the modern company as a mode of diversified ownership there has been a gradual shift of power from those who own to those who control or manage such companies. In many large public companies the top management have relatively small personal shareholdings.

10   F M Scherer *Industrial Market Structure and Economic Performance* (2nd edn, 1980), p 72.
11   See arts 85 and 86.
12   See Chapters 10 and 11, post.
13   See Chapter 33, post.
14   *Scherer*, op cit, p 558.
15   See *Berle and Means*, op cit; C S Beed (1966) 1 Journal of Economic Studies 29; J H Farrar 'Ownership and Control of Listed Public Companies: Revising or Rejecting the Concept of Control' in *Company Law in Change* (1987) (ed B Pettet), p 39 et seq.; JE Parkinson *Corporate Power and Responsibility* (1993), Ch 2.

On the other hand, they have functional control of the enterprise. This again is a central thesis of Berle and Means' analysis of US companies in 1930. Although as a theory it had been anticipated by Marx and others, Berle and Means were the first to give it empirical content. Berle and Means traced the development of the concept of *control* which they recognised to be somewhat amorphous. They identified five different types of control in the modern company:

(1)   control through almost complete ownership;
(2)   majority control;
(3)   control through legal devices without majority ownership eg pyramiding, the use of non-voting shares, voting trusts;
(4)   minority control; and
(5)   management control.

The first three rest on a legal base. The last two are extra-legal. The trend is to the last two because of the dispersion of share ownership in the larger public companies. With this divergence of ownership and control comes a divergence of interest. The shareholder is interested more in income and capital appreciation of his or her investment rather than the company as an enterprise. Management is interested in the enterprise for a diversity of motives ranging from professional pride to the most naked self-interest in the pursuit of power.

While some economists challenge the divergence of interest argument, most subsequent research has tended to confirm Berle and Means' major findings in substance. Those who subscribe to their separation theory are known as the school of Managerialists. This is a broad heading and there is considerable diversity within it. While Marxists agree on separation of ownership and control, they use the theory as part of a larger enquiry. As Michel de Vroey has written[16]: 'While Managerialists just ask the question "who ... rules the corporation?", Marxists' main question is: "For which class interests are the corporations ruled?"'. Thus to Marxists there is a dispersion of *legal* ownership but not economic ownership in the sense that the latter remains in the hands of the dominant class.

While much of the discussion has taken place at the level of theory, Berle and Means did test their theory against the evidence. In the UK, an empirical study by Sargent Florence in 1961 adopting several alternative criteria concluded that two-thirds of the large companies in 1951 were not owner-controlled[17]. A more recent study by S Nyman and A Silberston of Nuffield College, Oxford[18] is critical of these findings. They argue that the extent of managerial control is more limited than has been thought and there may not be an inexorable tendency to increase. However, the situation differs from industry to industry and this probably affects earlier empirical findings. They favour a flexible, more realistic approach to the concept of control, arguing that firms controlled by families, professional managers, other firms or by financial institutions may display different behavioural characteristics. In particular, they stress the need to accommodate potential control and what we call our fourth theme.

The fourth theme is the ever-increasing ownership of ordinary shares in UK companies by institutional investors, ie pension funds, insurance companies, unit trusts and investment trusts who manage other people's savings[19]. The combined holdings

---

16   (1975) 7 Review of Radical Political Economy 2.
17   Florence *Ownership, Control and Success of Large Companies* (1961).
18   (1978) 30 Oxford Economic Papers 74.
19   See eg R Dobbins and T W McRae *Institutional Shareholders and Corporate Management* (1975) but see also R C Clark 94 Harv L Rev 561 where he argues that there is a further stage beyond this — the age of the group savings planner through pension schemes. We subsume this under institutional investment.

of such bodies amounted to 54.1% of the market value of listed UK equities and 63.8% of listed UK company bonds in 1981[20]. In the past institutional investors have been reluctant to use their voting strength and be active at general meetings. This contrasts very sharply with the role of financial institutions in France and Germany where they play a more positive part in corporate governance. In the UK, such institutions came under some criticism by the Committee on the Functioning of Financial Institutions[1]. Recently there have been signs of a more active role by institutional investors as minority shareholders[2]. The full implications of this trend have not been worked out[3]. Obviously it represents a change in one's model of the typical shareholder. For management, it represents a possible institutional check on their abuses. On the other hand, it may represent a source of useful support in a takeover, in corporate planning and as a source of further funds for expansion. We deal with this question in detail in Chapter 35.

A fifth theme is the ever increasing amount of government intervention in corporate affairs. The early Companies Acts were a blend of intervention and laissez-faire. By providing for incorporation on registration they encouraged the growth of this form of business medium. On the other hand, they required disclosure of an increasing amount of information regarding the company. Disclosure[4] has long been recognised as the dominant philosophy of most modern systems. It is a sine qua non of corporate accountability. It can be justified on the following main policy grounds:

(1)   it leads to a better informed and consequently more efficient stock market;
(2)   it minimises the risk of fraud;
(3)   it prevents excessive secrecy and the distrust which this engenders; and
(4)   it facilitates equality of opportunity.

Counter arguments can be put forward in terms of confidentiality, lack of utility and excessive cost.

The UK corporate system is distinctive in that until recently the law and the government have been less involved in the regulation of public companies than in most other larger economies. This has been because of the strong tradition of self-regulation of the City of London financial institutions. The Stock Exchange, the Takeover Panel and other self-regulatory bodies have supplemented Parliament and the courts. Some have argued that the system was in need of root and branch reform and generally favoured the creation by legislation of a Securities Commission which would have public participation in its membership, rule formulation and procedures. The thinking behind the Financial Services Act 1986 was, however, to develop the present system of self-regulation within a statutory framework[5]. The system has been a pyramid of

---

20   *The Stock Exchange Fact Book*, cited by J Oakley and L Harris *The City of Capital* (1983), pp 106–7. A study by International Capital Markets Group in 1995 had 59.8% for institutions and 0.4% for banks. See Eddy Wymeersch 'Comparative Corporate Governance: Elements of Convergence', unpublished paper given at the National Corporate Law Teachers' Conference, Melbourne 1997.

1   Cmnd 7937 (1980).

2   See *Prudential Assurance Co Ltd v Newman Industries Ltd (No 2)* [1981] Ch 257, where the Prudential took action as a minority shareholder against a fraudulent management. However, the result was expensive and rather unsatisfactory.

3   See eg J H Farrar and M Russell (1984) 5 Co Law 107; P L Davies 'Institutional Investors in the United Kingdom' in DD Prentice and P R J Holland *Contemporary Issues in Corporate Governance* (1993), p 90; J Farrar, *Takeovers, Institutional Investors and the Modernisation of Corporate Laws* (1993); G P Stapledon *Institutional Shareholders and Corporate Governance* (1996).

4   For a valuable discussion of the concept of disclosure, see W Grover and J C Baillie in *Proposals for a Securities Market Law for Canada*, vol 3, p 350 ff.

5   See the Gower Report on Investor Protection (Cmnd 9125) 1984; *The Times*, 18 October 1984; the White Paper, *Financial Services in the United Kingdom* (Cmnd 9432) 1985.

power, descending from the Secretary of State for Trade and Industry through the Securities and Investments Board (SIB) to a number of self-regulatory agencies. The Director General of Fair Trading has had a watching brief to report on restrictive trade practices. In May 1997 the new Labour Government announced a radical new system of regulation. The new framework takes bank supervision away from the Bank of England and replaces it with an enhanced Securities and Investment Board (SIB). *The Economist* of 24 May 1997, at p 13, stated that 'later the plan is to fold into the SIB the existing array of city regulators (one for each main branch of the financial services industry), shifting from a regime based on self-regulation to one based on statute'. SIB is to have tougher powers as well as a wider remit. Building societies may also be put under its supervision later. On 28 October 1997, SIB changed its name to the Financial Services Authority (FSA).

Another area of government intervention, as we have seen, has been the regulation of concentration. Nationalisation took place in various sectors of the economy in the post-war period and, from time to time, government invested public money in companies in key sectors. However, the trend under the Conservative governments has been in the opposite direction, towards privatisation of public enterprises. Since 1973 the UK's membership of the European Union (EU) has meant that its laws are increasingly influenced by the EU institutions.

Sixth, a point related to increasing government intervention, is the increasing legal impact of economic integration through membership of the EU. Since 1973 the UK has been a member state of the EU which has adopted an elaborate programme for harmonisation of company law and securities regulation. Since 1973 this had had an important influence on domestic law reform.

Seventh, there has been the growth of multinational enterprises which in capital and power have begun to rival the nation state[6]. There is an increasing call in the OECD, United Nations and EU to lay down guidelines to regulate the activities of multinationals[7].

Historically the UK has been the headquarters of some of the early multinationals such as Imperial Chemical Industries plc, formed in 1926, which was designed from its incorporation to be multinational in its interests. Its objects were inter alia to 'extend the operations of the company to any foreign country, colony or state, by establishing and carrying on there all or any' of the businesses mentioned in its memorandum. ICI now has manufacturing companies in more than 40 countries and selling companies in more than 60. Since the end of the First World War we have seen the phenomenal growth and spread of American multinationals. The growth of multinational companies has had an impact on the corporate form, labour practices, the transfer of technology and on tax in the host countries. In macro-economic terms they have sometimes caused balance of payments problems for smaller countries and threatened the very sovereignty of those countries. A small country like New Zealand, for example, with a population of less than the size of London or Sydney is often not in a very strong position to regulate a multinational oil or aluminium corporation. This particular trend in company law, therefore, necessarily raises problems of international law.

Lastly, there have been the changes in the world economy from being international to transnational. The transnational economy is shaped by money flows as much as trade in goods and services[8]. Part of this transition has been the so-called international financial revolution[9]. The causes are many and complex (indeed some may be

6   There is a plethora of literature on this subject. See eg R Vernon *Sovereignty at Bay* (1971), N Fatemi et al *Multinational Corporations* (2nd edn revised, 1976) and R Eels *Global Corporations* (1972).
7   See *International Investment Guidelines for Multinational Enterprises* (Cmnd 6525).
8   See Peter Drucker *The New Realities* (1989), pp 115–116.
9   See A Hamilton *The Financial Revolution* (1986); J L Jones (1986) 7 Co Law 99.

effects)—the growth of the Eurodollar market and its consequences—the reduction of money to a commodity in its own right and the move towards deregulation of capital markets; the massive developments in technology and multimedia which provide ever more efficient information and communication systems; increasing competition in banking, brokerage and insurance—the whole marketing of financial services; and the breakdown of barriers between different financial markets. Today the monetary and tax policies of nation states increasingly react to movements in the transnational money and capital markets rather than try to shape them[10].

The principal beneficiaries of this revolution have been the larger listed companies, especially the multinational ones. Taking advantage of their status in the market place they are now able to achieve great flexibility through individual contracting in their financial affairs. It is a world of syndicated loans; futures, options; convertibles and swaps characterised by flexibility, diffusion of risk and the rapid trading of commercial paper. Some aspects of these developments are tax driven to take advantage of loopholes in national tax regimes and tax havens. Now, more than at any other time in the past, the financial world in which companies operate is fluid and the changes fast moving. The effects of this on conventional concepts of company law are yet to be assessed.

STAKEHOLDER INTERESTS

Underlying any discussion of company law and any rational debate about the policy of law reform is the question of the interests of the various stakeholders. By 'stakeholder' we mean those having a legitimate stake in the company, using that term in a broad sense. The limited liability company does not simply represent one interest. It represents an arena in which there is a potential clash of many interests. We may identify the following stakeholders':

(1) investors—share capital
   —loan capital
(2) outside creditors — commercial finance
   —trade creditors
(3) employees
(4) consumers
(5) the public.

Investors either provide share or loan capital to the company. Generally the former have a permanent stake in the profits of the business which they can nevertheless realise. The latter usually have a fixed income and are investors for a limited time. Their interest is often secured.

Outside creditors are principally trade creditors who are usually unsecured and concerned with the company as a credit risk. Commercial finance creditors are institutions such as banks who are invariably secured creditors but do not regard themselves as investors.

The employees are a species of creditor but with an interest in the company as a source of job security.

Consumers are members of the general public who are interested in the company as a source of products and service.

The public interest can embrace investor and consumer protection but also covers residual matters such as regional development, resource management and the national

10   Drucker, op cit, p 115.

interest. Under the law as it stands, the directors of a company primarily owe their duties to the company as an abstract entity. Since this abstract entity potentially covers all the interests mentioned above, directors have to weigh them up in practice and resolve the conflict between them. The law is unsatisfactory in that if the directors consider consumers and the public interest at the expense of investors and employees they may be held to have committed a breach of duty and yet pressure might have been put on them by the government to do this. Until the Companies Act 1980[11] they would have been in breach of duty by considering employees. The formulation of the duties of management of the modern company needs more thorough and realistic appraisal[12]. Modern business enterprise is often very large and complex. This size and complexity gives it considerable resources of power which can be used to control and influence others. Modern corporate governance is a vital matter of social control calling for a sensitive balancing of efficiency and fairness. It cannot be solved by any simple formula, economic or otherwise.

11   Sections 46 and 74.
12   See the classic article by E M Dodd (1932) 45 Harv LRev 1145 and Klaus Hopt and G Teubner (eds) *Corporate Governance and Directors' Liabilities* (1985). See Philip A Joseph (1980) 14 UBCLR 75 for a valuable discussion of the relationship of corporate management to labour. The issues of social responsibility and employee participation will be dealt with in more detail later. For a general critique see Mary Stokes 'Company Law and Legal Theory' in Sally Wheeler (ed) *A Reader on the Law of the Business Enterprise* (1994) 80. See also Lynne Dallas (1988) 22 U of Mich J of LR 104.

CHAPTER 2

A brief general history of English company law

To understand modern company law, one needs to know something of the economic, social and legal history of business enterprise. In some of the chapters which follow we will give more detailed discussion of the history of particular branches of company law where this is helpful to an understanding of the modern law, but we will start by giving a brief general survey[1]. The history can be divided into four main periods:

(1) from earliest times until the South Sea Bubble;
(2) from the Bubble Act until the first Companies Act 1844;
(3) from 1844 until the UK's accession to the Common Market; and
(4) from 1972 until the present day.

1 THE EARLY PERIOD UP TO THE SOUTH SEA BUBBLE

The simplest and earliest form of business organisation is the sole trader. In the Middle Ages the principal trades were regulated by the guilds of merchants which roughly resembled modern trade protection associations with the ceremonial and social activities of organisations such as City Livery Companies and the Free Masons[2]. The guilds regulated a broad branch of trade or conferred on their members a monopoly of dealing in a particular kind of commodity. Their regulations also covered apprenticeships and the employment of journeymen, ie qualified employees. The medieval guild was part of the structure of municipal organisation in England, closely linked with the borough[3], and thus existed as much for social as economic purposes. There was a fellowship between the members and a concern for welfare as well as business standards. It represented a closed economic group of sole traders characterised

---

1   See Sir William Holdsworth *A History of English Law* (1932), vol VIII, ch IV, para 4; R R Formoy *The Historical Foundations of Modern Company Law* (1923); C A Cooke *Corporation Trust and Company* (1950); W R Scott *Joint Stock Companies to 1720* (1912); A B DuBois *The English Business Company after the Bubble Act 1720–1800* (1938), H R Hahlo [1982] JR 139; Bishop Hunt *The Development of the Business Corporation in England 1800–1867* (1936); and L C B Gower *Principles of Modern Company Law* (6th edn, 1997) (ed Paul L Davies), chs 2 and 3.
2   *Gower*, op cit, p 20.
3   *Cooke*, op cit, ch 11.

by corporate monopoly and privilege, albeit usually of a local extent[4]. As with a modern cartel the standard of regulation was set by the least efficient economic unit[5]. The purpose of the guild was to ensure an adequate level of profit to the poorest business. The effect of this was necessarily to increase the wealth and power of the most efficient members. Through the guild and the borough merchants were able to throw off the feudal yoke. Through the craft guild and the trading company, associations of merchants were able to throw off local public control. The result of this was eventually to make the whole country the economic unit and to lead to national economic policies[6].

The two earliest business organisations which bear some resemblance to the modern partnership are the *Commenda* and the *Societas*[7]. The *Commenda*, which was found in Babylonian and Arabic as well as Western law[8], was a cross between a modern partnership and a loan and involved one person advancing money to a trader on terms that he should have a return which varied with the profits. Originally this was a temporary association for a particular transaction. The *Commenda* has largely disappeared from the English scene but still exists in the other Continental European members of the EU. The *Societas* was a more permanent association which was the forerunner of the modern partnership. As such it developed as a form of commercial agency and gradually the common law and equitable rules coalesced into specialised partnership principles. The reason given for the relative unimportance of *Commenda* and the development of *Societas* in England is that English business practice lagged behind that of Continental countries in book-keeping. 'If a limit to individual liability is to be operated it requires a separation of the accounts of the firm from the capital accounts of the capitalist partners'[9], *Commenda* is the earliest transaction in which we see a method of capitalistic accounting[10]. This type of accounting did not generally develop in England until much later. The normal convention was a simple division of profits and simple participation in the business with no capital account.

At common law, the only means of incorporation were by Royal Charter or statute although there is some suggestion that before the Reformation Papal Charters were recognised[11]. Incorporation by Royal Charter was relatively rarely given to traders. The original purpose of incorporation by Royal Charter seems to have been to confer protection and status[12]. The grant was often for charitable purposes such as the founding of a new college or incorporation of an existing college at Oxford or Cambridge. Later, in the Elizabethan period, the dominant purpose was to regulate a particular trade[13]. This became necessary when the guild system had declined and become the subject of abuse. Some of these grants amounted to monopolies. Underlying the grant, however, was the idea of public purpose. The concept of public purpose and benefit in incorporation declined due to a number of factors—the Stuart abuse of the Royal prerogative, the increase of trade and manufacture and the growth of overseas trade, originally as privateering expeditions. This is the beginning of the rise of capitalistic enterprise whose dominant characteristic is to produce a more open economic group[14], but this is to anticipate later events.

4   See Julien Freund *The Sociology of Max Weber* (1968), p 154 ff.
5   *Cooke*, op cit, p 22.
6   *Cooke*, op cit, p 34.
7   See *Holdsworth*, op cit, p 195 ff.
8   See *Max Weber on Law in Economy and Society* (1954) ed Max Rheinstein, p 148.
9   *Cooke*, op cit, p 46.
10   *Weber*, op cit.
11   For religious and educational bodies.
12   *Cooke*, op cit, p 52.
13   Ibid, p 53.
14   *Freund*, op cit.

With the development of overseas and especially colonial trade we see the rise of 'merchant ventures'. The merchant venturers gave rise to 'regulated companies' which extended the guild system into overseas trade. The pattern was for each member to trade on his own stock but as a member of the 'company'. From the beginning of the fifteenth century the Crown made extensive grants of privileges to companies of merchants trading overseas. Later these were Royal Charters providing for incorporation and a monopoly of trade in a particular region. The objects of such grants are to provide for proper organisation of the trade, to develop a new trade or colonisation. The interest of merchants was not in separate legal personality as such so much as the exercise of governmental power and trading privilege.

The next development is the concept of joint stock[15]. Historically this seems to have been linked with the grant of a monopoly. The grant is made to a 'company' of individuals who raise stock for the exploitation of the monopoly. Joint stock represents a combination of association and exploitation of a privilege. This concept was particularly useful with overseas trading ventures. At first each voyage was a separate venture but later more permanent accounting took place. The East India Company was the first to combine incorporation, overseas trade and joint stock raised from the general public. This development was summed up well by a Committee of the House of Commons in 1604. 'A whole Company', it said, 'by this means, is become as one man'[16]. Although some joint stock ventures obtained incorporation, many did not and were in essence partnerships describing themselves loosely as 'companies'. Stocks and shares in both incorporated and unincorporated ventures began to be dealt in on the developing stock market which Parliament found it necessary to regulate in 1696. By the beginning of the eighteenth century, therefore, there was considerable diversity in the forms of business organisation and added to this there was some trade in the charters of defunct chartered corporations.

Further, in 1694 in return for money lent to the government by a group of individuals, a Royal Charter incorporated the group as a joint stock company. This was the Governor and Company of the Bank of England[17]. Underlying this was the idea that the money lent to the state constituted a fund of credit on which loans could be made by the bank. It did not take long for the next stage to be reached whereby a company might venture to take over the whole national debt. Such a company would be granted trading privileges and exchange its shares for existing holdings of government stock. It is against this background that one must now consider the South Sea Bubble[18]. This had its origin in 1711 when a lawyer and financier, John Blunt, formed a company styled 'The Company of Merchants of Great Britain Trading to the South Seas'. The main object of the company was to secure the trade in the South Seas. The company prospered so much that in 1719 it offered to take over the National Debt, buying out either for cash or for shares all other creditors. The company proposed to pay £7.5 m for this privilege and to reduce the interest which the country was paying. At this time the National Debt stood at £31 m and rumours were circulating that the country was facing bankruptcy. The government of the day regarded the scheme as the answer to its problems. It did so all the more willingly as Blunt had bribed some of the ministers. The company persuaded Parliament to pass the South Sea Act which empowered the company to pay anyone who had a government annuity the amount which was due to

---

15   *Cooke*, op cit, ch IV.
16   Report of Committee on the Bill for Free Trade: Journals of the House of Commons I, p 218 in respect of the Muscovy Company.
17   For the background, see *Scott*, op cit, vol 1 and J Carswell *The South Sea Bubble* (1960), chs 1 and 2.
18   See *Scott*, op cit; L Melville, pseud (LS Benjamin) *The South Sea Bubble* (1921); *Carswell*, op cit, on which what follows is based. See also Charles P Kindleberger *Manias, Panics and Crashes* (3rd ed, 1996).

him. Payment was not, however, to be in cash, but in shares in the company. It was anticipated that the close connection with the government would act as great publicity for the company and inspire confidence in its business. For a time this was indeed the case. People were remarkably ignorant about trading in the South Seas but they were tremendously impressed by the size of the enterprise and its close connection with the government. Everyone—merchants, professors, doctors, clergymen and even the Canton of Berne—invested in the company. Within a few days the £100 shares went up to £1,000. Blunt and his colleagues made huge fortunes. The success of the South Sea Co led to numerous similar schemes with a rich variety of objects. These companies were floated to fatten elephants, fix quicksilver and even for 'a certain design which will hereafter be promulgated'. People's credulity knew no bounds and there was such an urge to invest in anything that resembled a share that stalls were set up in the streets. The size of this investment reached incredible proportions. At one time the amounts invested in such companies amounted to £500 m, twice the then value of all the land in England.

However, in 1720 the bubble inevitably burst. The immediate cause seems to have been proceedings against other joint stock companies. Whether these were instigated by or at the behest of the directors of the South Sea Co is a matter of controversy[19]. People began to realise that the shares could not possibly be worth the amount they had paid for them and they tried to get rid of them. The South Sea Co itself was unable to meet its liabilities and the whole tower came tumbling down. In the resulting confusion there was great fury and cries for vengeance. It was suggested that the directors of the South Seas Co should be given a Roman-style execution. A government enquiry was set up. A Bill was passed for the confiscation of the property of those guilty of fraud. A sum of £2 m was provided for compensation. A number of ministers were disgraced. The South Sea Bubble and the resulting Bubble Act set back the development of joint stock companies for some time.

2   THE PERIOD FROM 1720–1844

The Bubble Act (6 Geo 1, c 18) prohibited a company from acting as a body corporate and from raising transferable stocks and shares without the legal authority of a Royal Charter or Act of Parliament. Any scheme contravening the Act was illegal and void. On the other hand it exempted a number of undertakings *including the South Sea Co itself* and contained a proviso that nothing in the Act prohibited the carrying on of business in partnership. The Act is a poor commencement of English company legislation which Maitland said 'seems to scream at us from the Statute Book'[20]. However, only one prosecution under the Act is reported until the beginning of the nineteenth century[1]. Whether this was due to the prolixity of the Act or the popular distrust of the joint stock concept as a medium of investment is not clear. Maitland explained the matter thus: 'In its panic, Parliament had spoken much of mischief to the public, and judges, whose conception of the mischievous was liable to change, were able to declare that where there was no mischievous tendency there was no offence'[2]. In the resulting hiatus, given that Royal Charters and Acts of Parliament were difficult to obtain, much was left to the ingenuity of legal draftsmanship. The principal development was the 'deed of settlement company' drafted so as to comply

19   See L C B Gower (1952) 68 LQR 214.
20   F W Maitland *Collected Papers*, vol 3, 'Trust and Corporation', p 390.
1   *R v Cawood* (1724) 2 Ld Raym 1361.
2   *Maitland*, op cit, p 391.

with the Act[3]. This was a combination of trust and association. Its assets were held on trust by trustees but its business was managed by managers or directors. What the investor obtained was an interest in the trust fund. Attempts were made from time to time to make such interests transferable and the resultant provisions often attained through complexity the practical effect, if not the letter, of limited liability. However, deed of settlement companies were vulnerable to prosecution under the Bubble Act, despite the fact that they were becoming increasingly common in business. In the early nineteenth century, after a crop of cases on the Act, an enquiry was carried out into the working of the Act and it was eventually repealed in 1825 at the behest of the Board of Trade. There was nevertheless doubt as to the legality of deed of settlement companies at common law until 1843[4].

It is with the growth of the railway companies that we see a considerable impetus for legislative reform. Railways needed to raise capital from the public. It was cumbrous and expensive for such enterprises to obtain incorporation by Act of Parliament and they were not likely to obtain the grant of a Royal Charter. There were gradual and piecemeal reforms. An attempt to pass a general Companies Act in 1838 was defeated in the House of Lords by opposition led by Lord Brougham[5]. It is odd that in this respect Brougham should find himself at odds with John Austin[6] and John Stuart Mill[7]. The latter was to compare the English position very unfavourably with that of America in the 1840s. However, the immediate cause of the first Companies Act was business fraud. A Select Committee was set up in 1841 'to inquire into the State of the Laws respecting Joint Stock Companies (except for Banking), with a view to the greater Security of the Public'. This came under the chairmanship of William Gladstone in 1843 and reported in 1844 that there was a need for legislation providing for registration of deed of settlement documents with a public official. This was enacted as 7 & 8 Vict, c 110 and is the first modern Companies Act. The deed of settlement company, when registered, was invested with the qualities and incidents of corporations, although the full effect of this was not recognised until later in the nineteenth century. The effect of this legislation was to shift from the privilege of incorporation to the right of incorporation provided the statutory conditions were fulfilled[8]. Nevertheless, traces of the old privilege idea lingered on in the case law.

3   THE PERIOD FROM 1844–1972

In 1844, there were about 970 deed of settlement companies of which 170 were in insurance[9]. The 1844 Act provided for incorporation on registration. It did so by a system of provisional registration which was later made complete. Until then the company was not fully incorporated. It did not provide for limited liability nor for a separate regime for the winding up of companies. Between 1844 and 1856, 910 companies were registered under the Act of which 219 were in insurance, 211 in gas and water, 85 in markets and public halls, 46 in shipping and 41 in lending. The Act thus seems to have had relatively little effect on the organisation and financing of manufacturing industry. Only 106 such companies were registered, of which the largest group was 13 cotton companies.

3   See *Gower*, op cit, p 29 ff, for a useful discussion of such 'companies'.
4   See *Gower* op cit, p 36.
5   See P L Cottrell *Industrial Finance 1830–1914* (1980), p 44.
6   See (1825) Parliamentary History and Review 711.
7   See J S Mill *Principles of Political Economy* (1909), Book V, ch IX.
8   See J W Hurst *The Legitimacy of the Business Corporation in the US 1780–1970* (1970), p 58.
9   *Cottrell*, op cit, pp 44–45.

The introduction of limited liability

The companies formed under the 1844 legislation were unlimited companies in the sense that their shareholders still had unlimited liability for the debts of the company[10]. Limited liability could be the subject of individual contracting between the shareholders and the creditors. Indeed, complex drafting of deeds of settlement and cumbrous legal procedures produced the effect, if not the letter, of limited liability, since creditors had to sue each shareholder in a separate action and, in practice, sued the richest. There was a question about the validity of clauses purporting to create limited liability but such a clause was upheld in 1852 in *Hallett v Dowdall*[11]. The Court of Exchequer Chamber held that it was valid and could bind third parties with express notice.

After some debate, limited liability was introduced in the Limited Liability Act 1855. It was introduced by Bouverie, the Vice President of the Board of Trade, as a progressive reform measure which would help to vitalise British business. He argued that increasing numbers of companies were seeking incorporation under French and American laws to achieve limited liability. Twenty 'English' companies had been formed in France from 1853 to 1854[12].

Other arguments in favour were:

(1) it enabled small capital to be turned to profitable employment;
(2) it was a question of free trade against monopoly;
(3) unlimited liability was impracticable and impeded work such as railways, canals and docks;
(4) it prevented prudent men from becoming members of companies which were consequently being formed by the rash and reckless.

The main arguments against it were that:

(1) it was not a privilege to be given to partners but a right to be taken from creditors;
(2) it encouraged people to trade beyond their means;
(3) it led to speculation and fraud;
(4) there was adequate capital available without it[13].

Liability was limited to the amount unpaid on the shares in the case of members of companies which had:

(1) at least 25 members holding £10 shares, of which 20% had been paid up;
(2) three-quarters of their capital subscribed; and
(3) the word 'limited' after the company's name[14].

The first requirement was introduced in the House of Lords because of a reluctance to extend the principle of limited liability to small trading companies. The Act was rapidly replaced by the Joint Stock Companies Act 1856, a comprehensive measure which abolished the old system of provisional registration and introduced the modern form of constitution consisting of memorandum and articles of association and separate winding-up procedures. Incorporation and limited liability could be had by any company mustering seven subscribers. The safeguards of 1855 were brushed aside in

---

10   See H N Butler (1986) 6 International Review of Law and Economics 169.
11   (1852) 21 LJQB 98.
12   139 Official Report (3rd series) (1855), p 321.
13   See B C Hunt *The Development of the Business Corporation in England 1800–1867* (1936), ch VI; R R Formoy *The Historical Foundations of Modern Company Law* (1923), section V and (1855) XXIV Law Times 142.
14   18 & 19 Vict, c 133.

the name of laissez-faire. Only the label 'Limited' and the facility of searching the public register protected the public. From then on we see the growth of the modern companies legislation. The first modern Companies Act is said to be the Act of 1862 which was a more comprehensive measure than the earlier legislation and was described by Sir Francis Palmer, the Victorian company law expert, as the 'Magna Carta of co-operative enterprise'. It was a major act of consolidation and also introduced companies limited by guarantee and unlimited companies, as well as more detailed provisions on winding up. It is after this Act that we see the incorporation for the first time of many industrial enterprises.

It is possible, as Maitland[15] argued, that if limited liability had not been introduced as a matter of law, it would have developed as a matter of contract. Its importance from an economic point of view[16] was that it eliminated the need for a number of separate contracts and substituted the separate capital of the company for the private property of the individual shareholders who might constantly change. In doing so it cheapened transaction costs, reduced risk for investors by transferring it to trade creditors and thereby also cheapened the cost of credit. It thus facilitated the raising of large masses of capital and the development of new industries at home and abroad. The number of incorporations rose dramatically in the period after 1856.

Major trends in the law between 1862 and 1972

Since much of what followed will be dealt with in detail later, we shall concentrate on the major trends in the legislation and case law between 1862 and the present day. The practice developed of having major reviews and consolidation statutes approximately every 20 years. Thus there was major legislation in 1908, 1929 and 1948. This was broken in the period after 1948 when successive governments failed to implement the totality of the Jenkins Report. There was piecemeal reform but no major consolidation until 1985.

In this period there are two rival approaches to companies—what we might call the *utility* approach and the *responsibility* approach[17]. The 1844 and 1855 Acts were largely based on the utility approach—the recognition that the company performed rational economic and social ends and was to be encouraged. Consistent with this approach was the permission given to companies to reduce their capital, to alter their objects clauses, the recognition and privileges given to the private company and the gradual recognition of management autonomy and the parent and subsidiary relationship. In the case law the same trend is marked by the recognition of the floating charge as a flexible species of security over the undertaking of companies and the reluctance of the courts to overrule business judgments.

However, it is arguable that the trend towards responsibility has been even stronger. From the beginning there has been a policy of requiring disclosure by companies of basic data by registration with the Registrar of Companies. Today the disclosure obligations extend to a wide range of information. This is mainly statute law. In the case law, the trend towards responsibility is manifest in the ultra vires doctrine which restricted corporate activity to the objects in the objects clause and matters incidental thereto. In fact the justification of the doctrine contained some recognition of the privilege approach to incorporation. The trend towards responsibility can also be seen

---

15   *Maitland*, op cit, p 392.
16   See R Posner *Economic Analysis of Law* (3rd edn, 1986), ch 14; P Halpern, M Trebilcock and S Turnbull (1980) 30 U of TLJ 117; O E Williamson (1981) 19 J Econ Lit 1537.
17   *Hurst*, op cit, passim.

in the development as a protection for creditors of the capital maintenance doctrine which prohibited the watering down of share capital by transactions at patent undervalue, the trafficking by a company in its own shares and the distribution of improper dividends. Gradually the courts realised that minority shareholders in a small incorporated firm could be locked in and unable to curb the power of the majority within the orthodox decision-making framework. A balance was struck between the business judgment rule and the need for intervention to prevent manifest wrongdoing or an interference with private rights. The case law, however, did not provide a particularly satisfactory system of minority shareholder remedies and this was eventually supplemented by statute. Whereas shareholders generally have some part in the constitutional structure of the company, creditors do not. Their remedies are essentially contractual and centre around the presence or absence of security and the type of security which they hold. Creditors' remedies were improved by the modern system of winding up—a form of corporate bankruptcy—which started in 1856 and assumed its modern form ultimately in 1929.

Much modern reform legislation has been aimed at safeguarding the market for investment capital and more recently the market for control. The first is concerned with disclosure on public issues of securities, continuing disclosure and the prevention of fraudulent market practices. The second is concerned with the regulation of mergers and takeovers of companies. In both these areas the public interest is involved.

An important development in the post-war period was the growth of a sophisticated system of self-regulation which supplemented the legislation and case law[18]. Historically the burden of supervision has rested with The Stock Exchange which from its earliest period has evolved rules to deal with membership of the Exchange and market practice[19]. It has more recently formulated detailed regulations with which companies whose shares are listed or dealt in on The Stock Exchange must comply. These have been the subject of EU directives and the present law is set out in the Financial Services Act 1986. Also the Bank of England as the centre of the City of London's financial activities maintains a general oversight of the financial system, and in particular the financial securities markets. The Bank of England has taken a leading role in the development of self-regulation of the securities market. It was on the instigation of the Governor of the Bank of England that the City Working Party was set up in 1959 which led to the formulation of a City Code on Takeovers and Mergers and the establishment of a Panel on Takeovers and Mergers, the latter with an appellate structure. There are a number of other city institutions which represent various sectors of the securities industry. However, there has been growing dissatisfaction with the system and there has been a trend towards increased legal regulation[20], culminating in the Labour Government's proposal in 1997 for the Financial Services Authority.

4   1972 UNTIL THE PRESENT DAY

On 1 January 1973, the UK joined the European Economic Community, now the European Union (EU). This meant that it became subject to the provisions of the Treaty of Rome which dealt with the harmonisation and unification of company laws. We

---

18   See B Rider and E Hew (1977) 19 Mal L Rev 144.
19   See its evidence to the Committee to Review the Functioning of Financial Institutions.
20   The Gower Report on Investor Protection (Cmnd 9125) 1984; *The Times*, 18 October 1984; the White Paper, *Financial Services in the United Kingdom* (Cmnd 9432) 1985.

will discuss the relevant provisions of the Treaty and the various measures in Chapter 3, so here we shall be brief[1]. In s 9 of the European Communities Act 1972, the UK implemented the First Directive of the EU on company law harmonisation. The major effect of this was to add a complicated gloss to the ultra vires doctrine and directors' authority[2]. The Companies Act 1980 implemented the Second Directive of the EU which deals with share capital and classification of companies[3] and the Companies Act 1981 implemented the Fourth Directive on company accounts. The Stock Exchange (Listing) Regulations 1984[4] issued under the 1972 Act gave effect to three directives of the EU[5] to harmonise the law and practice of the grant and maintenance of listings on stock exchanges of member states. These are now consolidated in the Financial Services Act 1986. There are a number of further measures in the pipeline, prominent among which are worker participation in corporate decision making and the project for a European Company, which would be a genuine transnational company.

In 1985–86, the companies legislation was the subject of a major consolidation with an attempt to restate the law in a more rational shape and to modernise the language. The principal Act is now the Companies Act 1985. There are separate Acts dealing with business names and insider trading. An Insolvency Act was passed in 1985 which was consolidated in the Insolvency Act 1986. This legislation attempts to co-ordinate personal and corporate insolvency into the same statute. It does this by a mixture of consolidation and reform. In the Financial Services Act 1986 a new regime was set up to replace the CSI. This introduced a system of self-regulation within an over-arching legal framework. The system has been a pyramid of power descending from the Secretary of State for Trade and Industry through the Securities and Investments Board (SIB) to a cluster of self-regulatory agencies. The Financial Services Act requirements replace the earlier law contained in the Prevention of Fraud (Investment) Act 1958 and the Stock Exchange (Listing) Regulations 1984. In May 1997 the new Labour Government announced a radical new system of regulation. The new framework takes bank supervision away from the Bank of England and places it with an enhanced Securities and Investment Board (SIB). *The Economist* of 24 May 1997, at p 13, stated that 'later the plan is to fold into the SIB the existing array of city regulators (one for each main branch of the financial services industry), shifting from a regime based on self-regulation to one based on statute'. SIB is to have tougher powers as well as a wider remit. Building societies may also be put under its supervision later. On 28 October 1997 SIB changed its name to the Financial Services Authority (FSA).

As if to demonstrate the innate capacity of UK corporate laws to resist rational and systematic structure Parliament enacted the Companies Act 1989[6]. This implemented the Seventh EU Directive on Consolidated Accounts[7] and the Eighth Directive on Regulation of Auditors[8]. The remainder of the Act attempted to complete the reform of ultra vires and constructive notice, made interim reformed to company charges, strengthened the range of investigatory powers of the DTI, reformed the competition rules governing mergers, deregulates private companies, modifies the insolvency rules applicable to settlement and clearing systems on financial markets as well as making further amendments to the companies and financial services legislation. Apart from some deregulation of private companies inadequate attention seems to have been paid

---

1   See Chapter 3, post.
2   See Chapter 10, post.
3   See Chapter 4, post.
4   SI 1984/716.
5   See Sch 1 to SI 1984/716.
6   See C Swinson *A Guide to the Companies Act 1989* (1990).
7   26 OJL 193, 18 July 1983.
8   27 OJL 126, 12 May 1984.

to the transaction costs of compliance with UK corporate laws, as opposed to the achievement of small economies in the civil service.

Since 1989, there has been a number of amendments to the 1985 Act resulting from the implementation of the EU directives by statutory instrument. These include amendments relating to company accounts[9]; disclosure requirements for branches of oversea companies;[10] and disclosure of major shareholdings in listed companies[11]. In addition, there has been the introduction of the single member private limited company, implementing the Twelfth Directive by the Companies (Single Member Private Limited Companies) Regulations 1992[12].

There has been legislation to implement the directive on insider dealing[13]. This resulted in the repeal of the Company Securities (Insider Dealing) Act 1985 and its replacement by Part V of the Criminal Justice Act 1993. Currently, the Department of Trade and Industry is reviewing a number of areas of law including company charges, directors' duties and financial assistance in connection with the purchase of shares; and shareholder remedies. As will be seen in a later chapter, the Government has pursued a policy of removing unnecessary statutory burdens from small business. The matter of the law applicable to private companies was referred to the Law Commission for a feasibility study and consultations[14]. Further work has been done on resolutions of private companies[15] and simpler procedures for summary financial statements[16].

To add to the overall complexity, some parts of the legislation passed in 1985-6 and 1989 have not been brought into force. Thus, Part V of the Financial Services Act relating to issues of unlisted companies was not brought into force but was replaced by the Public Offers of Securities Regulations 1995. Part IV of the Companies Act 1989 which deals with registration of charges has also not been brought into force and is the subject of continuing consultation.

To sum up the overall situation, the attempt to rationalise the law by consolidation in 1985-86 has now been frustrated by subsequent developments which have made the law as complex as it has ever been. What is needed is further consolidation at the very least. Indeed, there is much to be said for adopting the approach of the more comprehensive reforms effected in Canada and New Zealand. In both cases the decision has been taken to reform the law, not only in its form, but in its substance, and to produce legislation which is user friendly, leaving the complexities arising from capital raising from the public to be dealt with by a separate regime. Australia has not gone so far and, if anything, has created legislation which is every bit as complex as the UK legislation, but more recently has attempted to temper this by a simplification project. The position of the UK is obviously now tied up with the EU and this has led to much of the recent complexity. Fortunately, there now seems to be something of a lull in the law making by the EU.[17]

---

9   Dir 90/604, [1990] OJ L317/57; implemented by the Companies Act 1985 (Accounts of Small and Medium-Sized Enterprises and Publication of Accounts in ECUS) Regulations 1992, SI 1992 No 2452.
10   Dir 89/666, [1989] OJ L395/36; implemented by the Overseas Companies and Credit and Financial Institutions (Branch Disclosure) Regulations 1992, SI 1992, No 3179.
11   Dir 88/629, [1988] OJ L348/62; implemented by the Disclosure of Interests in Shares (Amendment) Regulations 1993, SI 1993 No 1819.
12   SI 1992 No 1699.
13   Dir 89/592, [1989] OJ L334/30.
14   See *Company Law Review: The Law Applicable to Private Companies*, November 1994, a Consultative Document of the DTI (URN 94/529).
15   See *Resolutions of Private Companies*, February 1995, a Consultative Document of the DTI (URN 95/554).
16   See *Simpler Procedures for Summary Financial Statements*, a Consultative Document of the DTI.
17   Cf Adriaan Dorresteijn, Ina Kuiper and Geoffrey Morse *European Corporate Law* (1994), p 65-66.

If there is one characteristic which distinguishes UK and EU corporate laws from the US it is the level of sophistication of the discussion of policy issues. With rare exceptions[18] there is little sophistication in the law reform debate. The rules often seem to have a mind and will of their own, which, coupled with the increasing bureaucratisation of the reform process, makes formal and substantive rationalisation a difficult goal.

---

18   The Law Commission has recently been given responsibilities in this area. It is to be hoped that this
will improve the quality of the reform debate.

CHAPTER 3

Harmonisation of company law in the EU

There have been European influences on the development of English company law from an early date. The first concepts of corporateness and partnership, as well as the system of double entry bookkeeping, were derived from European ideas[1]. In the nineteenth century the adoption of the modern form of constitution was partly influenced by French ideas, and later the German reforms, which gave legal recognition to private companies, indirectly influenced the adoption of the private/public dichotomy in the UK[2]. Alarm at the rapid technological and scientific advances of Germany at the end of the century was the cause of the adoption of what is now s 4 of CA 1985, which enables a company to alter its objects clause[3]. Connected with these legal influences is the close geographic proximity of England to Europe and the inevitability of trade with Europe. Thus, even before 1973, a UK company such as ICI Ltd could find itself brought before the European Court for violation of the anti-trust laws of the EU[4].

ECONOMIC INTEGRATION UNDER THE TREATY OF ROME

On 1 January 1973, the UK became a member state of the European Communities. The Communities are the European Economic Community, the European Coal and Steel Community and the European Atomic Energy Community. It is with the EC, now the European Union (EU), that we are presently concerned. The EU, as Dr Walter Hallstein, the first President of the EEC Commission, wrote 'is a remarkable legal phenomenon. It is a creation of the law; it is a source of law; and it is a legal system ... The basic law of the European Economic Community, its whole philosophy, is liberal. Its guiding principle is to establish undistorted competition in an undivided market.'[5] In other words, it is equality of treatment between nationals of member states. This philosophy seems based on Adam Smith and Ricardo. The essential doctrine is that

---

1   See Cooke *Corporation, Trust and Company* (1950).
2   See Chapter 2, ante.
3   See *Re Jewish Colonial Trust (Juedische Colonial Bank) Ltd* [1908] 2 Ch 287.
4   Case 48/69: *ICI Ltd v EC Commission* [1972] ECR 619.
5   *Europe in the Making* (1973), p 30.

there is a general presumption in favour of customs unions and other forms of economic integration. Added to this is the more modern argument of increasing returns from economies of scale. However, the market economy is tempered by social welfare considerations, strong public control of agriculture and transport and a measure of public control over the economy[6]. The EU marks a number of steps on the road from a loose co-operation of nation states towards a federation. At the moment the EU remains far from being a single integrated unit and at the same time is faced with increasing international competition which is beginning to erode living standards. In 1985 the Commission published proposals to create a Single European Market. This was embedded in the Commission's White Paper on the Completion of the Single Market. This called for 300 regulatory changes leading to a complete elimination of trade barriers and to the free movement of goods, services, capital and people. This was reviewed by the governments of the member states who committed themselves to it through the package of reforms which were known as the Single European Act. Article 8a of the EC Treaty, as introduced by the Single European Act, set a deadline for completion of this program on 1 January 1993. Advocates of the Single Market wish to see an unobstructed market of great size governed by market forces, not politics or geography[7]. On 1 November 1993, following the Maastricht Treaty on European Union, the European Communities became the European Union (EU). On 1 January 1996 the 15-country-strong EU had a population of more than 370 million people and a land mass stretching from the Mediterranean to the Arctic.

The UK's membership resulted from Treaties of Accession which were given internal effect by the European Communities Act 1972. The 1972 Act provided for the recognition and enforcement of enforceable community rights created or arising by or under the treaties. Thus, we are concerned with the provisions of the Treaty of Rome, further treaties made thereunder or by way of amendment, and secondary legislation adopted by the appropriate institutions under the treaties[8]. Article 189 of the Treaty of Rome defines the principal secondary legislation. A regulation has general application. It is binding in its entirety and directly applicable in all member states. A directive is binding, as to the result to be achieved, upon each member state to which it is addressed, but leaves to the national authorities the choice of form and methods. A decision is binding in its entirety upon those to whom it is addressed, and recommendations and opinions have no binding force. It is further provided under art 190 that regulations, directives and decisions shall state the reasons on which they are based and shall refer to any proposals or opinions which are required to be obtained pursuant to the treaty. Under s 3(1) of the European Communities Act 1972, any question as to the meaning or effect of any of the treaties, or as to the validity, meaning or effect of any community legislation, is to be treated as a question of law and, if not referred to the European Court, be for determination in accordance with the principles laid down by and any relevant decision of the European Court. Section 3(2) provides that judicial notice shall be taken of the treaties, the Official Journal and of any decision or expression of opinion by the European Court. If a member state fails to comply with its obligations under the treaties, it can be brought before the European Court under arts 169 and 170. These articles provide for the action to be brought by the Commission or by another member state. A complicated jurisprudence has developed

6   See E Stein *Harmonization of European Company Laws* (1971), p 6. See too *Programme of the Commission for 1989* EEC Bull Supp 2/89, pp 7–8.
7   See generally Ernst and Whinney *Europe 1992: The Single Market* (1988); N Colchester and D Buchan *Europe Relaunched* (1990); M Silva and B. Sjögren *Europe 1992 and the New World Power Game* (1990).
8   For a useful discussion see T C Hartley *The Foundations of European Community Law* (2nd edn, 1988).

over the meaning of direct applicability and direct effect. If a provision of the treaty or secondary legislation has direct effect, then an individual or a company may have locus standi. This is a developing, complicated area of law with which it is not possible to deal in detail here[9].

One species of decision is judical decisions of the European Court of Justice. Many of these are only indirectly relevant to company law. However, there have been recently some decisions which have turned expressly on company law matters. In *Powell Duffryn plc v Wolfgang Petereit*,[10] the court decided that a choice of forum clause in the articles of association of a company dealing with disputes between the company and its shareholders was covered by art 17 of the Brussels Convention on Jurisdiction and Enforcement of Judgements in Civil Matters. The court held that the articles constitute a contract for this purpose. This applies even to shareholders who have acquired their shares subsequently, since they become bound by the contract once they are entered on the register of members. Of more general interest is *Marleasing SA v La Comercial Internacional de Alimentación SA*[11] In that case Spain had failed to implement the company law directives. As a result Spanish Law provided for more grounds of nullification of a company than allowed by the First Company Law Directive. The court held that national law had to be interpreted as containing only the nullity grounds allowed by the Directive. In that case the court decided that, in interpreting national law implementation of company law directives, the national courts are bound to interpret their law in the light of the text and purpose of the directive. This highlights the procedure under art 177 of the Treaty of Rome of applying to the European Court of Justice for preliminary rulings. The tendency at the moment, nevertheless, is for national courts to interpret the new laws in conformity to existing national law and to frustrate 'integration from below'. This has been criticised[12] but as Professor Andre Tunc has written, '...the law is now so bulky and changing so fast that one can be excused for concentrating his energy on keeping abreast of national developments.'[13]

The role of the European Court of Justice in relation to Company Law matters can be summed up as follows:

(1)   interpretation of the EC Treaty relevant to company law matters, eg Art 52;
(2)   interpretation of the company law directives;
(3)   remedies against failure to implement the directives.
(4)   company law matters in the context of the Brussels Convention.

Relevant provisions of the Treaty of Rome

Article 2 of the Treaty sets out the goals of the EU. These are, by establishing a common market and progressively approximating the economic policies of member states, to promote throughout the community a harmonious development of economic activities, a continuous and balanced expansion, an increase in stability, an accelerated raising of the standard of living and closer relations between the states belonging to it. Article 3 provides that for the purposes set out in art 2, the activities of the EU shall include, inter alia, (c) the abolition, as between member states of obstacles to freedom of

9   Ibid, ch 7.
10   Case C-214/89: [1992] ECR I-1745.
11   Case C-106/89: [1990] ECR I-4135.
12   See Klaus J Hopt 'European Community Legal Harmonisation and the Business Enterprise' in Klaus J Hopt and Eddy Wymeersch (eds) *European Company and Financial Law* (1991), p 22; *Corporate Law - The European Dimension* (1991).
13   'Corporate Law', Richard M. Buxbaum (ed) in *European Business Law* (1991), p 203.

movement for persons, services and capital, and (h) the approximation of the laws of member states to the extent required for the proper functioning of the common market.

The Treaty recognises certain basic freedoms. These include the right of establishment. Article 52 provides for the abolition of restrictions on the freedom of establishment of nationals of a member state in the territory of another. This includes freedom to set up and manage undertakings, in particular companies or firms within the meaning of art 58. Article 58 gives a broad definition of companies or firms. It means companies or firms constituted under civil or commercial law, including co-operative societies, and other legal persons governed by public or private law, save for those which are non-profit-making. Article 54 provides for the drawing up of a general programme for the abolition of existing restrictions on freedom of establishment within the Community. Under art 54(3)(g) the Council and the Commission are instructed to carry out their duties 'by co-ordinating to the necessary extent the safeguards which, for the protection of the interests of members and others, are required by member states of companies or firms within the meaning of the second paragraph of art 58 with a view to making such safeguards equivalent throughout the EU'.

Article 100 is a general provision on approximation of laws. It provides that the Council shall, acting unanimously on a proposal from the Commission, issue directives for the approximation of such provisions laid down by law, regulation or administrative action in member states and directly affect the establishment or functioning of the common market. The Parliament and the Economic and Social Committee shall be consulted in the case of directives whose implementation would, in one or more member states, involve the amendment of legislation. Articles 100A and 100B which were added by the Single European Act provide for qualified majorities in certain cases.

Article 220 provides that member states shall, so far as is necessary, enter into negotiations with a view to securing inter alia the mutual recognition of companies or firms within the meaning of the second paragraph of art 58, the retention of legal personality in the event of transfer of their seat from one country to another, and the possibility of mergers between companies or firms governed by the laws of different countries; the simplification of formalities governing the reciprocal recognition and enforcement of judgments of courts or tribunals and of arbitration awards. These negotiations will lead to international treaties which will supplement the existing treaties. An example is the 1968 convention on mutual recognition of companies. Article 221 provides for abolition of all discriminatory provisions in the laws of member states with respect to equity participation in companies.

Lastly, art 235 contains sweeping-up provisions. If action by the EU proves necessary to attain one of the objectives of the EU and the Treaty of Rome has not provided the necessary powers, the Council shall, acting unanimously on a proposal from the Commission and after consulting the Parliament, take the appropriate measures.

Patterns of legal integration

The three basic legal techniques of integration used are, therefore:

(1) the removal of all restrictions which discriminate on the basis of nationality including restrictions on freedom of establishment;

(2) the putting into effect of common rules and common policies;

(3) the approximation of national laws under art 3(h)[14].

---

14   *Stein*, op cit, pp 6–9. See also Richard Buxbaum and Klaus J Hopt *Legal Harmonisation and the Business Enterprise* (1988), chs 3 and 4.

The Treaty also uses the terms 'harmonisation', which English lawyers tend to prefer, and 'co-ordination', but there seems to be little consistency in the way in which they are used and there seems to be no meaningful difference between them[15]. All three terms fall short of unification.

The usual pattern is for drafts of proposals to be prepared by the Commission. They may then be discussed in a group convened by the Commission and consisting of 'experts' (ie officials) from member states and may be circulated by the Commission to interested outside bodies. After adoption by the Commission as formal proposals, they are sent to the European Parliament and the Economic and Social Committee for their opinions. In the light of these opinions the Commission may amend their proposals, before presenting them to the Council of Ministers for discussion in a working group of officials from the various member states. Such discussions are normally chaired by officials from the member state holding the Presidency of the Council of Ministers. They are subsequently referred to the Committee of Permanent Representatives (COREPER) which in turn refers them to the Council of Ministers itself for final decision[16].

Under the European Communities (Amendment) Act 1986, which implemented the Single European Act signed at Luxembourg and The Hague on 17 and 28 February 1986, proposals based on arts 7, 49, 54(2), 56(2) (second sentence), 57 (excluding the second sentence of para 2), 100A, 100B, 118A, 130E and 130Q(2) of the Treaty were made subject to qualified majority voting and to a new 'cooperation procedure' with the European Parliament. As a result of the Maastricht Treaty, the position of the European Parliament has been further strengthened and a 'codecision' procedure introduced which requires the assent of Parliament to certain matters which include steps to implement a single internal market. The relevance of the 'co-operation' and 'co-decision' procedures in relation to company law seems small.

PROGRESS TO DATE

Within the EU, some progress has been made on three broad fronts. First, there are the directives prepared under the provisions of art 54(3)(g); secondly, there are treaties drawn up under art 220, and thirdly, there is a draft regulation providing a statute for a European company drawn up under art 235. Let us look at each of these in turn.

The First Directive (68/151/EEC)[17]   This was adopted on 9 March 1968 and mainly provided for relief against the doctrine of ultra vires and limits on directors' authority as well as providing for some basic publicity. The Directive was implemented by the UK in s 9 of the European Communities Act 1972[18].

The Second Directive (77/91/EEC)[19]   This Directive provides for minimum requirements regarding the formation of companies and the maintenance, increase and

---

15   Ibid, p 9. On Community policy with regard to approximation of laws, see the lecture given by Dr C D Ehlermann, Director General of the Legal Service of the Commission published in App 3(b) of 'Approximation of Laws under Article 100 of the EEC Treaty' 22nd Report (1977–78) of the House of Lords Select Committee on the European Communities ('HLSC') (HL 131) (1977–78).
16   This summary of procedure is taken more or less verbatim from *The Single Market—Company Law Harmonisation* published by the Department of Trade and Industry.
17   OJ Special edition 1968(1), pp 41–45.
18   See D D Prentice (1973) 89 LQR 518; J H Farrar and D G Powles (1973) 36 MLR 270; J G Collier and L S Sealy (1973) CLJ 1. See now CA 1985, ss 35 and 35A.
19   20 OJ, L 26, 31 January 1977, pp 1–13.

reduction of capital. It provides, amongst other things, for a new classification of private and public companies and introduces compulsory valuation for non-cash consideration provided to a public company in consideration of its allotment of its shares. This Directive was implemented by the Companies Act 1980 in the UK[20].

The Third Directive (78/855/EEC)[1]   This provides for co-ordination of procedures applying to internal mergers within a member state. It only applies to public companies and to what in English company law are known as reconstructions. It will be applicable mainly where by means of a scheme of arrangement under s 425 of CA 1985 the assets and liabilities of company A are transferred to another, B, in consideration of the issue of shares in B issued to the shareholders of A. A is then dissolved. This procedure is rarely used and is mainly used on a merger of investment trusts. In some minor respects, it is stricter than English law and required changes in ss 425–430. The Directive[2] does not apply to a takeover by acquisition of shares. The Companies (Mergers and Divisions) Regulations 1987, SI 1987/1991 implement it by inserting s 427A and Sch 15A in the CA 1985.

The Fourth Directive (78/660/EEC)[3]   This deals with disclosure of financial information and the contents of a company's annual accounts. This Directive was revised in the light of the UK's membership and now contains a basic requirement that the accounts give 'a true and fair view'. The Directive was implemented in the UK by the Companies Act 1981[4].

Draft Fifth Directive[5]   This deals with the important topics of company structure and worker participation and has been the subject of much controversy[6]. The present position is that the Commission's modified proposal is under consideration by a Council Working Group of officials from member states and the Commission. It is anticipated that discussion of the draft will take several more years. The new draft provides for a distinction between directors of a public limited company who will be responsible for management and those responsible for their supervision. At the end of 1983, the Commission announced an alteration so that this distinction could be achieved either through a two-tier board or a conventional one-tier board as in the UK. On the one-tier board, there would be a division between executive directors who would manage, and non-executive directors who would supervise. The implementation of this distinction as a matter of law would require changes to English law.

Employee participation in corporate decision-making would be required to take one of the following forms.

(1)   through board representation at the supervisory level;
(2)   by means of a works council; or

20   See D D Prentice *The Companies Act 1980* (1980); J Tinnion *The Companies Act 1980* (1980).
1   21 OJ, L 295, 20 October 1978, pp 36–43.
2   See 'Implementation of the Third EC Directive on Company Law', and explanatory and commentative note by the Department of Trade, London 1982.
3   21 OJ, L 222, 14 August 1978, pp 11–31.
4   See G W Eccles and J Cox *Companies Act 1981* (1982).
5   This Directive was first proposed in 1972; see Official Journal of the European Communities 1972 No C 131/49. The current version is that put forward in 1991 (OJC 321/9 of 12 December 1991). See the Green Paper on Employee Participation and Company Structure in the European Communities, EEC Bull Supp 8/75. See C M Schmitthoff [1983] JBL 456 and the memoranda of the Law Society's Company Law Committee of March 1984 and April 1990. For useful recent discussion see J J Du Plessis and J Dine [1997] JBL 23.
6   See J Welch (1983) 8 ELR 83. See also W Kolvenbach (1990) 11 University of Pennsylvania J of International Business Law 709 at 720–733.

(3) through collective agreements giving the same rights as (1) or (2).

Further options are included in respect of employee participation in groups of companies.

In addition to these major provisions, the latest draft also includes provision in respect of (a) the duties and liability of directors; (b) the powers of the general meeting; (c) the rights of shareholders and in particular minority shareholders; (d) approval of annual accounts; and (e) the functions and liability of auditors. With regard to (a) there is a general provision for personal liability for loss suffered by the company as a result of breaches of law, the corporate constitution or other wrongful acts. Liability is to be joint and several which would involve a change in English law and arguably lead to more effective monitoring of management by management. An individual director may be exonerated if he can prove that no fault is attributable to him personally. The draft does not define the standard of care required of directors although the Commission's Explanatory Memorandum to the original proposal in 1972 suggested that 'other wrongful acts' might include negligence and would arguably go further than the current law. With regard to (b), shareholders are given slightly more rights in respect of the convening of meetings. As regards (c), arts 16–18 allow a minority shareholder to bring a derivative action on behalf of the company, even where the general meeting has expressly renounced its right to bring proceedings provided that the plaintiff shareholder voted against the resolution or made objection which was recorded in the minutes. Proceedings can be instituted by a simple majority of the shareholders or in the case of a derivative action by shareholders holding 5% of the issued capital or shares to the value of 100,000 ECUs. An unsuccessful shareholder who fails to establish reasonable grounds for commencing the proceedings may be ordered to pay costs. Presumably in English law, the new interlocutory procedures would protect him against this risk. Under the original art 19, a derivative action could also be brought by a creditor who was unable to obtain payment and such an action would not be affected by any waiver by the company of a breach of duty. This has been deleted and replaced by a vague provision which leaves the matter to be determined by the laws of the member state.

Other important provisions prevent a shareholder from voting on an issue where there is a conflict of interest between the company and him personally. This would go further than the existing English law. Another provision renders void shareholder agreements whereby a shareholder undertakes always to vote in a certain way. This would involve an alteration of the English law. There are provisions for compulsory reserves and appropriation of profits. The latter would have the effect of shifting the power to determine dividends to the general meeting. Both of these would involve a change in English law.

We will not comment on the detailed provisions in respect of auditors and accounts.

In addition there is Directive 94/95/EC of 22 September 1994 on the establishment of a European Works Council and also a draft Directive on procedures for informing and consulting employees which overlaps with the Fifth Directive[7]. This is sometimes known as the Vredeling Directive. It does not form part of the company law harmonisation programme as it applies to other employers as well as companies. It would require head offices of large companies to inform and consult employees of subsidiaries or separate establishments through local management. The Department of Employment and the Department of Trade and Industry issued a consultative document in November 1983 on both draft directives. The basic attitude of the government was in favour of voluntary rather than compulsory adoption. It took the view that the introduction of community-wide legislation in this area would contribute

7   26 OJ, C 217, 12 August 1983, pp 3–16.

nothing to the establishment of a common market in goods and services but would increase employers' costs and damage the competitive position of industry in the community. Legislation of this kind would do nothing to cope with rising unemployment but at the same time be likely to disrupt existing industrial relations practices. This undoubtedly overstates the case. Many of the proposals are attractive and would involve considerable improvement to English law. On the other hand, the cost factor must be weighed up and reforms should not be introduced if the costs are prohibitive.

The Sixth Directive (82/891/EEC)[8]   This was adopted on 17 December 1982 and deals with scissions or divisions. 'Scission' means the transaction whereby a public company ('plc') transfers to a number of public companies ('plcs') within the same member state which are already incorporated or yet to be formed, all its assets and liabilities in exchange for the issue of shares to the shareholders of the original company. It is the logical opposite of merger and might be termed demerger. The Directive should have been implemented by 1 February 1986 but this was delayed. It is now implemented by the Companies (Mergers and Divisions) Regulations 1987, SI 1987/1991.

The Seventh Directive (83/349/EEC)[9] This deals with group accounts and supplements the Fourth Directive. It was adopted on 13 June 1983 and was implemented by CA 1989.

The Eighth Directive (84/253/EEC)[10]   This deals with the qualifications and independence of auditors of both public and private companies[11] and was adopted on 10 April 1984. This was implemented by CA 1989.

Draft Ninth Directive   This draft, which has never been officially published in the Official Journal, deals with certain aspects of the group relationship[12]. The preliminary draft was greatly influenced by the German law relating to groups. A revised text was circulated informally to member states in December 1984. The revised text seeks to provide an organised legal structure for the 'unified management' of a plc which is controlled by any other undertaking (whether a company or not) and of that other undertaking. The Directive will also set out rules for the conduct of groups which are not subject to 'unified management' although in this case the rules would apply to the relations between the parent or dominant undertaking and those members of the group which are plcs. Unless the dominant undertaking formalises its relationship by one of the methods specified by the Directive it will be liable for any losses sustained by the dependent company resulting from that influence and attributable to a fault in management or to action which was not in its interests. There are to be two methods for constituting a group—the control contract or a unilateral declaration of control. In addition, the Directive would leave member states free to introduce other methods of achieving the same result. The revised text was the subject of a consultative document published in 1985 but no action is expected in the near future.

---

8   25 OJ, L 378, 31 December 1982, pp 47–54. See 'Company Law: Scissions' 43rd Report (1979–80) of the HLSC (HL 206) (1979–80).
9   26 OJ, L 193, 18 July 1983, pp 1–17. See 'Group Accounts' 18th Report (1981–82) of the HLSC (HL 214) (1981–82). See (1984) 9 ELR 143; S Turley (1986) 7 Co Law 10.
10   27 OJ, L 126, 12 May 1984, pp 20–26.
11   See 'Qualifications of Company Auditors', 12th Report (1979–80) of the HLSC (HL 60) (1979–80).
12   See F Woolridge *Groups of Companies* (1981); T Hadden *The Control of Corporate Groups* (1983), p 42; J Welch (1986) 7 Co Law 112; K. Gleichmann 'The Law of Corporate Groups in the EC' in D Sugarman and G Teubner (eds) *Regulating Corporate Groups in Europe* (1990).

Proposal for a Tenth Directive[13] This proposal is designed to facilitate on a Community-wide basis the type of merger between plcs dealt with in the Third Directive. Work on a draft convention on this subject started before the enlargement of the EC but was then suspended. Meetings were resumed in 1984 at which it was decided that the draft convention should be converted into a proposal for a Directive which was adopted by the Commission on 4 January 1985. The negotiations on this are currently blocked.

The Eleventh Directive[14]   The Commission has adopted a proposal for a directive dealing with disclosure requirements in respect of branches opened in a member state by certain types of companies governed by the law of another state. The directive was implemented in 1992.

The Twelfth Directive[15]   This allows private companies with only one member. This is permitted already in a number of jurisdictions.

Proposal for a Thirteenth Directive[16]   This deals with takeovers and is influenced by the City of London Takeover Code. It is dealt with in detail in Chapters 35 and 41. The proposal has been strongly attacked. The UK Government is concerned that it is too inflexible and may inhibit takeovers. On the other hand, other member states have criticised it because it opens the door to hostile takeovers by blocking certain takeover defences. The position regarding takeovers differs between member states. For example, in Germany the practice is for shares to be held by banks for their own account or for their clients and thus a takeover of a German listed company cannot be effected without the consent of the banks involved.[17] An amended proposal was issued in 1996.

Directives on prospectuses[18]   The first relates to the issue and contents of prospectuses and the object is to co-ordinate national requirements for the admission of securities to listing. This was implemented in the UK by The Stock Exchange (Listing) Regulations 1984[19] made under the European Communities Act 1972, together with further directives (79/279/EEC) and (82/121/EEC) which relate to admission to listing on a stock exchange and continuing disclosure. These are now consolidated in the Financial Services Act 1986. There is a further Directive adopted on 22 June 1987 providing for mutual recognition of listing particulars. This requires a prospectus and vetting by the competent authority[20] which in the UK is the Council of the Stock Exchange. Directive 90/211/EEC (OJL 112/24 of 3 May 1990) allows for recognition of a public offer prospectus as an admission prospectus in the case of a multi-jurisdiction offering. There is also the so-called 'Eurolist Directive' (Directive 94/18/EC of 30

13   Bull Supp 1985/3; 28 OJ, C 23, 25 January 1985, pp 11–15. See J Welch (1986) 7 Co Law 69.
14   32 OJ 1989, L 395, 30 December 1989.
15   32 OJ 1989, L 395/40, 30 December 1989.
16   32 OJ, C 64, 14 March 1989, pp 8–14; Amended Proposal (COM (90) 416 final), Sept 14 1990, OJC 162/5 of 6 June 1996. See LS Sealy 'The Draft Thirteenth EC Directive on Take-overs' in M Anderras and S Kenyon-Slade *EC Financial Market Regulation and Company Law* (1993), ch 9; J Dine (1996) 17 Co Law 248.
17   See Adriaan Dorresteijn, Ina Kuiper and Geoffrey Morse, *European Corporate Law* (1994), p 63; JMM Maeijer and K Green (eds) *Defensive Measures against Hostile Takeovers in the Common Market* (1990).
18   See 22 OJ, L 66, 16 March 1979, pp 21–32; 23 OJ, L 100, 17 April 1980, pp 1–26; 25 OJ, L 48, 20 February 1982, pp 26–29; 30 OJ, L 185, 4 July 1987, pp 81–83. See too 32 OJ, C 101, 22 April 1989, p 13; 32 OJ, L 124, 5 May 1989, pp 8–15.
19   SI 1984/716.
20   See also EEC Draft Directive for Prospectuses for Unlisted Securities (80/893) which is the subject of the 43rd Report (1980–81) of the HLSC (HL 271) (1980–81).

May 1994, OJL 135/1 of 31 May 1994) which amended the 1980 prospectus directive in relation to multi-jurisdictional admissions to listing. These have been implemented by the Public Offers of Securities Regulations 1995 (SI 1995 No 1537).

Amongst other matters that have been or are currently under consideration are European Economic Interest Groupings[1], takeover formalities and defences in different member states[2], liquidations, reservations of property clauses, insider trading and disclosure of substantial shareholdings. A European Economic Interest Grouping means a new legal form enabling undertakings in different member states to establish common, non-profit support activities with unlimited liability. The regulation came before the House of Lords Select Committee on the European Communities in 1984 and was adopted by the Council of Ministers on 25 July 1985[3]. This was supplemented by the European Economic Interest Grouping Regulations 1989 (SI 1989 No 638) and there are now over a hunderd registered at Companies House. Liquidations and reservation of property clauses are no longer on the agenda and action has now been taken in respect of inside trading and disclosure of substantial shareholdings.

On 29 February 1968, the original member states of the EU other than the Netherlands signed the convention on the mutual recognition of companies and legal persons[4]. The convention was to apply to all companies incorporated in any member state and would include an English partnership. Recognition was to be accorded when the company has its statutory registered office in one of the member states. This would be subject to certain exceptions based on the principle of the real seat. After much discussion, the member states have now decided to abandon the project. Mutual recognition occurs in practice anyway, without the necessity of a Convention.

A draft convention has been prepared dealing with bankruptcy, winding-up, arrangements, compositions and similar proceedings[5]. This supplements the convention on mutual recognition of judgments which has now been given internal effect by legislation[6]. It has undergone a great deal of revision, particularly as a result of UK membership. This in essence provides for the rationalisation of bankruptcy, winding up and analogous proceedings in the EU. First, it sets out detailed rules to enable bankruptcy jurisdiction to be vested in a single and appropriate national court. Secondly, it seeks to secure that the liquidator appointed by the court has extensive authority to administer the insolvent estate, wherever situated in the EU. Thirdly, it aims at simplification of the liquidator's duties in collecting assets and determining claims by a limited measure of harmonisation and identification of applicable law. Fourthly, it aims at simplification of the rules and reduction of the cost for a foreign creditor making a claim. The draft convention was debated in the House of Lords Select Committee on the EU in 1981 and a Council Working Group carried out a second reading of the text in 1984. The convention is likely to come into effect soon.

---

1   See 31 OJ, C 153, 11 June 1987, pp 8–10; S Israel (1988) 9 Co Law 14; 25th Report of the HLSC 1984.
2   See C Bradley (1986) 7 Co Law 131; J Dine (1988) 9 Co Law 56.
3   28 OJ, L 199, 31 July 1985, pp 1–9.
4   EEC Bull Supp 2/69; B Goldman *European Commercial Law* (1973), p 389; G K Morse [1972] JBL 195.
5   See Report of the Advisory Committee on the Draft Convention (Cmnd 6602). See also 'Bankruptcy Convention' 26th Report (1980–81) of the HLSC (HL 175) (1980–81). See M Hunter QC (1972) 21 ICLQ 682, (1976) 25 ICLQ 310; I Fletcher (1977) 2 ELR 15; J H Farrar [1977] JBL 320; F Dahan (1996) 17 Co Law 181.
6   The Convention on Jurisdiction and the Enforcement of Judgements in Civil and Commercial Matters, dated 27 September 1968 and amended on 9 October 1978 (1978) OJC 304, 30 October; (1979) OJC 59, 5 March.

A further draft convention dealing with international mergers of companies[7] has been superseded by the proposal for the Tenth Directive and considerable work has been done on harmonisation of the law relating to disclosure of information to employees on a merger[8]. An EU Mergers Regulation was adopted in 1990 to implement a new regime of competition law within the Community. This is dealt with in Chapter 42[9].

The last measure to be discussed is the most ambitious. This is the draft regulation for a European company[10]. The proposal goes beyond harmonisation and provides for an additional form of incorporation which will have registration with the Community. It will be available when two or more limited companies merge or form a joint holding or subsidiary company. Much work on this project was done by Professor Pieter Sanders of the Netherlands, although the French claim some responsibility for the paternity of the project. The project has been under debate for 25 years but acquired a momentum as part of the proposals for 1992. The Commission adopted an amended draft in April 1996 as a result of the report of a group of experts chaired by Etienne Davignon and this is the subject of a Consultative Document by the Department of Trade and Industry of July 1997. The draft is discussed in Chapter 42, post, when we consider cross-frontier mergers.

The European company may be compared with the European Economic Interest Grouping. The latter is to facilitate joint ventures and hence is very flexible. The European Company Proposal, after lying somewhat dormant, featured as part of the programme for 1992. It is seen as a vehicle for cross-frontier mergers.

THE FUTURE

The tactics employed by the Commission have in the past been described as 'salami tactics'. In other words, they approached the matter slice by slice. This approach was criticised on the basis that it was difficult to agree upon any particular directive without knowing, at least in broad terms, what else was to be done. The counter-argument was that elaboration of a complete uniform Companies Act would take a lot of time and bog down reform within the Community for a long time. In any event, it has been said that the statute for the European company would provide some sort of blueprint. Be that as it may, certain changes took place under the Jenkins presidency.

There was a suspension of work on certain projects and a determination to concentrate on certain key areas. Some real progress was made with company accounts and listing requirements. Work on the draft Fifth Directive has continued, although in its nature it is controversial. The key areas on which the Commission is currently engaged are disclosure, corporate governance and its relationship to the draft Fifth Directive and the statute for a European company. With regard to disclosure, the Commission has participated in the negotiations in the ad hoc expert group on

---

7   See 'International Mergers' 28th Report (1977–78) of the HLSC (HL 159) (1977–78).

8   See 'Employee Consultation' 37th Report (1980–81) of the HLSC (HL 250) (1980–81). See also 'Comparative survey of the protection of employees in the event of the insolvency of their employer in the Member States of the European Communities' Doc V/305/1/76 final (Professor G Schnorr).

9   (1990) OJ, L 257/13 in force 21 September 1990.

10   See *The European Company Statute*, A Consultative Document (July 1997, URN 97/786). See Report of the Select Committee on the EEC, HL. Session 1989–90, 19th Report (HL Paper 81-I); J Dine (1990); 11 Co Law 208. For some earlier discussion see 'Memorandum de la Commission de la CEE sur la création d'une société commerciale européenne' SEC (66) 1250 22 April 1966; 'Projet d'un statut des sociétés anonymes européennes' Doc 16. 205/IV/66, December 1966; See generally *Quo vadis, Jus Societatum?*, ed P Zonderland (1972) and Chapter 42, post.

accounting of the United Nations Centre on Multinationals. On groups the original draft, based heavily on German law, has been the subject of controversy in other member states. This and codetermination have presented obstacles to the implementation of a number of other proposals, including the European Company Proposal. Dorresteijn, Kuiper and Morse in *European Corporate Law*[11] argue that the overall achievements of the harmonisation programme have been impressive, particularly when compared with other areas such as taxation, social policy and competition. Nevertheless, there are questions as to how the particular instruments of harmonisation have been used. First, directives tend to be over-specific and sometimes do not fit too well with national laws. Secondly, some directives, like the fourth and seventh, contain too many options. Thirdly, the harmonisation so far achieved has mainly related to the external structure of the company. Attempts to co-ordinate provisions relating to the internal structure have been unsuccessful. The two striking examples are employee participation and the law of groups.

In considering harmonisation as a whole, remarkably little attention seems to have been paid to the US experience, where at first sight an effective market system seems to work without harmonisation of corporate laws. Indeed, there is said to be a market for corporation statutes. Certainly, there is diversity, but the extent of its importance can be exaggerated. Most of the major corporations are registered in Delaware and many others are incorporated in states which are based on the Model Business Corporation Act. Also, securities regulation is largely federal law.

Although, from time to time, strong criticisms are made of the effect of membership of the EU on reform of English company law, it is interesting to note that the UK is one of the member states which have been most effective in translating the directives into national law. In doing so, however, it is severing many of the traditional links with the US and the Commonwealth and losing many of the benefits of developments in those countries. As Dr Hans Claudius Ficker, a member of the Commission staff, argued expressing his personal view: 'the future development of the harmonised national law must be carried out in common, so that the member states lose their right to independent law reforms. Otherwise new disparities will arise obstructing all common efforts'[12]. The year of 1973 marked a change of direction in English company law reform, the full implications of which are only just beginning to be appreciated. At the moment it is unclear whether the EU will continue its harmonisation programme. The other alternatives are systems of mutual recognition such as have been employed for the financial sector and other less formal methods of unification through the activities of private bodies and systems of self-regulation.

---

11   Op cit pp 64-66.
12   'The EEC Directives on Company Law Harmonisation' in Clive M Schmittoff (ed) *The Harmonisation of European Company Law* (1973) 67. See also G Wolff 'The Commission's Programme for Company Law Harmonisation: The Winding Road to a Uniform European Company Law' in Anderras and Kenyon-Slade, op cit, ch 2.

CHAPTER 4

Classification of firms and companies

We saw in Chapter 1 how economists concentrate on the firm as a unit of ownership and production which comprehends sole traders, partnerships and companies and regard the company as a method of capital raising whereas lawyers put the emphasis on the particular legal forms. The lawyers' conferment of abstract legal personality on the company sometimes leads to strains and tensions in legal decision making. The logic of the former sometimes conflicts with the practicality and justice of the factual situation. It is useful at this stage to compare the economists' and lawyers' alternative systems of classification, since it would be puzzling if there was too wide a divergence between them and the difference would need to be explained. Indeed economic reasoning may sometimes afford a corrective to the abuses of legal logic. One must recognise that the *purposes* of classification may differ. Economics is concerned with a variety of purposes—analysis, explanation, prediction and evaluation—but mainly in the context of rational choice and allocation of scarce resources. Law is principally concerned with social control and regulation. A regulatory scheme should, however, proceed on a rational basis and economics in its new and broadest sense provides an instrumental approach which is compatible with the law pursuing non-economic objectives[1].

CLASSIFICATION OF FIRMS BY SIZE

Business firms are classified by economists in many ways. One obvious way is to attempt some kind of factual classification based on size, but this begs many questions relating to the criteria to be used to measure size. The amount of assets, the aggregate market value of shares, turnover or net income after tax, the return on capital, the number of employees and the number of shareholders[2] can be used, but they are all problematic. The use of assets for instance gives a disproportionate prominence to capital intensive industries, and consequently sales are often taken as an index for some companies. Businesses are roughly classified into small, medium or large, whatever

---

1   See Cento Veljanovski 'Legal Theory, Economic Analysis and the Law of Torts' in W Twining, *Common Law and Legal Theory* (1986), pp 215, 216.
2   See P I Blumberg *The Megacorporation in American Society* (1975), p 21.

criteria are used. Indeed some are so large that they transcend the corporate form and the nation state, as we shall see in Chapter 43. These are called multinationals. Thus there is considerable diversity in size. Coupled with this is diversity of production and organisational structure.

Most firms start as small firms and grow until they reach minimum efficient size. Some firms operate beyond minimum efficient size incurring diseconomies of scale. Some go through the progression to medium and then to large size but the particular events which lead to this and the speed of transition often differ greatly. Much depends on the capacity of the market to absorb new firms.

Small firms

Small firms are either run as sole traders, partnerships or companies. What is a small firm differs according to the type of industry concerned and this also seems to influence the use of the corporate form. In its feasibility study—*Reform of the Law Applicable to Private Companies*—the Law Commission pointed to the lack of consensus as to the meaning of 'small company' and set out nine definitions taken from different sources. These were as follows:[3]

Bolton Report [a]	less than 200 employees	
European Observatory for Small and Medium Size Enterprises	Small	11–100 employees
	Micro	0–10 employees
Banks	up to £1m debit turnover [b]	
Bank of England	up to £10m debit turnover	
VAT Registration Threshold	up to £45,000 turnover [c]	
VAT Threshold for Cash Accounting	up to £350,000 turnover	
Corporation Tax [d]	no more than £300,000 profit	
Companies Act	At least 2 of the following not exceeding	
	turnover	£2.8m
	balance sheet	£1.4m
	employees	50
EC Fourth Directive	At least 2 of the following not exceeding	
	turnover	£4.3m [e]
	balance sheet	£2.1m [f]
	employees	50

---

3   Appendix A of *Company Law Review: The Law Applicable to Private Companies*. A Consultative Document, Department of Trade and Industry, November 1994.

a   Report of the Committee of Inquiry on Small Firms: Small Firms (1971) Cmnd 4811 at p 1.
b   'Debit turnover' is a bank term for the amount spent through the bank.
c   'Turnover' is a business accounting term meaning sales recorded in the year.
d   Income and Corporation Taxes Act 1988, s 13, as amended.
e   5m ecus at 21 March 1994.
f   2.5m ecus at 21 March 1994.

Medium sized firms

The only definition of medium size we have is given in s 248(2) of CA 1985 for accounting purposes. A medium sized company must satisfy two out of the following three criteria:

(1) its turnover must not exceed £11.2 m;
(2) its balance sheet total must not exceed £5.6 m; and
(3) its average number of employees on a weekly basis must not exceed 250.

A medium sized firm is likely to be a private company or private group of companies. The 1985 Act allows such companies to file modified accounts with the Registrar.

Large firms

One could pursue the implicit logic of the 1985 Act and say that a large firm is one which satisfies two out of three of the following criteria:

(1) its turnover exceeds £8 m;
(2) its balance sheet total exceeds £3.9 m; and
(3) its average number of employees exceeds 250.

A large firm will almost certainly be incorporated as a limited liability company and is likely to be a public company. Indeed it will usually be a public company and approximately one fifth of public companies have securities which are listed on The Stock Exchange. If so, they will be subject to the Stock Exchange Listing Rules and provisions of the Financial Services Act 1986 in so far as the latter are not contained in the former. The Stock Exchange generally does not favour applications for listing from companies whose expected total capitalisation is less than £700,000 in the case of shares. Some large firms are multinationals and are dealt with in Chapter 43.

Large listed firms came into existence because entrepreneurs needed to raise capital from a relatively large number of investors. They are characterised by specialised management which tends to be separate from the capital investors and indeed performs a discrete economic function. It has also been argued[4] that limited liability flows logically from the concept of the company as a capital raising mechanism. It should, however, be noted that the argument is not that corporate personality per se entails limited liability but that the capital raising characteristic of public companies does so. It allows individuals to invest a small part of their savings without risking ruin if the company becomes insolvent. Such companies provide a market for investment capital and liquidity for investment through the buying and selling of their securities on the Stock Market. They are also active in the market for corporate control as the bidder or target for a takeover bid. The market for investment capital and the market for corporate control provide ways of monitoring performance of the management of such

4   See H G Manne (1967) 53 Virginia Law Review 259.

companies. The price of the company's securities reflects many factors, but prominent amongst these is the market's appraisal of the efficiency of management. If the price declines, particularly if it falls below asset valuation, it will attract the attention of a bidder who will feel that he or she can make more efficient use of the assets. These market forces all affect the relevant legal norms[5]. Large firms are thus essentially different from small firms in matters other than size.

It seems pretty obvious, therefore, that the size and capital-raising characteristics of a firm are useful starting points for legal classification since larger companies usually:

(1) have specialised management;
(2) have separation of ownership and control;
(3) provide a market for investment capital;
(4) participate in the market for corporate control more regularly.

It is patently unjust to subject a small firm to a disclosure regime appropriate to a large company or multinational[6]. Also the structural problems of such companies are vastly different, as we shall see in later chapters.

CLASSIFICATION OF FIRMS BY REFERENCE TO BASIS OF COMPETITION IN WHICH THEY OPERATE

For the purpose of economic analysis it is also useful to distinguish firms on the basis of the competitive situation in which they operate. Bigness in the economy is not necessarily synonymous with market concentration. There are in theory four basic types of situation: perfect competition, monopolistic competition, monopoly and oligopoly.

A firm operates in perfect competition when the price at which it can profitably sell its product is determined by market forces outside its control. Each business is so small in relation to the total sources of supply that its influence on the price is infinitesimal. Monopoly is the other side of the coin. Here a single seller occupies the whole market, and the product it sells cannot be replaced by close substitutes. Monopolistic competition puts the emphasis on each seller selling a differentiated but substitutable product. Oligopoly is where there are a few sellers in the market and these regard themselves as interdependent.

The common law dealt with competition by the doctrine of restraint of trade. This favours competition and prohibits unreasonable restraints of trade. Popular hostility to abuse of monopolies has been the case throughout much of English history. It is reflected in the classical economic writings of Adam Smith who thought that the principle underlying the successful functioning of a market economy was a pursuit of individual self-interest, controlled through competition. This was his famous 'invisible hand' which led individual self-interest to the common good[7]. We have seen in the previous chapter that early corporateness was associated with monopoly. It should be noted, however, that this was usually in relation to foreign trade and was an early means of social control. Smith was hostile to monopoly and suspicious of the joint stock company. His theory and indeed the common law have been affected by subsequent more complex economic conditions. This has led to monopolies and restrictive practice legislation in the post-war period. Added to this is EU law under arts 85 and 86 of the Treaty of Rome which regulate competition and prohibit abuse of a dominant position. We touch on these in a later chapter.

---

5   See *Hadden*, op cit, passim.
6   See Buchanan *The Economics of Corporate Enterprise* (1937), p 23.
7   *An Inquiry into the Nature and Causes of the Wealth of Nations* (1937).

Although some small firms are able to exploit a monopoly or oligopolistic position for a short time, high profits will attract new entrants, who will compete, given the absence of substantial barriers to entry. Since perfect competition does not exist, most small firms operate in an environment of effective competition in the real world. Indeed, the same is true of most medium sized and large firms. Some large companies and multinationals are, however, able to exploit an oligopolistic position. Competition affects the growth of the firm and the elimination of competition, economies of scale and access to capital are all motives in takeovers and mergers. Competition is also a factor in business failure.

LEGAL CLASSIFICATION OF COMPANIES UNDER THE COMPANIES ACTS

There are two basic systems of legal classification of companies under the Companies Acts, neither of which is now directly concerned with size, but both of which have some bearing on the raising of capital. These are (1) by reference to the liability of members and (2) the public/private dichotomy.

Dealing with (1), registered companies may be:

   (a)   companies limited by shares (this was introduced in 1855);
   (b)   companies limited by guarantee (this was introduced in 1862);
   (c)   unlimited companies (this is the oldest type of company and ultimately dates back to 1844).

In the case of (a), which is the most common type in practice, each member must contribute to the company's assets the amount unpaid on his or her shares. Under s 74(1) of the Insolvency Act 1986, past members are also liable if they were members within one year before the commencement of the winding up and it appears to the court that the existing members are unable to satisfy the contributions required of them; but past members are only liable to the extent unpaid on their former shares before they ceased to be members and for debts contracted before they ceased to be members. The limited liability of members effectively transfers the risk of business failure from them to the creditors. In practice this means trade creditors and involuntary creditors, since finance creditors usually take security and personal guarantees in the case of small firms. In the case of larger firms the limited liability greatly facilitates capital raising from the public.

In the case of (b), the member is contingently liable for the amount which he or she has undertaken to contribute in the event of insolvent winding up. In the case of (c) the member's liability is unlimited if the company is insolvent, although the company has legal personality.

In practice, (b) and (c) are rare. (b) is mainly used for educational or other charitable bodies as an alternative to the trust mechanism.

Until 1907, there was just one basic type of company under the Companies Acts. In that year the public/private dichotomy was introduced. The introduction of the private company was almost by accident. Originally the Loreburn Committee had simply intended it as the basis of exemption from the statement in lieu of prospectus but in the House of Lords it was successfully proposed that it should be exempt from filing a balance sheet. English law did not, like German law, recognise the private company as an institution, sui generis but simply as a species of the genus, limited company[8].

---

8   See C M Schmitthoff 'How the English Discovered the Private Company' in *Quo Vadis, Jus Societatum?* ed P Zonderland (1972), p 183.

The basis of the dichotomy was restrictions on offers to the public of its shares, share transfers and the number of shareholders. Thus to some extent size entered into the classification. The private company was intended for small businesses, the public company for large businesses. However, the method of capital raising was fundamental to the classification.

Because public companies are able to incorporate private companies as subsidiaries, the 1948 Act limited the privilege of not filing accounts to the exempt private company, which corresponded roughly to the small incorporated firm. This continued until the Companies Act 1967 abolished the concept. Apart from the accounting advantages conferred on small and medium sized companies by CA 1985, private companies have had basically the same disclosure obligations as a public company. However, the Companies Act 1989 has relaxed a number of the legal requirements as part of a policy of 'de-regulation'. We shall deal with the matter in more detail later.

The rational basis of classification of the 1900s was abandoned in 1980 in order to implement the Second Directive of the EU. Now CA 1985 defines a public company explicitly and a private company by exclusion. A public company is defined in s 1(3) as a company limited by shares or limited by guarantee and having a share capital (a) whose memorandum states that it is to be a public company and (b) which has complied with the provisions for registration of such a company. This means that its memorandum must be in the form specified by regulations under the Act by virtue of s 3 and it must have a minimum capital of at least £50,000. With effect from 22 December 1980, a company cannot be formed as or become a company limited by guarantee with a share capital. A private company is a company which is not a public company. The only provision still expressly concerned with size and capital raising is s 81 which makes it a criminal offence for a private company (other than a company limited by guarantee and not having a share capital) to offer its securities to the public directly or indirectly. This is now the only real disadvantage of incorporation as a private company which otherwise has substantial advantages over public companies.

The following is a list of the other legal differences between public and private companies:

(i)   public companies must have at least two directors whereas private companies need only have one (CA 1985, s 282(1));

(ii)   in the case of public companies, two or more directors cannot be appointed by a single resolution unless a resolution that it shall be so has first been agreed to without any vote being given against it (s 292);

(iii)   proxies appointed to attend and vote instead of a member of a private company have the same right to speak as the member;

(iv)   accounting records need only be kept for three years in the case of a private company whereas they must be kept for six years in the case of a public company (s 222(4));

(v)   the period for laying and delivering accounts by a private company is 10 months after the end of the account period whereas it is seven months for public companies (s 244(1));

(vi)   the company secretary of a public company must be suitably qualified (s 286);

(vii)   certain pre-emptive rights conferred by ss 89 and 90 may be excluded by a provision in the memorandum or articles of a private company (s 91);

(viii) the stringent rules for payment for shares which regulate non-cash consideration only apply to public companies (s 99 et seq);

(ix)   the obligation to convene an extraordinary general meeting in the event of a serious loss of capital only applies to a public company (s 142);

(x)   the rules relating to treatment of shares held by or on behalf of a company in itself only apply to public companies (s 146);

(xi)   the rules restricting liens and charges by a company on its shares only apply to public companies (s 150);

(xii)   the rules restricting payment of dividends to an amount which does not diminish a company's net assets below its called up share capital and undistributable reserves only apply to public companies (s 264);

(xiii) the directors of a private company are under fewer restrictions in their financial relationship to their company and need make less disclosure in the accounts (s 330 et seq);

(xiv)   the public company registered as such on its original incorporation must obtain a certificate before it carries on business or borrows. The principal significance of this is that the private company does not have to have a minimum capital;

(xv)   a private company may purchase or redeem its own shares out of capital (s 171 et seq);

(xvi)   a private company may provide financial assistance for the purchase of its own shares (s 155 et seq);

(xvii) private companies are not subject to the disclosure of interests in shares provisions of Pt VI of the Act.

(xviii) private companies have been 'deregulated' by CA 1989, ss 113, 116 by allowing written resolutions and elective resolutions to relax formalities in respect of authority to allot shares, laying accounts before general meetings, holding annual general meetings, short notice of meetings and dispensing with the annual appointment of auditors.

Patterns of registration

Table A shows the numbers of private and public companies on the register in Great Britain between 1992–93 to 1996–97[9]. From this it can be seen that public companies are a small percentage of the total population of registered companies.

TABLE A

	Thousands of companies				
	92–93	*93–94*	*94–95*	*95-96*	*96-97*
Public companies					
New incorporations	1.1	1.3	0.9	0.9	1.1
Conversions from private	2.3	2.6	2.9	3.1	3.4
Dissolved	1.1	0.8	1.1	0.9	1.3
In liquidation/course of removal	1.5	1.8	1.8	2.3	1.7
Effective number on register at end of period	11.7	12.0	11.9	11.5	11.7
Public companies as percentage of effective register	1.2%	1.2%	1.2%	1.1%	1.1%

9   *Companies in 1996/97.*

	Thousands of companies				
	92–93	*93–94*	*94–95*	*95-96*	*96-97*
Private companies					
New incorporations	107.6	114.0	130.9	145.7	169.1
Conversions from public	1.0	1.2	1.4	1.6	2.0
Dissolved	152.8	132.9	127.4	105.6	91.5
In liquidation/course of removal	174.3	161.1	140.6	124.4	150.4
Effective number on register at end of period	948.9	944.7	969.9	1,027.3	1,080.2
Of which: Unlimited	3.8	3.7	3.8	3.8	3.9
GB total of effective numbers of public & private companies	960.6	956.7	981.8	1,038.8	1,091.9

Table B shows an analysis of companies on the register at 31 March 1997 on the basis of amount of issued share capital which is a crude index of size and capitalisation[10].

TABLE B

	England & Wales		Scotland		Great Britain	
	No of companies	*Issued capital*	*No of companies*	*Issued capital*	*No of companies*	*Issued capital*
Issued share capital	*000s*	*£m*	*000s*	*£m*	*000s*	*£m*
No issued share capital	40.6	0.0	2.5	0.0	43.1	0.0
Up to £100	774.7	28.3	38.9	1.3	814.6	29.6
Over £100 & under £1,000	53.5	18.7	2.1	0.7	55.6	19.4
£1,000 & under £5,000	105.6	163.9	5.5	9.5	111.1	173.4
£5,000 & under £10,000	28.8	177.7	2.5	15.5	31.3	193.2
£10,000 & under £20,000	39.6	465.8	3.9	46.2	43.5	512.0
£20,000 & under £50,000	35.5	1,031.1	3.8	112.8	39.3	1,143.9
£50,000 & under £100,000	27.4	1,691.3	2.6	165.0	30.0	1,865.3
£100,000 & under £200,000	21.1	2,624.8	2.1	266.4	23.2	2,891.2
£200,000 & under £500,000	16.8	4,986.8	1.4	434.6	18.2	5,421.4
£500,000 and under £1m	9.0	5,896.8	0.7	474.7	9.7	6,371.5
£1m & over	23.1	556,436.0	1.3	21,881.8	24.4	585,317.8
Total	1,175.7	573,521.2	68.3	23,408.5	1,240.0	596,929.7

10   Nominal capital is simply the legal measure of the capital fund. It does not necessarily reflect the value of the fund.

Groups

Many companies and undertakings belong to a group. This introduces the further classification of companies and undertakings into parent or holding companies or undertakings and subsidiaries. The simplest group relationship is:

P controls S.

However, there can in practice be sub-holding companies and subsidiaries. Thus:

With the larger firms, group structures become increasingly complex and sometimes the legal picture is not an accurate reflection of the actual organisational structure. Some subsidiaries may be little more than shells or may be run as agents for other companies in the group. Some groups such as ICI operate a division structure which is superimposed on the legal group structure. Management may be organised on a divisional basis rather than a company basis. This may make the monitoring of management performance by external agencies more difficult. Both the group structure and the other more elaborate operational structures pose difficulties for outside creditors. Normally these only surface when the difficulties give rise to insolvency. Here the de jure separation of entities may be contradicted de facto both by business operations and the practice of finance creditors of taking group guarantees and security.

We examine the question of groups in Chapter 33.

Legislative reform

The reforms introduced by the Companies Act 1981 allowed modified accounts by small and medium sized companies. These were consolidated in Part VII of the CA 1985. Recently the CA 1989 allowed a measure of 'deregulation' in respect of private companies. Written resolutions are allowed as are elective resolutions to relax a number of company law formalities. Other reform proposals have been for a new simpler form of incorporation for small businesses[11]. Such reforms have taken place in South Africa and Australia. We discuss this in Chapter 31. A further reform which has been contemplated is a greater recognition of the single economic enterprise of a group of companies when a member of a group becomes insolvent. Such reforms have been introduced in New Zealand but the Cork Committee on Insolvency Law and Practice[12] made no recommendation of this kind, preferring to leave it to a general review of company law.

11   *A New Form of Incorporation for Small Firms*—A Consultative Document 1981. See also the useful report, *Alternative Company Structures for the Small Business* by A Hicks, R Drury and J Smallcombe, ACCA Research Report 42.
12   Cmnd 8558 (1882).

THE EMERGENCE OF A FACT-BASED JURISPRUDENCE

English law has traditionally been unconcerned with whether the private company was a *kapitalgesellschaft* or *personalgesellschaft*[13]. It was simply regarded as a species of limited liability company. The public/private dichotomy was almost exclusively regarded as the basis of statutory disclosure requirements and nothing else. However in the last 50 years there have been signs of the development of a more fact-based jurisprudence in the cases. The various trends can be summarised as follows:

(1) There has been a tendency to disregard the corporate form where the interests of justice require it. These cases are usually referred to as piercing the corporate veil[14].

(2) There is a trend towards recognition of something like a *personalgesellschaft*— a relationship of personal confidence with a network of equitable obligations— behind the corporate form in the case of small incorporated firms[15]. This development started under the just and equitable ground for winding up but has been used as the basis of control over a majority shareholder in two English and one Canadian case[16]. The *locus classicus* is a speech of Lord Wilberforce in *Ebrahimi v Westbourne Galleries Ltd*[17] in 1972 where he said[18]:

> ... a limited company is more than a mere judicial entity, with a personality in law of its own: ... there is room in company law for recognition of the fact that behind it, or amongst it, there are individuals, with rights, expectations and obligations inter se which are not necessarily submerged in the company structure. That structure is defined by the Companies Act and by the articles of association by which the shareholders agree to be bound. In most companies and in most contexts, this definition is sufficient and exhaustive, equally so whether the company is large or small. The 'just and equitable' provision does not, as the respondents suggest, entitle one party to disregard the obligation he assumes by entering a company, nor the court to dispense him from it. It does, as equity always does, enable the court to subject the exercise of legal rights to equitable considerations; considerations, that is, of a personal character arising between on individual and another, which may make it unjust, or inequitable, to insist on legal rights, or to exercise them in a particular way.

At the present time it is difficult to see how far this development will go. In a way it is a potentially wide doctrine which could change much of established company law as it relates to small and medium sized firms.

(3) In a number of cases starting with *Baroness Wenlock v River Dee Co*[19] in 1883 the courts have shown a willingness to bypass the strict legal formalities

---

13   Literally, capital company and personal company. See Schmitthoff, op cit.
14   See Chapter 7, infra.
15   See Chapters 32 and 28, infra.
16   *Clemens v Clemens Bros Ltd* [1976] 2 All ER 268; *Pennell v Venida Investments Ltd* (25 July 1974, unreported) discussed in (1981) 44 MLR 41; *Diligenti v RWMO Operations Kelowna Ltd* [1976] 1 BCLR 36.
17   [1973] AC 360, HL.
18   Ibid, at 379b–d.
19   (1883) 36 Ch D 675n. See also *Re George Newman & Co* [1895] 1 Ch 674, CA; *Re Express Engineering Works Ltd* [1920] 1 Ch 466, CA; *Re Oxted Motor Co Ltd* [1921] 3 KB 32; *Parker & Cooper Ltd v Reading* [1926] Ch 975; *Re Pearce Duff & Co Ltd* [1960] 3 All ER 222; *Re Duomatic Ltd* [1969] 2 Ch 365; *Re Moorgate Mercantile Holdings Ltd* [1980] 1 All ER 40; *Cane v Jones* [1981] 1 All ER 533. See J Birds (1981) 2 Co Law 68; C Baxter [1983] CLJ 96.

prescribed by the Companies Acts in the case of small incorporated firms. However, this is usually on the basis of unanimity or estoppel or waiver, which are established legal doctrines.

Thus in *Re Duomatic Ltd*[20] Buckley J said:

> I proceed on the basis that where it can be shown that all shareholders who had a right to attend and vote at a general meeting of the company assent to some matter which a general meeting of the company could carry into effect, that assent is as binding as a resolution in general meeting would be.

As we have seen this has now been allowed by the CA 1989 for all unanimous written resolutions of private companies as part of a scheme for 'deregulation'.

(4) In some, but not all, cases of groups of companies the courts have shown a willingness to look to the group enterprise as a whole in spite of conventional legal principles which emphasise the separate interests of individual companies.

In *DHN Food Distributors v London Borough of Tower Hamlets*[1] Lord Denning MR said:

> We all know that in many respects a group of companies are treated together for the purpose of general accounts, balance sheet and profit and loss account. They are treated as one concern. Professor Gower in his book on company law says: 'there is evidence of a general tendency to ignore the separate legal entities of various companies within a group, and to look instead at the economic entity of the whole group'. This is especially the case when a parent company owns all the shares of the subsidiaries, so much so that it can control every movement of the subsidiaries. These subsidiaries are bound hand and foot to the parent company and must do just what the parent company says.

It must be conceded, however, that there have been signs recently of a return to legal orthodoxy in the cases[2]. It is difficult to provide any general theoretical framework for these trends. Perhaps they represent no more than a reluctance by the judiciary to make a fetish of legal classification where this is too much at odds with economic theory and common sense. We shall return to this question in Chapter 32 when we look at small incorporated firms in more detail.

20   [1969] 2 Ch 365 at 373. See also *Cane v Jones* [1980] 1 WLR 1451.
1   [1976] 3 All ER 462 at 467, CA.
2   See Chapter 7, infra.

CHAPTER 5

Promotion and pre-incorporation contracts

PROMOTERS

Promoter, like company, is a word with a variety of meanings. It was the old name for a common informer and the technical term for the prosecutor of a suit in the ecclesiastical courts. We are, however, not concerned with those meanings nor with promotion at large, but simply with the promotion of a company. Speaking in general terms, the promoters of a company are those who are the leading lights in its formation or flotation or, to adopt the metaphor of an American writer, who are 'the midwife of the business'[1]. Before incorporation a company does not exist. Someone must act on its behalf. Formalities need to be attended to. Professionals need to be instructed and paid. The business proposition may need to be appraised. Initial finance may need to be arranged. The legal approach to these commercial facts has never fully crystallised. Promotion was not a legal term of art at common law and is not given an exhaustive statutory definition. Consequently the courts have been reluctant to pin themselves down to any precise definition, at the same time imposing strict obligations on those who fall within the category. The obligations have been built up by the courts relying on agency and trust principles supplemented from time to time by statute. On the whole, however, the legislative reforms have been piecemeal.

The small trader who takes steps to incorporate his business is engaged in promotion. From the seventeenth century onwards there have been people who have specialised in the promotion of public companies although in the early period they usually had a number of other interests as well. Thus Nicholas Barbone[2], son of Cromwell's General Praise-God Barbone, was a physician, member of Parliament and property developer, as well as promoter of a fire insurance company and bank. Most professional promoters of public companies have been connected with the City of London and have been men of repute, but in the period 1860–1920 there were a number of company promoters who perpetrated frauds which the courts sought to combat by means of the development of specific fiduciary duties. In recent years, most leading companies have started off

---

1   H G Henn and J A Alexander *Laws of Corporations* (3rd ed, 1983), p 237. Midwife of the birth of the company is perhaps more apt.
2   See E V Morgan and W A Thomas *The Stock Exchange: its History and Functions* (2nd edn, 1969), p 25. For a description of some of the professional promoters see ibid, pp 136–139, 206 ff.

life as private companies or unlisted public companies and then 'gone public' later after establishing a sound profit record. In this process they have been assisted by stockbrokers or specialist financial institutions known as issuing houses. An issuing house, which will usually be a merchant bank, organises the raising of capital by new issues of securities. The stockbrokers and issuing houses are promoters if they perform more than mere ministerial acts. In the nineteenth century, promoters were sometimes classified into three types—professional, occasional and ad hoc[3]. The issuing houses are professionals. The individual professional promoter of public companies has disappeared because he often considered the question whether the company would float rather than whether it would succeed as the question of greatest importance. Occasional promoters were persons of greater status who never took part in a scheme unless its bona fides and prospects were beyond question. They too are rare today as are ad hoc promoters. Issuing houses have taken over much of the new issue business and have improved standards. The Radcliffe Report said that some 60% of new issues were sponsored by issuing houses. Today the figure would be higher. 'In sponsoring an issue [an issuing house] accepts the responsibility for the bona fides of the company seeking listing. The public of course get to know those houses on whose reputation they can rely in their reputation for bringing sound companies to the market ... in a way a good issuing house provides its own guarantee of success in much the same way as the Good Housekeeping Seal of Approval does[4].' Thus changes in commercial practice have now rendered the case law on promoters largely of historical interest in the case of public companies but the principles are still relevant to private companies.

The concept of promotion

The concept has been judicially described but not exhaustively defined. The policy reasons for the lack of a definition are said to be four[5]:

(1) The cases coming before the courts involve misfortune or fraud which has brought the company into difficulties. In these circumstances the judges have been satisfied that the retention of secret profits would be inequitable and, therefore, by a process of ex post facto rationalisation they call the person who made them a promoter.

(2) It is thought that the term is best left as a business term.

(3) The lack of a precise definition makes evasion and avoidance of the legal rules difficult.

(4) The wide variety of companies promoted makes a unifying definition impossible.

Let us now examine the judicial descriptions.

In *Erlanger v New Sombrero Phosphate Co*[6] in 1878, Lord Blackburn said that the term was 'a short and convenient way of designating those who set in motion the machinery by which the Act ... enables them to create an incorporated company'. This is not enough. In *Whaley Bridge Calico Printing Co v Green*[7] in 1879, Bowen J was

---

3   This was the classification adopted by Sir Francis Palmer in his *Company Precedents* (1956–60).
4   Michael Richardson *Going Public* (1976), p 16.
5   See Joseph H Gross *Company Promoters* (1972) pp 19–20. This chapter was also published in (1970) 86 LQR 493 at 498.
6   (1878) 3 App Cas 1218, HL.
7   (1879) 5 QBD 109.

a little more explicit. He said: 'The term promoter is a term not of law, but of business, usefully summing up in a single word a number of business operations familiar to the commercial world by which a company is generally brought into existence'[8]. The trouble with this is that it begs the question of what those business operations are. In *Twycross v Grant*[9] the Court of Appeal in fact found that the defendants who had planned the formation of the company, found directors, paid the preliminary expenses, arranged contracts, and were to receive substantial remuneration from the vendors were undoubtedly promoters. Cockburn CJ said that the term meant 'one who undertakes to form a company with reference to a given project and to set it going, and who takes the necessary steps to accomplish the purpose'. The most comprehensive description was given by Lindley J in *Emma Silver Mining Co v Lewis & Son* where he said[10]:

> It is now clearly settled that persons who get up and form a company have duties towards it before it comes into existence: see *Bagnall v Carlton* (1877) 6 Ch D 371 and per Lord Cairns LC in *Erlanger v New Sombrero Phosphate Co* (1878) 3 App Cas 1218 at 1236. Moreover, it is in our opinion an entire mistake to suppose that after a company is registered its directors are the only persons who are in such a position towards it as to be under fiduciary relations to it. A person not a director may be a promoter of a company which is already incorporated, but the capital of which has not been taken up, and which is not yet in a position to perform the obligations imposed upon it by its creators.

This shows that promotion can in certain circumstances extend to subsequent flotation. In *Tracey v Mandalay Pty Ltd*[11] in 1953 the majority of the High Court of Australia (Dixon CJ, Williams and Taylor JJ) held that it was not only the persons who take an active part in the formation of a company and the raising of capital who were promoters. Persons who leave it to others to get up the company upon the understanding that they also will profit from the operation may become promoters.

Ultimately, however, the question is one of fact to be determined in the light of all the circumstances.

Examples of promotion

CLEAR CASES OF PROMOTION

The clearest case is the person who plans the scheme for the formation of a company, has the documents prepared and registered, finds the directors, negotiates the preliminary contracts and deals with the drafting, printing, registration and circulation of any prospectus[12]. He or she has done all the things one associates with promotion. It will, however, be sufficient to do some of these things in co-operation with others[13].

---

8   (1880) 5 QBD 109 at 111.
9   (1877) 2 CPD 469 at 541, CA.
10   (1879) 4 CPD 396 at 407. Followed in *Tracy v Mandalay Pty Ltd* (1952) 88 CLR 215.
11   (1952) 88 CLR 215.
12   *Emma Silver Mining Co v Grant* (1879) 11 Ch D 918; *Re Olympia Ltd* [1898] 2 Ch 153, CA; *Re Leeds and Hanley Theatres of Varieties Ltd* [1902] 2 Ch 809, CA.
13   *Emma Silver Mining Co v Grant* (1879) 11 Ch D 918.

LESS CLEAR CASES

A vendor of property may be and often is a promoter but he or she is not a promoter when he or she merely acts as vendor[14]. A person who assists in the flotation but took no part in the formation of a company may be a promoter[15]. People who appear at first sight to be acting as agents or employees of another may sometimes be held to be promoters if they share in the remuneration or have some say in the promotion[16]. Thus the director of a promoting company may be held to be a promoter if he or she acts otherwise than as a director of that company[17].

CASES OF NON-PROMOTERS

A person who acts as agent or servant of a promoter is not per se a promoter[18]. Thus the solicitor, accountant, printer, stockbroker and bank are not promoters provided they merely act in a ministerial way.

The fiduciary duties of promoters

A promoter is not an agent of the company which he or she is forming for the simple reason that it does not then exist[19]. Neither is he or she treated as a trustee in normal circumstances, despite the doctrinal possibility[20]. Upon incorporation he or she does, however, stand in a fiduciary position towards the company which begins when the promotion itself began and ends after the company is formed or the promotional plan is completed. It is often superseded by new fiduciary duties where the promoter becomes a director of the company. The essence of the promoter's fiduciary duties are good faith, fair dealing and full disclosure[1]. Lord Blackburn said in *Erlanger v New Sombrero Phosphate Co*[2] that the Companies Act gave to promoters 'an almost unlimited power to make the corporation subject to such regulations as they please, and for such purposes as they please, and to create it with a managing body whom they select, having such powers as they choose to give to those managers'. He continued: 'I think those who accept and use such extensive powers are not entitled to disregard the interests of that corporation altogether. They must make a reasonable use of the powers which they accept from the legislature ... and consequently they do stand, with regard to that corporation, when formed, in what is commonly called a fiduciary relation to some extent'. *Erlanger's* case was the first case to recognise the existence of a fiduciary relationship.

14   *Erlanger v New Sombrero Phosphate Co* (1878) 3 App Cas 1218.
15   *Emma Silver Mining Co v Lewis & Son* (1879) 4 CPD 396.
16   See Pearson J in *Lydney and Wigpool Iron Ore Co v Bird* (1885) 31 Ch D 328 at 339.
17   *Re Darby, ex p Brougham* [1911] 1 KB 95.
18   *Re Great Wheal Polgooth Co Ltd* (1883) 53 LJ Ch 42.
19   *Kelner v Baxter* (1866) LR 2 CP 174.
20   See *Re Leeds and Hanley Theatres of Varieties Ltd* [1902] 2 Ch 809 at 819, CA; *Rita Joan Dairies Ltd v Thomson* [1974] 1 NZLR 285 at 293; P D McKenzie (1973) 5 NZULR 117.
1   Cf H A Henn and J A Alexander *Corporations* (3rd edn, 1983), p 239.
2   (1878) 3 App Cas 1218 at 1236, 1268.

THE DUTIES

There are three basic fiduciary duties. These are owed to the company and are:

(1) a duty not to make a secret profit at the expense of the company. A profit is not secret if it is disclosed but the disclosure must be full and frank. It must be made to either:

    (a) an independent board of directors[3] *or*

    (b) the existing and intended shareholders[4].

Independence in (a) is a question of fact; (b) is satisfied where all the members of a private company are aware of the facts and there is no intention to 'go public'. It is satisfied in the case of a public company by full disclosure of the facts in the articles or a prospectus. It will also be satisfied where the company in a general meeting, at which neither the promoter nor the holders of any shares in which he or she is beneficially interested vote in favour of the transaction, elect not to rescind it[5]. Even if they do vote in favour of it this will probably be valid. In *Erlanger*'s case[6] a syndicate headed by Erlanger acquired a lease of an island in the West Indies said to contain valuable phosphates for £55,000 and then formed a company to acquire the lease and to work the mines. The lease was sold to the company through a bare nominee for the syndicate for £100,000 without the circumstances of the sale being disclosed. The facts were found out later when the first phosphate shipments had been a failure. The shareholders removed the old board and sought rescission. It was held that the syndicate were promoters and that since they had failed to disclose their secret profit the contract could be rescinded.

In *Salomon v A Salomon & Co Ltd*[7] the House of Lords recognised that where there was not an independent board there may be sufficient disclosure if all the original shareholders are told of the material facts. In *Gluckstein v Barnes*[8], however, it was held that the promoter will not be exonerated in these circumstances if the original shareholders are not independent and the scheme is designed as a fraud on the public. An eloquent moral indignation characterises the speech of Lord Macnaghten in that case. He said that where 'gentlemen set about forming a company to pay them a handsome sum for taking off their hands a property which they contracted to buy with that end in view ... appoint themselves sole guardians and protectors of this creature of theirs, half-fledged and just struggling into life, bound hand and foot while yet unborn by contracts tending to their private advantage, and so fashioned by its makers that it could only act by their hands and only see through their eyes', and the company goes to the public for share subscriptions '"Disclosure" is not the most appropriate word to use when a person who plays many parts announces to himself in one character what he has done and is doing in another. To talk of disclosure to the thing called the company, when as yet there were no shareholders, is a mere farce. To the intended shareholders there was no disclosure at all'[9].

3   *Erlanger*, supra; *Gluckstein v Barnes* [1900] AC 240, HL.
4   *Salomon v A Salomon & Co Ltd* [1897] AC 22, HL; *Larocque v Beauchemin* [1897] AC 358 at 364, PC.
5   *Lagunas Nitrate Co v Lagunas Syndicate* [1899] 2 Ch 392, CA. As to whether the promoter and his nominess should abstain, cf Ghana Companies Code, s 12(4)(c) and L C B Gower's discussion in his Report thereto.
6   (1878) 3 App Cas 1218, HL.
7   [1897] AC 22, HL.
8   [1900] AC 240, HL.
9   Ibid, at 248–249.

(2) When the promotion has started the promoter must account to the company for the benefit of any subsequent contract for the acquisition of property which he or she intends to sell to the company, since this belongs in equity to the company which can insist on taking it at cost[10]. Where the promoter acquired the property on his or her own account before the commencement of the promotion it belongs to him or her in law and equity and he or she can sell at a profit provided he discloses the facts[11]. If he or she does not make disclosure the contract is liable to be rescinded[12].

(3) A promoter must not exercise undue influence or fraud[13] and in particular must not hide his or her interest through a nominee[14].

REMEDIES OF THE COMPANY

The company's remedies are rescission, recovery of the secret profit and damages for breach of fiduciary duty or deceit.

Rescission   We have seen that in *Erlanger*'s case the company was entitled to rescind the contract for the purchase of the lease of the island. Rescission is an equitable remedy which involves unscrambling the contract and return of the consideration and will be lost:

(a) if the parties cannot be substantially restored to their original position[15] unless this is due to the fault of the promoter;

(b) if third parties have acquired rights for value[16].

In *Re Leeds & Hanley Theatres of Varieties Ltd*[16] promoters made a profit by selling through a nominee and failed to disclose the facts. Meanwhile a mortgagee sold the property. It was held that rescission was no longer possible but damages could be recovered.

Recovery of the secret profit   Where the company has affirmed the contract it can still sue the promoter to account for the secret profit. The action for recovery of the secret profit is either in equity on the basis of a constructive trust or at law as a claim for money had and received[17]. It can also be the subject of a misfeasance summons in the winding up of the company[18] and is provable in the bankruptcy of the promoter[19].

In *Gluckstein v Barnes*[20] Gluckstein and others, intending to buy the Olympia exhibition hall and promote a company, first bought up charges on the property at below par. They later bought the property and sold it to their new company at a profit. They also procured repayment of the charges at par. They then disclosed the profit on the sale but not on the charges. The House of Lords held that the company could recover

---

10   *Hichens v Congreve* (1829) 1 Russ & M 150; *Re Leeds and Hanley Theatres of Varieties Ltd* [1902] 2 Ch 809, CA; *Re Cape Breton Co* (1885) 29 Ch D 795, CA; *Jacobus Marler Estates Ltd v Marler* (1913) 85 LJPC 167n; *Tracy v Mandalay Pty Ltd* (1952) 88 CLR 215 at 239.
11   *Erlanger*'s case, supra.
12   *Ladywell Mining Co v Brookes* (1887) 35 Ch D 400, CA.
13   *Erlanger*'s case, supra; *Gluckstein v Barnes*, supra.
14   *Erlanger*'s case, supra; *Cavendish-Bentinck v Fenn* (1887) 12 App Cas 652 at 671, HL.
15   *Lagunas Nitrate Co v Lagunas Syndicate* [1899] 2 Ch 392, CA.
16   *Re Leeds and Hanley Theatres of Varieties Ltd* [1902] 2 Ch 809, CA.
17   L S Sealy *Cases and Materials in Company Law* (6th edn, 1996), p 25.
18   *Re Caerphilly Colliery Co, Pearson*'s case (1877) 5 Ch D 336, CA.
19   *Re Darby, ex p Brougham* [1911] 1 KB 95.
20   [1900] AC 240, HL.

the secret profit from the promoters who were jointly and severally liable. In computing the secret profit all bona fide expenses of the promotion can be deducted. Thus in *Emma Silver Mining Co v Grant*[1] a defendant was allowed sums expended in securing the services of directors and in payments to brokers and the press.

Damages for breach of fiduciary duty We have seen in *Re Leeds and Hanley Theatres of Varieties* (supra) that damages for breach of fiduciary duty may be awarded in lieu of rescission. Where property is acquired before the promotion commenced by the promoter in his or her own right but which he failed to disclose, the company cannot affirm the contract and claim damages or recover the secret profit[2]. The reason is that in this case the property does not belong in equity to the company and for the court to order damages or recovery of the secret profit would amount to variation of the contract. The law is that the promoter must not make a *secret* profit in respect of the sale of his or her own property, not that he or she should sell at a lower price.

Damages for deceit The facts will usually warrant an action in deceit against the promoter for a misrepresentation inducing the company to enter into the contract.

LIABILITY TO AND REMEDIES OF SHAREHOLDERS AND CREDITORS

In English law promoters do not owe fiduciary duties to shareholders and creditors[3] in the absence of special facts giving rise to such a relationship which go beyond the ordinary aspects of promotion[4]. The shareholders and creditors may, however, have actions at common law for deceit, misrepresentation or negligence. In addition there may be actions for compensation under ss 150–152 of the Financial Services Act 1986 in the case of listed securities and ss 166–168 in the case of unlisted securities against the persons responsible for the issue of the listing particulars or prospectus. We shall examine these remedies in more detail when we discuss raising capital, in Chapter 33.

THE IMPACT OF S 103

Section 103 provides that a public company must not allot shares as fully or partly paid for a consideration other than cash unless there has been a valuer's report by an independent person. The necessity for such a report will cut down the possibility of fraud by promoters but as we have seen the possibility for this in the case of promoters of companies whose shares are publicly quoted in practice is negligible anyway.

If the promoter is a subscriber to the memorandum and the transaction takes place within two years of receipt of the certificate to commence business under s 117, the further requirements of s 104 apply. These require approval by an ordinary resolution of the company as well as valuation.

1   (1879) 11 Ch D 918.
2   *Re Cape Breton Co* (1885) 29 Ch D 795, CA; *Jacobus Marler Estates Ltd v Marler* (1913) 85 LJPC 167n; *Tracy v Mandalay Pty Ltd* (1952) 88 CLR 215 at 239.
3   Cf American law. See *Henn and Alexander*, op cit, p 244.
4   Cf *Coleman v Myers* [1977] 2 NZLR 225, NZCA.

Remuneration of promoters

To claim remuneration the promoter must establish a contract under seal at least in respect of formation, since the consideration will be past consideration. The promoter cannot rely for this purpose on a provision in the articles[5] except perhaps if he or she is a member and claims the general right to have the company's business conducted in accordance with the articles[6].

Disclosure of the remuneration paid in the two preceding years must be made in any prospectus[7].

PRE-INCORPORATION CONTRACTS

Before the company is incorporated it is often necessary for the promoters to enter into negotiations with third parties on its behalf. If these proceed to the contract stage, the question arises, who is to be liable on the contract and in particular is the promoter personally liable? The position at common law is quite complicated but to some extent this has been superseded by s 9(2) of the European Communities Act 1972, now re-enacted with minor amendments in s 36C of CA 1985. The problems usually arise in connection with small private companies.

Let us first briefly consider the position at common law. This can be summed up in the following principles:

(1) Since the company was a non-existent principal at the time of the contract, it cannot be bound nor take any benefit under it[8].

(2) For the same reason ratification is impossible[8].

(3) There may be evidence of the substitution of a new contract by novation but merely accepting the old contract and carrying it into effect after incorporation does not give rise to novation[9]. On the other hand a variation of one of the terms may be sufficient[10].

(4) There will normally be a presumption of personal liability on the part of the agent although the matter is ultimately one of construction and personal liability may be rebutted[11].

(5) Even if the agent is not liable on the contract he or she may possibly be liable for breach of warranty of authority[12].

(6) The use of the trust device appears to be ineffective to bind the unborn company and to exonerate the agent from personal liability[13].

Article 7 of the First Directive of the EU provides that any person who enters into a transaction on behalf of a company 'which is in the process of formation', shall be personally liable on the transaction unless the company, on formation, assumes the

5   *Melhado v Porto Alegre Rly Co* (1874) LR 9 CP 503.
6   See p 122, post.
7   FSA 1986, s 144.
8   *Kelner v Baxter* (1866) LR 2 CP 174; *Newborne v Sensolid (GB) Ltd* [1954] 1 QB 45, CA.
9   *Re Northumberland Avenue Hotel Co Ltd* (1886) 33 Ch D 16, CA.
10   *Howard v Patent Ivory Manufacturing Co* (1888) 38 Ch D 156.
11   *Black v Smallwood* (1965) 117 CLR 52 (Aust HC); *Marblestone Industries Ltd v Fairchild* [1975] 1 NZLR 529.
12   *Black v Smallwood,* supra and *Lomax v Dankel* [1981] 29 SASR 68 but cf *Newborne v Sensolid* supra and *Hawke's Bay Milk Corpn Ltd v Watson* [1974] 1 NZLR 236 at 239.
13   *Rita Joan Dairies Ltd v Thomson* [1974] 1 NZLR 285.

obligation, or there is an agreement negating such liability. Section 36C of the CA 1985 (which replaces the old s 36(4) of that Act which in its turn replaced s 9(2) of the European Communities Act) provides:

36C. Pre-incorporation contracts, deeds and obligations
(1) A contract which purports to be made by or on behalf of a company at a time when the company has not been formed has effect, subject to any agreement to the contrary, as one made with the person purporting to act for the company or as agent for it, and he is personally liable on the contract accordingly.

Section 36C does not deal with case law rules (1), (2), (3), (5) and (6). It simply clarifies (4) in a very marginal way[14]. The scope of the subsection was explored by the Court of Appeal in *Phonogram Ltd v Lane*[15]. The material facts were that prior to the incorporation of a company called Fragile Management Ltd the defendant contracted with the plaintiff for a loan of £12,000 to finance a pop group, Cheap Mean and Nasty. The plaintiff wrote a letter to the defendant in which it referred to him undertaking to repay. He nevertheless was required to sign and return a copy 'for and on behalf of Fragile Management Ltd'. The company was, however, never formed. The group never performed under the contract and the defendant was held personally liable under s 9(2) to repay the amount advanced.

Ingenuous arguments based on the wording of art 7 of the Directive 'in the course of formation' and 'purport' were rejected. Lord Denning MR said that s 9(2) obliterated the old subtleties which turned on the wording adopted. It applied whatever formula was adopted. The reference to 'subject to any agreement to the contrary' means 'unless otherwise agreed'. Unless there is a clear exclusion of personal liability the subsection applies. Shaw LJ agreed. Oliver LJ did not think that the pre-1973 position depended on subtle verbal distinctions but on what was the real intent revealed by the contract. However, he agreed that the subsection had made the old cases irrelevant. As regards contracting out his Lordship did not think that an agreement to the contrary could be inferred by the fact that a contract was signed by a person acting as agent.

How marginal is the effect of s 36C as so construed on the case law? It is submitted that what was formerly a rebuttable presumption of construction is now a rule of law but one which can be excluded by a clear agreement to the contrary. Anything short of an express exclusion of liability will be insufficient in practice if not in theory.

The Jenkins Report[16] favoured a reform which not only dealt with the position of the agent but also enabled a company unilaterally to adopt contracts which purported to be made on its behalf or in its name prior to incorporation. Such a reform has now been adopted in Ghana, Ireland, Canada, Australia and New Zealand[17] and should be introduced in the UK to complete reform of this topic.

---

14 See D D Prentice (1973) 89 LQR 518 at 530–533 for a useful discussion of s 9(2) which predates *Phonogram Ltd v Lane* [1982] QB 938, CA.
15 [1982] QB 938, CA. See also *Cotronic (UK) Ltd v Dezonie* [1991] BCLC 721, CA; *Badgerhill Properties Ltd v Cottrell* [1991] BCLC 805, CA; *Rover International Ltd v Cannon Films Sales Ltd (No 2)* (1987) 3 BCC 369 and the unreported cases of *Bitar v Al Sanea* (27 April 1983, unreported) and *Janfred Properties Ltd v Ente Nationale Haliane etc* (14 July 1983, unreported) discussed by N N Green (1984) 47 MLR 671. See also A. Griffiths (1993) 13 LS 241.
16 Cmnd 1749 (1962) para 54(b).
17 See a useful summary of the various reforms in *Pre-incorporation Contracts*, Report No 8 of the Law Reform Commissioner of Victoria, p 9 ff.

CHAPTER 6

The mechanics of company formation

The Companies Act 1844 provided for incorporation by registration of deeds of settlement. The modern company is no longer formed in this way although vestiges of those days still survive in the form of subscription of the memorandum of association by the initial subscribers and the wording of s 14 of CA 1985 which refers to the corporate constitutional documents when registered as binding the company and its members to the same extent as if they respectively had been signed and sealed by each member. We shall examine this wording in detail in Chapter 11. Every public company must have at least two members[1]. Originally this was seven[2] but when the public/private dichotomy was introduced in 1907, private companies were allowed a statutory minimum of two[3]. The number was reduced to two in the case of public companies by the Companies Act 1980[4]. A private company (if a single member private limited company) need only have one member.[5] If a company falls below the statutory minimum and carries on business for more than six months, those members who know are personally liable for its debts[6]. This is an exception to the separate legal personality of the company and the limited liability of members of a company limited by shares.

CHOOSING THE APPROPRIATE FORM

Once the decision has been reached in principle to incorporate, the question arises what particular form of company to adopt.

The parties today will rarely seek incorporation by Royal Charter unless they are concerned with education or some other charitable or public purpose. This form is mainly used for new universities set up by the state and the recognition of the governing

---

1   Section 1(1) of CA 1985.
2   Joint Stock Companies Act 1856, s 3.
3   Companies Act 1907.
4   Section 2(1) of the Companies Act 1980.
5   S 1(1)(3A). As to the modification of the CA in the light of the single member company, see the Companies (Single Member Private Limited Companies) Regulations 1992 (SI 1992 No 1699).
6   Section 24.

bodies of certain key professions. It requires a petition addressed to the Crown accompanied by a draft charter[7] and is dealt with by the Privy Council.

It will also be rare today that the parties will choose to promote a statutory company which requires the passing of a specific public Act of Parliament[8]. This form is only used today for public corporations such as the nationalised industries and is usually conventionally regarded as constitutional rather than company law.

The most common form is to incorporate as a species of registered company under the Companies Acts. The basic choices here are (1) between an unlimited or a limited company, and (2) between a public and a private company. The unlimited company confers separate legal personality, but the members remain personally liable for its debts in full. This form in practice is usually only adopted by some professions who seek the administrative convenience of incorporation but who are subject to professional rules which do not allow them to limit their liability. A company can be limited by shares or by guarantee. A company limited by shares is one whose members are liable to pay up the full amount of the nominal value of their shares in the event of its winding up but no more[9]. These are by far the most common species of company. A company limited by guarantee is one whose members are liable to pay up the amount specified in their guarantee in the memorandum and no more. This form in practice is often used by educational bodies. Examples are the London School of Economics and the College of Law. Prior to the Companies Act 1980, companies limited by guarantee could also have a share capital for other purposes such as attributing votes to members. Since 22 December 1980, a company limited by guarantee may not be formed with a share capital but this does not affect existing companies which have such capital[10].

A further choice as far as limited companies are concerned is between public and private status. Under the law in force before 1980, the public/private dichotomy was worked out by reference to the definition of a private company in s 28 of the Companies Act 1948. A public company was one which was not a private company. A private company was characterised by three attributes:

(a) a restriction on the right to transfer its shares;
(b) a limit on its membership to 50, excluding employees and ex-employees;
(c) a prohibition on making an invitation to the public to subscribe for its shares or debentures.

This has now been repealed and s 1(3) of CA 1985 defines a public company as:

a company limited by shares or limited by guarantee and having a share capital, being a company—
(a) the memorandum of which states that it is to be a public company, and
(b) in relation to which the provisions of the Act or the former Companies Acts as to the registration or re-registration of a company as a public company have been complied with on or after 22 December 1980.

A public company must now have a minimum share capital of £50,000. The requirement of limited liability rules out unlimited companies and the requirement of

---

7   For the procedure, see Gower *Modern Company Law* (6th edn, 1997), pp 98-99.
8   See *Gower*, op cit, p 98.
9   This does not include any premium since this technically does not form part of the share capital: *Niemann v Smedley* [1973] VR 769.
10 Companies Act 1980, s 1(2) which came into force on 22 December 1980. See now s 1(4) of CA 1985.

a share capital excludes companies limited by guarantee formed on or after 22 December 1980.

A private company is a company which is not a public company.

In practice most companies will probably continue to be formed as private companies and will be converted into public companies only when they want to 'go public' ie to invite public investment in their shares or debentures. This will often precede a flotation of their shares or debentures on a Stock Exchange when the company's business has been built up to the requisite size.

THE FORMATION FORMALITIES

The modern company is formed by the registration of certain documents with the Registrar of Companies. There are separate registers for England and Wales, Scotland and Northern Ireland.

Name

STATUTORY RULES

Before this is done, prior to 1981, it was usual to apply for consent to the incorporation of the company with a particular name. The reason was that the Registrar had a discretion under s 17 of the Companies Act 1948 which stated quite simply that no company should be registered by a name which in the opinion of the Department of Trade was undesirable. Although the Act conferred a broad discretion the Registrar issued a practice direction describing the way in which he exercised his discretion. The main points were that the name must not be misleading or suggest a connection with the Crown, government departments, local authorities, statutory undertakings or foreign governments. In addition the use of certain words such as 'Bank', 'Insurance' and so on had to be justified as appropriate[11]. The Registrar normally made a search in the Register and in the Trade Marks Register and refused to consent if there was likely to be confusion.

Because of the element of uncertainty, incorporators usually proffered a number of alternative names. The rate of incorporations has increased considerably in recent years. The result of all this was a considerable volume of work for the Registrar's staff both prior to and on incorporation which resulted in delays.

Sections 17 and 18 of the Companies Act 1948 were repealed by s 119(5) of, and Sch 4 to, the Companies Act 1981. The present system, now set out in Pt I, Ch II of CA 1985, provides, first, that no name will be permitted if it is the same as a name on an index of names maintained by the Registrar or if the Secretary of State in certain circumstances objects, secondly, that certain specified words are unacceptable; and, thirdly, circumstances in which the Secretary of State may request a company to change its name.

The index referred to in s 26(1)(c) must include the names inter alia of:

(a) companies within the meaning of the Act;
(b) overseas companies (ie companies incorporated abroad who have filed documents with the Registrar under s 691 and which 'do not appear to the registrar of companies not to have a place of business in Great Britain'). The

---

11   For a fuller discussion see *Gower*, op cit, p 100 ff.

reason for the ugly double negative is to safeguard the Registrar from fly-by-night foreign companies which he may as a result keep on the Register (s 714(1)).

The purpose of the index is to enable the company itself to check whether its proposed name is the same as one already on the Register.

Unacceptable names are those:

(1) the use of which in the opinion of the Secretary of State constitutes a criminal offence (s 26(1)(d));
(2) which in his opinion are offensive (s 26(1)(e));
(3) which in his opinion are likely to give the impression that the company is connected with either government or a local authority (s 26(2)(a));
(4) which include a word or expression specified in regulations made under s 29 which necessitates prior approval of the Secretary of State or relevant body[12] (s 26(2)(b)).

The Secretary of State has power to exempt a company from (3) and (4).

Section 28 sets out three circumstances in which the Secretary of State may direct a company to change its name. These are:

(1) where it is the same as a name that appears or should have appeared at the time of registration in the index;
(2) where it is in the opinion of the Secretary of State 'too like' a name which is on, or should have appeared in, the index (s 28(2)(a) and (b));
(3) where the company provided misleading information in order to be registered with the name or gave undertakings which it has not fulfilled (s 28(3)).

Obviously (2) is a broad category.

Under s 18 of the Companies Act 1948, it was formerly necessary for a company to obtain consent for a change of name. This has now been abolished. All that the company need do is pass a special resolution; but of course if the name falls within the sections discussed above, the company may be required to effect a further change.

The result of these elaborate reforms, accompanied as they are by the abolition of the Business Names Registry, which kept a record of other business names, is to reduce staff and to 'privatise' this area. More obligations are cast upon companies, which ignore them at their peril. The law as opposed to the administrative practice of company names has increased in importance.

One organisation which has stepped in to fill the gap is sponsored by the principal Chambers of Commerce and provides a name check service which is based on the information on the public records which have been computerised.

THE TORT OF PASSING OFF

Any person who is aggrieved by the incorporation of a company with a name which is likely to cause confusion in relation to his goods may be able to bring proceedings for an injunction to prevent the tort of passing off[13]. The basis of the action is a right not so much in the name itself but in the goodwill engendered by the use of the name in

---

12   A regulation has been made entitled the Company and Business Names Regulations 1981, SI 1981 No 1685.
13   See J D Heydon *Economic Torts* (2nd edn, 1978) for a discussion of this tort.

connection with the plaintiff's business[14]. The existence of the goodwill is a question of fact. However, a person may carry on business under his or her own name even if it does cause confusion with competitors provided he or she does not intend to deceive the public in relation to the goods[15]. The courts may infer such an intent. Thus in *Ewing v Buttercup Margarine Co Ltd*[16] the plaintiff carried on an unincorporated business under the trade name Buttercup Dairy Co. The defendant company was incorporated to trade in similar products and had adopted the name innocently. The Court of Appeal held that nevertheless the plaintiff was entitled to an injunction since confusion must result. Where the name of a new company may lead to the suggestion that it has taken over an existing business, this may be the ground for an injunction. Thus the Manchester Brewery Co was granted an injunction against the North Cheshire and Manchester Brewery Co[17] on the basis that it was calculated to deceive. Where there is similarity as to name, there may be no risk of confusion because of different geographical areas in which the parties operate[18] or different areas of business. Where one company carried on specialised insurance business and the other general insurance business it was held in a Scottish case that no confusion was likely to result[19].

A company cannot claim a monopoly in a descriptive word even where it was the first to use it. Thus the British Vacuum Cleaner Co could not prevent a company called New Vacuum Cleaner Co from using the words 'vacuum cleaner'[20]. It is interesting to note that Parker J also held that the plaintiff company, by allowing subsidiary companies to be formed to work particular areas under names using the words 'vacuum cleaner', had admitted that another company with a name containing those words would not necessarily be confused with the plaintiff company. This seems very questionable.

It is not necessary to prove an intention to deceive, at least to obtain an injunction. The fact of passing off per se gives rise to a right to nominal damages if damage is probable but actual damage can be pleaded and recovered. In equity, relief could be obtained where the passing off was innocent whereas at common law it was necessary to prove fraud. The position since the Judicature Acts is not clear[1]. There are strong policy grounds for holding that fault should be necessary before the company is held liable in damages. On the other hand absence of fault need not bar the grant of an injunction.

LIMITED AND PUBLIC LIMITED COMPANY

The word 'limited' must appear at the end of the name of a private company and the words 'public limited company' at the end of the name of a public company. Section 19 of the Companies Act 1948 enabled a company to apply for dispensation from the obligation to put the word limited at the end of its name. Most companies which successfully applied were companies limited by guarantee. The dispensation was negated to some extent by s 9 of the European Communities Act 1972 which required

14   *Spalding & Bros v A W Gamage Ltd* (1915) 113 LT 198, HL; *Ad-Lib Club Ltd v Granville* [1971] 2 All ER 300. See also *Star Industrial Co Ltd v Yap Kwee Kor* [1976] FSR 256, PC.
15   *Hall-Gibbs Mercantile Agency Ltd v Dun* (1910) 12 CLR 84.
16   [1917] 2 Ch 1, CA.
17   *North Cheshire and Manchester Brewery Co v Manchester Brewery Co* [1899] AC 83, HL.
18   *Empire Typesetting Machine Co of New York v Linotype Co Ltd* (1898) 79 LT 8, CA. Cf, however, *Maxim's Ltd v Dye* [1978] 2 All ER 55.
19   *Scottish Union and National Insurance Co v Scottish National Insurance Co* 1909 SC 318.
20   *British Vacuum Cleaner Co Ltd v New Vacuum Cleaner Co Ltd* [1907] 2 Ch 312. See also *Aerators Ltd v Tollitt* [1902] 2 Ch 319 ('Aerators').
1   See *Heydon*, op cit.

· disclosure of the company's limited liability on its letter headings. Section 19 was repealed by the Companies Act 1981 and replaced by s 15 of that Act. Section 15 of the 1981 Act has now been re-enacted in s 30 of CA 1985, and s 9(3) of the European Communities Act 1972 in s 35(1) of the 1985 Act. In future private companies limited by guarantee and those companies limited by shares which had dispensation under s 19 on 25 February 1982 are exempt provided they satisfy the criteria set out in s 30(3)(a) and (b). These provide respectively:

(a) that the objects of the company are (or, in the case of a company about to be registered, are to be) the promotion of commerce, art, science, education, religion, charity or any profession, and anything incidental or conducive to any of those objects; and

(b) that the company's memorandum or articles of association
   (i)   require its profits (if any) or other income to be applied in promoting its objects,
   (ii) prohibit the payment of dividends to its members, and
   (iii) require all the assets which would otherwise be available to its members generally to be transferred on its winding up either to another body with objects similar to its own or to another body the objects of which are the promotion of charity and anything incidental or conducive thereto (whether or not the body is a member of the company)'.

The effect of these changes is to reduce the class of companies having dispensation.

The documents to be filed

The principal documents which are registered are the memorandum and articles of association which have superseded the deeds of settlement. The basic form of these dates back to the Joint Stock Companies Act 1856 and was influenced by the New York Business Corporations Act. The current forms are set out in regulations made by the Secretary of State under ss 3 and 8 of CA 1985[2]. The memorandum of association of a company limited by shares states the name and country in which the company's registered office is situated, its objects and powers, the basis of liability, the initial share capital and the number of shares into which it is divided. If the company is a public company, this too must be stated in the memorandum. It is subscribed by the original members of the company and states their name, address and the number of shares they subscribe. The main function of the memorandum of association is to describe the essential attributes of the particular company and its relationship with the outside world. Section 3 provides for the form to be set out in regulations made by the Secretary of State.

The articles of association deal with such matters as classes of shares, class rights, transfer and transmission of shares, procedures at general meetings and meetings of directors, and dividends—in other words, the internal organisation of the company. Most companies adopt a modified version of the model set out in Table A, formerly set out in Sch 1 to the Companies Act 1948 and now set out in regulations made under s 8. Section 7 provides that there may, in the case of a company limited by shares, and there shall, in the case of a company limited by guarantee or unlimited, be registered with the memorandum articles of association signed by the subscribers and prescribing regulations for the company. Section 8(1) provides that the articles may adopt the whole

2   The Companies (Table A–F) Regulations 1985, SI 1985 No 805.

or any part of Table A and s 8(2) provides that in the case of a company limited by shares:

> if articles are not registered or if articles are registered but do not exclude or modify Table A, Table A applies as in force at the date of the company's registration.

However, the statutory precedents are a guide, not a straitjacket. They indicate form or arrangement, not substance. They do not have to be followed literally. They are directory, not mandatory, forms[3]. Thus provisions which differ from them, or conflict with them, may still be valid.

Accompanying the memorandum and articles there must be a Declaration of Compliance[4] which is a statutory declaration made by the solicitor engaged in the formation or by a person named as the first director or secretary in the articles. The registration fee[5] must be paid and it is now obligatory to file the Particulars of Registered Office[6] and Particulars of Directors and Secretary[7] at this stage.

THE ROLE OF THE REGISTRAR

The role of the Registrar in respect of incorporation is administrative. He has to be satisfied that the documents are in order and that the formalities prescribed by the Companies Acts have been complied with. He has no power to conduct a judicial enquiry. Section 1(1) of CA 1985 requires the members to be associated 'for a lawful purpose'. In *R v Registrar of Joint Stock Companies, ex p More*[8] some Irishmen wanted to incorporate an English company to market Irish Sweepstake tickets. It was lawful to do this in Eire but not in the UK. The Registrar consequently refused registration and the Irishmen sought mandamus. The court refused to upset the Registrar's decision. On the other hand if the purpose is lawful and all the statutory conditions have been complied with, the Registrar must issue the certificate of incorporation and if he refuses to issue it, an order of mandamus will be made against him[9].

The certificate of incorporation

On the registration of the company the Registrar gives a certificate that the company is incorporated and, in the case of a limited liability company, that its liability is limited (s 13(1)). Under s 711(1)(a), the Registrar must advertise the issue of the certificate in the Gazette, the official newspaper. The effect of the certificate is specified in s 13(3) and (4).

---

3   Per Megarry J in *Gaiman v National Association for Mental Health* [1971] Ch 317 at 328.
4   Section 12(2). Form 41a.
5   Now a fixed flat rate fee; see Companies (Fees) Regulations 1991, SI 1991 No 1206, as amended. For a larger fee, registration can be completed on the same day if the documents are in order and there is no problem with the name.
6   Section 10(6).
7   Section 10(2).
8   [1931] 2 KB 197, CA.
9   *R v Registrar of Companies, ex p Bowen* [1914] 3 KB 1161.

From the date of incorporation the subscribers of the memorandum, together with people who subsequently become members, constitute a body corporate capable forthwith of exercising all the functions of an incorporated company but with such liability on the part of the members to contribute to its assets in the event of winding up as is provided by the Act. In the case of a public company an additional certificate under s 117 as to the amount of the allotted share capital must be obtained before it can commence business or borrow.

Section 13(7) provides that the certificate of incorporation is conclusive evidence (a) that the requirements of the Act in respect of registration and of matters precedent and incidental thereto have been complied with and that the association is a company authorised to be registered, and is duly registered under the Act; and (b) if the certificate contains a statement that the company is a public company, that the company is such a company. The ample scope of this provision is illustrated by *Jubilee Cotton Mills Ltd v Lewis*[10] where it was held that the certificate was conclusive as to the date of incorporation even though it was wrong. Also, in *Cotman v Brougham*[11], the House of Lords felt that an earlier provision to similar effect prevented them from vetoing a clause in a memorandum which they did not like. The clause in question treated every paragraph in the objects clause as a separate object and became known as a *Cotman v Brougham* clause which appears in most objects clauses today. We examine this question in detail in a later chapter. On the other hand the certificate is only conclusive that the formalities have been complied with and is not conclusive of the legality of the company's objects. In *Bowman v Secular Society Ltd*[12], it was held that the Attorney General could apply for certiorari to have the registration cancelled in the event of its object being unlawful[13].

The effect of the section is to exclude from English company law the doctrine of nullity of incorporation which exists in continental systems. This allows judicial annulment for irregularities in formation and was the subject of Section III of the First EU Directive[14].

One last matter to which we shall briefly refer is that it is possible to convert a company incorporated as a private company into a public company, and vice versa, provided the formalities set out in ss 43 and 53 respectively are complied with. In practice most public companies are incorporated as private companies. Under s 43, this means that a special resolution must be passed, an application made in the prescribed form accompanied by certain documents and the requirements of s 43(2) and (3) and ss 44 and 45 must be complied with.

There are also procedures laid down in ss 49 and 51 for converting from limited to unlimited form and vice versa but s 49(3) provides that no *public* company or a company previously registered as unlimited may apply to be re-registered as an unlimited company.

---

10   [1924] AC 958, HL.
11   [1918] AC 514, HL.
12   [1917] AC 406, HL.
13   See too the case of the incorporated prostitute *R v Registrar of Companies, ex p A–G* [1991] BCLC 476. Cf *Princess of Reuss v Bos* (1871) LR 5 HL 176.
14   On nullity see R R Drury (1985) 48 MLR 644.

CHAPTER 7

Corporate personality and limited liability

THE CONCEPT OF CORPORATE PERSONALITY

A company is a species of corporation which is a distinct kind of organisation. This means that it is 'a body of bodies; technically, an artificial person composed of natural persons'[1]. For the purposes of much legislation it ranks as a legal person along with natural persons unless the context otherwise requires[2].

The early companies legislation merely referred to the subscribers forming themselves into an incorporated company and did not spell out the consequences in any detail[3]. As a learned commentator in the Law Quarterly Review of 1897 stated: 'Our Legislature ... delivered itself on the Companies Acts in its usual oracular style, leaving to the Courts the interpretation of its mystical utterances'[4]. The separate legal personality of a limited liability company was firmly established by the House of Lords in the leading case of *Salomon v A Salomon & Co Ltd*[5], although the courts have subsequently, for reasons of policy, disregarded this personality in a minority of cases.

The facts of *Salomon v A Salomon & Co Ltd* were as follows: Aron Salomon was a boot and shoe manufacturer trading as a successful sole trader in the East End of London for over 30 years. There was family pressure to give them a share in the business and he wished to extend the business. He, therefore, formed a company and sold his business to the company. At the time the legislation required a company to have a minimum of seven members. A Salomon and Co Ltd had Salomon himself and six members of his family who held one share each as nominees. Thus the company was

1   Harry G Henn and J A Alexander *Corporations* (3rd edn, 1983), p 145. It should be noted, however, that sometimes the members are themselves companies but ultimately there will be natural persons at the end of the chain.
2   Interpretation Act 1978, s 5 and Sch 1.
3   Joint Stock Companies Act 1856, s 3.
4   (1897) 13 LQR 6. For useful recent discussions of the economic and legal background to the case, see P Ireland 'Triumph of the Company Legal Form 1856–1914' and G R Rubin 'Aron Salomon and his Circle' in *Essays for Clive Schmitthoff* ed J Adams (1983), pp 29 ff and 99 ff respectively. The case was also the subject of Lord Cooke of Thorndon's Hamlyn Lecture in 1996.
5   [1897] AC 22, HL. The principle was reaffirmed by the House of Lords in *JH Rayner (Mincing Lane) Ltd v Department of Trade and Industry* [1990] 2 AC 418, a case concerning the International Tin Council. The House of Lords held that, at common law, members were not liable for the debts of a corporate body.

in reality a 'one-man company'. The price paid by the company for the transfer of the business was on paper over £39,000, 'a sum which', Lord Macnaghten said, 'represented the sanguine expectations of a fond owner rather than anything that can be called a businesslike or reasonable estimate of value'[6]. Although worthy of comment, this fact ultimately had no bearing on the case in the House of Lords. The purchase price was to be paid as to £30,000[7] out of money as it came in, which Salomon immediately returned to the company in exchange for fully paid shares, £10,000 in debentures and the balance (except for £1,000) to be used to pay the debts. The debentures were an acknowledgement of indebtedness by the company secured on its property and effects. At the end of the day Salomon received about £1,000 in cash, £10,000 in debentures and half the nominal capital of the company in issued shares. The company fell upon hard times. There was a great depression in the trade and strikes of workmen. In view of the latter, contracts with public bodies on which the company relied were farmed out amongst a number of different firms. Salomon attempted various strategies to get the company back on its feet. He and his wife lent it money. He mortgaged his debentures to obtain the necessary funds which he loaned to the company. The mortgagee was registered as the holder of the debentures. Still the company did not prosper and it went into receivership and then liquidation. There was a forced sale of its assets. There was enough to enable the liquidator, if he wished, to pay the mortgagee but not enough to repay the debentures in full or the unsecured creditors. In the course of the liquidation the mortgagee of the debentures brought a claim under the debentures against the company. The liquidator attempted to resist the claim by arguing that the debentures were invalid on the ground of fraud. At first instance[8] Vaughan Williams J, a bankruptcy expert[9], looked upon the case with a jaundiced eye. He disapproved of the one-man company which was then a new practice[10] and thought he detected fraud. He held that the company was merely acting as Salomon's nominee and agent and therefore Salomon as principal had to indemnify the company's creditors himself. Salomon appealed to the Court of Appeal which turned down his appeal, but largely on the different ground that Salomon was a trustee for the company which was his mere shadow[11]. Both the first instance judge and the Court of Appeal thought that a one-man company was an abuse of the Companies Act. Salomon appealed to the House of Lords which totally rejected the rulings below. A one-man company was not an abuse of the Companies Act, all the relevant formalities had been complied with and the Act was silent on the question of beneficial interests and control. A Salomon and Co Ltd was different from Salomon as an individual. Lord Halsbury LC[12] saw the view of the Court of Appeal as involving a logical contradiction. Sometimes it regarded A Salomon and Co Ltd as a company and sometimes it did not. Lord Watson[13] mentioned a new point, namely that the creditors of the company could have searched the Companies Register to find out the name of the shareholders and their failure to do so should not impute a charge of fraud against Salomon. Lord Herschell[14] largely based his speech on the intention of the statute to protect shareholders by limiting their liability. The speech of Lord Macnaghten, which is more comprehensive, is a legal classic. He states at p 51 quite firmly that:

6   [1897] AC 22 at 49, HL.
7   Lord Macnaghten's speech (ibid) seems wrong on this point.
8   [1895] 2 Ch 323, CA.
9   He was author of *Williams on Bankruptcy*.
10   See Lindley LJ at [1895] 2 Ch 323 at 336, CA.
11   [1895] 2 Ch 323 at 336, CA.
12   [1897] AC 22 at 31, HL.
13   Ibid, at 40.
14   Ibid, at 45.

The company is at law a different person altogether from the subscribers to the Memorandum and, although it may be that after incorporation the business is precisely the same as it was before, and the same persons are managers, and the same hands receive the profits, the company is not in law the agent of the subscribers or trustee for them. Nor are subscribers as members liable, in any shape or form, except to the extent and in the manner provided by the Act. That is, I think, the declared intention of the enactment.

The House of Lords' decision in *Salomon* has been criticised as going too far. The contemporary comment of the Law Quarterly Review[15] was that the House of Lords had recognised that one trader and six dummies would suffice and that the statutory conditions were mere machinery. 'You touch the requisite button and the company starts into existence, a legal entity, an independent *persona*.' The decision recognised that the one-man company fell within the policy of the Act. There was nothing startling in that. Once limited liability was recognised the creditors must look at the capital— the limited fund—and that only. Nevertheless, from the point of view of statutory construction it was thought that such a decision would have been impossible 20 or 30 years earlier. The reference in the Act to the persons being 'associated' would then have predicated a partnership. A more drastic modern criticism was that of the late Professor Otto Kahn-Freund[16] who thought that the decision was 'calamitous'. The courts, while developing fiduciary principles to protect shareholders, had failed to mitigate 'the rigidities of the "folklore" of corporate entity in favour of the legitimate interests of the company's creditors'. Not only this but the incongruity permeated the whole of legal business life. He thought that the answer lay in:

(a) raising the cost of incorporation;
(b) the introduction of minimum capital for all companies not exempted by the Department of Trade and a minimum subscription on incorporation;
(c) the abolition of private companies;
(d) a general clause deeming those companies under the control of 10 persons to be the agents of those persons.

As we have seen, a minimum capital has now been introduced for public companies. Most of Professor Kahn-Freund's other suggestions are probably too draconian but variations on the theme of (d) received some consideration by the Insolvency Law Review Committee of the Department of Trade which preferred not to express a final view on the matter.

We saw in the first chapter how all legal personality is in a sense fiction—the creation of legal artifice. *Corporate* personality is essentially a metaphorical use of language clothing the formal group with a single separate legal identity by analogy with a natural person[17]. Metaphors in fact abound in this area of law, both to support and to reject the separate legal personality of the company. As Cardozo J said in the American case of *Berkey v Third Avenue Rly*[18]: 'Metaphors in law are to be narrowly watched, for starting as devices to liberate thought, they often end by enslaving it'. It is certainly the case that the application of the *Salomon* principle has on occasions led to some extreme results. Thus in the Northern Irish case of *Macaura v Northern*

15   (1897) 13 LQR 6.
16   (1944) 7 MLR 54.
17   There are advantages and disadvantages in doing this. These were brilliantly analysed by Martin Wolff (1938) 54 LQR 494.
18   244 NY 84 (1926) at 94–5.

Assurance Co Ltd[19] Macaura was the controlling shareholder of a company and effected fire insurance in his own name in respect of the property of the company. The question in issue was whether he had an insurable interest in the property of the company. The House of Lords held that only the company had an insurable interest in its property. Macaura had no insurable interest and, therefore, could not claim on the policies. This seems a rather harsh application of the principle although it may be that the House was influenced by the charges of fraud which had been unsuccessful in the earlier arbitration. Certainly there seems to have been less than a month between the taking out of one of the policies and the fire. The converse also applies. In the Canadian Supreme Court case of *Wandlyn Motels Ltd v Commerce General Insurance Co*[20] it was held that a company has no insurable interest in the assets of the principal shareholder.

A more humane application of the principle which really pushes it to its logical extreme is *Lee v Lee's Air Farming Ltd*[1]. This was a New Zealand appeal to the Privy Council. Lee was the controlling shareholder, sole governing director and chief pilot of the company. A governing director has all the powers of management vested in him. Lee died as a result of an air crash while top-dressing. The question was whether he was an employee of the company for the purpose of the workmen's compensation legislation. The New Zealand Court of Appeal had held that he was not, as he was not sufficiently separate from the company. The Privy Council overruled this, applying a strict application of the *Salomon* principle. The company and Lee were separate legal persons and it was possible for a controlling shareholder and governing director to have a contract with his company which could be the basis of a claim.

LEGITIMATE USE OF THE CORPORATE FORM AND PIERCING THE VEIL

The courts have on occasion not applied the *Salomon* principle. However, they have not done this in a systematic way by defining the proper ends of incorporation. Instead they have moved from case to case.

As Rogers AJA said in the New South Wales Court of Appeal in *Briggs v James Hardie & Co Pty Ltd*[2]:

> The threshold problem arises from the fact that there is no common, unifying principle, which underlies the occasional decision of courts to pierce the corporate veil. Although an ad hoc explanation may be offered by a court which so decides, there is no principled approach to be derived from the authorities …

It is difficult to start to rationalise the cases except under the broad, rather question-

after explanation

---

19 [1925] AC 619, HL. Cf however *Constitution Insurance Co of Canada v Kosmopoulos* (1987) 34 DLR (4th) 208 (Supreme Court of Canada) and *American Indemnity Co v Southern Missionary College* 260 SW 2d 269 (1953) which allowed claims in the case of a sole shareholder. In the *Kosmopoulos* case the court concentrated on the concept of insurable interest and did not regard itself as piercing the corporate veil. For earlier comment on the case see Jacob Ziegel (1984) 62 Can Bar Rev 95. It is always possible to insure the shares themselves. See *Paterson v Harris* (1861) 1 B & S 336; *Wilson v Jones* (1867) LR 2 Exch 139.

20 (1970) 12 DLR (3d) 605.

1 [1961] AC 12, PC.

2 [1989] 16 NSWLR 549 at 567. See also McKay J in *A-G v Equiticorp Industries Group Ltd* (*in statutory management*) [1996] 1 NZLR 528, 541 (piercing the corporate veil is not a principle but a process).

begging heading of policy and by describing the main legal categories under which they fall[3]. These are:

(1) agency;
(2) fraud;
(3) group enterprises;
(4) trusts;
(5) tort;
(6) enemy;
(7) tax;
(8) the companies legislation;
(9) other legislation.

We will deal with each of these in turn and then attempt a summing up.

1 Agency

The *Salomon* case held that a company was not automatically the agent of its shareholders. It did not exclude the possibility of there being an agent relationship in fact. Occasionally the courts have seemed willing to construe an express or implied agency of the company for its members[4]. It has, however, been held that a 98% controlling interest in a company by itself does not create or manifest an agency relationship[5]. The authorities were reviewed by Atkinson J in *Smith, Stone & Knight Ltd v Birmingham Corpn*[6] where he attempted, not particularly successfully, to identify the underlying principles. The facts of the case were that a company took over a business and continued it through a subsidiary company which was treated as a department. The parent company claimed compensation on the basis of injury by the corporation's use of its powers of compulsory acquisition over the subsidiary's land. Piercing the corporate veil was essential to the plaintiff's claim since the corporation would otherwise escape paying compensation altogether by virtue of s 121 of the Lands Clauses Consolidation Act 1845 which enabled purchasers to get rid of occupiers with short tenancies by giving them notice. Counsel for the parent company used agency and group arguments and Atkinson J accepted at the end of the day that the parent company could recover. He said that the overall question of whether the subsidiary was carrying on the business as the parent's business or its own was a question of fact. In answering it, six factors were to be weighed:

(a) were the profits of the subsidiary those of the parent company?
(b) were the persons conducting the business of the subsidiary appointed by the parent company?

---

3   See Murray Pickering (1968) 31 MLR 481; M Whincup (1981) 2 Co Law 158; Gower *Principles of Modern Company Law* (6th edn, 1997), Ch 8; *Henn and Alexander*, op cit, p 344 and the bibliography cited by the latter at pp 345–346. However, for attempts to break away from this unsatisfactory approach see P Carteaux (1984) 58 Tulane L Rev 1089; A Domanski (1986) 103 SALJ 224; A Beck 'The Two Sides of the Corporate Veil' in *Contemporary Issues in Company Law* (1987) (ed J H Farrar), 69; S. Ottolenghi (1990) 53 MLR 338. Dr Ottolenghi distinguishes between peeping behind, penetrating, extending and ignoring the corporate veil. See too JS Ziegel (1990) 31 Les Cahiers de Droit 1075 and Ruthven (1969) Jur Rev 1.
4   See *Rainham Chemical Works Ltd v Belvedere Fish Guano Co* [1921] 2 AC 465, HL; *Southern v Watson* [1940] 3 All ER 439, CA; *Clarkson Co Ltd v Zhelke* (1967) 64 DLR (2d) 457. For a detailed survey see R Flannigan (1986–7) 51 Sask Law Rev 23. Cf *Re Polly Peck International plc* [1996] 2 All ER 433.
5   *Kodak Ltd v Clark* [1903] 1 KB 505, CA; *Denis Wilcox Pty Ltd v FCT* (1988) 14 ACLR 156.
6   [1939] 4 All ER 116.

(c) was the parent company the 'head and brains' of the trading venture?

(d) did the parent company govern the adventure?

(e) were the profits made by the subsidiary company made by the skill and direction of the parent company?

(f) was the parent company in effective and constant control of the subsidiary?

Conceptually, this is an incoherent approach, (d), (e) and (f) cover very much the same ground. At the end of the day Atkinson J held that the subsidiary was the 'agent or employee; or tool or simulacrum of the parent'. For all its faults *Smith, Stone & Knight* was followed by Else-Mitchell J in the New South Wales Supreme Court case of *Hotel Terrigal Pty Ltd v Latec Investments Ltd (No 2)*[7] where His Honour disregarded a purported sale by a mortgagee company of the mortgaged property to its wholly owned subsidiary for an improper purpose. The emphasis in compulsory acquisition cases has shifted more recently to the group enterprise argument.

Is it possible to be more orderly in one's thinking in this area? Professor Otto Kahn-Freund in a note in [1940] 3 MLR 226 distinguished between two kinds of control, 'capitalist control' and 'functional control' and argued that the *Salomon* case was about capitalist control. 'Capitalist control', which means control by ownership of a company's share capital, does not necessarily mean there is an agency. Functional control is concerned with who is actually running the company and, therefore, is relevant to the determination of an agency. As can be seen most of the factors mentioned by Atkinson J are concerned with aspects of 'functional control'.

US corporation laws recognise functional control under the instrumentality doctrine. A clear statement of principle appears in the judgment of Alcorn J in *Zaist v Olson* 227 A 2d 552 (1967) at p 558 where he said:

> The instrumentality rule requires, in any case but an express agency, proof of three elements: (1) control, not mere majority or complete stock control, but complete domination, not only of finances but of policy and business practice in respect to the transaction attacked so that the corporate entity as to this transaction had at the time no separate mind, will or existence of its own; and (2) such control must have been used by the defendant to commit fraud or wrong, to perpetuate the violation of a statutory or other positive legal duty, or a dishonest or unjust act in contravention of plaintiff's legal rights; and (3) the aforesaid control and breach of duty must proximately cause the injury or unjust loss complained of ...

As we will see in a moment there is a link between agency in fact, instrumentality and the concept of the group enterprise.

2 Fraud

The courts are prepared to pierce the corporate veil to combat fraud. They will not allow the *Salomon* principle to be used as an engine of fraud. Fraud here covers criminal fraud but also includes equitable fraud. In *Gilford Motor Co Ltd v Horne*[8], a managing director of a company entered into a covenant in a service agreement not to solicit customers from his employers. Upon leaving the company's employment he formed

---

7 [1969] 1 NSWLR 676.

8 [1933] Ch 935, CA. See also *Creasey v Breachwood Motors Ltd* [1993] BCLC 480. As to criminal fraud see eg *Hare v Customs and Excise Comrs* (1996) 140 Sol Jo 67, CA.

a company to solicit customers. It was held by the Court of Appeal that his company was a mere sham to cloak his wrongdoings and, therefore, he could be restrained from committing a breach. Similarly, in *Jones v Lipman*[9] a man contracted to sell property but then changed his mind. In order to avoid an order for specific performance he transferred the property to a company. Russell J held that specific performance could be ordered against the company. It was 'the creature of the first defendant, a device and a sham, a mask which [he] held before his face to avoid recognition by the eye of equity'[10].

Again, in *Re Bugle Press Ltd*[11] the use of a company as a device to fall within the provisions of s 209 of the Companies Act 1948 was disallowed. Section 209 which is re-enacted in s 428 of CA 1985 enables a takeover bidder who falls within the section and has acquired the requisite proportion of shares to acquire the minority compulsorily. Here there were three shareholders, and two wanted to buy out the third, who refused. As things stood the facts did not fall within the section so the majority formed a company to make an offer for all the shares in order to bring the matter within the section. The Court of Appeal, looking to substance rather than form, disregarded the company as a mere sham or simulacrum. The minority shareholder, said Harman LJ, had only to shout and the walls of Jericho fell flat.

The timing of the switch to a different corporate entity is crucial. Where it occurs before the accrual of the cause of action the courts will not pierce the corporate veil but it is otherwise where the switch is made after the cause of action accrued. Thus in *Adams v Cape Industries Pty Ltd*[12] in 1990 the Court of Appeal refused to pierce the corporate veil where a subsidiary company was set up to reduce potential tortious liability but this was distinguished by the judge in *Creasey v Breachwood Motors Ltd* in 1993[13] where assets had been transferred to another company owned by the same individual in order to defeat a claim for unfair dismissal after that claim had arisen. In such cases as the latter the courts frequently use the terms 'device', 'facade' or 'sham'.[14]

There has in fact been an increasing tendency on the part of English courts and, on occasion, Commonwealth courts, to use the language of 'facade', 'sham' or 'cipher' echoing the earlier use of mask, cloak or simulacrum.[15]

Like much common law usage this is question begging or a category of illusory or circular reference[16] and better avoided. It does little more than imply a value judgment of disapprobation[17]. Most of the cases are in fact examples of fraud in the broadest sense. Beyond this they represent an inarticulate attempt to mark the limits of legitimate incorporation.

It should, however, be noted that the courts have not shown any great willingness to step in to protect creditors from abuse of the corporate form due to reckless as opposed to fraudulent trading. Where fraudulent trading has taken place, s 213 of the Insolvency Act 1986 enables the court to pierce the corporate veil. The Cork Report favoured an extension of this to wrongful trading, and this concept was introduced by

9   [1962] 1 All ER 442.
10   Ibid, at 445 c–d.
11   [1961] Ch 270, CA.
12   [1990] Ch 433.
13   [1993] BCLC 480.
14   See for example *Re H (Restraint order: realisable property)* [1996] 2 BCLC 500. For the use of such terms see Lord Cooke of Thorndon's Hamlyn Lecture.
15   See LCB Gower *Principles of Modern Company Law* (6th ed) 171. For recent discussion see Robert Walker J in *Re Polly Peck International plc* [1996] 2 All ER 433, 447 a–g. For Australian usage see eg *State Bank of Victoria v Parry* (1990) 8 ACLC 766, 775. For New Zealand see *A-G v Equiticorp Industries Ltd* [1996] 1 NZLR 528, 541.
16   See Julius Stone *Precedent and Law* (1985) chapter 4 for a restatement of his analysis in *The Province and Function of Law* (1946) and *Legal System and Lawyers' Reasonings* (1964).
17   See Robert Walker J in *Re Polly Peck International plc* [1996] 2 All ER 433 at 447b.

the Insolvency Act 1985, the relevant provision now being consolidated in s 214 of the Insolvency Act 1986.

3 Group enterprises

The courts have sometimes shown a willingness to look upon a group of companies as one economic unit[18]. This is done by the accounting and disclosure provisions of the companies legislation to some extent and is now carried on by the courts on occasion. Indeed the legislation has been used as a justification for the case law even though not strictly relevant. In *Littlewoods Mail Order Stores Ltd v McGregor*[19] Lord Denning stated that the doctrine laid down in *Salomon* had to be carefully watched. It has often been supposed to cast a veil over a limited liability company through which the courts could not see. This was not true. The courts can and often do draw aside the veil and look at what really lies behind. Parliament had shown the way: the courts should follow suit. A similar line was taken in *DHN Food Distributors Ltd v London Borough of Tower Hamlets*[20]. This was a case of compulsory acquisition. The facts were that one company in the group owned the freehold and another company which carried on the business on the premises was a bare licensee. The Court of Appeal was prepared to recognise the economic unit of the group as a single entity to enable them to recover their compensation. The different members of the Court of Appeal seem to have been influenced by different factors. Lord Denning MR referred to the fact that the subsidiaries were wholly owned, but thereafter lapsed into metaphor. Goff LJ made it clear that not every group would be treated in this way but pointed to ownership, no separate business operations and the nature of the question to be answered. Shaw LJ pointed to common directors, shareholdings and common interest.

This approach seems to go too far and is inconsistent with the view of the High Court of Australia in *Industrial Equity Ltd v Blackburn*[1] where it was said that the group account provisions did not operate to deny the separate legal personality of the company. The *DHN* case was not followed by the House of Lords in the Scottish appeal of *Woolfson v Strathclyde Regional Council*[2]. A similar approach again more consistent with *Salomon*'s case was taken by the New Zealand Court of Appeal in the case of *Re Securitibank Ltd (No 2)*[3]. This involved an in-house bill where the client drew a bill of exchange on Merbank which was then discounted by another member of the group, Commercial Bills. Counsel sought to argue that this involved an infringement of the money lending legislation because the essence of the transaction was a loan if one pierced the corporate veil. The Court of Appeal referred to the *Littlewoods* case and thought that it was putting the matter the wrong way round. The starting point should be the application of the *Salomon* principle and any departure from it must be looked

---

18   See *Gower*, op cit, p 166 ff. For an interesting recent analysis see H Collins (1990) 53 MLR 731. For recent case law discussion see *Adams v Cape Industries plc* [1990] Ch 433, CA. See too the discussion of Salomon, groups and undertakings in *Istituto Chemioterapico Italiano SpA and Commercial Solvents Corpn v EC Commission*: Case 6, 7/73 [1974] ECR 223, ECJ, Advocate General Warner at p 263. For the relationship with factual control and agency see above and *Adams v Cape Industries plc* (supra) and *Revlon Inc v Cripps and Lee Ltd* [1980] FSR 85, CA.

19   [1969] 3 All ER 855 at 860, CA.

20   [1976] 3 All ER 462, CA.

1   (1977) 137 CLR 567 at 577.

2   (1978) 38 P & CR 521, HL. See F Rixon (1986) 102 LQR 415. For discussion of recent Northern Irish cases see G Dee (1986) 7 Co Law 248. See also *Glasgow City District Council v Hamlet Textiles Ltd* 1986 SLT 415; *National Dock Labour Board v Pinn & Wheeler Ltd* (1989) 5 BCC 75; *Acatos & Hutchinson plc v Watson* [1995] 1 BCLC 218.

3   [1978] 2 NZLR 136.

at very carefully. *Woolfson v Strathclyde Regional Council* and *Re Securitibank Ltd* were considered by Young J in the New South Wales case of *Pioneer Concrete Services Ltd v Yelnah Pty Ltd*[4]. This was a case of a complicated commercial agreement involving a group of companies which had been entered into with full legal advice. His Honour held that the court would only pierce the corporate veil where it could see that there was in law or in fact a partnership between the companies or where there was a mere sham or facade. Here there was a good commercial reason for having separate companies perform different functions and the veil should not be pierced.

A conservative restatement of the English position was made by the Court of Appeal in *Adams v Cape Industries Pty Ltd*[5], a case involving a foreign judgment against a company. The court held that each company in a group is a separate entity, after a review of the earlier cases. It made the point that in many of the cases of 'simple economic unit' there was some justification in the wording of the particular statute or contract. DHN could be explained in this way.

In the New South Wales Court of Appeal decision of *Briggs v James Hardie & Co Pty Ltd*[6] Rogers AJA made an interesting analysis of what he called 'the unity of enterprise theory' relying on Commonwealth and US authorities. The majority gave a liberal interpretation to s 58 of the Limitation Act NSW 1969 to allow an extension of the limitation period in a case of multiple defendants and Rogers AJA said that the mere potential to exercise control over a subsidiary was not enough to justify piercing the corporate veil. The exercise of some control in fact was also insufficient. Dominance may be part of the test but Commonwealth company law was not settled on this or on the degree of control or the extent of reliance or under capitalisation. The Salomon principle had survived the growth of corporate groups, and domination and control were not per se sufficient to pierce the corporate veil. It is unfortunate that His Honour does not appear to have been referred to the US instrumentality doctrine which, when read in the context of the US approach overall, completes the picture. In *Re a Company*[7] in 1985 the Court of Appeal was prepared to pierce the corporate veil by granting an injunction restricted to companies controlled by the defendant where the evidence showed that the defendant had created a corporate network to dispose of his assets and there was an allegation of fraud.

One area where the courts have been particularly reluctant to recognise the concept of group entity is in relation to corporate debts. It is not usually possible in the absence of an agency or trust relationship or wrongful trading[8] to hold one group company liable for the debts of another. In the USA equitable doctrines are sometimes applied in this context and in New Zealand and the Irish Republic there is legislation giving the court power to order a pooling of assets. Sometimes, however, even in the UK the courts have been forced into this position due to the hopeless muddle which has faced them.[9]

4   [1986] 5 NSWLR 254. See also *National Dock Labour Board v Pinn and Wheeler Ltd* [1989] BCLC 647.
5   [1990] Ch 433. See also *Bank of Tokyo Ltd v Karoon* [1987] AC 45n at p 64, CA per Robert Goff LJ and recent Canadian cases, *Tridont Leasing (Canada) Ltd v Saskatoon Market Mall Ltd* (1996) 24 BLR 105 (Sask CA) and *Bow Valley Husky v Saint John Shipbuilding Ltd* (1996) 21 BLR (2d) 265 (Newf CA).
6   [1989] 16 NSWLR 549.
7   [1985] BCLC 333, CA.
8   For a case where a claim under s 332 of the 1948 Act failed see *Re Augustus Barnett & Son Ltd* (1986) 2 BCC 98, 904. Noted by D D Prentice (1987) 103 LQR 11. For a case where the House of Lords seemed willing to pierce the corporate veil or use the alter ego approach in equity, see *Winkworth v Edward Baron Development Co Ltd* [1987] 1 All ER 114, HL.
9   *Re Bank of Credit and Commerce International SA (No 3)* [1993] BCLC 1490, CA and *No 10* [1995] 1 BCLC 362.

4   Trust

Occasionally, the courts may pierce the corporate veil to look at the characteristics of the shareholders. In *Abbey Malvern Wells Ltd v Ministry of Local Government and Planning*[10] a school was carried on in the form of a company, but the shares were held by trustees on educational charitable trusts. The court was prepared to pierce the corporate veil and look at the terms on which the trustees held the shares.

5   Tort

Although there are isolated cases where English courts have used tort remedies to pierce the corporate veil, it is not common in Commonwealth jurisdictions outside Canada. In Canada, however, there is an increasing use of tort to bypass *Salomon's* case. Inducing a breach of contract[11], deceit[12] and conspiracy[13] have all been used in recent cases. Thus in the British Columbia Court of Appeal case of *BG Preeco I (Pacific Coast) Ltd v Bon Street Holdings Ltd*[14] the Court held that *Salomon's* case was to be adhered to but that there was a direct remedy in deceit against the principal directors and shareholders where they had misled the plaintiff by switching the name of a company with assets to a shell company. The end result turned out to be the same. There would appear to be potential here for undermining the rigour of the *Salomon*[15] principle and this perhaps reflects the fact that its application in the tort area has always been less justifiable than in contract. Many tort victims have no choice in the selection of tort feasor. Here domination and under-capitalisation seem particularly relevant to piercing the veil.

6   Enemy

In times of war the court is prepared to pierce the corporate veil to see who are the controlling shareholders of companies. This was done in *Daimler Co Ltd v Continental Tyre and Rubber Co (Great Britain) Ltd*[16] where shares in an English company were held by Germans in the First World War.

7   Tax

From time to time for reasons of fiscal policy tax legislation disregards the separate legal personality of companies. Also the courts are prepared to disregard the separate legal personality of companies in the case of tax evasion or over-liberal schemes of tax avoidance without any necessary legislative authority. In such cases the courts frequently dismiss the company as a mere sham[17]. The question of form and substance in tax law is quite complex and this is merely part of it.

10   [1951] Ch 728.
11   *McFadden v 481782 Ontario Ltd* (1984) 47 OR (2d) 134; *BG Preeco I (Pacific Coast) Ltd v Bon Street Holdings Ltd* (1989) 60 DLR (4th) 30.
12   *BG Preeco* (supra).
13   *Lehndorff Canadian Properties Ltd v Davis & Co* (1987) 10 BCLR (2d) 342.
14   (1989) 60 DLR (4th) 30. Cf *Trevor Ivory Ltd v Anderson* [1992] 2 NZLR 517, CA for a more conservative approach.
15   See Rogers AJA in *Briggs v James Hardie & Co Pty Ltd* [1989] 16 NSWLR 549 at 578, 580.
16   [1916] 2 AC 307, HL.
17   See *Gower*, op cit, p 164.

8   Companies legislation

LESS THAN STATUTORY MINIMUM MEMBERS

The Companies Act 1985 and the Insolvency Act 1986 contain provisions which pierce the corporate veil. Section 24 of the Companies Act 1985 provides that if a company carries on business for more than six months with less than the statutory minimum number of members, any person who is a member after that six months may be liable jointly and severally with the company for the payment of its debts. The statutory minimum number of members is not less than two except in the case of a single member private limited company where it is one. It would be logically impossible for the latter to have less than the statutory minimum number of members and yet be subject to the section since there would be no member to whom the liability could attach. It should be noted under these provisions that the company itself remains liable and that liability does not attach to the directors under this section.

FRAUDULENT AND WRONGFUL TRADING

Another important section which was formerly in the Companies Act but is now in the Insolvency Act 1986 is the fraudulent and wrongful trading provision. This is now contained in ss 213–215 of the Insolvency Act 1986. Originally the liability was limited to the persons who were party to the carrying on of the company's business with the intent to defraud creditors. The liability is now extended to wrongful trading which is a much broader concept. Wrongful trading is dealt with by s 214 and enables the court to make a declaration where a company has gone into insolvent liquidation. The declaration can be made against a person who at any time before the commencement of the winding up was a director of the company and knew or ought to have concluded at that time that there was no reasonable prospect that the company would avoid going into insolvent liquidation. The declaration is not to be made if the court is satisfied that the person took every step with a view to minimising the potential loss to the creditors that he ought to have taken. The standard applied is one of a reasonably diligent person having the general knowledge, skill and experience to be expected of a person carrying out his or her functions in relation to the company and the general knowledge, skill and experience that he or she in fact has.

Section 214 extends the term director to include shadow directors.[18] Shadow directors are persons in accordance with whose directions or instructions the directors of the company are accustomed to act. It may be that a parent company can constitute a shadow director for this purpose, since the definition in the Insolvency Act differs from that in the Companies Act itself.[19]

PHOENIX COMPANIES

The Insolvency Act 1986 also deals with certain abuses arising from the 'Phoenix Company' problem, whereby fraudsters walk away from an insolvent company and start another one with the same or a similar name. Section 216 provides for an offence for anyone who was a director or shadow director of a company at any time during the

---

18   Section 124(1) of the Insolvency Act cf Companies Act 1985, s 741(2).
19   See *Gower's Principles of Modern Company Law* (6th ed), pp 154 et seq.

12 months preceding its insolvent liquidation to be in any way concerned (without leave of the court) during the next five years in the formation or management of a company or business with a name by which an earlier company was known or is so similar as to suggest an association. Section 217 provides for personal liability jointly and severally with the company for the debts and liabilities of the original company.

ACTING WHILE DISQUALIFIED

Section 15 of the Company Directors Disqualification Act 1986 provides that a person acting in the management of a company when an order under that Act has been made against him or her and any person acting on his or her instructions knowing him or her to be disqualified are jointly and severally liable with the company for debts contracted during that period.

MISDESCRIPTION OF COMPANY

There are provisions in the Companies Act 1985 which deal with personal liability for misdescription of the company. Section 349(4) of the Companies Act 1985 provides that, if any officer of the company or any other person acting on its behalf signs or authorises to be signed on behalf of the company any bill of exchange, promissory note, endorsement, cheque or order for money or goods in which the company's name is not mentioned, he or she is liable to a fine and is also personally liable unless the company pays.

9   Other legislation

The locus classicus for legislation in general is perhaps the speech of Lord Diplock in *Dimbleby & Sons Ltd v National Union of Journalists*[20] where he said:

> My Lords, the reason why English statutory law, and that of all other trading countries, has long permitted the creation of corporations as artificial persons distinct from their individual shareholders and from that of any other corporation even though the shareholders of both corporations are identical, is to enable business to be undertaken with limited financial liability in the event of the business proving to be a failure. The 'corporate veil' in the case of companies incorporated under the Companies Acts is drawn by statute and it can be pierced by some other statute if such other statute so provides: but in view of its raison d'être and its consistent recognition by the courts since *Salomon v A Salomon & Co Ltd* [1897] AC 22, HL, one would expect that any parliamentary intention to pierce the corporate veil would be expressed in clear and unequivocal language. I do not wholly exclude the possibility that even in the absence of express words stating that in specified circumstances one company, although separately incorporated, is to be treated as sharing the same legal personality of another, a purposive construction of the statute may nevertheless lead inexorably to the conclusion that such must have been the intention of Parliament.

20   [1984] 1 WLR 427 at 435 B–G, HL.

In that case the House of Lords held that the phrase 'an employer who is a party to the dispute' did not extend to another company which had identical shareholdings and the same parent company as the actual employer.

Conclusion

It is difficult to sum up these exceptions except to say that the departures from the *Salomon* principle seem to be based on policy decisions. The general principle seems to be that *Salomon* will be applied until some strong reason to the contrary appears. There is a range from legitimate purposes where it will be applied to dishonest purposes where it will not be applied. Where there is unity of interest and ownership and the concept of separate legal personality is being used to defeat public convenience, justify wrong, protect fraud, or defend crime, the law will tend to regard the company as an association of the natural persons comprising it[1]. Reduction of potential tort liability (short of fraud) will not suffice[2]. In between are cases where the court might disregard it to achieve a just result. There seems to be a general reluctance to apply the principle in a pedantic way where the result will cause injustice. It should, however, be noted that the argument for piercing the corporate veil will not usually be the sole argument in the case. It will usually be incidental to some other argument of substance. A similar but not identical point was made by Stone J in the American case of *Re Clark's Will*[3], when he said:

> Many cases present avowed disregard of corporate entity ... But they all come to just this—courts simply will not let interposition of corporate entity or action prevent a judgment otherwise required. Corporate presence and action no more than those of an individual will bar a remedy demanded by law in application to facts. Hence the process is not accurately termed one of disregarding corporate entity. It is rather and only a refusal to permit its presence and action to divert the judicial course of applying law to ascertained facts. The method neither pierces any veil nor goes behind any obstruction, save for its refusal to let one fact bar the judgment which the whole sum of facts requires. For such reasons, we feel that the method of decision known as 'piercing the corporate veil' or 'disregarding the corporate entity' unnecessarily complicates decision. It is dialectically ornate and correctly guides understanding, but over a circuitous and unrealistic trail. The objective is more easily attainable over the direct and unencumbered route followed herein.

It is submitted, however, that this describes judicial policy rather than legal principle. To state a policy is not to provide a substitute for legal principle. However, as a frank avowal of judicial policy it is welcome.

---

1   *Henn and Alexander*, op cit, p 344.
2   See *Adams v Cape Industries plc* [1990] BCC 786, CA; *Walkovszky v Carlton* 18 NY 2d 414 (1966). For interesting law and economics analysis of *Walkovszky* see Halpern, Trebilcock and Turnbull (1980) 30 U Toronto LJ 117, 145–146.
3   204 Minn 574 (1939) at 578. See also Wilson J in *Constitution Insurance Co of Canada v Kosmopoulos* (1987) 34 DLR (4th) 208 at 213–14 and a note in (1982) 95 Harv L Rev 853. For a valuable empirical study of US practice see R Thompson (1991) 76 Cornell L Rev 1036.

CONSEQUENCES OF SEPARATE CORPORATE PERSONALITY

As a species of corporation the company has the following traditional and modern corporate attributes[4].

(1) It has perpetual succession. Until dissolved a company continues to exist and survives the death of its directors and shareholders. As Grant wrote in 1850 'This unbroken personality, this beautiful combination of the legal characters of the finite with essentials of infinity appears to have been the primary object of the invention of incorporations'[5].

(2) It owns its own property. The assets of a company do not belong to the shareholders. The only interest which they have in the assets of the company is indirectly through the medium of their shares. They have no proprietary rights to the underlying assets. Similarly creditors of the company are not creditors of the shareholders. The creditors must go against the company and it is only if the company is being wound up and there is some evidence of fraud that they may possibly have recourse against the shareholders.

(3) As a separate legal person the company can sue or be sued in its own name.

(4) A company can create a floating charge. This is a type of equitable security which can only be granted by companies and others who are empowered under specific legislation. The essence of a floating charge is that it floats over the undertaking or class of assets until an event occurs which causes it to crystallise, whereupon it becomes a fixed equitable charge. Until then the company can dispose of its assets in the ordinary course of business.

(5) Although it is not perhaps a logically necessary attribute of separate legal personality in modern law, the liability of the members of a limited company is limited and the two concepts are closely linked in practice.[6] Members are only liable for the amount unpaid on nominal value of their shares. In the case of a company limited by guarantee they are only liable for the amount of their guarantee.

(6) As the price of separate legal personality, the company must comply with the formalities of the Companies Acts. This requires payment of the registration fee, and the regular filing of documents and accounts with the Registrar of Companies. These are the costs of transacting business in this particular way.

THE RELATIONSHIP OF LEGAL PERSONALITY TO LIMITED LIABILITY

Although there is a tendency to equate the two, legal personality and limited liability are two separate concepts. A company can be a separate legal person but its shareholders may still have unlimited liability for its debts. Unlimited companies, which existed in England between 1844–1855 as the norm, still continue as the exception. Limited liability can be the subject of individual contracting between a company's shareholders and its creditors. Complex drafting of deeds of settlement and cumbrous legal procedures produced the effect if not the letter of limited liability before the 1855 Act. Creditors had to sue each shareholder in a separate action and in practice sued the

---

4   See *The Case of Sutton's Hospital* (1612) 10 Co Rep 1a at 23a and 30b and 1 Bl Comm 456 at 463–6; CA 1985, s 13(3), (4).

5   *Grant on Corporations* (1850) Butterworths, p 4.

6   Chartered corporations usually involved this. The first companies under the general Companies Acts did not. This status became possible in 1855.

richest. The latter had no recourse. The reforms in the Joint Stock Companies Winding Up Act 1848 put an end to this de facto limited liability and reduced the attractiveness of shares to smaller investors. However, in 1852 in *Hallett v Dowdall*[7] the validity of a limited liability clause was upheld by the Court of Exchequer Chamber and it was held to bind third parties with express notice. The result was widespread use of such clauses which may have accounted for the change in public opinion in favour of limited liability[8].

Alternatively the company might take out insurance to cover its liabilities, thereby adding to its costs which it will pass on to its consumers. The third possibility is that adopted from 1855 onwards of institutionalised limited liability under the Companies Acts.

Limited liability under the Companies Acts means that shareholders are under no obligation to the company or its creditors beyond their obligations on the par value of their shares or under their guarantee in the case of a company limited by guarantee. Limited liability arguably reduces the costs involved in the separation of ownership and control. Generally this will only be relevant in the case of public companies. First, limited liability reduces the need to monitor management and other shareholders. Secondly, limited liability and free transfer of shares with which it is arguably linked facilitate the market for control. This acts as an incentive to management to perform efficiently. Thirdly, limited liability, in adding to the marketability of shares, improves the information fed to the market place by the increased volume of transactions. Fourthly, limited liability allows shareholders to diversify their holdings. Fifthly, it facilitates optimal investment decisions since a positive attitude to risk taking will ensue[9].

English company law, unlike US corporation laws, does not link limited liability with adequate capitalisation of the company. In some cases in the US jurisdictions it has been suggested that inadequate capitalisation is in itself a sufficient basis for piercing the corporate veil[10]. However, the orthodox view is that it is only one factor[11]. US courts have been more willing than English courts to pierce the corporate veil in cases of insolvent one-man companies and groups prior to winding up. Underlying this is perhaps some idea that the corporate privilege must be used for legitimate business purposes. The problem with this is to define what such purposes are.

It has been argued by Meiners, Mofsky and Tollinson[12] that the primary reasons for the corporate form of business are not in fact related to the principle of limited liability. These reasons are said to be:

(1) the marketability of shares (although this is only the case in public listed companies)
(2) perpetual existence
(3) flexible financing methods
(4) specialisation of management
(5) majority rule.

These could exist without limitation of liability. The argument is a variation on the theme of Coase's theorem that if transaction costs are zero the ultimate use of the

7   (1852) 21 LJQB 98.
8   H N Butler (1986) 6 International Review of Law and Economics 169.
9   See F Easterbrook and D Fischel (1985) 52 U Chi L Rev 89, 94 et seq.
10   *Minton v Cavaney* 364 P (2d) 473 (1961). See generally Phillip Blumberg, *The Multinational Challenge to Corporation Law—The Search for a New Corporate Personality* (1993), ch 6 and his five volume treatise, *The Law of Corporate Groups*.
11   *Pearl v Shore* 17 Cal App 3d 608 (1971).
12   (1979) 4 Delaware Journal of Corporate Law 351.

property will not depend on the initial assignment of property rights. Here the argument is that free contracting will vitiate the impact of the rule of liability on credit terms. Such contract based arguments do not, however, deal with the immunity of shareholders from liability to *involuntary* creditors. This is seen as a question of allocation of risk. Limited liability for tort transfers the obligation to insure on to the consumer who arguably pays lower prices in consequence[13].

In recent years there has been an increased call for restriction of limited liability and inroads have been made into the concept by s 214 of the Insolvency Act 1986 which deals with wrongful trading and supplements the law on fraudulent trading. Other alternatives are to introduce effective minimum capital requirements or compulsory insurance for certain involuntary creditors[14].

MOTIVES FOR AND AGAINST INCORPORATION

In practice, the privilege of limited liability is whittled away to some extent by the requirement of banks that the controllers of small incorporated firms give a guarantee in respect of the company's indebtedness. The result of this is that commercially the corporate veil is pierced for financial creditors. The limitation of liability is, however, still very relevant as regards trade creditors and involuntary creditors such as claimants in tort. A second motive for incorporation is taxation although at the end of the day there are taxation arguments either for or against incorporation. The use of the corporate form is a useful means of spreading income amongst members of a family. It is also useful for spreading ownership of wealth. Shares in a company are convenient subjects for gifts by wealthy relatives to the junior members of their family. A third motive for incorporation is organisation. A business often outgrows a sole trader or partnership and there is a need for a more sophisticated administrative structure. However, it must be admitted that the legal structure envisaged by company law is rather simplistic and outdated in practice. Modern companies have developed a managerial structure and chain of command which give recognition to middle management and the work force in addition to the basic company law requirements. A fourth motive for incorporation is to take advantage of the floating charge. We have briefly discussed the nature of the floating charge above. It is understood that banks and other financial institutions put pressure on businesses to incorporate so that they can be granted a floating charge as security over stock in trade and book debts.

Incorporation is not without its price. First there is the cost of incorporation and of maintaining proper secretarial and accounting systems. Trading as an incorporated company involves constant disclosure although the amount has been reduced for small firms. As far as a proprietor of a solvent business is concerned, as a sole trader he or she owes no duties to anyone in respect of his or her control of his or her business except that he or she must pay his or her taxes and comply with other general legislation applicable to him or her. Once the business is incorporated and he or she becomes a director, he or she is a fiduciary, and owes duties not to make secret profits and not to use his or her powers for an improper purpose[15]. These duties can be enforced by the company in general meetings[16] by exercising its powers of removal and can be the subject matter of an investigation by the Department of Trade and Industry[17]. In

---

13 For a strong argument in favour of compulsory insurance *by companies* in respect of tort claims see B Pettet 'Limited Liability—A Principle for the 21st Century?' in (1995) 48 CLP Part 2, 125.
14 F Easterbrook and D Fischel (1985) 52 U Chi L Rev 89, 101 et seq; Pettet op cit.
15 See Chapter 26, post.
16 See Chapter 28, post.
17 See Chapter 30, post.

practice, shareholders in public companies are not active in monitoring management and prefer to vote with their feet by selling their shares rather than get involved in a corporate row. Also, the track record of the Department of Trade and Industry for investigating corporate fraud and mismanagement is not particularly impressive, as we shall see in a later chapter. Nevertheless, the market for control and the market for management provide some control over management behaviour. A mismanaged company may be taken over and management prefer to be associated with a winner rather than a loser. To that extent they may be self-policing. If the company goes into liquidation, a person who is party to wrongful trading may be made personally liable[18]. These are some of the costs which a person must pay if the corporate form is adopted.

18   See Chapter 40, post.

CHAPTER 8

The companies registration system and the concepts of constructive notice and official notification

THE COMPANIES REGISTRATION SYSTEM

Part of the price which the incorporators of a company pay for incorporation is a continuing obligation to file certain documents with the Registrar of Companies. This obligation is in addition to the obligation to keep proper books and records at the company's registered office. When the Registrar grants a certificate of incorporation he or she opens a file for the new company and allots it a number. (The name and number so allotted have to be disclosed on the company's letter headings[1].) The documents lodged on registration are placed in the file together with a copy of the certificate of incorporation. If the company has been incorporated as a public company the declaration made for the purposes of obtaining a certificate to carry on business under s 117 will also appear on the file.

An annual return has to be filed[2] which gives up-to-date particulars about the company and, unless the company is an exempted unlimited company, it must file its accounts.

Other important documents which must be filed include the following:

(1) notice of the situation of the registered office or any change[3];
(2) particulars of directors or secretary or any change[4];
(3) copies of all special and extraordinary resolutions and contain ordinary resolutions[5];
(4) copies of the memorandum or articles as altered by any statutory provision other than a special resolution under s 4[6];
(5) copies of any prospectus[7];
(6) the valuation of a non-cash consideration provided for the shares in a public company[8];

---

1   Section 351(1).
2   Section 363.
3   Section 10(6).
4   Section 10(2).
5   Sections 123, 380 (4)(a) and (b).
6   Section 18.
7   Section 149, Financial Services Act 1986.
8   Section 111.

(7) particulars of registrable charges[9];
(8) resignation of auditors[10];
(9) appointment of a receiver[11] or liquidator[12];
(10) office copy of an administration order[13].

This is not an exhaustive list but gives an idea of the range of information contained on the company's file.

The main office of the Registrar of Companies for England and Wales was formerly in City Road, Islington in London. Now the main office is in Cardiff, but a smaller office is still kept in London[14]. There are separate registries for companies incorporated in Scotland and Northern Ireland.

When a member of the public makes a search he or she obtains a microfiche copy of the company's file.

THE PURPOSES OF THE SYSTEM

The companies registration system has grown up in a piecemeal way but the original purpose in 1844 was that it was part of a constitutive act whereby a deed of settlement company was transformed into a body corporate[15]. It was a state formality which involved a degree of publicity. The Registrar's file was open to the public and thus provided a source of information about the company. The main worry that people had at that time was to ascertain the authority of people to bind such companies. Registration on a public file of the constitutional documents afforded the public the means of checking the authority of persons purporting to bind the company. On the other hand there was no express provision such as is found in the Law of Property Act 1925 providing that registration should amount to notice. However, Lord Wensleydale said in *Ernest v Nicholls*[16] in 1857:

> The Legislature then devised the plan of incorporating these companies in a manner unknown to the common law, with special powers of management and liabilities, providing at the same time that all the world should have notice who were the persons authorised to bind all the shareholders, by requiring the co-partnership deed to be registered, certified by the directors, and made accessible to all; and, besides, including some clauses as to the management, as in the Act 7 and 8 Vict c 110, s 7, etc. All persons, therefore, must take notice of the deed and the provisions of the Act. If they do not choose to acquaint themselves with the powers of the directors, it is their own fault, and if they give credit to any unauthorised persons they must be contented to look to them only, and not to the company at large. The stipulations of the deed, which restrict and regulate their authority, are obligatory on those who deal with the company; and the directors can make no contract so as to bind the whole body of shareholders, for whose protection the rules are made, unless they are strictly complied with.

9   Section 395.
10   Section 390(3).
11   Sections 53 and 54 of the Insolvency Act 1986.
12   Section 109(1) of the Insolvency Act 1986.
13   Section 21(2) of the Insolvency Act 1986.
14   There was much criticism of this move. See eg L S Sealy (1981) 2 Co Law 51 at 52.
15   For a discussion of the distinction between constitutive and declaratory effect, see E Stein *Harmonisation of European Company Laws* (1971), p 277.
16   (1857) 6 HL Cas 401 at 418–419. See also *Mahony v East Holyford Mining Co* (1875) LR 7 HL 869 at 893 per Lord Hatherley. See J Montrose (1934) 50 LQR 224 at 236 ff.

The company's file which started off life as part of a constitutive act became a definitive source of information about the company's powers and directors' authority. Persons who dealt with companies were affected with notice of all that was contained in the registered constitution and, not only that, they were taken to understand the documents according to their proper meaning. The latter point was no doubt due to the principle 'ignorance of the law is no excuse'. Most of the cases involve shareholders and in *Oakbank Oil Co v Crum* (1882) 8 App Cas 65 at 71 Lord Selborne LC described their position in this way:

> Each party must be taken to have made himself acquainted with the terms of the written contract contained in the articles ... and the Acts of Parliament, so far as they are important. He must also in law be taken (though that is sometimes different from what the fact may be) to have understood the terms of the contract according to their proper meaning; and that being so he must take the consequences, whatever they may be ...

Although the authorities are less clear it appears that a similar principle was applied to outsiders. Eventually, however, this was reduced to a form of estoppel and to a negative doctrine. It cut down the scope of apparent authority but could not be relied on by one who did not know of the terms of a particular article. This doctrine became known as the doctrine of constructive notice. Starting off life as a doctrine about the constitution, it was later extended to non-constitutional matters when registration of charges with the Registrar was introduced. Again there was no express provision for constructive notice and it had been held that registration under the Bills of Sale legislation did not give rise to it. When it came it was again as a result of judicial law-making[17]. Notice was, however, confined to the existence of a charge as disclosed in the registered particulars and not its contents. Copies of the charge do not appear on the Register; furthermore, although non-registration of a charge will invalidate it as against the liquidators and creditors, registration does not amount to a conclusive priority point for the charge. This is usually the date of creation. The system of registration of charges is thus an incomplete registration system. A complete registration system would conclusively determine all these questions.

We can sum up the purposes of the company registration system, therefore, as threefold:

(1) constitutional
(2) informational
(3) validatory.

It is possible to identify further purposes of the system of disclosure at large, such as monitoring corporate management but we shall discuss these in later chapters under those headings[18].

THE DOCTRINE OF CONSTRUCTIVE NOTICE

The doctrine of constructive notice was originally developed in equity in property cases. An intending purchaser or mortgagee had a duty to investigate deeds the existence of

---

17 See W J Gough *Company Charges* 2nd edn (1996), p 824.
18 See generally Sealy, op cit and *Hahlo's Cases and Materials on Company Law* (3rd edn, 1987) by H R Hahlo and J H Farrar, ch 8 and materials cited.

which was disclosed or which he discovered where such deeds could affect the title[19] otherwise he or she took subject to them. Historically it was different from the common law concept of actual knowledge which would be inferred where a person had been wilfully blind, although in practice the same facts could fall under both concepts. Constructive notice as applied to companies developed originally as a constitutional doctrine. Here one was not concerned with title but with capacity and authority. Constructive notice in this sense was originally an evidential rule concerning public documents. It was a necessary corollary of this that matters which could not be verified by a search could not bind a member of the public.

The doctrine was extended beyond the memorandum and articles and particulars of directors to special resolutions[20]. When registration of charges was introduced, the judges extended the doctrine of constructive notice to them, although here as we have seen the purpose of registration was different. Non-registration operated to invalidate charges. The doctrine of constructive notice of registered particulars of charges, however, operated (albeit inconclusively) to postpone subsequent charges and was thus similar to the original equitable doctrine.

Dr W J Gough in his book *Company Charges*[1] argues that the extension of the doctrine to registered charges was bogus since the original company law doctrine was a constitutional doctrine. This seems to take too rigid a view of company registration. The purposes of registration evolved as we have seen, and as they developed the doctrine of constructive notice changed. As it related to company charges, it assumed a character closer to the original equitable doctrine.

A further question remains. How far does the company doctrine extend? It is clear law that before 1973 it extended to the memorandum and articles and special resolutions[2]. It is also clear that it continues to apply to company charges[3]. It is submitted that for documents other than charges distinctions can be drawn between those documents which are constitutional and those non-constitutional documents whose validity nevertheless depends on registration on the one hand, and those documents which fall outside these categories and whose function is merely to supply information on the other hand[4]. In the latter category would fall accounts and annual returns.

Even before 1973 the rigours of constructive notice were mitigated by the rule in *Royal British Bank v Turquand*[5] whereby outsiders were not to be concerned with internal irregularities and could rely on the evidential maxim *omnia praesumuntur rite et solemniter esse acta*—everything is presumed to have been done properly and solemnly which ought to have been done so[6]. The doctrine was substantially abolished as far as constitutional matters were concerned by the European Communities Act 1972, s 9(1) which was consolidated in CA 1985, s 35. The reforms were completed by the CA 1989 which make further amendments to the ultra vires doctrine and then purported to abolish what the act calls 'deemed notice' by the insertion of a new s 711A in the CA 1985. This reads as follows:

---

19 See *English and Scottish Mercantile Investment Co Ltd v Brunton* [1892] 2 QB 700, CA and J H Farrar (1974) 38 Conv (NS) 315.
20 *Re London and New York Investment Corpn* [1895] 2 Ch 860.
1   Page 361.
2   *Irvine v Union Bank of Australia* (1877) 2 App Cas 366, PC; *Re London and New York Investment Corpn* [1895] 2 Ch 860.
3   *Re Standard Rotary Machine Co Ltd* (1906) 95 LT 829; *Wilson v Kelland* [1910] 2 Ch 306.
4   Cf *Palmer's Company Law* (24th edn, 1987) vol 1, para 21–02 (now deleted in recent editions) and W J Gough *Company Charges* 2nd edn (1996), p 821 which adopt a distinction between public documents and non-public documents.
5   (1856) 6 E & B 327.
6   Discussed in detail in Chapter 23, post.

711A   Exclusion of deemed notice   (1) A person shall not be taken to have notice of any matter merely because of its being disclosed in any document kept by the registrar of companies (and thus available for inspection) or made available by the company for inspection.

(2) This does not affect the question whether a person is affected by notice of any matter by reason of a failure to make such inquiries as ought reasonably to be made.

(3) In this section 'document' includes any material which contains information.

(4) Nothing in this section affects the operation of—

(a) section 416 of this Act (under which a person taking a charge over a company's property is deemed to have notice of matters disclosed on the companies charges register), or

(b) section 198 of the Law of Property Act 1925 as it applies by virtue of section 3(7) of the Land Charges Act 1972 (under which the registration of certain land charges under Part XII or Chapter III of Part XXIII, of this Act is deemed to constitute actual notice for all purposes connected with the land affected).

Section 711A(2) retains the doctrine of inferred actual knowledge on the basis of wilful blindness and section 711A(4) retains constructive or deemed notice for charges registered under CA 1985 or the property legislation.

Unfortunately, although enacted, s 711A has not been brought into force because of the delay over the charges provisions.

We discuss these reforms in Chapters 10 and 25, post.

OFFICIAL NOTIFICATION[7]

The 1972 Act, while partially abolishing constructive notice, introduced the additional formality of official notification for a subclass of registrable documents. The formalities are that *the Registrar* must give notice in the Gazette of the *issue* or *receipt* of the following documents specified in s 711(1) of CA 1985. These are:

(a) any certificate of incorporation of a company;

(b) any document making or evidencing an alteration in a company's memorandum or articles;

(c) any notification of a change among the directors of a company;

(d) any copy of a resolution of a public company which gives, varies, revokes or renews an authority for the purposes of s 80 (allotment or relevant securities);

(e) any copy of a special resolution of a public company passed under s 95(1), (2) or (3) (disapplication of pre-emption rights);

(f) any report under ss 103 or 104 as to the value of a non-cash asset;

(g) any statutory declaration delivered under s 117 (public company share capital requirements);

(h) any notification (given under s 122) of the redemption of shares;

(j) any statement or notice delivered by a public company under s 128 (registration of particulars of special rights);

---

7   For a discussion of the evolution of this doctrine and the influence of the German Commercial Code and case law see *Stein*, op cit, pp 278–279 and the German materials there cited. The provisions represent a series of political compromises and remind one of the definition of a camel as a horse designed by a committee.

(k)   any documents delivered by a company under s 241 (annual accounts);
(l)   a copy of any resolution or agreement to which s 380 applies and which—
    (i)   states the rights attached to any shares in a public company, other than shares which are in all respects uniform (for purposes of s 128) with shares previously allotted; or
    (ii)   varies rights attached to any shares in a public company; or
    (iii)   assigns a name or other designation, or a new name or designation, to any class of shares in a public company;
(m)   any return of allotments of a public company;
(n)   any notice of a change in the situation of a company's registered office;
(p)   any copy of a winding-up order in respect of a company;
(q)   any order for the dissolution of a company on a winding up;
(r)   any return by a liquidator of the final meeting of a company on a winding up.

[Provisions (i) and (o) are omitted from the statutory list.]

Official notification is not a constitutive act and does not give rise to constructive notice[8]; it is a source of information and failure to deliver such documents gives rise in some cases to a form of statutory estoppel under s 42(1) which prevents the company from relying on the relevant event against a third party who was unaware of it. This statutory estoppel is not quite the same as invalidity. The act in question is valid but the company cannot rely on it as against a person who could not have been aware of it. What we have in effect is a subclass of the subclass specified in s 711(1). Section 42(1) refers to:

(a)   the making of a winding-up order in respect of the company, or the appointment of a liquidator in a voluntary winding up of the company; or
(b)   any alteration of the company's memorandum or articles; or
(c)   any change among the company's directors; or
(d)   (as regards service of any document on the company) any change in the situation of the company's registered office.

Section 42(1) also provides that in any event there is a 15-day leeway period after gazetting during which the company cannot rely on the relevant event against a person who was unavoidably prevented from knowing of it during that period. It is not clear what 'unavoidably prevented' means here. Presumably it does not obligate a person to make a search.

In *Re Peek Winch & Tod Ltd*[9] it was held that a company and its receiver could not rely on the making of a winding-up order until it was gazetted and the statutory period had expired, as against a party who had no actual notice of it.

COMPANIES HOUSE, AN EXECUTIVE AGENCY

The Registry of Business Names was abolished and effectively superseded by a private system operating under the aegis of the principal Chambers of Commerce. There was an announcement on 24 November 1982 by the Minister of Consumer Affairs that he was considering 'privatising' the whole or part of the companies registration system[10].

---

8   See *Official Custodian for Charities v Parway Estates Developments Ltd* [1985] Ch 151, CA—official notification by gazetting of a winding-up order held not to give rise to notice or knowledge of the winding up.
9   (1980) 130 NLJ 116, CA.
10   For an attack on this see (1983) 4 Co Law 2.

The aim of this was to reduce government spending. It was later dropped in the absence of commercial interest. The main arguments for retention of the present system were:

(1) Company registration is treated as a public matter in all common law countries.
(2) It is basic to effective disclosure which runs throughout our company law.
(3) There needs to be public control over the creation of companies and access to information.
(4) Enforcement of the statutory disclosure requirements needs to be handled by a public official.
(5) The systems of constructive notice and official notification could not operate as part of a private system.

The main arguments in favour of 'privatisation' were:

(1) Many EU member states use chambers of commerce for a number of these purposes. We could do the same.
(2) The role of the Registrar need not be totally abolished but could be cut down to a formal receipt and policing function.
(3) The information carried by the companies registration systems needs to be computerised and the government is currently unwilling to invest this money whereas private enterprise might be. Computers can store the information more efficiently and cut down costs in the long run.
(4) If a system is centred on regional Chambers of Commerce as part of a computer link up, then searching can be decentralised to the advantage of consumers.
(5) Constructive notice has been abolished for constitutional matters. For charges what is needed is a complete registration system integrated with the land registration system. Official notification could continue as part of a more limited role for the Registrar of Companies.

On 3 October 1988 a compromise was reached. Companies House became an executive agency within the Department of Trade and Industry and the occasion was suitably marked by the unveiling of a commemorative slate plaque. The aim of the agency is 'to operate with a greater degree of autonomy, leading to the prospect of increased efficiency and the delivery of an improved service to the customer'[11].

In conclusion one can say that traditional assumptions of company law are being challenged. Economic rigour, like the prospect of being hanged, concentrates the mind. Increasingly our system of companies registration has seemed a costly and inefficient storage house of information whose practical relevance has often seemed small[12]. If the primary objective of the system is now seen as the provision of up-to-date and accurate information then the impact of information technology and the new developments in optical disc and imaging technology are an obvious prerequisite. The Department in *Companies in 1994–5*, p 2 states that 'a balance has to be struck between the deregulation approach which is most likely to benefit business, and the need to retain market and commercial confidence in the effectiveness of regulation'.

11   *Companies in 1988–89*, p 13.
12   See Sealy, op cit and *Company Law and Commercial Reality* (1986).

PART II

The corporate constitution

CHAPTER 9

Constitutional issues

The constitution of a modern company consists of two documents usually bound up as one—the memorandum and articles of association. These are all that is prescribed by law. Sometimes, however, they are supplemented by shareholders' agreements, and other similar arrangements. Overall there is considerable freedom of choice in the drafting of the original documents but this freedom is more restricted when it comes to constitutional change. In the case of the memorandum, there are considerable restrictions on change, but even in the case of the articles freedom is curtailed to protect minorities from oppression. Thus provisions which would be valid if in the original constitution, such as an exclusion of the rules of natural justice, may not subsequently be adopted or there will at least be a heavy onus on those seeking the change.

The purpose of the constitution is to provide for the distribution of *profit, risk* and *control* within the company. Profits will be distributed in accordance with shareholders' rights which may be specified in the memorandum but nowadays are more usually set out in the articles. The memorandum sets out the basis of liability of members—limited or unlimited and limited by shares or guarantee. Allocation of control between the company in general meeting and the board of directors is dealt with in the articles. However, profit and control and allocation of risk amongst the proprietors per se are often the subject matter of shareholders' agreements where these are used. Shareholders' agreements are mainly used in the case of private companies and joint ventures between larger companies.

In broad terms, the memorandum governs the relationship between the company and the outside world. The company identifies the name by which it is first incorporated and the purposes and objects for which it is formed. Originally incorporation was regarded as a privilege and there was a natural tendency on the part of the courts to restrict it. This led to the development of the ultra vires doctrine which protected some creditors at the expense of others. Shareholders and intra vires creditors were protected from unauthorised depletion of the capital fund. The history of the ultra vires doctrine is a history of a struggle between two competing models of incorporation—the *legal privilege model* and the *freedom of contract model*. Whereas the legal privilege model emphasised responsibility through restriction and the fulfilment of conditions, the contract model emphasises the utility of the right to incorporate and the freedom of choice of incorporators under a liberal economy state concerned with facilitating rather than restricting business. The legal privilege model is the oldest model of incorporation and dates back to the Middle Ages. Indeed, early business corporations were often regarded as arms of the state or means of extending state control. This model continued as the dominant model even after the liberal reforms of 1844–1856. The origins of the freedom of contract model perhaps lie in the 1844 Act, although some commentators stress that this represented state intervention as well. It grew in strength as a result of the Limited Liability Act 1855 and the adoption of the modern form of constitution in 1856. The reform of the 1890s which provided for alteration of objects and the growing liberalism of judicial decisions on ultra vires from the turn of the century added to this trend. It perhaps reached its logical extreme in 1972 when in *Ebrahimi v Westbourne Galleries Ltd* [1973] AC 360, the House of Lords allowed the contract greater significance than the legal constitution, an equitable doctrine which had some of its roots in the earlier jurisprudence of the substratum cases. This supremacy of the contract/equitable model, however, is at the moment limited to winding up on the just and equitable ground and the statutory minority shareholder's remedy and is of uncertain scope and significance elsewhere. It is a potentially wide doctrine which may need to be kept in check.

Recently the debate about the two models has taken a distinctly economic perspective in the USA as the result of an important symposium sponsored by the Columbia Law School Center for Law and Economic Studies, entitled 'Contractual Freedom in Corporate Law'[1]. It is impossible to do justice here to the sophistication of this debate and to understand it one must see it in its US context. There is no such thing as US company law. Each state has its own corporation law statute. In a sense there is a market for corporation law statutes. Business people are free to choose their state of incorporation. Some state statutes are more lax than others. There is diversity although many of the major corporations incorporate in Delaware, a small state which has a tradition of permissiveness and a pro-management attitude. People of the Chicago School argue the freedom of contract principle, relying on the law and economics analysis of the company as a nexus of contracts[2]. The primary function of corporate law should be to facilitate the private contracting process by providing a set of non-mandatory 'standard-form' provisions, leaving it to the parties to opt out. They argue that there is little convincing justification for many mandatory rules. This argument, which is simply made, has put more traditionally minded commentators on the defensive. To deal with the argument they maintain that to treat the company as a nexus of contracts is reductionist. The most effective spokesman is Professor Melvin Eisenberg[3] who argues that contract here does not mean contract but a modified and specialist conception of implicit contract taken from labour economics where it means neither contract nor even bargain. They are forms of private ordering but not contracts. Professor Eisenberg sees many of the rules of company law being determined by the unilateral action of corporate organs or officials, some by contract or other forms of agreement and others determined by law. He classifies the rules into *enabling rules, suppletory or default rules* and *mandatory rules*. The first gives legal effect to rules that corporate actors adopt. The second apply unless the corporate actors adopt other

1   See the November 1989 issue of the Columbia Law Review, especially the foreword by Lucian Bebchuk 'The Debate on Contractual Freedom in Corporate Law' 89 Col LR 1395 (1989).
2   Frank Easterbrook and Daniel Fischel 'The Corporate Contract' ibid 1416.
3   Melvin Eisenberg 'The Structure of Corporation Law' ibid 1461, for other useful analysis see John C Coffee Jr 'The Mandatory/Enabling Balance in Corporate Law: An Essay on the Judicial Role' Ibid 1618; Jeffrey Gordon 'The Mandatory Structure of Corporate Law' ibid 1529; see too Roberta Romano 'Answering the Wrong Question; the Tenuous Case for Mandatory Corporate Laws' ibid 1599; and for an over aggressive polemic which at times hides some sound criticisms see Fred McChesney 'Economics, Law and Science in Corporate Field: A Critique of Eisenberg' ibid 1530. For focus on the 'nexus of contracts' see William W Bratton Jr (1989) 74 Cornell L Rev 407.

rules. The third cannot be varied. Mandatory rules are only part of this complex picture. Examples of enabling rules are the provisions for the conferral of authority and the rules for increase or reduction of capital although all of these have mandatory aspects. Examples of suppletory rules are the regulations of Table A. Examples of mandatory rules are the rule against insider trading, the disclosure rules, the provisions for alteration of articles and the principal fiduciary duties. There is a justification for many mandatory provisions. Some are not totally mandatory in any event. They can be avoided by a restructuring of the transaction. It is, therefore, necessary to make a close study of each rule. Further, the libertarian argument conspicuously falls down in respect of constitutional change as opposed to the original adoption of the corporate constitution[4]. Freedom of contract here would lead to the tyranny of the majority.

The EU harmonisation programme relies heavily on mandatory rules and rejects the idea of a market for company law statutes. English and EU discussions of principle and policy pay too much attention to existing legal rules and often fail to take in the broader perspective. The policy issues raised by the US debate suggest that greater sophistication is needed in London and Brussels[5]. The issues are not clear cut and the problems are not necessarily solved by more intervention. Professor Eisenberg's analysis is helpful in coming to terms with the innate complexity of corporate law.

Reverting to domestic company law, not only is the memorandum a source of definition of the purpose and capacity of the company, it is sometimes used as a place in which to entrench class rights of shares. Before 1980, to insert such rights in the memorandum without a variation of rights clause rendered them immutable save by a scheme of arrangement under what is now s 425 of CA 1985. This was modified slightly by the Companies Act 1980.

Whereas the memorandum deals with the company's relationship with the outside world, the articles regulate the internal affairs of the company. The statutory regulation is permissive to a greater extent than in the case of the memorandum. This is particularly so in the case of constitutional change. The model articles in Table A are merely a guide and it is possible to contract out. The statutory model envisages a democratic board of directors and general meeting operating by majority rule. It does not mandate compliance with natural justice although occasionally the courts will imply it. It envisages the company's dirty linen being laundered within the company but on the whole is pretty silent on the matter of resolving disputes. Its approach to the board of directors is collegiate and egalitarian with the exception of the managing director's authority and the chairman's casting vote. The working democracy so constituted, however, grants no franchise to employees or creditors. The equitable concept of the good of the company which company law inherited from partnership as the yardstick at general meetings, has traditionally meant in practice the good of the shareholders, although the law is currently undergoing change. At the moment, however, English law has not developed a concept of fiduciary obligation on majority shareholders such as exists in the USA.

The articles are a source of rights, but only for members, and there is some complicated jurisprudence about their enforcement. Outsider rights in articles are difficult to enforce in the absence of an extrinsic contract which incorporates them. Where the rights constitute class rights and they are varied there is also a further degree of procedural complication involved.

---

4   Bebchuk, op cit, and his 'Limiting Contractual Freedom in Corporate Law: the Desirable Constraints on Charter Amendments' 102 Harv LR 1820 (1989).
5   See a similar plea by the Company Law Committee of the Law Society, 'The Reform of Company Law' (July 1991). Noted (1991) 12 Co Law 162.

From the point of view of legal theory, the corporate constitution represents a complicated area where public law joins agency, contract and equity. In the development of company law, ideas have been borrowed from each of these branches of law. However at the end of the day it must be recognised that the corporate constitution is sui generis. Mistakes can arise if any analogy is pushed to extremes. The corporate constitution serves a multiplicity of business organisations of differing size and with differing pressures. The statutory model although regarded by some economists as a standard form contract which rational contractors would independently adopt has proved rather limited in practice and has been supplemented by both judicial equity and self-help by incorporators and their legal advisers. Within the bounds set by illegality and public policy, the latter have been allowed considerable freedom. The greatest restriction on freedom of contract is the inability of a director as fiduciary to abuse his position. The fiduciary concept is perhaps the most potent modern weapon in the judicial armoury in spite of its intellectual limitations. Laskin J in the Canadian Supreme Court case of *Canadian Aero Service Ltd v O'Malley*[6] described this as:

> an updating of the equitable principle whose roots lie in the general standards that I have already mentioned, namely, loyalty, good faith and avoidance of a conflict of duty and self-interest. Strict application against directors and senior management officials is simply recognition of the degree of control which their positions give them in corporate operations, a control which rises above day [sic] accountability to owning shareholders and which comes under some scrutiny only at annual general or at special meetings. It is a necessary supplement, in the public interest, of statutory regulation and accountability which themselves are, at one and the same time, an acknowledgement of the importance of the corporation in the life of the community and of the need to compel obedience by it and by its promoters, directors and managers to norms of exemplary behaviour ...

This emphasises the public interest in the corporate constitution and the regulation of corporate and corporate executive conduct.

Even here certain aspects of the strict fiduciary principles have been relaxed in relation to directors contracting with their companies. The law is dealt with in Chapter 26 and to understand it fully one needs to know the tortuous path which has led the law from a strict trust rule to relaxation and then to restrictions on contracting out.

To sum up, law and economics writers, echoing the earlier debate on freedom of contract, argue that the fiduciary rules and principles are an elaborate standard form which obviates the need for individual contracting with its resulting transaction costs. A number of traditional scholars are prepared to accept this as a useful insight but are not prepared to countenance free contracting out of these particular rules and principles. These rules and principles are mandatory on the grounds of public policy. In the case of public listed companies shareholders would generally not be in a position to exercise informed choice and are subject to a contract of adhesion[7].

6　(1974) 40 DLR (3d) 371, 384.
7　V Brudney 'Corporate Governance, Agency Costs and the Rhetoric of Contract' 85 Col LR 1403 (1985); Melvin Eisenberg 'The Structure of Corporation Law' 89 Col LR 1461 at 1474 et seq (1989), but cf Henry Butler and Larry Ribstein 'Opting out of Fiduciary Duties: A Response to the Anti-Contractarians' 65 Wash LR 1 (1990). For recent comment see Douglas Branson 'The Death of Contractarianism and the Vindication of Structure and Authority in Corporate Governance and Corporate Law' in Lawrence Mitchell (ed) *Progressive Corporate Law* (1995) 93. The volume is also interesting for arguments in favour of 'communitaranism' and 'humanomics' in corporate law.

CHAPTER 10

The memorandum of association and the question of corporate capacity

THE EVOLUTION OF THE MODERN FORM OF MEMORANDUM

The first Companies Act of 1844 provided for incorporation by registration of deeds of settlement[1]. The modern form of memorandum of association, however, dates from the Joint Stock Companies Act 1856[2]. This legislation was introduced by Robert Lowe MP, then President of the Board of Trade, based on the model of the New York Business Corporation Act[3]. This modern form is different from a deed although, as we have seen, it still retains the old characteristic of subscription and s 14(1) of CA 1985 gives the memorandum effect as if it had been signed and sealed by each member and contained covenants on the part of each member to observe all its provisions. The basic legal requirements are set out in s 2 and Tables D and F[4]. These require the memorandum to state:

(1) the name of the company, which in the case of a private limited company must end with the word 'limited' and in the case of a public company the words 'public limited company';
(2) in the case of a public company, the fact that it is such a company;
(3) whether the registered office is to be situated in England and Wales or Scotland;
(4) the objects of the company;
(5) in the case of a company limited by shares or guarantee that the liability of its members is limited;
(6) in the case of a company limited by guarantee the amount of the guarantee;
(7) in the case of a company with a share capital the amount of the share capital with which the company proposes to be registered and its division (except in the case of an unlimited company).

Section 3A provides that where the memorandum states that the object of the company is to carry on business as a general commercial company—

(a) the object of the company is to carry on any trade or business whatsoever, and

---

1 See Chapter 2, ante.
2 Ibid, s 5 and Schedule Form A.
3 Hansard, vol CXL (1856), col 133.
4 The Companies (Tables A to F) Regulations 1985 (SI 1985 No 805) Schedule.

(b) the company has power to do all such things as are incidental or conducive to the carrying on of any trade or business by it.

The procedural requirements are:

(a) in the case of a company with a share capital, no subscriber of the memorandum may take less than one share and against his or her name must be shown the number of the shares he or she takes;
(b) the memorandum and articles must be signed by each subscriber in the presence of at least one witness who must attest the signature. The original is dated and filed with the Registrar of Companies.

CORPORATE CAPACITY AND THE RISE AND FALL OF THE ULTRA VIRES DOCTRINE

Conceptual questions

The memorandum of association governs the relationship between the company and the outside world. In particular it defines the capacity of the company. The Act of 1844 required a statement of the business or purpose of the company in the deed of settlement but this could be altered by the members. Section 25, however, defined its main powers and privileges which included power 'to perform all other Acts necessary for carrying into effect the Purposes of such Company, and in all respects as other Partnerships are entitled to do'. The latter words are important. The 'company' under the 1844 Act was still a partnership on which certain corporate attributes had been conferred. It was not subject to the ultra vires doctrine. However, the intention of the legislature from 1856 onwards was for capacity to be defined by the simple specification of an object which could not be changed. Object has never been defined in the legislation but the precedents set out in the Companies Acts seem to imply some notion of purpose[5] or the description of the nature of the company's trade or business in a broad generic way[6]. A distinction is drawn in the cases between objects and powers. Power has been defined as 'a legal ability by which a person may create, change or extinguish legal relations'[7]. Power is thus an aspect of capacity. It seems to be generally accepted that a power is something less than an object in the sense that it is a means, while the object is the end. Anything outside the objects and powers of a company is ultra vires. Sometimes it is also said to be illegal but this is a misuse of terms. This point was made clear by Lord Cairns LC in the leading case of *Ashbury Railway Carriage and Iron Co Ltd v Riche*[8] in 1875 where he said:

> I have used the expressions extra vires and ultra vires. I prefer either expression very much to one which occasionally has been used in the judgments in the present case, and has also been used in other cases, the expression 'illegality'.

5   See *Re Governments Stock Investment Co* [1891] 1 Ch 649, a case on alteration of objects. Chitty J discusses both terms at 655.
6   Section 7 of the 1844 Act referred to 'business or purpose'. Section 5 of the Joint Stock Companies Act 1856 used the term 'objects' and the form set out in the Schedule for the Eastern Steam Packet Company Ltd provided: The objects for which the company is established are, '"the Conveyance of Passengers and Goods in Ships or Boats between such Places as the Company may from Time to Time determine, and the doing of all such other Things as are incidental or conducive to the Attainment of the above Object"'.
7   Seavey (1920) 29 Yale LJ 859 at 861.
8   (1875) LR 7 HL 653 at 672.

In a case such as that which your Lordships have now to deal with, it is not a question whether the contract sued upon involves that which is *malum prohibitum* or *malum in se*, or is a contract contrary to public policy, and illegal in itself. I assume the contract in itself to be perfectly legal, to have nothing in it obnoxious to the doctrine involved in the expressions which I have used. The question is not as to the legality of the contract; the question is as to the competency and power of the company to make the contract.

A second sense in which the phrase ultra vires can be used was mentioned by Vinelott J in *Rolled Steel Products (Holdings) Ltd v British Steel Corpn*[9] when he referred to a wider sense where a transaction ostensibly within the scope of the powers of the company express or implied is entered into in furtherance of a purpose which is not authorised. Although this was perhaps a useful way of explaining earlier authority involving loans to companies it was potentially a dangerous doctrine capable of producing uncertainty in commercial transactions and the Court of Appeal did not accept it[10]. Sometimes the phrase 'ultra vires' is used in a third sense to refer to the acts of directors outside their authority. This usage is not improper, but undesirable. It is better to limit the phrase 'ultra vires' to the capacity of the company and use the term 'lack of authority' to refer to the directors to avoid equivocation.

The doctrine of ultra vires does not apply to chartered corporations. At common law chartered corporations seem to have been regarded as having all the powers of a natural person in spite of the practice of specifying express objects in the charter. From Coke onwards this seems to have been regarded as the law[11]. This does not mean, however, that a chartered corporation can never be stopped from acting outside its charter. In *Institution of Mechanical Engineers v Cane*[12], Lord Denning in the House of Lords thought that anyone injured thereby could apply for an injunction to prevent a chartered corporation acting outside its objects. The more orthodox view, however, is that only a member has locus standi[13]. In addition, the Attorney General can apply for revocation of the charter if the corporation persistently acts outside its objects[14].

The development of the doctrine of ultra vires in relation to registered companies[15]

THE BASIC RULE

Although the doctrine of ultra vires was modified by s 9(1) of the European Communities Act 1972 (now s 35 of CA 1985) it is still necessary to trace the development of the doctrine in order to understand the full implications of the reforms. In the eighteenth century there were occasional references to corporate assets being held on trust. There seems to have been an equation of corporate bodies with a trust[16]. However, this reflected the loose usage of that time and although it may have been

9   [1982] 3 All ER 1057 at 1076 and 1077.
10   [1984] BCLC 466.
11   See the case of *Sutton Hospital* (1612) 10 Co Rep 1a, 23a.
12   [1961] AC 696 at 724.
13   See *Jenkin v Pharmaceutical Society of Great Britain* [1921] 1 Ch 392; *Pharmaceutical Society of Great Britain v Dickson* [1970] AC 403, HL.
14   See *Jenkin v Pharmaceutical Society of Great Britain*, supra, at 398.
15   See *Brice on Ultra Vires* (3rd edn, 1893); *Street on Ultra Vires* (1930); Horrwitz (1946) 62 LQR 66; Hornsey (1949) 61 Jur Rev 263; Holt (1950) 66 LQR 493.
16   See CA Cooke *Corporation, Trust and Company* (1950), p 69 ff.

strictly accurate in relation to deed of settlement companies it ceased to have any relevance after 1856. In the early nineteenth century with the growth of statutory companies, the question arose as to whether they were to be treated in the same position as chartered corporations. After some fluctuation of opinion a view came to be accepted that they had the powers of a natural person except in so far as these were cut down by the legislation or their objects clause[17]. This view, however, was decisively rejected by the House of Lords in *Ashbury Railway Carriage and Iron Co Ltd v Riche*[18]. The facts of the case were that the company was incorporated under the Companies Act 1862 and had as its objects the following:

> The objects for which the company is established are to make and sell, or lend on hire, railway-carriages and wagons, and all kinds of railway plant, fittings, machinery, and rolling-stock; to carry on the business of mechanical engineers and general contractors; to purchase and sell, as merchants, timber, coal, metals, or other materials; and to buy and sell any such materials on commission, or as agents.

It entered into a contract to finance the building of a railway in Belgium by Riche but later wanted to get out of the contract. It consequently argued that it was ultra vires. In the courts below, much had turned on whether or not the transaction had been ratified because the company had an old deed of settlement clause in its articles which provided for extension of the objects by special resolution. The House of Lords held that the transaction was ultra vires. The company had only such objects as were specified in its objects clause. Benjamin QC had argued the ratification point but the House of Lords rejected this argument on the basis that the act was void and it was not possible to ratify a void act. This point was of considerable significance at the time as there was no possibility of altering an objects clause from 1856 until 1890. The immediate policy behind the decision seems to be that incorporation is a privilege only to be granted in respect of the objects specified. In other words, the court adopted the legal privilege model of incorporation. This is extremely unrealistic, as the company can choose its own objects. The underlying policy is far from clear-cut. There seem to be elements of investor protection, creditor protection and public interest. These interests are not necessarily reconcilable and have motivated the courts to different decisions at different times, as we shall see[19].

IMPLIED POWERS

Shortly after the *Ashbury* case, the House of Lords realised that its ruling had been somewhat draconian, and in the case of *A-G v Great Eastern Rly Co*[20], it relaxed the rule by recognising implied powers which were reasonably incidental to the carrying out of the express objects.

---

17   See *Taylor v Chichester and Midhurst Rly Co* (1867) LR 2 Exch 356, and *Riche v Ashbury Railway Carriage Co* (1874) LR 9 Exch 224.
18   (1875) LR 7 HL 653. For recent authority see *Halifax Building Society v Meridian Housing Association Ltd* [1994] 2 BCLC 540.
19   For a full discussion, see L Getz (1963) 3 UBCLR 30, and the Consultative Document of the Department of Trade and Industry, *Reform of the Ultra Vires Rule*, Pt II, Report by D D Prentice, Chapter III.
20   (1880) 5 App Cas 473, HL.

THE MAIN OBJECTS RULE OF CONSTRUCTION AND *COTMAN V BROUGHAM* CLAUSES

Businessmen, however, were not satisfied with the *Ashbury* case, even as relaxed in *A-G v Great Eastern Rly Co*. They required further protection. The practice grew up of extending the objects clause by a proliferation of objects and powers. The patronising and moralising attitude of some of the Chancery judiciary of the time to such practices can be seen from the speech of Lord Wrenbury in *Cotman v Brougham*[1] where he said:

> There has grown up a pernicious practice of registering memoranda of association which under the clause relating to objects contain paragraph after paragraph not specifying or delimiting the proposed trade or purpose, but confusing power with purpose and indicating every class of act which the corporation is to have power to do. The practice is not one of recent growth. It was in active operation when I was a junior at the Bar. After a vain struggle I had to yield to it, contrary to my own convictions. It has arrived now at a point at which the fact is that the function of the memorandum is taken to be, not to specify, not to disclose, but to bury beneath a mass of words the real object or objects of the company, with the intent that every conceivable form of activity shall be found included somewhere within its terms.

That these views were not universally held is made clear by Sir Francis Palmer in his *Company Precedents* where he wrote[2]:

> No doubt some persons have argued that what the Legislature really intended was that the principal objects should be specified—not the powers by which those objects are proposed to be attained—and proceeding from this premise maintain that once a main or primary 'object' is specified it is improper to set out in the memorandum further objects which merely confer 'powers'. But there is nothing in the Act to give colour to this contention, or to show an intention to discriminate between main objects and objects merely conferring powers. Every object stated, whether main or auxiliary, in effect endows the company with a power or powers. To exclude objects conferring powers is to nullify the Act.
>   Beside these critics there is another class who complain of what may be called the multifariousness of the contents of a memorandum of association. The objects clause, according to their view, ought to specify the leading objects, be they one or many; and that is enough! To go on and specify as an object anything which is implied or may possibly be implied as incidental, on a reasonable construction of the leading object or objects, is irregular and improper. There ought to be no overloading, overlapping, repetition or surplusage. But here again the answer is that it is a matter for the subscribers' discretion.

The courts reacted to this development by adopting the main objects rule of construction in *Re Haven Gold Mining Co*[3]. Under this rule, where the objects are expressed in a series of paragraphs, the courts seek for the paragraph which appears to contain the main or dominant object and treat all the other paragraphs, however generally expressed, as ancillary to this main object and limited thereby[4]. Businessmen were not happy with this at all and the practice grew up of including a clause at the

---

1   [1918] AC 514 at 523, HL.
2   *Palmer's Company Precedents* (11th edn, 1912) vol 1, pp 458–9.
3   (1882) 20 Ch D 151, CA. See also *Re German Date Coffee Co* (1882) 20 Ch D 169, CA.
4   See *Palmer*, op cit, p 470.

end of the objects clause providing that the objects set out should not be restrictively construed and that each of the paragraphs should be regarded as conferring a separate and independent object[5]. Such a clause was ignored in *Stephens v Mysore Reefs (Kangundy) Mining Co Ltd*[6] in 1902 by Swinfen Eady J who disapproved of the stringing together of wide powers. The validity of such a clause was raised in the leading case of *Cotman v Brougham*[7]. The facts of the case were that the company was a rubber company with a long objects clause ending with this clause. It underwrote an issue of shares by an asphalt company. The validity of the underwriting could be upheld by accepting that underwriting was a separate object. The House of Lords considered that it could not decide the issue of validity of the clause because the Act said that the Registrar's certificate was conclusive that the formalities had been complied with. This took the matter out of their hands. Numerous members of the House, in particular Lord Wrenbury, expressed strong disapproval of such clauses. Nevertheless, now known as *Cotman v Brougham* clauses, they have become standard form, and it is very unusual not to find one at the end of an objects clause of a modern company. In *Re Introductions Ltd*[8], however, we see perhaps a last ditch stand by the courts when a restrictive view was taken of the effect of a *Cotman v Brougham* clause. The company was incorporated to promote exhibitions at the time of the Festival of Britain. It later went into pig breeding and was unsuccessful. A bank had lent them money for the pigbreeding business and in the insolvency of the company the efficacy of the bank's security was raised. There was no reference to pig-breeding in the objects clause and to validate the security it was necessary to argue that the borrowing clause existed as an independent object by virtue of the *Cotman v Brougham* clause. The Court of Appeal held that it did not. A *Cotman v Brougham* clause could not convert something which was intrinsically a power into an object, and borrowing was intrinsically a power.

SUBJECTIVE OBJECTS CLAUSES

In addition to *Cotman v Brougham* clauses, draftsmen sometimes preceded the leading objects with the words 'as an independent object' or drafted the leading objects very widely. A further development which has taken place is the appearance of so-called subjective objects clauses. These provide for the carrying on of any business which the company or the directors think fit. The clause in the *Stephenson* case was an example. A common clause is 'To do all such other things as the company may think conducive to the attainment of the above objects or any of them'. Such a clause was accepted in *Peruvian Rlys Co v Thames and Mersey Marine Insurance, Re Peruvian Rlys Co*[9] where Cairns LJ said:

> Anything, therefore, which, in the opinion of the company (how to be expressed we shall see afterwards) is incidental or conducive to the main object of the company—which was the acquisition of concessions for railways—they may do. If, therefore, there comes to be a concession for a railway which is to be paid for by instalments, it is, I think, beyond all possibility of dispute, that if they think it incidental or conducive to the attainment of the concession, when the instalments become or are about to fall due, in place of making calls on their

5   The practice was probably started by Sir Francis Palmer in 1891. See op cit (5th edn, 1905) p 207.
6   [1902] 1 Ch 745.
7   [1918] AC 514, HL.
8   [1970] Ch 199, CA. Noted by Leigh (1970) 33 MLR 81.
9   (1867) 2 Ch App 617 at 624.

shareholders, they should give a bill of exchange, payable at a future day, for the amount of the instalments, they may do so. The words seem to me so wide that they necessarily include a power of that kind. This is a power which, of course, may require to be exercised by a general meeting of the shareholders, or it may be capable of being exercised by the directors.

There is some suggestion in the cases that such clauses may not have been adequate compliance with the Companies Acts[10]. However, the practice of the Registrar was to accept such clauses and in a number of modern cases they have been accepted as valid.

In *Bell Houses Ltd v City Wall Properties Ltd*[11] the validity of such a clause was upheld by the Court of Appeal. The facts were that a property development company had know-how and contacts in the financial world, and had agreed to introduce another company to financiers to enable it to obtain development finance. It charged a commission for the introduction which the other company having first accepted then refused to pay. The question of ultra vires was raised. The Court of Appeal, faced with this defence, recognised that the commission was valid on the basis of the subjective objects clause which read 'To carry on any other trade or business whatsoever which can, in the opinion of the board of directors, be advantageously carried on by the company in connection with or as ancillary to ... the general business of the company'. The court emphasised, however, that the transaction was ancillary to the existing business.

THE CORPORATE GIFTS AND GRATUITOUS TRANSACTIONS CASES

In practice, companies make gratuitous payments to charities, hospitals, and even to the Conservative Party[12]. These are regarded as being justified on the basis of social responsibility. In America, the validity of charitable payments is clearly recognised[13]. This is not necessarily the case in the UK, although their validity is assumed perhaps in s 235(3) of CA 1985, which requires disclosure in the directors' report. Indeed the case law on this topic has grown progressively more complex and has raised fundamental questions about the relationship of the ultra vires doctrine to directors' authority and duties and minority shareholders' remedies.

In *Hutton v West Cork Rly Co*[14] Bowen LJ said that there should be 'no cakes and ale except such as are required for the benefit of the company' and that 'charity has no business to sit at boards of directors qua charity'. In *Re Lee, Behrens & Co Ltd*[15] Eve J laid down three tests for the validity of corporate gifts. He said: 'Whether they be made under an express or implied power, ... the validity of such grants is to be tested ... by the answers to three pertinent questions: (1) Is the transaction reasonably incidental to the carrying on of the company's business? (2) Is it a bona fide transaction? and (3) Is it done for the benefit of and to promote the prosperity of the company?'.

10 See *Re Crown Bank* (1890) 44 Ch D 634.
11 [1966] 1 QB 207. Noted by Wedderburn (1966) 29 MLR 673; Polack [1966] CLJ 174; Baker (1966) 82 LQR 463. The case went back to Mocatta J to be tried on the facts and he decided in favour of City Wall because Bell Houses had never earned their commission. Bell Houses again appealed, this time unsuccessfully. The second hearing and appeal were never reported. We are grateful to Prof J Milnes Holden for this information. Prof Milnes Holden was junior counsel for City Wall.
12 Gifts by the League Against Cruel Sports, a company limited by guarantee, to the Labour Party were ruled ultra vires in *Simmonds v Heffer* [1983] BCLC 298. The matter was treated as one of construction. See P Davies [1983] JBL 485.
13 See H G Henn and J Alexander *Corporations* (3rd edn, 1983), p 350.
14 (1883) 23 Ch D 654, CA.
15 [1932] 2 Ch 46.

As can be seen (1) is the test of an implied power and it seems to be inappropriate to an express power (2) seems to be an ingredient in directors' duties, not corporate capacity and (3) seems to add nothing to (1) and (2). Nevertheless, these tests were applied in later cases which have only recently been considered at appellate level. In *Parke v Daily News Ltd*[16] the defendant company was proposing to close down its operation. The Cadbury family which held the majority of shares wished to make gratuitous payments to redundant employees. This was before the Redundancy Payments Act 1965 which made it compulsory to make such payments. The proposed payments were challenged by Parke who was a minority shareholder. Plowman J applied the *Lee Behrens* tests and held that the proposed redundancy payments were ultra vires. The immediate effect of *Parke v Daily News Ltd* was negated by ss 309 and 719 of CA 1985. Section 309 enables the directors of a company to have regard to the interests of employees as well as shareholders and s 719 gives power to the company to provide for employees on the cessation or transfer of a business. The tests were also applied in the case of *Re W & M Roith Ltd*[17]. In that case a director had no pension arrangements with the company. He fell ill and the company entered into a service agreement with him, making provision for his wife after his death. It was held, applying the *Lee Behrens* tests, that the agreement was ultra vires. This case has been criticised on the grounds that it was not really a case of ultra vires, but one of directors' breach of duty. The *Lee Behrens* tests were, however, rejected by Pennycuick J in the case of *Charterbridge Corpn Ltd v Lloyds Bank Ltd*[18]. This was a case involving a group guarantee. The bank had advanced money to the property development subsidiary in the group on condition that each other company in the group gave a guarantee of the indebtedness secured by a debenture on its assets. The question arose as to whether the guarantees and debentures given by the other companies were ultra vires. There was an express provision in their objects clauses providing for the giving of guarantees and securities. Pennycuick J rejected the *Lee Behrens* tests on the above grounds and said that where the transaction was expressly authorised, that was the end of the matter. He also expressed the basis of an alternative ratio by saying that if the motivation of the directors was relevant one need not see whether they had actually considered the transaction to be for the good of the company if an honest and reasonable director, standing in their shoes, would have believed that it was for the good of the company. There is much to commend in both the *Charterbridge* approaches. Two matters, however, arguably weaken the decision. *Parke* and *Roith* were not cited and, also, the judge did not consider the object/power distinction. Such transactions may be rejected on the basis that the power to give a guarantee or security cannot be an independent object. *Charterbridge* was followed in Scotland in *Thompson v J Barke & Co (Caterers) Ltd*[19] and a similar approach was taken by Oliver J in *Re Halt Garage (1964) Ltd*[20] when he held that once a transaction was intra vires the proper test lay in the genuineness and honesty of the transaction—was it a genuine exercise of the power?—not on some abstract test of the benefit of the company. If claims are made for remuneration the real question is—are the payments in question genuine remuneration? He said:

> I cannot help thinking, if I may respectfully say so, that there has been a certain confusion between the requirements for a valid exercise of the fiduciary powers

16   [1962] Ch 927.
17   [1967] 1 All ER 427.
18   [1970] Ch 62. Cf *Equiticorp Fiannce Ltd (in liquidation) v Bank of New Zealand* (1993) 11 ACLC 952.
19   1975 SLT 67.
20   [1982] 3 All ER 1016. Noted (1980) 2 Co Law 141 and (1983) 46 MLR 204.

of directors (which have nothing to do with the capacity of the company but everything to do with the propriety of acts done within that capacity), the extent to which powers can be implied or limits be placed, as a matter of construction, on express powers, and the matters which the court will take into consideration at the suit of a minority shareholder in determining the extent to which his interests can be overridden by a majority vote. These three matters, as it seems to me, raise questions which are logically quite distinct but which have sometimes been treated as if they demand a single, universal answer leading to the conclusion that, because a power must not be abused, therefore, beyond the limit of propriety it does not exist.

The matter was further reviewed this time by the Court of Appeal in *Re Horsley & Weight Ltd*[1]. This case is particularly interesting because the court included Buckley LJ who had also sat in *Re Introductions Ltd*. The issue was whether a pension policy for a director and employee was ultra vires and amounted to misfeasance by the director in question in the liquidation of the company. The court held that there was an express provision to grant pensions which constituted a *substantive object* and not merely an ancillary power. That being the case, the benefit and prosperity of the company were immaterial. The *Lee Behrens* tests and *Re W & M Roith Ltd* were doubted and *Charterbridge* approved. The policy was intra vires and there was no misfeasance.

Buckley LJ[2] said that the objects of a company need not be commercial; they could be charitable or philanthropic or whatever the original incorporators wished, provided they were legal. There was no reason why a company should not part with its funds gratuitously or for non-commercial reasons if this was within its declared objects.

All three judges were of the opinion that the scope of a paragraph in an objects clause was a matter of construction. The significance of this is highlighted by the later case of *Rolled Steel Products (Holdings) Ltd v British Steel Corpn*[3]. Here the facts were considerably more complicated but the essential issue was the validity of a guarantee and debenture given by a company which was in excess of the company's own indebtedness and stood to benefit others. There was a power to lend and advance money in the objects clause but Vinelott J held that as a matter of construction this was not a substantive object but an ancillary power. Not only that but he distinguished between powers conferred for the furtherance of commercial purposes and those which were not. Powers in the first category must be exercised for commercial purposes which overlapped if they did not in fact coincide with the *Lee Behrens* requirement of benefit and prosperity of the company. Vinelott J regarded the pension power in *Re Horsley & Weight Ltd* as an example of the first category although this seems at odds with what Buckley LJ had said.

The Court of Appeal[4] did not accept Vinelott J's classification but restated the law in the following principles. A clear distinction should be drawn between transactions which are beyond the capacity of the company and those which are in excess or an abuse of power of directors. The term ultra vires should be used for the former. The question of capacity of the company must depend on a true construction of the memorandum. Although each provision of the memorandum is to be given its full effect, a particular provision might by its very nature be incapable of constituting a substantive object or its wording might indicate that it was only intended to constitute

1   [1982] Ch 442, [1982] 3 All ER 1045, noted (1981) 2 Co Law 70. See also Wedderburn (1983) 46 MLR 204; McMullen [1983] CLJ 58.
2   [1982] Ch 442 at 450, [1982] 3 All ER 1045 at 1052.
3   [1982] Ch 478, [1982] 3 All ER 1057, noted by Birds (1982) 3 Co Law 123.
4   [1984] BCLC 466, CA. Noted (1986) 102 LQR 169.

a power ancillary to the other objects. However, even where a particular transaction was capable of being performed as something reasonably incidental to the attainment or pursuit of the company's objects, it will not be rendered ultra vires merely because the directors entered into it for purposes other than those set out in the memorandum. The transaction would be binding on the company on the basis of the apparent authority of the directors to bind the company unless the other party had notice or knowledge of the directors exceeding their authority. Such a person could be liable as constructive trustee of the company's property which came into his hands. Where a power is limited to be only exercisable for the purpose of the company or the company's business this does not put a third party on inquiry as to whether it has been so exercised.

Re Lee Behrens & Co Ltd (supra) was disapproved of and rejected. The tests laid down in that case have now been laid to rest as far as ultra vires is concerned. These principles are consistent with *Re Horsley & Weight Ltd* and add to the clarification of the law attempted in that case. Vinelott J's analysis had muddied waters which were beginning to clear.

In *Brady v Brady*[5] the Court of Appeal held that in the broadest terms a company could not give all its assets away. Theoretically it could reserve to itself such a power but in the real world of trading companies would not be likely to do so. The majority of the court put emphasis on the need to safeguard assets for the protection of the creditors and rejected an argument that it might be in the interests of the company to survive at any cost, including giving half its assets away. Such a transaction could not be justified on the basis of an express power which was not explicit nor as an implied power. The House of Lords, however, allowed an appeal holding that the transactions were expressly authorised by the objects clauses and did not involve misfeasance by the directors. There was no suggestion of fraud or bad faith. The case also involved the question of companies financing the purchase of their own shares and is considered later.

The modern English approach sits uneasily with a new approach which emanates from the Antipodes but whose origins lie in orthodox reasoning. This is the emerging doctrine of corporate benefit. It is established law that a company which is insolvent or nearly insolvent must not deal with its property to the detriment of creditors. Corporate property must be applied only for corporate purposes. Thus in *ANZ Executors & Trustee Co Ltd v Qintex Australia Ltd* (1990) 2 ACSR 676, where QAL covenanted with a trustee for holders of unsecured notes issued by QAL that it would at the request of the trustee procure its subsidiary companies to guarantee repayment, the Full Court of the Supreme Court of Queensland held that there could be no corporate benefit to an insolvent subsidiary in giving the guarantee. The idea of corporate benefit was linked by McPherson J in a masterly judgment with fundamental concepts of company law such as capital maintenance. The following passage from Nourse L J in *Brady v Brady* [1989] AC 755 at 777 was cited and followed:

'The integrity of a company's assets, except to the extent allowed by its constitution, must be preserved for the benefit of all those who are interested in them, most pertinently its creditors.'

Although the decision in *Brady* was reversed by the House of Lords no doubt was cast on this self evident proposition.

---

5   [1989] AC 755, [1988] 2 All ER 617, HL. See also *Aveling Barford Ltd v Perion Ltd* [1989] BCLC 626.

CONSEQUENCES OF ULTRA VIRES PRIOR TO 1973

In *Ashbury Railway Carriage and Iron Co Ltd v Riche*[6], it was held that an ultra vires act was void. This did not mean, however, that there was no possibility of relief. There could be the following relief:

(1) The person dealing with the company could enforce the transaction if he or she did not know of its ultra vires character[7]. This seems odd and it may be that the authorities which suggest this were not cases of ultra vires but cases of intra vires powers being used for an improper purpose by the directors[8] or alternatively ultra vires in the sense used by Vinelott J in the *Rolled Steel* case. In any event the scope of this was severely curtailed by the doctrine of constructive notice.

(2) A guarantor of the company's obligation might be liable depending on the wording of his or her guarantee[9].

(3) Directors who negotiated the transaction might be liable to the third party for breach of warranty of their authority[10], deceit[11] or negligent misstatement[12] provided the representation was in respect of fact, not law.

(4) Any payment could be recovered if it was possible to trace it in equity[13].

(5) By an equitable right akin to subrogation, any ultra vires loan which was applied to pay intra vires creditors conferred on the ultra vires lender a right to stand in the shoes of the intra vires creditors who had been paid except that he was not entitled to any securities which they had held[14].

It appears that the following could plead ultra vires[15]:

(a) the company[16];

(b) the other party to the transaction. There was some confusion in the cases but the better view seems to be that the other party could plead ultra vires except possibly where the contract had been performed by the company[17];

(c) a shareholder[18];

(d) a creditor generally could not unless he or she was a debenture holder whose security was threatened by the proposed payment[19];

(e) normally a stranger could not but in *Charterbridge Corpn Ltd v Lloyds Bank Ltd*[20] a purchaser of leasehold property, who was concerned to get a good title,

---

6   (1875) LR 7 HL 653.
7   *Re David Payne & Co Ltd, Young v David Payne & Co Ltd* [1904] 2 Ch 608, CA.
8   See Baxter [1970] CLJ 280.
9   *Garrard v James* [1925] Ch 616.
10   *Chapleo v Brunswick Permanent Building Society* (1881) 6 QBD 696, CA.
11   *Derry v Peek* (1889) 14 App Cas 337, HL.
12   *Hedley Byrne & Co Ltd v Heller & Partners Ltd* [1964] AC 465, HL.
13   *Sinclair v Brougham* [1914] AC 398, HL.
14   *Re Wrexham, Mold and Connah's Quay Rly Co* [1899] 1 Ch 440, CA; *Blackburn Building Society v Cunliffe Brooks & Co* (1882) 22 Ch D 61, CA; affd sub nom *Cunliffe Brooks & Co v Blackburn and District Benefit Building Society* (1884) 9 App Cas 857, HL.
15   See *Street on Ultra Vires*, p 30; Furmston (1961) 24 MLR 717; *Gore-Brown on Companies* (44th edn, 1985) by Boyle and Sykes, paras 3–18.
16   See Collier and Sealy [1973] CLJ 1, pp 2–3; Farrar and Powles (1973) 36 MLR 270, p 273 ff; Prentice (1973) 89 LQR 518, p 524 ff.
17   *Anglo-Overseas Agencies Ltd v Green* [1961] 1 QB 1; *Re KL Tractors Ltd (in liquidation)* (1960) 106 CLR 318 and *Bell Houses Ltd v City Wall Properties Ltd* [1966] 2 QB 656 at 694, CA.
18   *Parke v Daily News Ltd* [1962] Ch 927.
19   *Cross v Imperial Continental Gas Association* [1923] 2 Ch 553.
20   [1970] Ch 62.

was allowed to seek a declaration that the bank's mortgage was ultra vires the vendor company. The company was not even joined as a party to the action.

Approaches to the reform of ultra vires

It is generally accepted by law reform bodies that the doctrine of ultra vires is unsatisfactory[1]. It represents a pluralism of policies which are not easy to reconcile—investor protection, creditor protection and the public interest[2]. There are four basic approaches to the reform of the doctrine:

(1) Total abolition. This means that a company is given all the powers of a natural person either expressly or impliedly. As we have seen this is the position of chartered corporations at common law. This approach has been adopted in a number of overseas jurisdictions, notably Canada, New Zealand and Australia where it has been combined with (2).

(2) Abolition as regards third parties but retention as an internal doctrine. This means that third parties are protected but that an ultra vires act can be the subject of internal redress against the directors. This is the approach which was recommended by the Cohen Committee in 1945.

(3) Partial abolition as regards third parties, but retention as an internal doctrine. This involves the protection of a limited class of persons. The Jenkins Committee in 1962 recommended the protection of persons contracting with the company in good faith[3]. As we shall see, s 9 of the European Communities Act 1972 (now s 35 of CA 1985) adopted a solution on these lines.

(4) The specification of a list of ancillary objects and powers which are implied unless excluded. This was adopted in New Zealand[4], Australia[5] and Canada[6] and was also recommended by the Jenkins Committee[7]. It is only a partial solution to the problems created by the doctrine since the objects and powers are ancillary to the express objects and may not cover a particular transaction in any case.

There is much to be said for the first and second approaches which logically require the abolition or modification of the doctrine of public notice whereby everyone has constructive notice of documents in the public file. They guarantee the security of commercial transactions and leave no doubt about their operation. However, as we have seen, the UK, by becoming a member of the EU, was obliged to adopt the third approach which was in line with the recommendations of the Jenkins Report.

The effect of CA 1985, s 35

Section 9(1) of the European Communities Act 1972 was passed to implement art 9 of the First Directive of the Council of the EU, 9 March 1968. This directive was made

1   See Cohen Report (Cmd 6659) 1945, para 12; Jenkins Report (Cmnd 1749) 1962, para 35 ff.
2   See Farrar [1978] 8 NZULR 164.
3   Paragraph 42.
4   Companies Act 1955, Sch 2. However this now only applies to companies registered before 1 January 1984 which have not assumed the powers of a natural person—Companies Amendment (No 2) Act 1983, s 6.
5   Uniform Companies Act 1961, Sch 3, Powers, Companies Code 1981, Sch 2. Since repealed in 1983.
6   Iacobucci, op cit.
7   Paragraph 43.

under art 54(3)(a) of the Treaty of Rome to harmonise the protections afforded to members and others. Article 9 provides as follows:

(1) Acts done by the organs of the company shall be binding upon it even if those acts are not within the objects of the company, unless such acts exceed the powers that the law confers or allows to be conferred on those organs.

However, Member States may provide that the company shall not be bound where such acts are outside the objects of the company, if it proves that the third party knew that the act was outside those objects or could not in view of the circumstances have been unaware of it; disclosure of the statutes shall not of itself be sufficient proof thereof.

(2) The limits on the powers of the organs of the company, arising under the statutes or from a decision of the competent organs, may never be relied on as against third parties, even if they have been disclosed.

(3) If the national law provides that authority to represent a company may, in derogation from the legal rules governing the subject, be conferred by the statutes on a single person or on several persons acting jointly, that law may provide that such a provision in the statutes may be relied on as against third parties on condition that it relates to the general power of representation; the question whether such a provision in the statutes can be relied on as against third parties shall be governed by Article 3.

The text is set out in full so that comparisons may be made with CA 1985, s 35 which replaced s 9 of the 1972 Act. The original section 35 provided:

(1) In favour of a person dealing with a company in good faith, any transaction decided on by the directors is deemed to be one which it is within the capacity of the company to enter into, and the power of the directors to bind the company is deemed to be free of any limitation under the memorandum or articles.

(2) A party to a transaction so decided on is not bound to enquire as to the capacity of the company to enter into it or as to any such limitation on the powers of the directors, and is presumed to have acted in good faith unless the contrary is proved.

The effect of s 35 which was later reformed in the CA 1989 was to add a complicated gloss to the ultra vires doctrine[8]. It did not abolish the doctrine but simply protected a limited class of person dealing with the company. The company itself could not rely on it. In order to be protected the person had to (1) be dealing with the company, (2) be in good faith and (3) the transaction must be decided on by the directors. These three requirements gave rise to a number of problems of interpretation. It was not clear whether a broad or a narrow meaning was to be given to the word 'dealing'. Dealing normally predicates reciprocity and is capable of limitation to commercial transactions[9]. It can also be used in an extended sense. The Jenkins Report limited the protection to persons contracting with the company but as can be seen above, art 9 simply talks about third parties in general. There is no reference to dealing. Probably the better view is that 'dealing' was used in an extended sense[10]. Whether it is wide enough to cover

8   See Collier and Sealy, op cit; Farrar and Powles, op cit; Prentice, op cit; Wyatt (1978) 94 LQR 182; LCB Gower *Modern Company Law* (6th edn, 1997), p 207 ff.
9   See Farrar and Powles, op cit, pp 272–3; Prentice, op cit, p 525.
10 See Prentice, op cit, p 525; see too *Re Halt Garage (1964) Ltd* [1982] 3 All ER 1016. Cf *International Sales and Agencies Ltd v Marcus* [1982] 3 All ER 551.

a corporate gift or other gratuitous transaction was not clear. It was arguable that it should not. The whole purpose of the Directive, indeed the EU itself, is economic. The use of the word 'transaction' seems to presuppose reciprocity[11]. A pension such as in *Re Horsley & Weight Ltd* may be covered where there is a long-standing relationship, whereas a one-off gift may not be protected, certainly where the company is improperly used as the vehicle for another's generosity. The concept of good faith was not defined[12]. Unlike some other systems such as the German, good faith is not a general requirement of English commercial and company law. It occurs in different areas of law with differing meanings. Thus it is a requirement of English law that an insured must show uberrima fides. This means that he or she must make full disclosure. In equity, equitable interests are enforceable against all except a bona fide purchaser for value without notice. In the Bills of Exchange Act 1882[13], the Sale of Goods Act 1979[14], and the Law of Property Act 1925, good faith is used and defined. The term 'good faith' was not used in the final version of the Directive because its usage differed between member states[15]. Instead, art 9 talks about knowledge and what amounts to wilful blindness. In the context of s 35 it was not clear whether good faith simply meant without notice or imported some further requirement of fairness. Clearly, if a person had actual knowledge or notice of the lack of corporate capacity he or she would not be protected. It was arguable in the light of art 9(1) that he or she would also not be protected if he or she had been wilfully blind, ie shut his or her eyes to the need to make further inquiry. Constructive notice of the objects clause, however, no longer applied[16].

The requirement that the transaction had to be decided on by the directors gave rise to further difficulties[17]. It seemed to predicate the necessity for a board decision and it was arguable that the act of a single director, even one who is a managing director, did not confer the protection of the section unless he or she had been given a general authority by the board as a whole. Even in the latter case it was necessary to adopt a liberal construction of the wording. Here, art 9 does not really help. It refers to 'organs', which is an ambiguous term in English company law. English law has never fully received the organ theory of German law. It has been applied in the area of tort and crime, where, arguably, different policies apply. The phrase in s 35 seemed to cover (1) a decision of the majority of a duly constituted board meeting; (2) a transaction entered into by a duly authorised director; (3) a transaction entered into by a managing director[18]. In *International Sales and Agencies Ltd v Marcus*[19] Lawson J resolved some but not all of the above problems. The material facts of the case were that loans were made to a major shareholder in two companies. He became ill, and said his friend M would see the lender was repaid if he died. The shareholder died and M, who was a director and effectively controlled the two companies, repaid the lender with cheques

11   Farrar and Powles and Prentice, op cit.
12   See Collier and Sealy, pp 2–3; Farrar and Powles, p 273 ff; Prentice, p 524 ff.
13   Section 90.
14   Section 62.
15   See W Fikentschen and B Grosfield (1964–5) CML Rev 259.
16   Collier and Sealy, op cit, p 2; Farrar and Powles, op cit, p 272.
17   Collier and Sealy, op cit, pp 3–4; Farrar and Powles, p 273 ff; Prentice, op cit, p 526; S N Frommel (1987) 8 Co Law 11. See too *Friedrich Haaga GmbH*: Case 32/74 [1974] ECR 1201, [1975] 1 CMLR 32, ECJ. It has been argued by the Commission that the UK government has failed to implement fully the First Directive in not specifying which persons represent the company (OJ 1977, C289/1).
18   This would be consistent with art 9(3). See now *International Sales and Agencies Ltd v Marcus* [1982] 3 All ER 551; and *TCB Ltd v Gray* [1986] Ch 621 (agreement of all directors individually). Noted by J Birds (1986) 7 Co Law 104; J Collier [1986] CLJ 207. Upheld on appeal on other points (1987) 3 BCC 503.
19   [1982] 3 All ER 551, [1982] 2 CMLR 46. The former contains an error at p 559 ff.

drawn on the companies. The companies reclaimed the moneys. The lender claimed the protection of s 9(1), now s 35 of CA 1985. Lawson J held that (1) M was in breach of his fiduciary duty and was a constructive trustee of the moneys; (2) the payments were ultra vires; (3) the lender was liable as a constructive trustee of the moneys since he had actual notice that the moneys belonged to the companies and the payment was in breach of trust; and (4) the lender was not protected by s 9(1), now s 35, CA 1985, which did not affect the operation of a constructive trust. Lawson J[20] said:

> Whilst s 9(1) [now s 35, CA 1985] reflects 'if it proves that the third party knew the act was outside those objects', it does not directly reflect in so many words, the alternative 'or could not in view of the circumstances have been unaware of it'. Which seems to me very close to turning a blind eye. In my judgment I am entitled to look at the Council's Directive as an aid to the interpretation of s 9(1) of the Act. I conclude, firstly, that s 9(1) relates only to legal obligations of the company under transactions with third parties, whether or not they be within or without its powers; secondly, that s 9(1) is designed to give relief to innocent third parties entering into transactions with companies against the operation in England of the old ultra vires doctrine; thirdly, that the test of lack of good faith in somebody entering into obligations with a company will be found either in proof of his actual knowledge that the transaction was ultra vires the company or where it can be shown that such a person could not in view of all the circumstances, have been unaware that he was a party to a transaction ultra vires.

His Lordship said that the onus of proof was on the lender to establish a 'dealing' but on the companies to establish lack of good faith. There was no dealing with the company since M simply used the company as the vehicle of his generosity. Since M was sole effective director to whom all actual authority to act for the companies had been effectively delegated the transactions were decided on by the directors. The results of the *Marcus* case were thus:

(1)   The onus of proving 'dealing' was on the third party and there was no dealing where the companies' funds were wrongly used to the third party's knowledge.
(2)   A single effective director could constitute 'directors'.
(3)   Good faith was to be interpreted in the light of art 9 of the Directive.
(4)   The section did not protect a constructive trustee.

In *Barclays Bank Ltd v TOSG Trust Fund Ltd* in 1984 Nourse J considered the matter at first instance[1]. The case which went on appeal on other points involved complicated facts surrounding the collapse of holiday tour operators and an argument about double proof of debts in a winding up. Nourse J considered s 9(1) of the European Communities Act 1972 and found that the transactions in question were intra vires. In approaching the section he thought that he would only have recourse to the First Directive if the language of the Act was either ambiguous or doubtful in some other respect. With respect to his Lordship this is not strictly correct. The courts are on judicial notice of the contents of the Official Journal and this includes the text of the Directive[2] . His Lordship then went on to say that the expression 'in good faith' was one whose meaning

---

20   [1982] 3 All ER 551 at 559. Noted (1983) 46 MLR 204, [1982] CLJ 244. See too *Rolled Steel Products (Holdings) Ltd v British Steel Corpn* [1986] Ch 246, CA; *Barclays Bank Ltd v TOSG Trust Fund Ltd* [1984] BCLC 1; *International Factors (NI) Ltd v Streeve Construction Ltd* [1984] NIJB.
1   [1984] BCLC 1 at 17–18.
2   See also *Marleasing SA v La Commercial Internacional de Alimentation SA*: Case C-106/89 [1993] BCC 421—legislation to implement a directive must be construed so as to give effect to the purpose of the directive.

was well established and understood in the law and that it did not admit to any ambiguity or doubt. This statement is remarkable and it is difficult to see any rational basis for it. However, taking that view, his Lordship did not think it necessary to rely on the Directive and preferred to follow his own chauvinistic line. His general view of the section was that it had abolished the rule that a person who deals with a company is automatically affected with constructive notice and its objects clause but by retaining the requirement of good faith it ensured that a defence based on absence of notice should not be available to anyone who had not acted genuinely and honestly in his dealings with the company. Notice and good faith, although two separate concepts, were often inseparable. His Lordship went on to say that a person who deals with a company in circumstances where he ought to know that the company has no power to enter into the transaction will not necessarily act in good faith. A fortiori where he actually knew. His Lordship emphatically refuted the suggestion that reasonableness was a necessary ingredient of good faith. In his Lordship's view a person acted in good faith if he acted genuinely and honestly in the circumstances of the case. Reading his Lordship's judgment highlights the folly of the British government in seeking to implement this directive by the use of some part of the draft prepared by the Jenkins Committee. This leads the court into more subjective dimensions than were intended by the First Directive. It is submitted that the approach of Lawson J is preferable both as to resort to the Directive and also in the interpretation of the section. It is interesting to note that the Irish Republic has the same problems resulting from the earlier enactment of a reform influenced by the Jenkins Report[3].

Section 35 thus led to a most unsatisfactory reform of ultra vires.

The CA 1989 reforms

The topic of ultra vires and the related topic of directors' authority were the subject of a consultative document issued by the Department of Trade and Industry entitled 'Reform of the Ultra Vires Rule'[4]. This was prepared by Mr D D Prentice of Pembroke College, Oxford. The document itself reflected earlier consultation which Mr Prentice had with the public. Part V of the CA 1989 largely gives effect to the Prentice proposals. Section 108 of the Act enacts a new s 35 of the Companies Act 1985. Section 35(1)–(4) now reads as follows:

(1) The validity of an act done by a company shall not be called into question on the ground of lack of capacity by reason of anything in the company's memorandum.

(2) A member of a company may bring proceedings to restrain the doing of an act which but for subsection (1) would be beyond the company's capacity; but no such proceedings shall lie in respect of an act to be done in fulfilment of a legal obligation arising from a previous act of the company.

(3) It remains the duty of the directors to observe any limitations on their powers flowing from the company's memorandum; and action by the directors which but for subsection (1) would be beyond the company's capacity may only be ratified by the company by special resolution.

A resolution ratifying such action shall not affect any liability incurred by the directors or any other person; relief from any such liability must be agreed to separately by special resolution.

3   See P Ussher *Company Law in Ireland* (1985), pp 123 et seq.
4   See R R Pennington (1987) 8 Co Law 103; S N Frommel (1987) 8 Co Law; B Hannigan [1987] JBL 173.

(4) The operation of this section is restricted by section 30B(1) of the Charities Act 1960 and section 112(3) of the Companies Act 1989 in relation to companies which are charities; and section 322A below (invalidity of certain transactions to which directors or their associates are parties) has effect notwithstanding this section.

This achieves most of the major reforms effected by the Canadian federal reforms of 1975, which have influenced reforms in Australia and New Zealand as well as in other Canadian jurisdictions[5].

The new English section, like the original Ontario reform of 1970[6], still does not expressly confer on companies all the powers of a natural person, but it removes the effects of lack of capacity. It will no longer be necessary to resort to verbose drafting and in effect ultra vires now becomes more clearly a question of directors' authority. As in the Canadian reforms, it remains open to a member of the company to bring proceedings under s 35(2) to restrain a threatened ultra vires transaction as well as seek internal redress against the directors for exceeding their authority under s 35A(4) and (5) which distinguish between executory and executed contracts. However, the wording of the new s 35(2) is rather obscure. It provides inter alia that 'no such proceedings shall lie in respect of an act to be done in fulfilment of a legal obligation arising from a previous act of the company'. This seems to distinguish between contract and conveyance, a distinction not adopted in other systems but one which arguably has roots in the case law of ultra vires. If this is so then the use of the words 'to be done' instead of 'done' is unfortunate. An act by directors outside the capacity of the company can be ratified by *special* resolution and such resolution does not affect any underlying liability of the directors.

The new s 35A which is dealt with in detail in Chapter 25 deals with the lack of authority by directors and unfortunately reproduces some of the unsatisfactory wording of s 9(1) of the European Communities Act 1972 and the old section. The new section is dealt with in Chapter 25, post, but a few remarks will be made here. The section still only operates 'in favour of a person dealing with a company in good faith'. Thus, the unsatisfactory concept of good faith which was removed from the final wording of the first directive[7] is retained although there is now a provision in s 35(A)(2)(b) whereby a person is not to be regarded as acting in bad faith by reason of his knowing that an act is beyond the powers of the directors under the company's constitution. A new s 35(B) provides that a party to a transaction is not bound to inquire as to whether it is permitted by the company's memorandum or as to any limitation on the powers of the board of directors to bind the company or authorise others to do so.

However, the clarity of these reforms is obscured by a further provision in CA 1989, s 142, which deals with the abolition of the doctrine of what it calls 'deemed notice'. Section 142(1) purports to abolish the doctrine of 'deemed notice', by the insertion of a new s 711A in the CA 1985. Unfortunately, this does not appear to have been brought into force and in any event a further subsection provides that this does not affect the question whether a person is affected by notice of any matter by reason of a failure to make such inquiries as are reasonably to be made. In other words, even when s 711A comes into force there is still the possibility of actual knowledge and actual notice and this may in certain circumstances include inferred actual knowledge or notice at

---

5   Canada Business Corporations Act, s 15. See Ziegel, Daniels, Johnston & MacIntosh, op cit, pp 293 et seq.

6   Business Corporations Act 1970, s 16.

7   Vide supra; see too F Wooldridge (1989) 133 Sol J 714. Dr Wooldridge's article contains a useful critique of the legislation at bill stage in the House of Lords.

common law. The retention of this in the wording of the section is likely to strengthen the hand of a conservative judge who is unsympathetic to the reform. This is unfortunate and differs from the approach adopted in respect of company charges. Another distinctive characteristic of the new reforms is an express provision that a transaction in excess of authority entered into with parties which include directors of the company or its holding company, or any person connected with such a director or a company with whom such a director is associated, is voidable at the instance of the company. It is assumed that such persons should know of limitations and ensure compliance. This reform is provided for in a new s 322A of the CA 1985. There are exceptions in s 322A(5), which include the intervention of third party rights and ratification by *ordinary* resolution.

One is left with the unfortunate impression that the original reform proposals of Professor Prentice have been confused by the inability of the DTI to take a consistent and clear-headed approach to reform. The result is still a bit of a muddle.

ALTERATION OF THE MEMORANDUM OF ASSOCIATION

Section 2(7) of CA 1985 expressly forbids the alteration of the conditions contained in the memorandum 'except in the cases, in the mode and to the extent for which express provision is made by this Act'.

Firstly, under s 28(1) of CA 1985, a company may by special resolution change its name.

Secondly, a company may only with considerable difficulty alter the country in which its registered office is situated. Usually this involves formation of a new company in the other jurisdiction[8].

Thirdly, it is possible under s 4 to alter the objects clause by special resolution.

As we have seen, between 1856 and 1890 a company could not alter its objects clause. The only solution was to form another company which was not as burdensome as it sounds since this could usually be a subsidiary. The policy behind the Companies (Memorandum of Association) Act 1890 was not so much reform of ultra vires as to assist companies to develop their business along more efficient and technological lines[9]. Initially, the change which was effected by special resolution was limited to seven specified purposes and needed confirmation by the court. This was changed in 1948 to dispense with confirmation by the court unless the holders of not less than 15% of the nominal capital of the company or any class thereof or not less than 15% of the company's pre-1947 debenture holders[10] object. This is now contained in CA 1985, s 5, although CA 1989 removed the old limitation in s 4 that the alteration of objects had to be for one of the seven specified purposes[11]. In practice, few cases now go to court and there is little check on the company's power to alter its objects.

Fourthly, it is possible to alter the clause dealing with limitation of liability. Under the Act as we have seen in Chapter 6, it is possible for a limited liability company to become unlimited and vice versa[12].

Fifthly, it is possible to alter the company's share capital. Section 121(2)(a) of CA 1985 gives a general power to increase the capital[13]. On the other hand, generally

8   See further *Palmer's Company Law* vol 1, paras 2.510 et seq.
9   Per Eve J in *Re Jewish Colonial Trust (Juedische Colonial Bank) Ltd* [1908] 2 Ch 287 at 295.
10   The debentures must have been issued before 1 December 1947 (s 5(8)).
11   CA 1989, s 110(2).
12   Sections 49–52.
13   See eg Table A, reg 32(a).

speaking, a reduction of capital (other than by redemption or purchase under Pt V, Ch VII) can only take place with the consent of the court[14]. This is necessary to protect creditors and to achieve fairness between the different classes of shareholders.

Lastly, s 17 contains a rather odd provision which is not found in most other systems. This provides that any condition which could lawfully have been contained in the articles instead of the memorandum may be altered by special resolution. This is subject, however, to the following restrictions:

(1) It does not apply where the memorandum provides for or prohibits alteration of such conditions (s 17(1)(b)).
(2) It does not authorise the variation or abrogation of class rights (s 17(2)(b)).
(3) An application can be made to the court to cancel the alteration (s 17(1)).
(4) Nothing can be done to increase the liability of any member to contribute or subscribe without his consent (s 16).
(5) The power is subject to any restriction imposed by the court under s 459. Section 459 is the statutory remedy for minority shareholders and gives the court wide powers.

It should be noted that s 17 does not apply if the relevant provision has been inserted in the objects clause[15].

Since the only matter of this kind likely to be inserted is a class rights provision, s 17 is not very useful. As we shall see later, if class rights are set out in the memorandum it is difficult to alter them. Whether this is a good thing or not depends on the circumstances.

---

14   Section 136.
15   *Re Hampstead Garden Suburb Trust Ltd* [1962] Ch 806.

CHAPTER 11

Articles of association

THE SCOPE AND CONSTRUCTION OF THE ARTICLES

The articles of association are the domestic regulations of the company and govern its internal administration. They determine how the powers conferred on the company by the memorandum of association shall be exercised. The matter was put succinctly by Lord Cairns LC in *Ashbury Railway Carriage and Iron Co Ltd v Riche*[1] in 1875 when he said: 'The memorandum is, as it were, the area beyond which the actions of the company cannot go; inside that area the shareholders may make such regulations for their own government as they think fit.'

The articles are subordinate to the memorandum in the sense that they cannot confer wider powers than the memorandum. If there is any inconsistency between them the memorandum prevails and any alteration to the articles which conflicts with the memorandum is void to the extent of the conflict[2]. The articles cannot be resorted to fill in any gap in the memorandum in respect of any matter which by law is required to be in the memorandum[3]. The reason is that such conditions are introduced for the benefit of creditors and the outside public as well as the shareholders[4]. In this respect at least, the memorandum is dominant. This, for instance, covers objects but not powers since the former but not the latter are required to be specified in the memorandum[5]. On the other hand in other cases the articles must be read together with the memorandum so far as may be necessary to explain any ambiguity in the memorandum or to supplement it upon any matter as to which it is silent[6]. In Scotland[7] it was held prior to 1980 that it is permissible to refer to a variation of rights clause in the articles which were filed contemporaneously with the memorandum although this was not

---

1   (1875) LR 7 HL 653 at 671. See also Bowen LJ in *Guinness v Land Corpn of Ireland* (1882) 22 Ch D 349 at 379, CA.
2   *Ashbury v Watson* (1885) 30 Ch D 376, CA.
3   *Guinness v Land Corpn of Ireland* (1882) 22 Ch D 349, CA.
4   Per Bowen LJ at 381.
5   Ibid at 383–4.
6   *Angostura Bitters (Dr JGB Siegert & Sons) Ltd v Kerr* [1933] AC 550 at 554, PC.
7   *Re Oban and Aultmore-Glenlivet Distillers Ltd* (1903) 5 F 1140; *Marshall, Fleming & Co Ltd* 1938 SC 873. See also *Harrison v Mexican Rly Co* (1875) LR 19 Eq 358 at 365, but cf *Guinness v Land Corpn of Ireland,* supra, at 377, 381.

referred to in the memorandum itself. Both cases involved applications to the court to confirm reduction of capital which had been approved by the shareholders so arguably they do not establish a general principle and in any event the English courts did not go so far[8]. However, s 125(4)(a) of CA 1985 adopts the Scots solution. If the class rights are set out exhaustively in the memorandum and this contains no variation of rights clause, such rights are unalterable except by unanimous consent of all the members of the company under s 125(5) or by a scheme of arrangement under s 425 which requires application to the court[9]. In practice it is rare to insert class rights in the memorandum today. The subject of class rights is dealt with in detail in Chapter 18.

The first set of articles in the modern form were set out in Table B of the Schedule to the Joint Stock Companies Act 1856 and most modern companies now have articles which are based to some extent on the form set out in Table A. There are express provisions in the Act dealing with articles. Section 7 provides that there may, in the case of a company limited by shares, and there shall, in the case of a company limited by guarantee or unlimited, be articles registered with the memorandum. Section 8(1) provides that the articles of association may adopt all or any of the regulations contained in Table A and s 8(2) provides that in the case of the company limited by shares, if articles are not registered or if articles are registered, in so far as the articles do not exclude or modify Table A, the regulations of Table A as in force at the date of the company's registration shall constitute the company's articles. Section 8(4) provides that the articles of companies limited by guarantee with and without share capital, and an unlimited company having a share capital, shall be respectively in the forms set out in Tables D, C and E as prescribed in regulations made by the Secretary of State or as near that form as circumstances admit. The statutory forms are directory, not mandatory. They are intended as models, not strait-jackets[10] and there is a greater measure of choice in the content of the articles than in the memorandum.

The courts regard articles as commercial documents and apply a liberal construction to them. Jenkins LJ in *Holmes v Keyes*[11] described their approach as follows:

> I think that the articles of association of a company should be regarded as a business document and should be construed so as to give them reasonable business efficacy, where a construction tending to that result is admissible in the language of the articles, in preference to a result which would or might prove unworkable.

This is important because the articles cannot be rectified by the courts[12]. The power to alter is purely statutory. Any alteration must be effected by special resolution of the company under s 9 subject to the case law and reforms outlined in Chapter 4. If there is any inconsistency between different parts of the articles, the courts will follow the ordinary canons of construction and look to the whole, seeking to achieve harmony between the different provisions and compliance with the law[13]. The relationship of

---

8   See eg *Duncan Gilmour & Co Ltd v Inman* [1952] 2 All ER 871.
9   The Jenkins Report 1962 (Cmnd 1749) para 190 recommended the adoption of the Scots rules.
10 *Gaiman v National Association for Mental Health* [1971] Ch 317, 328.
11 [1959] Ch 199 at 215, CA. Such construction may lead the court to imply terms—see *Mutual Life Insurance Co of New York v Rank Organisation Ltd* [1985] BCLC 11, at 21. However, the particular terms were arguably simply a paraphrase of the existing law. See also *Re Hartley Baird Ltd* [1955] Ch 143 at 146.
12 *Scott v Frank F Scott (London) Ltd* [1940] Ch 794 at 801–3, CA. Nor will the court imply a term to give business efficacy to the articles—see *Bratton Seymour Service Co Ltd v Oxborough* [1992] BCLC 693, CA.
13 *Oakbank Oil Co v Crum* (1882) 8 App Cas 65, HL. Cf *Elderslie SS Co v Borthwick* [1905] AC 93 at 96, HL, a case on bills of lading where the ordinary canons of construction are discussed by Lord Halsbury LC at 96.

express articles to the statutory model in Table A can give rise to problems of construction if the articles are not well drafted. Thus, in the New Zealand case of *McNeil v McNeil's Sheepfarming Co Ltd*[14] the company's own articles provided for one man, one vote, but the Table A provision of one vote per share also applied. The court held that the express article took precedence. On the other hand, the mere fact that the articles deal with the matter in question does not necessarily exclude Table A. In *Fischer v Black & White Publishing Co*[15] the articles provided that the company's profits available for dividend should be applied in a certain order between different classes of shareholders. Some regulations of Table A were excluded, but the Court of Appeal held that the regulations of Table A which allowed directors to set aside reserves out of profits before paying any dividend at all, applied. Sometimes the commercial construction adopted by the court is so liberal that it almost amounts to rectification. Thus in *Rayfield v Hands*[16] the judge interpreted an article referring to directors as if it referred to members to enable a provision requiring them to buy the plaintiff's shares at fair value to take effect. The court may resort to the memorandum to resolve ambiguities in the articles but if there is a conflict between the two the memorandum prevails[17].

The articles must not contain anything which is illegal or contrary to public policy. Thus in the Australian case of *Re Victoria Onion and Potato Growers' Association Ltd v Finnigan, Ryan and Farrell*[18] an article was held void as being in unreasonable restraint of trade[19]. In theory this should be rejected by the Registrar, but in practice this seldom happens.

THE LEGAL EFFECT OF THE ARTICLES

Section 7 of the 1844 Act required a deed in the form specified in the section and Sch A under the hand and seals of the members. This had to contain 'a Covenant on the Part of every Shareholder, with a Trustee on the Part of the Company to pay up the Amount of the Instalments on the share taken by such Shareholder and to perform the several Engagements in the Deed contained on the Part of the Shareholders'. This meant there was an actual contract. Section 26 required any new shareholder to execute the deed or a deed referring thereto. This constituted novation. As we have seen in Chapters 2 and 6, the modern form of memorandum and articles was adopted by the Joint Stock Companies Act 1856. Sections 7 and 10 of that Act catered for the transition from registered deed of settlement to the modern form, by providing that the memorandum and articles, when registered, bound the company and the shareholders 'to the same Extent as if each Shareholder had subscribed his Name and affixed his Seal thereto or otherwise executed the same, and there were in such Articles contained, on the Part of himself, his Heirs, Executors and Administrators, a Covenant to conform to all the Regulations of such Articles, subject to the Provisions of this Act'. This obviated the

---

14   [1955] NZLR 15.
15   [1901] 1 Ch 174, CA.
16   [1960] Ch 1. See the comments of L C B Gower (1958) 21 MLR 401 at 657 and K W Wedderburn [1958] CLJ 148. See also *Re Caratti Holding Co Pty Ltd* (1975) 1 ACLR 87 but cf *Cohen & Sons Pty Ltd v Brown* [1969] 2 NSWR 593.
17   *Duncan Gilmour & Co Ltd v Inman* [1952] 2 All ER 871.
18   [1922] VLR 384.
19   See also *Otaraia Co-operative Co v Flynn* [1930] GLR 74; *Heron v Port Huon Fruitgrowers Co-operative Association Ltd* (1922) 30 CLR 315; *Parker & Co Ltd v Woollands* (1924) 26 WALR 172; *Tasmanian Hopgrowers Pool Ltd v Wilton* (1926) 22 Tas LR 16; *St Johnstone Football Club Ltd v Scottish Football Association Ltd* 1965 SLT 171. See also *Invercargill Sports Depot Ltd v Patrick* [1939] NZLR 161 which dealt with alteration of articles.

need for every incoming member to execute the memorandum and articles. Although the 1856 Act provided for incorporation, the consequences of the separate legal personality of the company were not fully appreciated at the time and this is probably the reason for the wording[20]. The modern wording is contained in s 14(1) of CA 1985, which provides that, subject to the provisions of the Act, the memorandum and articles, when registered, bind the company and its members to the same extent as if they respectively had been signed and sealed by each member, and contained convenants on the part of each member to observe all the provisions of the memorandum and of the articles. Section 14(2) provides that all money payable by any member to the company under the memorandum or articles shall be a debt due from him to the company, and in England and Wales, of the nature of a specialty debt. The reason for s 14(2) is most likely to have been to resolve any doubt as to whether money payable by a *subsequent* member was a debt at all[1]. The wording of s 14 sometimes produces some strange results. In *Re Compania de Electricidad de la Provincia de Buenos Aires Ltd*[2] Slade J drew attention to the fact that the section did not say that the articles took effect as if they had been sealed by the company. There was deemed to be a contract and the company was bound but the contract was only under seal as far as members were concerned. This had the effect that money owed by members to the company was a specialty debt as s 14(2) in fact states but money owed by the company was a simple contract debt. The period of limitation is consequently different—12 years in the first case, six years in the second. The position of the company has been explained by Jordan CJ in *Australian Coal and Shale Employers' Federation v Smith*[3]. He said that it can be regarded as an application of the equitable principle that a party who takes the benefit of a deed is bound by it although he does not execute it.

The nature of the statutory contract created by s 14(1) has been much discussed by the courts and legal commentators. The following principles and contradictions arise from the cases.

(1)   The articles of association constitute a statutory contract with its own distinctive features[4]. It has been held that the articles constitute a 'social contract[5]' but this is just a sophisticated way of saying that they constitute the constitution of an association[6]. The statutory contract has some rather odd characteristics. First, the section says that it is subject to the provisions of the Act. These provisions include s 9 which gives the company unilateral power to alter the contract by special resolution. Secondly, the normal remedies for breach of contract do not necessarily apply[7]. Thus articles are not defeasible on the grounds of misrepresentation, undue influence or duress and cannot be rectified on the grounds of mistake[8]. It is generally accepted that the remedies of a member for external redress are limited to an injunction or a declaration although

---

20   See Gower *Modern Company Law* (6th edn, 1997), p 116; Pennington *Company Law* (7th edn, 1995), ch 2.

1   3 Blackstone's Com 153 states that a debt is a sum due by certain and express agreement.

2   [1978] 3 All ER 668 at 697g–698a.

3   (1937) 38 SRNSW 48 at 55. See too *Bailey v NSW Medical Defence Union* (1995) 184 CLR 399 (HCA). See MJ Whincop (1997) 19 Sydney LR 314.

4   See *Bratton Seymour Service Co Ltd v Oxborough* [1992] BCLC 693, CA.

5   See the Australian cases of *Dutton v Gorton* (1917) 23 CLR 362 at 395; *Wood v W and G Dean Pty Ltd* (1929) 43 CLR 77; *Bailey v NSW Medical Defence Union Ltd* (1995) 184 CLR 399.

6   Cf *Re Chas Jeffries & Sons Pty Ltd* [1949] VLR 190 at 194 where it was described by Fullagar J as 'A Rousseau-esque synonym for the articles of association'. Indeed the phrase is perhaps as meaningless here as it is in the context of society as a whole.

7   See Gower, op cit, p 116.

8   *Bratton Seymour Service Co Ltd v Oxborough* [1992] BCLC 693, CA per Steyn LJ at 698.

in the case of *Moffatt v Farquhar*[9], Mallins VC directed an inquiry as to damages where directors acting in excess of their powers refused to register share transfers. Although it has been held that rectification is not available we have seen the commercial construction adopted by the courts sometimes achieves a similar result by a different means. However the courts will not go outside the articles and imply a term from extrinsic circumstances since this would prejudice third parties, namely potential shareholders who are entitled to look to and rely on the articles as registered[10].

(2)   The articles bind members qua members only. It has been held that the articles create a contract binding each member of the company but that the member is only bound qua member. In the leading case of *Hickman v Kent or Romney Marsh Sheep-Breeders' Association*[11], the articles provided for reference of disputes between members and the company to arbitration. The plaintiff brought an action against the company in connection with his expulsion from the company. Astbury J held that the company was entitled to have the action stayed because the articles amounted to a contract between the company and the member and referred such matters to arbitration[12]. In *Beattie v E & F Beattie Ltd*[13] there was a dispute between a director and his company. The director sought to have the dispute referred to arbitration under one of the articles. The Court of Appeal, following *Hickman* regarded this as a dispute qua director not member, and refused although it has been suggested that since the director was also a member it fell within the articles and his right as a member to have the company's business conducted in accordance with the articles[14].

(3)   Although the section does not provide that the articles bind the company and the members as if they had been sealed by the company, it has been held in numerous cases that the section gives rise to a contract binding the company to the members on which it can sue and be sued. In *Pender v Lushington*[15] the articles limited a shareholder's vote at a general meeting to 100 in all. Certain shareholders before a meeting transferred shares to nominees to increase their voting power. The chairman ruled the latter out of order and the plaintiff's votes were rejected on this ground. The court held that he was entitled to an injunction against the directors because he had a right to have his vote recorded. In substance, his claim appears to have been against the company although he technically joined the company as a co-plaintiff.

(4)   The articles constitute a contract between individual members. Normally this will be enforceable through the company but it may be possible in certain circumstances to have direct redress. *Hickman's* case left open the question as to whether the articles constitute a contract between the members inter se. In *Welton v Saffery*[16], Lord Herschell dissenting said: 'It is quite true that the articles constitute a contract between each

---

9   (1878) 7 Ch D 591.
10   *Bratton Seymour Service Co Ltd v Oxborough* [1992] BCLC 693, CA; *Stanham v National Trust of Australia* (1989) 15 ACLR 87,90; *Mutual Life Insurance Co of New York v Rank Organisation Ltd* [1985] BCLC 11.
11   [1915] 1 Ch 881; *Bailey v NSW Medical Defence Union* (1995) 184 CLR 399. See also the authorities cited below and *Gore Bros v Newbury Dairy Co Ltd* [1919] NZLR 205; Chantler (1976) 12 UWAL Rev 333; Bastin [1977] JBL 17. See too *Williams v MacPherson* 1990 SLT 279.
12   Cf *St Johnstone Football Club Ltd v Scottish Football Association Ltd* 1965 SLT 171 where it was held that an article prohibiting a member from taking legal proceedings against the company was contrary to public policy and void.
13   [1938] Ch 708, CA.
14   Wedderburn [1957] CLJ 193.
15   (1877) 6 Ch D 70.
16   [1897] AC 299 at 315, HL.

member and the company, and that there is no contract in terms whatever between the individual members of the company; but the articles do not any the less, in my opinion, regulate their rights inter se. Such rights can only be enforced by or against a member through the company ...'. The same view was expressed by Scott LJ in *London Sack and Bag Co v Dixon and Lugton Ltd*[17] and by Harman J in *Re Greene, Greene v Greene*[18]. On the other hand in *Wood v Odessa Waterworks Co*[19] Stirling J said that the articles took effect between each individual shareholder and every other, although the issue before him was an application by shareholders for an injunction against the company and its directors. In *Rayfield v Hands*[20], Vaisey J adopted the latter view and allowed direct enforcement without joinder of the company. There, the articles of a private company provided that any member intending to transfer his shares should inform the directors who should take the shares equally between them at fair value. Vaisey J adopting a commercial construction regarded the reference to directors as a reference to members and held that the article was directly enforceable. The cases cited above which appear to require enforcement through the company were cited but his Lordship gave them short shrift. The decision has been criticised as going too far[1] but can perhaps be justified on the basis that (1) it appears to have been an innocent drafting error of a mechanical kind and the intention was clear; (2) the company in question was analogous to a partnership; and (3) (more convincingly) the action is explicable as being an example of a personal right being infringed which is one of the recognised exceptions to the rule in *Foss v Harbottle* which requires an action to be brought through the company[2].

(5)   The articles do not per se constitute an enforceable contract between a company and an outsider[3]. This is no doubt due to privity of contract and lack of mutuality. Outsider means a person who is not a member or a member acting in a capacity other than that of a member. Even a director is normally treated as an outsider for this purpose[4]. Any right claimed by an outsider must be conferred by a separate contract or relationship outside the articles. In *Eley v Positive Government Security Life Assurance Co Ltd*[5] an agreement was made between a promoter and the plaintiff that the latter should advance the costs of formation and in return be appointed permanent solicitor. The plaintiff advanced £200 and prepared the articles. The articles provided that the plaintiff should be the solicitor of the company and should not be removed except for misconduct. He was allotted 200 shares in satisfaction of the advance made by him. His employment as solicitor was terminated and he sued for damages for breach of contract. It was held he could not claim as a solicitor relying on the articles. There are two important points about this case. First, the court did not like the original

---

17   [1943] 2 All ER 763 at 765, CA.
18   [1949] Ch 333 at 340.
19   (1889) 42 Ch D 636 at 642.
20   [1960] Ch 1.
1   See Gower (1958) 21 MLR 401, 657; Wedderburn [1958] CLJ 148.
2   See Chapter 28.
3   *Hickman v Kent or Romney Marsh Sheep-Breeders' Association* [1915] 1 Ch 881 at 897, 903. Cf *Bailey v NSW Medical Defence Union* (1995) 18 ACSR 521 as to 'special contracts' outside the articles. See also *Woodlands Ltd v Logan* [1948] NZLR 230 for a case where enforcement by legal proceedings was unnecessary. It is arguable that this rule does not apply to New Zealand law in any event because of s 4 of the Contracts (Privity) Act 1982 which abolishes the doctrine of privity of contract subject to certain exceptions.
4   See *Beattie v E & F Beattie Ltd,* supra.
5   (1876) 1 Ex D 88, CA. This was followed in *Browne v La Trinidad* (1887) 37 Ch D 1, CA. See the analysis of *Eley* in *Cumbrian Newspapers Group Ltd v Cumberland and Westmorland Herald Newspaper and Printing Co Ltd* [1986] 3 WLR 26 at 36–7.

arrangements and second, there had been insufficient disclosure of it to shareholders. An extrinsic contract may be made by the company with an outsider on the basis of the articles and such a contract may even be inferred from the conduct of the parties. In *Eley's* case the court said that there was nothing but the fact of employment in favour of such a view and this was insufficient. However, in *Swabey v Port Darwin Gold Mining Co*[6], *Re International Cable Co*[7], and *Re New British Iron Co, ex p Beckwith*[8], the courts were prepared to imply an extrinsic contract from service upon the terms of the article. *Swabey* was a Court of Appeal decision. There the directors had served the company without any express service contract. An article provided for remuneration at a fixed rate per annum. The company purported to reduce this by a retrospective special resolution. A director sued. The Court of Appeal held that although the articles did not themselves form a contract one could nevertheless get from them the terms upon which the director was serving. This was followed by Stirling J in *Re International Cable Co*[9] and a similar approach was adopted by Wright J in *Re New British Iron Co*[10] where the two earlier cases were not cited. Such a contract will be on the basis that the article as a term can be unilaterally changed by the company by special resolution under s 9 but such alteration must not be retrospective[11].

(6)   It is sometimes maintained that in any event there is a roundabout way of enforcing outsider rights on the basis of every member of a company having a right to have the company's business conducted in accordance with the articles[12]. However, clear authority for this proposition is somewhat limited[13]. In *Richmond Gate Property Co Ltd*[14] the argument was used to defeat a director's claim. This was a case of a claim in contract or quasi contract for remuneration as a director[15]. There was no express service agreement. There was a provision in the articles that directors' remuneration was to be fixed by the Board. None had been fixed. Indeed there had been an understanding that none would be paid to the managing director until the company got on its feet. Plowman J held that there was no claim in quantum meruit. For quantum meruit there must be no contract. Here there was a contract — the contract constituted by the articles. Under the terms of that contract, the remuneration was to be fixed by the directors. It had not been fixed. Therefore, there was no claim to remuneration. This decision can be criticised on two grounds. First, it seems to ignore the fact that this was using the contract argument in an outsider right situation and second, it is then using the argument to defeat the outsider's claim. This seems to be wrong in principle and unjust in effect although the decision can be justified on its facts.

It is arguable that this roundabout way of enforcement rests on the questionable proposition that all outsider rights conferring articles are true articles. Although Table A is directory, not mandatory, the further one gets from it the harder it is to justify the provision as an article. There is some authority to the effect that provisions in articles

---

6   (1889) 1 Meg 385, CA.
7   (1892) 66 LT 253.
8   [1898] 1 Ch 324.
9   (1892) 66 LT 253.
10 [1898] 1 Ch 324.
11 *Swabey v Port Darwin Gold Mining Co* (1889) 1 Meg 385, CA.
12 See Wedderburn [1957] CLJ 193.
13 See *Quin & Axtens Ltd v Salmon* [1909] AC 442, HL and *Re H R Harmer Ltd* [1958] 3 All ER 689, CA. See also *Kraus v J G Lloyd Pty Ltd* [1965] VR 232 at 235–6; *Hogg v Cramphorn Ltd* [1967] Ch 254 and *Bamford v Bamford* [1970] Ch 212, CA. But see too *Ram Kissendas Dhanuka v Satya Charan Law* (1949) LR 77 Ind App 128, PC. See P Smart [1989] JBL 143.
14 [1964] 3 All ER 936.
15 See Wedderburn (1965) 28 MLR 347 and Evans (1966) 29 MLR 608.

conferring commercial rights in a capacity other than that of a member derive no binding force from s 14(1). Any binding force which they have must be derived from a separate contract outside the articles[16]. This view is consistent with what Astbury J said in *Hickman's* case. The matter has been the subject of an interesting but inconclusive academic debate. The argument that since every member has a right to have the company's business conducted in accordance with the articles a member can indirectly enforce outsider rights qua member was first developed by Lord Wedderburn in 1957[17]. Professor Gower put forward the more orthodox view that s 14 gives the articles contractual effect only in so far as they confer rights or obligations on the member in his or her capacity as member but acknowledged the force of Wedderburn's argument[18]. Mr Goldberg tacked a middle course[19]. An outsider right can only be enforced if this is incidental to the enforcement of the member's contractual right under s 14(1) to have the company's affairs conducted by the particular organ of the company specified in the Act or the memorandum or articles. A refinement of this was put forward by Mr G N Prentice[20]. He argues that:

(1) it is misleading solely to ask whether a member sues qua member or qua outsider;
(2) it is not enough to shift the emphasis on to the organ of the company concerned;
(3) it is necessary to go one stage further and ask whether the provision in question affects the power of the company to function in the circumstances in question and it is only where there is some interference with the power of the company to function that a member will have a remedy.

Robust support for Wedderburn is provided by R Gregory who argues that there is more basis in the authorities for the thesis than had been thought. The cases on which he relies mainly involve directors[1] and it must be admitted that it seems rather absurd to regard directors as outsiders since they stand in a fiduciary relationship to the company which in part is defined by the articles. To sum up, a member qua member has rights which are either (1) personal rights covering the incidents of his shares or (2) constitutional rights to have the company function properly in accordance with the basic statutory scheme. Any other rights are not within s 14(1) and must be the subject of an extrinsic contract. The position of directors is, however, somewhat problematic. In some cases they have been allowed to sue on the articles[2]. In other cases such as *Swabey v Port Darwin Gold Mining Co* the courts have readily implied an extrinsic contract. In other cases they have been denied redress[3]. The position is most unsatisfactory particularly since directors are clearly bound by the articles qua

---

16 See *London Sack and Bag Co Ltd v Dixon and Lugton Ltd* [1943] 2 All ER 763, CA; *Eltham Co-operative Dairy Factory Co Ltd v Johnson* [1931] NZLR 216; *Black, White and Grey Cabs Ltd v Gaskin* [1971] NZLR 552 and *Ryans Cartage Services Ltd v Connor* (1981–3) 1 NZCLC 95–071.
17 [1957] CLJ 193.
18 Gower *Modern Company Law* (6th edn, 1997), p 121 et seq where he reformulates the argument and favours a new statutory version similar to the Australian Corporations Law, s 180 (1).
19 (1972) 35 MLR 362. See too (1985) 48 MLR 158.
20 (1980) 1 Co Law 179.
1 (1982) 44 MLR 526 citing *Orton v Cleveland Fire Brick and Pottery Co Ltd* (1865) 3 H & C 868; *Pulbrook v Richmond Consolidated Mining Co* (1878) 9 Ch D 610; *Imperial Hydropathic Hotel Co, Blackpool v Hampson* (1882) 23 Ch D 1, CA; *Hayes v Bristol Plant Hire Ltd* [1957] 1 All ER 685. See also *Breckland Group Holdings Ltd v London & Suffolk Properties Ltd* [1989] BCLC 100 noted by Wedderburn (1989) 52 MLR 401.
2 See cases cited in 1 and Gower, op cit, 121.
3 (1889) 1 Meg 385, CA.
4 *Browne v La Trinidad* (1887) 37 Ch D 1 at 14–15, CA.

directors and it seems odd to say that they have obligations but not rights under the articles[5].

(7)   A clause providing for exclusion, if in the original articles, will be regarded as falling within the contract and the rules of natural justice will not necessarily be implied. In *Gaiman v National Association for Mental Health*[6] Megarry J recognised that there can be such a power which need not conform with the principles of natural justice. It is also possible to provide in the articles expressly that the rules of natural justice shall not apply[7]. However, it is one thing to adopt such a provision on incorporation and another to attempt to alter the articles to adopt such a provision. In the latter case it may be rejected by the courts as not being for the good of the company[8]. Also it may be that where the company is an entity such as a football club or association and seeks to operate the provision to deprive a person of his livelihood, the courts will import a requirement of natural justice[9].

ALTERATION OF ARTICLES

Under s 9, subject to the provisions of the Act and to the conditions contained in its articles, a company may by special resolution alter its articles. There are a number of rules and principles which have been introduced either by the Companies Acts or by the cases which regulate the exercise of this power. These were conveniently summarised in the judgment of Latham CJ in the Australian case of *Peter's American Delicacy Co Ltd v Heath* in 1939[10]. We shall follow His Honour's basic analysis. The rules and principles are as follows:

(1)   A company cannot deprive itself of its statutory power to alter its articles either by agreement or by provision in its articles. Any provision to that effect is void[11]. It is, however, possible to put an entrenched provision in the memorandum of association and if this provides for class rights which are not to be alterable then the provision is immutable except by unanimous consent of all the members or a scheme of arrangement under s 425.

(2)   The contract constituted by the articles must be regarded as containing a provision that the articles may be altered by special resolution under s 9. Such an alteration may amount to a breach of an extrinsic contract but this does not invalidate the resolution[12].

(3)   Subject to compliance with class rights procedures and s 127, it is possible to alter members' rights in this way[13] and the fact that the alteration prejudices or

---

5   For yet another view—this time using relational contract analysis—see R R Drury [1986] CLJ 219.
6   [1971] Ch 317. Noted by Prentice (1970) 33 MLR 700. See also H H Mason (1975–6) 1 ABLR 226.
7   *Thorborn v All Nations Club* (1975) 1 ACLR 127. Cf *McNab v Auburn Soccer Sports Club Ltd* [1975] 1 NSWLR 54 at 59.
8   See p 128.
9   See *Enderby Town Football Club Ltd v Football Association Ltd* [1971] 1 All ER 215 at 219, CA.
10   (1938-9) 61 CLR 457, 479-482. Compare the more philosophical discussion by Dixon J at 496 et seq and the recent High Court of Australia decision in *Gambotto v WCP Ltd* (1995) 182 CLR 432.
11   *Malleson v National Insurance and Guarantee Corpn* [1894] 1 Ch 200; *Allen v Gold Reefs of West Africa Ltd* [1900] 1 Ch 656, CA; *Russell v Northern Bank Development Corp Ltd* [1992] BCLC 1016, HL.
12   *Allen's* case, supra, at 672.
13   *Allen's* case, supra; *Sidebottom v Kershaw, Leese & Co Ltd* [1920] 1 Ch 154, CA; *Shuttleworth v Cox Bros & Co (Maidenhead) Ltd* [1927] 2 KB 9, CA.

diminishes the rights of some members is not per se a ground for attacking the validity of the alteration[14].

(4)   The power to alter must, however, be exercised bona fide for the benefit of the company as a whole[15]. This is a concept inherited by company law from partnership law where it is used as a curb on a majority exercising a power of expulsion[16]. Its nature was described but its scope not defined by Lindley MR in *Allen v Gold Reefs of West Africa Ltd*[17] where he said:

> Wide, however, as the language of Section 10 is, the power conferred by it must, like all other powers, be exercised subject to those general principles of law and equity which are applicable to all powers conferred on majorities and enabling them to bind minorities. It must be exercised, not only in the manner required by law, but also bona fide for the benefit of the company as a whole, and it must not be exceeded. These conditions are always implied, but are seldom, if ever, expressed.

Thus in *Allen*'s case an article was altered in such a way as to prejudice one shareholder. The articles gave a lien on partly-paid shares for debts of members. Zuccani owed money in respect of unpaid calls on partly-paid shares but was the only holder of fully-paid shares. After his death insolvent, an alteration was made to give the company a lien on fully-paid shares as well. The court held that it was for the benefit of the company to recover moneys due to it and the alteration in its terms related to all holders of fully-paid shares. The fact that Zuccani was the only member of that class at that moment did not invalidate it.

In *Greenhalgh v Arderne Cinemas Ltd*[18] Evershed MR explained the test in the following way:

> I think it is now plain that 'bona fide for the benefit of the company as a whole' means not two things but one thing. It means that the shareholder must proceed upon what, in his honest opinion, is for the benefit of the company as a whole ... the phrase, 'the company as a whole', does not (at any rate in such a case as the present) mean the company as a commercial entity, distinct from the corporators: it means the corporators as a general body. That is to say, the case may be taken of an individual hypothetical member and it may be asked whether what is proposed is, in the honest opinion of those who voted in its favour, for that person's benefit.

(5)   It is not for the court to impose on a company its ideas as to what is for the benefit of the company. It is for the shareholders to determine whether the alteration is or is not for the benefit of the company subject to the proviso that the court will step in if the decision is such as no reasonable man could have reached. In other words, this is a prima facie general rule, not an absolute rule[19]. The courts will interfere if the alteration is 'so oppressive as to cast suspicion on the honesty of the persons responsible for it,

---

14   *Sidebottom*'s case, supra; *Shuttleworth*'s case, supra.
15   *Allen*'s case, supra. See F Rixon (1986) 49 MLR 446 for a lucid analysis of the concept. Cf the implied terms as regards exercise of the powers of the directors which overlap but also include fairness between shareholders—see *Mutual Life Insurance Co of New York v Rank Organisation Ltd* [1985] BCLC 11.
16   *Blisset v Daniel* (1853) 10 Hare 493.
17   Discussed in *Shuttleworth v Cox Bros & Co (Maidenhead) Ltd* [1927] 2 KB 9, CA.
18   [1951] Ch 286 at 291, CA.
19   *Carruth v ICI Ltd* [1937] AC 707, HL.

or so extravagant that no reasonable man could really consider it for the benefit of the company'. The test is thus analogous to that which a court of appeal applies in quashing the verdict of a jury[20]. It is probably easier to approach it by phrasing it in the negative — the majority must not exercise their powers so that the result will be contrary to the interest of the company, and to instance cases of the latter[1]. Evershed MR in *Greenhalgh v Arderne Cinemas Ltd* put the matter thus:

> I think that the matter can, in practice, be more accurately and precisely stated by looking at the converse and by saying that a special resolution of this kind would be liable to be impeached if the effect of it were to discriminate between majority shareholders and the minority shareholders, so as to give to the former an advantage of which the latter were deprived. When the cases are examined in which the resolution has been successfully attacked, it is on that ground.

On the other hand the court in that case took a narrow view of discrimination. The letter of the rights remained the same and the court did not consider the question of the enjoyment of the rights.

(6)   The benefit of the company cannot be regarded as a criterion which is capable of solving all the problems in this branch of law. An alteration which is made bona fide and for the benefit of the company, if otherwise within the power, will be good. But it is not the case that it is necessary that the shareholders should always have the benefit of the company in view. In cases where the question which arises is simply a question as to the relevant rights of different classes of shares, the problem cannot be solved in any event by regarding merely the benefit of the company[2]. The shareholders are not trustees for the company or for one another, nor are they to be regarded as partners[3]. A shareholder can vote in his or her own interests but the power to alter articles must not be exercised fraudulently or for the purpose of oppressing a minority[4]. It is thus not enough to prove tax and administrative savings if what is involved is expropriation of a member's interest even for fair value[5].

(7)   When the validity of a resolution altering the articles is challenged the onus of showing that the power has not been properly exercised is on the person complaining. The courts will not presume fraud or oppression or other abuse of power[6].

Let us now consider some of the cases in which these principles have been applied. In *Brown v British Abrasive Wheel Co*[7] the company had two distinct groups of shareholders. One group had a large majority and was prepared to inject more money into the company on condition that the articles were changed to get rid of the recalcitrant

---

20   Per Bankes LJ in *Shuttleworth*'s case, supra, at 18.
1   Cf JL Austin *Sense and Sensibilia*. The concept of the benefit of the company as a whole is probably a 'trouser word' in that the negation of the concept 'wears the trousers' ie controls the definition.
2   *Pender v Lushington* (1877) 6 Ch D 70 at 75, 76; *Mills v Mills* (1938) 60 CLR 150. For a lucid analysis of the concept of the good of the company see F Rixon (1986) 49 MLR 446. For increasing criticism of the concept by the High Court of Australia see *Gambotto v WCP Ltd* (1995) 182 CLR 432. It is suggested that a better test would be 'is the alteration beyond any purpose contemplated by the articles or oppressive as that expression is understood in the law relating to corporations?' (p 425).
3   *Phillips v Manufacturers' Securities Ltd* (1917) 116 LT 290, CA.
4   *Cook v Deeks* [1916] 1 AC 554 at 564, PC; *Menier v Hooper's Telegraph Works* (1874) 9 Ch App 350; *Shuttleworth*'s case, supra, at 27; *Carruth v ICI Ltd* [1937] AC 707, HL.
5   *Gambotto v WCP Ltd* (1995) 182 CLR 432, HC of Australia.
6   *Peter's American Delicacy Co Ltd v Heath* (1939) 61 CLR 457 at 482. See P Xuereb (1985) 6 Co Law 199, 206 et seq; Rixon, op cit.
7   [1919] 1 Ch 290.

minority. The alteration was challenged by the minority and the court held that it was not for the good of the company. Similarly in *Dafen Tinplate Co Ltd v Llanelly Steel Co (1907) Ltd*[8] a power to buy out a minority at fair value was held to be not for the good of the company. On the other hand in *Sidebottom v Kershaw, Leese & Co Ltd*[9] one of the shareholders was a competitor of the company and the others wanted to get rid of him. They consequently proposed an alteration of the articles providing for the compulsory purchase at a fair price of the shares of any members who competed with the business of the company. The Court of Appeal held that this was for the good of the company. Lord Sterndale MR held that the question whether the directors introduced the alteration for the benefit of the company was ultimately one of fact. Evidence of malicious motive and discrimination would negate the bona fides. Similarly, in *Shuttleworth v Cox Bros & Co (Maidenhead) Ltd*[10] the articles contained a provision for one person to be a permanent director of the company. He failed to account to the company for moneys belonging to the company and failed to resign when called upon to do so. The company passed a special resolution altering the articles providing for terminating of office by the permanent directors on a request in writing by all the other directors. The Court of Appeal held that this was for the good of the company.

In *Gambotto v WCP Ltd*[11] in 1995 WCP proposed an alteration to its articles which would require its minority shareholders to sell their shares to the majority shareholders. This would have made WCP a wholly owned subsidiary of IEL, resulting in tax and administrative advantages to WCP. The price offered was above market value but two shareholders resisted the buyout. Gambotto representing himself succeeded in the High Court of Australia which rejected the benefit of the company test and opted for the following two fold approach:

(a) an alteration for a purpose other than expropriation of shares is valid unless it is ultra vires, beyond any purpose contemplated by the articles or oppressive;

(b) an alteration for the purpose of expropriation of shares is valid only if it is for a proper purpose and it is fair.

Fairness has two aspects. First, the process must be fair and secondly the buyout price must be fair. This goes beyond market value. It is for the company to establish that the change is for a proper purpose. Tax and administrative gains were insufficient. It would be a proper purpose if the object was to save the company from significant detriment or harm. Examples were the buyout of a competing shareholder or where the membership resulted in a loss of business.

One cannot help but think that it was a great mistake for the High Court to attempt a restatement of principle in this complex area without the benefit of counsel for the appellant. The result is not a significant improvement and the result bears an ill-defined relationship with other areas of company law[12]. It is uncertain whether the reasoning will be followed in the UK.

8   [1920] 2 Ch 124.
9   [1920] 1 Ch 154, CA.
10 [1927] 2 KB 9, CA.
11 (1995) 182 CLR 432. Noted by D D Prentice (1996) 112 LQR 194. *Gambotto* involved a clash of interest between two groups of shareholders. Quaere if there is a third category which covers non clash of interest cases eg. administrative article changes where the good of the company test is still applicable even if *Gambotto* is followed in the UK.
12 See *Gambotto v WCP Ltd: Its Implications for Corporate Regulation* Ian Ramsay(ed) (1996). See also S Kevans (1996) 18 Sydney LR 110. For earlier analysis see S Fridman (1994) 22 Federal LR 205; V Mitchell (1994) 6 Bond LR 92; M Whincop (1995) 23 ABLR 276 (an updated version of the last appears in the 1996 collection).

In *Greenhalgh v Arderne Cinemas Ltd*[13] the Court of Appeal upheld an alteration as being for the good of the company which discriminated in fact if not in law. The company had a nominal capital of £31,000 divided into 21,000 10 shilling preference shares and 205,000 2 shilling ordinary shares. The plaintiff held 4,213 ordinary shares. The articles contained a pre-emption clause. The majority shareholder agreed to sell ordinary shares to an outsider and a notice of meeting was sent out proposing the alteration of the articles by the addition of a clause authorising a sale to a transferee if sanctioned by an ordinary resolution. The court rejected the plaintiff's claim that it was not for the good of the company since it negated his enjoyment of his rights. *Greenhalgh* represents a harsh decision but one which nevertheless is consistent with the cases on variation of class rights as we shall see in Chapter 17. The court seems to concentrate on form and ignore substance.

Occasionally the courts have had resort to mainstream principles of the law of contract. Thus in the New Zealand case of *Invercargill Sports Depot Ltd v Patrick*[14] the adoption of a proposed article restricting competition was held to be invalid for reasons of restraint of trade. This seems to go beyond the concept of the good of the company and in some ways to be inconsistent with it. The company exists for an economic rationale which may be served by restrictions on trade. Activities which are in restraint of trade may be for the good of the company in an economic sense. On the other hand there is no reason why parties should be in any preferential position under the general law of contract merely because they have assumed the corporate form for their particular arrangements.

The sixth principle laid down by Latham CJ in the *Peters Delicacy* case must now be regarded as subject to a possible qualification. His Honour said that shareholders are not trustees for the company or one another. In New Zealand it was held as long ago as 1879 in *Stanford v Gillies*[15] that where a shareholder entered into a secret agreement with an intending purchaser of the company's property to be paid a sum of money to use his influence with the other shareholders to promote the sale at a certain price, the agreement was founded on an illegal consideration, and fraudulent, and the shareholder was a trustee for the company in respect of the money received. In this case the shareholder was active in getting shareholder approval in general meeting and was in league with another shareholder who was also a director. Although they were two of the largest shareholders they only held 91 out of a total of 300 shares. The court largely based its decision on cases involving co-owners and *Menier v Hooper's Telegraph Works*[16] but it can also perhaps be explained in terms of constructive trust. The shareholder was knowingly a party to the director's breach of duty. In the USA, the courts have developed a doctrine of fiduciary obligations on controlling shareholders to the other shareholders[17] in certain circumstances and in *Clemens v Clemens Bros Ltd*[18] and *Estmanco (Kilner House) Ltd v Greater London Council*[19] there is perhaps some limited support for that doctrine. The facts of *Clemens* were

13   [1951] Ch 286, CA.
14   [1939] NZLR 161.
15   (1880) OB & F (SC) 91.
16   (1874) 9 Ch App 350.
17   See eg *Jones v Ahmanson & Co* 460 P 2d 464 (1969).
18   [1976] 2 All ER 268. Noted by D Prentice (1976) 92 LQR 502; and see G R Sullivan (1978) 41 MLR 169. See also L S Sealy 'Equitable and Other Fetters on the Shareholder's Freedom to Vote', *The Cambridge Lectures 1981* (1981) ed Eastham & Krivy, p 80 ff, especially pp 84–85. See also the unreported case of *Pennell v Venida Investments Ltd* in 1974 discussed by S Burridge (1981) 44 MLR 40.
19   [1982] 1 All ER 437. See R Gregory (1982) 45 MLR 584.

that the plaintiff held 45% and her aunt 55% of the shares in the defendant company. Thus she had negative control in the sense that she could block a special resolution which required a three-quarters majority. There was a pre-emption provision in the articles under which the plaintiff would in the normal course get complete control of the company on her aunt's death. The aunt and four non-shareholders were the directors. The directors proposed a capital increase which would result in the non-shareholder directors getting shares and the balance going to a trust for employees. The requisite ordinary resolutions were duly passed. The effect of this was to dilute the plaintiff's holdings and to remove her present negative and future actual control. The plaintiff challenged the resolutions on the ground of oppression. The case did not involve an actual alteration of the articles but an effective de facto negation of the plaintiff's rights. It raised the question of the aunt's duties as director and majority shareholder. At the end of the day, Foster J thought it unwise to try to formulate a principle 'since the circumstances of each case are infinitely varied'. He was prepared to say, however, that the aunt was not 'entitled as of right to exercise her votes as an ordinary shareholder in any way she pleases'. The right was subject to equitable considerations which might make it unjust to exercise it in a particular way. He cited Evershed MR in *Greenhalgh v Arderne Cinemas Ltd* and equated the niece with the hypothetical shareholder for whose benefit the power must be exercised. This seems an improper use of Evershed MR's rather impractical test. In the *Estmanco* case the GLC owned a block of flats which it decided to sell on long leases. A management company was formed and one share was to be allocated to each flat. The shares were to have voting rights when all the flats had been sold but until then all voting rights vested in the GLC. After 12 flats had been sold, the GLC decided to let the remainder to council tenants. The company issued a writ to prevent this. The GLC in an extraordinary general meeting used its votes to obtain a resolution instructing the directors to withdraw the action. A minority shareholder brought an action and Megarry VC allowed the action to proceed. The case, like *Stanford v Gillies* and *Clemens*, is not an alteration of articles case but Megarry VC said some interesting things about the alteration of articles cases and their relevance to a minority shareholder's action. He held that:

Although a majority shareholder, unlike a director, owed no fiduciary duty to the company and was entitled to vote in his own interest, that did not give him an unrestricted right to pass a resolution depriving a minority shareholder of its rights or property merely because the majority shareholder reasonably believed that his actions were in the best interests of the company.

He drew attention to the difficulty of wedding the alteration of articles cases to the fraud on the minority exceptions to the rule in *Foss v Harbottle*. The cases indeed are more consistent with the rule which equates the company with the majority than with the exceptions. He said at p 444 g–j:

Now the question is how far authorities such as these on the validity of making alterations in the articles fit in with the rule in *Foss v Harbottle* (1843) 2 Hare 461, 67 ER 189, and its exceptions; for counsel for the council accepted, as he had to, that the line of authority on altering the articles has not yet been applied to the rule in *Foss v Harbottle* and its exceptions. I do not think that counsel ever succeeded in answering that question satisfactorily. Plainly there must be some limit to the power of the majority to pass resolutions which they believe to be in the best interests of the company and yet remain immune from interference by the courts. It may be in the best interests of the company to deprive the minority of some of their rights or some of their property, yet I do not think that this gives the majority an unrestricted right to do this, however unjust it may be, and however much it may harm shareholders whose rights as a class differ from those of the majority. If a case falls within one of the exceptions from *Foss v Harbottle*, I cannot see why the right of the minority to sue under that exception should be taken away from them merely because the majority of the company reasonably believe it to be in the best interest of the company that this should be done. This is particularly so if the exception from the rule falls under the rubric of 'fraud on a minority'.

Clemens shows the difficulty of applying the good of the company test to a private company and the need to resort to some broader conception of fairness between shareholders. In the past this has generally been limited to classes of shares but in a two shareholder company it seems appropriate since the fact that there are two shareholders with different holdings give them a de facto position analogous to different classes. This was the approach adopted in *Re Hellenic and General Trust Ltd*[20] in relation to the concept of class for the purposes of the scheme of arrangement procedures in s 425. Equitable considerations enable one to transcend the legal form of the company on such occasions. As we shall see such considerations arise on a petition to wind up the company on the just and equitable ground under s 122(1)(g) of the Insolvency Act 1986. Indeed Foster J in the *Clemens* case relied on the leading case in that area, *Ebrahimi v Westbourne Galleries Ltd*[1]. *Ebrahimi* was not cited in *Estmanco* but the decision is consistent with it. What *Estmanco* reveals is the difficulty of fitting together the alteration of articles cases with the fraud on the minority exception to the rule in *Foss v Harbottle*. It seems to follow from this that an alteration may be validly effected but still capable of being regarded as fraud on the minority and the subject of a minority shareholder's action. *Stanford v Gillies, Clemens* and *Estmanco* do not, however, go as far as the American cases. There is not yet full recognition of fiduciary duties on controlling shareholders as such. Nevertheless the jurisprudence of fairness which is emerging from equitable principles of restraints on powers and the statutory remedies under s 459, CA 1985 and s 122(1)(g) of the Insolvency Act 1986 are leading courts in that direction. It will be easier for the courts to think in fiduciary terms in the case of a quasi partnership company than in the case of a listed public company. We look in more depth at the special problems of the latter in Chapter 34[2].

It is interesting to see that the draft Fifth EU Directive contains articles which prevent a shareholder from voting on an issue where there is a conflict of interest between the company and him personally (art 34) and for avoiding shareholder agreements which fetter a shareholder's vote (art 35). While these fall short of general fiduciary obligations on controlling shareholders, they will prevent many of the abuses in practice.

Sometimes a proposed alteration of the articles involves class rights. Professor Gower has described class rights as rights relating to dividends, voting and surplus assets on a winding up[3]. In *Cumbrian Newspapers Group Ltd v Cumberland and Westmorland Herald Newspaper and Printing Co Ltd*[4] in 1986 Scott J defined rights or benefits contained in articles into three different categories. First, there are rights

---

20   [1975] 3 All ER 382.
1   [1973] AC 360, HL.
2   See further J H Farrar 'Duties of Controlling Shareholders' in *Contemporary Issues in Company Law* (1987) ed J H Farrar, pp 185–202.
3   Op cit, pp 562–3.
4   [1986] 3 WLR 26 at 36–7. Noted by J Birds (1986) 7 Co Law 202; K Polack [1986] CLJ 399.

or benefits which are annexed to particular shares. He regarded, as classic examples of these, dividend rights and rights to participate in surplus assets on a winding up. Secondly, there are rights or benefits conferred on individuals, not in the capacity of members or shareholders of the company, but for ulterior reasons, connected with the administration of the company's affairs or the conduct of its business. These are the outsider rights discussed above. Thirdly, there was an intermediate category of rights or benefits which, although not attached to any particular shares, are nevertheless conferred on the beneficiary in the capacity of member or shareholder of the company. His Lordship thought that the first and third categories were 'rights attached to a class of shares' for the purposes of s 125, CA 1985. It is usual for a company to have an express variation of rights clause. Where there is no such clause s 125 now sets out procedures to be complied with. The procedures must be followed by members of the class prior to the general meeting at which the special resolution is proposed. The question arises, must the variation of rights procedure be complied with before there can be a valid alteration of articles? On this, prior to the statutory reforms of 1980 now contained in s 125, there were two conflicting Australian decisions. In *Fischer v Easthaven Ltd*[5] the judge held that articles can be freely altered by special resolution in spite of a variation of rights clause. On the other hand in *Crumpton v Morrine Hall Pty Ltd*[6] the judge came to the opposite conclusion and was prepared to restrain the company from acting on an alteration which did not comply with the variation of rights clause. In an earlier English decision in *Lord St Davids v Union Castle Mail SS Co*[7] in 1934 which was never fully reported, Clauson J appears to have thought that the variation of rights clause must be complied with and in *Rights and Issues Investment Trust Ltd v Stylo Shoes Ltd*[8], Pennycuick J appeared to take the same view. Section 125 now seems to make that view the law in all cases in future. We shall examine this question in more detail in Chapter 18.

The effect of articles and alterations to articles on contracts[9]

There are three main possibilities. First, the articles may be the only form of legal relationship between a company and a member. Second, there may be an extrinsic contract between the company and a member which refers to the articles. Third, there may be an extrinsic contract between the company and an outsider which refers to the articles.

WHERE THE ARTICLES ARE THE ONLY LEGAL RELATIONSHIP WITH A MEMBER

In this first case the articles are freely alterable under s 9, subject to the alteration being for the good of the company and complying with class rights procedures.

---

5   [1964] NSWR 261.
6   [1965] NSWR 240.
7   (1934) 78 Sol Jo 877; see also *Australian Fixed Trusts Pty v Clyde Industries Ltd* [1959] SRNSW 33.
8   [1965] Ch 250.
9   See generally M J Trebilcock [1967] 31 Conv (NS) 95 and L G S Trotman, 'Articles of Association and Contracts' in *Contemporary Issues in Company Law* (1987) ed J H Farrar. See too the recent High Court of Australia decision in *Bailey v NSW Medical Defence Union* (1995) 184 CLR 399.

WHERE THE MEMBER HAS AN EXTRINSIC CONTRACT WITH THE COMPANY WHICH REFERS TO THE ARTICLES

In this case the case law is rather complex. In *Punt v Symons & Co Ltd*[10] Byrne J held that a company cannot by contract—even an extrinsic contract—exclude the power to alter its articles and no injunction would be granted to restrain it from effecting the alteration. In the House of Lords case of *Southern Foundries (1926) Ltd v Shirlaw*[11], which technically involved an outsider, there is some limited support for this proposition. The facts of the case were that a man was appointed managing director of the company under an express service agreement for 10 years. There was a provision that he would cease to be managing director if he ceased to be a director. The company altered the articles to allow a principal shareholder to remove directors. The House of Lords held by a majority of three to two that the managing director was entitled to damages for wrongful dismissal. The House of Lords recognised that a company could always alter its articles and could not contract out of that power but it also recognised that to do so may make it liable to a claim for damages if the terms of the contract are such that the alteration amounts to a breach. Lord Porter said obiter that the courts will not grant an injunction to prevent the adoption of new articles. On the other hand there is earlier authority which is inconsistent with this. In *Baily v British Equitable Assurance Co*[12] the Court of Appeal held that a company cannot by altering its articles alter an extrinsic contract and could be restrained by declaration from adopting articles which infringed the profit-sharing rights of its policy holders. That decision was reversed by the House of Lords on a point of construction on the basis that the terms of the articles were incorporated into the contract in question and consequently the statutory power to alter them. The Court of Appeal's decision was, however, followed in *British Murac Syndicate Ltd v Alperton Rubber Co Ltd*[13] by Sargeant J, who mistakenly thought that *Punt v Symons* had been overruled by *Baily's* case. He therefore granted an injunction. In *Cumbrian Newspapers Group Ltd v Cumberland & Westmorland Herald Newspaper & Printing Co Ltd*[14] Scott J said obiter that if a company had agreed that its articles would not be altered he could see no reason why it should not 'in a suitable case' be injuncted from initiating the calling of a general meeting with a view to the alteration of the articles. However, he thought that this should not be granted to prevent a company from discharging its statutory obligations to call a general meeting on a members' requisition, for example under s 368, CA 1985. As His Lordship's reasoning is premised on the right to alter being a right of the members, not the company, this seems logical. However, his initial premise seems questionable. It is not a right of the members. It is a corporate power exercisable by the appropriate majority of the members.

In *Russell v Northern Bank Development Corpn Ltd*,[15] the House of Lords held that an agreement between four shareholders of a private company not to vote in favour of an increase in share capital unless they had agreed in writing was valid. They emphasised that the company was not bound by the agreement but that, nevertheless, it was valid between the shareholders. The part of the agreement purporting to bind

---

10   [1903] 2 Ch 506.
11   [1940] AC 701, HL. See too *Cumbrian Newspapers Group Ltd v Cumberland and Westmorland Herald Newspaper and Printing Co Ltd* [1986] 3 WLR 26 at 43–44 where Scott J obiter agreed with Lord Porter's obiter dicta. Cf *Carrier Australasia Ltd v Hunt* (1939) 61 CLR 534 (High Court of Australia).
12   [1904] 1 Ch 374, CA.
13   [1915] 2 Ch 186.
14   [1986] 3 WLR 26 at 43. See also *Harman v BML Group Ltd* [1994] 2 BCLC 674.
15   [1992] BCLC 1016. For useful analysis see L S Sealy [1992] CLJ 437; G. Shapira (1993) 109 LQR 210; B.J. Davenport QC (1993) 109 LQR 553; Eilis Ferran [1994] CLJ 343.

the company was void as an attempt to fetter the company's statutory power to alter its articles but was severable. The agreement between the shareholders was a personal agreement and did not run with the shares to bind their successors. The House of Lords granted a declaration because in the circumstances an injunction was not sought. The decision confirms the absolute prohibition on a direct contracting out of the statutory power but allows it effectively to be circumvented by agreement between shareholders. This is hardly a satisfactory state of the law and represents another example of the triumph of form over substance in the law.

A distinction can perhaps be drawn between granting an injunction to stop a company from altering its articles and granting an injunction to stop a company from acting in breach of contract under an altered article[16]. Whereas it is possible to argue that no injunction will be granted to stop a company from altering its articles, an injunction may possibly still lie to prevent a company acting in breach of contract. However, against this can be argued that to grant an injunction to stop a company from acting in accordance with the altered article so far negates the exercise of the power to alter the articles that it almost negates the power itself. To this argument perhaps there is a rejoinder to the effect that this does not stop the company acting on the article in respect of persons other than the other party to this particular contract.

WHERE THE COMPANY HAS AN EXTRINSIC CONTRACT WITH AN OUTSIDER WHICH REFERS TO THE ARTICLES

An extrinsic contract between the company and an outsider is governed by normal contract principles. Complications arise when the contract in some way is affected by the articles or incorporates them.

We have seen that the articles per se cannot give rise to a contract with an outsider[17] but may be evidence of an implied contract[18]. If the articles are a term of the contract the matter is largely one of construction. If the article was incorporated qua article the court may say that the original contract has impliedly incorporated the statutory power to alter it[19] but an alteration cannot be made retrospectively. The effect of this is that the company has a unilateral power of variation of the contract or at least that term of the contract[20]. The position is rather analogous to members of a club. One joins the club subject to the rules for the time being.

In *Read v Astoria Garage (Streatham) Ltd*[1] a managing director was appointed under the articles but without any extrinsic service agreement. Article 68 of Table A, which applied, enabled the company to dismiss him without notice by resolution in general meeting. It was held by the Court of Appeal that a term as to reasonable notice was not to be implied. A different construction, however, was reached in *Shindler v Northern Raincoat Co Ltd*[2] where there was an extrinsic service agreement which expressly provided for a term of 10 years. Diplock J held that there was an implied term that the company would not do anything of its own motion to put an end to that

---

16   Cf M J Trebilcock [1967] 31 Conv (NS) 95 at 114.
17   *Hickman v Kent or Romney Marsh Sheep-Breeders' Association* [1915] 1 Ch 881.
18   *Re New British Iron Co, ex p Beckwith* [1898] 1 Ch 324; *Bailey v NSW Medical Defence Union* (1995) 184 CLR 399.
19   See *Swabey v Port Darwin Gold Mining Co* (1889) 1 Meg 385, CA; *Bailey v NSW Medical Defence Union* (1995) 184 CLR 399.
20   See *Malleson v National Insurance and Guarantee Corpn* [1894] 1 Ch 200.
1   [1952] Ch 637, CA. Noted by L C B Gower (1953) 16 MLR 82.
2   [1960] 2 All ER 239.

state of affairs. This latter view is consistent with *Nelson v James Nelson & Sons Ltd*[3] and reconcilable with *Southern Foundries (1926) Ltd v Shirlaw* (supra). It was held by the Court of Appeal in *Nelson v James Nelson & Sons Ltd* that where the company had entered into a service agreement with a managing director for a fixed term the company could not rely on an article which enabled them to revoke such appointment at will or otherwise than in accordance with the agreement. It is to be noted that here the article in question was already there. There was no question of alteration. What the court was holding was that the company relying on one provision in the articles to enter into a commitment could not later renege relying on another provision. Nevertheless, neither *Shindler* nor *Nelson* were cases of alteration of articles and the company cannot exclude its statutory power to alter its articles by special resolution although as we have seen a particular alteration may give rise to an action for damages for breach of contract by the outsider. The principles are the same as those we have discussed above in relation to an extrinsic contract with a member.

CONCLUSION

This rather brief discussion of the cases indicates that it is important to distinguish between the statutory 'contract' on the one hand and all other contracts on the other. The statutory contract is a deemed contract governed by the principles of company law. Other contracts are ordinary contracts governed by the law of contract. One should not perhaps let the fact that some of the terms of an ordinary contract are found in the articles confuse the issue. As far as possible the latter should be governed by the ordinary principles of the law of contract[4].

3   [1914] 2 KB 770, CA.
4   See Trotman, op cit, for a more detailed and convincing argument along these lines. For a recent application of similar principles see *Bailey v NSW Medical Defence Union* (1995) 184 CLR 399 especially at 439 per McHugh and Gummow JJ. The problem arises when the courts rely on the concept of implied contract in respect of the latter. See also M Whincop (1997) 19 Syd LR 314.

CHAPTER 12

Supplementing the statutory constitution

Since 1856, the Companies Acts have provided for a constitution in the form of memorandum and articles of association. The proprietors of a company sometimes wish to supplement these for a variety of reasons. Although they value the limitation of personal liability as regards the outside world they wish to agree among themselves how risk, profit and control shall ultimately be distributed. Let us first examine some of their reasons and then some of the methods of supplementation.

REASONS FOR SUPPLEMENTATION[1]

First, it may be felt in the case of an incorporated partnership or joint venture company that the statutory form provides an inadequate record of their understanding. Some additional agreement is necessary to deal with the composition of the board, removal of directors, the entitlement of members to office, the exercise of corporate powers to borrow, pay dividends or wind up and the right of a shareholder to be bought out given the absence of a ready market for shares in such companies.

Secondly, it may be necessary to supplement the statutory methods of resolution of disputes. The statutory model provides a simple model. Disputes are resolved by majority decision in general meetings, although certain matters require a three-quarters majority, such as a change of the constitution. A supplementary arrangement may provide for arbitration, rights of pre-emption or voluntary winding up in such circumstances.

Thirdly, in the past the rights of minority shareholders to bring an action for oppression were severely curtailed by the rule in *Foss v Harbottle* and the limitations of the statutory remedy under s 459 of CA 1985. A supplementary agreement can expressly provide against oppression and breach of the agreement will carry all the

---

1   See P Finn [1978] ABLR 97, 102–4; B N Apple QC *Special Lectures on Law Society of Upper Canada 1968* (1968), pp 41–64. G Stedman and J Jones *Shareholders Agreements* (2nd ed); L S Sealy 'Enforcement of Partnership Agreements, Articles of Association and Shareholders' Agreements' in P D Finn (ed) *Equity and Commercial Relationships* (1987), 89-113. See also F Hodge O'Neal *Close Corporations* (3rd edn, 1988), vol 1, ch 5; and C M Roose (1971) 15 Scandinavian Studies in Law 163 and B Gomard (1972) 16 Scandinavian Studies in Law 97; V Goldwasser (1994) 22 ABLR 265; A Rutabanzibwa (1996) 17 Co Law 194.

normal contractual remedies. However, there is the risk that the court may say that it defines the relationship of the parties to the exclusion of other factors.

Since the House of Lords decision in *Ebrahimi v Westbourne Galleries Ltd*[2] the courts are prepared to consider a broad range of issues in order to assess whether one or more of the proprietors are reneging on their equitable obligations. Whereas previously there was some wisdom in opting for a supplementary agreement the recent case law on s 459 gives reason for doubt. It can be a two-edged sword.

One Swedish jurist attempted to categorise the basic types of supplementary arrangement as (1) those which concentrate control (2) those which distribute control and (3) those which transfer control. However, not all such arrangements are necessarily concerned with control unless the term is used in the broadest possible sense. Dispute resolution, for instance, is not a matter of control except in the sense of social control[3].

METHODS OF SUPPLEMENTATION

There are four methods of supplementation which have found favour[4] —shareholders' agreements, voting trusts, irrevocable proxies and management agreements. We deal with each of these in turn although only shareholders' agreements are common in the UK.

1   Shareholders' agreements

Shareholders' agreements are usually one of three kinds:

(a) an agreement between the company and the members collateral and supplementary to the articles;

(b) an agreement between all the shareholders inter se;

(c) an agreement between some of the shareholders.

(A)   AGREEMENT BETWEEN THE COMPANY AND THE MEMBERS

Here the position was described with characteristic lucidity by Salmond J in the New Zealand case of *Shalfoon v Cheddar Valley Co-operative Dairy Co Ltd*[5] in 1924 where he said:

There are two distinct ways in which an obligation may come into existence as between a company and one of its shareholders. In the first place, it may have its source in a regulation validly made by the company and inserted in the articles of association ... In the second place, it may have its source in a contract made between the company and the individual shareholder. This distinction is of practical importance for several reasons. In the first place, an obligation imposed by a regulation is not merely personal, but is appurtenant to the shares of the company so as to run with those shares in the hands of successive owners and to

2   [1973] AC 360, HL.
3   Roose, op cit, p 166.
4   *O'Neal*, op cit; M Pickering (1965) 81 LQR 248; NCSC Commentary, 'Regulation on the Use of Proxies, Voting Trusts and Arrangements' in the *NCSC* (Australia) *Manual:* Release 404; P Xuereb (1987) 8 Co Law 16.
5   [1924] NZLR 561.

bind all shareholders for the time being; but a contractual obligation is purely personal and binds only the individual shareholder who has become a party to the contract, and cannot be made to run with the shares as appurtenant thereto in the hands of successive owners. In the second place, a regulation can always be altered or repealed by the company, and the rights and obligations created thereby may be thus modified or destroyed; whereas a contract between the company and a shareholder can only be altered or cancelled by the mutual consent of both parties. In the third place, a regulation to be valid must be within the scope of the legislative authority given by the Companies Act to a company over its shareholders; whereas a contract made between a company and a shareholder is subject merely to the general provisions of the law of contract, a company being entitled to make any contract with a shareholder which it might lawfully make with an outsider. A shareholder may therefore take upon himself by contract with the company many obligations which could not be imposed upon him by the company by the making of regulations.

The existence and importance of this distinction between a contract and a regulation are not affected by the circumstances that the regulations of a company have themselves the effect of a contract between the company and the shareholders by virtue of section [14].

Thus an agreement between the company and its member can range wider than the articles and cover outsider rights but this remains personal to the particular members and only binds their transferees if there is a novation. A collateral agreement between the company and *all* its members is perfectly legitimate. However, in the USA recently some large companies are entering into what are called 'standstill agreements' with major shareholders. Such agreements are long-term contracts in which the contracting shareholder generally agrees that it will not buy or sell any of the company's stock without management's written approval and will vote as they direct on certain issues. In exchange the contracting shareholder gets its nominee on the board of directors and may be given other rights. In so far as standstill agreements involve a sale of the contracting shareholder's votes they may be illegal and void under US laws as contrary to public policy. We examine the latter question in (b) below. The risk of such agreements—even informal agreements—is that they may effectively disenfranchise other shareholders.

(B)   AGREEMENT BETWEEN ALL THE SHAREHOLDERS INTER SE[6]

Such agreements are often used to supplement the articles and usually relate to participation in management, the right to be bought out and the circumstances in which the company will be put into voluntary liquidation.

While there is nothing improper in all the shareholders agreeing to vote in a particular way at general meeting such agreements are of doubtful efficacy if they:

(i)   provide for a pecuniary benefit to a particular shareholder for voting in a particular way;

(ii) purport to bind members qua directors as to how they should vote as directors;

(iii) purport to fetter the company's power to alter its articles.

---

6   P Finn [1978] ABLR 97; G Hornstein (1950) 59 Yale LJ 1040. However, see now the latest provisions of the Fifth Directive of the EU discussed in Chapter 3. These would avoid many such agreements.

In addition they may be held to be limited in terms of time to a reasonable time or the length of time the shares are held[7]. In the USA, in certain states, a maximum period has been stipulated[8]. Professor Finn has argued that type (i) is illegal either on the basis that they constitute a bribe or that they amount to a fraud on other shareholders[9] but that these bases do not seem to be relevant if the shareholders' agreement is an open one supported primarily or solely by mutual promises. The case he cites is *Elliott v Richardson*[10] in 1870 which was an agreement between two shareholders A and B in a company which was being wound up compulsorily that in consideration of A agreeing to use his influence to postpone a call about to be made and to support B's claim as a creditor of the company B would pay all calls on A's shares. It was held that the agreement was contrary to the policy of the winding-up provisions of the Companies Acts and void. Willes J also expressed the opinion that the agreement to support B's claim was void as being against the spirit of the law against maintenance. It is submitted, however, that while there is a well-established body of law against contracting out of the winding-up scheme and against fraud on creditors, the mere passing of a money consideration should not invalidate such an agreement in a situation where there is no winding up. It is established that a member's vote is an item of personal property and he is entitled to consider his own interests without regard to the interests of other shareholders[11] subject to a duty on the majority voting in a general meeting to consider the interests of the company as a whole. Where the consideration is part of a sale of the shares[12] or a mortgage advance on the security of the shares[13] the member has been obliged to honour his agreement. Also where instead of providing for a consideration for voting in a particular way the agreement provides a penalty for not voting in a particular way, it has been upheld[14].

On the other hand it has been held in New Zealand in *Stanford v Gillies*[15] that a shareholder who enters into a secret agreement with a purchaser of the company's assets to receive a bribe to promote the sale with the other shareholders is liable as a trustee for the company. In the particular case the shareholder was in league with another shareholder who was also a director. Together they were two of the largest shareholders holding 91 out of 300 shares. The four significant features of this case were the secrecy, the bribe, the active promotion of the sale in general meeting and the complicity in a breach of duty by the director. The shareholder was in effect a constructive trustee.

Article 35 of the draft Fifth Directive of the EU avoids agreements whereby a shareholder undertakes to vote in one of the following ways:

(a) always to follow the instructions of the company or one of its organs;
(b) always to approve the proposals of the company or one of its organs;
(c) to vote in a specified manner or abstain in consideration of special advantages.

Except in the case of puppet shareholders, (a) and (b) will be rare in practice. (c) is the most far reaching and covers the situation which we have discussed above. It arguably goes further than *Elliott v Richardson* in making such agreements void. It is

---

7   *Greenhalgh v Mallard* [1943] 2 All ER 234, CA.
8   See O'Neal *Close Corporations* (3rd edn, 1988), vol 1, para 5–09.
9   Op cit, p 99.
10 (1870) LR 5 CP 744.
11 *Coronation Syndicate Ltd v Lilienfeld and New Fortuna Co Ltd* 1903 TS 489 at 497.
12 *Greenwell v Porter* [1902] 1 Ch 530; *Thorby v Goldberg* (1964) 112 CLR 597.
13 *Puddephatt v Leith* [1916] 1 Ch 200. See S Kruger (1978) 94 LQR 557, (1981) 10 Anglo American LR 73 for a comparison with US law.
14 *Ringuet v Bergeron* (1960) 24 DLR (2d) 449 (Supreme Court of Canada). The penalty here was a transfer of the shares of the defaulting shareholder.
15 (1880) OB & F (SC) 91.

questionable whether such a provision ought to apply where a voting arrangement is part of an agreement for sale of shares or a mortgage advance.

Type (ii) agreements (above) are proscribed on the basis of the fiduciary duties of a director[16]. Where a shareholders' agreement binds them in their capacity as a director, it is invalid as constituting a fettering of their discretion although valid portions of the agreement may be severed and remain in force[17]. For this reason an agreement requiring unanimity by the directors in every decision is void[18]. On the other hand, if, when a contract is negotiated on behalf of a company the directors bona fide think it in the interests of the company as a whole that the transaction should be entered into, they may bind themselves by the contract to do whatever is necessary to effectuate it[19]. The limits of this latter doctrine are hard to define although it appears to have been adopted in Australia and England. In the unreported English case of *Pennell v Venida Investments Ltd*[1] in 1974, Templeman J appears to have accepted that an oral shareholders' agreement existed to perpetuate an existing status quo with regard to the ratio of shareholdings within a 'quasi-partnership' company and this could not be unilaterally altered by the majority shareholder and its nominee directors. This goes further than the Australian authority.

Type (iii) has given rise to more case law which we have already considered in the previous chapter. Basically, a company cannot contract out of its power to alter its articles although to act on the alteration may amount to a breach of contract.

In *Russell v Northern Bank Development Corpn Ltd*,[2] the House of Lords held that an agreement between four shareholders of a private company not to vote in favour of an increase in share capital unless they had agreed in writing was valid. They emphasised that the company was not bound by the agreement but that, nevertheless, it was valid between the shareholders. The part of the agreement purporting to bind the company was void as an attempt to fetter the company's statutory power to alter its articles but was severable. The agreement between the shareholders was a personal agreement and did not run with the shares to bind their successors. The House of Lords granted a declaration because in the circumstances an injunction was not sought. The decision confirms the absolute prohibition on a direct contracting out of the statutory power but allows it effectively to be circumvented by agreement between shareholders. This is hardly a satisfactory state of the law and represents another example of the triumph of form over substance in the law.

(C)   AGREEMENT BETWEEN SOME OF THE SHAREHOLDERS[3]

The principles are the same as in (b) above but the exercise of the contractual provisions can work oppressively on members who are not parties to the contract and may for that reason give rise to minority shareholder remedies[4] although the wronged shareholder will face problems of proof.

---

16   Finn, op cit, p 100; Delaney (1950) 50 Col LR 52.
17   *Motherwell v Schoof* [1949] 4 DLR 812.
18   *Atlas Development Co Ltd v Calof and Gold* (1963) 41 WWR 575.
19   *Thorby v Goldberg* (1964) 112 CLR 597.
1   (25 July 1974, unreported). See the valuable article by Susan Burridge (1981) 44 MLR 40.
2   [1992] BCLC 1016. For useful analysis see L S Sealy [1992] CLJ 437; G Shapira (1993) 109 LQR 210; B J Davenport QC (1993) 109 LQR 553; Eilis Ferran [1994] CLJ 343.
3   Finn, op cit.
4   See Chapter 28, infra.

2   Voting trusts

A voting trust involves the voting rights of all or some of the shares in a company being settled upon trust[5]. The shares are usually transferred as there is doubt as to whether votes can be separated from ownership of the shares. Such a trust can be a very flexible instrument of control. The trustees may be given a free hand or a very limited discretion. 'In effect a voting trust confers a joint irrevocable proxy with general or restricted powers[6]'. It is, however, a more formal device than a shareholders' agreement since the trustees get title to the shares. This can sometimes have disadvantages for the original shareholder who may lose his membership rights and not be able to control the trustees.

Voting trusts are much more common in the USA than in the UK although it was formerly common here to settle shares on trustees as part of a settlement. Voting trusts are still used where there is need to maintain a particular tradition or viewpoint eg in a newspaper. The use of voting trusts has been restricted by specific state legislation in the USA where trust has an 'antitrust' connotation in the sense that they were used to further monopolies and restrictive trade practices.

3   Irrevocable proxies

A proxy is an authority to exercise voting rights given by a member to another person to act on his behalf. Unlike the voting trust a proxy does not have the title to the shares vested in him.

In order to be irrevocable the grant of the proxy must be coupled with an interest and to secure the interest. 'Interest' is a rather vague concept which Bentham said was a primitive term with no known genus and it may be sufficient if the proxy is given for valuable consideration[7]. If the latter is the case then it can be regarded as a species of voting agreement.

It is uncertain whether a proxy can be compelled to attend company meetings and vote as directed[8]. In *Second Consolidated Trust Ltd v Ceylon Amalgamated Tea and Rubber Estates Ltd*[9] it was held by Uthwatt J that a chairman at a meeting holding proxies was under an obligation to use them to demand a poll to ensure that the real sense of a meeting was given effect. In *Oliver v Dalgleish*[10] Buckley J said obiter that the principal might be in a position to complain if the proxy did not perform the duty.

It is common for companies to send out proxy forms in favour of the board but the Listing Rules of The Stock Exchange direct the despatch of two-way proxy forms for companies whose shares are listed on a Stock Exchange. These enable the shareholder to mandate the proxy to vote for or against a resolution.

5   M Pickering (1965) 81 LQR 248 at 257; *O'Neal*, op cit, para 5.31.
6   Pickering, ibid.
7   See Pickering, op cit, p 262; *O'Neal* op cit, para 5.36. See also R Powell *The Law of Agency* (2nd edn, 1961), p 392 but cf *Bowstead on Agency* (16th edn, 1996), art 135.
8   Pickering, op cit, p 263.
9   [1943] 2 All ER 567.
10   [1963] 3 All ER 330.

4   Management agreements[11]

It is possible for a company itself to delegate the whole or part of its management to a member or an outsider under an express agreement. This is common in relation to investment trusts and companies carrying on business abroad[12]. Another similar mechanism is the appointment of a governing director where the general authority to manage the company's affairs is vested in one man. This gives rise to problems of definition of the responsibilities of the other members of the board. Both mechanisms are to be distinguished from a delegation of *part* of their functions by the board of directors to a committee or individual where final power is left with the board.

In the USA management contracts have sometimes been impugned on the basis of violation of a statutory provision whereby management is vested in the board of directors or the board not having authority to bind the corporation to a long-term contract on such matters. The validity of a management contract seems to depend to a large extent on the number and importance of the powers delegated and the length of time involved[13]. In the only English authority where such a contract was considered, *Investment Trust Corpn Ltd v Singapore Traction Co Ltd*[14], it was for so long as the company was entitled under a local law to operate the undertaking and was assumed by the Court of Appeal to be valid. The case, however, was concerned with whether a substantial payment for termination was intra vires.

Other non-constitutional methods of control

In addition to these quasi-constitutional arrangements, it is possible for control to be exercised by:

(1) a group structure
(2) cross-holding of shares[15]
(3) circular holdings of shares.

We shall discuss the group relationship in Chapter 33. It exists where one company called the parent company is a member of and controls other companies which are called subsidiaries. Cross-holdings normally involve two or more companies which hold a majority of each other's shares. If the directors are common to all the companies or have some agreement to act together their position is impregnable. This can be represented thus:

11   Pickering, op cit, pp 267–268; *O'Neal*, op cit, para 5.39.
12   Such an agreement was regarded as valid in *Investment Trust Corpn Ltd v Singapore Traction Co Ltd* [1935] Ch 615 at 626 where the Court of Appeal held that it was not ultra vires the company to enter into a proposed agreement to terminate the management contract. See also *Ram Kissendas Dhanuka v Satya Charan Law* (1949) LR 77 Ind App 128, PC.
13   *O'Neal*, op cit, para 5.39.
14   [1935] Ch 615, CA. See also *Ram Kissendas Dhanuka v Satya Charan Law* (supra).
15   See Pickering, op cit, pp 265–6 on which this is based.

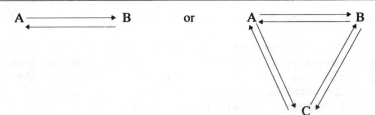

Circular holdings differ from cross-holdings of the second type in that shares in one company are normally only held by one other company. This can be represented thus:

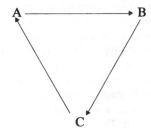

THE LEGITIMACY OF SUPPLEMENTARY DEVICES

We have considered the question of the legal validity of particular methods. The ultimate policy question remains—should such variation of the statutory constitution be allowed?[16]

The main reasons why people attempt to do this are either that they are individual shareholders in a private company and desire to be shareholders to the outside world but partners among themselves[17] or that they are companies in a joint venture enterprise who wish to keep their arrangements secret. The first highlights a defect in the present law in the way it fails to cater for such businesses, a matter to which we shall return in Chapter 31. In the absence of such a provision, it is arguably justifiable to supplement the present statutory scheme in this way, provided outsiders do not suffer. The latter represents a legitimate business goal which the law should protect.

A final question remains: granted the legitimacy of the reasons for such supplementation, should the proprietors be allowed to use illegitimate devices to achieve their ends? The answer to this is clearly 'No'. Bribery, fraud, distortion of the facts and evasion of statutory obligations to outsiders should not be countenanced. The ends do not justify the means.

16   Pickering, op cit, p 272 ff.
17   See Bradley 'Toward a More Perfect Close Corporation—Need for More and Improved Legislation' (1966) 54 Geo LJ 1145 at 1148.

CHAPTER 13

Constitutions and the company as a legal actor in contract, criminal law and tort

Corporate constitutions and the companies legislation do not exist in a vacuum. They have to fit into the framework of the Common Law and other statute law. The Common Law has developed its principles of liability on the basis of individualism and personal responsibility with limited recognition of the social group personality and liability. Where recognition of the group has taken place it has been done on the basis of analogy, metaphor or fiction. As we shall see in Chapter 33 the problem is compounded when we introduce the concept of the corporate group.

Sir John Salmond, the distinguished New Zealand judge and jurist, summed this up with his usual lucid dogmatism in the following passages from the last edition of his *Jurisprudence* which he wrote in 1924.[1]

> A society is not a person, but a number of persons. The so-called will of a company is in reality nothing but the wills of a majority of its directors or shareholders. Ten men do not become in fact one person, because they associate themselves together for one end, any more than two horses become one animal when they draw the same cart. The apparent absurdity of holding that a rich and powerful joint-stock company is a mere fiction of the law, and possesses no real existence, proceeds not from the fiction-theory, but from a misunderstanding of it. No one denies the reality of the company (that is to say, the group of shareholders). What is in truth denied is the reality of its personality. A group or society of men is a very real *thing*, but it is only a fictitious *person*.
>
> ... Although corporations are fictitious persons, the acts and interests, rights and liabilities, attributed to them by the law are those of real or natural persons, for otherwise the law of corporations would be destitute of any relation to actual fact and of any serious purpose.

A company is thus a potentially complex organisation which is assimilated into the pre-existing individualistic framework of the law by pursuit of fiction and analogy with a natural person.[2] This approach is at the risk of ignoring its distinctive social and

---

1   Seventh Edition; 342-3. These passages were dropped by more recent editors.
2   H L A Hart (1954) 70 LQR 37.

legal characteristics.[3] As Sir John Salmond stated, a company must act by human hands in the real world. This raises questions such as whose acts are regarded as the acts of the company. Normally this is solved by reference to the constitution and the rules of agency and vicarious liability. In the case of criminal law the approach has been first to deny corporate criminal liability then to base it on identification of certain persons as the alter ego of the company. In some offences this is mitigated by excuses based on lack of fault. Most recently this has been subsumed under a general concept of attribution which provides a path through the mists of metaphysics of fictitious personality. Other approaches are based on the ideas of aggregation and organisational liability.

Lord Hoffmann, in the New Zealand appeal to the Judicial Committee of the Privy Council in *Meridian Global Funds Management Asia Ltd v Securities Commission*[4] echoes some of Salmond's dogmatic views and engaged in the following general analysis:

> A company exists because there is a rule (usually in a statute) which says that a *persona ficta* shall be deemed to exist and to have certain of the powers, rights and duties of a natural person. But there would be little sense in deeming such a persona ficta to exist unless there were also rules to tell one what acts were to count as acts of the company. It is therefore a necessary part of corporate personality that there should be rules by which acts are attributed to the company. These may be called 'the rules of attribution'.
>
> The company's primary rules of attribution will generally be found in its constitution, typically the articles of association, and will say things such as 'for the purpose of appointing members of the board, a majority vote of the shareholders shall be a decision of the company' or 'the decisions of the board in managing the company's business shall be the decisions of the company'. There are also primary rules of attribution which are not expressly stated in the articles but implied by company law, such as 'the unanimous decision of all the shareholders in a solvent company about anything which the company under its memorandum of association has power to do shall be the decision of the company': see *Multinational Gas and Petrochemical Co v Multinational Gas and Petrochemical Services Ltd* [1983] 2 All ER 563, [1983] Ch 258.

His Lordship then recognised the limits of corporate law to provide in itself a comprehensive framework. He continued:

> These primary rules of attribution are obviously not enough to enable a company to go out into the world and do business. Not every act on behalf of the company could be expected to be the subject of a resolution of the board or a unanimous decision of the shareholders. The company therefore builds upon the primary rules of attribution by using general rules of attribution which are equally available to natural persons, namely, the principles of agency. It will appoint servants and agents whose acts, by a combination of the general principles of agency and the company's primary rules of attribution, count as the acts of company. And having done so, it will also make itself subject to the general rules by which liability for the acts of others can be attributed to natural persons, such as estoppel or ostensible authority in contract and vicarious liability in tort.[5]

3   Meir Dan-Cohen, *Rights, Persons and Organisations – A Legal Theory for Bureaucratic Society*, 14. For a useful modern survey see Celia Wells *Corporations and Criminal Responsibility* (1993).
4   [1995] 3 WLR 413, 418.
5   Ibid.

His Lordship then made the following interesting philosophical remark pointing to the implausibility of the law's characteristic mode of approaching companies:

> Judges sometimes say that a company 'as such' cannot do anything; it must act by servants or agents. This may seem an unexceptionable, even banal remark. And of course the meaning is usually perfectly clear. But a reference to a company 'as such' might suggest that there is something out there called the company of which one can meaningfully say that it can or cannot do something. There is in fact no such thing as the company as such, no 'ding an sich', only the applicable rules. To say that a company cannot do something means only that there is no one whose doing of that act would, under the applicable rules of attribution, count as an act of the company.[6]

This approach which at this last point is somewhat narrower than that of Sir John Salmond contrasts with that of Professor Meir Dan-Cohen in his interesting monograph, *Rights, Persons and Organisations*.[7] Dan-Cohen refers to the limits of the traditional approaches and the legal personality of corporation when confronted by the reality of the separation of ownership and control in large companies. He sees such entities as examples of organisations, characterised by large, goal-oriented, permanent, complex, formal, decisionmaking, functional structures. The problem is that whole areas of law such as contract, tort and criminal law have been built up on the premise of individual autonomy. The result is that Dan-Cohen treats organisations such as corporations as entities for ontological purposes but aggregates for normative purposes. This is a problematic compromise. The advantage of Lord Hoffmann's speech is that it enables us to deal with this through a flexible rule based approach,[8] and to overcome some but not all of the problems which the law has sought to face using either the agency or organic approach to organisations. Let us examine each of traditional approaches before considering Lord Hoffmann's approach and the gaps which remain and how they might be filled.

AGENCY RULES APPLICABLE TO COMPANIES

The basic principles of agency apply with some modifications to companies. These principles are:

(a) a principal is bound by the contracts of an agent acting within the scope of express, implied or apparent (or ostensible) authority.

(b) a principal may also be vicariously liable for the torts committed by an agent in certain circumstances.

Authority presupposes corporate capacity and while the doctrine of ultra vires applied in its full vigour the question of ultra vires had to be resolved first. Next, there was the doctrine of constructive notice whereby the public were deemed to have notice of constitutional restraints. This led in turn to the so called indoor management rule which protected bona fide third parties from internal irregularities not verifiable by

---

6 Ibid.
7 *Rights, Persons and Organisations* (1986). For a penetrating review of this book see R B Stewart (1987-8) 101 Harv L Rev 371 especially at 377 for the ontological/normative distinction. See Wells op cit chap 7. For another interesting approach see G Teubner 'Enterprise Corporation: New Industrial Policy and the "Essence" of the Legal Person' in Sally Wheeler (ed) *A Reader on the Law of the Business Enterprise* (1994), 51.
8 Consistently with Hart (1954) 70 LQR 37.

reference to the public file. This rule known as the Rule in *Royal British Bank v Turquand* (1856) 6 E & B 327 overlapped with the agency principles in a confusing way until relatively recently. The judicial attempt to clarify the law has now been partially superseded by statutory reform but a few ghostly relics of the old law remain to haunt and confuse us.

We have already seen in Chapter 10 that the CA 1989 sought to abolish the ultra vires doctrine, at least in so far as outsiders are concerned, thus ensuring the validity of transactions entered into by the company despite any limitations on the company's capacity in the memorandum of association.

Of course, for many third parties difficulties arise, not from any lack of capacity, given the width of most objects clauses, but from a lack of authority, perhaps on the part of the board but more commonly on the part of an individual director or officer with respect to a particular transaction.

It has always been open to the company in general meeting, or to the board, if appropriate, to ratify a transaction entered into in breach of authority.[9] However, on occasion third parties were faced with companies wishing to disown onerous obligations by alleging that the director or directors responsible had no authority to enter into the transaction. Any reforms designed to increase the security of third parties dealing with companies had necessarily to address these questions of lack of authority in addition to issues of capacity and this the 1989 Act did, as far as the board was concerned, by inserting new ss 35A and 35B into the CA 1985. These statutory provisions replace much of the old law in this area but in so doing raise many new uncertainties, both in terms of the wording of s 35A and its relationship with the existing law. The whole of this is dealt with in depth in Chapter 25.

THE ALTER EGO APPROACH

An alternative approach to corporate liability based on agency principles is the organic or alter ego approach which has been mainly applied in criminal law and tort. The leading case is *Lennard's Carrying Co Ltd v Asiatic Petroleum Co Ltd*[10] in 1915 which concerned a cargo claim which Lennards sought to defend by arguing s 502 of the Merchant Shipping Act 1894 which exonerated the owner from losses arising without his actual fault. The House of Lords held that they could not rely on that defence since the fault of the appropriate organ such as the board of directors or managing director could be attributed to the company. Viscount Haldane, drawing on his knowledge of German Law and philosophy said:[11]

> My Lords, a corporation is an abstraction. It has no mind of its own any more than it has a body of its own; its active and directing will must consequently be sought in the person of somebody who for some purposes may be called an agent, but who is really the directing mind and will of the corporation, the very ego and centre of the personality of the corporation. That person may be under the direction of the shareholders in general meeting; that person may be the board of directors itself, or it may be, and in some companies it is so, that that person has an authority co-ordinate with the board of directors given to him under the articles of association, and is appointed by the general meeting of the company, and can only be removed by the general meeting of the company.

9   See *Irvine v Union Bank of Australia* (1877) 2 App Cas 366, PC; *Grant v United Kingdom Switchback Railways Co* (1888) 40 Ch D 135, CA.
10   [1915] AC 705 HL.
11   Ibid at p 713.

The doctrine attributes to the company the mind and will of the natural person or persons who manage and control its affairs. As Millett J said in *El Ajou v Dollar Land Holdings Plc* [1993] BCLC 735 at 760:

> Their minds are its mind; their intention its intention; their knowledge its knowledge.

It is nevertheless necessary, not to consider management in the round, but to identify the natural person or persons having actual management and control in relation to the act or omission in question. The formal constitutional position, though highly relevant, is not necessarily conclusive and the question is to some extent pragmatic – what is the actual practice in the particular company?

In the Court of Appeal in the same case Hoffmann LJ said:[12]

> It is well known that Viscount Haldane derived the concept of the 'directing mind' from German law (see *Gower Principles of Modern Company Law* (5th edn, 1992) p 194, n 36) which distinguishes between the agents and organs of the company. A German company with limited liability (GmbH) is required by law to appoint one or more directors (Geschäftsführer). They are the company's organs and for legal purposes represent the company. The knowledge of any one director, however obtained, is the knowledge of the company (Scholz, *Commentary on the GmbH Law* (7th edn, 1986), s 35.) English law has never taken the view that the knowledge of a director ipso facto imputed to the company: *Powles v Page* (1846) 3 CB 16, 136 ER 7; *Re Carew's Estate Act* (1862) 31 Beav 39, 54 ER 1051. Unlike the German Geschäftsführer, an English director may as an individual have no powers whatever. But English law shares the view of the German law that whether a person is an organ or not depends upon the extent of the powers which in law he has express or implied authority to exercise on behalf of the company.

An employee who acts for the company in the course of his or her employment will usually bind the company and his or her knowledge will be attributed to the company because he or she is the company for the purpose of the transaction in question.

This is so even if the employee is acting dishonestly or against the interests of the company or contrary to orders but it is not so where the company is the victim.[13] This is to avoid an obvious contradiction.

PRACTICAL PROBLEM OF IDENTIFICATION

In *Tesco Supermarkets Ltd v Nattrass* in 1972,[14] the defendant company was charged under s 11(2) of the Trade Descriptions Act 1968 with advertising goods at a price less than that at which they were in fact available. The store branch had run out of specials and had replaced them by similar items at the normal price. The employee in question should have notified the store manager but had failed to do so. The manager therefore failed to discharge his responsibilities. The defendant company had in place

12   [1994] 1 BCLC 464. There are, however, limits to this see for example *Deutsche Genossenschaftsbank v Burnhope* [1995] 4 All ER 717, 727,HL.
13   *R v Roziek* [1996] 3 All ER 281, 286, CA.
14   [1972] AC 153, [1971] 2 All ER 127, HL.

·an extensive system designed to ensure compliance with the Act. Section 20 of the Act provided:

> where an offence under this Act which has been committed by a body corporate is proved to have been committed with the consent and connivance of, …any director, manager, secretary or other similar officer of the body corporate, …he as well as the body corporate shall be guilty of that offence …

Section 24 of the Act provided the following defence:

> In any proceedings for an offence under this Act it shall, …be a defence for the person charged to prove – (a) that the commission of the offence was due to …the act or default of another person ….and (b) that he took all reasonable precautions and exercised all due diligence to avoid the commission of such an offence …

The defendant company successfully pleaded the defence. Lord Reid said:[15]

> Normally the board of directors, the managing director and perhaps other superior officers of a company carry out the functions of management and speak and act as the company. Their subordinates do not. They carry out orders from above and it can make no difference that they are given some measure of discretion. But the board of directors may delegate some part of their functions of management giving to their delegates full discretion to act independently of instructions from them. I see no difficulty in holding that they have thereby put such a delegate in their place so that within the scope of the delegation he can act as the company. It may not always be easy to draw the line but there are cases in which the line must be drawn.

Not only is the line drawn but also the law has hitherto avoided liability based on *aggregation* of individual faults into a concept of organisational liability or responsibility.

VICARIOUS LIABILITY

Vicarious liability is an extension of individual liability based on the responsibility to meet losses which arises out of control and the benefit from the employee's acts.

Vicarious liability requires three things —

(1) a tortious act or omission;
(2) some relationship between the wrongdoer and the defendant; and
(3) a nexus between the act and that relationship.[16]

Vicarious liability developed at the same time as the growth of corporations.[17]

There is a need to distinguish vicarious from personal liability. Using the organic theory a company can be liable personally for acts by its 'controlling mind and will'. Vicarious liability is in addition to such liability but it is only in criminal law that the distinction has much significance.

15   [1972] AC at p 170.
16   P Atiyah *Vicarious Liability in the Law of Torts* (1967), p 3.
17   Ibid, p 38.

In general, excepting the common law offences of public nuisance and criminal libel, criminal law in the United Kingdom and Commonwealth has rejected vicarious liability on the basis that it would be unjust to impose such liability in the absence of personal fault. However, statute law has made inroads into this on occasion and a different rule applies in the US federal courts and in South Africa.[18]

THE POLICY BASIS OF CORPORATE LIABILITY

Professor Glanville Williams[19] stated that the liability of corporations exemplifies utilitarian theory in the criminal law and is based not on the theory of justice but upon the need for deterrence. It may help to keep the company as an organisation up to the mark. It is arguable that strict liability does not create the same problems of justice as with human defendants and it may help to overcome the problem of tracing the individual in the organisation ultimately responsible or the problem of aggregating individual actions or states of mind.

Nevertheless some offences allow exemptions to strict liability based on 'passing on' the blame to someone else including an employee or on proving due diligence. Indeed in many areas of regulation today there is often a due diligence defence which exonerates the company which can prove that it used all due diligence to secure compliance. This usually involves proof of having a workable system in place to ensure compliance. However, in the absence of such a defence, steps taken to prevent a prohibited matter are only a matter of mitigation, not excuse. This even extends to the law of contempt. Thus in *Re Supply of Ready Mixed Concrete (No 2) Director General of Fair Trading v Pioneer Concrete (UK) Ltd,*[20] the House of Lords held the respondent companies in contempt for giving effect to an agreement registrable under the Restrictive Trade Practice Act 1976 which had not been registered. The actions were actions of local managers without express or ostensible authority and without knowledge of the respondent companies' management.

ATTRIBUTION

A fresh approach to corporate liability based on attribution was adopted as we saw earlier by the Judicial Committee of the Privy Council in *Meridian Global Funds Management Asia Ltd v Securities Commission* in 1995.[1] In that case two employees of Meridian, Koo, a former management director but presently its chief investment officer, and Ng, a senior portfolio manager, had improperly used their authority to purchase in the name of the company a substantial interest in Euro-National Corp Ltd ('ENC'), a New Zealand listed company. Under the New Zealand Securities Amendment Act 1988, Meridian was required to give notice of its acquisition to ENC and the Stock Exchange. Koo and Ng knew this but the board and the managing director of Meridian did not. No notice was given. The Privy Council upheld the New Zealand court in ruling that Meridian had contravened the law, holding that the knowledge of Koo was to be attributed to Meridian.

---

18   See E. Colvin (1995) 6 Criminal Law Forum 1.
19   *Textbook of Criminal Law* (1978), 950. See also the important article by John Coffee Jr (1981) 79 Michigan L Rev 386 and the recent work by Celia Wells, *Corporations and Criminal Liability* (1993); G Sullivan (1995) 15 OJLS 281; C Clarkson (1996) 59 MLR 557.
20   [1995] 1 All ER 135, especially at 142 per Lord Templeman.
1   [1995] 2 AC 500, [1995] 3 All ER 918.

Lord Hoffmann delivering the opinion of the Board said[2]:

> The company's primary rules of attribution together with the general principles of agency, vicarious liability and so forth are usually sufficient to enable one to determine its rights and obligations. In exceptional cases, however, they will not provide an answer. This will be the case when a rule of law, either expressly or by implication, excludes attribution on the basis of the general principles of agency or vicarious liability. For example, a rule may be stated in language primarily applicable to a natural person and require some act or state of mind on the part of that person 'himself', as opposed to his servants or agents. This is generally true of rules of the criminal law, which ordinarily impose liability only for the actus reus and mens rea of the defendant himself. How is such a rule to be applied to a company?'

His Lordship then considered the potentially complex situations where the law may be ambiguous in its application to companies. He continued:

> One possibility is that the court may come to the conclusion that the rule was not intended to apply to companies at all; for example, a law which created an offence for which the only penalty was community service. Another possibility is that the court might interpret the law as meaning that it could apply to a company only on the basis of its primary rules of attribution, ie if the act giving rise to liability was specifically authorised by a resolution of the board or a unanimous agreement of the shareholders. But there will be many cases in which neither of these solutions is satisfactory; in which the court considers that the law was intended to apply to companies and that, although it excludes ordinary vicarious liability, insistence on the primary rules of attribution would in practice defeat that intention. In such a case, the court must fashion a special rule of attribution for the particular substantive rule. This is always a matter of interpretation: given that it was intended to apply to a company, how was it intended to apply? Whose act (or knowledge, or state of mind) was *for this purpose* intended to count as the act etc of the company? One finds the answer to this question by applying the usual canons of interpretation, taking into account the language of the rule (if it is a statute) and its content and policy[3].

The advantage of this approach[4] is that it provides a comprehensive approach to corporate liability which is aware of the complications of applying law often premised on individual autonomy to companies and other organisations.

CORPORATE CULTURE LEADING TO NON COMPLIANCE

In recognition of these complexities, there is an increasing tendency in some jurisdictions to consider law reform imposing liability, particularly criminal liability, on institutions for having a corporate culture which directed, encouraged, tolerated or

2   Ibid, p 418
3   Ibid, p 418
4   See L S Sealy [1995] CLJ 507; S Robert-Tissot (1996) 17 Co Law 99; Celia Wells (1995) NLJ 1326; G R Sullivan (1995) 15 OJLS281; [1996] CLJ 515; C M V Clarkson (1996) 59 MLR 557. For economic arguments against the very concept of corporate criminal liability see D R Fischel and A O Sykes (1996) 25 J Legal Stud 319 and V S Khanna (1996) 109 Harv L Rev 1477. For a useful comparative study see H de Doelder and K Tiedemann *Criminal Liability of Corporations* (1996).

led to non compliance with the law. This is a form of organisational responsibility. This has arisen out of dissatisfaction with derivative forms of criminal liability in the aftermath of disasters such as the sinking of 'The Herald of Free Enterprise' where organisational sloppiness was insufficient because corporate liability depended on an individual's criminal liability[5]. The need has been felt for some kind of organisational liability. The Law Commission in its draft Involuntary Homicide Bill introduces the new offence of corporate killing. Clause 4 of the draft bill provides inter alia:

(1) A corporation is guilty of corporate killing if–
  (a) a management failure by the corporation is the cause or one of the causes of a person's death; and
  (b) that failure constitutes conduct falling far below what can reasonably be expected of the corporation in the circumstances.
(2) For the purposes of subsection (1) above–
  (a) there is a management failure by a corporation if the way in which its activities are managed or organised fails to ensure the health and safety of persons employed in or affected by those activities; and
  (b) such a failure may be regarded as a cause of a person's death notwithstanding that the immediate cause is the act or omission of an individual.

(3) A corporation guilty of an offence under this section is liable on conviction on indictment to a fine.

(4) No individual shall be convicted of aiding, abetting, counselling or procuring an offence under this section but without prejudice to an individual being guilty of any other offence in respect of the death in question.

There are special provisions extending these rules to cases where injury takes place on a British ship or aircraft.

The court is to be given power to make remedial orders and a failure to comply will give rise to a fine.

Similar general provisions now appear in the Criminal Code Act 1995 (Australia). 'Corporate culture' is defined by s 12.3(6) of that Act in broad terms. It is 'an attitude, policy, rule, course of conduct or practice existing within the body corporate generally or within the area of the body corporate in which the relevant activities take place.' Two specific factors are mentioned as being relevant – whether authority or permission to commit a similar offence had previously been given by a high managerial agent of the body corporate and whether the person who actually committed the offence reasonably believed that a high managerial agent would have authorised or permitted the commission of the offence. 'High managerial agent' is defined as a person whose role in the body corporate is such that his or her conduct can be taken to represent corporate policy[6].

---

5   See *R v HM Coroner for East Kent* (1987) 88 Cr App Rep 10; *R v P & O Europeam Ferries (Dover) Ltd* (1990) 93 Cr App Rep 72. See also *Seaboard Offshore Ltd v Secretary of State for Transport* [1992] 2 All ER 99. But see *R v Kite and OLL Ltd* (9 December 1994, unreported), Winchester Crown Court; *R v Tam Ping-Cheong and Kwong Tim-yau* (1996) Hong Kong High Court, Crim Action No 355 of 1995, 12 June for recent successful prosecutions of corporations for manslaughter. See the useful articles by Celia Wells (1995) 6 Criminal Law Forum 16 and Melanie Pritchard (1997) 27 Hong Kong LJ 40.

6   For a very useful discussion of these trends see E Colvin (1995) 6 Criminal Law Forum 1. See also *Legislating the Criminal Code – Involuntary Manslaughter* (Law Com No 237), Parts VI and VIII (recommending the new offence of corporate killing).

RESIDUAL QUESTION OF PERSONAL LIABILITY OF OFFICER

Lennards, Tesco and *Meridian* were all concerned with establishing the existence of liability on the part of the defendant company, not with proving the *absence* of liability of the company employee. In the case of the tort of negligence for example an individual tort feasor is essential to establish corporate liability. But it is difficult to argue that a liability based on identification with another can at the same time be treated as inconsistent with the liability of that other.[7] The doctrine of identification has been no more than a fiction for establishing the state of mind of the company. It does not address the state of mind of the director or his or her personal liability. Whether the courts should go behind the separate legal personality of the company and hold an individual director liable is a question of policy assuming that factors such as proximity and foreseeability are established. Into the policy analysis will enter factors such as control, identification and assumption of responsibility. In the New Zealand Court of Appeal decision in *Trevor Ivory Ltd v Anderson*[8] in 1992, the plaintiffs contracted with Ivory, the principal shareholder of Trevor Ivory Ltd for expert advice in the management of a raspberry orchard. There was no contact with Ivory personally. Ivory gave negligent advice about spraying which led to destruction of the plants. The trial judge held both the company and Ivory liable. The Court of Appeal overturned the finding that Ivory was personally liable. Each of the three judges held that Ivory had not assumed responsibility for the advice given. Assumption of responsibility, however, like intentional wrong doing, will lead to personal liability. It will not be enough simply to trade as a one person company or directly or indirectly to direct or procure the act or omission. The test is the degree and kind of personal involvement by which the director or officer makes the tortious act his or her own.[9] The state of mind of the director or officer might be relevant where it is a necessary ingredient in proving the commission of the particular wrong but different considerations may apply where the state of mind of the tort feasor is not relevant.[10]

---

7   See also S M D Todd (1993) 9 PN2, 54; Mary-Anne Simpson 'The Tort Liability of Corporate Participants' an LLM thesis at the University of Canterbury (NZ).

8   [1992] 2 NZLR 517. See G Fridman (1992) 5 Cant L Rev 41; D Wishart (1992) C & SLJ 363; M Simpson [1995] NZLJ 6. *Trevor Ivory* was followed by the Court of Appeal in *Williams v National Life Health Food Ltd* [1997] 1 BCLC 131. Noted by R Grantham [1997] CLJ 259.

9   See *Fairline Shipping Corpn v Adamson* [1975] QB 180; *Mentmore Merchandising Co Ltd v National Merchandising Manufacturing Co Ltd* (1978) 89 DLR (3d) 195; *C Evans & Sons Ltd v Spritebrand Ltd* [1985] 2 All ER 415, CA.

10   *C Evans & Sons Ltd v Spritebrand Ltd* [1985] 2 All ER 415, 424d-e. See JH Farrar (1997) 71 ALJ 20 for a discussion of this and recent Australian cases.

PART III

Financial structure and membership

CHAPTER 14

The concept of capital and the financing of companies

THE ECONOMIC CONCEPT OF CAPITAL

There is probably no concept in economics which is quite so ambiguous and confusing as capital. According to the context the word may mean wealth, a factor or means of production, the value of those means of production, the net worth of a business enterprise, the present value of a future sequence of receipts, money, the money value of assets, and possibly other things as well. Capital is thus thought of in physical terms, in value terms and in money terms[1], an ambiguity which has sometimes been carried over into law, as we shall see in a later chapter.

The etymology of the word seems to be the Latin 'caput' meaning head or principal. In medieval Latin, there are references to *capitalis pars debiti*, that is, the principal sum as distinct from interest. Originally the term seems to be confined to loans of money. Later it took in other assets and acquired a wider meaning than loan. The word is then said by some to be an adjective used elliptically as a substantive[2]. The full phrase is said to be capital stock. Capital was used for capital stock at least as early as 1635[3]. Dyche and Pardon's *English Dictionary* in 1735 had an entry on capital—'Chief, head, or principal; it relates to several things, as the capital stock in trading companies it is the fund or quantity of money they are by their charter allowed to employ in trade'[4]. To understand this transition in usage one needs to examine the history. In the Guild system there was little need for capital stock[5]. The principal asset of the business was the skill and connection of the tradesman. The only capital he needed was to build or rent a house, purchase tools or stock and set himself up. These funds could usually be acquired by savings as a journeyman working for another established trader. By the sixteenth century, however, with the expansion of the money supply there is a growth of a distinctly capitalist class and with them the concept of capital as a fund of money. The removal of the prohibitions on usury facilitated this development. For a time such

---

1   See N S Buchanan *The Economics of Corporate Enterprise* (1940); A A Alchian and W R Allen *University Economics* (3rd edn, 1974), p 387.
2   Murray's *New English Dictionary* (1888–1928).
3   See Dafforne *Merchant's Mirrour* Ex No 96.
4   For an interesting discussion of the history of the concept of capital see *The New Palgrave Dictionary of Economics* (1987) vol 1—Capital as a Factor of Production, 328 et seq.
5   See C A Cooke *Corporation, Trust and Company* (1950) p 39 ff, on which this paragraph is based.

capitalists ran the risk of being held to be partners. The *commenda* never gained a strong foothold in English law because of the backwardness of English accounting methods. Nevertheless certain accounting developments took place. First, there was the idea of the value of a business as a going concern and not just as a chain of single instances. Secondly, there was the growth of double entry book-keeping which enabled a separation of the accounts of the business from those of the capitalists. The concept of the business as a separate accounting unit reached a more sophisticated stage of development in the joint stock company. The penultimate stage of the development was when the company was regarded as a separate legal person and the ultimate stage was when the liability of the members was limited and the fund of share capital was regarded at the end of the day as the company as far as creditors were concerned.

THE MODERN LEGAL CONCEPT OF CAPITAL

As Latham CJ said in the Australian case of *Incorporated Interest Pty Ltd v Federal Commission of Taxation* (1943) 67 CLR 508 at 515: 'It is impossible to say that "capital" has a single technical meaning which prima facie should be attributed to the word in any statutory provision'.

The legal concept of capital crops up in the law of trusts and revenue law as well as company law. In trust law it describes the original trust fund and any assets which replace the items in the original fund. A distinction is drawn between capital and income and problems arise with some borderline cases. On the whole the trust law concept of capital is a relatively simple one since the legal title to the fund vests in the trustees and the beneficiaries have reasonably well defined interests in the equitable ownership of the fund[6]. In revenue law, there is the same capital/income distinction. Here the distinction is resolved by reference to accounting principles and the authorities. The distinction was formerly crucial as most capital gains were not taxable at all. That is no longer the case but the distinction is still of some consequence as the taxation of the two is different.

Capital is used in modern company law to cover:

(1) *share* capital—the funds subscribed by members;
(2) *loan* capital—the fund provided by commercial finance providers and investors holding debentures or debenture stock;
(3) all funds whether provided by members, creditors or by retention of profits; and
(4) the assets in which all the funds have been invested.

The memorandum specifies the initial *authorised* share capital of the company. This is sometimes known as the *nominal* capital. The whole or part of this may be *paid-up*. Hence the terms fully-paid and partly-paid share capital. Thus we have the legal measure of the fund and the amount actually subscribed by investors. This money or other value transferred does not usually lie idle. It is invested in assets for the purposes of the company's business. This is sometimes called *real* capital from the Latin 'res' meaning 'a thing'.

In the Canadian case of *St Michael Uranium Mines Ltd v Rayrock Mines Ltd*[7] Le Bel, JA distinguished between the various meanings of capital in the following dictum:

> I think ... it is right to say that there is confusion commonly existing regarding the meaning of the term capital in corporation financing. To the economist it

---

6   R R Pennington *Company Law* (7th edn, 1995), ch 6.
7   (1958) 15 DLR (2d) 609, Ont CA.

usually signifies tangible instruments of production, that is, physical assets used in the creation of other goods or of services. The average man frequently thinks of 'money' as 'capital' and uses the terms synonymously, and bankers often use the word capital, in the sense of net worth. However, in business parlance the term ordinarily means the investment in an enterprise, which from the legal point of view, may be thought of as being represented by money or by money's worth consisting of property and valuable tangible assets the corpus of the corporate business.... . And capital and share capital are not the same: *Re Ontario Express and Transportation Co* (1894) 21 OAR 646, CA.

Although share capital is represented by real capital the value of shares does not always correspond to that of the underlying net assets. The value of shares depends on the number of shares offered by sellers and sought by buyers at any particular time[8]. Where the shares represent control of a company which is a small incorporated firm, the shares will tend to reflect the net asset value of the business. A minority holding in such a company will not generally have as high a value[9]. For most articles of such companies, there will be a pre-emption clause enabling the other shareholders to buy at fair value to be certified by the auditor. In the case of companies whose shares are listed in a recognised stock exchange the value will be at or around the current list price although such quotations are sometimes unreliable[10]. There are a number of criteria used by investment analysts and accountants in valuing shares. These include capital cover, dividend yield, the price:earnings ratio and discounted cash flows[11]. Capital cover is not the same as an assets valuation. It is a calculation based on the extent to which net assets are sufficient to repay share capital. It is merely a factor, not a conclusive factor, since the other criteria might compensate for inadequate capital cover. Dividend yield is calculated by reference to the price and is affected by government restraints on dividends. The price:earnings ratio puts the emphasis on profitability not dividend yield. Discounted cash flow puts the emphasis on the present value of a future income flow. The question of the value of the share capital is thus potentially a more complicated question than the question of the value of the underlying real capital used in the business.

We saw above that the original usage of the word 'capital' referred to a loan. Capital in modern company law is used to cover not only share capital provided by the proprietors but also the loan capital provided by creditors. Whereas the former represents a right in the company the latter represents a right *against* the company[12]. The debt may be unsecured or secured. If there is at least a written acknowledgment of the debt it is usually called a debenture[13]. The value of debentures will depend on a number of factors—security, the position of the company, the interest rate and the date of repayment. Debentures listed in the Stock Exchange stand at a figure below par. This represents the discount which the loan creditor takes for the company's use of his or her money. Thus the company pays or suffers the discount and has to pay interest on the par value of the loan capital.

8   *R R Pennington*, op cit, ch 6. This contains a useful analysis of the fundamentals of valuation of shares. See too V Krishna (1987) 8 Co Law 66; (1987) 13 Can Bus LJ 132.
9   See, however, *Re Bird Precision Bellows Ltd* [1984] Ch 419; normally there is no such discount in valuation for purposes of s 459. See Chapter 28, post.
10   A V Adamson *The Valuation of Company Shares and Businesses* (5th edn, 1975) Law Book Co, Sydney, pp 138–140.
11   See *Lusk v Archive Security Ltd* (1991) 5 NZCLC 66,979, 66,992.
12   See L C B Gower *Modern Company Law* (6th edn, 1997) at p 321.
13   See Chapter 20, post.

The real capital into which both share and loan capital is invested is divided by economists into *fixed* and *circulating* capital. The distinction which has been traced back as far as the Physiocrats[14] and was adopted by Smith, Mill and Marx, was said by Ricardo to be not 'essential', and one in which the line of demarcation cannot be accurately drawn[15]. In other words they are relative terms. Hayek in *The Pure Theory of Capital*[16] thought that such a simple dichotomy probably does more harm than good. Nevertheless the courts have adopted the distinction which seems to have passed into law as a result of Sir Horace Davey's argument in a leading case[17]. In *Ammonia Soda Co v Chamberlain*[18] in 1918, Swinfen Eady LJ said fixed capital was:

> That which a company retains, in the shape of assets upon which the subscribed capital has been expended, and which assets either themselves produce income, independent of any further action by the company, or being retained by the company are made use of to produce income or gain profits.

Circulating capital was:

> A portion of the subscribed capital of the company intended to be used by being temporarily parted with and circulated in business, in the form of money, goods or other assets, and which, or the proceeds of which, are intended to return to the company with an increment, and are intended to be used again and again, and to always return with some accretion. Thus the capital with which a trader buys goods circulates; he parts with it, and with the goods bought by it, intending to receive it back again with profit arising from the resale of the goods ... It must not, however, be assumed that the division into which capital thus falls is permanent ... The terms 'fixed' and 'circulating' are merely terms convenient for describing the purpose to which the capital is for the time being devoted when considering its position in respect to the profits available for dividend.

As we shall see in the next chapters, the usage in the Companies Acts and the cases is loose and it is often difficult to say in which sense the word capital is being used. This has led to confusion in the past although the reforms in the Companies Act 1980 (now contained in Pt VIII of the CA 1985) settle much of the earlier confusion in the law of company dividends.

SOURCES OF CAPITAL[19]

Share capital and loan capital such as debentures are usually sources of long-term capital for the company. Once started it will hopefully generate profits and these can be used in whole or in part as a source of internal finance.

For the smaller company[20] bank borrowing on a short-to medium-term basis and trade credit are common methods of financing. The problems about bank borrowing

---

14   See J Gold (1945) 6 UTLJ 14 at 26.
15   D Ricardo *The Principles of Political Economy and Taxation* (1926) (Everyman edn), p 19n.
16   (1941) p 323.
17   See *Lee v Neuchatel Asphalte Co* (1889) 41 Ch D 1, 7, 13, CA.
18   [1918] 1 Ch 266, CA.
19   See generally Richard A Brearley and Stewart C Myers *Principles of Corporate Finance* (5th edn, 1996), ch 14 et seq.
20   See J Bates *The Financing of Small Business* (2nd edn, 1971), chs 7 and 8 and M Chesterman *Small Businesses* (2nd edn, 1982), ch 4.

are that banks generally require a fixed and floating charge and personal guarantees by directors, and the company to some extent can be subject to the vagaries of bank policy. Trade credit can also be an unreliable source since it can be affected by the pressures on suppliers from their creditors in turn.

To improve their cash flow position, an increasing number of companies factor their trade debts, which means that they receive payment in advance but at a discount from a credit factor who then collects the debts.

Hire purchase is a common method of buying goods on credit but the cost is expensive. An increasingly common method of obtaining the use of plant and machinery without the capital outlay is plant hire. The assets are simply hired rather than purchased and the cost of hire is a trading expense for tax purposes.

In this book we shall concentrate on share and loan capital and look at each in turn in the following chapters, but first let us examine elementary canons of financial prudence. A high risk firm will have to pay a higher return on loan capital than a lower risk firm. This is usually called a risk premium and varies according to the lender's perception of the risk. Obviously payment of the premium does not eliminate the risk but on average the losses from default should be offset against the gains from the receipt of risk premiums. Loan capital servicing is a first charge on profits. Share capital represents a residual return although the entitlement to the residue will differ where there are different classes of shares. The interest of the shareholder is to receive an income return, capital appreciation and a surplus on a solvent winding up. Internal financing by retention of profits which is sometimes together with share capital referred to as equity finance is not free of cost. There is opportunity cost to the shareholders which may be reflected ultimately in a lower market price of the shares because shareholders have decided to liquidate their investment in the company[1].

Mainly for taxation reasons, loan capital tends to be a cheaper source of finance for a company than share capital. Also in the long term, equity shareholders will require a higher return than creditors since they are always at risk in the event of a decline in profits or insolvency[2]. Nevertheless according to traditional thinking the advantages of loan capital can only be carried up to a point. This is because of the concept of gearing. Gearing[3] (called leverage in the USA) means the relationship between fixed interest capital and capital with variable remuneration. The greater the proportion of the former, the higher the gearing. If gearing becomes too high, both types of investor will demand a higher return to compensate for the risk of insolvency. The levels of gearing beyond which it is imprudent to go differ according to time and the particular sector.

Another view is that put forward by Modigliani and Miller[4] in 1958, where they argued that what counts is the future earnings stream of the company, not how it is financed. The total market value of a company is independent of its capital structure since investors can through market operations eliminate differences in value. However their theory is predicated on certain assumptions such as there being no corporation taxes and perfect capital markets. When the institutional facts to the contrary are taken into account and allowance is made for transaction costs in arbitrage, we seem to be back to the traditional approach[5].

1   See J Freear *The Management of Business Finance* (1980), ch 6.
2   Royal Commission on the Distribution of Income and Wealth Report No 2, *Income from Companies and its Distribution* (Cmnd 6172), p 73.
3   Royal Commission on the Distribution of Income and Wealth, Background paper No 1, *The Financing of Quoted Companies in the United Kingdom*, p 13.
4   F Modigliani and M Miller (1958) 48 Am Econ Rev 261.
5   See R Posner and K Scott *Economics of Corporation Law and Securities Regulation* (1980), p 235 and the materials there cited.

Apart from the question of gearing there is the additional point that for smaller businesses, long-term debt is unpopular because of the fear of loss of independence. Directors of unlisted companies generally prefer to finance their activities where possible out of retained earnings.

In addition to traditional concepts of share and debt capital there are now an increasing number of derivative products which are available to larger companies. These are specialist topics outside the scope of this book but a brief appendix summarises the main types and their role in corporate finance. The increasing flexibility conferred by these instruments makes the simple dichotomy into share and loan capital seem dated. Institutionally, however, company law has still to absorb these consequences of deregulation and the international financial revolution. Company law structures exist like a Procrustean bed from which smart people seek to escape by contract.[6]

---

6   See Richard A Brearley and Stewart C Myers *Principles of Corporate Finance* (5th edn, 1996), ch 14, especially at 362-364.

CHAPTER 15

Share capital

This Chapter will consider share capital looking in particular at the rules governing payment for share capital and the doctrine of capital maintenance. Here the rules are predominantly statutory and originated in the Companies Act 1980 which implemented the requirements of the Second EC Directive in this regard[1].

NOMINAL CAPITAL

The memorandum of association of a company having a share capital must state the amount of the share capital with which the company proposes to be registered and the division of the share capital into shares of a fixed amount[2]. This is known as the nominal or authorised capital. For example, a company may decide to have a share capital of £100 divided into 100 £1 shares so the nominal or authorised share capital is £100 and each share has the nominal or par value of £1. The company may issue up to 100 shares. If the company wishes to go beyond that figure, and if so authorised by its articles[3], it may alter the limit set in the memorandum by an ordinary resolution and increase its share capital by new shares of such amount as it thinks expedient[4].

MINIMUM AUTHORISED CAPITAL OF PUBLIC COMPANIES

Private companies in the UK do not have to have a minimum share capital although this is common in continental systems. We saw in Chapter 4, however, that public companies do have to have a minimum share capital. Indeed it is a feature of many of

---

1   The Second EC Directive of 13 December 1976, EC Council Directive 77/91, OJ L 26, 31.1.77, p 1 addresses the formation of public limited liability companies and the maintenance and alteration of their capital with a view to ensuring minimum equivalent protection for both shareholders and creditors of such companies: implemented initially by the Companies Act 1980 and now by the Companies Act 1985. It was subsequently amended by EC Directive 92/101, OJ L 347, 28.11.92, p 64.
2   CA 1985, s 2(5)(a). There is no such requirement in the case of an unlimited company: ibid.
3   See Table A, art 32.
4   CA 1985, s 121(1), (2)(a). See further Chapter 17.

the capital rules, as we shall see, that stricter requirements are imposed on public companies.

The origin of the requirement of a minimum authorised share capital for public companies is art 6 of the Second EC Directive[5] which requires a minimum capital of not less than 25,000 ecus. It was felt that discrepancies between the various member states on this question would affect freedom of establishment and attract capital to countries with the most liberal regimes. Requiring a minimum capital also reflects an expectation that public companies should possess a greater measure of substance than the typical £100 private company. Requiring a minimum authorised capital does not ensure, of course, that the capital will remain intact for it may well be lost in trading.

When a memorandum of association delivered to the registrar of companies states that the company is to be registered as a public company, the amount of the share capital stated in the memorandum to be that with which the company proposes to be registered must not be less than the authorised minimum as defined by the Companies Act 1985[6]. The 'authorised minimum' is defined as £50,000 or such other sum as the Secretary of State may specify by order made by statutory instrument[7].

In addition, a company registered as a public company on its original incorporation[8] must not do business or exercise any borrowing powers unless the registrar of companies has certified that he is satisfied that the nominal value of the company's allotted share capital is not less than the authorised minimum[9] or the company is re-registered as a private company[10]. A certificate to this effect in respect of a company is conclusive evidence that the company is entitled to do business and exercise any borrowing powers[11].

If a company does business or exercises any borrowing powers without this certificate, then the company and any officer in default is liable to a fine[12] but the validity of any transaction entered into by the company is not affected[13]. If, however, a company enters into a transaction in contravention of this requirement and fails to comply with its obligations in that connection within 21 days of being called upon to do so, the directors of the company are jointly and severally liable to indemnify the other party to the transaction in respect of any loss or damage suffered by him by reason of the company's failure to comply with those obligations[13]. This provision is of little significance for few public companies are likely to attempt to trade without this certificate and it would be difficult, in any event, to establish that the loss or damage suffered was by reason of the company's failure to comply with these obligations.

Serious loss of capital by public company

Where a public company has suffered a serious loss of capital so that its net assets are half or less of its called-up share capital, the directors must call an extraordinary general

---

5   See note 1 supra.
6   CA 1985, s 11.
7   Ibid, s 118(1). Despite the power to alter this figure, the minimum figure remains at the level set in 1980.
8   As to the position when a private company re-registers as a public company, see ibid, s 45(2).
9   A statutory declaration to this effect in the prescribed form and signed by a director or secretary of the company must be filed with the registrar: ibid, s 117(2), (3); and the registrar may accept a statutory declaration so delivered to him as sufficient evidence of the matters stated in it: s 117(5).
10 Ibid, s 117(1), (2).
11 Ibid, s 117(6). Note that a public company registered as such on its original incorporation which has not obtained a s 117 certificate and more than a year has expired since it was registered as a public company may be wound up by the court: Insolvency Act 1986, s 122(1)(b).
12 CA 1985, s 117(7).
13 Ibid, s 117(8).

meeting to consider whether any, and if so what, steps should be taken to deal with the situation[14].

NOMINAL OR PAR VALUE

As noted above, the amount of the nominal share capital will be divided into shares of fixed nominal or par value, a figure which will usually be set quite low, for example, £1, 50p or 25p. If the company's nominal share capital is £100 divided into 100 shares of £1 each, £1 is the nominal or par value of each share and a shareholder must pay at least £1 for each share allotted to him by the company. The relevance of par value to the shareholder is that the company may not issue its shares for less than the par value, something which is discussed in greater detail below, hence the need to pay at least £1.

Companies used to have shares of a high par value but today lower par values are preferred as they are seen to increase the marketability of the shares and are preferred by investors. Many other jurisdictions have dispensed with the idea of par value and shares of no par value are allowed, for example, in the USA and Canada[15]. The Gedge Committee in 1954 and the Jenkins Committee in 1962 recommended that no par value shares be permitted in the UK but no action was taken[16]. The objection to par value is that it is misleading to unsophisticated investors for it quickly ceases to have any relevance to the market value of the shares[17]. No par value shares, on the other hand, can be issued for such consideration as the directors decide is in the best interests of the company. Shareholders would simply hold a number of shares whose value would depend, as now, on the value of the company and the market's perception of that value but without being confused by the historical figure of nominal value.

On 1 January 1999, the euro is expected to be introduced alongside (and subsequently to replace) national currencies in European Union member states which join the single currency. Although the UK is very unlikely to join in the first group of member states, it is thought likely that many UK companies may start to conduct some or all of their business in euros from that date. In anticipation of such developments, the Department of Trade and Industry is consulting as to possible changes to the Companies Act 1985 to facilitate the redenomination of the nominal or par value of shares into the euro or other currencies.[17a]

ISSUE AT A PREMIUM

While the initial subscribers to the memorandum may take their shares at the nominal or par value, it is quite common thereafter for shares to be issued at a premium, ie at more than par value. So a share with a par value of £1 may subsequently be issued for £1.30, £1.50 or any higher figure which the market will bear.

---

14   Ibid, s 142. As to extraordinary general meetings, see Chapter 23.
15   See Clark *Corporate Law* (1986), pp 707 – 715; Welling *Corporate Law in Canada* (1984), pp 577 – 580.
16   Cmnd 9112 and Cmnd 1749, respectively. An attempt to introduce such reforms in the Companies Act 1967 failed.
17   See Sealy *Cases and Materials in Company Law* (6th edn, 1996), p 383 where he makes the point that if shares were originally issued at a premium or in exchange for a non-cash consideration, the shares may never have been worth their face value and after issue their market value will never again bear any resemblance to the historic figure once ascribed to it.
17a See DTI *The Euro: redenomination of Share Capital, A Consultative Document* (January 1998).

Shares issued for a consideration other than cash are issued at a premium if the value of the assets in consideration of which they are issued is more than the nominal value of the shares. The point arose in *Henry Head & Co Ltd v Ropner Holdings Ltd*[18] where there was an amalgamation of two shipping companies through the formation of a new holding company. There was a one-for-one exchange of shares by the shareholders of the two companies for shares in the holding company. The assets of the companies were undervalued and were worth £5m more than the nominal value of the shares in the new holding company. The question was whether it was correct for the holding company to transfer £5m to a share premium account. The court found that it was necessary for a transfer to be made to the share premium account and this decision was followed in *Shearer (Inspector of Taxes) v Bercain Ltd*[19] although its effects have been mitigated by Companies Act 1985, ss 131–134, noted below.

There is no requirement for companies to issue shares at a premium[20]. It depends on the circumstances of each case whether it will be prudent or even possible to do so, and it is a question for the directors to decide[1]. An example of a situation where the company will forgo some of the available premium is where the company makes a rights issue to raise further capital from its shareholders and does so, as is normally the practice, at a price which is at a discount to the market price. It is in the interests of the company to make the price attractive to encourage the shareholders to take up further shares in the company. Rights issues are discussed in detail below. In some circumstances, however, directors may be in breach of their duties to the company in not obtaining the greatest financial return from the shares[2].

The share premium account

Subject to various provisions granting relief[3], when a company issues shares at a premium, whether for cash or otherwise, a sum equal to the aggregate amount or value of the premiums on those shares must be transferred to an account called 'the share premium account'[4].

As regards the use which may be made of share premium, the position had been that the company could distribute the premium as a dividend since it was not share capital[5]. That rule was changed by statute and the legislation now requires that share premium be treated in most respects as share capital. It is therefore subject to many of the statutory constraints imposed on the use of share capital by the company[6].

The share premium account may be applied by the company:

(i)   in paying up unissued shares to be allotted to members as fully paid bonus shares (discussed below); or

---

18   [1952] Ch 124, [1951] 2 All ER 994.
19   [1980] 3 All ER 295.
20   *Hilder v Dexter* [1902] AC 474; *Lowry (Inspector of Taxes) v Consolidated African Selection Trust Ltd* [1940] AC 648, [1940] 2 All ER 545.
1   *Hilder v Dexter* [1902] AC 474 at 480, per Lord Davey.
2   *Hilder v Dexter* [1902] AC 474 at 481, per Lord Davey, as where in a particular case the arrangement is open to challenge as improvident or an abuse or in excess of the powers of management committed to the directors. See also *Lowry (Inspector of Taxes) v Consolidated African Selection Trust Ltd* [1940] AC 648 at 679, [1940] 2 All ER 545 at 565.
3   See CA 1985, ss 131–134.
4   Ibid, s 130(1).
5   *Drown v Gaumont-British Picture Corpn Ltd* [1937] Ch 402, [1937] 2 All ER 609.
6   Note that the provisions of the Companies Act 1985 relating to the reduction of a company's share capital apply as if the share premium account were part of its paid-up share capital: ibid, s 130(3). See also ss 160(2), 171(5).

   (ii) in writing off (a) the preliminary expenses of the company; or (b) the expenses of, or the commission paid or discount allowed on, any issue of shares or debentures of the company; or

   (iii) in providing for the premium payable on redemption of debentures of the company[7].

Exceptions to this requirement to transfer any premium to a share premium account are provided by Companies Act 1985, ss 131 – 134 which set out certain circumstances in which either a share premium account is not required or only a limited amount need be transferred to such an account. This is in response to the decisions in *Henry Head & Co Ltd v Ropner Holdings Ltd*[8] and *Shearer (Inspector of Taxes) v Bercain Ltd*[9], noted above, and the net effect is to allow certain reconstructions and mergers to take place without a transfer to a share premium account so releasing certain assets which may be distributed as a dividend.

PROHIBITION ON ISSUE AT DISCOUNT

While a company can issue shares for a premium, it cannot issue shares at a discount, ie for less than the nominal value[10]. In the leading case *Ooregum Gold Mining Co of India v Roper*[11], a company purported to issue £1 preference shares credited with 15 shillings paid up, leaving only five shillings to be paid on allotment. The House of Lords held that there was no power under the Companies Acts to do this and the allotment was ultra vires with the allottees liable to pay the full amount of £1 on each of their shares. In his speech Lord Macnaghten made the point that in a limited liability company shareholders purchase immunity from liability beyond the amount due on their shares on the basis that they remain liable up to that limit: 'Nothing but payment and payment in full, can put an end to the liability'[12].

This basic rule is now reflected in the legislation which provides that a company's shares must not be allotted at a discount[13]. If shares are allotted in contravention of the provision, the allottee is liable to pay the company an amount equal to the amount of the discount, with interest at the appropriate rate[14]; the company and any officer of it who is in default is liable on conviction on indictment to a fine, or on summary conviction to a fine not exceeding the statutory maximum[15].

A limited exception to the no discount rule is that which permits companies to pay underwriting commissions, provided such payments are authorised by the articles and the amount involved does not exceed specified limits[16]. Underwriting involves the use

---

7   Ibid, s 130(2).
8   [1952] Ch 124, [1951] 2 All ER 994.
9   [1980] 3 All ER 295.
10 *Ooregum Gold Mining Co of India v Roper* [1892] AC 125, HL; *Re Eddystone Marine Insurance Co* [1893] 3 Ch 9, CA; *Welton v Saffery* [1897] AC 299. The rule cannot be evaded by issuing convertible debentures at a discount which are capable of being immediately converted to ordinary shares: *Mosely v Koffyfontein Mines Ltd* [1904] 2 Ch 108, CA.
11 [1892] AC 125, HL.
12 [1892] AC 125 at 145. Equally, the company cannot thereafter increase the member's liability to contribute to the company's share capital without his consent: CA 1985, s 16.
13 Ibid, s 100(1).
14 Ibid, s 100(2). Directors who allot shares at a discount are guilty of a breach of duty to the company and are liable to pay the amount of the discount and interest to the company if that amount cannot be recovered from the allottee or holder of the shares, as where the shares have passed into the hands of a bona fide purchaser for value from the original allottee: *Hirsche v Sims* [1894] AC 654, PC.
15 CA 1985, ss 114, 730, Sch 24.
16 Ibid, s 97.

of professional intermediaries (such as merchant banks and institutional investors) by companies seeking to raise funds from the public by the issue of shares. These intermediaries undertake, in return for a fee, to subscribe or procure subscriptions for those shares to the extent that the public or other persons do not subscribe for them. This fee could be prohibited as a discount on the shares were it not for this explicit provision permitting such payments.

Finally, it should be noted that while a company may not allot shares at less than the nominal value, it may accept as payment for those shares money or money's worth[17]. Where money's worth is received and the company is a private company, the courts will not inquire into the adequacy of the consideration unless it is illusory or manifestly inadequate. In such circumstances, it is possible that the shares are issued at a discount. This issue is considered further below.

PAID-UP SHARE CAPITAL

Shares may be fully or partly paid-up. In the latter case the company can make calls on the shareholder up to the amount of the share price which has not been paid[18]. So if a share is a £1 share of which 50p is paid up, the company can later call up the balance of 50p.

It is uncommon today to find companies with partly-paid capital as they prefer to obtain from the outset the capital which they have raised and to avoid the administrative burden of making calls on shareholders.

Public companies, in any event, must not allot a share except as paid up at least as to one-quarter of its nominal value and the whole of any premium[19]. If this rule is contravened the allotment is still valid and the share allotted in contravention is to be treated as if one-quarter of its nominal value together with the whole of any premium on it had been received but the allottee is liable to pay the company the minimum amount which should have been received in respect of the share less any consideration actually applied in payment, with interest at the appropriate rate[20].

ISSUED AND ALLOTTED SHARE CAPITAL

Shares are taken to be allotted, for the purposes of the Companies Act 1985, when a person acquires the unconditional right to be included in the company's register of members in respect of those shares[1]. The term 'issue' is not defined in the companies legislation but means something distinct from allotment and imports that some subsequent act has been done whereby the title of the allottee has been completed[2]. The allotment creates an enforceable contract for the issue of the shares and the shares

---

17   Ibid, s 99(1).
18   A limited company may by special resolution resolve that it will not call up any uncalled capital except in the event of winding up: ibid, s 120. The creation of such reserve capital is unusual.
19   Ibid, s 101(1).
20   Ibid, s 101(3), (4).
1   Ibid, s 738.
2   *National Westminster Bank plc v IRC* [1995] 1 AC 119, [1994] 3 All ER 1, HL; *Clarke's Case* (1878) 8 Ch D 635 at 638, CA. It would seem that the meaning of 'issue' depends on the context of the enactment in which the word occurs: *National Westminster Bank plc v IRC* [1995] 1 AC 119, [1994] 3 All ER 1, HL.

are issued when an application to the company has been followed by allotment and notification to the purchaser and completed by entry on the register of members[3].

BONUS ISSUE

A bonus issue of shares occurs where the company capitalises profits or revenue reserves or some other permissible fund[4] and applies the proceeds in paying up bonus shares which normally go to existing members in proportion to their entitlement to dividend[5]. The process involves the use of the funds mentioned above to provide the shareholders with additional fully paid (usually) shares in the company[6]. It is essentially an accounting exercise as the company's reserves are reduced but its share capital fund is increased.

From the point of view of the shareholders, calling the issue a bonus issue is somewhat misleading for the company is still worth the same as before the bonus issue and the total value of their shareholding has not altered[7]. All that has happened is that each shareholder holds more shares but each share is worth less than before.

One advantage as far as the company and shareholders are concerned is that a bonus issue is not a distribution[8] for the purposes of the distribution rules[9] so funds which would not be available for distribution as dividends may be used for this purpose.

RIGHTS ISSUE

A rights issue occurs where the company offers a new issue of shares to its existing shareholders in proportion to their existing shareholdings. Such pre-emption rights, if taken up, enable the existing shareholders to retain their proportionate shareholdings in the company and prevents the dilution of their holdings which would occur if the company could by-pass its existing shareholders and offer shares directly to the public or other selected groups of investors. As such issues are usually offered at a discount to the market price[10], requiring the company to offer the shares to the existing shareholders also means that they get the benefit of that discount rather than outsiders.

In the continental European Union states, companies are generally obliged to offer their shares to their existing shareholders before going outside the company. In the UK, this requirement became a statutory requirement for all companies in the

---

3   *National Westminster Bank plc v IRC* [1995] 1 AC 119, [1994] 3 All ER 1, HL (tax relief to investors in shares in companies set up under the business expansion scheme was altered in respect of shares 'issued' after 16 March 1993: here shares had been allotted prior to that date but registration took place after the date: held (3–2 majority) shares were 'issued' after 16 March 1993).

4   The company may also use its share premium account (CA 1985, s 130(2)) or capital redemption reserve (s 170(4)) to finance a bonus issue.

5   See Table A, art 110; note also *Re Cleveland Trust plc* [1991] BCC 33 where a bonus issue was declared void on the ground of common mistake when the directors and shareholders were mistaken as to the availability of profits which could be capitalised.

6   As this appears to be a case of the company allotting shares without receiving money or money's worth, it would seem to fall foul of CA 1985, s 99(1) but, as noted above, s 99(4) specifically provides that s 99(1) does not prevent the company from making a bonus issue.

7   Of course, it is not strictly accurate to say that there is no difference in value before and after a bonus issue, for the market may respond favourably to a bonus issue so the shares may gain a little in value but essentially the shareholder's position does not alter.

8   CA 1985, s 263(2)(a).

9   Ibid, ss 263–281; discussed in Ch 16.

10 A rights issue, although at a discount to the market, does not infringe the no discount rule because it is not a discount on the nominal value.

Companies Act 1980 which implemented art 29 of the Second EC Company Law Directive[11] requiring pre-emption rights whenever shares were to be offered for a cash consideration. The current provisions are in Companies Act 1985 ss 89–96 which are considered below.

The general rule

The general rule is that a company proposing to allot equity securities:[12]

(i)   must not allot any of them on any terms to any person unless it has first made an offer to each person holding relevant shares[13] to allot to him on the same or more favourable terms, a proportion of those securities which is as nearly as practicable equal to the proportion in nominal value held by him of the relevant shares[14]; and

(ii) must not allot any of those securities to a person unless the period during which any such offer may be accepted has expired or the company has received notice of the acceptance or refusal of every offer so made[15].

The effect of the definitions of 'equity securities' and 'relevant shares' is that this general rule applies to:

• any allotment by a company of shares which are not subscriber shares or bonus shares; and

• where the allotment is to any shareholder other than a shareholder holding shares which as respects dividends and capital carry a right to participate only up to a specified amount in a distribution, or shares which are held or, are to be allotted, in pursuance of an employees' share scheme[16].

Any such allotment must be done on a pro rata basis in accordance with the statute. Any pro rata offer must be in writing and must be made to a holder of shares either personally or by sending it by post to him[17]. The offer must state a period of not less than 21 days during which it may be accepted and the offer must not be withdrawn before the end of that period[18].

Exceptions

It would seem therefore that practically all allotments must be on a pro rata basis. However, there are a large number of instances when the general rule does not apply.

---

11   EC Council Directive 77/91, OJ L 26, 31.1.77, p 1. As to the scope of art 29, see *Siemens AG v Nold*: Case C-42/95 [1997] 1 BCLC 291.

12   'Equity security', in relation to a company, means a relevant share in the company (other than a share shown in the memorandum to have been taken by a subscriber to the memorandum, or a bonus share) or a right to subscribe for, or to convert securities into, relevant shares in the company: CA 1985, s 94(1), (2). For the meaning of 'relevant share' see note 13 infra.

13   'Relevant shares', in relation to a company, means shares in the company other than (1) shares which as respects dividends and capital carry a right to participate only up to a specified amount in a distribution; and (2) shares which are held by a person who acquired them in pursuance of an employees' share scheme or, in the case of shares which have not been allotted, are to be allotted in pursuance of such a scheme: ibid, s 94(1), (5).

14   Ibid, s 89(1)(a).

15   Ibid, s 89(1)(b).

16   See notes 12, 13 supra.

17   CA 1985, s 90(2) unless the holder cannot be contacted when a notice in the *Gazette* will suffice: ibid, s 90(5).

18   Ibid, s 90(6).

It does not apply to:

(1) an allotment of equity securities which is on a pre-emption basis to a class of shares in pursuance of a class right to that effect[19]. In this instance the general rule imposing statutory pre-emption rights does not apply because there is an internal provision applying a pre-emption right in any case. If the holder of those shares or anyone in whose favour he has renounced his right to their allotment accepts the offer, then the general rule has no application and the company may allot accordingly[20]. If they are not so accepted then any subsequent offer of those shares has to be in accordance with the general rule, ie on a pre-emption basis to the rest of the shareholders rather than to the general public[20]. In these cases, therefore, the order of allotment is to the holder of the class of shares or anyone in whose favour he has renounced, then to the existing shareholders generally, and only then to the general public;

(2) a particular allotment of equity securities if these are, or are to be, wholly or partly paid up otherwise than in cash[1]. This obviously offers an easy method of avoiding pre-emption rights for so long as any part of the consideration is paid otherwise than in cash then the general rule does not apply;

(3) an allotment of securities which would, apart from a renunciation or assignment of the right to their allotment, be held under an employees' share scheme[2];

(4) allotments by a private company of equity securities or to such allotments of a particular description, where the general requirement of pre-emption has been excluded by a provision contained in the memorandum or articles of that company[3]. A requirement or authority contained in the memorandum or articles of a private company, if it is inconsistent with the general requirement of pre-emption, has effect as a provision excluding that requirement[4]. However, a class right of pre-emption is not to be treated as being inconsistent with the general requirement that offers to shareholders be made on a pre-emption basis;

(5) an allotment of equity securities by any company, if the general rule has been disapplied in accordance with the statutory provisions and the directors authorised to allot on a non-rights basis[5]. Disapplication is discussed in detail below.

Disapplication of pre-emption rights

The legislation provides for two situations:

(1) Where the directors of a company are generally authorised to allot relevant securities[6], they may be given power by the articles, or by a special resolution

---

19   Ibid, ss 89(2) and (3). A reference to a class of shares is to shares to which the same rights are attached as to voting and as to participation, both as respects dividend and as respects capital, in a distribution: ss 94(1), (6).

20   Ibid, s 89(3).

1   Ibid, s 89(4); as to when a share is deemed allotted for cash, see s 738(2). On this point, see *Siemens AG v Nold*: Case C-42/95 [1997] 1 BCLC 291, ECJ.

2   CA 1985, s 89(5).

3   Ibid, s 91(1).

4   Ibid, s 91(2).

5   Ie in accordance with ibid, s 95.

6   Ie generally authorised under ibid, s 80(1). In this instance 'relevant securitites' is defined in ibid, s 80(2).

of the company, to allot equity securities[7] pursuant to that authority as if the pre-emptive basis of allotment[8] did not apply, or as if it applied to the allotment with such modifications as the directors may determine[9];

(2) Where the directors of a company are authorised to allot relevant securities[9a] (whether generally or otherwise), the company may by special resolution resolve either that the pre-emptive basis shall not apply to a specified allotment of equity securities to be made pursuant to that authority, or that that basis shall apply to the allotment with such modifications as may be specified in the resolution[10].

Head (1) is a general disapplication whereas head (2) allows for a more limited disapplication done on an individual basis with regard to a specified allotment. A special resolution under head (2) must be recommended by the directors and they must circulate to the shareholders, with the notice of the meeting at which the resolution is proposed, a written statement setting out their reasons for making the recommendation, the amount to be paid to the company in respect of the equity shares to be allotted and the directors' justification of that amount[11].

The power referred to above under head (1) and (2) ceases to have effect when the authority to which it relates is revoked or would (if not renewed) expire; but if the authority is renewed, the power or (as the case may be) the resolution may also be renewed, for a period not longer than that for which the authority is renewed, by a special resolution of the company[12].

LISTED COMPANIES AND PRE-EMPTION RIGHTS

Where shareholders give their authorisation to a general disapplication of pre-emption rights in accordance with head (1) above, the Listing Rules require that that general disapplication is for a fixed period of time which must terminate no later than fifteen months after the passing by the shareholders of the relevant special resolution[13].

---

7   'Equity security', in relation to a company, means a relevant share in the company (other than a share shown in the memorandum to have been taken by a subscriber to the memorandum, or a bonus share) or a right to subscribe for, or to convert securities into, relevant shares in the company: ibid, s 94(1), (2). 'Relevant shares', in relation to a company, means shares in the company other than (1) shares which as respects dividends and capital carry a right to participate only up to a specified amount in a distribution; and (2) shares which are held by a person who acquired them in pursuance of an employees' share scheme or, in the case of shares which have not been allotted, are to be allotted in pursuance of such a scheme: ibid, s 94(1), (5).

8   Ie the general requirement discussed above and contained in ibid, s 89(1).

9   Ibid, s 95(1).

9a   Ie authorised under ibid, s 80. In this instance 'relevant securities' are defined in ibid, s 80(2).

10   Ibid, s 95(2). For the meaning of 'equity security', see note 7 supra.

11   Ibid, s 95(5). Where a private company wishes to proceed by written resolution, this requirement as to the circulation of a written statement by the directors with a notice of the meeting does not apply but such a statement must be supplied to each relevant member at or before the time at which the resolution is supplied to him for signature: s 381A(7), Sch 15A, para 3. As to written resolutions, see Ch 23. A person who knowingly or recklessly authorises or permits the inclusion in a statement so circulated of any matter which is misleading, false or deceptive in a material particular is liable to imprisonment or a fine, or both: s 95(6).

12   Ibid, s 95(3).

13   The Listing Rules, r 9.20; see also r 14.8. Details of issues for cash other than on a pre-emptive basis under a general disapplication must also be included in the annual report and accounts: Listing Rules, r 12.43(o). This requirement is in addition to the disclosure required by CA 1985, Sch 4, para 39.

This effectively means that listed companies are obliged to ask their shareholders at each annual general meeting to renew the authority to allot equity securities for cash otherwise than to the existing shareholders in proportion to their existing holdings[14].

Consequences of breach of pre-emption requirements

If there is a contravention of the provision that equity securities must be offered to shareholders on a pre-emption basis[15], or of the provisions relating to the communication of pre-emption offers[16], the company, and every officer of it who knowingly authorised or permitted the contravention, are jointly and severally liable to compensate any person to whom an offer should have been made for any loss, damage, costs or expenses which the person has sustained or incurred by reason of the contravention[17]. This is subject to a two-year limitation period[18]. A failure to comply with the pre-emption provisions may also be grounds for a petition alleging unfairly prejudicial conduct[19].

QUASI-CAPITAL

In addition to share capital properly so-called there are two notional funds which are by law required to be created and which appear in the balance sheet of a company as a kind of quasi-capital. Subject to certain exceptions, they can only be distributed or returned to shareholders in the same restricted way as share capital. The two notional funds are the share premium account and the capital redemption reserve. The former is required when shares are issued at a higher price than their par value and was discussed above: the latter is required where shares are redeemed or purchased by a company in certain circumstances and is discussed in Chapter 16.

CAPITAL MAINTENANCE

Having considered the basic concepts, it is necessary to consider the detailed rules concerning payment for share capital.

---

14 Institutional investors are anxious to prevent any dilution of their statutory rights and so set limits to their support for resolutions disapplying the pre-emption provisions. The institutions will not oppose resolutions which seek to disapply pre-emption rights in respect of ordinary share capital provided the resolution is restricted to an amount of shares not exceeding 5% of the issued ordinary share capital at the relevant time. This is subject to a cumulative limit of 7.5% in any rolling three-year period. The discount available when shares are allotted on a non pre-emptive basis is also limited.
15 Including any breach of a class pre-emption right under CA 1985, s 89(3): s 92(1).
16 Ie ibid, s 90(1)–(5), (6).
17 Ibid, s 92(1). No provision is made for improper allotments to be set aside but see *Re Thundercrest Ltd* [1995] 1 BCLC 117 where the court did set aside an allotment by directors in their own favour which was made in breach of the statutory requirements.
18 CA 1985, s 92(2).
19 Under ibid, s 459 discussed in detail in Chapter 28. See *Re a Company (No 005134 of 1986), ex p Harries* [1989] BCLC 383 at 396. Indeed an allotment on a pre-emption basis in accordance with the statutory provisions may even be the subject of a s 459 petition, see *Re a Company* [1985] BCLC 80.

The doctrine of capital maintenance

To understand the rules concerning payment for share capital, they must be placed against the background of the capital maintenance doctrine.

With the advent of limited liability, the courts' concern at the end of the last century turned to the protection of creditors. To that end the courts developed the doctrine of capital maintenance. This doctrine regards the company's share capital as a fund which is a safeguard for creditors. As Jessel MR explained in *Re Exchange Banking Co, Flitcroft's Case*[20]:

> The creditor has no debtor but that impalpable thing the corporation, which has no property except the assets of the business. The creditor, therefore, I may say, gives credit to that capital, gives credit to the company on the faith of the representation that the capital shall be applied only for the purposes of the business, and he has therefore a right to say that the corporation shall keep its capital and not return it to the shareholders, though it may be a right which he cannot enforce otherwise than on a winding up.

Of course, the courts cannot guarantee that this capital fund will be intact when the creditors need to resort to it and this was recognised in those early decisions. Lord Watson in *Trevor v Whitworth*[1] noted:

> Paid-up capital may be diminished or lost in the course of the company's trading; that is a result which no legislation can prevent; but persons who deal with, and give credit to a limited company, naturally rely upon the fact that the company is trading with a certain amount of capital already paid ... and they are entitled to assume that no part of the capital which has been paid into the coffers of the company has been subsequently paid out, except in the legitimate course of business.

Nevertheless, within the limits of what the law can achieve, the courts set about developing a set of rules concerning the establishment and maintenance of share capital which have since been modified by the Companies Acts. Whether the protection afforded by such rules is real or illusory is another matter.

There are essentially two aspects to the capital maintenance doctrine which consists of:

(i)   rules concerned with raising share capital;
(ii) rules ensuring that capital once raised is not returned to the shareholders ahead of a winding up.

If share capital is to be a creditors' fund then every care must be taken to ensure appropriate payment is received by the company for the shares and this Chapter considers that aspect of the doctrine. Having raised capital, it is important that the company does not return that capital to the shareholders, as where the company purchases back the shares, or funds the original purchase by providing financial assistance to the purchaser, or simply depletes the company's assets through improper

---

20   (1882) 21 Ch D 519 at 533. See also *Ooregum Gold Mining Co of India v Roper* [1892] AC 125 at 133, per Lord Halsbury LC, HL.
1   (1887) 12 App Cas 409 at 423-424. In this case the company purported to purchase back its own shares. The court held that it had no power under the Companies Acts so to do.

dividends, funded not out of profits but out of capital. All of these aspects are discussed in Chapter 16. Finally, stringent procedures must be followed if a company wishes formally to reduce its capital fund and this is considered in Chapter 17.

Payment for shares – the basic rules

The starting point, as noted above, is that a company cannot make a gratuitous allotment of its shares[2] nor an allotment at a discount[3]. The allottee must pay in full at least the nominal value of the shares and will probably pay a premium as well.

MONEY OR MONEY'S WORTH

While the company must receive at least the nominal value of the shares, the shares allotted by a company, and any premium on them, may be paid up in money or money's worth (including goodwill and know-how)[4].

Obviously where a company obtains cash as consideration for an allotment of shares, it is clear whether or not the shares have been issued at a discount to the nominal value. A share in a company is deemed paid up in cash or allotted for cash if:

(i) the consideration for the allotment or payment up is cash received by the company, or

(ii) is a cheque received in good faith which the directors have no reason for suspecting will not be paid, or

(iii) is a release of a liability of the company for a liquidated sum, or

(iv) is an undertaking to pay cash to the company at a future date[5].

Note also that shares taken by a subscriber to the memorandum of a public company in pursuance of an undertaking of his in the memorandum, and any premium on the shares, must be paid up in cash[6].

The position may be less clear where the company accepts a non-cash consideration. If the non-cash consideration is worth less than the nominal value, then the company will have issued its shares at a discount which is prohibited[7]. This practice of allotting shares for an undervalue by accepting non-cash assets is known in America as stock watering. It is damaging to the creditors and to the other shareholders as it dilutes the value of the capital fund and their shares.

In considering the question of non-cash consideration, the rules distinguish between public and private companies.

---

2 *Re Wragg Ltd* [1897] 1 Ch 796; *Ooregum Gold Mining Co of India v Roper* [1892] AC 125; *Re Eddystone Marine Insurance Co* [1893] 3 Ch 9, CA.
3 CA 1985, s 100(1); *Ooregum Gold Mining Co of India v Roper* [1892] AC 125.
4 CA 1985, s 99(1) although this requirement does not prevent the company from allotting bonus shares: ibid, s 99(4).
5 Ibid, s 738(2). For the purpose of determining whether a share is or is to be allotted for cash, or paid up in cash, 'cash' includes foreign currency: s 738(4). An assignment of a debt is not an undertaking to pay cash at a future date for these purposes, see *Systems Control plc v Munro Corporate plc* [1990] BCLC 659.
6 CA 1985, s 106.
7 Ibid, s 100.

Private companies

The position as far as a private company is concerned is that such a company is entitled to issue fully paid-up shares in return for a non-cash consideration. As Lindley LJ noted in *Re Wragg Ltd*[8]:

> Provided a limited company does so honestly and not colourably, and provided that it has not been so imposed upon as to be entitled to be relieved from its bargain, it appears to be settled ... that agreements by limited companies to pay for property or services in paid-up shares are valid and binding on the companies and their creditors.

The question whether the consideration is colourable is one of fact in each case[9]. There is a danger in these situations, of which the courts are aware, that the company may over-value the consideration so that the transaction is essentially the issue of shares at a discount.

> The Court would doubtless refuse effect to a colourable transaction, entered into for the purpose or with the obvious result of enabling the company to issue its shares at a discount; but it has been ruled that, so long as the company honestly regards the consideration given as fairly representing the nominal value of the shares in cash, its estimate ought not to be critically examined. That state of the law is certainly calculated to induce companies who are in want of money, and whose shares are unsaleable except at a discount, to pay extravagant prices for goods or work to persons who are willing to take payment in shares. The rule is capable of being abused and I have little doubt that it has been liberally construed in practice[10].

It is only where the consideration is illusory or it is manifest on the face of the instrument that the shares are issued at a discount that the court will be prepared to consider the adequacy of the consideration. This judicial attitude is in keeping with the courts' traditional reluctance to interfere in business matters. The result, given that the vast majority of companies are private companies, is that there are no real constraints on issuing shares at a discount provided the consideration is money's worth rather than cash[11].

Public companies

Many continental jurisdictions countered such abuses arising from the issue of shares for a non-cash consideration by requiring expert valuation reports and this requirement was adopted for public companies in art 10 of the Second EC Directive. The Companies Act 1985 reflects that provision and imposes stringent requirements on public companies in a number of respects.

---

8   [1897] 1 Ch 796 at 830. See also *Mosely v Koffyfontein Mines Ltd* [1904] 2 Ch 108; *Re White Star Line Ltd* [1938] Ch 458.
9   *Re Innes & Co Ltd* [1903] 2 Ch 254 at 262.
10   *Ooregum Gold Mining Co of India v Roper* [1892] AC 125 at 137, per Lord Watson.
11   The inconsistency between prohibiting a discount but allowing payment in money's worth was noted by Lindley LJ in *Re Wragg Ltd* [1897] 1 Ch 796 at 831 who accepted that the difference between issuing shares at a discount and issuing them at a price put upon property or services by the vendor and agreed to by the company may not always be very apparent in practice. In his opinion, however, the two transactions were essentially different, and while the one was ultra vires the other was intra vires.

ALLOTMENTS FOR CONSIDERATION OTHER THAN CASH

A public company must not allot shares as fully or partly paid up (as to their nominal value or any premium on them) otherwise than in cash[12] unless:

(a) the consideration for the allotment has been independently valued[13]; and

(b) a report with respect to its value has been made to the company by a person appointed by the company (in accordance with the statutory provisions) during the six months immediately preceding the allotment of the shares; and

(c) a copy of the report has been sent to the proposed allottee[14].

Note that the consideration need not be wholly in non-cash assets but may be part cash and part non-cash.

These requirements do not apply to an allotment of shares in connection with:

(a) a share exchange for the shares of all the holders of shares in another company or of a particular class of shares[15]; or

(b) a proposed merger[16] of the company with another[17].

The section also makes clear that bonus issues are not caught by these provisions[18].

If a company allots shares in contravention of the above requirements and either the allottee has not received the valuer's report required to be sent to him, or there has been some other contravention of the above requirements or the provisions as to valuation which the allottee knew or ought to have known amounted to a contravention, the allottee is liable to pay the company an amount equal to the aggregate of the nominal value of the shares and the whole of any premium (or, if the case so requires, so much of that aggregate as is treated as paid up by the consideration) with interest at the appropriate rate[19].

A copy of the report must be filed by the company with the registrar of companies at the same time as it files the return of allotment of those shares by the company[20].

Independent valuation and report

The statutory provisions governing the independent valuation and report were described by Harman J in *Re Ossory Estates plc*[1] as curious and arcane.

The valuation of the non-cash consideration and the report required thereon must be made by an independent person ('the valuer'), that is to say a person qualified at the time of the report to be appointed, or continue to be, an auditor of the company[2]. The company's existing auditor may be appointed as the valuer for these purposes.

---

12 See earlier discussion in text as to when a share in a company is deemed paid up in cash, or allotted for cash; CA 1985, s 738(2).

13 Under ibid, s 108.

14 Ibid, s 103(1).

15 Ibid, s 103(3), (4).

16 See ibid, s 103(5) which defines 'merger' for these purposes.

17 Ibid, s 103(5).

18 Ibid, s 103(2).

19 Ibid, s 103(6). The effect is to create an immediate liability as if the allottee had agreed to take up the shares for cash: *Re Bradford Investments Ltd* [1991] BCLC 224 at 233. These penalties can be onerous, see *Re Ossory Estates plc* [1988] BCLC 213; *Re Bradford Investments plc (No 2)* [1991] BCLC 688 but may be mitigated by the court's powers under CA 1985, s 113 to give relief.

20 Ibid, s 111(1). The filing of a return of allotment is required by s 88(2) within one month of the allotment.

1 [1988] BCLC 213 at 215.

2 CA 1985, s 108.

Where, however, it appears to the valuer to be reasonable for the valuation of the consideration, or any part of it, to be made (or for him to accept a valuation made) by another person who appears to him to have the requisite knowledge and experience to value the consideration or that part of it, and who is not a connected person of the company in any of the ways specified[3], he may arrange for or accept the other person's valuation[4].

The valuer's report must state:

(a) the nominal value of the shares to be wholly or partly paid for by the consideration in question;

(b) the amount of any premium payable on the shares;

(c) the description of the consideration and, as respects so much of the consideration as he himself has valued, a description of that part of the consideration, the method used to value it and the date of the valuation;

(d) the extent to which the nominal value of the shares and any premium are to be treated as paid up by the consideration or in cash[5].

Where the valuation is by a person other than the valuer, the latter's report must state that fact and must also state:

(a) the former's name, knowledge and experience; and

(b) describe so much of the consideration as was valued by the other person, and the method used to value it, and specify the date of the valuation[6].

In all cases the valuer's report must state that:

(a) the method of valuation (and any delegation of responsibility) was reasonable in all the circumstances;

(b) it appears to the valuer that there has been no material change in the value of the consideration since the valuation; and

(c) the value of the consideration together with any cash by which the nominal value of the shares or any premium payable on them is to be paid up, is not less than so much of the aggregate of the nominal value and the whole of any such premium as is treated as paid up by the consideration and any such cash[7].

A person carrying out a valuation or making a report with respect to any consideration proposed to be accepted or given by a company is entitled to require from the officers of the company such information and explanation as he thinks necessary to enable him to carry out the valuation or make the report[8].

Any person who knowingly or recklessly makes a statement which is misleading, false or deceptive in a material particular in connection with the preparation of such report commits an offence[9].

---

3   Ibid, s 108(2)(b). To be independent the person must not be an officer or servant of the company or any other body corporate which is that company's subsidiary or holding company or a subsidiary of that company's holding company, or a partner or employee of such an officer or servant: s 108(2)(b). The company's existing auditor is not included in the categories of excluded persons: s 108(3) and so may act as the valuer for these purposes.

4   Ibid, s 108(2).

5   Ibid, s 108(4).

6   Ibid, s 108(5).

7   Ibid, s 108(6).

8   Ibid, s 110(1).

9   Ibid, ss 110(2), 730, Sch 24.

TRANSFER TO PUBLIC COMPANY OF NON-CASH ASSET IN INITIAL PERIOD

For a period of two years from the date of the certificate of entitlement to do business[10], any transfer[11] of non-cash assets[12] from a subscriber to the company's memorandum for a consideration equal in value to 10% or more of the nominal value of the company's issued share capital at that time will be void unless the following conditions are met:

(a) the consideration to be received by the company, and any consideration other than cash to be given by the company, must have been independently valued by a valuer in the same way as outlined above and a report[13] on the consideration must have been made to the company during the six months immediately preceding the date of the agreement; and

(b) the terms of the agreement must have been approved by an ordinary resolution of the company[14].

Copies of the resolution and report must have been available before the meeting to the members of the company and to the other party to the agreement if not then a member of the company[15].

These requirements do not apply to (i) acquisitions of assets in the ordinary course of business, a potentially wide category, or (ii) acquisitions as a result of a court order or under court control[16].

There is clearly a degree of overlap between the requirement for a non-cash consideration to be valued before an allotment of shares (s 103) discussed above and these provisions governing the transfer to a public company of non-cash assets in the initial period (s 104) and it is important to appreciate the difference between the scope of the provisions. Section 103 applies whenever a public company accepts a non-cash consideration from anyone as consideration for an allotment of shares. Section 104 applies to any transfer of a non-cash asset from a subscriber to a public company within the first two years, whether the consideration for the transfer is an allotment of shares or something else. There are also different exceptions to each provision.

It is possible for both provisions to be applicable in the same instance since the provisions are not mutually exclusive. Thus any allotment of shares for a non-cash consideration to a subscriber within the two year period is potentially within both provisions which is not unduly burdensome as each requires a similar independent valuation and report. However, in addition, s 104 requires transactions within its ambit to be approved by the company in general meeting by an ordinary resolution. In other words, the informed consent of the shareholders will have to be sought.

As we will see later, the general meeting has lost much of its authority as an effective monitor of this type of transaction as a result, in larger companies, of the directors' control of proxy votes and the indifference of the average shareholder; and, in smaller

---

10 Ie the certificate required by ibid, s 117, discussed above.
11 See ibid, s 739(2): a reference to the transfer or acquisition of a non-cash asset includes the creation or extinction of an estate or interest in, or a right over, any property and also the discharge of any person's liability, other than a liability for a liquidated sum.
12 Defined in ibid, s 739(1) as meaning any property or interest in property other than cash.
13 The contents of the report are set out in ibid, s 109 and are essentially the same as those required under s 108 outlined above.
14 Ibid, s 104(2), (4). The section also applies to a private company which is re-registered as a public company, in which case it applies to persons who were members of the company on the date of re-registration and any transfer of non-cash assets between them and the company within two years beginning with that date: s 104(3).
15 Ibid, s 104(4). Copies of the report and the resolution must also be filed with the registrar of companies within 15 days of passing the resolution: s 111(2).
16 Ibid, s 104(6).

companies, because of the identity of interest between directors and shareholders. Nevertheless, many provisions in the Companies Act still require matters such as this to be presented for the shareholders' approval. There is another loophole, however, namely that s 104 does not apply where it is part of the company's ordinary business to acquire such assets as have been transferred. This may exclude the vast majority of suspect transactions from s 104 and leaves them subject solely to the valuation and report procedures of s 103.

The type of transaction which is within s 104 but not within s 103 is where the transaction does not involve an allotment of shares but is simply a transfer of non-cash assets by a subscriber to the company within the two-year period. That transfer is subject to independent valuation and requires the consent of the company in general meeting unless it can be shown, as will frequently be the case, that it is part of the company's business to acquire assets of that description. So even in this instance s 104 can be sidestepped, all of which suggests it may be of little more than nuisance value.

UNDERTAKINGS TO DO WORK OR PERFORM SERVICES

A public company must not accept at any time, in payment up of its shares or any premium on them, an undertaking given by any person that he or another should do work or perform services for the company or any other person[17]. If a public company accepts such an undertaking in payment up of its shares or any premium on them, the holder of the shares when they or the premium are treated as paid up (in whole or in part) by the undertaking is liable (1) to pay the company in respect of those shares an amount equal to their nominal value, together with the whole of any premium or, if the case so requires, such proportion of that amount as is treated as paid up by the undertaking; and (2) to pay interest at the appropriate rate on the amount payable under head (1) above[18].

If a company contravenes any of the above provisions, the company and any officer of it who is in default is liable on conviction on indictment to a fine, or on summary conviction to a fine not exceeding the statutory maximum[19]. Despite any contravention of these provisions, any undertaking given by any person to do work or perform services or to do any other thing remains enforceable by the company[20].

RESTRICTION ON LONG-TERM UNDERTAKING

A public company must not allot shares as fully or partly-paid as to their nominal value or any premium on them if the consideration for the allotment is or includes an undertaking which is to be, or may be, performed more than five years after the date of the allotment[1]. In the event of breach, the allottee is liable to pay the company an

---

17   Ibid, s 99(2).
18   Ibid, s 99(3). This restriction does not prevent a company from allotting bonus shares to its members or from paying up, with sums available for the purpose, any amounts for the time being unpaid on any of its shares, whether on account of the nominal value of the shares or by way of premium: ibid, s 99(4).
19   Ibid, ss 114, 730, Sch 24.
20   Ibid, s 115 which is subject to s 113.
1   Ibid, s 102(1). The provision equally applies to a contract which did not originally contravene this provision but is subsequently varied and results in a contravention. In such cases the variation is void; equally caught is the situation where an undertaking was to have been performed within five years but was not: ss 102(3) and (5).

amount equal to the aggregate of the nominal value and the whole of any premium due[2].

Consequences of breach of the rules as to payment for shares

The consequences of breach of any of the payment and valuation rules is relatively uniform.

As a general rule, the allottee remains liable to pay an amount equal to the nominal amount and any premium due together with interest[3]. Subsequent holders are jointly and severally liable unless they are purchasers for value and did not have actual notice of the contravention or they took from a holder who was not himself liable under these provisions[4].

These penalties can be quite onerous. In *Re Ossory Estates plc*[5] property was sold to a company and the vendor received as part of the consideration eight million shares in the company. As this was an allotment of shares for a non-cash consideration, an independent valuation and report was required. No such report was ever made with the result that the allottee, despite having transferred his property to the company, was liable to pay the company £1.76m as the price of the shares. Not surprisingly, this was described by Harman J as a somewhat startling conclusion[6].

However, provision is made for a person so liable to make an application to the court to be exempted in whole or in part from the liability[7]. If such liability arises in relation to payment in respect of any shares, the court may exempt the applicant from the liability only if and to the extent that it appears to the court just and equitable to do so having regard to the matters mentioned below[8]. The matters to be taken into account by the court are whether:

(1) the applicant has paid, or is liable to pay, any amount in respect of any other liability arising in relation to those shares under any of the relevant provisions, or of any liability arising by virtue of any undertaking given in or in connection with payment for those shares;

(2) any person other than the applicant has paid or is likely to pay (whether in pursuance of an order of the court or otherwise) any such amount; and

(3) the applicant or any other person has performed, in whole or in part, or is likely so to perform any such undertaking, or has done or is likely to do any other thing in payment or part payment for the shares[9].

In determining whether it should exempt the applicant in whole or in part from any liability, the court must have regard to the following overriding principle[10], namely

---

2   Ibid, s 102(2).
3   The effect is to create an immediate liability as if the allottee had agreed to take up the shares for cash: see *Re Bradford Investments plc* [1991] BCLC 224 at 233.
4   CA 1985, s 112.
5   [1988] BCLC 213, noted Birds (1989) 10 Co Law 67.
6   [1988] BCLC 213 at 214.
7   CA 1985, s 113(1).
8   Ibid, s 113(2). Note *Re Bradford Investments plc (No 2)* [1991] BCLC 688 at 693 where Hoffmann J thought that in the light of CA 1985, s 113(5) (see below) these matters were not intended to be an exhaustive statement of the matters to which the court should or may have regard.
9   Ibid, s 113(3).
10 See *Re Bradford Investments plc (No 2)* [1991] BCLC 688 at 694 where Hoffmann J thought that the designation 'overriding principle' did not oblige the court to refuse relief unless the company had received at least the nominal value of the allotted shares and any premium: had that been the intention the requirement would have been framed as a rule.

that a company which has allotted shares should receive money or money's worth at least equal in value to the aggregate of the nominal value of those shares and the whole of any premium or, if the case so requires, so much of that aggregate as is treated as paid up[11].

In *Re Ossory Estates plc*[12], noted above, relief was granted as the company had sold some of the property transferred to it in consideration for the allotment at a substantial profit and had undoubtedly received at least money or money's worth equal in value, and probably exceeding, the aggregate of the nominal value of the shares and any premium. It was just and equitable that the allottee should be relieved from any further liability.

This can be contrasted with *Systems Control plc v Munro Corporate plc*[13] where the court said there was no prospect of relief being granted when there was absolutely no evidence that the company had received the minimum amount; and *Re Bradford Investments plc (No 2)*[14] where the applicants failed to discharge the burden of showing that the company had received value for its shares.

Where a person is liable to a company as a result of the transfer to a public company of a non-cash asset in the initial period[15], the court may, on application, exempt him in whole or in part from that liability if and to the extent that it appears to the court just and equitable to do so having regard to any benefit accruing to the company by virtue of anything done by him towards the carrying out of the agreement for transfer[16].

In addition to the civil consequences, where there is a breach of these provisions, the company and officers in default are also guilty of an offence and liable to a fine[17]. Directors may also be in breach of duty and liable to make good any damage suffered by the company as a result of these contraventions[18].

Conclusion

Having considered the payment rules, it will be apparent that the statutory provisions seek to cover every conceivable eventuality and in the process submerge the basic principles beneath a welter of detail. As Professor Sealy has noted, this is a pretty large sledgehammer to crack a fairly small nut[19].

In any event, as *Re Harmony and Montague Tin and Copper Mining Co, Spargo's Case*[20] made clear many years ago, rules regulating the allotment of shares for non-cash assets are easily evaded by the simply process of dividing the transaction into two stages. First, the individual sells assets to the company and the company becomes indebted to him for a stated amount. Secondly, the company allots fully-paid shares to him and in return the company is released from the liability to pay the stated sum. The transaction is no longer an allotment of shares for a non-cash consideration but an allotment of shares for cash. In *Spargo's Case*, Sir W M James LJ explained that it

---

11   CA 1985, s 113(5)(a); see also s 113(5)(b).
12   [1988] BCLC 213.
13   [1990] BCLC 659.
14   [1991] BCLC 688.
15   The restrictions on such transfers were discussed above and are contained in CA 1985, s 104; the liability in consequence arises under s 105(2).
16   Ibid, s 113(8).
17   Ibid, s 114.
18   *Hirsche v Sims* [1894] AC 654.
19   Sealy *Cases and Materials in Company Law* (6th edn 1996), p 386.
20   (1873) 8 Ch App 407.

is not necessary that the formality should be gone through of the money being handed over and taken back again. If the two demands are set off against each other, the shares have been paid in cash[1]. The point is confirmed by the statute which provides that a share is allotted for cash if the consideration for the allotment is, inter alia, the release of a liability of the company for a liquidated sum.[2]

1   (1873) 8 Ch App 407 at 412
2   CA 1985, s 738(2).

CHAPTER 16

The capital maintenance doctrine, share dealings and distributions

Having considered the rules relating to the payment of share capital, this Chapter looks at the statutory provisions which attempt to prevent the return of that capital in various ways to the shareholders ahead of a winding up.

The capital maintenance rules originally developed by the courts have now been expanded and modified through legislation, in some cases strengthening, in others diminishing, the doctrine of capital maintenance.

In this Chapter we consider the rules governing:

(i)   the purchase and redemption by companies of their own shares;
(ii) the giving of financial assistance by companies to purchasers of their shares;
(iii) the payment of dividends.

PURCHASE AND REDEMPTION OF THEIR OWN SHARES

Background

One of the landmark cases in company law is the decision of the House of Lords in *Trevor v Whitworth*[1] in 1887 where it was held that a company had no power under the Companies Acts to purchase its own shares, even if so authorised by its articles of association. Lord Macnaghten said:

It appears to me that the notion of a limited company taking power to buy up its own shares is contrary to the plain intention of the [Companies] Act of 1862, and inconsistent with the conditions upon which, and upon which alone, Parliament has granted to individuals who are desirous of trading in partnership the privilege of limiting their liability[2].

---

1   (1887) 12 App Cas 409. For an interesting overview of its importance, see the judgment of Harman J in *Barclays Bank plc v British and Commonwealth Holdings plc* [1996] 1 BCLC 1 at 6–10, Ch D; affd [1996] 1 BCLC 1, CA. See also *Aveling Barford Ltd v Perion Ltd* [1989] BCLC 626.
2   (1887) 12 App Cas 409 at 433.

The objections to the purchase by a company of its own shares were based on a need to protect creditors from a reduction of capital in this way without the company adhering to the statutory provisions on reduction of capital which require any reduction to be confirmed by the court[3]. Creditors took the risk of a company losing its capital in trading but had a right to rely on the company not diminishing its capital by returning any part of it to its shareholders[4]. As Lord Watson noted:

> Paid-up capital may be diminished or lost in the course of the company's trading; that is a result which no legislation can prevent; but persons who deal with, and give credit to a limited company, naturally rely upon the fact that the company is trading with a certain amount of capital already paid, as well as upon the responsibility of its members for the capital remaining at call; and they are entitled to assume that no part of the capital which has been paid into the coffers of the company has been subsequently paid out, except in the legitimate course of its business[5].

As Professor Sealy has noted:

> This case settled a controversy which had existed, at least potentially, ever since the passing of the 1856 [Joint Stock Companies] Act. It was only slowly recognised that the issue was not a domestic matter concerned with compliance with the articles, or even a question of vires dependent upon the powers set forth in the memorandum, but a matter of legality under the Companies Act itself[6].

Opposition to companies purchasing their own shares remained an element of company law thereafter and was ultimately included in statutory form in the Companies Act 1980. The Companies Act 1985 now provides that a company limited by shares may not acquire its own shares, whether by purchase, subscription or otherwise[7]. In cases of breach, the company will be liable on conviction to a fine, every officer of the company who is in default will be liable to imprisonment or a fine, and the purported acquisition will be void[8].

However, the prohibition on purchase of its own shares does not apply in relation to:

(a)   the redemption or purchase of shares in accordance with the statutory scheme, discussed below;

(b)   the acquisition of shares in a reduction of capital duly made[9];

---

3   See CA 1985, s 135. Reduction is discussed in Chapter 17.
4   *Trevor v Whitworth* (1887) 12 App Cas 409 at 415, per Lord Herschell.
5   *Trevor v Whitworth* (1887) 12 App Cas 409 at 423, 424.
6   Sealy *Cases and Materials in Company Law* (6th edn, 1996), p 378.
7   CA 1985, s 143(1). This does not prohibit a company (A) from acquiring the shares of another company (B) in circumstances where the sole asset of the acquired company B is shares in the acquiring company A: *Acatos & Hutcheson plc v Watson* [1995] 1 BCLC 218. It was argued in this case that if A could not, without authorisation, purchase its own shares then equally it could not purchase a company whose sole asset was A's shares. The court agreed with counsel that in law what A was purchasing was B and not the assets of that company which were A's shares. The acquisition did not therefore contravene the prohibition on a company acquiring its own shares. Note also in this context Companies Act 1985, s 23 which generally prohibits a company from being a member of its holding company, discussed in greater detail in Chapter 19.
8   CA 1985, s 143(3).
9   Ie a reduction in accordance with the statutory scheme (ibid, s 135) governing reduction which is discussed in Chapter 17.

   (c) the purchase of shares in pursuance of an order of the court under certain statutory provisions[10]; or

   (d) the forfeiture[11] of shares, or the acceptance of shares surrendered in lieu, in pursuance of the articles, for failure to pay any sum payable in respect of the shares[12].

The dramatic shift in heading (a) above away from the rule in *Trevor v Whitworth*[13] was brought about by the Companies Act 1981 which permitted companies to issue redeemable shares, to purchase back their own shares and, in the case of private companies, to purchase back out of capital.

Redemption involves the redemption by the company of shares which are issued on the basis that they are redeemable at the option of the company or the shareholder. A purchase back scheme involves the purchase back by the company of its own shares and it can apply to any shares, whether or not they are issued as redeemable. The power to issue redeemable shares was not new in 1981 as companies had been able from 1929 to issue redeemable preference shares. The purchase powers, however, were entirely novel. Before considering the statutory requirements in detail, it is useful to consider why the rule in *Trevor v Whitworth*[14] was relaxed in this way.

REASONS FOR THE CHANGE OF APPROACH

The statutory provisions allowing companies to issue redeemable shares and to purchase back their own shares were just one of a series of measures introduced in the early 1980s which were designed to encourage equity investment in small businesses[15]. The difficulties which small companies face in trying to raise equity investment have been well documented[16]. Many small businesses are family concerns where the individuals concerned, much as they might welcome an injection of capital, are reluctant to raise it through an issue of shares for fear of losing control of the business to an outsider. Outsiders, for their part, are reluctant to contribute their capital to an enterprise whose shares are not easily marketable and where they risk being locked in. Any scheme to assist such companies would have to be flexible enough to increase the marketability of the shares without necessarily depriving the existing owners of control and without jeopardising the position of the company's creditors[17].

---

10   Ie under ibid, s 5 (proceedings objecting to a proposed alteration of objects), see Chapter 10; s 54 (proceedings objecting to resolution for public company to be re-registered as private), see Chapter 6; or s 459 (seeking relief on the grounds of unfair prejudice to members), see Chapter 28.

11   Forfeiture is discussed in Chapter 17.

12   CA 1985, s 143(3).

13   (1887) 12 App Cas 409.

14   (1887) 12 App Cas 409.

15   Another example would be the various tax incentives offered under schemes such as the Business Expansion Scheme (subsequently abolished) to make equity investment more attractive for individuals.

16   See *The Financing of Small Firms, Interim Report of the Committee to Review the Functioning of Financial Institutions* (the Wilson Committee), (Cmnd 7503, 1979); *The Report of the Committee of Inquiry on Small Firms* (the Bolton Committee) (Cmnd 4811, 1971); Chesterman *Small Businesses* (2nd edn, 1982), Ch 4. Also CBI *A share in the future, Building the UK's smaller quoted company sector* (1996).

17   For an interesting discussion of the difficulty in reconciling all the interested parties in purchase back schemes, see Dugan in Farrar (ed) *Repurchase of own shares for New Zealand* in *Contemporary Issues in Company Law* (1987); also Harris and Ramsay, 'An Empirical Investigation of Australian Share Buy-Backs' (1995) 4 Australian Journal of Corporate Law 393.

These are just the advantages which are seen to come from a company having the power to issue redeemable shares and the power to purchase back its own shares as Professor Gower outlined in the consultative document, *The Purchase by a Company of its Own Shares*, which preceded the legislative changes[18]. The provisions complement one another and together provide a flexible equity capital structure for such companies.

A company may issue redeemable shares, envisaging from the outset that the shareholder's commitment will be a short-term one or at least for a definite period. The company will have the use of the capital for this period while the investor knows that he will not be locked in. The purchase-back powers, on the other hand, enable the company at some point in the future to buy back shares without having to anticipate that eventuality at the time of issue. As far as investors are concerned, the possibility that the company itself will purchase the shares reduces the chances of their being locked in to the company.

It was also thought that these new powers might accommodate family re-arrangements, for example, by enabling founding shareholders to resign and realise their investment without the remaining family members being required personally to fund the purchase back of their shares. The provisions might offer a means of dealing with the holdings of deceased members or buying out discontented shareholders. Such schemes might also be used to provide employee shareholdings which the company could purchase back when the employment was terminated.

All of these factors pointed towards these powers being of greatest use in private companies. Indeed Professor Gower found it difficult to identify reasons why public companies would need these powers, questions of marketability and equity finance gaps being irrelevant there[19]. The reasons suggested were that these powers would enable such companies to use up surplus funds and, in the case of unlisted public companies, would provide shareholders with a purchaser for their shares. Overall the provisions would give these companies a more flexible capital structure.

In fact, listed public companies have made considerable use of these provisions, particularly in recent years, and it is now very common for public companies to seek authority from their shareholders to purchase back their own shares. There are a number of reasons why public companies are now using these powers. Many of these companies have openly conceded that buy-backs, as they are called, are a means of enhancing earnings per share when market conditions make this difficult otherwise. In addition, cash-rich companies have returned capital to shareholders to enable the shareholders to make their individual investment decisions with regard to that capital. Such a strategy can be seen as indicative of a management lacking ideas or, alternatively, as indicative of sensible management resisting unsuitable diversifications simply to reduce their cash holdings. Many companies which were cash-rich at the end of the 1980s used the cash in unsuitable takeover bids which subsequently turned into disastrous investments. Buy-backs are seen as a sign that management has resisted the temptation to pursue such policies in the mid-1990s. Buy-backs can also prove attractive to institutional shareholders who, because of the size of their holdings, find it difficult to offload their holdings in the market in the normal way.

One concern with buy-back powers is that public companies might use these powers to buy up shares in the market which might otherwise be available to a would-be bidder so providing a defensive mechanism against takeover bids. This possibility is restricted by the Takeover Code which prevents any redemption or purchase by an offeree (target) company of its own shares without shareholder approval during the course of an offer

---

18   Cmnd 7944, 1980.
19   Cmnd 7944, 1980, para 16.

or even before the date of the offer if the board of the offeree company has reason to believe that a bona fide offer might be imminent[20].

The potential for abuse of the provisions by public and private companies was recognised from the outset by Parliament and dealt with by the imposition of very stringent procedural requirements which are set out in the statutory provisions. These are designed to ensure that the powers can only be exercised in certain circumstances, using certain funds and in the full glare of publicity. A final point to remember is that the exercise of these powers may have tax consequences for both the company and the shareholders involved[1] and that factor will weigh heavily in any decision to use these provisions.

The statutory scheme

The statutory provisions are extremely detailed and complex so it may be useful to start with a brief summary of the position. The provisions governing redemption and purchase are practically identical and so will be considered together.

Basically, redemption or purchase back must be authorised by the articles and must be carried out by way of a special or ordinary resolution (although private companies may use the written resolution procedure). Only certain specified funds may be used to finance the scheme and there are numerous disclosure requirements to ensure that the transaction is done openly. On purchase or redemption, the shares are cancelled so reducing the company's issued capital. However, because of the requirement to establish a capital redemption reserve (discussed below), a reduction of capital does not occur save in the exceptional case where a private company purchases back or redeems out of capital.

Strict adherence to the procedures is required for it is only purchase or redemption in accordance with the statutory provisions which are permissible. Any non-compliance with the statutory requirements will not be treated as a mere procedural irregularity capable of being waived or dispensed with or validated by unanimous agreement of all members entitled to vote at meetings of the company[2] but will be a breach of the general prohibition on a company acquiring its own shares[3]. The company will be liable on conviction to a fine, every officer of the company who is in default will be liable to imprisonment or a fine, and the purported acquisition will be void[4].

---

20   Takeover Code, r 37.3. There is an exception for redemption or purchase in pursuance of a contract entered into earlier than the offer.

1   For a discussion of the tax position, see *Butterworths UK Tax Guide 1997–98* (1998); *Butterworths Simon's Direct Tax Service* D 2.507–512.

2   See *Acatos & Hutcheson plc v Watson* [1995] 1 BCLC 218; also *Re SH & Co (Realisations) 1990 Ltd* [1993] BCLC 1309 at 1316 (here the court considered the statutory scheme relating to the giving of financial assistance by a company for the purchase of its own shares which is very similar to the scheme governing redemption and purchase of shares); *Precision Dippings Ltd v Precision Dippings Marketing Ltd* [1986] Ch 447 at 456–457, [1985] 3 WLR 812 at 816–817 (failure to comply with the statutory procedures governing auditors' reports when the company proposed to make a distribution on the basis of qualified accounts). However, an error which is so insignificant that no one could be thought to be prejudiced by its correction will not invalidate the whole scheme: *Re Willaire Systems plc* [1987] BCLC 67.

3   Ie that contained in CA 1985, s 143(1).

4   Ibid, s 143(3).

GENERAL REQUIREMENTS

In order for a company to purchase or redeem its own shares, it must be authorised to do so by its articles[5]. Redeemable shares cannot be issued unless the company has other shares in issue which are not redeemable[6] and, after a purchase-back scheme has been effected, the company must have other shares in issue at least some of which are not redeemable[7]. The company must be left with at least two members unless it is a private company when one will suffice[8]. Subject to the statutory provisions, the redemption of shares may be effected on such terms and in such manner as may be provided by the company's articles[9]. Details of the terms of issue of redeemable shares must be included in a note to the accounts[10].

Shares to be redeemed or purchased must be fully paid up (otherwise the creditors would loose a valuable asset on liquidation, namely uncalled capital) and payment to the shareholders must be made at the time when the shares are purchased or redeemed[11]. This is to prevent companies from oppressing shareholders by redeeming or purchasing their shares so depriving them of their status as members but without actually paying over the proceeds. This requirement also resolves difficulties of timing and valuation.

More specific requirements apply depending on whether the share purchases are 'off-market' or 'market' purchases.

OFF-MARKET AND MARKET PURCHASES

A purchase by a company of its own shares is 'off-market' if the shares either:

(i)   are purchased otherwise than on a recognised investment exchange[12]; or
(ii) are purchased on a recognised investment exchange but are not subject to a marketing arrangement[13] on that investment exchange[14].

5   Ibid, ss 159(1) and 162(1). Standard provisions are contained in Table A, arts 3 and 35.
6   CA 1985, s 159(2).
7   Ibid, s 162(3).
8   Ibid, s 24.
9   Ibid, s 160(3). Note that s 160(3) only applies to redemption and not to purchase schemes. In response to concerns as to the matters to be dealt with in the articles, the Department of Trade and Industry decided to repeal s 160(3) and to add a new provision (s 159A inserted by Companies Act 1989, s 133(2)) which would have required matters relating, for example, to the date of redemption, the circumstances of redemption, and the amount payable on redemption to be laid down in the articles. Subsequent consultation suggested that s 159A was inflexible and would create more problems than it would solve. The Department has now indicated that s 159A (which has never been brought into force) will be repealed when the next legislative opportunity arises: *Company Law Review: Terms and Manner of Redemption of Redeemable Shares. Sections 159A and 160(3) of the Companies Act 1985* (November 1993, DTI). This leaves s 160(3) as the governing provision.
10 Ibid, Sch 4, para 38(2).
11 Ibid, ss 159(3), 162(2).
12 'Recognised investment exchange' means a body (other than an overseas investment exchange) declared by an order of the Secretary of State for the time being in force to be a recognised investment exchange for the purposes of the Financial Services Act 1986: CA 1985, s 163(4).
13 For this purpose, a company's shares are subject to a marketing arrangement on a recognised investment exchange if either (1) they are listed under Part IV of the Financial Services Act 1986, or (2) the company has been afforded facilities for dealings in those shares to take place on that investment exchange without prior permission for individual transactions from the authority governing that investment exchange and without limit as to the time during which those facilities are to be available: CA 1985, s 163(2).
14 Ibid, s 163(1).

A purchase by a company of its own shares is a 'market purchase' if it is a purchase made on a recognised investment exchange, other than a purchase which is on a recognised investment exchange but not subject to a marketing arrangement on that exchange[15]. Essentially private companies and unlisted public companies will make off-market purchases while public listed companies will normally be subject to the market purchase regime although in some instances they may transact off-market purchases.

The purpose behind this distinction is to impose a lower level of regulation on market purchases in recognition of the fact that the market authorities, essentially the Stock Exchange, impose their own regulatory requirements[16] which coupled with the higher degree of publicity attaching to such purchases should be sufficient to deter any abuses.

Thus, in relation to an off-market purchase, a specific contract of purchase must be approved in advance by the company in general meeting[17]. Before the contract is entered into, the terms of the proposed contract must be authorised by a special resolution of the company[18]. The authority conferred by the company in general meeting may be varied, revoked or from time to time renewed by a further special resolution[19]. In the case of a public company, the authority must specify a date on which it is to expire and in a resolution conferring or renewing authority that date must not be later than 18 months after that on which the resolution is passed[20].

It should be noted with respect to off-market purchases that the special resolution to confer, vary, revoke or renew authority is not effective if any member of the company holding shares to which the resolution relates exercises the voting rights carried by any of those shares in voting on the resolution and the resolution would not have been passed if he had not done so[1]. Such a resolution is not effective unless (if the proposed contract is in writing) a copy of the contract or (if not) a written memorandum of its terms is available for inspection by members of the company both at the company's registered office for not less than 15 days ending with the date of the meeting at which the resolution is passed, and at the meeting itself[2].

Private companies may deal with these matters by way of a unanimous written resolution[3] instead of by resolution in general meeting and consequential changes are then made to the procedures[4]. First, the disenfranchisement referred to above does not apply because it would mean that unanimity could not be achieved. Instead the member holding shares to which the resolution relates is not for these purposes regarded as a member who would be entitled to attend and vote[5]. He does not count therefore for the purpose of achieving unanimity. Secondly, instead of details of the proposed contract being available before and at the meeting, details must have been supplied to each member at or before the time when the resolution was supplied to him for signature[6].

In the case of market purchases, the company may not make a market purchase unless the purchase has first been authorised by an ordinary resolution in general

---

15   Ibid, s 163(3).
16   See The Listing Rules, ch 15, the requirements of which mainly relate to notification of proposed and actual purchases.
17   CA 1985, s 164(1).
18   Ibid, s 164(2).
19   Ibid, s 164(3).
20   Ibid, s 164(4).
1   Ibid, s 164(5).
2   Ibid, s 164(6).
3   See ibid, s 381A.
4   Ibid, s 381A(7), Sch 15A, para 5.
5   Ibid, Sch 15A, para 5(2).
6   Ibid, Sch 15A, para 5(3).

meeting[7]. The authority may be general or limited to the purchase of shares of any particular class or description and may be conditional or unconditional[8]. The authority must specify the maximum number of shares which may be acquired, determine both the maximum and minimum price which may be paid for the shares[9] and specify a date on which the authority is to expire which must in any event be not later than 18 months from the date of the resolution[10]. Any resolution conferring, varying, revoking or renewing such an authority to purchase must be sent to the registrar of companies within 15 days[11].

No question of disenfranchising any shares arises in this context since the authority is not specifically aimed at any particular shares but is a general authority.

FINANCING OF REDEMPTION AND PURCHASE-BACK SCHEMES

A crucial element in any redemption or purchase-back scheme, obviously, is the source of the funding which will pay for it. Here the danger to creditors is that capital will be returned to the shareholders leaving a shell with inadequate assets to pay off the company's creditors in full. The legislation attempts to prevent that happening by providing, subject to one major exception, that companies must fund redemption or purchase-back:

(i) out of distributable profits[12]; or the proceeds of a fresh issue of shares made for the purpose; and

(ii) any premium payable on redemption or purchase must be paid out of distributable profits of the company[13].

Essentially, the company must use funds (distributable profits) which could have gone to the shareholders anyway in the form of dividend, or must substitute for the capital which they are repaying, new capital brought in by a fresh issue of shares. Neither has any impact on the company's creditors so there is no erosion of the capital maintenance doctrine. Furthermore, to ensure that this is in fact the case, the company must set up a capital redemption reserve fund.

Where shares of a company are redeemed or purchased wholly out of the company's profits, the amount by which the company's issued share capital is diminished on cancellation of the shares redeemed or purchased must be transferred to a reserve called 'the capital redemption reserve'[14].

If the shares are redeemed or purchased wholly or partly out of the proceeds of a fresh issue and the aggregate amount of those proceeds is less than the aggregate nominal value of the shares redeemed or purchased, the amount of the difference must

---

7   Ibid, s 166(1).
8   Ibid, s 166(2).
9   The price may be determined either by specifying a particular sum or providing a basis or formula for calculating the price in question without reference to any person's discretion or opinion: ibid, s 166(6). This is to ensure that the directors are not in a position to enter into transactions at varying prices, depending on their relationship with the vendors.
10   Ibid, s 166(3), (4).
11   Ibid, s 166(7). This is an exception to the general rule that ordinary resolutions do not have to be filed with the registrar of companies.
12   Ie profits out of which it could lawfully make a distribution within the meaning of ibid, s 263(2): s 181(a).
13   Ibid, ss 160(1), 162(2). This is subject to certain exceptions where the shares redeemed or purchased back were originally issued at a premium in which case the proceeds of a fresh issue may be used to pay the premium to a limited extent: see ss 160(2), 162(2).
14   Ibid, s 170(1).

be transferred to the capital redemption reserve[15]; but this does not apply if the proceeds of the fresh issue are applied by the company in making a redemption or purchase of its own shares in addition to a payment out of capital[16].

The provisions of the Companies Act 1985[17] relating to the reduction of a company's share capital apply as if the capital redemption reserve were paid-up share capital of the company, except that the reserve may be applied by the company in paying up its unissued shares to be allotted to members of the company as fully paid bonus shares[18].

CONSEQUENCES OF A FAILURE TO REDEEM OR PURCHASE

If, having agreed to do so, a company fails to purchase or redeem shares, the company is not liable in damages in respect of any such failure[19]. Specific performance may still be available but not if the company shows that it is unable to meet the costs of redeeming or purchasing the shares in question out of distributable profits[20].

CANCELLATION

Shares once purchased or redeemed are treated as cancelled thus reducing the company's issued (but not authorised) capital[1]. This is designed to prevent companies trafficking in their shares and to reduce the impact which purchase-back schemes can have within the company. For example, the directors are not able to retain the shares and vote them as they see fit although they are able to re-issue shares, of course, up to the authorised limit. Cancellation should increase the earnings of the remaining shares although this depends on factors such the market's perception of the wisdom of redemption or purchase, the price paid and whether there has been a fresh issue of shares.

DISCLOSURE REQUIREMENTS

Within 28 days of any shares purchased (whether on or off-market) being delivered to the company, a return must be delivered to the registrar of companies stating the number and nominal value of the shares and the date on which they were delivered to the company[2]. In the case of a public company, further details relating to the aggregate amount paid by the company for the shares, and the maximum and minimum paid by the company for shares of each class purchased have to be included[3]. A copy of any contract of purchase (whether on or off-market), or a written memorandum of its terms,

---

15   Ibid, s 170(2).
16   Ibid, s 170(3). Payments out of capital are discussed below.
17   Ie ibid, ss 135–141. Reduction of capital is discussed in Chapter 17.
18   Ibid, s 170(4).
19   Ibid, s 178. The section is concerned with direct claims for damages as a result of a breach by the company of its duty to redeem the shares. It does not preclude the recovery of damages claimed by a plaintiff against the company for breach of a financing agreement even though the measure of damages for that breach may well be the equivalent of damages for failure to redeem: *Barclays Bank plc v British and Commonwealth Holdings plc* [1996] 1 BCLC 1, CA.
20   CA 1985, s 178(3). As to the position where the company goes into winding up, see s 178(4)–(6).
1   Ibid, ss 160(4), 162(2).
2   Ibid, s 169(1).
3   Ibid, s 169(2).

must be kept at the company's registered office for 10 years from the date of purchase[4] and must be available for inspection by any member of the company and, if it is a public company, by any other person[5]. Details of any purchases must also be given in the directors' report[6].

Private companies – redemption or purchase out of capital

A provision which potentially has a significant impact on creditors is that which allows private companies in certain circumstances to redeem or purchase back shares out of capital. Given the potential danger to creditors, it is not surprising that the statutory provisions surround such purchases with even more stringent requirements than those already noted.

CONDITIONS FOR PAYMENT OUT OF CAPITAL

A private company must be specifically authorised by its articles to redeem or purchase its own shares otherwise than out of its distributable profits or the proceeds of a fresh issue of shares[7].

As for the amount which may be paid out of capital, the company must first use any available distributable profits[8] and the proceeds of any fresh issue made for the purpose of purchase or redemption before resorting to capital with the amount then needed being described as the permissible capital payment[9].

Any payment out of capital must be approved by a special resolution[10]. The resolution is ineffective if any member of the company holding shares to which the resolution relates exercises the voting rights carried by any of those shares in voting on the resolution and the resolution would not have been passed if he had not done so[11]. The resolution is also ineffective unless the required statutory declaration and auditors' report (discussed below) are available for inspection by members of the company at the meeting at which the resolution is passed[12].

Private companies may deal with these matters by way of a unanimous written resolution[13] instead of by resolution in general meeting with consequential changes to the procedure[14]. First, the disenfranchisement referred to above does not apply because it would mean that unanimity could not be achieved. Instead the member holding shares to which the resolution relates is not, for these purposes, regarded as a member who is

---

4 Ibid, s 169(4).
5 Ibid, s 169(5).
6 Ibid, Sch 7, Part II.
7 Ibid, s 171(1). An authority to purchase is insufficient; the article must specifically make provision for purchase out of capital. See Table A, art 35.
8 Defined in this instance in accordance with CA 1985, s 172 rather than ss 270–275 which apply generally.
9 Ibid, s 171(3). See s 171(4)–(6) as to the necessary transfers to or reduction of the capital redemption reserve in these cases.
10 Ibid, s 173(2). The resolution must be passed on or within the week immediately following the date on which the directors make the required statutory declaration under s 173(3) (see below) and the actual payment out of capital must be made no more than five and not later than seven weeks after the date of the resolution: s 174(1).
11 Ibid, s 174(2).
12 Ibid, s 174(4).
13 See ibid, s 381A.
14 Ibid, s 381A(7), Sch 15A, para 6.

entitled to attend and vote[15]. He simply does not count for the purposes of achieving unanimity in the written process. Secondly, instead of the statutory declaration and auditors' report, discussed below, being available before and at the meeting, details must have been supplied to each member at or before the time when the resolution was supplied to him for signature[16].

STATUTORY DECLARATION AND AUDITORS' REPORT

The company's directors must make a statutory declaration specifying the amount of the permissible capital payment for the shares in question and stating that, having made full inquiry into the affairs and prospects of the company, they have formed the opinion:

(1) as regards its initial situation immediately following the date on which the payment out of capital is proposed to be made, that there will be no grounds on which the company could then be found unable to pay its debts[17], and

(2) as regards its prospects for the year immediately following that date that, having regard to their intentions with respect to the management of the company's business during that year and to the amount and character of the company's financial resources which will in their view be available to the company during that year, the company will be able to continue to carry on business as a going concern (and will accordingly be able to pay its debts as they fall due) throughout that year[18].

This emphasis on the issue of solvency reflects the overriding concern that creditors must be protected from injudicious use of purchase-back schemes.

Annexed to this declaration must be a report by the company's auditors stating that:

(a) they have inquired into the company's state of affairs;

(b) the amount specified in the declaration as the permissible capital payment for the shares in question is in their view properly determined in accordance with the relevant statutory provisions; and

(c) they are not aware of anything to indicate that the opinion expressed by the directors in their declaration is unreasonable in all the circumstances[19].

Any director who makes this statutory declaration without having reasonable grounds for the opinion expressed in it is liable to imprisonment or a fine or both[20].

More significant, however, is the potential liability where a company is being wound up and it has made a payment out of capital in respect of purchase or redemption of any of its own shares and the aggregate of its assets and the amounts paid by way of contribution to its assets are not sufficient for the payment of its debts and liabilities and the expenses of winding up[1]. In those circumstances, if the winding up commenced within one year of the date on which the relevant payment out of capital was made, then:

15 Ibid, Sch 15A, para 6(2).
16 Ibid, Sch 15A, para 6(3).
17 Ibid, s 173(3)(a). In forming their opinion for these purposes, the directors must take into account the same liabilities (including contingent and prospective liabilities) as would be relevant under Insolvency Act 1986, s 122 to the question whether a company is unable to pay its debts: CA 1985, s 173(4).
18 Ibid, s 173(3)(b).
19 Ibid, s 173(5).
20 Ibid, ss 173(6), 730, Sch 24.
1   See Insolvency Act 1986, s 76(1).

    (i)   the person from whom the shares were redeemed or purchased; and
    (ii) the directors who signed the statutory declaration;

are, so as to enable the insufficiency to be met, liable to contribute to the company's assets[2].

A person from whom any of the shares were so redeemed or purchased is liable to contribute an amount not exceeding so much of the relevant payment as was made by the company in respect of his shares; and the directors are jointly and severally liable with that person to contribute that amount[3]. A director will be excused liability if he shows that he had reasonable grounds for forming the opinion set out in the declaration[4]. Presumably he will claim that he was justified in relying on the auditors who, after all, agreed with his opinion.

DISCLOSURE REQUIREMENTS

Various disclosure requirements also apply here which are aimed at bringing the proposed payment to the attention of creditors who may wish to apply to the court for an order prohibiting payment.

Within the week immediately following the date of the resolution for payment out of capital, the company must cause to be published in the *Gazette* a notice;

    (a) stating that the company has approved a payment out of capital for the purpose of acquiring its own shares by purchase or redemption (as the case may be);
    (b) specifying the amount of the permissible capital payment and the date of the special resolution;
    (c) stating that the directors' statutory declaration and the auditors' report are available for inspection at the company's registered office; and
    (d) stating that any creditor of the company may at any time within the five weeks immediately following the date of the resolution for payment out of capital apply to the court for an order prohibiting payment[5].

A similar notice must be published in a national newspaper or a notice in writing to that effect must be given to each creditor[6]. A copy of the directors' statutory declaration and the auditors' report must also be sent to the registrar of companies at the same time[7].

OBJECTIONS BY CREDITORS OR MEMBERS

In recognition of the potential for abuse when companies are permitted to redeem or purchase back out of capital and the fact that this essentially allows companies to reduce capital without the sanction of the court[8], provision is made for an application by an objecting creditor or member to the court for cancellation of the resolution. It should be noted that no such procedure is available in respect of purchase or redemption in any other instance.

---

2   Ibid, s 76(2).
3   Ibid, s 76(3).
4   Ibid, s 76(2)(b).
5   CA 1985, s 175(1).
6   Ibid, s 175(2).
7   Ibid, s 175(5).
8   As would be required by ibid, s 135.

An application must be within five weeks of the date on which the resolution was passed and may be made by any member of the company other than one who consented to or voted in favour of the resolution; or by any creditor of the company[9].

No minimum shareholding or debt is required but obviously the more insignificant the amounts, the less weight is likely to be attached to the objections. The difficulty for those objecting, particularly if they are members, is to persuade the court to set aside something which, in the case of an off-market purchase, has been approved by a special resolution, ie by 75% of those voting not including the interested shareholders. The courts in such circumstances tend to refuse redress, stating that the members know best and that it is not for the court to interfere in what is essentially a difference as to business policy[10]. Dissentient members may prefer, given that this will be a private company, to present their objections, if possible, within the context of a more broadly based petition seeking relief against unfairly prejudicial conduct[11].

The jurisdiction of the court on any application is open-ended. The court may adjourn the proceedings in order that an arrangement can be made for the purchase of the interests of dissentient members or for the protection of dissentient creditors (as the case may be)[12]. Without prejudice to such powers, the court must make an order[13] on such terms and conditions as it thinks fit either confirming or cancelling the resolution. The court's order may, in particular, provide for the purchase by the company of the shares of any members and for the reduction of the company's capital accordingly[14].

FINANCIAL ASSISTANCE BY A COMPANY FOR THE ACQUISITION OF ITS OWN SHARES

Background

Having prohibited companies from purchasing their own shares, it soon became apparent that an equally unacceptable practice was that of companies giving financial assistance to enable other persons to buy the company's shares. The classic abuse was for a takeover bidder to borrow money from a bank, make a successful bid for a company and then to repay the bank out of the company's funds after the takeover. The Greene Committee reporting in 1927[15] recommended an extension to the prohibition on companies purchasing their own shares to cover the giving of financial assistance and this was introduced in the Companies Act 1929. The Jenkins Committee in 1962 in turn recommended that the provisions should be retained and strengthened[16]. It explained its concerns about this sort of practice as follows:

> If people who cannot provide the funds necessary to acquire control of a company from their own resources, or by borrowing on their own credit, gain control of a company with large assets on the understanding that they will use funds of the

9   Ibid, s 176(1).
10 The position would not be dissimilar to that of shareholders trying to persuade the court not to confirm a reduction of capital sanctioned by special resolution. They have usually been unsuccessful. See the discussion of reduction of capital in Chapter 17.
11 Ie under CA 1985, s 459, discussed in detail in Chapter 28.
12 Ibid, s 177(1).
13 Within 15 days of any order being made, or such longer period as the court may direct, the company must deliver an office copy of the order to the registrar of companies: ibid, s 176(3)(b).
14 Ibid, s 177(3).
15 Report of the Company Law Amendment Committee (Cmnd 2657).
16 Report of the Company Law Committee (1962, Cmnd 1749), para 173.

company to pay for their shares, it seems to us all too likely that in many cases the company will be made to part with its funds either on inadequate security or for an illusory consideration[17].

It then noted that when the facts are ultimately discovered, the company's remedies against the bidder will be worthless, either because he has disappeared, or has disposed of his assets, or is insolvent, and minority shareholders and creditors suffer accordingly[18]. This is the classic asset-stripping type of financial assistance.

Another type of abuse arising from financial assistance which has attracted comment in recent years is the use of company funds to fund share support schemes as an element of a takeover strategy.[18a] In the 1980s many takeovers of companies were carried out on a share-for-share basis with shareholders in the target company being offered shares in the bidder company rather than cash for their shares. For the scheme to work, the value of the shares in the bidder company had to be maintained at a level which made them attractive to the shareholders in the target. This might be done by generating purchases of the bidder's shares by giving financial assistance to persons to buy shares in the bidder or by indemnifying purchasers against any loss incurred on their purchases. The result is to deceive the market as to the true nature of the purchases and so manipulate the company's share price. In this wider context, therefore, financial assistance can distort the equity markets.

The statutory scheme

The original statutory provision governing financial assistance was s 45 of the Companies Act 1929 which was replaced by s 54 of the Companies Act 1948 which made it an offence for a company to give financial assistance for the purpose of or in connection with the acquisition, by purchase or subscription, of its own shares. Concerns arose as to the scope of this provision[19] and it was repealed and replaced by the Companies Act 1981. The current statutory provisions are to be found in the Companies Act 1985 ss 151–158.

BASIC POSITION

Subject to certain exceptions noted below, where a person is acquiring or is proposing to acquire any shares in a company, it is not lawful for the company or any of its subsidiaries[20] to give financial assistance directly or indirectly for the purpose of that acquisition before or at the same time as the acquisition takes place[1]. Equally, where a person has acquired shares in a company and any liability has been incurred (by that or any other person) for the purpose of that acquisition, it is not lawful for the company

---

17   See Cmnd 1749, para 173.
18   See Cmnd 1749, para 176.
18a   For an account of one of the most controversial share suport schemes, see the *Report of the Inspectors into Guinness plc, Investigation under ss 432(2) and 442 of the Companies Act 1985* (HMSO, 1997); also *Saunders v United Kingdom (Case 43/1994/490/572)* [1997] BCC 872, ECtHR.
19   See *Belmont Finance Corpn Ltd v Williams Furniture Ltd (No 2)* [1980] 1 All ER 393 at 402 which queried whether a transaction entered into in the ordinary course of business, even if for fair value, might be caught if any part of the purpose for the transaction was to provide financial assistance.
20   The prohibition applies only to subsidiaries registered under the Companies Act 1985 and therefore a foreign subsidiary of an English parent company can give financial assistance for the acquisition of the latter's shares: *Arab Bank plc v Merchantile Holdings Ltd* [1994] Ch 71, [1994] 2 All ER 74.
1   CA 1985, s 151(1).

or any of its subsidiaries to give financial assistance directly or indirectly for the purpose of reducing or discharging any liability so incurred[2].

If a company acts in contravention of this section, it is liable to a fine and every officer in default is liable on conviction to imprisonment or a fine or both[3]. The civil consequences are discussed below.

Financial assistance is widely defined[4] to include, inter alia, financial assistance given by way of gift, guarantee, security or indemnity[5], or by way of release or waiver, or by way of a loan or any other agreement under which any of the obligations of the person giving the assistance are to be fulfilled at a time when in accordance with the agreement, any obligation of another party to the agreement remains unfulfilled, or any other financial assistance given by a company the net assets[6] of which are thereby reduced to a material extent or which has no net assets[7].

In *Charterhouse Investment Trust Ltd v Tempest Diesels Ltd*[8] Hoffmann J said that the commercial realities of the transaction as a whole must be considered in deciding whether a transaction can properly be described as the giving of financial assistance by the company, bearing in mind that the section is a penal provision and should not be strained to cover transactions which are not fairly within it[9].

The key elements are the acquisition of shares in the company and the giving of financial assistance by a company or any of its subsidiaries, directly or indirectly, for the purpose of the acquisition, before or at the same time as the acquisition, or to reduce any liability incurred in the acquisition[10].

Among the forms which financial assistance might take is the purchase of an asset at an overvalue so putting the vendor in funds with which to acquire the company's shares[11]. The payment of a debt owed by the company itself cannot be financial

---

2   Ibid, s 151(2). A reference to a company giving financial assistance for the purpose of reducing or discharging a liability incurred by a person for the purpose of the acquisition of shares includes its giving such assistance for the purpose of wholly or partially restoring his financial position to what it was before the acquisition took place: s 152(3)(b).

3   Ibid, ss 151(3), 730, Sch 24. Sealy *Cases and Materials in Company Law* (6th edn, 1996), p 390 makes the point that the draftsman has thoughtlessly made liable the very company whose protection it is his concern to promote.

4   See CA 1985, s 152(1)(a).

5   Each of the terms used here (guarantee, security, indemnity, release, waiver) can properly be described as a legal term of art: *Barclays Bank plc v British and Commonwealth Holdings plc* [1996] 1 All ER 381 at 395, [1996] 1 BCLC 1 at 39, CA.

6   Net assets is defined as the aggregate of the company's assets less the aggregate of its liabilities: CA 1985, s 152(2). Contrast this with the definition of net assets in ibid, s 154(2) and see *Parlett v Guppys (Bridport) Ltd* [1996] 2 BCLC 34 at 42 on this point.

7   See *Parlett v Guppys (Bridport) Ltd* [1996] 2 BCLC 34 at 45 where the suggestion was made that a reduction of 5% or more would be material for these purposes. Nourse LJ noted that there can be no rule of thumb, it is a question of degree to be answered on the facts of the particular case.

8   [1986] BCLC 1.

9   [1986] BCLC 1 at 10 (referring to CA 1948, s 54 but his comments are equally valid in relation to CA 1985, s 151); see also *Barclays Bank plc v British and Commonwealth Holdings plc* [1996] 1 BCLC 1 at 40, CA: '… the section requires that there should be assistance or help for the purpose of acquiring shares and that that assistance should be financial.'

10 As the facts in many financial assistance schemes can be extremely complex, it may be useful to keep in mind Lord Denning's comments in *Wallersteiner v Moir* [1974] 3 All ER 217 at 238, [1974] 1 WLR 991 at 1014, where he said: 'You look at the company's money and see what has become of it. You look at the company's shares and see into whose hands they have gone. You will then soon see if the company's money has been used to finance the purchase.' In the more complex cases, the use of nominee shareholders may cloud the picture but nevertheless this general approach is a good starting point when considering a financial assistance scheme.

11 See *Belmont Finance Corpn Ltd v Williams Furniture Ltd* [1979] Ch 250, [1979] 1 All ER 118, CA.

assistance for that is a mere discharge of a debt[12] but the payment off of a parent company's debt by a subsidiary in order to facilitate an acquisition of the parent company's shares may constitute such assistance[13]. The payment of a dividend does not constitute financial assistance[14].

Where an agreement is capable of being performed in alternative ways, one lawful and one in breach of the provisions on financial assistance, it is to be presumed that the parties intend to carry out the agreement in a lawful and not an unlawful manner[15].

The basic scheme of the provisions then is tolerably clear even if, as we shall see, the detail gives rise to many difficulties of interpretation. Moreover, the legislation does provide for a large number of circumstances when the prohibition does not apply.

EXCEPTIONS

The exceptions fall into three distinct categories:

(i) the 'purpose' exceptions designed to ensure that the width of the prohibition does not inadvertently catch genuine commercial transactions which are in the best interests of the company;

(ii) transactions specifically identified as not being within the prohibition: most are subject to other statutory provisions;

(iii) exemptions provided for those companies whose business it is to give financial assistance in the ordinary course of business and various exemptions designed to facilitate employees' share schemes.

(i)   The 'purpose' exceptions
The 'purpose' category is the one which causes most difficulty. The prohibition against providing financial assistance for the acquisition of shares in a company does not prohibit a company from giving such assistance for the purpose of an acquisition of shares in it or its holding company if:

(1) the company's principal purpose in giving that assistance is not to give it for the purpose of any such acquisition; or

(2) the giving of the assistance for that purpose is but an incidental part of some larger purpose of the company;

and the assistance is given in good faith in the interests of the company[16].

Likewise, the prohibition against providing financial assistance directly or indirectly for the purpose of reducing or discharging a liability which has been incurred in the acquisition of shares in the company does not prohibit the company from giving such assistance if:

(1) its principal purpose in giving the assistance is not to reduce or discharge any

---

12   *Spink (Bournemouth) Ltd v Spink* [1936] Ch 544, [1936] 1 All ER 597.
13   *Armour Hick Northern Ltd v Armour Trust Ltd* [1980] 3 All ER 833, sub nom *Armour Hick Northern Ltd v Whitehouse* [1980] 1 WLR 1520. Note that the assistance does not have to be given to the purchaser, it is financial assistance to whomsoever given provided that it is for the purpose of the purchase of those shares.
14   *Re Wellington Publishing Co Ltd* [1973] 1 NZLR 133. See CA 1985, s 153(3)(a).
15   *Neilson v Stewart* [1991] BCC 713. See also *Brady v Brady* [1989] AC 755, [1988] 2 All ER 617, HL; *Parlett v Guppys (Bridport) Ltd* [1996] 2 BCLC 34.
16   CA 1985, s 153(1).

liability incurred by a person for the purpose of the acquisition of shares in the company or its holding company; or

(2) the reduction or discharge of any such liability is but an incidental part of some larger purpose of the company;

and the assistance is given in good faith in the interests of the company[17].

This 'purpose' exception was considered in detail by the House of Lords in *Brady v Brady*[18].

The facts of this case were extremely complicated but essentially revolved around a scheme of reorganisation of a group of companies which was designed to enable two brothers to split a family business after disagreements between them meant it was impossible to continue as a joint venture. Without going into the labyrinthine complexities of the scheme, it suffices for our purposes to say that M purchased all of the shares in B from O and therefore incurred a liability in so doing, namely the purchase price. That liability was then partly reduced by the transfer of half of B's assets to O. So a liability incurred by M on the acquisition of B's shares was partly reduced or discharged by B's assets.

The question was whether this prima facie case of financial assistance was saved by being within the 'purpose' exception outlined above. What was the principal purpose for the transfer of the assets ? Was the discharge of the liability but an incidental part of a larger purpose ? In either case, was it in the best interests of B ? The Court of Appeal, for varying reasons, thought that the purpose element was satisfied in one way or another but did not accept that the assistance was given in good faith in the interests of the company[19]. The House of Lords, for its part, would have accepted that the assistance was given in good faith in the interests of the company but would not accept that the purpose element had been satisfied.

The starting point, the House of Lords said, was the statutory wording:

(1) its principal purpose in giving the assistance is not to reduce or discharge any liability incurred by a person for the purpose of the acquisition of shares in the company or its holding company; or

(2) the reduction or discharge of any such liability is but an incidental part of some larger purpose of the company;

and the assistance is given in good faith in the interests of the company[20].

It was clear, Lord Oliver said, that this provision contemplated two alternative solutions[1]. The first envisaged a principal and a subsidiary purpose. In Lord Oliver's view, on the facts here the principal purpose of the financial assistance was simply and solely to reduce the indebtedness incurred by M in acquiring B and therefore the transaction was not saved under the first part of the provision. As for the second part, here it was not suggested that the financial assistance was intended to achieve any object other than the reduction or discharge of the indebtedness but that result, it was said, was merely incidental to some larger purpose. The key to being within that element, in Lord Oliver's opinion, was finding some larger overall corporate purpose in which the resultant reduction or discharge of liability was merely incidental. In construing purpose in the context of this provision, he noted:

17   Ibid, s 153(2).
18   [1989] AC 755, [1988] 2 All ER 617, HL; revsg [1988] BCLC 20, CA. See Greaves and Hannigan (1989) 10 Co Law 135, also noted (1988) CLJ 24, 359; [1988] JBL 65, 412. See also *Plaut v Steiner* (1988) 5 BCC 352.
19   See Greaves and Hannigan (1989) 10 Co Law 135 at 137 on the Court of Appeal position.
20   CA 1985, s 153(2).
1   [1989] AC 755 at 778, [1988] 2 All ER 617 at 632.

... there has always to be borne in mind the mischief against which s 151 is aimed. In particular, if the section is not, effectively, to be deprived of any useful application, it is important to distinguish between a purpose and the reason why a purpose is formed. The ultimate reason for forming the purpose of financing the acquisition may, and in most cases probably will, be more important to those making the decision than the immediate transaction itself. But 'larger' is not the same thing as 'more important' nor is 'reason' the same as 'purpose'[2].

The House of Lords thus concluded that the purpose of the transaction was to assist in the financing of the acquisition of the shares although the reason for the transaction was to facilitate a break up of the business which would divide it equally between the two brothers and leave each with a viable business.

In approaching the transaction in this manner the House of Lords focused narrowly on the immediate transaction itself without regard to the financial and commercial advantages in the wider context which were considered by their Lordships to be mere by-products of the scheme[3]. The transaction did therefore amount to the giving of financial assistance which was not saved by the 'purpose' exception. However, as the company was a private company, the parties could have used the statutory provisions which permit private companies to give financial assistance in certain circumstances. This is discussed further below.

Finally, it must be remembered that there is a further limb to the 'purpose' exception, namely that the assistance is given in good faith in the interests of the company. On this aspect, Lord Oliver stated that the words 'in good faith in the interests of the company' form a single composite expression and require that those responsible for procuring the company to provide the assistance act in the genuine belief that it is being done in the company's interests[4]. This was undoubtedly the case in *Brady* where the scheme was necessary to save the company from probable liquidation and so was properly perceived as calculated to advance Brady's corporate and commercial interests and the interests of its employees. It was in the company's interest that it should continue under proper management unhampered by insoluble differences between the directors. As the company was solvent, there was no risk to the interests of present creditors and their position in the long term would be further improved by the restructuring[5]. However, this was not sufficient to save the scheme.

(ii) Transactions identified as permissible

The prohibitions on the giving of financial assistance do not apply to:

(1) a distribution of a company's assets by way of dividend lawfully made[6] or a distribution made in the course of the company's winding up;
(2) the allotment of bonus shares[7];
(3) a reduction of capital duly confirmed by the court[8];

---

2   [1989] AC 755 at 779, [1988] 2 All ER 617 at 633.
3   [1989] AC 755 at 780, [1988] 2 All ER 617 at 633.
4   *Brady v Brady* [1989] AC 755 at 777, [1988] 2 All ER 617 at 632, HL. The time at which this is to be considered is the time at which the assistance is given: *Brady v Brady* supra. If the company was insolvent at that time the assistance could not be given in good faith in the interests of the company: *Plaut v Steiner* (1988) 5 BCC 352.
5   [1989] AC 755 at 778, [1988] 2 All ER 617 at 632.
6   See discussion below.
7   As to bonus shares see discussion in Chapter 15.
8   Ie under CA 1985, s 135. See Chapter 17.

(4)   a redemption or purchase of shares made in accordance with the statutory provisions[9];

(5)   anything done in pursuance of an order of the court under the provisions dealing with compromises and arrangements with creditors and members[10];

(6)   anything done under an arrangement made in pursuance of the statutory provisions enabling liquidators in winding up to accept shares as consideration for the sale of property[11]; or

(7)   anything done under an arrangement[12] made between a company and its creditors which is binding on the creditors by virtue of the statutory provisions relating to such arrangements when made by a company about to be or in the course of being wound up[13].

The prohibition of financial assistance is essentially based on the need to protect creditors against a return of capital to shareholders ahead of a winding up and to prevent the company from having its assets misused[14]. All of the schemes mentioned are subject to statutory requirements designed to ensure the protection of creditors and prevent the misuse of assets and in a number of cases the schemes require the confirmation of the court. There is no need therefore to subject such transactions to the prohibition on financial assistance.

(iii)   Lending in the ordinary course of business and employees' share schemes

This third category provides exemptions for those companies where the lending of money is part of the ordinary business of the company[15] and various exemptions designed to facilitate employees' share schemes[16]. It should be noted that the exemptions in this category may only be relied on by a public company if the company has net assets which are not thereby reduced or, to the extent that those assets are thereby reduced, the financial assistance is provided out of distributable profits[17].

Financial assistance by private companies

As we have already seen, the statutory provisions governing redemption and purchase of a company's own shares are relaxed for private companies[18] and this is also the position regarding financial assistance[19]. This relaxation of the prohibition has proved

---

9   Ie under ibid, ss 159–181, discussed above.
10   Ie under ibid, s 425.
11   Ie under the Insolvency Act 1986, s 110.
12   Ie under ibid, Pt I (ss 1–7).
13   CA 1985, s 153(3).
14   *Wallersteiner v Moir* [1974] 3 All ER 217 at 239, [1974] 1 WLR 991 at 1014, per Denning LJ.
15   CA 1985, s 153(4)(a); see *Steen v Law* [1964] AC 287, [1963] 3 All ER 770.
16   CA 1985, s 153(4)(b), (bb), (c). For the definition of 'employees' share scheme', see s 743.
17   Ibid, s 154(1).
18   As noted above, only private companies are entitled to fund redemption or purchase back out of capital: ibid s 171.
19   The Jenkins Committee Report (1962, Cmnd 1749), paras 178–187 would have applied the relaxations to all companies. This would have avoided many of the complex questions of interpretation which arise under ss 151–153 but it is not possible now with regard to public companies in the light of the requirements of the Second EC Directive, art 23; Second Council Directive of 13 December 1976 (77/91/EEC) OJ C 31.1.1977, 1–13. Article 23(1) provides that a company may not advance funds, nor make loans, nor provide security, with a view to the acquisition of its shares by a third party.

of great importance in practice, particularly in terms of facilitating management buy-outs which have become quite common in recent years[20].

A private company may give financial assistance for the acquisition of its own shares[1] only if the company has net assets[2] which are not thereby reduced or, to the extent that they are reduced, if the assistance is provided out of distributable profits[3]. In other words, if the net assets are to be reduced then the financial assistance must come out of the fund which would otherwise be available to the shareholders for dividends, namely distributable profits. This ensures that creditors cannot be disadvantaged in such circumstances.

The procedural requirements are extensive and in many respects identical to those already considered in relation to redemption or purchase of a company's own shares out of capital. Non-compliance with these statutory requirements will not be treated as a mere procedural irregularity capable of being waived or dispensed with or validated by unanimous agreement of all members entitled to vote at meetings of the company[4]. Non-compliance will mean that the relaxation provisions will not apply and there will be a breach of the statutory prohibition on the giving of financial assistance with all the consequences of unenforceability and liability to penal sanctions which that entails[5].

GENERAL REQUIREMENTS

The giving of financial assistance must be approved by special resolution of the company in general meeting[6] or the company may opt to use the written resolution procedure[7]. Any such special resolution must be passed on the date on which the directors of that company make the statutory declaration referred to below, or within the week immediately following that date[8].

STATUTORY DECLARATION AND AUDITORS' REPORT

The directors of the company proposing to give financial assistance must make a statutory declaration which must:

---

20 See Lumsden (1987) JBL 111.
1 A private company may also give financial assistance for the acquisition of shares in its holding company, if that company is a private company: ibid, s 155(1); but a subsidiary may not give financial assistance for the acquisition of shares in the holding company if the subsidiary is also a subsidiary of a public company which is itself a subsidiary of the holding company: s 155(3).
2 Defined ibid, ss 154(2), s 155(2).
3 Ibid, s 155(2).
4 *Re S H & Co (Realisations) 1990 Ltd* [1993] BCLC 1309 at 1316; see also *Precision Dippings Ltd v Precision Dippings Marketing Ltd* [1985] BCLC 385 at 388–389.
5 *Re S H & Co (Realisations) 1990 Ltd* [1993] BCLC 1309 at 1317. The very severity of the consequences of non-compliance may encourage some leniency on the part of the court towards errors in compliance: see *Re S H & Co (Realisations) 1990 Ltd* [1993] BCLC 1309 at 1319. See also *Re Willaire Systems plc* [1987] BCLC 67.
6 CA 1985, s 155(4), except where the company proposing to give the financial assistance is a wholly-owned subsidiary when no resolution is required. Where the financial assistance is to be given by a company in a case where the acquisition of shares is an acquisition of shares in its holding company, that holding company and any other company which is both the company's holding company and a subsidiary of that other holding company (except in any case a company which is a wholly owned subsidiary), must also approve by special resolution in general meeting the giving of the financial assistance: s 155(5). 'Holding company' is defined in s 736.
7 Ibid, s 381A.
8 Ibid, s 157(1).

(1) contain such particulars of the financial assistance to be given, and of the business of the company of which they are directors, as may be prescribed[9] and must identify the person to whom the assistance is to be given; and

(2) state that the directors have formed the opinion[10], as regards the company's initial situation immediately following the date on which the assistance is proposed to be given, that there will be no ground on which it could then be found to be unable to pay its debts, and either:

    (a) if it is intended to commence the winding up of the company within 12 months of that date, that the company will be able to pay its debts in full within 12 months of the commencement of the winding up, or

    (b) in any other case, that the company will be able to pay its debts as they fall due during the year immediately following that date[11].

Annexed to this declaration must be a report by the company's auditors stating that they have inquired into the company's state of affairs and that they are not aware of anything to indicate that the opinion expressed by the directors in their declaration as to any of the matters specified is unreasonable in all the circumstances[12]. Any director who makes this statutory declaration without having reasonable grounds for the opinion expressed in the declaration is liable on conviction to imprisonment or a fine or both[13].

The special resolution is not effective unless the statutory declaration, together with the auditors' report, is available for inspection by members of the company at the meeting at which the resolution is passed[14]. Where a private company uses the written resolution procedure then these documents must be made available to the member at or before the time at which the resolution is supplied to him for signature[15].

Strict time limits must be complied with and the financial assistance must not be given before the expiry of the period of four weeks beginning with the date on which the special resolution is passed unless every member of the company who is entitled to vote at general meetings of the company voted in favour of the resolution[16]. This is to allow any objecting shareholders time to apply to the court for cancellation of the resolution.

Equally, the financial assistance must not be given after the expiry of the period of eight weeks beginning with the date on which the directors of the company proposing to give the assistance made their statutory declaration[17]. This is to prevent the assistance being given when the statutory declaration has become out of date.

9   The legislation does not state how detailed the particulars must be but the prescribed form refers to the form of assistance and the principal terms on which it is given: see the Companies (Forms) Regulations 1985, SI 1985/854, Sch 3. If information sufficient to address those requirements is included in the statutory declaration, the fact that other matters are omitted does not prevent the particulars from being reasonably and fairly described as particulars of the form and principal terms of financial assistance: *Re S H & Co (Realisations) 1990 Ltd* [1993] BCLC 1309.

10   In forming their opinion for these purposes, the directors must take into account the same liabilities, (including contingent and prospective liabilities) as would be relevant under s 122 of the Insolvency Act 1986 to the question whether the company is unable to pay its debts: CA 1985, s 156(3).

11   Ibid, s 156(2).

12   Ibid, s 156(4).

13   Ibid, ss 156(7), 730, Sch 24. However, unlike the case of redemption or purchase out of capital, no civil liability attaches under the Insolvency Act 1986 in the event of insolvency within 12 months of the payment of the financial assistance.

14   CA 1985, s 157(4). The statutory declaration and auditors' report must also be delivered to the registrar of companies together with any special resolution required to be passed: s 156(5).

15   Ibid, s 381A(1),(7), Sch 15A, para 4.

16   Ibid, s 158(2).

17   Ibid, s 158(4).

OBJECTING MEMBERS

Where a special resolution has been passed authorising the giving of financial assistance by a private company, an application for its cancellation may be made to the court within 28 days by the holders of not less than 10% in nominal value of the company's issued share capital or any class thereof[18]. Such an application cannot be made by any person who consented to or voted in favour of the resolution[19]. It should be noted that this procedure is not available to creditors who are already adequately protected by the restrictions on the funds which may be used and the need for a statutory declaration by the directors supported by the auditors.

At the hearing the court has wide powers. It must make an order either cancelling or confirming the resolution and may, if it thinks fit, adjourn the proceedings in order that an arrangement may be made for the purchase of the interests of dissentient members and may give such directions and make such orders as it thinks expedient for facilitating such arrangements[20]. Where the court's order provides for the purchase by the company of any member's shares it may provide accordingly for the reduction of the company's capital[1]. Notice of any application to the court must be given forthwith to the registrar of companies and notice of any court order must be given within 15 days of the making of it[2]. No financial assistance can be given where an application has been made by a member until the final determination of the application unless the court orders otherwise[3].

For the reasons noted above in relation to members objecting to private companies redeeming or purchasing shares out of capital, it is difficult to see shareholders enjoying much success under this provision. They may have a greater chance of success if they can present their objections within the context of a more broadly based petition seeking relief against unfairly prejudicial conduct[4].

It must not be forgotten that the other exemptions already outlined above do apply to private companies so it is not necessary to follow this statutory scheme. However, the great advantage in using the statutory scheme is that companies do not face the uncertainties noted above as to the scope of the 'purpose' exception. Despite the procedural requirements, therefore, it is much the preferred method of proceeding.

Consequences of breach of the financial assistance provisions

As already noted, if a company acts in contravention of the provisions on financial assistance, it is liable on conviction to a fine and every officer in default is liable to imprisonment or a fine or both[5]. The statutory provisions do not deal, however, with the civil consequences which remain a matter for the common law.

A director who authorises the giving of financial assistance in breach of the statutory provisions will be in breach of his duties to the company and liable to make good any sums paid by the company unlawfully[6].

18   Ibid, s 157(2). Such applications are governed by the procedure laid down in s 54: s 157(3).
19   Ibid, s 157(2).
20   Ibid, s 54(5).
1   Ibid, s 54(6).
2   Ibid, s 54(4), (7).
3   Ibid, s 158(3).
4   Ie under ibid, s 459, discussed in detail in Chapter 28.
5   Ibid, ss 151(3), 730, Sch 24.
6   *Selangor United Rubber Estates Ltd v Cradock (a bankrupt) (No 3)* [1968] 2 All ER 1073, [1968] 1 WLR 1555; see also *Wallersteiner v Moir* [1974] 3 All ER 217, [1974] 1 WLR 991; *Steen v Law* [1964] AC 287, [1963] 3 All ER 770.

A shareholder may seek an injunction to restrain the giving of financial assistance in breach of the statutory provisions but once the transaction is completed then he can only bring a derivative action on behalf of the company to recover the sums expended[7].

The involvement of third parties such as bankers is often crucial to the carrying out of an illegal financial assistance scheme. A liability in equity to make good any resulting losses to the company will attach to any such third party who dishonestly procures or assists the directors in a breach of their fiduciary duties to the company[8]. In this context, acting dishonestly means simply not acting as an honest person would in the circumstances; and for the most part dishonesty is to be equated with conscious impropriety[9]. The court when called upon to decide whether a person was acting honestly will look at all the circumstances known to the third party at the time[10].

Equally, a third party who receives company funds may be liable to the company as a constructive trustee if he receives the funds with knowledge of the directors' breach of duty, whether it be actual knowledge or knowledge in the sense that he wilfully shut his eyes to the obvious or wilfully and recklessly failed to make the type of inquiries which an honest and reasonable man would have made[11].

Another issue which has arisen is whether a transaction entered into in pursuance of the illegal financial assistance scheme is itself invalid. For example, if the financial assistance takes the form of a debenture given by a company as security for money lent to enable a person to purchase shares in the company, is the debenture enforceable? This question was considered in *Victor Battery Co Ltd v Curry's Ltd*[12] where Roxburgh J held that it was. The case was much criticised[13] and in *Heald v O'Connor*[14], on similar facts, the court refused to follow the earlier decision and found the debenture to be void and unenforceable. The court noted that such a result best furthered the policy of the legislation in that it would deter potential lenders from lending money on security which might be held to contravene the statute.

---

7   See *Smith v Croft (No 2)* [1988] Ch 114, [1987] 3 All ER 909; the derivative action is discussed in detail in Chapter 28.

8   *Royal Brunei Airlines Sdn Bhd v Tan* [1995] 2 AC 378, [1995] 3 All ER 97, PC; see also *Barnes v Addy* (1874) 9 Ch App 244; *Agip (Africa) Ltd v Jackson* [1990] Ch 265 at 293, [1992] 4 All ER 385 at 405; *Eagle Trust plc v SBC Securities Ltd* [1992] 4 All ER 488 at 499, [1993] 1 WLR 484 at 495; *Polly Peck International plc v Nadir (No 2)* [1992] 4 All ER 769 at 777, [1992] 2 Lloyd's Rep 238 at 243.

9   *Royal Brunei Airlines Sdn Bhd v Tan* [1995] 2 AC 378 at 389, [1995] 3 All ER 97 at 106, PC.

10   *Royal Brunei Airlines Sdn Bhd v Tan* [1995] 2 AC 378 at 381, [1995] 3 All ER 97 at 107, PC.

11   *Selangor United Rubber Estates Ltd v Cradock (a bankrupt) (No 3)* [1968] 2 All ER 1073, [1968] 1 WLR 1555; *Eagle Trust plc v SBC Securities Ltd* [1992] 4 All ER 488; *Re Montagu's Settlement Trusts* [1987] Ch 264, [1992] 4 All ER 308; *Polly Peck International plc v Nadir (No 2)* [1992] 4 All ER 769, [1992] 2 Lloyd's Rep 238; *Cowan de Groot Properties Ltd v Eagle Trust plc* [1992] 4 All ER 700; *Eagle Trust plc v SBC Securities Ltd (No 2)* [1996] 1 BCLC 121. The whole issue of the type of knowledge required in these 'knowing receipt' cases has been the subject of extensive and inconclusive judicial and academic debate: see Gardiner (1996) 112 LQR 56. It may be helpful to recall the point made by Knox J in *Cowan de Groot* supra at 761: '... it may well be that the underlying broad principle which runs through the authorities regarding commercial transactions is that the court will impute knowledge, on the basis of what a reasonable person would have learnt, to a person who is guilty of commercially unacceptable conduct in the particular context involved'.

12   [1946] Ch 242, [1946] 1 All ER 519.

13   The case was doubted in *Selangor United Rubber Estates Ltd v Cradock (No 3)* [1968] 2 All ER 1073, [1968] 1 WLR 1555 and in many overseas jurisdictions. See *Heald v O'Connor* [1971] 2 All ER 1105 at 1109, [1971] 1 WLR 497 at 501, 502 where Fisher J outlines the history of the *Victor Battery* decision.

14   [1971] 2 All ER 1105, [1971] 1 WLR 497.

Where the illegal element of the transaction can be severed, the court will do so[15]. In *Carney v Herbert*[16] the Privy Council was of the view that the nature of the illegality is not such as to preclude severance on the grounds of public policy so severance can take place provided that the financial assistance is ancillary to the overall transaction and its elimination would leave unchanged the subject matter of the transaction[17]. In this case, the illegal financial assistance (in the form of mortgages) was severed from an agreement for the sale of shares which could then be enforced between the parties in the ordinary way.

Reform

It will be clear from the preceding discussion that the provisions on financial assistance are complex and technical. Despite the reforms introduced by the Companies Act 1981 there are still difficulties of interpretation, as was evident from *Brady v Brady*[18]. Practitioners remain concerned, particularly when dealing with the acquisition of other companies, about the uncertainty surrounding the scope of the provisions. These concerns prompted the Law Society's Standing Committee on Company Law to make submissions to the Department of Trade and Industry urging the DTI to resolve some of the present uncertainties[19].

As part of a wider review of company law announced in 1992, the DTI set up a working party of business people, members of the legal and accountancy professions and DTI officials to examine the statutory provisions with a view to reform. A consultation document followed in October 1993 suggesting that the current prohibition be replaced with a two-tier structure[20].

The first tier would prohibit, for public companies only, the types of assistance within the scope of art 23 Second Council Directive (77/91/EEC)[1]. Article 23(1) provides that a company may not advance funds, nor make loans, nor provide security, with a view to the acquisition of its shares by a third party. A second tier would apply to all financial assistance except that covered by the first tier, ie all financial assistance by public companies not within the scope of art 23 and all financial assistance by private companies. This would enable the existing exemptions for private companies to apply more broadly across this second tier. The 'purpose' exemption might also be re-drafted in the light of the *Brady* judgment.

Since 1993 the DTI has undertaken further consultation with interested parties[2]. It seems that the response to the consultation in October 1993 has prompted a complete rethink by the Department which is likely to proceed with much simpler reforms than originally envisaged. There would only be limited technical amendments to the public

---

15 *Spink (Bournemouth) Ltd v Spink* [1936] Ch 544, [1936] 1 All ER 597; *South Western Mineral Water Co Ltd v Ashmore* [1967] 2 All ER 953, [1967] 1 WLR 1110; *Carney v Herbert* [1985] AC 301, [1985] 1 All ER 438, PC; *Neilson v Stewart* [1991] BCC 713, HL.
16 [1985] AC 301, [1985] 1 All ER 438, PC.
17 [1985] AC 301 at 314, [1985] 1 All ER 438 at 446, PC.
18 [1989] AC 755, [1988] 2 All ER 617.
19 See The Law Society's Standing Committee on Company Law, *Section 151 Companies Act 1985* (Memorandum No 233, September 1990).
20 *Company Law Review: Proposals for Reform of Sections 151–158 of the Companies Act 1985* (October 1993, DTI). For the response of The Law Society's Committee on Company Law to the proposals, see *Company Law Reform: Proposals for Reform of ss 151–158 of the Companies Act 1985* (Memorandum No 293, January 1994).
1 Second Council Directive of 13 December 1976 (77/91/EEC) OJ C 31.1.1977, 1–13.
2 See the Law Society Company Law Committee, *Financial Assistance by a Company for the Acquisition of its Own Shares* (Memorandum No 310, November 1994; Memorandum No 344, January 1997).

company regime. The effect of the decision in *Brady* would be reversed by replacing the principal and larger purpose test with a new 'predominant reason' test. Financial assistance would not be prohibited where the company's predominant reason for entering into the transaction was not to give financial assistance. Criminal penalties would be retained but the company itself would no longer be guilty of an offence and the transaction would not be automatically void at common law. The provisions applicable to private companies would be revised to provide a clearer general prohibition on financial assistance coupled with a simpler gateway procedure and an exemption for small transactions. As any reform will require primary legislation, the timing of the introduction of any of these proposals remains uncertain. In any event, the Department has indicated that it expects to consult further on detailed legislative proposals.[2a]

DIVIDENDS

Background

The particular problem which the rules attempt to address in this area is the risk that directors and shareholders will attempt to create fictitious profits in order to swell the dividend fund and so distribute the company's assets during its lifetime thus depleting the capital of the company to the ultimate detriment of the company's creditors who, on liquidation, will find the company stripped of its assets. Its significance in the context of capital maintenance is obvious.

Before 1980 the position was governed entirely by the common law which, while prohibiting the payment of a dividend out of capital[3], was in other respects rather lax[4]. For example, the rules permitted dividends to be paid out of current trading profits without making good losses in fixed capital[5] or trading losses in previous years[6]; allowed dividends to be paid out of an unrealised capital gain resulting from a bona fide revaluation of fixed assets[7]; and did not require companies to provide for depreciation[8]. Many of these legal rules were commercially unwise and contrary to good accounting practice but the courts were reluctant to interfere with the directors' discretion as men of business[9].

The position altered with the Companies Act 1980 which displaced in most instances the old common law rules. Now the provisions of Companies Act 1985 Part VIII govern this area. The result is a series of statutory requirements which curb the more dubious dividend practices for the protection of creditors generally[10].

2a   DTI *Companies in 1996-97* (1997), para 4, p 2.
3   *Re Exchange Banking Co, Flitcroft's Case* (1882) 21 Ch D 519; *Verner v General and Commercial Investment Trust* [1894] 2 Ch 239.
4   For an interesting account of the historical development of the dividend rules, see Yamey 'Aspects of the Law relating to Company Dividends' (1941) 4 MLR 273.
5   *Lee v Neuchatel Asphalte Co* (1889) 41 Ch D 1; *Verner v General and Commercial Investment Trust* [1894] 2 Ch 239.
6   *Ammonia Soda Co v Chamberlain* [1918] 1 Ch 266; *Re National Bank of Wales Ltd* [1899] 2 Ch 629.
7   See *Dimbula Valley (Ceylon) Tea Co Ltd v Laurie* [1961] Ch 353 at 371–373, [1961] 1 All ER 769 at 779–781.
8   *Lee v Neuchatel Asphalte Co* (1889) 41 Ch D 1; *Bolton v Natal Land and Colonization Co* [1892] 2 Ch 124.
9   See *Lee v Neuchatel Asphalte Co* (1889) 41 Ch D 1 at 18, 21.
10   See *Precision Dippings Ltd v Precision Dippings Marketing Ltd* [1986] Ch 447 at 455, [1985] 3 WLR 812 at 815, per Dillon LJ. However, a creditor does not have locus standi to seek an injunction to prevent an unlawful dividend, only a shareholder can do that: *Hoole v Great Western Rly Co* (1867) 3 Ch App 262; *Mills v Northern Rly of Buenos Ayres Ltd* (1870) 5 Ch App 621; *Lawrence v West Somerset Mineral Rly Co* [1918] 2 Ch 250.

If a company does not have distributable profits as defined by these provisions, then it cannot declare a dividend. Even if it has distributable profits, it should be remembered that the rules lay down the minimum requirements which must be met before a company may declare a dividend and there may be further restrictions on the directors' freedom of action in the memorandum and articles of association[11]. In the exercise of the power to recommend the payment of dividends, the directors must act bona fide in the interests of the company as a whole and prudent financial management may require putting a certain percentage of the funds to reserves rather than distributing the entire amount[12]. Business and taxation considerations will have to be taken into account and the position will also vary as between public and private companies, and between public listed and unlisted companies.

In practice, it is unusual for private companies to declare dividends. Many such companies are small family concerns where all the shareholders also act as the directors. Such companies will distribute profits by way of directors' remuneration instead of by way of formal declaration of dividends. In the past, this practice was dictated by taxation requirements but the position has now altered and there is no longer the tax disincentive against distributions which previously existed. Indeed there may now be tax savings to be made by paying dividends thus avoiding, for example, paying national insurance contributions on salary. The question of dividends or salary is therefore a matter to be determined in the light of the individual's position rather than by any general taxation requirements.

Problems can arise where profits are distributed by way of remuneration but not all the shareholders are directors. This can be a source of considerable tension, particularly if the directors' remuneration is generous. In such cases, a persistent failure to pay dividends when funds are available, coupled with high levels of directors' remuneration, may amount to unfairly prejudicial conduct[13].

Shareholders in public companies are much less likely to be directors and therefore would expect that dividend payments would be made in the usual way when profits are available. For listed public companies, a failure to maintain a significant level of dividend pay out each year can have a serious impact on their share price and might expose the company to potential takeover bids. It is also likely to be unpopular with institutional investors who are the predominant category of shareholders in listed companies. That type of market pressure for dividend payments has been criticised as contributing to the 'short-termism' problem in British companies[14]. It is argued that the need to focus on short-term strategies designed to give immediate shareholder returns and maintain the company's share price is detrimental to longer term planning which would be to the advantage of the company and the economy.

---

11   See CA 1985, s 281.
12   This may include in some circumstances an obligation to have regard to the interests of creditors (discussed in Chapter 26) which may preclude the payment of a dividend: see *Hilton International Ltd v Hilton* (1988) 4 NZCLC 64,721. The Draft Fifth EC Directive on Company Law, art 49, would have required the compulsory transfer of at least 5% of the profits in each financial year to a statutory reserve until that reserve amounted to not less than 10% of the subscribed capital but that Directive is unlikely to be adopted: see discussion in Chapter 3.
13   Under CA 1985, s 459. See *Re Sam Weller & Sons Ltd* [1990] Ch 682, [1989] 3 WLR 923; *Re a Company (No 00370 of 1987), ex p Glossop* [1988] BCLC 570.
14   See Stapledon, *Institutional Shareholders and Corporate Governance* (1996), pp 222–227; also discussion in Chapter 35.

The statutory scheme

AVAILABLE PROFITS

The basic rule is that a company must not make a distribution except out of profits available for the purpose[15].

By distribution we usually mean the payment of a dividend but the term is defined to apply to every description of distribution of a company's assets to its members, whether in cash or otherwise, except distributions by way of:

(a) an issue of shares as fully or partly paid bonus shares (discussed in Chapter 15);

(b) the redemption or purchase of any of the company's own shares out of capital (including the proceeds of any fresh issue of shares) or out of unrealised profits in accordance with the statutory provisions (discussed above);

(c) the reduction of share capital by extinguishing or reducing the liability of any of the members on any of the company's shares in respect of share capital not paid up, or by paying off paid-up share capital (discussed in Chapter 17); and

(d) a distribution of assets to members of the company on its winding up (discussed in Chapter 40)[16].

The distributions identified in headings (a)–(d) are subject to other statutory provisions so it is unnecessary to apply the provisions of Part VIII to them.

The profits available for distribution are defined as the company's accumulated realised profits, so far as not previously utilised by distribution or capitalisation, less its accumulated realised losses, so far as not previously written off in a reduction or reorganisation of capital duly made[17].

The key point is that it is only *realised* profits or losses[18] which enter the equation. In *Re Oxford Benefit Building and Investment Society*[19] it was said that 'realised profits' must have its ordinary commercial meaning, which if not equivalent to 'reduced to actual cash in hand' must at least be 'rendered tangible for the purpose of division'. The reason for this requirement is to prevent companies from relying on estimated or expected profits which might never actually materialise. This statutory requirement that the profit be realised reverses the much criticised common law rule laid down in *Dimbula Valley (Ceylon) Tea Co Ltd v Laurie*[20] which enabled a company to declare a dividend on an unrealised profit occurring on a revaluation of assets. Equally, depreciation, for which formerly no provision was made[1], must be treated as a realised loss[2]. On the other hand, unrealised losses are not taken into account unless the company is a public company (see below).

Equally crucial is the requirement that the amount of *accumulated* realised losses must be deducted before any distribution can be made. This abrogates the old common law rule, noted above, that losses made in previous accounting periods did not have to be made good. Now accounting periods can no longer be regarded in isolation from

---

15   CA 1985, s 263(1).
16   Ibid, s 263(2).
17   Ibid, s 263(3).
18   References to profits and losses are to revenue and capital profits and losses: ibid, s 280(1), (3).
19   (1886) 35 Ch D 502. For criticism of this definition see Noke [1989] JBL 37 at 42.
20   [1961] Ch 353, [1961] 1 All ER 769.
1   *Lee v Neuchatel Asphalte Co* (1889) 41 Ch D 1; *Bolton v Natal Land and Colonization Co* [1892] 2 Ch 124.
2   CA 1985, s 275 (1) subject to an exception where the value of a fixed asset is diminished in a revaluation of all fixed assets or all fixed assets other than goodwill.

one another. Hence the need in many cases to write off losses by way of a reduction of capital duly made[3] before resuming the payment of dividends.

PUBLIC COMPANIES

There are further requirements as far as public companies are concerned. This is in keeping with the approach generally in the Companies Act 1985 which, reflecting the provisions of the Second EC Directive[4], commonly imposes more stringent requirements on public companies.

In addition to having profits available for distribution as outlined above, a public company must satisfy two further conditions before it makes a distribution.

A public company may only make a distribution at any time:

(a)   if at that time, the amount of its net assets is not less than the aggregate of its called-up share capital and undistributable reserves, and

(b)   if, and to the extent that, the distribution does not reduce the amount of those assets to less than that aggregate[5].

For these purposes, net assets are defined as meaning the aggregate of the company's assets less the aggregate of its liabilities[6]. Called-up share capital is widely defined to include capital to which a company will become entitled but which it has not received and situations where a call has been made but not paid[7].

For these purposes, a company's undistributable reserves are:

(a)   the share premium account;

(b)   the capital redemption reserve;

(c)   the amount by which the company's accumulated unrealised profits (so far as not previously utilised by any capitalisation) exceeds its accumulated unrealised losses (so far as not previously written off in a reduction or re-organisation of capital duly made); and

(d)   any other reserve which the company is prohibited from distributing by any enactment or by its memorandum or articles[8].

RELEVANT ACCOUNTS

All of these matters must be determined in accordance with the company's accounts, ie the company's last annual accounts prepared in accordance with the requirements of the Companies Act, which accounts must have been duly laid before the general meeting[9]. If the auditors have qualified the accounts, then they must state in writing whether, in their opinion, the substance of the qualification is material for determining

---

3   Reduction of capital is discussed in Chapter 17.
4   Second Council Directive of 13 December 1976 (77/91/EEC) OJ C 31.1.1977, 1–13. See discussion in Chapter 3.
5   CA 1985, s 264(1). This reflects the Second EC Directive (77/91/EEC), art 15.
6   CA 1985, s 264(2).
7   Ibid, s 737(1).
8   Ibid, s 264(3).
9   Ibid, s 270(1), (3). If the company is a private company which has elected to dispense with the laying of accounts and reports before the company in general meeting, then the accounts must have been sent to the members: s 252(3).

the legality of the proposed dividend and a copy of that statement must also have been laid before the company in general meeting[10].

The significance of this statement by the auditors was considered by the Court of Appeal in *Precision Dippings Ltd v Precision Dippings Marketing Ltd*[11]. In this case no auditors' statement had been made although the accounts had been qualified. A dividend of £60,000 was paid and the company (Dippings) later went into liquidation. The auditors at that stage issued a written declaration to the effect that the qualification in their report did not affect the validity of the dividend payment. The liquidator tried to recover the amount of the dividend from the recipient (Marketing).

In defence to the claim, it was argued, that this requirement of an auditors' statement was a mere procedural requirement and so the failure to comply with it did not invalidate the payment. The court rejected this argument, stating that it was not a mere procedural requirement but an important part of the scheme provided by the statutory provisions as a major protection for creditors[12]. The wording of the provision showed that the auditors' statement had to be available to the shareholders before the distribution was made. As it had not been so available then the statutory provisions had been contravened. The consequences of contravention are considered below.

Liability where an improper dividend is paid

Where a distribution is made in contravention of the requirements of Part VIII, any member who, at the time of the distribution, knew or had reasonable grounds for believing that it was so made is liable to repay the distribution to the company[13]. This statutory liability is without prejudice to any obligation imposed apart from the statutory provisions on a member to repay a distribution unlawfully made to him[14].

Returning to the decision in *Precision Dippings Ltd v Precision Dippings Marketing Ltd*[15], noted above, the court having found the dividend payment to be in breach of the statutory requirements turned to the issue of liability. The only directors and shareholders of Marketing were also the directors of Dippings. Marketing, as the recipient of the dividend, claimed that, while it knew all the facts concerning the payment of the dividend, it did not know the terms of the statutory provisions and therefore did not have the requisite knowledge to incur liability to repay the distribution. The Court of Appeal decided that it was unnecessary to examine the question of knowledge since it was possible to impose liability quite apart from the statutory provision. The payment of the dividend in breach of the statutory provisions was an ultra vires act of the company. Marketing, when it received the money, had notice of the facts and held the £60,000 dividend on constructive trust for the company which was entitled to repayment[16]. Directors who recommend dividends in breach of the provisions are liable to account to the company for the sums paid out[17].

10   Ibid, s 271(4). If the company is a private company which has elected to dispense with the laying of accounts and reports before the company in general meeting, then the statement must have been sent to the members: s 252(3).
11   [1986] Ch 447, [1985] 3 WLR 812.
12   [1986] Ch 447 at 451, [1985] 3 WLR 812 at 817.
13   CA 1985, s 277(1).
14   Ibid, s 277(2).
15   [1986] Ch 447, [1985] 3 WLR 812.
16   [1986] Ch 447 at 458, [1985] 3 WLR 812 at 818, per Dillon LJ, applying *Rolled Steel Products (Holdings) Ltd v British Steel Corpn* [1986] Ch 246, [1985] 3 All ER 52. See also *Re Cleveland Trust plc* [1991] BCLC 424.
17   *Re Exchange Banking Co, Flitcroft's Case* (1882) 21 Ch D 519; *Re Oxford Benefit Building and Investment Society* (1886) 35 Ch D 502.

Declaration and payment of dividends

Assuming that a company does have distributable profits as determined in accordance with the statutory provisions, the next question is whether this automatically entitles the shareholders to a dividend. It will do so if the memorandum or articles expressly provide for the payment of a fixed dividend where the company has distributable profits[18]. More commonly, the articles will require a declaration of a dividend by the company in general meeting by ordinary resolution following a recommendation by the directors[19]. It is common practice to declare a dividend as so many pence per share.

Only when a dividend has actually been declared does it become payable and due to the members[20]. As a rule a dividend must be paid in cash and if a non-cash consideration is to be provided, eg in the form of additional shares[1], then specific authorisation to that effect must be included in the articles[2]. A dividend paid in the form of additional shares is known as a scrip dividend.

---

18   See *Evling v Israel and Oppenheimer* [1918] 1 Ch 101.
19   See Table A, art 102. The general meeting may decrease but not increase the amount to be distributed. The directors have power to declare an interim dividend: art 103.
20   *Bond v Barrow Haematite Steel Co* [1902] 1 Ch 353.
1   See Table A, art 110.
2   *Wood v Odessa Waterworks Co* (1889) 42 Ch D 636.

CHAPTER 17

Share capital alteration

The amount of a company's share capital and the division thereof is set out on incorporation in the company's memorandum of association[1] and a company may not alter the conditions contained in the memorandum except in the cases, in the mode and to the extent, for which express provision is made by the Companies Act[2]. A company is therefore limited in the ways in which it can alter its share capital.

ALTERATION OF SHARE CAPITAL

A company limited by shares or a company limited by guarantee and having a share capital, if so authorised by its articles, may alter the provision in its memorandum regarding share capital in any of the following ways[3]:

The company may:

(a) increase its share capital by new shares of such amount as it thinks expedient;
(b) consolidate and divide all or any of its share capital into shares of larger amount than its existing shares;
(c) convert all or any of its paid-up shares into stock, and re-convert that stock into paid-up shares of any denomination;
(d) sub-divide its shares, or any of them, into shares of smaller amount than is fixed by the memorandum[4];
(e) cancel[5] shares which, at the date of the passing of the resolution to cancel them, have not been taken or agreed to be taken by any person, and diminish the amount of the company's share capital by the amount of the shares so cancelled[6].

---

1 As required by CA 1985, s 2(5)(a).
2 Ibid, s 2(7).
3 Ibid, s 121(1).
4 See also ibid, s 121(3).
5 A cancellation of shares in this way does not for the purposes of the Act constitute a reduction of capital: ibid, s 121(5).
6 Ibid, s 121(2).

Various procedural points common to all these categories should be noted before considering each in turn. First, the company's articles must authorise the alteration in question[7].

Secondly, the powers conferred by the legislation must be exercised by the company in general meeting[8].

Thirdly, notice of any of the above alterations (other than an increase of share capital) must be given to the registrar of companies within one month of the alteration[9]. In the case of an increase of share capital, notice must be given within 15 days of the passing of the resolution authorising the increase[10]. In all cases, the company must send to the registrar a copy of the memorandum as altered[11]. In cases of breach of these requirements, the company and any officer in default is liable to a fine[12].

Increasing share capital

This is the most common alteration. Its purpose is to lift the ceiling on the company's share capital imposed by the terms of the memorandum. After a number of years in business, a company may find that the limit originally set, for example £500,000 divided into 500,000 £1 shares, is inappropriate given the size to which the company has grown and does not allow for the further expansion of the business. The company may wish to increase that capital figure to £1m divided into one million £1 shares so as to enable it to issue another 500,000 shares.

It should be noted that the passing of a resolution to increase the authorised share capital does not operate as a grant of authority to the directors to proceed to allot those shares. Authority to allot is a separate matter and the directors will need authority from their shareholders in general meeting or in the company's articles[13]. The allotment of shares is discussed in detail in Chapter 15.

The House of Lords in *Russell v Northern Bank Development Corpn Ltd*[14] held that any provision in the articles purporting to fetter the power of the company to increase its share capital is void although shareholders may reach an agreement outside of the articles as to how they would exercise their voting rights on any resolution to increase capital[15]. They may agree therefore not to support any increase in capital although such a provision may not be put in the articles.

---

7   A common provision is that contained in Table A, art 32. The one omission from art 32 is any provision in respect of (c) above which reflects the fact that it is rare now for companies to convert their shares into stock.

8   CA 1985, s 121(4). A meeting need not actually be held as anything which in the case of a private company may be done by a resolution in general meeting may be done, without a meeting, by a resolution in writing signed by or on behalf of all the members of the company: ibid, s 381A. The written resolution procedure is explained in detail in Chapter 23.

9   Ibid, s 122(1).

10   Ibid, s 123(1).

11   Ibid, s 18(2).

12   Ibid, ss 122(2), 123(4), 18(3).

13   Under ibid, s 80(1).

14   [1992] 3 All ER 161, [1992] 1 WLR 588, HL.

15   See also *Welton v Saffery* [1897] AC 299, HL. The company may not be a party to the agreement: *Russell v Northern Bank Development Corpn Ltd* [1992] 3 All ER 161, [1992] 1 WLR 588, HL.

Consolidation

Consolidation means combining a number of shares into a new share of commensurate nominal value. Thus 10 £1 shares may be consolidated into one £10 share. This process is less common now as investors prefer shares of lower rather than higher nominal value but it is sometimes used as an element of a capital re-arrangement scheme where that scheme has left the company with shares of an unwieldy nominal value. Thus 12.5p shares may be consolidated into 50p or £1 shares. This exercise has no financial impact on the shareholders who now hold fewer shares but of greater nominal value.

Conversion of shares into stock

Provision is made for the conversion of shares into stock and vice versa although this is of limited significance now for it is rare for UK companies to convert in this way[16]. Stock cannot be issued directly by the company[17] but arises from a conversion of fully-paid shares into stock. There were two reasons, in particular, for converting shares in this way. First, shares could not (and cannot) be dealt with in fractions whereas stock may be. Secondly, shares have to be numbered but stock does not. However, these supposed advantages are less significant now. While stock may be dealt with in fractions, in practice a company's articles will prescribe the minimum dealing unit which is usually the same as one share so stock is not necessarily any more flexible than shares. Equally, the administrative advantages of unnumbered stock are available in respect of shares, for numbers may be dispensed with where all the issued shares in a company, or of a particular class, are fully paid up and rank pari passu for all purposes[18].

Subdivision

This is quite a common process and is simply the opposite process to consolidation which was described above. Subdivision involves dividing a share into a number of new shares and is usually done to increase the marketability of shares where companies feel their nominal value is too high. Thus £1 shares can be subdivided in four 25p shares or ten 10p shares.

Cancellation

A company may cancel shares which, at the date of the relevant resolution, have not been taken or agreed to be taken by any person. For example, a company may have been incorporated with a share capital of £200,000 divided into 200,000 £1 shares. The company's plans prove over-optimistic and it is trading only in a limited way for which share capital of £50,000 is adequate. The company might wish to cancel £100,000 of that outstanding capital since it cannot envisage ever raising that amount

---

16   The Jenkins Committee on Company Law (1962, Cmnd 1749), para 472 noted that the advantages of conversion seemed to be negligible and recommended that steps be taken to phase out the use of stock but this was never acted upon. The limited significance of conversion explains why provision for conversion is omitted from Table A, art 32.

17   *Re Home and Foreign Investment and Agency Co Ltd* [1912] 1 Ch 72.

18   See CA 1985, s 182(2).

of share capital. The only effect of this is to reduce the scope for issuing further shares but power to do so can be restored at any time by simply increasing the share capital back to £200,000 if circumstances so warrant.

This alteration results in the reduction of the company's authorised capital but not its issued capital[19] and is therefore to be distinguished from such a reduction which is discussed below. A reduction of issued capital may have implications for a company's creditors as they look to the share capital as a creditors' fund whereas a cancellation of capital not yet taken up or agreed to be taken up has no effect on creditors. Given its limited significance, this power is rarely used other than again as part of an overall scheme of reconstruction.

REDUCTION OF CAPITAL

Here the issue is the reduction of share capital previously raised by the company. Given the overriding concern with share capital as a creditors' fund, it is not surprising that it is a basic principle of company law that capital cannot be returned by a company to its members save by a reduction of capital sanctioned by the court. The position was explained by Lord Watson in *Trevor v Whitworth*[20] as follows:

> ...the effect of these statutory restrictions is to prohibit every transaction between a company and a shareholder, by means of which the money already paid to the company in respect of his shares is returned to him, unless the Court has sanctioned the transaction. Paid up share capital may be diminished or lost in the course of the company's trading; that is a result which no legislation can prevent; but persons who deal with, and give credit to a limited company, naturally rely upon the fact that the company is trading with a certain amount of capital already paid, as well as upon the responsibility of its members for the capital remaining at call; and they are entitled to assume that no part of the capital which has been paid into the coffers of the company has been subsequently paid out, except in the legitimate course of its business ... [1].

Lord Herschell was equally clear on the position:

> ... whatever has been paid by a member cannot be returned to him. In my opinion ... the capital cannot be diverted from the objects of the society. It is, of course, liable to be spent or lost in carrying on the business of the company but no part of it can be returned to a member so as to take away from the fund to which the creditors have a right to look as that out of which they are to be paid.[2]

Having said that, business realities require that there should be provision for a number of exceptional circumstances when capital may be reduced. These must be considered against the background of the general prohibition, however, so that reduction is

---

19 A point explicitly made in ibid, s 121(5).
20 (1887) 12 App Cas 409, HL. For an example of a breach of the basic principle that capital may not be returned, see *Aveling Barford Ltd v Perion Ltd* [1989] BCLC 626: disguising the transaction as a sale (at a gross undervalue) of an asset to a company controlled by a shareholder did not hide the true nature of the transaction which was an unauthorised return of capital to that shareholder. See also Harman J in *Barclays Bank plc v British and Commonwealth Holdings plc* [1996] 1 BCLC 1 at 10–11, Ch D, affd on different grounds [1996] 1 BCLC 1 at 27, CA.
1   (1887) 12 App Cas 409 at 423–424.
2   (1887) 12 App Cas 409 at 419–420.

permitted only in limited instances and surrounded by measures designed to ensure that the interests of creditors are properly safeguarded.

A reduction of capital may occur in the following ways:

(i) reduction in accordance with the statutory scheme for the reduction of capital[3], discussed in detail below;

(ii) reduction as a consequence of a redemption or a purchase back of shares by a private company out of capital[4] (discussed in Chapter 16) which has the effect of a reduction of capital for such companies. Creditors and members are protected in such circumstances, however, by the extensive statutory provisions governing such schemes;

(iii) reduction as a consequence of a court order for the purchase by the company of shares held by an objecting member under a variety of provisions[5];

(iv) reduction as a result of forfeiture or surrender by members, discussed below.

This Chapter will concentrate on the statutory scheme for reduction of capital.

Types of reduction of capital

A reduction of capital may be effected only in accordance with the Companies Act 1985 which provides that, subject to confirmation by the court, a company limited by shares or a company limited by guarantee and having a share capital may, if so authorised by its articles, by special resolution reduce its share capital in any way[6].

In particular, and without prejudice to the above power[7], the company may:

(i) extinguish or reduce the liability on any of its shares in respect of share capital not paid up; or

(ii) either with or without extinguishing or reducing liability on any of its shares, cancel any paid-up share capital which is lost or unrepresented by available assets; or

(iii) either with or without extinguishing or reducing liability on any of its shares, pay off any paid-up share capital which is in excess of the company's wants;

and the company may, if and so far as is necessary, alter its memorandum by reducing the amount of its share capital and of its shares accordingly[8].

---

3   Under CA 1985, s 135.

4   Reduction does not occur in the case of redemption or purchase otherwise than out of capital for, in those instances, an amount equivalent to the amount redeemed or purchased must be transferred to the capital redemption reserve which, for most purposes, is treated as if it were share capital: ibid, s 170(4).

5   For example, under ibid, s 54(6) (objection to public company being re-registered as a private company); s 157(3) (objection to private company giving financial assistance for the purchase of its own shares); s 177(3) (objection to purchase or redemption of shares by private company out of capital); and s 461(2) (relief for unfairly prejudicial conduct).

6   Ibid, s 135(1).

7   The courts have emphasised on many occasions that there is no question of limiting or controlling the power available to the company to reduce its capital in any way as provided by ibid, s 135(1): *British and American Trustee and Finance Corpn v Couper* [1894] AC 399; *Poole v National Bank of China Ltd* [1907] AC 229; *Re Thomas de la Rue & Co Ltd and Reduced* [1911] 2 Ch 361; *Ex p Westburn Sugar Refineries Ltd* [1951] AC 625, [1951] 1 All ER 881.

8   CA 1985, s 135(2).

EXTINCTION OR REDUCTION OF LIABILITY ON SHARES NOT PAID UP

Reduction in this instance appears to endanger creditors for it extinguishes a liability, namely the obligation on the part of the holders of partly-paid shares to pay the amount due on those shares, which would be a valuable asset to the creditors in the event of a winding up[9]. In practice, however, this category is rarely used for it is unusual now for shares to be issued as partly-paid. It is seldom therefore that there is any question of there being any unpaid share capital outstanding.

CANCELLATION OF PAID-UP SHARE CAPITAL WHICH IS LOST OR UNREPRESENTED BY AVAILABLE ASSETS

The cancellation of paid-up share capital which is lost or unrepresented by available assets appears to have an impact on creditors for it reduces the minimum level of assets which must be maintained by the company. However, reduction in this instance will usually be an exercise to restore reality to the company's accounts. If a company had at one time a paid-up share capital of £200,000 but, following trading losses, its net assets now amount only to £50,000, little is achieved by maintaining the figure of £200,000 in the accounts as the capital yardstick.

Reduction will also be crucial to the company's ability to make or resume dividend payments to its shareholders and it is important to appreciate the impact of the dividend rules, discussed in detail in Chapter 16, in this context. The net effect of the dividend rules and, in particular, the need to have regard to accumulated profits and losses means that it will be necessary for the company to reduce capital to take account of losses and to reorganise its balance sheet so as to be in a position to resume the payment of dividends.

The court must be satisfied that the capital is lost and that that loss is permanent, for if it is not permanently lost then a cancellation of paid-up share capital will prejudice the interests of the creditors. In *Re Jupiter House Investments (Cambridge) Ltd*[10], where the loss could not be proved to be permanent[11], the court confirmed the reduction subject to an undertaking by the company which ensured that if the loss of capital was in fact recovered, it would not be distributed as dividends but would be placed to a capital reserve. On the other hand, in *Re Grosvenor Press plc*[12] the court was loath to require such an undertaking, noting that there were already statutory safeguards[13] to protect the interests of future creditors and shareholders and there was no need, except in special circumstances, for the court to require a reserve to be set aside indefinitely.

PAYMENT OFF OF ANY PAID-UP SHARE CAPITAL IN EXCESS OF THE COMPANY'S WANTS

As for the payment off of paid-up share capital in excess of the company's needs, this clearly poses no risk to creditors and may simply reflect a shrinking of the company's activities. It might be noted that it is only in this instance that capital is actually returned

9   Assuming that those shareholders were in a position to meet their liability on those shares.
10 [1985] 1 WLR 975, [1985] BCLC 222; noted Milman (1986) 7 Co Law 68.
11 The loss arose from defects in a substantial building which the company owned. The company had been advised that it had more than an even chance of recovering the loss by an action for damages against a third party.
12 [1985] 1 WLR 980, [1985] BCLC 286; noted Milman (1986) 7 Co Law 68.
13 Creditors and shareholders were protected by the publicity requirements surrounding the reduction and the need for the company's accounts to give a true and fair view of the state of its affairs.

to the shareholders. In (i) above, the capital has never been received and in (ii) above, the capital is lost.

It is not necessary that the shareholders should actually receive cash; non-cash assets may be used instead[14] and in that case there need not be an exact correlation between the capital reduced and the value of the assets transferred[15]. This may appear to offer some opportunity for abuse but the courts have indicated that the important matter is not how much is returned to the shareholders but how much is retained for the protection of creditors[16].

Procedure for reduction

A company must be authorised by its articles to reduce capital. Table A states that, subject to the provisions of the Companies Act, the company may by special resolution reduce its share capital, any capital redemption reserve and any share premium account in any way[17]. This is frequently qualified in public companies by providing that the reduction must not have the effect of reducing the share capital below the authorised minimum for a public company[18].

A special resolution in general meeting is required subject to the availability now of a written resolution in the case of private companies[19]. When the company has passed the special resolution then it may apply to the court for an order confirming the reduction[20] which the court may make on such terms and conditions as it thinks fit[1], subject to the position of the company's creditors having been safeguarded, as discussed below.

In practice, assuming that the procedures have been followed properly and the necessary special resolution passed, the court's role is little more than to endorse the company's plans. The creditors' consent will usually have been secured by the company and the company's position will usually be such that shareholders will have little interest in objecting other than in the context of a variation of class rights, which is discussed below.

---

14   *Ex p Westburn Sugar Refineries Ltd* [1951] AC 625, [1951] 1 All ER 881; *Re Thomas de la Rue & Co Ltd and Reduced* [1911] 2 Ch 361. It might also be noted that a distribution whether of cash or assets in a reduction of capital is not a distribution for the purposes of CA 1985, s 263(2); hence there is no need to have distributable profits as therein defined.

15   In *Ex p Westburn Sugar Refineries Ltd* [1951] AC 625 at 631, [1951] 1 All ER 881 at 885, Lord Reid made the point that this must be the position because in many cases it is impossible to make any exact valuation of the non-cash assets. It is therefore possible that the shareholder may receive more or less than the value of his capital but if what is offered to the shareholder is illusory then the court will refuse to confirm the reduction: *Re Thomas de la Rue & Co Ltd and Reduced* [1911] 2 Ch 361.

16   See, for example, Lord Normand in *Ex p Westburn Sugar Refineries Ltd* [1951] AC 625 at 630, [1951] 1 All ER 881 at 884.

17   Table A, art 34. The share premium account and the capital redemption reserve are treated as share capital and so are subject to the same constraints on reduction: see CA 1985, ss 130(3) and 170(4) respectively.

18   Such a provision does not rule out a reduction by a company which momentarily reduces the company's capital to nil before following it with an increase in capital to above that minimum: *Re MB Group Ltd* [1989] BCLC 672. The authorised minimum is £50,000: CA 1985, s 118. As to the position when a reduction does result in the capital of a public company falling below the authorised minimum, see ibid, s 139 noted below.

19   Ibid, s 381A. This removes the doubts expressed in *Re Barry Artists Ltd* [1985] 1 WLR 1305, [1985] BCLC 283 as to whether written resolutions are acceptable for reduction of capital schemes.

20   CA 1985, s 136(1).

1   Ibid, s 137(1). The court can confirm a resolution even if there is a factual error in it, provided that it is so insignificant that no one could be thought to be prejudiced by its correction: *Re Willaire Systems plc* [1987] BCLC 67. See also *Re European Home Products plc* [1988] BCLC 690 where a more significant error occurred but the court reluctantly confirmed the reduction as creditors were not affected and no shareholder regarded the mistake as being of such importance as to seek the court's refusal.

Protection of creditors

In recognition of the potential risk to creditors when companies exercise a power to reduce share capital, specific statutory provision is made for their protection.

Where the proposed reduction involves either a diminution of liability in respect of unpaid share capital or the payment of any paid-up share capital to a shareholder, and in any other case if the court so directs, then every creditor of the company whose claim would be admissible to proof in a winding up is entitled to object to the reduction of capital[2].

If there are creditors so entitled to object then a list of such creditors must be settled[3] and the court has to be satisfied that any such creditor has either consented to the reduction, or his debt or claim has been discharged or has been determined, or has been secured, before it makes an order confirming the reduction on such terms and conditions as it thinks fit[4]. This is subject to a power vested in the court to dispense with this procedure[5]. This provision is limited to these two categories of reduction and while the court could direct a settling of creditors in this way in any other case, prima facie creditors are not supposed to be concerned in questions of reduction where no diminution of unpaid capital or repayment to shareholders of paid-up capital is involved[6].

In practice, because reduction is frequently part of an overall reconstruction, the company will usually have reached an agreement with its creditors who have either consented to the scheme subject to bank guarantees being forthcoming covering amounts due to them or who have been paid off. Applications to dispense with the settling of the list are therefore very common and invariably granted.

Protection of shareholders

There are no specific statutory provisions dealing with the shareholders' position and objecting shareholders must persuade the court not to confirm the reduction.

Confirmation by the court

The court has a discretion whether or not to confirm a reduction[7] and the main question for the court is whether the proposed reduction is fair and equitable as between the different classes of shareholders[8].

---

2   CA 1985, s 136(2), (3).
3   Ibid, s 136(4).
4   Ibid, s 137(1).
5   Ibid, s 136(6). In considering whether to dispense with the list of creditors, the court will consider whether a company holds sufficient cash and gilt-edged securities to cover all provable liabilities with a reasonable margin of safety as well as the amount which it is proposed to be returned to the shareholders: see *Re House of Fraser plc* [1987] BCLC 293; *Anderson Brown & Co Ltd, Petitioners* 1965 SC 81; *Re Lucania Temperance Billard Halls (London) Ltd* [1966] Ch 98, [1965] 3 All ER 879.
6   See *Re Meux's Brewery Co Ltd* [1919] 1 Ch 28 at 36.
7   *British and American Trustee and Finance Corpn v Couper* [1894] AC 399; *Re Thomas de la Rue and Co Ltd and Reduced* [1911] 2 Ch 361.
8   *British and American Trustee Corpn and Finance v Couper* [1894] AC 399; *Re Thomas de la Rue and Co Ltd and Reduced* [1911] 2 Ch 361; *Poole v National Bank of China Ltd* [1907] AC 229; *Wilsons and Clyde Coal Co Ltd v Scottish Insurance Corpn* 1948 SC 360; affd sub nom *Scottish Insurance Corpn Ltd v Wilsons and Clyde Coal Co Ltd* [1949] AC 462, HL; *Ex p Westburn Sugar Refineries Ltd* [1951] AC 625, [1951] 1 All ER 881.

Speaking generally, a reduction of capital need not be spread equally or rateably over all the shares of the company[9]. If there is nothing unfair or inequitable in the transaction, the shares of one or more shareholders may be extinguished without affecting other shares of the same or a different class[10]. However, a reduction which does not provide for uniform treatment of shareholders whose rights are similar is narrowly scrutinised[11].

Some of the earlier cases suggested that the court should have regard to the interests of creditors, shareholders and to the interests of those members of the public who may be induced to take shares in the company[12] but the court appears to give little weight to such considerations now[13] for in the absence of special circumstances creditors and future shareholders are adequately protected by the statutory safeguards.

So long as creditors and shareholders are not prejudiced, wider public concerns do not influence the court and it is not concerned with any ulterior purpose for the reduction provided it is lawful. Thus reduction schemes for reasons of tax avoidance (as opposed to evasion) or to avoid some of the consequences of nationalisation have in the past been approved[14].

The general approach of the courts and the nature of the jurisdiction to confirm a reduction is set out most clearly in Lord Cooper's (dissenting) judgment in *Wilsons and Clyde Coal Co Ltd v Scottish Insurance Corpn*[15]:

> In the early days the courts took this jurisdiction very seriously and refused to confirm many reductions, often on the dubious ground that they were ultra vires. This tendency was corrected in *British and American Trustee Corpn*[16], *Balmenach-Glenlivet Distillery*[17], *Poole v National Bank of China*[18], and *Caldwell & Co*[19], which progressively narrowed the court's powers and inaugurated in company practice what might be called an era of self determination and laissez-faire. Nevertheless, emphasis was again and again laid by the House of Lords upon the proposition that the courts had a 'discretion' to confirm or not to confirm, which it was their duty to apply in 'every proper case', and that this discretion fell to be exercised by reference to the test of whether the scheme would be 'fair and equitable', 'just and equitable', 'fair and reasonable', or 'not unjust or inequitable', expressions sometimes qualified and explained by the

9   *Re Agricultural Hotel Co* [1891] 1 Ch 396; *Re Floating Dock Co of St Thomas Ltd* [1895] 1 Ch 691; *Re London and New York Investment Corpn* [1895] 2 Ch 860; *British and American Trustee and Finance Corpn v Couper* [1894] AC 399.

10   *British and American Trustee and Finance Corpn v Couper* [1894] AC 399 at 406, 415, 417, HL; *Bannatyne v Direct Spanish Telegraph Co* (1886) 34 Ch D 287, CA; *Re Direct Spanish Telegraph Co* (1886) 34 Ch D 307; *Re Thomas de la Rue & Co Ltd and Reduced* [1911] 2 Ch 361.

11   In *Re Robert Stephen Holdings Ltd* [1968] 1 All ER 195n, [1968] 1 WLR 522, it was stated that the better practice in cases where one part of a class are to be treated differently from another part of the same class (unless all the shareholders consent) is to proceed by way of a scheme of arrangement under what is now CA 1985, s 425 as this affords better protection to a non-assenting minority. In this case the court did confirm the reduction despite it affecting shareholders of the same class in different ways but no shareholder appeared to oppose the confirmation.

12   *Poole v National Bank of China Ltd* [1907] AC 229 at 239, HL; *Caldwell & Co v Caldwell* 1916 SC (HL) 120 at 121; *Ex p Westburn Sugar Refineries Ltd* [1951] AC 625 at 630, [1951] 1 All ER 881 at 884.

13   See *Re Grosvenor Press plc* [1985] 1 WLR 980, [1985] BCLC 286.

14   *Ex p Westburn Sugar Refineries Ltd* [1951] AC 625, [1951] 1 All ER 881.

15   1948 SC 360; affd sub nom *Scottish Insurance Corpn Ltd v Wilsons and Clyde Coal Co Ltd* [1949] AC 462, [1949] 1 All ER 1068, HL.

16   [1894] AC 399.

17   (1906) 8 F 1135.

18   [1907] AC 229.

19   1916 SC (HL) 120.

addition of the words 'in the ordinary sense of the term' or 'as a matter of business'. ... it is abundantly plain from these decisions that the court's jurisdiction is a discretionary one, not confined to verifying the technical correctness of the formal procedure, nor even to determining according to strict law the precise rights of the contending parties, but involving an application of broad standards of fairness, reasonableness and equity ...[20].

Having established the discretionary nature of the jurisdiction to confirm a reduction, involving the application of broad standards of fairness and equity, he continued:

Nothing could be clearer and more reassuring than these formulations of the duties of the court. Nothing could be more disappointing than the reported instances of their subsequent exercise. Examples abound of the refusal of the courts to entertain the plea that a scheme was not fair or equitable, but it is very hard to find in recent times any clear and instructive instance of the acceptance of such an objection. The explanations may be that the modern company meeting never deviates by a hair's breadth from fairness and equity, and that the "proper case" for the exercise of the court's discretionary control never nowadays occurs; but I find it difficult to regard this explanation as convincing[20].

So despite the existence of this broad equitable jurisdiction vested in the courts, it is rare for the courts to refuse to confirm a reduction. Lord Cooper went on to indicate why he thought this was the case:

It is important to observe that nearly all the cases in which the court has refused to listen to the complaint of a minority have been marked by one or both of two significant features: (a) that the dissentient minority was very small and usually merely obstructive, and (b) that the company was a going concern, recasting its capital structure in the general interests of the company as a trading entity, or staving off the threat of ruin in the interests of all concerned. When such features are present it is easy to understand the hint dropped by Eve J (*Thomas de la Rue & Co*)[1] that in ninety-nine cases out of a hundred the court should not interfere, and to appreciate the importance rightly attached by Stirling LJ (*Welsbach Incandescent Gas Light Co*)[2] to the bona fide judgment of businessmen on a matter of business in which they themselves are largely interested[3].

These arguments are a familiar response to objecting shareholders. The scheme in question is always supported by a large majority of the shareholders (necessarily so for the statute requires a special resolution) and raises issues of internal management and business judgement which are for the company to decide upon and not the courts[4].

Little has changed in the more recent cases with Harman J in *Re Ratners Group plc*[5] noting:

---

20   1948 SC 360 at 376.
1   [1911] 2 Ch 361.
2   [1904] 1 Ch 87.
3   1948 SC 360 at 376–377.
4   See *Poole v National Bank of China Ltd* [1907] AC 229 at 236, per Lord Loreburn: '... it is no part of the business of a court of justice to determine the wisdom of a course adopted by a company in the management of its own affairs.'
5   [1988] BCLC 685. See also *Re Thorn EMI plc* [1989] BCLC 612. The other qualification on the court's discretion noted by Harman J in both of these cases was that the court must not be asked to confirm a reduction which was for no discernible purpose but was a hollow and pointless act.

The court has over the years established... three principles on which the court will require to be satisfied. Those principles are, first, that all shareholders are treated equitably in any reduction. That usually means that they are treated equally, but may mean that they are treated equally save as to some who have consented to their being treated unequally, so that counsel's word 'equitably' is the correct word which I adopt and accept. The second principle to be applied is that the shareholders at the general meeting had the proposals properly explained to them so that they could exercise an informed judgment on them. And the third principle is that creditors of the company are safeguarded so that money cannot be applied in any way which would be detrimental to creditors.[5a]

It was noted above that in many instances the creditors, shareholders and the company are in complete agreement about the proposal and the court's role is limited to endorsing their plans. It will equally be appreciated, in the light of the judicial attitude outlined above, that even the presence of dissentient shareholders is unlikely to alter the court's willingness to approve such schemes.

What has troubled the courts to a slightly greater degree in some of the cases has been a claim by preference shareholders that the effect of a proposed reduction of capital is to vary or abrogate their class rights and so requires their consent before it can be confirmed by the courts.

Reduction of capital and class rights

A particular area of difficulty has concerned schemes for the reduction of capital which have involved paying off the preference shareholders. Preference shareholders are often reluctant to be 'expelled' from the company in this way, particularly when it means an end to high dividend returns which are no longer available in the market. The question is whether the court should confirm such reductions or whether it is a variation of class rights (so requiring the consent of the class) to eliminate a class of preference shareholders in this way on a reduction of capital.

The approach of the courts has been to look at what the class rights would have been in a winding up and to compare that with the position which would arise under the proposed reduction. If what is proposed is in accordance with the class rights on a winding up, then there is no variation requiring the consent of the class.

Thus, if capital has been lost or is unrepresented by available assets and the classes rank pari passu, then prima facie the loss should be borne equally[6] but if there are preference shares which have priority as to a return of capital on a winding up, then the ordinary shares must bear the loss as they would do if the company was being wound up[7].

Alternatively, if surplus capital is being returned, it will normally be returned to the preference shareholders who will usually have priority as to repayment of capital in a winding up[8].

5a   [1988] BCLC 685 at 687.
6   See *Bannatyne v Direct Spanish Telegraph Co* (1886) 34 Ch D 287, CA where the preference shareholders had no preference as to capital, only as to dividend.
7   *Re Floating Dock Co of St Thomas Ltd* [1895] 1 Ch 691.
8   *Re Chatterley-Whitfield Collieries Ltd* [1948] 2 All ER 593; affd sub nom *Prudential Assurance Co Ltd v Chatterley-Whitfield Collieries Ltd* [1949] AC 512, [1949] 1 All ER 1094, HL; *Wilsons and Clyde Coal Co Ltd v Scottish Insurance Corpn* 1948 SC 360; affd sub nom *Scottish Insurance Corpn Ltd v Wilsons and Clyde Coal Co Ltd* [1949] AC 462, [1949] 1 All ER 1068, HL; *Re Fowlers Vacola Manufacturing Co Ltd* [1966] VR 97; *Re Saltdean Estate Co Ltd* [1968] 3 All ER 829, [1968] 1 WLR 1844; *House of Fraser plc v ACGE Investments Ltd* [1987] AC 387, [1987] 2 WLR 1083, HL.

The issue arose in *House of Fraser plc v ACGE Investments Ltd*[9] where the ordinary shareholders in general meeting passed a special resolution approving the paying off of the whole of the preference share capital of the company as being in excess of the wants of the company. No class meetings of the preference shareholders were held to approve the reduction. The company's articles provided that the special rights attached to any class of shares could only be modified, commuted, affected or dealt with, with the consent of the holders of the class of shares. The preference shareholders argued that the failure to obtain their consent meant that the court could not confirm the reduction.

The House of Lords accepted that the issue had been definitively addressed by Buckley J in *Re Saltdean Estate Co Ltd*[10], a case on almost identical facts:

> It has long been recognised that at least in normal circumstances where a company's capital is to be reduced by repaying paid-up share capital, in the absence of agreement or the sanction of a class meeting to the contrary, that class of capital should first be repaid which would be returned first in a winding up of the company (see *Re Chatterley-Whitfield Collieries Ltd*[11], per Lord Greene) ... In the present case the preference shareholders are entitled to prior repayment of capital in a winding up and, consequently, if the company has more paid up capital than it needs and wishes to repay some part of it, the first class of capital to be repaid should prima facie be the preferred shares.
>
> ...it is said that the proposed cancellation of the preferred shares will constitute an abrogation of all the rights attached to those shares which cannot validly be effected without an extraordinary resolution of a class meeting of preferred shareholders under art 8 of the company's articles. In my judgment, that article has no application to a cancellation of shares on a reduction of capital which is in accord with the rights attached to the shares of the company. Unless this reduction can be shown to be unfair to the preferred shareholders on other grounds, it is in accordance with the right and liability to prior repayment of capital attached to their shares. The liability to prior repayment on a reduction of capital, corresponding to their right to prior return of capital in a winding up, is a liability of the kind to which Lord Greene in the passage I have referred to, said that anyone has only himself to blame if he does not know it. It is part of the bargain between the shareholders and forms an integral part of the definition or delimitation of the bundle of rights which make up the preferred share. Giving effect to it does not involve the variation or abrogation of any rights attached to such shares[12].

Buckley J concluded:

> The fact is that every holder of preferred shares of the company has always been at risk that his hope of participating in undrawn or future profits of the company might be frustrated at any time by a liquidation of the company or a reduction of capital properly resolved upon by a majority of his fellow members. This vulnerability is, and has always been, a characteristic of the preferred shares.

9   [1987] AC 387, [1987] 2 WLR 1083, HL.
10   [1968] 3 All ER 829, [1968] 1 WLR 1844.
11   [1948] 2 All ER 593 at 596.
12   [1968] 3 All ER 829 at 831–832, [1968] 1 WLR 1844 at 1849–1850.

Now that the event has occurred, none of the preferred shareholders can, in my judgment, assert that the resulting state of affairs is unfair to him[13].

Applying that approach in the *House of Fraser* case, the House of Lords found that the proposed reduction of capital involved an extinction of preference shares in strict accordance with the contract embodied in the articles of association, to which the holders of the preference shares were party. The preference shareholders had a right to a return of capital in priority to other shareholders and that right was not affected, modified, dealt with or abrogated but was given effect to[14].

This is so in any instance where the preference shareholders have priority as to a return of capital, even if they also have further rights of participation as regards dividend[15]. It is not clear whether preference shares which are participating as to surplus on a winding up could be dealt with in this way although *Re William Jones & Sons Ltd*[16] suggests that they can. In that instance, however, the preference shareholders raised no objection to being paid off, probably because they were to be paid off in full although the shares stood at less than par. Moreover, there was no present prospect of the company being wound up so any enjoyment of surplus on a winding off would not occur for many years.

Preference shareholders must appreciate the impact which the company's ability to reduce capital may have on their position. It is important to bear in mind that it is possible to avoid the danger of a restrictive interpretation of what constitutes a variation by the court by identifying in the terms of issue those matters which are deemed to be a variation or abrogation of the rights attached to that class[17].

In *Re Northern Engineering Industries plc*[18] such a provision was included. The articles stated that the rights of any class were to be deemed to be varied by the reduction of the capital paid up on those shares. The company proposed to reduce its capital by paying off its preference shares and cancelling them without obtaining the consent of the class. The company argued that the provision in the articles only applied to a 'reduction' and a 'reduction' was something which involved a diminution or lessening from one number to a smaller number. It did not apply to a reduction to zero.

The Court of Appeal rejected this argument finding that the provision in the articles must be construed in the light of its purpose, namely the protection of the shareholders of the class affected. It applied both where there was a piecemeal reduction of capital and where there was complete repayment of their investment. A reduction of capital without the consent of the class affected could not therefore be confirmed.

If a scheme of reduction does vary or abrogate class rights, despite the generality of the court's power to confirm (and some suggestions to the contrary in older cases[19]), it is unlikely that the court would now confirm a reduction without the appropriate class consent having been obtained[20].

---

13 [1968] 3 All ER 829 at 833–834, [1968] 1 WLR 1844 at 1849–1852. See also *Bannatyne v Direct Spanish Telegraph Co* (1886) 34 Ch D 287, CA; *Wilsons and Clyde Co Ltd v Scottish Insurance Corpn* 1948 SC 360; affd sub nom *Scottish Insurance Corpn Ltd v Wilsons and Clyde Coal Co Ltd* [1949] AC 462 at 487, [1949] 1 All ER 1068 at 1077–1078, per Lord Simonds, HL.
14 [1987] AC 387 at 393, [1987] BCLC 478 at 484.
15 *Re Saltdean Estate Co Ltd* [1968] 3 All ER 829, [1968] 1 WLR 1844.
16 [1969] 1 All ER 913, [1969] 1 WLR 146.
17 See *Re Northern Engineering Industries plc* [1994] 2 BCLC 704, CA.
18 [1994] 2 BCLC 704, CA.
19 See *Re William Jones & Sons Ltd* [1969] 1 All ER 913, [1969] 1 WLR 146.
20 See *Re Northern Engineering Industries plc* [1994] 2 BCLC 704 at 713, CA.

Procedure following confirmation by the court

Once the court confirms the reduction, a copy of the court order and of a minute approved by the court setting out the alteration to the company's capital must be filed for registration with the registrar of companies and the reduction is not effective until this has been done[1]. The registrar then certifies the registration and this certificate of registration is conclusive evidence that all the requirements with respect to the reduction of share capital have been complied with and the court minute sent to the registrar is deemed to be substituted for the corresponding part of the memorandum[2].

Where the court makes an order confirming a reduction of a public company's capital which has the effect of bringing the nominal value of its allotted share capital below the authorised minimum, the registrar of companies must not register the order unless the court otherwise directs, or the company is first re-registered as a private company[3].

FORFEITURE AND SURRENDER

The articles of association of a company may provide that shares may be forfeited for non-payment of calls in respect of sums remaining unpaid on the shares[4]. This does not fall foul of the prohibition on a company acquiring its own shares[5]. Such forfeiture provisions are regarded as penal provisions and must be construed strictly[6]. Subject to the provisions of the Act, a forfeited share may be sold, re-allotted or otherwise disposed of on such terms and in such manner as the directors determine[7].

A person whose shares have been forfeited ceases to be a member and must surrender to the company for cancellation the share certificate in respect of those shares but remains liable to the company for all moneys which at the date of forfeiture were payable by him to the company in respect of those shares, although the directors may waive payment wholly or in part[8].

In the case of a public company, unless the shares are previously disposed of, the company must not later than the end of three years from the date of their forfeiture, cancel them and diminish the amount of share capital by the nominal value of the shares[9]. The company must not exercise any voting rights in respect of the shares and any purported exercise of those rights will be void[10].

A company's articles may also provide for the surrender of shares and it is common to find a provision for surrender in lieu of forfeiture. A surrender of shares in a public company is governed by the same rules as those applying to forfeiture[11].

---

1   CA 1985, s 138(1) and (2).
2   Ibid, s 138(4) and (5).
3   Ibid, s 139. The authorised minimum is set at £50,000: s 118(1).
4   See Table A, arts 18–22.
5   CA 1985, s 143(3)(d).
6   *Johnson v Lyttle's Iron Agency* (1877) 5 Ch D 687, CA.
7   Table A, art 20.
8   Table A, art 21.
9   CA 1985, s 146(2)(a); see also ibid, s 146(2)(b).
10   Ibid, s 146(4).
11   Ibid, s 146(1).

CHAPTER 18

Classes of shares and class rights

BACKGROUND

In the early period of modern company law, from the mid 1850s to the early 1880s, it was common to have shares of only one class. These were usually of high nominal value but were only partly paid[1]. From about 1880, fashions changed with the rise of the small shareholder interested in investing in the company but not in participating in its affairs. We see in this period the issue of shares of smaller nominal value on which a higher proportion of the price was paid up on issue. Up to this point nearly all the shares issued were ordinary shares but here we also see the rise of the preference share as a fashionable hybrid between ordinary shares and debentures[2]. It suited the needs of those who were more interested in a fixed yield and proved useful to those companies which wished to raise further capital without risking a loss of control by the existing equity shareholders.

Since the 1920s there has been a trend towards greater simplicity in share structures. Private companies usually restrict themselves to ordinary shares while public companies often have two classes of shares, ordinary and preference, with possibly several forms of each. More sophisticated structures may be found in public listed companies.

THE CONCEPT OF A CLASS AND CLASS RIGHTS

It is common for the articles of association to give a company complete freedom to issue shares with such rights and restrictions as the company may by ordinary resolution determine[3]. Formerly, it was thought that this power should be reserved from incorporation[4] but it is clear that such a provision can be adopted at any time provided that there is no conflict with the memorandum[5].

---

1   See G H Evans *British Corporation Finance 1775–1850* (1936).
2   See Cottrell *Industrial Finance 1830–1914* (1979), ch 4.
3   See Table A, art 2.
4   *Hutton v Scarborough Cliff Hotel Co Ltd* (1865) 2 Drew & Sm 521.
5   *Andrews v Gas Meter Co* [1897] 1 Ch 361, CA.

Where particular rights are annexed to certain shares, these are described as class rights. A class can probably be defined as 'those persons whose rights are not so dissimilar as to make it impossible for them to consult together with a view to their common interest'[6]. Different classes of shares will have differing rights concerning, in particular, the right to vote and attend meetings, to receive a dividend, and to a return of capital on a winding up.

In *Cumbrian Newspapers Group Ltd v Cumberland and Westmorland Herald Newspaper and Printing Co Ltd*[7], Scott J broadened the classification of class rights in an unorthodox way to include rights conferred on a member of the company in his capacity as a member which rights were not attached to any particular class of shares. The plaintiff in that case had been given by name certain rights of pre-emption and the right to appoint a director and to transfer shares. Scott J thought that the shares for the time being held by that member constituted a class for the purposes of the statutory procedure for variation of class rights[8]. The purpose of the articles, he found, was to enable the plaintiff, in its capacity as a shareholder in the company, to obstruct an attempted takeover:

> In my judgment, a company which, by its articles, confers special rights on one or more of its members in the capacity of member or shareholder thereby constitutes the shares for the time being held by that member or members a class of shares for the purposes of s 125 [the statutory provision governing variation of class rights]. The rights are class rights[9].

The value of a right being classified as a 'class right' is that, in general, it cannot be varied without the consent of the class. The precise method of variation is discussed in detail below. A provision in the articles which does not amount to a class right, on the other hand, can be altered by a special resolution under the statutory authority to alter the articles of association[10]. A class right can therefore be a valuable element in the protection of minority shareholders or any other special interests. For example, the Government protects its special interests in retaining an element of control in some of the privatised companies through a so-called 'golden share', discussed below, which is nothing more than a separate class of share consisting of one £1 share held by the relevant Secretary of State.

Class rights may be set out in the memorandum or articles or in the resolution creating them. In practice, they are usually set out in the articles. In any case of conflict between rights in the memorandum and those in the articles or the resolution authorising the issue, the memorandum prevails[11]. If class rights are created other than by the memorandum, articles, or a resolution requiring registration[12], then details of those

---

6   *Sovereign Life Assurance Co v Dodd* [1892] 2 QB 573 at 583, per Bowen LJ, CA. See also *Re Hellenic & General Trust Ltd* [1975] 3 All ER 382, [1976] 1 WLR 123.

7   [1987] Ch 1, [1986] 2 All ER 816.

8   [1987] Ch 1 at 16, [1986] 2 All ER 816 at 830. See Polack [1986] CLJ 399; *Palmer's Company Law* (25th edn, 1992), para 6.007: 'It is submitted ... that this decision is incorrect'; cf *Gower's Principles of Modern Company Law* (6th edn, 1997), p 720: 'This decision is greatly to be welcomed ...'.

9   [1987] Ch 1 at 22, [1986] 2 All ER 816 at 830. See also *Re Blue Arrow plc* [1987] BCLC 585 at 590 (a right conferred on an individual unrelated to any shareholding in any way cannot be described as a class right).

10   Ie under Companies Act 1985, s 9.

11   *Guinness v Land Corpn of Ireland Ltd* (1882) 22 Ch D 349, CA.

12   Ie under Companies Act 1985, s 380.

class rights must be notified to the registrar of companies[13]. Where all the shares fall within the one class, there are no class rights but only shareholder rights.

RULES OF CONSTRUCTION

Certain rules of construction have been developed by the courts to assist them in identifying the rights attaching to each class, given that they vary from company to company. However, it must be stressed that each case ultimately turns on the particular terms of issue[14].

A presumption of equality

There is a presumption of equality as between shareholders with all shareholders being deemed to be entitled to the same proportionate part in the capital of the company[15]. This presumption is easily rebutted by an issue of shares on terms which give special rights with respect to dividends, to the return of capital, or to voting at meetings of the company, to a class or classes of shareholders. Preference shareholders typically will have a preferential right to a dividend and to a return of capital on a winding up.

Rights granted are deemed to be exhaustive

There is a presumption that any rights which are attached to a share are deemed to be exhaustive[16]. The position was clearly expressed by Sargant J in *Re National Telephone Co*[17] where he said:

> ... the weight of authority is in favour of the view that, either with regard to dividend or with regard to the rights in a winding up, the express gift or attachment of preferential rights to preference shares, on their creation, is, prima facie, a definition of the whole of their rights in that respect, and negatives any further or other right to which, but for the specified rights, they would have been entitled.

In *Will v United Lankat Plantations Co Ltd*[18] the attachment of preferential dividend rights to preference shares was presumed to be exhaustive as to their dividend rights. This had the effect of negating any right to further participation in any surplus profits of the company. This presumption of exhaustive rights can be rebutted by expressly declaring the shares to be participating preference shares with a right of participation

---

13   Ibid, s 128(1). A similar requirement applies to variations of such rights and to the assignment of a new name or designation to any class of members: s 128(3), (4).
14   The Jenkins Committee (1962, Cmnd 1749), para 196 considered but rejected the idea of a schedule to the Companies Act listing the particular rights which would attach to preference shares in the absence of a contrary provision. The Committee questioned the wisdom of attempting to define by statute the basic rights of preference shares given that there are so many varieties.
15   *Birch v Cropper, Re Bridgewater Navigation Co Ltd* (1889) 14 App Cas 525 at 543, HL, per Lord Macnaghten.
16   *Re National Telephone Co* [1914] 1 Ch 755.
17   [1914] 1 Ch 755 at 774.
18   [1914] AC 11.

in surplus profits after a certain percentage of dividend has been paid to the ordinary shareholders[19].

Likewise where preference shares are given an express priority to a return of capital on a winding up, this negates any right to participate in surplus assets in a winding up[20]. Again, the terms of issue may enable preference shareholders to share in surplus assets with the other shareholders after their capital had been repaid but it is for preference shareholders to show that they are entitled to share in this way[1].

A cumulative dividend

Prima facie, preference shares are entitled to a cumulative dividend, even in the absence of any such provision in the terms of issue[2]. This means that the preference shareholders will be entitled to have any deficiencies made up from the profits of subsequent years before anything is distributed to other shareholders. Alternatively, preference shares may be issued as non-cumulative but this must be clearly stated to ensure that the presumption does not apply[3].

On a winding up, if the company is solvent, a question concerning the payment of arrears of dividend may arise. There is a prima facie presumption that dividends and arrears thereof are only payable while the company is a going concern and are therefore no longer payable once winding up has begun[4]. That inference is rebuttable where there are express words in the terms of issue to the contrary or a definition in the right to dividend which is inconsistent with it[5].

The net effect of these rules of construction is that class rights are usually spelt out in great detail in the terms of issue to avoid falling foul of one or other presumption.

CLASSES OF SHARES

Ordinary shares

Ordinary shares, often called equities, carry the residual rights of participation in the income and capital of the company which have not been granted to other classes. Ordinary shareholders have no right to any fixed dividend but after the payment of any dividends to preference shareholders, the ordinary shareholders enjoy the remainder of the surplus actually distributed as dividend by the directors. In difficult times, the ordinary shareholders run the risk that the profits available for distribution will be inadequate and will not extend beyond (or indeed to) the payment of the dividend due on the preference shares but in prosperous times, while the preference shareholders will be restricted to their fixed dividend, the ordinary shareholders will enjoy all of the surplus distributable profits.

19   *See Re Isle of Thanet Electric Supply Co Ltd* [1950] Ch 161, CA.
20   *Scottish Insurance Corpn Ltd v Wilsons and Clyde Coal Co Ltd* [1949] AC 462, [1949] 1 All ER 1068; *Prudential Assurance Co Ltd v Chatterley-Whitfield Collieries Ltd* [1949] AC 512, [1949] 1 All ER 1094, HL.
1   *Re Isle of Thanet Electric Supply Co Ltd* [1950] Ch 161, CA; *Scottish Insurance Corpn Ltd v Wilsons and Clyde Coal Co Ltd* [1949] AC 462, [1949] 1 All ER 1068, HL.
2   *Webb v Earle* (1875) LR 20 Eq 556.
3   *Staples v Eastman Photographic Materials Co* [1896] 2 Ch 303, CA (the terms of issue referred specifically to dividends paid out of the profits of each year).
4   *Re Crichton's Oil Co* [1902] 2 Ch 86.
5   *Re E W Savory Ltd* [1951] 2 All ER 1036 (reference to the ranking of the preference shares must have been a reference to what would happen on winding up); *Re Walter Symons Ltd* [1934] Ch 308.

Ordinary shareholders will have a right to a return of capital ranking after the preference shares but, in the same way as with the payment of dividends, ordinary shares will claim the pool of surplus assets in a solvent winding up after the return of capital to all other shareholders. Sometimes, however, preference shares have a right to participate in surplus assets.

Ordinary shares will usually carry one vote per share although companies may attach such voting rights as they choose. As preference shares have only a restricted right to vote, ordinary shares will carry voting control in general meetings. Non-voting ordinary shares can be issued but they are not common and are disapproved of by The Stock Exchange although capable of being listed. In recent years many of the small number of listed companies which did have non-voting shares have restructured their capital so as to enfranchise the non-voting shares.

Preference shares

Typically, a preference share will have a fixed preferential cumulative dividend[6], a priority as to a return of capital on a winding up and will be non-participating as to surplus both while the company is a going concern and on a winding up. Preference shares can be participating as to dividend and/or capital which means that they are sometimes given a further right to participate in profits or assets.

Preference shares usually have restricted voting rights limited to matters which affect their rights such as when their dividends are in arrears.

In some ways, the position of preference shareholders is akin to creditors. Indeed preference shares are often regarded as a hybrid between equity or share capital and loan capital[7]. Their fixed dividend resembles the fixed interest payable on loan capital and their priority to a return of capital in a winding up resembles the creditor's right to a return of the capital sum; although it is only a priority over other shareholders and, as shareholders, the preference shareholders rank after secured and unsecured creditors.

Redeemable shares

As already discussed in Chapter 16, a company limited by shares or limited by guarantee and having a share capital may, if authorised to do so by its articles, issue shares which are to be redeemed or are liable to be redeemed at the option of the company or the shareholder.

Convertible shares

It is possible for a company to issue preference shares which are convertible into ordinary shares either on a set date or at the option of the shareholders or, in some circumstances, at the option of the company.

---

6   The payment of dividends is still dependent on the company having distributable profits as required by Companies Act 1985 Part VIII but if there are such profits then the terms of issue of preference shares usually require the payment of a dividend on fixed dates.

7   See Pickering (1963) 26 MLR 499; note also Gower's *Principles of Modern Company Law* (6th edn, 1997) p 318: 'Suspended midway between true creditors and true members they [preference shareholders] may get the worst of both worlds, unless the instrument creating the preference shares is carefully drafted.'

Golden shares

Over the past decade the Government has privatised a number of businesses which previously operated in the public sector. This was achieved essentially by the Government selling its shareholding in these companies to the public. However, in a number of cases the Government wished to retain some control over the company, for example, to prevent a foreign takeover or to prevent individual shareholders building up too large a stake. In some cases the restrictions have been imposed indefinitely, in others the Government sought to retain some powers only for a limited period of time. To have placed such restrictions in the articles of association would not have been sufficient as the articles could then have been altered by the shareholders once the company had been privatised.

The method used instead to entrench these provisions was to create a class of special preference share, usually made up of a single £1 share held by the relevant Secretary of State. Whatever restriction which the Government wished to impose was then specified in the articles and it was stated that any attempt to vary those provisions required the consent of the special preference class[8]. Hence the so-called golden share, a single £1 share which gave the power to veto certain changes within the company[9].

VARIATION OF CLASS RIGHTS

The variation of class rights is governed by statute which provides that rights attached to a class can only be varied or abrogated in certain ways[10]. In *Re House of Fraser plc*[11] the Court of Session noted that variation presupposes the continuance of rights in a varied state while abrogation presupposes termination of rights without satisfaction or fulfilment. Where either occurs, the statute broadly speaking requires either compliance with the statutory scheme (ie the consent in writing to the variation of the holders of 75% in nominal value of the issued shares of the class or an extraordinary resolution passed at a separate general meeting of the holders of the class sanctioning the variation) or adherence to a variation provision in the company's constitution which will usually be in broadly similar terms[12]. However, the statutory protection only applies if what has occurred does amount to a variation or abrogation of class rights and the courts have restricted the application of the section (and equivalent provisions in the articles) by interpreting 'variation' and 'abrogation' quite restrictively.

---

8   It is interesting to consider the terms of issue of these shares although they vary from company to company. In the context of the regional electricity companies, the notes to the accounts of Southern Electric plc explained what the special share entailed: 'The special share is a special rights redeemable preference share redeemable at par at any time before 31 March 1995 at the option of the Secretary of State after consulting the Company. Unless so redeemed the special share will be redeemed at par on 31 March 1995. This share, which may only be held by the Secretary of State or another person acting on behalf of HM Government, does not carry any rights to vote at general meetings but entitles the holder to attend and speak at such meetings. Certain matters, in particular the alteration of specified sections of the articles of association of the company (including the article relating to limitations that prevent a person from owning or acquiring an interest in 15% or more of the ordinary shares in Southern Electric plc) require the prior written consent of the holder of the special share. The special share confers no right to participate in capital or profits of the company, except that on a winding up the special shareholder is entitled to repayment of £1 in priority to other shareholders: Southern Electric plc *Annual Report and Accounts 1994*, p 36.

9   See Prosser *Privatising Public Enterprises* (1991); Veljanovski *Selling the State* (1987), pp 127–128; Graham and Prosser 'Privatising Nationalised Industries' (1987) 50 MLR 16.

10   Companies Act 1985, s 125.

11   [1987] BCLC 293 at 301.

12   Companies Act 1985, s 125(2).

In approaching the question of whether a variation or abrogation has occurred, the courts have drawn a very artificial distinction between matters affecting the rights attaching to each share, and matters affecting the enjoyment of those rights. Only in the former category is it necessary to adhere to the variation provision. Where only the enjoyment of the right is affected then the shares may be commercially less valuable but their rights remain what they always were[13].

A typical case is *White v Bristol Aeroplane Co Ltd*[14] where an issue of further preference shares which would dilute the control of the existing preference shareholders was held not to be a variation. All the new shares were to be issued to the existing ordinary shareholders and paid for out of the reserves of the company. The company's articles provided that all or any of the rights or privileges attached to any class of shares forming part of the capital for the time being of the company might be affected, modified, varied, dealt with or abrogated in any manner with the sanction of an extraordinary resolution passed at a separate meeting of the members of that class. It was argued by the plaintiff preference shareholder that the word 'affect' was wide and must be taken to cover a transaction which though not necessarily modifying or varying rights would in some way otherwise affect them.

Evershed MR concluded that the new issue did not affect the rights or privileges of the existing preference shareholders which remained exactly as they were before. They might be affected as a matter of business by reason of the new preference stock which would be in the possession of the ordinary shareholders and which would have a majority over the existing preference stock. This, however, would only affect the enjoyment of the rights and not the rights themselves.

Romer LJ drew a distinction between rights on the one hand and the result of exercising the rights on the other hand:

> The rights, as such, are conferred by resolution or by the articles, and they cannot be affected except with the sanction of the members on whom those rights are conferred; but the results of exercising those rights are not the subject of any assurance or guarantee under the constitution of the company, and are not protected in any way[15].

Similarly in *Greenhalgh v Arderne Cinemas Ltd*[16] a subdivision of a class of ten shilling ordinary shares into two shilling shares was held not to vary the rights of Mr Greenhalgh, a holder of the existing two shilling ordinary shares, although the result of the sub-division was to alter control of the company. Lord Greene noted:

> ... I agree, the effect of this resolution is, of course, to alter the position of the two shilling shareholders. Instead of Greenhalgh finding himself in a position of control, he finds himself in a position where the control has gone, and to that extent the rights of the two shilling shareholders are affected, as a matter of business. As a matter of law, I am quite unable to hold that, as a result of the transaction, the rights are varied; they remain what they always were – a right to have one vote per share pari passu with the ordinary shares for the time being issued which include the new two shilling shares resulting from the subdivision[17].

13   See *Greenhalgh v Arderne Cinemas Ltd* [1946] 1 All ER 512; *Re John Smith's Tadcaster Brewery Co Ltd* [1953] Ch 308, [1953] 1 All ER 518.
14   [1953] Ch 65, CA.
15   [1953] Ch 65 at 82, CA.
16   [1946] 1 All ER 512, CA.
17   [1946] 1 All ER 512 at 518, CA.

A particular area of difficulty has concerned schemes for the reduction of capital which have usually involved paying off the preference shareholders. The question is whether it is a variation of class rights to eliminate a class of preference shareholders in this way on a reduction of capital. As discussed above in Chapter 17, it is clear that far from regarding reduction as a variation of class rights, the court regards it as a fulfilment of the rights of a preference shareholder, provided that the reduction is consistent with the preference shareholders' rights as to a return of capital on a winding up[18].

It is important to bear in mind that it is possible to avoid the danger of a restrictive interpretation of what constitutes a variation by the court by identifying in the terms of issue those matters which are deemed to be a variation or abrogation of the rights attached to a class so triggering the variation mechanism[19]. In *Re Northern Engineering Industries plc*[20] the articles stated that the rights of any class were to be deemed to be varied by the reduction of the capital paid up on those shares. The company proposed to reduce its capital by paying off its preference shares and cancelling them without obtaining the consent of the class. The company argued that the provision in the articles only applied to a reduction which involved a diminution or lessening from one number to a smaller number. It did not apply to a reduction to zero.

The Court of Appeal rejected this argument finding that the provision in the articles must be construed in the light of its purpose, namely the protection of the shareholders of the class affected. It applied both where there was a piecemeal reduction of capital and where there was complete repayment of their investment. A reduction of capital without the consent of the class affected could not therefore be confirmed.

METHODS OF VARIATION

Assuming that what is proposed is indeed a variation or abrogation of class rights, it is necessary to ensure that the proper variation procedure is followed.

The statutory scheme is intended to provide a comprehensive code setting out the manner in which rights attached to any class of shares can be varied[1]. It is quite complicated but it will usually require the consent of the holders of 75% in nominal value of the issued shares of that class in writing or an extraordinary resolution of the class approving the variation at a separate class meeting[2]. At a class meeting so held, the shareholders must have regard to what is in the best interests of the class[3].

---

18 See *Re Floating Dock Co of St Thomas Ltd* [1895] 1 Ch 691; *Re Chatterley-Whitfield Collieries Ltd* [1948] 2 All ER 593; affd sub nom *Prudential Assurance Co Ltd v Chatterley-Whitfield Collieries Ltd* [1949] AC 512, [1949] 1 All ER 1094, HL; *Wilsons and Clyde Coal Co Ltd v Scottish Insurance Corpn* 1948 SC 360; affd sub nom *Scottish Insurance Corpn Ltd v Wilsons and Clyde Coal Co Ltd* [1949] AC 462, [1949] 1 All ER 1068, HL; *Re Saltdean Estate Co Ltd* [1968] 3 All ER 829, [1968] 1 WLR 1844; *House of Fraser plc v ACGE Investments Ltd* [1987] AC 387, [1987] 2 WLR 1083, HL. See generally Chapter 17.
19 See *Re Northern Engineering Industries plc* [1994] 2 BCLC 704.
20 [1994] 2 BCLC 704.
1 *Cumbrian Newspapers Group Ltd v Cumberland and Westmorland Herald Newspaper and Printing Co Ltd* [1987] Ch 1 at 14, [1986] 2 All ER 816 at 824, per Scott J.
2 Companies Act 1985, s 125(2).
3 *British America Nickel Corpn v M J O'Brien Ltd* [1927] AC 369; *Re Holders Investment Trust Ltd* [1971] 2 All ER 289, [1971] 1 WLR 583; see also *Re Hellenic & General Trust Ltd* [1975] 3 All ER 382, [1976] 1 WLR 123. But see Sealy *Cases and Materials in Company Law* (6th edn, 1996), p 469: 'If taken literally, the rule [that members voting at a class meeting must act in the interest of the class as a whole] as so interpreted would not allow a class to subordinate its own interests to those of the company as a whole, and class rights could never be varied except to the holders' advantage. This cannot surely have been intended.'

However, the statute provides a number of permutations which depend on:

(i)　the origin of the class rights (ie whether they are contained in the memorandum or articles or elsewhere); and
(ii)　whether specific provision has been made by the company for their variation.

Class rights set out in the memorandum

If the rights are set out in the memorandum and there is no provision for variation (whether in the memorandum or in the articles), then the rights may only be varied by unanimous agreement of all members of the company (not the class)[4]. This result could also be achieved by a scheme of arrangement[5].

If the rights are set out in the memorandum and there is an express prohibition on variation in the memorandum, the rights cannot be altered except by a scheme of arrangement.

If the rights are set out in the memorandum and there is a provision for variation in the memorandum or in the articles (which provision in the articles was included in the articles at the time of the company's original incorporation), it is necessary to adhere to the provision for variation[6] unless the variation is concerned with the giving, variation, revocation or renewal of authority for allotment[7] or with a reduction of capital[8]. In those cases, it is necessary to comply with the statutory procedure, ie 75% of the class must consent, and with any additional requirements imposed by the variation clause in the memorandum or articles[9].

Class rights set out in the articles

If the class rights are set out in the articles and there is no provision for variation in the articles, then the statutory scheme must be used, ie 75% of the class must consent, and any additional requirement (however imposed) must be complied with[10].

If the class rights are set out in the articles or elsewhere and there is a provision for variation in the articles then it is necessary to adhere to the provision in the articles[11] unless the variation is concerned with the giving, variation, revocation or renewal of authority for allotment[12] or with a reduction of capital[13]. In those cases, it is necessary to comply with the statutory procedure, ie 75% of the class must consent, and with any additional requirements imposed by the variation clause in the articles[14].

Finally, note that the alteration of an existing variation provision or the insertion of a variation procedure is itself a variation of class rights and subject to the statutory scheme[15].

4　CA 1985, s 125(5). Note ibid, s 17(2)(b) in this context.
5　Under ibid, s 425.
6　Ibid, s 125(4).
7　Ie under ibid, s 80.
8　Ie under ibid, s 135.
9　Ibid, s 125(3).
10　Ibid, s 125(2).
11　Ibid, s 125(4).
12　Under ibid s 80.
13　Under ibid, s 135.
14　Ibid, s 125(3).
15　Ibid, s 125(7).

OBJECTIONS TO VARIATIONS

Where a class has duly consented to a variation, the holders of not less in the aggregate than 15% of the issued shares of that class, provided that they did not consent to or vote for the variation, may apply to the court within 21 days after the date on which the resolution was passed to have the variation cancelled[16]. Where such an application is made, the variation will not take effect until it has been confirmed by the court[17]. The court on hearing the application may, if satisfied having regard to all the circumstances of the case, that the variation would unfairly prejudice the shareholders of the class represented by the applicant, disallow the variation; otherwise, it shall confirm it[18].

In practice, this provision is rarely used, not least because it is unlikely that a court will overturn a variation which has already been agreed to by 75% of the class. A member of a class who feels aggrieved may try to bring a more broadly based case under the unfairly prejudicial remedy[19].

16   Ibid, s 127(1)–(3).
17   Ibid, s 127(2).
18   Ibid, s 127(4).
19   Ie under ibid, s 459, discussed in Chapter 28.

CHAPTER 19

Legal incidents of membership

INTRODUCTION

The terms 'member' and 'shareholder' are often used interchangeably and in most cases a member is a shareholder. However, this may not always be the case. For example, a company limited by guarantee without a share capital has members but no shareholders while the holder of a bearer share warrant is a shareholder but not a member because his name has not been entered on the company's register of members which, as we shall see, is decisive in determining who is a member.

RESTRICTIONS ON MEMBERSHIP

As a general rule, anyone may be a member but there are restrictions imposed on some classes of persons.

Minors

There is no prohibition on minors[1] being shareholders although the company may refuse to accept a minor as a shareholder[2]. Applying ordinary contract law rules, a contract to purchase shares is voidable by a minor before or within a reasonable time of attaining his majority. If the minor repudiates the contract, he will not be liable for future calls but cannot recover the purchase price unless there has been a total failure of consideration[3], which is unlikely to be the case. Given that shares are normally issued as fully paid, there is little reason now for repudiation and it is rare for problems with minors to arise, unlike in the late nineteenth century when there were many cases of heirs and heiresses seeking to repudiate contracts for shares. Until the minor repudiates, the minor has full rights of membership.

1　That is anyone under 18 years of age in England and Wales: Family Law Reform Act 1969, s 1.
2　*Re Asiatic Banking Corpn, Symons' Case* (1870) 5 Ch App 298.
3　*Steinberg v Scala (Leeds) Ltd* [1923] 2 Ch 452, CA.

Companies and subsidiary companies

A company cannot be a member of itself, a point originally established in *Trevor v Whitworth*[4] and now included in the statute which provides that any purported acquisition by a company of its own shares is void and an offence by the company and any officer in default[5]. The prohibition does not apply where a company acquires any of its own fully paid shares otherwise than for valuable consideration; or on a redemption or purchase of its own shares or on a reduction of capital properly authorised; or as a result of the forfeiture of shares or the surrender of shares in lieu of forfeiture under the articles; or pursuant to a court order[6].

The legislation further provides that, subject to certain exceptions, a company cannot be a member of its holding company and any allotment or transfer of shares in a company to its subsidiary is void[7]. The policy behind this prohibition is to reinforce the rule in *Trevor v Whitworth*[8] and prevent any reduction of capital. The prohibition cannot be avoided by using a nominee for the prohibition applies to a nominee acting on behalf of a subsidiary as to the subsidiary itself[9].

However, there are a number of exceptional circumstances when a subsidiary may hold shares in its holding company:

(i)   where the subsidiary is concerned only as personal representative or trustee unless, in the latter case, the holding company or a subsidiary of it is beneficially interested under the trust[10];

(ii)   where shares in the holding company are held by the subsidiary in the ordinary course of its business as an inermediary[11] (which essentially means carrying on a bona fide business of dealing in securities);

(iii)   where the subsidiary held the shares before 1 July 1948; or held the shares between 1 July 1948 and 20 October 1997 in circumstances in which these provisions (prohibiting membership) as they then had effect did not apply, but at any time after 20 October 1997 falls within the prohibition in respect of those shares (because of changed definitions of holding and subsidiary companies), it may continue to be a member of the holding company (and to receive bonus issues in respect of its holding) but it has no right to vote those shares in general or class meetings[12];

(iv)   where a company becomes a holder of shares in another company on or after 20 October 1997 and subsequently becomes a subsidiary of that other company, it may continue to hold those shares (and receive bonus issues in respect of them) but may not vote those shares at general or class meetings[13].

---

4   (1887) 12 App Cas 409, HL.
5   CA 1985, s 143(1), (2).
6   Ibid, s 143(3); see also ss 144-145 as to the position where the company's nominee acquires the shares. A public company acquiring its own shares in certain circumstances (particularly on forfeiture and surrender) is required to disenfranchise such shares and to cancel them within a certain period (generally three years) if not previously disposed of: see s 146.
7   Ibid, s 23(1). 'Holding company' and 'subsidiary' are defined by s 736.
8   (1887) 12 App Cas 409, HL.
9   CA 1985, s 23(7).
10   Ibid, s 23(2).
11   Ibid, s 23(3), as amended by the Companies (Membership of Holding Company) (Dealers in Securities) Regulations 1997, SI 1997 No 2306.
12   Ibid, s 23(4), (6), as amended.
13   Ibid, s 23(5), (6), as amended.

Subject to these cases, a company can be a member of another company and may appoint a corporate representative[14] to attend meetings.

NOMINEE HOLDINGS

Nominee shareholdings, ie holdings registered in the name of someone holding the shares directly or indirectly on behalf of the true owner, are valid and common. This is particularly the case in public companies where nominees can be used to amalgamate large numbers of small holdings although they can also be used to mask the identity of those holding shares in a company. This may be for reasons of privacy and commercial convenience but it may also be a means of disguising undesirable practices such as insider dealing and share support schemes contrary to the statutory provisions[15] and of camouflaging would-be bidders for the company who may be trying to evade the requirements of the City Code on Takeovers and Mergers[16].

The Companies Act 1985 Part VI contains a number of provisions aimed at curbing such abuses. These include an obligation to notify the company of any known interests in voting shares in a public company within two days of the obligation arising[17]. A notifiable interest for this purpose essentially means a material interest equal to 3% or more of the nominal value of the share capital of the company[18]. There is also a requirement to notify particulars of certain family and corporate interests[19]; and notification of interests of persons acting together[20]. A register of interests in shares must be kept by every public company[1] and the company has power to require information with respect to interests in its voting shares[2]. These provisions are supplemented by the powers of investigation conferred on the Department of Trade and Industry which are discussed in Chapter 30.

DEFINITION OF MEMBER

The statute provides that:

(1) the subscribers of a company's memorandum are deemed to have agreed to become members of the company, and on its registration must be entered as such in its register of members.

(2) Every other person who agrees[3] to become a member of a company, and whose name is entered in its register of members, is a member of the company[4].

It should be noted that entry on the register of members is essential to membership in all cases save that of the subscribers[5].

---

14   Under ibid, s 375(1).
15   Ie contrary to ibid, ss 151-158.
16   Discussed in detail in Chapter 36.
17   CA 1985, ss 198, 202. The requirements of Part VI are considered in Chapters 35 and 36.
18   Ibid, s 199(2)(a); in some circumstances the threshold is 10%, see s 199(2)(b).
19   See ibid, s 203.
20   See ibid, s 204.
1   Ibid, s 211.
2   Ibid, s 212.
3   This requirement is satisfied when a person assents to become a member and it does not require that there should be a binding contract between the person and the company: *Re Nuneaton Borough Association Football Club Ltd* [1989] BCLC 454, CA.
4   CA 1985, s 22.
5   See *Re Florence Land and Public Works Co, Nicol's Case, Tufnell and Ponsonby's Case* (1885) 29 Ch D 421, CA.

There are four methods of becoming a shareholder:

(i)   by subscribing to the memorandum;
(ii) by taking up an allotment of shares by the company;
(iii) by a transfer of shares from an existing member;
(iv) by a transmission of shares on the death or bankruptcy of a member.

MEMBERSHIP – SUBSCRIBERS TO THE MEMORANDUM

·The subscribers to the company's memorandum are deemed to have agreed to become members and on registration of the memorandum they must be entered as such in the company's register of members[6]. The memorandum will indicate the number of shares which the subscribers have undertaken to purchase and every subscriber in the case of a company having a share capital must take at least one share[7]. It is rare now for any problems to arise with regard to subscribers.

MEMBERSHIP – ALLOTMENT OF SHARES

The allotment of shares by the company to existing or new investors is a matter for the directors, subject to certain statutory constraints. The duties of directors in this regard are discussed in Chapter 26 while the statutory constraints have already been discussed in Chapter 15. In Chapter 34 we shall examine in more detail the mechanics of allotment by public companies. It is sufficient to note here that the final requirement in all cases is entry on the company's register of members.

MEMBERSHIP – TRANSFER OF SHARES

The shares of any member in a company are personal estate and are transferable in the manner provided by the company's articles[8]. Notwithstanding anything in the articles, it is not lawful for a company to register a transfer of shares unless a proper instrument of transfer has been delivered to the company[9]. A person may acquire shares from an existing member by purchase or gift but in either case the transferee does not become a member until he is entered on the register[10].

The basic position on share transfer, set out in *Re Smith, Knight & Co, Weston's Case*, is that a shareholder has a prima facie right to transfer his shares and directors

---

6   CA 1985, s 22(1).
7   Ibid, s 2(5). Shares taken by a subscriber to the memorandum of a public company in pursuance of an undertaking of his in the memorandum, and any premium on the shares, must be paid up in cash: s 106.
8   Ibid, s 182(1); subject to the Stock Transfer Act 1963 (which enables securities of certain descriptions to be transferred by a simplified process) and to regulations made under the Companies Act 1989, s 207 (which enable title to securities to be evidenced and transferred without a written instrument): CA 1985, s 182(1)(b).
9   Ibid, s 183(1) or the transfer is an exempt transfer within the Stock Transfer Act 1982 or is in accordance with the Uncertificated Securities Regulations 1995, SI 1995/3272, discussed below.
10 CA 1985, s 22(2).

have no discretionary powers, independent of any powers given to them by the articles, to refuse to register a transfer[11].

The articles need not impose any restrictions on transfer although restrictions are usually justified in a private company on the basis that they ensure that the existing members have control over who is admitted to the company, something which is regarded as essential given that many private companies are small family concerns or quasi-partnership type ventures[12]. With respect to listed public companies, the listing rules of the London Stock Exchange require that listed securities be freely transferable[13].

Typical restrictions on transfer

Table A allows directors to refuse to register the transfer of a share which is not fully paid to a person of whom they do not approve; and they may refuse to register the transfer of a share on which the company has a lien[14].

The directors may also refuse to register a transfer unless:

(a) it is lodged at the office or at such other place as the directors may appoint and is accompanied by the certificate for the shares to which it relates and such other evidence as the directors may reasonably require to show the right of the transferor to make the transfer;

(b) it is in respect of only one class of shares; and

(c) it is in favour of not more than four transferees[15].

These are very limited provisions and it is customary to adopt an additional provision which provides that the directors may, in their absolute discretion and without assigning any reason therefor, decline to register any transfer of any share, whether or not it is a fully paid share[16].

In addition to these provisions giving the directors a discretion to refuse to register transfers, some type of pre-emption provision is commonly included which ensures that existing members have the opportunity to buy any shares which may be for disposal before they are offered for sale outside of the company.

Usually a member wishing to sell will be permitted to transfer his shares to an existing member without restriction but where he seeks to transfer to an outsider then a pre-emption provision will come into effect. This will normally require the intending transferor to give notice to the company secretary who must notify the other members that there are shares available for purchase. If the other members then make an offer for the shares, the transferor may accept or reject their offer but, if he rejects it, he is precluded normally from proceeding with the transfer of the shares to an outsider. If the shares are not taken up by the other shareholders, then the transferor is usually entitled at that stage to offer his shares to an outside purchaser, subject to the proviso that the directors may refuse to register a transfer in such circumstances.

---

11 (1868) 4 Ch App 20; and the right is not to be cut down by uncertain language or doubtful implications: *Re Smith & Fawcett Ltd* [1942] Ch 304, [1942] 1 All ER 542.

12 See *Re Smith & Fawcett Ltd* [1942] Ch 304, [1942] 1 All ER 542. Until 1980 it was mandatory for private companies to include a restriction on the transfer of their shares in the articles: CA 1948, s 28 repealed by CA 1980, Sch 4. See generally Hannigan (1990) 11 Co Law 170.

13 See *The Listing Rules* r 3.15.

14 Table A, art 24.

15 Table A, art 24.

16 This provision was contained in the previous Table A, see CA 1948, Sch 1, Table A, Pt II, art 3.

Any scheme of transfer laid down by the articles must be adhered to and the directors have no power to authorise registration in circumstances where there is a breach of the articles[17].

Triggering a pre-emption provision

The first step in the pre-emption process normally involves establishing that a shareholder wishes/desires/intends to transfer his shares. An issue is whether such a provision in the articles will only cover an attempt to transfer the legal title to the shares or whether it is sufficiently all encompassing to include dealing with the beneficial interests attached to the shares so that such dealing triggers the mechanism provided by the articles.

The point was considered in *Safeguard Industrial Investments Ltd v National Westminster Bank Ltd*[18] where the defendant bank, as the executor of a deceased shareholder, had been registered in respect of the deceased's holding. The bank held the shares as trustee for two beneficiaries to whom, for the moment at least, it did not propose to transfer the shares. The articles provided that any member who desired to transfer his shares (the proposing transferor) had to give notice to the company which would then notify the existing members who could then purchase the shares.

One of the existing members who wished to acquire some of these shares argued that the bank's position (it could at any moment be required to transfer the shares to the beneficiaries) was such that it was under a duty to serve a transfer notice.

The Court of Appeal disagreed. 'Transfer' in the articles only embraced the transfer of the legal title and was inapt to apply to the transfer of beneficial interests. The mere fact that there was someone who could make an immediate demand for the transfer of the shares did not make the existing member (the bank in this case) a proposing transferor for these purposes.

The court distinguished the position in *Safeguard* from that which had arisen in an earlier case, *Lyle and Scott Ltd v Scott's Trustees*[19]. In that case, a number of shareholders entered into an agreement with a third party under which they received £3 per share and bound themselves, inter alia, to vote as he desired so putting him as fully in control of the company as they could without actually presenting transfers for registration. It was alleged that they were desirous of transferring and so the pre-emption provision in the articles came into effect.

In this instance the House of Lords agreed. Having agreed to sell and having received the purchase price, the vendors held the shares as trustees for the purchasers. They were bound to do everything to perfect the title of the purchaser. It was impossible that they could have done as they did unless they desired to transfer[20].

Oliver LJ in *Safeguard* thought the two cases were clearly distinguishable. In *Lyle* the parties had entered into an unconditional agreement to sell which obliged the

---

17   *Tett v Phoenix Property and Investment Co Ltd* [1986] BCLC 149, CA. See also *Curtis v J J Curtis & Co Ltd* [1986] BCLC 86, NZCA.
18   [1982] 1 All ER 449, [1982] 1 WLR 589, CA.
19   [1959] AC 763, [1959] 2 All ER 661; noted Sealy (1960) CLJ 38.
20   [1959] AC 763 at 774, [1959] 2 All ER 661 at 665, HL. See also *Re Macro (Ipswich) Ltd* [1994] 2 BCLC 354 where two shareholders had entered into a sale agreement in favour of a third and had executed declarations of trusts of the shares. They had delivered the share certificates and forms of transfer duly executed in blank and had agreed as to the receipt of dividends and the exercise of voting rights. The court found they had done more than deal in the beneficial interests and nothing remained to be done by them with the result that they did desire to sell their shares and had triggered the pre-emption provision in the articles requiring them to offer the shares to all the existing members.

shareholders to transfer when requested on payment of the price, which price had been paid and which agreement remained uncancelled and unrepudiated at the time of the hearing. This, in his opinion, was a long way from the position in *Safeguard*[1]. The fact that the bank in *Safeguard* was under a duty to transfer the shares on request did not mean that it had the necessary desire to transfer for the purpose of the articles.

Another example of dealing with beneficial interests in a way which does not trigger the pre-emption mechanism is to be found in *Theakston v London Trust plc*[2].

In theory the transfer under scrutiny was from one member of the company (London Trust) to another (Paul) so avoiding the pre-emption provision contained in the articles. However, the transfer was being financed by an outsider, Matthew Brown (MB). MB also paid the stamp duty due and gave Paul certain tax indemnities. The agreement provided that Paul would: (i) endeavour to have the shares registered in MB's name; (ii) charge the shares in favour of MB; (iii) vote the shares as directed by MB; (iv) account to MB with respect to any distributions received in connection with the shares; (v) accept any offer for the shares as and when made by MB and endeavour to have MB registered as the owner of the shares; and (vi) not accept any other offer for any shares in the company.

The question was whether the effect of this agreement was such that the transfer from London Trust to Paul was really a transfer to MB (an outsider) so triggering the pre-emption provisions.

Harman J accepted as a fact that London Trust had sold its shares to Paul. He in turn had charged the shares to MB. In other words, in keeping with the *Safeguard* position, the court looked to see what had happened to the legal title to the shares. Moving on from that conclusion, the next suggestion was that, given the relationship between Paul and MB, Paul should be regarded as proposing to transfer his shares to MB so triggering the mechanism at this second stage.

Having reviewed *Lyle* and *Safeguard*, Harman J thought the agreement did not make Paul a person who proposed to transfer the shares. Some further steps would need to be taken under the agreement before the question of triggering the mechanism could arise and any steps taken would have to be examined to see whether they were sufficiently unequivocal to indicate that he was then proposing to transfer[3].

The effect of these decisions, as Lord Sorn anticipated in *Lyle*[4], is to leave open the obvious manoeuvre of dealing in the beneficial interest thus defeating the draftsman's attempt to ensure that control of the company is retained by the existing shareholders[5].

NOTIFICATION TO THE COMPANY

Where a shareholder has triggered the mechanism, the next requirement is to notify the company, probably through the company secretary, indicating the number of shares

---

1   [1982] 1 All ER 449 at 454, [1982] 1 WLR 589, CA.
2   [1984] BCLC 390.
3   See also *Re a Company (No 005685 of 1988), ex p Schwarcz (No 2)* [1989] BCLC 427 where a conditional agreement to sell subject to several events occurring (which were not within the control of either party to the agreement) did not constitute a present and unequivocal desire to transfer or dispose of shares.
4   1958 SC 230 at 250.
5   As Vinelott J stressed at first instance in *Safeguard*, this gap in the articles cannot be filled by construction and if the parties wish to preclude dealing in the beneficial interests in this way then they must do so expressly: see [1980] 3 All ER 849 at 860.

which the member wishes to transfer[6]. The company secretary in turn will notify those members who are entitled under the pre-emption provision to make an offer to purchase the shares in question. The articles may also provide a means of determining the price to be paid, often simply that the price is to be the fair value[7] as certified by the company's auditor whose opinion is binding and conclusive. This sometimes creates problems as the transferor may be dissatisfied with the figure determined under this method. The courts are reluctant to permit challenges to such valuations save in exceptional circumstances as where the valuers have departed from their instructions in a material respect[8].

Directors' power to refuse to register a transfer

It is frequently the case that having gone through the various stages outlined above, a share transfer is then blocked by a refusal by the directors to register the transfer. The significance of entry on the register of members has already been noted.

As far as the directors' power to refuse registration is concerned, there are two possibilities:

(i)   the directors have an absolute discretion to refuse to register; or

(ii) the directors have a limited power to refuse to register.

AN ABSOLUTE DISCRETION

With regard to an absolute discretion, here the typical provision will state that the directors may, in their absolute discretion, decline to register any transfer of any share. The leading authority on this provision is *Re Smith & Fawcett Ltd*[9] where the Court of Appeal accepted that where the articles contain a provision such as this, drafted in the widest possible terms, there is no limitation on the exercise by directors of that power other than the standard requirement that, as a fiduciary power, it must be exercised bona fide in what they consider – and not what a court may consider – to be in the interests of the company, and not for any collateral purpose[10]. Subject to that qualification, an article in this form gives the directors an absolute and uncontrolled discretion. It enables them to take into account any matter which they consider to be in the interests of the company. Obviously, in such instances, it is very difficult to challenge a refusal to register, particularly as the directors cannot be required to give reasons to justify their decision[11] and the onus of proof is on those challenging the directors[12].

---

6   Notification operates as an invitation to treat, subject to any provision in the articles, and it is for would-be purchasers to make an offer to purchase, leaving the transferor to decide whether to accept or not: *Tett v Phoenix Property and Investment Co Ltd* [1986] BCLC 149, CA. However, if the transferor refuses an offer from an existing shareholder, he may be precluded by the articles from then offering the shares to an outsider.

7   See *Re Howie and Crawford's arbitration* [1990] BCLC 686 on the meaning of fair market value.

8   *Jones v Sherwood Computer Services plc* [1992] 2 All ER 170, [1992] 1 WLR 277. See also *Macro v Thompson* [1997] 1 BCLC 626.

9   [1942] 1 All ER 542.

10 [1942] Ch 304 at 306, [1942] 1 All ER 542 at 543. See also *Re Bell Bros, ex p Hodgson* (1891) 7 TLR 689; *Re Coalport China Co* [1895] 2 Ch 404; *Popely v Planarrive Ltd* [1997] 1 BCLC 8.

11 *Re Gresham Life Assurance Society, ex p Penney* (1872) 8 Ch App 446; *Berry and Stewart v Tottenham Hotspur Football and Athletic Co Ltd* [1935] Ch 718; *Duke of Sutherland v British Dominions Land Settlement Corpn Ltd* [1926] Ch 746.

12 See *Popely v Planarrive Ltd* [1997] 1 BCLC 8 at 16. The unfairly prejudicial remedy (CA 1985, s 459) may provide relief: see Chapter 28.

A LIMITED POWER

The directors' power to refuse to register may be a more limited power and the provisions vary greatly from company to company. For example, the articles might provide that the directors may refuse to register any transfer: (a) where the company has a lien on the shares; (b) where it is not proved to their satisfaction that the proposed transferee is a responsible person; (c) where the directors are of the opinion that the proposed transferee is not a desirable person to admit to membership[13]. Here the basic obligation is that the directors must act bona fide in what they consider to be in the interests of the company and not for any collateral purpose. More specifically, they must act within the limits laid down by the provisions in the articles which will be strictly construed for the prima facie right to transfer is not to be cut down by uncertain language or doubtful implications[14].

In *Re Bede Steam Shipping Co Ltd*[15] the articles provided that the directors might decline to register a transfer if, in their opinion, it was contrary to the interests of the company that the proposed transferee should be a member thereof. The directors admitted that no inquiry had been made as to the fitness of the transferees. The transfers in question had been rejected because a majority of the board objected to the transferor disposing of single shares or small lots of shares to individuals with a view to increasing the number of shareholders who would support him. The Court of Appeal found that the articles required the directors to focus on the qualities of the transferee and identify reasons why he was unsuitable. The particular objections which the directors had focused on were more concerned with the motives and attitudes of the transferor. These were not grounds provided for by the articles and so the transferees should be registered.

TIME LIMITS

Registration may be secured as a result of the failure of the directors to exercise their discretion to refuse registration within the requisite time period. There are two requirements in this context. The first is that the directors must actively exercise their discretion and decide to refuse to register a transfer for otherwise the prima facie right to transfer will prevail[16]. Secondly, the decision by the directors must be taken within a reasonable time and a reasonable time for these purposes is within two months of the transfer being lodged with the company[17]. If that period has elapsed then the directors will no longer be able to exercise their discretion[18] and an application can be made to have the register rectified by the inclusion of the name of the transferee[19].

---

13   See *Re Coalport China Co* [1895] 2 Ch 404. Other examples can be found in *Re Gresham Life Assurance Society, ex p Penney* (1872) 8 Ch App 446; *Berry and Stewart v Tottenham Hotspur Football and Athletic Co Ltd* [1935] Ch 718.

14   *Re Smith & Fawcett Ltd* [1942] 1 All ER 542.

15   [1917] 1 Ch 123. See also *Re Bell Bros, ex p Hodgson* (1891) 7 TLR 689; *Re Ceylon Land and Produce Co Ltd, ex p Anderson* (1891) 7 TLR 692.

16   *Re Hackney Pavilion Ltd* [1924] 1 Ch 276; *Moodie v W and J Shepherd (Bookbinders) Ltd* [1949] 2 All ER 1044; *Re Swaledale Cleaners Ltd* [1968] 3 All ER 619, [1968] 1 WLR 1710; CA 1985, s 183(5). Where the directors take a decision but fail to notify the transferee of the refusal to register, the failure to notify does not nullify the decision: *Popely v Planarrive Ltd* [1997] 1 BCLC 8.

17   *Re Swaledale Cleaners Ltd* [1968] 3 All ER 619, [1968] 1 WLR 1710; this period is effectively dictated by CA 1985, s 183(5) which requires that notice of rejection be given within two months.

18   This is not required by ibid, s 183(5) which simply imposes a fine for default (see s 183(6)) but it was accepted in *Re Swaledale Cleaners Ltd* [1968] 3 All ER 619, [1968] 1 WLR 1710 that this can be the only consequence of requiring the power to be exercised within a reasonable time.

19   Under CA 1985, s 359.

Where the directors have correctly exercised their discretion so making the decision to refuse unimpeachable, there remains the question as to the position between the vendor and the purchaser of the shares who cannot now complete the transaction by having the purchaser registered. The position on a sale of shares is that the equitable title to the shares passes to the purchaser once the contract is made and payment received and the legal title passes on completion and registration by the company[20]. Unless the contract so provides, the vendor does not promise to secure registration and, if the directors do refuse to register the transfer, he is not liable in damages for breach although he will hold the shares as bare trustee for the purchaser[1]. Where the parties are agreeable to such an outcome, then they can negate the effect of the directors' refusal to register.

MEMBERSHIP – TRANSMISSION OF SHARES

Transmission arises by operation of law on the death or bankruptcy of a member. On the death of a shareholder, the shares are transmitted to his personal representative and the production of the grant of probate of the will or letters of administration of the estate must be accepted by the company as sufficient evidence of the grant notwithstanding anything in the articles to the contrary[2]. Whether the personal representative can actually be registered as a member depends on the provisions of the articles but in any event a personal representative may transfer the shares even though he is not registered[3]. In the case of bankruptcy, the beneficial interest in the shares vests in the trustee in bankruptcy whose position is similar to that of the personal representative.

The position is generally governed by articles similar to those in Table A which provides that a person becoming entitled to a share in consequence of death or bankruptcy may elect either to become a holder of the share or to have someone else registered as the transferee[4]. In either case, under the Table A provisions, the decision takes effect as a decision to transfer by the member as if death or bankruptcy had not occurred. In other words, the election by the personal representative or trustee in bankruptcy to be registered or to have someone else registered has the effect of triggering any pre-emption provisions which may exist[5].

On being registered, the personal representative or trustee in bankruptcy enjoys the same rights as any other holder. Before that occurs, they enjoy the same rights as any other holder except the right to attend and vote at general or class meetings[6].

---

20   *Hawks v McArthur* [1951] 1 All ER 22.
1   *Stevenson v Wilson* 1907 SC 445.
2   CA 1985, s 187.
3   Ibid, s 183(3). Further s 459(2) enables a person to whom shares have been transmitted to apply to the court to grant relief where the affairs of the company are being conducted in a manner which is unfairly prejudicial. This could cover the case where the directors unfairly refuse registration.
4   Table A, art 30.
5   In *Safeguard Industrial Investments Ltd v National Westminster Bank Ltd* [1982] 1 All ER 449 at 451, Oliver LJ made the point that had the company's articles in that case contained this Table A provision on transmission on death which treats an election by a personal representative to be registered as an event triggering any provisions applicable on transfer, the bank would have been required to serve a transfer notice. As it was, the company had excluded such a provision from its articles and so the bank was entitled as personal representative to be registered without any restriction coming into play; see also *Scott v Frank F Scott (London) Ltd* [1940] Ch 794.
6   Table A, art 31.

THE REGISTER OF MEMBERS

Every company must keep a register of members giving details of the names, addresses and holdings of its shareholders[7]. Entry on the register is essential to membership in all cases save that of subscribers to the memorandum[8] and the register is prima facie but not conclusive[9] evidence of any matters directed or authorised by the Companies Act to be inserted in it[10].

The register provides creditors and investors with information as to the identity of those behind the corporate form which may affect any decision to invest or provide credit. It is also constantly monitored by public companies in order to detect bidders for the company building up a stake with which to launch a takeover bid.

Contents

The register must disclose the date of entry on the register as a member and the date of ceasing to be a member[11], dates which may be of considerable significance with regard to voting and dividend rights. If the number of members of a private company limited by shares or by guarantee falls to one or increases from one to two or more members, there must upon the occurrence of that event be entered in the company's register of members with the name and address of the sole member: (1) a statement that the company has only one member, or has ceased to have only one member, as the case may be; and (2) the date on which the company became a company having only one member or the date on which it ceased to have only one member[12].

Location and inspection of register

A company's register of members must be kept at the registered office, except that:

(a) if the work of making it up is done at another office of the company, it may be kept there; and

(b) if the company arranges with another person to make it up on behalf of the company, it may be kept at the office of that person provided in both cases the latter office is not outside the country of registration[13].

The registrar of companies must be notified of the place where the register is kept[14]. The register may be inspected during business hours by members without charge and by any other person on payment of a fee[15]. Copies of the register or part of it may also be obtained[16].

---

7   CA 1985, s 352. In the case of a company having a share capital, where the shares are numbered, the numbers must be given; where there are separate classes of shares, the class must be specified; and the amount paid up or agreed to be considered as paid up must be disclosed: ibid, s 352(3).
8   Ibid, s 22.
9   See *Reese River Silver Mining Co v Smith* (1869) LR 4 HL 64 at 80, per Lord Cairns; also *Re Briton Medical and General Life Association* (1888) 39 Ch D 61 at 71, per Stirling J.
10   CA 1985, s 361.
11   Ibid, s 352(2)(b), (c).
12   Ibid, s 352A.
13   Ibid, s 353(1).
14   Ibid, s 353(2).
15   Ibid, s 356; The Companies (Inspection and Copying of Registers, Indices and Documents) Regulations 1991, SI 1991/1998. The register may be closed for not more than 30 days in each year after notice has been published in a newspaper: CA 1985 s 358.
16   Ibid, s 356(3).

Rectification

The details in the register of members can be challenged, for instance on the grounds of mistake, but any shareholder wishing to challenge an entry must act promptly[17].
Where

(a) the name of any person is, without sufficient cause, entered in or omitted from the register; or

(b) default is made, or unnecessary delay takes place, in recording the fact that a person has ceased to be a member;

the person aggrieved, or any member of the company, or the company may apply to the court[18] for rectification[19]. The court has a discretion to refuse the application or order rectification and the payment by the company of any damages sustained[20]. There is no necessity to show any wrongdoing by the company and any question of omission by error or entry by error can be raised.

The power to rectify has been exercised where there was no valid allotment of shares[1]; or the allotment is irregular[2]; or where a transfer of shares has been improperly registered or registration has been refused[3].

The jurisdiction to rectify the register was considered in *Re Piccadilly Radio plc*[4]. In this instance, shares in a radio company were transferred without obtaining the consent of the Independent Broadcasting Authority (IBA) as required by the articles of association. Other shareholders in the company, with a view to preventing certain proposals being agreed to at a general meeting, sought rectification of the share register by deleting the names of the transferees and restoring the name of the original transferor. Millett J, despite finding that there had been a breach of the articles, refused rectification. The statutory procedure, he noted, provided a discretionary remedy and the court must consider the circumstances in which and the purpose for which the relief

---

17   *Re Scottish Petroleum Co* (1883) 23 Ch D 413 at 434, CA.

18   The directors of a company may rectify the register of members without any application to the court, if there is no dispute, and the circumstances are such that the court would order rectification: *Re London and Mediterranean Bank, Wright's Case* (1871) 7 Ch App 55; *Reese River Silver Mining Co v Smith* (1869) LR 4 HL 64 at 74; *Hartley's Case* (1875) 10 Ch App 157; *First National Reinsurance Co v Greenfield* [1921] 2 KB 260 at 279; but ordinarily the protection of the court's order is essential to any rectification by the removal of the name of a registered holder of shares: *Re Derham and Allen Ltd* [1946] Ch 31 at 36.

19   CA 1985, s 359(1).

20   Ibid, s 359(2). See Gower *Principles of Modern Company Law* (6th edn, 1997), p 332 which makes the point that 'compensation' would be a better word than 'damages'.

1   *Re Homer District Consolidated Gold Mines, ex p Smith* (1888) 39 Ch D 546 at 551; *Re Portuguese Consolidated Copper Mines Ltd* (1889) 42 Ch D 160, CA.

2   *Re Homer District Consolidated Gold Mines, ex p Smith* (1888) 39 Ch D 546; *Re Cleveland Trust plc* [1991] BCLC 424, [1991] BCC 33 (register rectified by deletion of bonus shares after bonus issue mistakenly made); *Re Thundercrest Ltd* [1995] 1 BCLC 117 (register rectified by cancellation of allotment to two members who were also directors when the third member of the company, to their knowledge, had not received a provisional letter of allotment of those shares to him, a letter which was in any event defective as it allowed insufficient time for acceptance).

3   *Re Copal Varnish Co Ltd* [1917] 2 Ch 349; *Welch v Bank of England* [1955] Ch 508, [1955] 1 All ER 811 (restoration of status quo after forged transfers); *International Credit and Investment Co (Overseas) Ltd v Adham* [1994] 1 BCLC 66 (restoration of status quo: no proper share transfers were executed merely entries made in share register purporting to deprive the true owner of his entire holding); *Re New Cedos Engineering Co Ltd* [1994] 1 BCLC 797 (on their true construction, a right to be registered existed under the articles); *Stothers v William Steward (Holdings) Ltd* [1994] 2 BCLC 266 (directors purported to exercise discretion to refuse registration which power, on the true construction of the articles, they did not possess).

4   [1989] BCLC 683.

was sought. The circumstances here did not warrant rectification for a number of reasons. The applicants had no interest in the shares and were not seeking to have their own names restored to the register. They were searching for a means to disenfranchise opposition to certain proposals to be put to the general meeting and had seized on a breach of an article of which the IBA itself did not complain. The transferor did not seek rectification and the company did not support the application. A less meritorious claim was difficult to imagine.

Notice of trusts

A company registered in England and Wales is not concerned with trusts over its shares[5]. No notice of any trust, express, implied or constructive, must be entered on the register or be receivable by the registrar in the case of companies registered in England and Wales[6]. The articles may provide that, except as required by law, no person shall be recognised by the company as holding any share upon any trust and (except as otherwise provided by the articles or by law) the company shall not be bound by or recognise any interest in any share except an absolute right to the entirety thereof in the holder[7]. The company is consequently not liable to beneficiaries in the case of breach of trust.

The only way a beneficiary can protect his position is by means of a stop notice[8]. A stop notice is effected by filing an affidavit of the facts and a notice in the right form with the court and serving office copies of the affidavit and notice on the company[9]. The effect of a stop notice is that the company may not register a transfer of the shares affected or take any other steps restrained by the stop notice until 14 days after sending notice thereof to the person on whose behalf the stop notice was filed. Where a stop notice has been filed then the company must act as stated but in all other respects the company treats the trustee as if he were the outright owner of the shares and in the same position as any other member.

SHARE CERTIFICATES

Unless the conditions of issue of the shares otherwise provides, every company must issue a share certificate within two months of the allotment of any shares or the lodging of a transfer of any shares[10].

The certificate is prima facie (but not conclusive) evidence of title[11] and the presumption arising from it can be rebutted but the company may be estopped from denying the facts stated in the certificate. In *Re Bahia and San Francisco Rly Co*[12] the court noted:

> The power of giving certificates is ... for the benefit of the company in general; and it is a declaration by the company to all the world that the person in whose

---

5   *Société Générale de Paris and Colladon v Walker* (1885) 11 App Cas 20.
6   CA 1985, s 360.
7   Table A, art 5.
8   Stop notices are governed by the Charging Orders Act 1979 and RSC Ord 50, rr 11 -15.
9   RSC Ord 50, rr 11-15.
10   CA 1985, s 185(1). Note also ibid, s 185(3), (4). See also the discussion of CREST below.
11   Ibid, s 186(1).
12   (1868) LR 3 QB 584.

name the certificate is made out, and to whom it is given, is a shareholder in the company, and it is given by the company with the intention that it shall be so used by the person to whom it is given, and acted upon in the sale and transfer of shares[13].

For example, if the company issues certificates which describe shares as fully paid up when they are not and a third party relies on the certificate, then the company is estopped from denying that they are fully paid[14]. In *Bloomenthal v Ford*[15] a lender to a company took shares in the company as collateral security. The certificate stated that he was the holder of 10,000 fully-paid ordinary shares when the shares were not in fact fully paid. It was held by the House of Lords that the company was estopped from denying the certificate. The lender could have found out the true position by enquiry but there was no actual notice and he had acted in good faith.

If a share certificate is issued following the presentation of a forged transfer then the company is not estopped from denying its validity. This is because the person presenting the transfer impliedly warrants the authenticity of the transfer[16]. A purchaser from such a person is in a better position and can claim compensation from the company if he is displaced by the true owner since he relied not on the forged transfer but on the certificate issued by the company[17].

A forged share certificate is a nullity and does not bind the company[18].

CREST – electronic settlement for listed securities

A major change in the way in which shares are transferred and certificates issued has occurred as a result of the CREST project allowing for the electronic transfer of listed securities. The reason for changing from paper records to an electronic method of recording transfers is to ensure that London has a fast, efficient and economic method of recording transactions which will enable it to remain as the leading equity market within the European time zone.

The scheme originally proposed by the Stock Exchange was TAURUS (Transfer and Automated Registration of Uncertificated Stock) but with that project behind schedule and over-budget, the Bank of England stepped in to develop a simpler and cheaper system called CREST.

CREST became operational in July 1996 and the provisions of the Companies Act 1985 providing for instruments of transfer and share certificates have had to be amended to accommodate these changes. This has been done by the Uncertificated Securities Regulations 1995[19].

---

13   (1868) LR 3 QB 584 at 595.
14   See *Burkinshaw v Nicolls* (1878) 3 App Cas 1004. Where there is a subsequent transfer and the transferor has acquired a good title by estoppel, the transferee acquires a good title even if he had actual notice that the shares were only partly paid: *Re Stapleford Colliery Co, Barrow's Case* (1880) 14 Ch D 432, CA. Cf *Re London Celluloid Co* (1888) 39 Ch D 190 at 197, CA.
15   [1897] AC 156, HL.
16   *Sheffield Corpn v Barclay* [1905] AC 392; *Yeung Kai Yung v Hong Kong and Shanghai Banking Corpn* [1981] AC 787, [1980] 2 All ER 599.
17   *Re Bahia and San Francisco Rly Co* (1868) LR 3 QB 584; *Balkis Consolidated Co v Tomkinson* [1893] AC 396; *Dixon v Kennaway & Co* [1900] 1 Ch 833.
18   *Ruben v Great Fingall Consolidated* [1906] AC 439; on this case see Sealy *Cases and Materials in Company Law* (6th edn, 1996), p 485.
19   The Uncertificated Securities Regulations 1995, SI 1995/3272. CA 1989, s 207 provided that the Secretary of State might make provision by regulations for enabling title to securities to be evidenced and transferred without a written instrument.

Before considering the regulations, it is important to bear in mind that one of the main features of the CREST scheme is that investors are able to have holdings outside CREST, ie retaining share certificates, if they so choose. The scheme is permissive rather than mandatory although, as more companies join the scheme, there will be pressure to be within it. Individual investors are expected to find that the costs of dealing in certificated shares will be higher than in uncertificated securities. The net effect for individual investors is likely to be that they will switch to holding uncertificated holdings through nominees, such as brokers and fund managers. Those nominees will appear on the company's register of members[20] and they will maintain a holding on behalf of any number of private investors.

UNCERTIFICATED SECURITIES REGULATIONS 1995

The regulations enable title to shares to be evidenced otherwise than by a certificate and transferred otherwise than by a written instrument in accordance with a computer-based system know as a relevant system[1]. The Operator of such a system must be approved by the Treasury and is regulated by the Securities and Investment Board[2] (recently renamed the Financial Services Authority).

A company's shares may be held in uncertificated form and transferred by means of a relevant system where the company's articles so allow[3] or where the directors have resolved that title to the shares may be transferred by a relevant system[4]. Provision is made for the members of the company to prevent or reverse such a directors' resolution by ordinary resolution[5].

A company must enter on its register of members in respect of any class of shares which is a participating security, how many shares each member holds in uncertificated form and certificated form respectively[6].

Subject to certain exceptions, an entry on such a register which records a person as holding shares in uncertificated form is evidence of such title to the shares as would be evidenced if the entry on the register related to shares in certificated form[7].

Provision is made for the conversion of shares from uncertificated into certificated form[8] and from certificated to uncertificated[9] and for the issue of new shares in uncertificated form[10]. However, shares cannot be converted from certificated to uncertificated except in the specified circumstances which require the company to have

---

20   CREST-sponsored membership is available allowing individuals access to the electronic settlement process and enabling them to remain named on the register of members but, at this early stage, it is not clear how many individuals will take advantage of that option. A corporate governance concern has emerged over the potential effect which CREST may have on the widening communication gap between companies and their shareholders: see DTI, Treasury *Private Shareholders: Corporate Governance Rights, A Consultative Document* (November 1996).

1   The Uncertificated Securities Regulations 1995, SI 1995/3272, reg 2(1).

2   SI 1995/3272, regs 2(3), 11. The system Operator is CRESTCo Ltd, a private company owned by a number of City institutions.

3   SI 1995/3272, reg 15(1). The articles must be consistent with (i) the holding of shares of that class in uncertificated form and (ii) the transfer of those shares by means of a relevant system and (iii) the Uncertificated Securities Regulations 1995.

4   SI 1995/3272, reg 16(2). This resolution will override any conflicting provisions in the articles.

5   SI 1995/3272, reg 16(6).

6   SI 1995/3272, reg 19(1).

7   SI 1995/3272, reg 20(1); see also reg 23(7).

8   SI 1995/3272, reg 26.

9   SI 1995/3272, reg 27.

10   SI 1995/3272, reg 28.

received a request in writing on the appropriate form from the shareholder together with the relevant certificate[11].

TRANSFERS OF SECURITIES

Subject to a number of exceptions, a company must register on the register of members a transfer of title to an uncertificated share following an instruction from the operator to do so[12]. A transferee acquires an equitable interest in the requisite number of shares in question from the time an operator instruction is generated which requires a company to register a transfer of title on the register of members until the time that the transferee is entered on the register in respect of the transfer of shares to him[13].

Where forged or unlawful instructions are given so that any person's name is removed or omitted or entered in error on a register of members, or the number or description of shares is altered, and that person suffers loss as a result, he may apply to the court for an order that the operator compensate him for any loss[14].

MORTGAGES OF SHARES

There are two species of share mortgage: legal and equitable. A legal mortgage, which affords the greatest security, is effected by a transfer of the shares followed by registration of the mortgagee as the holder of the shares. The mortgagor's equity of redemption cannot be noted by the company and the only protection which the mortgagor can obtain is by use of a stop notice, a process outlined above. Otherwise the mortgagee is treated by the company as the absolute owner of the shares. When the mortgage is repaid, the shares are retransferred. Despite the security offered by a legal mortgage there are drawbacks involved. If the company's articles contain restrictions on transfer then that mechanism will be triggered by the attempt to have the mortgagee registered. Equally, if the mortgagee is registered in respect of partly-paid shares, then the mortgagee as holder of the shares is liable to pay any calls which the company may make in respect of those shares.

An equitable mortgage, which is much more common, is effected by delivery of the share certificate and a blank transfer executed by the mortgagor. Once the mortgagee is in possession of these documents, he may exercise a power of sale in the event of default without having to apply to the court for an order for sale[15]. It is common for the parties also to draw up a memorandum setting out the basis on which the shares have been charged and dealing with such matters as dividend and voting rights. The memorandum will frequently contain an irrevocable power of attorney authorising the mortgagee to complete the share transfer form in the event of foreclosure or to exercise a power of sale on default.

---

11   See SI 1995/3272, reg 27(2).
12   See SI 1995/3272, reg 23. Note that any purported registration of a transfer of title to an uncertificated share other than in accordance with this Regulation is of no effect: reg 23(7).
13   SI 1995/3272, reg 25(1).
14   SI 1995/3272, reg 30. This is without prejudice to any right of the operator to recover from a third party any sum that he may be ordered to pay.
15   *Stubbs v Slater* [1910] 1 Ch 632.

LIENS ON SHARES

At common law a company has no lien on the shares of its members but the articles may provide that the company shall have a lien for unpaid calls and other debts. Under English law, such a lien takes effect as an equitable charge[16].

The position regarding liens varies depending on whether the company is public or private. If it is a private company, then its articles may provide that the company shall have a first and paramount lien over a member's shares in respect of amounts due in respect of the shares[17]. Alternatively, provision may be made for the company to have a lien in respect of any indebtedness of the shareholder to the company. As regards enforcement, the articles normally grant the directors an express power of sale.

A lien or other charge of a public company on its own shares is void unless it falls within the following categories:

(1)   liens on partly-paid shares for any sums payable in respect of those shares;
(2)   liens which are in the ordinary course of business of a lending or credit company;
(3)   liens created by private companies which were in existence prior to re-registration as public companies[18].

Categories (2) and (3) are obviously very restricted in their application, leaving (1) as the most common kind of lien but even it is of limited importance as public companies rarely have partly-paid shares.

16   *Everitt v Automatic Weighing Machine Co* [1892] 3 Ch 506.
17   See Table A, arts 8-11. Article 8 provides that the company shall have a first and paramount lien on every share, not being a fully-paid share, for all moneys (whether presently payable or not) payable at a fixed time or called in respect of that share. Complicated questions can arise with regard to priorities as between a lien and other charges: see *Bradford Banking Co v Briggs, Son & Co Ltd* (1886) 12 App Cas 29.
18   CA 1985, s 150.

CHAPTER 20

Debt capital—debentures, debenture stock and new developments

In this chapter we are concerned with medium- and long-term debt capital, not short-term debt such as trade credit and hire purchase. However, within the concept of debt capital, we include bank overdrafts which in practice if not in theory often represent medium-term financing for healthy companies in normal credit conditions in addition to term loans. There are three important characteristics which have traditionally distinguished debt from share capital. First, debt capital represents a set of rights against the company, not rights in the company. Secondly, the rights arise out of a relationship of debtor and creditor, and thirdly, although debt is common enough with natural persons there are certain legal forms which are only employed by companies. Let us examine each of these characteristics in a little more detail.

Since the creditor's rights are against the company, he or she has only limited control over the company's affairs. He or she is not a member of the company. Such controls as he or she can exercise arise contractually from the loan agreement until default. After default, these are augmented by the normal creditors' remedies which are often extended by contract. The most common remedy is the appointment of a receiver and manager. Sometimes loan capital is 'convertible' into share capital, that is the investor can require his or her loan to be applied in the purchase of shares. Thereafter he or she has such rights of participation as the shares themselves confer.

The essence of the legal relationship is debt, although loan creditors fall into two main categories, commercial finance providers and investors. The first covers financial institutions who are conventionally not regarded as investors. Investment creditors cover a wide range of people and institutions whose common link is that in fact they invest for a safe fixed return since loan capital does not produce capital appreciation for the loan creditor. Their investment is usually remunerated at a fixed rate of interest. There is often flexibility as to when the debt must be repaid. The debt constitutes a prior charge on the profits of the company and on its assets in a liquidation in the sense that the claims of the loan creditor must be met before shareholders are paid. Since debt capital is debt, not share, capital, it is not subject to the share capital maintenance rules. It can be issued at a discount and be repurchased by the company and reissued. Interest on it may be paid out of capital.

Debt capital is a common method of financing business enterprise and for successful companies, particularly listed companies, there is an increasing variety of debt capital available. Much of this is handled privately by financial institutions and does not involve public listing on stock exchanges. Listed debt capital is thus becoming less common.

What is distinctive about corporate debt is the frequent use of the debenture stock trust deed and floating charge. By the former, we mean that instead of having a large number of individual creditors with their separate rights and remedies, larger companies often enter into a trust deed with a financial institution as trustee, creating debenture stock. The investor takes up the stock and his or her rights are enforced through the trustee. This form has been common since the end of the nineteenth century and avoids the difficulties which would arise from having thousands of individual debenture holders. By a floating charge, we refer to a species of equitable charge which relates but does not specifically affix to a class of assets. The company can dispose of particular assets in the ordinary course of business until crystallisation when the floating charge attaches as a fixed equitable charge. We shall consider the floating charge in more detail later in Part VI.

THE HISTORICAL DEVELOPMENT OF DEBT CAPITAL

In the seventeenth century the share capital of the leading companies was oversubscribed, and the number of shareholders relatively small and mainly concentrated in the merchant classes. Such companies made increasing use of debt capital. The advantages of this were:

(1) the debt capital could be issued at an interest rate below the expected yield on the shares; and

(2) this concentrated the profits in the hands of a small number of investors.

The nature of the debt capital at this time was bonds and annuities. Scott[1] described bonds, which were an acknowledgement of debts under seal, as 'a striving towards the modern debenture'. Originally bonds were short-term loans repayable at three or six months or at call. Later, although they retained this nominal character in practice, they were rolled over and became longer-term capital. There was an advantage from the company's point of view in that it could renegotiate the interest rate from time to time. Terms were often extended or the bonds replaced by a new issue. Annuities which gave the investor a right to a fixed annual payment were popular with the government and the main companies at this time. Consols—the Consolidated Annuity of the Bank of England—date from the eighteenth century. The East India Company, for example, traded heavily in such loan capital[2].

Bonds were popular with 'persons not familiar with the wayward habits of the embryo stock market', especially women[3]. Women held only about 2–4% of India stock but about 20% of India bonds in 1685. The figures for the African Company were 10% and 20% respectively. Trustees and even a few institutions such as the Drapers Company, a City livery company, held bonds. This is a pattern which continues to the present day.

1   *Constitution and Finance of English, Scottish & Irish Joint Stock Companies to 1720* (1910–1912) vol 1, p 304.

2   'Britannia Languens' in *A Select Collection of Early English Tracts on Commerce* (1953) ed J R McCulloch, p 341.

3   K G Davies 'Joint Stock Investment in the Later Seventeenth Century' in *Essays in Economic History* (1954) ed E M Carus-Wilson, vol II, p 289.

Turning next to the eighteenth century, there is difficulty in distinguishing between investment and trade creditors since the ordinary trade creditor often received a sealed obligation. The methods of raising loan capital varied. An issue could be made by a direct public offer or an offer for sale to one person who then sold to the public. The African Company left a broad discretion to the directors as to choice of method. Sometimes it was provided that the interest on particular bonds would be paid in preference to all other debts of the company.

Mr DuBois in *The English Business Company After the Bubble Act 1720–1800* states: 'In general during the eighteenth century, the differentiation between the creditors' and the proprietors' position was not always clearly defined'[4]. He cites[5] a proprietor at a general court of the East India Company on 9 August 1732 which was considering a reduction of the dividend on the stock arguing for a reduction of the interest on bonds on the basis: 'This Company consists of two sorts of proprietors, to wit, Stock Proprietors and Bond Proprietors; but why should the Burden be all laid on the stock?'. It was thought necessary in 32 Geo 3 c 101 (1792) which incorporated the Company of Proprietors of the Lancaster Canal Navigation to provide expressly: 'that no Person to whom any such Mortgage or Assignment shall be made or transferred as aforesaid shall be deemed a Proprietor ... or capable of acting or voting for or on Account of ... such Mortgage or Assignment'. Sometimes there was an option given to bondholders to become stockholders and sometimes bonds were repaid in stock.

As regards investor protection, the creditor could sue for default in payment of interest or principal. In addition, he or she could petition one of the Houses of Parliament for the appointment of a committee of investigation. Petitions were made in respect of the York Buildings Company, the Charitable Corporation in 1733 and the Royal African Company in the 1740s. Such petitions maintained that this was their only remedy in the absence of bankruptcy provisions for chartered corporations[6]. It is clear, however, that creditors were in a weaker position than stockholders in not having a representative in the active management of the company. From time to time committees of creditors grew up on an ad hoc basis[7]. Creditors of deed of settlement companies were generally in a better position in that they could in theory sue the stockholders but in practice this was curtailed by complex drafting. They also lacked participation in management and adequate representation.

On the whole, bondholders seem to have recovered their loans if the company foundered, but with the industrial revolution came a vast expansion of credit for current transactions. When companies failed, bondholders often found they were one of a number of competing unsecured creditors. Investment creditors then began to insist on security and this raised the question of what security the company could give[8]. Loan capital was still usually issued for relatively short terms, no more than five years. It was not until the 1880s that long-term loan capital became common.

Let us look first of all at the rights of a bondholder, prior to 1862. The bond was a chose in action which could not be assigned at law. In equity it could be assigned, but only subject to equities. This made the title to the debentures vulnerable and restricted their marketability.

---

4   *DuBois* (1938, reprinted 1971), p 372.
5   Ibid, p 429.
6   Ibid, p 431.
7   Ibid.
8   See R R Pennington (1960) 23 MLR 630.

From the 1860s onwards, steps were taken to achieve negotiability in the case of bearer debentures and freedom from equities in the case of other debentures. The Judicature Act reforms improved the position by allowing legal assignment of choses in action.

From the point of view of security at common law, the company could only give a legal mortgage of land and a pledge of chattels. Equity was more flexible and the floating charge was developed in the 1870s as an equitable security over an undertaking or class of assets whose members changed in the course of business. Professor Pennington[9] has argued that there were three influences at work—equity, railway undertaking mortgages and insurance policy clauses, although the influence of the latter was problematic. Dr W J Gough[10] argues that the only influence was the equitable assignment of future property cases which allowed transfer of future assets by a present act which was later completed by identification or appropriation. The floating charge was conceptualised in the period 1870 to 1910 but unfortunately largely in the language of metaphor. To say that a floating charge 'floats' and does not attach to any specific assets until crystallisation and yet is a present charge and present security over shifting assets, is potentially contradictory. This use of metaphorical language, rather than sharp analytical terms, has led to conceptual confusion which we shall explore later in Part VI. By the end of the nineteenth century, companies found it useful to adopt a debenture stock trust deed for large scale issues. The advantages of the deed were that it enabled the company to create one security and it provided clear procedures during the subsistence of the security and on default.

There have been further developments in this century. Debt capital has become popular due to tax advantages—the interest being deductible against gross profits and only taxable in the hands of the recipients. Added to this is the substantial increase in the number of flexible types of debt financing offered by international financial institutions, particularly for the larger companies. Nevertheless the risks attaching to high gearing are driving some companies back to equity financing or to greater use of convertibles.

FORMS OF LOAN CAPITAL

Debentures

Nearly every document evidencing indebtedness by a company is commercially called a debenture, although it would be a mistake to equate the two completely. The term is not usually applied to routine correspondence. Also, loan capital can be raised by means of bills of exchange and other negotiable instruments which evidence debt but these are not usually called debentures. This is a matter of convention. We shall not deal with such instruments here. Generally, if not always, there will also be a covenant or agreement to repay[11].

Although it is an ancient term[12], there is no precise legal form of a debenture. Various forms of instruments are usually called debentures. There are mortgage debentures which create a charge on some kind of property. There are bonds which are under seal. There are others which are nothing more than a formal acknowledgement of

9   (1960) 23 MLR 630.
10   Gough *Company Charges* (2nd edn), p 102 ff.
11   *Topham v Greenside Glazed Fire-Brick Co* (1887) 37 Ch D 281 at 292 per North J.
12   See the historical usage discussed in *Palmer's Company Precedents*, Pt III (Debentures) (16th edn, 1956–1960) p 1.

indebtedness. They all seem to have the common characteristic that they are documents which either create or acknowledge a debt[13]. The use of the term is not necessarily conclusive as to the nature of the instrument. A debenture can be issued singly or in a series. The statutory definition contained in s 744 of CA 1985 provides that the term 'debenture' *includes* debenture stock, bonds and any other securities of a company, whether constituting a charge on the assets of the company or not. The word security is used here in a narrow sense. Debenture covers a mortgage issued to a single mortgagee[14].

Debenture stock

A debenture is an instrument evidencing a debt with or without security. There are two parties—the company and the loan creditor. Debenture stock is not an instrument but an equitable interest under an instrument (generally a debenture stock trust deed) which evidences a collective debt divided into units. Debenture stock is 'borrowed capital consolidated into one mass for the sake of convenience'[15]. Whereas a single debenture is only usually transferable in its entirety, a holding of debenture stock may be disposed of in whole or in part like a holding of shares. Sometimes the debenture stock trust deed or terms of issue restrict transfers to particular multiples of stock. The trust deed contains covenants by the company with the trustee to repay the capital sum and interest, and to observe and perform other covenants relating to the conduct of its business. It also usually contains security in the sense of a fixed or floating charge or both and the normal mortgage provisions. It invariably contains administrative provisions dealing with such matters as transfer of stock and meetings of stockholders.

The early forms of debenture trust deed supplemented individual debentures but usually contained the security offered by the company. The modern form replaces individual debentures and the holder of loan stock is now not usually a direct creditor of the company[16]. He or she is a beneficiary under the trust by which the trustee holds the debt. Most trust deeds provide for action to be taken by the trustee and pre-empt individual action by a stockholder whose main remedy is against the trustee, to compel it to exercise its powers under the trust deed.

Redeemable and irredeemable debentures

Debentures may be redeemable at the option of the company or irredeemable. At common law, when a debenture was redeemed or transferred to the company, the debt was discharged and the debenture ceased to exist. Now where debentures have been redeemed, s 194 enables the company to reissue them or issue other debentures in their place:

(a) unless any express or implied provision to the contrary is contained in the articles or in any contract entered into by the company; or

---

13 *British India Steam Navigation Co v IRC* (1881) 7 QBD 165 at 172–173; *Edmonds v Blaina Furnaces Co* (1887) 36 Ch D 215 at 219–221; *Levy v Abercorris Slate and Slab Co* (1887) 37 Ch D 260 at 263–264; *Union Bank of Australia Ltd v South Canterbury Building and Investment Co Ltd* (1894) 13 NZLR 489 at 512; *Lemon v Austin Friars Investment Trust Ltd* [1926] Ch 1, CA; *R v Findlater* [1939] 1 KB 594 at 599, CA.
14 *Knightsbridge Estates Trust Ltd v Byrne* [1940] AC 613, HL.
15 *Palmer's Company Law* (24th edn, 1987), vol 1, para 44–04.
16 R R Pennington *Company Law* (7th edn, 1995), ch 12.

(b) unless the company has, by passing a resolution to that effect or by some other act, manifested its intention that the debentures should be cancelled.

On a reissue of redeemed debentures, s 194(2) provides that a person entitled to the debentures has the same priorities as if the debentures had never been redeemed.

Formerly, there was some doubt about whether a company could issue irredeemable debentures or debentures payable at a long time in the future. It was thought that this might involve a clog on the equity of redemption. To remove doubts, s 193 contains a provision which was first introduced in 1907. This provides that, notwithstanding any rule of equity to the contrary, a condition in a debenture should not be invalid by reason only that the debentures are thereby made (a) irredeemable or (b) redeemable on a contingency or (c) on the expiration of a period (however long)[17].

It has been held by the House of Lords in *Knightsbridge Estates Trust Ltd v Byrne*[18] that a mortgage of land to a single mortgagee by a company is within the section. In practical terms, it is unlikely that a lender will wish to have his or her money out on mortgage for so long at least if the interest rate is fixed. Even where it is variable by reference to some index, like the minimum lending rate of a particular bank, a lender will lose the benefit of capital appreciation of his or her investment in this kind of long-term loan.

Issue of debentures and debenture stock

We saw in Chapter 15 that a company cannot issue shares at a discount. Debentures may be issued at a discount unless the memorandum or articles forbid it. Indeed, they usually are issued at a discount in the case of large scale issues by public companies. However, it is not possible to use convertible debentures to avoid the rule applicable to shares. Thus in *Mosely v Koffyfontein Mines Ltd*[19] in 1904 a debenture issued at a discount provided for immediate conversion into fully paid shares equal to par. It was held to be objectionable.

Debentures may be issued payable to registered holder or to bearer. The latter have been rare in the last 30 years because of exchange control restrictions, but since these have recently been lifted, we may see a return to this type of security.

Issues of debentures are subject to the provisions of the Financial Services Act 1986 which we will deal with later in Chapter 34. They are also subject to the Stock Exchange listing rules where a listing is sought.

There is now no loan capital duty on the issue of debentures. This was abolished by the Finance Act 1973, s 49(2).

In equity, an agreement to issue a debenture by way of charge gives rise to a charge[20] since equity looks on that as done which ought to be done. The agreement must, however, be registered under s 395 as we shall see. Specific performance of a contract to make a loan will not normally be granted. The policy is that the borrower can borrow elsewhere. While this will generally be so, it may not be so in the case of an agreement to make a substantial advance or to enter into an offer for sale of debenture stock when the market subsequently declines. For these reasons s 195 makes specific performance available to a company. It will be lost, however, where the company has forfeited the debentures.

---

17   Note the limits of the section. Other provisions may in fact and in equity constitute a clog.
18   *Knightsbridge Estates Trust Ltd v Byrne* [1940] AC 613, HL.
19   [1904] 2 Ch 108, CA.
20   *Levy v Abercorris Slate and Slab Co* (1887) 37 Ch D 260.

ISSUES IN A SERIES AND PARI PASSU CLAUSES

Debentures are sometimes issued in a series. When this is done and the debentures do not contain a pari passu (ie equality) clause they rank according to the date of issue or if all issued on the same day, by their numbering. This negatives their marketability. It is usual, therefore, to set out a pari passu clause on the following lines[1]: 'The debentures of this series are all to rank pari passu in point of charge without any preference or priority one over another.'

The effect of this is to place all the debentures on the same level as to security so that if it is enforced, the proceeds are divided pro rata amongst the debentureholders according to the amount paid up, and if more interest is due on some of the debentures, in proportion to the total amount due in respect of principal and interest. When debenture stock is issued, such a clause is not strictly necessary in view of the nature of the stockholder's interest but in practice it is usual to include such a clause in the trust deed.

Although the precedents usually mention a maximum fixed sum for the series it is more common today in the case of public issues of debenture stock to have a formula in the debenture stock trust deed rather than a fixed amount[2].

SUBORDINATION OF DEBENTURES

Sometimes debentures contain express provision for subordination of debts. Obviously there are problems of privity of contract as far as the benefiting creditors are concerned. These can probably be overcome either by a separate deed to which they are parties or by an express covenant in the debenture in favour of the company and the creditors intended to benefit or by arguing a trust or agency by the company in their favour. A further argument might be possible on the ground of waiver and estoppel if it can be proved that the new creditors suffered a detriment by relying on the purported subordination[3]. We look at subordinated debt later in this chapter as a new form of loan capital.

Transfer of debentures and debenture stock

A debenture is a species of chose in action. Section 183 requires a proper instrument of transfer to be delivered to the company except in cases of transmission by operation of law.

Debentures which are fully paid registered debentures are usually transferred by means of a form under the Stock Transfer Act 1963 or, if they are dealt in on the Stock Exchange, by the CREST (computersied securities settlement) system which we have discussed in relation to shares. Bearer debentures are transferable by delivery. Otherwise the form of transfer will often be specified in the terms of issue.

A transfer of a debenture which is not a bearer debenture takes place subject to equities unless the terms of issue provide that transfers shall be free of equities. Thus in *Re Rhodesia Goldfields Ltd*[4], A, a debenture stockholder transferred stock to B who

---

1   Taken from *Palmer's Company Law* (24th edn, 1987), Vol 1, para 44–16.
2   See *Pennington*, op cit, ch 12.
3   See *Pennington*, op cit, ch 12. Cf *Gough*, op cit, p 415 and R M Goode *Legal Problems of Credit and Security* (2nd edn, 1988), pp 95 et seq.
4   [1910] 1 Ch 239.

was registered. A was also a director and the company had a claim against him for money had and received. It was held that B had to suffer a deduction of the company's claim against A before he could be paid. It is usual, however, to provide for payment of principal and interest to the registered holder free of equities. This amounts to a contract by the company that it will not rely on such equities. In a case somewhat similar to *Re Rhodesia Goldfields Ltd,* but where the debentures contained such a clause, a transferee from a delinquent director was held entitled to payment in full[5]. On the usual wording, it will be necessary for the transferee to be registered to obtain the benefit of the clause[6].

It has been held[7] that bearer debentures are negotiable instruments. Although bearer debenture stock has not been the subject of a court decision it is treated by commercial custom as negotiable[8].

Redemption

The terms of the particular debenture stock trust deed usually specify a procedure for redemption. The three most common methods are (i) out of a sinking fund set aside for the purpose, (ii) by annual drawings normally done by lot, and (iii) by purchase in the market or by tender[9]. In addition, the debentures can be redeemed out of the proceeds of a fresh issue of shares or debentures although there are certain problems in this method due to the difficulty of getting the timing and pricing right.

NEW DEVELOPMENTS IN CORPORATE DEBT FINANCING

Reference has been made in earlier chapters and at the beginning of this chapter to developments in international finance. In the context of corporate debt financing there is a decreasing separation of long-term and short-term lending and between debt and equity. The emphasis is on flexibility through individual contracting. Short-term debt can be rolled over into medium-term finance, bonds can be converted into equity and interest separated from principal. It is a world of syndicated loans, convertibles and swaps characterised by flexibility, diffusion of risk and rapid trading of commercial paper. Some of these developments are tax driven to take advantage of loopholes in national tax regimes and tax havens. Three common forms taken by the new corporate debt financing are negative pledges, debt defeasance and subordinated debt.

A *negative pledge* is a restrictive clause which does not appear in a debenture or floating charge. Indeed its logical character is the opposite of security. It is an agreement not to give security to anyone, or at least anyone other than certain specified lenders. In the US there have been arguments that certain forms of negative pledge can give rise to an equitable lien. Thus in *Connecticut Co v New York, NH and HRR Co*[10] bonds issued by a railway company contained a covenant whereby if the company should subsequently mortgage any of its present property the bonds would participate in such security. The court held that the bonds created an equitable lien or charge which would

5   *Re Goy & Co Ltd* [1900] 2 Ch 149.
6   *Re Palmer's Decoration and Furnishing Co* [1904] 2 Ch 743.
7   *Bechuanaland Exploration Co v London Trading Bank Ltd* [1898] 2 QB 658.
8   See *Pennington,* op cit, p 483.
9   See further *Palmer's Company Law* (24th edn), vol 1, para 44–43.
10   107 A 646 (1919).

attach on the making of a new mortgage. Indeed in a Californian case in 1964[11] it was held that an equitable lien might arise if a negative pledge was broken even if it did not provide for the creation of equal security. However, this seems to go too far. In English law the most that one can say is that it may be possible in certain circumstances to establish either an equitable charge or an equitable mortgage[12]. Normally the agreement will do no more than give a future and contingent charge and until this contingency occurs there is no charge and no need for registration. It might also be possible to argue that the torts of inducing a breach of contract or conspiracy and even equitable fraud apply in appropriate circumstances[13].

Debt defeasance is a concept sometimes linked with the negative pledge[14]. The lender under a negative pledge will usually be unhappy to see an earlier debenture or debenture stock trust deed continue to exist. Debt defeasance provides one possible solution. It involves the borrower company not necessarily discharging the prior debenture but setting aside securities to provide cash flow to service the debt and adequate cover for satisfaction of the debt. As well as providing a solution in the case of a negative pledge the company may wish to engage in debt defeasance (a) to improve reported profits, (b) to provide greater freedom to deal with its assets, (c) to use up cash so that a 'crown jewel' is removed to thwart a hostile takeover bid. There are two main types of debt defeasance—legal defeasance and 'in substance' defeasance. Legal defeasance is where the original debt is released. 'In substance' defeasance is where there is no formal release but satisfactory arrangements are made using the mechanism of a trust or some contractual undertaking by third parties to be responsible for the debt. The latter is sometimes known as the 'assumption' method. There is no legal regulation of debt defeasance at the moment in the UK. In the US the Financial Accounting Standards Board in consultation with the SEC issued a practice statement outlawing some of the more extreme forms of 'in substance' defeasance. Now in the US there needs to be a release or the use of a trust over cash or other essentially risk free monetary assets.

Brief reference was made earlier in this chapter to subordination of debt. *Subordinated debt* is increasingly popular as an alternative to equity capital. English law is less tolerant of subordination than US laws. There seems to be no great problem while the debtor company is solvent but on insolvency subordinated debt runs foul of the pari passu principle. It is arguable that subordination arrangements purport to contract out of the statutory scheme applicable in winding up and for that reason are contrary to public policy. However, much depends on how the documents are drawn up. It may be possible to provide for subordination after winding up to take the form of arrangements which only take effect after the statutory procedures have been completed. Also it may be possible to use the mechanism of a trust to operate outside the winding-up scheme in any event. While a trust over book debts may possibly require registration as a covert charge on book debts, a trust over dividends accruing on winding up is not a charge on book debts and there is no need for registration[15].

On the whole the new forms of corporate debt financing operate outside the scheme of the CA 1985. It can be argued that there is a need for registration of details to complete the picture of a company's finances. It would, however, be difficult to introduce such legislation while the practice is in a state of flux.

11   *Coast Bank v Minterhout* 392 P (2d) 265 (1964).
12   *Re Gregory Love & Co* [1916] 1 Ch 203.
13   See J H Farrar 'Negative Pledges, Debt Defeasance and Subordination of Debts' in *Contemporary Issues in Company Law* (1987) ed J H Farrar, pp 35 et seq; Tan [1996] SJLS 415.
14   For further detailed discussion see Farrar, op cit, p 142.
15   For further detailed discussion see Farrar, op cit, pp 155–6.

CHAPTER 21

The taxation of companies

CONCEPTS

It is a fundamental concept of company law that a company is a legal entity distinct from its shareholders, and company law textbooks concentrate on the rights and obligations of a company as an independent legal person. However, the starting point to an understanding of company taxation is economics, not law. Although taxes may be imposed on, and paid by, legal entities such as trusts or companies, tax is ultimately borne by individuals. Concentration on corporation tax as solely a tax on companies without considering its implications for shareholders and others will result in a misleading overall picture. For example, assume a tax system which has no corporation tax and a company which makes profits of £100,000. Subsequently tax is introduced at 50%. One of the effects of the new tax is to reduce from £100,000 to £50,000 the funds available for distribution to shareholders or, if the company retains rather than distributes its profits, to reduce the increase in the market value of the shares which would otherwise have occurred. Corporation tax has therefore had a direct effect on individuals, the shareholders. It is an oversimplification to assume that only shareholders are affected by the imposition of, or alteration to the rates of, corporation tax, as a company may seek to pass on the burden of corporation tax in a number of ways. It may increase its prices to customers in an attempt to maintain its post-tax profits at pre-tax levels; it may reduce, or restrain an increase in, the prices it is prepared to pay its suppliers for goods or services, and it may reduce or restrain the wages it is prepared to pay its employees. The exact interaction of these different methods of shifting the burden of corporation tax is a matter for argument among economists[1], but it is at least clear that corporation tax is ultimately borne by individuals and that one of the groups of individuals affected is the company's shareholders. Any consideration of corporation tax would therefore be incomplete without a discussion of the related tax implications for individual shareholders.

1   See eg Kay and King *The British Tax System* (5th edn, 1990), pp 153–163; *First Report of the Irish Commission on Taxation* (July 1982), paras 24.2–24.9; *Report of the Canadian Royal Commission on Taxation* (the Carter Commission, 1966), vol 4, pp 19–27; *1955 British Royal Commission on the Taxation of Profits and Income* (Cmnd 9474), paras 44–57; A R Prest 'The Select Committee on Corporation Tax' [1972] BTR 15; S Cnossen 'Corporation Taxes in OECD Member Countries' [1984] Bulletin International Bureau of Fiscal Documentation 483.

In the UK the principal direct taxes paid by individuals are income tax, capital gains tax, and inheritance tax. Income tax is imposed on the worldwide income of a UK resident and domiciled individual, after deduction of authorised expenditure such as gifts to charity of £250 or more, and personal allowances[2]. For 1998/99, the first £4,300 of taxable income is taxed at 20% (the lower rate), the next £22,800 is taxed at 23% (the basic rate) with any excess being taxed at a single higher rate of 40%[3]. Capital gains tax on chargeable gains, computed after deducting an annual exemption, used to be imposed at a flat rate of 30%, so that a higher rate income tax payer saved tax if he could realise profits as capital gain rather than as income. However, in the March 1988 Budget the Chancellor, Nigel Lawson, announced two major changes of policy which were implemented by the 1988 Finance Act. First, after deducting an annual exemption, which is currently the first £6,800 of chargeable gains[4], the excess gains are added to the taxpayer's income and taxed as if they were the top slice of his income[5]. Thus a higher rate income taxpayer now pays CGT at 40%, and the tax advantage in receiving a profit as capital gain rather than as income has largely been removed. Second, to prevent capital gains tax being a tax on gains due solely to the effects of inflation, the tax was rebased to 31 March 1982, so that only gains accruing since that date are now taxed[6]. Additionally the taxpayer can claim an inflation indexation allowance the effect of which is that the 31 March 1982 market value of the asset, or its cost if it was acquired after that date, is increased by the percentage increase in the retail prices index from 31 March 1982, or the date of acquisition if later, to the date the asset is disposed of or to April 1998, if earlier[7]. For periods of ownership after 5 April 1998 indexation relief is replaced by a taper relief under which, after a minimum period of ownership of one year for business assets or three years for non business assets, a portion of any gain is exempt from tax. The portion increases with the length of ownership, and is higher for business assets than for non-business assets[7a]. Thus, for example, if a non-business asset is owned for more than ten years after 5 April 1998, 40% of the gain will be exempt from tax[7b].

No capital gains tax is payable on assets transferred on a death, but the donee acquires the assets at their market value on the date of death[8], thus effectively exempting any gain accruing to the deceased from CGT.

Transfers of capital may also be subject to inheritance tax. Apart from a number of exempt transfers, such as the transfer of assets between husband and wife[9], the first £223,000 of the deceased's chargeable estate is taxed a a nil rate, and any excess value is taxed at 40%[10]. Inter vivos gifts are now generally exempt from inheritance tax provided the gift is an outright gift with no reservation of benefit to the donor[11]. However, gifts made within the seven years preceding the taxpayer's death remain taxable as part of his estate[12]. They are taxed in the order in which they were made,

2   Relief for some expenditure (eg qualifying mortgage interest) and personal allowances (eg married couple's allowance) is now given as a 10 or 15% tax credit to restrict the value of the relief.
3   ICTA 1988, s 1(2).
4   TCGA 1992, s 3(2). References to current tax legislation are to the original legislation as amended and in force for 1998/99. The amended legislation is contained in Butterworths *Yellow and Orange Tax Handbooks* for 1998/99.
5   TCGA 1992, s 4.
6   Ibid, s 35(2).
7   Ibid, ss 53 and 54.
7a   TCGA 1992, s 2A.
7b   Ibid, s 2A(5).
8   Ibid, s 62(1).
9   ITA 1984, s 18(1).
10   ITA 1984, s 7(1) and Sch 1.
11   ITA 1984, s 3A(4).
12   ITA 1984, s 3A(4).

and are entitled to tapering relief varying with the length of time the donor has survived the transfer[13]. Certain inter vivos gifts, such as transfers into discretionary trusts[14] and the alteration of share capital in a close company[15], remain taxable when made, but with the benefit of the £223,000 nil rate band, and the rate of tax chargeable is 20% (half the death rate)[16]. If such transfers are made within seven years prior to the donor's death they are cumulated with his estate, and are charged to the higher of the inter vivos rate or the death rate, with credit being given for any inter vivos tax paid[17]. All inter vivos gifts, whether initially chargeable, or chargeable only because the donor dies within seven years, are entitled to an annual exemption of £3,000 in computing the value transferred[18].

Additionally, there are substantial inheritance tax reliefs for business and farming assets. These reliefs were significantly extended by the 1992, 1995, and 1996 Finance Acts, so that now a proprietor of a business or a farmer is effectively exempt from inheritance tax on the value of his interest in the business, whether the business is incorporated or unincorporated. Subject to certain conditions[19], 100% relief can be claimed against the value of interests in unincorporated businesses[20], shareholdings in unquoted companies[1], including companies listed on the Unlisted Securities Market and the Alternative Investment Market[2], and against the value of land used for agriculture[3]. FA 1995 extended the 100% relief to the value to the landlord of the reversion of land let for agricultural purposes[4] for tenancies granted on or after 1 September 1995. For earlier tenancies 100% relief is only available if the landlord has the right to possession within 12 months[5]. If 100% relief is not available, 50% relief can be claimed against the value of shares in a quoted company of which the taxpayer had control[6], and against the value of any land, building, machinery or plant owned by the taxpayer but used for the business of a company in which he had a controlling interest, or by a partnership in which he was a partner[7]. 50% relief may also be available for interests in agricultural land which do not qualify for 100% relief[8].

When considering corporation tax, it is therefore necessary to keep in mind:

(1) tax paid by a company on corporate profits;
(2) tax paid by a company on corporate capital gains;
(3) income tax paid by an individual shareholder on distributions from a company;
(4) capital gains tax paid by individual shareholders on the disposal of shares;
(5) to a lesser extent, inheritance tax payable by individual shareholders on the transfer of shares.

13   Eg, if the donor survives four years only 60% of the inheritance tax otherwise due will be levied, ITA 1984, s 7(4).
14   ITA 1984, s 3, not excluded by s 3A.
15   ITA 1984, s 98. Gifts by close companies also remain chargeable, ibid, s 94 with s 3A(6).
16   Ibid, s 7(2).
17   Ibid, s 7(4) and (5).
18   Ibid, s 19.
19   Including a minimum ownership period of seven years for let farmland and two years for other assets.
20   ITA 1984, s 104(10)(a) and s 105(1)(a).
1   Ibid, s 104(1)(a) and 105(1)(b) and (bb). For transfers prior to 6 April 1996, there was a minimum shareholding requirement of 25.1%, with shareholdings of 25% or less attracting 50% relief. The minimum shareholding requirement was abolished by FA 1996, s 184.
2   IR press release, para 3, [1995] Simon's Tax Intelligence (STI) 1833.
3   ITA 1984, s 115(2) and 116(2).
4   Ibid, s 116(2) as amended by FA 1995, s 155(1).
5   Ibid, s 116(2)(a).
6   Ibid, s 105(1)(cc).
7   Ibid, s 105(1)(d). Relief is also available for equivalent assets held in a trust in which the taxpayer has an interest in possession (s 105(1)(e)).
8   ITA 1984, s 116(2).

HISTORICAL BACKGROUND TO CORPORATION TAX

Until as recently as 1965, the UK had no separate corporation tax. Originally, companies were taxed like trusts and paid standard rate income tax on their profits. When these profits were distributed as dividend, a shareholder was taxed on a gross dividend of the cash amount he received grossed up by the standard rate of tax[9], but was credited with having paid this standard rate tax. Thus, at least to the extent that profits were distributed, the tax rate on companies was effectively a payment in advance of the shareholders' income tax liability. As there was no capital gains tax, retained profits suffered only standard rate income tax[10]. To fund an armaments build up before the Second World War, a National Defence Contribution of 5% of company profits was imposed in 1937. In 1939, this was supplemented by an excess profits tax. Neither of these taxes was credited to shareholders if profits were distributed. After the war these taxes were replaced by a profits tax designed to encourage the retention of profits to finance the post-war regeneration of British industry[11]. Thus, under the system which existed in 1955 when the Royal Commission on the Taxation of Profits and Income[12] reported, companies paid standard rate income tax on their profits, plus an additional 22.5% profits tax on profits in excess of £2,000. If profits were retained, profits tax at the rate of 20% was refunded. If profits were distributed, there was no refund of profits tax but the shareholder, while taxed on the dividend grossed up at the standard rate, was credited with having paid standard rate tax, thus leaving the profits tax as an unrecoverable tax on distributed profits[13]. This tax system encouraged the retention, rather than the distribution, of profits, with a further incentive being the absence of a capital gains tax on the disposal of shares. The 1955 Royal Commission recommended no change in the basic system of company taxation[14], although they did recommend the abolition of non-distribution relief for profits tax[15], a recommendation implemented in the 1958 Finance Act[16]. However, the Royal Commission Report contained a minority report by G Woodcock, H L Bullock and N Kaldor which recommended the introduction of a capital gains tax[17] and a separate tax on company profits, distributed or retained, with shareholders paying income tax on dividends but receiving no credit for the underlying corporation tax paid by the company[18]. The minority recommendations became Labour Party policy and were implemented in the 1965 Finance Act.

Corporation tax was imposed at a flat rate of 40% on company profits, whether retained or distributed. If a dividend was paid the company deducted, and paid over to the Revenue, standard rate tax at 41.25% of the gross dividend. The shareholder was then subject to income tax on the gross dividend, but was credited with having paid

---

9   Which tax had already been paid by the company as income tax on its profit.
10   For historical background to corporation tax, see eg Boydon's *Modern Income Tax and Surtax Practice* (1933); *1955 Royal Commission Report* (Cmnd 9474), paras 49 and 50; R White 'The Changing Face of Taxation – Corporation Tax' [1981] BTR 349; 1982 Green Paper on the Reform of Corporation Tax (Cmnd 8456), App 1.
11   See *1955 Royal Commission Report*, paras 518–540.
12   Cmnd 9474.
13   *1955 Royal Commission Report*, paras 47 and 48. The profits tax was not levied on non-corporate businesses, and thus some differentiation in the taxation of companies existed prior to 1965.
14   Ibid, para 553.
15   Ibid, para 540.
16   FA 1958, s 25(1).
17   Ibid, p 365 ff.
18   Ibid, p 382 ff.

the 41.25% tax withheld[19]. This system of company taxation, which is known as the classical system, had the advantage of maintaining the company law demarcation between the company and the shareholder, but also had the economic disadvantage of discriminating in favour of retained profits and against distributed profits. £100 profits were subject to £40 tax if retained in the company but to £64.75 tax if distributed to a standard rate taxpayer, the whole of this tax being paid by the company. Although retention of profits did not normally confer significant tax advantages on shareholders other than high rate taxpayers, as capital gains tax at 30% was now imposed on any gain on the disposal of shares, it was thought to distort the capital market by encouraging inefficient as well as efficient companies to retain profits, rather than distribute them and enable shareholders to reinvest in more productive companies[20].

In 1971, the Conservative Government issued a Green Paper, 'The Reform of Corporation Tax'[1], which discussed three alternative systems of corporation tax all of which were designed to preserve neutrality between tax on retained and distributed profits. The first alternative was a return to the pre-1965 system, which the government rejected (because, without complex provisions, it could result in the crediting of shareholders with payments of tax which had never been received from the company). The remaining two were the two-rate system of corporation tax, then operated by West Germany, and the partial imputation system, then operated by France[2]. Under a two-rate system[3] a company pays corporation tax at, say. 50% on its profits. If it distributes profits it withholds and pays over to the Revenue tax at the basic rate of income tax on the gross dividend, but pays a reduced rate of corporation tax (37.5% if the basic rate is 25%) on the profits it has distributed. The shareholder pays income tax on the gross dividend, but is credited with having paid the income tax withheld by the company. The net effect is that the company pays 50% tax to the Revenue whether its profits are retained or distributed, with no additional tax charge to a basic rate shareholder if profits were distributed. Under a partial imputation[4] system, a company pays tax at a flat rate of, say, 50% on its profits, whether distributed or retained. but is not required to withhold income tax on payment of a dividend. A shareholder in receipt of a dividend is taxed on the cash dividend received grossed up by a portion of the underlying corporation tax, but is credited with having paid this tax. In practice, grossing up is normally at a rate of income tax which is lower than the corporation tax rate, and hence the title 'partial imputation' rather than 'full imputation' as a shareholder is only being credited with part, and not the whole, of the underlying corporation tax paid by the company. Again the net effect is that a company pays 50% tax on its profits, whether retained or distributed, and there is no additional tax charge to a basic rate taxpayer if profits are distributed.

If international considerations could be ignored, the two-rate and partial imputation systems are identical in their practical effect. Under both the company has the same

---

19   The rates quoted are those effective for 1965/66. A detailed outline of the 1965 corporation tax provisions is contained in an Inland Revenue booklet on corporation tax issued in February 1966 under reference no 570 (1966).

20   Chancellor of the Exchequer Mr Barber's Budget Statement for 1971, 814 HC Official Report (5th series) (1970–71). See also evidence of Alan Lord to the House of Commons Select Committee established to review the 1971 Green Paper on Corporations Tax, HC 622, HMSO.

1   Cmnd 4630, March 1971.

2   For a summary of Corporation tax systems operated by a number of other countries, including Germany and France, see App 7 of the 1982 Green Paper on the Reform of Corporation Tax (Cmnd 8456) and see also Thomas Knatz 'Corporation Tax Systems' [1972] BTR 33; S N Frommel 'The New German Imputation System and Foreign Investors' [1976] BTR 269; S Cnossen 'Corporation Taxes in OECD Member Countries' [1984] Bulletin International Bureau of Fiscal Documentation 483.

3   See 1971 Green Paper (Cmnd 4630), paras 15–38.

4   See ibid, paras 39–42.

total burden whether it retains or distributes profits, and under both there is no additional tax charge to a basic rate shareholder on distributed profits. In 1971 the Government initially favoured the two-rate system[5] but a House of Commons Select Committee established to consider the Green Paper recommended firmly in favour of the partial imputation system[6]. The recommendation was accepted by the Government and legislation implementing a partial imputation system was contained in the Finance Act 1972 and took effect on 1 April 1973. A major reason for the change of mind was the international implications of the two systems[7]. Business is increasingly conducted by multinational groups of companies, and foreign countries also impose corporation tax. To ensure that there is no unnecessary net loss to the UK of tax, or of national income, when foreign companies repatriate the profits of a UK subsidiary in comparison with the repatriation by UK parent companies of the profits of foreign subsidiaries, there must be no significant difference between the total tax imposed by a foreign country on a UK-owned foreign subsidiary as compared with the UK tax imposed on the profits of a foreign-owned UK subsidiary. In practice it was thought easier to achieve this balance with an imputation system, which retains the same (high) rate of corporation tax whether profits are retained or distributed, than with the two-rate system which charges a lower rate of corporation tax if profits are distributed, thus potentially benefiting foreign parent companies.

In 1973, the UK joined the European Economic Community. One of the objectives of the European Commission is to harmonise the corporation tax systems of member countries as an aid towards the free flow of profits and capital within the Community. To this end, the Commission submitted to the Council of Ministers on 1 August 1975[8] a draft directive recommending that all member states should adopt a partial imputation system of corporation tax similar to that then operated by France and the UK. However, the directive made no subsequent progress, so that the Irish Commission on Direct Taxation, which reported in July 1982 and recommended a full imputation tax system for Ireland[9], said that they did not consider the EEC draft directive to be a significant constraint on their recommendation[10]. In January 1982, the UK Conservative Government issued a further Green Paper[11] on the reform of corporation tax which made virtually no mention of the need to harmonise corporation tax within the EEC. In the light of these and other developments the European Commission have therefore recommended to the Council and the European Parliament that it is not now appropriate to proceed with proposals for major reforms of company taxation within member states to bring the systems more closely in line with one another[12].

Sir Geoffrey Howe, then Chancellor of the Exchequer, announced in his March 1983 budget[13] that, in the light of representations received on the Green paper, no major change in the structure of the tax was now envisaged. However, after the June 1983

---

5   See 1971 Green Paper (Cmnd 4630), para 10.
6   Report of the Select Committee on Corporation Tax, Session 1970/71, HC 622, HMSO, November 1981. See also A R Prest 'The Select Committee on Corporation Tax' [1972] BTR 15; R White 'The Changing Face of Taxation – Corporation Tax' [1981] BTR 349.
7   Report of the Select Committee on Corporation Tax, supra. .
8   Official Journal of the European Communities 5/11/1975 No C 253/2, and see J Chown 'The Harmonisation of Corporation Tax in the EEC: The Commission's Programme' [1981] BTR 329 at 337.
9   First Report of the Commission on Taxation, July 1982, para 27.35. In so recommending they agreed with a similar recommendation of the Canadian Royal Commission on Taxation, 1966, vol 4, p 83.
10 First Report of the Commission on Taxation, supra, para 29.22.
11 Corporation Tax 1982 (Cmnd 8456). The Green Paper provides an excellent analysis of the current corporation tax system and its effect.
12 'Guidelines on Company Taxation' (SEC (90) 601 final).
13 39 HC Official Report (6th series) col 149 (1982–83).

general election, Nigel Lawson was appointed Chancellor of the Exchequer and in his March 1984 budget, while retaining the imputation system, he announced a number of important changes[14]. First, he considered the then current 52% rate of corporation tax to be much too high, penalising profits and discouraging commercial risk-taking. The rate was therefore progressively reduced to 35% with the reduction fully implemented from 1 April 1986. The rate for small companies was reduced to 30% immediately and thereafter in practice further reduced in line with reductions in the basic rate of income tax. Secondly, two significant corporation tax reliefs, stock relief and first year capital allowances (or accelerated depreciation), were withdrawn, either immediately or progressively. In 1991 the main rate of corporation tax was further reduced to 33%[15] and, in 1993, for reasons explained later in this chapter, significant changes were made to the corporation tax and income tax consequences of the payment of a dividend[16]. For 1997/98 the forecast corporation tax receipts are £27.2bn, or 11.67% of total tax receipts, which compares with £8.2bn, or 9.22% of tax receipts, in 1984/85 and £13.4bn, or 13.66% of tax receipts, in 1986/87[17].

In July 1997, in the first budget of the new Labour Government, the main rate of corporation tax was reduced to 31%, with retrospective effect to 1 April 1997, and in the March 1998 Budget a further reduction to 30% was announced, with effect from 1 April 1999. Further significant changes were made to the tax treatment of dividend income by precluding pension funds and companies from reclaiming tax credits on dividends paid on or after 2 July 1997. Other shareholders are not affected until 1999/2000, when the tax credit attaching to dividends will be reduced to 10%, but with an adjustment to the income tax treatment of dividends, so that individual shareholders should pay no more income tax than at present.

UK IMPUTATION CORPORATION TAX[18]

Legislation on income tax and corporation tax is contained in a succession of annual Finance Acts. Periodically these Acts are consolidated. the most recent consolidation is the Income and Corporation Taxes Act 1988, which took effect on 6 April 1988 for individuals, and for accounting periods ended after 5 April 1988 for companies[19]. Corporation tax is imposed annually in a Finance Act for a financial year. A financial year runs from 1 April–31 March[20], and should be contrasted with the tax year for individuals, the fiscal year, which runs from 6 April to 5 April[1]. Thus the 1998 Financial year runs from 1 April 1998 to 31 March 1999. From the inception of the imputation system of corporation tax in 1973, until the financial year 1982, the rate of corporation tax was 52%, but this rate has now been progressively reduced to 31%, and will be further reduced to 30% in April 1999[2]. For ease of exposition, the remainder of this chapter will assume a rate of corporation tax of 31%, the rate in force for the financial year ended 31 March 1999.

---

14   [1984] Simon's Tax Intelligence (STI) 196; 56 HC Official Report (6th series) col 295 (1983–84).
15   FA 1991, s 24.
16   FA 1993, ss 77–81.
17   Figures taken from the Financial Statement and Budget reports for 1985/86, 1987/88, and 1997/98.
18   For a more detailed exposition see eg *Simon's Taxes*, vol D (Butterworths) and Bramwell *The Taxation of Companies and Company Reconstructions* (6th edn, 1994).
19   ICTA 1988, s 843(1).
20   ICTA 1988, s 834(1).
1   Ibid, s 2(2).
2   F (No 2) B 1998, cl 29(1).

Traditionally, the corporation tax rate has been higher than the basic rate of income tax, currently 23%[3], and this might be considered to discriminate against the conducting of a small business through a company rather than as a sole trader or in partnership. Small companies therefore pay corporation tax at a reduced rate, known as the small companies rate. This rate remained at 42% from 1973–1978, reduced to 40% for 1979–1981, and to 38% for the financial year 1982. As part of the general reduction of corporation tax rates, it was reduced to 30%, the same as the basic rate of income tax, for the financial year 1983[4], was then further reduced in line with the fall in the basic rate of income tax, and in July 1997 was reduced below the basic rate of income tax to 21% for the financial year 1997[5]. From April 1999, the rate will be 20%.[5a]

However, to call it a rate for small companies is something of a misnomer, as the criterion is the amount of a company's profits, not the value of its assets or the number of its shareholders or employees. For the financial year 1998, if a company's profits, which have an extended definition for this purpose, do not exceed £300,000[6] the whole of its taxable profits are taxed at 21%. If its profits exceed £1,500,000[7] the whole of its taxable profits are taxed at 31% with no relief for the first £300,000 profits. The income of a company with profits between £300,000 and £1,500,000 is taxed under a formula[8] the approximate effect of which is to tax the first £300,000 at 21% with the excess over £300,000 being taxed at 31%[9]. If a company has associated companies the limits are divided by one plus the number of associated companies[10]. If a company has an accounting period of less than 12 months, the limits are proportionately reduced[11]. The practical significance of the small companies rate has been considerable. The 1982 Green Paper estimated that about 95% of companies either took advantage of the small companies rate provisions or paid no tax at all, all but 3% or 4% of them having profits below £80,000, the then lower limit for the small companies rate[12]. Conversely the top 5% of all active companies contributed over 85% of the total corporation tax yield[13]. In 1998 the Revenue estimated that, out of 700,000 companies within the charge to corporation tax, only about 400,000 actually have to pay it. Around 85% of tax paying companies pay tax at the small companies' rate. About 10% of taxpaying companies pay tax at the full rate, but contribute 85% of the total corporation tax yield[14].

Computation of taxable profits

Corporation tax is imposed by reference to accounting periods[15]. A company's first accounting period begins when a company first comes into charge to corporation tax and ends with the earliest of the following events[16]:

3   FA 1997, s 55. The rate was reduced from 24% to 23% for 1997/98.
4   FA 1984, s 20.
5   F (No 2) A 1997, s 18. The rate is unchanged for 1998.
5a   F (No 2) B 1998, cl 29.
6   ICTA 1988, s 13(3).
7   Ibid.
8   ICTA 1988, s 13(2).
9   The greater the gap between the main CT rate and the small companies rate, the greater is the tax on profits in excess of £300,000.
10   Ibid, s 13(3)(b).
11   Ibid, s 13(6).
12   Cmnd 8456, para 16(6).
13   1982 Green Paper on Corporation Tax (Cmnd 8456) App 4, para 10.
14   Revenue press release, [1998] STI 400, paras 1-4.
15   ICTA 1988, ss 8(3) and 12(1).
16   Ibid, s 12(3).

  (a) 12 months after its commencement;

  (b) the company's own termination date for its accounting period;

  (c) the company ceasing to trade, to be resident in the UK, or to be liable to corporation tax;

  (d) the commencement of the winding up of the company, when a new accounting period starts[17].

If a company's own accounts are prepared for a period exceeding 12 months, the first 12 months constitute one accounting period, with the balance of the period being a separate accounting period for tax purposes[18]. For companies who regularly prepare accounts to the same financial year end, the accounting period for corporation tax will coincide with the period covered by their own accounts. Where an accounting period straddles two financial years, the profits are apportioned on a time basis and taxed at the appropriate rate for each financial year[19]. Thus a company preparing annual financial accounts to 31 December 1998 will have one-quarter of the taxable profits of that account taxed at the corporation tax rate for the financial year ended 31 March 1998 and three-quarters taxed at the rate for the financial year ended 31 March 1999.

    Companies resident in the UK are liable to corporation tax on their worldwide profits[20], although credit may be given against their UK tax liability for foreign tax paid on foreign income[1]. Non-resident companies are only liable to UK corporation tax on their profits from a branch or agency in the UK[2], or on income, such as interest or dividends, from sources within the UK. Prior to 15 March 1988 the test for company residence was based solely on case law and depended on where the company was centrally managed and controlled. A company was only resident in the UK for tax purposes if it was centrally managed and controlled here irrespective of its country of incorporation[3].

    As from 15 March 1988, a company is resident in the UK for corporation tax purposes if *either*

  (a) it is centrally managed and controlled in the UK, *or*

  (b) it is incorporated in the UK[4].

However, if a company is resident in both the UK (eg because it is incorporated here) and in a foreign country (eg because it is centrally managed and controlled there), and is allocated the foreign country as its country of residence for the purposes of a double tax treaty between the UK and the foreign country, then it is not resident in the UK for corporation tax purposes[5].

    Transitional relief may still be available for companies which are incorporated in the UK but which were centrally managed and controlled abroad before, or shortly after, 15 March 1988. A company which, prior to 15 March 1988, was carrying on a business and had ceased to be resident in the UK in pursuance of a Treasury consent,

17   Ibid, s 12(7).

18   Ibid, s 12(2) and (3).

19   ICTA 1988, s 8(3).

20   Ibid, s 8(1) and s 11(1).

1   Ibid, ss 788–816. The credit is limited to the UK corporation tax which would otherwise have been payable on the income.

2   Ibid, s 11(1), (2), (3).

3   Bramwell *Taxation of Companies and Company Reconstructions* (4th edn, 1988), paras 12.02–12.05; *De Beers Consolidated Mines Ltd v Howe (Surveyor of Taxes)* [1906] AC 455, HL; *Unit Construction Co Ltd v Bullock (Inspector of Taxes)* [1960] AC 351, HL; and see Inland Revenue Statement of Practice SP 1/90, and Sheridan 'The Residence of Companies for Taxation Purposes' [1990] BTR 78.

4   FA 1988, s 66(1).

5   FA 1994, s 249.

will remain non-resident until the later of 15 March 1993 or the date it ceases to carry on business or, if the consent was a general consent, it ceases to be taxable in a foreign country[6]. If a UK-incorporated company ceased to be resident after 15 March 1988 in pursuance of a Treasury consent and was carrying on business immediately after 15 March 1988, it retains non-resident status until the later of 15 March 1993 or the date it ceases to carry on business[7]. Any other UK incorporated company which was non-resident under the central management and control test on 15 March 1988 became resident in the UK from 15 March 1993[8], unless it had assumed actual residence on an earlier date[9].

Prior to 15 March 1988 it was a criminal offence for a company which was resident in the UK to become non-resident without the consent of the Treasury, which would almost certainly have been refused if the purpose of the change of residence was tax avoidance[10]. As from 15 March 1988, the criminal sanction against companies becoming non-resident has been repealed[11], but they must first notify the Revenue and make arrangements to pay any outstanding tax liabilities[12]. Additionally, the company will be deemed to have disposed of all its assets, with a consequent possible charge to corporation tax on capital gains[13].

A UK-resident company computes its profits for corporation tax in the same way as an individual computes his income for income tax[14]. The assessable profits of a company are those actually earned in an accounting period[15]. Apart from trading profits, assessable profits include income from land, interest received, and dividends from foreign companies. They do not include dividends from other UK-resident companies, technically known as franked investment income, which have already borne corporation tax and are not charged to this tax again if received by a resident company[16]. Additionally, a company is charged to corporation tax on its post-31 March 1982 capital gains less any allowable capital losses[17]. Companies are entitled to the indexation allowance in computing their chargeable gains[18], but do not receive the £6,800 annual exemption[19]. Capital gains made by companies, and retained in the company rather than distributed, will increase the value of a company's shares, but, unless the company is a unit or investment trust[1], a shareholder is given no relief for the potential double taxation of the same capital gain initially to the company and subsequently to the shareholder on disposal of his shares. It may therefore be sensible tax planning for small family companies to keep appreciating assets, such as land, outside the company

---

6   FA 1988, Sch 7, para 1.
7   Ibid, Sch 7, para 2.
8   Ibid, Sch 7, paras 3 and 4.
9   FA 1988, Sch 7, paras 1(3), 2(3) and 4(2).
10   ICTA 1988, s 765(1)(a). In *R v HM Treasury, ex p Daily Mail and General Trust plc* [1988] STC 787, the European Court held that this provision did not offend European Law in so far as it affected transfers to other EC countries.
11   FA 1988, ss 105(b), 148 and Sch 14, Pt IV.
12   Ibid, s 130 and s 131, and see SP 2/90 which provides guidance on the arrangements for emigrating companies.
13   TCGA 1992, s 185.
14   ICTA 1988, s 9(1).
15   Ibid, ss 8(3), 70(1).
16   Ibid, s 208.
17   TCGA 1992, s 8.
18   Ibid, s 53. An indexation allowance cannot create or increase a loss, TCGA 1992, s 53(1)(b). Companies continue to get indexation allowance after April 1998 and do not get taper relief.
19   The section conferring the exemption, TCGA 1992, s 3(1), refers only to individuals.
1   Investment and unit trusts are exempt from tax on capital gains which they make on the disposal of investments (TCGA 1992, s 100(1)), but a share or unit holder is chargeable to CGT on any gains he makes on the disposal of his shares or units.

to avoid this double taxation[2]. Alternatively the company should consider distributing its realised capital gains as dividend, rather than retain them. The gains will effectively remain liable to corporation tax, but double taxation will be avoided unless the shareholder is liable to higher rate income tax.

From its gross profits a company may deduct charges[3], which include interest paid on loans, including debentures, which have been used for business purposes[4]. A deduction as a charge on income can be claimed for gifts to charity under a deed of covenant which is capable of lasting for more than three years[5]. Provided certain formalities are complied with, a deduction is also available for single donations to charity[6]. For a company which is not a close company, there is no lower or upper limit to the amount of a donation on which tax relief can be claimed. If the company is a close company the minimum net of tax payment is £250[7], there is no maximum amount, and there must be no collateral conditions or right to repayment attached to the gift[8].

The balance of gross profits less charges is then subject to corporation tax. For accounting periods ended on or after 1 October 1993[9] companies pay corporation tax under a system called 'pay and file'. Not later than nine months after the end of its accounting period a company must estimate its corporation tax liability for the period and pay that liability to the Inland Revenue[10]. If requested by a Revenue officer to do so, it must then file its corporation tax return not later than 12 months after the end of the relevant accounting period[11], and it is subject to automatic penalties if it fails to do so without reasonable excuse[12]. The Revenue then assess the corporation tax liability for the period. If the assessment is more than the company's initial estimate, the excess is payable to the Revenue together with interest computed from the original due date of nine months after the end of the accounting period. If the estimated payment was too high, the excess is refunded with interest computed from the normal due date, or the date of actual payment, whichever is the later[13].

From 1996/97 self-assessment for income tax has been introduced[14]. Under this system, a taxpayer liable to income tax is required both to return his income for a year of assessment and to compute his tax liability for the year based on his return[15]. Self-assessment is being extended to companies[16], for accounting periods which end on or after 1 July 1999[17].

For most companies, the most significant item in their corporation tax computation is trading profit. A company's taxable trading profit is initially computed applying

2   Although other tax considerations may militate against this eg the inability to obtain roll-over relief if an unincorporated business is being transferred to a company, see p 289, and a possible reduction of inheritance tax business property relief from 100% to 50% of the value of the asset.
3   ICTA 1988, s 338(1).
4   Ibid, s 338(3) and (6).
5   Ibid, s 338(2), (3) and (5), with s 339(8).
6   Ibid, ss 338(2)(b) and 339.
7   Ibid, s 339(3A),
8   ICTA 1988, s 339(3B)–(3E).
9   SI 1992 No 3066.
10 ICTA 1988, s 10(1)(a).
11 TMA 1970, s 11(4).
12 Ibid, s 54.
13 ICTA 1988, s 826(1) and (2).
14 The main provisions are in FA 1994, ss 178–199.
15 A tax return filed before 30 September following the tax year can require the Revenue to compute the tax liability, but the assessment is treated as if it had been done by the taxpayer (new TMA 1970, s 9(2) and (3), inserted by FA 1994, s 179).
16 F (No 2) B 1998, cl 115 and Sch 18.
17 F (No 2) B 1998 cl 115(4) and (5), with IR Press Release 25 November 1997 [1997] STI 1532.

normal commercial accounting principles, but is then subject to adjustment[18]. Only the historical cost method of preparing accounts is currently recognised for tax purposes[19]. This system gives little or no recognition to the proportion of a company's profits attributable solely to inflation, and therefore tends to result in an overstatement of real profit and an increased tax burden on companies. This failure to permit a system of inflation accounting for tax purposes has had a significant impact on the real tax burden borne by companies. The 1982 Green Paper on corporation tax estimated that the effective rate of UK tax on company income of UK-based industrial and commercial companies, excluding those engaged on North Sea oil and gas production, earned over the period of 1976 to 1980 averaged roughly 25%[20] on the basis of historical cost profits but roughly 65% on the basis of inflation adjusted profits[1]. For financial companies, the figures were 30% and 40% respectively[2]. As yet the accountancy bodies have made only limited progress in agreeing on an acceptable system of inflation accounting[3], and the Revenue have been unwilling to accept any system other than historical cost accounting without it first being agreed and generally implemented as standard accounting practice[4].

The principal adjustments made to historical cost accounting profits for tax purposes involve the disallowance of some expenditure items properly deducted in computing accounting profit, such as the entertainment of customers[5], donations to political parties[6] and, most significantly, depreciation[7]. Depreciation is disallowed because technically it is the write-off of capital expenditure, which is itself disallowable for tax purposes. The total disallowable expenditure increases the taxable profit. From this increased profit, a number of deductions are authorised, of which the most significant are capital allowances.

Capital allowances are, in effect, statutory depreciation. Not all capital expenditure qualifies for capital allowances[8], but prior to 1984 the rate of allowance for expenditure

---

18 See, eg, *BSC Footwear Ltd v Ridgway (Inspector of Taxes)* [1972] AC 544, HL; *Gallagher v Jones (Inspector of Taxes)* [1993] STC 537, CA; *Johnston (Inspector of Taxes) v Brittania Airways Ltd* [1994] STC 763; and see generally a series of articles in [1995] British Tax Review 433–524.

19 *Lowe v IRC* [1983] STC 816, PC, a New Zealand case, but the same decision would almost certainly be reached in the UK.

20 This apparently low rate is explained largely by the effect of tax reliefs attributable to capital allowances and stock relief.

1   1982 Green Paper on Corporation Tax (Cmnd 8456) App 6, para 6.

2   Ibid, App 6, para 7.

3   A Statement of Standard Accountancy Practice (SSAP 16) required, for an experimental period, that large companies should include a statement showing the effect of inflation on profit for accounting periods beginning on or after 1 January 1980 applying a method known as current cost accounting. The standard has been the subject of considerable criticism and a revised proposed standard 'Accounting for the effects of changing prices' (ED 35) was issued by the Accounting Standards Committee of the Joint Accounting Bodies in July 1984. The revised proposals were themselves the subject of controversy and have now been abandoned. SSAP 16 was made voluntary in June 1985 by all CCAB bodies. They have since proposed that the standard be withdrawn, but support further work towards a new standard (*Accountancy* (November 1986) p 153). The lower inflation rates of recent years have, however, made the problem less urgent.

4   The Irish Commission recommended against the use of inflation accounting for tax purpose until appropriate principles have been recommended for universal application by the accountancy bodies; Irish Commission on Direct Taxation, para 26.37, July 1982. The British government has adopted the same approach: see the Chancellor of the Exchequer's Budget statement 1983, 39 HC Official Report (6th series), col 151 (1982–83).

5   ICTA 1988, s 577.

6   See the Chancellor of the Exchequer's statement, 460 HC Official Report (5th series), col 25 (18 January 1949).

7   *Forder (Surveyor of Taxes) v Handyside* (1876) 45 LJQB 809, and see J R Edwards 'Tax Treatment of Capital Expenditure and the Measurement of Accounting Profit' [1976] BTR 300.

8   For example, no relief is given for the construction of buildings which are not industrial buildings.

which does qualify was substantially greater than the depreciation charged in a company's commercial accounts, because successive governments used capital allowances to encourage industry to increase its capital investment by permitting a rapid write-off of the expenditure for tax purposes. This was achieved by a combination of generous initial or first year allowances with an annual writing down allowance for any expenditure remaining unrelieved. Thus, until the 1984 Budget, a company which erected or acquired a new industrial building was permitted to claim an initial allowance of 75% of the expenditure[9], with the balance being written off annually at the rate of 4% of the total cost of the building.[10] Similarly, a company which purchased plant or machinery was entitled to a first year allowance of 100%[11] of the cost. The company was free to disclaim this allowance[12], in which case it received a writing down allowance of 25% per year of the declining balance of expenditure not yet written off[13]. In his 1984 budget, the Chancellor of the Exchequer stated that he considered this policy of high initial write-off of capital expenditure for tax purposes to have been misguided because it encouraged the purchase of assets which tax allowances made appear profitable, but which did not generate a good commercial return[14]. In a major change of policy, initial and first year allowances for industrial buildings and plant and machinery have therefore been progressively withdrawn so that, for expenditure after 1 April 1986[15], only an annual writing down allowance is given[16].

It was announced in the July 1997 budget that writing down allowances in the first year for expenditure incurred by small and medium-sized businesses on most plant and machinery in the year ended 1 July 1998 would be doubled from 25% to 50%.[16a] The Revenue estimated that more than 99% of all businesses would qualify for the increased relief.[16b] For the year from 2 July 1998 – 1 July 1999 first year allowance for small and medium-sized businesses is 40%.[16c]

Distributions

THE TAX POSITION OF THE DISTRIBUTING COMPANY

It will be recalled that under the UK imputation system of corporation tax, company profits are taxed at 31%, or at 21% of the small companies rate applies. If profits are subsequently distributed to a shareholder a portion of the corporation tax paid is attributed to the shareholder who is subject to income tax on the actual dividend received plus the tax attributed, but is credited with having already paid the tax attributed. In effect the corporation tax has become an advance payment of income tax. If a company's pre-tax accounting profit and its profit for tax purposes were always

---

9   Capital Allowances Act 1968, s 1(2), as in effect for 1983/84.
10   Ibid, s 2(2).
11   FA 1971, ss 41 and 42 as in effect for 1983/84.
12   Ibid, s 41(3).
13   Ibid, s 44.
14   56 HC Official Report (6th series) cols 295, 6 (1983/94).
15   FA 1984, s 8 and Sch 12. The capital allowances legislation has since been consolidated in the Capital · Allowances Act 1990 with effect for chargeable periods ended after 5 April 1990.
16   In a limited number of cases, such as qualifying buildings in enterprise zones, generous initial allowances are still available. For expenditure incurred between 1 November 1992 and 31 October 1993 an initial/first year allowance of 20% for industrial buildings and 40% for plant and machinery was reintroduced as a temporary measure to encourage capital investment.
16a F (No 2) A 1997, s 42.
16b Inland Revenue Press Release, 2 July 1997 [1997] STI 907.
16c CAA 1990, s 22.

identical, distributions would pose no problems. The company would pay corporation tax and be left with a net of tax profit which could then be distributed to shareholders to the extent desired with no further tax implications for the company. But, in practice, profits for tax purposes may be materially lower than its distributable profits for company law purposes. The consequent reduction of the corporation tax bill may be further increased if a company has foreign income, as foreign tax paid on the foreign income will generally be creditable against any UK tax liability on the same income, thus reducing the amount of UK corporation tax that the company has to pay. The Revenue consider it to be a fundamental principle that they should not be required to credit a shareholder in receipt of a dividend with having paid tax unless they have actually received that tax from the distributing company. In the absence of further provisions, this could not be guaranteed as a company may well have distributable profits for company law purposes but have little or no UK corporation tax liability.

To deal with the problem, a system of advance corporation tax has been added to the basic imputation corporation tax structure. Advance corporation tax is payable where a company makes a distribution which is also a 'qualifying distribution'[17]. Distributions are widely defined to include not only dividends but distribution of capital profits and the transfer of assets other than as a return of capital on liquidation[18]. The capitalisation of profit followed by the issue of bonus shares does not constitute a distribution, although a shareholder may be liable to income tax if he is given the option to receive either a dividend or bonus shares[19]. With very limited exceptions, such as a bonus issue of redeemable share capital, all distributions are also qualifying distributions[20]. On, or within a short time after making a qualifying distribution, a company is required to pay over to the Revenue advance corporation tax (ACT) at a rate related to the lower rate of income tax[1] and which is currently 20/80 of the amount distributed.

Prior to 1993/94 the rate was fixed at a rate equivalent t the basic rate of income tax on an amount equivalent to the actual distribution plus the ACT, and a shareholder was credited with having paid basic rate tax income tax on the gross dividend. From 1994/95, for reasons explained subsequently, the rate is linked to the 20% lower rate of income tax on an amount equal to the actual distribution plus the ACT on it[2], with the shareholder being credited with having paid an equivalent amount of income tax. However, it needs to be emphasised that there is no necessary connection between the rate of ACT paid by a company on distributed profits and the amount of income tax which a shareholder is credited with having paid. Indeed, in 1993/94 the rate of ACT was 22.5% of the gross distribution, whereas most shareholders were only credited with having paid 20% income tax, and under changes announced in the July 1997 budget the rate of ACT payable by companies is unaltered, even though not all shareholders are entitled to an equivalent tax credit.

So far as the company making a qualifying distribution is concerned, ACT is not a withholding of income tax. It is an advance payment of the company's liability for corporation tax for the year in which the qualifying distribution is made. Accordingly, a company may deduct any ACT actually paid from its corporation tax liability for the year, but this right to deduct is subject to important limitations[3]. The deduction

---

17   ICTA 1988, s 14(1).
18   Ibid, s 209.
19   Ibid, s 249.
20   Ibid, s 14(2).
1   Ibid, s 14(3). Distributions between 1 and 5 April, the overlap between the corporation tax and income tax year, continue to attract the previous year's rate of ACT (ICTA 1988, s 246(6)).
2   Ibid, s 14(3).
3   ICTA 1988, s 239(1).

may not exceed the amount of ACT which would have been payable by a company, had it distributed an amount which, together with the ACT on it, equals the company's profits, including capital gains, for the period[4].

Example
For an accounting period a company has taxable profits of £1,800,000. During the period it paid cash dividends of £1,600,000. Its tax liability for the year is as follows, assuming a corporation tax rate of 31% and an ACT rate of 20/80.

(a) Payment of ACT on payment of dividends

    £1,600,000 x 20/80   £400,000

(b) Corporation tax liability

Taxable profits	£1,800,000
Corporation tax @ 31%	£558,000
Less ACT, restricted to £1,440,000 x 20/80	(360,000)
(£1,440,000 + £360,000 = £1,800,000	
the company's profits for the period)[5]	
Mainstream corporation tax	£198,000

The company has therefore paid £598,000 (£400,000 + £198,000) tax to the Revenue of which £558,000 is its corporation tax liability for the year, and £40,000 is unrelieved ACT.

The system ensures that the Revenue is always paid tax which it has to credit to shareholders. Unrelieved ACT may be carried back for six years and set against mainstream corporation tax of prior accounting periods, taking later periods before earlier periods[6], and carried forward indefinitely against corporation tax due on profits of future accounting periods[7]. However, carry forward of unutilised ACT will be denied if within any period of three years there is both a major change of ownership of the company and a major change in the nature of the company's trade[8]. This is to prevent the purchase of companies with unutilised ACT solely for the purpose of utilising the ACT against the future profits of a quite different trade, and follows rules which disallow the carry forward of trading losses where there is a change of ownership of a company and a change of trade[9]. For changes of ownership occurring on or after 16 March 1993, and within a three-year period of a major change in the company's trade, unutilised ACT arising after the change of ownership may not be carried back to periods prior to the change of ownership[10].

Despite the ability of a company to carry back or carry forward unrelieved ACT, the inability of a number of companies to get full relief for ACT paid when dividends are paid to shareholders has proved to be a significant problem for the UK imputation

---

4   Ibid, s 239(2).
5   Put another way, £1,440,000 is the amount which, with ACT on it of £360,000, equals the company's profits of £1,800,000. The maximum ACT credit against the company's mainstream CT liability is therefore £360,000.
6   Ibid, s 239(3).
7   Ibid, s 239(4).
8   Ibid, s 245. A similar rule applies if a trade becomes negligible and there is a change of ownership before it revives. For what is meant by 'a major change in the nature or conduct of the company's trade' see s 245(4) and IR Statement of Practice SP 10/91.
9   Ibid, s 768.
10 Ibid, s 245(3A) and (3B).

system of corporation tax. In November 1993 the Revenue reported that the total amount of unrelieved ACT was estimated to be about £5.5bn, with a current net rate of increase of £0.7bn a year[11]. Companies caught in an unrelieved ACT trap effectively pay more corporation tax on their profits than Parliament intends. Companies most liable to suffer from the problem are UK-resident companies which trade abroad and derive a substantial amount of their profits or income in foreign countries where they have had to pay tax. The UK normally gives double tax relief by crediting foreign tax paid on foreign profits against the UK corporation tax liability on the same profits. If the foreign tax paid exceeds the UK tax liability, no UK corporation tax is payable. However, for company law purposes the company is perfectly entitled to pay a dividend out of its foreign profits, and ACT normally has to be paid on any such dividend. In computing a company's corporation tax liability for a year, double tax relief is deducted before deducting ACT. Where foreign tax liabilities are substantial there may simply not be enough mainstream UK corporation tax liability left against which to credit ACT on dividends paid during the accounting period. If the company continues to have substantial foreign interests, there may be no practical prospect of relieving ACT, thus unfairly discriminating against companies which operate abroad in comparison with those which operate in the UK.

A number of steps have therefore been taken to alleviate the problem. First, it became attractive for companies quoted on the Stock Exchange who had substantial unrelieved ACT to offer shareholders an 'enhanced stock dividend' as an alternative to a cash dividend. This took the form of bonus shares in the company the market value of which was significantly (as much as 50%) higher than the cash dividend alternative. The attraction to the company was that ACT does not have to be paid on a stock dividend, and there were also cash flow advantages. A shareholder liable to income tax had no additional tax to pay if he was a lower or basic rate taxpayer, but if he was a higher rate taxpayer he was liable to 15% tax (the excess of the 40% higher rate income tax over the 25% basic rate in force prior to 1993/94, when these schemes were most popular) on the market value[12] of the shares received grossed up at the basic rate[13]. Nevertheless, he would still normally be better off than if he had opted for the cash dividend. Shareholders who were exempt from income tax, such as charities and pension funds, could be worse off under the enhanced stock dividend option, as there was no tax credit to reclaim[14], but they remained free to choose to receive a cash dividend.

The remaining solutions, provided by the Chancellor of the Exchequer Norman Lamont, were:

(a) a reduction in the rate of ACT;
(b) an option to declare a 'foreign income dividend' free of ACT;
(c) special relief for international headquarters companies.

For 1993/94 the rate of ACT on dividends was reduced to 22.5% of the gross dividend, and was further reduced to 20% in 1994/95 where it has since remained. However, as will be seen in the next section, this was accompanied by reductions in the tax credits available to shareholders, which have considerably complicated the income tax system, and have made exempt shareholders such as pension funds and charities worse off. For companies which are unable to obtain full relief for ACT when they pay a dividend, the advantage of the change is that there is now less tax on which they cannot get relief.

11 Revenue press release, [1993] STI 1517, para 4.
12 ICTA 1988, s 251(2)(b).
13 Since 1993/94 grossing up is at the lower rate of income tax. Prior to that, grossing up was at the basic rate.
14 ICTA 1988, s 249(4)(b).

Companies with substantial foreign income or profits may elect to treat a cash dividend as a foreign income dividend (FID) paid out of their foreign profits[15]. On paying an FID the company pays ACT in the normal way. But if it later turns out that the ACT exceeds the company's UK tax liability on the foreign profits, the unrelieved ACT will be repaid to the company or set off against its corporation tax liability[16]. An individual shareholder who is liable to lower, basic, or higher rate tax is taxed in the same way as if a normal dividend had been received[17], but a shareholder who is not liable to tax cannot claim any tax refund, and is therefore worse off than if a normal dividend was paid[18]. For corporate shareholders, a foreign income dividend is not franked investment income[19], and cannot give rise to a tax credit[20], but may be used to frank foreign income dividend payments by the company which has received the dividend[1]. Anti-avoidance provisions exist to stop companies targeting foreign income dividends at shareholders who are liable to income tax[2]. It was announced in the July 1997 budget that these rules for the payment of foreign income dividends will cease to apply from 6 April 1999, and the effect of the changes which will take place from 6 April 1999 are discussed subsequently.

An international headquarters company is elaborately defined in ICTA 1988, s 246S, but is basically a foreign-owned company with a maximum of 20% of its ordinary share capital owned by UK-resident non-corporate shareholders, and with no shareholder owning less than 5% of its share capital. An IHC can pay a foreign income dividend without paying any ACT[3]. However, if it later turns out that the company has some mainstream corporation tax liability on its foreign source income because, for example, foreign taxes imposed on the foreign income are lower than UK corporation tax on the same income, the company is liable to pay ACT of the lower of the full ACT on the foreign income dividend or its residual corporation tax liability on the foreign income out of which the dividend is paid[4]. The due date for payment of this ACT liability is significantly earlier than the normal due date for payment of a normal residual mainstream corporation tax liability[5]. Relief for international headquarters companies was left unaltered in the July 1997 budget.

THE TAX TREATMENT OF THE RECIPIENT SHAREHOLDER

The tax treatment of qualifying distributions in the hands of UK-resident[6] shareholders depends on whether the recipient is an individual (or other person liable to income tax such as a trustee) or a company. The tax treatment of individuals was greatly complicated by changes made in 1993/94, and explained in the previous section, to deal with the problem for companies of unrelieved advance corporation tax. The Inland Revenue have never been prepared to refund to shareholders through a tax repayment claim more tax than they have actually received from the company paying a dividend.

---

15   Ibid, ss 246A–246R.
16   Ibid, s 246N(2). Speaking in February 1996, Michael Jack, the Financial Secretary, stated that, to that date, about 800 companies had paid FIDs, Hansard, Standing Committee E, 15th sitting, col 484.
17   Ibid, s 246D.
18   Ibid, s 246D(2)(b).
19   Ibid, s 246E.
20   Ibid, s 246C.
1   Ibid, s 246F.
2   See eg ibid, s 246A(3)–(10).
3   Ibid, s 246T(2).
4   Ibid, s 246U.
5   Ibid, s 246U(2).
6   Special rules may apply if the recipient shareholder is not resident in the UK.

Consequently the reduction in the rate of company ACT from the equivalent of 25% to 20% of the gross dividend meant corresponding adjustments to the income tax treatment of dividends.

An individual, or other person liable to income tax, is treated as having received income taxable under Sch F of the amount of the actual distribution plus the tax credit attached to it[7], but is credited with having paid income tax of the amount of the tax credit[8]. The tax credit is currently 20/80[9] x the dividend, or an amount which is equivalent to the 20% lower rate of income tax on the dividend plus the tax credit. Thus an individual in receipt of a dividend of £80 will also have a tax credit of £20 (20/80 x £80), and will be taxed on £100 gross income on which he is treated as having already paid £20 tax.

From 6 April 1999, the tax credit for individual shareholders will be reduced to 10%. This reduced credit will not be repayable to a non-taxpayer, but the income tax treatment for lower, basic and higher rate taxpayers will be adjusted so that no more tax is payable than under the current system. These changes are discussed more fully in the next section.

Prior to 2 July 1997, a taxable person which was exempt from income tax, such as a pension fund or a charitable trust, could reclaim the 20% tax credit, although the reduction in the rate of credit from the basic rate to the lower rate reduced the amount that could be reclaimed. In a significant change of policy, it was announced in the July 1997 budget that, for dividends paid on or after 2 July 1997, pension funds and most UK corporate shareholders will no longer be able to claim repayment from the Revenue of dividend tax credits. Charities can continue to claim repayment until 6 April 1999. From that date no repayments will be made, but for a five-year transitional period charities will receive a cash payment from the Treasury to compensate for their loss of the repayment of tax credits[9a]. The compensation will be computed as a reducing percentage of their actual dividend income, ranging from 21% in 1999/2000 to 4% in 2003/2004 [10].

An individual liable to lower rate income tax has no additional tax to pay on dividend income. Theoretically, a basic rate taxpayer should be liable to an additional 3% tax, but to avoid the Revenue having to make a large number of small assessments, dividend income is only liable to the 20% lower rate of income tax provided it is not liable to higher rate income tax[11]. This also provided a step towards the Conservative Government's long-term objective of reducing the basic rate of income tax on all income to 20%. For the purpose of determining the extent to which a dividend is liable to higher rate income tax, it is to be treated as the highest part (top slice) of a taxpayer's income[12]. A higher rate taxpayer is liable to 40% income tax on the dividend plus the tax credit, but is credited with having paid 20% tax, thus effectively leaving a further 20% to pay[13].

The new system can result in a taxpayer's marginal rate of income tax (the rate paid on the top slice of income) falling as income increases, and is one of the disadvantages of the new system. The following example, which illustrates the point, is adapted from a Revenue example provided when the provisions were originally introduced[14]:

7   ICTA 1988, s 20(1).
8   Ibid, s 231(1).
9   Ibid, s 231(1).
9a   F (No 2) A 1997, s 19.
10   IR press release, 2 July 1997, [1997] STI 900.
11   ICTA 1988, ss 51A and 1A(2).
12   Ibid, s 1A(5).
13   This is equivalent to an additional liability of 25% of the actual dividend.
14   See a Revenue example at [1993] STI 452.

'An individual has taxable income of £29,000 of which £5,000 is dividend income (including the tax credit). For 1998/99 he will be liable to tax
- at 20% on the first £4,300
- at 23% on the next £19,700 of non-dividend income.

The dividend income will then be taxed
- at 20% to the extent that it falls below the basic rate limit of £27,100, so £3,100 is taxed at 20%.
- at 40% on the remaining £1,900.'

Qualifying distributions received by companies are not liable to corporation tax in the hands of the recipient company[15]. The qualifying distributions plus the tax credit are together known as franked investment income[16]. From 2 July 1997 this tax credit is not normally repayable to the recipient company[17]. Franked investment income is primarily used to cover qualifying distributions made by the recipient company, so that when a recipient company makes a qualifying distribution of its own it is only required to pay ACT to the extent that its franked payments (qualifying distributions plus related ACT) exceed its franked investment income[18]. The practical effect is to flow through the distribution from the first company to the shareholders of the recipient company in priority to the distribution of other profits of the recipient company.

Changes taking effect in 1999

From 6 April 1999 major changes take effect on the taxation of company dividends and other distributions. Legislation dealing with the changes is contained partly in the F(No 2)A 1997, which followed the July 1997 Budget, partly in the 1998 Finance Bill (subsequently Finance Act), and partly in Regulations. The changes have largely been motivated by a continuing attempt to deal with the problem of companies whose mainstream corporation tax liability is insufficient to enable them to absorb ACT on dividends. They were also motivated by a desire to stop major tax exempt shareholders such as pension funds from claiming tax refunds of the tax credit attaching to dividends, a consequence of which was that a slice of company profits effectively escaped paying any tax. This perceived defect was removed in respect of dividends paid on or after 2 July 1997 by prohibiting pension funds from claiming a refund of the tax credit[19].

For dividends paid on or after 6 April 1999 companies will no longer have to deduct and account for ACT[20]. Hence no additional unused ACT can arise after that date. As a consequence of this change, the principal reason for enabling companies to pay foreign income dividends disappears, and they are therefore abolished[1]. To deal with unrelieved ACT accumulated by companies prior to 6 April 1999, estimated as in the region of £7bn[2], it is intended to have a system of 'shadow ACT'. The purpose of this system is to give companies relief in the future for unrelieved ACT resulting from fluctuations in the trading cycle, but to deny relief for structural unrelieved ACT, as where most of a company's profits are earned abroad, so that its credit for foreign taxes

---

15   Ibid, s 208.
16   Ibid, s 238(1).
17   July 1997 Budget, [1997] STI 903. F (No 2) A 1997, ss 19-20.
18   Ibid, s 241.
19   F(No 2)A 1997, s 19.
20   F(No 2)B 1998, cl 31(1).
1   F(No 2)A 1997 s 36(1).
2   Revenue consultative document A modern system for corporation tax payments, November 1997, para 3.4.

means that it only ever has a small UK mainstream corporation tax liability[3]. From 6 April 1999, while no company will be required to pay ACT, a computation will be made of how much ACT would have been payable had the system remained unchanged. A company will be assumed to have deducted this ACT from its corporation tax liability for the year, but without any actual deduction being made. To the extent that the notional deduction is less than 20% of its mainstream liability, real unrelieved ACT being carried forward may be deducted from the company's corporation tax liability, thus reducing the amount payable. If the shadow ACT equals or exceeds 20% of the company's mainstream corporation tax liability, no deduction will be permitted for unrelieved ACT, and it will continue to be carried forward[4]. It may be that, at some stage in the future, the Government will decide that ACT which has not been relieved by that time is inherently structural, and the possibility of claiming relief for it will finally be withdrawn.

The abolition of the requirement on companies to pay ACT also has implications for shareholders, as the original purpose of ACT was to ensure that the Government did not have to make tax repayments to shareholders in respect of dividends unless it was certain that it had first received the tax from the company. From 6 April 1999 individual shareholders in receipt of dividends are assumed to have received dividends plus a notional tax credit equal to one ninth of the actual dividend, or 10% of the dividend plus the tax credit[5]. The shareholder is taxable under Sch F on the dividend plus the tax credit, in the same was as under the current system. This also preserves the concept of a partial imputation system of corporation tax under which, when a company distributes profits, part of the corporation tax paid by the company is flowed through to, and treated as paid by, a shareholder.

However, unlike the current system, the 10% tax credit will not be repayable to a non-taxpayer[6], and dividends will resemble the composite rate income tax which used to apply to building society interest, but was abolished in 1990/91, mainly to take account of the introduction of the independent taxation of a husband and wife. The 10% tax credit will discharge the income tax liability of lower and basic rate taxpayers, who will have no additional tax to pay[7], but, as under the current system, higher rate income tax payers will have additional tax to pay. To preserve the existing system, under which higher rate income tax payers effectively pay additional tax of 25% of the cash dividend, a new top rate of tax on dividends is being introduced of 32.5% of the dividend plus the tax credit[8]. From this liability a taxpayer can deduct the 10% tax credit, leaving additional tax to pay of 22.5% of the dividend plus the tax credit, which is equivalent to 25% of the actual dividend.

Dividend income received by a corporate shareholder will continue to be exempt from corporation tax, although the need to use dividend income to frank dividend payments will no longer be relevant[9]. The tax credit attaching to dividends is now not normally repayable to corporate shareholders and pension funds. However, to provide some relief for charities, which would otherwise be adversely affected by the changes as they have been entitled to reclaim the tax credit on dividends, transitional relief will be given until 2003/04, ranging from a refund of 21% of the cash dividend in 1999/00 to 4% of the cash dividend in 2003/04[10].

3   Notes on clauses, F(No 2)B 1998, cl 32.
4   Revenue press release *A modern system for corporation tax payments*, 17 March 1998, para 12 ([1998] STI 403). The detailed rules will be contained in regulations authorised by F(No 2)B 1998, cl 32.
5   F(No 2)A 1997, s 30(3).
6   F(No 2)A 1997, s 30(5).
7   F(No 2)A 1997, s 31(3) and (5).
8   F(No 2)A 1997, s 31(3) and (5).
9   It is abolished by F(No 2)B 1998, cl 31(2) and (3).
10   F(No 2)A 1997, s 35.

With the introduction of self-assessment for companies for accounting periods ending on or after 1 July 1999, the way in which companies pay corporation tax is also to change. Small and medium sized companies, broadly companies with profits less than £1.5m, will pay tax in one instalment due nine months after the end of their accounting period. However large companies will pay tax in four equal instalments. For companies with a 12 month accounting period, the first payment will be due in the seventh month of the year, and the last will be due in the fourth month after the end of the year[11]. The profits on which the tax payments must be based are the current year's profits, which will not be known precisely when the first payment is due. Large companies are likely to have accounting systems which enable a reasonably accurate projection of profits, and the only consequence for honest, but mistaken, estimates will be an interest charge or refund, with only a small difference between the rate of interest charged for underpayments of instalments and the rate of interest paid by the Revenue on overpayments. In a reversal of normal policy, interest paid by a company on tax underpayments will be tax deductible, and interest received from the Revenue will be taxable[12]. To stop excessive tax payments in early years, the new payment arrangements for large companies are to be phased in over a four year period[13].

Groups of companies

It is common for an organisation with a number of different businesses to use separate companies for each business. For company law purposes, each company is a legal entity distinct from other companies in the group, but this legal demarcation could have considerable disadvantages from a tax viewpoint with, for example, losses in one company not being available for deduction from profits of another company in the group. The corporation tax legislation therefore contains provisions which enable a group of companies to be taxed as if they were one entity, but care must be taken in applying the provisions as not all inter-group transactions are covered, and the definition of a group may vary from one provision to another. It is a basic principle of all the reliefs that they only apply to a group of UK-resident companies, so that they will not apply, for example, to a wholly-owned UK subsidiary of a foreign parent company. The application of this principle to consortium relief has recently been confirmed by the House of Lords in *ICI plc v Colmer (Inspector of Taxes)*[14], but it referred to the European Court the issue of whether this is discriminatory under EC law where some relevant subsidiaries are resident in the UK and other subsidiaries are resident in other EC countries. The principal reliefs are outlined in the following paragraphs.

Under the ICTA 1988, s 240 a UK-resident parent company may surrender to UK-resident subsidiaries in which it has more than 50% of the share capital[15] all or any part of ACT which it has paid on dividends, but not on other qualifying distributions[1]. ACT may be surrendered even if the parent company has a corporation tax liability and, where there are a number of subsidiaries, in such proportions as may be desired[2].

---

11   Revenue press release *A modern system for corporation tax payments*, 17 March 1998, para 2 ([1998] STI 402). The detailed rules will be contained in regulations authorised by F(No 2)B 1998, cl 30.
12   F(No 2)B 1998, cl 33 & cl 34.
13   Revenue press release *A modern system for corporation tax payments*, 17 March 1998, para 3 ([1998] STI 402).
14   [1996] STC 352.
15   ICTA 1988, s 240(10) – indirect shareholdings through non-resident companies are excluded, as are shareholdings which are trading stock of any company. Anti-avoidance provisions exist to prevent the relief from being abused (ibid, s 240(11)).
1   Ibid, s 240(1).
2   Ibid, s 240(1)(b).

Surrendered ACT may be used to reduce the subsidiary's mainstream corporation tax liability[3]. It may not be carried back, although it is relieved in priority to any ACT actually paid by the subsidiary[4]. It may be carried forward indefinitely against the subsidiary company's future mainstream corporation tax liability provided that, throughout the relevant accounting period, it remained a subsidiary of the surrendering parent company[5]. If it ceases to be a subsidiary, the benefit of any surrendered but unutilised ACT is lost unless both surrendering and receiving companies remain subsidiaries of a third company[6]. As from 13 March 1989 the ability of the subsidiary company to carry forward surrendered ACT is lost if there is both a change of ownership of the subsidiary company and a major change in the business of the surrendering company within three years before, or three years after, the change of ownership[7]. A recipient company may make a payment to the surrendering company up to the value of the ACT surrendered without the payment being taken into account for corporation tax purposes[8]. Apart from ensuring relief for ACT, the surrender rules may provide a useful mechanism for the transfer of funds within the group.

In the absence of special provisions, whenever a subsidiary company paid a dividend, or made an annual payment, to a parent company it would have to account for ACT or withhold income tax[9], leaving the parent to utilise the ACT or recover the income tax from the Inland Revenue. Relieving provisions are therefore contained in ICTA 1988, s 247 to deal with the transfer of 'group income'. These provisions apply to transfers between 51% subsidiaries and a parent company[10], but ownership of more than 50% of the share capital is only sufficient if the parent is also beneficially entitled to more than 50% of the profits available for distribution and more than 50% of the assets of the subsidiary were it to be wound up[11]. The provisions also apply to consortia[12]. A consortium exists for the purposes of s 247 if 75% or more of the ordinary share capital of a trading or holding company is owned by UK-resident companies with no company needed to make up the 75% owning less than 5% of the shares or entitled to less than 5% of the distributable profits or the assets available for distribution on a winding up[13]. A trading or holding company does not qualify for consortium relief if it is a 75% subsidiary of another company, or arrangements exist under which it could become one[14]. A holding company is a trading company, or a company the business of which consists wholly or mainly in the holding of shares or securities of trading companies which are its 90% subsidiaries[15].

If s 247 applies, payer and recipient may jointly elect that dividends, but not other qualifying distributions, should be paid without accounting for ACT but, even if an election for group income is in force, the payer company remains entitled to give notice

3   Ibid, s 240(2).
4   Ibid, s 240(4).
5   Ibid, s 240(5).
6   Ibid, s 240(5).
7   Ibid, s 245A. The Revenue's interpretation of a major change in the business is discussed in Statement of Practice SP 10/91.
8   Ibid, s 240(8).
9   Although annual payments are normally tax deductible to a company, it must usually withhold and pay over to the Revenue under ICTA 1988, s 349 basic rate income tax on the gross payment, which is then treated as having been paid by the recipient.
10   ICTA 1988, s 247(1)(a).
11   ICTA 1988, s 247(8A) and Sch 18, applied by s 247(9A).
12   Ibid, s 247(1)(b).
13   Ibid, s 247(1)(b), s 247(9)(c) and Sch 18, applied by s 247(9A).
14   ICTA 1988, s 247(1)(b) and s 247(1A).
15   Ibid, s 247(9)(a).

that it will account for ACT on all or part of the dividend[16]. When ACT is abolished on 6 April 1999, the group income provisions become superfluous, and the ability to pay a dividend without accounting for ACT is therefore repealed.[16a] Similar provisions apply to authorise the payment gross of annual payments, such as interest, by a subsidiary[17] but these provisions are extended to include annual payments from a parent company to its 51% subsidiary[18], although not from a member of a consortium to a consortium subsidiary in which it has less than a 51% interest. If the payer company wishes to revert to accounting for income tax, the election for group annual payments must be revoked[19].

Perhaps the most economically significant group relief provisions are those in ss 402 and 403 of the ICTA 1988, which enable losses of one member of a group or consortium to be set against the profits of another, and allow loss relief for consortia, but the definition of a group or consortium is more restricted than under the ACT surrender or group income provisions. A group comprises a UK-resident parent company plus UK-resident[20] subsidiaries in which it has 75% interest[1]. 'Interest' for this purpose means ownership of 75% of the ordinary share capital plus entitlement to 75% of the profits available for distribution to equity holders plus entitlement to 75% of the assets of the subsidiary on its winding up[2]. A consortium exists if 75% of the share capital of a relevant company is owned by UK-resident companies, with none of the members of the consortium owning less than 5%[3].

A relevant company is a trading company which is owned by the consortium but is not a 75% subsidiary of any single company[4]. Alternatively, it may be a trading company which is a 90% subsidiary of a holding company which is owned by the consortium and which is not a 75% subsidiary of any other company[5], or is a holding company owned by the consortium and not a 75% subsidiary of another company[6]. A holding company is defined as a company whose business consists wholly or mainly of holding shares in companies which are trading companies and which are its 90% subsidiaries[7]. Relief is only given if companies are members of a qualifying group or consortium throughout the whole or relevant accounting periods of both surrendering and claimant companies[8].

In *ICI plc v Colmer (Inspector of Taxes)*[9] the House of Lords held, reversing the decision of the High Court and the Court of Appeal, that the relevant subsidiary companies must be resident in the UK. Thus a consortium which held shares in a holding company with 23 subsidiary companies, only four of which were resident in the UK, was not entitled to consortium relief for losses of one of the four UK subsidiary companies. The main business of the holding company was not the holding of shares in UK resident trading companies which were its 90% subsidiaries. However, as this interpretation would preclude consortium relief where the non-UK resident subsidiaries

---

16   Ibid, s 247(1), (2), (3).
16a F (No 2) B 1998, Sch 3, para 18(2).
17   Ibid, s 247(4)(a).
18   Ibid, s 247(4)(b).
19   There is no equivalent of ICTA 1988, s 247(3), which applies only to dividends.
20   ICTA 1988, s 413(5).
1   Ibid, s 413(3)(a).
2   Ibid, s 413(7).
3   Ibid, s 413(6)(a).
4   Ibid, s 402(3)(a).
5   Ibid, s 402(3)(b).
6   Ibid, s 402(3)(c).
7   Ibid, s 413(3)(b).
8   ICTA 1988, s 409(1).
9   [1996] STC 352.

were all resident in other EC countries, the House of Lords referred their interpretation to the European Court for a decision on whether it was inconsistent with European law.

If the conditions for claiming consortium relief are satisfied, trading losses[10], unutilised capital allowances given otherwise than as a deduction in computing trading profit or loss[11], and unrelieved charges on income[12] may be transferred up or down, and set against the profits of the claiming member of the group or consortium for its corresponding accounting period[13]. The claimant company is required to utilise other available relief before group relief[14] and, in the case of a consortium claim, only a fraction of losses appropriate to the consortium member's interest in the subsidiary may be transferred up or down[15]. Where a loss-making company is both a member of a consortium and a member of a group it may surrender any loss for which group relief is unavailable to members of the consortium[16]. Further, if a consortium member is in receipt of a loss under consortium relief which it cannot use, and is itself the member of a group, it may surrender the loss to other members of its group[17]. A consortium company's interest in a subsidiary is the lower of its percentage entitlement to share capital, or profits, or assets on a winding up[18]. Anti-avoidance provisions exist to prevent the group relief provisions being abused[19]. A payment may be made by the claimant company and, to the extent that it does not exceed the loss surrendered, it may be ignored for corporation tax purposes[20].

Relief from tax on capital gains exists where assets are transferred between companies which are members of a 75% group[1]. A 75% group exists if a parent company, the principal company, owns more than 75% of the ordinary share capital of a subsidiary[2]. If the subsidiary in turn has a 75% subsidiary, all the companies are members of a group, with the top company as the principal company[3]. Additionally, each subsidiary must be a 51% effective subsidiary[4]. By this is meant that the parent must be beneficially entitled to more than 50% of the distributable profits of the subsidiary and more than 50% of its assets on a winding up[5]. A company can only be a member of one group, and TCGA 1992, s 170(6) provides tests to determine to which group a company should be allocated if it would otherwise be a member of more than one group.

Assets transferred within the group are deemed to be transferred on a basis which ensures no gain or loss to the transferor company[6], but the transferee company takes over the asset at the transferor's cost base and date of acquisition[7]. If the recipient

10   Ibid, s 403(1), (2).
11   Ibid, s 403(3).
12   Ibid, s 403(7).
13   Ibid, s 403(1). 'Corresponding accounting period' is defined in s 408.
14   Ibid, s 407(1)(b).
15   Ibid, s 403(9).
16   Ibid, s 405(1)–(3).
17   Ibid, s 406.
18   Ibid, s 413(8).
19   Ibid, s 410, and s 403A, inserted by F (No 2) A 1997, Sch 7.
20   Ibid, s 402(6).
1   TCGA 1992, ss 170–181.
2   Ibid, s 170(3)(a).
3   Ibid, s 170(3)(a).
4   Ibid, s 170(3)(b).
5   Ibid, s 170(7) with ICTA 1988, Sch 18, applied by TCGA 1992, s 170(8).
6   Ibid, s 171(1). Where the asset is not trading stock of one company but was or becomes trading stock of the other, the transfer will give rise to a notional disposal and reacquisition for the purposes of CGT and the computation of trading profit (s 173).
7   Ibid, s 171(1); s 174(4).

company leaves the group within six years, otherwise than on a liquidation, still retaining the asset, or a replacement asset into which the gain has been rolled over, there is a notional disposal of the asset for the purposes of the tax on capital gains[8]. Under the capital gains tax code, where business assets are replaced, any gain on the asset disposed of can generally be 'rolled over' into the new asset, so that a chargeable gain is deferred until the new asset is ultimately disposed[9]. For this purpose all the trades carried on by members of a 75% group of companies are treated as if they were carried on by one company, unless the acquisition or disposal is from or to another company in the same group[10].

Anti-avoidance provisions exist to prevent a company milking its subsidiaries of assets, disposing of the shares in the subsidiary, and claiming a capital loss on the disposal[11], and these anti-avoidance provisions apply even if one of the relevant companies is non-resident[12]. Anti-avoidance provisions also exist in ICTA 1988, s 770 to prevent artificial prices being placed on transfers of trading stock between associated companies (roughly members of a 51% group but including foreign companies) unless both are resident in the UK[13]. Such a provision against artificial inter-company pricing is needed to ensure that profits earned in the UK are not transferred to a foreign country by the simple expedient of placing artificially low or high prices on goods transferred to or from foreign companies in the group. For periods of account ending on or after 1 July 1999, associated companies will be required to use arm's length pricing for the transfer of goods, services and other assets between them without, as at present, any prior direction from the Revenue for them to do so.[13a]

Close companies and close investment-holding companies

Since 1922 there have been special rules to ensure that conducting business through, or holding investments in, a small family company (called a close company in the tax legislation) does not confer significant tax advantages in comparison with the conduct of the same activities without incorporation[14]. Historically the reason for such rules has mainly been the difference between income tax rates and corporation tax rates. For example, in 1976/77 the top marginal rate of income tax on unearned income was 98% and on earned income 83%, whereas the main rate of corporation tax was 52% and the small companies rate was 42%. Prior to 1989/90, if a company was a close company and did not distribute a required proportion of its profits to shareholders, the Revenue were entitled to apportion the undistributed profits among shareholders and tax them as if the company had distributed a dividend of the amount apportioned. With the reduction in income tax rates from 1979, the apportionment provisions were repealed for trading companies by FA 1980 but remained for non-trading companies, with different distribution requirements for income from trading and land and for other income. With the subsequent reduction in income tax rates to almost the same level as corporation tax rates, and the taxation of capital gains realised by an individual at his marginal rate of income tax, in his March 1989 budget the Chancellor announced that the apportionment provisions had outlived their usefulness and would be repealed.

---

8   Ibid, s 178(1)–(3) and s 179(1)–(3).
9   Ibid, ss 156–158.
10   Ibid, s 175(1).
11   Ibid, ss 176 and 177.
12   Ibid, ss 176(7) and 177(4).
13   ICTA 1988, s 770.
13a New ICTA 1988, ss 770, 770A and Sch 28AA.
14   FA 1922, s 21.

However, special provisions would still be needed for the small minority of close companies, estimated at less than 5% of the total[15], which were largely concerned with passive investments. This type of company is termed a close investment-holding company. The repeal of the apportionment provisions did not affect other anti-avoidance legislation which applies to close companies, so that now there are provisions which apply to all close companies and provisions which only apply to close companies which are also investment-holding companies.

Under the current law a company is a close company if it satisfies one of the following conditions and is not otherwise exempt:

(a) it is controlled by five or fewer participators[16]. Control is widely defined in ICTA 1988, s 416 as general control over the company's affairs, including entitlement to a majority of the share capital, or share capital which confers entitlement to a majority of the distributable income of the company, or of its assets on a winding up. 'Participator; is defined in ICTA 1988, s 417(1) to include a shareholder and a loan creditor[17] and, in counting the shares or interests of a participator, there has to be included any shares or interests in the company owned by the participator's 'associates'. A participator's associates include his spouse, parents, grandparents, children, brothers and sisters, partners, and trustees of related trusts[18]. No double counting is permitted, so that a wife's shares must either be counted as her own or her husband's, but if any combination results in five or fewer people having control, the company is close;

(b) it is controlled by its directors[19], however many[20];

(c) five or fewer participators, or the directors, have rights, whether or not arising through their ownership of share capital, which would entitle them on a winding up of the company to the majority of its assets[1].

Even if any of these tests is satisfied, a company is not a close company in any of the following circumstances[2]:

(a) it is controlled by an 'open' company[3];

(b) it is non-resident[4];

(c) it is a quoted company which satisfied the conditions that[5]:
   (i) its shares have been quoted on a UK stock exchange in the past 12 months[6]; and
   (ii) the shares quoted have been dealt with in the last 12 months[7]; and
   (iii) 35% of the voting stock excluding preference shares are held by the public[8], and have been quoted and dealt with as in (i) and (ii)[9]; and

15   See IR press release [1990] STI 202.
16   ICTA 1988, s 414(1).
17   Which is itself defined in s 417(7).
18   Ibid, s 417(3) and (4).
19   Defined in s 417(5).
20   Ibid, s 414(1).
1   Ibid, s 414(2).
2   This list of circumstances is not exhaustive, but includes the principal exemptions.
3   Ibid, s 414(5).
4   Ibid, s 414(1)(a).
5   Ibid, s 415.
6   Ibid, s 415(1)(b).
7   Ibid, s 415(1)(b).
8   Ibid, s 415(1)(a).
9   Ibid, s 415(1)(b).

(iv) 85% of the stock is not held by five or fewer principal members[10].

A close company is also a close investment-holding company unless throughout the whole of the relevant accounting period it exists wholly or mainly for one or more of the following purposes[11]:

(a) the carrying on of a trade on a commercial basis[12];

(b) making investments in land which is not let to anyone connected with the company or a relative[13];

(c) as a holding company for one or more companies which satisfy either of the first two conditions, or to co-ordinate the administration of two or more such companies[14];

(d) to facilitate a trade carried on on a commercial basis by a company which is not a close investment-holding company, or is its parent company[15];

(e) to facilitate the investment in land within (b) by a company which is not a close investment-holding company, or is its parent company[16].

If a company is a close company, whether or not it is also a close investment-holding company, the following special rules apply. First, if it provides for a participator or his associate[17] any living accommodation, entertainment, domestic or other services, or any other benefits of whatever nature, the expense incurred by the company, less any amount reimbursed, is treated as a distribution[18]. The expense is therefore not tax deductible to the company; ACT has to be paid on it[19], and the value of the benefit plus the tax credit[20] is taxed as income of the participator. The rules do not apply if the participator is also a director or higher paid employee of the company[1] as the payment will then be treated as additional pay taxable under Sch E[2]. For living accommodation the exemption extends to all employees[3], as the benefit will be taxed under ICTA 1988, s 145.

Secondly, if a close company·makes a loan to a participator, otherwise than in the course of a normal lending business, it must pay to the Revenue an amount equivalent to ACT on the loan[4]. The provision normally does not apply to loans to a participator who is also a director or employee provided the loan does not exceed £15,000 *and* the borrower does not have a material interest (roughly 5%) in the share capital of the company[5]. For loans made in an accounting period ending after 30 September 1993 and prior to 31 March 1996, the tax was payable not later than 14 days after the end of the accounting period in which the loan was made[6]. If the loan was repaid, the tax was

---

10   Ibid, s 415(2) and (6).
11   Ibid, s 13A.
12   Ibid, s 13A(2)(a).
13   Ibid, s 13A(2)(b).
14   Ibid, s 13A(2)(c) and (d).
15   Ibid, s 13A(2)(e).
16   Ibid, s 13A(2)(f).
17   Ibid, s 418(8).
18   Ibid, s 418(2).
19   Because the distribution is not excluded from being a qualifying distribution (ICTA 1988, s 14(2)).
20   Ibid, ss 20(1) and 231(1).
1   Ibid, s 418(3)(a).
2   Ibid, s 153 or s 154.
3   Ibid, s 418(3)(b).
4   Ibid, s 419(1). An equivalent provision will apply after 5 April 1999, F (No 2) B 1998, Sch 3, para 23.
5   Ibid, s 420(2)(a).
6   Ibid, s 419(1) and (3), before amendment by FA 1996, s 159(2). For accounting periods ended on or before 30 September 1993, the due date was 30 days after the notice of assessment, but for the purpose of the running of interest, it could effectively be earlier if the taxpayer's neglect had caused the late raising of an assessment.

refunded, but if the tax was not paid by the due date it remained payable even if the loan had been repaid before the Revenue assessed the tax[7]. The practical implication of this was that, although payment of tax would not be required if the loan had been repaid, interest was payable on the tax which should have been paid from the due date of payment until the date of repayment of the loan[8]. This created a trap for companies which unwittingly made loans to participators, for example through an overdrawn director's account where the director was also a substantial shareholder. Accordingly, for loans first made in an accounting period ending on or after 31 March 1996[9], tax due on loans or advances to participators is not due until nine months after the end of the accounting period in which the loan is made[10]. However, if the loan has not been repaid before that date, the tax is payable, and cannot be refunded until nine months after the end of the accounting period in which the loan is repaid[11].

If the loan is written off, the participator is treated as having received unearned income of the amount written off plus the related ACT, but on which non-refundable income tax at the lower rate of 20% has been paid. The gross amount is not liable to lower or basic rate income tax, but may become liable to higher rate tax income tax[12]. The notional ACT paid by the company is never credited against its mainstream corporation tax liability.

Thirdly, if a close company transfers assets to any person for less than their market value under a bargain which is not at arm's length, the difference between the market value and the actual transfer value is apportioned among the shareholders and reduces the cost of their shares for CGT purposes[13]. Finally, companies are not normally liable to inheritance tax, but if a close company makes a gift of assets, inheritance tax may be charged on the company or, if it fails to pay, on the participators or recipients proportionate to their respective interests in the company. There is no tax charge in respect of anyone to whom the total amount apportioned does not exceed 5% of the total value transferred[14]. An inheritance tax charge may also arise if there is an alteration to a close company's share capital resulting in a transfer of value from some shareholders to others[15].

If a close company is also a close investment-holding company, it is not entitled to claim the small companies' rate of corporation tax[16], and will consequently be taxed at 31% on its taxable profits, including chargeable gains. Provisions also counteract the effect of a close investment-holding company paying dividends to particular shareholders primarily to enable them to reclaim from the Revenue the tax credit attaching to the dividends[17]. For example, in the absence of anti-avoidance provisions, child shareholders could be allocated shares with limited voting rights but high entitlement to dividend, so that company profits distributed to them which did not exceed their personal allowance would be free of income tax. If arrangements exist to achieve this objective, any repayment of the tax credit to a shareholder may be restricted to the extent that is just and reasonable[18]. The anti-avoidance provisions do not apply

7   Ibid, s 419(3), before amendment by FA 1996, s 159(2).
8   *Joint (Inspector of Taxes) v Bracken Developments Ltd* [1994] STC 300; *Earlspring Properties Ltd v Guest (Inspector of Taxes)* [1993] STC 473.
9   FA 1996, s 159(6).
10 ICTA 1988, s 419(3), as amended by FA 1996, s 159(2).
11 Ibid, s 419(4A).
12 Ibid, s 421(1).
13 TCGA 1992, s 125.
14 ITA 1984, s 94.
15 Ibid, s 98.
16 ICTA 1988, s 13(1)(b).
17 Ibid, s 231(3)–(3D).
18 Ibid, s 231(3A).

if, throughout the relevant accounting period, the company had only one class of shares and no shareholder waived his entitlement to dividends[19].

Business reorganisations

One of the objectives discernible in tax legislation is that some attempt should be made to ensure that a business reorganisation which is merely a change of form without a significant change of substance should not attract adverse tax consequences. The achievement of this objective is inevitably patchy, and in practice it is important that, once a business decision of substance has been reached, a tax specialist should be consulted to ensure that the implementation of that decision attracts the most favourable tax treatment. The following paragraphs give some indication of the reliefs which may be available, but each relief contains qualifying conditions and it is vital to study the actual legislation before reliance can be placed on its availability in a given situation.

Under ICTA 1988, s 343 where one company ceases to carry on a trade or part of a trade which is then taken over by another company, the trade may be treated as a continuous trade for corporation tax purposes, if, at the time of the transfer or within two years thereafter, at least three-quarters of both the old and new trades are in common ownership. For this purpose, shareholders in a company are treated as owners of a trade carried on by the company in proportion to their shareholdings[20]. No relief is available under this section for the transfer of a trade by an individual to a company, and relief may be restricted if the transferor company is insolvent at the time of the transfer[1].

If, as part of a company reorganisation or amalgamation, the business of a UK-resident company is transferred to another UK-resident company[2], any chargeable gain on the assets transferred may be deferred until the assets are disposed of by the acquiring company, providing the transferring company receives no consideration for the transfer other than the assumption of its liabilities by the acquiring company[3]. This relief is available where a company is put into liquidation and the liquidator agrees to transfer the old business or part of it to a new company and issues shares in the new company directly to the shareholders of the old company.

If a company disposes of a chargeable capital asset used in its trade and, within one year before or three years after the disposal, acquires another chargeable asset for use in its trade, it will often be able to defer any CGT liability arising on the disposal of the original asset[4]. For the purposes of this relief, all trades carried on by a company and its 75% UK-resident subsidiaries are treated as a single trade[5]. Both the disposed and acquired assets must be within a list of 'approved' assets[6] which comprises land and buildings, fixed plant and machinery, ships, aircraft and hovercraft, satellites, space stations and spacecraft, and milk and potato quotas[7].

Relief for demergers is available under ICTA 1988, ss 213–218. If a UK-resident trading company or member of a trading group[8] distributes to its shareholders the shares

---

19   Ibid, s 231(3B).
20   ICTA 1988, s 344(2).
1   Ibid, s 343(4).
2   A company which is non-resident by virtue of a tax treaty and exempt from CGT does not qualify, TCGA 1992, s 139(1)(b).
3   TCGA 1992, s 139.
4   Ibid, s 152.
5   Ibid, s 175(1).
6   Ibid, s 152(1).
7   Ibid, s 155.
8   ICTA 1988, s 213(4) and (5).

in one or more of its 75% subsidiaries[9], which must also be a trading company or holding company of a trading company[10], the distribution is not treated as a distribution of profit for corporation tax purposes[11], and neither is it treated as a disposal for CGT[12]. Instead it is treated as a reorganisation of share capital[13] so that the cost of a shareholder's shares in the distributing company is apportioned between those shares and the shares received on the demerger, and a CGT charge will only arise on the subsequent disposal of any of the shares[14]. Similar relief may be available where a distributing company transfers a trade or trades, or shares in a 75% trading subsidiary company, to another company, and shares in that other company are in return issued to the members of the distributing company[15].

The reorganisation of a company's share capital, such as the creation of separate classes of ordinary shares, the issue of bonus shares, or the issue of shares under a rights issue, has few if any CGT consequences[16]. The cost of the original holding is merely apportioned to the revised holdings[17], although money paid by a shareholder to acquire shares under a rights issue will increase the cost base of his total shareholding[18]. If bonus shares are offered as an alternative to a dividend, both company and shareholder are taxed as if there had been a distribution of revenue profits equivalent to the amount of the cash dividend which could have been claimed, or the market value of the bonus shares issued if significantly different[19]. Apart from this, reorganisations of share capital normally have no income tax consequences, but any attempt to use a reorganisation to distribute income to shareholders disguised as capital is liable to be caught by anti-avoidance provisions in ICTA 1988, s 703, a section which is designed to counteract artificial devices used to turn revenue profit into capital distributions. It is important to check this section if any capital reorganisation is contemplated. It is a defence to an assessment under ICTA 1988, s 703, that a transaction was carried out for bona fide commercial reasons which did not have as their main object, or one of their main objects, the avoidance of tax[20], and it is possible to obtain advance clearance from the Revenue that they will not seek to charge a particular transaction under s 703[1].

Tax relief exists to assist an individual currently carrying on business as a sole trader or in partnership who wishes to transfer the trade to a company. Provided all the assets of the business, or all the assets other than cash, are transferred to the company, any gain on the assets transferred may be deducted from the value of the shares received in exchange[2], thus deferring a CGT charge until the shares are disposed of. If the transferor receives consideration additional to shares in the new company, the chargeable gain is apportioned between the shares and the other consideration, and only the CGT on the portion attributed to the shares may be deferred[3]. A drawback of

---

9   Ibid, s 213(3)(a).
10   Ibid, s 213(5).
11   Ibid, s 213(2).
12   TCGA 1992, s 192(2)(a).
13   Ibid, s 192(2)(b).
14   Ibid, ss 126–131.
15   ICTA 1988, s 213(3)(b) with CGT relief being provided by TCGA 1992, s 192(3) and (4), although on an apparently more limited basis than for demergers within s 313(3)(a).
16   TCGA 1992, ss 126–131.
17   Ibid, s 127.
18   Ibid, s 128(1).
19   ICTA 1988, s 249.
20   ICTA 1988, s 703(1).
1   Ibid, s 707.
2   TCGA 1992, s 162.
3   Ibid, s 162(2), (3) and (4).

this relief is that it requires all the assets except cash to be transferred[4], thus precluding, if the relief is to be claimed, the retention of land outside the company which might be desirable for other tax reasons. There is no equivalent relief for income tax purposes, so that the transfer of a trade to a company will be taxed as the termination of one trade and the commencement of a new one[5]. However, if the old trade has unrelieved losses these losses may, subject to certain conditions, be carried forward and deducted from future income that the proprietor of the business takes from the company[6]. Although some reliefs exist to assist the incorporation of a business there are no equivalent reliefs to assist disincorporation. The demerger provisions only give tax reliefs where groups of companies are broken down into smaller units. They do not give relief where a company disincorporates with its business thereafter being carried on by the shareholders either as sole traders or in partnership. With the increased volume of companies legislation, and the resulting increased administrative and compliance burdens imposed on companies, the proprietors of many small companies may wish now to disincorporate their business to avoid the company law obligations of incorporation. Currently tax considerations militate against this.

Business incentives

Since the advent of a Conservative Government in 1979, it has been Government policy to provide tax incentives to encourage investment in, and the expansion of, small businesses, and the Labour Government are continuing this policy. Under the Business Expansion Scheme (BES), which applied to expenditure incurred from 6 April 1983 to 31 December 1993[7], a person unconnected with a trading company could subscribe for new shares in the company and, subject to a number of conditions being satisfied, could obtain an income tax deduction for the amount he paid for the shares. Any capital gain on eventual disposal of the shares was tax free. Initially, the scheme only applied to companies which could broadly be described as trading companies, but in 1988 it was extended to companies formed to provide private rented housing under assured tenancies. In 1992 the Government announced that BES relief would cease for all investments made after 31 December 1993[8]. It was not then intended to put anything in its place, but subsequently the Government brought forward and enacted three separate reliefs: (a) the enterprise investment scheme; (b) venture capital trusts; and (c) reinvestment relief. In addition to these reliefs for investment, the capital gains tax legislation gives retirement relief from CGT for proprietors of businesses, and this relief has been significantly extended in recent years. In the July 1997 budget, it was announced that the operation of enterprise investment schemes and venture capital trusts would be reviewed to ensure that they remain properly targeted. In particular, the Government wished to remove relief from schemes which were largely asset backed, or which involved an investor in little financial risk. Changes resulting from the review was announced in the March 1998 Budget and will be enacted in the 1998 Finance Act.

---

4   Ibid, s 162(1).
5   ICTA 1988, s 113(1). It may still be possible to elect under ICTA 1988, s 100(1C) for trading stock to be transferred at original acquisition cost, but otherwise it will be transferred at market value (ICTA 1988, s 100(1A)(b)).
6   ICTA 1988, s 386.
7   It developed out of the Business Start-Up Scheme, which was introduced in 1981.
8   March 1992 Budget statement, see Revenue press release [1992] STI 311.

Under the enterprise investment scheme (EIS) an investor may obtain 20% tax relief for new equity investment in qualifying trading companies[9]. The relief may be withdrawn if the shares are not retained for at least five years[10]. The minimum investment qualifying for relief in any year is £500[11] and, if an investment exceeds £150,000, no relief will be given on the excess[12]. Any capital gain on the eventual disposal of the shares is exempt provided the shares have been held for at least five years[13], and there may also be relief if the shares are disposed of at a loss[14]. To qualify for relief, an investor must not be connected with the company in which he is investing[15]. Broadly this means that he must not be an employee or a director of the company[16] or own more than 30% of its share capital[17]. However, the exclusion does not extend to an unpaid director[18] or an investor who becomes a director of the company after, and normally in consequence of, the purchase of the shares[19].

A company in which an EIS investment can be made must be an unquoted company carrying on a qualifying trade or the parent company of a trading group[20]. A qualifying trade is any trade other than one dealing in land; dealing in shares or financial futures; dealing in goods other than as a wholesaler or retailer; banking; oil extraction; leasing; legal and accountancy services; and providing services to an excluded trade[1]. From 17 March 1998 also excluded are property development; farming or market gardening; commercial woodlands and forestry; hotels; and residential nursing homes.[1a] Companies providing private rented housing on assured tenancies do not qualify for EIS relief. The company's assets must not exceed £10m before, or £11m after, the share issue[2], and the finance must be raised by the issue of new ordinary shares[3].

The EIS is primarily targeted at individuals with substantial amounts to invest who are prepared to make their own investment decisions. It does not readily enable an individual investor to spread his investment risk across a range of companies, and a direct investment in an unquoted company may be difficult to sell after the five-year retention period has expired. Introduced by FA 1995 with effect from 1995/96[4], venture capital trusts (VCTs) are designed to deal with these problems. VCTs are companies which are quoted on the Stock Exchange[5] and which are similar to investment trusts, and aim to raise money from many investors which can then be pooled and invested in a range of companies. The overall success of the VCT will then depend on the success

---

9   ICTA 1988, s 289A(2). This relief is less generous than under the BES, where a taxpayer with a marginal income tax rate of 40% obtained 40% tax relief on his investment.
10   Ibid, s 299 with s 312(1A)(a).
11   Ibid, s 290(1).
12   Ibid, s 290(2). The limit was increased from £100,000 for shares issued on or after 6 April 1998, F (No 2) B 1998, s 74(1), (3) and Sch 13, para 4.
13   TCGA 1992, s 150A(2).
14   TCGA 1992, s 150A(1) first requires any capital loss to be reduced by the initial income tax relief, but if there is still a loss it may be relieved for either capital gains tax or income tax (ICTA 1988, s 305A, applying s 574).
15   ICTA 1988, s 291(1)(b).
16   Ibid, s 291(2).
17   Ibid, s 291B(1).
18   Ibid, s 291A(1)–(3).
19   Ibid, s 291A(4) and (5).
20   Ibid, s 289(1) and s 293(1) and (2). A trading group is elaborately defined in s 293(3A)–(3F).
1   Ibid, s 289(2) and s 297(1) and (2).
1a   F (No 2) B 1998, Sch 12, para 1(1).
2   Ibid, s 293(6A), inserted by F (No 2) B 1998, Sch 13, para 9.
3   Ibid, s 289(7).
4   FA 1995, ss 70–73. In July 1997 the Revenue announced that, by that date, the first 18 venture capital trusts had raised over £350m, [1997] STI 918.
5   ICTA 1988, s 842AA(2)(e).

of all the companies in which it invests, and it will be less vulnerable to a failure by one company. As the company is quoted on the Stock Exchange, investing shareholders should have little difficulty in selling their shares.

To gain Revenue approval as a VCT, a company must be quoted on the Stock Exchange and must derive its income wholly or mainly from owning shares. At least 70% of its investments must be in qualifying companies, with at least 30% of its qualifying holdings being in ordinary shares, with not less than 10% of its shareholding in each company being in ordinary shares. No more than 15% of its total investments may be in any one company, and the maximum amount of dividend income that it can retain is 15%[6]. Qualifying companies in which a VCT may invest are unquoted trading companies carrying on qualifying trades and unquoted parent companies of a trading group[7]. Qualifying trades are defined in the same way as for the EIS[8]. The gross assets of the trading company or trading group must be less than £10m[9], and the maximum annual investment in any one company is £1m[10].

An individual over 18 who subscribes for *new* ordinary shares in a VCT is entitled to income tax relief of 20% of the investment, subject to an annual maximum investment of £100,000, provided the shares are held for at least five years[11]. Purchases on the stock market of issued VCT shares attract no initial relief. For both initial investors and subsequent purchasers, dividend income received from a VCT is tax free[12], and any profit on disposal of the shares is free of capital gains tax provided the company was a VCT at the date of both the acquisition and the disposal[13]. The VCT is exempt from corporation tax on capital gains on a disposal of shares in companies in which it invests[14], and any dividends it receives are treated as franked investment income, so that there will be no additional tax to pay. Any interest which it receives is subject to corporation tax.

The third relief, reinvestment relief, is designed to encourage people who have sold assets and realised a chargeable capital gain to reinvest at least part of the sale proceeds in EIS companies (whether or not income tax relief is also available), or venture capital trusts. The relief applies to any chargeable gain realised on the disposal of any asset[15]. To the extent that the gain is reinvested in newly-issued shares in an EIS company or a venture capital trust[16], any capital gains tax liability is deferred until the reinvestment shares are ultimately sold[17]. The purchase of reinvestment shares in an EIS company must normally take place not more than one year before, nor later than three years after, the disposal which gives rise to the chargeable gain[18]. For the purchase of shares in a VCT the period is shorter, from one year before to one year after the relevant disposal[19].

6   The qualifying conditions are set out in ICTA 1988, s 842AA(2).
7   ICTA 1988, Sch 28B paras 1 and 2. Amendments adapting the relief for trading groups were made by FA 1997, Sch 9, with effect from 26 November 1996.
8   Ibid, Sch 28B, para 4.
9   Ibid, Sch 28B, para 8(1).
10   Ibid, Sch 28B, para 7(2).
11   ICTA 1988, Sch 15B, paras 1–6.
12   Ibid, Sch 15B, para 7. The individual must be over 18, and the annual acquisition of VCT shares qualifying for relief is £100,000, Sch 15B, paras 7(2), 7(3)(a)(ii) and 8.
13   TCGA 1992, s 151A(1).
14   Ibid, s 100(1) as amended by FA 1995, s 72(2).
15   TCGA 1992, Sch 5B, para 1, and Sch 5C, para 1.
16   Ibid, Sch 5B, para 1(2) and Sch 5C, para 1(2).
17   Ibid, Sch 5B, para 2, and Sch 5C, para 2.
18   Ibid, Sch 5B, para 1(3).
19   Ibid, Sch 5C, para 1(3).

Reinvestment relief may be combined with EIS relief or VCT relief.[20] Thus if, in 1998/99, a taxpayer liable to 40% tax on chargeable gains reinvests a £10,000 chargeable gain in a VCT, he will effectively gain 60% initial tax relief on the investment – 40% through deferring the tax that would otherwise have been payable on the gain, and 20% VCT relief for his investment of £10,000. The deferred CGT liability will, however, ultimately become payable when the VCT shares are sold, as it is not covered by the CGT exemption for sales of VCT shares.

The EIS and VCT reliefs outlined above are aimed primarily at investors, and not owners of businesses. Reinvestment relief helps both outside investors and the owner of a business who wishes to sell his shares in one trading company and invest the proceeds in a company carrying on a completely different business. However, the Conservative Government was also concerned to ensure that entrepreneurs who build up the value of an unquoted company should be able to retain the economic benefit without it being seriously eroded by tax. This has been achieved by the business property reliefs for inheritance tax, outlined earlier, and by a generous capital gains tax relief known as retirement relief, although retirement is not a pre-condition for the relief.

Retirement relief applies to both unincorporated and incorporated businesses[1]. For it to apply to reduce the capital gains tax that would otherwise be payable on the sale of shares in a company, there must be a disposal of the shares by a individual who is over 50 at the time of the disposal, or who has been forced to retire at an earlier age on the grounds of ill health[2]. The shares must be shares in the individual's personal company[3], defined as a company in which the individual has at least 5% of the voting rights[4]. Additionally, for at least a year before the disposal, the personal company must either have been a trading company or the holding company for one or more trading companies, and the transferor must have been a full-time working officer or employee of the company, or a company within the trading group[5].

If these minimum conditions are satisfied, any gain on the disposal of shares in the personal company must be apportioned in the ratio that the company's chargeable business assets bears to its total chargeable assets[6]. Any gain apportioned to non-business assets gets no relief. Gains apportioned to chargeable business assets qualify for retirement relief. For qualifying disposals in 1998/99, the maximum relief is 100% relief from the CGT that would otherwise be payable on gains up to £250,000 and 50% relief on gains which exceed £250,000 but which do not exceed £1m[7]. However, the maximum relief is only available if the qualifying condition that the shares should be shares in a personal company and that the transferor should be a full-time employee have been satisfied for 10 years prior to the disposal. If the qualifying conditions have been satisfied for at least a year, the minimum period, but less than 10 years, the maximum relief is reduced pro rata[8]. Thus, if a transferor only satisfies the minimum one-year period, there is 100% relief for the first £25,000 of gains, and 50% relief for gains between £25,000 and £100,000.

For years after 1998/99 retirement relief is to be progressively withdrawn, as the Government believes that the new taper relief for capital gains tax will provide a

20   TCGA 1992, Sch 5B and Sch 5C.
1   TCGA 1992, s 163(2).
2   Ibid, s 163(1).
3   Ibid, s 163(2) with s 163(5)(b).
4   Ibid, Sch 6, para 1(2).
5   Ibid, s 163(5)(b).
6   TCGA 1992, Sch 6, para 7(1) and (2).
7   Ibid, Sch 6, para 13(1).
8   Ibid, Sch 6, para 13(1).

sufficient substitute albeit that, under taper relief, at least 25% of any gain on the disposal of business assets will remain taxable whereas, under retirement relief, the whole of any qualifying gain up to £250,000 is exempt. The withdrawal of the relief will take place over a four year period from 1999/00 to 2002/03. In 1999/00 the maximum 100% relief is limited to gains up to £200,000, and 50% relief on any excess gains up to a maximum of £800,000. By 2002/03 this reduces to 100% relief on gains up to £50,000 and 50% relief on excess gains up to £200,000, with no retirement relief available in 2003/04.[9]

Further protection against loss for an investor in an unquoted company is provided by ICTA 1988, s 574. This section enacts that if an individual subscribes for shares in a qualifying company, basically an unquoted trading company, and subsequently disposes of those shares at loss, he may claim to deduct the loss for income tax purposes[10]. To avoid double relief under the enterprise incentive scheme provisions and this section, any capital loss must be reduced by any relief claimed for an EIS investment[11].

One disadvantage of investing in shares of an unquoted company is that the shares may prove difficult to resell. The Companies Act therefore contains provisions[12] authorising companies to repurchase their own shares in specified circumstances. In the absence of special provisions, such a repurchase might have tax disadvantages as the purchase price would be treated as a distribution by the company and would be liable to income tax in the hands of the shareholder[13]. Relieving provisions are therefore contained in ICTA 1988, ss 219–229. Provided a number of conditions are satisfied, the purchase price will be treated as a capital receipt, with any profit liable to CGT rather than income tax[14]. The most important conditions are that the acquiring company must be an unquoted trading company[1], it must make the purchase to benefit its trade[2] or to enable the vendor to pay inheritance tax[3], and it must acquire substantially the whole of the investor's shareholding[4]. The investor must be resident and ordinarily resident in the UK[5], and must have owned the shares for at least five years[6].

TAX ADVANTAGES AND DISADVANTAGES OF INCORPORATION

Prior to the changes made in the 1980s to the structure of both income tax and corporation tax there were significant tax advantages to be gained by conducting business through a company. The top rates of corporation tax were much lower than the top rates of income tax, thus enabling more profits to be retained for reinvestment in the business if it was incorporated. However, the tax system is now more neutral, and considerations other than tax are more likely to determine whether the incorporation of a business is desirable. The following tax considerations remain relevant to any decision on incorporation versus non-incorporation.

9   F (No 2) B 1998, cl 138.
10   ICTA 1988, s 574(1). Amendments to the rules are made by F (No 2) B 1988, cl 80.
11   TCGA 192, s 150A(1) with ICTA 1988 ss 305A and 574.
12   Companies Act 1985, ss 162ff.
13   The possible tax disadvantages have been considerably reduced now that capital gains are taxed at income tax rates.
14   ICTA 1988, s 219(1).
1   Ibid, s 219(1), or an unquoted holding company of a trading group.
2   Ibid, s 219(1)(a).
3   Ibid, s 219(1)(b).
4   Ibid, s 221.
5   Ibid, s 220(1).
6   Ibid, s 220(5).

If a business is conducted outside a company the proprietor is liable to higher rate income tax of 40% to the extent that his taxable income, including business profits, exceeds £27,100[7]. He is liable to Class II National Insurance contributions of £6.35 a week plus Class IV contributions of 6% on profits between £7,310 and £25,220[8]. The maximum tax deductible amount he can contribute to a pension scheme is 17.5% of his earnings until he attains the age of 36, when the percentage gradually increases to 40% from the age of 61[9]. The maximum earnings in respect of which tax deductible pension contributions may be made may be limited to £87,600[10]. The proprietor of a business is liable to capital gains tax at his top rate of income tax on capital gains from the disposal of business assets, subject to an annual exemption of £6,800[11], generous retirement relief if he is over 50[12], and the right to defer a charge if the disposal proceeds are reinvested in new qualifying business assets[13]. However, equivalent capital gains tax rates and reliefs are available for the disposal of shares by a proprietor in his personal business company.

If a business is incorporated and its profits do not exceed £300,000 they are taxed at the small companies rate of 21%[14], thus apparently conferring a tax advantage over non-incorporation for profits in excess of £27,100. However, if profits are distributed they will be taxed at the proprietor's appropriate rate of income tax. If they are retained the proprietor will eventually be taxed at income tax rates on the capital gain accruing to his shares, subject to any available relief such as retirement relief or reinvestment relief. The difference in tax rates is thus not as great as might at first sight appear.

If a proprietor takes money out of a company as salary the amount paid will be taxed as his income rather than as the company's[15], but Class I National Insurance contributions will be payable both by the proprietor and by the company. If the proprietor is in a contracted out pension scheme his contributions are 2% on the first £64 weekly earnings and 8.4% on weekly earnings from £64 to £485, the maximum amount on which employees have to pay Class I NI contributions. The company must pay at rates up to 7% on earnings up to £485 per week and 10% on any excess with no upper limit[16]. Total national insurance contributions are therefore likely to be higher than if the business was unincorporated. If profit is taken out of the company as dividend rather than as salary it is effectively only taxed as the income of the proprietor provided the company's profits remain below £300,000 and so taxable at the small companies' rate, and no National Insurance contributions are payable. However, this method of withdrawing profits from the company may restrict the pension which the proprietor can receive on retirement. Pension scheme arrangements for company employees are, in general, more generous than for the self-employed because payments by a company to an employee pension scheme are tax deductible to the company, but not taxable income of the employee, to the extent that they are designed to produce a retirement pension not exceeding two-thirds of the employee's final salary[17]. If an employee is elderly this can result in tax relief being available for much larger payments than if he had remained self-employed. Capital gains realised by a company which are retained in the company are subject to a double tax charge, first to the company when the gains

7   ICTA 1988, s 1(2)(b).
8   [1997] STI 1590.
9   ICTA 1988, s 640.
10   Ibid, s 640A.
11   TCGA 1992, s 3(2).
12   Ibid, s 163, although the relief is being withdrawn and replaced by a less generous tax relief.
13   Ibid, s 152.
14   ICTA 1988, s 13.
15   Because it will be deductible in computing the company's taxable profit.
16   [1997] STI 1590, which gives the rates for 1998/99 for both employees and employers.
17   ICTA 1988, s 590(3)(a).

are realised and later to the proprietor when he disposes of his shares in the company, which will have increased in value to reflect the gain. However this double charge can be eliminated if the company is liable to tax at the small companies' rate and the capital gain is distributed as dividend, although the proprietor will not then have the benefit of the exemption of the first £6,800 chargeable gains.

Corporate power and its regulation

CHAPTER 22

Corporate governance: the distribution and regulation of power in a company

We saw in Chapter 1 how some economists look at a company as legal recognition of a nexus of contracts by a group of persons pooling their capital and delegating management to specialist managers who agree to work for a given salary[1]. This represents a particular sophisticated network. The members of this group possess an underlying investment interest and a vote which bear a complex relationship to each other as we saw in Part III. They are not only individual owners of rights but they also share in the less tangible legal personality of the company, a metaphysical relationship which plagues the law and generates many contradictions. They are all members of the one body, as St Paul said.of the Christian Church. Another way of looking at a company is in relation to the accumulation and distribution of power and control both de jure and de facto. In the classic small private company, ownership and control are often vested in the same people. In such companies there is a natural tendency to informality, with a blurring of managerial and shareholder functions. This raises few problems unless there is conflict within the company or pressure from a loan creditor. In the larger company there is frequently a separation of ownership and control and a wide dispersal of share ownership. This gives management considerable scope for the exercise of power by virtue of their strategic position and control over the proxy machinery for general meetings. On the other hand, the ever increasing extent of institutional investment means that there is a potentially countervailing power.

THE CONCEPT OF CORPORATE GOVERNANCE

Corporate governance is a term which has been much in vogue in the last 10 years. It suffers, nevertheless, from a lack of precision[2]. Corporate governance is about the process of direction of a company, the relationship between the board of directors and management. It is also ultimately about regimes of accountability[3]. There is a core of

---

1   It should be noted, however, that directors have no right to be paid for their services in the absence of authority under the articles—*Re George Newman & Co* [1895] 1 Ch 674 at 686, CA.
2   See J H Farrar (1993) 6 CBLJ 1.
3   See Robert Monks and Nell Minow *Corporate Governance* (1995); Robert Tricker *International Corporate Governance* (1994), *Maw on Corporate Governance* (1994) by N Maw, Lord Lane and Sir Michael Craig-Cooper; Bob Garratt *The Fish Rots from the Head* (1996).

certainty in the sense of the law relating to directors' duties and the conduct of general meetings. In addition, there is a penumbra of standards and practices which are extra legal. Some of these are expressed in codes of practice which sometimes approximate to law. The following diagram gives some indication of the underlying relationships covered by the concept[4].

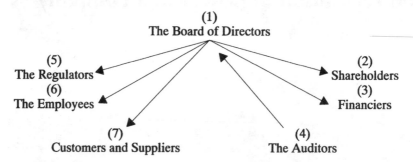

From this it can be seen that the board of directors is central to the concept. The board is appointed by the members entitled to vote and the underlying theory is that shareholders monitor the board. The reality is more complex. The main monitoring that is done in the case of publicly listed companies is by institutional investors who represent an increasing proportion of holders of ordinary shares of such companies. The performance of the board is also monitored by the terms on which the company acquires its debt finance. This has already been dealt with in Chapter 20. The law requires public companies to have auditors. The main role of these is in relation to accounts, although some of the aspects of auditing go further.

The performance of company directors is increasingly subject to legal and self regulation. This includes the Department of Trade and Industry and bodies such as the Monopolies and Mergers Commission and the Office of Fair Trading and the proposed new competition commission. In addition, there are bodies such as the Stock Exchange and the Panel on Takeovers and Mergers. The board has also certain responsibilities to the workforce under specific industrial relations legislation.

Although organically employees are not part of the decision-making process in the company, the Companies Acts do refer to them in a number of ways. Thus, it is appropriate for the board to consider the interests of employees in a redundancy situation. The European Union has long had proposals for greater worker participation in corporate governance but so far this has been resisted by the UK.

Although company law does not directly recognise it, economic reality requires the board to give careful attention to the interests of consumers of the company's products. At the end of the day, this is the market which provides the ultimate discipline for company directors.

As *Corporate Practices and Conduct*[5], a code of good practice produced by a Working Group of leading Australian institutions chaired by Henry Bosch, states:

> There is no simple universal formula for good governance. Companies vary so greatly in size, complexity, ownership structure and other characteristics that

---

4   Based on *Maw on Corporate Governance*, p 3.
5   3rd edn (1995), p 7. This work draws on UK, Australian, Canadian, US and Hong Kong material, including the UK Cadbury Report and Code.

what is ideal in some cases may be inappropriate in others. Moreover, as companies and industries change, ways of governing may need to adapt. Tried and proven structures and processes can help to improve governance, and can play an important role in building shareholder confidence in the soundness of their investments and thus a company's ability to attract capital. However, it is essential that all involved, and particularly boards of directors, should adopt the practices best suited to the good governance of their organisations in their particular circumstances.

THE RECEIVED LEGAL MODEL

The received legal model of the company is a closed system of corporate governance. The two organs of the company recognised by company law are the general meeting of shareholders (which may not necessarily include all the shareholders, since some shares may not carry votes and preference shareholders may have limited voting rights) and the board of directors. The board of directors manages the company and makes business policy decisions and the general meeting of the shareholders as a body elects the board and decides on organic change. Company officers are answerable to the board but the board is only answerable to the company as a whole not the shareholders as such. This is at any rate the received general legal theory[6] although it is belied to some extent by the market for control. Dissatisfied shareholders may sell and this may depress the share price in the case of a listed company. They will also be inclined to accept a takeover offer.

In the case of the larger companies with debenture stock, there will usually be debenture stockholders' meetings and class meetings of the various classes of shares but the status of both of these is largely contractual and ad hoc. There is no recognition of the workforce in the organic structure of the company although the board may now legitimately consider their interests in making decisions. This latter reform perhaps marks a closer equation by the law of the company with the economic concept of the firm. Collective bargaining nevertheless operates outside the company structure. Government and community pressures are also outside the corporate system. However, the reality of corporate decision-making is that it must be open to outside influences in order to survive particularly in a time of recession. Trade union negotiations, the activities of competitors, the constraints of government and local authorities, the pressures of international trade are all influences on corporate decision-making in the real world[7].

Active and latent control[8]

When companies are controlled by owner managers, active power and control are merged. For instance, the early coal and steel companies in the later part of the

---

6   M A Eisenberg *The Structure of the Corporation; a Legal Analysis* (1976).
7   See F Hilmer (ed) *Strictly Boardroom* (1993) para 2.19.
8   Edward Herman *Corporate Control, Corporate Power* (1981), ch 4.

nineteenth century were run like this. The general tendency in the larger companies is for ownership and control to separate. The separation of ownership and control, instead of producing pure management control because of the dispersal of shareholding, has often resulted in the continuation of significant non-managerial ownership, which frequently is in the hands of financial institutions. Where this is the case the extent of control is often hard to assess and has been labelled by one American writer as latent power[9]. Such power is usually negative in nature. It rests on powers of veto in loan agreements or the power of constraint by influence on the board. The concept of control is considered further in Chapter 35. Although the general body of shareholders may be said to have latent power in the sense of certain residual rights of intervention and control, differences between shareholders in wealth, tax position, and investment objectives as well as the lack of a countervailing institutional framework parallel to that of management all tend to weaken this power in practice[10].

THE STRATEGIC POSITION OF THE BOARD

Although in the nineteenth century management was frequently thought of as the agent of the company in general meeting which could be controlled by the general meeting, the change of wording in the standard form of article by the early twentieth century vested wider powers in the board of directors and curtailed the rights of the general meeting to interfere[11]. In a word it legitimated centralised management[12].

As Henry Manne has put it:

Management is a discrete economic service or function and the selection of individuals to perform that function, whether undertaken at the outset or during the later life of a company, is a part of the entrepreneurial job. Centralising management serves simply to specialise these various economic functions, and to allow the system to operate more efficiently[13].

Control of management then rests with the board of directors which in theory must act as a collegiate body. In practice much authority is delegated to a managing director and other executives. The law has not fully come to terms with the variety of management structures and practices in modern companies. Although there is evolving a sensible law based on a modern view of agency principles this sometimes seems a little over-simplified and remote from reality. As we saw in Chapter 13 the law relating to the authority of an individual director and a manager to bind the company is not very satisfactory. Another conceptual approach which in the past has been mainly adopted in tort and criminal law is the attribution to the company of the acts of certain officers as its alter ego. This approach, known also as the organic theory, has been developed more fully in German law. Both the agency and organic approaches have recently been subsumed under a general attribution approach. There are signs of a new approach developing of specifically corporate responsibility based on the bad habits of a corporate culture which led to non-compliance.[14]

9   Ibid.
10   Ibid, p 23.
11   See L C B Gower *Modern Company Law* (6th edn, 1992), p 148.
12   See H G Manne (1967) 53 Virginia LR 259.
13   Ibid.
14   See E Colvin (1995) 6 Criminal Law Forum 1.

The practice of appointing non-executive directors particularly in larger companies is becoming standard practice and they are increasingly taking a proactive role to enhance shareholder value in companies.

Control by the board of the proxy machinery has important strategic consequences, since few shareholders turn up at general meetings. However, the Stock Exchange requirements of two-way proxies which enable the shareholder to mandate the directors to give effect to his wishes curtail this somewhat.

Given that management usually has strategic control, in whose interests is it exercised? Obviously where there is ownership and control vested in the same hands there is no great problem unless the proprietors sacrifice the interests of creditors by wrongful trading. It is thought that in publicly-held companies, management generally runs company affairs without regard to its own self interest as far as business decisions are concerned. On the other hand when it comes to structural decisions such as a merger or takeover, conflicts of interest arise[15]. Management and shareholders do not then necessarily have the same interest[16]. Management reward is frequently unconnected with share ownership and in any event is only one of the operative motives of managerial conduct. These motives include the urge to power and prestige and the desire for security.

THE ECONOMICS OF THE RIGHT TO VOTE[17]

Voting rights exist because someone must have residual power to act where the contracts are incomplete[18]. The contractual nexus cannot cover every future contingency expressly. Decisions may have to be made which are felt by the law or the founders to need the backing of investors. The rights, however, usually attach to the ordinary shares as the residual claimants to the company's income. They receive most of the marginal gains and suffer most of the marginal costs. Hence it is felt that they are the appropriate group to exercise voting rights.

Ordinary shareholders normally have one vote per share at general meetings. Preference shareholders usually have only limited voting rights. Debenture holders have no right to vote at general meetings. Voting in any case is not compulsory and for many shareholders there is a strong disincentive to vote. To attend a meeting in person may be expensive. The exercise of one's votes does not give one any privileges unless one has control or one's votes can be decisive. Given the cost, the difficulty and the uncertainty of outcome many investors rely on the market and tend to spread their risks by investing in a number of companies. On the other hand, the right to vote is not without value. The value is at a minimum when the need to exercise it is remote and rises to a maximum when the exercise of voting rights assumes significance. Also

15   *Eisenberg*, op cit, ch 4.
16   Cf however, George J Benston (1973) 63 Am Econ Rev 132, who argues that the evidence does not support this conclusion.
17   See M S Rix *Stock Exchange Economics* (1954), p 53; F H Easterbrook and D R Fischel (1983) 26 J of Law & Econ 395; R Hessen *Defence of the Corporation* (1979), ch 5, cf R Nader *Taming the Giant Corporation* (1976). For a discussion of share voting in mergers see H Manne 'Some Theoretical Aspects of Share Voting' in *The Economics of Legal Relationships* (1975) ed H Manne, p 534.
18   Easterbrook and Fischel, op cit, p 403.
19   Manne, op cit.

the market recognises that shares can have a nuisance value. Thus, even in the case of winding up or a major reconstruction, shares carrying votes will have some value depending on what the support or opposition of the holders is thought to be worth.

THE LEGAL AND SELF REGULATION OF MANAGEMENT

The legal regulation of management can be broadly divided into a free enterprise approach and a public interventionist approach. The first, which is the product of case law augmented by statute, is represented by two tiers of protection. The director owes a mixture of case law and statutory duties to the company. Some of these are characterised as fiduciary obligations and are owed to the company, not the individual shareholders or creditors of the company. For wrongs done to the company, the company is the proper plaintiff. The majority generally represents the company. The purpose of this latter doctrine was to curb the number of suits, and it is perhaps implicit in the economics of public companies. As Henry Manne has argued, the function of the shareholder is to put money at risk for use by entrepreneurs and managers: 'Apart then from having the shareholders' funds used in the corporation's interest and his contracted-for return paid ... economics suggests no other relationship between investors and managers.' Manne later equates the concept of centralised management with majority rule. It is not that management necessarily owns a majority of shares but that it has the means of control of them. There are, however, exceptions to the proper plaintiff rule when a minority shareholder is allowed to sue and to these can be added the statutory remedy under s 459 and winding up on the just and equitable ground. These remedies are somewhat draconian and less important in the policing of management behaviour than market forces, particularly in the market for securities and the market for corporate control. Unless a public company whose shares are listed is efficiently managed, the price of its shares will decline and this will lower the price at which an outsider can take over the company[19]. Small firms, however, are not subject to the same market forces since the market for a minority interest will usually only be the majority. In the case of both types of company the rights of loan creditors to intervene depend on their contract with the company, their security and the general law.

The public interventionist approach is largely concerned with policing disclosure and commercial fraud. The Department of Trade and Industry has a number of statutory powers of investigation and inspection. Added to these are the specialist powers of the Director General of Fair Trading and the EU Commission in respect of monopolies and restrictive practices which we shall consider in the next part of the book. The legal regulation of management has recently come under attack by some economists. It is said to be based on the largely unproven empirical assumptions that the separation of ownership and control is not economically optimal and that the legal treatment of the problem reduces or eliminates the inefficiencies at a cost less than the benefits obtained. The whole elaborate structure is thought to be built up on guesswork. Another unproven hypothesis is that market controls are not sufficient to police management shirking and abuse of discretion. Such critics argue[20]:

20   See eg N Wolfson (1980) 34 Univ of Miami LR 959; E Fama 'Agency Problems and the Theory of the Firm' (1980) 88 Journal of Political Economy 288; M C Jensen and W H Meckling 'Theory of the Firm; Managerial Behaviour, Agency Costs and Ownership Structure' (1976) 3 Journal of Financial Economics 305.

(1) Separation of ownership and control is simply another example of joint effort and the inevitability of 'agency costs'. These costs include the cost of monitoring to deter shirking and abuse by management.

(2) Monitoring is worthwhile only when the costs of monitoring management behaviour are less than the benefits derived.

(3) Government intervention might force the incurring of monitoring costs which exceed the benefits derived.

(4) Market forces will cause managements to seek to prove that they are honest and efficient. This will encourage investment in the company, ward off a takeover and improve their own marketability.

(5) It is better to think of shareholders not as owners but as risk takers, since this more accurately analyses their position.

These arguments provide a valuable perspective and powerful critique of the law. They suffer, however, from one signal weakness. The law is not exclusively concerned with economic factors. Certain goals are thought worthy of public pursuit which are not necessarily cost effective. This is because of the close interface of law and social morality. Even if the benefits of policing management fraud were outweighed by the costs we should still feel obliged to incur them. Whether this applies to lack of care and inefficiency in management is more problematic. Although to some limited extent it affects the public interest, it is probably better left to private law enforcement by the shareholders through the company.

The UK has a long history of self regulation. The City of London Takeover Code is a classic example. More recently there has been the Report of the Committee on the Financial Aspects of Corporate Governance chaired by Sir Adrian Cadbury. This proposed a new system of self regulation of publicly listed companies mainly concerned with financial reporting of corporate governance. The resulting code which came into effect on 30 June 1994 will be dealt with in later chapters. In January 1995 it was announced that Sir Richard Greenbury would chair a private sector group representing business and investors to examine the framework within which pay and conditions for directors of PLCs are determined and disclosed. The report was published in July 1995. Many of its recommendations are being implemented by changes to the Stock Exchange Listing Rules. The Hampel Committee has reviewed the impact of the Cadbury and Greenbury codes and reported on 28 January 1998.

In May 1997 the new Labour Government announced a radical new system of regulation. The new framework takes bank supervision away from the Bank of England and places it with an enhanced Securities and Investment Board (SIB). *The Economist* of 24 May 1997, at p 13, stated that 'later the plan is to fold into the SIB the existing array of city regulators (one for each main branch of the financial services industry), shifting from a regime based on self-regulation to one based on statute'. SIB is to have tougher powers as well as a wider remit. Building societies may also be put under its supervision later. SIB was renamed the Financial Services Authority on 28 October 1997.

A Green Paper is foreshadowed for Spring 1998.

CHAPTER 23

Company general meetings

DO GENERAL MEETINGS MATTER?

General meetings of the company are meetings of the shareholders. Their importance is partly because company law reserves certain decisions in the running of the company to be taken by the shareholders in general meeting.[1] But general meetings also provide an opportunity for shareholders to call to account the board of directors and to ask questions about the board's performance and future plans. In this respect general meetings can be seen as one of the mechanisms company law provides for ensuring the accountability of the board of directors to the shareholders.

Despite this in large public companies general meetings play a relatively unimportant part in securing the accountability of management. This is partly because of inertia and lack of interest from shareholders in attending and voting at general meetings. This has led management to feel that they are able to secure support for whatever resolution they put forward which in turn leads to greater apathy among shareholders who feel unable to influence events. Attendance at meetings and voting need to be considered separately because voting rights can be exercised by proxy and need not entail attending the meeting.[2] So far as voting is concerned there are signs that institutional shareholders are increasingly recognising the importance of voting as part of their role in responsible corporate governance.[3] To aid them both the National Association of Pension Funds and the Association of British Insurers run voting services for their members which identify when contentious issues arise. Alternatively pension funds may belong to Pensions Investment Research Consultants Ltd which produces detailed reports on all meetings of companies in the FTSE 350 and, unlike the NAPF and ABI, not only identifies contentious issues but gives advice on which way to vote.[4] As regards attendance at meetings it has become rare for institutional shareholders to

---

1   See Chapter 25 below.
2   The increasing tendency for both institutional and private shareholders to hold shares via nominees places a further obstacle to the exercise of voting rights. For a review of the practicalities of institutional shareholders voting, see Stapledon *Institutional Shareholders and Corporate Governance* (1996), pp 88–92. As regards private shareholders see DTI Consultative Document *Private Shareholders: Corporate Governance Rights* (1996) URN 96/983.
3   See Stapledon *Institutional Shareholders and Corporate Governance* (1996), pp 92–98.
4   Ibid, pp 98–100.

attend meetings. If they wish to discuss the company's plans they will tend to do so in private meetings with the management.[5] Nevertheless there is increasing pressure on insitutional shareholders to attend meetings of companies in which they hold shares. This, coupled with the growth in numbers of private individual shareholders resulting largely from privatisation, has led to a resurgence of interest in the function of general meetings of shareholders and how they can be made most effective.[6]

At the opposite end of the corporate spectrum a quite separate development concerning meetings and resolutions is the programme for deregulation of private companies.[7] Following suggestions made in a report published by the Institute of Directors[8] two procedures were introduced in the Companies Act 1989 designed to ease the burden of running a small private company. One allows shareholders by unanimous 'elective resolution'[9] to disapply certain Companies Act formalities. The other introduced a statutory procedure for passing resolutions by written agreement[10].

One final word of introduction. The conduct of company meetings, although affected by statutory provisions, is very much a matter of the company's own regulations. Frequent reference will therefore be made in this chapter to the provisions of Table A as illustrating the most common practice in this area. In addition the Stock Exchange Listing Rules contain some provisions affecting meetings of listed companies and these too will be referred to when appropriate.

ANNUAL GENERAL MEETING

Every company must hold at least one general meeting each calendar year[11] which it must designate in notices calling the meeting its annual general meeting[12]. There is no limit to the number of general meetings a company may hold each year but it must hold at least one, called the annual general meeting. The articles will usually provide for the meeting to be called by the directors[13] but if they fail to do so then any member of the company can ask the Department of Trade and Industry to call, or direct the calling, of a meeting.[14]

---

5   Ibid, pp 101–106. For an example of the problems this can create arising from the possible disclosure of inside information see *Mackie v H M Advocate* 1995 SLT 110. The Stock Exchange has published a document giving advice to companies having such meetings: *Guidance on Dissemination of Price Sensitive Information* (1995).
6   See Donald Butcher 'Reform of the General Meetings' in (Sheikh and Rees eds) *Corporate Governance and Corporate Control* (1995) ch 11. The Institute of Chartered Secretaries and Administrators has published *A Guide to Best Practice for Annual General Meetings* (1996). See also the Cadbury Report on *The Financial Aspects of Corporate Governance* (1992), pp 48–52 and the Report of a joint City/Industry working group *Developing a Winning Partnership* (1996 edition), pp 12–13.
7   Once a more coherent classification of public and private companies was introduced by the Companies Act 1980 it was to be expected that there would be an increasing divergence in the legislation relating to each type of company. Deregulation should be seen as a part of this process.
8   'Deregulation for Small Private Companies' (1986).
9   See p 321 below.
10 See pp 327-328 below.
11 *Gibson v Barton* (1875) LR 10 QB 329.
12 Section 366(1). This is one of the provisions the members of a private company may elect to disapply. Under s 366A a private company may, by elective resolution, dispense with holding an annual general meeting unless required to do so by a member.
13 See Table A, art 37. If the articles make no provision for the calling of meetings then a minimum number of members may do so: s 370(3).
14 Section 367(1).

The minimum period of notice that must be given of an annual general meeting is 21 days and the company's articles cannot provide for any shorter period.[15] However, if all the members entitled to attend and vote at an annual general meeting agree, the period of notice laid down in the Act or, if longer, in the company's articles can be waived[16]. Although there are no items of business which the Companies Act requires to take place at the annual general meeting, certain items are by convention usually dealt with, such as declaring a dividend, consideration of the accounts, balance sheets and the reports of the directors and auditors, the election of directors in place of those retiring and the appointment and remuneration of the auditors.[17]

The difficulty for members seeking to propose resolutions at an annual general meeting is that notice must be given to every member and in a large public company with a widely dispersed shareholding, this is likely to prove impractical and expensive. The company may, of course, be willing to circulate members' resolutions with the notice calling the meeting but the company can now be compelled to do so[18] by members holding not less than 5% of the voting rights or 100 members holding an average paid up capital of £100 per member[19]. The members requisitioning the resolution must give notice to the company at least six weeks before the annual general meeting is due to take place[20]. They must also pay the company's expenses unless the company resolves otherwise, and may be required to deposit a sum to cover these expenses in advance[1].

Apart from proposing resolutions shareholders may also secure discussion of an issue at the annual general meeting by asking a question. Under common law the question must relate to the subject matter of the resolution under discussion but in practice public companies usually hold a time for open questions.[2] To avoid questions being asked by individuals which are irrelevant to the majority of shareholders at the meeting it has been suggested that shareholders should be encouraged to submit their questions in advance and that questions specific to an individual and not of general

---

15   Section 369(1), (2). See also Table A, art 38. Reference to a number of days' notice means clear days, ie excluding the day notice is given and the day the meeting is held: *Re Railway Sleepers Supply Co* (1885) 29 Ch D 204; *Re Hector Whaling Ltd* [1936] Ch 208 (cf the Scottish case of *Re Neil M'Leod & Sons Ltd, Petitioners* 1967 SC 16 which allowed the day of the meeting to be counted). Table A expressly refers to 'clear' days and defines this as excluding both the day notice is given or deemed to be given and the day the meeting is held: art 1. In calculating the precise period of notice, therefore, it is also necessary to take account of any provision as to when notice is deemed to be given. Under Table A notices are deemed to be given 48 hours after posting: art 115. For the problems raised by a postal strike, see *Bradman v Trinity Estates plc* [1989] BCLC 757.

16   Section 369(3)(a). The attention of members must be drawn to the fact that the required notice has not been given for their consent to be valid: *Re Pearce, Duff & Co Ltd* [1960] 3 All ER 222, [1960] 1 WLR 1014.

17   Under the Stock Exchange Listing Rules the items mentioned in the text, plus resolutions under s 80, disapplying s 89, conferring authority for a company to purchase its own shares or continuing an existing authority to issue a scrip dividend as an alterative to cash, are designated ordinary business of an annual general meeting. If any other business is transacted the company must send an explanatory circular accompanying the notice of meeting: Listing Rules 14.17.

18   Section 376(1)(a). Based on recommendations by the Cohen Committee (1945) Cmd 6659 para 128.

19   Section 376(2).

20   Section 377(1)(a)(i).

1   Section 377(1)(b). The question whether companies should be required to pay for circulating shareholders' resolutions is canvassed in the DTI Consultative Document *Shareholder Communication at the Annual General Meeting* Section 2 (1996) URN 96/685. For some recent examples of resolutions proposed by shareholders, both private and institutional, rather than by the directors see ibid, Appendix C.

2   In a recent survey 85% of companies surveyed normally received at least three questions at the annual general meeting and 38% of companies at least 10 questions: Roger Hussey *Shareholder Questions at the AGM* (Touche Ross)(1995).

interest should be referred to the relevant director for a response after the meeting.[3] The issue of shareholders' questions is not governed by legislation and the government has raised for discussion the possibility that statute should require companies to make provision for shareholders questions or alternatively give shareholders the specific right to table questions at the annual general meeting.[4]

EXTRAORDINARY GENERAL MEETINGS

The articles of association of a company will usually provide for the directors to convene meetings apart from the annual general meeting[5]. These additional meetings are commonly referred to as extraordinary general meetings[6]. Of course, if the members' views are to be heard, a meeting will be necessary for the views to be formulated and resolutions passed and if the directors suspect those views will be critical they may be unwilling to call a meeting. It is important, therefore, that since 1900, provided they have sufficient support, shareholders have been able to requisition the directors to convene an extraordinary general meeting[7]. The requisition must state the objects of the meeting[8] and must be supported by holders of not less than 10% of the voting paid up capital or, in the case of a company with no share capital, by members representing not less than 10% of the voting rights in the company.[9] If there is a valid requisition, the directors must convene a meeting within 21 days, otherwise the requisitionists may themselves convene one[10]. Formerly the section did not specify a time within which the meeting convened by the directors had to take place and, provided a meeting was convened within 21 days, the requisitionists were prevented from calling one themselves[11]. It is now provided[12] that the meeting convened by the directors must take place not more than 28 days[13] after the notice convening it.

The minimum period of notice for extraordinary general meetings laid down by the Act is 14 days[14] unless the meeting is one at which a special resolution is to be proposed in which case at least 21 days' notice must be given[15]. The company's articles cannot provide for any shorter period but the minimum periods, whether those laid down by the Act or longer periods specified in the company's articles, can be waived if sufficient of the members entitled to attend and vote at the meeting agree[16]. There

3   Report of a City/Industry working group: *Developing a Winning Partnership* (2nd edn, 1996), pp 12–13 URN 95/551. The ISCA *Guide to Best Practice at Annual General Meetings* (1996) recommends that shareholders be invited to submit questions in advance but companies should not use this to restrict the ability of shareholders to raise questions at the AGM: pp 18–19.
4   DTI Consultative Document *Shareholder Communications at the Annual General Meeting* Section 3 (1996) URN 96/685.
5   See Table A, art 37. If the articles make no provision for the calling of meetings then a minimum number of members may do so: s 370(3).
6   Ibid, art 36.
7   Section 368.
8   Section 368(3).
9   Section 368(2).
10   Section 364(4).
11   Re *Windward Islands Enterprises (UK) Ltd* [1983] BCLC 293.
12   Section 368(8), inserted by the Companies Act 1989, Sch 19, para 9.
13   The maximum permissible time between receipt of the requisition and the holding of the meeting is thus seven weeks. Table A, art 37 allows a maximum of eight weeks and will therefore need amending.
14   Section 369(1), (2). This will normally mean clear days: see note 15 above.
15   Section 378(2). Likewise as to clear days, see note 15 above (p 310). Under Table A, if a resolution appointing a director is to be proposed then 21 clear days' notice is required: art 38.
16   Sections 369(3)(b) and (4) and 378(3). As to drawing the members' attention to such consent, see note 16 above (p 310). A private company may by elective resolution reduce the 95% majority needed for consent to short notice under these provisions, but to not less than 90%.

must be a majority in number of such members who must together hold at least 95% in nominal value of the shares giving a right to attend and vote at the meeting.[17]

POWER OF THE COURT TO CALL MEETINGS

Despite the number of provisions relating to the calling of meetings, it may still happen that it is impracticable to call a meeting or to conduct one in the manner prescribed by the articles or the Act. In these circumstances, the court may order a meeting to be held and conducted in such manner as the court thinks fit[18]. This power has existed since 1862 and has been used to overcome difficulties such as the company being left without any directors able validly to convene a meeting, or, proper notice of a meeting being unable to be given because, for example, the records of the membership have been destroyed.[19] As a result of a recommendation by the Cohen Committee the section has since 1948 expressly authorised the court to direct that one member of the company present in person or by proxy shall constitute a meeting.[20] This has been used on several occasions to overcome so-called quorum tactics in which the minority refuses to attend meetings thus making any meeting called by the majority shareholder inquorate and preventing the majority shareholder exercising voting rights. In such cases the court orders a meeting to be held on terms that by-pass the quorum requirement.[1] But it has been held that the jurisdiction does not extend to altering the balance of power between shareholders and thus the court refused to make an order that would overcome a deadlock between two equal shareholders.[2] Likewise the court refused to make an order where the quorum provision was part of a negotiated structure for the protection of a particular shareholder or group of shareholders[3].

NOTICES RELATING TO MEETINGS

To whom must notice be given

Unless the articles otherwise provide, notice of general meetings must be given to every member of the company[4]. Thus, although members without votes at general meetings

---

17   Ibid.
18   Section 371(1). The court may exercise this power either of its own motion or on the application of any director of the company or of any member of the company who would be entitled to vote at the meeting.
19   *Harman v BML Group Ltd* [1994] 1 WLR 893 at 896; [1994] 2 BCLC 674 at 677 per Dillon LJ. The most far-reaching use of the court's power was in a case where the court deemed it to be impracticable to call a meeting because of a fear that it would be disrupted by violence. The court ordered that a meeting be convened to be attended only by the executive committee with the rest of the members voting by postal ballot: *Re British Union for the Abolition of Vivisection* [1995] 2 BCLC 1.
20   Section 371(2).
1   See *Re El Sombrero Ltd* [1958] 3 All ER 1; *Re HR Paul & Son Ltd* (1973) 118 Sol Jo 166; *Re Opera Photographic Ltd* [1989] 1 WLR 634; *Re Sticky Fingers Restaurant Ltd* [1992] BCLC 84; *Re Whitchurch Insurance Consultants Ltd* [1993] BCLC 1359.
2   *Ross v Telford* [1998] 1 BCLC 82, CA.
3   *Harman v BML Group Ltd* above, note 19.
4   Section 370(2). Notice must also be given to the auditors who are entitled to attend general meetings of the company and to be heard at general meetings on matters concerning them as auditors: s 390(1). Table A also requires notice to be given to all persons entitled to a share in consequence of the death or bankruptcy of a member and to the directors: art 38. Note that under Table A directors are entitled to attend and speak at meetings, even if they are not members: art 44. It is not entirely clear what happens if notice is not given to a director or if a director is prevented from attending and speaking in

normally have no right to attend[5] they will normally have the right to receive notice of any meetings. Again, except in so far as the articles otherwise provide, the manner in which notice of meetings must be served is that laid down by Table A as for the time being in force[6]. At common law, a meeting cannot be held unless every member entitled to receive notice has done so[7]. It is usual therefore for articles[8] to provide that accidental omission to give notice or the non-receipt of notice shall not invalidate proceedings at the meeting[9].

Contents of notices

Apart from indicating the time and place at which a meeting is to be held, the notice of a meeting[10] must also give members a sufficient indication of the business to be transacted at the meeting as will enable them to decide whether they need to attend or not. The notice will therefore also set limits on what may be decided at a meeting and if a resolution is passed of which proper notice was not given a member will be entitled to a declaration that it was invalid[11]. It is normally sufficient for the notice to indicate the general nature of the business to be transacted at the meeting[12] but certain resolutions may need to be set out in full. Thus a notice of a meeting called to pass an extraordinary, special or elective resolution must specify that the resolution is to be proposed as such[13] and must set out either the text or the entire substance of the resolution[14]. Similarly, the notice of an annual general meeting must set out the exact text of any resolution to be proposed as a result of a requisition by shareholders[15]. Finally, as part of the directors' duty to ensure that the members are fully aware of what is to be discussed at the meeting, the notice must disclose any benefit the directors will obtain as a result of the passing

---

breach of the relevant Table A articles. A director who is not also a member of the company will not be a party to the contract in the articles and so will not be able to raise the breach of the articles as a breach of contract. Although another member might be entitled to challenge the meeting on the grounds of breach of the articles, none might be bothered to do so. And yet failure to give notice of a meeting to all those entitled to it can have serious consequences for the validity of the meeting and what takes place there: see notes 7 and 8 below.

5   *Re Mackenzie & Co Ltd* [1916] 2 Ch 450.
6   Section 370(2). The relevant provisions of Table A are arts 111–116. Article 115 provides that proof of posting is conclusive evidence that the notice was given. This avoids the problem that arises where notices are returned because, for example, shareholders have not told the company of a new address. Cf *Re Thundercrest Ltd* [1995] 1 BCLC 117 at 129–131 noted by Davenport (1995) 111 LQR 193
7   *Smyth v Darley* (1849) 2 HL Cas 789.
8   See Table A, art 39. This covers inadvertently not sending a notice to a member (*Re West Canadian Collieries Ltd* [1962] Ch 370, [1962] 1 All ER 26) but not deliberately not giving someone notice because of a mistaken view that they were not entitled to it (*Musselwhite v CH Musselwhite & Son Ltd* [1962] Ch 964, [1962] 1 All ER 201).
9   This is another way of avoiding the problem highlighted in footnote 6 above where notices are returned undelivered.
10 This section deals with notices of meetings but note that under Table A where, at a general meeting, a person is to be appointed director or re-appointed (unless retiring by rotation) a notice including the person's name, address, nationality and other directorships must be given to all those entitled to notice of the meeting between 7 and 28 days before the meeting: art 77.
11 *MacConnell v E Prill & Co Ltd* [1916] 2 Ch 57.
12 See Table A, art 38. Where the articles of a company distinguish between ordinary and special business, the effect is usually to enable a company to transact the ordinary business of that meeting without any notice of the items of business at all. Thus a company could, simply by giving notice of its annual general meeting, transact any items designated as ordinary business of the annual general meeting.
13 Sections 378(1), (2) and 379A(2).
14 *MacConnell v E Prill & Co Ltd* [1916] 2 Ch 57; *Re Moorgate Mercantile Holdings Ltd* [1980] 1 All ER 40, [1980] 1 WLR 227; *Re Willaire Systems plc* [1987] BCLC 67, CA.
15 Section 376(3).

of any resolution[16]. This rule has been made statutory for meetings of members and creditors considering a scheme of arrangement[17] and the obligation in such cases extended to require the disclosure of any interests held by trustees for debenture holders[18]. The Jenkins Committee thought that the whole topic of the contents of notices of meetings should be the subject of a general provision declaratory of the existing law to 'serve as a reminder to directors and other officers of duties of which they may not be fully aware', but no such provision has been enacted[19].

Special notice

Three types of resolution referred to in the Companies Act require what is called special notice. This means that the persons intending to move such a resolution must give *to the company* at least 28 days' notice before the meeting at which the resolution is to be moved[20]. The company must then give notice of the resolution to the members at the same time, and in the same manner, as the notice of the meeting. If that is not practicable, for example because notices of the meeting have already been sent out, the company must give notice either by advertisement or in any other mode allowed by the articles in which case the notice must be given at least 21 days before the meeting[1]. The three types of resolution for which special notice are needed are:

(1)   to remove a director by ordinary resolution[2];
(2)   to appoint an auditor in certain circumstances or to remove an auditor from office[3]; and
(3)   to allow a director to serve beyond retiring age[4].

CIRCULARS

Besides sending a notice of meeting to the members, the directors have a common law duty to give members such explanations and additional information as may be necessary to understand the implications of any proposed transactions. Provided the directors honestly believe that the policy they are promoting is in the best interests of the company, they will be entitled to exhort members to vote in support of the board and to pay for any circulars or advertisements involved out of company funds[5].

The ability to use the machinery and money of the company to make their views known to the members places the directors in a strong position compared to that of members who are critical of the board's policy. In order to help critics get their views

---

16   *Kaye v Croydon Tramways Co* [1898] 1 Ch 358, CA; *Tiessen v Henderson* [1899] 1 Ch 861; *Baillie v Oriental Telephone and Electric Co Ltd* [1915] 1 Ch 503, CA.
17   Section 426(2).
18   Section 426(4).
19   Report of the Company Law Committee (Cmnd 1749), paras 465–467. The proposal was included in the Companies Bill 1973, cl 74.
20   Section 379(1). The company might try and invalidate the notice by convening a meeting to take place in less than 28 days so it is provided that if this is done, notice shall be deemed to have been properly given: s 379(3).
1   Section 379(2). *Fenning v Fenning Environmental Products Ltd* [1982] LS Gaz R 803. But notice that the section cannot be used as a way of enabling members to have a resolution they wish to propose notified to all members: *Pedley v Inland Waterways Association Ltd* [1977] 1 All ER 209.
2   Section 303(2).
3   Sections 388(3) and 391A(1).
4   Section 293(5).
5   *Peel v London and North Wester Rly Co* [1907] 1 Ch 5, CA; *Campbell v Australian Mutual Provident Society* (1908) 77 LJPC 117.

across, there is a provision whereby a certain proportion of members can require the company to circulate a statement not exceeding 1,000 words relating to the business of a meeting[6]. The proportion of members supporting the requisition must either represent not less than 5% of the total voting rights or be not less than 100 members holding shares in the company on which an average of at least of £100 per member is paid up[7]. The requisition must reach the company at least one week before the meeting and the company may require the requisitionists to deposit a sum reasonably sufficient to meet the company's expenses[8]. The company will then be obliged to circulate the statement to all members entitled to notice of meetings in the same manner and at the same time as the notice of meeting (a crucial provision if the members are to hear the critics' views before they send in their proxies) or as soon as practicable thereafter[9]. The word limit and the fact that the critics can be required to pay the company's expenses mean that they are still at a considerable disadvantage compared to the board of directors. Whether, if the critics are ultimately successful and their policy is accepted as being in the best interests of the company, they are entitled to be reimbursed by the company is as yet undecided but there are at least two US decisions supporting the view that they are[10]. It may sometimes happen that an argument as to the policy to be adopted by a company results from a split in the boardroom itself. Although in such a case boards of directors normally act by majority decision, it is arguable that both sets of directors have a duty to advise shareholders on what they honestly believe to be the best interests of the company and are therefore entitled to spend the company's money in doing so.

PROXIES

One reason why the circulars sent to members are so important is that if members vote at all, they are far more likely to do so via the proxy voting machinery than to attend in person at the meeting and vote there. The information members receive before the meeting will be crucial therefore in persuading them to vote in a particular way. In fact, as we shall see, the proxy voting machinery may further reinforce the advantage held by the board in seeking support for their policy.

The term 'proxy' refers both to the instrument of appointment and to the person so appointed. Any member of a company with a share capital may appoint a proxy who need not be a member of the company[11] and any notice calling a meeting of such a company must include a statement of this right.[12] The board of directors could try and prevent the opposition case being heard if it could require proxies to be returned to the company before the opposition has had a chance to mobilise. To prevent this, it is provided that any provision requiring proxies to be returned to the company more than 48 hours before the meeting is void[13]. The Companies Act does not require companies to send out proxy forms but the Stock Exchange does require listed companies to do

---

6   Section 376(1)(b).
7   Section 376(2).
8   Section 377(1).
9   Section 377(3)–(5).
10 *Steinberg v Adams* 90 F Supp 604 (1950); *Rosenfield v Fairchild Engine and Airplane Corpn* 309 NY 168 (1955).
11 Section 372(1). The Jenkins Committee recommended extending the right to appoint proxies to companies without a share capital: Report of the Company Law Committee (Cmnd 1749), para 462. Despite being included in the Companies Bill 1973, cl 75(1) this has not been enacted.
12 Section 372(3).
13 Section 372(5).

so and they must be two-way proxies giving shareholders the equal opportunity to vote for or against resolutions[14]. It is perfectly permissible, provided directors honestly believe this is in the best interests of the company, to use the company's money to pay for the cost of sending out and returning proxy forms, even if they only invite members to appoint one of the directors to vote in favour of the board's policy[15]. The only control over this is that if invitations to appoint proxies are issued at the company's expense, they must be sent to every member entitled to notice of and to vote by proxy at the meeting[16]. The directors cannot just send invitations to those people they think will support them.

Proxies have the right to attend all meetings[17] but they may vote on a show of hands only if the articles permit[18]. They may, however, always vote on a poll and may be counted towards any minimum demand necessary for a poll[19]. In a private company, proxies have the same right to speak as the appointing member but in a public company the right to speak will depend on the articles[20]. If the appointment of a proxy is an entirely gratuitous transaction, the proxy will not, however, be under any duty to the appointing member actually to vote. The authority to vote in a particular way by implication excludes any authority to vote in a different way but does not impart an obligation actually to attend and vote. It will be different if the proxy is under a contractual obligation or an equitable obligation arising from a fiduciary duty, and it may be that where proxies are given to the chairman of a meeting, part of the chairman's duty of ensuring that the will of the meeting is heard entails exercising proxies vested in the chairman[1].

A proxy appointment is conditional on the member not attending the meeting in person and if the member does so the proxy is ineffective[2]. A proxy may also be determined at any time[3], and will be determined automatically in certain circumstances[4]. Since this may happen without the company or other shareholders being aware of it, it is common for the articles to provide that despite any determination of authority, a vote cast by a proxy shall be valid unless the company has been notified in writing before the meeting, adjourned meeting or time appointed for taking a poll[5]. Such provision will not affect the position as between the member and the proxy, but it will protect the company if it treats as valid a vote cast by a proxy whose authority, unknown

---

14   Listing Rules 9.26 and 13.28.
15   *Peel v London and North Western Rly Co* [1907] 1 Ch 5, CA. The importance of whether the company supplies proxy voting cards and whether they are pre-paid is illustrated by Midgley (1974) 114 Lloyds Bank Review 24. He found one company where reply-paid proxies had produced an average of 1,700 returns each year; when no cards were supplied only one proxy was submitted and when proxy cards were supplied but not pre-paid, 300 were returned. The resistance of shareholders to paying to return proxies is illustrated by another company where proxies were not pre-paid and although 820 were returned, 343 shareholders had failed to put a stamp on! It is not obvious that companies should supply pre-paid proxy cards. As Midgley points out, most business is routine and non-contentious and is decided by a show of hands without the proxy votes ever even being looked at.
16   Section 372(6).
17   Section 372(1).
18   Section 372(2). Table A does not permit proxies to vote on a show of hands: see art 59.
19   Section 372(2). Where a poll is taken on a procedural motion, a proxy will be entitled to vote: *Re Waxed Papers Ltd* [1937] 2 All ER 481, CA.
20   Section 372(1).
1   *Second Consolidation Trust Ltd v Ceylon Amalgamated Tea and Rubber Estates Ltd* [1943] 2 All ER 567 at 570.
2   *Cousins v International Brick Co Ltd* [1931] 2 Ch 90, CA.
3   Unless the proxy has been given to protect some interest of the appointee, for example where share certificates are deposited as security for a loan.
4   For example by the death of the member.
5   See Table A, art 63.

to the company, had ended. Such a clause does not, however, prevent a member from attending and voting in person, in which case the company must count the member's votes and not the proxy's[6].

Corporate representatives

A corporation as an artificial legal person obviously cannot attend meetings in person. It could appoint a proxy but as we have seen proxies are subject to various disabilities compared to members attending in person[7]. So the Companies Act provides for the directors or other governing body of corporate members to appoint representatives who can exercise all the powers of individual members[8]. Appointments may be made in respect of meetings of members, classes of members or creditors (including debenture holders) and, unlike the appointment of a proxy, at least under Table A articles, they do not need to be notified to the company holding the meeting[9].

QUORUM

For business to be validly transacted at a meeting the meeting must be quorate. Unless the articles provide otherwise, the quorum for a company is two members[10] personally present[11] but it is common to provide that two members present in person or by proxy will suffice[12]. The question has arisen whether the latter formulation allows one member holding a proxy from another member, or one person holding proxies from two different members, to constitute a quorate meeting. The answer has always been 'no', because of the common law rule that there must be at least two people present for a meeting to take place at all[13] and that one person's presence on behalf of two people does not

---

6   *Cousins v International Brick Co Ltd* [1931] 2 Ch 90, CA.
7   For example they cannot normally vote on a show of hands or speak at meetings of public companies.
8   Section 375. Representatives can, for example, be counted towards a quorum: *Re Kelantan Coconut Estates Ltd and Reduced* [1920] WN 274; see also Table A, art 40. A corporate shareholder may only appoint one representative which creates a problem for a company which is nominee for many different beneficial owners because it will be unable to reflect the views of different beneficial owners. The representative could attend as proxy for each beneficial owner, in which case it could reflect the different instructions of beneficial owners but suffers the disadvantages of being unable to vote on a show of hands or speak at meetings of public companies. This has the led to suggestions that either corporate shareholders should be permitted to appoint more than one representative or the restrictions on proxies should be repealed: DTI Consultative Document *Shareholder Communications at the Annual General Meeting* Section 4 (1996) URN 96/685.
9   See *Maori Development Corpn Ltd v Power Beat International Ltd* [1995] 2 NZLR 568 where this point was critical.
10   Except that in a private limited company having only one member, one member present in person or by proxy shall be a quorum: s 370A.
11   Section 370(4). Although there is no specific provision that only members with votes at the meeting may be counted towards the quorum, it has been described as 'a practical absurdity' if members without votes could be counted, per Kekewich J in *Young v South African and Australian Exploration and Development Syndicate* [1896] 2 Ch 268 at 277. Under Table A, only members entitled to vote can be counted towards the quorum: art 40.
12   See Table A, art 40.
13   There seems to be no reason why the two people present need to be in each other's presence physically. It has been recognised that for a meeting everyone does not need to be face to face; it suffices if electronically they can hear and be heard and see and be seen by the others attending: *Byng v London Life Association Ltd* [1990] Ch 170 at 183, [1989] 1 All ER 560 at 565, CA. In that case there was more than one person in each room but the principle should enable a meeting to take place between persons none of whom is in the same room.

suffice[14]. It ought to be possible for a company's articles to exclude the common law rule and to provide instead that one person can constitute a meeting and to provide for a quorum of one[15]. This would not only avoid problems of dual capacity but also remove one of the devices whereby the minority can thwart the wishes of the majority[16]. If, on the other hand, the articles provide for a quorum of *more* than two members present in person or by proxy, it is thought that, provided there were at least two people present to constitute a meeting at common law, any person present could be counted for the purposes of the quorum as representing the number of members for whom that person held proxies[17].

At common law, if a meeting becomes inquorate, it is dissolved but Table A provides[18] that in such circumstances, or, if the quorum has not been reached within 30 minutes of the time when the meeting should have started, it stands adjourned to the same day of the following week at the same time and place or to such time and place as the directors decide[19]. Finally, it should be noted that at a class meeting in connection with the variation of class rights, the quorum at such a meeting, other than an adjourned meeting, is two persons holding or representing by proxy one-third in nominal value of the issued shares of the class[20]. At an adjourned meeting, the quorum is one person holding shares of the class in question present in person or by proxy[1]. Since it is perfectly possible for one member to hold the whole of one class of shares, references to class meetings must be construed accordingly and it has been held that a member holding all the shares in one class may constitute a valid meeting[2].

CHAIRMAN

Unless the articles make provision for the appointment of a chairman of the meeting the members may elect one of their number to be chairman[3]. Table A provides for the chairman of the board of directors or, in his absence, some other director nominated by the directors to be chairman at general meetings[4]. If the chairman or any such nominee is more than 15 minutes late, or unwilling to act, then the directors present may elect one of their number to be chairman[5]. If no director is willing or they are all more than 15 minutes late then the members present and entitled to vote may appoint one of themselves chairman[6].

---

14   *Sharp v Dawes* (1876) 2 QBD 26, CA where the only member to turn up took the chair and having conducted the meeting resolved 'that a vote of thanks be given to the chairman'! *Re Sanitary Carbon Co* [1877] WN 223; *Re Prain & Sons Ltd* 1947 SC 325; *Re M J Shanley Contracting Ltd (in voluntary liquidation)* (1989) 124 Sol Jo 239.
15   But in *Re Prain & Sons Ltd* 1947 SC 325 it was stated obiter that this would not be possible.
16   See cases cited at p 312 footnote 1, above.
17   See *Re Neil M'Leod & Sons Ltd, Petitioners* 1967 SC 16.
18   Table A, art 41.
19   As to the exercise of the directors' discretion, see p 319, below.
20   Section 125(6)(a).
1   Ibid.
2   *East v Bennett Bros Ltd* [1911] 1 Ch 163; *Re RMCA Reinsurance Ltd* [1994] BCC 378.
3   Section 370(5).
4   Table A, art 42.
5   Ibid.
6   Table A, art 43.

ADJOURNMENTS

One of the questions most likely to land the chairman in controversy is that of adjourning the meeting. At common law, the power to dissolve or adjourn meetings rests with the members[7]. However, the chairman has power to do so where it is impracticable for the members to pass a resolution. This has been held to apply where unruly conduct prevented the continuation of business[8]. It has also been applied where a meeting was unable to proceed to business at all because the venue was not large enough for all those entitled to attend to take part in the debate and to vote[9]. More mundanely, it also allows the chairman to suspend a meeting where a poll has been demanded on a motion to adjourn and the poll cannot be taken forthwith[10]. The chairman is not prevented from exercising this common law power by a provision in the articles authorising the chairman to adjourn 'with the consent of the meeting'. Such a power can only apply where it is practicable to obtain the consent of the meeting and therefore does not exclude the chairman's common law power where it is impracticable to obtain such consent[11]. Even where the articles empower the chairman to dissolve or adjourn meetings with the consent of the meeting, it has been held that the chairman may refuse to do so even against the wishes of the meeting[12]. Hence it is common to provide that the chairman is not only empowered to adjourn the meeting with its consent, but is also obliged to do so if the meeting directs[13].

In exercising the common law power a chairman must not only act in good faith but must act reasonably in the light of the purposes for which the power exists[14]. At a company meeting a member is entitled not only to vote but also to hear and be heard in the debate. Accordingly, the impact of the proposed adjournment on those seeking to attend the original meeting and the other members must be a central factor in considering the validity of the chairman's decision to adjourn[15].

MINUTES

Minutes of all proceedings at general meetings must be entered in books kept for the purpose[16] and members have statutory rights to inspect and to request copies of them[17].

7   *National Dwellings Society v Sykes* [1894] 3 Ch 159.
8   *John v Rees* [1970] Ch 345, [1969] 2 All ER 274. Megarry J's decision was that the disorder was not sufficient to warrant an adjournment. 'Certainly there was noise, disorder, and, in a few cases, bodily contact; but whatever affronts to dignity there may have been, there was nothing that could really be called violence:' at 383, 294.
9   *Byng v London Life Association Ltd* [1990] Ch 170, [1989] 1 All ER 560, CA. The cinema at which the meeting was to take place could accommodate 300. Over 800 turned up and when one of the doors of the cinema was forced open it let in a 'muted roar' from the foyer!
10   *Jackson v Hamlyn* [1953] Ch 577, [1953] 1 All ER 887.
11   *Byng v London Life Association Ltd*, note 9 above.
12   *Salisbury Gold Mining Co Ltd v Hathorn* [1897] AC 268, PC.
13   See Table A, art 45, which also provides that if a meeting is adjourned for 14 days or more, fresh notices must be served, whereas at common law no notice of an adjourned meeting is necessary: *Wills v Murray* (1850) 4 Exch 843.
14   *Byng v London Life Association Ltd*, note 9 above, at 188–191, 569–571. Quaere whether any such requirement of reasonableness applies to adjournment decisions taken by the meeting itself.
15   *Byng v London Life Association Ltd*, note 9 above, it was held not reasonable to adjourn to a larger venue two hours later when the chairman knew that several members would be unable to attend, despite the fact that had the meeting begun on time and merely carried on into the afternoon the same members would presumably be unable to stay. This decision is probably, therefore, restricted to cases where the meeting as originally convened was unable to proceed to business. In such a case a member is effectively denied any opportunity to attend any part of the meeting.
16   Section 382(1).
17   Section 383.

If the minutes are signed by the chairman of that meeting or of the next succeeding meeting they constitute evidence of the proceedings[18] and where minutes have been duly made, it raises a rebuttable presumption that the meeting was properly convened, that all proceedings were properly conducted and all appointments of directors, managers or liquidators valid[19].

RESOLUTIONS

There are four types of resolution referred to in the Act: ordinary, extraordinary, special and elective.

Ordinary resolutions

An ordinary resolution, apart from being specified on certain occasions, will also suffice whenever the Act does not specify any other type of resolution or require any particular majority. It is passed by a simple majority of votes cast in person or by proxy. There are no particular requirements as to notice of an ordinary resolution. Amendments at the meeting are therefore permissible provided they fall within the scope of the notice of the original resolution and are not such as would have caused any member to decide differently about attending the meeting[20].

Extraordinary and special resolutions

An extraordinary or a special resolution is passed by a majority of not less than 75% of the votes cast in person or by proxy at a general meeting of which notice specifying the intention to propose the resolution as an extraordinary or special resolution was given[1]. The difference between them is that in the case of a special resolution at least 21 days' notice of the meeting must have been given[2]; for an extraordinary resolution no special period of notice is required so it will be 21 days or 14 days according to whether the meeting is an annual or an extraordinary general meeting. Since in the case of an extraordinary general meeting, the requirement for 14 days' notice can be waived by a sufficient majority of members and the same majority can waive the 21-day period required for a meeting at which a special resolution is to be passed[3], it will be apparent there is today very little difference between extraordinary and special resolutions. Before 1929 there was a considerable difference because a special resolution had to be confirmed by a separate meeting but since that requirement was repealed there is now no justification for keeping extraordinary resolutions and the

---

18 Section 382(2).
19 Section 382(4).
20 *Choppington Collieries Ltd v Johnson* [1944] 1 All ER 762, CA.
1   Section 378(1) and (2). These sub-sections refer to a three-quarters majority of members who vote but they have been drafted on the basis of a show of hands. On a poll, the appropriate majority is three-quarters of the votes cast: s 378(5).
2   Section 378(2).
3   Section 369(3) and (4) and s 378(2).

Jenkins Committee recommended their replacement by special resolutions[4]. Because notice must be given of the resolution where it is to be proposed as either an extraordinary or special resolution, it has been held that no amendment which will alter the substance of the resolution can be allowed at the meeting[5]. What will be permitted are corrections to grammatical or clerical errors, reducing the words of the notice into formal language or reducing it into the form of a new text but provided in each case that the substance remains identical[6].

Elective resolutions

An elective resolution is a procedure by which a private company can disapply certain Companies Act requirements. The idea originated in a report from the Institute of Directors[7] suggesting that shareholders could be permitted to dispense with certain formalities and requirements where this would not affect creditors or other outside parties. At present there are five provisions which private companies can elect to disapply[8], although the Secretary of State has power to extend elective resolutions to cover other areas of internal administration or procedure[9]. Eventually it may be possible to pass a single resolution adopting the entire deregulation package or 'elective regime'[10] but for the time being separate elective resolutions are needed to disapply each provision.

The key principle governing shareholders' decisions to opt for a more deregulated regime is that unanimous consent is required: an elective resolution therefore requires that all the members entitled to attend and vote at the meeting must agree, either in person or by proxy[11]. At least 21 days' notice in writing must be given of the meeting, stating that an elective resolution is to be proposed and stating the terms of the resolution[12]. Companies do not need any authority in their articles to pass elective resolutions and an elective resolution overrides any contrary provision in the articles[13]. An elective resolution may be revoked by an ordinary resolution[14].

4   Report of the Company Law Committee (Cmnd 1749), para 461. The nearest this came to implementation was inclusion in the Companies Bill 1973, cl 77(4).
5   *Re Moorgate Mercantile Holdings Ltd* [1980] 1 All ER 40, [1980] 1 WLR 227.
6   Ibid at 54 and 242; *Re Willaire Systems plc* [1987] BCLC 67, CA.
7   'Deregulation for Small Private Companies' (1986).
8   Section 379A(1). They relate to (i) the duration of authority to issue shares, (ii) dispensing with laying accounts before a general meeting, (iii) dispensing with an annual general meeting, (iv) reducing the majority needed to consent to short notice of meetings, (v) dispensing with the annual appointment of auditors.
9   Companies Act 1989, s 117.
10 As the Institute of Directors suggested it should be called.
11 Section 379A(2)(b). It follows that although the new regime is available to all private companies in practice it will be closely-held private companies and wholly-owned subsidiaries which will benefit from it most. A measure of deregulation already existed before the Companies Act 1989 in that private companies were able to exclude the provisions governing new issue pre-emption rights (s 91), provide financial assistance in the acquisition of shares in the company (s 155) and redeem or purchase shares in the company out of capital (s 171). Ironically these provisions are of far greater significance for shareholders than those that can be disapplied by elective resolutions and yet only a special resolution is required in these cases: ss 91(1), 155(4), (5) and 173(2).
12 Section 379A(2)(a). The members entitled to attend and vote at the meeting can unanimously agree to waive the 21 days' notice: s 379A(2A). An elective resolution may also be passed by unanimous written resolution: s 381A(1), (6).
13 Section 379A(5).
14 Section 379A(3).

REGISTRATION OF RESOLUTIONS

Certain resolutions or agreements then need to be registered with the Registrar of Companies. This involves the company forwarding a copy of the resolution or agreement to the Registrar within 15 days of it being passed or entered into, which the Registrar then records[15]. This requirement applies to all elective, special and extraordinary resolutions[16] and any resolution or agreement agreed to by all the members which would otherwise have had to be passed as a special or extraordinary resolution[17]. It also applies to any resolution or agreement of a class of members which has the effect of binding all the members of the class even though some may not have agreed to it[18]. Registration is also required of ordinary resolutions in seven circumstances: voluntary winding up[19]; increasing the authorised share capital[20]; giving, varying, revoking or renewing authority to the directors to issue shares[1]; making a market purchase of the company's own shares[2]; approving certain acquisitions from subscribers to the company's memorandum of associations[3]; revoking an elective resolution[4]; or treating a meeting called by the Secretary of State as the annual general meeting[5]. Failure to register gives rise to criminal penalties[6] but does not make the resolution invalid although the company may be prevented from relying on the passing of certain resolutions against other persons until they are officially notified which process includes registration[7].

VOTING

The normal practice in company meetings is for a vote to be taken first on a show of hands and then, if a valid demand is made, for a poll to be held. The difference is crucial because on a show of hands each member present will have one vote irrespective of the number of shares held[8]; on a poll, members can cast all the votes attached to all the shares they own[9]. A poll therefore will be a far more accurate reflection of the voting strength among the members. It is also provided that, on a show of hands, a proxy cannot vote unless the articles allow this[10] and even if a proxy is allowed to vote on a show of hands the proxy can record only one vote even though acting as proxy for more than one member[11]. On a poll, a proxy may always vote, a right which

---

15   Section 380(1).
16   Section 380(4)(a) (b) and (bb).
17   Section 380(4)(c).
18   Section 380(4)(d).
19   Section 380(4)(j).
20   Section 123(3).
1   Section 380(4)(f).
2   Section 380(4)(h),
3   Section 111(2).
4   Section 380(4)(bb).
5   Section 367(4). Four resolutions of the board of directors also require registration: s 380(4)(e), (g) (k) and (l).
6   Sections 380(5), 123(4), 111(4) and 367(5).
7   Section 42.
8   See Table A, art 54.
9   The number of votes carried by each share on a poll depends on the memorandum or articles of association or the terms on which the shares were issued but if no other provision is made each share is presumed to carry one vote: s 370(6). See also Table A, art 54.
10   Section 372(2)(c). Table A, art 54 does not allow proxies to vote on a show of hands.
11   *Ernest v Loma Gold Mines Ltd* [1897] 1 Ch 1, CA.

cannot be excluded by the articles[12]. Furthermore, on a poll members or proxies may split their votes so that they may vote in favour, and against, and abstain on the same resolution, a power which enables proxies or nominee shareholders representing more than one beneficial owner to reflect accurately their instructions[13].

Because of the potential for different results on a show of hands, and a poll, the right to demand a poll is very important. At common law, any member could demand a poll when the result of a show of hands was declared[14] but the articles could exclude or limit that right[15]. The Act therefore now provides[16] that notwithstanding anything in the articles, except on a resolution to elect a chairman or to adjourn the meeting, a poll must be held if demanded by any of the following: not less than five members having a right to vote at the meeting[17]; members holding not less than 10% of all voting rights that could be cast at the meeting; members holding shares conferring a right to vote at the meeting on which the aggregate sum paid up equals not less than 10% of the total sum paid up on all such shares. Under Table A, the minimum number of members who may demand a poll is reduced from five to two[18]. It is also provided that the chairman may demand a poll[19], a right which must be exercised to give effect to the real sense of the meeting so that the chairman must demand a poll if there is any reason to believe the result on a poll would differ from the result on a show of hands[20]. Table A also permits a poll on the election of a chairman and the adjournment of a meeting[1] and allows a demand for a poll to be made before any show of hands[2], thus permitting a show of hands to be dispensed with[3]. Finally the Act provides that proxies may always join in the demand for a poll[4] and logically proxies should be able to count for this purpose as representing as many members as they hold proxies for.

The articles of association will usually empower the chairman to direct how a poll is to be conducted, and when[5]. If the meeting is adjourned for a poll to be held then an article allowing proxies to be lodged 'before a meeting or adjourned meeting' will allow further proxies to be lodged. But if the meeting is not adjourned but the holding of the poll merely deferred, such an article will not allow further proxies to be lodged[6] and hence Table A is now drafted so as to allow proxies to be deposited with the company 'not less than 24 hours before the time appointed for the taking of the poll'[7].

12 Section 372(1).
13 Section 373(3).
14 *R v Wimbledon Local Board* (1882) 8 QBD 459, CA.
15 See for example the articles of association in *Punt v Symons & Co Ltd* [1902] 2 Ch 506 which provided that a poll could only be demanded by at least five members.
16 Section 373(1). On a resolution in connection with an off-market purchase of a company's own shares any one member may demand a poll: s 164(5)(b). Note also that at a class meeting in connection with the variation of class rights, any holder of shares of that class present in person or by proxy may demand a poll: s 125(6)(b).
17 This would have enabled the majority to demand a poll in *Punt & Symons & Co Ltd* above note 15 , and thus prevented the problem in that case arising.
18 Table A, art 46.
19 Ibid.
20 *Second Consolidated Trust Ltd v Ceylon Amalgamated Tea and Rubber Estates Ltd* [1943] 2 All ER 567.
1 Table A, art 51.
2 Table A, art 46.
3 Per Jenkins LJ in *Holmes v Lord Keyes* [1959] Ch 199 at 212, [1958] 2 All ER 129 at 136, CA.
4 Section 373(2).
5 See Table A, arts 49, 51 and 52. It seems likely, at any rate under articles which say 'votes may be given either personally or by proxy' as Table A, art 59 does, that it is not open to the chairman to direct that a postal ballot be held: cf *McMillan v Le Roi Mining Co Ltd* [1906] 1 Ch 331.
6 *Shaw v Tati Concessions Ltd* [1913] 1 Ch 292; *Jackson v Hamlyn* [1953] Ch 577, [1953] 1 All ER 887.
7 Table A, art 62(b). This applies in the case of a poll taken more than 48 hours after it was demanded; otherwise the proxy must be delivered at the meeting at which the poll was demanded: art 62(c).

At common law, members may vote on a poll even though they did not attend and were not represented at the original meeting[8].

If the show of hands or poll results in a tie, then at common law such a result stands[9] but articles commonly give a casting vote to the chairman in such circumstances in addition to any vote he or she may be entitled to as a member[10]. It is also common for articles to attempt to reduce so far as possible uncertainty attending the result of a vote. Thus Table A provides that no objection may be made to the qualification of any voter except at the meeting at which the vote is tendered[11]. If no objection is made, or it is overruled, then the vote is valid. This ties in with the common law rule that if no objection is taken to a form of proxy before the proxy votes are cast, although it may be possible to object to the proxy afterwards, the votes themselves are valid[12]. Under Table A, any objection which is made is referred to the chairman whose decision is final and conclusive[13] and can only be challenged on the grounds of fraud or misconduct[14]. The possibility of uncertainty over the result of a show of hands is particularly acute. As regards special or extraordinary resolutions, the Act itself therefore provides that, unless a poll is demanded, the declaration of the chairman shall be conclusive evidence of the result[15], with the effect that it can only be challenged on the grounds of fraud[16] or that it is wrong on the face of it[17]. Table A extends this principle to ordinary resolutions by providing that unless a poll is demanded, a declaration of the result of a show of hands plus an entry to that effect in the minutes shall be conclusive evidence of the result of the vote[18].

WRITTEN AND INFORMAL RESOLUTIONS

In the case of companies with a small number of members, the reality of how members decide matters may not reflect very closely the technical requirements of meetings and resolutions outlined above. Provided all the members know about and agree to a decision that is within the capacity of the company, then it is sensible to treat that as binding on the members and the company even though the formal requirements for passing resolutions have not been complied with. This is recognised by an express provision in Table A that a resolution in writing signed by all the members entitled to notice of and to attend and vote at general meetings shall be as effectual as if the resolution had been passed at a general meeting[19].

---

8   *R v D'Oyly* (1849) 12 Ad & El 139.
9   But a chairman who has not yet cast any vote to which he or she may be entitled as a member may do so to resolve a tie: *Nell v Longbottom* [1894] 1 QB 767.
10   See Table A, art 50.
11   Table A, art 58.
12   *Colonial Gold Reef Ltd v Free State Rand Ltd* [1914] 1 Ch 382; *Marx v Estates and General Investments Ltd* [1975] 3 All ER 1064, [1976] 1 WLR 380.
13   Table A, art 58.
14   *Wall v London and Northern Assets Corpn* [1899] 1 Ch 550; *Wall v Exchange Investment Corpn* [1926] Ch 143, CA.
15   Section 378(4).
16   *Re Hadleigh Castle Gold Mines Ltd* [1900] 2 Ch 419; *Arnot v United African Lands Ltd* [1901] 1 Ch 518, CA.
17   *Re Caratal (New) Mines Ltd* [1902] 2 Ch 498.
18   Table A, art 47. See *Kerr v John Mottram Ltd* [1940] Ch 657, [1940] 2 All ER 629.
19   Table A, art 53.

But the common law has developed the principle further, without any need for written resolutions. If it is shown that all the members know of and acquiesce in a decision, they and the company will be bound[20]. At first the principle depended on the members actually having met together[1] but this is no longer necessary provided all of them know of and agree to the decision[2]. As with written resolutions, it will be sufficient if only those members with the right to attend and vote at meetings consent, unless the matter to be decided is one where the Act specifies that others must be notified as well. Thus a payment to a director under s 312 must be disclosed to all members including, therefore, non-voting preference shareholders and will not be valid just because the voting shareholders know of and agree to it[3].

In an interesting article[4] Ross Grantham explains the unanimous consent rule as reflecting "the assumption that there is between the company and its shareholders such a unity of interest and ownership that the company can be identified with its shareholders. Once this premise is recognised it follows quite naturally that the law should give effect to the plainly expressed will of the shareholders however that will is expressed."[5] This explains why the same rule does not apply to decisions by the board of directors.[6] It also suggests the doctrine should be approached with more caution where the unanimous consent of the shareholders is to the ratification of a decision which constitutionally it is for the board of directors to make.[7]

The principle of unanimous agreement, whether written or informal, has several times been held to bind the company in matters which would otherwise need to be passed by special or extraordinary resolution. Although under s 380(4)(c) such resolutions or agreements should be registered, failure to register does not make them invalid though in certain cases it may prevent the company relying on them against other parties[8]. The principle of unanimous assent is non-controversial where it merely cures a procedural irregularity in the passing of a special or extraordinary resolution[9]. It becomes more complicated where the agreement is to do something for which the

---

20   *Re Express Engineering Works Ltd* [1920] 1 Ch 466, CA. Acquiescence in a procedural irregularity may be inferred in certain circumstances from a failure to use an opportunity to object (*Re Bailey, Hay & Co Ltd* [1971] 3 All ER 693, [1971] 1 WLR 1357) but not where the irregularity could mislead or prejudice the members concerned (*Imperial Bank of China, India and Japan v Bank of Hindustan, China and Japan* (1868) LR 6 Eq 91).

1   *Re George Newman & Co* [1895] 1 Ch 674, CA; *Re Lee, Behrens & Co Ltd* [1932] 2 Ch 46.

2   *Parker & Cooper Ltd v Reading* [1926] Ch 975; *Re Duomatic Ltd* [1969] 2 Ch 365, [1969] 1 All ER 161; *Re Halt Garage (1964) Ltd* [1982] 3 All ER 1016.

3   *Re Duomatic Ltd* [1969] 2 Ch 265, [1969] 1 All ER 161.

4   "The Unanimous Consent Rule in Company Law" [1993] CLJ 245.

5   Ibid p 258.

6   Ibid pp 254–256.

7   Ibid p 271.

8   Section 42(1).

9   *Re Oxted Motor Co Ltd* [1921] 3 KB 32 (failure to give notice that resolution to be proposed as an extraordinary resolution); *Re Pearce, Duff & Co Ltd* [1960] 3 All ER 222, [1960] 1 WLR 1014 (notice one day short); *Re Bailey, Hay & Co Ltd* [1971] 3 All ER 693, [1971] 1 WLR 1357 (notice one day short). Grantham [1993] CLJ 245 at pp 253–254 explains that unanimous, as opposed to majority, consent is needed in relation to waiving the formalities of meetings because notice of the meeting, the right to vote and the right to influence the views of others, are personal rights of each shareholder. Once these personal rights are waived the principle of majority rule should prevail as regards the substance of the matter decided. Thus in *Re Bailey, Hay & Co Ltd*, above where two shareholders abstained on a resolution to put the company into liquidation for which insufficient notice had been given it was correct for the court to find that the abstainers waived the insufficient notice point but arguably not necessary to find that they had also thereby agreed to the winding-up: see Grantham ibid p 253 fn 55.

Act prescribes a special or extraordinary resolution, and no such resolution has been proposed, let alone passed. One approach is to treat a unanimous agreement among shareholders, whether written or informal, as taking effect as a special or extraordinary resolution; alternatively unanimous agreement is sometimes regarded as a separate means by which shareholders can make decisions which would otherwise require to be made by special or extraordinary resolutions.[10] The latter approach was the one adopted in *Cane v Jones*[11] where the court held that a unanimous written agreement had the effect of altering the articles notwithstanding that no special resolution had been passed. The provision in the Companies Act that "a company may by special resolution alters its articles"[12] was held not to mean that the articles could *only* be altered by special resolution – rather it laid down a procedure whereby *some only* of the shareholders could validly alter the articles.

This approach works in cases like alteration of the articles where the Act's requirement of a special resolution can be read as being merely facilitative, that is making it possible to do by special or extraordinary resolution what could in any case be done by unanimous agreement. It breaks down, however, where the provision of the Companies Act is constitutive, that is enabling the company to achieve something which would otherwise not be possible even with unanimous consent. An example is alteration of the objects because the Act prohibits a company from altering the conditions in its memorandum "except in the cases, in the mode and to the extent, for which express provision is made by this Act."[13] When, therefore, the Act provides that "A company may by special resolution alter its memorandum with respect to the objects of the company"[14] that is the *only* way in which the objects can be changed. Thus in *Re Home Treat Ltd*[15] where the court accepted that unanimous informal assent of members had the effect of changing the objects it is submitted that that must be on the basis that such assent took effect as a special resolution, that being the only way in which the objects can be altered.[16] It is submitted that this is also the position where a written resolution is passed under Table A, art 53 which says that such resolution shall be as effectual as if it had been passed at a general meeting.[17]

Written resolutions in private companies

Although the procedures for written and informal resolutions discussed above are only likely to be relevant to a company with a small number of members, they are applicable

---

10   See Higginson 'Waiver of Requirements of the Companies Act' (1983) 80 LS Gaz 3085.
11   [1981] 1 All ER 533, [1980] 1 WLR 1451.
12   Section 9(1).
13   Section 2(7).
14   Section 4(1).
15   [1991] BCLC 705.
16   See also *Re Barry Artists Ltd* [1985] BCLC 283 where a unanimous written agreement by shareholders to a reduction of capital must be regarded as taking effect as a special resolution required by s 135(1) because s 135 is constitutive of the company's power to reduce capital, not facilitative.
17   Even this is not certain, however. The 1985 Table A was based on a draft submitted to the DTI by the Law Society and the original draft for what became art 53 contained the further sentence: "If the resolution in writing is described as a special resolution or an extraordinary resolutions it shall have effect accordingly." The DTI dropped the sentence because they did not feel it appropriate to determine in drafting Table A a matter on which differing views were held.

to public as well as private companies. Following a report by the Institute of Directors[18] a statutory procedure for passing unanimous written resolutions in private companies was introduced by the Companies Act 1989. With two exceptions[19] anything which a private company may do by a resolution of a general or class meeting may instead be done by written resolution[20]. The procedure is that a written resolution has to be signed by or on behalf of all members who, at the date of the resolution, would be entitled to attend and vote at such a meeting[1]. The signatures may be on separate documents, provided each sets out the terms of the resolution[2]. Once agreed to in this manner a written resolution is as effective as if it had been passed at the appropriate meeting, although no meeting at all need be held and no previous notice of the resolution need be given[3]. It is specifically provided that this statutory written resolution procedure can be used to pass any sort of resolution, whether ordinary, special, extraordinary or elective[4].

There are two requirements in relation to the statutory written resolutions procedure which do not apply to the procedure under the articles, at least not under Table A, art 53. The first is the requirement that in relation to a company which has auditors, a copy of the proposed resolution must be sent to them or they must be otherwise notified of its contents at or before the time the resolution is supplied to a member for signature.[5] Until 1996 the auditors then had up to seven days to decide if the resolution affected them as auditors and if it did to require the resolution to be put to a meeting. In the meantime the resolution could not take effect. This cumbersome obligation was repealed in 1996[6] and the surviving requirement to give the auditors notice of the resolution simply corresponds to the requirement to give auditors all notices of, and other communications relating to, any general meeting which a member is entitled to receive.[7] It is also clear since the amendments in 1996 that while the company's memorandum and articles cannot exclude or modify the statutory written resolution procedure any provision for a separate written resolution procedure, such as Table A, art 53, remains valid.[8]

The second respect in which the statutory written resolution procedure differs from that under the articles is that statutory written resolutions which have effect as if agreed by the company in general meeting must be recorded in the same way as minutes of a general meeting.[9] This does not apply to written resolutions passed under a procedure laid down by the articles, at least not under Table A, art 53. By their very nature

18 'Deregulation for Small Private Companies' (1986).
19 Schedule 15A, para 1. The exceptions relate to removal of directors or auditors from office before the expiry of their term of office under ss 303 and 391 respectively. The reason for these exceptions is that the director or auditor has the right to make representation at a general meeting of the company: ss 304 and 391(4).
20 In extending to class meetings this is a wider power than conferred by Table A art 53 which does not cover resolutions of class meetings.
1 Section 381A(1).
2 Section 381A(2).
3 Section 381A(1) and (4). Consequential amendments as to formalities needed for valid resolutions in certain cases are set out in Sch 15A, Pt II.
4 Section 381A(6). This therefore avoids the question that arises under unanimous agreement at common law, whether under the articles or the doctrine of acquiescence, of whether such agreement is an alternative to a special or extraordinary resolution or takes effect as a special or extraordinary resolution: see p 326 above.
5 Section 381B(1) as substituted from 19 June 1996.
6 Deregulation (Resolutions of Private Companies) Order 1996 SI 1996 No 1471.
7 Section 390(1)(2).
8 Section 381C.
9 Section 382A.

decisions arrived at through the process of unanimous acquiescence are unlikely to be susceptible to being minuted although where the sole member of a single-member private limited company takes any decision which may be taken by the company in general meeting and has effect as if agreed by the company in general meeting, the member must provide the company with a written record of that decision.[10]

10   Section 382B.

CHAPTER 24

Company officers

DIRECTORS

The business of the company is managed by the directors who are expected to act collectively as a board although the articles of association may also provide for the delegation of extensive powers to smaller committees or individual directors[1]. The proceedings of the board are regulated by the articles which will contain detailed rules covering such matters as voting, the required quorum and the calling of meetings[2]. Minutes must be kept of all board meetings[3].

'Director' as such is not defined in the Companies Act 1985 which provides simply that 'director' includes any person occupying the position of director, by whatever name called[4]. It is possible therefore for someone to be a director though described as a manager or governor. Equally, companies may describe employees as, for example, technical directors, without their occupying the position of director in law.

Appointment

The first directors may be named in the articles but more usually are appointed by the subscribers to the memorandum and named as such in a statement delivered to the registrar of companies on incorporation[5]. Thereafter the power to appoint directors is

---

1   See Table A, arts 70, 72. The powers of the board and of individual directors are discussed in Chapter 25.
2   See Table A, arts 88–89.
3   CA 1985, s 382(1). There is no provision, however, for inspection of such minutes. The minutes of general meetings are available for inspection by any member: s 383(1).
4   Ibid, s 741(1). See Browne-Wilkinson V-C in *Re Lo-Line Electric Motors Ltd* [1988] Ch 477 at 488, [1988] 2 All ER 692 at 699: 'In my judgment the words "by whatever name called" show that the subsection is dealing with nomenclature; for example where the company's articles provide that the conduct of the company is committed to "governors" or "managers".'
5   CA 1985, s 10(2), (3).

commonly vested by the articles in the company in general meeting[6] although the board will have power to fill casual vacancies[7]. Such an appointment is held only until the next following annual general meeting when the appointee can be re-elected[8]. It is not the case that a director must necessarily be an individual and a company may be appointed[9]. Every company must keep at its registered office a register of its directors, giving such details as their names, addresses, nationalities, business occupations, any other directorships held by a director in the preceding five years and their dates of birth[10]. This register must be open to inspection by members of the company, free of charge, and by the public for such fee as may be prescribed[11].

In the case of a public company, each proposed director must be voted on individually unless there is unanimous consent to a block resolution[12]. This is to ensure that shareholders can express their disapproval of any particular director without having to reject the entire board. Failure to comply with this requirement means that the resolution is void[13].

The acts of a director or manager are valid notwithstanding any defect which may afterwards be discovered in his appointment or qualification[14]. This covers the situation where there has been some technical breach of the requirements regarding appointment with the result that the appointment is defective but it does not validate the acts of someone who has never been appointed at all but who simply purports to fill the office of director[15], nor can it assist a party having knowledge of the facts giving rise to the defect or a party who is put on inquiry but does not inquire[16]. In some circumstances, however, the company may still be bound by the acts of a person purporting to fill the office of director[17]. Note also that a company cannot rely against other persons on any change among the company's directors if that change has not been notified in the *London Gazette*[18].

6   Note *Wilton Group plc v Abrams* [1991] BCLC 315, [1990] BCC 310 where board representation was made a contractual term on a sale of shares. The court found such a term objectionable in relation to a public listed company although it accepted that the position would be different in a private company where all the shareholders agreed. Board appointments are a matter for the company, not for the private disposition of vendors and purchasers.

7   See Table A, arts 73–80. A casual vacancy is defined as 'any vacancy not occurring by effluxion of time, that is any vacancy occurring by death, resignation or bankruptcy': *York Tramways Co v Willows* (1882) 8 QBD 685 at 694, per Lord Coleridge CJ.

8   Table A, art 79.

9   *Re Bulawayo Market and Offices Co Ltd* [1907] 2 Ch 458. The register of directors must include the corporate name and registered office of any company holding the office of director: CA 1985, s 289(1)(b).

10   Ibid, ss 288(1), 289(1). The contents of the register are under review: DTI *Disclosure of Directors' and Company Secretaries' Particulars* (1997).

11   Ibid, s 288(3).

12   Ibid, s 292(1).

13   Ibid, s 292(2).

14   Ibid, s 285; and this is so even in the case of an appointment which is void under s 292(2) (appointment of directors of a public company to be voted on individually).

15   *Morris v Kanssen* [1946] AC 459, [1946] 1 All ER 586; *British Asbestos Co Ltd v Boyd* [1903] 2 Ch 439; *Dawson v African Consolidated Land and Travel Co* [1898] 1 Ch 6.

16   See *Re New Cedos Engineering Co Ltd* [1994] 1 BCLC 797 at 812; *British Asbestos Co Ltd v Boyd* [1903] 2 Ch 439.

17   As where the company holds him out to third parties as having authority to act on its behalf, see discussion of authority in Chapter 25.

18   CA 1985, s 42(1). The effect of the section is purely negative. It does not entitle the company to treat the gazetting of an event as notice to all the world: *Official Custodian for Charities v Parway Estates Developments Ltd* [1985] Ch 151, [1984] 3 All ER 679.

Number

A private company need have only one director whereas a public company must have at least two[19]. The number of directors may, from time to time, be increased by ordinary resolution[20].

Age

A person aged 70 or more cannot be appointed, and a person reaching the age of 70 must retire, as a director of a public company or of a private company which is a subsidiary of a public company unless the appointment is or was made or approved by the company in general meeting[1]. These restrictions are all subject to the provisions of the company's articles which may permit the appointment and retention of directors over the age limit[2]. There are no age restrictions in relation to private companies which are not subsidiaries of public companies.

Share qualification

The articles may provide that an individual cannot be appointed as a director unless he holds a certain (usually very small) number of shares in the company. The number required will be determined by the company in general meeting and unless and until so fixed no qualification is required. A share qualification is usually justified on the ground that it ensures that the directors have a personal commitment to the company and its well-being[3]. In fact, managerial commitment is more likely to be ensured by their remuneration packages than by any share qualification requirement designed to induce a sense of 'ownership'.

If the company's articles do impose a share qualification, then the shares must be obtained within two months of the director's appointment or within such shorter time as may be fixed by the articles[4]. The office of director is vacated if the director does not within two months of his appointment (or within such shorter time as may be set by the articles) obtain his qualification; or if, having initially acquired his qualification, the director thereafter ceases to hold the shares[5]. If the company increases the amount of shares to be held, the office of director is not immediately vacated but if the director in question continues as a director, he is deemed to have contracted to acquire the necessary shares within a reasonable time[6]. If a director continues to act despite being unqualified, by virtue of not holding the requisite shareholding, then he is liable to a fine[7].

---

19 CA 1985, s 282; unless the public company was incorporated before 1 November 1929 in which case one director will suffice. Note Table A, art 64 which provides that the number of directors shall be not less than two.

20 See Table A, arts 64, 75, 78, 79.

1   CA 1985, s 293. Special notice must be given of any resolution appointing or approving the appointment of any such director and the notice of the resolution must give the age of the person to whom it relates: s 293(5).

2   Ibid, s 293(7).

3   *Re North Australian Territory Co, Archer's Case* [1892] 1 Ch 322 at 337, per Lindley MR.

4   CA 1985, s 291(1). The two-month period runs from the date of ascertaining the result of the poll electing the director: *Holmes v Lord Keyes* [1959] Ch 199, [1958] 2 All ER 129.

5   CA 1985, s 291(3).

6   *Molineaux v London, Birmingham and Manchester Insurance Co Ltd* [1902] 2 KB 589.

7   CA 1985, s 291(5).

TYPES OF DIRECTOR

As the number of shareholders in a company increases, it is obviously impossible for all to be involved in the management and control of the company's affairs, so a separation will develop between those who own the company (the shareholders) and those who manage it (the directors). Problems can arise from this separation of ownership and control as distance from the day-to-day running of the business makes it difficult for shareholders to deal with incompetent or self-dealing management. In the worst cases, poor management may run the company into insolvency with serious consequences for shareholders, creditors, employees and the economy.

The way in which companies are governed and the relationship between management and shareholders are issues at the heart of the corporate governance debate[8] which has come to prominence in recent years following concerns about declining standards in the wake of the much publicised collapses of companies such as the Maxwell group and Polly Peck.

It is unlikely that any single mechanism can provide an answer to the problems presented by the separation of ownership and control but one area which has been the subject of considerable attention is the composition of the board. In this regard much work has focused on the role of the non-executive director.

As we have seen, the directors are appointed either by the subscribers to the memorandum, the board or by the company in general meeting. These directors may be executive or non-executive directors although neither classification is to be found in the Companies Act 1985. Essentially the executive directors are those directors concerned with the actual management of the company. They will have extensive management powers delegated to them by the articles and will usually also have separate service contracts with the company which together with the articles will delimit their powers and responsibilities[9]. Non-executive directors are more commonly found in larger companies and have an advisory and supervisory role.

Non-executive directors

From the early 1980s onwards there was a growing awareness of the role of non-executive directors and bodies such as PRO NED (then sponsored by the Bank of England, the CBI and the Institutional Shareholders' Committee) had argued for increased use of non-executive directors[10]. But the real impetus in this regard comes from the more recent work of the Cadbury Committee.

THE CADBURY COMMITTEE

In response to the growing concerns about corporate governance, noted above, a Committee on The Financial Aspects of Corporate Governance, chaired by Sir Adrian

---

8   On corporate governance see generally Stapledon *Institutional Shareholders and Corporate Governance* (1996); Sheikh & Rees *Corporate Governance and Corporate Control* (1995); Maw *Maw on Corporate Governance* (1994); Dimsdale & Prevezer (eds) *Capital Markets and Corporate Governance* (1994); Charkham *Keeping Good Company: a study of corporate governance in five countries* (1994); Parkinson, *Corporate Power and Responsibility* (1993); Prentice & Holland (eds) *Contemporary Issues in Corporate Governance* (1993).

9   *Harold Holdsworth & Co (Wakefield) Ltd v Caddies* [1955] 1 All ER 725, [1955] 1 WLR 352.

10   See generally Institutional Shareholders Committee *The Role and Duties of Directors – A Statement of Best Practice* (1991); Association of British Insurers *The Role and Duties of Directors, A Discussion Paper* (1990); Charkham *Corporate Governance and the market for companies: aspects of the shareholders' role* Bank of England Discussion Paper No 44 (1989).

Cadbury, was set up in May 1991 by the Financial Reporting Council, the London Stock Exchange and the accountancy profession. Its terms of reference included, inter alia, to consider and to make recommendations on good practice in respect of the responsibilities of executive and non-executive directors for reviewing and reporting on performance to shareholders and other financially interested parties[11]. While strictly speaking the Cadbury Committee's remit was to review those aspects of corporate governance specifically related to financial reporting and accountability, its conclusions were a contribution to the broader debate on corporate governance as a whole[12].

The Cadbury Committee, as it is commonly known, reported in December 1992. Its central recommendation was that the boards of all listed companies registered in the UK should comply with a Code of Best Practice and as many other companies as possible should aim at meeting its requirements[13]. The Committee also recommended that listed companies should make a statement in their reports and accounts about their compliance with the Code and identify and give reasons for any areas of non-compliance[14]. A company's statement of compliance should be reviewed by the auditors before publication[15].

The Code of Best Practice[16] was widely welcomed and the publication of this statement of compliance, reviewed by the auditors, was made a continuing obligation of listing by the Stock Exchange[17].

The Code states that the board should meet regularly, retain full and effective control over the company and monitor the executive management. The board should include non-executive directors of sufficient calibre and number for their views to carry weight in the board's decisions. Non-executive directors should bring an independent judgement to bear on issues of strategy, performance, resources, including key appointments, and standards of conduct[18].

The key element is that the non-executive directors should be independent. On this issue the Code states that the majority of non-executive directors should be independent of management and free from any business or other relationship which could materially interfere with the exercise of their independent judgement, apart from their fees and shareholding[19]. They should be appointed for specific terms and reappointment should not be automatic[20]. Non-executive directors should be selected through a formal process and both this process and their appointment should be a matter for the board as a whole[1].

In terms of the actual functions which non-executive directors would undertake, the Cadbury Committee concentrated on their roles with respect to remuneration and audit committees. This focus reflected matters of concern at the time of the Cadbury Committee's deliberations. There was, and still is, much public debate on the issue of directors' remuneration. Here the Code stated that executive directors' pay should be subject to the recommendations of a remuneration committee made up wholly or mainly

---

11   See Report of the Committee on the Financial Aspects of Corporate Governance (1992) (hereafter the Cadbury Committee Report), Appendix 1.
12   See the Cadbury Committee Report, para 1.2.
13   The Cadbury Committee Report, para 3.1. See also Cadbury 'Highlights of the Proposals of the Committee on Financial Aspects of Corporate Governance' in Prentice & Holland (eds) *Contemporary Issues in Corporate Governance* (1993), pp 45–55; Finch 'Corporate Governance and Cadbury: self regulation and alternatives' [1994] JBL 51; Finch 'Board Performance and Cadbury on Corporate Governance' [1992] JBL 581.
14   The Cadbury Committee Report, para 3.7.
15   The Cadbury Committee Report, para 3.9.
16   The full text of the Code is set out in the Cadbury Committee Report at pp 58–59.
17   See The Listing Rules, 12.43(j). The annual report and accounts must contain the statement of compliance.
18   See the Cadbury Committee Report, para 4.11.
19   See the Cadbury Committee Report, para 4.12.
20   See the Cadbury Committee Report, para 4.16.
1   See the Cadbury Committee Report, para 4.15.

of non-executive directors[2]. Much of the Cadbury Committee's work in this area has been superseded now by the work of the Greenbury Committee[3] which is discussed below.

Likewise there were concerns both as to the quality of audits and as to the relationship within a company between the board and the company's auditors. Many of the corporate collapses in the late 1980s had been preceded by unqualified audit reports which had failed to detect anything amiss. In an attempt to improve channels of communication and to provide for greater scrutiny of financial matters, the Cadbury Committee favoured the use of audit committees. The Code states that the board should establish an audit committee of at least three non-executive directors with written terms of reference which deal clearly with its authority and duties[4].

THE HAMPEL COMMITTEE

The Cadbury Report and Code of Best Practice have now become an accepted piece of the corporate landscape[5] and, allowing for a few sceptical rumblings, the Code is generally seen as a positive contribution to the corporate governance debate.

A successor committee under the chairmanship of Sir Ronald Hampel was set up in November 1995 to review the impact of the Code[6] and, more broadly, 'to keep under review the role of directors, executive and non-executive, recognising the need for board cohesion and the common legal responsibilities of all directors'[7]. The Hampel Committee also considered the work of the Greenbury Committee on directors' remuneration and that aspect of its work is discussed below.

The Hampel Committee produced a preliminary report in August 1997[8] and its final report followed in January 1998[9]. The report endorsed the overwhelming majority of the findings of the Cadbury and Greenbury Committees[10]. The Committee did attempt, however, to reposition the debate on corporate governance which by concentrating on accountability, it said, had tended to obscure a board's first responsibility – to enhance the prosperity of the business over time[11].

It noted that good corporate governance is not just a matter of prescribing particular corporate structures and complying with a number of hard and fast rules, the 'box ticking' approach, as the Committee described it[12]. Instead there is a need for broad principles which, the Committee hoped, will command general agreement and which can be applied flexibly and with common sense to the varying circumstances of individual companies[13]. In adopting this approach, the Hampel Committee emphasised that there is a distinction between principles of corporate governance and more detailed

---

2　See the Cadbury Committee Report, paras 4.40–4.46.
3　See Directors' Remuneration, Report of a Study Group chaired by Sir Richard Greenbury (1995).
4　See the Cadbury Committee Report, paras 4.33–4.38.
5　See Cadbury 'The Response to the Report of the Committee on the Financial Aspects of Corporate Governance' in Patfield (ed) *Perspectives on Company Law* (1995) pp 23-33.
6　Indeed it was a specific recommendation of the Cadbury Committee that a successor committee should examine how compliance with the Code of Best Practice had progressed and whether it needed updating: see Cadbury Committee Report, para 3.12.
7　See the Hampel Committee Report (1998) p 66 for the terms of reference of the Committee.
8　*Committee on Corporate Governance: Preliminary report* (1997).
9　*Committee on Corporate Governance: Final report* (1998) hereafter referred to as the Hampel Committee Report.
10　See the Hampel Committee Report, para 1.7.
11　See the Hampel Committee Report, para 1.1.
12　See the Hampel Committee Report, paras 1.11-1.14.
13　See the Hampel Committee Report, paras 1.11, 1.20.

guidelines such as the Cadbury and Greenbury Codes. 'With guidelines, one asks "How far are they complied with?"; with principles, the right question is "How are they applied in practice ?" '[14].

The main elements of the Hampel *principles* as they apply to the board[15] are set out below:

- Every listed company should be headed by an effective board which should lead and control the company.
- There are two key tasks at the top of every public company – the running of the board and the executive responsibility for the running of the company's business. A decision to combine these two roles in one individual should be publicly explained.
- The board should include a balance of executive and non-executive directors (including independent non-executives) such that no one individual or small group of individuals can dominate the board's decision taking.
- The board should be supplied in a timely fashion with information in a form and of a quality appropriate to enable it to discharge its duties.
- There should be a formal and transparent procedure for the appointment of new directors to the board.
- All directors should be required to submit themselves for re-election at regular intervals and at least every three years.

Turning to a more detailed consideration of the directors' role, the Committee concluded that[16]:

- Executive and non-executive directors should continue to have the same duties under the law.
- Management has an obligation to provide the board with appropriate and timely information and the chairman has a particular responsibility to ensure that all directors are properly briefed.
- The majority of non-executive directors should be independent, and the board should disclose in the annual report which of the non-executive directors are considered to be independent.
- To be effective, non-executive directors need to make up at least one third of the membership of the board.
- Separation of the roles of chairman and chief executive is to be preferred, other things being equal, and companies should justify a decision to combine the roles.
- Whether or not the roles of chairman and chief executive are combined, a senior non-executive director should be identified in the annual report, to whom concerns can be conveyed.
- All directors should submit themselves for re-election every three years.
- There should be no fixed rules for the length of service or age of non-executive directors.
- Each company should establish an audit committee of at least three non-executive directors, at least two of whom are independent.

The main difference emerging from the previous reports is this emphasis on the *independent* non-executive director. While independence had been stressed in the Cadbury Report[17], many companies have appointed non-executive directors who have previously held executive posts with the company or have been their professional advisers. So while these boards have non-executive directors, they do not necessarily

14 See the Hampel Committee Report, para 2.1.
15 See the Hampel Committee Report, paras 2.1-2.8.
16 See the Hampel Committee Report, Ch 3.
17 See the Cadbury Committee Report, para 4.12.

have sufficient distance from the company. Hampel hopes to address that issue by stressing the need for the majority of non-executive directors to be independent.

The Hampel Committee recommended that its broad principles together with the Cadbury and Greenbury Codes of Practice should be combined in a single code which will operate alongside the Listing Rules. This aspect of the project has been referred to the London Stock Exchange which is consulting as the content of the proposed 'supercode' which will combine the work of all three committees.

It is anticipated that the final code will be published by mid-1998 when it will be included in the Stock Exchange's Listing Rules as best practice but it will not form part of the Listing Rules as such. The new code will be supported by a compliance statement in the Listing Rules which will require companies to provide in the annual reports a statement of how they have applied the principles and complied with the guidelines set out in the new code.

De facto directors

In a number of recent cases, mainly involving disqualification, the courts have consider the position of de facto directors. Disqualification orders (which are discussed in detail below) can be sought, inter alia, against individuals who were directors of companies which went into insolvent liquidation in cases where their conduct has shown them to be unfit to be concerned in the promotion, formation or management of a company. In these cases it emerged that the individual in question was never formally appointed to the board and so was not a de jure director. Nevertheless it was alleged that he was a de facto director and as such within the scope of the disqualification provisions.

In *Re Hydrodam (Corby) Ltd*[18] Millett J suggested the following (non-exhaustive[19]) definition of a de facto director:

> A de facto director is a person who assumes to act as a director. He is held out as a director by the company, and claims and purports to be a director, although never actually or validly appointed as such. To establish that a person was a de facto director of a company, it is necessary to plead and prove that he undertook functions in relation to the company which could properly be discharged only by a director. It is not sufficient to show that he was concerned in the management of the company's affairs or undertook tasks in relation to its business which can properly be performed by a manager below board level[20].

It can be difficult in practice to distinguish between functions which can properly be discharged only by a director and functions which can be performed below board level. It is often unclear whether what the person did was referable to an assumed directorship or to some other capacity such as manager, shareholder or consultant[1]. In the context of disqualification, given its consequences, the person in question is to be given the benefit of the doubt[2].

---

18   [1994] 2 BCLC 180, [1994] BCC 161. This case was not a disqualification case but was brought in respect of wrongful trading under Insolvency Act 1986, s 214.

19   See *Re Richborough Furniture Ltd* [1996] 1 BCLC 507 at 522; *Re Moorgate Metals Ltd* [1995] 1 BCLC 503 at 517.

20   [1994] 2 BCLC 180 at 183, [1994] BCC 161 at 163.

1   See *Re Sykes (Butchers) Ltd, Secretary of State for Trade and Industry v Richardson* [1998] BCLC 110; *Re Richborough Furniture Ltd* [1996] 1 BCLC 507; *Secretary of State for Trade and Industry v Hickling* [1996] BCC 678; *Secretary of State for Trade and Industry v Morrall* [1996] BCC 229.

2   See *Re Richborough Furniture Ltd* [1996] 1 BCLC 507 at 524; *Secretary of State for Trade and Industry v Hickling* [1996] BCC 678; *Secretary of State for Trade and Industry v Morrall* [1996] BCC 229.

Shadow directors

A number of provisions in the Companies Act 1985 and the Insolvency Act 1986[3], particularly those requiring disclosure and regulating certain types of transactions by directors, also apply to a shadow director. This extension of these provisions is designed to prevent the easy evasion of legal liabilities and responsibilities by persons who control companies but who take care not to be appointed to their boards in the hope of evading any liabilities which might attach to directors.

A shadow director is defined as a person in accordance with whose directions or instructions the directors of a company are accustomed to act[4]. In *Re Hydrodam (Corby) Ltd*[5] Millett J reviewed the key elements of this definition. He stated:

To establish that a defendant is a shadow director of a company, it is necessary to allege and prove:
   (i)   who are the directors of the company, whether de facto or de jure;
   (ii) that the defendant directed those directors how to act in relation to the company or that he was one of the persons who did so;
   (iii) that those directors acted in accordance with such directions;
   (iv) that they were accustomed so to act.
   What is needed is, first, a board of directors claiming and purporting to act as such; and, secondly, a pattern of behaviour in which the board did not exercise any discretion or judgment of its own but acted in accordance with the directions of others[6].

A key requirement, and one of most difficult to establish, is that in heading (iv) above, of 'accustomed so to act'. The directors must act on the directions or instructions of the shadow director as a matter of regular practice over a period of time and as a regular course of conduct[7].

Controlling shareholders are obviously most at risk of being classified as shadow directors. However, the category is not restricted to controlling shareholders and it is a question of considering the particular facts to see whether a person has fallen within the definition. The courts have heard argument as to secured creditors[8] and bankers[9] being so classified but the courts have yet to be persuaded.

Another situation which may give rise to a shadow directorship is the relationship between parent and subsidiary companies[10]. In *Re Hydrodam (Corby) Ltd*[11] a liquidator

---

3   See for example CA 1985, ss 317(8), 319(7), 320(3); IA 1986, ss 206(3), 214(7); see Pennington *Company Law* (7th edn, 1995), p 711 for a full list of the relevant provisions.
4   CA 1985, s 741(2). However, a person is not deemed a shadow director by reason only that the directors act on advice given by him in a professional capacity: ibid.
5   [1994] 2 BCLC 180, [1994] BCC 161.
6   [1994] 2 BCLC 180 at 183, [1994] BCC 161 at 163.
7   See *Re Unisoft Group Ltd (No 3)* [1994] 1 BCLC 609 at 620, [1994] BCC 766 at 775.
8   See *Re PFTZM Ltd, Jourdain v Paul* [1995] 2 BCLC 354, [1995] BCC 280. The court noted here that the alleged shadow directors were not accustomed to give directions, they simply tried to rescue what they could from the company using their undoubted rights as secured creditors, see [1995] 2 BCLC 354 at 367, [1995] BCC 280 at 290–291.
9   See *Re a Company (No 005009 of 1987), ex p Copp* [1989] BCLC 13 at 21, 4 BCC 424 at 431. Subsequent stages of the action are reported as *Re M C Bacon Ltd* [1990] BCLC 324, [1990] BCC 78 by which time the liquidator in this case had abandoned his original claim that a bank was a shadow director of a company, see [1990] BCLC 324 at 326, [1990] BCC 78 at 79. See generally Financial Law Panel, *Shadow Directorships* (1994).
10 Note the limited exemption for holding companies in CA 1985, s 741(3).
11 [1994] 2 BCLC 180, [1994] BCC 161.

alleged unsuccessfully that directors of a parent company were shadow directors of a subsidiary company so as to bring them within the reach of the wrongful trading provisions in the Insolvency Act 1986[1]. On the facts this could not be established but the case contains an interesting discussion of the possibilities in this context. There are two main scenarios. First, it may be possible to establish that the board of a parent company as a collective body gave instructions to the directors of a subsidiary and that the directors of the subsidiary were accustomed to act in accordance with those instructions. In that case, where the instructions have come from the appropriate organ of the parent company, this would constitute the parent company but not the individual directors as shadow directors of the subsidiary. A second possibility, and one which in practice is much more likely, is that the directors of the parent company or some of them individually and personally gave directions or instructions to the board of the subsidiary so rendering themselves personally liable as shadow directors of the subsidiary[2].

Finally, note that in *Re Hydrodam (Corby) Ltd*[3] Millett J cautioned against confusing shadow directors with de facto directors. In his view, in most and perhaps all cases these categories are mutually exclusive:

> ... in my judgment an allegation that a defendant acted as a de facto or shadow director, without distinguishing between the two, is embarrassing. It suggests ... that the liquidator takes the view that de facto or shadow directors are very similar, that their roles overlap, and that it may not be possible to determine in any given case whether a particular person was a de facto or a shadow director. I do not accept that at all. The terms do not overlap. They are alternatives, and in most and perhaps all cases they are mutually exclusive[4].

Alternate directors

The articles may provide for the appointment of alternate directors. Such a director is appointed by a director and is entitled generally to perform all the functions of his appointer as a director in his absence[5].

DIRECTORS' REMUNERATION

The mere holding of office by itself does not entitle a director to remuneration[6] but the articles will invariably provide that remuneration for the directors shall from time to time be determined by the company in general meeting[7]. More commonly, the power to settle remuneration for executive directors for their services will be delegated to

---

1   Ie under IA 1986, s 214.
2   See [1994] 2 BCLC 180 at 184, [1994] BCC 161 at 164.
3   [1994] 2 BCLC 180, [1994] BCC 161.
4   [1994] 2 BCLC 180 at 182–183, [1994] BCC 161 at 163.
5   See Table A, arts 65–69.
6   *Hutton v West Cork Rly Co* (1883) 23 Ch D 654.
7   See Table A, art 82; and the general meeting may resolve to pay a director for the mere holding of office, even if he undertakes no specific duties: *Re Halt Garage (1964) Ltd* [1982] 3 All ER 1016. If there is a provision in the articles which requires either the general meeting or the directors or a committee of the directors to determine the amount of the remuneration and the correct body has not done so, then the director has no claim for payment under the articles: *Guinness plc v Saunders* [1990] 2 AC 663, [1990] 1 All ER 652, HL.

the board[8]. In larger public companies, as we have seen, the task is frequently delegated to a remuneration committee composed mainly of non-executive directors, the role of which is discussed further below.

Executive directors invariably will have a service contract with the company which will set out the appropriate level of remuneration. This is necessary as a director cannot rely on the articles as constituting a contract between himself and the company[9] although it may be possible for a director to pursue a claim to recover payment on the basis of an implied extrinsic contract[10].

Exceptionally a director may seek to claim on a quantum meruit basis for services rendered and accepted by the company[11] or on the basis of an equitable allowance[12] although the courts are very reluctant to allow such claims by directors[13].

Where remuneration is paid, the court will not normally concern itself with the quantum of that remuneration and will not attempt to compare the market value of the services rendered with the amount of remuneration actually paid[14]. However, the court will wish to ensure that the payment is genuinely remuneration and not a sham transaction masking an improper return of capital to the shareholders[15]. Excessive payments at a time when the company is in financial difficulties may be challenged by a liquidator[16] and may form part of the evidence of unfitness to be a director when a disqualification order is sought[17].

Problems can also arise from the payment of (usually large) sums of money to directors as compensation on the loss of, or retirement from, office. Such payments are often called 'golden handshakes'. It is not lawful for a company to make to a director of the company any payment by way of compensation for loss of office, or as consideration for or in connection with his retirement from office, without particulars of the proposed payment (including its amount) being disclosed to members of the

---

8   See Table A, art 84.
9   *Hickman v Kent or Romney Marsh Sheep-Breeders' Association* [1915] 1 Ch 881; see discussion in Chapter 11.
10   See *Re New British Iron Co, ex p Beckwith* [1898] 1 Ch 324.
11   *Craven-Ellis v Canons Ltd* [1936] 2 KB 403, [1936] 2 All ER 1066; but there will be no room for a quantum meruit claim by a director when the articles have already made express provision for special remuneration for a director: *Guinness plc v Saunders* [1990] 2 AC 663, [1990] 1 All ER 652, HL.
12   See *Boardman v Phipps* [1967] 2 AC 46, [1966] 3 All ER 721.
13   The position on quantum meruit and equitable allowance claims was restrictively stated in *Guinness plc v Saunders* [1990] 2 AC 663, [1990] 1 All ER 652, HL; see Beatson & Prentice (1990) 106 LQR 365; Hopkins [1990] CLJ 220; Birks [1990] LMCLQ 330. Directors are precluded from contracting with their companies for their services except in the circumstances authorised by the articles of association; likewise there should be no remuneration for their services except as provided by the articles of association. To allow otherwise might encourage fiduciaries to put themselves in a position where there is a conflict between their personal interests and their duties as fiduciaries.
14   See *Re Halt Garage (1964) Ltd* [1982] 3 All ER 1016 at 1039, per Dillon J: '... assuming that the sum is bona fide voted to be paid as remuneration, it seems to me that the amount, whether it be mean or generous, must be a matter of management for the company to determine in accordance with its constitution which expressly authorises payment for directors' services. Shareholders are required to be honest but ... there is no requirement that they must be wise and it is not for the courts to manage the company.'
15   *Re Halt Garage (1964) Ltd* [1982] 3 All ER 1016.
16   For example under the IA 1986, s 212 (misfeasance); or s 238 (a transaction at an undervalue); see also *Re Halt Garage (1964) Ltd* [1982] 3 All ER 1016.
17   See discussion of disqualification on the grounds of unfitness post; also *Secretary of State for Trade and Industry v McTighe (No 2)* [1996] 2 BCLC 477; *Secretary of State for Trade and Industry v Van Hengel* [1995] 1 BCLC 545, [1995] BCC 173; *Re Ward Sherrard Ltd* [1996] BCC 418; *Re Firedart Ltd, Official Receiver v Fairall* [1994] 2 BCLC 340; *Re Moorgate Metals Ltd* [1995] 1 BCLC 503, [1995] BCC 143.

company and the proposal being approved by the company[18]. This only applies to payments to directors in connection with their office as directors and does not apply, for example, to payments to them in respect of any post they may have as employees of the company. It applies to gratuitous, uncovenanted, payments and does not cover any payments which the company is contractually bound to make[19], nor does it apply to any bona fide payments by way of damages for breach of contract or by way of pension in respect of past services[20]. These exceptions are wide enough to ensure that few of these payments need the approval of the general meeting.

Details of directors' remuneration and compensation for loss of office must be included in notes to the accounts[21] and details of service contracts must be available for inspection by any member at the company's registered office[22].

Remuneration committees and the Greenbury Report

As noted above, one of the key functions of non-executive directors as envisaged by the Cadbury Committee was that they should form a remuneration committee which would set appropriate levels of remuneration for the executive directors[23]. As was also noted above, the work of the Cadbury Committee in this regard was soon superseded by that of the Greenbury Committee.

The Greenbury Committee was set up in January 1995 on the initiative of the CBI in response to public and shareholder concerns about the remuneration of company directors. The Committee was chaired by Sir Richard Greenbury and its terms of reference were to identify good practice in determining directors' remuneration and to prepare a Code of such practice for use by public companies. Its report and Code of Best Practice were published in July 1995[24].

As with the Cadbury Report, the Greenbury Report recommended that all listed companies should comply with a Code of Best Practice to the fullest extent practicable and should make an annual compliance statement to shareholders which should also explain any areas of non-compliance. The Stock Exchange has made an annual compliance statement a continuing obligation for listed companies[1].

The key emphasis in the Greenbury Code of Best Practice is on accountability and transparency and this is reflected in the provisions dealing with the composition of the remuneration committee and on disclosure.

The Code's requirements include:

- boards of directors should set up remuneration committees of non-executive directors to determine on their behalf, and on behalf of shareholders, within agreed terms of reference, the company's policy on executive remuneration and specific remuneration packages for each of the executive directors including pension rights and any compensation payments;

---

18   CA 1985, s 312. Similar provisions apply where a payment is made in a take-over situation: ss 313–316.
19   *Taupo Totara Timber Co Ltd v Rowe* [1978] AC 537, [1977] 3 All ER 123.
20   CA 1985, s 316(3). 'Pension' here includes any superannuation allowance, superannuation gratuity or similar payment.
21   Ibid, s 232 and Sch 6, Part 1; as amended by the Company Accounts (Disclosure of Directors' Emoluments) Regulations 1997 SI 1997 No 570.
22   CA 1985, s 318; or at any other appropriate place specified in s 318(3).
23   See the Cadbury Committee Report, noted supra, paras 4.40–4.46.
24   Directors' Remuneration, Report of a Study Group chaired by Sir Richard Greenbury (1995). The Code of Best Practice is set out at pp 13–18.
1   See The Listing Rules, r 12.43(w), (x).

- remuneration committees should consist exclusively of non-executive directors with no personal financial interest other than as shareholders in the matters to be decided, no potential conflicts of interest arising from cross-directorships and no day-to-day involvement in running the business;
- the company's annual report and accounts each year should include a report from the remuneration committee to the shareholders on behalf of the board;
- the report should set out the company's policy on executive directors' remuneration, including levels, comparator groups of companies, individual components, performance criteria and measurement, pension provision, contracts of service and compensation commitments on early termination;
- the report should include full details of all elements in the remuneration of each individual director by name, such as basic salary, benefits in kind, annual bonuses, long-term incentive schemes including share options and pension entitlements earned by each director during the year;
- any service contracts which provide for, or imply, notice periods in excess of one year (or any provisions for predetermined compensation on termination which exceed one year's salary and benefits) should be disclosed and the reasons for the longer notice periods explained.

The main result of the Greenbury Report has been a vast increase in the information available to shareholders as to directors' remuneration. Whether the shareholders can make sensible use of that volume of information is one question; another is whether companies will continue to be willing to support the bureaucracy involved in supplying such detailed information.

As noted above, one of the terms of reference of the Hampel Committee on Corporate Governance was to 'pursue any relevant matters arising' from the Greenbury Report[2]. As also noted, the Hampel Committee's Report has proceeded by identifying principles which listed companies should apply. On the issue of directors' remuneration, the Committee suggested the following broad principles[3]:

- Levels of remuneration should be sufficient to attract and retain the directors needed to run the company successfully. The component parts of remuneration should be structured so as to link rewards to corporate and individual performance.
- Companies should establish a formal and transparent procedure for developing policy on executive remuneration and for fixing the remuneration packages of individual executive directors.
- The company's annual report should contain a statement of remuneration policy and details of the remuneration of each director.

Turning to a more detailed consideration of the issues raised by the Greenbury report, the Committee noted that it is too early to judge how the Greenbury Code is working in practice or to consider the case for possible changes in it[4]. However, there were a number of issues on which the Committee did wish to comment. The Committee considered that[5]:

- Boards should set as their objective the reduction of directors' contract periods to one year or less but the Committee recognises that this cannot be achieved immediately.
- Boards should establish a remuneration committee, made up of independent

2   See the Hampel Committee Report, p 66.
3   See the Hampel Committee Report, paras 2.9-2.12.
4   See the Hampel Committee Report, para 4.1.
5   See the Hampel Committee Report, Ch 4.

> non-executive directors, to develop policy on remuneration and devise remuneration packages for individual executive directors.
- The requirement to include a statement on remuneration policy in the annual report should be retained and these statements should be made more informative.
- Disclosure of individual remuneration packages should continue but this has become too complicated and should be simplified.
- While agreeing that shareholder approval should be sought for new long-term incentive plans for directors, companies should not be obliged to seek shareholder approval for the remuneration report.

RETIREMENT, RESIGNATION, VACATION AND REMOVAL OF DIRECTORS

Retirement

The articles will normally provide for the retirement of all the directors at the first annual general meeting and thereafter may provide for the rotation of directors with a selected number retiring each year, although they remain eligible for re-election and retiring directors are automatically reappointed in default of another appointment[6].

Resignation

A director may resign at any time. The articles will normally require notice in writing to the board and on so doing the director is deemed to have vacated his office[7].

Vacating office

The articles would normally indicate a number of instances in which a director is deemed to have vacated his office including, for example, resignation, becoming a bankrupt, or being prohibited by law from being a director[8]. A standard provision is one which provides that the office of a director is to be vacated if a director is requested in writing by all his co-directors to resign. That power, effectively to expel a director, must be exercised in the best interests of the company[9].

Removal from office

A company may by ordinary resolution remove a director before the expiration of his period of office notwithstanding anything in its articles or any agreement between him and the company[10]. Special notice[11] of the resolution must be given and the director concerned is entitled to be heard at the meeting where it is proposed to remove him[12].

---

6   See Table A, arts 73–80. Private companies will frequently dispense with rotation.
7   See Table A, art 81(d).
8   See Table A, art 81.
9   *Lee v Chou Wen Hsien* [1985] BCLC 45.
10   CA 1985, s 303(1).
11   Defined ibid, s 379.
12   Ibid, ss 303(2), 304(1).

He may also require the company to circulate his representations in writing to the members[13] unless this right is being abused to secure needless publicity of defamatory material[14].

There are a number of issues which a company must consider before exercising this power of removal. In particular, the company must consider the amount of damages which may be payable to a dismissed director as the power to remove a director granted by the statute does not deprive a person removed thereunder of compensation or damages payable in respect of the termination of his appointment as director[15].

Problems are most likely to arise when the company attempts to dismiss an executive director with a service contract. If a managing director is appointed by contract for a fixed term and the company exercises its power to remove him as a director before that term expires, then the company will be liable in damages as the courts will imply a term that the company undertakes to do nothing of its own accord (for example, by terminating his post as a director) to bring to an end the circumstances necessary to enable a person to act as managing director[16].

Where a director does not have a separate service contract and has simply been appointed under the articles then his position can be terminated at any time and he cannot recover any damages[17]. Indeed the company may specifically alter its articles to facilitate the removal of such a director and he will not be entitled to any relief[18]. It is clear then that a director without a service contract will be in a somewhat vulnerable position.

A major problem for shareholders wishing to remove directors was that they found that the directors had such lengthy service contracts with the company that the cost of removing them was exorbitant. In practice therefore such directors were irremovable.

To curb this practice, shareholder approval is now required of any provision whereby a director is to be employed[19] for a period exceeding five years[20] and the contract cannot be determined by the company by notice or it can be so terminated only in specified circumstances[1]. Lengthy service contracts then must be approved by the company in general meeting[2] after the shareholders have had an opportunity to inspect a memorandum setting out the proposed agreement and identifying the period for which it is to run[3]. If a term is included in contravention of this section and without the approval of the general meeting, then that term is void and the agreement will become one determinable by the giving of reasonable notice[4].

13   Ibid, s 304(2).
14   Ibid, s 304(4).
15   Ibid, s 303(5).
16   *Shindler v Northern Raincoat Co Ltd* [1960] 2 All ER 239, [1960] 1 WLR 1038; *Southern Foundries (1926) Ltd v Shirlaw* [1940] 2 All ER 445, HL.
17   *Read v Astoria Garage (Streatham) Ltd* [1952] Ch 637, [1952] 2 All ER 292.
18   *Shuttleworth v Cox Bros & Co (Maidenhead) Ltd* [1927] 2 KB 9.
19   Employment is defined as including employment under a contract for services, so consultancy services are caught by the provision: CA 1985, s 319(7)(a).
20   Ibid, s 319(2) provides for the aggregation of periods in certain circumstances so that the provision cannot be avoided by a string of contracts. However, the rather obscure wording of that provision offers scope for avoidance.
1   Ibid, s 319(1); shadow directors are included: s 319(7). The section does not apply if the company in question is a wholly-owned subsidiary: 319(4). Note in this context the recommendations of the Greenbury Committee, above, as to the duration of service contracts.
2   Of course, the directors' ability to control the general meeting means that they will not be unduly worried by this provision although it does mean exposing their arrangements to the full glare of publicity.
3   CA 1985, s 319(5). The memorandum must be available at the registered office for 15 days before the meeting and at the meeting itself.
4   Ibid, s 319(6).

In appropriate circumstances removal of a director, particularly in small quasi-partnership type companies, may warrant winding up the company on the just and equitable ground[5]. In practice, an order for winding up on this basis is unlikely to be sought now, given the availability of more tailored relief by petitioning in such cases on the grounds of unfair prejudice[6]. The scope of these remedies is considered in detail in Chapter 28.

Directors can protect themselves to some extent against the possibility that at some date in the future the general meeting will seek to remove them from the board. One method is the inclusion of a provision in the articles entitling the director to weighted votes on any resolution to remove him from the board, a practice permitted by the House of Lords in *Bushell v Faith*[7]. In that case the articles of the company provided that on a resolution to remove a particular director, his shares would carry three times the number of votes they normally carried. As a consequence, it was impossible for the other shareholders to pass the required ordinary resolution. Ungoed-Thomas J at first instance refused to permit the practice saying that it made a mockery of the Act but the Court of Appeal and the House of Lords approved it[8] and it remains a valid method of entrenchment for directors.

DISQUALIFICATION OF DIRECTORS

One of the major concerns of Parliament in passing the Insolvency Act 1985 (subsequently consolidated as the Insolvency Act 1986) was to curb the activities of directors who shelter behind the corporate form and who having put a company into insolvent liquidation, promptly set up in business immediately thereafter and start the whole cycle again[9].

The Cork Committee noted:

> It has been made evident to us that there is a widespread dissatisfaction at the ease with which a person trading through the medium of one or more companies with limited liability can allow such a company to become insolvent, form a new company, and then carry on trading much as before, leaving behind him a trail of unpaid creditors, and often repeating the process several times[10].

The Companies Act 1985 already provided for disqualification on certain grounds but it was decided to strengthen and extend those provisions. This was done in the

---

5   Under IA 1986, s 122(1)(g); see *Ebrahimi v Westbourne Galleries Ltd* [1973] AC 360, [1972] 2 All ER 492.
6   Ie under CA 1985, s 459.
7   [1969] 2 Ch 438, [1969] 1 All ER 1002, CA; affd [1970] AC 1099, [1970] 1 All ER 53, HL.
8   See [1970] AC 1099 at 1109, [1970] 1 All ER 53 at 57, per Upjohn LJ: 'Parliament has never sought to fetter the right of a company to issue shares with such rights or restrictions as it thinks fit.' Note Schmitthoff [1970] JBL 1: '... one of the most remarkable instances of judicial interpretation defeating the clear intention of the legislature.' See *Palmer's Company Law* (25th edn, 1992), para 8.033 where it is suggested that the decision can be justified in the case of private companies of a quasi-partnership nature but that its ratio does not extend to public companies.
9   The Cork Committee reporting in 1982 had found widespread concern at the apparent inability of the law to deal adequately with such individuals: see the Report of the Review Committee on Insolvency Law and Practice, Cmnd 8558, chs 43, 45.
10 The Report of the Review Committee on Insolvency Law and Practice (the Cork Committee), Cmnd 8558, para 1813.

Insolvency Act 1985 and the provisions were subsequently consolidated and re-enacted as the Company Directors Disqualification Act 1986[11].

Grounds for disqualification

The grounds for disqualification are:

(a) convicted of an indictable offence;
(b) persistent default;
(c) fraud;
(d) disqualification when made personally liable;
(e) undischarged bankrupts;
(f) failure to pay county court administration order;
(g) directors found to be unfit following an investigation;
(h) unfit directors of insolvent companies.

By far the most important category is that in heading (h) which addresses the concerns raised by the Cork Committee as to whether directors of companies which have gone into insolvent liquidation should continue to be afforded the privilege of running their businesses through limited liability companies.

(A) CONVICTED OF AN INDICTABLE OFFENCE

The court may make a disqualification order against a person where he is convicted of an indictable offence (whether on indictment or summarily) in connection with the promotion, formation, management, liquidation or striking off of a company, or with the receivership or management of a company's property[12]. This provision is widely drafted and covers any offence 'in connection with' any aspect of the birth, life and death of the company and extends to the conduct of both the internal and external affairs of the company[13].

In *R v Goodman*[14] a director had been disqualified following a conviction for insider dealing in his company's shares while in possession of unpublished information regarding the company's trading position. He argued that he should not be disqualified since the insider dealing offence was not an offence committed in connection with the management of the company. The Court of Appeal found it was not necessary to establish that the offence related to the management of the company itself but only that the offence did have some relevant factual connection with the management of the company. On the facts, the insider dealing offence of which he was convicted was an offence in connection with the management of the company and he was properly disqualified.

---

11 Hereafter referred to as the CDDA 1986. On disqualification see generally Mithani and Wheeler *Disqualification of Company Directors* (1995); Sealy *Disqualification and Personal Liability of Directors* (4th edn, 1993); Milman (1992) 43 NILQ 1; Dine (1991) 12 Co Law 6; Finch (1990) 53 MLR 385.
12 CDDA 1986, s 2.
13 *R v Austen* (1985) 7 Cr App Rep (S) 214. See also *R v Corbin* (1984) 6 Cr App Rep (S) 17; *R v Georgiou* (1988) 4 BCC 322.
14 [1993] 2 All ER 789, [1994] 1 BCLC 349, CA.

(B)   PERSISTENT DEFAULT

The court may make a disqualification order against a person where it appears that he has been persistently[15] in default in relation to provisions of the companies legislation requiring any return, account or other document to be filed with, delivered or sent, or notice of any matter to be given, to the registrar of companies[16].

The fact that a person has been persistently in default may, without prejudice to its proof in any other manner, be conclusively proved by showing that in the five years ending with the date of the application he has been adjudged guilty (whether or not on the same occasion) of three or more defaults[17] in relation to those provisions[18].

(C)   FRAUD

The court may make a disqualification order against a person if, in the course of the winding up of a company, it appears that he has been guilty of an offence of fraudulent trading[19] for which he is liable (whether he has been convicted or not) or has otherwise been guilty, while an officer[20] or liquidator of the company or receiver or manager of its property, of any fraud in relation to the company or of any breach of his duty as such officer, liquidator, receiver or manager[1].

(D)   DISQUALIFICATION WHEN MADE PERSONALLY LIABLE FOR FRAUDULENT OR WRONGFUL TRADING

The court may, regardless of whether any application is made or not, disqualify any person against whom a contribution order has been made under the fraudulent trading or wrongful trading provisions[2]. Fraudulent trading involves trading with intent to defraud creditors. Wrongful trading occurs if a company goes into insolvent liquidation and at some time before the commencement of the winding up of the company, a director or shadow director knew or ought to have concluded that there was no reasonable prospect that the company would avoid going into insolvent liquidation. In both cases a person may be required to make such contribution to the company's assets as the court thinks proper. Disqualification is an additional penalty in such cases.

(E)   UNDISCHARGED BANKRUPTS

The one instance when disqualification is automatic is in the case of an undischarged bankrupt who is prohibited from acting as a director of, or directly or indirectly taking

---

15   'Persistent' means nothing more than that there should be some degree of continuance or repetition: *Re Arctic Engineering Ltd (No 2)* [1986] 2 All ER 346, [1986] 1 WLR 686.
16   CDDA 1986, s 3.
17   Ibid, s 3(3) defines the circumstances in which a person will be adjudged guilty of a default.
18   Ibid, s 3(2). See *Re Civica Investments Ltd* [1983] BCLC 456; *Re Arctic Engineering Ltd (No 2)* [1986] 2 All ER 346, [1986] 1 WLR 686. Note also CDDA 1986, s 5.
19   Ie under CA 1985, s 458.
20   'Officer' includes a shadow director: CDDA 1986, s 4(2); and a director, manager or secretary: ibid, s 22(6) applying CA 1985, s 744.
1   CDDA 1986, s 4.
2   Ibid, s 10. Liability can arise under IA 1986, ss 213 or 214 respectively.

part in or being concerned in the promotion, formation or management of, a company save with the leave of the court by which he was adjudged bankrupt[3].

(F)   FAILURE TO PAY UNDER COUNTY COURT ADMINISTRATION ORDER

Where a court revokes an administration order[4] against an individual, it may order that that person may not, except with the leave of the court which made the order, act as a director or liquidator of, or directly or indirectly take part in or be concerned in the promotion, formation or management of, a company for such period not exceeding two years which may be specified in the order[5].

(G)   DISQUALIFICATION AFTER INVESTIGATION

Where it appears to the Secretary of State from any report made or information or documents obtained under the powers relating to the investigation of companies[6] or under the powers exercisable for the purposes of assisting an overseas regulatory authority[7], that it is expedient in the public interest that a disqualification order should be made against any person who is or has been a director or shadow director of any company, he may apply[8] to the court for such an order to be made against that person[9]. The court may make such an order where it is satisfied that that person's conduct in relation to the company makes him unfit to be concerned in the management of a company[10].

In *Re Looe Fish Ltd*[11] an investigation by the Department of Trade and Industry had revealed an abuse of power by a director who had allotted shares in such a way as to ensure that he retained control of the company rather than a rival faction. The court held that, in using the power to allot shares in the way he did, the director displayed a clear lack of commercial probity and was unfit to be concerned in the management of a company. He was disqualified for two and a half years.

(H)   UNFIT DIRECTORS OF INSOLVENT COMPANIES

As noted above, the most commonly relied on ground for disqualification is that the director of an insolvent company has been found to be unfit. This was a new ground brought into being by the Insolvency Act 1985 and designed to address the concerns

3   CDDA 1986, s 11. Note that this offence is one of strict liability: *R v Brockley* [1994] 1 BCLC 606 (where the bankrupt unsuccessfully pleaded that he genuinely thought that he had been discharged from his bankruptcy).
4   Ie under County Courts Act 1984, Part VI.
5   CDDA 1986, s 12; IA 1986, s 429.
6   Ie under the Companies Act 1985, Part XIV; Financial Services Act 1986, ss 94, 105, 177; Criminal Justice Act 1987, s 2.
7   Ie under Companies Act 1989, Part III.
8   Where the Secretary of State decides not to make such an application, the court can properly interfere only if the facts demonstrated that the only possible course open to the Secretary of State was to make an application to the court: *R v Secretary of State for Trade and Industry, ex p Lonrho plc* [1992] BCC 325.
9   CDDA 1986, s 8(1).
10   Ibid, s 8(2); see *Re Samuel Sherman plc* [1991] 1 WLR 1070, [1991] BCC 699. In determining unfitness for these purposes the court will have regard, in particular, to the matters specified in CDDA 1986, Sch 1, s 9(1); see discussion below under heading (H).
11   [1993] BCLC 1160.

of the Cork Committee noted above. The applicable provisions are now found in the Company Directors Disqualification Act 1986.

Over 5,000 disqualification orders have been made since these provisions came into force in 1986 and a substantial body of case law has grown up around them. Before considering that case law and, in particular, how the courts have defined 'unfit', it may be helpful to have a broad overview of the scheme.

The overall scheme

When a company becomes insolvent, defined to encompass liquidation, administration and administrative receivership[12], and it appears to an official receiver, liquidator, administrator or administrative receiver (collectively referred to as the office-holder) that the conditions mentioned below are satisfied in respect of a person who is or has been a director of that company, then the office-holder must forthwith report the matter to the Secretary of State[13].

The conditions which must be met are that:

(i)   that person is or has been a director[14] of a company which has become insolvent, and

(ii)   his conduct as a director of that company (either taken alone or taken together with his conduct as a director of any other company or other companies[14a]) makes him unfit to be concerned in the management of a company[15].

Following a report from the office-holder, the Secretary of State may apply for a disqualification order if it appears to him expedient in the public interest that an order should be made against any person[16]. Alternatively, if the Secretary of State so directs, the application may be brought by the official receiver in the case of a person who is or has been a director of a company which is being wound up by the court in England and Wales[17].

Except with the leave of the court, such an application by the Secretary of State may not be made more than two years after the day on which the company became insolvent[18]. In deciding whether to grant leave to commence disqualification proceedings out of time, the court will take into account (i) the length of the delay; (ii)

---

12   See CDDA 1986, s 6(2).
13   Ibid, s 7(3). In practice the report is made to the Disqualification Unit of the Insolvency Service which is an executive agency of the Department of Trade and Industry. Such reports are not covered by legal professional privilege and their discovery may be sought by a director who is the subject of disqualification proceedings: *Re Barings plc, Secretary of State for Trade and Industry v Baker* [1998] 1 All ER 673, [1998] 1 BCLC 16.
14   Or a shadow director: CDDA 1986, s 6(3); or a de facto director: *Re Lo-Line Electric Motors Ltd* [1988] 2 All ER 692, [1988] BCLC 698; see also *Re Moorgate Metals Ltd* [1995] 1 BCLC 503, [1995] BCC 143; *Re Richborough Furniture Ltd, Secretary of State for Trade and Industry v Stokes* [1996] 1 BCLC 507, [1996] BCC 155; *Secretary of State for Trade and Industry v Hickling* [1996] BCC 678.
14a   See *Secretary of State for Trade and Industry v Ivens* [1997] 2 BCLC 334, [1997] BCC 801 on the question of the director's conduct in such other companies.
15   CDDA 1986, s 6(1).
16   Ibid, s 7(1)(a).
17   Ibid, s 7(1)(b).
18   Ibid, s 7(2). This means two years from the happening of the first of the insolvent events specified in s 6(2): *Re Tasbian Ltd* [1990] BCC 318, CA; see Fletcher [1989] JBL 365 at 375; Finch (1990) 53 MLR 385 at 390. Where a company has gone into compulsory winding up, the two-year period runs from the date of the court order and not from the date of presentation of the winding-up petition: *Re Walter L Jacob & Co Ltd, Official Receiver v Jacob* [1993] BCC 512.

the reasons for the delay; (iii) the strength of the case against the directors; and (iv) the degree of prejudice caused to the director by the delay[19].

Once an application has been made to the court, the court must make a disqualification order against a person where it is satisfied that he is unfit to be concerned in the management of a company[20].

In *Secretary of State for Trade and Industry v Gray*[1] the Court of Appeal emphasised that the question whether a director's conduct makes him unfit is to be determined by reference to the matters and evidence in the application for the disqualification order and not by reference to whether, at the date of the hearing, the future protection of the public might or might not require a period of disqualification. It is not a question of whether a director is unfit at the time of the hearing but rather whether his conduct as set out in the application for the disqualification order had fallen below the appropriate standard[2].

In all cases an application for disqualification must be made to the court and this has given rise to considerable pressure on court resources, given the number of disqualification orders now being sought. In December 1995 the Vice-Chancellor of the Chancery Division recommended to the Secretary of State that he give consideration to the possibility of introducing amending legislation under which an agreement between a director and the Secretary of State or the Official Receiver as to the disqualification period to be applied to the director be given the same effect as a court order imposing a disqualification period[3].

This proposal is an extension of the procedure initiated in *Re Carecraft Construction Co Ltd*[4] where it was agreed that where there is no dispute about material facts and no dispute about the appropriate period of disqualification and the director accepts, in substance, his unfitness, a disqualification case might be dealt with by the court in a summary fashion. The summary procedure initiated by *Carecraft* has since been endorsed by the Court of Appeal in *Secretary of State for Trade and Industry v Rogers*[5] which accepted that it enables disqualification proceedings to be dealt with expeditiously and with a substantial saving of costs. The court rejected concerns that the procedure presents the judge with a virtual fait accompli as it cannot oblige the judge actually to make a disqualification order and cannot bind him as to the period of disqualification to be imposed[6].

---

19   See *Re Probe Data Systems Ltd (No 3), Secretary of State for Trade and Industry v Desai* [1992] BCLC 405, [1992] BCC 110, CA; also *Secretary of State for Trade and Industry v Cleland, Re Stormont Ltd* [1997] 1 BCLC 437; *Secretary of State for Trade and Industry v Davies (No 2)* [1997] 2 BCLC 317, [1997] BCC 235; *Secretary of State for Trade and Industry v Morrall, Re Westmid Packing Services Ltd (No 2)* [1996] BCC 229; *Re NP Engineering and Security Products Ltd* [1994] 2 BCLC 585, [1995] BCC 1052; *Re Cedar Developments Ltd* [1994] 2 BCLC 714, [1995] BCC 220; *Secretary of State for Trade and Industry v McTighe, Re Copecrest Ltd* [1994] 2 BCLC 284, [1993] BCC 844, CA; *Re Crestjoy Products Ltd* [1990] BCLC 677; *Re Cedac Ltd* [1990] BCC 555; revsd in part on other grounds [1991] BCLC 543.

20   CDDA 1986, s 6(1).

1   [1995] 1 BCLC 276, [1995] BCC 554.

2   [1995] 1 BCLC 276 at 285, [1995] BCC 554 at 574, CA although his later conduct may have a bearing on the question of leave and the period of disqualification; see also *Re Pamstock Ltd* [1994] 1 BCLC 716.

3   See *Practice Note* [1996] 1 All ER 442.

4   [1993] 4 All ER 499, [1994] 1 WLR 172; see also *Secretary of State for Trade and Industry v Banarse* [1997] 1 BCLC 653.

5   [1996] 2 BCLC 513, [1997] BCC 155.

6   [1996] 2 BCLC 513 at 518, [1997] BCC 155 at 159; although the court acknowledged that it would be rare for the court to have doubts – after all the parties will have agreed on disqualification and the appropriate period.

A further refinement on the *Carecraft* procedure was an offer by a director of undertakings similar in scope to a disqualification order in return for the disqualification proceedings being stayed. But in *Re Blackspur Group plc, Secretary of State for Trade and Industry v Davies*[6a] the Court of Appeal rejected the use of undertakings in this way. The Parliamentary scheme laid down in the Company Directors Disqualification Act 1986 for the protection of the public provided for the making of a disqualification order on a factual basis sufficient to justify the judicial finding that the respondent was unfit to be a director of a company. This might arise, as we have seen, either through a hearing or through the *Carecraft* procedure, but the Act did not provide for the disposal of proceedings on the basis of undertakings made without an admission of unfitness.

Penal or civil proceedings

The starting point for the courts is that disqualification is designed to protect the public against the future conduct of companies by persons whose past records as directors of insolvent companies have shown them to be a danger to creditors and others[7]:

> It is beyond dispute that the purpose [of the statutory power to disqualify unfit directors of insolvent companies] is to protect the public, and in particular potential creditors of companies, from losing money through companies becoming insolvent when the directors of those companies are people unfit to be concerned in the management of a company[8].

That this is the key element is evident from the wording of the statute itself which authorises an application to be made for disqualification where it appears that it is expedient in the public interest for the director to be disqualified[9].

It is frequently asserted by the courts that disqualification is not intended as a punitive measure although the courts recognise that removing the privilege of trading through a limited liability company does involve a substantial interference with the freedom of the individual[10]. The debate as to the boundary between civil and penal proceedings carries over to discussions as to the appropriate burden of proof. In *Re Living Images Ltd*[11] Laddie J, while accepting that disqualification proceedings were

---

6a   [1998] BCC 11, CA, affg [1997] 2 BCLC 96, [1997] BCC 488, Ch D. Cf *Secretary of State for Trade and Industry v Cleland* [1997] 1 BCLC 437, [1997] BCC 473; *Re Homes Assured Corpn plc* [1996] BCC 297 where disqualification proceedings were stayed when the court did accept undertakings by directors similar in scope to a disqualification order. Those cases were distinguished on the grounds of the particular circumstances in those cases: see [1998] BCC 11 at 21, CA; also [1997] 2 BCLC 96 at 107, [1997] BCC 488 at 497, Ch D.

7   See *Re Lo-Line Electric Motors Ltd* [1988] Ch 477 at 486, [1988] 2 All ER 692 at 696, per Browne-Wilkinson V-C; also *Re Sevenoaks Stationers (Retail) Ltd* [1991] Ch 164, [1991] 3 All ER 578.

8   *Re Sevenoaks Stationers (Retail) Ltd* [1991] Ch 164 at 176, [1991] 3 All ER 578 at 583. See the National Audit Office Report *The Insolvency Service Executive Agency: Company Directors Disqualification* (1993) which was critical of the Service for allowing a number of unfit directors to fall through the net. The report noted that a failure to pursue all unfit directors suggested that the Service was not fully meeting the protective objectives laid down in the legislation. Since then there has been a significant increase in the number of disqualification orders sought.

9   See CDDA 1986, s 7(1).

10   See *Re Lo-Line Electric Motors Ltd* [1988] Ch 477 at 478, [1988] 2 All ER 692 at 696, per Browne-Wilkinson V-C; also *Re Crestjoy Products Ltd* [1990] BCLC 677 at 681, [1990] BCC 23 at 26. See Finch (1990) 53 MLR 385 who argues that there is a significant punitive element in many of these decisions. Also Dine [1994] JBL 325, (1988) 9 Co Law 213.

11   [1996] 1 BCLC 348.

civil proceedings and therefore the appropriate standard of proof was the balance of probabilities, went on to say:

> However disqualification does involve a substantial interference with the freedom of the individual ... Furthermore some of the allegations made by the Official Receiver may involve serious charges of moral turpitude. ... In such cases the court must bear in mind the inherent unlikeliness of such serious allegations being true. The more serious the allegation, the more the court will need the assistance of cogent evidence .... I should add that the court must also be alert to the dangers of hindsight[12].

Unfitness

In deciding whether a person is unfit the court must have regard in particular to the matters specified in Sch 1 to the Company Directors Disqualification Act 1986, Part I of which is applicable in all cases, Part II of which is applicable only if the company has become insolvent[13].

Part I requires the court to have regard to:

(i) any misfeasance or breach of any fiduciary or other duty by the director in relation to the company;

(ii) any misapplication or retention by a director of, or any conduct by the director giving rise to an obligation to account for, any money or other property of the company;

(iii) the extent of the director's responsibility for the company entering into any transaction liable to be set aside under the Insolvency Act 1986[14];

(iv) the extent of the director's responsibility for the company's failure to comply with various disclosure requirements[15];

(v) the extent of the director's responsibility for any failure by the directors of the company to comply with the provisions relating to the preparation of annual accounts or the approval and signature of the accounts[16].

Part II requires the court to have regard to:

(i) the extent of the director's responsibility for the causes of the company becoming insolvent;

(ii) the extent of the director's responsibility for any failure by the company to supply any goods or services which have been paid for, in whole or in part;

(iii) the extent of the director's responsibility for the company entering into any transaction at an undervalue or giving any preference which is liable to be set aside[17];

(iv) the extent of the director's responsibility for any failure by the directors to comply with the requirements of the Insolvency Act 1986 in relation to creditors' meetings[18];

---

12 [1996] 1 BCLC 348 at 355–356.
13 CDDA 1986, s 9(1). The Schedule is not exclusive and the Secretary of State retains the power to alter it by statutory instrument: s 9(4)–(5). It is possible to seek disqualification on the grounds of unfitness in cases where the company has not become insolvent, for example following an investigation by the DTI. In that case only Part 1 of the Schedule would be relevant.
14 Ie under IA 1986, Part XVI.
15 Ie under CA 1985, ss 221, 222, 288, 352, 353, 363, 399, 415.
16 Ie under ibid, ss 226, 227, 233.
17 Ie under IA 1986, ss 127, 238–240.
18 Ie under ibid, s 98.

(v)   any failure by the director to supply any statement of affairs or attend meetings, or to co-operate with any office-holder under the Insolvency Act 1986[19].

The standards required of directors

An initial formulation as to the standard of behaviour evidencing unfitness was that it had to be conduct which amounted to a breach of commercial morality[20]. Most frequently cited was the dictum of Browne-Wilkinson V-C in *Re Lo-Line Electric Motors Ltd*[1] that the conduct complained of must display a lack of commercial probity. However, in *Re Sevenoaks Stationers (Retail) Ltd*[2] the Court of Appeal cautioned against treating such guidance as judicial paraphrases of the statute. Dillon LJ noted that:

> The test laid down ... is whether the person's conduct as a director of the company or companies in question makes him unfit to be concerned in the management of a company. These are ordinary words of the English language and they should be simple to apply in most cases. It is important to hold to those words in each case[3].

At one end of the scale, there is the dishonest conduct of a company's affairs, the cynical exploitation of the privilege of trading through limited liability, which would certainly indicate a lack of commercial probity and warrant disqualification. On the other hand, an ordinary commercial misjudgment is in itself not sufficient to justify disqualification[4]. Between these two points, it is for the court to decide on the evidence presented whether the conduct of the director, viewed cumulatively and taking into account any extenuating circumstances, has fallen below the standards of probity and competence appropriate for persons fit to be a director[5].

There may be no dishonesty but nonetheless irresponsible and incompetent management evidencing unfitness to be concerned in the management of a company[6]. This has been the greatest change in emphasis brought about by disqualification as directors in the past have been accustomed to very low standards of competence being tolerated. Now incompetence may render a director unfit and warrant disqualification.

---

19   Ie under ibid, ss 22, 47, 99, 131, 234, 235.
20   *Re Dawson Print Group Ltd* [1987] BCLC 601 at 606, 3 BCC 322 at 324, per Hoffmann J.
1   [1988] Ch 477 at 486, [1988] 2 All ER 692 at 696. See also *Re Keypak Homecare Ltd* [1990] BCLC 440, [1990] BCC 117.
2   [1991] Ch 164, [1991] 3 All ER 578.
3   [1991] Ch 164 at 176, [1991] 3 All ER 578 at 583; See also *Re Park House Properties Ltd* [1997] 2 BCLC 530; *Re Firedart Ltd, Official Receiver v Fairall* [1994] 2 BCLC 340; *Secretary of State for Trade and Industry v Van Hengel* [1995] 1 BCLC 545, [1995] BCC 173; *Re Dominion International Group plc (No 2)* [1996] 1 BCLC 572 at 575–576.
4   *Re Lo-Line Electric Motors Ltd* [1988] Ch 477 at 486, [1988] 2 All ER 692 at 696, per Browne-Wilkinson V-C; also *Re McNulty's Interchange Ltd* [1989] BCLC 709; *Re Douglas Construction Services Ltd* [1988] BCLC 397.
5   *Secretary of State for Trade and Industry v Gray* [1995] 1 BCLC 276 at 284, [1995] BCC 554 at 574, per Hoffmann LJ.
6   See *Secretary of State for Trade and Industry v Van Hengel* [1995] 1 BCLC 545, [1995] BCC 173; *Re Linvale Ltd* [1993] BCLC 654; *Re Sevenoaks Stationers (Retail) Ltd* [1991] Ch 164, [1991] 3 All ER 578; *Re Chartmore Ltd* [1990] BCLC 673; *Re DJ Matthews (Joinery Design) Ltd* (1988) 4 BCC 513; *Re Lo-Line Electric Motors Ltd* [1988] Ch 477, [1988] 2 All ER 692. Of course, the absence of dishonesty may affect the period of disqualification imposed and may persuade the court to grant leave to act despite being disqualified, discussed further below.

The process involves two stages: first, a consideration of whether the director was incompetent; secondly, whether such incompetence justifies a finding of unfitness[6a].

In *Re Continental Assurance Co of London plc*[7] a non-executive director of an insurance company, who was also a non-executive director of its parent company, was found unfit as a result of the insurance company having made transfers of assets to the parent company in breach of the provisions of the Companies Act 1985 governing financial assistance for the purchase of a company's own shares[8]. The director, who was a corporate financier, did not know of the giving of financial assistance but it was evident from the parent company's accounts. The only conclusion open to the court, Chadwick J said, was that the director did not trouble to read the accounts which would have given him the necessary information. He failed to appreciate what was required of someone in his position, in this case that a director who was a corporate financier should be prepared to read and understand the statutory accounts and to satisfy himself that transactions between the companies were properly reflected in the accounts. Had he done so, he would have recognised the improper financial assistance.

Any competent director in his position, the court said, would have known what was going on and his failure to know displayed serious incompetence or neglect[9]. He was disqualified for three years[10].

The role which disqualification plays in raising the standards expected of directors was emphasised by the Court of Appeal in *Secretary of State for Trade and Industry v Gray*[11]:

> The concept of limited liability and the sophistication of our corporate law offers great privileges and great opportunities for those who wish to trade under that regime. But the corporate environment carries with it the discipline that those who avail themselves of those privileges must accept the standards laid down and abide by the regulatory rules and disciplines in place to protect creditors and shareholders ... The Parliamentary intention to improve managerial safeguards and standards for the long term good of employees, creditors and investors is clear[12].
>
> ... Those who trade under the regime of limited liability and who avail themselves of the privileges of that regime, must accept the standards of probity and competence to which the law requires company directors to conform[13].

Applications for disqualification typically focus on one or more of the following factors:

- poor accounting records usually coupled with a failure to file annual accounts and returns to Companies House;

6a   *Re Continental Assurance Co of London plc* [1997] 1 BCLC 48 at 56, [1996] BCC 888 at 895, *Re Park House Properties Ltd* [1997] 2 BCLC 530 at 555.

7   [1997] 1 BCLC 48, [1996] BCC 888.

8   Ie contrary to CA 1985, s 151.

9   [1997] 1 BCLC 48 at 56, 58, [1996] BCC 888 at 895, 896. See also *Secretary of State for Trade and Industry v Laing* [1996] 2 BCLC 324 at 342; *Secretary of State for Trade and Industry v Van Hengel* [1995] 1 BCLC 545, [1995] BCC 173; *Re Burnham Marketing Services Ltd, Secretary of State for Trade and Industry v Harper* [1993] BCC 518; *Re Austinsuite Furniture Ltd* [1992] BCLC 1047; *Re Melcast (Wolverhampton) Ltd* [1991] BCLC 288.

10   It is clear that the court would have disqualified him for longer had the Secretary of State not indicated that he would be content with three years: see [1997] 1 BCLC 48 at 60, [1996] BCC 888 at 897–898.

11   [1995] 1 BCLC 276, [1995] BCC 554, CA; see also *Re Park House Properties Ltd* [1997] 2 BCLC 530.

12   [1995] 1 BCLC 276 at 288, [1995] BCC 554 at 577, per Henry LJ.

13   [1995] 1 BCLC 276 at 289, [1995] BCC 554 at 577, per Neill LJ.

- continued trading whilst insolvent without regard to creditors' interests;
- personal benefits accruing to directors including excessive remuneration.

It is rare for a case to consist of only one of these headings and usually all three are present to a greater or lesser degree. Where there are a number of allegations, the correct approach is for the judge to consider each matter and to decide whether that matter amounts to misconduct and if so whether alone or in conjunction with other such matters it indicates that the respondent is unfit to be concerned in the management of a company[14].

Failure to maintain accounting records and file annual accounts and returns

In many cases the directors will have failed to maintain adequate accounting records as they are required to do[15] and consequently usually also fail to comply with their statutory obligations regarding filing annual accounts and returns with the registrar of companies[16].

Such failures are viewed very seriously for disclosure is part of the price to be paid for the privilege of trading through the limited liability company. A failure to maintain proper records means that the directors do not know the company's financial position with accuracy and so cannot appreciate the need to take steps to protect their creditors[17]. A failure to file information with the registrar deprives creditors of information which would influence their behaviour[18].

The position was clearly stated by the Court of Appeal in *Secretary of State for Trade and Industry v Ettinger, Re Swift 736 Ltd*[19]:

> Those who take advantage of limited liability must conduct their companies with due regard to the ordinary standards of commercial morality. They must also be punctilious in observing the safeguards laid down by Parliament for the benefit of others who have dealings with their companies. They must maintain proper books of account and prepare annual accounts; they must file their accounts and returns promptly; and they must fully and frankly disclose information about deficiencies in accordance with the statutory provisions. Isolated lapses in filing documents are one thing and may be excusable. Not so persistent lapses which show overall a blatant disregard for this important aspect of accountability. Such lapses are serious and cannot be condoned even though, and it is right to have this firmly in mind, they need not involve any dishonest intent[20].

The court noted that the seriousness with which this conduct is viewed is evident from the fact that Parliament included this item specifically in Sch 1 to the Company Directors Disqualification Act 1986, as noted above. The court went on[20]:

---

14   *Secretary of State for Trade and Industry v McTighe (No 2)* [1996] 2 BCLC 477, CA.
15   Ie under CA 1985, s 221.
16   As required by ibid, ss 242, 363.
17   See *Secretary of State for Trade and Industry v Arif* [1997] 1 BCLC 34; also *Re Firedart Ltd, Official Receiver v Fairall* [1994] 2 BCLC 340 at 352 ; *Re Hitco 2000 Ltd* [1995] 2 BCLC 63 at 70, [1995] BCC 161 at 167; *Re New Generation Engineers Ltd* [1993] BCLC 435.
18   See *Re Park Properties Ltd* [1997] 2 BCLC 530; also Re *Pamstock Ltd* [1994] 1 BCLC 716, [1994] BCC 264; *Re Tansoft Ltd* [1991] BCLC 339. See also *Secretary of State for Trade and Industry v Banarse* [1997] 1 BCLC 653, [1997] BCC 425 (directors negligently permitted materially inaccurate accounts to be circulated).
19   [1993] BCLC 896, [1993] BCC 312, CA.
20   [1993] BCLC 896 at 899–900, [1993] BCC 312 at 315, per Nicholls V-C.

Those who persistently fail to discharge their statutory obligations in this respect can expect to be disqualified ... The business community should be left in no doubt on this score. It may be that ... there is still a lingering feeling in some quarters that a failure to file accounts and so forth is a venial sin. If this is still so, the sooner the attitude is corrected the better it will be. Judicial observations to this effect have been made before but they bear repetition.

Continued trading whilst insolvent in disregard of creditors' interests

One of the problems which the Cork Committee identified and which is common in these cases is that the directors continue to trade after a point in time when the company's financial position becomes hopeless instead of putting the company into insolvent liquidation. This simply increases the number of creditors and the amount of the deficiency when the company does collapse. In so doing the directors are taking unwarranted risks with creditors' money and merit disqualification[1].

For example, in *Re Living Images Ltd*[2] the court found that the three directors were aware by late 1989 at the latest that the company was extremely unlikely to avoid liquidation yet they kept the company going until the end of April 1990. The company was ultimately wound up with a deficiency in excess of £1.5m. The directors believed that there was a chance that they might be able to secure one or more of the very large projects which appeared from time to time in their line of business but they were fully aware that the chance was small. The court found that they refused to bow to the inevitable and kept the company going as long as there was the barest flicker of a possibility that a large contract might come in. During this period the company continued to incur further substantial losses. The court concluded that the directors in effect used the cover of limited liability to suck in more creditors to prop up an obviously moribund company[3]. Two of the directors were disqualified for six years; the third for two and a half years.

In many instances when the company becomes unable to pay all its debts, the directors adopt a policy of paying only those creditors who press for payment or paying only those who need to be paid in order to keep the business going. In *Re Sevenoaks Stationers (Retail) Ltd*[4] Dillon LJ accepted that the adoption of such a policy merits a

---

1   See *Re Synthetic Technology Ltd, Secretary of State for Trade and Industry v Joiner* [1993] BCC 549; also *Secretary of State for Trade and Industry v Lubrani, Re Amaron Ltd* [1997] 1 BCLC 115; *Secretary of State for Trade and Industry v Laing* [1996] 2 BCLC 324; *Secretary of State for Trade and Industry v McTighe (No 2)* [1996] 2 BCLC 477; also *Re Richborough Furniture Ltd* [1996] 1 BCLC 507, [1996] BCC 155; *Re Hitco 2000 Ltd* [1995] 2 BCLC 63, [1995] BCC 161; *Re Ward Sherrard Ltd* [1996] BCC 418; *Secretary of State for Trade and Industry v Gray* [1995] 1 BCLC 276, [1995] BCC 554; *Re Firedart Ltd, Official Receiver v Fairall* [1994] 2 BCLC 340; *Re Linvale Ltd* [1993] BCLC 654. Cf *Secretary of State for Trade and Industry v Van Hengel* [1995] 1 BCLC 545, [1995] BCC 173 where the court accepted that the continued trading was in the genuine belief that fresh capital and changed trading circumstances would enable the company to survive. See also *Secretary of State for Trade and Industry v Gash* [1997] 1 BCLC 341 (also reported as *Re CS Holidays Ltd* [1997] BCC 172) as to whether a director who failed to resign once he found that the company was trading at the risk of creditors was unfit. Cf *Re Park House Properties Ltd* [1997] 2 BCLC 530 (inactive directors who left everything to another director who ran the company in an inappropriate way were unfit by virtue of their sheer inactivity).
2   [1996] 1 BCLC 348, [1996] BCC 112.
3   [1996] 1 BCLC 348 at 367, [1996] BCC 112 at 126.
4   [1991] Ch 164, [1991] 3 All ER 578.

finding of unfitness[5] and this has proved a common charge in disqualification cases[6]. The result of such a policy is that the company while insolvent is unfairly using as working capital money which ought to be paid to creditors[7].

Another feature of these cases is that often a significant proportion of the deficiency on liquidation consists of Crown debts, essentially sums sue to the Revenue in the form of PAYE, National Insurance and VAT receipts. In many instances, it is the Inland Revenue which ultimately petitions for the compulsory winding up of the company. Initially the courts regarded the non-payment of Crown debts as particularly culpable[8]. This approach was justified as arising from the involuntary nature of the Crown as a creditor and the fact that the failure to pay over these sums might have a prejudicial effect on the employees[9].

In *Re Sevenoaks Stationers (Retail) Ltd*[10], however, the Court of Appeal rejected this approach finding that the Crown's position is as it is because of its administrative practice of not pursuing these debts and that employees are not prejudiced because, as far as they are concerned, the Crown treats the sums as paid. Dillon LJ concluded that Crown debts were not in a different class from other debts and non-payment of Crown debts could not automatically be relied on as evidence of unfitness. It is necessary instead to see what, if any, is the significance of that non-payment. It may be part of a deliberate decision by the directors only to pay those creditors who pressed for payment and to retain sums which should have been paid to creditors (be they the Crown or otherwise) to fund the company's continued trading[11]. As noted above, that in itself is evidence which will support a finding of unfitness.

Part of the 'juggling' required to continue trading in this way usually involves the issuing of numerous cheques to creditors hoping that the account will be within limits when they are presented for payment. In many cases, of course, the cheques are subsequently dishonoured. In *Re Hitco 2000 Ltd*[12] the court accepted that regularly drawing cheques in the hope that the account will be within limits when the cheques are presented is misuse of a bank account and is conduct which is certainly capable of evidencing unfitness. Whether it does so in any particular case is a matter depending on all the evidence in the case.

A further factor is usually the inadequate capitalisation of the company throughout its trading history. The absence of any required minimum share capital for private companies means that many companies commence business with a share capital of £100 or less. It may also be difficult for the company to borrow money in the absence of a trading record. The net result is that many of these companies have a negligible

---

5   [1991] Ch 164 at 183, [1991] 3 All ER 578 at 589.
6   See also *Secretary of State for Trade and Industry v McTighe (No 2)* [1996] 2 BCLC 477; *Secretary of State for Trade and Industry v Laing* [1996] 2 BCLC 324 at 342; *Re New Generation Engineers Ltd* [1993] BCLC 435; *Re GSAR Realisations Ltd* [1993] BCLC 409; *Re Melcast (Wolverhampton) Ltd* [1991] BCLC 288.
7   See *Re GSAR Realisations Ltd* [1993] BCLC 409 at 412, per Ferris J.
8   See *Re Lo-Line Electric Motors Ltd* [1988] Ch 477 at 488, [1988] 2 All ER 692 at 698, per Browne-Wilkinson V-C; agreeing with Vinelott J in *Re Stanford Services Ltd* [1987] 3 BCLC 607, 3 BCC 326.
9   See *Re Lo-Line Electric Motors Ltd* [1988] Ch 477 at 487–488, [1988] 2 All ER 692 at 697–698; *Re Stanford Services Ltd* [1987] BCLC 607 at 617, 3 BCC 326 at 334.
10   [1991] Ch 164, [1991] 3 All ER 578. ·
11   [1991] Ch 164 at 183, [1991] 3 All ER 578 at 589–590. See also *Re Richborough Furniture Ltd* [1996] 1 BCLC 507 at 518, [1996] BCC 155 at 164; *Re GSAR Realisations Ltd* [1993] BCLC 409 at 412, per Ferris J; *Re Austinsuite Furniture Ltd* [1992] BCLC 1047.
12   [1995] 2 BCLC 63, [1995] BCC 161. See also *Re Pamstock Ltd* [1994] 1 BCLC 716, [1994] BCC 264.

financial base from which to trade and so from the outset they trade at the risk of their suppliers, bankers and the Crown[13].

It is also common for the directors to have been involved in the management of a number of companies which have gone into insolvent liquidation one after the other. Again this is the scenario about which the Cork Committee expressed particular concern. In *Re Swift 736 Ltd*[14], for example, the court noted that two of the directors had set up six companies which carried on the business of making shirts. The pattern was that each company in succession became insolvent and immediately upon its insolvency the next company took over the same business and at the same premises. Hoffmann J noted:

> That form of trading, where one had a succession of companies which no doubt pay a salary to their principal directors and are then allowed to sink, having lived on involuntary credit provided by the Crown, is the very thing which the provisions for disqualification of directors is intended to prevent ...[15].

Similarly in *Re Travel Mondial (UK) Ltd*[16] Browne-Wilkinson V-C stated:

> This was an attempt to carry on the same business at the same premises, leaving behind the creditors of the old business. This is exactly the kind of behaviour by directors that is most to be deplored in that it is the use of the fabric of a limited company to deprive creditors of their money and simply to change the cloak in which that is done from one company to the next. It is in my judgment a serious case of unfitness to be a director[17].

Personal benefits for directors

In addition to taking unwarranted risks with creditors' money and the other breaches of duty outlined above, in many of the cases the directors will have continued, despite looming insolvency, to pay their own remuneration and to obtain other personal benefits. Misconduct identified by the courts has included the granting of preferences to themselves and personal friends[18]; the transfer or use of the company's assets for inadequate consideration or without security for the sale price[19]; undisclosed conflicts of interest resulting in personal gain[20]; and the award of excessive remuneration[1].

---

13   See *Re Ipcon Fashions Ltd* (1989) 5 BCC 773 at 774. Also *Re Ward Sherrard Ltd* [1996] BCC 418; *Re Austinsuite Furniture Ltd* [1992] BCLC 1047; *Re Chartmore Ltd* [1990] BCLC 673.

14   [1993] BCLC 1, [1992] BCC 93. The case was subsequently appealed on a different point see [1993] BCLC 896, [1993] BCC 312, CA. See also *Secretary of State for Trade and Industry v McTighe (No 2)* [1996] 2 BCLC 477.

15   [1993] BCLC 1 at 3, [1992] BCC 93 at 95.

16   [1991] BCLC 120.

17   [1991] BCLC 120 at 123. See also *Re Linvale Ltd* [1993] BCLC 654.

18   See *Re Firedart Ltd, Official Receiver v Fairall* [1994] 2 BCLC 340; *Secretary of State for Trade and Industry v Gray* [1995] 1 BCLC 276, [1995] BCC 554; *Re Living Images Ltd* [1996] 1 BCLC 348, [1996] BCC 112.

19   See *Re Park House Properties Ltd* [1997] 2 BCLC 530; *Secretary of State for Trade and Industry v McTighe (No 2)* [1996] 2 BCLC 477; *Secretary of State for Trade and Industry v Arif* [1997] 1 BCLC 34, [1996] BCC 586; *Secretary of State for Trade and Industry v Gray* [1995] 1 BCLC 276, [1995] BCC 554; *Re Keypak Homecare Ltd* [1990] BCLC 440, [1990] BCC 117.

20   *Re Dominion International Group plc (No 2)* [1996] 1 BCLC 572; *Re Godwin Warren Control Systems plc* [1993] BCLC 80.

1   See *Secretary of State for Trade and Industry v Lubrani, Re Amaron Ltd* [1997] 2 BCLC 115; *Secretary of State for Trade and Industry v McTighe (No 2)* [1996] 2 BCLC 477; *Re Ward Sherrard Ltd* [1996] BCC 418; *Secretary of State for Trade and Industry v Van Hengel* [1995] 1 BCLC 545, [1995] BCC 173; *Re Moorgate Metals Ltd* [1995] 1 BCLC 503, [1995] BCC 143; *Re Firedart Ltd, Official Receiver v Fairall* [1994] 2 BCLC 340.

The effect of a disqualification order

If a disqualification order is made, then the person concerned may not, without leave of the court:

(a) be a director of a company; or
(b) be a liquidator or administrator of a company; or
(c) be a receiver or manager of a company's property; or
(d) in any way, whether directly or indirectly, be concerned or take part in the promotion, formation or management of a company

for a specified period beginning with the date of the order[2].

Note that the order must prohibit the person from all of these activities and it is not possible simply to specify that he shall not act as a director leaving it open to him to act, for example, as a receiver and manager[3].

In *R v Campbell*[4] a disqualified person was found to be acting as a management consultant to a company and tried to argue that this did not fall within the scope of the prohibition as he was not in control of the decision-making process within the company. The Court of Appeal found that the wording of the prohibition is widely cast and comprehensively designed to make it impossible for persons to be part of the management and central direction of the company's affairs, and that included acting as a management consultant to the company.

LEAVE TO ACT

It is possible for a disqualified director to apply to the court for leave to act[5]. Before granting leave to act the court must be satisfied that there is a need for the order and that the public will remain adequately protected[6]. Granting leave to act in this way rather diminishes the force of a disqualification order but can be justified if the overriding principle is protection of the public, for leave is usually granted subject to conditions designed to insulate the public from any possible financial mismanagement by the disqualified director[7].

In *Re Lo-Line Electric Motors Ltd*[8], having disqualified a director on the grounds of unfitness for a period of three years, the court then gave him leave to be a director of two named family companies which were solvent and trading profitably. Leave was granted subject to conditions relating to the control of those companies and the appointment of a finance director.

In *Re Majestic Recording Studios Ltd*[9] leave was granted to act in respect of one particular company in view of the fact that the director was the moving spirit behind

2 CDDA 1986, s 1(1). See also Table A, art 81 which provides that a director must vacate his office in the event of being disqualified.
3 *Re Gower Enterprises Ltd (No 2)* [1995] 2 BCLC 201, [1995] BCC 1081 agreeing with Lindsay J obiter in *Re Polly Peck International plc (No 2), Secretary of State for Trade and Industry v Ellis* [1994] 1 BCLC 574 at 581–582, [1993] BCC 890 at 897; see also *Re Brian Sheridan Cars Ltd* [1996] 1 BCLC 327; *Re Seagull Manufacturing Co Ltd (No 3)* [1996] 1 BCLC 51.
4 [1984] BCLC 83.
5 CDDA, ss 1(1), 17.
6 *Re Cargo Agency Ltd* [1992] BCLC 686 at 692, [1992] BCC 388 at 393, per Harman J. See also *Re Gibson Davies Ltd* [1995] BCC 11; *Re Chartmore Ltd* [1990] BCLC 673.
7 See *Re Gibson Davies Ltd* [1995] BCC 11 where 10 conditions were attached to leave; *Re Godwin Warren Control Systems plc* [1993] BCLC 80; also note *Secretary of State for Trade and Industry v Palfreman* [1995] 2 BCLC 301, [1995] BCC 193 as to whether conditions should be imposed.
8 [1988] Ch 477, [1988] 2 All ER 692.
9 [1989] BCLC 1, (1989) 4 BCC 519.

the business and without him the jobs of 55 employees would be in jeopardy. Leave was granted subject to the appointment to the board of an independent chartered accountant approved by the court.

In *Re Godwin Warren Control Systems plc*[10] leave was granted to permit the disqualified director to continue to act as chief executive of two companies provided that the order of the court and the reasons for it were brought to the attention of the boards of those companies.

The position where a director disregards the conditions of leave was considered in *Re Brian Sheridan Cars Ltd, Official Receiver v Sheridan*[11]. The conditions (which had not been adhered to) specified the appointment of other directors and approved auditors and the service of the court's judgment on various interested third parties.

In a thorough review of the position regarding the granting of leave to act, the court noted that a person who was granted leave was being accorded a privilege or indulgence by the court which was liable to be withdrawn if he was casual in any way in relation to his conduct as a director or with regard to any aspect of the proceedings[12].

Where a person was permitted to act as a director on specific terms, it was of cardinal importance that those terms were strictly observed. A failure to observe those terms scrupulously meant that, in acting as a director, that person was not acting pursuant to the leave granted to him and was contravening the Company Directors Disqualification Act 1986 which rendered him liable to criminal penalties and personal liability[13] for the company's debts[14]. Where a disqualified person continued to act as a director in breach of the terms of the order granting him leave to act, then other persons involved with the management of a company also faced similar potential personal liability[15] for the company's debts[16].

The period of disqualification

Where a person is disqualified on the grounds of persistent default, or on conviction of an indictable offence by a court of summary jurisdiction, or on conviction of summary offences in relation to returns to the registrar of companies, then the maximum period of disqualification is five years[17]. In any other case, the maximum period is 15 years[18]. If the court makes a disqualification order on the grounds of unfitness in the case of a director of an insolvent company[19] then a minimum period of two years is prescribed[20]. Any period of de facto disqualification suffered by a person while disqualification proceedings are pending is not a relevant consideration and cannot be used to reduce what would be the appropriate disqualification period[1].

---

10   [1993] BCLC 80.
11   [1996] 1 BCLC 327, [1995] BCC 1035.
12   [1996] 1 BCLC 327 at 346, [1995] BCC 1035 at 1050.
13   Ie under CDDA 1986, ss 13, 15 discussed below.
14   [1996] 1 BCLC 327 at 346, [1995] BCC 1035 at 1050.
15   Ie under CDDA 1986, s 15.
16   [1996] 1 BCLC 327 at 346, [1995] BCC 1035 at 1050.
17   CDDA 1986, ss 3(5), 2(3)(a), 5(5) respectively.
18   Ibid, ss 2(3)(b), 4(3), 6(4), 8, 10.
19   Ie under ibid, s 6.
20   Ibid, s 6(4).
1   *Secretary of State for Trade and Industry v Arif* [1997] 1 BCLC 34, [1996] BCC 586. However, such a period of de facto disqualification may be a relevant consideration when deciding whether to grant leave to act as a director of a particular company or companies pursuant to an application under CDDA 1986, s 17, discussed above.

Guidelines as to the appropriate period of disqualification were laid down by the Court of Appeal in *Re Sevenoaks Stationers (Retail) Ltd*[2]. Dillon LJ divided the possible periods of disqualification into three brackets:

(a)   the top bracket of 10-15 years should be reserved for particularly serious cases such as where a director has previously been disqualified;

(b)   the middle bracket of 6-10 years should apply to serious cases which do not merit the top bracket;

(c)   the bottom bracket of 2-5 years should be applied where, though disqualification is mandatory, the case is, relatively, not very serious[3].

It is open to the Secretary of State to appeal both against a failure to disqualify[4] and against the length of an order[5].

Consequences of acting while disqualified

It is a criminal offence to act in breach of a disqualification order, the penalty for which is imprisonment or a fine or both[6]. Personal liability may be imposed not only on any person who acts in breach of a disqualification order[7] but also on any person who acts or is willing to act on the instructions of a disqualified person[8].

Any disqualified person who is involved in the management of a company becomes personally responsible for such debts and liabilities as are incurred at the time when he was so involved[9]. For these purposes, a person is involved in the management of a company if he is a director or if he is concerned, whether directly or indirectly, or takes part in the management of a company[10].

Liability also extends to any person who is involved in the management of the company and who acts or is willing to act[11] on instructions given without leave of the court by a person whom he knows at that time to be the subject of a disqualification order or to be an undischarged bankrupt[12]. Liability in this case is for such debts and other liabilities of the company as are incurred at the time when that person was acting or willing to act on instructions so given[13]. In each case liability is joint and several[14].

---

2   [1991] Ch 164, [1991] 3 All ER 578. See also *Practice Note* [1996] 1 All ER 445.

3   [1991] Ch 164 at 174, [1991] 3 All ER 578 at 581. The question of leave to act should be considered separately after a period of disqualification has been fixed; and the power to grant leave to act is irrelevant to determining the proper period of disqualification: *Secretary of State for Trade and Industry v Griffiths* (1997) Times, 29 December, CA.

4   See *Secretary of State for Trade and Industry v Gray* [1995] 1 BCLC 276, [1995] BCC 554; *Re Hitco 2000 Ltd* [1995] 2 BCLC 63, [1995] BCC 161.

5   See *Secretary of State for Trade and Industry v McTighe (No 2)* [1996] 2 BCLC 477 (Eight and four year periods increased to twelve and six years respectively); *Secretary of State for Trade and Industry v Ettinger, Re Swift 736 Ltd* [1993] BCLC 896, [1993] BCC 312, CA; on appeal from [1993] BCLC 1 (three years increased to five years).

6   CDDA 1986, s 13.

7   Including any undischarged bankrupt who is automatically disqualified under ibid, s 11.

8   CDDA 1986, s 15(1). Hicks [1988] JBL 27 at 45 notes that this self-enforcing device is probably a far greater inducement to compliance than the remote risk of being prosecuted for acting while disqualified.

9   Ibid, s 15(1), (3)(a).

10   Ibid, s 15(4).

11   Note the presumption that a person who has acted on the instructions of a person whom he knew to be disqualified is presumed, unless the contrary is shown, to have been willing at any time thereafter to act on any instructions given by that person: ibid, s 15(5).

12   Ibid, s 15(1).

13   Ibid, s 15(3)(b).

14   Ibid, s 15(2).

Register of disqualification orders

Court officers are required to provide the Secretary of State with details of cases in which a disqualification order is made or varied or ceases in force or where the court has granted leave to act[15]. Companies House in turn maintains a register of such information which is available for inspection by the public[16].

THE COMPANY SECRETARY

All companies are required to have a company secretary and a sole director cannot also act in that capacity[17]. The company secretary is appointed by the directors[18] and in the case of a public company, the directors must take all reasonable steps to secure that the secretary is a person who appears to them to have the requisite knowledge and experience to discharge that position[19]. That person must fall within one of six specified categories which covers persons with experience as a company secretary and members of various professions such accountants, chartered secretaries, solicitors and barristers. Equally, the directors may appoint someone who appears to them to be capable of discharging the functions of secretary[20].

The duties of a company secretary are mainly of an administrative nature, in particular ensuring compliance by the company with the disclosure and information requirements of the Companies Acts and adherence by the board to the proper procedures. They are not mere clerks but officers of the company who may have extensive duties and responsibilities and even authority to enter into contracts on behalf of the company, at least on the administrative side of the company's affairs[1].

Recognising the importance of the company secretary's role, the Cadbury Committee's Code of Best Practice which is addressed to listed companies states that all directors should have access to the advice and services of the company secretary and any question of the removal of the company secretary should be a matter for the board as a whole[2].

15   Ibid, s 18(1).
16   Ibid, s 18(2), (4).
17   CA 1985, s 283(1), (2).
18   See Table A, art 99.
19   CA 1985, s 286(1).
20   Ibid, s 286(1)(e).
1   *Panorama Developments (Guildford) Ltd v Fidelis Furnishing Fabrics Ltd* [1971] 2 QB 711, [1971] 3 All ER 16.
2   See the Report of the Committee on the Financial Aspects of Corporate Governance (1992), Code of Best Practice, noted above, para 1.6.

CHAPTER 25

The distribution of power within a company

In theory, at least, a company acts through two bodies. One is the company in general meeting, ie the shareholders; the other is the board of directors which is elected by the general meeting and usually entrusted with the management of the company. This chapter will consider the division of power between these two bodies and the position when the powers granted are exceeded.

A number of points need be borne in mind when examining this theoretical division of power. The division of power in this way between the board and the general meeting is inappropriate to the smaller private company where the individuals concerned may act both as shareholders and directors without differentiating particularly between those capacities, a fact which is not always reflected in the legal regulation of such companies. At the other end of the spectrum, in large public companies, the board's role in practice will be supervisory rather than managerial with extensive powers delegated to individual directors and to professional executive managers, a group largely ignored by the legal structure[1]. Moreover, the extent to which the shareholders can realistically be regarded as electing the directors in that type of company, given the board's control of the proxy machinery, must be open to question. In fact such boards tend to be self-perpetuating.

THE DIVISION OF POWER BETWEEN THE BOARD AND THE GENERAL MEETING

Authority to manage the business

Any discussion must start with the company's articles of association, for it is clearly established that the relationship between the board and the general meeting is a contractual one based on the articles which determine the extent of the management

---

1   See Berle and Means *The Modern Corporation and Private Property* (1932); Eisenberg *The Structure of the Corporation* (1976) pp 140–148; Parkinson *Corporate Power and Responsibility* (1993), ch 2.

powers conferred on the board[2]. Normally these powers will be extensive with very few matters retained exclusively by the company in general meeting. Some powers will be retained by virtue of the Companies Act 1985 such as the right to alter the memorandum and articles[3], or to increase or reduce the share capital[4], and the right to petition for a voluntary winding up[5]. Other powers, such as the power to determine the number of directors[6], are customarily given to the general meeting by the articles.

As the extent of the powers conferred on the board is purely a contractual matter, it is open to a company to adopt whatever form of management article it pleases. In practice art 70 of Table A is normally adopted. It provides that:

> Subject to the provisions of the Act, the memorandum and the articles and to any directions given by special resolution, the business of the company shall be managed by the directors who may exercise all the powers of the company.

This provision replaced art 80 of the 1948 Table A[7] which provided that the business of the company should be managed by the directors who might exercise all the powers of the company subject to such regulations (not being inconsistent with the provisions of the articles) as might be prescribed by the company in general meeting.

Although this wording suggested that shareholders could exercise control over the directors by way of an ordinary resolution[8], the courts consistently interpreted it to mean that the general meeting could only interfere with the exercise by directors of their management powers by way of a special resolution or by altering the articles and the mandate which those articles gave to the directors[9]. The position was stated in *John Shaw & Sons (Salford) Ltd v Shaw*[10]:

> A company is an entity distinct alike from its shareholders and its directors. Some of its powers may, according to its articles, be exercised by directors, certain other powers may be reserved for the shareholders in general meeting. If powers of management are vested in the directors, they and they alone can exercise these powers. The only way in which the general body of the shareholders can control the exercise of the powers vested by the articles in the directors is by altering the articles, or ... by refusing to re-elect the directors of whose actions they disapprove. They cannot themselves usurp the powers which by the articles are vested in the directors any more than the directors can usurp the powers vested by the articles in the general body of shareholders.

---

2 *Automatic Self-Cleansing Filter Syndicate Co Ltd v Cuninghame* [1906] 2 Ch 34, CA; *Gramophone and Typewriter Ltd v Stanley* [1908] 2 KB 89, CA; *Salmon v Quin & Axtens Ltd* [1909] 1 Ch 311, CA; affd sub nom *Quin & Axtens Ltd v Salmon* [1909] AC 442, HL; *Breckland Group Holdings Ltd v London & Suffolk Properties Ltd* [1989] BCLC 100.

3 See CA 1985, ss 4, 9.

4 See ibid, ss 121, 135. Note also that the power to issue shares is vested in the company in general meeting although the company may restore that power to the directors, either by the articles or by an ordinary resolution: s 80.

5 See IA 1986, s 84(1)(b).

6 See Table A, art 64.

7 See CA 1948, Sch 1.

8 See Goldberg (1970) 33 MLR 177; Sullivan (1977) 93 LQR 569; Mackenzie (1983) 4 Co Law 99; *Marshall's Valve Gear Co Ltd v Manning, Wardle & Co Ltd* [1909] 1 Ch 267.

9 See *Automatic Self-Cleansing Filter Syndicate Co Ltd v Cuninghame* [1906] 2 Ch 34, CA; *Gramophone and Typewriter Ltd v Stanley* [1908] 2 KB 89, CA; *Quin & Axtens Ltd v Salmon* [1909] AC 442, HL; *John Shaw & Sons (Salford) Ltd v Shaw* [1935] 2 KB 113, CA; *Scott v Scott* [1943] 1 All ER 582; *Breckland Group Holdings Ltd v London & Suffolk Properties Ltd* [1989] BCLC 100.

10 [1935] 2 KB 113 at 134, per Greer LJ, CA.

Article 70 now reflects that approach and permits interference by the shareholders with the directors' freedom to manage the business only if shareholders holding a sufficiently large stake in the company feel strongly about a particular matter. The division of power then is predominantly in favour of the board at the expense of the general meeting. The board in turn is usually given power by the articles to delegate any of its powers to any committee consisting of one or more directors or to any managing director or any director holding any other executive office[11].

Authority of the general meeting

It is clear then that very little managerial power is retained by the company in general meeting apart from certain powers conferred by statute and some limited concessions in the articles. The general meeting may alter the directors' mandate by way of special resolution either:

(i)   on an ad hoc basis, by giving particular directions; or
(ii) on a more permanent basis, by altering the articles.

The shareholders also possess the power, in theory at least, to remove the directors[12].

In certain limited circumstances, the courts are prepared to hold that there is a residual power of management in the general meeting. For this residual power to arise the board must be deadlocked[13] or unable to act[14] or for all practical purposes has ceased to exist[15]. As Warrington J noted in *Barron v Potter*[16]:

> ... I am not concerned to say that in ordinary cases where there is a board ready and willing to act it would be competent for the company to override the power conferred on the directors by the articles except by way of special resolution for the purpose of altering the articles. But the case which I have to deal with is a different one. For practical purposes there is no board of directors at all.

Faced with such inability on the part of the board to act, it is not surprising that the courts look to the other corporate organ to resolve the problem. This the general meeting may do, for example, by appointing another director[17], or commencing proceedings[18]. Once a functioning board is again in operation the powers of management revert to it.

---

11   See Table A, art 72. See *Mitchell & Hobbs (UK) Ltd v Mill* [1996] 2 BCLC 102: there must be an actual delegation under art 72 if a director is to claim internally that he has powers of management separate from the collective board; externally a third party may be able to rely on the appearance of authority: see discussion of actual and apparent authority below.
12   Ie under CA 1985, s 303.
13   *Barron v Potter* [1914] 1 Ch 895. Such deadlock would justify winding up the company on the just and equitable ground under IA 1986 s 122(1)(g); see *Re Yenidje Tobacco Co Ltd* [1916] 2 Ch 426, CA.
14   *Foster v Foster* [1916] 1 Ch 532.
15   *Barron v Potter* [1914] 1 Ch 895.
16   [1914] 1 Ch 895 at 902.
17   See *Barron v Potter* [1914] 1 Ch 895.
18   See *Alexander Ward & Co Ltd v Samyang Navigation Co Ltd* [1975] 2 All ER 424, HL, noted Wedderburn (1976) 39 MLR 327.

INITIATING LITIGATION

Before leaving this discussion, one remaining issue must be considered, namely which body controls the commencement of litigation in the company's name.

This matter was the subject of a lengthy debate following *Marshall's Valve Gear Co Ltd v Manning, Wardle & Co Ltd*[19] which permitted the general meeting to commence litigation despite the opposition of the board to whom powers of management had been delegated. It had been thought that this decision could be explained by accepting that there was some sort of parallel authority vested in the board *and* the general meeting[20]. However, in *Breckland Group Holdings Ltd v London & Suffolk Properties Ltd*[1] Harman J refused to countenance such interference by the shareholders with the management powers of the board. He refused to permit the majority shareholder to continue litigation which it had initiated in the company's name when the company's articles vested management power in the board of directors. He stated:

> The principle, as I see it, is that [the article] confides the management of the business to the directors and in such a case it is not for the general meeting to interfere ... If the board do not adopt it [the unauthorised litigation], a general meeting would have no power whatever to override that decision of the board and to adopt it for itself[2].

Breckland indicates that this issue is no different from any other management matter which under the articles is vested in the board so precluding shareholder intervention in the absence of directions by special resolution or alteration of the articles[3]. As far as *Marshall's Valve Gear* was concerned, Harman J thought it was overwhelmed by the weight of authority against it[4]. However, the power of the majority in general meeting to institute litigation in the name of the company against the wishes of the board must of necessity be retained where the directors are themselves the wrongdoers[5]. It would be inconsistent with the rule in *Foss v Harbottle*[6] for the majority to be precluded from bringing an action against wrongdoing directors by the fact that the articles had delegated management powers to those very wrongdoers[7]. This power in the general meeting could be treated as an exercise of a residual power of management, for where the wrongdoers are the board then there is no board in existence capable of exercising the power to commence litigation[8]. Alternatively, as Professor Sealy notes, it could be justified on the basis that the exclusive powers granted to the board under an article such as art 70 relate only to powers to manage the business of the company

---

19   [1909] 1 Ch 267.
20   See Gower *Principles of Modern Company Law* (5th edn, 1992) p 152; Wedderburn (1976) 39 MLR 327.
1   [1989] BCLC 100, noted Wedderburn (1989) 52 MLR 401; Sealy (1989) CLJ 26.
2   [1989] BCLC 100 at 106.
3   Note also *Mitchell & Hobbs (UK) Ltd v Mill* [1996] 2 BCLC 102 where an action against a company secretary initiated on behalf of the company by its managing director was struck out as the articles were in the form of art 70 and intended to vest power to manage the affairs of the company in the board of directors as a whole.
4   [1989] BCLC 100 at 105.
5   See Sealy (1989) CLJ 26 at 28; Partridge (1987) CLJ 122 at 130, fn 58.
6   (1843) 2 Hare 461.
7   See Wedderburn (1957) CLJ 194 at 201-202; Palmer's *Company Law* (25th edn, 1992), para 8.801; Sealy *Cases and Materials in Company Law* (6th edn, 1996), pp 213–214.
8   See *Alexander Ward & Co Ltd v Samyang Navigation Co Ltd* [1975] 2 All ER 424, HL, noted Wedderburn (1976) 39 MLR 327; also Wedderburn (1989) 52 MLR 402.

and do not apply to a matter which is not simply a matter of business but involves an intra-corporate dispute[9]. In practice, of course, the majority shareholders would probably remove the wrongdoing directors and have the new board initiate litigation against them.

To sum up, the proper approach to the issue of commencing litigation in the company's name is that the starting point is the rule in *Foss v Harbottle*[10] which essentially provides that where a wrong is done to the company then the company is the proper person to sue. Which organ of the company should take that decision depends on the company's constitution. Where the articles are in the standard form (ie art 70) then the matter is vested in the board which may decide as a matter of management not to sue. This is subject to the general meeting intervening in the ways outlined above and to the general meeting being the appropriate decision-making body when the directors are themselves the wrongdoers. Where the wrongdoers control both the board and the general meeting then the matter may be the subject of a derivative action by an individual shareholder[11].

ACTS BY CORPORATE AGENTS IN EXCESS OF AUTHORITY

In Chapter 10 we noted that the reform of the ultra vires doctrine has benefited third parties by ensuring the validity of transactions entered into by the company despite any limitations on the company's capacity in the memorandum of association. In any event, difficulties regarding capacity rarely arise in view of the width of most modern objects clauses.

For third parties difficulties may instead arise from a lack of authority, perhaps on the part of the board, more commonly on the part of an individual director or officer, with respect to a particular transaction. A company may try to disown an onerous obligation by alleging that the director or directors responsible had no authority to enter into the transaction. The reforms implemented by the Companies Act 1989, designed as they were to increase the security of third parties dealing with companies, had necessarily to address these questions of lack of authority in addition to issues of corporate capacity.

Authority of the Board (CA 1985 s 35A)

The statute provides:

> In favour of a person dealing with a company in good faith, the power of the board of directors to bind the company, or authorise others to do so, shall be deemed to be free of any limitation under the company's constitution[12].

9   See *Cases and Materials in Company Law* (5th edn, 1996), p 508.
10 (1843) 2 Hare 461.
11 Subject to *Smith v Croft (No 2)* [1988] Ch 114, [1987] 3 All ER 909 which enables a majority of independent shareholders to block a derivative action where they believe that litigation is not in the best interests of the company. This decision is discussed in detail in Ch 28.
12 CA 1985, s 35A(1) inserted by CA 1989, s 108. Note that the application of the section is modified by CA 1985, s 322A where the parties to the transaction include a director of the company or of its holding company, or a person connected with such a director or a company with whom such a director is associated: s 35A(6). Section 322A is discussed in greater detail in Ch 27. See also s 36A (in favour of a purchaser in good faith for valuable consideration, a document is deemed to have been duly executed by a company if it purports to be signed by a director and the secretary of the company or by two directors of the company).

In good faith

The provision operates in favour of persons dealing with a company in good faith[13] and the statutory provisions ensure that it is very difficult for a person to be in bad faith. First, a person is presumed to have acted in good faith unless the contrary is proved[14]. Secondly, a person is not to be regarded as acting in bad faith by reason *only* of his knowing that an act is beyond the powers of the directors under the company's constitution[15]. To establish bad faith, it would be necessary to show something in addition to knowledge such as malicious intent or collusion by the third party in the breach by the directors although the precise factors which the courts will take to be indicative of bad faith remain to be identified. Furthermore, a party to a transaction with a company is not bound to enquire as to any limitation on the powers of the board to bind the company or authorise others to do so[16].

Third parties dealing with the board of directors are deemed under the doctrine of constructive notice to have notice of the company's memorandum and articles of association and various public documents and any limitations contained therein[17] but this is irrelevant here since even actual knowledge of itself does not establish bad faith.

Limits on powers of board may be disregarded

Assuming that a person is dealing with a company in good faith, the effect of this is that limitations imposed by the company's constitution on the powers of the board of directors to bind the company or authorise others to do so may be disregarded. The focus of the provision is on limits to the *powers of the board.*

The limitations on the powers of the board of directors which may be set aside are those arising under the memorandum and articles of association but also limitations deriving:

(a) from a resolution of the company in general meeting or a meeting of any class of shareholders, or

(b) from any agreement between the members of the company or of any class of shareholders[18].

The types of limitations which would be covered would include provisions such as those expressly prohibiting the directors from dealing with a particular matter or requiring directors to execute a transaction in a particular manner. The question then arises as to whether it is valid to regard other requirements, such as those relating to quorum requirements or the location of board meetings, as constitutional limitations on the powers of the directors to act which might be ignored by a third party dealing in good faith. Lord Wedderburn in the House of Lords debates as the Companies Bill

---

13   For these purposes a person deals with a company if he is a party to any transaction or other act to which the company is a party: ibid, s 35A(2)(a). This ensures that the provision applies to gratuitous as well as commercial transactions.

14   Ibid, s 35A(2)(c).

15   Ibid, s 35A(2)(b). See HL Debs, vol 505, cols 1273-74, 6 April 1989; vol 512, col 682, 7 November 1989 on this aspect of the provision.

16   CA 1985, s 35B. Note that s 35B refers to a party to a transaction whereas s 35A is wider and covers dealing with a company defined as any transaction and other acts to which the company is a party.

17   See *Ernest v Nicholls* (1857) 6 HL Cas 401; *Mahony v East Holyford Mining Co* (1875) LR 7 HL 869; *Irvine v Union Bank of Australia* (1877) 2 App Cas 366, PC. The doctrine of constructive notice was to have been abolished by CA 1985, s 711A to be inserted by CA 1989, s 142 but drafting problems meant that CA 1985, s 711A was never brought into force.

18   Ibid, s 35A(3).

was going through Parliament argued strongly that such requirements are limitations. However, the Government's position was that rules as to quorum, for example, are not limitations on the powers of the board of directors but deal with the logically prior question of what constitutes a board of directors and are therefore not within the provision[19].

The point may be debatable as far as the interpretation of CA 1985, s 35A is concerned but in any event the answer to whether third parties can hold the company to transactions which are in breach of such requirements may lie in the existing law, namely the rule in *Royal British Bank v Turquand*[20], discussed below.

In the discussion above concerning the division of power as between the board and the general meeting, it was noted that, as it is a contractual matter, it is possible for the general meeting to reserve to itself certain powers. For example, the consent of the company in general meeting might be needed to authorise the sale of a particular asset, or the articles may limit the power of the board to delegate, or the general meeting might issue special directions to the board by way of special resolution in accordance with art 70. All of these limitations on the powers of the board of directors may be ignored as far as persons dealing in good faith are concerned as a result of CA 1985, s 35A. The company will be bound by the transaction despite the board lacking authority to enter into it and it is binding without any need for ratification by the company in general meeting.

This obviously increases the security of third parties and expands the authority of the board but it further diminishes what little power had been retained by the company in general meeting by denying shareholders the option of disowning such unauthorised transactions. The statute in recognition of this does go on to offer shareholders some redress although the practical value of these provisions is open to question.

Shareholder protection

First, a member may bring proceedings to restrain the doing of an act which is beyond the powers of the directors although no such proceeding may lie in respect of an act to be done in fulfilment of a legal obligation arising from a previous act of the company[1]. For example, an injunction cannot be obtained to restrain the execution of an executory contract. The obvious difficulty for the members, of course, is finding out about the proposed transaction at an early enough stage to seek injunctive relief.

Given the inability to disown a transaction as a result of s 35A, it might be thought that shareholders will have an incentive to monitor the conduct of the board in order to ensure that the directors do not exceed the limitations, such as they are, imposed on the board under the company's constitution. The practical difficulties of doing this, and the natural inertia of many shareholders, mean that this is unlikely to occur in practice and so injunctive relief may be irrelevant.

Secondly, the validity conferred on the transaction does not affect any liability incurred by the directors, or any other person, by reason of the directors exceeding their powers[2]. This raises the possibility of the company, despite being unable to disown the transaction, suing the directors in respect of it and possibly seeking to hold a third

19   See HL Debs, vol 512, cols 685–687, 7 November 1989.
20   (1855) 5 E & B 248.
1   See HL Debs, vol 512, col 681, 7 November 1989 where Lord Wedderburn argues that this formula means that there will almost never be a case where the proposed right of the shareholder to seek an injunction can operate. By the time the shareholder tries to act, there will always have been an act which creates some legal obligation.
2   CA 1985, s 35A(5).

party liable as a constructive trustee[3]. It is unclear whether it is possible to hold a third party liable as a constructive trustee where he is within the statutory provision and able to hold the company to the transaction.

This issue arose with respect to the previous provision (prior to the Companies Act 1989 reforms) in *International Sales and Agencies Ltd v Marcus*[4] where Lawson J decided that liability as a constructive trustee can arise separately from and distinct from the statute. The statutory provision, he noted, did not affect the principles of constructive trust in relation to the recipients of companies' moneys knowingly paid in breach of trust[5]. It would seem that the same is true of s 35A. On the point being raised by Lord Wedderburn in the House of Lords debate (in the context of s 35 but the position is the same under s 35A), the Government stated that it would not wish to uphold the constructive trusteeship approach where it arose because the third party knew the directors were exceeding limitations imposed on them. This would confound the purpose of the new provisions for it would in effect be saying that knowledge could prejudice the position of the third party when that is what the sections seek to exclude. As Lord Wedderburn pointed out, in the absence of express wording in the section to limit the application of constructive trusteeship in this way, this is not necessarily the interpretation which a court would adopt[6].

As for actions against the directors after the event, the difficulties involved in pursuing such an action and the reluctance of companies to sue wrongdoing directors are discussed in Chapter 28. Another possible sanction, again more theoretical than practical, is for the shareholders to remove a board which does not observe the limitations imposed on its activities but, as we saw in Chapter 24, removing directors is itself a difficult exercise.

THE RULE IN TURQUAND'S CASE

As mentioned earlier, the relationship between s 35A and the existing common law rules is not altogether clear and that is particularly true of the rule in *Turquand's* case. The rule provides that third parties are not obliged to inquire into the internal proceedings of a company but can assume that all acts of internal management had been properly carried out, save where an outsider knows or ought to know of the failure to adhere to procedures[7]. As Lord Simonds explained in *Morris v Kanssen*[8]:

> The wheels of business will not go smoothly round unless it may be assumed that that is in order which appears to be in order.

3   See *Rolled Steel Products (Holdings) Ltd v British Steel Corpn* [1986] Ch 246, [1985] 3 All ER 52, CA.
4   [1982] 3 All ER 551, [1982] 2 CMLR 46.
5   [1982] 3 All ER 551 at 559–560, [1982] 2 CMLR 46 at 58.
6   See HL Debs, vol 505, cols 1243–1247, 6 April 1989.
7   *B Liggett (Liverpool) Ltd v Barclays Bank Ltd* [1928] 1 KB 48; *Morris v Kanssen* [1946] AC 459, [1946] 1 All ER 586, HL; *Rolled Steel Products (Holdings) Ltd v British Steel Corpn* [1986] Ch 246, [1985] 3 All ER 52, CA. Insiders, ie persons holding positions within the company, are prevented from relying on the rule as they are in a position to know whether there has been compliance with the internal requirements: *Morris v Kanssen* [1946] AC 459, [1946] 1 All ER 586, HL; *Howard v Patent Ivory Manufacturing Co* (1888) 38 Ch D 156; cf *Hely-Hutchinson v Brayhead Ltd* [1968] 1 QB 549, [1967] 3 All ER 98. A further refinement to the rule is that it does not apply if the document which the outsider seeks to rely on is a forgery although this limitation is criticised: see *Ruben v Great Fingall Consolidated* [1906] AC 439, HL; also *Kreditbank Cassel GmbH v Schenkers Ltd* [1927] 1 KB 826, CA. See Prentice, *The Rule in Turquand's Case* (1991) 107 LQR 14, noting the decision in *Northside Developments Pty Ltd v Registrar-General* (1990) 93 ALR 385, H Ct Aust.
8   [1946] AC 459 at 475, [1946] 1 All ER 586 at 592.

In *Royal British Bank v Turquand*[9] the board of directors had borrowed money without having the transaction authorised by a resolution of the company in general meeting as required by the deed of settlement. The court held that the company was bound by the borrowing as the resolution was a matter of internal management which the third party could assume had been correctly carried out.

And the party here, on reading the deed of settlement, would find, not a prohibition from borrowing but a permission to do so on certain conditions. Finding that the authority might be made complete by a resolution, he would have a right to infer the fact of a resolution authorising that which on the face of the document appeared to be legitimately done.

In *Mahony v East Holyford Mining Co*[10] a bank was entitled to accept cheques drawn and signed by the directors in the manner authorised by the articles and was not obliged to query whether the individuals signing the cheques were validly appointed as directors.

Obviously s 35A (enabling a third party to ignore limitations on authority arising from the memorandum, articles, resolutions in general meeting or shareholders' agreements) is much broader in its application than the rule in *Turquand's* Case and this will reduce the need for third parties to fall back on the rule. For example, the situation in *Royal British Bank v Turquand*[11] itself would now be within s 35A involving as it did a limitation on the board's authority to act. However, cases do remain, such as those involving inquorate boards or invalidly appointed directors, which will be outside s 35A (not being limitations on the board's power to act) and there will still be a need to have recourse to the rule. It remains narrower than s 35A in that notice of the defect will prevent the third party relying on *Turquand*[12] whereas knowledge of limitations on the powers of the board does not preclude reliance on s 35A.

RATIFICATION

Finally, it should be remembered that an act in excess of the board's authority can be ratified by ordinary resolution of the general meeting even though an alteration to the board's powers would require a special resolution[13].

Authority of individual directors

So far our discussion has focused on the statutory provision removing limits to the authority of the board. In practice the management articles adopted by companies give the board an almost open-ended authority to manage the company's business and so problems of authority are rare.

---

9   (1856) 6 E & B 327.
10   (1875) LR 7 HL 869.
11   (1856) 6 E & B 327.
12   See *B Liggett (Liverpool) Ltd v Barclays Bank Ltd* [1928] 1 KB 48; *Morris v Kanssen* [1946] AC 459, [1946] 1 All ER 586, HL; *Rolled Steel Products (Holdings) Ltd v British Steel Corpn* [1986] Ch 246, [1985] 3 All ER 52, CA.
13   See *Irvine v Union Bank of Australia* (1877) 2 App Cas 366, PC; *Grant v United Kingdom Switchback Railways Co* (1888) 40 Ch D 135, CA. This is subject to the usual limitations on ratification discussed in Ch 28 below.

What remains a problem is the situation where a third party deals with an individual director whose authority to act on behalf of the company is disputed. The position of third parties dealing with individual directors is not directly addressed by the statute and their position remains subject to the rules of agency to which we now turn.[13a]

A third party may have an action for damages for breach of an implied warranty of authority against the director who contracts without authority[14] but he is usually more concerned with holding the company to the transaction. To do that, it will be necessary for the third party to show that the individual director with whom he dealt had authority, actual or apparent, to bind the company in this way. Diplock LJ noted in *Freeman and Lockyer v Buckhurst Park Properties (Mangal) Ltd*[15] that:

> Actual authority and apparent authority are quite independent of one another. Generally they co-exist and coincide but either may exist without the other and their respective scopes may be different … it is upon the apparent authority of the agent that the contractor normally relies in the ordinary course of business when entering into contracts.

We need to consider each type of authority in turn.

ACTUAL AUTHORITY

Actual authority may be express or implied actual authority. Little need be said about express actual authority which arises from an explicit conferring of authority on a director. This would frequently be recorded in the board minutes. Implied actual authority arises from the position which the individual holds. If, for example, an individual is appointed as a managing director then implied authority will authorise him to do all such things as fall within the usual scope of that office[16].

In *Hely-Hutchinson v Brayhead Ltd*[17] a director who was the chairman of the company also acted as its de facto managing director. He entered into contracts on the company's behalf on his own initiative and subsequently reported them to the board which acquiesced in this practice. In this instance, the board refused to honour an undertaking which the director had given to a third party to repay certain moneys and to indemnify the third party against loss.

The Court of Appeal found that the director lacked express actual authority. Also there was no implied actual authority on the basis of his post as chairman of the company as that office of itself did not carry the authority to enter into contracts without the sanction of the board. However, as de facto managing director, he did have implied actual authority. This would be implied from the circumstance that the board by their conduct over many months had acquiesced in his acting as managing director and committing the company to contracts without the necessity of sanction from the board[18].

13a   See Hannigan 'Contracting with Individual Directors' in Rider (ed) *The Corporate Dimension* (1998).

14   *Hely-Hutchinson v Brayhead Ltd* [1968] 1 QB 549, [1967] 3 All ER 98, CA.

15   [1964] 2 QB 480 at 502, [1964] 1 All ER 630 at 644, CA.

16   See *Hely-Hutchinson v Brayhead Ltd* [1968] 1 QB 549, [1967] 3 All ER 98, CA.

17   [1968] 1 QB 549, [1967] 3 All ER 98, CA.

18   [1968] 1 QB 549 at 584, [1967] 3 All ER 98 at 103, CA. Cf *Mitchell & Hobbs (UK) Ltd v Mill* [1996] 2 BCLC 102 where the court found that a managing director only had such powers to manage the business as were delegated to him. This is correct as regards the narrow issue in that case which involved an internal dispute as to the commencement of litigation in the company's name when powers of management were vested in the board collectively. Of course, as regards his dealings with a third party, a managing director will have extensive authority, actual and apparent.

APPARENT AUTHORITY

Apparent (or ostensible) authority, on the other hand, is the authority of an agent as it appears to others[19] and it can operate both to enlarge actual authority[19] and to create authority where no actual authority exists[20].

In *Freeman and Lockyer v Buckhurst Park Properties (Mangal) Ltd*[1] the director in question managed the company's property and acted on its behalf and in that role employed the plaintiff architects to draw up plans for the development of land held by the company. The development ultimately collapsed and the plaintiffs sued the company for their fees. The company denied that the director had any authority to employ the architects.

The court found that while he had never been appointed managing director (and therefore had no actual authority, express or implied) his actions were within his apparent authority and the board had been aware of his conduct and had acquiesced in it[2].

Diplock LJ identified four factors which must be present before a company can be bound by the acts of an agent who has no actual authority to do so. It must be shown that:

(1) a representation that the agent had authority to enter on behalf of the company into a contract of the kind sought to be enforced was made to the contractor;

(2) such representation was made by a person or persons who had 'actual' authority to manage the business of the company either generally or in respect of those matters to which the contract relates;

(3) he (the contractor) was induced by such representation to enter into the contract, ie that he in fact relied upon it; and

(4) under its memorandum or articles of association the company was not deprived of the capacity either to enter into a contract of the kind sought to be enforced or to delegate authority to enter into a contract of that kind to the agent[3].

The agent must have been held out by someone with actual authority to carry out the transaction and an agent cannot hold himself out as having authority[4]. Where the third party is relying on a holding out by the board, his position is enhanced by CA 1985 s 35A (provided that he is in good faith) since he can ignore limits on the powers of the board to authorise others to bind the company.

The acts of the principal must constitute a representation that the agent had a particular authority and must be reasonably so understood by the third party[5]. In

---

19   *Hely-Hutchinson v Brayhead Ltd* [1968] 1 QB 549 at 583, [1967] 3 All ER 98 at 102, CA, per Lord Denning.

20   See *First Energy (UK) Ltd v Hungarian International Bank Ltd* [1993] BCLC 1409.

1   [1964] 2 QB 480, [1964] 1 All ER 630, CA.

2   It is difficult to distinguish this case from *Hely-Hutchinson*, above, where the court found the director had implied actual authority. Indeed Diplock LJ in *Freeman and Lockyer* thought the trial judge might have concluded that there was actual authority, see [1964] 2 QB 480 at 501, [1964] 1 All ER 630 at 643, CA. See *Bowstead & Reynolds on Agency* (16th edn, 1996), paras 3-001–3-005; the distinction essentially is between authority arising from the relationship between the principal and agent (as in *Hely-Hutchinson*) and authority arising from the relationship as the principal allows it to appear to third parties.

3   [1964] 2 QB 480 at 505, [1964] 1 All ER 630 at 646.

4   *Freeman and Lockyer v Buckhurst Park Properties (Mangal) Ltd* [1964] 2 QB 480, [1964] 1 All ER 630, CA; *British Bank of the Middle East v Sun Life Assurance Co of Canada (UK) Ltd* [1983] BCLC 78, [1983] 2 Lloyd's Rep 9, HL; *Armagas Ltd v Mundogas SA* [1986] AC 717, [1986] 2 All ER 385, HL.

5   *Egyptian International Foreign Trade Co v Soplex Wholesale Supplies Ltd, The Raffaella* [1985] BCLC 404 at 411, [1985] 2 Lloyd's Rep 36 at 41, CA, per Browne-Wilkinson V-C.

determining whether the principal had represented his agent as having authority to enter into the particular transaction, the court has to consider the totality of the principal's conduct[5].

The commonest form of holding out is permitting the agent to act in the conduct of the principal's business[6] and in many cases the holding out consists solely of the fact that the company has invested the agent with a particular office, eg 'managing director' or 'secretary'[7].

In *Panorama Developments (Guildford) Ltd v Fidelis Furnishing Fabrics Ltd*[8] the company secretary as the chief administrative officer of the company was found to have apparent authority to enter into contracts connected with the administrative side of the company's affairs.

In *First Energy (UK) Ltd v Hungarian International Bank Ltd*[9] a senior manager of a bank had no actual or apparent authority to make an offer of credit facilities to a customer; nor did he have any actual authority to communicate any offer of credit facilities from the head office in London to the customer. However, the court found that his position gave him apparent authority to communicate to the customer an offer of credit facilities from the head office in London. Therefore the bank was in breach of contract when it refused credit facilities to the customer after the customer had accepted an offer so communicated. In this case the apparent authority arose from the position which the senior manager held. By putting him in that position, the bank conferred on him the trappings of authority[10].

Finally, the apparent authority which has arisen from the representation which has been made by someone with actual authority and which the third party has relied on must not be cut down by anything in the memorandum or articles of association which would deprive the company of the capacity either to enter into a contract of the kind sought to be enforced or to delegate authority to enter into a contract of that kind to the agent.

To a large extent the statutory reforms, discussed above, have diminished the significance of this fourth requirement as identified by Diplock LJ in *Freeman* above. Limitations on the company's capacity are no longer relevant following the enactment of CA 1985, s 35 abolishing the ultra vires doctrine which was discussed in Chapter 10. Limitations on the board's power to delegate are no longer relevant following CA 1985, s 35A, discussed above.

However, notwithstanding the statutory reforms, apparent authority cannot be relied upon where the third party is aware of some limitation (other than a limitation on the board's power to delegate since that is within s 35A) which prevents the authority arising, or is put on inquiry as to the extent of the individual's authority[11]. For example,

6   *Freeman and Lockyer v Buckhurst Park Properties (Mangal) Ltd* [1964] 2 QB 480 at 505, [1964] 1 All ER 630 at 645, per Diplock LJ.

7   *Egyptian International Foreign Trade Co v Soplex Wholesale Supplies Ltd, The Raffaella* [1985] BCLC 404 at 411, [1985] 2 Lloyd's Rep 36 at 41, CA, per Browne-Wilkinson V-C.

8   [1971] 2 QB 711, CA.

9   [1993] BCLC 1409, [1993] 2 Lloyd's Rep 194.

10   [1993] BCLC 1409 at 1424, [1993] 2 Lloyd's Rep 194 at 204. The decision is not without its critics: see *Bowstead & Reynolds on Agency* (16th edn, 1996), para 8-023. Cf *British Bank of the Middle East v Sun Life Assurance Co of Canada (UK) Ltd* [1983] BCLC 78, [1983] 2 Lloyd's Rep 9, HL: a branch manager of an insurance company had no authority by virtue of his title to bind the company to a third party.

11   *A L Underwood Ltd v Bank of Liverpool* [1924] 1 KB 775, CA; *B Liggett (Liverpool) Ltd v Barclays Bank Ltd* [1928] 1 KB 48; *Morris v Kanssen* [1946] AC 459, [1946] 1 All ER 586, HL; *Rolled Steel Products (Holdings) Ltd v British Steel Corpn* [1986] Ch 246, [1985] 3 All ER 52, CA. Remember that the doctrine of constructive notice has not been abolished and so third parties are affected with knowledge of the company's constitution which may restrict (although it is unlikely) the powers of an individual director.

the very nature of a proposed transaction may put a person on inquiry[12]. In *A L Underwood Ltd v Bank of Liverpool*[13], for example, a director paid cheques drawn in favour of the company into his own personal bank account. Whether a person dealing with the director is put on inquiry will depend on all the circumstances. Section 35B, freeing a third party from any obligation to enquire, does not assist the third party in this instance since it only applies with respect to limitations on the powers of the board of directors to bind the company or authorise others to do so.

THE RULE IN TURQUAND'S CASE

The rule in *Turquand's* case, noted above, does not enable a third party to hold the company to an unauthorised transaction entered into by a director. It allows a third party to assume that a transaction within the authority of the directors has been properly carried out but it requires the third party to establish the fact of authority, actual or apparent, in the first place.

RATIFICATION

It is always open to the board to ratify an unauthorised contract entered into by a director or officer.

MONITORING MANAGEMENT

The corporate structure envisages a strict division of power between the board and the general meeting with extensive power vested in the hands of the former which in turn delegates to individual directors and professional managers. The legal recognition of the concentration of power in the hands of management is consistent with the separation of ownership and control hypothesis and the concept of the corporation as a device for raising large amounts of capital[14]. The problem is that, having accepted this division of power, the law must find ways of monitoring the exercise of that power and curbing abuses arising from it in order that individuals who contribute capital are not exposed to undue risk. The law's response is to be found in a number of differing approaches:

(i) *Reform of the board*   Many proposals for reform are directed towards re-enforcing the composition of company boards and place considerable emphasis on the role of non-executive directors. The position of non-executive directors was considered in Chapter 24.

(ii) *Returning power to the general meeting*   A number of powers are returned by the statute to the general meeting. For example, the power to issue shares is vested in the general meeting[15]; shareholder approval is required of any purchase of the company's own shares[16]; shareholders must approve of

---

12   See Prentice (1991) 107 LQR 14.
13   [1924] 1 KB 775, CA.
14   See Berle & Means *The Modern Corporation and Private Property* (1932); Manne (1967) 53 Va L Rev 259; Parkinson *Corporate Power and Responsibility* (1993), ch 2.
15   See CA 1985, s 80; this is subject to the ability of the general meeting to return this power to the directors: see s 80(1).
16   Ibid, ss 164–166.

directors' service contracts for more than five years and any substantial property transactions with the company[17]. This increased monitoring by shareholders is imposed notwithstanding the widely held view that shareholders have only a limited interest in monitoring directors' behaviour.

Given the inertia, apathy and lack of expertise of individual investors, it has been suggested that this vacuum might be filled by the institutional investors who now own roughly 60% of listed UK equities. Their role has been the subject of much debate in the UK, both in terms of their contribution to short-termism in British industry rather than long-term planning, and in terms of their contribution to corporate governance[18]. Throughout the last decade, the institutions had focused on specific, relatively narrow, issues such as non-voting shares, pre-emption rights and directors' remuneration, and relied on takeovers to resolve problems of managerial incompetence (or worse)[19]. The suggestion is that they should seek a closer relationship with the companies in which they invest and should press, in particular, for well-constructed boards of directors with the requisite level of non-executive directors, separate posts of chairmen and chief executive, and appropriate remuneration and audit committees. The question of institutional investment raises a number of issues which are discussed in Chapter 35.

(iii) *Fiduciary duties*   An extensive range of fiduciary duties apply to company directors and officers and are used to control the exercise by them of their powers. These duties are discussed in Chapters 26 and 27. As a rule the company is the proper plaintiff in the event of a breach of those duties but in certain circumstances a minority shareholder can sue. Shareholders' remedies are discussed in Chapter 28.

(iv) *Disclosure*   Proceeding on the assumption that the full glare of publicity will make directors more circumspect in their activities and will assist shareholders in monitoring those activities, a variety of disclosure requirements are imposed on companies. Recently the tide has turned against disclosure as part of a general drive to reduce the regulatory burden on companies, especially smaller companies. Disclosure is considered in Chapter 29.

(v) *Public regulation and investigation*   The maintenance of confidence in the proper conduct of business and the protection of investors and others may require the Department of Trade and Industry to exercise its powers to investigate companies and their affairs. The powers of the Department are discussed in Chapter 30.

(vi) *The market for corporate control*   Finally, the market itself may operate as a constraining force as inefficient management leaves itself open to takeovers which enable shareholders to displace inadequate managers with those better able to run the business. The possibility of such displacement, in theory, encourages existing management to maximise their efforts on behalf of the company and so provides the necessary incentive for efficient management. Others would argue that the use of takeovers to regulate management increases the short-term pressures on management and hinders overall long-term economic growth. The role and regulation of takeovers is discussed in detail in Chapter 36.

17   Ibid, ss 319, 320.
18   See generally Stapledon *Institutional Shareholders and Corporate Governance* (1996); Davies *Institutional Investors in the UK* in Prentice, Holland (eds) *Contemporary Issues in Corporate Governance* (1993).
19   See Stapledon *Institutional Shareholders and Corporate Governance* (1996), ch 4.

CHAPTER 26

Directors' duties

DIRECTORS AS FIDUCIARIES

Having sanctioned the granting of practically unlimited powers to the board of directors, the next issue is to devise some means of controlling the directors in the exercise of those powers. A balancing act is required: management must not be stifled but neither can unfettered, unsupervised, absolute discretion be permitted. The law's response has been to apply strict fiduciary principles designed to ensure certain minimum standards of behaviour from directors with potentially severe penalties in the event of breach[1]. These rules are backed up by disclosure requirements designed to prevent directors shrouding their transactions in secrecy. This response by the legal system can be seen as the means by which the law fills in the otherwise standard contract which is commonly adopted as between directors and their shareholders[2]. Critics would argue that there is no need for such strict rules as the markets for management and control will effectively constrain managerial discretion within reasonable limits and in a more cost-effective way than the legal rules[3].

While directors have been regarded as trustees[4], or partners[5], or agents[6], in reality 'directors of a limited company are the creatures of statute and occupy a position

---

1   See *Regal (Hastings) Ltd v Gulliver* [1967] 2 AC 134n, [1942] 1 All ER 378; *Boardman v Phipps* [1967] 2 AC 46, [1966] 3 All ER 721.
2   See generally Easterbrook and Fischel *The Economic Structure of Corporate Law* (1991), chs 1, 4.
3   See generally Parkinson *Corporate Power and Responsibility* (1993), ch 4.
4   See *Great Eastern Rly Co v Turner* (1872) 8 Ch App 149 at 152, per Lord Selborne; *Re Lands Allotment Co* [1894] 1 Ch 616 at 631, per Lindley LJ; *Selangor United Rubber Estates Ltd v Cradock (a bankrupt) (No 3)* [1968] 2 All ER 1073 at 1091–1094, [1968] 1 WLR 1555 at 1574–1577, per Ungoed-Thomas J. See Sealy 'The Director as Trustee' (1967) CLJ 83.
5   See *Re Forest of Dean Coal Mining Co* (1878) 10 Ch D 450 at 453, per Jessel MR.
6   See *Great Eastern Rly Co v Turner* (1872) 8 Ch App 149 at 152, per Lord Selborne; *Ferguson v Wilson* (1866) 2 Ch App 77 at 89; *Aberdeen Rly Co v Blaikie Bros* (1854) 1 Macq 461.

peculiar to themselves'[7]. All that can safely be said is that they are fiduciaries[8] and as such they are subject to the following duties[9]:

- the directors must act bona fide in the interests of the company and must not exercise their powers for any collateral purpose;
- a director who, by use of his position, makes a profit is liable to account for that profit;
- where a director finds himself in a position where his duty to the company and his personal interests conflict, any contract concerned is voidable at the instance of the company.

In addition, a director must exercise reasonable care and such skill as might reasonably be expected of a person of his knowledge and experience. Attempts over the years to reduce these duties to statutory form have come to nothing[10].

Directors owe their duties to the company and not to individual shareholders[11]. The leading authority is *Percival v Wright*[12] where the directors purchased shares from existing shareholders without disclosing that they were in the process of negotiating a takeover bid at a higher price. It was held that since the directors owed no fiduciary duties to the shareholders, they could not be liable for the non-disclosure. The decision in this case has been much criticised and is limited to its facts[13]. However, the principle stands: directors owe their duties to the company and not to individual shareholders. Equally, while a director may be appointed as a nominee of a particular shareholder or class of shareholders, his overriding responsibility remains to the company as a whole[14].

As regards creditors, the orthodox position was stated in *Multinational Gas and Petrochemical Co v Multinational Gas and Petrochemical Services Ltd*[15]:

> The directors indeed stand in a fiduciary relationship to the company, as they are appointed to manage the affairs of the company and they owe fiduciary duties

7   *Regal (Hastings) Ltd v Gulliver* [1967] 2 AC 134n at 147, [1942] 1 All ER 378 at 387, per Lord Russell; *Great Eastern Rly Co v Turner* (1872) 8 Ch App 149 at 152, per Lord Selborne: 'The directors are the mere trustees or agents of the company, trustees of the company's money and property and agents in the transactions which they enter into on behalf of the company'.

8   See Finn 'The Fiduciary Principle' in Youdan (ed) *Equity, Fiduciaries and Trusts* (1989), ch 1; Finn *Fiduciary Obligations* (1977), ch 1 (directors are the most complex fiduciary office); Shepherd *The Law of Fiduciaries* (1981), pp 347–348: 'Nowhere are fiduciary principles applied in a more difficult or complex context than the modern corporation – any attempt to build tidy little theoretical cubbyholes in the corporate context is doomed to failure'; Sealy 'Fiduciary Obligations' (1962) CLJ 69.

9   More accurately, duties and disabilities: see *Movitex Ltd v Bulfield* [1988] BCLC 104 and discussion in Chapter 27.

10   See the Companies Bill 1973, cls 52–53; the Companies Bill 1978, cls 44–46. The DTI in 1993 announced the setting up of a working party to review the law relating to directors' duties and an initial consultation document was expected by the end of 1994. However, although a draft report was completed, it has not been published and there does not appear to have been any recent progress on this project: see DTI *Companies in 1993–94* (1994), p 2; DTI *Companies in 1994–95* (1995), p 3. See generally Arden 'Codifying Directors' Duties' in Rawlings (ed) *Law, Society and Economy* (1997).

11   See generally Davies 'Directors' Fiduciary Duties and Individual Shareholders' in McKendrick (ed) *Commercial Aspects of Trusts and Fiduciary Obligations* (1992).

12   [1902] 2 Ch 421.

13   The shareholders had approached the directors and had named the price at which they wished to sell. Also the court was not satisfied that the board ever intended to accept the takeover offer in any event. Indeed the negotiations were ultimately aborted, see [1902] 2 Ch 421 at 426. See also Rider and Ffrench *The Regulation of Insider Trading* (1979), p 147; *Coleman v Myers* [1977] 2 NZLR 225; *Re Chez Nico (Restaurants) Ltd* [1992] BCLC 192 at 208.

14   *Scottish Co-operative Wholesale Society Ltd v Meyer* [1959] AC 324, [1958] 3 All ER 66, HL; *Boulting v ACTT* [1963] 2 QB 606, [1963] 1 All ER 716, CA. See Boros (1989) 10 Co Law 211, (1990) 11 Co Law 6 for an interesting discussion of the difficulties facing nominee and multiple directors.

15   [1983] Ch 258, [1983] 2 All ER 563.

to the company though not to the creditors, present or future, or to individual shareholders[16].

Of course, the shareholders may specifically appoint the directors as their agents in any matter, in which case the directors will then owe them the ordinary fiduciary duties arising from that agency relationship[17], or the circumstances of a particular transaction may place the directors in a fiduciary position vis-à-vis the shareholders[18].

In a number of cases concerning takeover bids, the courts have had to consider the relationship between the directors and their shareholders in that context. Where a takeover bid has been made, the directors must give sufficient information to the shareholders and refrain from misleading them[19]. In the case of competing bids, the directors must do nothing to prevent the shareholders from choosing to take the best price[20] but the courts do not accept that the board must inevitably be under a positive duty to recommend and take all steps within its power to facilitate whichever is the highest offer[1]. These cases might seem to raise the possibility of directors owing fiduciary duties directly to shareholders but their true relevance is succinctly explained in *Dawson International plc v Coats Paton plc*[2]:

> If ... directors take it on themselves to give advice to current shareholders, the cases ... show clearly that they have a duty to advise in good faith and not fraudulently, and not to mislead whether deliberately or carelessly. ... However, these cases do not, in my view, demonstrate a pre-existing fiduciary duty to the shareholders but a potential liability arising out of their words or actions which can be based on ordinary principles of law. This, I may say, appears to be a more satisfactory way of expressing the position of directors in this context than by talking of a so-called secondary fiduciary duty to the shareholders[3].

Equally, directors may by agreement or representation assume a special duty to creditors[4].

Our main concern then is with duties owed by directors to the company[5]. The significance of this is that if there is a breach of duty then the wrong is done to the

16   [1983] Ch 258 at 288, [1983] 2 All ER 563 at 585, per Dillon LJ.
17   *Allen v Hyatt* (1914) 30 TLR 444; *Briess v Woolley* [1954] AC 333, [1954] 1 All ER 909.
18   *Coleman v Myers* [1977] 2 NZLR 225; *Re Chez Nico (Restaurants) Ltd* [1992] BCLC 192 at 208.
19   *Re a Company (No 008699 of 1985)* [1986] BCLC 382; *Gething v Kilner* [1972] 1 All ER 1166, [1972] 1 WLR 337. Also note the requirements of the Takeover Code, General Principal 9 of which states: 'Directors of an offeror and the offeree company must always, in advising their shareholders, act only in their capacity as directors and not have regard to their personal or family shareholdings or to their personal relationships with the companies. It is the shareholders' interests taken as a whole, together with those of employees and creditors, which should be considered when the directors are giving advice to shareholders. Directors of the offeree company should give careful consideration before they enter into any commitment with an offeror (or anyone else) which would restrict their freedom to advise their shareholders in the future. Such commitments may give rise to conflicts of interest or result in a breach of the directors' fiduciary duties'.
20   *Heron International Ltd v Lord Grade* [1983] BCLC 244.
1   *Re a Company (No 008699 of 1985)* [1986] BCLC 382.
2   [1989] BCLC 233, CS (Outer House).
3   [1989] BCLC 233 at 244, per Lord Cullen.
4   See *Kuwait Asia Bank EC v National Mutual Life Nominees Ltd* [1990] 3 All ER 404 at 421, [1990] BCLC 868 at 889. An assumption of a duty of care, for example, is not limited to creditors but could extend in appropriate circumstances to other third parties including, possibly, would-be takeover bidders: see *Morgan Crucible Co plc v Hill Samuel & Co Ltd* [1991] Ch 295, [1991] 1 All ER 148.
5   While, as a matter of convenience, the discussion throughout will refer to directors, the fiduciary duties discussed apply equally to officers of the company authorised to act on its behalf and in particular to those acting in a managerial capacity: see Gower *Principles of Modern Company Law* (6th edn, 1997), pp 600-601 approved in *Canadian Aero Service v O'Malley* (1974) 40 DLR (3d) 371 at 381, per Laskin J.

company and the company is the proper person to sue in respect of it. This is the rule in *Foss v Harbottle*[6] (discussed in detail in Chapter 28) which generally precludes actions by individual shareholders in respect of wrongdoing by directors. When considering the extent of the duties owed by directors, therefore, it must be borne in mind that those duties cannot easily be enforced.

THE DUTY TO ACT BONA FIDE IN THE INTERESTS OF THE COMPANY

It is clearly established that directors are under a duty to act bona fide in what they consider, and not what a court may consider, is in the interests of the company and not for any collateral purpose[7].

The overriding nature of this obligation was stressed in two cases concerning takeover bids. In *Dawson International plc v Coats Patons plc*[8] the court accepted that an agreement between a target company and a bidder company which provided that the board of the target company would recommend the bid, and would not encourage or co-operate with any other bidder which might emerge, was subject to an implied qualification derived from the law which defines directors' overriding duties to their company and their shareholders. The qualification was that, if circumstances altered materially, the board could decide in fulfilment of their continuing duty to the company and its shareholders not to implement the agreement. In *John Crowther Group plc v Carpets International plc*[9] the court likewise accepted that an agreement to recommend one particular bid had to be read in the light of the fact, known to all parties, that directors owe a fiduciary duty to act in the interests of the company. The bidders were not therefore entitled to damages when the board recommended that their bid should be set aside after a rival bidder made a more attractive offer.

This issue was addressed by the Court of Appeal in *Fulham Football Club Ltd v Cabra Estates plc*[10] where the directors of a company had entered into undertakings to support, and to refrain from opposing, planning applications by another party for the development of certain land. The directors subsequently wanted to give evidence to a planning inquiry opposing the development and sought a declaration that they were not bound by the undertakings and were entitled to give such evidence to the inquiry as they considered to be in the best interests of the company.

The Court of Appeal held that since the undertakings given by the directors were part of contractual arrangements which conferred substantial benefits on the company, the directors had not improperly fettered the future exercise of their discretion by giving those undertakings. Nor was there any scope for the implication of a term into those undertakings that the directors would not be required to do anything that would be inconsistent with their fiduciary duties to the company.

The distinction which must be drawn is between directors fettering their discretion (which is prohibited)[11] and directors exercising their discretion in a way which restricts their future conduct (which is permissible). In *Thorby v Goldberg*[12] the directors of a

---

6   (1843) 2 Hare 461.
7   *Re Smith & Fawcett Ltd* [1942] Ch 304 at 306; [1942] 1 All ER 542 at 543, per Lord Greene. See generally Heydon 'Directors' Duties and the Company's Interests' in Finn (ed) *Equity and Commercial Relationships* (1987).
8   [1990] BCLC 560. See also *Rackham v Peek Foods Ltd* [1990] BCLC 895.
9   [1990] BCLC 460.
10   [1994] 1 BCLC 363; noted Griffiths (1993) JBL 576.
11   *Motherwell v Schoof* [1949] 4 DLR 812 (Alta SC); *Selangor United Rubber Estates Ltd v Cradock (a bankrupt) (No 3)* [1968] 2 All ER 1073, [1968] 1 WLR 1555.
12   (1964) 112 CLR 597 (Aust HC). See Prentice (1977) 89 LQR 107 at 111–113.

company agreed as part of a transaction to allot shares in a particular manner at a later date. They failed to do as they had promised and in an action to force them to make the allotment, they pleaded that it was an invalid fettering of their discretion on their part. The court rejected this argument, holding that the time for exercising their discretion was at the time of entering into the agreement and, provided they had considered the best interests of the company at that time, the agreement was valid. It was not the case that they had wrongly fettered their discretion rather that they had already exercised it[13].

In *Fulham Football Club Ltd v Cabra Estates plc*[14] the Court of Appeal emphatically endorsed the approach taken in *Thorby v Goldberg*[15] as the true rule. The directors had exercised their discretion at the time when they gave the undertakings not to oppose the planning applications and therefore it was not a case of fettering their discretion but rather a case that they had already exercised it. Moreover, the Court of Appeal went on to note that in so far as cases such as *John Crowther Group plc v Carpets International plc*[16] could be read as laying down a general proposition that directors can never bind themselves as to the future exercise of their fiduciary powers, they would be wrong[17].

It is clear then that the directors' overriding duty is to act bona fide in the interests of the company but the time at which they exercise that judgment is a matter for them depending on the particular transaction involved. There are many transactions where the proper time for the exercise of their discretion will be at the time of the negotiation of the contract and not the time at which the contract is to be performed[18].

Shareholders' interests

Traditionally, this obligation to act bona fide in the interests of the company has been defined as an obligation to act in the interests of the shareholders and it is the directors' subjective opinion as to the interests of the corporators as a general body, balancing the short-term interests of the present members against the long-term interests of future members, which counts[19].

Notwithstanding this subjective test, a decision by the directors may be set aside if it is such that no reasonable man could consider it to be bona fide in the interests of the company[20] but the courts rarely interfere and the overall emphasis on a subjective test can be criticised as entrenching management to an unacceptable degree[1].

It can be seen therefore that while directors may not owe any fiduciary duties to shareholders as such, the position is redressed to some extent by defining the directors'

---

13   (1964) 112 CLR 597 at 618, per Owen J.

14   [1994] 1 BCLC 363.

15   (1964) 112 CLR 597.

16   [1990] BCLC 460.

17   [1994] 1 BCLC 363 at 393. See Gower *Principles of Modern Law* (6th edn, 1997) p 609.

18   See *Thorby v Goldberg* (1964) 112 CLR 597 at 605–606.

19   Second Savoy Hotel Investigation, Report of the Inspector (1954, HMSO); *Gaiman v National Association for Mental Health* [1971] Ch 317 at 330, per Megarry J. Sometimes only the interests of the current shareholders will be relevant, as where the directors are considering rival takeover bids: see *Heron International Ltd v Lord Grade* [1983] BCLC 244 at 265.

20   See *Re Smith & Fawcett Ltd* [1942] Ch 304, [1942] 1 All ER 542; *Heron International Ltd v Lord Grade* [1983] BCLC 244.

1   If the article conferring the particular power is drafted widely enough, and if a subjective test is applied to the exercise of that power by the directors, then the result can be to confer an absolute and uncontrolled discretion on the directors: see *Re Smith & Fawcett Ltd* [1942] Ch 304, [1942] 1 All ER 542.

duty to act bona fide in the interests of the company in terms of the interests of shareholders, albeit according to the directors' view of those interests.

Normally the duty requires directors to treat all shareholders equally. For example, they cannot make calls on some members while payment is outstanding on other members' shares[2]. However, where there are different classes of shareholders so decisions may adversely affect the interests of one class and benefit another, the question is not so much one of the interests of the company as one of what is fair as between different classes of shareholders[3] and fairness does not always require identity of treatment[4]. In *Mutual Life Insurance Co of New York v Rank Organisation Ltd*[5] the directors were not in breach of their duty to act fairly when they decided that it was in the best interests of the company to make a rights issue to only some of the holders of ordinary shares. That decision by the directors excluded the company's American and Canadian shareholders from the rights issue and was done in order to avoid the onerous regulatory requirements of those jurisdictions. In *Re BSB Holdings Ltd (No 2)*[6] the requirement to act fairly meant that the directors when undertaking a complex financing agreement should have considered the effect of the proposals on the different groups of shareholders within the company[7]. The fact that the decision ultimately taken by the directors also benefits themselves as shareholders does not necessarily mean it is invalid for directors are not required to live in 'an unreal region of detached altruism'[8].

Where the company is one of a group of companies, the directors must continue to act in the interests of that company and not look solely to the overall interests of the group. This is not to deny, of course, that the interests of the group may be relevant to deciding what is in the interests of the company[9]. The proper approach is to consider whether an intelligent and honest man in the position of the director of the company concerned could, in the whole of the existing circumstances, have reasonably believed that the transaction was for the benefit of the company[10].

Creditors' interests

The orthodox position, as we have seen, is that directors owe their fiduciary duties to the company though not to the creditors, present or future[11]. However, there is support for treating creditors in the same manner as shareholders, ie for defining the duty to

2   *Galloway v Hallé Concerts Society* [1915] 2 Ch 233.
3   *Mills v Mills* (1938) 60 CLR 150 at 164, per Latham CJ; *Howard Smith Ltd v Ampol Petroleum Ltd* [1974] AC 821 at 835, [1974] 1 All ER 1126 at 1134.
4   *Mutual Life Insurance Co of New York v Rank Organisation Ltd* [1985] BCLC 11.
5   [1985] BCLC 11.
6   [1996] 1 BCLC 155.
7   This case was brought as a petition under CA 1985, s 459 (the unfairly prejudicial remedy) and on the facts the court concluded that while the directors had failed to act fairly by considering the impact of the proposed scheme on different groups of shareholders, that failure did not amount to unfairly prejudicial conduct as required by s 459: see [1996] 1 BCLC 155 at 254.
8   *Mills v Mills* (1938) 60 CLR 150 at 164, per Latham CJ.
9   See *Nicholas v Soundcraft Electronics Ltd* [1993] BCLC 360.
10   *Charterbridge Corpn Ltd v Lloyds Bank Ltd* [1970] Ch 62 at 74, [1969] 2 All ER 1185 at 1194. See also *Walker v Wimborne* (1976) 50 ALJR 446.
11   *Multinational Gas and Petrochemical Co v Multinational Gas and Petrochemical Services Ltd* [1983] Ch 258 at 288, [1983] 2 All ER 563 at 585. See also *Kuwait Asia Bank EC v National Mutual Life Nominees Ltd* [1990] 3 All ER 404, PC. Cf *Winkworth v Edward Baron Development Co Ltd* [1987] 1 All ER 114 at 118, [1987] BCLC 193 at 197, per Lord Templeman – robustly criticised by Sealy (1988) CLJ 175.

act bona fide in the interests of the company as encompassing creditors' interests in some circumstances[12].

This approach has its origins in dicta in a number of Australian and New Zealand decisions[13]. In *Walker v Wimborne*[14] the company's directors, in breach of their duties to the company and its creditors, guaranteed loans of another company in the group at a time when the company was itself in serious financial difficulties. The court found the transaction exposed the company to the probable prospect of substantial loss and was undertaken in accordance with a policy adopted by the directors in total disregard of the interests of the company and its creditors. Mason J noted:

> ... it should be emphasised that the directors of a company must take account of the interest of its shareholders and its creditors. Any failure by the directors to take into account the interests of creditors will have adverse consequences for the company as well as for them[15].

The New Zealand Court of Appeal considered the issue in *Nicholson v Permakraft (NZ) Ltd*[16] where Cooke J noted:

> ... the duties of directors are owed to the company. On the facts of particular cases this may require the directors to consider inter alia the interests of creditors. For instance creditors are entitled to consideration, in my opinion, if the company is insolvent, or near-insolvent, or of doubtful solvency, or if a contemplated payment or other course of action would jeopardise its solvency[17].

Such an extension of duties to creditors, restricted in the way outlined, could be justified, he said, on the basis that limited liability is a privilege which can be used to the prejudice of creditors and that is a mischief to which the courts should be alive[18]. Equally, he noted that a balance has to be struck and there is no good reason for cultivating a paternal concern to protect business people perfectly able to look after themselves[19]. Creditors are best able to protect themselves, of course, through appropriate contractual provisions.

12   See generally Furey 'The Protection of Creditors' Interests in Company Law' in Feldman & Meisel (eds) *Corporate and Commercial Law: Modern Developments* (1996); Prentice 'Directors, Creditors and Shareholders' in McKendrick (ed) *Commercial Aspects of Trusts and Fiduciary Obligations* (1992); Grantham 'The Judicial Extension of Directors' Duties to Creditors' (1991) JBL 1; Prentice 'Creditors' Interests and Directors' Duties' (1990) 10 OJLS 265; Farrar 'The Responsibility of Directors and Shareholders for a Company's Debts' (1989) 4 Canta L R 12; Heydon 'Directors' Duties and the Company's Interests' in Finn (ed) *Equity and Commercial Relationships* (1987); Dawson 'Acting in the Best Interests of the Company – For whom are Directors"Trustees"?' (1984) 11 NZULR 68.

13   See generally Farrar 'The Responsibility of Directors and Shareholders for a Company's Debts' (1989) 4 Canta L R 12.

14   (1976) 50 ALJR 446, noted Barrett (1977) 40 MLR 226.

15   (1976) 50 ALJR 446 at 449.

16   [1985] 1 NZLR 242, noted (1985) JBL 413; (1986) 7 Co Law 39.

17   [1985] 1 NZLR 242 at 249.

18   [1985] 1 NZLR 242 at 250. Somers J agreed that directors must have regard to the interests of creditors where the company is insolvent while Richardson J preferred to reserve to another day what he considered to be the controversial question of the nature and scope of the duties owed to creditors. All three judges were clear that no duty to have regard to creditors' interests arises where the company is solvent.

19   [1985] 1 NZLR 242 at 250.

Support for this inclusive approach can be found in *West Mercia Safetywear Ltd v Dodd*[20] where Dillon LJ approved the following statement of the position by the New South Wales Court of Appeal in *Kinsela v Russell Kinsela Pty Ltd*[1]:

> In a solvent company the proprietary interests of the shareholders entitle them as a general body to be regarded as the company when questions of the duty of directors arise. If, as a general body, they authorise or ratify a particular action of the directors, there can be no challenge to the validity of what the directors have done. But where a company is insolvent the interests of the creditors intrude. They become prospectively entitled, through the mechanism of liquidation, to displace the power of the shareholders and directors to deal with the company's assets. It is in a practical sense their assets and not the shareholders' assets that, through the medium of the company, are under the management of the directors pending either liquidation, return to solvency, or the imposition of some alternative administration[2].

In the *West Mercia* case, a director organised payment by an insolvent company of a debt in respect of which he had given a personal guarantee. The court found him to be in breach of his duty to the company by acting in disregard of the interests of the general creditors of the company.

There has been some debate as to the value of the judicial approach outlined above. Professor Sealy, in particular, has been robust in his criticisms of 'well-meant but ill-focused dicta'[3]. His point being that if the cases are looked at in detail the conduct in question comes within some existing well-defined rule of law such as the law imposing liability for misfeasance, the expropriation of corporate assets or fraudulent preference.

This is correct and it is true that such action as might be taken to enforce the duty will be taken not by an individual creditor but by a liquidator in the usual way under existing provisions in the Insolvency Act 1986. There might therefore seem no need for the changed judicial emphasis and no value in it but in reality this change is part of a broader picture, one shaped by statutory developments in the form of the Insolvency Act 1986 and the Company Directors Disqualification Act 1986.

A number of provisions in the Insolvency Act 1986 assess directors' conduct on a company going into insolvency in the light of the effect of that conduct on the company's creditors. For example, a director's liability for wrongful trading will depend on whether he took every step with a view to minimising the potential loss to the company's creditors as he ought to have taken[4]. A director may also be liable if he was knowingly a party to the carrying on of any business of the company with intent to defraud creditors[5]. Any misfeasance or breach of any fiduciary or other duty by a director may be the subject of misfeasance proceedings brought on the application of,

---

20   [1988] BCLC 250. See also *Brady v Brady* [1989] AC 755, [1988] 2 All ER 617, HL; *Lonrho Ltd v Shell Petroleum Co Ltd* [1980] 1 WLR 627 at 634; *Re Horsley & Weight Ltd* [1982] Ch 442 at 454–455, [1982] 3 All ER 1045 at 1055–56.
1   (1986) 4 ACLC 215 at 223, per Street CJ.
2   [1988] BCLC 250 at 252.
3   See Sealy (1988) CLJ 175 at 177.
4   IA 1986, s 214(3). Wrongful trading essentially involves continuing to trade when the director knew or ought to have concluded that there was no reasonable prospect that the company would avoid going into insolvent liquidation. See Chapter 38.
5   Ie under ibid, s 213.

inter alia, any creditor[6]. Provisions governing vulnerable transactions are also designed to protect the position of creditors[7].

The Company Directors Disqualification Act 1986 also focuses on the creditors' position. A director must be disqualified if the court is satisfied that his conduct as a director of an insolvent company makes him unfit to be concerned in the management of a company[8]. In determining unfitness the court must have regard to the matters specified in the Schedule to the Act which include the extent of the director's responsibility for the causes of the company becoming insolvent together with various other factors relevant to the director's conduct vis-à-vis the creditors[9]. The need to protect creditors has been a consistent theme in the disqualification cases and directors who take unwarranted risks with creditors' money are disqualified[10]. As the Court of Appeal noted in *Secretary of State for Trade and Industry v Gray*[11]:

> The concept of limited liability and the sophistication of our corporate law offers great privileges and great opportunities for those who wish to trade under that regime. But the corporate environment carries with it the discipline that those who avail themselves of those privileges must accept the standards laid down and abide by the regulatory rules and disciplines in place to protect creditors and shareholders ... The Parliamentary intention to improve managerial safeguards and standards for the long term good of employees, creditors and investors is clear[12].

All of these factors have combined to influence the common law to move to recognise that creditors are an important constituency within a company and, where the company is insolvent, their interests must be reflected in the directors' duty to act bona fide in the interests of the company.

Employees' interests

The matters to which the directors of a company are to have regard in the performance of their functions have been expanded by statute to include the interests of the company's employees in general as well as the interests of its members[13]. In the light of that wording, however, it would be very difficult to establish that the directors have

6   Ie under ibid, s 212. See *Re Halt Garage (1964) Ltd* [1982] 3 All ER 1016; *Re Horsley & Weight Ltd* [1982] Ch 442 at 454–455, [1982] 3 All ER 1045 at 1055.
7   IA 1986, ss 238–246.
8   CDDA 1986, s 6.
9   Ibid, s 9.
10 See *Re Synthetic Technology Ltd, Secretary of State for Trade and Industry v Joiner* [1993] BCC 549; also *Secretary of State for Trade and Industry v Lubrami, Re Amaron Ltd* [1997] 1 BCLC 115; *Secretary of State for Trade and Industry v Laing* [1996] 2 BCLC 324; *Secretary of State for Trade and Industry v McTighe (No 2)* [1996] 2 BCLC 477; *Re Richborough Furniture Ltd* [1996] 1 BCLC 507, [1996] BCC 155; *Secretary of State for Trade and Industry v Gray* [1995] 1 BCLC 276, [1995] BCC 554; *Re Firedart Ltd, Official Receiver v Fairall* [1994] 2 BCLC 340. For a detailed discussion of disqualification see Chapter 24.
11 [1995] 1 BCLC 276, [1995] BCC 554, CA.
12 [1995] 1 BCLC 276 at 288, [1995] BCC 554 at 577, per Henry LJ.
13 CA 1985, s 309 (originally CA 1980, s 46); see Prentice *Companies Act 1980* (1980), ch 17. At common law directors were not entitled to have regard to employees' interests: *Parke v Daily News Ltd* [1962] Ch 927, [1962] 2 All ER 929 reversed by CA 1985, s 719. A rare reference to CA 1985, s 309 can be found in *Re Saul D Harrison & Sons plc* [1995] 1 BCLC 14 where directors justified their decision to continue to run the company rather than to sell the business and realise the assets for the shareholders on the basis, inter alia, that they had to have regard to the interests of their 100 employees who were unlikely to find other employment. See also *Re Welfab Engineers Ltd* [1990] BCLC 833.

failed to comply with the requirements of the section. In any event, as the duty is owed only to the company[14] the rule in *Foss v Harbottle*[15] will come into play and enforcement of the duty will be at the discretion of the company[16]. It is a statutory provision without teeth but nevertheless it represents a tentative step towards recognising the employees' role in the enterprise[17].

Stakeholders' interests

Another issue much debated recently is whether a company should adopt a more inclusive approach and consider the interests not just of its shareholders, employees and creditors but also broader constituencies such as its suppliers, customers and the community[18]. This has been described as the stakeholder debate, the idea being to identify those groups of interests which have stakes in a company and whose position should be reflected in the way in which management conducts its responsibilities. Little concrete progress has been made on this idea and such social responsibility as is enforced arises through legislation governing such matters as planning and environmental controls. Given the reluctant recognition of those groups most intimately connected with the company, namely the employees and creditors, it is not surprising that company law has been slow to embrace broader stakeholder concerns.

The Report of the Hampel Committee on Corporate Governance, discussed above in Chapter 24, considered these issues briefly before concluding that:

> ... to redefine the directors' responsibilities in terms of the stakeholders would mean identifying all the various stakeholder groups; and deciding the nature and extent of the directors' responsibility to each. The result would be that the directors were not effectively accountable to anyone since there would be no clear yardstick for judging their performance. This is a recipe neither for good governance nor for corporate success.[18]

Ultimately, of course, regardless of what the legal rules are, the directors will want to balance the differing interests of shareholders, employees, creditors, consumers and society at large, having regard to the nature and size of the company and the interests most affected by any particular transaction or decision.

---

14   CA 1985, s 309(2).
15   (1843) 2 Hare 461.
16   As to the problems of enforcement, see Prentice *Companies Act 1980* (1980) pp 138–139.
17   Major reform of the employees' position had been promised by the draft Fifth EC Company Law Directive but, after many years of opposition (mainly by the UK) to those proposals, that Directive appears to have been shelved. See Chapter 3; also Docksey 'Information and Consultation of Employees: The UK and the Vredeling Directive' (1986) 49 MLR 281; Clough 'Trying to make the Fifth Directive Palatable' (1982) 3 Co Law 109. See generally Milman 'From Servant to Stakeholder: Protecting the Employee Interest in Company Law' in Feldman & Meisel (eds) *Corporate and Commercial Law: Modern Developments* (1996); Wedderburn 'Companies and Employees: Common Law or Social Dimension?' (1993) 109 LQR 220; Parkinson *Corporate Power and Responsibility* (1993), ch 12; Wedderburn 'The Legal Development of Corporate Responsibility' in Hopt & Teubner (eds) *Corporate Governance and Directors' Liabilities* (1985).
18   See generally RSA Inquiry *Tomorrow's Company* (1995); Parkinson *Corporate Power and Responsibility* (1993), ch 9; Hopt & Teubner (eds) *Corporate Governance and Directors' Liabilities* (1985). A large number of very useful papers on the stakeholder debate can be found at (1993) 43 U Tor LJ 297–796. For a broad overview of the debate, see Plender *A Stake in the Future, The Stakeholding Solution* (1997).

Indeed the Hampel Committee did concede that the directors can meet their legal duties to shareholders, and can pursue the objective of long-term shareholder value successfully, only by developing and sustaining these stakeholder relationships.[19]

The proper purpose doctrine

It will be recalled that the directors' duty to act in what they consider to be the best interests of the company is qualified by the proviso that they must not act for any collateral purpose[21]. The powers given by the articles to the directors are held in trust for the company and must not be exercised for any purpose other than that for which the power was conferred. If they are so exercised, the transaction may be set aside notwithstanding the directors' assertions that they honestly believed it to be in the best interests of the company[22].

So while directors may have wide managerial powers conferred on them by the articles and may only be constrained by a subjective bona fides test, some measure of control is regained by the use of a proper purpose doctrine which examines objectively the directors' purpose while giving due credit to their business judgement[1]. The requirement that they must not exercise their powers for an improper purpose applies to the exercise by the directors of any of their powers, be it the power to make calls on shares[2], to refuse to register transfers[3], to order the forfeiture of shares[4], or to expel a member[5]. The wider the power, however, the more difficult it is to restrain the directors[6].

Often the directors' self-interest is evident and the courts have little difficulty in invalidating the exercise of a particular power. In *Lee Panavision Ltd v Lee Lighting Ltd*[7] the court found that it was unconstitutional and beyond the powers of outgoing directors, however much they may have thought it in the company's best interests, to commit the company to a management agreement with a third party (with whom the outgoing directors were closely associated) which would have deprived the incoming directors of all management powers. In *Neptune (Vehicle Washing Equipment) Ltd v Fitzgerald (No 2)*[8] a sole director was not acting in the best interests of the company

19 See the Hampel Committee Report, para 1.17.
20 See the Hampel Committee Report, para 1.18.
21 *Re Smith & Fawcett Ltd* [1942] Ch 304, [1942] 1 All ER 542. It is sometimes argued that there should be no test other than the genuineness of the directors' motives. Once they have acted bona fide and have reasonable grounds for their belief then that should end the matter, see *Teck Corpn Ltd v Millar* (1972) 33 DLR (3d) 288; also Sealy (1967) CLJ 33.
22 *Punt v Symons & Co Ltd* [1903] 2 Ch 506; *Piercy v S Mills & Co* [1920] 1 Ch 77; *Hogg v Cramphorn Ltd* [1967] Ch 254, [1966] 3 All ER 420; *Howard Smith Ltd v Ampol Petroleum Ltd* [1974] AC 821, [1974] 1 All ER 1126; *Lee Panavision Ltd v Lee Lighting Ltd* [1992] BCLC 22; *Bishopsgate Investment Management Ltd v Maxwell (No 2)* [1993] BCLC 1282.
1 See generally Sealy, '"Bona Fides" and "Proper Purposes" in Corporate Decisions' (1989) 15 Mon ULR 265.
2 *Galloway v Hallé Concerts Society* [1915] 2 Ch 233; *Alexander v Automatic Telephone Co* [1900] 2 Ch 56.
3 *Re Smith & Fawcett Ltd* [1942] Ch 304, [1942] 1 All ER 542; *Re Bede Steam Shipping Co Ltd* [1917] 1 Ch 123.
4 *Re Agriculturist Cattle Insurance Co, Stanhope's Case* (1866) 1 Ch App 161.
5 *Gaiman v National Association for Mental Health* [1971] Ch 317, [1970] 2 All ER 362. See Prentice (1970) 33 MLR 700.
6 See *Gaiman v National Association for Mental Health* [1971] Ch 317, [1970] 2 All ER 362; *Re Smith & Fawcett Ltd* [1942] Ch 304, [1942] 1 All ER 542. See Prentice (1970) 33 MLR 700.
7 [1992] BCLC 22, CA.
8 [1995] BCC 1000. Cf *Runciman v Walter Runciman plc* [1992] BCLC 1084 where the court accepted that the directors had acted bona fide and in the interests of the company in extending a director's service contract for five years.

when he procured the company to make a payment to him of £100,000 on termination of his service contract with the company.

Most controversy has centred on the exercise by the directors of the power to allot shares, a power which is now restricted by statute which provides that the power to allot shares must not be exercised by the directors unless they are authorised to do so by the company in general meeting or by the articles[9].

Many attempts by directors to use this power to consolidate their control or prevent a rival body from taking over the company have been held to be invalid, notwithstanding the asserted belief of the directors that they were acting in the best interests of the company[10]. In *Punt v Symons & Co Ltd*[11] an injunction was granted to prevent the company from holding a meeting when an improper allotment had been made for the purpose of securing the passing of a resolution at that meeting; in *Piercy v S Mills & Co*[12] an allotment made for the purpose of destroying the voting control of the existing majority shareholders was held to be invalid; in *Hogg v Cramphorn Ltd*[13] an allotment was invalid where its primary purpose was to ensure control of the company by the directors and their supporters; and in *Bamford v Bamford*[14] an allotment made with an eye primarily on the exigencies of a takeover and not with a single eye to the benefit of the company was held to be invalid.

This uncompromising stance by the UK courts has not been followed by Commonwealth authorities[15] which regard such an approach as too inflexible, and in fact contrary to the test in *Re Smith & Fawcett Ltd*[16], in that it prevents directors who bona fide believe that a takeover is not in the best interests of the company (perhaps because the offeror is a well-known corporate looter) from doing anything about it[17]. In *Mills v Mills*[18] the court favoured a broader consideration of the motivating factors at work in any particular instance with an emphasis on what was the moving cause of the directors' actions rather than whether any element of personal advantage or benefit was present[19]. In *Teck Corpn Ltd v Millar*[20] the court permitted an allotment to defeat a takeover even though the allotment was made against the wishes of the existing majority shareholder and deprived that shareholder of control of the company. The court was satisfied that the directors had simply been concerned to obtain the best possible deal for the company[1]. In *Harlowe's Nominees Pty Ltd v Woodside (Lake Entrance) Oil Co*[2] the court permitted an allotment of shares which was made in order

9   CA 1985, s 80(1).
10   See *Fraser v Whalley* (1864) 2 Hem & M 10; *Punt v Symons & Co Ltd* [1903] 2 Ch 506; *Piercy v S Mills & Co* [1920] 1 Ch 77; *Ngurli Ltd v McCann* (1953) 90 CLR 425; *Hogg v Cramphorn Ltd* [1967] Ch 254, [1966] 3 All ER 420; *Bamford v Bamford* [1970] Ch 212, [1969] 1 All ER 969; *Howard Smith Ltd v Ampol Petroleum Ltd* [1974] AC 821, [1974] 1 All ER 1126.
11   [1903] 2 Ch 506.
12   [1920] 1 Ch 77.
13   [1967] Ch 254, [1966] 3 All ER 420.
14   [1970] Ch 212; see also *Winthrop Investments Ltd v Winns Ltd* [1975] 2 NSWLR 666.
15   See *Mills v Mills* (1938) 60 CLR 150; *Harlowe's Nominees Pty Ltd v Woodside (Lake Entrance) Oil Co* (1968) 121 CLR 483; *Teck Corpn Ltd v Millar* (1972) 33 DLR (3d) 288, noted Slutsky (1974) 37 MLR 457.
16   [1942] Ch 304, [1942] 1 All ER 542.
17   See *Teck Corpn Ltd v Millar* (1972) 33 DLR (3d) 288 at 312, per Berger J, S Ct BC.
18   (1938) 60 CLR 150.
19   'It would be setting up an impossible standard to hold that if an action by a director was affected in any degree by the fact that he was a preference or ordinary shareholder, his action was invalid and should be set aside': (1938) 60 CLR 150 at 164, per Latham CJ.
20   (1972) 33 DLR (3d) 288, S Ct BC; noted Ziegel [1974] JBL 85.
1   'If they (the directors) decide, on reasonable grounds, a takeover will cause substantial damage to the company's interests, they are entitled to use their powers to protect the company. That is the test that ought to be applied in this case.': (1972) 33 DLR (3d) 288 at 317.
2   (1968) 121 CLR 483 (Aust HC).

to secure the financial support of a large oil company although a consequence of the allotment was to block a would-be takeover by an existing shareholder.

HOWARD SMITH LTD V AMPOL PETROLEUM LTD

The Privy Council in *Howard Smith Ltd v Ampol Petroleum Ltd*[3] subsequently lent support to this more flexible doctrine.

The proper approach, Lord Wilberforce said, is:

> ... to start with a consideration of the power whose exercise is in question, in this case a power to issue shares. Having ascertained, on a fair view, the nature of this power, and having defined as can best be done in the light of modern conditions the, or some, limits within which it may be exercised, it is then necessary for the court, if a particular exercise of it is challenged, to examine the substantial purpose for which it was exercised, and to reach a conclusion whether that purpose was proper or not[4].

The first step then is to construe the article conferring the power in order to ascertain the nature of the power and the limits within which it may be exercised[5]. In theory, the article could be limitless, permitting the allotment of shares (or indeed the exercise of any other power) for any purpose[6].

Having established the limits, if any, to the power, the second step is to determine the actual purpose or purposes for which it was exercised. This is not always easy to decide and may involve a very detailed examination of the facts. Here–

> the court ... is entitled to look at the situation objectively in order to estimate how critical or pressing, or substantial or, per contra, insubstantial an alleged requirement may have been. If it finds that a particular requirement, though real, was not urgent, or critical, at the relevant time, it may have reason to doubt, or discount, the assertions of individuals that they acted solely in order to deal with it, particularly when the action they took was unusual or even extreme[7].

The Privy Council accepted that there are difficulties of proof here which would require crediting the bona fide opinion of the directors if such is found to exist and respecting their judgement as to matters of management[8]. Having done so, the ultimate conclusion must be as to the side of a fairly broad line on which the case falls[8].

---

3   [1974] AC 821, [1974] 1 All ER 1126, PC. See Birds (1974) 37 MLR 580.

4   [1974] AC 821 at 835, [1974] 1 All ER 1126 at 1136. See Farrar (1974) CLJ 221 at 223: '... substantial purpose is of course a crypto value judgement of the kind which the courts find useful but which produces flexibility at the price of certainty'.

5   See Sealy *Cases and Materials in Company Law* (6th edn, 1996), pp 318–319 who suggests that instead of regarding the matter as one of construction and focusing on the scope of the power, it would have been better to have regarded the question (as to which shareholder or group of shareholders should gain control) as a constitutional issue within the control of the general meeting and not within the powers of the directors at all.

6   See *Re Smith & Fawcett Ltd* [1942] Ch 304 at 308, [1942] 1 All ER 542 at 545, per Lord Greene; also Prentice (1970) 33 MLR 700.

7   *Howard Smith Ltd v Ampol Petroleum Ltd* [1974] AC 821 at 832, [1974] 1 All ER 1126 at 1131–1132.

8   *Howard Smith Ltd v Ampol Petroleum Ltd* [1974] AC 821 at 835, [1974] 1 All ER 1126 at 1134.

On the facts in *Howard Smith* it was unconstitutional for the directors to use their fiduciary powers over the shares in the company for the purpose of destroying an existing majority or creating a new majority. The directors' primary objective was to alter the majority shareholding and the allotment was invalid.

This approach requires that, having identified the substantial purpose for the particular exercise of a power, that purpose must be measured against the permissible purposes for the exercise of that power as indicated by the articles or ascertained by the court. Provided that that substantial purpose is a proper purpose, then the exercise of the power will not be invalidated by the presence of some other improper, but insubstantial, purpose. For example, some incidental benefit obtained by a director will not invalidate the exercise of the power unless his self-interest was the substantial purpose for the exercise of the power[9].

Some commentators have suggested that, realistically, it is almost impossible for the courts to determine which is the substantial and which the insubstantial purpose[10]. In the light of the difficulties of establishing the purposes for which the power was exercised and placing those within some hierarchy of permitted purposes, any exercise of a power, it is argued, should be set aside once any improper purpose is established. Anything less than such a strict approach will reduce what little control shareholders have over management. Such an approach while it has the merit of certainty is inflexible and gives little credit to the judiciary's ability to weigh up the case before them and to modify and refine the doctrine as need be to protect shareholders. So in *Whitehouse v Carlton Hotel Pty Ltd*[11] the Australian High Court noted that where there are competing permissible and impermissible purposes, the preferable view is that regardless of whether the impermissible purpose was the dominant one or but one of a number of significant contributing causes, an allotment will be invalidated if the impermissible purpose was causative in the sense that *but for* its presence the power would not have been exercised[12].

As far as a power to allot shares is concerned, it seems that such a power is not restricted to cases where the company requires additional capital but can be used (unless the articles otherwise provide) to defeat a corporate looter[13], to foster business connections[14], or indeed to ensure that the company has the requisite number of shareholders to exercise its statutory functions[15]. On the other hand, it can never be used solely to destroy an existing majority or create a new one[16].

RATIFICATION

In *Hogg v Cramphorn Ltd*[17], having decided that the directors had exercised their powers for an improper purpose, the court did not set aside the allotment but instead adjourned the proceedings to enable a general meeting to be held which duly ratified

9   *Ngurli Ltd v McCann* (1953) 90 CLR 425 at 440; *Mills v Mills* (1938) 60 CLR 150 at 164–165; *Hirsche v Sims* [1894] AC 654 at 660–661.
10   See Burridge (1981) 44 MLR 40; Birds (1974) 37 MLR 580.
11   (1987) 5 ACLC 421 at 427.
12   Citing Dixon J in *Mills v Mills* (1938) 60 CLR 150.
13   *Teck Corpn Ltd v Millar* (1972) 33 DLR (3d) 288, S Ct BC; noted Ziegel [1974] JBL 85.
14   *Harlowe's Nominees Pty Ltd v Woodside (Lake Entrance) Oil Co* (1968) 121 CLR 483 (Aust HC).
15   See *Punt v Symons & Co Ltd* [1903] 2 Ch 506.
16   *Howard Smith Ltd v Ampol Petroleum Ltd* [1974] AC 821, [1974] 1 All ER 1126; *Piercy v S Mills & Co* [1920] 1 Ch 77.
17   [1967] Ch 254, [1966] 3 All ER 420. See Wedderburn (1967) 30 MLR 77.

the directors' conduct. Support for this approach followed in *Bamford v Bamford*[18] where Harman LJ noted that ratification was 'a perfectly good "whitewash" of that which up to that time was a voidable transaction'[19]. Of course, it is ratification by the general meeting as it was constituted prior to the invalid allotment which is required, not ratification by the new majority created by the attempted allotment.

In *Re a Company (No 005136 of 1986)*[20] Hoffmann J found that an exercise by directors of their fiduciary powers for an improper purpose in this fashion, while technically a wrong done to the company, is substantially a complaint by a shareholder that his personal rights as a shareholder have been infringed. The basis of the complaint is that the allotment is an improper and unlawful exercise of the powers granted to the board by the articles of association which constitute a contract between the company and its members. An abuse of power in this way is therefore an infringement of a member's contractual rights under those articles. If that is the case then questions of ratification do not arise and a shareholder will have a personal cause of action[1]. Abuse of power by directors may also form the basis of a petition alleging unfairly prejudicial conduct[2]. That remedy is discussed in detail in Chapter 28.

THE DUTY OF CARE AND SKILL

City Equitable Fire Insurance Co

The law on this issue is dominated by the decision in *Re City Equitable Fire Insurance Co Ltd*[3] in 1925 where an insurance company suffered large losses as a result of the fraudulent activities of its managing director, a person described by the court as 'a daring and unprincipled scoundrel'[4]. In considering the conduct of the remainder of the board[5], the court reviewed many of the older authorities, some dating back to the previous century, and concluded that it was impossible to describe the duty of directors in general terms because of the wide variety of companies and functions which would have to be encompassed[6]. However, Romer J did think that some general propositions did seem to be warranted by the reported cases. These are discussed in detail below.

Many of the older cases in this area are from a time when directors were part-time officers, adornments to the corporate Christmas tree[7], without any specific obligations

---

18   [1970] Ch 212, [1969] 1 All ER 969; see also *Winthrop Investments Ltd v Winns Ltd* [1975] 2 NSWLR 666.
19   [1970] Ch 212 at 238, [1969] 1 All ER 969 at 973.
20   [1987] BCLC 82 (also reported as *Re Sherborne Park Residents Co Ltd* (1986) 2 BCC 99,528).
1   Support for this approach can be found in the Australian case *Residues Treatment and Trading Co Ltd v Southern Resources Ltd* (1988) 6 ACLC 1,160 (S Ct S A).
2   Ie under CA 1985, s 459.
3   [1925] Ch 407.
4   [1925] Ch 407 at 474. The managing director, Bevan, had been convicted and sentenced in respect of the fraud which had involved the granting of unsecured loans and the making of dividend payments out of capital. The court noted that he was one of the greatest authorities on finance in the City of London:'In reputation and credit he stood second to none.': see [1925] Ch 407 at 445.
5   Some of the other directors were found to have been negligent but were protected by an exemption clause in the company's articles. Such a clause would be invalid now, see CA 1985, s 310 discussed in detail in Ch 27. Companies may purchase insurance for their officers or auditors in respect of negligence: s 310(3), see Ch 27; also Finch 'Personal Accountability and Corporate Control: The Role of Directors' and Officers' Liability Insurance' (1994) 57 MLR 880.
6   [1925] Ch 407 at 426.
7   Mace *Directors Myth and Reality* (1971), p 107.

or responsibilities[8]. In keeping with that state of affairs, the courts regarded directors as pleasant, if sometimes incompetent, amateurs who did not possess any particular executive skills and upon whom it would be unreasonable to impose onerous standards of care and skill[9]. After all, it was the shareholders who elected the directors and if they decided to appoint incompetent amateurs then that was a matter for them. Obviously the modern position must be considered against the backdrop of a different commercial world, a recent emphasis on improved corporate governance[10] and an increasing number of disqualification orders made on the grounds of unfitness, a concept which, as we saw in Chappter 24, encompasses incompetence and negligence.

PROPOSITION 1

> A director need not exhibit in the performance of his duties a greater degree of skill than may reasonably be expected from a person of his knowledge and experience[11].

This is a subjective test of skill with the nature and extent of the duty depending on the nature of the business and the particular knowledge and experience of the individual director[12]. So a non-executive director who was a corporate financier and who failed to read and understand the company's statutory accounts was found to have fallen below the minimum standard of competence expected of him[13]. However, while the degree of skill expected will vary according to the individual, the standard of care required is such care as an ordinary man might be expected to take in the same circumstances on his own behalf[14].

Directors do not exercise a reasonable amount of care if they blindly accept all documents placed before them. In *Re City Equitable Fire Insurance Co Ltd*[15] Romer J found that the directors should have reviewed the company's investments and ought not to have been guided as to the value of their company's assets merely by the assurances of their chairman, however apparently distinguished and honourable, nor with the expression of belief of the auditor, however competent and trustworthy. In *Dorchester Finance Co Ltd v Stebbing*[16] the court rejected the argument that non-

---

8   See *Overend Gurney & Co v Gibb* (1872) LR 5 HL 480; *Lagunas Nitrate Co v Lagunas Syndicate* [1899] 2 Ch 392; *Re Brazilian Rubber Plantations and Estates Ltd* [1911] 1 Ch 425.

9   Dwight (1907) 17 Yale LJ 33 at 35 noted the atmosphere of good-humoured tolerance which pervaded the decisions on directors: 'From the gingerly manner in which the question of liability is discussed, one would suppose that directors were all trustees of charitable institutions giving freely of their services and engaged in the most self-denying tasks'.

10   See Finch 'Company Directors: Who Cares about Skill and Care?' (1992) 55 MLR 179; also Hicks (1994) 110 LQR 390.

11   *Re City Equitable Fire Insurance Co Ltd* [1925] Ch 407 at 428, per Romer J; see also *Dorchester Finance Co Ltd v Stebbing* [1989] BCLC 498; *Norman v Theodore Goddard (a firm)* [1991] BCLC 1028.

12   *Re City Equitable Fire Insurance Co Ltd* [1925] Ch 407 at 428; See also *Re Brazilian Rubber Plantations and Estates Ltd* [1911] 1 Ch 425.

13   *Re Continental Assurance Co of London plc* [1997] 1 BCLC 48, [1996] BCC 888, discussed in Chapter 24. For an interesting Australian review of the position of, and duties owed by, non-executive directors, see *Daniels v AWA Ltd* (1995) 13 ACLC 614, 16 ACSR 607; also Stapledon 'The AWA Case: Non-Executive Directors, Auditors and Corporate Governance Issues in Court' in Prentice & Holland (eds) *Contemporary Issues in Corporate Governance* (1993).

14   See *Overend Gurney & Co v Gibb* (1872) LR 5 HL 480; *Re Forest of Dean Coal Mining Co* (1878) 10 Ch D 450; *Re Brazilian Rubber Plantations and Estates Ltd* [1911] 1 Ch 425; *Re City Equitable Fire Insurance Co Ltd* [1925] Ch 407; *Dorchester Finance Co Ltd v Stebbing* [1989] BCLC 498.

15   [1925] Ch 407 at 474.

16   [1989] BCLC 498.

executive directors could rely on the competence and diligence of the auditors and do nothing themselves[17].

When signing cheques, a director is only required to satisfy himself that the cheque has been authorised by the board. He need not verify that the money is in fact required for the particular purpose specified or is indeed expended on that purpose, assuming that the cheque comes before him for signature in the regular way having regard to the usual practice of that company[18]. Signing blank cheques is, of course, negligent[19].

In *Re D'Jan of London Ltd*[20] a director signed a simple insurance proposal form without reading it. It contained inaccurate information and the insurance company subsequently repudiated liability on the policy when the company's stock was damaged by fire. The director was found not to have shown reasonable diligence when he signed the form without reading it.

PROPOSITION 2

A director is not bound to give continuous attention to the affairs of his company. His duties are of an intermittent nature to be performed at periodical board meetings, and at meetings of any committee of the board upon which he happens to be placed. He is not, however, bound to attend all such meetings, though he ought to attend whenever, in the circumstances, he is reasonably able to do so[1].

Executive directors appointed under service agreements will usually be required to give exclusive attention to the affairs of their companies while non-executive directors, certainly in public companies, would be expected to attend board meetings although private companies will operate a more relaxed regime[2].

In *Dorchester Finance Co Ltd v Stebbing*[3] no board meetings were held and two of the three directors rarely attended at the company's premises. All three directors, including the two inactive directors who had acted bona fide throughout, were liable for losses incurred when unsecured loans were made by the third director which subsequently turned out to be irrecoverable. The inactivity of the two directors was such that they had failed to perform any duty at all as directors of Dorchester. Complete inactivity in relation to, and complete uninvolvement with, the running of a company, in the absence of special circumstances, may warrant a finding of unfitness justifying disqualification.[3a]

However, a director is not under any obligation to undertake a definitive part in the conduct of the company's business and his role will vary from company to company[4]. As Hoffmann LJ noted obiter in *Bishopsgate Investment Management Ltd v Maxwell*

---

17 [1989] BCLC 498 at 505.
18 *Re City Equitable Fire Insurance Co Ltd* [1925] Ch 407 at 452.
19 See *Dorchester Finance Co Ltd v Stebbing* [1989] BCLC 498.
20 [1994] 1 BCLC 561.
1   *Re City Equitable Fire Insurance Co Ltd* [1925] Ch 407 at 429, per Romer J. See *Re Cardiff Savings Bank, Marquis of Bute's Case* [1892] 2 Ch 100; *Re Denham & Co* (1883) 25 Ch D 752.
2   It should be noted that, if the articles are in the form of Table A, a director is deemed to have vacated his office if he is absent for six months from directors' meetings without consent and the directors resolve that his office be vacated: art 81(e).
3   [1989] BCLC 498.
3a See *Re Park House Properties Ltd* [1997] 2 BCLC 530 at 556. Disqualification is discussed in Chapter 24. See also *Secretary of State for Trade and Industry v Arif* [1997] 1 BCLC 34 (director who failed to ensure that company maintained adequate accounting records disqualified as unfit). Cf *Secretary of State for Trade and Industry v Gash* [1997] 1 BCLC 341 (director who failed to stop company trading while insolvent was not unfit because he failed to resign).
4   *Re Brazilian Rubber Plantations and Estates Ltd* [1911] 1 Ch 425 at 437, per Neville J; *Re City Equitable Fire Insurance Co Ltd* [1925] Ch 407.

(No 2)[5], the existence of a duty to participate must depend upon how a particular company's business is organised and the part which the director could reasonably be expected to play[6].

PROPOSITION 3

> In respect of all duties that having regard to the exigencies of business and the articles of association, may properly be left to some other official, a director is, in the absence of grounds for suspicion, justified in trusting that official to perform such duties honestly[7].

It is obvious that a company could not hope to run its business in an efficient manner if the directors were required to do everything themselves and were not permitted to delegate on a wide scale. An intelligent devolution of labour must be possible[8]. Having permitted delegation, the law does not require that the directors should distrust and constantly supervise those to whom tasks have been delegated for this would defeat the whole purpose.

In *Huckerby v Elliott*[9] a director of a gaming club was not negligent in failing to check whether the club had the appropriate licence when the task of obtaining it had been delegated to someone else. In *Dovey v Cory*[10] the director of a banking company was not negligent in relying on the assertions of the chairman and general manager of the company, whose integrity, skill and competence he had no reason to doubt, with the result that dividends were paid out of capital and advances made on improper security. The court did not accept that the director should have watched either the inferior officers of the bank or verified the calculations of the auditors himself; nor was he required to examine the entries in the company's books[11]. In *Norman v Theodore Goddard*[12] a director who relied on information regarding the company's investments supplied to him by a solicitor and who did not check on the safety and security of the investments was not in breach of his duty of care to the company. The solicitor was a partner in an eminent firm of City solicitors who had misappropriated the money rather than investing it on the company's behalf. Hoffmann J, citing Romer LJ in *Re City Equitable Fire Insurance Co Ltd*[13], noted:

> … 'Business cannot be carried on upon principles of distrust' and men in responsible positions may be trusted until there is reason to distrust them[14].

The director was not negligent for the solicitor was someone whose honesty the director had no grounds to suspect.

A statutory statement

A modern statutory approach to the issue of care and skill can be found in the wrongful trading provision in the Insolvency Act 1986 which judges a director's conduct by

5   [1993] BCLC 1282.
6   [1993] BCLC 1282 at 1285.
7   *Re City Equitable Fire Insurance Co Ltd* [1925] Ch 407 at 429, per Romer J.
8   *Dovey v Cory* [1901] AC 477 at 485; *Huckerby v Elliott* [1970] 1 All ER 189.
9   [1970] 1 All ER 189.
10   [1901] AC 477.
11   [1901] AC 477 at 486, 493. See also *Re Denham & Co* (1883) 25 Ch D 752.
12   [1991] BCLC 1028.
13   [1925] Ch 407.
14   [1991] BCLC 1028 at 1031.

objective and subjective standards for the purpose of ascertaining whether he knew or ought to have known or concluded that the company was wrongfully trading[15]. Wrongful trading involves continuing to trade when there is no reasonable prospect of avoiding insolvent liquidation. Here it is necessary to judge the director's conduct against the conduct that might be expected of a reasonably diligent person having both:

   (a) the general knowledge, skill and experience that may reasonably be expected of a person carrying out the same functions as are carried out by that director in relation to the company, and

   (b) the general knowledge, skill and experience that that director has[16].

That this provision accurately states the modern position regarding the duty of care and skill was accepted by Hoffmann J in *Norman v Theodore Goddard*[17] and *Re D'Jan of London Ltd*[18], neither of which involved wrongful trading. However, this approach is open to question on the grounds that the court is converting a test imposed by a statutory provision for one purpose, wrongful trading, into a provision of general application. Also, in neither case was there a thorough review of the authorities relating to directors' duties of care and skill.

   In any event, it is interesting to note that the outcome of both cases would have been the same at common law. *Norman v Theodore Goddard*[19] was a case of justified reliance on a person whose honesty the director had no grounds to doubt. The negligence in *D'Jan*[20] was a failure to meet the standard of care which an ordinary man would take in such circumstances on his own behalf. An ordinary man in such circumstances would have appreciated the importance of full and accurate disclosure on an insurance form.

Enforcement of the duty

Breach of a director's duty of care and skill will be a wrong done to the company and in respect of which the company should sue. This is the rule in *Foss v Harbottle*[1]. If the company decides not to proceed then a shareholder can only bring an action on behalf of the company if he can bring himself within the fraud on the minority exception to the rule in *Foss v Harbottle*. The rule and the exception are discussed in detail in Chapter 28. However, it can be noted here that mere negligence on the part of the directors is not sufficient to bring a case within the fraud on the minority exception[2] although an action may be brought in the case of self-serving negligence[3]. Where the shareholders have authorised the allegedly negligent activity then no action can be taken against the directors[4]. Negligence in the management of the company's affairs may justify a petition alleging unfairly prejudicial conduct[5].

---

15   IA 1986, s 214. See Hicks (1994) 110 LQR 390.
16   IA 1986, s 214(4).
17   [1991] BCLC 1028.
18   [1994] 1 BCLC 561.
19   [1991] BCLC 1028.
20   [1994] 1 BCLC 561.
1   (1843) 2 Hare 461; see Chapter 28.
2   See *Pavlides v Jensen* [1956] Ch 565, [1956] 2 All ER 518.
3   See *Daniels v Daniels* [1978] Ch 406, [1978] 2 All ER 89.
4   *Multinational Gas and Petrochemical Co v Multinational Gas and Petrochemical Services Ltd* [1983] Ch 258, [1983] 2 All ER 563; see Wedderburn (1984) 47 MLR 87. However, the shareholders must have mandated or ratified the act, informally or formally, and it is not enough that they probably would have ratified it if they had known or thought about it: *Re D'Jan of London Ltd* [1994] 1 BCLC 561 at 564, per Hoffmann LJ.
5   Ie under CA 1985, s 459; see discussion of the unfairly prejudicial remedy in Ch 28 below.

CHAPTER 27

Self-dealing by directors

THE NO-CONFLICT RULE

General principle

... it is a rule of universal application that no one, having such [fiduciary] duties to discharge, shall be allowed to enter into engagements in which he has, or can have, a personal interest conflicting, or which possibly may conflict, with the interests of those whom he is bound to protect[1].

Where directors place themselves in a position where their duties and their personal interests conflict, any contract involved is voidable at the instance of the company[2]. It is not necessary to prove that there is an actual conflict of interest but there must be a real possibility of a conflict and not just some theoretical or rhetorical conflict[3].

This long-established rule of equity is inflexible and the court will not enquire as to the fairness or otherwise of the transaction[4]. The right to avoid the contract will be lost, however, if: (i) the company delays unduly before rescinding; or (ii) restitutio in integrum becomes impossible; or (iii) the rights of bona fide third parties intervene[5].

---

1   *Aberdeen Rly Co v Blaikie Bros* (1854) 1 Macq 461 at 471–472, per Lord Cranworth. This applies equally where the conflict is between the duty which a director owes to the company and the duty which he owes to another: *Transvaal Lands Co v New Belgium (Transvaal) Land and Development Co* [1914] 2 Ch 488.

2   *Aberdeen Rly Co v Blaikie Bros* (1854) 1 Macq 461; *Bray v Ford* [1896] AC 44 at 51, per Lord Herschell; *Transvaal Lands Co v New Belgium (Transvaal) Land and Development Co* [1914] 2 Ch 488; *Boulting v Association of Cinematograph, Television and Allied Technicians* [1963] 2 QB 606 at 635, [1963] 1 All ER 716 at 728, per Upjohn LJ; *Guinness plc v Saunders* [1990] 2 AC 663, [1990] 1 All ER 652.

3   See *Boulting v Association of Cinematograph Television and Allied Technicians* [1963] 2 QB 606 at 637–638, [1963] 1 All ER 716 at 730 per Upjohn LJ; *Boardman v Phipps* [1967] 2 AC 46, [1966] 3 All ER 721; *Transvaal Lands Co v New Belgium (Transvaal) Land and Development Co* [1914] 2 Ch 488; see also *Cowan de Groot Properties Ltd v Eagle Trust plc* [1991] BCLC 1045 at 1116; *Re Dominion International Group plc (No 2)* [1996] 1 BCLC 572 at 597.

4   *Aberdeen Rly Co v Blaikie Bros* (1854) 1 Macq 461 at 471–472.

5   *Hely-Hutchinson v Brayhead Ltd* [1968] 1 QB 549, [1967] 3 All ER 98.

In addition to setting aside the contract, the company can call upon the director to account for any gains which he has made.

It is commonly stated that directors must not place themselves in a position of conflict but, as Vinelott J made clear in *Movitex Ltd v Bulfield*[6], directors are not under a duty not to place themselves in a position of conflict. It is simply that, if they do, then the contract is voidable and they may be called to account. Their position as fiduciaries obliges them to act bona fide in the best interests of the company and consequently places them under certain disabilities.

The leading authority on directors' conflicts of interest is *Aberdeen Rly Co v Blaikie Bros*[7] where a company was entitled to set aside a contract for the purchase of equipment entered into between it and a partnership when it transpired that the chairman of the directors was also the managing partner of the partnership. The danger is obvious: the director is obliged to purchase goods on behalf of the company at the lowest possible price while as a member of the partnership he wishes to sell the goods at the highest price. Where such a conflict exists, the law recognises that the director, despite his best intentions, may be swayed by his own self-interest.

There are advantages in applying such a strict no-conflict principle. There is certainty resulting from the absolute prohibition and savings in terms of the time and money which would otherwise be expended if the courts had to be satisfied as to the fairness of each transaction. But there are also disadvantages. Prohibition may force a company to incur costs as where the company is forced to contract with an outsider when an insider is the sole or most favourable source of the goods or services which the company requires[8]. In addition, individuals are often appointed as directors in order to foster business relations between two companies and so a possible conflict will exist from the outset. Bearing in mind these disadvantages and the fact that the rule is imposed essentially for the protection of those to whom fiduciary duties are owed, it is not surprising that the persons entitled to the benefit of the rule may relax it[9]. Thus a director may enter into a transaction in which he has a conflict of interest with the informed consent of the shareholders in general meeting and a company by its articles may permit directors to be interested in contracts with the company or in which the company is otherwise interested[10]. It is extremely common for companies to use the articles in this way as it eliminates the need to present every contract in which the directors are interested to the general meeting.

Provisions in the articles – art 85, Table A

The standard provision for these purposes is art 85 of Table A which provides:

> Subject to the provisions of the Act, and provided that he has disclosed to the directors the nature and extent of any material interest of his, a director notwithstanding his office–

6   [1988] BCLC 104.
7   (1854) 1 Macq 461.
8   See *Boulting v Association of Cinematograph, Television and Allied Technicians* [1963] 2 QB 606 at 637, [1963] 1 All ER 716 at 730; also generally Brudney 'The Independent Director – Heavenly City or Potemkin Village ?' (1982) 95 Harv L Rev 597 at 624.
9   See *Boulting v Association of Cinematograph, Television and Allied Technicians* [1963] 2 QB 606 at 636, [1963] 1 All ER 716 at 729, per Upjohn LJ; *Bray v Ford* [1896] AC 44 at 51, per Lord Herschell; *Imperial Mercantile Credit Association v Coleman* (1871) 6 Ch App 558.
10 See Table A, art 85 discussed below; *Imperial Mercantile Credit Association v Coleman* (1871) 6 Ch App 558; *Boulting v Association of Cinematograph, Television and Allied Technicians* [1963] 2 QB 606, [1963] 1 All ER 716; *Movitex Ltd v Bulfield* [1988] BCLC 104.

    (a) may be a party to, or otherwise interested in, any transaction or arrangement with the company or in which the company is otherwise interested;

    (b) may be a director or other officer of, or employed by, or a party to any transaction or arrangement with, or otherwise interested in, any body corporate promoted by the company or in which the company is otherwise interested; and

    (c) shall not, by reason of his office, be accountable to the company for any benefit which he derives from any such office or employment or from any such transaction or arrangement or from any interest in any such body corporate and no such transaction or arrangement shall be liable to be avoided on the ground of any such interest or benefit[11].

Such a provision comprehensively excludes the no-conflict rule where the director has disclosed his interest[12].

Statutory disclosure – CA 1985, s 317

In addition to disclosure under the articles, the statute also provides that it is the duty of a director who is in any way, whether directly or indirectly, interested in a contract or proposed contract, transaction or arrangement[13], with the company to declare the nature of his interest at a meeting of the directors of the company[14].

In the case of a proposed contract, the declaration must be made at the meeting of the directors at which the question of entering into the contract is first taken into consideration; or if the director only subsequently became interested in the proposed contract, at the next meeting of directors held after he became so interested[15]. In a case where a director becomes interested in a contract after it is made, the declaration must be made at the first meeting of directors held after he becomes so interested[15].

For these purposes, a director may give a general notice to the directors to the effect that he is a member of a specified company or firm and is to be regarded as interested in any contract which may, after the date of the notice, be made with that company or firm; or he may give a general notice to the effect that he is to be regarded as interested in any contract which may, after the date of the notice, be made with a specified person who is connected[16] with him[17]. However, no such notice is of effect unless either it is given at a meeting of the directors or the director takes reasonable steps to secure that it is brought up and read at the next meeting of the directors after it is given[18].

---

11   The interested directors are normally prohibited from voting in respect of such contracts and from being counted in the quorum present at the meeting: Table A, arts 94, 95 but note also art 96.

12   See *Movitex Ltd v Bulfield* [1988] BCLC 104 at 114.

13   Whether or not that transaction or arrangement constitutes a contract: CA 1985, s 317(5); included within 'transaction or arrangement' are all the transactions described in s 330, ie loans, quasi-loans, credit transactions etc, whether made by the company for a director or a person connected with such a director: s 317(6).

14   Ibid, s 317(1). This section also applies to shadow directors and in that case disclosure is by notice in writing to the board: s 317(8). Details of any transaction or arrangement in which a director has a material interest must be included in a note to the accounts by virtue of s 232, Sch 6, Pt II.

15   Ibid, s 317(2).

16   Within the meaning of ibid, s 346.

17   Ibid, s 317(3).

18   Ibid, s 317(4).

RELATIONSHIP BETWEEN ART 85 AND CA 1985, S 317

The statute does not define the relationship between this statutory requirement of disclosure and provisions in the articles such as art 85. But the position was clearly established by the Court of Appeal in *Hely-Hutchinson v Brayhead Ltd*[19]: the statutory provision merely creates a statutory duty of disclosure and imposes a fine for non-compliance[20]. Accordingly, a breach of the statutory provision, or indeed compliance with it, has no effect on the issue of the validity of a contract entered into in disregard of the no-conflict rule. That issue is determined by whether the articles have relaxed the self-dealing rule and whether there has been strict compliance with the articles. This approach was endorsed by Lord Goff in *Guinness plc v Saunders*[1].

However, art 85 makes no provision for the manner of disclosure of a conflict of interest by a director although it is stated that the article is subject to the provisions of the Companies Act. This has allowed the courts to read into art 85 the requirements of s 317 as to the manner and timing of disclosure[2] although they have been reluctant to explore fully the relationship between these provisions[3]. The position is not helped by the fact that the judgments in the cases tend to move between the requirements of the statute and the articles as if they were interchangeable and part of one common requirement[3]. As the judgment in *Hely-Hutchinson v Brayhead Ltd*[4] noted above, makes clear, compliance with the articles is the key to the validity of the contract whereas compliance with s 317 is necessary to avoid a fine.

Disclosure to the directors

Given the inflexible nature of the over-riding equitable principle, strict compliance with the requirements of the articles is essential if a director is to free himself effectively of the disability which arises from the no-conflict rule.

Disclosure must be to the board at the meeting when the contract first falls to be considered and disclosure to a committee of directors would be insufficient[5]. The

---

19 [1968] 1 QB 549 at 595, [1967] 3 All ER 98 at 109, per Lord Pearson.
20 Note CA 1985, s 317(9): Nothing in the statutory provision precludes the operation of any rule of law restricting directors of a company from having an interest in contracts with the company.
1   [1990] 2 AC 663 at 697, [1990] 1 All ER 652 at 665. Lord Templeman's 'surprising observation' to the contrary [1990] 2 AC 663 at 694, [1990] 1 All ER 652 at 662 (see Harman J in *Lee Panavision Ltd v Lee Lighting Ltd* [1991] BCLC 575 at 583) was clearly wrong. See also *Cowan de Groot Properties Ltd v Eagle Trust plc* [1991] BCLC 1045 at 1113.
2   See *Lee Panavision Ltd v Lee Lighting Ltd* [1991] BCLC 575 at 583; *Runciman v Walter Runciman plc* [1992] BCLC 1084. This is made easier by the fact that many articles repeat the statutory provision.
3   See, for example, the comments of Dillon LJ in *Lee Panavision Ltd v Lee Lighting Ltd* [1992] BCLC 22 at 33; and of Simon Brown J in *Runciman v Walter Runciman plc* [1992] BCLC 1084 at 1093, 1096.
4   See [1968] 1 QB 549 at 595, [1967] 3 All ER 98 at 109, per Lord Pearson.
5   *Guinness plc v Saunders* [1990] 2 AC 663, [1990] 1 All ER 652, HL; also [1988] 2 All ER 940 at 944, [1988] 1 WLR 863 at 868, CA. It is not clear whether disclosure to a committee of directors would suffice even if the articles so provided because of the uncertainty as to the precise relationship between article 85 and CA 1985 s 317. On one interpretation, articles excluding the no-conflict rule are subject to the provisions of the Act and s 317 requires disclosure to the board. Another interpretation would be that the exclusion of the no-conflict rule is a matter for the shareholders to regulate and if they are satisfied with disclosure to a committee, then that would suffice for the purposes of excluding the no-conflict rule although such disclosure would be inadequate for the purposes of CA 1985 s 317.

disclosure required is full and frank disclosure as to the nature of the transaction so that the other directors can see what the director's interest is and how far it extends[6].

Disclosure at a formal board meeting may be required even though all of the directors are aware informally of the conflict of interest but there are conflicting views on this point. In *Lee Panavision Ltd v Lee Lighting Ltd*[7] Dillon LJ noted, obiter, that he would have been loath to regard a technical non-declaration of an interest in this way as having an adverse effect on any agreement[8]. In *Runciman v Walter Runciman plc*[9] Simon Brown J queried, obiter, whether in all commonsense a formal declaration of interest is required where all the board would have been aware of the conflict[10].

The merits of a formal declaration at a board meeting were stressed by Lightman J in *Neptune (Vehicle Washing Equipment) Ltd v Fitzgerald*[11] where he had to consider the question of disclosure in the case of a company with a sole director. The plaintiff company had dispensed with the services of its sole director and sought recovery of £100,000 paid to him by the plaintiff company on the termination of his employment. This payment was pursuant to resolutions passed by the defendant as the sole director. Lightman J considered the objects of disclosure, namely: that all the directors should know or be reminded of the interest of any director; that the making of the declaration should be the occasion for a statutory pause for thought about the existence of the conflict of interest and the duty to prefer the interests of the company; and that the disclosure or reminder should be a distinct happening at a meeting and be recorded in the minutes[12]. It followed that, even in the case of a sole director, a formal disclosure of the conflict of interest must take place[13].

Not everyone would agree with this approach. Vinelott J in *Movitex Ltd v Bulfield*[14] doubted, obiter, whether disclosure can sensibly occur where there is only one director since, in his view, 'disclosure imports the concept of informing someone of something of which he would not otherwise be aware'[15]. In *Neptune (Vehicle Washing Equipment) Ltd v Fitzgerald (No 2)*[16], the court reluctantly applied Lightman J's approach even though the trial judge had 'doubts about its correctness'[17]. A better approach would be to require that disclosure by a sole director should be to the shareholders in general meeting[18].

FAILURE TO DISCLOSE

A failure to comply strictly with the requirements of the articles will deprive the director of the protection afforded by them and will result in the application of the general no-conflict rule with the result that the contract is voidable and the director may be called

---

6   See *Movitex Ltd v Bulfield* [1988] BCLC 104 at 121; *Imperial Mercantile Credit Association v Coleman* (1873) LR 6 HL 189 at 205.
7   [1992] BCLC 22, CA.
8   [1992] BCLC 22 at 33. The non-disclosure in question was a failure to disclose formally at a board meeting a conflict which was known to and common to all the directors.
9   [1992] BCLC 1084.
10 [1992] BCLC 1084 at 1095. In this case the interest in question was the interest of a director in his own service contract which had been varied by the board.
11 [1995] 1 BCLC 352.
12 [1995] 1 BCLC 352 at 359.
13 See [1995] 1 BCLC 352 at 360 as the manner of disclosure where the director is a sole director.
14 [1988] BCLC 104.
15 [1988] BCLC 104 at 116.
16 [1995] BCC 1000.
17 [1995] BCC 1000 at 1003.
18 See *Neptune (Vehicle Washing Equipment) Ltd v Fitzgerald (No 2)* [1995] BCC 1000 at 1003.

to account[19]. It will also necessarily mean a failure to comply with the statutory disclosure requirement for which the penalty is a fine[20].

The court will not permit a director who has placed himself in a position of conflict to claim payment from the company either on a quantum meruit basis or as an equitable allowance for services rendered. In *Guinness plc v Saunders*[1] a committee of the board of Guinness, without authority, awarded remuneration of £5.2m to one of the Guinness directors (Ward) in return for his services. There was a clear conflict of interest and so potentially a voidable contract on the basis outlined above, namely the no-conflict rule would apply rendering the contract voidable in the absence of due compliance with the disclosure requirements contained in the Guinness articles. However, the House of Lords concluded that the contract was in fact void for want of authority. Ward sought to retain all or some of the £5.2m on the basis of quantum meruit or as an equitable allowance in respect of the services rendered. This was rejected by the House of Lords.

Lord Goff noted that directors must not put themselves in a position where there is a conflict between their personal interests and their duties as fiduciaries and so they are for that reason precluded from contracting with the company for their services except in circumstances authorised by the articles of association[2]. It would be inconsistent, he said, with this long-established principle to award remuneration in such circumstances as of right on the basis of a quantum meruit claim although the principle does not altogether exclude the possibility that an equitable allowance might be made in respect of services rendered. This equitable jurisdiction could be exercised, however, only if it did not conflict with the policy underlying the rule, ie if it did not provide any encouragement to fiduciaries to put themselves in a position where their duties as fiduciaries conflicted with their interests[3]. There was no possibility of granting such an allowance in this case for Ward's interests were in stark conflict with his duty as a director of Guinness.

Guinness plc v Saunders[4] is a strong affirmation by the House of Lords of the importance of the rule of equity which prohibits a fiduciary from placing himself in a position of conflict except as expressly authorised by the articles. This stance is particularly important in the company context where directors are frequently faced with conflicts which can produce significant personal gain.

The interests of the company

Finally, it should be noted that disclosure in itself will not validate a transaction where it is entered into by a director in breach of his duty to act bona fide in the interests of the company as a whole and not for a collateral purpose.

In *Neptune (Vehicle Washing Equipment) Ltd v Fitzgerald (No 2)*[5] (discussed above) the court held that, even if it had been satisfied that there had been due compliance

19 *Hely-Hutchinson v Brayhead Ltd* [1968] 1 QB 549, [1967] 3 All ER 98; *Aberdeen Rly Co v Blaikie Bros* (1854) 1 Macq 461; *Guinness plc v Saunders* [1990] 2 AC 663, [1990] 1 All ER 652.
20 CA 1985, s 317(7).
1 [1990] 2 AC 663, [1990] 1 All ER 652; noted Hopkins (1990) CLJ 220; Beatson & Prentice (1990) 106 LQR 365; Birks (1990) LMCLQ 330. For an account of the fascinating background to the transaction at issue in this case, see DTI *Guinness plc Report of the Investigation under ss 432(2) and 442 of the Companies Act 1985* (1997) Ch 7.
2 [1990] 2 AC 663 at 700, [1990] 1 All ER 652 at 666.
3 [1990] 2 AC 663 at 701, [1990] 1 All ER 652 at 667. Lord Goff went on to query whether any such allowance might ever be granted in the case of a director of a company (Lord Templeman thought not [1990] 2 AC 663 at 694, [1990] 1 All ER 653 at 662). See also *Re Neptune (Vehicle Washing Equipment) Ltd v Fitzgerald (No 2)* [1995] BCC 1000 at 1021.
4 [1990] 2 AC 663, [1990] 1 All ER 652.
5 [1995] BCC 1000.

with the company's articles which had excluded the no-conflict rule, that did not entail that the director was relieved from his other obligations to the company including his duty to act bona fide in the company's interests.

On the facts, the defendant had acted in breach of his fiduciary duties to the company in passing resolutions and procuring the payment to himself of £100,000. He was not acting in what he honestly and genuinely considered to be in the best interests of the company but rather was acting exclusively to further his own personal interests.

The court went on to note that when the no-conflict rule has been excluded, the court must scrutinise the transaction with great care to determine whether in carrying out the transaction the director truly has managed to avoid the temptation of putting his personal interests before that of the company[6].

Specific financial transactions

It is clear from the foregoing discussion that the strict no-conflict rule gives way in practice to a more relaxed regime requiring disclosure to the board under the articles. In order to curb some of the more blatant abuses arising from this permissive regime, it has been necessary to make statutory provision for certain types of transactions, in particular for loans and related transactions and substantial property transactions.

These transactions in favour of directors and connected persons are the subject of extensive statutory prohibitions. However, each statutory prohibition also contains numerous exceptions and, as the various exceptions are not mutually exclusive, careful planning should still enable a director to obtain substantial financial benefits from his association with his company.

In addition to the statutory requirements, directors must consider any more restrictive provisions included in the company's articles and, in entering into any such transactions, must bear in mind their overriding duty to act in the best interests of the company[7].

LOANS

A company must not make a loan to a director or shadow director of the company or of its holding company[8]. Loans to directors of subsidiary companies are not affected provided that the director is not also a director of the holding company.

In addition to the basic prohibition, a relevant company[9], ie a public company or a company which is part of a group which contains a public company, is prohibited from making a loan to a person connected with such a director[10]. The prohibitions were extended in this way because over the years DTI inspectors' reports have shown that the greatest abuse of loans and related transactions occurs in public companies and,

---

6   [1995] BCC 1000 at 1017.
7   See, for example, *Neptune (Vehicle Washing Equipment) Ltd v Fitzgerald (No 2)* [1995] BCC 1000; also Ch 26.
8   CA 1985, s 330(2)(a), (5). 'Loan' is not defined but see *Champagne Perrier-Jouet SA v HH Finch Ltd* [1982] 3 All ER 713 at 717, [1982] 1 WLR 1359 at 1363 where Walton J adopted the definition from the *Shorter Oxford English Dictionary*: a loan is a sum of money lent for a time to be returned in money or money's worth.
9   Defined CA 1985, s 331(6). It was felt that the potential for abuse was much greater in public companies where the directors do not usually combine their managerial functions with a significant degree of ownership: HC Official Report, Standing Committee A, Session 1979–80, vol I, col 436, 29 November 1979.
10 CA 1985, s 330(3)(b).

of course, in such companies the shareholders are more vulnerable given their greater number and distance from the company's management. There is no prohibition on private companies, which are not relevant companies, making loans to persons connected with the directors.

A person is connected with a director of a company if, but only if, he (not being himself a director of it), is:

(i) that director's spouse, child or step-child; or

(ii) except where the context otherwise requires, a body corporate with which the director is associated[11]; or

(iii) a person acting in his capacity as trustee of any trust the beneficiaries of which include the director or (i) or (ii) above or of a trust whose terms confer a power on the trustees that may be exercised for the benefit of the director or (i) or (ii) above; or

(iv) a person acting in his capacity as a partner of that director or a partner of any person who by virtue of (i), (ii) or (iii) above is connected with that director[12].

There are a number of exceptions to the general prohibitions.

Small amounts

A loan may be made to a director of a company or of its holding company provided the aggregate of the relevant amounts does not exceed £5,000[13]. It should be noted that this does not permit a relevant company to make a loan to a person connected with a director. That remains totally prohibited.

The aggregate of the relevant amounts is determined essentially by adding together the value of the proposed transaction or arrangement and the value of any existing transaction or arrangement of that particular type in favour of the person in respect of whom it is proposed to make the new transaction or arrangement[14]. These provisions are designed to prevent attempts to circumvent the legislation by breaking up a transaction into a number of smaller transactions.

The value of a transaction or arrangement will vary according to the nature of the transaction. For example, if the transaction is a loan then it is the principal of the loan[15]. Where the value of a transaction or arrangement cannot for any reason be expressed as a specific sum of money, the value is deemed to exceed £100,000[16].

Intra-group transactions

Where a relevant company is a member of a group of companies, then it is not prohibited from making a loan to another member of the group by reason only that a director of one member of the group is associated with another[17]. A company may also make a loan in favour of its holding company[18]. These exceptions were thought necessary if

11 Defined ibid, s 346(4). Essentially a director is associated with a body corporate if the director and persons connected with him together are interested in at least one-fifth of the equity share capital of that company or are entitled to exercise or control the exercise of more than one-fifth of the voting power at any general meeting. The circumstances in which a director is deemed to control a company are set out in s 346(5).

12 Ibid, s 346(2).

13 Ibid, s 334.

14 Ibid, s 339.

15 Ibid, s 340(1), (2) .

16 Ibid, s 340(7).

17 Ibid, s 333.

18 Ibid, s 336(a).

intra-group business was not to be unduly hampered[19]. Without this exception, the following transaction would have been prohibited: where X is a director of Company A (which is a relevant company) and owns 40% of the shares in Company B, another member of the group, Company A could not have made a loan to Company B as Company B is a connected person of X, being a body corporate with whom X is associated.

Money-lending companies

Where a company is a money-lending company[20] then it may make a loan to any person, notwithstanding the general prohibitions, provided certain conditions are met[1]. The loan must be made in the ordinary course of the company's business and the amount of the loan must be no greater than, nor the terms more favourable than, those which it is reasonable to expect the company would have offered to a person of the same financial standing but unconnected with the company[2]. In the case of a relevant company (unless it is a banking company[3]), the aggregate of the relevant amounts must not exceed £100,000[4].

A money-lending company may also make a loan to one of its directors or a director of its holding company to enable such a person to purchase their only or main residence, to improve their dwelling house, or in substitution for a loan provided by a third party for any of those purposes, provided that loans of that type are ordinarily made by the company to its employees on terms no less favourable[5]. The aggregate of the relevant amounts must not exceed £100,000[6].

QUASI-LOANS

A relevant company must not make a quasi-loan to one of its directors or to a director of its holding company, or to a person connected with such a director[6]. The circumstances in which a person is regarded as connected with a director are set out above. There are no restrictions on private companies (which are not relevant companies) entering into quasi-loan transactions.

A quasi-loan is defined as a transaction whereby payments are made by a creditor (the company) on behalf of the borrower (the director) on terms that the borrower or a person on his behalf will reimburse the creditor or in circumstances giving rise to a liability on the part of the borrower to reimburse the creditor[7]. This would include, for example, the provision by a company of a credit card to a director who uses it on the basis that the company will pay the bill initially and the director will reimburse the company later. The provision of goods or services on a receive now, pay later, basis is open to abuse hence the need in the case of relevant companies to extend the prohibitions to such transactions.

There are a number of exceptions to the general prohibitions.

---

19 See HC Official Report, Standing Committee A, Session 1979–80, vol I, col 448, 29 November 1979.
20 Defined as a company whose ordinary business includes the making of loans or quasi-loans or the giving of guarantees in connection with loans or quasi-loans: CA 1985, s 338(2).
1   Ibid, s 338(1)(a).
2   Ibid, s 338(3).
3   Defined as a company which is authorised under the Banking Act 1987: CA 1985, s 744.
4   Ibid, s 338(4).
5   Ibid, s 338(6).
6   Ibid, s 330(3)(a), (b).
7   Ibid, s 331(3).

Small amounts

A relevant company may make a quasi-loan to one of its directors or a director of its holding company (but not to persons connected with such a director) provided the quasi-loan contains a term requiring repayment of the expenditure by the director or a person on his behalf to the company within two months of its being incurred and the aggregate of the relevant amounts does not exceed £5,000[8]. This would permit the use of the credit card outlined above.

Intra-group transactions

Where a relevant company is a member of a group of companies then it is not prohibited from making a quasi-loan to another member of that group by reason only that a director of one member of the group is associated with another[9]. A company may also make a quasi-loan to its holding company[10].

Money-lending companies

A company which is a money-lending company[11] may make a quasi-loan to any person, notwithstanding the general prohibitions, provided certain conditions are met[12]. The loan must be made in the ordinary course of the company's business and the amount of the loan must be no greater than, nor the terms more favourable than, those which it is reasonable to expect the company would have offered to a person of the same financial standing but unconnected with the company[13]. In the case of a relevant company (unless it is a banking company[14]), the aggregate of the relevant amounts must not exceed £100,000[15].

CREDIT TRANSACTIONS

A relevant company must not enter into a credit transaction as creditor for a director of the company, or a director of its holding company, or a person so connected[16]. There are no restrictions on private companies which are not relevant companies.

A credit transaction is a transaction under which one party (the creditor):

(a) supplies any goods or sells any land under a hire-purchase agreement or a conditional sale agreement;

(b) leases or hires any land or goods in return for periodical payments; or

(c) otherwise disposes of land or supplies goods or services on the understanding that payment, in whatever form, is to be deferred[17].

An example would be where the company (the creditor) leases a car for use by a director of the company for a specific period, upon the expiry of which the car is returned to

8   Ibid, s 332(1).
9   Ibid, s 333.
10   Ibid, s 336(a).
11   Defined as a company whose ordinary business includes the making of loans or quasi-loans or the giving of guarantees in connection with loans or quasi-loans: ibid, s 338(2).
12   Ibid, s 338(1)(a).
13   Ibid, s 338(3).
14   Defined as a company which is authorised under the Banking Act 1987: CA 1985, s 744.
15   Ibid, s 338(4).
16   Ibid, s 330(4)(a).
17   Ibid, s 331(7).

the lessor. The danger is presumably that payment will be deferred for a very long time and that the other terms of the agreement will be overly favourable to the director.

There are a number of exceptions to the general prohibitions.

Small amounts
Credit transactions are permitted provided the aggregate of the relevant amounts does not exceed £10,000[18].

Intra-group transactions
A company may enter into a credit transaction as a creditor for its holding company[19].

Ordinary course of business
Credit transactions are permitted if the company enters into the transaction in the ordinary course of its business and the value of the transaction is no greater and the terms are no more favourable than those which it is reasonable to expect the company to have offered to a person of the same financial standing but who is unconnected with the company[20].

RELATED TRANSACTIONS

Back-to-back transactions
A company must not take part in any arrangement whereby another person enters into a transaction which, if it had been entered into by the company, would have been a prohibited loan, quasi-loan, credit transaction, guarantee, security or assignment[1], and that other person, in pursuance of the arrangement, has obtained or is to obtain any benefit from the company or its holding company or a subsidiary of the company or its holding company[2]. The prohibition was thought necessary in order to prevent company assets being used indirectly to assist or procure financial transactions for a director[3].

The provision is designed to cover what are called back-to-back transactions, for example where Company A makes a loan to X, a director of Company B, in return for Company B making a loan to Y, a director of Company A. The benefit conferred by Company A must be a quid pro quo for the facility obtained by its director Y and must not be merely incidental to a transaction.

Thus it would not cover the situation where Company A banks with Super Bank plc and a director of Company A receives a personal loan from Super Bank. It does cover the situation where the director is a customer of Super Bank plc and negotiates a loan from the bank on favourable terms in return for his instructing the company to bank with Super Bank plc. It is the element of reciprocity which brings the back-to-back provisions into play.

---

18   Ibid, s 335(1).
19   Ibid, s 336(b).
20   Ibid, s 335(2).
1   Ie within ibid, s 330(2), (3), (4), (6).
2   Ibid, s 330(7).
3   See HC Official Report, Standing Committee A, Session 1979–80, vol I, col 438, 29 November 1979.

Assignment/assumption of liabilities

A company must not arrange for the assignment to it, or the assumption by it, of any rights, obligations or liabilities under a transaction which, if it had been entered into by the company, would have been a prohibited loan, quasi-loan, credit transaction, guarantee or security[4]. This is to prevent the situation where, for example, A makes a loan to B, a director of Company C, and the company either buys A's interest in the loan or takes over the rights and liabilities of Z who is the guarantor of B's loan. The net effect of these transaction is the company becomes a creditor of a director just as if it had advanced the loan in the first place[5]. It was felt that there was too much scope for collusive agreements in these cases[5].

Guarantees/security

The overall position in respect of a company entering into any guarantee[6] or providing any security in respect of any loan, quasi-loan or credit transaction entered into by a director is that if the company is prohibited from entering into the transaction in respect of which the security is sought, then the company is also prohibited from giving a guarantee or providing security in respect of that transaction[7]. If the company is permitted to enter into the transaction then, as a general rule, it will also be permitted to give any guarantee or provide security[8].

Expenditure incurred for the purposes of the company

A company may do anything, notwithstanding the statutory prohibitions, to provide a director (but not the directors of its holding company) with funds to meet expenditure incurred or to be incurred by him for the purposes of the company or for the purpose of enabling him properly to perform his duties as an officer of the company; and the company is not prohibited from doing anything to enable a director to avoid incurring such expenditure[9]. In the case of a relevant company, the aggregate of the relevant amounts in respect of each director must not exceed £20,000[10]. This would, for example, permit the company to make a bridging loan to a director where he was required to move residence in the course of his duties.

The assistance provided must be approved in advance by the company in general meeting, at which meeting the purpose of the expenditure, the amount to be provided by the company and the extent of the company's liabilities under the transaction must be disclosed[11]. Alternatively, approval can be sought at the next following annual general meeting but, if approval is not given, then the loan must be repaid or any other liability incurred must be discharged within six months from the conclusion of that meeting[12].

4   Ie prohibited by CA 1985, s 330(2), (3) or (4): s 330(6).
5   See HC Official Report, Standing Committee A, Session 1979–80, vol I, col 438, 29 November 1979.
6   Defined to include any indemnity: CA 1985, s 331(2).
7   Ibid, ss 330(2)(b), (3)(c), (4)(b).
8   Ibid, ss 333 (inter-company loans in same group), 336 (transactions at behest of holding company) and 338 (loan or quasi-loan by money-lending company).
9   Ibid, s 337(1), (2).
10   Ibid, s 337(3).
11   Ibid, s 337(3), (4).
12   Ibid, s 337(3)(b).

CONSEQUENCES OF BREACH

Civil remedies

Where a company enters into a transaction or arrangement in breach of the general prohibitions on loans etc outlined above, the transaction or arrangement is voidable at the instance of the company unless:

(a) restitution of any money or any other asset which is the subject matter of the arrangement or transaction is no longer possible; or the company has been indemnified by the parties involved for the loss or damage suffered by it; or

(b) any rights acquired bona fide for value and without actual notice of the contravention by a person other than the person for whom the transaction or arrangement was made would be affected by its avoidance.[13]

Any director and any person connected with such a director for whom a prohibited transaction or arrangement was entered into, together with any other director of the company who authorised the transaction or arrangement, is liable:

(a) to account to the company for any gain which he has made directly or indirectly by the arrangement or transaction; and

(b) to indemnify the company for any loss or damage resulting from the arrangement or transaction[14].

This is so whether or not the company has avoided the transaction and without prejudice to any liability which might arise at common law[15].

A director who is liable as a result of the company entering into a transaction with a person connected with the director can escape liability under the statute if he can show that he took all reasonable steps to secure the company's compliance with the statutory requirements[16]. There is no such defence when the transaction in question has been entered into between the company and himself.

In respect of any prohibited transaction where liability falls on a person connected with a director or on any director who authorised the transaction, that person or director can escape liability if he shows that, at the time the arrangement or transaction was entered into, he did not know the relevant circumstances constituting the contravention[17].

Criminal penalties

Criminal penalties have been imposed in respect of breaches of the provisions by relevant companies and their directors. This reflects the much tougher line taken in respect of those companies where there has been most abuse of the loan provisions in the past.

A relevant company which enters into a transaction or arrangement for one of its directors or for a director of its holding company in contravention of the statutory provisions is guilty of an offence unless it can show that, at the time the transaction or arrangement was entered into, it did not know the relevant circumstances[18].

---

13   Ibid, s 341(1). See *Tait Consibee (Oxford) Ltd v Tait* [1997] 2 BCLC 349.
14   Ibid, s 341(2).
15   Ibid, s 341(2), (3).
16   Ibid, s 341(4).
17   Ibid, s 341(5).
18   Ibid, s 342(2), (5).

A director of a relevant company who authorises or permits the company to enter into a transaction or arrangement knowing or having reasonable cause to believe that the company was thereby contravening the statutory provisions is guilty of an offence[19]. In addition, any person who procures a relevant company to enter into a transaction or arrangement knowing or having reasonable cause to believe that the company was contravening the statutory provisions is guilty of an offence[20].

DISCLOSURE

Any transaction or arrangement of the type discussed above (loan, quasi-loan, credit transaction) made by a company for a director of the company or a person connected with such a director, whether prohibited or not, is treated as a transaction or arrangement in which that director is interested and it must be disclosed at a meeting of the directors of the company[1]. Details of such transactions must also be included in a note to the company's accounts[2].

Substantial property transactions

The greatest possibility of abuse of position arises when directors purchase assets from, or sell assets to, their companies or companies in which they have an interest. The statutory provisions in this regard requiring the approval of the shareholders in general meeting are the legislative response to a problem which was highlighted by a series of DTI inspectors' reports on fraudulent asset stripping by directors in the 1970s[3]. It must be borne in mind that the approval required under these provisions is in addition to complying with the requirements laid down in the company's articles for excluding the no-conflict rule[4] and complying with the statutory requirements for disclosure of material interests to the board of directors[5]. In addition, in entering into any such transaction, the directors must have regard to their duty to act in the best interests of the company.

Subject to certain exceptions, a company must not enter into an arrangement:

(a) whereby a director of the company or its holding company, or a person connected with such a director[6], acquires or is to acquire one or more non-cash assets[7] of the requisite value (see below) from the company; or

(b) whereby the company acquires or is to acquire one or more such non-cash assets from such a director or a person so connected;

unless the arrangement is first approved by a resolution of the company in general meeting; and if the director or connected person is a director of the company's holding company or a person connected with such a director, then

---

19 Ibid, s 342(1).
20 Ibid, s 342(3).
1 Ibid, s 317(1), (6).
2 Ibid, s 232, Sch 6, Pt II.
3 Ibid, ss 320–322; initially introduced by CA 1980, s 48. See Sealy *Cases and Materials in Company Law* (6th edn, 1996), p 288 who criticises the 'very crude overlap' between this section and the common law position.
4 Ie under art 85 Table A.
5 Ie under CA 1985, s 317. Disclosure must also be made in the notes to the company's accounts: s 232, Sch 6, Pt II.
6 Defined ibid, s 346(2).
7 Defined as any property or interest in property other than cash: ibid, s 739(1).

the arrangement must be approved by a resolution in general meeting of the holding company[8].

In *Re Duckwari plc, Duckwari plc v Offerventure Ltd*[9] a company (Offerventure) owned by C and his wife entered into a contract with a third party to purchase a property for £495,000. Having paid the deposit, Offerventure then offered to pass the property on to Duckwari in return for Duckwari repaying the deposit to Offerventure and undertaking to pay the remaining purchase price. C was a director of Duckwari. The transaction therefore was an agreement by a company (Duckwari) to acquire from a person connected with one of its directors (Offerventure) a non-cash asset. In this case, the asset was the right of Offerventure to call for completion of the contract and conveyance of the property on the payment of a sum of money. Hence the transaction was within, and approval was required under, the statutory provisions.

The purpose of the provision is to provide the members of a company with an opportunity to check on any potential abuse of position by directors and it allows a matter to be more widely considered and a more objective decision to be reached[10]. However, the section does not prohibit the interested director from voting as a shareholder in favour of the arrangement at the general meeting[11].

The provision is broadly drafted with 'arrangement' being deliberately chosen with a view to catching a range of transactions other than a direct contract between a company and one of its directors. For example, it would encompass any scheme whereby an asset was first transferred to a third party and subsequently to a director or a connected person but not any bona fide transaction which ultimately had this outcome.

There are a number of exceptions to the requirement that approval be obtained.

Minimum amounts

Approval is required only if the requisite value of the non-cash asset, at the time the arrangement is entered into, exceeds £100,000 or 10% of the company's asset value (in which case it must exceed £2,000)[12]. The company's asset value means the value of the company's net assets determined by reference to its last annual accounts, or if no such accounts have been so prepared and laid, the amount of its called-up share capital[12]. Where it is alleged that there is a contravention of the statutory provision, the onus is on the person alleging the contravention to prove that the value of the non-cash asset exceeds the requisite value[13].

---

8   Ibid, s 320(1); including shadow directors: s 320(3). For an example of the importance of securing the approval of the shareholders, see *British Racing Drivers' Club Ltd v Hextall Erskine & Co* [1997] 1 BCLC 182.
9   [1997] 2 BCLC 713, [1995] BCC 89, Ch D and CA.
10   See *British Racing Drivers' Club Ltd v Hextall Erskine & Co* [1997] 1 BCLC 182 at 198.
11   See *North-West Transportation Co Ltd and Beatty v Beatty* (1887) 12 App Cas 589 at 593, PC; *Northern Counties Securities Ltd v Jackson & Steeple Ltd* [1974] 2 All ER 625, [1974] 1 WLR 1133; directors may not vote, however, to make a present of corporate assets to themselves: *Cook v Deeks* [1916] 1 AC 554.
12   CA 1985, s 320(2).
13   *Niltan Carson Ltd v Hawthorne* [1988] BCLC 298.

Certain companies

No approval is required unless the company is a company within the meaning of the CA 1985 or is registered under that Act[14], nor is approval required in the case of wholly-owned subsidiaries[15].

Intra-group transactions

A feature of all these statutory provisions, as we have seen, has been exemptions designed to permit unhindered intra-group activity. Here again transactions between two companies could be within the prohibitions because one of the companies is a connected person of a director[16] and as such is within the general provision.

Approval is not required in the case of intra-group transactions involving:

(i) the acquisition of assets by a holding company from any of its wholly-owned subsidiaries; or

(ii) the acquisition of assets from a holding company by any of its wholly-owned subsidiaries; or

(iii) the acquisition of assets by a wholly-owned subsidiary of a holding company from another wholly-owned subsidiary of that same holding company[17].

Winding up

Approval is not required if the arrangement is entered into by a company which is being wound up[18] since if the company is being wound up the shareholders will have little interest in the disposal of its assets. If transactions of this nature with directors were prohibited, the liquidator might be unduly hampered in the execution of his duties. This exception does not apply if the winding up is a members' voluntary winding up because in that case the shareholders will retain an interest in the disposal of the company's assets[18].

Members

Approval is not required if the arrangement is one whereby a person is to acquire an asset from a company of which he is a member, if the arrangement is made with that person in his character as a member[19]. Note that this exemption does not cover the acquisition of a non-cash asset by the company from a member.

CONSEQUENCES OF BREACH

Any arrangement entered into by the company without having first obtained the approval of the company in general meeting and any transaction entered into in pursuance of the arrangement, whether by the company or by any other person, is voidable at the instance of the company[20].

14 Ie registered under CA 1985, s 680.
15 Ibid, s 321(1).
16 Ie within ibid, s 346(2).
17 Ibid, s 321(2)(a).
18 Ibid, s 321(2)(b).
19 Ibid, s 321(3). See Leigh and Edey *Companies Act 1981* (1981), para 376 who express misgivings about this exemption and question whether it is possible in such circumstances to ignore a member's status as a director.
20 CA 1985, s 322(1).

A company will lose its right to avoid the transaction if:

(a)   restitution of the subject matter of the arrangement or transaction is no longer possible or the company has been indemnified by any other person for the loss or damage suffered by it; or

(b)   any rights acquired bona fide for value and without actual notice of the contravention by any person who is not a party to the arrangement or transaction would be affected by its avoidance; or

(c)   the arrangement is, within a reasonable period, affirmed by the company in general meeting[1].

Regardless of whether the company exercises its right to avoid the transaction, the director who entered into the arrangement and any person connected with him and any director who authorised the transaction is liable:

(a)   to account to the company for any gain which he has made directly or indirectly by the arrangement or transaction; and

(b)   to indemnify the company for any loss or damage resulting from the arrangement or transaction[2].

The scope of the obligation to indemnify the company was considered in *Re Duckwari plc (No 2), Duckwari plc v Offerventure Ltd (No 2)*[3] where a company bought a property from a connected person in 1989 for £495,000. There was no evidence that the property had been under or over-valued at the time of purchase. By May 1993 when the property was valued for the purposes of the proceedings, and following the collapse of the property market, it was valued at £90,000. As it was no longer possible to avoid the transaction, the company sought an indemnity under these provisions.

The case revolved around the point in time at which the loss or damage caused by the transaction should be measured. The court found that where the company cannot avoid or elected not to avoid a transaction, the recoverable loss would certainly include the difference between the market value at the date of the transaction and the price paid or received as the case may be. However, it would not include compensation for loss of value as between the date of the transaction and some subsequent date such as the date of the proceedings or the date of the hearing.

This was because the court thought that the only mischief which the statutory provision addresses is acquisition by the company at an inflated value or disposals by the company at an undervalue[4]. It is the terms of the acquisition which lead to liability under the statute and therefore the correct date is the date of the acquisition. On the facts, there was no recoverable loss at that date.

If the arrangement is between a company and a connected person, the director to whom he is connected is not liable to account or indemnify if he shows that he took all reasonable steps to secure the company's compliance with the statutory requirements[5]. In any case, a person so connected and any director who authorised the transaction is not so liable if he can show that, at the time the arrangement was entered into, he did not know the relevant circumstances constituting the contravention[6].

1   Ibid, s 322(2); or affirmed by the holding company if necessary, see s 320(1).
2   Ibid, s 322(3), (4); the liability to indemnify the company is joint and several with any other person so liable; and is without prejudice to any liability at common law: s 322(4).
3   [1997] 2 BCLC 729, [1997] BCC 45, Ch D. This case is the sequel to *Re Duckwari plc, Duckwari plc v Offerventure Ltd* [1997] 2 BCLC 713, [1995] BCC 89 noted above in the text.
4   [1997] BCC 45 at 49.
5   CA 1985, s 322(5).
6   Ibid, s 322(6).

Invalidity of certain transactions involving directors

A further restriction on transactions between a company and its directors or connected persons is imposed by CA 1985, s 322A. This provision is designed to prevent the use of ss 35 and 35A, discussed above, to validate transactions between a company and such persons. The effect of those provisions, as we saw, is that a company may be bound by transactions even though the board exceeds some limitation on their powers under the company's constitution[7]. The potential for abuse where the directors are party to the transaction is such that it was thought that such parties should not be able to avail of the protection afforded by those provisions[8].

Section 322A applies where a company enters into a transaction to which the parties include a director of the company or its holding company, or a person connected with such a director[9], or a company with whom such a director is associated[10]; and the board of directors, in connection with the transaction, exceed any limitation on their powers under the company's constitution[11].

Such transactions are voidable at the instance of the company[12] unless:

(a) restitution of the subject matter is no longer possible, or the company is indemnified for any loss or damage resulting from the transaction; or

(b) rights acquired bona fide for value and without actual notice of the directors' exceeding their powers by a person who is not party to the transaction would be affected by its avoidance; or

(c) the transaction is ratified by the company in general meeting, by ordinary or special resolution or otherwise as the case may require[13].

Whether or not the transaction is avoided, any such party as is specified above and any director of the company who authorised the transaction is liable to account to the company for any gain which he has made directly or indirectly by the transaction and to indemnify the company for any loss or damage resulting from the transaction[14]. Any person other than a director of the company may escape such statutory liability by showing that at the time the transaction was entered into he did not know that the directors were exceeding their powers[15]. Liability at common law is retained and nothing in this provision is to be construed as excluding the operation of any other enactment or rule of law by virtue of which the transaction may be called in question or any liability to the company may arise[16].

Where the transaction is between the company and two other parties, only one of whom is within s 322A, so that the transaction may be valid under s 35A with respect to one party and voidable under s 322A with respect to another party, then the court has a discretion to make such order affirming, severing, or setting aside the transaction on such terms as appear to be just[17].

---

7 See discussion in Chapter 10 (s 35); Chapter 25 (s 35A).
8 See CA 1985, ss 35(4), 35A(6); see Furey *The Companies Act 1989* (1990), para 4.24.
9 Defined CA 1985, s 346(2).
10 Defined ibid, s 346(4).
11 Ibid, s 322A(1).
12 Ibid, s 322A(2).
13 Ibid, s 322A(5).
14 Ibid, s 322A(3).
15 Ibid, s 322A(6).
16 Ibid, s 322A(4).
17 Ibid, s 322A(7).

Contracts of employment

As previously noted, lengthy service agreements can be abused by directors and used to defeat the members' power to remove them by an ordinary resolution[18]. Hence shareholder approval is required of any term of an agreement whereby a director is to be employed[19] for a period exceeding five years[20] during which the employment cannot be terminated by the company by notice or it can be so terminated only in specified circumstances[1]. The term must be approved by the company in general meeting[2] after the shareholders have had an opportunity to inspect a memorandum setting out the proposed agreement and identifying the period for which it is to run[3]. If a term is included in contravention of this section, then that term is void and the agreement is deemed to be one determinable by the giving of reasonable notice[4].

Competing directorships

It might have been expected that competing directorships would be prohibited but that is not the case and there is no principle preventing one person from being a director of two companies which are wholly or partly engaged competitively in the same trade[5]. Whatever the theory, in practice the problems are obvious and a director will find it difficult to serve two masters at once[6]. Of course, a company can always make provision in the articles precluding directors from occupying directorships in competing companies[7] and directors with service contracts may be subject to an implied contract term of good faith and fidelity which would prevent them from working for a competitor[8].

---

18   Ie under ibid, s 303. Lengthy service contracts make it too expensive for the company to exercise its statutory powers of removal: see Ch 24.

19   'Employment' is defined as including employment under a contract for services so consultancy services are caught by the provision: ibid, s 319(7)(a).

20   See ibid, s 319(2) which provides for the aggregation of periods in certain circumstances so that the provision cannot be avoided by a string of contracts. However, the rather obscure wording of that provision does offer scope for avoidance.

1   Ibid, s 319(1); shadow directors are included: s 319(7).

2   In the case of a director of a holding company, the approval of that company in general meeting is required: ibid, s 319(3).

3   Ibid, s 319(5). The memorandum must be available at the registered office for 15 days before the meeting and at the meeting itself. No approval is required if the company in question is a wholly-owned subsidiary: s 319(4).

4   Ibid, s 319(6).

5   See *London and Mashonaland Exploration Co Ltd v New Mashonaland Exploration Co Ltd* [1891] WN 165; approved in *Bell v Lever Bros Ltd* [1932] AC 161, HL; *Berlei Hestia (NZ) Ltd v Fernyhough* [1980] 2 NZLR 150. For criticism of this approach, see Christie 'The Director's Fiduciary Duty not to Compete' (1992) 55 MLR 506.

6   See *Scottish Co-operative Wholesale Society Ltd v Meyer* [1959] AC 324 at 368, [1958] 3 All ER 66 at 88, HL; *Abbey Glen Property Corpn v Stumborg* (1978) 85 DLR (3d) 35.

7   See *Berlei Hestia (NZ) Ltd v Fernyhough* [1980] 2 NZLR 150.

8   See *Hivac Ltd v Park Royal Scientific Instruments Ltd* [1946] Ch 169, [1946] 1 All ER 350, CA where employees were prevented from working for a competitor in their spare time.

THE NO-PROFIT RULE

General principle

Another inflexible rule of equity is that a person who is in a fiduciary position is not, unless otherwise expressly provided, entitled to profit from that position; where he does so he is liable to account[9]. The rule is often regarded as an element of the no-conflict rule but each rule exists independently of the other although the same fact situation may result in both rules applying in a particular case[10]. If a director profits from a conflict of interest disclosed in the manner discussed above then he will be able under the articles to retain that profit and is not required to account. Therefore our main concern is with secret profits.

The no-profit rule has its origins in the leading trust case of *Keech v Sandford*[11] but the most famous application of the principle in company law is *Regal (Hastings) Ltd v Gulliver*[12].

The company (Regal) was the owner of a cinema and wished to acquire a further two cinemas with a view to selling all three as a group. A subsidiary company was established to acquire the additional cinemas. The owner of these cinemas was only willing to grant a lease to the subsidiary company if the authorised share capital of £5,000 was fully paid up or if the directors of Regal would give personal guarantees in respect of the rent. Regal was unable to raise more than £2,000 of the £5,000 required and the directors were unwilling to give personal guarantees. In the circumstances it was decided that the directors themselves would subscribe for the remaining shares. Eventually the transaction was carried out by means of a sale of the shares in Regal and the subsidiary. The directors personally made a profit of almost £3 per share on their shares. The new controllers of Regal successfully sued the former directors to recover those profits.

The House of Lords found that the directors had obtained their profits by reason of and in the course of the execution of their office as directors of Regal[13]. They had entered, in the course of their management, into a transaction in which they utilised the position and knowledge possessed by them in virtue of their office as directors[14]. They were thus liable to account, notwithstanding the fact that they had acted bona fide throughout:

> The rule of equity which insists on those, who by use of a fiduciary position make a profit, being liable to account for that profit, in no way depends on fraud, or absence of bona fides; or upon such questions or considerations as whether the profit would or should otherwise have gone to the plaintiff, or whether the

---

9   *Keech v Sandford* (1726) Sel Cas Ch 61; *Ex p James* (1803) 8 Ves 337; *Parker v McKenna* (1874) 10 Ch App 96; *Boston Deep Sea Fishing and Ice Co v Ansell* (1888) 39 Ch D 339, CA; *Bray v Ford* [1896] AC 44 at 51, HL, per Lord Herschell; *Cook v Deeks* [1916] 1 AC 554, PC; *Regal (Hastings) Ltd v Gulliver* [1967] 2 AC 134n, [1942] 1 All ER 378, HL; *Guinness plc v Saunders* [1990] 2 AC 663, [1990] 1 All ER 652. See generally Austin 'Fiduciary Accountability for Business Opportunities' in Finn (ed) *Equity and Commercial Relationships* (1987), pp 141–185.

10   See, for example, *Regal (Hastings) Ltd v Gulliver* [1967] 2 AC 134n, [1942] 1 All ER 378, HL (the no-profit rule); *Guinness plc v Saunders* [1990] 2 AC 663, [1990] 1 All ER 652, HL (the no-conflict and no-profit rule).

11   (1726) Sel Cas Ch 61.

12   [1967] 2 AC 134n, [1942] 1 All ER 378, HL.

13   [1967] 2 AC 134n at 147, [1942] 1 All ER 378 at 389, per Lord Russell.

14   [1967] 2 AC 134n at 153, [1942] 1 All ER 378 at 391, per Lord Macmillan. For a case where directors profited but not from their positions see *Framlington Group plc v Anderson* [1995] BCC 611.

profiteer was under a duty to obtain the source of the profit for the plaintiff, or whether he took a risk or acted as he did for the benefit of the plaintiff, or whether the plaintiff has in fact been damaged or benefited by his action. The liability arises from the mere fact of a profit having, in the stated circumstances, been made. The profiteer, however honest and well-intentioned, cannot escape the risk of being called upon to account[15].

Each of their Lordships in this case used slightly different formulations of the no-profit duty, as noted above. Lord Russell emphasised that the directors had obtained their profits by reason of and in the course of the execution of their office as directors of Regal while their remaining Lordships emphasised that the key was that persons occupying a fiduciary relationship must not make a profit by reason thereof.[15a] While Lord Russell's dicta have been much cited, the latter formulation better reflects the width of this equitable jurisdiction which prohibits a fiduciary from profiting from his position.

We shall consider two particular instances of profit making by directors:

(i)   corporate opportunities;
(ii) insider dealing.

Corporate opportunities

A corporate opportunity is regarded as a corporate asset which the directors cannot therefore appropriate to their own use[16]. A classic corporate opportunity case is *Cook v Deeks*[17]. Here three out of four directors of a Canadian railway company diverted a contract in which the company was interested to another company which they had formed. The Privy Council found that the opportunity to obtain this contract had come to the directors in their capacity and by virtue of their position as directors of the company. While still retaining that position, while still acting as managers, and with their duties to the company entirely unchanged, they had proceeded to negotiate in reality on their own behalf[18]. The contract was one which in equity belonged to the company and they were therefore bound to hold it on behalf of the company and were not entitled to make a present of it to themselves[19].

Likewise in the Canadian case, *Canadian Aero Service v O'Malley*[20], the president and executive vice-president of a company were held liable where, having actively pursued a contract on behalf of the company, they resigned, formed a new company and acquired it for the new company.

Such cases are relatively straightforward. The companies were actively seeking the contracts, the opportunities, which their directors instead obtained for themselves. In

---

15   [1967] 2 AC 134n at 144, [1942] 1 All ER 378 at 386, per Lord Russell. The actual decision in *Regal* has been much criticised: see Gower *Principles of Modern Company Law* (6th edn, 1997), p 617: '... carrying equitable principles to an inequitable conclusion'; also Jones (1968) 84 LQR 472 at 497. Note Sullivan (1979) 42 MLR 71 who points out that the directors had a would-be purchaser in mind throughout and that there were other shareholders in *Regal* who could have put up some of the money required but who were not invited to do so. See also *Boardman v Phipps* [1967] 2 AC 46, [1966] 3 All ER 721, HL.

15a See, for example, [1967] 2 AC 134 n at 158, [1942] 1 All ER 378 at 395, per Lord Porter.

16   See generally Austin 'Fiduciary Accountability for Business Opportunities' in Finn (ed) *Equity and Commercial Relationships,* (1987), pp 141–185.

17   [1916] 1 AC 554, PC.

18   [1916] 1 AC 554 at 559–560.

19   [1916] 1 AC 554 at 564.

20   (1973) 40 DLR (3d) 371, noted Prentice (1974) 37 MLR 464; see Beck 'The Quickening Fiduciary Obligation: Canadian Aero Service v O'Malley' (1975) 53 Can Bar Rev 771.

such situations, the directors are caught clearly by the no-profit rule. The question is whether directors and officers are prohibited from taking all profit opportunities which come their way or whether a more limited corporate opportunity doctrine applies.

Two further scenarios must be considered: (i) where the company could not have secured the opportunity from which the director has profited; and (ii) where the company rejected the opportunity from which the director subsequently profited.

(I) COMPANY IS UNABLE TO SECURE AN OPPORTUNITY

In considering profiting from the taking of corporate opportunities, the courts have concentrated on the capacity of the profiteers, applying Lord Russell's dictum in *Regal* that the profit/opportunity must have been acquired by the directors by reason of their positions as directors and in the course of their fiduciary relationship[1], rather than engaging in any examination of the nature of the opportunity and whether the no-profit rule requires that the director should account. Where the director has profited from his position, the fact that the company could not have secured the opportunity for itself is irrelevant, as *Regal* makes clear.

In *Industrial Development Consultants Ltd v Cooley*[2] a director was held liable to account to his former company for the benefits he received under a contract which he had entered into with the Eastern Gas Board. Cooley had been employed as managing director by IDC which was hopeful of obtaining contracts from the Gas Board. He was actively involved in ongoing negotiations to secure these contracts for the company when the Gas Board indicated to him that they were not prepared, under any circumstances, to contract with IDC but they were willing to deal with him personally. He promptly resigned and took the contract offered by the Gas Board[3]. Roskill J held that he was liable to account as he had one capacity and one capacity only at that time and that was as managing director of the plaintiff company[4]. Information which came to him while he was managing director and which was of concern to the plaintiff and was relevant to the company to know was information which it was his duty, because of his fiduciary position, to pass on to the company.

An alternative, more flexible, approach can be seen in *Canadian Aero Service v O'Malley*[5] (discussed above) where Laskin J preferred to have regard to a number of different factors and to consider whether or not, in the light of all the circumstances, a director was in breach of his fiduciary duties. It was a mistake, he said, to try to encase the no-profit rule (along the lines of *Regal*) in the strait-jacket of special knowledge acquired while acting as directors, let alone limiting it to benefits acquired by reason of and during the holding of that office[6]. Instead the general standards of loyalty, good faith and avoidance of a conflict of duty and self-interest to which the conduct of a director must conform must be tested in each case by many factors. These would include the position or office held, the nature of the corporate opportunity, its ripeness, its

1 [1967] 2 AC 134n at 147, [1942] 1 All ER 378 at 389, per Lord Russell.
2 [1972] 2 All ER 162, [1972] 1 WLR 443; see Prentice 'Directors' Fiduciary Duties – The Corporate Opportunity Doctrine' (1972) 50 Can Bar Rev 623.
3 Cooley deceived the company into thinking he was resigning because of ill health. As this case makes clear, a director's fiduciary duty does not necessarily come to an end when he ceases to be a director: see also *Island Export Finance Ltd v Umunna* [1986] BCLC 460; *Canadian Aero Service v O'Malley* (1973) 40 DLR (3d) 371. It is also important that it was Cooley who was conducting the negotiations: see also *Furs Ltd v Tomkies* (1936) 54 CLR 583; *Framlington Group plc v Anderson* [1995] BCC 611.
4 [1972] 2 All ER 162 at 173, [1972] 1 WLR 443 at 451.
5 (1973) 40 DLR (3d) 371.
6 (1973) 40 DLR (3d) 371 at 390.

specific nature and the director's relationship to it, the amount of knowledge possessed, the circumstances in which it was obtained and whether it was special or even private information and the circumstances under which the relationship was terminated[7].

The varying approaches were considered in *Island Export Finance Ltd v Umunna*[8]. Umunna was the managing director of IEF Ltd, a company which specialised in seeking business in West Africa. In 1976 he secured a contract for IEF Ltd from the Cameroon postal authorities. In 1977 he resigned from the company and subsequently obtained orders from the Cameroon postal authorities for his own company. IEF Ltd alleged that this was a breach of the fiduciary duty he owed to it and that he must account for the profits derived from the contracts. Hutchison J found no breach of fiduciary duty and in his judgment combined elements of the existing English and overseas authorities in a more flexible corporate opportunities doctrine than had previously been applied in this jurisdiction.

The court found that while Umunna may in a general way have contemplated on resignation that the Cameroon authorities might be a good source of business for his own company, the exploitation of that opportunity was not his primary or indeed an important motive in his resignation. Moreover, neither when Umunna resigned nor when he got the orders was IEF actively pursuing further business with the Cameroon authorities. At most it had a hope of obtaining further orders but that could not in any realistic sense be said to be a maturing business opportunity[9]. As it was not a maturing business opportunity of IEF's, then it was open to Umunna to take it on his own account.

This decision combined both approaches in that it considered Umunna's capacity as IEF's former managing director but also examined the nature of the opportunity which IEF was claiming as a corporate opportunity. In so doing, the court endorsed the more wide-ranging and flexible approach favoured by Laskin J in *Canadian Aero Service v O'Malley* (set out above) which involves going beyond an examination of the capacity of the individual concerned and examining more precisely whether the no-profit duty requires that the director be prohibited from exploiting a particular opportunity.

(II)   COMPANY CONSIDERS AND REJECTS AN OPPORTUNITY

A further scenario is where a director exploits an opportunity which the company has been offered but which the board, after due consideration, has rejected. *Regal* clearly precludes directors from exploiting such an opportunity but Commonwealth authorities are more flexible on this point.

In *Peso-Silver Mines Ltd v Cropper*[10] a mining company was offered an opportunity to acquire certain mineral claims. The opportunity was turned down by the board because of the company's strained finances and because it felt that the company already had enough land. Three of the Peso directors then personally acquired the claims at the price for which the claims had been offered to Peso. On a subsequent change of management at Peso, an action was brought by the company against the three directors calling on them to account for their gains. The Supreme Court of Canada, while accepting that the directors were in a fiduciary relationship with Peso, refused to hold

---

7   (1973) 40 DLR (3d) 371 at 391; see *Island Export Finance Ltd v Umunna* [1986] BCLC 460 at 481.
8   [1986] BCLC 460.
9   [1986] BCLC 460 at 482.
10   (1966) 58 DLR (2d) 1, noted Prentice (1967) 30 MLR 450. See Beck 'The Saga of Peso Silver Mines: Corporate Opportunity Reconsidered' (1971) 49 Can Bar Rev 80.

them accountable[11]. The decision by the board of directors of Peso to reject the opportunity had been taken bona fide and for sound business reasons in the interests of Peso. The opportunity then ceased to be one which they acquired by reason of, and in the course of, the execution of their office as directors of Peso and it was open to them as individuals to acquire the opportunity for themselves[12].

Support for this type of approach can be found in the Australian High Court in *Queensland Mines Ltd v Hudson*[13]. A company (Queensland) was formed to exploit mining licences. Hudson, the managing director of the company, was negotiating with the government for the licences when the company ran into severe financial difficulties. Hudson took the licence in his own name, subsequently resigned as managing director, formed his own company to exploit the licences and eventually made considerable profits. The company then sought to hold him to account for those profits. The Privy Council held that he was not liable as he had fully discussed the situation and what he proposed to do with the Queensland board which had resolved not to proceed further in pursuit of the licences[14].

The major criticism of this type of approach is that it requires a determination by the court as to whether the board's rejection of the opportunity was bona fide[15]. The evidence, moreover, which would establish the financial ability or inability of the company to take the opportunity is solely within the control of those who will benefit personally if the company decides to reject the opportunity[16]. It is preferable that they should direct all their energies to obtaining the finance for the company as opposed to preparing to take the opportunity themselves if and when the company rejects it. Anything less than an absolute rule, it is argued, will tempt the directors to be less than totally committed to obtaining the opportunity on behalf of the company. In any event, while rejection by the board may mean that it is no longer a corporate

---

11   See the strong dissenting judgment in the lower court of Norris J where he argued convincingly that the complexities of modern business life and the possibility of abuse required the application of strict principles: (1966) 56 DLR (2d) 117 at 139 (BCCA). See also Beck 'The Saga of Peso Silver Mines: Corporate Opportunity Reconsidered' (1971) 49 Can Bar Rev 80. For the opposite view, see Oakley *Constructive Trusts* (2nd edn, 1987), p 75 '... approach [in *Peso*] seems preferable in every way to that adopted by the House of Lords in *Regal*'.

12   The Canadian Supreme Court reached this decision by relying on dicta of Lord Greene in the Court of Appeal in *Regal* to the effect that it was carrying duties of directors too far to suggest that if the board bona fide rejected an opportunity that an individual director could not acquire it: see (1966) 58 DLR (2d) 1 at 9. In the House of Lords in *Regal*, Lord Russell declined to state a view on Lord Greene's approach (see [1967] 2 AC 134n at 152, [1942] 1 All ER 378 at 391) which the Canadian court read as indicating that he did not quarrel with that position. However, they did not consider Lord Wright's categoric rejection of that approach as 'dead in the teeth of the wise and salutary [no-profit] rule so stringently enforced in the authorities' (see [1967] 2 AC 134n at 156, [1942] 1 All ER 378 at 394).

13   (1978) 52 ALJR 399, PC.

14   See Sullivan (1979) 42 MLR 711. The case can also be explained on the basis that as all the shareholders were completely appraised of the facts throughout, it is simply an example of the general meeting unanimously releasing a director from his liability to account; see *New Zealand Netherlands Society Oranje Inc v Kuys* [1973] 2 All ER 1222, PC.

15   The courts themselves are sceptical about their ability to determine the directors' motives: see *Regal (Hastings) Ltd v Gulliver* [1967] 2 AC 134n at 154, [1942] 1 All ER 378 at 392, HL, per Lord Wright; *Ex p James* (1803) 8 Ves 337 at 345: 'no court is equal to the examination and ascertainment of the truth in these cases'. See also Beck 'The Saga of Peso Silver Mines: Corporate Opportunity Reconsidered' (1971) 49 Can Bar Rev 80; Bishop & Prentice 'Legal and Economic Aspects of Fiduciary Remuneration' (1983) 46 MLR 289.

16   See *Regal (Hastings) Ltd v Gulliver* [1967] 2 AC 134n at 154, [1942] 1 All ER 378 at 392, HL, per Lord Wright; Beck 'The Saga of Peso Silver Mines: Corporate Opportunity Reconsidered' (1971) 49 Can Bar Rev 80.

opportunity, the basic conflict of interest remains and the directors should be liable to account[17].

Perhaps the most appropriate solution to the problems in this area is that suggested by Brudney and Clark[18], namely that different rules should apply depending on whether the company is a public company or a close corporation (a small private company). Public companies should be covered by a categorical rule in view of, inter alia, their widely dispersed shareholdings and the adequate managerial compensation schemes in those companies. Private companies, on the other hand, should be free to regulate this problem as a matter of contract between the parties, given that the people involved are likely to be a closer, more intimate, group and lavish managerial compensation plans are not as common. Another suggestion is that in fact no rules are required at all; instead the market will regulate managerial wrongdoing with executives who deflect corporate assets to themselves soon being removed by the shareholders and being identified as wrongdoers in the market.

Re-stating the general principle

At the time of the decision in *Island Export Finance Ltd v Umunna*[19] it might have been thought that this heralded a move to an 'opportunity' rather than 'capacity' orientated doctrine with the possibility that this might open the door to Peso-like decisions here with the courts working to develop and refine what is encompassed within a 'maturing business opportunity'. In other words, there would be a shift towards the Commonwealth authorities and away from the strictness of *Regal*. However, *Island Export* increasingly looks to be very much restricted to its facts with the House of Lords in more recent cases such as *Guinness plc v Saunders*[20] and (as the Privy Council) in *A-G for Hong Kong v Reid*[1] adopting an uncompromising stance on the importance of the strict application of fiduciary obligations to curb abuses by directors and others.

In the light of those decisions, it is very unlikely that the House of Lords would be persuaded of the merits of anything other than a rigid application of the uncompromising position as stated in *Regal*. The more recent cases herald a return to the position, as expressed in *Keech v Sandford*[2], that the no-profit rule must be strictly pursued and not in the least relaxed[3]. The words of James LJ in *Parker v McKenna*[4] 100 years ago epitomise the current approach:

> … it appears to me very important that we should concur in laying down again and again the general principle that in this Court no agent in the course of his agency, in the matter of his agency, can be allowed to make any profit without the knowledge of his principal; that that rule is an inflexible rule, and must be applied inexorably by this Court which is not entitled, in my judgment, to receive evidence, or suggestion, or argument as to whether the principal did or did not suffer any injury in fact by reason of the dealing of the agent; for the safety of

17   See Prentice (1967) 30 MLR 450.
18   Brudney & Clark 'A New Look at Corporate Opportunities' (1981) 94 Harv L Rev 997. See Austin 'Fiduciary Accountability for Business Opportunities' in Finn (ed) *Equity and Commercial Relationships* (1987) pp 166–171 who argues that the case for having different standards has not been made.
19   [1986] BCLC 460.
20   [1990] 2 AC 663, [1990] 1 All ER 652, HL.
1   [1994] 1 AC 324, [1994] 1 All ER 1, PC.
2   (1726) Sel Cas Ch 61.
3   (1726) Sel Cas Ch 61 at 62, per Lord King LC.
4   (1874) 10 Ch App 96.

mankind requires that no agent shall be able to put his principal to the danger of such an inquiry as that[5].

Insider dealing

One particular form of profit making which has been made a criminal offence is insider dealing[6]. Basically this entails the use by an insider of inside information (known to him but not generally and which he has acquired by virtue of his position) to trade to his advantage in the securities of a company. This practice is not limited to directors and can be engaged in by anyone who has access to this type of information. It is convenient, however, to consider insider dealing here since directors have easy access to this type of information and are most likely to deal or 'tip' other persons to deal on the strength of it.

Initially regulated by the Companies Act 1980 and subsequently by the Company Securities (Insider Dealing) Act 1985, the adoption of an EC Directive Co-ordinating Regulations on Insider Dealing in 1989[7] meant that the legislation had to be redrafted to meet the requirements of the Directive. The relevant provisions are now found in the Criminal Justice Act 1993, Part V.

Only individuals who have information as insiders are subject to the prohibitions laid down in the legislation. A person has information as an insider if and only if (i) he has inside information and he knows it is inside information; (ii) he has it from an inside source and he knows it is an inside source[8].

Inside information is information which:

(i)   relates to particular securities or to a particular issuer of securities or to particular issuers of securities, and it must not relate to securities generally or to issuers of securities generally;
(ii) is specific or precise;
(iii) has not been made public[9]; and
(iv) if it were made public would be likely to have a significant effect on the price of any securities[10].

Typically the information will relate to a takeover bid; or a new acquisition; or an increase in profits; or the loss of a contract or of an important executive.

A person has information from an inside source if and only if (a) he has it through (i) being a director, employee or shareholder of an issuer[11] of securities; or (ii) having access to the information by virtue of his employment, office or profession; or (b) the direct or indirect source of his information is a person within (a) above[12]. An example of insider dealing by a director can be found in *R v Dickinson*[13] where the defendant was the managing director of a subsidiary company who took out an option contract on shares in the parent company ahead of an impending takeover.

---

5   (1874) 10 Ch App 96 at 124–125.
6   See Hannigan *Insider Dealing* (2nd edn, 1994); Rider & Ashe *Insider Crime: the new law* (1993).
7   Council Directive of 13 November 1989 co-ordinating regulations on insider dealing (89/592 EEC), OJ L 334/30 18.11.1989.
8   Criminal Justice Act 1993, s 57(1).
9   A non-exhaustive definition of when information is made public is contained in ibid, s 58.
10 Ibid, s 56(1).
11 An 'issuer', in relation to any securities, means any company, public sector body or individual by which or by whom the securities have been or are to be issued: ibid, s 60(2).
12 Ibid, s 57(2).
13 Unreported but noted (1982) 3 Co Law 1985.

An individual who has information as an insider is prohibited from dealing in price-affected securities[14], encouraging another person to deal[15] and disclosing the information, other than in the proper performance of the functions of the insider's employment, office or profession, to another person[16]. Any individual guilty of insider dealing is liable to a fine or to imprisonment or to both[17]. Various defences are included in the legislation and an individual is not guilty of insider dealing if he shows that he did not expect the dealing to result in a profit attributable to the information; or that he believed on reasonable grounds that the information had been disclosed widely enough; or that he would have dealt in any event[18]. No contract is void or unenforceable by reason only of insider dealing[19]; and the statute makes no provision for civil remedies which remain a matter for the common law.

In fact very few insider dealing prosecutions have been brought since the matter was first made a criminal offence in 1980 and even fewer convictions have been secured[20]. Where a conviction has been obtained the actual fines imposed have been modest and the courts have been loath to impose a sentence of imprisonment, if they do it is almost invariably suspended. In one case, in addition to being the first person actually sentenced to jail for insider dealing, a company chairman was disqualified from acting as a company director for 10 years[1].

Liability for breach of the no-profit rule

A director who makes a secret profit from his position is liable to account to the company and where the profit arises from a use or misappropriation of corporate assets he will hold that profit as a constructive trustee for the company[2].

The importance of the constructive trust remedy in this context is clear from the decision of the Privy Council in *A-G for Hong Kong v Reid*[3], a case which concerned

---

14   Ie securities listed in Criminal Justice Act 1993 Sch 2: s 54(1). The dealing must take place on a regulated market or relying on or acting as a professional intermediary: s 52(1), (3).
15   In the circumstances specified in ibid, s 52(2)(a).
16   Ibid, s 52(1), (2).
17   Ibid, s 61. The penalty on conviction on indictment is a fine or imprisonment for a term not exceeding seven years or both: s 61(1)(b).
18   Ibid, s 53(1); see also s 53(2), (3). Further specialist defences for market makers etc are contained in Sch 1.
19   Ibid, s 63(2).
20   See statistics and cases noted in Hannigan *Insider Dealing* (1994, 2nd edn), pp 118–124.
1   Disqualification was imposed under Company Directors Disqualification Act 1986, s 2 (disqualification when convicted of an indictable offence): see *R v Goodman* [1992] BCC 625. Goodman was sentenced to 18 months' imprisonment with nine months suspended. He had sold shares in his company ahead of the disclosure of significant losses which caused the share price to fall.
2   *Keech v Sandford* (1726) Sel Cas Ch 61; *Parker v McKenna* (1874) 10 Ch App 96; *Cook v Deeks* [1916] 1 AC 554, PC; *Boardman v Phipps* [1967] 2 AC 46, [1966] 3 All ER 721; *Regal (Hastings) Ltd v Gulliver* [1967] 2 AC 134n, [1942] 1 All ER 378, HL; *Guinness plc v Saunders* [1990] 2 AC 663, [1990] 1 All ER 652; although the line between an accounting for profits and the imposition of a constructive trust is frequently blurred in the cases and it is often difficult to identify the basis on which a particular remedy was granted. See generally Austin 'Fiduciary Accountability for Business Opportunities' in Finn (ed) *Equity and Commercial Relationships* (1987), pp 141–185; Goode 'The Recovery of a Director's Improper Gains: Proprietary Gains for Infringement of Non-Proprietary Rights' in McKendrick (ed) *Commercial Aspects of Trusts and Fiduciary Obligations* (1992); Millett 'Bribes and Secret Commissions' [1993] RLR 7.
3   [1994] 1 AC 324, [1994] 1 All ER 1, PC; noted Allen (1995) 58 MLR 87; Pearce [1994] LMCLQ 189; Crilly [1994] RLR 57; Watts (1994) 110 LQR 178; Smith (1994) 110 LQR 180. The court doubted the much-criticised decision in *Lister & Co v Stubbs* (1890) 45 Ch D 1 to the effect that, with respect to bribes and secret commissions, the relationship between the agent and his principal was that of debtor and creditor and not that of trustee and *cestui que trust*. Birks summarises the debate about *Lister* at [1993] LMCLQ 30; see also Millett 'Bribes and Secret Commissions' [1993] RLR 7.

a fiduciary who had accepted bribes. The court found that a bribe was a secret benefit which the fiduciary had derived from trust property or obtained from knowledge which he acquired in the course of acting as a fiduciary. As soon as the bribe was received, the fiduciary was accountable under a constructive trust to the person to whom the fiduciary duty was owed under the equitable principle that equity considered as done that which ought to have been done. If the property representing the bribe increased in value or a cash bribe was invested advantageously, the fiduciary was accountable not only for the original amount or value of the bribe but also for the increased value of the property representing the bribe. The attraction of this remedy is clear from the facts of *Reid* where the principal was able to recover properties which had been purchased with the bribes.

The decision in *Reid* is important in the general context of secret profit making by fiduciaries as a modern affirmation that fiduciary obligations will be strictly enforced and the widest remedies will be available in respect of any breach of such duties[4]. The ready imposition of a constructive trust rather than a mere accounting is also consistent with the strict line taken in respect of company directors by the House of Lords in *Guinness plc v Saunders*[5].

A dishonest agreement by directors to impede a company in the exercise of its right of recovery of any secret profits made by them may constitute a conspiracy to defraud[6].

A liability in equity to make good any resulting losses to the company will attach to any third party who dishonestly procures or assists the directors in a breach of their fiduciary duties to the company[7]. In this context, acting dishonestly means simply not acting as an honest person would in the circumstances; and for the most part dishonesty is to be equated with conscious impropriety[8]. The court when called upon to decide whether a person was acting honestly will look at all the circumstances known to the third party at the time[9].

Equally, a third party who receives company funds may be liable to the company as a constructive trustee if he receives the funds with knowledge of the directors' breach of duty, whether it be actual knowledge or knowledge in the sense that he wilfully shut his eyes to the obvious or wilfully and recklessly failed to make the type of inquiries which an honest and reasonable man would have made[10].

4   For a contrary view see Crilly 'A Case of Proprietary Overkill' [1994] RLR 57.
5   [1990] 2 AC 663, [1990] 1 All ER 652.
6   *Adams v R* [1995] 1 WLR 52, [1995] 2 BCLC 17, PC.
7   *Royal Brunei Airlines Sdn Bhd v Tan* [1995] 2 AC 378, [1995] 3 All ER 97, PC; see also *Barnes v Addy* (1874) 9 Ch App 244; *Agip (Africa) Ltd v Jackson* [1990] Ch 265 at 293, [1992] 4 All ER 385 at 405; *Eagle Trust plc v SBC Securities Ltd* [1992] 4 All ER 488 at 499, [1993] 1 WLR 484 at 495; *Polly Peck International plc v Nadir (No 2)* [1992] 4 All ER 769 at 777, [1992] 2 Lloyd's Rep 238 at 243.
8   *Royal Brunei Airlines Sdn Bhd v Tan* [1995] 2 AC 378 at 389, [1995] 3 All ER 97 at 106, PC.
9   *Royal Brunei Airlines Sdn Bhd v Tan* [1995] 2 AC 378 at 391, [1995] 3 All ER 97 at 107, PC.
10   *Selangor United Rubber Estates Ltd v Cradock (a bankrupt) (No 3)* [1968] 2 All ER 1073, [1968] 1 WLR 1555; *Eagle Trust plc v SBC Securities Ltd* [1992] 4 All ER 488; *Re Montagu's Settlement Trusts*; [1987] Ch 264, [1992] 4 All ER 308; *Polly Peck International plc v Nadir (No 2)* [1992] 4 All ER 769, [1992] 2 Lloyd's Rep 238; *Cowan de Groot Properties Ltd v Eagle Trust plc* [1992] 4 All ER 700; *Eagle Trust plc v SBC Securities Ltd (No 2)* [1996] 1 BCLC 121. The whole issue of the type of knowledge required in these 'knowing receipt' cases has been the subject of extensive and inconclusive debate: see Gardiner (1996) 112 LQR 56. It may be helpful to recall the point made by Knox J in *Cowan de Groot supra* at 761: '... it may well be that the underlying broad principle which runs through the authorities regarding commercial transactions is that the court will impute knowledge, on the basis of what a reasonable person would have learnt, to a person who is guilty of commercially unacceptable conduct in the particular context involved'.

Authorisation to make or retain a profit

One of the most difficult issues is the extent to which a director may be permitted to make or retain a profit and the manner of authorisation which is required[11].

THE SHAREHOLDERS

It is clear that the company in general meeting acting unanimously can permit a director to profit from his position following full disclosure of all relevant information[12].

The position is not so clear-cut where the shareholders purport to ratify such profit-making by a simple majority. It was assumed in *Regal (Hastings) Ltd v Gulliver*[13] that the directors could, had they wished, have protected themselves by a resolution of the company in general meeting[14]. It is difficult to reconcile this view with *Cook v Deeks*[15] where the Privy Council refused to accept a purported ratification of profit making by the directors which amounted to the misappropriation by the directors of a contract which belonged in equity to the company. The cases can be reconciled, perhaps, by regarding *Regal* as an instance of merely incidental profit-making by directors who acted bona fide throughout while *Cook v Deeks* represents the other end of the spectrum, the actual misappropriation of corporate assets, which is not ratifiable[16].

A further question is whether a director as a shareholder could vote to ratify such incidental profit-making. As a general rule a director as a shareholder may vote on any question in general meeting though he has a personal interest in the subject matter opposed to or different from the general or particular interests of the company[17]. However, it is difficult to believe that the courts would accept that a director should be able to cast his vote as a shareholder to approve of incidental profit-making by him in breach of his fiduciary duty[18].

THE BOARD OF DIRECTORS

Whether the board can permit a director to profit from his position is debatable. Obviously it can in the context of a disclosed conflict of interest under article 85 but here we are concerned with whether there is a broader power vested in the board to permit a director to profit from his position.

---

11   For an excellent review of these issues, see Cranston 'Limiting Directors' Liability: Ratification, Exemption and Indemnification' [1992] JBL 197.
12   *New Zealand Netherlands Society 'Oranje' Inc v Kuys* [1973] 2 All ER 1222, [1973] 1 WLR 1126, PC; *Parker v McKenna* (1874) 10 Ch App 96; *Regal (Hastings) Ltd v Gulliver* [1967] 2 AC 134n, [1942] 1 All ER 378, HL. Note also *Queensland Mines Ltd v Hudson* (1978) 52 ALJR 399, PC.
13   [1967] 2 AC 134n, [1942] 1 All ER 378, HL.
14   [1967] 2 AC 134n at 150, [1942] 1 All ER 378 at 389, HL, per Lord Russell.
15   [1916] 1 AC 554, PC; see also *Menier v Hooper's Telegraph Works* (1874) 9 Ch App 350.
16   See Gower *Principles of Modern Company Law* (6th edn, 1997), p 647. It is arguable that *Regal* was a case where the directors appropriated to themselves the opportunity to subsequently profit from the sale of the shares. Note Sealy *Cases and Materials in Company Law* (6th edn, 1996), p 297 who says that unless the finding of bona fides is thought to be crucial, it is difficult to say why the impropriety in *Regal* was capable of ratification while that in *Cook v Deeks* was not.
17   *North-West Transportation Co Ltd and Beatty v Beatty* (1887) 12 App Cas 589, PC; but the directors may not vote to make a present of company assets to themselves: *Cook v Deeks* [1916] 1 AC 554.
18   See Vinelott J in *Prudential Assurance Co Ltd v Newman Industries Ltd (No 2)* [1980] 2 All ER 841 at 862.

Some support might be found in *Queensland Mines Ltd v Hudson*[19] (discussed above) where the board had been fully aware of what the director proposed to do and had resolved that the company would not proceed to exploit the mining licences in question; or in *Peso-Silver Mines Ltd v Cropper*[20] where the board rejected the opportunity which the directors subsequently exploited. However, these cases can be explained as examples of the broader corporate opportunity approach being developed in the Australian and Canadian authorities. The result is that there is no breach of duty at all as the opportunity is regarded as one which is not a corporate opportunity[1]. *Queensland Mines Ltd v Hudson*[2], in any event, may be seen as an example of profit-making which is permitted by the unanimous approval of the shareholders for throughout all of the shareholders were aware of the director's intentions[3].

As was suggested above, the decisions in recent cases such as *Guinness plc v Saunders*[4] and *A-G for Hong Kong v Reid*[5] support an uncompromising stance on the strict application of fiduciary obligations to curb abuses by directors and others. In that climate, the court is unlikely to accept that the board is the appropriate organ to release a director from those stringent obligations. Having said that, the courts do permit profit-making via a disclosed conflict of interest, disclosed to the board under articles such as art 85. This leads us to the question of the extent to which the no-profit rule might be modified by the articles.

THE ARTICLES

We have already noted the extent to which the no-conflict principle is modified by companies adopting provisions similar to art 85 of Table A. The question is whether the articles could permit derogations from the no-profit rule in a similar way.

Companies had developed the practice of including in their articles widely drafted exemption clauses relieving their officers from liability arising from breaches of their duties save in the case of wilful negligence or default[6] until the Greene Committee on Company Law recommended that this practice be prohibited[7]. Hence CA 1985, s 310 which provides that any provision, whether contained in the articles or in any contract with the company or otherwise[8], for exempting any officer of the company from, or indemnifying him against, any liability which by virtue of any rule of law would otherwise attach to him in respect of any negligence, default, breach of duty or breach of trust of which he may be guilty in relation to the company, is void[9]. This is subject

---

19   (1978) 52 ALJR 399, PC.
20   (1966) 58 DLR (2d) 1.
1   See Prentice (1967) 30 MLR 450; Sullivan (1979) 42 MLR 711; also *Island Export Finance Ltd v Umunna* [1986] BCLC 460.
2   (1978) 52 ALJR 399, PC.
3   See Sullivan (1979) 42 MLR 711.
4   [1990] 2 AC 663, [1990] 1 All ER 652, HL.
5   [1994] 1 AC 324, [1994] 1 All ER 1, PC.
6   See *Re Brazilian Rubber Plantations and Estates Ltd* [1911] 1 Ch 425; *Re City Equitable Fire Insurance Co Ltd* [1925] Ch 407.
7   The Greene Committee on Company Law (1929, Cmnd 2657), paras 46–47. The prohibition was introduced by CA 1929, s 152, now CA 1985, s 310.
8   The words 'or otherwise' are to construed eiusdem generis with the preceding words 'whether contained in the company's articles or in any contract with the company', the genus being any arrangement between the company and its officers: *Burgoine v London Borough of Waltham Forest* [1997] 2 BCLC 612, [1997] BCC 347.
9   CA 1985, s 310(1). This only applies to indemnities given by the company concerned and not to indemnities given by third parties: *Burgoine v London Borough of Waltham Forest* [1997] 2 BCLC 612, [1997] BCC 347.

to certain exceptions, the most important being that it does not prevent a company taking out liability insurance for its directors[10]. Insurance is discussed below.

Much debate has taken place as to the impact which this statutory prohibition has on provisions such as art 85[11]. The issue was addressed in *Movitex Ltd v Bulfield*[12] where the argument before the court was that a provision such as art 85 permitting a director to enter into a transaction despite a conflict of interest is one which exempts a director from a liability arising from a breach of duty and is therefore void under the statutory provision.

Vinelott J thought it would be startling, or at the lowest very paradoxical, to find that there was a conflict between the statute and the articles contained in Table A, given they are both legislative provisions[13]. Accordingly, it was necessary to seek a construction which would allow the provisions to co-exist. The solution, in his view, lay in the judgment of Megarry V-C in *Tito v Waddell (No 2)*[14] which identified the self-dealing rules not as part of the duties of trustees but as disabilities affecting trustees and other fiduciaries. Directors are not under a duty not to place themselves in a position of conflict; rather if they do so then certain consequences follow[15].

Provisions in the articles, such as art 85, simply exclude or modify the application of the no-conflict principle but they do not exempt a director from a duty or from the consequences of a breach of a duty owed to the company[16]. An attempt to modify a duty would infringe the statute[17].

So provided the rule can be classified as a disability subjecting the director to certain consequences in certain situations, rather than a duty owed to the company, provisions such as art 85 are permissible. The question is which of the obligations of directors are disabilities and which are duties. Clearly the no-conflict rule, itself the subject of *Movitex Ltd v Bulfield*, is a disability. On the other hand, Vinelott J himself seemed to rule out the application of that classification to the duty to exercise care and skill[18], or to the duty to act in the best interests of the company[19]; nor would it appear appropriate

10   See CA 1985, s 310(3). The section does not prevent a company from indemnifying any such officer against any liability incurred by him in successfully defending any civil/criminal proceedings or in connection with any application under s 144 (acquisition of shares by innocent nominee) or s 727 (general power to grant relief in case of honest and reasonable conduct) in which relief is granted to him by the court: s 310(3)(b).

11   See Baker 'Disclosure of Directors' interests in Contracts' [1975] JBL 181; Birds 'The Permissible Scope of Articles Excluding the Duties of Company Directors' (1976) 39 MLR 394; Parkinson 'The Modification of Directors' Duties' (1981) JBL 335; Gregory 'The Scope of the Companies Act 1948, Section 205' (1982) 98 LQR 413.

12   [1988] BCLC 104, noted Sealy (1987) CLJ 217; Birds (1987) 8 Co Law 31.

13   [1988] BCLC 104 at 117.

14   [1977] Ch 106, [1977] 3 All ER 129.

15   See Cranston 'Limiting Directors' Liability: Ratification, Exemption and Indemnification' [1992] JBL 197.

16   *Movitex Ltd v Bulfield* [1988] BCLC 104 at 120.

17   [1988] BCLC 104 at 121. One view, prior to *Movitex*, was that literally interpreted CA 1985, s 310 only restricted clauses which attempted to relieve directors of the consequences of their breaches of duty but it did not prevent the inclusion of terms which modified or excluded the duty itself: see Birds 'The Permissible Scope of Articles Excluding the Duties of Company Directors' (1976) 39 MLR 394. This interpretation was expressly rejected by Vinelott J: see [1988] BCLC 104 at 117–118; also Gregory 'The Scope of the Companies Act 1948, Section 205' (1982) 98 LQR 413.

18   [1988] BCLC 104 at 117.

19   [1988] BCLC 104 at 121. See Birds (1987) 8 Co Law 31 who makes the point that it is possible to derogate from the proper purpose doctrine since that arises from the articles itself and so can be modified by the articles; also Sealy (1987) CLJ 217.

to the no-profit obligation[20]. The net effect would appear to be simply to validate those provisions modifying the application of the no-conflict rule[1].

Insurance

Much attention in recent years had focused on the effect of CA 1985, s 310 (discussed above) on directors' and officers' liability insurance. On a strict interpretation of that section, such policies might well have been found to be void. The uncertainty was resolved by an amendment by the Companies Act 1989 which makes clear that the statutory prohibition in CA 1985, s 310 does not prevent a company from purchasing and maintaining for any officer such liability insurance[2].

Court's power to grant relief

The court has power under the Companies Act 1985 to relieve a director from liability in certain circumstances. If in any proceedings for negligence, default, breach of duty or breach of trust, it appears to the court that the director[3] is or may be liable in respect of the negligence, default, breach of duty or breach of trust, but that he has acted honestly and reasonably, and that having regard to all the circumstances of the case, he ought fairly to be excused, the court may relieve him, either wholly or partly, from his liability on such terms as it thinks fit[4].

Relief under this provision was sought, rather optimistically, in *Guinness plc v Saunders*[5] (discussed above) but the court held that there could be no question of relief where a director was found to be retaining £5.2m paid to him by the company under a void contract. In *Neptune (Vehicle Washing Equipment) Ltd v Fitzgerald (No 2)*[6] (discussed above) relief was refused where the defendant had acted in breach of his fiduciary duties to the company in passing resolutions and procuring the payment to himself of £100,000.

Relief was also refused in *Dorchester Finance Co Ltd v Stebbing*[7] where the directors were negligent in failing to carry out their duties and in signing blank cheques which allowed another director to do as he pleased. They had failed to show that they had acted reasonably and ought fairly to be excused. Relief was granted, however, in *Re D'Jan of London Ltd*[8] where a director in breach of his duty of care had signed an

---

20 See Sealy (1987) CLJ 217 who describes the no-profit rule as a complex of rules which would not admit of any ready classification; also Birds (1987) 8 Co Law 31.
1   See Cranston 'Limiting Directors' Liability: Ratification, Exemption and Indemnification' [1992] JBL 197.
2   For a comprehensive review of the issues in this area: see Finch 'Personal Accountability and Corporate Control: The Role of Directors' and Officers' Liability Insurance' (1994) 57 MLR 880. See also Turnbull and Edwards 'Companies Act 1989: Directors and Officers' Liability Insurance' (1990) 134 Sol Jo 768.
3   The provision extends to any officer of the company and any auditor whether or not an officer of the company.
4   CA 1985, s 727(1).
5   [1990] 2 AC 663, [1990] 1 All ER 652, HL.
6   [1995] BCC 1000; see also *Re Duckwari plc (No 2), Duckwari plc v Offerventure Ltd (No 2)* [1997] 2 BCLC 729 at 737, [1997] BCC 45 at 52 (director not liable but had it been necessary to consider CA 1985, s 727, the court would have held that where a director has a direct or indirect personal interest in a substantial property transaction and intends to profit from it, it is not a case where he ought fairly to be excused from the liability for loss or damage resulting from it).
7   [1989] BCLC 498; see discussion of this case in Ch 26.
8   [1994] 1 BCLC 561; see discussion of this case in Ch 26. See also *Re Welfab Engineers Ltd* [1990] BCLC 833.

insurance form without reading it. Had he done so, he would have discovered the inaccurate information which subsequently caused the insurance company to repudiate liability under the policy. Although he was careless, he had acted honestly and reasonably and what had happened could have happened to any busy man. Hoffmann LJ noted:

> It may seem odd that a person found to have been guilty of negligence, which involves failing to take reasonable care, can ever satisfy a court that he acted reasonably. Nevertheless, the section clearly contemplates that he may do so and it follows that conduct may be reasonable for the purposes of [the provision] despite amounting to a lack of reasonable care at common law[9].

On the other hand, in *Re Produce Marketing Consortium Ltd*[10] the court refused to accept that relief might be granted in cases where liability arose under the Insolvency Act 1986 in respect of wrongful trading[11]. Knox J decided that the statutory provisions were mutually exclusive in that if the court imposed liability for wrongful trading, it did so as a result of an objective assessment of the conduct of the director in question and a conclusion that he had failed to take every step to minimise loss to creditors. Having reached those conclusions, it was not open to the court then to re-assess the director's conduct subjectively for the purpose of relieving him of liability.

---

9   [1994] 1 BCLC 561 at 564.
10   [1989] 3 All ER 1, [1989] 1 WLR 745.
11   Ie under IA 1986, s 214. See also *Re DKG Contractors Ltd* [1990] BCC 903.

CHAPTER 28

Shareholder remedies

ACTIONS BY SHAREHOLDERS

There are a number of obstacles in the path of any shareholder who decides to pursue an action against wrongdoing directors, whether on his own behalf or on behalf of the company[1]. Often the suspect transactions are of a complicated financial nature which the shareholder cannot easily unravel. It may be difficult therefore to establish precisely what the transaction involves and who are the beneficiaries. The board, if questioned at the general meeting, will usually refuse to disclose any information on the basis that the matter is confidential and unsuited to discussion at a public meeting. The non-wrongdoing directors may take a back seat although, as we have seen, there is increasing pressure on directors to take a more active role in their company's affairs. Removing wrongdoing directors, as we have also seen, is not always an available option[2]. In any event, the directors' control of the proxy machinery, and in smaller companies their close identification with the majority shareholders, will normally ensure that the appropriate resolution cannot be passed. Even if a shareholder does decide to proceed, he must also overcome the judiciary's traditional reluctance to second-guess the business judgement of directors or to interfere in the internal management of a company[3]. Add to this the significant costs involved, in terms of time and money, and it is little wonder that few shareholders can be persuaded to proceed[4].

For dissatisfied shareholders, the best option is not litigation but simply to withdraw their investment from the company by selling their shares. If the company is a public

---

1   For an excellent account of the difficulties faced by minority shareholder litigants, see Sealy, 'Problems of Standing, Pleading and Proof in Corporate Litigation' in Pettet (ed) *Company Law in Change* (1987), cited hereafter as Sealy (1987).

2   Discussed in Ch 24.

3   As Lord Eldon LC stated in *Carlen v Drury* (1812) 1 Ves & B 154: 'the court could not undertake the management of every brewhouse and playhouse in the kingdom'. See also *Burland v Earle* [1902] AC 83 at 93, per Lord Davey; *Hogg v Cramphorn Ltd* [1967] Ch 254 at 268, [1966] 3 All ER 420 at 428, per Buckley J; Sealy (1985) 6 Co Law 21; Sealy (1987).

4   It had been hoped that the institutional shareholders might take up the challenge but the Court of Appeal was unenthusiastic about such moves in *Prudential Assurance Co Ltd v Newman Industries Ltd (No 2)* [1982] Ch 204, [1982] 1 All ER 354; see Stapledon *Institutional Shareholders and Corporate Governance* (1996), p 132.

company, this is quite easily done. If the company is a private one[5], then the shareholders' position is more difficult as there is no readily available market for such shares and so they may find it difficult to obtain a purchaser[6].

If a shareholder does decide to proceed, there are three types of action which he may bring.

A personal action

A shareholder may bring a personal action where some personal individual right has been infringed. It must be remembered that only limited personal rights are recognised by the courts[7].

A representative action

A representative action may be brought by a shareholder on behalf of a group of shareholders where the same personal right of a number of shareholders has been infringed.

A derivative action

A derivative action may be brought by a member of the company in respect of a wrong done to the company where the wrongdoers are in control and prevent the company itself from suing. This is permitted only in exceptional circumstances for the general rule is that the proper plaintiff in an action brought in respect of a wrong done to the company is the company itself. This is the rule in *Foss v Harbottle*[8] which is discussed below. Where a derivative action is brought the entire benefit of the proceedings will go to the company and not to the shareholder who brings the action.

It should be noted at this point that this entire subject of shareholders' actions is a complex and obscure area of company law where inconsistencies abound[9]. Moreover there is an element of overlap between these categories of actions with the same act on occasion giving rise to a personal action and a derivative action[10]. Equally, a derivative action is a representative action brought by one shareholder as representative of all the shareholders in the company other than those who are made defendants.[10a]

THE RULE IN FOSS v HARBOTTLE

There are two elements to the rule, the classic statement of which is to be found in the judgment of Jenkins LJ in *Edwards v Halliwell*[11]:

5   Private companies make up 98.9% of the companies on the register of companies: see DTI *Companies in 1996–97* (1997), Table A2, p 26.
6   In any event there may well be restrictions in the company's articles on a member's right to transfer his shares: see Ch 19. In theory the position has been eased to some extent by the statutory provisions which now permit companies to purchase their own shares: CA 1985, ss 162 ff; but it is unlikely that the majority shareholders will agree to the exercise of those powers for the benefit of the minority.
7   See discussion below; also Ch 11.
8   (1843) 2 Hare 461.
9   Much has been written in an attempt to resolve the inconsistencies in this area but the classic exposition of the rule remains Wedderburn, 'Shareholders' Rights and the Rule in Foss v Harbottle' (1957) CLJ 194, (1958) CLJ 93.
10   See *Pender v Lushington* (1877) 6 Ch D 70.
10a   See *Cooke v Cooke* [1997] 2 BCLC 28, [1997] BCC 17.
11   [1950] 2 All ER 1064.

First, the proper plaintiff in an action in respect of a wrong alleged to be done to a company or association of persons is prima facie the company or the association of persons itself. Secondly, where the alleged wrong is a transaction which might be made binding on the company or association and on all its members by a simple majority of the members, no individual member of the company is allowed to maintain an action in respect of that matter for the simple reason that, if a mere majority of the members of the company or association is in favour of what has been done, then cadit quaestio[12].

The rule, therefore, is basically quite simple. The proper plaintiff is prima facie the company. Where the wrong or irregularity might be made binding on the company by a simple majority of its members, no individual shareholder is allowed to maintain an action in respect of that matter[13].

The first proposition is based on the separate legal personality of the company and derives from *Foss v Harbottle*[14] itself where the court refused to permit two shareholders to bring an action on behalf of the company against the directors and promoters who had sold property to the company at an inflated value. The court found that it was not open to individual members to assume to themselves the right of suing in the name of the company. The company was the proper person to sue and while that was a rule that could be departed from, it should not be, save for very urgent reasons.

The second proposition is based on the principle of majority rule and derives from the decision in *Mozley v Alston*[15] where two shareholders tried unsuccessfully to restrain four directors of the company from acting as such when they should have retired in rotation under the articles. The court refused to permit the shareholders to bring their action on the basis that if the alleged wrong is a transaction which might be made binding on the company and all its members by a simple majority then no action will lie. As the court explained in *MacDougall v Gardiner*[16]:

> ... if the thing complained of is a thing which in substance the majority of the company are entitled to do ... there can be no use in having litigation about it, the ultimate end of which is only that a meeting has to be called, and then ultimately the majority gets its wishes[17].

There are a number of advantages to the rule. First, it is more convenient that the company should sue in respect of a wrong done to it instead of having any number of suits started and subsequently discontinued by individual shareholders. It eliminates wasteful litigation where the only outcome can be that the majority pass a resolution at the next meeting approving the 'wrongdoing'. It prevents vexatious actions started by troublesome minority shareholders trying to harass the company.

But there is a major drawback. The company is the proper person to sue but a company can only act through its human agents, usually the board of directors, and the directors may well be the actual wrongdoers. They may therefore decide not to sue, a decision which may be approved by the company in general meeting where the wrongdoers may likewise control a majority of the votes. The net outcome would be

---

12   [1950] 2 All ER 1064 at 1066. See also *Burland v Earle* [1902] AC 83 at 93, per Lord Davey.

13   See *Barrett v Duckett* [1995] 1 BCLC 243 at 249–250.

14   (1843) 2 Hare 461. See also *Prudential Assurance Co Ltd v Newman Industries Ltd (No 2)* [1982] Ch 204 at 223–224, [1982] 1 All ER 354 at 367.

15   (1847) 1 Ph 790.

16   (1875) 1 Ch D 13.

17   (1875) 1 Ch D 13 at 25, per Mellish LJ.

that the wrongdoers would go unpunished and the minority shareholders would be at the mercy of the majority who could loot the company with impunity[18]. This could not be tolerated and so the fraud on the minority exception (discussed below) has been developed whereby, notwithstanding the rule, an individual shareholder may sue by way of a derivative action. This is done in order to give a remedy for a wrong which would otherwise escape redress[19].

STATUTORY REMEDIES

Statutory alternatives open to an aggrieved shareholder include petitioning for relief on the grounds that the affairs of the company are being or have been conducted in a manner which is unfairly prejudicial to the interests of its members generally or of some part of its members[20], or petitioning to have the company wound up on the just and equitable ground[1], both of which are discussed in greater detail later.

Before proceeding to consider each of the remedies in turn, it is worth noting the following principles which the Law Commission has suggested as the guiding principles for the law on shareholder remedies[2]:

- *Proper plaintiff* – the proper plaintiff rule entails that normally the company should be the only party entitled to enforce a cause of action belonging to it. Accordingly, a member should be able to maintain proceedings about wrongs done to the company only in exceptional circumstances.
- *Internal management* – an individual member should not be able to pursue proceedings on behalf of a company about matters of internal management, that is, matters which the majority are entitled to regulate by ordinary resolution.
- *Commercial decisions* – the court should continue to have regard to the decision of the directors on commercial matters if the decision was made in good faith, on proper information and in the light of the relevant considerations, and appears to be a reasonable decision for the directors to have taken.
- *Sanctity of contract* – a member is taken to have agreed to the terms of the memorandum and articles of association when he became a member, whether or not he appreciated what they meant at the time. The law should continue to treat him as so bound unless he shows that the parties have come to some other agreement or understanding which is not reflected in the articles or memorandum. Failure to do so will create unacceptable commercial uncertainty. The corollary is that the best protection for a shareholder is appropriate protection in the articles themselves.
- *Freedom from unnecessary shareholder interference* – shareholders should not be able to involve the company in litigation without good cause, or where they intend to cause the company or the other shareholders embarrassment or harm rather than genuinely pursue the relief claimed.
- *Efficiency and cost effectiveness* – all shareholder remedies should be made as efficient and cost effective as can be achieved in the circumstances.

18   See *Wallersteiner v Moir (No 2)* [1975] QB 373 at 395, [1975] 1 All ER 849 at 862.
19   See *Burland v Earle* [1902] AC 83 at 93–94, per Lord Davey; *Smith v Croft (No 2)* [1988] Ch 114, [1987] 3 All ER 909.
20   Ie under CA 1985, s 459.
1   Ie under IA 1986, s 122(1)(g).
2   See Law Commission *Shareholder Remedies* (1997, Cm 3769) Law Com No 246, para 1.9.1.

PERSONAL ACTIONS

The three categories noted below (illegal and ultra vires acts; acts requiring a special majority and personal rights) are usually treated as exceptions to the rule in *Foss v Harbottle*. However, they are equally usually said not to be true exceptions to the rule in *Foss v Harbottle*, being wrongs done to the member's personal rights as opposed to wrongs done to the company. In that case, it seems clearer to group them under the heading of personal actions rather than to continue to assert that they are exceptions (but not true exceptions) to the rule in *Foss v Harbottle*. This treatment is also in line with the Law Commission's recommendations on reform of the derivative action discussed below[3].

Illegality and ultra vires

Actions to restrain threatened ultra vires or illegal actions are outside the rule in *Foss v Harbottle* and matters for personal actions[4]. An individual shareholder may obtain an injunction to restrain the company proceeding with an ultra vires or illegal act. This is subject to the statutory qualification that no such proceedings may lie in respect of an ultra vires act to be done in fulfilment of a legal obligation arising from a previous act of the company[5]. The position as regards illegal transactions is unaffected.

It had been thought that an action by a shareholder to recover money or property on behalf of the company in respect of an ultra vires or illegal transaction could equally be a personal action[6]. However, in *Smith v Croft (No 2)*[7] it was decided that where what is sought is compensation for the company for the loss caused by the transaction, the wrong is done to the company and the company is the proper plaintiff. Any action by a shareholder therefore must be a derivative one.

Furthermore, as far as ultra vires transactions are concerned, the shareholders may by special resolution specifically relieve the directors from personal liability arising from an ultra vires transaction[8].

Special majorities

The rule in *Foss v Harbottle* does not apply and a member may seek redress where the matter is one which could validly be done or sanctioned not by a simple majority of the members but by some special majority.

This covers the situation where the articles specify a particular procedure which must be followed in respect of a particular transaction. If that procedure is not followed, the majority cannot ratify such conduct for that would be to deny the minority the

---

3   See Law Commission *Shareholder Remedies* (1997, Cm 3769) Law Comm No 246, paras 6.56-6.57.
4   See *Simpson v Westminster Palace Hotel Co* (1860) 8 HL Cas 712; *North-West Transportation Co Ltd and Beatty v Beatty* (1887) 12 App Cas 589; *Parke v Daily News Ltd* [1962] Ch 927, [1962] 2 All ER 929.
5   CA 1985, s 35(2).
6   See Wedderburn (1957) CLJ 194 at 206 who noted that 'In claims relating to ultra vires acts, however, the plaintiff appears to have, in most cases, a free choice as to the form in which he sues and many actions have been personal.'
7   [1988] Ch 114, [1987] 3 All ER 909. See Prentice (1988) 104 LQR 341.
8   CA 1985, s 35(3); note that the company can ratify the ultra vires act by a special resolution. There is nothing preventing the directors as shareholders voting in favour of the resolution: *North-West Transportation Co Ltd and Beattly v Beatty* (1887) 12 App Cas 589, PC; but shareholders may not ratify something which is fraudulent or illegal: *Cook v Deeks* [1916] 1 AC 554, PC.

protection afforded by the initial provision. The majority must follow the procedure laid down in the articles or, alternatively, alter the articles[9]. Where they simply purport to ratify the transaction by an ordinary resolution, the minority shareholder can bring an action to restrain them. In *Edwards v Halliwell*[10] two members of a trade union successfully restrained an attempt by a delegate meeting to increase the members' contribution without obtaining the two-thirds majority required under their rules. In *Quin and Axtens Ltd v Salmon*[11] the articles of association provided that certain transactions could not be entered into without the consent of both managing directors. In this instance one of the directors dissented but the company in general meeting nevertheless tried to authorise the transaction without that director's consent. It was held that the shareholders could not do so. It was an attempt to alter the terms of the contract between the parties by an ordinary rather than a special resolution. But note the inconsistency between these cases and *Grant v United Kingdom Switchback Railways Co*[12] and *Irvine v Union Bank of Australia*[13] where the courts permitted the majority in general meeting to ratify conduct in breach of the articles. These cases are supposedly distinguishable on the ground that they involved only minor internal irregularities and were not attempts to alter for all time the terms of the contract. Drawing the line between the two categories is not easy.

Personal rights

Obviously if a member can point to the infringement of some personal right then he need not be concerned with the rule in *Foss v Harbottle* at all[14]. Here the wrong will be done to him and not to the company and the rule will not apply. Again this category overlaps to some extent with the previous one: *Edwards v Halliwell*[15] involving the personal right of a member not to have his contribution increased without a special resolution being passed; and *Quin & Axtens Ltd v Salmon*[16] involving the personal right of a member to have the procedures followed which are specified in the articles.

The crucial issue is to identify those membership rights which will give rise to a personal action if infringed. Membership rights can arise in a number of ways, from the articles, from statute, or from a separate shareholders' agreement. But it is primarily with rights arising from the articles that we are concerned, for that is the grey area where the conflict between shareholder protection and majority rule is most acute.

To determine the extent of the membership rights provided by the articles it is necessary to consider the nature of the contract established between the company and the members. Many commentators have argued for a liberalisation of the personal rights category since ultimately that would make the rule in *Foss v Harbottle* redundant. One suggestion has been that all the articles should be regarded as conferring personal rights

---

9 *Automobile Self-Cleansing Filter Syndicate Co Ltd v Cunninghame* [1906] 2 Ch 34; *Quin & Axtens Ltd v Salmon* [1909] AC 442.
10 [1950] 2 All ER 1064. See also *Cotter v National Union of Seamen* [1929] 2 Ch 58; *Baillie v Oriental Telephone and Electric Co Ltd* [1915] 1 Ch 503.
11 [1909] AC 442.
12 (1888) 40 Ch D 135.
13 (1877) 2 App Cas 366.
14 See Wedderburn (1957) CLJ 194, (1958) CLJ 93; Sealy *Cases and Materials in Company Law* (6th edn, 1996), p 517.
15 [1950] 2 All ER 1064.
16 [1909] AC 442.

on the shareholders except for those articles which have already been clearly identified by case law as concerning internal procedures only[17].

However, it would seem clear that a member does not have a right to have all the articles observed, notwithstanding Wedderburn's arguments to the contrary[18]. Membership rights are more limited than that but include such rights as the right to have your vote recorded[19]; to have a dividend paid in cash if the articles so specify[20]; to enforce a declared dividend as a legal debt[1]; and to have the articles observed if they specify a particular procedure to be followed in a particular instance[2]. On the other hand, a member does not have a right to have accounts prepared in accordance with the requirements of the Companies Act[3]; nor to have directors retire in accordance with the articles[4]; nor does a member have the right to recover damages merely because the company in which he is a shareholder has suffered damage[5].

The precise scope of a member's personal rights may be of diminishing importance as actions to enforce personal rights in this way have to a large extent been eclipsed by the broader statutory action alleging unfairly prejudicial conduct[6].

DERIVATIVE ACTIONS

A derivative action is brought by a shareholder on behalf of the company in respect of a wrong done to the company. This is the only true exception to the rule in *Foss v Harbottle*[7] which establishes that the company is the proper plaintiff in respect of wrongs done to the company. To bring a derivative action a shareholder must establish (i) fraud on the minority[8] and (ii) wrongdoer control which prevents the company itself bringing an action in its own name[9].

As a preliminary matter the court will require that the plaintiff shareholder establish a prima facie case that the company is entitled to the relief claimed and that the action

---

17 See Wedderburn (1957) CLJ 194 at 214–215. Note that the Law Commission has rejected the idea of drawing up a list identifying those personal rights which are enforceable: see Law Commission *Shareholder Remedies* (1997, Cm 3769) Law Comm No 246, paras 7.8-7.11.1.
18 See Wedderburn (1957) CLJ 194; also Drury (1986) CLJ 219.
19 *Pender v Lushington* (1877) 6 Ch D 70.
20 *Wood v Odessa Waterworks Co* (1889) 42 Ch D 636.
1   *Mosely v Koffyfontein Mines Ltd* [1904] 2 Ch 108, CA.
2   *Edwards v Halliwell* [1950] 2 All ER 1064, CA. See generally Wedderburn (1957) CLJ 194 at 210–211.
3   *Devlin v Slough Estates Ltd* [1983] BCLC 497.
4   *Mozley v Alston* (1847) 1 Ph 790.
5   *Prudential Assurance Co Ltd v Newman Industries Ltd (No 2)* [1982] Ch 204 at 222–223, [1982] 1 All ER 354 at 366–367, CA. The position in *Prudential* was one where the shareholder had no independent right of action distinct from that of the company. See likewise *Stein v Blake* [1998] 1 All ER 724, CA (shareholder had suffered no less distinct from that suffered by the company). The position is different where the shareholder does have a distinct (and perhaps the only) right of action: see *George Fischer (Great Britain) Ltd v Multi Construction Ltd* [1995] 1 BCLC 260, CA (plaintiff had an unquestionable right of action for damages for breach of contract against defendant and could recover damages for the loss on value of its shares in a subsidiary company where that loss was a direct and foreseeable result of the breach of contract. See also *Barings plc v Coopers & Lybrand* [1997] 1 BCLC 427, CA (where parent company and subsidiary company each had an independent right of action).
6   Ie under CA 1985, s 459 discussed below. See also Law Commission *Shareholder Remedies, A Consultation Paper* (1996, No 142), para 7.10.
7   (1843) 2 Hare 461.
8   As Wedderburn (1958) CLJ 93 notes this should more properly be described as a fraud on the company.
9   An attempt to broaden the category to permit a shareholder to bring an action where the justice of the case so required was accepted by Vinelott J in *Prudential Assurance Co Ltd v Newman Industries Ltd (No 2)* [1980] 2 All ER 841 at 877 but rejected as an impractical test by the Court of Appeal [1982] Ch 204 at 221, [1982] 1 All ER 354 at 366. See also *Estmanco (Kilner House) Ltd v Greater London Council* [1982] 1 All ER 437 at 444, [1982] 1 WLR 2 at 11.

falls within the proper boundaries to the rule in *Foss v Harbottle*[10]. The court will also have to be satisfied that the plaintiff is a proper person to bring the action, that his conduct has not been so tainted as to bar equitable relief, and that there has not been an unacceptable delay in bringing the action[11]. If the action is brought for an ulterior motive or if another adequate remedy is available the court will not allow the derivative action to proceed[12].

Fraud on the minority

Fraud in this context includes not just fraud at common law but also fraud in the wider equitable sense of an abuse or misuse of power[13]. Certain categories of misbehaviour are ratifiable by the majority (and so cannot be the subject of a derivative action) while others are not ratifiable. The difficulty is deciding into which category the conduct in question falls.

APPROPRIATION OF CORPORATE PROPERTY

It is clearly established that the majority cannot 'appropriate to themselves money, property or advantages which belong to the company or in which the other shareholders are entitled to participate'[14]. Such conduct amounts to a fraud on the minority and cannot be ratified[15]. This clearly covers misconduct such as that in *Cook v Deeks*[16] where the directors appropriated to themselves a contract which the company was actively pursuing. The Privy Council refused to permit the general meeting to ratify such conduct noting that:

> ... a resolution that the rights of the company should be disregarded in this matter would amount to forfeiting the interests and property of the minority shareholders in favour of the majority and that by the votes of those who are interested in securing the property for themselves. Such use of voting power has never been sanctioned by the courts[17].

---

10   *Prudential Assurance Co Ltd v Newman Industries Ltd (No 2)* [1982] Ch 204 at 221–222, [1982] 1 All ER 354 at 366; *Smith v Croft (No 2)* [1988] Ch 114 at 145, [1987] 3 All ER 909 at 922. See RSC Ord 15, r 12A: a plaintiff must make a preliminary application to a Master before proceeding with his action beyond the issue of the writ; where a defendant has given notice of intention to defend, the plaintiff must apply to the court for leave to continue the action.

11   *Towers v African Tug Co* [1904] 1 Ch 558; *Nurcombe v Nurcombe* [1985] 1 All ER 65, [1985] 1 WLR 370; *Barrett v Duckett* [1995] 1 BCLC 243.

12   *Barrett v Duckett* [1995] 1 BCLC 243.

13   *Estmanco (Kilner House) Ltd v Greater London Council* [1982] 1 All ER 437 at 445, [1982] 1 WLR 2 at 12, per Sir R Megarry.

14   *Burland v Earle* [1902] AC 83 at 93, see Lord Davey.

15   *Cook v Deeks* [1916] 1 AC 554 at 564. See also *Atwool v Merryweather* (1867) LR 5 Eq 464n; *Menier v Hooper's Telegraph Works* (1874) 9 Ch App 350; *Estmanco (Kilner House) Ltd v Greater London Council* [1982] 1 All ER 437, [1982] 1 WLR 2. See also *Aveling Barford Ltd v Perion Ltd* [1989] BCLC 626 – sale of property to the controlling shareholder at a gross undervalue amounted to an unauthorised return of capital which was ultra vires and could not be ratified.

16   [1916] 1 AC 554.

17   [1916] 1 AC 554 at 564, per Lord Buckmaster.

The difficulty in distinguishing such unratifiable misappropriation of corporate assets from the apparently ratifiable profit making in *Regal (Hastings) Ltd v Gulliver*[18] has already been considered[19].

NEGLIGENCE

Mere negligence on the part of the controllers is not sufficient to bring a case within the fraud on the minority exception. In *Pavlides v Jensen*[20] the sale of a corporate asset, a mine, at a gross undervalue (for £182,000 when it was allegedly worth £1m) was held to be ratifiable. However, self-serving negligence is not ratifiable. In *Daniels v Daniels*[1] the board sold an asset at a gross undervalue to one of the directors. The court found that such use by directors of their powers, intentionally or unintentionally, fraudulently or negligently, in a manner which benefits themselves at the expense of the company was within the fraud on the minority exception and so a minority shareholder could bring an action against them on behalf of the company. Essentially the transaction amounted to a misappropriation of corporate assets.

ABUSE OF POWER

Another difficult area is where directors act other than bona fide in the interests of the company as a whole or for a collateral purpose. Certainly a mala fide exercise of their powers is not ratifiable[2] although a bona fide exercise of their powers for a collateral purpose is ratifiable, as we saw in *Hogg v Cramphorn Ltd*[3] and *Bamford v Bamford*[4].

One final point to consider is whether a wrongdoer director can vote, as a shareholder, to ratify his own misconduct where that wrongdoing is ratifiable. The answer is that he can for:

> Every shareholder has a perfect right to vote upon any such question, although he may have a personal interest in the subject matter opposed to or different from the general or particular interest of the company[5].

Voting, however, to deprive the company of an asset as in *Menier v Hooper's Telegraph Works*[6] and *Estmanco (Kilner House) Ltd v Greater London Council*[7] is in itself a fraud on the minority.

---

18   [1967] 2 AC 134n, [1942] 1 All ER 378.
19   See discussion ante Ch 27.
20   [1956] Ch 565, [1956] 2 All ER 518.
1   [1978] Ch 406, [1978] 2 All ER 89.
2   *Cook v Deeks* [1916] 1 AC 554.
3   [1967] Ch 254, [1966] 3 All ER 420: see Ch 26.
4   [1970] Ch 212, [1969] 1 All ER 969: see Ch 26.
5   *North-West Transportation Co Ltd and Beatty v Beatty* (1887) 12 App Cas 589 at 593, per Sir R Baggally; *Pender v Lushington* (1877) 6 Ch D 70; *Burland v Earle* [1902] AC 83. However, the company in general meeting cannot ratify something which is illegal or fraudulent: *Cook v Deeks* [1916] 1 AC 554.
6   (1874) 9 Ch App 350.
7   [1982] 1 All ER 437, [1982] 1 WLR 2. See also *Cook v Deeks* [1916] 1 AC 554.

Wrongdoer control

The second element which must be established before a member can come within the fraud on the minority exception is wrongdoer control which prevents the company bringing an action in its own name[8]. It is necessary therefore to make some attempt to persuade the company to sue and it is not sufficient simply to allege that the wrongdoers are in control. Wrongdoer control will exist if the wrongdoer has a majority of the votes, or the majority has actually approved a fraud on the minority, or the company has otherwise shown that it is not willing to sue[9]. In *Prudential Assurance Co Ltd v Newman Industries Ltd (No 2)*[10] the Court of Appeal recognised that control embraces a broad spectrum extending from an overall absolute majority of votes at one end to a majority of votes at the other end made up of those likely to be cast by the delinquent himself plus those voting with him as a result of influence or apathy[11].

Abandoning or compromising a claim

Once a shareholder has established a prima facie case of fraud on the minority and wrongdoer control, this would normally be the end of the issue and he would have established standing to sue. However, in *Smith v Croft (No 2)*[12] the court held that it did not follow from establishing standing to sue that the minority shareholder necessarily had an individual and indefeasible right to prosecute the action on the company's behalf. Knox J found a clear distinction between the impossibility of ratification and the possibility of abandoning or compromising or not pursuing rights of action. He went on:

> Ultimately the question which has to be answered in order to determine whether the rule in *Foss v Harbottle* applies to prevent a minority shareholder seeking relief as plaintiff for the benefit of the company is: Is the plaintiff being prevented improperly from bringing these proceedings on behalf of the company ? If it is an expression of the corporate will of the company by an appropriate independent organ that is preventing the plaintiff from prosecuting the action he is not improperly but properly prevented and so the answer to the question is No.
> ... I remain unconvinced that a just result is achieved by a single minority shareholder having the right to involve a company in an action for recovery of compensation for the company if all the other minority shareholders are for disinterested reasons satisfied that the proceedings will be productive of more harm than good[13].

In deciding whether the decision not to sue was an independent decision, votes should be disregarded if, but only if, the court is satisfied either that the vote or its equivalent is actually cast with a view to supporting the defendants rather than securing

---

8   *Pavlides v Jensen* [1956] Ch 565, [1956] 2 All ER 518; *Birch v Sullivan* [1958] 1 All ER 56, [1957] 1 WLR 1247.
9   *Russell v Wakefield Waterworks Co* (1875) LR 20 Eq 474 at 482, per Jessel MR. See Law Commission *Shareholder Remedies, A Consultation Paper* (1996, No 142), paras 4.13–4.16 on the difficulty of identifying wrongdoer control.
10   [1982] Ch 204, [1982] 1 All ER 354, CA.
11   [1982] Ch 204 at 219, [1982] 1 All ER 354 at 364, CA.
12   [1988] Ch 114 at 177, [1987] 3 All ER 909 at 950.
13   [1988] Ch 114 at 185, [1987] 3 All ER 909 at 956.

benefit to the company, or that the situation of the person whose vote is considered is such that there is a substantial risk of that happening[14].

On the facts in *Smith v Croft (No 2)*[15] the view of the majority of the shareholders who were independent of the wrongdoers was that, for disinterested reasons, they did not wish proceedings to continue[16]. In such a case the plaintiff minority shareholder would not be permitted to proceed.

This decision renders it even more unlikely that derivative actions will be brought[17]. Time, costs, inconvenience, managerial disruption and natural inertia must combine to dictate that, save in the most extreme cases, the tendency will be for the independent shareholders to decide that litigation is not in the best interests of the company.

Costs

As noted earlier, one of the greatest obstacles to shareholder litigation is the enormous costs which it entails. The position in respect of derivative action was alleviated by the decision of the Court of Appeal in *Wallersteiner v Moir (No 2)*[18] to the effect that where a shareholder has, in good faith and on reasonable grounds, sued as plaintiff in a minority shareholder's action, the benefit of which if successful will accrue to the company and only indirectly to the plaintiff as a member of the company and which it would be reasonable for an independent board of directors to bring in the company name, then the court may order the company to pay the plaintiff's costs[19].

Reform

A half-hearted attempt to outflank the rule in *Foss v Harbottle* can be found in the statutory provision which permits the court, if satisfied that the petitioner has been unfairly prejudiced[20], to authorise civil proceedings to be brought in the name and on behalf of the company, by such person or persons and on such terms as the court may direct[21]. This provision seems rarely, if ever, to have been used, not least because a successful petitioner on the grounds of unfairly prejudicial conduct can obtain a direct personal remedy and is unlikely to be interested in commencing litigation on behalf of the company[22].

In 1995 the Law Commission was requested by the Lord Chancellor and the Department of Trade and Industry to carry out a review of shareholder remedies with

---

14 [1988] Ch 114 at 186, [1987] 3 All ER 909 at 958.
15 [1988] Ch 114, [1987] 3 All ER 909.
16 The defendants essentially were the main assets of the company and to sue them might result in their leaving the company thus jeopardising the investment of the shareholders.
17 See Sealy (1987) CLJ 398; Prentice (1988) 104 LQR 341.
18 [1975] QB 373, [1975] 1 All ER 849.
19 [1975] QB 373 at 403–404, [1975] 1 All ER 849 at 868–869, per Buckley LJ. In *Smith v Croft* [1986] 1 WLR 580 Walton J suggested that it is for the plaintiff to show that he did not have sufficient resources to finance the action and that he genuinely needed an indemnity from the company; see Prentice [1987] Conv 167. This more restrictive approach to *Wallersteiner* orders was not followed in *Jaybird Group Ltd v Greenwood* [1986] BCLC 319 at 327.
20 Ie under CA 1985 s 459.
21 Ibid, s 461(1)(c).
22 The draft Fifth EC Directive on Company Law would have permitted an action to be brought against defaulting board members on behalf of the company by one or more shareholders holding 10% of the subscribed capital of a public company. The last version of the Directive was put forward in 1983: OJEC 1983 C240/2. No progress has been made on it for many years and it is unlikely ever to be adopted.

particular reference, inter alia, to the rule in *Foss v Harbottle*. It published a consultation paper in 1996 setting out its provisional recommendations in this regard[23]; and this was followed by its final report in October 1997[1].

The Law Commission concluded that the rule in *Foss v Harbottle* was complicated and unwieldy with much of it derived from old case law; the scope of the exceptions to the rule was uncertain and the procedural difficulties were such that simply establishing standing to sue could amount to a mini-trial[2]. The Law Commission therefore recommended that there should be a new derivative procedure with more modern, flexible and accessible criteria for determining whether a shareholder can pursue the action[3]; and a new statutory provision to that effect should be included in the Companies Act[4]. This would replace entirely the common law derivative action, ie the existing true exception to the rule in *Foss v Harbottle* covering fraud on a minority. The position noted above relating to personal actions would be unaffected[5].

The proposal is that the new procedure should only be available if:

> the cause of action arises as a result of an actual or threatened act or omission involving (a) negligence, default, breach of duty or breach of trust by a director of the company, or (b) a director putting himself in a position where his personal interests conflict with his duties to the company[6].

A shareholder wishing to bring a derivative action would be required to serve a notice on the company at least 28 days before the commencement of the proceedings[7], specifying the grounds of the proposed derivative action[8].

The leave of the court to maintain the action would have to be sought at an early stage in the proceedings[9]. In considering whether or not to grant leave the court would have regard to all relevant circumstances without limit including[10]:

(i)   whether the applicant is acting in good faith[11] (however, the good faith of the applicant should not be a prerequisite to the grant of leave);

(ii) whether the proceedings are in the interests of the company[12] (however, the court should refuse leave if it is satisfied that the proceedings are not in the interests of the company);

---

23   Law Commission *Shareholder Remedies, A Consultation Paper* (1996, No 142) (hereafter Law Commission Consultation Paper).

1   Law Commission *Shareholder Remedies* (1997, Cm 3769), Law Com No 246 (hereafter Law Commission Report).

2   See Law Commission Report, para 6.4; Law Commission Consultation Paper, paras 14.1-14.4.

3   See Law Commission Report, para 6.15; Law Commission Consultation Paper, para 14.13.

4   See Law Commission Report, paras 6.16-6.21.

5   See Law Commission Report, paras 6.51-6.57; Law Commission Consultation Paper, para 16.14.

6   See Law Commission Report, paras 6.23-6.49; Law Commission Consultation Paper, paras 16.7-16.11.

7   In part this would allow the company time to take remedial action so rendering the proceedings unnecessary: see Law Commission Consultation Paper, para 16.16.

8   See Law Commission Report, paras 6.58-6.59; Law Commission Consultation Paper, paras 16.15-16.17.

9   See Law Commission Report, paras 6.66-6.69; Law Commission Consultation Paper, para 16.18.

10   See Law Commission Report, paras 6.70-6.74; Law Commission Consultation Paper, paras 16.20-16.25. The Law Commission, while not wanting to limit the scope of the court's review of all relevant circumstances, believes the specification of certain matters relevant to the issue of whether leave should be granted will be helpful to advisers who might otherwise be unsure as to the types of matters which might be relevant: see Law Commission Consultation Paper, para 16.44.

11   See Law Commission Report, paras 6.75-6.76; Law Commission Consultation Paper, paras 16.27-16.31.

12   See Law Commission Report, paras 6.77-6.79; Law Commission Consultation Paper, paras 16.32-16.34.

(iii) whether the wrong has been, or may be, approved by the company in general meeting[13] (however, effective ratification should continue to be a complete bar to the continuation of a derivative action[14]);

(iv) whether the general meeting has resolved not to pursue the cause of action (as opposed to ratifying the wrongdoing)[15];

(v) the views of an independent organ[16]; and

(vi) the availability of alternative remedies[17] (however, their availability should not necessarily be conclusive on the issue of whether or not leave should be granted).

The remedy obtained would remain a remedy for the company and it would not be possible for the court to order a personal remedy under any new derivative procedure[18].

WINDING UP ON THE JUST AND EQUITABLE GROUND

A statutory remedy available to shareholders is the ability to petition to have the company wound up on the just and equitable ground[19], a provision regarded by the courts as providing a very wide discretionary jurisdiction[20].

Procedural matters

APPLICATIONS BY CONTRIBUTORIES

An application to the court for a winding-up order may be made by a contributory[1] defined as every person liable to contribute to the assets of a company in the event of its being wound up[2]. For example, a partly paid-up shareholder who remains liable to contribute the amount unpaid on his shares in the event of the company being wound up is a contributory. A fully paid-up member must establish that he has a tangible interest in the winding up, defined as a prima facie probability of surplus assets

---

13 See Law Commission Report, paras 6.80-6.86; Law Commission Consultation Paper, paras 16.35-16.37.

14 This approach may disappoint those who feel that any reform in this area which fails to address the uncertainties surrounding what is a ratifiable and unratifiable wrong is incomplete. But the Law Commission notes: "Given that the project is only concerned with remedies and not, for example, with directors' duties, we do not consider that it would be within our terms of reference to consider substantive changes to the law of ratification.": see Law Commission Report, para 6.84.

15 See Law Commission Report, para 6.87.

16 See Law Commission Report, paras 6.88-6.90; Law Commission Consultation Paper, para 16.38. By independent organ is meant a group of persons within the company essentially independent of the wrongdoers, in the sense used by Knox J in *Smith v Croft (No 2)* [1988] Ch 114 at 186, [1987] 3 All ER 909 at 958.

17 Law Commission Report, para 6.91; Law Commission Consultation Paper,   paras   16.39-16.40.

18 See Law Commission Report, para 6.108; Law Commission Consultation Paper, paras 16.48 -16.50.

19 Ie under IA 1986, s 122(1)(g). Various other parties (including the directors and creditors) may also petition for a winding up: see Ch 40. Here we deal only with petitioning shareholders.

20 See *Re Yenidje Tobacco Co Ltd* [1916] 2 Ch 426; *Loch v John Blackwood Ltd* [1924] AC 783; *Re Wondoflex Textiles Pty Ltd* [1951] VLR 458; *Ebrahimi v Westbourne Galleries Ltd* [1973] AC 360, [1972] 2 All ER 492.

1 IA 1986, s 124(1).

2 Ibid, s 79(1). See also s 74(1) which provides that every present and past member is included in the definition; see also s 74(2)(d).

remaining after the creditors have been paid for distribution among the shareholders[3]. An exception may be made where the ground for seeking a winding-up order is the management's failure to disclose information, for in such a case it is unlikely that the shareholder will be able to determine whether or not there will be surplus assets[4].

A contributory is not entitled to present a winding-up petition unless either:

(i)   the number of members is reduced below two; or
(ii) the shares held by him were originally allotted to him, or have been held by him for at least six months during the 18 months before the commencement of the winding up, or have devolved to him through the death of a former holder[5].

This provision is designed to prevent individuals from purchasing shares with a view to winding up a company although a six-month period seems inadequate for this purpose.

CLEAN HANDS

The jurisdiction to wind up a company on the just and equitable ground requires the petitioner to come with clean hands[6]. If the breakdown in the conduct of the company's affairs is a result of the petitioner's own misconduct[7], or the petitioner has acquiesced in the conduct of which he now complains[8], then the court will refuse the application. On the other hand, if the petitioner can establish sufficient grounds for petitioning, the fact that he also has an ulterior, perhaps personal, motive for pursuing the matter does not render those grounds insufficient[9].

EXISTENCE OF AN ALTERNATIVE REMEDY

The court will not order a winding up if there is some alternative remedy available and the petitioner is acting unreasonably in not pursuing that alternative[10].

3   *Re Rica Gold Washing Co* (1879) 11 Ch D 36; *Re Expanded Plugs Ltd* [1966] 1 All ER 877, [1966] 1 WLR 514; *Re Othery Construction Ltd* [1966] 1 WLR 69; *Re Bellador Silk Ltd* [1965] 1 All ER 667. See also *Re Chesterfield Catering Co Ltd* [1976] 3 All ER 294 at 299, [1976] 3 WLR 879 at 885 where Oliver J suggested that 'tangible interest' is not limited to surplus assets but could cover where, as a member of the company, the shareholder will achieve some advantage or avoid or minimise some disadvantage which would accrue to him by virtue of his membership of the company.
4   See *Re Newman and Howard Ltd* [1962] Ch 257, [1961] 2 All ER 495; *Re Commercial and Industrial Insulations Ltd* [1986] BCLC 191; *Re Wessex Computer Stationers Ltd* [1992] BCLC 366. The petition for winding up will not therefore be struck out on the ground that the petitioner has failed to establish that he has a tangible interest.
5   IA 1986, s 124(2). A private company limited by shares or by guarantee is permitted now to have a sole member and, therefore, for such companies, a membership below two is not a ground for winding up: Companies (Single Member Private Limited Companies) Regulations 1992, SI 1992 No 1699.
6   See *Ebrahimi v Westbourne Galleries Ltd* [1973] AC 360 at 387, [1972] 2 All ER 492 at 507, per Lord Cross.
7   *Vujnovich v Vujnovich* [1990] BCLC 227 at 231–232, PC.
8   *Re Fildes Bros Ltd* [1970] 1 All ER 923, [1970] 1 WLR 592.
9   *Bryanston Finance Ltd v De Vries (No 2)* [1976] Ch 63, [1976] 1 All ER 25.
10   IA 1986, s 125(2).

Petition for relief on unfairly prejudicial grounds

A common alternative will be to petition for relief on the ground that the affairs of the company are being conducted in an unfairly prejudicial manner[11]. That option also offers flexibility in the relief which the court might order. An immediate issue is whether the existence of the unfairly prejudicial remedy means that a petitioner seeking a winding-up order on the just and equitable ground will be found to be acting unreasonably in not pursuing that more flexible alternative. In *Re a Company (No 001363 of 1988), ex p S-P*[12] the court accepted that the availability of relief, possibly wider relief, under the provisions governing the unfairly prejudicial remedy does not of itself make it plainly unreasonable to seek a winding-up order so as to justify striking out the petition.

More recently, however, in *Re a Company (No 004415 of 1996)*[13] the court struck out a petition for winding up on the just and equitable grounds where the parties had also petitioned for relief under the unfairly prejudicial remedy.

The petitioners alleged that three companies had been run for the benefit of the majority shareholders and directors by means of paying unduly high directors' fees and declaring low dividends which combination amounted to conduct unfairly prejudicial to the interests of the non-director shareholders. The companies had consistently traded profitably and had distributable reserves of almost £9m of which some £5.7m was in cash.

The court found that the allegations made by the petitioners regarding dividends and remuneration as unfairly prejudicial conduct were fairly arguable in which case by far the most likely form of relief the petitioner would obtain from the court would be an order that the respondents purchase the petitioners' shares in the companies. Since the court would set a fair price for the petitioners' shares taking into account that dividends had been kept at an unreasonably low level, if that were found to be the case, it would be unreasonable for the petitioners to seek to have the companies wound up instead of pursuing their buy-out remedy. The winding-up petition would be struck out.

This decision reaffirms the general judicial approach which is that winding up is a remedy of last resort while the unfairly prejudicial remedy is a jurisdiction of great width which is well able to do justice between the parties. As the width of that jurisdiction and its flexibility have become more established, it has become increasingly unlikely that a winding-up petition will be permitted in this type of dispute[14].

Provisions in the company's articles

Another alternative remedy may be set out in the company's articles which frequently provide a mechanism enabling shareholders to sell their shares and leave the company where they are dissatisfied with the way in which it is being conducted. Initially the courts regarded a refusal to use that mechanism in the articles as a ground for refusing a winding up petition. In *Re a Company*[15] the refusal of the petitioner to accept an offer by the other shareholders to purchase his shares at a fair value to be determined by an independent expert was found to be unreasonable and the petition was struck

---

11   Ie petition under CA 1985, s 459.
12   [1989] BCLC 579. See also *Re Copeland and Craddock Ltd* [1997] BCC 294, CA.
13   [1997] 1 BCLC 479.
14   Of course, there may be some cases where it will be appropriate to seek both remedies. For example, cases where there may be a failure on the facts to establish unfairly prejudicial conduct: see *Re R A Noble & Sons (Clothing) Ltd* [1983] BCLC 273; see the discussion below on the relationship between the two remedies.
15   [1983] 2 All ER 854, [1983] 1 WLR 927.

out, a decision followed in a number of other cases[16]. However, in *Virdi v Abbey Leisure Ltd*[17] the Court of Appeal found that the petitioner's refusal in that case to use the mechanism for purchase of a member's shares set out in the articles was not unreasonable, given that the value of his shares might be discounted under that scheme when the company's assets were held in cash and therefore a discount was inappropriate[18]. Balcombe LJ further indicated that, given the just and equitable nature of the jurisdiction, it may be equitable to ignore provisions in the articles obliging the petitioner to sell his shares at a price fixed by the company's auditors and instead permit the petitioner to proceed to a winding up[19].

So the fact that there is a possibility of relying on a provision for a sale of shares in the articles does not of itself mean that a petitioner is acting unreasonably in seeking winding up. It will all depend on the circumstances and in particular whether the mechanism provided by the articles is a fair method of dealing with the dispute.

Grounds for the petition

Various attempts have been made in the past to categorise the grounds on which a petition will be granted but this has been criticised, most notably by Lord Wilberforce in the leading case, *Ebrahimi v Westbourne Galleries Ltd*[20], who took the view that general words must remain general and should not be reduced to the sum of particular instances[1]. Certainly the categories of conduct within the 'just and equitable' ground are not, and should not, be regarded as closed. Nevertheless the courts had developed certain recognised headings within the jurisdiction although all must now be considered in the light of *Ebrahimi v Westbourne Galleries Ltd*[2] which is discussed in detail below.

Quasi-partnership

An important basis for winding up on the just and equitable ground was where the court decided that the company in question was really an incorporated or quasi-partnership and the personal relationship between the parties had broken down so making continuation of the business impossible. Generally the company would have a small number of shareholders, most if not all of whom participated in the management of the company and who were prevented by restrictions in the articles from freely transferring their shares[3].

The classic example of this category is *Re Yenidje Tobacco Co Ltd*[4]. Here the relationship between the two shareholders (who were also the directors) had completely broken down. They refused to talk to one another and all communications were through

---

16 *Re a Company (No 004377 of 1986)* [1987] BCLC 94 at 103; *Re a Company (No 003843 of 1986)* [1987] BCLC 562; *Re a Company (No 003096 of 1987)* (1987) 4 BCC 80; *Re a Company (No 005685 of 1988), ex p Schwarcz (No 2)* [1989] BCLC 427 at 452.
17 [1990] BCLC 342, CA.
18 [1990] BCLC 342 at 349. See also *Re a Company (No 001363 of 1988), ex p S-P* [1989] BCLC 579: the petitioner's refusal to accept an offer for his shares was not unreasonable when there was a dispute as to the number of shares to which he was actually entitled.
19 [1990] BCLC 342 at 350.
20 [1973] AC 360, [1972] 2 All ER 492.
1   [1973] AC 360 at 374, [1972] 2 All ER 492 at 496.
2   [1973] AC 360, [1972] 2 All ER 492, HL.
3   See Chesterman (1973) 36 MLR 129; Prentice (1973) 89 LQR 107.
4   [1916] 2 Ch 426. See also *Symington v Symington Quarries Ltd* 1906 SC 121; *Re Davis and Collett Ltd* [1935] Ch 693; *Re Wondoflex Textiles Pty Ltd* [1951] VLR 458.

a third party. The court found that the company was in essence a partnership and that there was such a state of animosity between the parties as to preclude all reasonable hope of reconciliation or friendly co-operation[5]. In such circumstances the court would order that it be wound up.

It was sometimes argued that a separate ground for winding up was deadlock but, as it mainly arose in the quasi-partnership cases, being a factor which clearly signified the breakdown of the personal relationship between the parties, it is convenient to mention it here. It was unlikely to be accepted as a ground for winding up companies which did not fall within the quasi-partnership category since in those companies the general meeting would be in a position to exercise its residual powers to resolve any deadlock which might arise[6].

LACK OF PROBITY

The classic statement of this ground is to be found in *Loch v John Blackwood Ltd*[7]:

It is undoubtedly true that at the foundation of applications for winding up on the 'just and equitable rule' there must lie a justifiable lack of confidence in the conduct and management of the company's affairs. But this lack of confidence must be grounded on conduct of the directors, not in regard to their private life or affairs, but in regard to the company's business. Furthermore the lack of confidence must spring not from dissatisfaction at being outvoted on the business affairs or on what is called the domestic policy of the company. On the other hand, whenever the lack of confidence is rested on a lack of probity in the conduct of the company's affairs, then the former is justified by the latter and it is, under the statute, just and equitable that the company be wound up.[8]

Here the directors failed to hold general meetings or submit accounts or recommend a dividend. Instead the majority shareholder treated the business as if it was his own business and ran it down with a view to forcing the minority shareholder to sell out at an undervalue. The court ordered that the company be wound up[9].

LOSS OF SUBSTRATUM

This category provided that if it was or became impossible or illegal to achieve the main objectives for which a company was formed, then the company would be wound up. The theory was that a member had subscribed to the company on the basis of it carrying on a particular business and where the company proposed to pursue some other object, then that member had not agreed to his money being used for that purpose, or to being subjected to the risk of loss in that venture, and he was entitled to recover it by having the company wound up[10].

5   [1916] 2 Ch 426 at 430, per Cozens Hardy MR.
6   See *Barron v Potter* [1914] 1 Ch 895; *Foster v Foster* [1916] 1 Ch 532.
7   [1924] AC 783.
8   [1924] AC 783 at 788, per Lord Shaw.
9   See also *Re Blériot Manufacturing Air Craft Co Ltd* (1916) 32 TLR 253; *Re Newbridge Sanitary Steam Laundry Ltd* [1917] 1 IR 67.
10   The doctrine originated in *Re Suburban Hotel Co* (1867) 2 Ch App 737. See also *Re Haven Gold Mining Co* (1882) 20 Ch D 151; *Re German Date Coffee Co* (1882) 20 Ch D 169; *Re Red Rock Gold Mining Co Ltd* (1889) 61 LT 785; *Re Baku Consolidated Oilfields Ltd* [1944] 1 All ER 24; *Re Kitson & Co Ltd* [1946] 1 All ER 435.

Modern drafting techniques ensure·that companies have very varied objects and it would be very unusual now for a company to be wound up for loss of substratum.

THE MODERN JURISDICTION

The definitive modern case on the just and equitable jurisdiction is the decision of the House of Lords in *Ebrahimi v Westbourne Galleries Ltd*[11].

Ebrahimi (E) and Nazar (N), having originally traded as a partnership selling oriental carpets, set up a company to take over the business. They became the only directors and shareholders, each holding 500 shares. Nazar's son George (G) subsequently joined the business and E and N both transferred 100 shares to him. G also became a director. Eventually the parties fell out and E was removed from the board by N and G and excluded from the day-to-day management of the company. As all profits of the company were distributed by way of directors' remuneration and not by way of dividend, the effect was to deprive E of any return on his investment. E petitioned for a winding-up order on the just and equitable ground[12].

The House of Lords found that, as a matter of law, N and G had acted completely within their rights, within the provisions of the articles, and the Companies Act in removing E in this way. But the just and equitable jurisdiction was not limited to proven cases of mala fides and the legal correctness of their conduct did not make it unassailable. In certain instances, the courts would subject the exercise of legal rights to equitable considerations, ie considerations of a personal character arising between one individual and another which might make it unjust or inequitable to insist on strict legal rights or to exercise them in a particular way[13].

The words 'just and equitable' were:

> ... a recognition of the fact that a limited company is more than a mere judicial entity, with a personality in law of its own: that there is room in company law for recognition of the fact that behind it, or amongst it, there are individuals, with rights, expectations and obligations inter se which are not necessarily submerged in the company structure[13].

In this instance E and N had together formed the company on the basis that the character of the association and, in particular, their joint participation in the management would as a matter of personal relation and good faith remain the same[14]. N and G were not entitled in all the circumstances therefore to exercise their undoubted legal power to remove E as a director and, having done so, the only just and equitable course was to dissolve the association[14].

This is not to say that every exercise of majority power will be restrained by the imposition of equitable considerations. In the vast majority of cases compliance with the Companies Act and the articles of association will ensure the validity of the act (in the absence of bad faith or fraud or any other invalidating ground) but there will be

11   [1973] AC 360, [1972] 2 All ER 492.
12   A winding-up order was granted at first instance [1970] 3 All ER 374, [1970] 1 WLR 1378; revsd by the Court of Appeal [1971] Ch 799, [1971] 1 All ER 561; and reinstated by the House of Lords [1973] AC 360, [1972] 2 All ER 492. Ebrahimi also petitioned unsuccessfully under CA 1948, s 210 (the remedy in cases of oppression). He failed because of the restrictive approach adopted by the courts to that provision, in particular their insistence that the petitioner be oppressed *qua* member which Ebrahimi was not since his complaint was about being removed as a director and being excluded from management: see *Re Westbourne Galleries Ltd* [1971] Ch 799, [1971] 1 All ER 561.
13   [1973] AC 360 at 379, [1972] 2 All ER 492 at 500.
14   [1973] AC 360 at 380, [1972] 2 All ER 492 at 501.

some instances where the rights of the members will not be exhaustively defined in the articles and so equitable considerations may come into play[15]. Such considerations will not arise simply because the company is a small private company, for there are many small private companies which are run on strictly commercial lines. Lord Wilberforce suggested that one or more of the following factors should be present:

(i) an association formed or continued on the basis of a personal relationship, involving mutual confidence;

(ii) an agreement or understanding that all or some of the shareholders shall participate in the conduct of the business; and

(iii) restrictions on the transfer of the members' interest in the company[16].

The approach taken by the House of Lords in *Ebrahimi's* case has since been applied in many instances although, as we shall see later in this Chapter, its influence has been greatest outside the sphere of winding up.

In *Re Zinotty Properties Ltd*[17] the court found as evidence of breach of the required trust and confidence that: (i) A had not been appointed as a director as he was entitled to expect; (ii) the company had not been dissolved when the project was completed as had been originally planned; (iii) there had been interest-free loans to a company in which another of the shareholders was interested; (iv) certain other financial matters needed investigating; and (v) the company had not held general meetings and the accounts had not been prepared in time. In all the circumstances, the court felt it was just and equitable that the company be wound up.

In *Re A and BC Chewing Gum Ltd*[18] the minority shareholder[19] was entitled under the articles and by virtue of a separate shareholders' agreement to appoint one director to the board yet the majority refused to give effect to the appointment. The court, relying on *Ebrahimi*, held that the company should be wound up as the majority had repudiated the minority's right to participate in the management of the company, a right which was the underlying basis of their participation in the company.

An interesting application of the *Ebrahimi* principles is to be found in the New Zealand case *Re North End Motels (Huntly) Ltd*[20]. Here the court, relying on *Ebrahimi*, ordered the company to be wound up where a minority shareholder/director was being constantly outvoted at board meetings and so had little say in the running of the company. The court found that while it was true that a minority shareholder/director accepts and runs the risk of being constantly outvoted, in this case the petitioner had had no outside advice before joining the company and had little business experience. Moreover, were he to sell his shareholding, the majority shareholder was to be the final arbiter of its value. In the circumstances, the court felt that a winding-up order was warranted[1].

It is clear that most of the old cases, in particular those dealing with quasi-partnership, deadlock and lack of probity, can all be subsumed within a more general

---

15   *Re Cuthbert Cooper & Sons Ltd* [1937] Ch 392 was disapproved of because of the undue emphasis placed therein on the articles as being exhaustive of the parties' rights: see [1973] AC 360 at 377, [1972] 2 All ER 492 at 498.

16   [1973] AC 360 at 379, [1972] 2 All ER 492 at 500.

17   [1984] 3 All ER 754, [1984] 1 WLR 1249.

18   [1975] 1 All ER 1017, [1975] 1 WLR 579.

19   The minority shareholder in this case was in fact an American public company, a reason perhaps for not applying *Ebrahimi*: see Womak (1975) CLJ 208.

20   [1976] 1 NZLR 446.

1   It will be recalled that mere dissatisfaction at being outvoted was not justification for making an order under the old headings (*Loch v John Blackwood Ltd* [1924] AC 783) although here the court seemed to find the entire transaction something of an unconscionable bargain: see Shapira (1977) 93 LQR 22.

Ebrahimi category; as indeed could the loss of substratum cases on the basis that they involve the destruction of some underlying fundamental commitment upon which the company was based.

The decision in *Ebrahimi* clearly strengthened the position of minority shareholders and for some years it established winding up as the only effective statutory remedy for aggrieved shareholders. The significance of winding up as a remedy has diminished considerably, however, as the jurisdiction to petition on the ground of unfair prejudice has come to the fore although that jurisdiction, as we shall see, itself builds on the approach laid down in *Ebrahimi*.

THE UNFAIRLY PREJUDICIAL REMEDY

The unfairly prejudicial remedy contained in Companies Act 1985, s 459[2] has proved invaluable to minority shareholders seeking redress in the courts[3].

The section provides:

> A member of a company may apply to the court by petition for an order ... on the ground that the company's affairs are being or have been conducted in a manner which is unfairly prejudicial to the interests of its members generally or of some part of its members (including at least himself) or that any actual or proposed act or omission of the company (including an act or omission on its behalf) is or would be so prejudicial[4].

The conduct complained of must relate to the conduct of the affairs of the company of which the petitioner is a member and a remedy is not available where the conduct complained of is merely that of an individual shareholder acting in a personal capacity[5].

---

2   This provision (and its predecessor CA 1980, s 75) replaced CA 1948, s 210 which provided relief for members where the company's affairs were being conducted in an oppressive, ie burdensome, harsh and wrongful, manner: see *Scottish Co-operative Wholesale Society Ltd v Meyer* [1959] AC 324, [1958] 3 All ER 66; *Re HR Harmer Ltd* [1958] 3 All ER 689, [1959] 1 WLR 62. This provision was interpreted very restrictively by the courts and was of little use to minority shareholders: see generally Prentice (1972) Current Legal Problems 124; Wedderburn (1966) 29 MLR 321.

3   See generally Boros *Minority Shareholders' Remedies* (1995); Prentice 'Protecting Minority Shareholders' Interests' in Feldman & Meisel (eds) *Corporate and Commercial Law: Modern Developments* (1996); Riley (1992) MLR 782; Hannigan [1988] LMCLQ 60; Prentice (1988) 8 Ox J L S 55.

4   CA 1985, s 459(1). For these purposes, 'member' includes persons to whom shares have been transferred or transmitted by law, ie personal representatives and trustees in bankruptcy: s 459(2). As to membership of a company, see s 22. A petition may also be presented by the Secretary of State: s 460. This power has never been exercised.

5   *Re a Company (No 005685 of 1988), ex p Schwarcz (No 2)* [1989] BCLC 427 at 437; also *Re Saul D Harrison & Sons plc* [1995] 1 BCLC 14, CA. See *Re Unisoft Group Ltd (No 3)* [1994] 1 BCLC 609 (allegations concerned activities of shareholders and alleged breach of shareholders' agreement); *Re Estate Acquisition & Development Ltd* [1995] BCC 338 (offer by one shareholder to another to purchase his shares cannot be treated as part of the conduct of the company's affairs); *Re Leeds United Holdings plc* [1996] 2 BCLC 545 (dispute as to agreemeent between shareholders over the sale of their shares does not relate to the company's affairs).

The interests of the members as members

The focus of the provision is on conduct which is unfairly prejudicial to the interests of the members as members[6]. When considering a member's interests, the court takes a broad view and has regard, where appropriate, to wider equitable considerations[7] in the same manner as was suggested by Lord Wilberforce in *Ebrahimi v Westbourne Galleries Ltd*[8], discussed above.

A member's interests are not necessarily limited, therefore, to his strict legal rights under the articles and the Companies Acts but can extend also to legitimate expectations as to the conduct of the company's affairs arising from the nature of the company and agreements and understandings between the parties[9]. This more flexible approach allows the court to recognise that behind a limited company, or among it, are individuals with rights, expectations and obligations inter se which are not necessarily submerged in the company structure[10]. Although, in most cases, the basis of association will be adequately and exhaustively laid down in the articles, there may be cases in which further equitable considerations might arise. Such cases would typically present one, or probably more, of the following features: a personal relationship between the shareholders involving mutual confidence; an agreement that some or all should participate in the conduct of the business; and restrictions on the transfer of shares which would prevent a member from realising his investment[10]. Companies which reflect these features are often referred to as quasi-partnerships[10].

Shareholders in such small private companies tend to be a close-knit group, actively involved in many instances in the day-to-day operation of the business and financially and personally committed to the company. Here the scope for legitimate interests and expectations beyond strict legal rights is obviously greatest. However, as Lord Wilberforce stressed in *Ebrahimi v Westbourne Galleries Ltd*[11], the case for giving effect to equitable considerations must be made in each instance and it is not sufficient simply to assert that the company is small or private, for in many cases the basis of the relationship will be adequately and exhaustively laid down in the articles.

A typical case is *Re Ghyll Beck Driving Range Ltd*[12] where a father and son and two others set up a company to run a golf range. Each was an equal shareholder and each was a director. The company was incorporated in December 1990 but by June 1991 the parties had fallen out over the funding and the direction of the business with one of the shareholders (the petitioner) increasingly isolated, as he told the court. There was a scuffle between himself and the father on the company's premises and thereafter the business was run without reference to the petitioner. The court concluded that he was unjustifiably excluded from a joint venture which it was contemplated would be managed by all four of the participators for the benefit of all of them.

6   *Re a Company (No 004475 of 1982)* [1983] Ch 178 at 189, [1983] 2 All ER 36 at 44, per Lord Grantchester; *Re a Company (No 005685 of 1988), ex p Schwarcz (No 2)* [1989] BCLC 427; *Re a Company (No 00314 of 1989), ex p Estate Acquisition & Development Ltd* [1991] BCLC 154; *R & H Electric Ltd v Haden Bill Electrical Ltd* [1995] 2 BCLC 280.
7   This approach is justified by the use of the word 'unfairly' in the provision: *Re Saul D Harrison & Sons plc* [1995] 1 BCLC 14, CA; also *Re a Company* [1986] BCLC 376; *Re Posgate & Denby (Agencies) Ltd* [1987] BCLC 8; *Re Blue Arrow plc* [1987] BCLC 585; *Re a Company (No 005685 of 1988), ex p Schwarcz (No 2)* [1989] BCLC 427; *Re Tottenham Hotspur plc* [1994] 1 BCLC 655.
8   [1973] AC 360, [1972] 2 All ER 492, HL.
9   *Re Saul D Harrison & Sons plc* [1995] 1 BCLC 14, CA; *Re a Company* [1986] BCLC 376; *Re Posgate & Denby (Agencies) Ltd* [1987] BCLC 8; *Re a Company (No 005685 of 1988), ex p Schwarcz (No 2)* [1989] BCLC 427; *R & H Electric Ltd v Haden Bill Electrical Ltd* [1995] 2 BCLC 280.
10   *Ebrahimi v Westbourne Galleries Ltd* [1973] AC 360 at 379, [1972] 2 All ER 492 at 500.
11   [1972] AC 360 at 379, [1973] 2 All ER 492 at 500.
12   [1993] BCLC 1126.

In *R & H Electric Ltd v Haden Bill Electrical Ltd*[13] a company was set up by four parties in 1989. By 1993 relations between the parties had broken down and three of the shareholders joined together to vote the fourth (who had provided the financial backing for the business) off the board. The court found that the company had been set up on the basis of mutual trust as between the parties which gave the fourth shareholder a legitimate expectation of being able to participate in the management for at least as long as he provided significant loan capital to the company. His summary exclusion therefore was unjustified and the court ordered that he be bought out.

In *Re a company (No 00709 of 1992)*[14] the Court of Appeal noted that in approaching these cases, the first step would be to ask: were the interests of the petitioner which were unfairly prejudiced his interests as a member of the company or his interests in some other capacity? 'In general, where the company is a quasi-partnership of which the petitioner is a member and no other relevant capacity can be attributed to him, the answer can only be his interests as a member'[15].

In this case, the trial judge had declined to find that the petitioner had been unfairly prejudiced *as a member*. The petitioner complained of being removed as managing director, and of the majority shareholder reneging on an agreement to share profits, and that the petitioner had been deprived of an expectation that in due course he would secure 50% of the shares in the company. The trial judge found that the petitioner had joined the company as an employee and later progressed to a directorship[16] and his complaint was that the respondent had reneged on the terms of appointment to the directorship. The trial judge could not see, therefore, any relationship between the petitioner's complaints and his position as a member of the company[17]. The judge emphasised that this was not a case where the petitioner and respondent had come together to form a company intending it to be a partnership; nor was it case of someone putting capital into a business on the basis that he would be allowed to work for it[18].

The Court of Appeal, adopting a more generous analysis, found that while the petitioner did not subscribe for his shares in the company nor bring any capital into the company, nevertheless within two years of his having joined the company, it did represent an association continued on the basis of a personal relationship involving mutual confidence.

At all times thereafter the petitioner did have a legitimate entitlement to 50% of the profits and, later, a legitimate expectation that he would receive 50% of the shares. When the majority shareholder reneged on the agreement regarding the profits, so dashing his expectation as to the 50% of the shares, and effectively forcing the petitioner out of the company, that amounted to conduct unfairly prejudicial to his interests as a member[19].

The interests of shareholders in larger private and public companies are likely to be quite different from, and considerably more restricted than, those of shareholders in quasi-partnerships[20]. In these larger companies there is usually no underlying

13   [1995] 2 BCLC 280.
14   [1997] 2 BCLC 739, CA.
15   [1997] 2 BCLC 739 at 768, per Nourse LJ.
16   Although the trial judge did accept that the relationship beween the parties did exhibit the elements of a quais-partnership identified by Lord Wilberforce in *Ebrahimi*, discussed above: see [1997] 2 BCLC 7739 at 756.
17   [1997] 2 BCLC 739 at 758.
18   [1997] 2 BCLC 739 at 758-759.
19   [1997] 2 BCLC 739 at 769-770. Leave to appeal to the House of Lords has been granted.
20   Equally it should not be forgotten that in time the parties' relationship may change, see *Re a Company (No 005134 of 1986), ex p Harries* [1989] BCLC 383 where a company started off as a quasi-partnership but the relationship between the parties changed to a more commercial footing so ending any expectations as to participation in management.

personal relationship, employment is rarely an issue and the shareholders are more interested in such matters as dividend yield and capital appreciation than involvement in the day-to-day running of the company. If they become dissatisfied, especially if it is a public company, they can sell their shares and withdraw from the company. In these companies there is little room for finding further legitimate expectations beyond the strict legal rights as provided by the articles[21].

For example, in *Re Blue Arrow plc*[22] the petitioner failed to establish any expectation that the company's articles would not be altered so as to enable her to remain in office as the president of the company. As it was a listed public company, outside investors were entitled to expect that the whole of the parties' relationship was contained in the articles. Likewise in *Re Tottenham Hotspur plc*[23], another listed public company, the court found that there were no understandings between the parties beyond those contained in the company's constitution.

If no such interests or expectations exist then, as the Court of Appeal made clear in *Re Saul D Harrison & Sons plc*[24], a petitioner must show some abuse by directors of their powers or an infringement of the member's strict legal rights under the company's constitution or the companies legislation.

Unfairly prejudicial conduct

The test of whether the company's affairs are being or have been conducted in a manner which is unfairly prejudicial to the petitioner's interests is an objective, and not a subjective, one[25] and the petitioner does not have to show that the persons controlling the company have acted deliberately in bad faith or with a conscious intent to treat him unfairly[25]. The conduct complained of must be prejudicial in the sense of causing prejudice or harm to the relevant interest of the member and also unfairly so and it is not sufficient if the conduct satisfies only one of these tests[26].

In *Re R A Noble & Sons (Clothing) Ltd*[1] the company was a quasi-partnership formed on the basis that the petitioner would provide capital while the respondent would be responsible for the conduct of the company's affairs. The petition alleged that the petitioner had been excluded from the running of the company. By way of defence, it was argued that while the petitioner might have been excluded, the respondent had not done so deliberately. He had simply got on with running the business as he had always run it. The court found that the issue was not whether the respondent intended to harm the petitioner but whether a reasonable bystander observing the consequences

21 See *Re Posgate & Denby (Agencies) Ltd* [1987] BCLC 8; *Re Elgindata Ltd* [1991] BCLC 959 (relationship negotiated at arms' length); *Re Estate Acquisition & Development Ltd* [1995] BCC 338 (no evidence of any expectations); *Re Saul D Harrison & Sons plc* [1995] 1 BCLC 14 (no evidence of any expectations); *Re a Company (No 005685 of 1988), ex p Schwarcz (No 2)* [1989] BCLC 427 (the relationship between the parties was governed by detailed professionally drawn agreements and service contracts). But see *Re a company (No 002015 of 1996)* [1997] 2 BCLC 1 (the mere existence of complex written agreements does not necessarily exclude the possibility of some other arrangements on understanding between the parties so as to justify striking out a s 459 petition).
22 [1987] BCLC 585.
23 [1994] 1 BCLC 655.
24 [1995] 1 BCLC 14.
25 *Re R A Noble & Sons (Clothing) Ltd* [1983] BCLC 273; *Re Elgindata Ltd* [1991] BCLC 959; *Re Macro (Ipswich) Ltd* [1994] 2 BCLC 354; *Re Saul D Harrison & Sons plc* [1995] 1 BCLC 14, CA; *Re Little Olympian Each-Ways Ltd (No 3)* [1995] 1 BCLC 636.
26 *Re Saul D Harrison & Sons plc* [1995] 1 BCLC 14; *Re R A Noble & Sons (Clothing) Ltd* [1983] BCLC 273.
1   [1983] BCLC 273.

of the conduct complained of would regard it as having unfairly prejudiced the petitioner's interests[2]. On the facts, such a reasonable bystander might well have thought that the conduct complained of was prejudicial but would not have regarded it as unfair, for the petitioner by his disinterest in the running of the company had partly brought it on himself.

In *Re Saul D Harrison & Sons plc*[3] the Court of Appeal stressed that in deciding what is fair or unfair for these purposes, it must be borne in mind that fairness is being used in the context of a commercial relationship, the contractual terms of which are set out in the articles of association[4]. The starting point is to ask whether the conduct of which the shareholder complains is in accordance with the articles and the powers which the shareholders have entrusted to the board. However, a finding that conduct was not in accordance with the articles does not necessarily mean that it was unfair, as trivial or technical infringements of the articles were not intended to give use to petitions under s 459. Conduct may also be unfair without being unlawful where it does not accord with the understandings upon which the shareholders are associated. Thus the personal relationship between a shareholder and those who control the company may entitle him to say that it would in certain circumstances be unfair for them to exercise a power conferred upon the board or the company in general meeting[5].

CONDUCT OF THE PETITIONER

There is no independent requirement that it should be just and equitable to grant relief or that the petitioner should come with clean hands[6]. However, the conduct of the petitioner may be relevant in a number of ways: as where the conduct complained of is found to be prejudicial but not unfair in the light of the petitioner's conduct[7]; or it may affect the relief granted by the court[8].

Examples of unfairly prejudicial conduct

It is clear from the cases that most complaints fall into certain well-defined categories, such as exclusion and removal from the board, self-dealing by the directors, abuse of power and mismanagement of the company's affairs. However, the categories of what constitutes unfairly prejudicial conduct are not closed[9].

As to removal and exclusion, it had been the position under the previous oppression remedy[10] that where the petitioner was essentially complaining of removal from the board and exclusion from management, he was not entitled to relief for he was not oppressed 'qua member'[11]. However, in numerous instances the courts have found that

---

2   [1983] BCLC 273 at 290; also *Re a Company (No 005134 of 1986), ex p Harries* [1989] BCLC 383.
3   [1995] 1 BCLC 14, CA. See *Re Macro (Ipswich) Ltd* [1994] 2 BCLC 354 at 404 (the concept of unfairness involves the balancing of many considerations).
4   [1995] 1 BCLC 14 at 17, CA.
5   [1995] 1 BCLC 14 at 18, CA.
6   *Re London School of Electronics Ltd* [1986] Ch 211, [1985] 3 WLR 474.
7   *Re R A Noble & Sons (Clothing) Ltd* [1983] BCLC 273.
8   *Re London School of Electronics Ltd* [1986] Ch 211, [1985] 3 WLR 474; *Re Bird Precision Bellows Ltd* [1986] Ch 658, [1985] 3 All ER 523, CA (affg [1984] Ch 419, [1984] 3 All ER 444).
9   *Re BSB Holdings Ltd (No 2)* [1996] 1 BCLC 155.
10 Ie CA 1948, s 210.
11 See *Elder v Elder & Watson Ltd* 1952 SC 49; *Re Lundie Bros Ltd* [1965] 2 All ER 692; *Re Westbourne Galleries Ltd* [1970] 3 All ER 374.

members in smaller companies have an interest in continued participation in the management of the company and removal from that position in circumstances where there is an expectation of participation can be unfairly prejudicial to their interests as members[12]. In the absence of such an expectation, every director is subject to the possibility of removal and has no right to remain in office[13].

Another recurring complaint is the diversion of business to another company in which the majority shareholder holds a greater interest[14]. In *Re Little Olympian Each-Ways Ltd (No 3)*[15] the directors disposed of the company's business at a substantial undervalue (in the region of £2m) to another company as part of a transaction from which they benefited significantly. Likewise in *Re Full Cup International Trading Ltd*[16] the directors disposed of the company's stock for an inadequate consideration to a company which they controlled. In both cases, the court had little difficulty in finding such conduct of the company's affairs to be unfairly prejudicial to the petitioner's interests.

Often the majority shareholder/director awards excessive financial benefits to himself[17]. In *Re Elgindata Ltd*[18] the court noted that the majority shareholder/director used the company's money for the personal benefit of himself, his family and friends. The court held that the misapplication of the company's assets by those in control of the company's affairs for their own benefit or for the benefit of their family and friends is conduct which is unfairly prejudicial to the interests of the minority shareholders[19]. Another common complaint is that the company fails to maintain a reasonable level of dividend payout while maintaining significant benefits for the majority shareholders/directors. This too could amount to unfairly prejudicial conduct[20].

In a small company the proportionate shareholding held by each shareholder is often of great importance. The ability to allot shares to alter that proportionate holding is a power which is open to abuse by the directors. A rights issue, even one made on a pro rata basis at an advantageous price, is capable of amounting to unfairly prejudicial treatment if it is known that the objecting member did not have sufficient funds to take up the offer and it was made for that reason, or where the objecting member was engaged in litigation with the majority and the offer was designed to deplete the resources available to him to finance such litigation. In *Re a Company (No 002612 of*

---

12 See *R & H Electric Ltd v Haden Bill Electrical Ltd* [1995] 2 BCLC 280; also *Re a Company* [1986] BCLC 376; *Re Cumana Ltd* [1986] BCLC 430; *Re Ghyll Beck Driving Range Ltd* [1993] BCLC 1126; *Quinlan v Essex Hinge Co Ltd* [1996] 2 BCLC 417; also *Ebrahimi v Westbourne Galleries Ltd* [1973] AC 360, [1972] 2 All ER 492.

13 *Re Estate Acquisition and Development Ltd* [1995] BCC 338; *Re a Company (No 005134 of 1986), ex p Harries* [1989] BCLC 383 (company changed from a quasi-partnership to commercial footing so ending expectation as to participation); *Re a Company (No 005685 of 1988), ex p Schwarcz (No 2)* [1989] BCLC 427; *Re Blue Arrow plc* [1987] BCLC 585; *Re Tottenham Hotspur plc* [1994] 1 BCLC 655.

14 See *Re Cumana Ltd* [1986] BCLC 430, CA; *Re London School of Electronics ltd* [1986] Ch 211, [1985] 3 WLR 474. These cases are being brought under CA 1985 s 459 to obtain a personal remedy for what are effectively breaches of fiduciary duty: see Law Commission *Shareholders Remedies, A Consultation Paper* (1996, No 142), para 9.40. This further erodes the significance of the derivative action.

15 [1995] 1 BCLC 636.

16 [1995] BCC 682 at 690–691; affd sub nom *Antoniades v Wong* [1997] 2 BCLC 419, CA.

17 See *Re Cumana Ltd* [1986] BCLC 430, CA; *Re Brenfield Squash Racquets Club* [1996] 2 BCLC 184.

18 [1991] BCLC 959.

19 [1991] BCLC 959 at 1004.

20 See *Re a Company (No 004415 of 1996)* [1997] 1 BCLC 479; *Quinlan v Essex Hinge Co Ltd* [1996] 2 BCLC 417 at 427; *Re Sam Weller & Sons Ltd* [1990] BCLC 80; *Re a Company, ex p Glossop* [1988] BCLC 570.

1984)[1] Harman J granted an injunction to restrain a proposed rights issue which had followed immediately on the presentation by the minority shareholder of a s 459 petition. Had it gone ahead it would have reduced his 33% holding to 0.33%. An allotment of shares secretly made in breach of the statutory provisions governing allotments for the improper purpose of increasing the majority's holding and decreasing the minority is also unfairly prejudicial conduct. In *Re a Company (No 005134 of 1986), ex p Harries*[2] there was a unilateral and secret exercise by a director of a power of allotment so as to increase his own shareholding from 60% to 96% and to reduce the petitioner's holding from 40% to 4%. That was unfairly prejudicial conduct.

The passing of a special resolution to alter the company's articles of association may be unfairly prejudicial conduct, for example if an alteration will affect the petitioner's legitimate expectation that he would control the management of the company, and even a proposal that such a resolution be passed may amount to unfairly prejudicial conduct[3]. But, in the absence of such special circumstances involving an abuse of the rights of the majority, a change in the articles is one of the ordinary incidents to which a member of a company cannot validly object[4].

Repeated failures to hold annual general meetings and to lay accounts before the members so depriving members of their right to know and consider the state of the company's affairs is conduct unfairly prejudicial to their interests, as is holding an extraordinary general meeting on incorrect notice so invalidating an allotment of shares made at the meeting[5].

Although in *Re Macro (Ipswich) Ltd*[6] it was accepted that it is open to the court to find that serious mismanagement of a company's business constitutes conduct that is unfairly prejudicial to the interests of the shareholders, the court will normally be very reluctant to accept that managerial decisions can amount to unfairly prejudicial conduct[7]. In *Re Macro (Ipswich) Ltd*[8] it was possible to point to specific acts of mismanagement repeated over many years causing financial loss to the company. The company had a substantial portfolio of properties which had been mismanaged by the sole director who was the 83-year-old father of the petitioners in this case. For example, he failed to institute a proper maintenance system for the properties or to ensure that they were properly let and rents duly paid. In *Re Elgindata Ltd*[9], on the other hand, the complaint was a broad complaint where the shareholder was simply disappointed as to the poor quality of the management[10]. That was insufficient as a basis for an allegation of unfairly prejudicial conduct.

1 [1985] BCLC 80; see *Re Cumana Ltd* [1986] BCLC 430, CA. Cf *Re a Company* [1986] BCLC 362 where the rights issue was motivated by a genuine desire to raise needed capital.
2 [1989] BCLC 383.
3 *Re Kenyon Swansea Ltd* [1987] BCLC 514; cf *Re Blue Arrow plc* [1987] BCLC 585 (no such expectations existed). Quaere if an alteration which involved the adoption of the provisions of Table A could ever be unfairly prejudicial to the members' interests for these purposes: *Re Estate Acquisition & Development Ltd* [1995] BCC 338 at 351.
4 *Re Estate Acquisition & Development Ltd* [1995] BCC 338; *Re a Company (No 005685 of 1988), ex p Schwarcz (No 2)* [1989] BCLC 427.
5 *Re a Company (No 00789 of 1987), ex p Shooter* [1990] BCLC 384.
6 [1994] 2 BCLC 354.
7 See *Re Elgindata Ltd* [1991] BCLC 959 at 993–994; *Re Macro (Ipswich) Ltd* [1994] 2 BCLC 354; *Re Saul D Harrison & Sons plc* [1995] 1 BCLC 14, CA.
8 [1994] 2 BCLC 354.
9 [1991] BCLC 959 at 993–994.
10 The allegations included that the majority shareholder/director took long lunches and played too much golf. The general impression, the court said, was that his management lacked vigour and purposefulness.

Court orders

Orders generally

If the court is satisfied that a petition under these provisions is well founded[11], it may make such order as it thinks fit for giving relief in respect of the matters complained of[12]. In *Re a Company (No 00789 of 1987), ex p Shooter*[13] the court rejected the suggestion that this requires the court to confine itself to remedying what had gone wrong. The provision is extremely flexible and the court will consider such relief as is appropriate at the time of the hearing[14]. The court's discretion as to the relief it may order extends to the refusal of specific relief where the court is unable to devise relief which would constitute an appropriate remedy or where some other course of action seems to be preferable[15].

Without prejudice to the generality of the court's powers, the order may:

(1) regulate the conduct of the company's affairs in the future[16];

(2) require the company to refrain from doing or continuing an act complained of by the petitioner, or to do an act which the petitioner has complained it has omitted to do[17];

(3) authorise civil proceedings to be brought in the name and on behalf of the company by such person or persons and on such terms as the court may direct[18];

(4) provide for the purchase of the shares of any members of the company by other members or by the company itself, and in the case of a purchase by the company itself, the reduction of the company's capital accordingly[19].

Purchase orders

The most commonly sought relief is a purchase order requiring the respondents to purchase the shares of the petitioner so enabling the petitioner to recover his investment

---

11 There must be a finding of unfair prejudice before the court can make any order for relief: *Re Bird Precision Bellows Ltd* [1986] Ch 658, [1985] 3 All ER 523, CA; *Re a Company (No 007623 of 1984)* [1986] BCLC 362. An order may be made in favour of the company: *Lowe v Fahey* [1996] 1 BCLC 262.

12 CA 1985, s 461(1).

13 [1990] BCLC 384.

14 *Re Hailey Group Ltd* [1993] BCLC 459; *Re Little Olympian Each-Ways Ltd (No 3)* [1995] 1 BCLC 636; *Lowe v Fahey* [1996] 1 BCLC 262.

15 This might be because the company has gone into receivership: see *Re Hailey Group Ltd* [1993] BCLC 459; or because it would be better for the company to go into winding up: see *Re Full Cup International Trading Ltd* [1995] BCC 682; affd sub nom *Antoniades v Wong* [1997] 2 BCLC 419, CA.

16 In *R & H Electric Ltd v Haden Bill Electrical Ltd* [1995] 2 BCLC 280 the court ordered, inter alia, that the petitioner's shares should be purchased by the majority shareholders and that the company repay as soon as possible loans made to it by the petitioner.

17 See *McGuinness v Bremner plc* [1988] BCLC 673 where the court ordered an extraordinary general meeting to be held on a set date.

18 This provision was designed to extend the causes of action open to a minority shareholder by allowing him to petition under CA 1985, s 459 for permission to commence a derivative action: see Jenkins Committee *Report of the Company Law Committee* (1962, Cmnd 1749), para 206. It is highly unlikely that any successful petitioner under CA 1985, s 459 who is then in a position to obtain a direct personal remedy would ask the court for permission to commence a derivative action.

19 CA 1985, s 461(2).

and depart from the company[20]. The valuation of the petitioner's shares under such a purchase order is a difficult question which contributes considerably to the length and complexity of s 459 proceedings.

The basis of valuation

The overall approach of the courts to the question of valuation was established in *Re Bird Precision Bellows Ltd*[1]. In determining what is the proper price to be paid for the petitioner's shares, there is a wide discretion in the court to do what is fair and equitable in the circumstances[2]. There is no rule that the shares have to be bought on a pro rata basis but nor is there a general rule that they have to be bought on a discounted basis to reflect the fact that they are a minority holding. It all depends on the circumstances of the case. In general, however, the court would distinguish between two types of shareholding in small private companies.

Where the sale is of a holding acquired in what is essentially a quasi-partnership and the sale is being forced on the holder because of the unfairly prejudicial manner in which the majority have conducted the affairs of the company then, as a general rule, the correct course would be to fix the price pro rata according to the value of the shares as a whole and without any discount[3]. This would be the only fair method of compensating an unwilling vendor of the equivalent of a partnership share.

Where a minority shareholding is acquired as an investment, different considerations apply and the price fixed will normally be discounted to reflect the fact that it is a minority holding[4].

In *Re Bird Precision Bellows Ltd*[5] the facts showed a forced sale in a quasi-partnership. Accordingly, the price to be paid was fixed on a pro rata basis without any discount to reflect the fact that the shares constituted a minority holding. A case where a pro rata basis was not required was *Re a Company (No 005134 of 1986), ex p Harries*[6] where the relationship between the parties had started off as a quasi-partnership but subsequently changed to a more commercial footing.

The date of valuation

As the value of the shares may fluctuate throughout the period in question, the choice of date of valuation will be of great importance to the parties. Prima facie, the shares

---

20   Very exceptionally the court may order the respondents to sell to the petitioner. See *Re a Company (No 00789 of 1987), ex p Shooter* [1990] BCLC 384 where the court found that the unfairly prejudicial manner in which the majority shareholder had conducted the company's affairs showed that he was unfit to control the company and he should sell to the petitioner; also *Re Brenfield Squash Racquets Club Ltd* [1996] 2 BCLC 184; *Re a Company (No 00836 of 1995)* [1996] 2 BCLC 192 at 205.

1   [1984] Ch 419, [1984] 3 All ER 444; affd [1986] Ch 658, [1985] 3 All ER 523, CA.

2   *Re Bird Precision Bellows Ltd* [1984] Ch 419, [1984] 3 All ER 444; affd [1986] Ch 658, [1985] 3 All ER 523, CA; *Re Elgindata Ltd* [1991] BCLC 959; *Re Little Olympian Each-Ways Ltd (No 3)* [1995] 1 BCLC 636.

3   *Re Bird Precision Bellows Ltd* [1984] Ch 419, [1984] 3 All ER 444; affd [1986] Ch 658, [1985] 3 All ER 523, CA; *Re London School of Electronics Ltd* [1986] Ch 211, [1985] 3 WLR 474; *Re Ghyll Beck Driving Range Ltd* [1993] BCLC 1126; *Quinlan v Essex Hinge Co Ltd* [1996] 2 BCLC 417.

4   *Re Elgindata Ltd* [1991] BCLC 959; *Re Bird Precision Bellows Ltd* [1984] Ch 419 at 430, [1984] 3 All ER 444 at 450, per Nourse J; *Re a Company (No 005134 of 1986), ex p Harries* [1989] BCLC 383.

5   [1984] Ch 419, [1984] 3 All ER 444; affd [1986] Ch 658, [1985] 3 All ER 523, CA.

6   [1989] BCLC 383.

should be valued at the date of the order for purchase[7] but, given the overriding requirement to do what is fair in the circumstances, the valuation may be directed to take place at the date of the presentation of the petition[8] or even at a date before such presentation[9].

Relationship between unfairly prejudicial provision and other shareholder remedies

It might be thought that the very width of the unfairly prejudicial remedy means that the jurisdiction to wind up companies on the just and equitable ground[10] is unimportant. It is not redundant, however, as in a particular case it may be that the facts are inadequate to support a petition on unfairly prejudicial grounds but would warrant a winding up order on the just and equitable ground. In *Re R A Noble & Sons (Clothing) Ltd*[11] a businessman excluded from the management of a company failed to obtain relief under s 459 for the court found that while his exclusion may have been prejudicial it was not unfair for he had effectively brought it on himself. However, a winding-up order was granted because the mutual trust and confidence which was the basis of the company had been destroyed. It may be that while unfairly prejudicial conduct can be established, no appropriate relief can be devised under s 459 and a winding-up order is a more appropriate remedy.[11a]

Equally, the facts may be inadequate to support a petition for winding up on the just and equitable ground but indicate arguable grounds for a petition alleging that the company's affairs are being carried on in an unfairly prejudicial manner[12].

It remains the case that there is a need for both remedies and the increasing use of s 459 does not render the winding-up jurisdiction obsolete. However, that is not to say that both remedies should be sought. Winding up is a remedy of last resort and, as was made clear in the 1990 Practice Direction[13], a petitioner should not seek relief under s 459 *and* winding up unless winding up is the relief which the petitioner prefers or if it is considered that it may be the only relief to which he is entitled. This approach is reinforced by the recent decision of Sir Richard Scott V-C in *Re a Company (No 004415 of 1996)*[14] to strike out a petition for winding up which had been combined with a petition for relief under s 459. The Law Commission has made recommendations for the further streamlining of these remedies and those recommendations are discussed at the end of this Chapter.

The fact that the petitioner could have brought a derivative action with respect to the alleged conduct does not preclude him seeking relief under the unfairly prejudicial

---

7   See *Re London School of Electronics Ltd* [1986] Ch 211, [1985] 3 WLR 474; *Re a Company (No 005134 of 1986), ex p Harries* [1989] BCLC 383; *Re Elgindata Ltd* [1991] BCLC 959; *Re Ghyll Beck Driving Range Ltd* [1993] BCLC 1126.

8   *Re London School of Electronics Ltd* [1986] Ch 211, [1985] 3 WLR 474 (unfair to value shares at date of judgment); *Re Cumana Ltd* [1986] BCLC 430, CA.

9   See *Re Cumana Ltd* [1986] BCLC 430 at 436 (date before petition might be permissible where wrongdoers took steps to depreciate shares in anticipation of presentation of petition); also *Re a Company* [1983] BCLC 151 at 162, [1983] 1 WLR 927 at 937; *Re OC (Transport) Services Ltd* [1984] BCLC 251; *Re London School of Electronics Ltd* [1986] Ch 211, [1985] 3 WLR 474.

10   Ie under IA, s 122(1)(g).

11   [1983] BCLC 273. See also *Jesner v Jarrad Properties Ltd* [1993] BCLC 1032, (CS).

11a   See *Re Full Cup International Trading Ltd* [1995] BCC 682; affd on appeal which is reported as *Antoniades v Wong* [1997] 2 BCLC 419, CA.

12   See *Re a Company (No 00314 of 1989), ex p Estate Acquisition and Development Ltd* [1991] BCLC 154.

13   *Practice Direction (Chancery 1/90)* [1990] 1 All ER 1056.

14   [1997] 1 BCLC 479, discussed above.

provision[15]. However, where a majority shareholder could remove from office the directors who are allegedly conducting the company's affairs in a manner unfairly prejudicial to that shareholder's interests, he should not seek the assistance of the court[16].

Relationship with the articles of association

A difficult issue has been the relationship between s 459 and the articles of association.

IDENTIFYING THE SCOPE OF A MEMBER'S INTERESTS

We have already noted that the width of the unfairly prejudicial jurisdiction allows the courts to look at a member's interests which extend beyond his strict legal rights as set down in the articles and the Companies Act[17]. Equally, we have seen that if the articles are very detailed, if they are supplemented by other written agreements, or if the company is a public company then the court may not find that there are any interests or expectations beyond the articles[18]. To that extent therefore the articles, by detailing and encapsulating the entire relationship between the parties, can cut down the potential for a disgruntled shareholder subsequently to bring a petition under s 459. The member in that case would be restricted to showing breaches of the articles or other duties[19].

AN APPROPRIATE REMEDY

The second issue involves purchase orders. As we have noted the most commonly sought remedy is a purchase order as the petitioner wishes to exit from the company.

Many private companies have articles which contain provisions which apply when a member wishes to sell. Typically they will state that a member wishing to sell should offer his shares to the existing members at a price to be determined by the company's auditor whose decision is binding and who shall not give reasons for his valuation. In some of the earlier s 459 cases, it was argued that where what the petitioner was seeking was an exit route from the company, he should be required to use the mechanism provided by the articles rather than resorting to a court valuation by way of an unfairly prejudicial petition.

---

15   *Re a Company (No 005287 of 1985)* [1986] 1 WLR 281, [1986] BCLC 68; *Re Little Olympian Each-Ways Ltd* [1995] 1 BCLC 636 at 665; *Lowe v Fahey* [1996] 1 BCLC 262. However, where the only substantive relief being sought was a claim on behalf of the company against a third party, the court would not necessarily allow the claimant to proceed by petition instead of by derivative action: *Lowe v Fahey*, supra. Note also *Cooke v Cooke* [1997] 1 BCLC 28 (not sensible to allow derivative action and s 459 petition raising substantially the same issues to proceed independently: derivative action stayed and proceedings continued under s 459). See Law Commission *Shareholder Remedies, A Consultation Paper* (1996, No 142), para 16.6; Law Commission *Shareholder Remedies* (1997, Cm 3769), p 75 n 27.

16   *Re Baltic Real Estate Ltd (No 2)* [1993] BCLC 503.

17   *Re Saul D Harrison & Sons plc* [1995] 1 BCLC 14, CA; *Re a Company* [1986] BCLC 376; *Re Posgate & Denby (Agencies) Ltd* [1987] BCLC 8; *Re a Company (No 005685 of 1988), ex p Schwarcz (No 2)* [1989] BCLC 427; *R & H Electric Ltd v Haden Bill Electrical Ltd* [1995] 2 BCLC 280.

18   See *Re Blue Arrow plc* [1987] BCLC 585; *Re Tottenham Hotspur plc* [1994] 1 BCLC 655; *Re a Company (No 005685 of 1988), ex p Schwarcz (No 2)* [1989] BCLC 427. But see *Re a Company (No 002015 of 1996)* [1997] 2 BCLC 1.

19   *Re Saul D Harrison & Sons plc* [1995] 1 BCLC 14, CA.

That argument was accepted in quite a number of the early authorities which decided that when it was plain that the appropriate solution to a breakdown of relations was for the petitioner to sell his shares at a fair price and the articles contained provisions for an independent determination of a fair price, or a fair offer had been made for the shares, the presentation or maintenance of a petition under CA 1985, s 459 would ordinarily be an abuse of process[20].

However, in *Re a Company (No 00330 of 1991), ex p Holden*[1] the court concluded that a petitioner was not necessarily acting unreasonably in seeking to have his shares valued pursuant to a court order under the unfairly prejudicial provision rather than relying on a valuation under provisions in the company's articles of association[2]. The court relied on the decision of the Court of Appeal in *Virdi v Abbey Leisure Ltd*[3], discussed above, which in effect overruled the earlier authorities. Harman J noted[4]:

> That decision [in *Abbey Leisure*] in my judgment has altered the balance against the view that shareholders who enter into a company with articles allowing for compulsory transfer are bound to go through compulsory transfer provisions rather than exercising their statutory rights and are unreasonable if they do not accept the transfer provisions. Such a view of the legal position is no longer, to my mind, the guiding principle. There must be questions of fact. In some cases the petitioner may be held to be unreasonable because it can be seen that it would be unreasonable to refuse to follow the contractual term, in other cases it will not. But the broad brush approach that it is always reasonable to insist upon the articles and it is always unreasonable to refuse so to do is no longer, as I understand *Abbey Leisure*, the law as it must be applied.

The key issue is whether the valuation provided for in the articles is fair. In *Re a Company (No 00836 of 1995)*[5] the court stayed a s 459 petition as an abuse of process on the ground that the majority shareholder had made a pro rata offer to buy out the minority on a valuation to be provided by an independent accountant. The court found that such an offer gave the petitioner all the relief that he could realistically expect to obtain on his petition and it would therefore be an abuse to continue with the litigation.

Impact of s 459

It is clear from the foregoing discussion that the unfairly prejudicial provision has developed into an extremely valuable remedy for the minority shareholder, particularly but not exclusively for those in the quasi-partnership type of company. The provision has effectively provided a code of conduct for those involved in a quasi-partnership in terms of identifying the obligations as between majority and

---

20 *Re a Company (No 007623 of 1984)* [1986] BCLC 362; *Re a Company (No 004377 of 1986)* [1987] BCLC 94; *Re a Company (No 003843 of 1986)* [1987] BCLC 562; *Re a Company (No 003096 of 1987)* (1988) 4 BCC 80; *Re a Company (No 006834 of 1988), ex p Kremer* [1989] BCLC 365; *Re Boswell & Co (Steels) Ltd (Re a Company No 001562 of 1987)* (1989) 5 BCC 145; *Re Castleburn Ltd* [1991] BCLC 89.

1 [1991] BCLC 597, CA. See Law Commission *Shareholder Remedies, A Consultation Paper* (1996, No 142), paras 9.49–9.52.

2 [1991] BCLC 597, [1991] BCC 241. On the facts here the petitioner's decision was not unreasonable because of the many difficulties in an expert's determination of valuation under the articles.

3 [1990] BCLC 342, CA.

4 [1991] BCLC 597 at 604.

5 [1996] 2 BCLC 192.

minority shareholders and has significantly curtailed the ability of the majority to ride roughshod over the expectations of the minority. For example, the majority shareholders may use their voting power to exclude a minority shareholder from involvement in the management of the company but if they do so unfairly, then the petitioner will be entitled to relief under s 459.

The very width and scope of the jurisdiction may mean that use of the section has to be carefully controlled in order to prevent it being used as a means of oppression by a dissident shareholder[6] but to date there has been little evidence of undeserving minority shareholders acting in this way.

The section also provides a method of side-stepping many of the difficulties surrounding the rule in *Foss v Harbottle*[7] and the derivative action while it offers more appropriate relief than winding up on the just and equitable ground. The range of conduct covered and the flexibility of the relief offered means that it has rapidly become the most attractive solution for a dissatisfied shareholder.

REFORM OF UNFAIRLY PREJUDICIAL REMEDY

The terms of reference of the Law Commission's work on shareholder remedies (noted above with respect to the rule in *Foss v Harbottle)* included a review of the unfairly prejudicial remedy[8]. In that regard, the main concerns which emerged about s 459 related not so much to the scope of the provision but to the length and complexity of the proceedings[9]. The Law Commission found, for example, that the hearing of the petition in *Re Elgindata Ltd*[10] lasted 43 days, costs totalled £320,000 and the shares, originally purchased for £40,000, were finally valued at only £24,600[11]. As Scott V-C noted in *Re a Company (No 004415 of 1996)*[12], the tendency in s 459 cases is for the litigation to become a Chancery version of a bitterly contested divorce with grievances from the history of the marriage dredged up and hurled about in an attempt to blacken the opposing party.

In many ways these complaints about length and costs are complaints about civil litigation generally and are not problems peculiar to s 459 petitions. Bearing that in mind the Law Commission, drawing on the recommendations of Lord Woolf on the Civil Justice System[13], has concentrated on procedural issues and, in particular, on the importance of active case management of s 459 petitions[14].

---

6   See *Re a Company (No 007623 of 1984)* [1986] BCLC 362 at 367, per Hoffmann J; also *Re a Company (No 00314 of 1989)* [1990] BCC 221; *Re Castleburn Ltd* (1989) 5 BCC 652; *Re a Company (No 005685 of 1988), ex p Schwarcz (No 2)* [1989] BCLC 427; *Re a Company (No 007623 of 1984)* [1986] BCLC 362.

7   (1843) 2 Hare 461.

8   See Law Commission *Shareholder Remedies* (1997, Cm 3769), Law Com No 246 (hereafter Law Commission Report); also Law Commission *Shareholder Remedies, A Consultation Paper* (1996, No 142) (hereafter Law Commission Consultation Paper).

9   The applicants tend to put in issue anything remotely relevant resulting in complex factual investigations and costly cumbersome litigation: see Law Commission Report, paras 2.1-2.2; Law Commission Consultation Paper, para 14. 5.

10   [1991] BCLC 959.

11   See Law Commission Report, para 1.6, n14.

12   [1997] 1 BCLC 479, Ch D.

13   Access to Justice, The Final Report to the Lord Chancellor on the Civil Justice System in England and Wales (1996), commonly referred to as the Woolf Report; see also Law Commission Report paras 1.28-1.30; Law Commission Consultation Paper, para 11.4.

14   See Law Commission Report, Part 2; Law Commission Consultation Paper, Part 17. Case management involves reviewing and addressing such issues as the court's powers to order preliminary issues to be heard, to make orders for security for costs, to impose costs sanctions, and to exclude issues from

More substantively, the Law Commission recommended making provision for certain (rebuttable) presumptions in proceedings under s 459[15].

There would be a rebuttable presumption that, in certain circumstances,

(i) where a shareholder has been excluded from participation in the management of the company, the conduct will be presumed to be unfairly prejudicial by reason of the exclusion; and

(ii) if the presumption is not rebutted and the court is satisfied that it ought to order a buy out of the petitioner's shares, it should do so on a pro rata basis (ie without any discount to reflect the fact that the petitioner's holding is a minority holding)[16].

The presumptions would only apply to a private company limited by shares where all, or substantially all, of the members of the company are directors[17]; and where, immediately before the exclusion from participation, the petitioner held shares in his sole name giving him not less than 10% of the right to vote at general meetings of the company on all or substantially all matters[18]. The petitioner must have been removed as a director or has been prevented from carrying out all or substantially all of his functions as a director[19].

Surveys of s 459 proceedings consistently show this type of fact pattern and the outcome in the vast majority of cases is invariably that the court regards exclusion from participation in these circumstances as being unfairly

prejudicial and the respondent must purchase the petitioner's shares at a pro rata price. If that is the case, then there is little point in having long and expensive litigation to reach an outcome which can be predicted at the outset. The Law Commission itself conducted a review of 233 unfairly prejudicial petitions lodged in the High Court in 1994 – 1996 and found that 96% of the cases related to private companies; 82% of which had five or fewer shareholders; 64% contained allegations of exclusion from management; and in 69% of cases the remedy sought was a purchase order[20].

SECTION 459 AND THE WINDING-UP REMEDY

A further recommendation was that winding up should be added to the remedies specified in CA 1985 s 461 as available to a successful petitioner under s 459, in the interests of streamlining shareholders proceedings and giving the courts maximum flexibility[1].

However, in order to prevent petitioners from seeking a winding-up order in order to put pressure on the other side, a petitioner who intends to seek a winding-up remedy under s 459 will require the court's leave to do so[2]. Equally, a petitioner who intends

---

determination: see Law Commission Report paras 2.4-2.5. In other words, the whole emphasis is on the judiciary having a greater hand in controlling the progress of litigation: see Law Commission Consultation Paper, paras 11.29-11.33.

15 See Law Commission Report, paras 3.26-3.30 (a draft s 459A is included in Appendix A); the recommendation in the Report differs significantly from that originally proposed in Consultation Paper; see Law Commission Report, paras 3.2-3.25.

16 See Law Commission Report, paras 3.26-3.30; 3.54-3.62.

17 See Law Commission Report, paras 3.38-3.39; 3.48.

18 See Law Commission Report, paras 3.44-3.53.

19 See Law Commission Report, paras 3.40-3.43.

20 See Law Commission Report, para 3.13, Appendix J.

1 See Law Commission Report, paras 4.24-4.35.

2 See Law Commission Report, paras 4.39-4.41.

to petition for winding up on the just and equitable ground[3] in conjunction with an application under s 459 should also require the leave of the court to apply for the winding-up order[4].

EXIT ARTICLES

The Law Commission also recommended that an exit article should be included in Table A which would encourage shareholders to provide in advance for what is to happen if there is a dispute[5]. Such a provision would facilitate the exit of a shareholder from a company without having to litigate under s 459. However, as with the remainder of Table A, such provisions could still be excluded by the parties.

The main features of the proposed exit article are[6]:

- exit rights must be conferred by an ordinary resolution;
- every shareholder who is to have or be subject to exit rights must be named in the resolution and must consent to it;
- the resolution must set out the events in which the exit rights are to be exercisable[7];
- when an exit right is exercisable, the shareholder entitled to the right may require other shareholders named in the resolution to buy his shares at a 'fair price';
- those shares must be shares he held when the resolution was passed or shares acquired in right of them, eg on a bonus issue[8];
- the resolution must state how the 'fair price' is to be calculated[9];
- if the shares require to be valued, the resolution must say how the valuer is to be appointed[10];
- the purchase must be completed within three months;
- the resolution comes to an end when one of the named shareholders dies or disposes of his shares;
- the company cannot amend the resolution or the regulation without the consent of the named shareholders.

The Law Commission Report emphasises that the drafting of the regulation in this way requires the shareholders to make positive choices about, in particular, the basis of valuation and the choice of valuer. This is an attempt to meet concerns that such a regulation could operate unfairly[11].

The drawback with this provision is that it may seem too complex for the very small companies which are often involved in shareholder disputes. However, its inclusion in Table A may at least prompt the parties, or more likely their advisers, to consider whether a shareholders' agreement might be appropriate[12].

---

3   Ie under Insolvency Act 1986, s 122(1)(g), discussed above.
4   See Law Commission Report, para 4.42.
5   See Law Commission Report, paras 5.1-5.2.
6   See Law Commission Report, paras 5.11-5.32; the full text of the proposed regulation for inclusion in Table A is set out at Appendix C to the Report.
7   For example, the exit right could be exercisable by personal representatives on the death of a named shareholder.
8   The exit right would not apply to other shares which were transferred to him later.
9   See Law Commission Report, para 5.27.
10   See Law Commission Report, para 5.26.
11   See Law Commission Report, para 5.10.
12   See Law Commission Report, para 5.31.

CHAPTER 29

Public regulation by disclosure of information concerning companies

THEMES UNDERLYING DISCLOSURE OF INFORMATION

Disclosure of information by companies is one of those topics in company law where there is a danger of being overwhelmed by the volume of detailed statutory requirements. It is helpful, therefore, in looking at such a topic to keep in mind certain underlying instrumental themes which can impose some order on the mass of detail[1].

Disclosure as a means of influencing behaviour

The first theme is that the assumption behind many disclosure requirements is that behaviour can be influenced merely by requiring it to be disclosed, without the need of negative prohibition or positive regulation. If those who invest in, or manage, companies know that their activities will be subjected to public scrutiny, their behaviour will be modified to avoid public disapproval[2]. So runs the idea, although in several instances provision for ex post facto disclosure has had to be supplemented by requirements for prior approval by the parties affected or even by outright prohibition. Thus, concern over the terms of directors' service contracts seems to have been the motivation behind a provision introduced in 1967 that companies must keep a copy of any written service contract or, if not in writing, a written memorandum of its terms, available for inspection by members of the company[3]. If the members could see how the directors were providing for themselves, they might be more restrained in their generosity. Perhaps directors are not modest about their worth, however, for in 1980,

---

1   This chapter is mainly concerned with disclosure via a company's annual report and accounts, although other aspects of disclosure are referred to in this introductory section.
2   See, for example, Company Law Reform (Cmnd 5391), para 10 'openness in company affairs is the first principle in securing responsible behaviour' and para 165 'disclosure of information is the best gurantee of fair dealing and the best antidote to mistrust'. For a less enthusiastic view, see Sealy (1981) 2 Co Law 51–56. See also Loss 'Disclosure as Preventive Enforcement' in Hopt and Teubner (eds) *Corporate Governance and Directors' Liability* (1985), pp 327–335, Stevenson *Corporations and Information – Secrecy, Access and Disclsoure* (1980), pp 79–94 and 157–176 and Grover and Baillie *Proposals for a Securities Market Law for Canada: Vol 13 – Disclosure Requirements*, pp 378–389.
3   Section 318.

following a lead given some years earlier by the Stock Exchange, a requirement was introduced for prior approval by the general meeting of any director's service contract which the company might not be able to terminate within five years[4]. Likewise, the provisions requiring directors to disclose dealings in securities of their company and for the company to maintain a register of such dealings represent the earliest legislative attempt to discourage insider dealing[5]. The theory is that if members of the public generally can see that directors sold shares in the company shortly before a large loss was announced, the directors will feel so embarrassed they will desist from the sale. One of the problems, however, in relying on disclosure to affect behaviour is that the individuals concerned may not even know about the disclosure requirement. At any rate insider dealing on the Stock Exchange has since been made subject to specific prohibitions with criminal penalties for breach.

The type of information to be disclosed

The second underlying theme concerns the type of information that is required to be disclosed. Until 1967, it was invariably information that could be regarded as being of interest to investors in the company whether as shareholders or creditors. It was all information about the financial state of the company and the topic was treated in company law textbooks as one of investor protection. In the Companies Act 1967, provisions were first introduced requiring companies to disclose information that was more obviously in the public interest although still of relevance to investors. Since then requirements have been added for disclosure of information of particular interest to employees and arguments have been put forward for disclosure of information that would more fully reflect companies' social responsibilities[6]. Such information might relate to the interests of consumers of a company's products or of those who live in the locality where a company operates. Disclosure requirements can be seen, therefore, as reflecting, more clearly perhaps than anywhere else in company law, recognition of new interests, besides those of investors, in the way companies operate[7].

Disclosure to whom

Closely related to developments regarding what information must be disclosed are developments regarding to whom the information must be disclosed. This represents a third underlying theme. The main legislative requirements are for disclosure to shareholders and registration at Companies House. Although when the Companies

---

4   Section 319.
5   Sections 323–328 and Sch 13. These sections must not be confused with somewhat similar rules (in ss 198–220) which require public companies to be informed about and maintain a register of any dealings in any class of shares by holders of 3% or more of the class concerned. These were designed to stop substantial stakes in public companies being acquired in secret, a practice often known as warehousing.
6   For two excellent articles setting out detailed proposals, see 'The Case for a Social Audit' *Social Audit*, vol 1, no 1, p 4 and Imberg and Macmahon 'Company Law Reform' *Social Audit*, vol 1, no 2, p 3. See also Gray, Owen and Maunders *Corporate Social Reporting* (1987). As regards environmental reporting see: *Financial Reporting 1991–92* pp 53–76; ICAEW *Environmental Issues in Financial Reporting* (1996); KPMG *Annual Survey on Environmental Reporting*; Seventh Progress Report of the Advisory Committee on Business and the Environment (1997).
7   Persons with such interests will often be encompassed within the term stakeholders but that term seems limited to those with something to gain from the company's activities. People who live in the vicinity of a polluting factory may gain nothing from the company's activity yet have a clear interest in the way the company operates.

Registration Office was set up in 1844 there was a requirement for an audited balance sheet to be registered and thus disclosed to the public,[8] this was repealed in 1856[9] and even the preparation of accounts and the presentation of them to shareholders became optional[10]. The present legislative requirements relating to disclosure began in 1900 with an implicit requirement that an audited balance sheet be presented to the company in general meeting[11]. In 1907, the requirement for registration of an audited balance sheet reintroduced the idea of public disclosure of financial information[12].

The requirements have been added to in most if not all subsequent Companies Acts. The purpose of mandatory disclosure to the shareholders is to promote efficient management by requiring the management to account for their stewardship of the company[13]. In this respect disclosure is just one of a number of techniques used by company law to ensure the accountability of management to shareholders. It should be viewed alongside other techniques designed to facilitate the same end, such as the regulation of the relationship of the board of directors to the general meeting, the power of appointment and removal of directors[14], and the duty of directors to act in the best interests of the company and to exercise care and skill[15].

Assuming that the shareholders' interest lies in the most productive use of the company's resources, promoting the accountability of management to shareholders will indirectly serve the public interest in the creation of wealth for society. This public interest is in part the justification for disclosure via registration at Companies House. It seems likely though that this has more to do with prevention of fraud and creditor protection in view of the fact that only limited liability companies are obliged to file their accounts with the registrar of companies[16]. In addition to financial information, all registered companies are obliged to file information about the company's constitution, the officers of the company, the address of the registered office, the share capital, charges on company property and an annual return.

In the case of listed companies the Stock Exchange also imposes disclosure requirements[17]. A series of financial collapses, frauds and concern about levels of directors' remuneration led to the establishment of three ad hoc committees, each of which has made recommendations aimed at improving corporate governance in listed companies. Each of the committees is referred to by the name of its chairman. The Cadbury Committee[18] was set up in 1991 because of 'the perceived low level of

8   7 & 8 Vict c 110 (1844) s 43.
9   By the Joint Stock Companies Act 1856.
10 Provisions were included in the model regulations for management of the company contained in the Schedule to the Joint Stock Companies Act 1856. It has been suggested that the justification for apparently giving shareholders less protection may have been the provisions for Board of Trade Inspectors to be appointed at the request of shareholders that the Act also introduced. See Edey and Panitpakdi 'British Company Accounting and the Law: 1844–1900' in Littleton and Yamey (eds) *Studies in the History of Accounting* (1956), pp 356–379.
11 Companies Act 1900, s 23.
12 Companies Act 1907, s 21.
13 This view is supported by the evidence about the background to the changes in disclosure implemented in the 1948 consolidation. See Bircher (1988) 18 Accounting and Business Research 107.
14 Representation on the board of directors is a further technique and current demands for inclusion of non-executive directors on the boards of public companies and clarification of their role via the establishment of audit committees are a reflection of this. See [1987] Bank of England Quarterly Bulletin 252 and [1988] Bank of England Quarterly Bulletin 242. One way to encourage such practices is via disclosure: Stevenson *Corporations and Information—Secrecy, Assets and Disclosure* (1980), pp 171–176.
15 Takeovers or the threat of takeovers also serve to keep the management responsive to shareholders' interests. See ch 36 below.
16 Unlimited companies are exempted: s 254.
17 Listing Rules, ch 12.
18 *The Financial Aspects of Corporate Governance* (1992).

confidence both in financial reporting and in the ability of auditors to provide the safeguards which users of company reports sought and expected'[19]. It defined corporate governance as 'the system by which companies are directed and controlled' which encompasses the role of the shareholders and the auditors as well as the board of directors. Its main recommendation, as with the Greenbury Committee[20] on directors' remuneration, was for a Code of Best Practice with which listed companies would be expected to comply, whereas the Hampel Committee[1] preferred to rely on statements of broad principle rather than codes of practice. For each of the committees, however, increased disclosure of information is a key part of their recommendations for securing more responsible management in the interests of both shareholders and the public.

Apart from additional obligations in respect of reports to shareholders the Stock Exchange also requires disclosure to the Exchange immediately of any information necessary to enable holders of the companies listed securities and the public to appraise the position of the company and to avoid the establishment of a false market in its listed securities[2]. The purpose of this form of disclosure is to aid the efficiency of the securities market. Whether it does so or not has been a matter of dispute among economists[3]. It is, however, important to appreciate the difference in function between this form of immediate disclosure to the market[4] and other forms of financial disclosure which are more a matter of record and are intended to serve the other purposes outlined in previous paragraphs.

One other group whose interest in the activities of companies may be reflected in future legislative requirements for disclosure of information is employees. Already, several items to be included in the directors' report reflect the interests of employees, but as yet there is no legal requirement to provide any form of annual report to the employees[5]. The Industrial Relations Act 1971 contained a provision[6] requiring companies employing more than 350 people to issue an annual statement to each employee covering matters to be specified in regulations by the Secretary of State. The section was never brought into force and following the repeal of the Industrial Relations Act has not been re-enacted. Nevertheless among large companies the practice of supplying a special report to employees is increasingly common[7].

19 Ibid, para 2.1. For a blunt statement about the state of UK financial reporting at the end of the 1980s see the report by Chairman of the Accounting Standards Board reviewing the first five years of its operation: Financial Reporting Council 1995 Progress Report, p 12.
20 *Directors Remuneration* (1995).
1   *Committee on Corporate Governance* (1998).
2   Listing Rules 9.1-9.2.
3   See the material cited in Stevenson *Corporations and Information—Secrecy, Access and Disclosure* (1980), p 210, footnotes 18 and 19 and by Meier-Schwartz (1986) 8 Journal of Comparative Business and Capital Market Law 219. Useful extracts are contained in Posner and Scott *Economics of Corporation Law and Securities Regulation* (1980), chs 10 and 11. See also Keane *Efficient Markets and Financial Reporting* (1987) who suggests certain characteristics a worthwhile disclosure policy in relation to stock markets should possess.
4   This aspect of disclosure relates more to the issues discussed in chapter 34 on raising capital from the public than it does to the issues discussed in this chapter.
5   The Labour Government in 1977 was in favour of requiring companies to send the full report and accounts to employees. See The Conduct of Company Directors (Cmnd 7037), para 5. The Conservative Government elected in 1979 preferred to allow companies to choose whether and how information should be given to employees. See Company Accounting and Disclosure (Cmnd 7654), p 8.
6   Industrial Relations Act 1971, s 57.
7   *Financial Reporting 1990–91*, pp 113–133.

Disclosure according to type of company

We have seen that listed companies are subject to additional disclosure requirements imposed by the Stock Exchange. Gradually the fact that listed companies represent a discrete category with special problems requiring special solutions is also becoming recognised in legislative disclosure requirements. This is just one example of a more general proposition, that disclosure requirements will tend to vary according to the type and size of company and the needs of users of the information. This represents a fourth angle from which to look at disclosure requirements.

SOURCES OF OBLIGATIONS

The most important disclosure of information by companies is that contained in the financial statements and auditors' and directors' reports that together constitute the annual report and accounts. Historically, and in terms of extent of coverage, the most important influence on the content of these documents is the companies legislation which in turn now reflects the impact of the Fourth[8] and Seventh[9] Directives on the harmonisation of legislation on company and group accounts in the EC. The Fourth Directive was implemented in 1981 and the Seventh Directive in the Companies Act 1989. Because of the scale of the changes involved, the Companies Act 1989 not only reformed the law but also consolidated the changes with the existing law on company accounts. This has the advantage that all the relevant legislation is together in one statute. However, the Act also reinserted the consolidated material back into Part VII of the Companies Act 1985. Some care still needs to be taken to make sure that a reference to a section in that Part of the 1985 Act (ss 221–262A) is to the legislation as substituted in 1989. Throughout this chapter any references to sections will be to the substituted legislation unless otherwise made clear.

In addition to legislative requirements, however, there is a growing body of professional accounting requirements affecting the content of company accounts[10]. The professional accountancy bodies first began issuing Recommendations on Accounting Principles in 1942. In 1970 the Accounting Standards Steering Committee was formed, becoming the Accounting Standards Committee in 1975, responsible for issuing Statements of Standard Accounting Practice. The importance of these may be gauged from the fact that any significant departure from them must be disclosed and explained in the financial statements and if the auditors agree with the departure they must be in a position to justify it[11]. Doubts, however, arose about the ability of the Accounting Standards Committee to respond quickly and with enough authority to new developments in accounting including the increasing use of creative accounting techniques which some companies and their advisers were prepared to justify by reference to observing the letter of accounting rules while ignoring the purpose behind them[12]. In response to this a committee was appointed, under the chairmanship of Sir Ronald Dearing, to review the process of setting accounting standards, the relationship of standards to company law and the procedures for monitoring compliance with, and

---

8   EEC Council Directive 78/660, OJ 1978 L 222/11.
9   EEC Council Directive 83/349, OJ 1983 L 193/1.
10   A third source of obligations for companies listed on the Stock Exchange is provided by the Listing Rules, ch 12.
11   See the Foreword to Accounting Standards in *Accounting Standards* published by the ICAEW. *Financial Reporting 1988–89* Pt I contains an interesting review of developments in financial reporting during the period 1968–1988 showing the influence of accounting standards.
12   See Whittington (1989) 19 Accounting and Business Research 195.

enforcement of, standards. As a result of the committee's recommendations[13] a new institutional framework was set up. At the top, responsible for determining overall policy, is the Financial Reporting Council. Below the Council is the Accounting Standards Board which took over from the Accounting Standards Committee responsibility for issuing what are now called Financial Reporting Standards[14]. It has a number of advantages over its predecessor. It has a full-time chairman and full-time technical officer; it is not reliant solely on the accountancy profession for funding; it can issue new standards on its own initiative without first having to obtain the consent of the six professional accountancy bodies. Its authority is further enhanced by the existence of a third body recommended by the Dearing Committee. This is the Financial Reporting Review Panel which examines material departures from accounting standards by large companies, whether public or private, involving issues of principle or which might result in accounts not giving a true and fair view.

ACCOUNTING REFERENCE PERIOD, ACCOUNTING REFERENCE DATE AND FINANCIAL YEAR

Before discussing the statutory obligations regarding company accounts there are three terms that need to be defined. The first is the company's *accounting reference period* which is the period between successive accounting reference dates[15]. In the case of a company incorporated on or after 1 April 1996 its *accounting reference date* will be the last day of the month in which the anniversary of its incorporation falls[16]. It is by reference to the end of its accounting reference period that the time limit for the company's obligation to circulate accounts to shareholders, present them to the general meeting and deliver them to the registrar is calculated[17]. The period for which the accounts themselves are drawn up is called the *financial year*[18]. This must end on, or within seven days either side of, the company's accounting reference date, the precise timing being chosen by the directors[19]. The new financial year then begins immediately after the end of the previous one[20]. The effect of this is that, unless the company changes its accounting reference date, the accounting reference period which fixes the obligation to present accounts to the shareholders and registrar remains static, while directors have a limited degree of flexibility in fixing the financial year in respect of which accounts must be drawn up.

13 *The Making of Accounting Standards* (1988).
14 Accounting Standards (Prescribed Body) Regulations 1990, SI 1990 No 1667. For discussion of what role accounting standards should fill in the light of current problems in accounting, see Tweedie and Whittington (1990) 21 Accounting and Business Research 87. One of the long-term tasks for the Accounting Standards Board is likely to be involvement in harmonising international accounting standards. In 1995 the European Commission abandoned the idea of creating European accounting standards in favour of International Accounting Standards to be developed by the International Accounting Standards Committee: see Financial Reporting Council 1996 Progress Report. For a review of the new institutional reporting structure, see *Financial Reporting 1993–94*, pp 33–50.
15 Section 224(4), (5).
16 Section 224(3A). In the case of companies incorporated before 1 April 1996 see s 224(3). A company may alter its accounting reference date: s 225
17 Section 244.
18 Section 226(1).
19 Section 223.
20 Section 223(3).

PRESENTATION TO SHAREHOLDERS AND REGISTRATION

This is a matter which is governed by the Companies Act. The Act requires four documents to be presented to the shareholders and delivered to the registrar each year: the balance sheet, the profit and loss account, the auditors' report and the directors' report[1]. The content of each is discussed below but the disclosure obligations relating to them are linked. Within a specified time after the end of a company's accounting reference period a copy of each document must be laid before the general meeting[2] and, at least 21 days before that general meeting, a copy of every such document must be sent to each member and debenture holder in the company[3]. Also, within the time specified for laying the accounts before the general meeting, limited companies must file with the Registrar of Companies a copy of every document comprised in the accounts required to be registered by that category of company[4]. Unlimited liability companies are exempt from the obligation to file accounts[5] and the advantage of secrecy which this offers must be the main reason why a business opting for the corporate form might nevertheless opt for unlimited liability. The specified time for laying accounts before the general meeting and filing them with the Registrar is 10 months after the end of the accounting reference period for a private company and seven months for a public company[6]. The Stock Exchange, however, requires listed companies to issue accounts within six months of the period to which they relate[7].

THE BALANCE SHEET AND PROFIT AND LOSS ACCOUNT

Every company must prepare a profit and loss account for each financial year[8] and a balance sheet as at the last day of the year[9]. The profit and loss account is essentially a record of the financial fortunes of the company during the period of the account. It will show, therefore, not only the company's trading record for the period but also income received on investments and interest the company has had to pay out to its creditors. The balance sheet, on the other hand, is an indication of the financial state of affairs of the company at a particular date, showing the net assets of the company

---

1   The chairman's report, which has become a standard feature of company reports and accounts, is not a matter of statutory obligation.

2   Section 241(1). This enables shareholders to discuss the accounts; there is no statutory requirement that shareholders vote on the accounts. As part of the deregulation of private companies the members of a private company may by unanimous elective resolution dispense with laying accounts before the general meeting unless required by a member or the auditors to do so: s 252.

3   Section 238(1). As to the right of companies listed on the Stock Exchange to offer their members summary financial statements in place of the accounts and directors' report, see below pp 492-493. Where a private company has dispensed with laying reports and accounts before a general meeting they must be sent to shareholders at least 28 days before what would otherwise be the expiry of the period for laying the accounts before the general meeting: s 253(1).

4   Section 242(1). Which category a company is in depends on its size according to criteria based on turnover, assets and number of employees. See below p 494.

5   Section 254.

6   Section 244. Following complaints by the Public Accounts Committee in 1984 that only 42% of companies were up to date with filing their annual accounts, Companies House mounted an enforcement campaign. By 1990 around 86% of accounts were filed on time. In 1992 civil penalties for late filing were introduced: s 242A. The compliance rate is now around 95%: see the Department of Trade and Industry's Annual Report on Companies.

7   Listing Rules 12.42(e).

8   Section 226(1)(b).

9   Section 226(1)(a).

and how they are financed[10]. The profit and loss account and balance sheet must comply with detailed requirements of Sch 4[11]. They must also, since 1948, give 'a true and fair view' of the company's profit or loss for the financial year and of the state of affairs of the company as at the end of the year respectively[12].

There are three major issues that arise in relation to the drawing up of a balance sheet and profit and loss account: (i) content, ie what must be included; (ii) format, ie how must the material be presented; and (iii) valuation, ie what rules of measurement must be used. Broadly speaking, legislative requirements until 1981 concentrated on matters of content, leaving companies themselves to decide questions of format and valuation. In the Companies Act 1981, the UK implemented the Fourth Directive on the harmonisation of company accounts. Not only did the Fourth Directive require changes in the content of the accounts but for the first time legislation was required to prescribe the format of the balance sheet and profit and loss account and to include valuation rules. The result is that companies[13] must now prepare balance sheets in accordance with one of two alternative formats and profit and loss accounts in accordance with one of four alternative formats[14]. Moreover the items to be entered must follow the order of the chosen format[15]. Finally, accounting principles are prescribed with alternatives allowing for current cost accounting as well as or instead of historical cost accounting[16]. It should be noted, however, that the obligation to present a true and fair view prevails over the detailed statutory requirements so that if the requirements are insufficient to give a true and fair view additional information must be provided or, in special circumstances, the statutory requirements themselves may be departed from[17].

One of the problems raised by the phrase 'a true and fair view' is whether applicable Financial Reporting Standards must be followed for the accounts to show a true and fair view[18]. Accounting standards are not legally enforceable although professional practice requires that 'any material departure from an accounting standard, the reasons for it and its financial effects should be disclosed in the financial statements'[19]. The Dearing Committee[20] discussed whether accounting standards should be legally enforceable and concluded for two main reasons that they should not[1]. First, there would be a danger that companies and their advisers might seek ways round the precise letter

---

10 This refers to how the assets are represented in terms of funds attributable to the shareholders in the form of called-up share capital, share premium account, capital redemption reserve, non-distributable reserves and reserves in the form of accumulations of trading profit.

11 Section 226(3).

12 Section 226(2). See Lasok and Grace (1989) 10 Co Law 13; Evans [1990] LMCLQ 255; McGee (1991) 54 MLR 874.

13 There are special provisions applicable to banking and insurance companies contained in ss 255–255D and Schs 9 and 9A.

14 Schedule 4, Pt 1, s B.

15 Schedule 4, para 1.

16 Schedule 4, paras 9–34. Under historical cost accounting the value of assets is taken to be their cost or book value less any provision for depreciation. In times of high inflation, the profits of a company can appear overstated if no account is taken of the true cost of replacing assets. If a current cost basis is chosen, however, any information necessary to calculate the historical cost figures must also be supplied

17 Section 226(4), (5).

18 As to the impact on interpretation of 'a true and fair view' of the fact that having begun life as a provision of the Companies Act 1948 it is now contained in the Fourth and Seventh Directives, see Lasok and Grace [1988] JBL 235.

19 See the Foreword to Accounting Standards issued by the Accounting Standards Board (1993), para 19.

20 *The Making of Accounting Standards* (1988).

1 Ibid, para 10.2.

of legal requirements while ignoring the spirit of the provisions[2]. Secondly, keeping accounting standards not legally enforceable enables them to be drafted in more general terms and makes it possible to respond to new developments in accounting more quickly than would be the case if statutory changes were involved. The Committee did, however, recommend that there should be a legal requirement for public and large private companies to disclose particulars of and the reasons for any material departure from applicable accounting standards[3] and this has now been enacted[4].

The Dearing Committee also recommended that there should be a statutory rebuttable presumption to the effect that compliance with accounting standards is necessary to give a true and fair view[5]. Thus, if there were a material departure from accounting standards the onus would be on those arguing that the accounts nevertheless gave a true and fair view to show that they did. Their recommendation, however, was not enacted because it came too close to giving accounting standards legal force with the disadvantages of excessive legalism that might entail. In any case it is doubtful whether such a statutory presumption would make all that much difference. In an opinion given to the Accounting Standards Committee in 1983 leading counsel stated that 'the courts will treat compliance with accepted accounting principles as prima facie evidence that the accounts are true and fair. Equally, deviation from accepted principles will be prima facie evidence that they are not'. This was reinforced by a further opinion in 1993[6] which emphasised that the recognition of accounting standards in the companies' legislation as a result of changes made by the Companies Act 1989 increased 'the likelihood... that the Courts will hold that in general compliance with accounting standards is necessary to meet the true and fair requirement'[7].

Group accounts

Where a business is carried on through subsidiary companies an accurate impression of the overall financial position of the business will not be achieved unless the accounts of all the separate companies are looked at together. In 1948, therefore, legislation was introduced requiring the preparation of group accounts where a company had subsidiaries[8]. The legislation was revised as a result of the implementation in the Companies Act 1989 of the Seventh Directive[9] on the harmonisation of group accounts. Because the Directive requires the inclusion of unincorporated subsidiaries the terms now used are parent and subsidiary undertaking. Any company which has one or more subsidiary undertakings must prepare group accounts[10] unless the group qualifies as a small or medium-sized group[11], the parent is itself a subsidiary and is included in the

---

2   The Foreword to Accounting Standards, para 17, states that 'In applying accounting standards it is important to be guided by the spirit and reasoning behind them'.
3   Ibid, para 10.4. The Committee saw three purposes in this requirement: first, to bring to the attention of the whole board of directors any proposed material departure from accounting standards; secondly, to help the user to understand the accounts; thirdly, to facilitate the task of monitoring compliance with accounting standards.
4   Schedule 4, para 36A.
5   *The Making of Accounting Standards* paras 15.14–15.17.
6   Published as an Appendix to the Foreward to Accounting Standards.
7   See also Bird [1984] JBL 480 and *Lloyd Cheyham & Co Ltd v Littlejohn & Co* [1987] BCLC 303.
8   Interesting background to the introduction of group accounting is given by Bircher (1988) 19 Accounting and Business Res 3.
9   EEC Council Directive 83/349. OJ 1983 L 193/1.
10   Section 227(1).
11   Sections 248 and 249.

accounts of a larger group[12] or all a parent's subsidiaries are excluded from the group accounts for one reason or another[13].

Group accounts must consist of a consolidated balance sheet and profit and loss account[14]. The detailed requirements as to the form and content are set out in Sch 4A[15] but as with individual company accounts the overriding requirement is to give a true and fair view of the state of affairs as at the end of the financial year and of the profit or loss for the financial year[16].

Under the definition of holding and subsidiary companies that was laid down in 1948 there were three ways in which one company(S) became the subsidiary of another (P): first, if P was a member of S and controlled the composition of its board of directors; secondly, if P held more than half in nominal value of S's equity share capital. Thirdly, any subsidiary of S was also a subsidiary of P. The major problem with this definition, in practice, was that it could exclude situations where one company controlled another which factually, though not legally, would be described as its subsidiary. This led to disagreement as to whether, in order to give a true and fair view, group accounts should reflect the substance of the relationship between companies rather than the formal legal relationship. In 1980 a successful prosecution was mounted against a company for including in its consolidated accounts the results of a company which it factually controlled but which did not legally become its subsidiary until after the end of the financial year[17]. The DTI then reminded auditors that emphasis on substance should never be at the expense of formal legal requirements[18]. Relying on this, companies justified making deliberate use of controlled non-subsidiaries as a means of keeping assets or liabilities off the consolidated balance sheet[19].

As a result of implementation of the Seventh Directive there is now a completely new definition of parent and subsidiary undertakings for accounting purposes. The Seventh Directive provides for mandatory implementation by member states of tests based on legal control[20] while tests based on factual control are optional[1]. However, to help deal with the problem of off-balance sheet financing described above, the UK has implemented the tests based on factual control as well as those based on legal control[2]. There are now six ways in which an undertaking may be a parent undertaking (P) in relation to a subsidiary undertaking (S). These are where:

   (i)   P holds a majority of the voting rights[3] in S[4]. This may be contrasted with the previous test of holding a majority of the equity share capital which might or might not have voting rights attached;

  (ii)   P is a member of S and controls alone a majority of the voting rights[5] pursuant to an agreement with other shareholders or members[6];

---

12   Section 228.
13   Section 229(5).
14   Section 227(2).
15   Section 227(4).
16   Section 227(3). For a review of consolidated accounts see *Financial Reporting 1991–92*, pp 29–51.
17   See (1981) 2 Co Law 275.
18   See *Tolley's Company Law*, Appendix 3.
19   See Bird [1986] JBL 132.
20   EEC Council Directive 83/349, art 1(1)(a), (b), (d).
1   Ibid, art 1(1)(c), (2).
2   See McBarnet and Whelan (1991) 54 MLR 848 who discuss this in the context of the general debate concerning 'form versus substance'. They point out how the accountants' view based on financial substance differs from the lawyers' view based on legal substance.
3   For the meaning of voting rights, see Sch 10A, para 2.
4   Section 258(2)(a).
5   See fn 3.
6   Section 258(2)(d).

(iii) P is a member of S and has the right to appoint or remove directors who have a majority of the voting rights at board meetings[7]. This may be contrasted with the previous test of controlling the composition of the board of directors but not necessarily controlling the majority of votes cast at board meetings;

(iv) P has the right to exercise a dominant influence over S by virtue of a provision in S's memorandum or articles or by virtue of a control contract[8]. The phrase 'the right to exercise a dominant influence' is not defined in the Act. It is, however, laid down by statute that it must at least involve P having the right to direct the operating and financial policies of S and the directors of S being obliged to comply with such directions whether or not they are for the benefit of S[9]. A 'control contract' is a contract in writing which confers on P the right to exercise a dominant influence over S and which is both expressly authorised by the memorandum or articles of S and permitted by the law under which S is established[10]. Such provisions for control of one undertaking by another are almost completely unknown in the UK and so this test is not likely to be of great significance where the putative subsidiary is incorporated in the UK. This test for establishing the relationship of parent and subsidiary is in fact optional so far as member states are concerned under the Seventh Directive. It has been implemented in the UK, however, because it might be useful if the putative subsidiary is established in, say, Germany, where provisions for control of one undertaking by another are recognised by law[11]. There is also, under discussion in Brussels, a proposed Ninth Directive to harmonise the treatment of groups in areas of company law besides that of consolidated accounts. The Ninth Directive, if it is ever issued, is likely to provide for control contracts to be recognised by member states and including this provision in the accounting legislation could prove helpful in preparing the ground for the Ninth Directive;

(v) P holds a participating interest in S and either actually exercises a dominant influence over S, or P and S are managed on a unified basis[12]. A 'participating interest' means an interest in the shares of S held[13] on a long-term basis for the purpose of securing a contribution to the activities of any undertaking in the group or of the group as a whole[14]. Neither the term 'dominant influence' nor the term 'managed on a unified basis' is defined in the Act. In particular the statutory provision regarding the interpretation of the phrase 'the right to exercise a dominant influence' referred to above does not apply here[15]. The terms are taken straight from the Seventh Directive and are deliberately left undefined. This test for establishing a parent subsidiary relationship is also an option for member states in the Seventh Directive. It has been implemented in the UK in the hope that it will curb the use of off-balance sheet financing whereby assets or liabilities are acquired by controlled non-subsidiaries with the intention of keeping them off the consolidated balance sheet. Any statutory definition of the relevant terms would merely encourage attempts at evasion;

---

7   Section 258(2)(b).
8   Section 258(2)(c).
9   Schedule 10A, para 4(1).
10 Ibid, para 4(2).
11 See Wooldridge *Groups of Companies – The Law and Practice in Britain, France and Germany* (1981), pp 5–7.
12 Section 258(4).
13 By or on behalf of P or any of its subsidiary undertakings: s 260(4), (5)(a).
14 Section 260(1).
15 Schedule 10A, para 4(3).

(vi) Where P is a parent undertaking of S, it is treated as a parent undertaking in relation to all S's subsidiary undertakings[16].

The inclusion of tests for establishing a parent/subsidiary relationship based on factual control should help to curb the use of off-balance sheet financing and resolve some of the 'substance versus form' disputes between accountants and lawyers. However, there may continue to be cases of undertakings which are in fact controlled by the parent but do not fall within the new definition of subsidiary. It may be necessary to give more information about such undertakings than will be shown using the equity method of accounting in order to give a true and fair view of the state of affairs of those undertakings which are included in the group accounts. In such circumstances, in order to comply with the true and fair view requirements, the parent company effectively has two options. It may either give any necessary additional information by way of notes to the accounts[17]; or, in special circumstances, it may override the statutory provisions and include the controlled non-subsidiary in the group accounts[18].

As well as introducing a new definition of parent and subsidiary undertaking for accounting purposes the Companies Act 1989 also revised the definition of holding and subsidiary company for non-accounting purposes[19]. Under the non-accounting definition there are four ways in which a holding company/subsidiary company relationship can be established. Apart from using the terms company instead of undertaking and holding company instead of parent the four ways mirror four of the tests of parent/subsidiary relationship set out above[20]: the first three plus the sixth (the equivalent of the grandparent/grandchild relationship). It will be noticed that these are the tests of legal control and are capable of relatively precise application. The two tests based on factual control are not included in the definition for non-accounting purposes because they depend too much on an element of judgment about the relationship between the two companies. They were included in the accounting definitions because they were important to help control off balance sheet financing for which definitions that enabled the true substance of a relationship to be identified were necessary. In non-accounting contexts the need is far more for precision and certainty.

CASH FLOW STATEMENT

This statement is not required by either the Companies Act or the Stock Exchange but is required by accounting practice[1] for nearly all companies. The main exceptions are companies entitled as small companies to the exemptions from filing accounts with the Registrar of Companies[2] and subsidiary undertakings where at least 90% of the voting rights are controlled within the group and consolidated financial statements in which those subsidiaries are included are publicly available. Cash flow information is said to show the quality of the profit made by a company by showing the relationship

---

16   Section 258(5).
17   Section 227(5).
18   Section 227(6).
19   Sections 736 and 736A.
20   Pages 472–474.
1   Financial Reporting Standard 1. Cash flow statements replaced, as from 1991, statements of source and application of funds previously required by Statement of Standard Accounting Practice, No 10.
2   See below p 494.

between profitability and cash-generating ability. It also provides information with which to assess the liquidity, solvency and financial adaptability of the company[3].

VALUE ADDED STATEMENT

It is not only by using different bases for valuation that the financial position of a company can be shown in a different perspective. The profit and loss account is only one form in which the income generated by a business can be stated. It is moreover a form which can give the impression that the only point of a company's activities is to generate profits for the shareholders or proprietors. It identifies as profit, or accretions to shareholders' funds, the surplus the business has generated after deducting from the total receipts of the company all the outgoings the company has had to pay except dividends and funds retained for reinvestment. An alternative way of looking at the income generated by a company is to calculate the value added in the course of the company's business. This can be done by subtracting from the gross amount received on sale of the company's products, whether they are goods or services, the sum paid by the company to buy in goods or services from outside, but not deducting the cost of labour, ie wages and salaries, nor of capital, ie dividends and interest. The resulting figure is the value added or wealth created by the business during the year. The way in which this wealth or value is then divided among employees in the form of wages or salaries, providers of capital in the form of interest or dividends, the government in the form of taxation or is retained in the business for re-investment can then also be shown. This form of account thus views the company's operations as a combined effort by the providers of capital and labour although there is, as yet, no legal or accounting requirement to publish a value added statement[4].

NOTES TO THE ACCOUNTS

Apart from laying down the format and contents of the profit and loss account and balance sheet, the schedules also list various items that must be included in notes to the accounts. Many of these amplify or explain items in the profit and loss account or balance sheet but others require disclosure of information that goes beyond what would be regarded as being primarily relevant to an appreciation of the financial position of the company. Some of these are discussed below but this is not a comprehensive list.

Information about related undertakings   Under Sch 5 companies must include details of interests of the company or its group in subsidiaries, associates, joint ventures and other entities.

Disaggregation   Where a company has diversified into more than one business, it may be very helpful to users of the accounts to know the relative contribution different businesses make to the company's overall performance. The first legislative requirement[5] to include any form of disaggregation was in the Companies Act 1967 which required the directors' report to show the proportion of turnover and profitability

---

3 It has been suggested that had a cash flow statement been included in the 1989 accounts of Polly Peck International plc analysts might have identified the financial difficulties that became apparent in September 1990: see Pijper *Creative Accounting* (1994). For a review of cash flow statements see Financial Reporting 1992–93, pp 53–67.
4 Cf The Future of Company Reports (Cmnd 6888), paras 13–17.
5 The Stock Exchange introduced a requirement for listed companies in 1964.

in each class of business.[6] As required by the Fourth Directive[7], this obligation was transferred to the notes to the accounts (the effect being that it is now audited) and was extended to require an analysis of turnover by geographical area[8].

Directors' emoluments   One of the perennial concerns of company law is seeking to regulate directors' remuneration and the principle method used is to require disclosure of various aspects of directors' emoluments[9]. Since 1929 many Companies Acts have added to the disclosure requirements but the disquiet associated with the remuneration levels of directors in newly privatised utilities caused the matter to be looked at once again. The Greenbury Committee on Directors' Remuneration recommended far greater levels of disclosure of all forms of emoluments of directors of listed companies and these are now reflected in the Stock Exchange Listing Rules[10]. The statutory requirements[11] were then amended to underpin the Listing Rules and avoid duplication of them. At the same time amendments were made to the statutory disclosure requirements for unlisted companies, broadening the range of items required to be disclosed but reducing the detail of some items already required to be disclosed. Apart from salary, fees and expenses the range of items now covers the exercise of share options, benefits under long-term incentive schemes, pension contributions and benefits, compensation for loss of office and sums due to third parties for making available the services of any director. Listed companies are required to show the remuneration of individual named directors; unlisted companies are required to show the remuneration of the highest paid director if the aggregate of directors' remuneration exceeds £200,000.

Particulars of staff   In 1967, a requirement was introduced for the directors' report to disclose the average number of employees and their aggregate remuneration.[12] In accordance with a provision in the Fourth Directive[13] such information must now be given in the accounts (the effect being, as with figures for disaggregation, that it is now audited) and must include aggregate social security contributions and aggregate pension contributions and funding[14].

Loans, quasi-loans or credit transactions[15]   Detailed particulars[16] of transactions or agreements to enter into transactions involving loans, quasi-loans or credit transactions of a type described in s 330 must be disclosed in notes to the accounts[17], whether or not the transaction or arrangement was prohibited by that section[18]. As regards credit

---

6   Companies Act 1967, s 17.
7   EEC Council Directive 78/660, art 43.1(8).
8   Schedule 4, para 55. For an analysis of disaggregation in published accounts, see *Financial Reporting 1987–88*, pp 139–160.
9   The theory being that disclosure would moderate directors' generosity towards themselves. There may be some justification for thinking that instead it led to a leap-frogging exercise. See the observations by Sealy *Company Law and Commercial Reality* (1984), pp 28–29.
10   Listing Rules 12.43(x).
11   Schedule 6, paras 1–14.
12   Companies Act 1967, s 18.
13   EEC Council Directive 78/660, art 43.1(9).
14   Schedule 4, paras 56 and 94.
15   The provisions outlined under this heading and the next, contained in Sch 6, Pts II and III, supplement Pt X of the Act which deals with enforcement of fair dealing by directors. Plans to amend and clarify Sch 6 Pts II and III were published in a DTI Consultative Document in 1991 but have not so far been enacted.
16   Schedule 6, para 22.
17   Schedule 6, paras 15 and 16.
18   Schedule 6, para 19.

transactions, no disclosure is needed if the aggregate value of the credit granted to the director concerned or persons connected with such director did not exceed £5,000[19]. In addition the aggregate amount of any loans, quasi-loans or credit transactions to officers other than directors must be disclosed, except where the aggregate amount outstanding does not exceed £2,500[20].

Other transactions involving directors   Detailed particulars[1] of other transactions in which a director had a material interest must also be disclosed in notes to the accounts[2] unless the aggregate value of such transactions did not exceed £1,000, or, if it did, did not exceed the lesser of 1% of net assets or £5,000[3]. Every transaction between a company and a director of the company or its holding company or a person connected with such a director is deemed to be one in which the director is interested[4]. It is, however, open to a majority of the directors, other than the director interested, when preparing the accounts, to decide that the interest is not material[5].

SECURING COMPLIANCE WITH OBLIGATIONS IN PREPARATION OF ACCOUNTS[6]

Following recommendations made by the Dearing Committee[7] a new set of procedures for dealing with failure to comply with accounting requirements was introduced by the Companies Act 1989. The Committee recognised that the overriding objective should be to ensure that good accounting information is ultimately produced, rather than the punishment of transgressors. Accordingly, the criminal offence of laying before the general meeting or delivering to the registrar accounts which do not comply with the Companies Act was repealed. It is, however, appropriate for the criminal law to be involved where there has been a deliberate attempt to mislead and a new offence was introduced where directors approve annual accounts which they know do not comply with the requirements of the Act or they are reckless as to whether they comply or not[8].

The more important changes, however, were the introduction of new civil procedures for securing compliance with the accounting requirements. The procedures are based on three stages. First, directors now have an opportunity voluntarily to prepare revised annual accounts or a directors' report[9]. Since it cannot simply be open to directors to change their minds about something and prepare revised accounts, the

---

19 Schedule 6, para 24.
20 Schedule 6, Pt III.
1   Schedule 6, para 22.
2   Schedule 6, paras 15(c) and 16(c).
3   Schedule 6, para 25.
4   Schedule 6, para 17(1).
5   Schedule 6, para 17(2). An incentive is thereby given to directors to disclose their interests to their fellow directors.
6   A minority shareholder is not entitled to bring proceedings to enforce the provisions of the Companies Act as to the form and content of the accounts: *Devlin v Slough Estates Ltd* [1983] BCLC 497. The company may, of course, decide not to object to proceedings where there is a point of construction it wants resolved: *Henry Head & Co Ltd v Ropner Holdings Ltd* [1952] Ch 124, [1951] 2 All ER 994. See also *Tomberger v Gebruder von der Wettern GmbH* [1996] 2 BCLC 457, ECJ where a point of construction arising under the Fourth Directive was referred to the European Court of Justice in proceedings brought by a shareholder in a German company challenging the manner in which the company's accounts had been drawn up.
7   *The Making of Accounting Standards* (1988), ch 15.
8   Section 233(5).
9   Section 245.

revisions must be confined to those aspects in which the previous accounts and reports did not comply with the Act, plus any necessary consequential amendments[10]. Although compliance with accounting standards is not referred to, in so far as the annual accounts fail to comply with the statutory requirement to give a true and fair view because of failure to follow applicable accounting standards, the directors are permitted to make revisions in order to comply with accounting standards.

It may seem strange that if directors have realised the annual accounts or directors' report do not comply with the Act it is not compulsory for them to prepare revised versions. The hope is that by leaving it as a voluntary matter more directors will be encouraged to act in an openly responsible manner. However, the second stage in the new procedure empowers the Secretary of State, where there appears to him to be a question whether a company's annual accounts (but not, it seems, the directors' report) comply with the Act, to require the directors to give an explanation of the accounts or prepare revised accounts[11]. If neither a satisfactory explanation nor revised accounts are produced then under the third stage of the new procedure the Secretary of State may apply for a court order to the directors to prepare revised accounts[12]. The Secretary of State may authorise other bodies to make court applications in respect of defective accounts[13] and the Financial Reporting Review Panel has been so authorised[14]. The Review Panel has been authorised to apply to the court in respect of the accounts of any class of company but by agreement with the Department of Trade and Industry it concentrates on the accounts of large companies public and private[15]. In practice this includes all listed companies. Matters come to the attention of the Review panel from three broad sources: qualified audit reports or disclosed non-compliance with accounting standards or other requirements; referrals by individuals or companies; and press comment. By the end of 1996 the Review Panel had completed actions in 148 cases, in 37 of which some form of remedial action by the company was called for. In all cases the company has taken the action required by the Review Panel voluntarily so that the Panel has not, so far, had to seek any court orders under s 245B. Apart from requiring remedial action by companies the Panel's work also reveals areas of uncertainty or deficiencies in coverage in accounting standards which it draws to the attention of the Accounting Standards Board.

THE DIRECTORS' REPORT

The requirement for directors to make a report to the members was introduced in the Companies Act 1929. The principal purpose of the report remains its original one of reviewing the progress of the company's business. It is, however, the changes in the contents of the directors' report since 1967, more than changes in any of the other reports and financial statements, which have reflected the recognition of new interests, besides those of shareholders and creditors, in the activities of companies.

---

10   Section 245(2). See also the Companies (Revision of Defective Accounts and Report) Regulations 1990, SI 1990 No 2570 dealing with such matters as the audit of the revised accounts and whether the same auditors can be used, the manner in which changes in the revised accounts are indicated and explained, and the circumstances in which revised accounts need to be circulated to all shareholders.
11   Section 245A.
12   Section 245B.
13   Section 245C.
14   Companies (Defective Accounts) (Authorised Person) Order 1991, SI 1991 No 13.
15   The information that follows in the text is drawn from the annual report of the chairman of the Financial Reporting Review Panel published as part of the annual report of the Financial Reporting Council.

Contents

Information about directors   As well as the names of the directors,[16] the extent of any directors' interest in shares or debentures of the company or any holding or subsidiary company must be given[17] unless such information is given in the profit and loss account or balance sheet[18].

Information about the company's business   The report must state the principal activities of the company and any subsidiaries including any significant changes in those activities during the year[19]. It must also contain a fair review of the development of the business of the company and its subsidiaries and of their position as at the end of the financial year[20]. The directors' report is also useful as a place where companies can be required to amplify information in their balance sheets but in a manner which allows directors flexibility to reflect their companies' particular circumstances. If the market value of any interests in land held by the company differs substantially from its balance sheet value that must be disclosed if the directors think it is significant enough to require the attention of members and debenture holders being drawn to it[1]. As a result of a requirement in the Fourth Directive[2] the directors' report is now also used to draw attention to important events affecting the company or any of its subsidiaries since the date of the balance sheet[3].

Despite the fact that traditionally the accounts are regarded as reports to investors in the company and future prospects are very important to investors, there has until recently been no legal or regulatory requirements for companies to report any forecast of future prospects. A small step in that direction has now been taken, again as a result of a Fourth Directive requirement[4]. Directors' reports must now include an indication of likely future business developments[5] and of any research and development activities of the company and its subsidiaries[6]. Expenditure on research and development is of interest to shareholders not least because it represents an application of money which would otherwise generally be available to them[7]. This can be regarded, therefore, as complementary to the information directors' reports have always had to contain about the amount recommended as dividend[8].

Information about employment   Expenditure on research and development is also of interest to employees since such expenditure is likely to play a large part in maintaining

---

16   Section 234(2).
17   Section 234(3) and Sch 7, paras 2, 2A and 2B. For companies listed on The Stock Exchange this information must be brought up to date to a date not more than one month before the notice of meeting at which the accounts are to be presented: Listing Rules 12.43 (k).
18   Schedule 7, para 2(1).
19   Section 234(2).
20   Section 234(1)(a).
1   Schedule 7, para. 1.
2   EEC Council Directive 78/660, art 46.2(a).
3   Schedule 7, para 6(a).
4   EEC Council Directive 78/660, art 46.2(b) and (c).
5   Schedule 7, para 6(b) and (c).
6   Ibid.
7   It has been suggested that companies should be required to disclose actual expenditure on research and development. It is envisaged that disclosure would encourage such expenditure and help to counteract any tendency of management to concentrate on short-term profitability. See D W Budworth *Rewinding the Mainspring* (1987). For an analysis of present disclosure practices, see *Financial Reporting 1987–88*, pp 125–138. SSAP 13 dealing with accounting for research and development was revised in 1989.
8   Section 234(1)(b).

the competitiveness of the company and hence the future employment prospects it offers. The first requirement to report information specifically related to employment was a requirement introduced in 1967 to show the average number of employees and their aggregate remuneration[9]. Then, in 1974, the Health and Safety at Work etc Act[10] provided for the Secretary of State to make regulations for the disclosure of the company's arrangements for securing the health, safety and welfare at work of employees and for protecting other persons against risk to health and safety arising out of or in connection with the activities at work of those employees. This is an example of how disclosure could be used to back up and indirectly enforce observance of existing regulations. There is, after all, a good deal of legislation governing health and safety at work and the law provides for liability for injury arising from negligently produced goods or negligent production processes. But if the board of directors, in drafting their report, were obliged to consider the company's safety record and perhaps disclose the number of industrial accidents, days lost through such accidents, and successful prosecutions for breaches of health and safety legislation, it might result in companies giving more attention to health and safety matters. The exercise would not be expensive since the information will already be available to companies. It is sometimes suggested that information of this sort, not directly related to the financial performance of the company, will not be read by anyone but it is hard to imagine trade unions, consumers' organisations and an army of investigative journalists ignoring it. These arguments obviously appeal more to this writer than they did to successive governments from 1974 onwards because no regulations were ever made to implement the provision and it was repealed in 1996.

The belief that compelling directors to report on a matter may concentrate their minds on it is behind a requirement, introduced in 1980, for directors' reports in companies with over 250 employees to contain a statement of the companies' policy about employment of disabled persons[11]. The statement must deal with the company's policy on recruitment of disabled persons, employment and retraining for employees who become disabled and generally with the training, career development and promotion of disabled persons employed by the company.

Another addition to the statutory contents of the directors' report which reflects the changing interests in companies' activities is a requirement that where a company has over 250 employees, the directors' report must contain a statement describing the action taken during the year to promote employee involvement[12]. Specifically the statement must deal with arrangements for providing relevant information to employees, for consulting employees or their representatives on matters likely to affect their interests, for encouraging involvement of employees in the company's performance through an employees' share scheme or by some other means, and for achieving a common awareness on the part of all employees of the financial and economic factors affecting the performance of the company.

---

9   Companies Act 1967, s 18. This now has to be given in notes to the accounts (CA 1985, Sch 4, para 56).

10   Health and Safety at Work etc Act 1974, s 79 adding what became CA 1985, Sch 7, Pt IV until it was repealed in 1996.

11   Schedule 7, Pt III. The Government had announced that it did not intend to introduce legislation requiring the inclusion of detailed employment information in company accounts (Company Accounting and Disclosure (Cmnd 7654), p 5, para 2). It was persuaded to include this requirement for a more general statement, however, by the widespread support for it that emerged in the House of Commons during the Manpower Services Commission's review of the quota system for the employment of disabled people under the Disabled Persons (Employment) Act 1944.

12   Schedule 7, Pt V introduced by the Employment Act 1982, s 1.

Charitable and political donations   Provided the payment is intra vires[13] the directors of companies may use the companies' assets to make charitable or political donations without reference to the shareholders. Until 1967, there was no requirement even to inform shareholders about such payments[14]. In that year a provision was introduced whereby, if such payments exceeded a certain annual sum, this had to be reported in the directors' report. Currently donations must be disclosed if the aggregate amount exceeds £200 per annum. The purpose of the payment must be stated and in the case of payments for political purposes the recipient must be identified[15].

Particulars of acquisition of a company's own shares   As a result of a requirement in the Fourth Directive[16], directors' reports must now include particulars of any acquisition by the company of its own shares, whether through purchase, gift, forfeiture or surrender[17]. In addition, particulars must be given if the company acquires a beneficial interest in, or a lien or other charge on, its own shares[18]. In the case of a purchase of shares, the particulars must include the aggregate amount of the consideration paid by the company and the reasons for the purchase[19].

Policy and practice in paying trade creditors   An example of how disclosure is used as a regulatory technique in company law is provided by the additions to the statutory requirements for inclusion in the directors' report made in 1996 and 1997. Public companies, and any private company in a group headed by a public company unless the private company qualifies as small or medium-sized, must now include in the directors' report a statement of the company's policy on the payment of suppliers and must also disclose the company's payment practice by means of a formula which allows comparison between companies in terms of the length of time taken to pay trade creditors' invoices[20].

Auditing of the directors' report

In contrast to the profit and loss account, the balance sheet and the notes attached to those documents, the directors' report is not audited. Where the report consists of interpretation of or commentary in narrative form on the activities of the company, auditing is not necessary, nor would it be practicable. But increasingly the directors' report is required to include factual information and auditing would help to ensure not only the accuracy of the information but establish uniform methods of presentation that would enable comparisons to be made between different companies. A step has

13   If the payment is reasonably incidental to the company's business then the company will have an implied power to make it. If it is not the company will need an express power coupled with an independent objects clause and trust that if challenged the court will not rule it incapable of being an independent object. See *Simmonds v Heffer* [1983] BCLC 298 and *Evans v Brunner, Mond & Co Ltd* [1921] 1 Ch 359.

14   Proposals are from time to time introduced into Parliament for companies to be obliged to set up political funds which shareholders could contract out of, analogous to the position governing trade unions. See the debate on the clause proposed to the Companies Bill 1978: HC Official Report, SC F, 15 February 1979, cols 642–689. The debate identified many company law difficulties in making such a clause operate fairly and effectively which had been taken into account when the clause was proposed again to the Companies Bill 1980: see 980 HC Official Report (5th series), cols 58–64.

15   Schedule 7, paras 3–5.

16   EEC Council Directive 78/660, art 46.2(d).

17   Schedule 7, para 7(a).

18   Schedule 7, para 7(b) and (c).

19   Schedule 7, para 8(a).

20   Schedule 7, para 12.

been taken in this direction as a result of a requirement in the Fourth Directive[1]. Now the auditors must at least check whether information given in the directors' report relating to the financial year in question is consistent with that given elsewhere in the company's accounts[2].

THE AUDITORS' REPORT

Although the 1844 Joint Stock Companies Act[3] required that registered companies appoint auditors, that the auditors report on the balance sheet to the shareholders and that the balance sheet and report be registered, the Act was repealed in 1856[4]. The provisions about accounts and auditing became optional provisions in the model regulations for the management of company[5]. From 1867 railway companies, and from 1879 limited liability banking companies, were obliged to appoint auditors; but it was not until 1900 that the obligation was re-introduced for all registered companies[6].

Duties of auditors

The main statutory duty on the auditors is to report to the members of the company on the company's accounts[7]. The report must state whether the accounts of the company concerned are prepared in accordance with the Companies Acts and whether they give a true and fair view of the state of the company's affairs as at the end of its financial year and of the profit or loss for the financial year[8].

In preparing their report, the auditors must consider whether proper accounting records have been kept, proper returns adequate for their audit have been received from branches not visited by them, and whether the balance sheet and profit and loss account are in agreement with the accounting records and returns[9]. If they find that any of these circumstances is not the case, this must be stated in the report[10]. To enable them to prepare their report, auditors are given a right of access at all times to the books and accounts of the company[11]. They may also require any necessary information or

---

1   EEC Council Directive 78/660, art 51.
2   Section 235(3).
3   7 and 8 Vict, c 110 (1844), ss 34–43.
4   Joint Stock Companies Act 1856.
5   Ibid, Sch, Table B.
6   Companies Act 1900, s 21.
7   Section 235(1). See Lee 'A Brief History of Company Audits 1840–1940' in Lee and Parker (eds) *The Evolution of Corporate Financial Reporting* (1979), p 153. Following a recommendation in the report of the *Inquiry into the Supervision of the Bank of Credit and Commerce International* (1992) auditors of businesses in the regulated sector are under a statutory duty to report fraud or other material misconduct to the appropriate regulatory authority: Accountants (Banking Act 1987) Regulations 1994, SI 1994 No 524; Building Societies (Auditors) Order 1994, SI 1994 No 525; Auditors (Financial Services Act 1986) Rules 1994, SI 1994 No 526; Auditors (Insurance Companies Act 1982) Regulations 1994, SI 1994 No 449; Friendly Societies (Auditors) Order 1994, SI 1994 No 132.
8   Section 235(2). If the auditors qualify their report on either of these two grounds and the accounts are used as the basis for a distribution, the auditors must state, either in their report or in a separate statement at the time or subsequently, whether in their opinion the qualification is material in determining whether the distribution is lawful: s 271(3),(4). See *Precision Dippings Ltd v Precision Dippings Marketing Ltd* [1986] Ch 447, CA.
9   Section 237(1).
10   Section 237(2).
11   Section 389A(1).

explanations not only from officers of the company itself[12] but also, despite forebodings about the difficulties this might cause[13], from subsidiary companies, if incorporated in Great Britain, and their auditors[14]. If the auditors fail to obtain all the information and explanations necessary for the audit, this too must be stated in the report[15]. Although the directors' report is not audited, the auditors must consider whether information given in the directors' report relating to the financial year in question is consistent with the audited accounts and, if it is not, that fact must be stated in the auditors' report[16].

Apart from the obligations to report on the accounts, the auditors are also under a duty, so far as they reasonably can, to supply certain information if they find the company has failed to supply it. The categories of information relate to the emoluments of directors and certain transactions or arrangements between the company and its officers[17]. Any information which the auditors give in these categories must be included in their report.

As with the accounting requirements for companies, the duties of auditors are laid down by a combination of legislative provisions and professional practice requirements. The latter emanate from the Auditing Practices Board which was established in 1991 by the Consultative Committee of Accounting Bodies comprising the six principal accountancy bodies in the UK and Republic of Ireland[18]. Thus the auditors must state whether the audit was conducted in accordance with approved Auditing Standards. If the company is one which is obliged by accounting practice to produce a cash flow statement, the statement must be audited and the auditors' report must refer to whether it gives a true and fair view of such matters. Also, if the company's accounting procedures involve any departure from any of the Financial Reporting Standards, which the auditors do not regard as justified, that fact must be stated in their report. The wording of qualifications in auditors' reports is also governed by an auditing standard. The aim here is to indicate by a consistent use of language whether the qualification relates to a matter of uncertainty or disagreement and whether it is material, in the sense that knowledge of it would be likely to influence the user of the accounts, or fundamental, in the sense that it renders the accounts either meaningless or misleading[19].

Qualifications of auditors

The importance of the auditors' role has been emphasised by developments over the last century and a half designed to ensure their professional competence and independence. In 1844, when for a brief period auditors were first made compulsory for registered companies, it was common practice for the auditors to be shareholders in the company[20]. In 1900, when auditors were again made obligatory for registered companies, it was provided, in an attempt to ensure the auditors' independence from the management, that the auditor should not be an officer of the company[1]. This has been extended to disqualify as auditor of a company anyone who is, or is in partnership

---

12 Ibid.
13 Report of the Company Law Committee (Cmnd 1749), para 431.
14 Section 389A(3). If a subsidiary undertaking is not a body incorporated in Great Britain the auditors may require the parent company to take steps to obtain necessary information: s 389A(4)
15 Section 237(3).
16 Section 235(3).
17 Section 237(4) and Sch 6.
18 The Auditing Practices Board issues Statements of Auditing Standards which contain basic principles and essential procedures which are mandatory where relevant.
19 See Statement of Auditing Standard 600 *Auditors Reports on Financial Statements.*
20 Hadden *Company Law and Capitalism* (2nd edn, 1977), p 137.
1 Companies Act 1900, s 21(3).

with or is the employee of, an officer or employee of the company[2]. In 1929, companies ceased to be eligible for appointment as auditors but it was not until 1948 that a legislative requirement that auditors possess professional qualifications was introduced.

The legislation on the qualification of auditors was revised as a result of the implementation, in the Companies Act 1989, of the Eighth Directive[3] harmonising the rules for approval of persons to act as auditors of limited liability companies[4]. In order to be eligible for appointment as a company auditor, persons must be members of a recognised supervisory body[5] and be eligible under its rules to be appointed as company auditor[6] which in turn requires that they be independent of the company concerned[7] and hold appropriate qualifications[8]. As under the previous legislation, certain relationships with the company concerned which are fundamentally likely to be incompatible with independence are prohibited outright[9]. The Secretary of State is, however, given a new power to make regulations specifying other connections between auditors and clients that would make a person ineligible[10]. Independence will also be secured by the requirement that recognised supervisory bodies have rules designed to prevent persons from being appointed auditors in circumstances in which they have any interest likely to conflict with the proper conduct of the audit[11].

One of the most significant changes resulting from the implementation of the Eighth Directive allows corporate bodies to act as auditors[12]. Where a firm (which in the Act covers a partnership[13] or a corporate body[14]) is appointed company auditor it is the firm which must be a member of a recognised supervisory body and be eligible for appointment as company auditor under the rules of the relevant body. In terms of holding appropriate qualifications this means that the individuals within the firm responsible for audit work must hold appropriate qualifications and the firm must be controlled by qualified persons[15]. The controllers themselves may, of course, be individuals or firms and 'qualified' in this context means, for an individual, holding appropriate qualifications, and for a firm, being eligible for appointment as company auditor[16]. A firm is then 'controlled by qualified persons' if, but only if, a majority of

2   Companies Act 1989, s 27(1).
3   EEC Council Directive 84/253, OJ 1984 L 126/20.
4   The European Commission has also published a discussion paper on *The Role, Position and Liability of the Statutory Auditor within the EU* OJ 1996, c321/1.
5   Companies Act 1989, s 25(1)(a). As to recognised supervisory bodies, see ibid, s 30 and Sch 11.
6   Ibid, s 25(1)(b).
7   Ibid, s 27.
8   Ibid, Sch 11, paras 4 and 5. As to the meaning of appropriate qualification, see ibid, ss 31, 32 and Sch 12.
9   See text at fn 2 above.
10 Companies Act 1989, s 27(2). No regulations have yet been made but it is possible that a corporate auditor will be prohibited from auditing a company which is one of its shareholders.
11 Ibid, Sch 11, para 7. There have from time to time been suggestions that auditors who receive a lot of non-audit work from their audit clients could find their independence jeopardised. The Companies Act 1989 does not restrict non-audit work being undertaken by auditors but auditors' fees for both audit and non-audit work must now be disclosed separately in notes to the accounts: s 390A(3) and Companies Act 1985 (Disclosure of Remuneration for Non-Audit Work) Regulations 1991, SI 1991 No 2128.
12 Companies Act 1989, ss 25(2) and 53(1).
13 Where a partnership which is not a legal person is appointed as company auditor, the appointment is (unless a contrary intention appears) an appointment of the partnership as such and not of the partners: ibid, s 26(2).
14 Ibid, s 53(1).
15 Ibid, Sch 11, para 4(1)(b).
16 Ibid, Sch 11, para 5(2).

its members and members of its management body are qualified persons[17]. These are minimum requirements and there is nothing to stop a recognised supervisory body imposing more stringent conditions if it wishes[18]. Firms must also have arrangements to prevent individuals who do not hold appropriate qualifications and persons who are not members of the firm being able to exert influence over the conduct of the audit in a way which might affect the independence or integrity of the audit[19].

Appointment, removal and resignation of auditors

The Companies Act 1989 also made a number of changes to other rules affecting auditors. As with the accounts provisions, these changes were consolidated with the existing law and then reinserted into the Companies Act 1985. As before references to the Companies Act 1985 are to the new section numbers as inserted by the Companies Act 1989.

As befits a person whose function is to report to the members and who originally was frequently also a member, the auditor has always been appointed by the members[20]. Apart from the period between 1948 and 1976, when annual reappointment was not necessary, every general meeting at which accounts are presented has had to appoint an auditor to serve until the next such meeting[1]. This is still likely to be the most common method of appointment and is the only one open to public companies. However, as a consequence of the programme of deregulation of private companies two alternative methods of appointment are available to private companies[2]. First, a private company may by elective resolution dispense with laying accounts before a general meeting[3] in which case it must make an annual appointment at a general meeting held within 28 days of sending out the accounts[4]. Secondly, a private company may by elective resolution dispense with annual reappointment of auditors altogether[5] in which case the auditors are automatically deemed to be reappointed[6]. This possibility is open to a private company whether or not it has elected to dispense with laying accounts before a general meeting. It is a particular advantage, however, to a company which has made such an election since it obviates the need to call a meeting at all in connection with the accounts and auditors.

As far as the removal[7], replacement[8] or resignation of auditors is concerned, the legislative provisions reflect a trend towards strengthening the position of auditors vis-à-vis the management so that the auditors are in a better position to promote the accountability of management to the shareholders and indirectly thereby to serve the

---

17   Ibid, Sch 11, para 5(3)–(6). If a firm consists of only two members, therefore, both of them must be qualified. However, in the case of the management body, if that consists of only two persons, it is sufficient if one of them is qualified: para 5(3)(b).
18   See *Ownership and Control of Firms of Auditors under the Companies Act 1989* a Consultation Paper published by the Department of Trade and Industry in December 1989.
19   Companies Act 1989, Sch 11, para 7(2).
20   Section 385(2).
1   Ibid.
2   Certain categories of small company and dormant companies are exempt from having their accounts audited and thus exempt from the requirement to appoint auditors: s 388A(1).
3   Section 252.
4   Section 385A(2). If a general meeting to consider the accounts is validly demanded under s 253(2), the appointment is made at that meeting.
5   Section 386(1).
6   Section 386(2). As to terminating the appointment of auditors where such an election is in force, see s 393.
7   In this context this refers to removing auditors before the expiration of their term of office.
8   In this context this refers to appointing as auditor a person other than a retiring auditor.

public interest by ensuring the efficient use of the company's assets. Although auditors may always be removed by ordinary resolution[9], any resolution to remove or replace auditors requires special notice[10]. Furthermore auditors who for any reason cease to hold office[11] must deposit with the company a statement setting out any relevant circumstances[12] which they consider should be brought to the attention of members or creditors, or, if there are none the statement must say so[13]. If the statement does set out relevant circumstances the company must send a copy to everyone entitled to receive the accounts[14]. If auditors are being removed or replaced a general meeting will necessarily be held but if auditors resign and state that there are relevant circumstances they may requisition a general meeting[15]. Prior to any such meeting the auditors may require the company to circulate a statement[16]. Auditors due to be replaced will have the right to attend and speak at the meeting by virtue of still being auditors until they are replaced[17]. This right is specifically extended to auditors who have been removed[18], or who have resigned[19] notwithstanding that they are no longer in office.

Liability of auditors for negligence[20]

The standard of care and skill auditors must exhibit in carrying out their tasks is that of the ordinary reasonable auditor[1]. The most famous statement about what that standard entails is that of Lopes LJ that an auditor 'is a watchdog but not a bloodhound'[2]. In other words, auditors are entitled to trust the officers and employees of the company they are auditing and to rely on the figures presented to them. If, however, they have reason to be suspicious of any information presented they should make personal inquiries or checks[3]. In view of the professional qualifications now required, and the increased rights to inspect records and demand information and explanations, it may be doubted whether a standard based on nineteenth century case law is still appropriate. There is increasing support for the view that auditors should take on a more active role[4]. In a case involving auditors, although not in relation to the annual accounts, Lord

9   Section 391(1).
10 Section 391A(1).
11 Whether the auditors have been removed, replaced or have resigned.
12 That is, connected with their ceasing to hold office.
13 Section 394(1). Any resignation by auditors is ineffective unless accompanied by a s 394 notice: s 392(1).
14 Section 394(3). The company may instead apply to the court for a direction that the statement need not be sent out on the grounds that it secures needless publicity for defamatory matter: s 394(6).
15 Section 392A(2).
16 Where auditors are being removed or replaced: s 391A(3)–(6); where auditors are resigning: s 392A(3)–(7).
17 Section 390.
18 Section 391(4).
19 Section 392A(8).
20 In October 1994, the ICAEW issued a valuable guidance note on 'Managing the Professional Liability of Accountants'. See also *Professional Liability: Report of the Study Teams* ('The Likierman Report') published by the Department of Trade and Industry (1989), pp 17–40.
1   *Re London and General Bank (No 2)* [1895] 2 Ch 673 at 682–3, CA. On the duty to comply with FRSs Woolf J has said, 'While they are not conclusive so that a departure from their terms necessarily involves a breach of the duty of care, … they are very strong evidence as to what is the proper standard which should be adopted and unless there is some justification, a departure from this will be regarded as constituting a breach of duty': *Lloyd Cheyham & Co Ltd v Littlejohn & Co* [1987] BCLC 303 at 313.
2   *Re Kingston Cotton Mill (No 2)* [1896] 2 Ch 279 at 288, CA.
3   *Re Thomas Gerrard & Son Ltd* [1968] Ch 455, [1967] 2 All ER 525.
4   Baxt (1970) 33 MLR 413.

Denning said that an auditor must approach his task 'with an inquiring mind—not suspicious of dishonesty, I agree—but suspecting that someone may have made a mistake somewhere and that a check must be made to ensure there has been none'[5].

Although the auditors make their report to the members, they will owe a contractual duty of care to the company itself and this is the most likely way in which a negligent audit may give rise to liability. A typical situation might be where profits have been overstated in audited accounts and, as a result, tax or dividends have been wrongly paid by the company. If the wrongful payment is to the shareholders in the form of dividends but the company is still solvent a question may arise as to whether the company has truly suffered any loss[6]. If the company goes into insolvent liquidation it may claim that if the accounts had been accurate it would have ceased trading earlier and not incurred such a large deficiency by the time it was finally wound up. However, in *Galoo Ltd v Bright Grahame Murray*[7] it was held that, although the negligent audit of the accounts gave the company the opportunity to continue to incur trading losses, in terms of legal causation it did not cause the losses.

Although the auditors may be liable to the company for negligence in the auditing of the company's accounts, directors or senior employees of the company may also have contributed to causing the company's loss through dishonest or unauthorised dealing or concealment of matters from the auditors. Under the present rules of joint and several liability each party liable for contributing to causing the company's loss is liable for 100% of that loss, but with a right of contribution against the others who are also liable. In practice, however, it is the auditors who are sued because of their insurance cover. Following a recommendation of the Likierman Report[8], the Law Commission investigated the introduction of a system of proportionate liability whereby each party contributing to causing the company's loss would be liable to the company only for their proportionate share of the loss. The Law Commission, however, concluded there were more disadvantages than advantages in such a reform and recommended retaining the present rule[9].

Where the company is vicariously liable for the defaulting directors or employees the auditors may be able to plead contributory negligence against the company itself. After some uncertainty it is now accepted that contributory negligence can be a defence in breach of contract where the duty in contract is co-extensive with a parallel duty in tort[10]. Where the auditors' negligence is failure to identify and report dishonest or unauthorised dealing by directors or employees of the client company it has been argued that to hold the client company contributorily negligent is inconsistent with the function of auditors to report to shareholders on management; but this argument has not been accepted.[11] Often the same conduct of the directors or employees could be pleaded as

---

5   *Fomento (Sterling Area) Ltd v Selsdon Fountain Pen Co* [1958] 1 All ER 11 at 23, [1958] 1 WLR 45 at 61, HL.
6   In *Segenhoe Ltd v Akins* (1990) 1 ACSR 691, NSW Supr Ct, it was held the company had suffered a loss just as if the money had been paid to a third party. But in that case the shareholders received the dividend as part of a takeover package in which they all then sold their shares to the purchaser who was now in control of the plaintiff company. It might be different if the same shareholders who received the dividend were now causing the company to sue the auditors on the grounds the dividend should not have been paid.
7   [1995] 1 All ER 16, [1994] 1 WLR 1360, CA. See also *Bank of Credit and Commerce International (Overseas) Ltd v Price Waterhouse (No 3)* (1998) Times, 2 April.
8   *Professional Liability: Report of the Study Teams* (1989).
9   *Feasibility Investigation of Joint and Several Liability* (1996).
10 *Forikringsaktieselskapet Vesta vButcher* [1989] AC 852, [1988] 2 All ER 43, CA. Marshall and Beltrami [1990] LMCLQ 416, 417–420.
11 *Daniels v AWA Ltd* (1995) 16 ACSR 607, NSW Court of Appeal at 719–726. *Dairy Containers Ltd v NZI Bank Ltd* [1995] 2 NZLR 30, New Zealand High Court at 74–83. Compare Stapledon (1995) 13 Co & Secs LJ 513.

giving rise to either contributory negligence by the company or a third party contribution claim. It has been held that it must be considered in relation to contributory negligence first because the quantum of the auditors' liability must be established before any claim for contribution is assessed[12]. The conduct giving rise to the claim for third party contribution could be that of the very shareholders to whom the auditors' report is addressed if, for example, the shareholder is a parent company which has been giving instructions to its nominees on the board of its subsidiary[13].

Since 1929 what is now s 310 has prevented auditors limiting or excluding their liability, or being indemnified against liability, by contract with the company[14]. The Likierman Report[15] recommended that companies and their auditors should be able to agree a limit on the auditors' potential negligence liability which would then be subject to the test of reasonableness under the Unfair Contract Terms Act 1977[16]. The only change, however, has been to make clear that it is not contrary to s 310 for companies to effect insurance in respect of their auditors' liability in relation to the company[17]. The Companies Act 1989 did, however, make it possible for auditing firms to adopt the form of limited liability companies[18]. The government is also considering allowing the formation of limited liability partnerships which, unlike the present limited partnership, will allow all partners the benefit of limited liability and will allow limited liability partners to participate in management without losing the protection of limited liability[19]. However, adopting the form of a limited liability company or limited liability partnership will still not prevent the individuals performing the audit from being personally liable for breach of any duty of care imposed on them under the law of tort.[20]

Since the House of Lords' decision in *Hedley Byrne & Co Ltd v Heller & Partners Ltd*[1] the possibility of a wider duty of care in tort has opened up. Although by statute, the auditors' report is specifically made to the members of the company it does not follow that the auditors owe a duty of care to the members[2]. Even if a duty of care is established, if the loss suffered by the members is in reality just a reflection of a loss suffered by the company it is not recoverable by individual members in actions against the auditors[3]. If, for example, as a result of negligently audited accounts the company paid too much tax, although the company might well have an action against the auditors,

12   *Daniels v AWA Ltd*, above fn 11, at 726–735. *Dairy Containers Ltd v NZI Bank Ltd*, above fn 11 , at 85–87.

13   *Dairy Containers Ltd v NZI Bank Ltd*, above fn 11 at 87–98.

14   This would not affect exclusions of liability in relation to non-audit work. See Dugdale and Stanton *Professional Negligence* (2nd edn, 1989), pp 443–444.

15   *Professional Liability: Report of the Study Teams.*

16   Unfair Contract Terms Act 1977, s 11.

17   Section 310(3)(a).

18   Companies Act 1989, Sch 11, para 13.

19   *Limited Liability Partnership* DTI Consultation Paper (1997) URN 97/597. Such partnerships would not, in England and Wales, have corporate personality but this possibility is likely to be suggested by the Law Commission in a review of partnership law it is undertaking.

20   For analogous cases involving the personal liability of directors: *Fairline Shipping Corpn v Adamson* [1975] QB 180, [1974] 2 All ER 967; *Thomas Saunders Partnership v Harvey* (1989) 30 Con LR 103; *Kuwait Asia Bank EC v National Mutual Life Nominees Ltd* [1991] 1 AC 187 at 217F–220E, [1990] 3 All ER 404 at 420b–422f, PC; *Williams v Natural Life and Health Food Products Ltd* [1998] 2 All ER 577, HL. See also Dugdale and Stanton *Professional Negligence* (2nd edn, 1989), ch 27.

1   [1964] AC 465, [1963] 2 All ER 575, HL. See Baxt (1973) 36 MLR 42.

2   In *Barings plc v Coopers & Lybrand* [1997] 1 BCLC 427, CA, the parent company alleged a duty was owed by the auditors of its subsidiary arising from the circumstances in which work was done and information supplied relating to the preparation of consolidated group accounts. In *Bank of Credit and Commerce International (Overseas) Ltd v Price Waterhouse*, [1998] 15 LS Gaz R 32, CA, one company in a group alleged a duty of care was owed to it by auditors of other companies in the group.

3   *Caparo Industries plc v Dickman* [1990] 2 AC 605 at 626, [1990] 1 All ER 568 at 580, HL.

it does not follow that if the value of shares in the company fell as a result, individual shareholders could recover any loss suffered[4].

On the other hand, negligently audited accounts may well be relied on by investors in deciding whether to buy shares in or grant credit to the company. Although any loss suffered by such investors is a purely economic loss the decision in *Hedley Byrne & Co Ltd v Heller & Partners Ltd*[5] recognises that a duty of care to avoid such losses may be owed where a relationship of sufficient proximity can be established. The problem, in the words of Cardozo CJ in *Ultramares Corpn v Touche*,[6] is that 'if liability for negligence exists, a thoughtless slip or blunder, the failure to detect a theft or forgery beneath the cover of deceptive entries may expose accountants to a liability in an indeterminate amount for an indeterminate time to an indeterminate class'. The House of Lords emphasised in *Caparo Industries plc v Dickman*[7] that in deciding whether auditors owe a duty of care to persons who rely on the published accounts in buying shares the proximity of the relationship is vital and this requires more than just foreseeability of reliance[8]. It must be shown that the auditors knew the accounts or any statement made in connection with them would be communicated to the investor, either as an individual or as a member of an identifiable class, specifically in connection with a particular transaction, or transactions of a particular kind, and that the investor would be very likely to rely on them for the purpose of deciding whether or not to enter that transaction or a transaction of that kind[9]. The mere fact that a company is vulnerable to a takeover and that bidders usually rely on the accounts in deciding to launch a bid is not enough to establish proximity; nor is the fact that the bidder is already a shareholder in the company[10]. A duty of care has been found, however, where the price of shares to be transferred was fixed as a multiple of profits as shown in audited accounts to be procured jointly by vendor and purchaser[11] and in another case where an auditor assumed responsibility for the accuracy of audited accounts in statements made to a prospective purchaser knowing this was the final hurdle in the purchaser deciding whether to bid[12]. In contrast no duty of care existed in two cases where the

---

4   The principle is similar to one of those behind the rule in *Foss v Harbottle* (1843) 2 Hare 461, that the loss is suffered by the company and it is the company therefore that is the only proper plaintiff in any action, thus preventing a multiplicity of actions. Exceptions, allowing shareholders to sue for their share of the company's loss, have been recognized where the company itself is unable to sue: *George Fischer (Great Britain) Ltd v Multi Construction Ltd* [1995] 1 BCLC 260, CA, and where the company had settled its claim but the shareholders had not agreed to and were not bound by the terms of the settlement: *Christensen v Scott* [1996] 1 NZLR 273, NZ Court of Appeal. Distinguishing shareholders' losses from those of the company is one of the issues in *Barings plc v Coopers & Lybrand* [1997] 1 BCLC 427 CA.

5   See fn 1 above.

6   174 NE 411 at 450, 255 NY 170 at 179 (1931).

7   [1990] 2 AC 605, [1990] 1 All ER 568, HL.

8   The High Court of Australia expressed a similar view in *Esande Finance Corpn Ltd v Peat Marwick Hungerfords* (1997) 23 ACSR 71 a case concerning a creditor relaying on published accounts.

9   As to whether these factors are more easily shown to be present if in a contested takeover bid under the rules of the City Code on Takeovers and Mergers, after an identified bidder has emerged, express representations are made with a view to influencing the bidder to offer a higher price, see *Morgan Crucible Co plc v Hill Samuel Bank Ltd* [1991] Ch 295, [1991] 1 All ER 148 CA.

10   Thus the majority decision of the Court of Appeal in New Zealand in *Scott Group Ltd v McFarlane* [1978] 1 NZLR 553, that a duty of care was owed to a person making a take over bid for a company 'rich in assets but unimpressive in earnings' which meant that the auditors should have realised there was 'a plain risk of takeover and the virtual certainty that in such an event the accounts would be relied on by the offeror' (at 582), would not be followed in the UK nor it seems in Australia.

11   *Galoo Ltd v Bright Grahame Murray* [1995] 1 All ER 16, [1994] 1 WLR 1360, CA, as regards the initial purchase of shares in 1987.

12   *ADT Ltd v BDO Binder Hamlyn* [1996] BCC 808.

accounts were only draft unaudited accounts prepared to assist the vendors in negotiations where as all parties knew the purchasers would be expected to rely heavily on their own advisers.[13]

ADDITIONAL DISCLOSURE PROVISIONS APPLICABLE TO LISTED COMPANIES

Apart from complying with the statutory disclosure requirements and requirements of professional accounting practice, companies listed on the Stock Exchange must also comply with various additional disclosure obligations contained in the Listing Rules. Thus listed companies, besides producing an annual report and accounts required by statute, must also produce half-yearly or interim reports on their activities and profit or loss for the first six months of each financial year.[14] The report is not required to be audited but where it has been the auditors report including any qualifications must be reported in full.[15]

As regards the content of the annual report and accounts there are various additional requirements imposed by the Listing Rules on listed companies. For example listed companies must disclose the existence of any major shareholding, ie those of 3% or more.[16] In practice many listed companies go further and provide a breakdown of the relative size of shareholdings in the company and the number of shareholders in different categories, eg pension funds, insurance companies, bank nominees, individuals etc.[17]

Corporate governance reports

The most important aspect of additional disclosure required from listed companies stems from the debate on corporate governance. The principle recommendation of the Cadbury Committee was that directors of listed companies should abide by a Code of Best Practice[18] and the Listing Rules require that listed companies state in their annual report the extent of their compliance with the Code, identifying and giving reasons for any area of non-compliance[19]. Under the Code boards of listed companies are also required to include in the annual report a number of more specific reports. In one of these, that should appear immediately before the auditors' report, the directors must explain their responsibility for preparing the accounts.[20] The Cadbury Committee were concerned to correct any misapprehension that may have developed, partly as a result of the number of negligence actions against auditors, that auditors were the people responsible for the company accounts. Under the Companies Act it is the directors who are responsible if the company does not keep proper accounting records[1] and it is

---

13   *James McNaughton Papers Group Ltd v Hicks Anderson* [1991] 2 QB 113, [1991] 1 All ER 134, CA. *Peach Publishing Ltd v Slater & Co* [1998] BCC 139, CA.
14   Listing Rules 12.46–12.59. Interim reports by listed companies are the subject of an EEC harmonisation directive the contents of which are reflected in the Listing Rules: EEC Council Directive 82/121: Official Journal of the European Communities 1982 L 48/26.
15   Listing Rules 12.54.
16   Ibid, 12.43(1)
17   For an analysis of such disclosure practices, see *Financial Reporting* 1984–85, pp 1–12.
18   *The Financial Aspects of Corporate Governance* (1992).
19   Listing Rules 12.43 (j). The Cadbury Committee published a report on *Compliance with the Code of Best Practice* (1995). See also *Financial Reporting* 1995–96, pp 105–129.
20   Cadbury Committee *Code of Best Practice*, para 4.4. In the full report see para 4.28 and Appendix 3.
1   Section 221 (1), (5).

the directors who are obliged to prepare the balance sheet and profit and loss account[2]. The statement required by the Cadbury Code of Best Practice is designed, therefore, to bring home to directors that the accounts are first and foremost their responsibility.

The Cadbury Code of Best Practice also requires that directors of listed companies report on the effectiveness of the company's system of internal control[3]. This requirement was supplemented by Guidance from the Working Group on Internal Control which provided a set of criteria for assessing the effectiveness of internal financial controls and outlined the minimum requirements for directors' statements on the matter[4]. It was accepted by the Cadbury Committee that this would amount to compliance with the Code even though the directors' statement is limited to internal *financial* controls, thus excluding issues of efficiency, value for money and legal and regulatory compliance issues. The Guidance also only requires directors to state that they have reviewed the effectiveness of internal financial controls and does not require that they disclose any conclusions from that review. Most recently the Hampel Committee has recommended dropping the word 'effectiveness' from the Code of Best Practice altogether but that internal controls should extend beyond financial controls to include operational and compliance controls and risk management.[5]

A requirement that was originally contained in the Cadbury Code of Best Practice[6] but is now a separate provision of the Listing Rules is that directors of listed companies report that the business is a going concern, with supporting assumptions and qualifications as necessary[7]. The statutory requirement for all companies in drawing up their accounts is that they do so on the basis that the company shall be presumed to be carrying on business as a going concern[8] and so this additional requirement is designed to focus the board's attention on how legitimate this presumption is. The Hampel Committee pronounced itself satisfied with the present situation, commenting only that it seemed further legislation on this matter, which had been contemplated by the Cadbury Committee, now seemed unnecessary[9].

Another issue touched on by the Cadbury Committee was the question of greater disclosure of directors' remuneration[10] but this topic was then the subject of a separate report by another committee. The Greenbury Committee also promulgated a Code of Best Practice concerning various matters relating to directors' remuneration[11]. The Code is annexed to the Listing Rules[12] and listed companies are required to state whether or not they have complied with Section A of the Code (concerning the establishment and operation of remuneration committees) and to explain and justify any areas of non-compliance[13]. In addition listed companies must publish a report of the remuneration committee, if there is one, or of the whole board, if there is not, setting out the company's policy on remuneration, including whether it has given full consideration to Section B of the Code of Best Practice (concerning remuneration policy, service contracts and compensation). More significantly the report must give

2   Section 226.
3   Cadbury Committee *Code of Best Practice*, para 4.5.
4   *Internal Control and Financial Reporting: Guidance for Directors of Listed Companies* (1994) Working Group on Internal Control.
5   *Report of the Committee on Corporate Governance* (1998), paras 6.11–6.13.
6   Cadbury Committee *Code of Best Practice* para 4.6. In the full report see para 5.22.
7   Listing Rules 12.43 (v). See also *Going Concern and Financial Reporting: Guidance for Directors of Listed Companies* (1994) Working Group on Going Concern.
8   Schedule 4, para 10.
9   *Report of the Committee on Corporate Governance* (1998), para 6.17.
10   *The Financial Aspects of Corporate Governance* (1992), para 4.40.
11   *Directors Remuneration* (1995), ch 2.
12   It appears at the end, after the Schedules and before the index.
13   Listing Rules 12.43(w)

the amount of each of various specified elements in the remuneration package of each named director which information must also be audited.[14]

Summary financial statements

A quite separate development in relation to listed companies was the introduction by the Companies Act 1989 of the possibility for listed companies to offer .their shareholders a summary financial statement instead of the full report and accounts[15], provided certain conditions are satisfied[16]. Listed companies which wish to take advantage of this possibility must ascertain from each of their shareholders whether they wish to receive full accounts before sending them only a summary financial statement[17]. If shareholders were asked to opt for either full accounts or a summary financial statement the likelihood is that the majority would not opt for either—in a few cases by deliberate choice but in most cases through inertia. The legislation, however, does not go that far. It does though entitle companies to assume that shareholders who fail to respond are content to receive the summary financial statement[18]. The consultation that invites shareholders to express a preference must therefore warn them that, unless the company is notified, only a summary financial statement will be sent in future[19]. There are two methods of consultation. The original method which is still permissible involves sending shareholders a set of full accounts and a summary financial statement for the same financial year so that shareholders can see for themselves what the differences are[20]. A simpler method was introduced in 1995 whereby the company sends shareholders a notice describing the contents of a summary financial statement[1]. Shareholders are entitled at any time to request a full set of reports and accounts free of charge and all summary financial statements must contain a reminder to this effect[2].

The form and content of a summary financial statement is laid down by regulations[3]. These represent the minimum contents and companies are free to include more information subject to the overriding requirement that all the information is derived from the company's annual accounts and directors' report[4]. Certain statements are also required by statute including one by the auditors as to whether the summary financial statement is consistent with the full accounts and report and complies with the legislative requirements[5]. Companies are free to issue summary financial statements as part of a more wide ranging document which can therefore include information not

---

14   Ibid, 12.43 (x).
15   Section 251.
16   A company does not need to have authority in its memorandum or articles to send out a summary financial statement but it cannot do so if there is a prohibition or if there is a requirement that full accounts and report be sent to members: Companies (Summary Financial Statement) Regulations 1995, SI 1995 No 2092, reg 3.
17   Ibid, reg 4 (1).
18   Ibid, reg 4(2)(b).
19   Ibid, regs 5 (1)(a) and 6 (2)(a).
20   Ibid, reg 6. As summary financial statements are not registered at Companies House it is not possible to be certain how many companies offer them but by 1995 it was probably not more than 30: *Summary Financial Statements – The Way Forward* (1996) ICAEW.
1   Companies (Summary Financial Statement) Regulations 1995, SI 1995 No 2092, reg 5.
2   Section 251(2) and Companies (Summary Financial Statement) Regulations 1995, SI 1995 No 2092, reg 7(3).
3   Ibid, regs 7–10 and Sch 1 and 2.
4   Section 251(3).
5   Section 251(4).

derived from the annual accounts and directors' report; but it must be clear which part is the summary financial statement and which is not.

The main pressure for the introduction of summary financial statements came from companies, particularly recently privatised ones, which have a very large number of small shareholders and for which it may represent a cost saving. However, summary financial statements may also give an opportunity to present information in a way which is more readily understood and more meaningful to the majority of shareholders[6]. The restriction to listed companies is because the inequality of information that arises if some shareholders receive full accounts and others receive a summary matters far less where there is an active market in the shares. The information contained in a company's report and accounts is normally assimilated by the market and reflected in the share price very quickly so that shareholders are unlikely to be prejudiced if they choose to receive only the summary financial statement.

REDUCED DISCLOSURE OBLIGATIONS FOR PRIVATE COMPANIES

There are four levels at which private companies have been granted exemption in relation to disclosure requirements: first, at the level of content, ie what information must be included in the annual accounts; secondly in relation to whether or not the accounts should be audited; thirdly in regard to disclosure to shareholders; and fourthly in relation to the obligation to publish their accounts via registration at Companies House.

Historical developments

When the classification of private company was introduced in 1907 the principal advantage of adopting private company status was that fewer of its financial affairs had to be disclosed via registration at Companies House. With each successive Companies Act the advantage to private companies was whittled away until following the 1967 Companies Act only unlimited liability companies were left without the obligation to register, and thus publicly disclose, their accounts. After 1967 both public and private limited companies were subject to the same disclosure requirements and the advantage of adopting private company status had to all intents and purposes disappeared. It was against this background, under threat of the Second Directive applying to all UK limited companies, that the present definition of public and private companies was introduced in 1980. The implementation in 1981 of the Fourth Directive raised again the possibility of exempting private companies from the full disclosure obligations because the Fourth Directive contained provisions allowing member states to grant exemptions at the levels of content[7], audit[8] and registration[9] to private companies classified as small or medium-sized[10]. At first advantage was taken only of exemptions from registration requirements but in 1992 exemptions as regards content and in 1994 exemptions as regards audit were also introduced.

---

6   It is a comparable development in many ways to the use of mini prospectuses. Both developments reflect disclosure requirements being tailored to the needs of the user.
7   EEC Council Directive 78/660, arts 11, 27, 44, 45 and 46.
8   Ibid, art 51(2). This is only available to small companies.
9   Ibid, art 47(2)(3).
10 Under the Seventh Directive small and medium-sized groups may be exempted from preparing group accounts: EEC Council Directive 83/349, art 6.

Present exemptions

To qualify as small or medium-sized a company must satisfy two or more requirements concerning size of turnover, value of assets and number of employees[11]. For a small company the requirements are that its turnover does not exceed £2,800,000, its gross assets do not exceed £1,400,000 and its average number of employees does not exceed 50. For a medium-sized company the conditions are that its turnover does not exceed £11,200,000, its gross assets do not exceed £5,600,000 and its average number of employees does not exceed 250. Certain companies, however, are ineligible for the exemptions: public companies, banking or insurance companies, companies which are authorised persons under the Financial Services Act 1986 and any company in a group which includes an ineligible company[12].

Content The exemptions regarding the content of a company's financial statements and directors' report are available only to small companies[13] although small or medium-sized groups are also exempted from the obligation to prepare group accounts[14].

Audit Apart from dormant companies, which have been exempted from audit since 1981[15], it is only a sub-category of small companies, those with a turnover not exceeding £350,000, which are exempted from the obligation to have their accounts audited[16]. As a protection for minority shareholders, holders of 10% of the issued share capital, or 10% of the members where the capital is not divided up into shares, may require the company to have its accounts for the year audited[17].

Laying before the general meeting The shareholders in all private companies, whatever the size of the company, have had the right since 1989, by unanimous elective resolution to dispense with the requirement that the accounts and reports be presented to a general meeting[18]. Where such an election is in force, however, each member and the auditor of the company has the right to require that the accounts and reports are laid before a general meeting[19].

Registration The most extensive exemptions are those which apply to registration of reports and accounts at Companies House. First unlimited liability companies have never been required to file any accounts and thus have the same advantage of keeping their affairs confidential which unincorporated associations like partnerships possess[20]. Secondly since 1981 small-sized companies are only required to file an abbreviated balance sheet with many items aggregated together; they need not file profit and loss accounts or directors' reports at all and they are exempt from most of the requirements as to notes to the accounts[1]. Thirdly the exemptions permitted for medium-sized

11 Section 247(3)
12 Section 247A.
13 Section 246(1)–(4). The content requirements for small company accounts are now set out separately in Sch 8. A separate comprehensive Financial Reporting Standard for Smaller Entities was also published in November 1997.
14 Sections 248, 248A and 249.
15 Section 250. Since 1996 it has been possible for public as well as private companies to be dormant.
16 Section 249A(1), (3). For companies which are charities more restrictive conditions apply: ss 249A(2), (3A), (4), 249C and 249D.
17 Section 249B(2).
18 Section 252.
19 Section 253.
20 Section 254.
1   Section 246(5), (6).

companies are that they may file profit and loss accounts in which certain items are aggregated and need not disclose disaggregated figures for turnover[2].

FUTURE DEVELOPMENTS

The classification of private companies into small and medium-sized and the introduction of summary financial statements and corporate governance disclosure for listed companies is a recognition that companies cannot simply be classified as public and private, limited and unlimited as the Companies Acts have tended to do in the past. Companies of different sizes raise different problems requiring different solutions. The developments in the 1980s in relation to disclosure recognised this and have provided a framework for possible further changes.

If statutory obligations are introduced to produce financial statements covering cash flow and value added, it may well be appropriate to apply them, initially, to public and large or medium-sized private companies. The largest companies could also more easily accommodate developments in social responsibility reporting, allowing the gradual introduction of further disclosure requirements not related to purely financial matters. Already additional disclosure obligations relating to employment apply to companies with more than 250 employees. These could well be extended, for example, to require information about sex discrimination, equal pay or the employment of minority racial groups and, ultimately, to require such companies to circulate a special annual report to all employees.

---

2   Section 246A(3). In the 12 months to 31 March 1997 43.5% of accounts registered were full accounts, 0.6% were for medium-sized companies, 38% were for small companies; 1.8% were group accounts and 16% were in respect of dormant companies.

CHAPTER 30

Investigations and inspections

DTI INVESTIGATION POWERS

The main regulatory authority as far as companies are concerned is the Department of Trade and Industry acting under powers contained in the Companies Act 1985, the Financial Services Act 1986 and the Companies Act 1989[1].

These provisions enable the DTI to carry out investigations in a wide variety of circumstances. For example, the Department may investigate the affairs of a company; significant investigations in recent years have included investigations into Atlantic Computers, Barlow Clowes, Astra Holdings, House of Fraser Holdings, Guinness, Blue Arrow and London United Investments. Alternatively, the Department may focus more narrowly on a company's membership or on share dealings by directors or on insider dealing. Its powers also extend to the investigation of insurance companies and the conduct of investment businesses.

A common scheme is adopted under the various statutes which generally allow for investigations at two levels. The Department may appoint inspectors, frequently barristers and accountants, with extensive powers under the legislation[2]. In less complex or serious cases inspectors may not be required and it may be sufficient to require the production of documents and records for examination by DTI officials[3]. In fact the vast majority of investigations are conducted at this level (see table below).

On receiving a request for an investigation, the Department will make an initial assessment as to whether to proceed to a more formal consideration of the matter. Requests may be refused at the initial stage or subsequently because the matter does not come within the criteria for investigation, or the matter is shown to be one where an adequate civil remedy is available to the complainant, or where it is established that another body (such as the Serious Fraud Office) has begun or is about to start its own enquiries[4].

---

1   In addition, the Department has special powers of investigation and intervention under the Insurance Companies Act 1982.
2   Under CA 1985, s 432.
3   Under ibid, s 447.
4   See DTI *Companies in 1996–97* (1997), para 5, p 10.

In recent years the Department has made greater use of these investigation powers as can be seen from the table below. While appointments of inspectors are rare, the cases where they are used tend to be high profile instances where the sums of money involved may be enormous and the scale of the wrongdoing significant. The costs involved in using inspectors are also very high[5].

	1991–92	1996–97
Requests for investigation	1,563	3,294
Public as source of requests[6]	65%	55%
Accepted for formal consideration	850	1,297
Merited investigation	177	417
Investigation by Departmental officers under CA 1985, s 447	155	395
Investigation by inspectors under CA 1985, s 432	4	–

Source: DTI *Companies in 1995–96* (1996), Tables 1, 2, pp 9–10.

INVESTIGATIONS OF THE AFFAIRS OF A COMPANY

The Secretary of State for Trade and Industry may at his discretion appoint inspectors to investigate a company's affairs in certain circumstances[7]. This is the broadest enquiry into a company's business and as such is usually reserved for the most serious cases with the result that the very announcement of the appointment of inspectors will itself have an adverse impact on the company. The initiative for an appointment may come from the company but more usually comes from the Department.

The appointment of inspectors

An appointment may be made:

- in the case of a company having a share capital, on the application either of not less than 200 members or of members holding not less than one-tenth of the shares issued;
- in the case of a company not having a share capital, on the application of not less than one-fifth in number of the persons on the company's register of members; and
- in any case, on application of the company[7a].

An appointment may also be made if it appears to the Secretary of State that there are circumstances suggesting:

(1) that the company's affairs are being or have been conducted with intent to defraud its creditors or the creditors of any other person, or otherwise for a

---

5   For example, the costs of the investigation in the case of Atlantic Computers plc were £6.5m; Barlow Clowes, £6.25m; Blue Arrow plc, £3.5m; Astra Holdings, £2.2m; London United Investments, £2.2m. See DTI *Companies in 1995–96*; *Companies in 1994–95*; *Companies in 1993–4*; *Companies in 1992–93*.

6   The second major source of requests are DTI Directorates and Agencies, such as Companies Investigation Branches, the Insolvency Service, Companies House and Insurance Directorate: DTI *Companies in 1996–97* (1997), p 11.

7   CA 1985, ss 431, 432.

7a   Ibid, s 431(2).

fraudulent or unlawful purpose, or in a manner which is unfairly prejudicial to some part of its members; or

(2) that any actual or proposed act or omission of the company, including an act or omission on its behalf, is or would be so prejudicial, or that the company was formed for any fraudulent or unlawful purpose; or

(3) that persons concerned with the company's formation or the management of its affairs have in connection therewith been guilty of fraud, misfeasance or other misconduct towards it or towards its members; or

(4) that the company's members have not been given all the information with respect to its affairs which they might reasonably expect[8].

The Department is obliged to appoint inspectors only in the very rare instance where the court by order declares that a company's affairs ought to be investigated by inspectors[9]. Otherwise, appointment is at the discretion of the Department.

The Secretary of State must exercise the power to appoint inspectors in good faith but it is not incumbent upon him to disclose the material he has before him or the reasons for the inquiry[10], nor is he required to desist from making an appointment because it may involve investigating fraudulent or criminal activity which should be investigated by the police or the Serious Fraud Office[11]. The Department's investigation powers in the companies legislation are separate from, even if they overlap with, the investigation powers of other bodies[12].

Powers of inspectors

Once inspectors have been appointed, it is the duty of all officers and agents[13] (past and present) of the company[14] being investigated:

- to produce all documents[15] of or relating to the company:
- to attend before the inspectors when required to do so; and
- otherwise to give the inspectors all assistance in connection with the investigation which they are reasonably able to give[16].

The inspectors may extend these requirements to officers, agents or any other person who they consider is or may be in possession of information relating to a matter which they believe to be relevant to the investigation[17].

A person may refuse to disclose information on grounds of legal professional privilege[18] which essentially protects oral and written communications between legal

---

8   Ibid, s 432(2).
9   Ibid, s 432(1).
10   *Norwest Holst Ltd v Secretary of State for Trade* [1978] Ch 201, [1978] 3 All ER 280, CA.
11   *Re London United Investments plc* [1992] Ch 578, [1992] 2 All ER 842, CA.
12   *Re London United Investments plc* [1992] Ch 578 at 594, [1992] 2 All ER 842 at 849, CA.
13   For these purposes, 'agents' includes the company's bankers, solicitors and auditors: CA 1985, s 434(4).
14   If inspectors think it necessary for the purposes of their investigation to investigate also the affairs of another body corporate which is or at any relevant time has been the company's subsidiary or holding company, or a subsidiary of its holding company or a holding company of its subsidiary, they have power to do so: ibid, s 433(1).
15   For these purposes, 'documents' includes information recorded in any form; and, in relation to information recorded otherwise than in legible form, the power to require its production includes power to require the production of a copy of the information in legible form: ibid, s 434(6).
16   Ibid, s 434(1).
17   Ibid, s 434(2).
18   Ibid, s 452(1)(a).

advisers and clients, made in confidence, for the purpose of obtaining or giving legal advice. There is also a limited exemption regarding banking information. A person is not required to disclose any information or produce any document in respect of which he owes an obligation of confidence by virtue of carrying on the business of banking unless:

(a) the person to whom the obligation of confidence is owed is the company under investigation, or

(b) the person to whom the obligation is owed consents to the disclosure or production, or

(c) the Secretary of State authorises the inspectors to require the disclosure or production of the information[19].

In addition to the powers granted to the inspectors to demand the production of documents, the Secretary of State may seek a search warrant where there are reasonable grounds for believing that there are on any premises documents whose production has been required and which have not been produced[20]. A warrant may also be sought where there are reasonable grounds for believing that an offence has been committed[1], and that there are on any premises documents relating to whether the offence has been committed, and that the production of the documents could be sought but that, if production was so required, the documents would be removed or destroyed[2]. It is a criminal offence for an officer of a company to destroy or falsify documents relating to the company's affairs unless he proves that he had no intention to conceal the state of the company's affairs or to defeat the law[3].

The conduct of the investigation

Inspectors are masters of their own procedures and the responsibility for the conduct of the investigation is theirs alone[4]. Their functions are investigatory and not judicial[5] and the basic requirement is that the inspectors must act fairly and give people an opportunity to respond before criticising them[6]. If they are minded to criticise a person then they should put to him the substance of the evidence against him and their intended criticisms and give him an opportunity to respond, either at an interview or further interview or in writing if he so wishes[7].

Inspectors need not provide a witness with transcripts of witness statements against him nor will he be allowed to cross-examine witnesses. A transcript of his own evidence

---

19   Ibid, s 452(1A). This exemption does not apply if the bank itself is the company under investigation: s 452(1B).

20   Ibid, s 448(1). A warrant authorises a constable to enter and search the specified premises, to take possession of such documents, to take copies of any such documents, and to require any person named in the warrant to provide an explanation of them or to state where they may be found: s 448(3).

1   The offence must be one for which the penalty on conviction on indictment is imprisonment for a term of not less than two years: ibid, s 448(2)(a).

2   Ibid, s 448(2).

3   Ibid, s 450(1).

4   DTI *Investigation Handbook* (1990), Appendix B: Notes for the Guidance of Inspectors Appointed under the Companies Act 1985, para 1.

5   *Re Pergamon Press Ltd* [1971] Ch 388, [1970] 3 All ER 535, CA; *Maxwell v Department of Trade and Industry* [1974] QB 523, [1974] 2 All ER 122, CA.

6   *Re Pergamon Press Ltd* [1971] Ch 388, [1970] 3 All ER 535, CA.

7   See *Re Pergamon Press Ltd* [1971] Ch 388, [1970] 3 All ER 535, CA; *Maxwell v Department of Trade and Industry* [1974] QB 523, [1974] 2 All ER 122, CA.

will normally be supplied to him at an appropriate time during the course of the enquiry. Witnesses may be accompanied by legal advisers.

All persons may be examined on oath by the inspectors[8] and the statute provides that answers given by a person to a question put to him in exercise of these powers may be used in evidence against him[9]. The use of such evidence in criminal proceedings, following the outcome of the *Saunders* litigation, is discussed below. In general, evidence given by a person to inspectors is admissible in civil proceedings also[10] although this is subject to a qualified duty of confidence owed to the witness who must be given an opportunity to object to disclosure of the transcript[11].

If anyone fails to assist the inspectors or refuses to answer any question put to him for the purposes of the investigation or fails to produce any document then the inspectors may certify that fact in writing to the court which may punish the offender in like manner as if he had been guilty of contempt of court[12].

THE RIGHT OF SILENCE

While the denial of the right of silence which these provisions impose has been controversial, it had been thought that such powers are necessary if inspectors are to get to the root of serious financial and corporate malpractices. Indeed the Royal Commission on Criminal Justice in 1993 effectively endorsed such powers, noting that the powers operate in the interests of justice without unfairness to those being questioned who are persons in responsible positions with ready access to legal advice, charged with sophisticated offences which might otherwise go not merely unpunished but undetected[13].

The courts took a similar line. In *Re London United Investments plc*[14] the Court of Appeal held that as the common law privilege against self-incrimination had been impliedly excluded by the statutory provisions governing investigations, those subject to investigation were not entitled to rely on the privilege as entitling them to refuse to answer the inspectors' questions[15]. Likewise in *R v Seelig*[16] the court rejected a challenge to the admissibility as evidence in criminal proceedings of admissions made to DTI inspectors conducting an investigation of a company's affairs.

However, the position must be reviewed now in the light of the decision in the *Saunders* case.

---

8   CA 1985, s 434(3).
9   Ibid, s 434(5).
10   See *London & County Securities Ltd v Nicholson* [1980] 3 All ER 861, [1980] 1 WLR 948 (transcripts of statements to inspectors by auditors of insolvent company were admissible in civil proceedings brought by liquidator against the auditors for negligence).
11   *Soden v Burns, R v Secretary of State for Trade and Industry, ex p Soden* [1996] 3 All ER 967, [1996] 1 WLR 1512, Ch D.
12   CA 1985, s 436. For an example of a case where inspectors did certify a refusal to the court under similar (but not identical) provisions governing investigations into insider dealing (Financial Services Act 1986, ss 177, 178(1)): see *Re an Inquiry under the Company Securities (Insider Dealing) Act 1985* [1988] AC 660, [1988] 1 All ER 203, HL.
13   Report of the Royal Commission on Criminal Justice (Cm 2263, 1993), para 30, p 57.
14   [1992] Ch 578, [1992] 2 All ER 842, CA.
15   See also *R v Saunders* [1996] 1 Cr App Rep 463, 140 Sol Jo LB 22, CA; *R v Seelig* [1991] 4 All ER 429, [1992] 1 WLR 148, CA; *R v Harris* [1970] 3 All ER 746, [1970] 1 WLR 1252.
16   [1991] 4 All ER 429, [1992] 1 WLR 148, CA.

Saunders v United Kingdom

Saunders had been the chief executive of Guinness, a major listed public company, which had taken over Distillers in a highly controversial takeover in the mid-1980s. Inspectors were subsequently appointed by the DTI to investigate the affairs of Guinness and the outcome was criminal proceedings against a number of people, including Saunders, with respect to an illegal share support scheme uncovered by the inspectors which had been used to secure the takeover of Distillers.[16a] Saunders was convicted of various offences in a trial where the prosecution relied heavily on the transcripts of interviews between him and the inspectors. He brought a case against the UK Government under the European Convention on Human Rights challenging the use of such evidence in criminal proceedings on the grounds that it was a breach of the due process provisions of the Convention.

The European Court of Human Rights found that aspects of his trial did depart from the basic principles of fair procedure[17]. The unfairness arose from the use in the criminal trial of information disclosed by Saunders when questioned by DTI inspectors. He had been compelled to answer their questions, there being no right of silence in such circumstances, and was in effect compelled to incriminate himself. This was a violation of art 6.1 of the European Convention on Human Rights which provides that in the determination of any criminal charge, everyone is entitled to a fair hearing by an independent and impartial tribunal. The public interest in combating fraud could not be invoked to justify the use of answers compulsorily obtained in a non-judicial investigation to incriminate him at his trial.

The Department of Trade and Industry is studying the impact of this decision on its investigation powers generally under the Companies Act 1985 and related Acts. Its actual impact may in fact be limited[18]. As noted above, the *Saunders* case deals solely with the issue of the use of inspectors' transcripts in subsequent criminal cases and, in anticipation of the decision[19], the DTI had for some time ceased to use such material in that way. The Department may feel therefore that the position is not significantly altered and the powers of the Companies Act 1985 are still valuable in obtaining information and in directing investigators to other sources of information which might be used in any subsequent criminal prosecution. This effectively puts the Department on the same footing as the Serious Fraud Office[20].

On the other hand, there is a body of opinion that criminal proceedings are in any event an inappropriate method of dealing with corporate fraud. This decision, if it renders criminal proceedings more difficult, may lend support to the view that corporate

---

16a See DTI *Guinness plc Report of the Inspectors following Investigations under ss 432(2) and 442 of the Companies Act 1985* (HMSO, 1997).

17 *Saunders v United Kingdom* (Case 43/1994/490/572) [1997] BCC 872. The European Court did not award any damages to Saunders (he had sought approximately £5m) nor did it speculate on whether the outcome of the criminal trial would have been any different had the prosecution not made use of the incriminating statements. The Court of Appeal prior to this ruling had upheld his conviction: *R v Saunders* [1996] 1 Cr App Rep 463, [1996] Crim LR 420, CA.

18 Although the statutory provision, CA 1985, s 434(5), will require amendment. See *R v Morrissey, Staines* (1997) Times, 1 May, CA: it is for Parliament to amend the statute and the courts have no power to give effect to the judgment of the European Court of Human Rights.

19 The European Commission on Human Rights had concluded in 1994 that there had been a violation of art 6.1 of the Convention so the decision of the Court did not come as a surprise.

20 Under the Criminal Justice Act 1987, s 2, the Serious Fraud Office can compel witnesses to answer questions but the answers cannot be used later against witnesses unless they change their story. This power assists with the detection of the offence but the evidence to prove it in court must be obtained by a different route: see Report of the Royal Commission on Criminal Justice (Cm 2263, 1993), para 28, p 56. See the guidelines issued by the Attorney General on the use of compelled answers (1998) NLJ, 13 February.

wrongdoing is better dealt with by civil sanctions and fines rather than criminal proceedings.

Inspectors' reports

As they conduct their investigations, the inspectors must keep the Department informed as to progress and may, and in certain cases must, make interim reports[1]. If it appears to the Secretary of State that criminal matters have come to light and those matters have been referred to the appropriate prosecuting authority, he may direct the inspectors to take no or only limited further steps in the investigation[2]. The purpose here is to avoid unproductive and unnecessary enquiries. Once their investigation is completed, the inspectors will prepare a final report for the Department[3].

The publication of inspectors' reports is left to the discretion of the DTI and it is the policy of the Department to publish reports if it is in the public interest where these relate to public companies[4]. The Department can appoint inspectors on the basis that their reports will not be published[5] and, in that case, it is Departmental practice not to announce their appointment[6].

In other cases, the Secretary of State may, if he thinks fit, forward a copy of the report to the company's registered office[7] and may furnish a copy on request and on payment of the prescribed fee to certain persons such as any member of the company which is the subject of the report, or any person whose conduct is referred to in the report, or the auditors of the company, or the applicants for the investigation[8].

The Secretary of State may, if he thinks fit, cause any such report to be printed and published[9]. In exercising his discretion as to whether to publish the report, the Secretary of State is required to act in the public interest after taking such advice as he considers appropriate[10]. In particular, he is entitled to take the view that early publication might be prejudicial to further inquiries and possible criminal proceedings[10].

Inspectors' reports are frequently highly critical of named individuals encouraged, perhaps, by Lord Denning's comments in *Re Pergamon Press Ltd*[11]:

> They [inspectors] should be subject to no rules save this: they must be fair. This being done, they should make their report with courage and frankness, keeping nothing back. The public interest demands it.

The DTI Investigation Handbook advises inspectors that they should exercise restraint when making critical comment and should do so only to the extent that it is necessary for a proper appreciation of their report[12].

---

1   CA 1985, ss 437(1), 437(1A).
2   Ibid, s 437(1B).
3   Ibid, s 437(1). In the very rare case where inspectors are appointed following an order of the court then the Secretary of State must furnish a copy of any report to the court: s 437(2).
4   DTI *Companies in 1995–96* (1996), para 17, p 12.
5   CA 1985, s 432(2A).
6   DTI *Companies in 1995–96* (1996), para 17, p 13.
7   CA 1985, s 437(3)(a).
8   Ibid, s 437(3)(b).
9   Ibid, s 437(3)(c).
10 *Lonrho plc v Secretary of State for Trade and Industry* [1989] 2 All ER 609, sub nom *R v Secretary of State for Trade and Industry, ex p Lonrho plc* [1989] 1 WLR 525, HL.
11 [1971] Ch 388 at 400, [1970] 3 All ER 535 at 540, CA.
12 DTI *Investigation Handbook* (1990), Appendix B: Notes for the Guidance of Inspectors Appointed under the Companies Act 1985, para 34, p 44.

In *Fayed v United Kingdom*[13] the European Court of Human Rights rejected a claim that publishing highly critical reports without allowing the individuals concerned to vindicate their position in a court of law was a breach of the due process provisions of the European Convention on Human Rights. The court found that the investigation procedure was an investigation carried out in the public interest to ensure the proper conduct of the affairs of public companies. It was not an adjudication and the procedure adopted was surrounded by considerable safeguards to ensure fair procedures. The court also thought that directors of large companies must tolerate wider limits of acceptable criticism than private individuals[14].

In the light of this endorsement of the process by the European Court of Human Rights, it is regrettable that the Department of Trade and Industry seems less inclined of late to publish reports and has taken a power to appoint inspectors on the basis that their report will not be published[15]. As noted above, the practice is then not to announce that inspectors have been appointed at all.

The announcement of investigations and the publication of reports serve a valuable public function in a number of ways. Reports inform the public that the Department charged with responsibility for the regulation of companies in the public interest is discharging that responsibility. They have a deterrent effect on other companies and directors who may be acting in a similar way. They inform investors, creditors, analysts and the financial media as to the method of operation employed in companies which have collapsed or lost significant sums of money and alert them as to sharp practices. Reports have shown not just incompetence and dishonesty on the part of executive directors but also how auditors, non-executive directors, bankers and lawyers have on occasion not performed in an altogether satisfactory manner. Criticisms of the publication of reports have come from sectors which perhaps have most to fear from reports disclosing how they have discharged their duties. To paraphrase Lord Denning in *Re Pergamon Press* quoted above, the Department should publish these reports with courage and frankness, holding nothing back. The public interest demands it.

A copy of any report of inspectors is admissible in any legal proceedings as evidence of the opinion of the inspectors in relation to any matter contained in the report[16] and is admissible in proceedings brought by the Secretary of State under the Company Directors Disqualification Act 1986[17] as evidence of any fact stated therein[18]. Also the contents of inspectors' reports may properly be taken into account by the court when considering a petition for the winding up of a company brought by the Secretary of State on the just and equitable ground[19].

---

13   (1994) 18 EHRR 393, ECtHR. This case concerned the report into the takeover by the Fayeds of the House of Fraser, the content of which has always been disputed by the Fayeds.

14   *Fayed v United Kingdom* (1994) 18 EHRR 393 at 433, ECtHR. See also *Saunders v UK* (Case 43/1994/490/572) [1997] BCC 872 at 887.

15   CA 1985, s 432(2A) inserted by CA 1989, s 55.

16   CA 1985, s 441(1).

17   Ie under Company Directors Disqualification Act 1986, s 8 (application by the Secretary of State for a disqualification order on grounds of unfitness following investigation).

18   CA 1985, s 441(1); this includes evidence in the form of third party statements: *Re Rex Williams Leisure plc* [1994] Ch 350, [1994] 2 BCLC 555, CA (a case under CA 1985, s 447, discussed below). This is an implied statutory exception to the hearsay rule.

19   Ie under IA 1986, s 124A. This too is an implied statutory exception to the hearsay rule: see *Re SBA Properties Ltd* [1967] 2 All ER 615, [1967] 1 WLR 799; *Re Armvent Ltd* [1975] 3 All ER 441, [1975] 1 WLR 1679; *Re St Piran Ltd* [1981] 3 All ER 270, [1981] 1 WLR 1300; *Savings and Investment Bank Ltd v Gasco Investments (Netherlands) BV* [1984] 1 All ER 296, [1984] 1 WLR 271. A contributory may also rely on the report to support a winding-up petition: *Re St Piran Ltd* [1981] 3 All ER 270, [1981] 1 WLR 1300.

Outcome of an investigation

There are a number of possible outcomes to any investigation. As noted above, the Department may petition to have the company wound up on public interest grounds[20]. This power is used relatively frequently, particularly to close down companies which are attracting considerable amounts of capital from the public such as unauthorised insurance or investment companies. Recent examples have involved companies offering exceptional returns to investors in ostriches and pyramid selling schemes.

The Department may seek a disqualification order under the Company Directors Disqualification Act 1986[1].

Criminal proceedings may also be instituted, subject now to the inability to make use in criminal proceedings of evidence obtained in witness interviews by inspectors following the finding by the European Court of Human Rights in the *Saunders* case discussed above.

The Secretary of State is also empowered to take civil action on behalf of the company[2] or to petition the court for relief under the unfairly prejudicial provision[3] but in practice these powers are never used.

The DTI may take no direct action itself but will pass the report and information obtained by the inspectors to other regulatory bodies such as the Bank of England, the Securities and Investments Board (now renamed the Financial Services Authority) and the Treasury as well as professional bodies such as the Law Society and the Institute of Chartered Accountants[4].

PRODUCTION OF DOCUMENTS

As noted above, the appointment of inspectors is reserved for the most serious cases. In most instances, the Department of Trade and Industry prefers to use its powers to secure the production of documents for examination[5] unless they are inadequate because of the nature of the case. Investigations of this nature are usually carried out by the Department's own officials[6]. They are not announced by the Department and there is no provision for the publication of any reports of such investigations. This power enables the Department to embark on discreet and speedy fact-finding investigations with minimum fuss and publicity[7]. It also ensures that the company concerned is not the subject of adverse speculation before an investigation has determined whether any wrongdoing has actually occurred.

---

20   Ie under IA 1986, s 124A.
1   Ie under CDDA 1986, s 8. A failure to apply for a disqualification order following a critical report can only be challenged if the Secretary of State's refusal to apply was perverse, i.e. if the facts demonstrated that the only possible course open was to apply: *R v Secretary of State for Trade and Industry, ex p Lonrho plc* [1992] BCC 325.
2   CA 1985, s 438.
3   Ibid, s 460.
4   Ibid, s 451A. See DTI *Companies in 1996–97* (1997), para 28, p 16.
5   Ie under CA 1985, s 447.
6   Provision is made in the statute for the power to be exercised by the Department's officials or 'any other competent person': ibid, s 447(3). This enables the Department to use external investigators, usually from accountancy firms, in order to smooth the workload and minimise backlogs in the Department: see DTI *Companies in 1996–97* (1997), para 10, p 12.
7   The Department aims to complete such investigations within 90 days: DTI *Companies in 1996–97* (1997), para 11, p 12.

The extent of the power to require the production of documents

The Secretary of State may at any time, if he thinks there is good reason to do so, give directions to a company requiring it, at such time and place as may be specified in the directions, to produce such documents[8] as may be so specified[9]. The Secretary of State may also at any time, if he thinks there is good reason to do so, authorise an officer of his or any other competent person[6], to require a company to produce forthwith any documents which the officer or other competent person may specify[10]. These powers also extend to any person who appears to be in possession of the documents[11].

The DTI Investigation Handbook notes that there is no statutory definition of 'good reason' for these purposes but it is taken to include grounds for suspicion of fraud, misfeasance, misconduct, conduct unfairly prejudicial to shareholders or a failure to supply shareholders with information which they may reasonably expect to obtain[12].

The power to require the production of documents includes the power to take copies of them, and to seek explanations of them from any person, and where the documents are not produced, to require the person who was required to produce them to state where they are[13].

A failure to produce the documents or provide an explanation when required is an offence[14]. In the case of non-production of any documents, it is a defence for a person in default to prove that the documents were not in his possession or under his control and it was not reasonably practicable for him to comply with the requirement to produce them[15]. A statement made by a person in compliance with a requirement to produce documents may be used in evidence against him[16] subject now to the decision in *Saunders v United Kingdom*, discussed above.

As before with regard to inspections, provision is made for non-disclosure where the document would be covered by legal professional privilege[17]. As far as bank confidentiality is concerned, production of documents relating to the affairs of a bank customer is not required unless it is necessary to do so for the purpose of investigating the bank or the customer is a person subject to the requirement to produce documents for examination[18].

The provisions governing the use of search warrants[19] and making it an offence to destroy or falsify documents[20], noted above in relation to inspections, apply also with regard to the production of documents.

---

8   For these purposes 'documents' includes information recorded in any form; and, in relation to information recorded otherwise than in legible form, the power to require its production includes power to require the production of a copy of the information in legible form: CA 1985, s 447(9).

9   Ibid, s 447(2).

10   Ibid, s 447(3).

11   Ibid, s 447(4).

12   DTI *Investigation Handbook* (1990), para 31, p 13. See also *R v Secretary of State for Trade, ex p Perestrello* [1981] QB 19, [1980] 3 All ER 28: the powers must not be exercised for any ulterior motive.

13   CA 1985, s 447(5). It is an offence for a person, in purported compliance with any requirement to provide an explanation or make a statement, to provide or make an explanation or statement which he knows to be false in a material particular or to recklessly provide or make an explanation or statement which is so false: s 451.

14   Ibid, s 447(6).

15   Ibid, s 447(7).

16   Ibid, s 447(8).

17   CA 1985, s 452(2).

18   Ibid, s 452(3); or subject to the equivalent provision relating to insurance companies.

19   Ie ibid, s 448.

20   Ie under ibid, s 450.

Security of information obtained

No document or information obtained under these powers may be disclosed without the consent of the company to which it relates, except to a competent authority[1], and unauthorised publication or disclosure is an offence[2]. However, there are numerous exceptions to this prohibition on publication or disclosure.

First, the information may be disclosed to a competent authority. The competent authorities for these purposes are listed in the statute and range from the Secretary of State at the Department of Trade and Industry to any inspector or authorised person appointed under the companies, financial services or insurance legislation, the Treasury, the Bank of England, the Director of Public Prosecutions and any constable[3]. The Inland Revenue is not included.

Secondly, a large number of gateways are set out in the legislation[4] which authorise publication or disclosure where it is required, inter alia:

- with a view to the institution of, or otherwise for the purposes of, criminal proceedings;
- with a view to the institution of, or otherwise for the purposes of, any proceedings under certain provisions of the Company Directors Disqualification Act 1986;
- for the purposes of enabling or assisting any inspector appointed under the Companies Act 1985, Part XIV, or under certain provisions of the Financial Services Act 1986, to discharge his functions;
- for the purpose of enabling the Secretary of State to exercise any powers conferred on him by the enactments relating to companies, insurance companies or insolvency;
- for the purpose of enabling an official receiver to discharge his functions under the insolvency legislation;
- with a view to the institution of, or otherwise for the purposes of, any disciplinary proceedings relating to the exercise by a solicitor, auditor, accountant, valuer or actuary of his professional duties;
- with a view to the institution of, or otherwise for the purposes of, any disciplinary proceedings relating to the discharge by a public servant of his duties;
- for the purpose of enabling or assisting an overseas regulatory authority to exercise its regulatory functions.

Thirdly, the restriction on publication or disclosure does not preclude publication or disclosure for the purpose of enabling or assisting any public or other authority so designated by statutory instrument to discharge its functions.[4a] A large number of authorities, including the Insolvency Practitioners Tribunal, the Panel on Takeovers and Mergers, the Director General of Fair Trading and the Monopolies and Mergers Commission, have been so designated[5].

---

1 Ibid, s 449(1).
2 Ibid, s 449(2).
3 Ibid, s 449(3).
4 See ibid, s 449(1)(a)–(1)(m).
4a Ibid, s 449(1B).
5 See Financial Services (Disclosure of Information) (Designated Authorities No 2) Order 1987, SI 1987/ 859; Companies (Disclosure of Information) (Designated Authorities) Order 1988, SI 1988/1334; Financial Services (Disclosure of Information) (Designated Authorities) (No 6) Order 1989, SI 1989/ 2009.

Outcome of an investigation of documents

As is clear from the large number of gateways noted above, the information obtained following a requirement to produce documents may be used in similar ways to information gathered by inspectors. The Secretary of State may use the information obtained to petition for a winding up on the just and equitable ground[6] or to apply for a disqualification order under the disqualification legislation[7]. Criminal proceedings may be instituted[8] and information passed to other regulatory and professional bodies.

INVESTIGATIONS INTO MEMBERSHIP

The DTI also has power to investigate company membership, again either by appointing inspectors or by using departmental officials[9]. In practice these powers are rarely used[10].

Power to appoint inspectors

The Secretary of State, where there is good reason to do so, may appoint one or more inspectors to investigate and report on the membership of any company, and otherwise with respect to the company, for the purpose of determining the true persons who are or have been financially interested in the success or failure (real or apparent) of the company or able to control or materially to influence its policy[11]. In this instance, the appointment of the inspectors may define the scope of their investigation and in particular may limit the investigation to matters connected with particular shares or debentures[12].

Many of the provisions noted above in relation to inspections apply here also[13]. The investigation can extend to subsidiaries and other companies in the group[14]; witnesses must produce documents, attend before the inspectors when required to do so, and assist the inspectors with the possibility that their statements may be used in evidence against them[15], subject now to the decision in *Saunders v United Kingdom*, noted above; a failure to assist may be punished as a contempt of court[16]; reports of inspectors may be published subject to the right of the Secretary of State to omit certain elements[17]. The standard provisions relating to legal professional privilege and bankers' confidentiality apply[18]; provision is made for search warrants where necessary[19]; and it is an offence to falsify or destroy any documents[20].

These provisions apply to officers and agents of the company and to all persons who are or have been, or whom the inspector has reasonable cause to believe to be or

6   Ie under IA 1986, s 124A.
7   See *Re Rex Williams Leisure plc* [1994] Ch 350, [1994] 2 BCLC 555, CA; *Re Looe Fish Ltd* [1993] BCLC 1160, [1993] BCC 348; *Re Samuel Sherman plc* [1991] 1 WLR 1070, [1991] BCC 699.
8   Subject to the constraints imposed by the decision in *Saunders v United Kingdom* noted above.
9   Ie under CA 1985, ss 442, 444.
10 See DTI *Companies in 1996–97* (1997), Table 2, p 11. Inspectors have not been appointed since 1992-93; and departmental officials were used on one occasion in 1995-96.
11 CA 1985, s 442(1).
12 Ibid, s 442(2).
13 See ibid, s 443.
14 Ibid, ss 443(1), 433(1).
15 Ibid, ss 443(1), 434(1), 434(5).
16 CA 1985, ss 443(1), 436.
17 Ibid, ss 443(3), 437.
18 Ibid, s 452(1), (1A).
19 Ibid, s 448(1).
20 Ibid, s 450.

have been, financially interested in the success or failure of the company, or able to control or materially influence its policy, including persons concerned only on behalf of others; and any other person whom the inspector has reasonable cause to believe possesses information relevant to the investigation[1].

These provisions reinforce the powers granted to a public company to serve a notice requiring any person who is or has been interested in its share capital to disclose the nature and extent of that interest[2]. An exercise of these investigation powers by the DTI may arise from a request from a company following a failure by the company to obtain information through the use of its powers. Frequently, inspectors appointed under these provisions will be asked to investigate the existence of concert parties[3]. Concert parties are considered in Chapter 36.

Members of a company, provided they are sufficient in number to meet the statutory thresholds noted above in relation to inspections[4], can require the Secretary of State to appoint inspectors to investigate the membership[5] although the Secretary of State can decline to appoint if the application is vexatious[6]. He can also limit the scope of the inspectors' investigation and require security for costs to an amount not exceeding £5,000[7]. Alternatively, he can decide that the use of his powers to obtain information, discussed below, rather than the appointment of inspectors, is sufficient[8].

Power to obtain information

Where it appears that there is good reason to investigate the ownership of any shares in or debentures of a company but it is unnecessary to appoint inspectors for the purpose, the Secretary of State may require any person whom he has reasonable cause to believe to have or to be able to obtain any information as to the present and past interests in those shares or debentures to give any such information to the Secretary of State[9].

Penalties for failing to assist

One of the most important provisions relating to investigations of membership is the power given to the Secretary of State to freeze shares which are the subject of the investigation although these provisions can be relaxed where they unfairly affect the rights of third parties[10].

If in connection with an investigation into membership[11] it appears to the Secretary of State that there is difficulty in finding out the relevant facts about any shares, he may by order direct that the shares shall until further order be subject to certain

---

1   Ibid, s 443(2).
2   Ie under ibid, s 212.
3   See ibid, s 442(4).
4   Ie in the case of a company having a share capital, on the application either of not less than 200 members or of members holding not less than one-tenth of the shares issued; in the case of a company not having a share capital, on the application of not less than one-fifth in number of the persons on the company's register of members: ibid, s 442(3).
5   Ibid, s 442(3).
6   Ibid, s 442(3A).
7   Ibid, s 442(3A), (3B).
8   Ibid, s 442(3C).
9   Ibid, s 444(1). A failure to give information as required or the making of any false statement in a material particular or the reckless making of any statement which is false in a material particular is an offence: s 444(3).
10   Ibid, s 445(1A); The Companies (Disclosure of Interests in Shares) (Orders imposing restrictions on shares) Regulations 1991, SI 1991/1646.
11   Whether under CA 1985, s 442 or s 444.

restrictions[12]. These restrictions, generally known as freezing orders, are designed to force the registered holders to reveal the true owners of the shares.

A freezing order involves restrictions on the transfer of the affected shares and on the exercise of voting rights attached to the shares[13]. Shareholders affected cannot take advantage of any rights issue or accept a takeover offer and are not entitled to dividends[14]. The shares can be freed from these restrictions only in a limited number of ways.

An application can be made to the court by any person aggrieved for an order removing the restrictions on the shares[14]. Where the court is satisfied that a freezing order unfairly affects the rights of third parties then the court may direct on an application so made that such acts by such persons and for such purposes as may be set out in the order will not constitute a breach of the restrictions[15].

The court or the Secretary of State may direct that the shares be freed from the restrictions on being satisfied that the relevant facts have been disclosed and no unfair advantage has accrued to any person as a result of the failure to disclose[16]. Alternatively, the shares will be freed from these restrictions where the shares are to be transferred for valuable consideration and the court or the Secretary of State approves the transfer[17] (which approval may not be forthcoming unless the information has been disclosed[18]).

The court may also order the sale of the shares on the application of the Secretary of State or the company with the proceeds being paid into court to await an application by any persons claiming to be beneficially entitled to them[19].

Disclosure of information obtained

Information obtained from investigations into a company's membership may be disclosed to the parties specified and for the purposes noted above with regard to the security of information obtained from the exercise of the powers to require the production of documents[20]. Information obtained, other than by the appointment of inspectors[1], may also be disclosed to the company whose ownership was the subject of the investigation, any member or auditor of the company, any person whose conduct was investigated and any person whose financial interests appear to be affected by matters covered by the investigation[2].

INVESTIGATIONS OF DIRECTORS' SHARE DEALINGS

The Secretary of State may appoint inspectors, with similar powers to those outlined above, to investigate whether directors or their immediate families have contravened

---

12   Ibid, s 445(1).
13   Ibid, s 454(1).
14   Ibid, s 456(1), (2).
15   Ibid, s 456(1A).
16   Ibid, s 456(3)(a).
17   Ibid, s 456(3)(b). See *Re Ricardo Group plc* [1989] BCLC 566; *Re Lonrho plc* [1988] BCLC 53, 3 BCC 265.
18   *Re Geers Gross plc* [1988] 1 All ER 224, [1987] 1 WLR 1649, CA.
19   CA 1985, ss 456(4), 457.
20   Ie as under ibid, s 449: s 451A (1), (2).
1   Ie under ibid, s 444.
2   Ibid, s 451A(5).

certain provisions of the Companies Act 1985[3] requiring disclosure of their interests in their own company's shares and prohibiting dealing in certain share options by directors[4]. This provision is rarely used[5].

INVESTIGATIONS UNDER THE FINANCIAL SERVICES ACT 1986

The Financial Services Act 1986 contains provisions modelled on the companies legislation which allow for the appointment of inspectors to investigate any person carrying on an investment business[6] and to investigate and report on the affairs of any unit trust scheme or collective investment scheme[7]. Provision is also made for the appointment of inspectors to investigate insider dealing[8]. The powers of these inspectors are very similar to those outlined above in relation to the investigation of a company's affairs.

Investigations of insider dealing

If it appears to the Secretary of State that there are circumstances suggesting that there may have been a contravention of the insider dealing legislation, he may appoint one or more competent inspectors to carry out such investigations as are requisite to establish whether or not any such contravention has occurred and to report the results of their investigations to him[9]. Appointments in insider dealing cases are not usually announced and there is no power to publish reports of such investigations.

Many of the provisions noted above in relation to inspections apply here also. Witnesses may be examined on oath[10] and must produce documents, attend before the inspectors when required to do so, and assist the inspectors[11] with the possibility that their statements may be used in evidence against them[12], subject to the decision in *Saunders v United Kingdom*, discussed above. Legal professional privilege is protected[13] and there is limited protection for the banker/customer relationship[14].

Where any person fails to co-operate with the inspectors, the inspectors may certify that fact in writing to the court[15]. The court, if it is satisfied that the individual in question did without reasonable excuse refuse to co-operate, may punish him in like manner as if he had been guilty of contempt of court; or direct that the Secretary of State may exercise his powers in respect of him[16].

---

3   Ie under ibid, ss 323, 324, or 328(3)–(5).
4   Ibid, s 446.
5   These powers were exercised on three occasions between 1991–92 and 1996–97; see DTI *Companies in 1996–97* (1997), Table 2, p 11.
6   FSA 1986, ss 105, 106.
7   Ibid, s 94.
8   Ibid, Part VII. See generally Hannigan *Insider Dealing* (2nd edn, 1994), ch 2.
9   FSA 1986, s 177(1). The number of cases in which inspectors are appointed is small but steadily increasing, for example inspectors were appointed five times in 1993/94; six times in 1994/95; 13 times in 1995/96; and 21 times in 1996/97: DTI *Companies in 1996–97* (1997), Table 8, p 14.
10   FSA 1986, s 177(4).
11   Ibid, s 177(3).
12   Ibid, s 177(6).
13   FSA 1986, s 177(7).
14   Ibid, s 177(8).
15   Ibid, s 178(1).
16   Ibid, s 178(2). See *Re an inquiry under the Company Securities (Insider Dealing) Act 1985* [1988] AC 660, [1988] 1 All ER 203, HL.

These powers are most effective where the unco-operative individual is an authorised person carrying on an investment business under the Financial Services Act 1986. In that case, the Secretary of State may cancel that individual's authorisation, disqualify him from becoming authorised, restrict his authorisation in a particular way, or prohibit him from entering into certain types of business[17]. The Secretary of State may also limit the ability of authorised persons to transact business with or behalf of any person who fails to co-operate[18].

The information obtained by inspectors is treated as restricted information[19] and disclosure is prohibited save to the extent permitted by the statute which includes for the purpose of instituting criminal proceedings[20].

INVESTIGATIONS TO ASSIST OVERSEAS REGULATORY AUTHORITIES

Increasingly, the investigation of corporate fraud requires international co-operation and new powers to accommodate these developments were provided by the Companies Act 1989. The DTI may undertake investigations, and interview witnesses on oath, and seek material in this jurisdiction to assist an overseas regulatory authority[1]. In deciding whether to give the assistance sought, regard must be had to the considerations laid down in the statute and in particular to whether reciprocal assistance would be forthcoming[2].

---

17   FSA 1986, s 178(3).
18   Ibid, s 178(5).
19   Ibid, s 179.
20   Ibid, s 180.
1   CA 1989 s 82. See generally DTI *Companies in 1996–97* (1997), p 16 for details of collaboration between the DTI and overseas regulators.
2   CA 1989, s 82(4).

PART V

Structural problems and change

CHAPTER 31

Structural problems and change—the issues

Almost all companies start small. Why they are started is arguably a matter for psychological and sociological rather than legal analysis; why they manage to survive is primarily an economic question—the availability of a local market, specialism, sometimes the development of a new idea. The small incorporated business is usually a one man or family concern with many of the characteristics of the sole trader or partnership. Unlike the public listed company, it is not peculiarly a capital-raising device but a means of organising production and limiting liability[1]. Although theoretically possessed of limited liability for its shareholders, in practice as a result of contract this does not extend to liability to commercial finance providers. As an economic unit it is vulnerable.

If the company survives and grows, it will usually adopt a group structure of parent and subsidiary companies with the proprietors holding shares in the former. This new relationship engenders complications of its own. To whom does the management of parent and subsidiaries owe duties? Whose interests should prevail? Can the parent company allow a subsidiary to go to the wall? What measure of disclosure should be required in relation to the group? From the point of view of a commercial finance provider, what security should it take[2]?

Whether or not a company adopts a group structure, problems of organisation tend to increase with size. Communication and co-ordination prove more difficult as the firm expands and an appropriate management control system is needed. The basic choice is between a highly centralised pyramidical structure or a decentralised system. Much will depend on the historical development of the firm, the technology involved and the management philosophy adopted. The law has little to say on these questions.

Another stage of growth will be where the company considers a listing of its shares on the Stock Exchange. The main reasons for doing this are principally to obtain finance for expansion from the market for investment capital and to enable the proprietors to realise some of their investment in the company. This represents a time of dispersal of share ownership, and a subjection of management to additional legal regulation and the self-regulatory controls. The trend in the UK is increasingly moving from self-regulation to legal regulation.

---

1   H G Manne (1967) 53 Va L Rev 259.
2   J M Landers (1975) 42 U Chi L Rev 589; cf R A Posner's comment (1976) 43 U Chi L Rev 499.

The company or group may expand further by vertical or horizontal integration. Vertical integration, as we saw in Chapter 1, is where the two companies occupy adjacent stages in some vertical chain of production and distribution. Horizontal integration is where the companies are actual competitors in some relevant market. Conglomerate integration is where the companies are in essentially unrelated fields. The company participates in the market for control by merging with or taking over or being the target of a bid by another company. There are various reasons for expansion — the availability of mass markets, economies of scale in production, marketing and financing, the desire to diversify the companies with strong cash flows, international competition and sometimes managerial ambitions[3]. The first discernible period of growth by merger was in the late nineteenth century, which was a period of rapid technological change, declining profits and growing international competition. After the First World War there was an increase in mergers due to depression and the need to reduce competition and rationalise production. In this period there was the emergence of the High Street banks, the four main railway companies and ICI. In the late 1960s and 1970s, there was a big increase in mergers due to rapid technological change and economic growth followed by recession due to the oil crises. During this latter period, there was increased government intervention to encourage mergers. The benefits or detriments of mergers have been the subject of much debate. Those in favour tend to stress the benefits to consumers, employees and the community by the more efficient reallocation of resources. These benefits will occur with economies of scale in production by greater specialisation in plant, plant scale economies enabling particular plant to operate to optimum size, and marketing economies through a reduction of advertising costs and distribution outlets[4]. On a larger plain, mergers affect allocative efficiency by transferring resources from one industry to another to ensure that the right type and quantity of goods are produced. Growth by merger will be faster. It is easier to buy an established business than to expand an existing one or to diversify — the structure is already there. It is arguably safer to do so since there is an existing track record. The larger unit[5] gives greater market power and access to finance. Those against mergers stress the insufficient competition for control or the detriment from particular mergers[6]. The first arises largely because the stock market is essentially a market for minority parcels of shares and reflects expectations of earnings rather than asset values. The second arises because some mergers have failed due to managerial shortcomings, and with others growth sometimes leads to a contraction in the market which may result in higher prices, inefficiencies and curtailment of choice[7]. There are, however, contradictions in the arguments for and against industrial expansion and this no doubt accounts for the differing government policies over the years[8].

The law had developed three main procedures for dealing with mergers — the takeover bid, amalgamation and reconstruction, although the historical evolution was in reverse order. Takeover bids whereby a bidder can if necessary appeal over the heads of a hostile management are the most common method in practice and are the subject of both legal and self-regulation of the securities market. An elaborate code of self-regulation and institutional framework was evolved by the City of London financial

---

3   See Edith T Penrose *The Theory of the Growth of the Firm* (1959) ch VIII; D A Hay and D J Morris *Industrial Economics, Theory and Evidence* (1979) ch 14.
4   K D George and C Joll *Industrial Organisation* (3rd edn, 1981), p 71 ff.
5   Ibid.
6   See New Zealand Securities Commission *Company Take-overs—A Review of the Law and Practice* (1983), vol 1, p 31.
7   A Singh *Takeovers* (1971); G Meeks *Disappointing Marriage: A Study of the Gains from Merger* (1977).
8   See *George and Joll*, op cit, ch 14.

bodies, whereas in many other English-speaking countries it is left to a system of legal regulation through a securities commission. As a result of the Financial Services Act 1986 there was a system of self-regulation within a statutory framework and now there is the proposal to give much greater powers to the Financial Services Authority which will become a kind of securities commission. Reconstructions whereby there is a merger of undertakings or businesses rather than companies are the oldest method in English law and still the most common method in Europe. Amalgamation, whereby two companies of approximately equal standing join together to form a third which becomes their holding company, was very common in the inter-war period but is less common today.

The main benefits of legal regulation of mergers are first, to promote confidence in the market, secondly, to promote competition for control and thirdly, by the pricing mechanism to achieve a rational reallocation of resources. The main costs are, first, loss of freedom and flexibility in the market place for some market participants, secondly, the risk of reducing the number of takeovers and thirdly, the administrative costs borne by participants or the community at large[9].

One American study found that the transaction costs of making a take-over by tender offer in the USA were on average 13% of the post-offer market price of the shares[10] and another study shows how the costs have increased as a result of a recent federal reform[11].

Sometimes a company may wish to reorganise its capital structure—for instance, it may wish to replace loan capital by shares or vice versa. Originally it was necessary to wind up the company, and start again. Later, companies were given the power to reduce their share capital, as we saw in Chapter 17. In addition, a procedure which was originally introduced as a means of enabling a company in financial difficulties to enter into a scheme with its creditors was later extended to cover arrangements with shareholders. The resulting provision, now s 425 of CA 1985, is very flexible and is used for a wide variety of purposes. Another structural change which may take place is where the original company has served its purpose or has become undesirable because of fiscal rules. Here, provided the company is not insolvent, it can be put into members' voluntary winding up which gives the members control over the initiation of the proceedings and choice of a liquidator. The ultimate stage of dissolution is the corporate equivalent of death. Winding up by the court is also possible but is rare in the case of a solvent company unless it is the result of a petition to wind up the company on the just and equitable ground. This has been dealt with already as a minority shareholder's remedy in Chapter 28. The whole topic of company insolvency is dealt with later in Part VI.

---

9   New Zealand Securities Commission, op cit.
10   R Smiley (1976) 58 Rev Econ & Stat 22.
11   D R Fischel (1978) 57 Tex L Rev 1.

CHAPTER 32

Small incorporated firms

Most companies start as small businesses although the majority of small businesses do not in fact incorporate. They remain as sole traders or partnerships[1]. The extent to which the corporate form is used depends on the sector of industry in which the business operates. According to the research findings of the Bolton Report, in manufacturing industry over 80% of small firms were incorporated, whereas in non-manufacturing, only 33% were incorporated and these were dominated by construction and wholesale distribution. In May 1995, there were nevertheless some 870,000 small private companies out of 957,000 companies on the register and the number of new incorporations per 1000 of the human population had increased from 0.4 in 1968 to 2.3 in 1989-90.

We are not concerned here with the problems of small firms in general but only with the problems which are solved or exacerbated by the use of the corporate form[2]. Small firms are characteristically managed by the people who own them which takes them outside the Berle and Means hypothesis of corporate development. In Marxist terms, the separation of ownership and control is the natural development of capitalism and small businesses represent an anachronism[3]. It is certainly true that small business has declined over the last hundred years and continues to do so at a death rate of 24% in the £1-14,000 turnover band to around 4% over the £100,000 threshold[3a] despite some assistance from the government. Those who support small business either rest their case largely on it as the source of innovation and capitalist development or on the broader social grounds of the greater contribution of small business to the community at large. Some argue that it is in the world of small business that Britan can best start to move from an adversarial society to a collaborative society with improved performance. Small firms surveyed by Bolton employed 4.4 million people

---

1   See 'Small Firms—Report of the Committee of Inquiry on Small Firms', Cmnd 4811 (1971) (the Bolton Report), p xv. For a valuable update see J Stanworth and C Gray *Bolton 20 Years On - The Small Firm in the 1990's* (1991).
2   For useful discussions of those problems, see the Bolton Report and M Chesterman *Small Business* (2nd edn, 1982) *and Stanworth and Gray*, op cit, chs 3-6 and 11.
3   *Chesterman*, op cit, pp 39, 40.
3a   *Stanworth and Gray*, op cit, 10-11.

which was over 30% of the persons employed in the industries surveyed and it was estimated that small business as a whole gave employment to 25% of the total employed population[4]. A more recent statistic shows that they still represent 20% of the gross national product[5]. The classic legal problems of small firms are choice of an appropriate legal structure, financing, coping with government requirements, and providing for continuity in the ownership and control of the business. Looked at from an economic point of view small incorporated firms have common characteristics with sole traders and moderately sized partnerships—they have relatively few managers who tend to be the largest shareholders; they need to restrict the alienability of a business interest; they lose the benefit of specialisation of function; the proprietors lack a public market for their business interest. The lack of a public market makes valuation difficult; it may lead to problems over distributions; and it precludes the use of the market as a monitoring device on management[6]. We shall examine each of these problems in turn looking at the matter primarily from a company law perspective[7].

DEFINING SMALL INCORPORATED FIRMS[8]

So far we have spoken fairly generally. Let us be a little more precise. While one should not make a fetish of definition and much depends on the immediate purpose of defining, it will be helpful if we at least take our bearings by reference to existing nomenclature. The Bolton Committee identified three characteristics of small firms—a relatively small share of the market, personal management by the owners, and independence. They then adopted shifting relativist criteria for different sectors of industry. In manufacturing industry there was widespread use of the corporate form which increased with the number of employees. In non-manufacturing, the trend was not so pronounced. Catering small firms tended not to use the corporate form and the two sectors which did— construction and wholesale distribution—probably did so because of the risks involved. In this chapter we shall concentrate on those small firms which are incorporated. Since 90% of incorporated small firms according to Bolton are close companies, the kind of company we are considering is the UK-resident company controlled by five or fewer persons or by its directors, provided at least 35% of its voting power is not held by the public and listed and dealt in on a stock exchange. However, we are only concerned with a subclass of close company which is characterised by independence and owner/ management.

THE USE OF THE CORPORATE FORM FOR SMALL FIRMS

Although the majority of small firms are not incorporated, a sufficient number are for us to consider what motivates the adoption of the corporate form and whether the present legal form is appropriate.

The traditional reasons given for choosing the corporate form have been limited liability of members and the capacity to create a floating charge. However, recent

---

4 Bolton Report, pp 33 and XIX; *Stanworth and Gray*, op cit, 9-10.
5 *The Times*, 27 January 1983, p 15. In the USA, the figure is 40%.
6 See Frank Easterbrook and D Fischel (1986) 38 Stanford L Rev 271.
7 See generally S J Naude (1982) 4 Modern Business Law 6; D S Ribbens (1982) TSAR 49, (1983) TSAR 118; M C Sheehan (1985) 2 Canta LR 374.
8 See the Bolton Report, ch 1; *Chesterman*, op cit, ch 2. Also see the Law Commission's Feasibility Study on Reform of Private Companies 1995 Appendix A.

research conducted by Andrew Hicks, Robert Drury and Jeff Smallcombe indicates a greater range of reasons. A table showing their valuable research findings is shown below[9].

Table of reasons given by directors or their advisers for the information of companies

Reasons for forming a limited company	*Reasons given* (Total)	*Reasons given by advisers*	*Directors reasons without advice*
Limited liability	58%	56%	61%
Prestige/credibility	13%	3%	20%
Tax reasons	13%	22%	9%
Defines each member's interest in the business	9%	0%	14%
Easier transfer of interest	3%	0%	5%
Facilitate raising capital from outside investors	2%	0%	4%
Easier to obtain credit	1%	0%	2%
Protection of business name	1%	0%	2%
To offer floating security to bank	0%	0%	0%
Difficulties with partnership form	2%	0%	4%
Corporate form necessary for professional or trading purposes	3%	0%	5%
To reflect size of business	4%	6%	4%
To run business through separate legal entity	3%	0%	5%
To continue original status and name of the business after its purchase	3%	0%	5%
Discipline of running business through company beneficial	2%	6%	0%
No considered reason	2%	0%	4%
Other reasons	4%	6%	4%
Number of respondents	90	32	56
Missing cases	2		

The early Companies Acts were probably not intended to be used by small businesses. The statutory minimum number of members was prescribed at seven and it was not until the decision of the House of Lords in *Salomon v A Salomon & Co Ltd*[10] that the legitimacy of the use of six nominees or dummy shareholders was recognised[11]. Prior to that date the practice had been adopted and the term 'private company' was occasionally used to describe in commercial language the incorporated small business[12]. That term was later adopted as a term of art in the Companies Act 1907 (later embodied in the Companies (Consolidation) Act 1908) to exempt them from certain requirements of publicity including the obligation to file accounts. The criteria of a private company

---

9   See *Alternative Company Structures for the Small Business* by A Hicks, R Drury and J Smallcombe ACCA Research Report 42, p 17.
10   [1897] AC 22.
11   See L C B Gower (1953) 18 Law & Contemporary Problems 535 at 538.
12   Thus Sir Francis Palmer, the Victorian company law specialist, first published his book on private companies in 1877. See also judicial usage in *Re British Seamless Paper Box Co* (1881) 17 Ch D 467 at 478, CA.

were originally a restriction on the transfer of shares, basically 50 members and a prohibition on raising capital from the public. Out of this class was created the subclass of exempt private company by the Companies Act 1948 as a result of the Cohen Report, and this alone of limited companies continued to enjoy the old privileges of not filing accounts and of making loans to directors. The definition of exempt private company was complex and produced anomalies. It was abolished by the Companies Act 1967. Now all private companies whose members' liability is limited by shares must file accounts. In the Companies Act 1980, s 1(1) a new definition of private company was introduced which involved not being a public company. The principal characteristics of a public company under s 1(3) of CA 1985 are a provision in its memorandum to that effect and compliance with the requirements of the Companies Acts. These include having a minimum share capital, a common requirement in Europe for private companies as well.

This approach of defining a private company by negation is even more unsatisfactory than the old approach of defining a public company by negation. It is arguable that private companies, particularly those which are small incorporated firms, have definite characteristics which need to be recognised. These characteristics are not adequately defined by not being public companies especially when the definition of the latter is so patently inept. Small incorporated firms have more in common with sole traders and partnerships than this approach recognises. Size is one important factor. The absence of capital raising from the public is the other.

The Companies Act 1981 introduced the new concept of small company for the purpose of filing modified financial statements which need not comply with all the provisions of the Companies Acts. Under s 247(1) (as amended), a company qualifies as a small company if it satisfies for that financial year any *two* of the following *three* conditions:

(a) the amount of its turnover is not more than £2.8m;
(b) the balance sheet total is not more than £1.4m;
(c) the average number of employees employed by the company in the financial year does not exceed 50.

It can be seen that (a) at least is a reasonably generous figure although in some businesses, turnover is high but profit margins low. This shift from an a priori general approach to classification to a more pragmatic relativist approach based on size as far as accounts are concerned is welcome. With this can be compared some overseas reforms such as the Canada Business Corporations Act[13] and the New Zealand Companies Act 1993 which have abandoned the public/private dichotomy altogether in favour of a variety of different definitions depending on the circumstances in which it is thought appropriate to draw distinctions between different types of company. The main distinctions are between those raising capital from the public and those which do not, although some jurisdictions have adopted specific close corporation provisions on US lines. These pay particular attention to the needs of small incorporated firms which are closed held and recognise the unity of management and ownership. The ways in which this has been done are:

(a) to relax procedures;
(b) to allow special redeemable shares;
(c) to allow and in some cases require pre-emption provisions;
(d) to introduce appraisal rights to prevent fundamental changes without consent;

---

13   See Iacobucci, Pilkington and Prichard *Canadian Business Corporations* (1977), p 75 ff.

(e) to allow unanimous shareholder agreements which also fetter directors' discretions; and

(f) to provide for application to the court for dissolution as in the case of a partnership.

The most relaxed procedure is perhaps contained in the Delaware statute in the USA and in s 10 of the Statutory Close Corporation Supplement to the Model Business Corporation Act in the US[14]. This allows direct shareholder management. The corporation need not elect directors but may be managed by shareholders who are deemed to be directors. This in effect is a subclass of close corporation and would suit the incorporated partnership type of company. (b) was facilitated in English law by the 1981 Act reforms. (c) is permissible and for new issues the rule unless excluded. (d) would involve a change in English law in so far as it allows fettering of directors' discretion although there is some latitude under the case law already[15]. (e) would be in addition to winding up on the just and equitable ground and might prejudice the interests of employees and creditors.

Given that all or some of these are desirable reforms, one is still left with the threshold problem of definition unless one adopts the approach of the Canadian and New Zealand reforms. It is difficult to produce a definition which is much better than the 1948 Act definition of private company, possibly reducing the number of members to less than 15.

In Chapter 4 we mentioned certain trends in the case law which indicated that the courts are beginning to recognise distinctive traits of the small incorporated firm. These were:

(1) the tendency to pierce the veil where the interests of justice required it;

(2) the trend to recognition of something like a *personellgesellschaft*;

(3) the willingness to bypass strict legalities;

(4) in some, but not all, cases, the willingness to look at a group of associated companies as a whole.

It is difficult to give conceptual unity to these trends but there are perhaps two alternative ways in which they can at least be partially explained. One is by reference to contract, the other by reference to equity. One can ask, what was the basic contract agreed between the parties and of which the company is the expression? Do the company constitution and machinery give adequate reflection to it? This helps to explain (2) and (3) but not necessarily (1) and (4). (4) in fact will be relatively rare although it is surprising how often problems arise because there is not a group in the strict sense but a motley collection of small incorporated firms owned by the same person or persons. The equity approach is capable of covering most of the field. Many instances of (1) are cases where it would be inequitable to enforce the strict letter of *Salomon's* principle although it is noteworthy that the courts have not readily disregarded the corporate form in favour of creditors. (2) arises because of the recognition of equitable considerations under the just and equitable formula in winding up. There have been a few faltering steps taken by first instance courts in the Commonwealth to extend this to non-winding-up situations. Many instances of (3) can be explained in terms of acquiescence, waiver or estoppel which can be the subject of equitable intervention. (3) and (4) can be explained in terms of equity's regard for the substance rather than the form in legal transactions. Of course, to say that these

---

14   Ibid, p 80; see Report of the Committee on Corporate Laws 'Proposed Statutory Close Corporation Supplement to the Model Business Corporation Act' (1981) 37 Bus Law 269–311; (1983) 38 Bus Law 1031. Cf the South African Close Corporations Act 1984, ss 42 and 46.

15   See Chapter 25, ante.

trends can be explained by reference to equity begs the question of why there has been equitable intervention. It is submitted that there are two reasons—first, the traditional personal equity which is rooted in a concept of conscience or fairness and secondly, and perhaps more importantly, what might be described as commercial equity—the willingness to look to the substance and not the form of legal transactions. Sometimes this is simply described as commercial construction but it seems to have been of equitable origin either in equity properly so called or the Law Merchant. However, there are limits. There is no general doctrine of small firms which overrides established equitable doctrines such as fiduciary obligations. There are certain things, to use Churchill's powerful phrase in another context, 'up with which' equity 'will not put'. The blurring of function between shareholder and director, for instance, while the most natural thing in the world for small incorporated firms, is frowned upon if it amounts to a fetter of the director's discretion although there is an increasing tendency in the cases to adopt a restricted approach to the doctrine[16]. Where greater latitude has been felt necessary, it has resulted from statutory reforms in the USA and Canada. English law has not yet found the impetus in either the case law or statute to recognise the full implications of the small incorporated firm.

The financing of small incorporated firms

Small firms are at a greater disadvantage than larger firms in raising finance[17]. External equity finance is difficult to find although the power to issue redeemable shares and to purchase its own shares may now assist the small incorporated firm. Nevertheless the terms will often be unfavourable. Loan capital is more expensive and the security requirements are more onerous.

According to the Bolton Report[18] a smaller proportion of the finance of small business comes from external borrowings than is the case with larger firms. Long-term debt together with bank loans and overdrafts provided finance for about 14% of total assets for the firms surveyed compared with 19% for quoted companies. A substantial number of small firms do not borrow at all. There are variations between sectors of industry. According to a survey by ICFC, faster growing firms rely to a much greater extent on external borrowing than slower growing firms. Bank credit nevertheless forms the greater part of the *external* finance for small businesses. Many small businesses are financed by the owners either out of their own capital or by ploughed back profits. Additionally further finance may be raised in the family.

Another important source of finance is trade credit, although in a time of recession suppliers are insisting on accounts being settled in shorter periods. For small businesses with some growth potential there are specialist City of London financial institutions who often mix equity and loan participation. Hire purchase and plant hire is indirectly a source of finance.

The disadvantages faced by small firms do not necessarily represent any distinct bias against them. The cost to the finance provider is higher and the risks more difficult to assess. The Wilson Committee[19] thought that if any bias did exist it might be in the banks' excessive caution in assessing risk, particularly where the customer had no capital of his own.

16 Ibid.
17 Wilson Report (Cmnd 7937), App 2.
18 Bolton Report, ch 17. See now *Stanworth and Gray*, op cit, *Chapter 4.*
19 See the Wilson Report, op cit. See now *Stanworth and Gray*, op cit, especially 56, for changes in banking policy.

Recently, there has been an attempt at reshaping the financing of small firms[20]. Some of this is tied in with regional development, some with more information and advice, while government guarantees and tax concessions have been given to investors and the relevant thresholds for corporation tax and VAT have been increased. The high street banks have set up specialist departments and specialist firms have grown up in the City. Sometimes one is left with the impression that there is now a bewildering range of choice open to small firms. It is remarkable, however, how this diminishes at the point of contact. A lot of the change is cosmetic.

Disclosure and the small incorporated firm

We have already dealt with disclosure in Chapter 29. We shall briefly recapitulate. The private company was exempt from many disclosure requirements until 1948. Between 1948 and 1967, exempt private companies were exempt from filing accounts. Between 1967 and 1981, all private limited companies had to file accounts but had a limited relaxation of certain disclosure requirements. Since 1981, small companies have been subject to a more lenient regime as regards financial reports. Since 1994, so-called 'micro companies' have exemption from the audit requirement. This arose as a consequence of the dissatisfaction with additional costs of audit arising from full requirements on auditors' qualifications.

Some would argue that even this does not go far enough and that we should have a return to the pre-1967 days but this seems undesirable from the point of view of creditor protection. We have seen in earlier chapters how the corporate form can be abused. Obligations to file accounts afford some, albeit an imperfect, index of solvency. The availability of public accounts makes credit reporting easier and cheaper[1].

Transitional problems of small incorporated firms

Small firms perhaps more than larger firms are fraught with transitional problems. These centre on the death or retirement of the founder or controller shareholder, expansion, disputes between the controllers and financial instability and insolvency[2].

Some small incorporated firms are in reality 'one man companies'—incorporated sole traders. Other small firms have been called 'little business' by an American writer[3]. They are really forms of self-employment where employees other than the proprietor are members of his family. When he dies or wishes to retire the impetus might disappear. The alternatives are that the business is; (1) sold, (2) wound up, or (3) is taken over by another member of the family. Where (1) occurs there will either be an agreement to sell the shares in the company or its undertaking and assets. (2) will be a members' voluntary winding up unless the company is insolvent. (3) will involve a member of the family taking over the proprietor's shares. Another alternative now made possible is for the employees or the company itself to buy the proprietor's shares. This has been possible since the Companies Act 1981.

20   *Chesterman*, op cit; *Stanworth and Gray*, op cit.
1   Bolton Report, ch 17.
2   For a useful discussion of this, see *Chesterman*, op cit, ch 7. See also Frank Easterbrook and Daniel Fischel (1986) 38 Stanford L Rev 271.
3   Edward D Hollander *The Future of Small Business* (1979).

Many small incorporated firms are in reality incorporated partnerships where the corporate form has been used primarily for reasons of limiting liability to third parties. Disputes can arise between the proprietors in innumerable ways. Michael Chesterman in his useful study, *Small Businesses*, includes the following as examples[4]:

1   dismissal of one of the proprietors from his position as director, manager or employee;
2   expulsion;
3   setting up a rival enterprise;
4   denying access to books and accounts;
5   failure to give notice of meetings;
6   denying a vote at meetings;
7   payment of excessive remuneration to others;
8   refusal to pay dividends;
9   issuing shares to others at less than full value;
10   refusal to register a person as member.

The remedies available to the injured party in such a case are to bring an action under one of the exceptions to the rule in *Foss v Harbottle* or under s 459 of CA 1985 or to petition to wind up the company on the just and equitable ground under s 122(1)(g) of the Insolvency Act 1986. Many of the cases discussed in Chapter 28 concerned small incorporated firms. Indeed *Ebrahimi v Westbourne Galleries Ltd*[5] laid down principles which seem to be based on a paradigm of such a company. Lord Wilberforce said:

It would be impossible, and wholly undesirable, to define the circumstances in which these considerations may arise. Certainly the fact that a company is a small one, or a private company, is not enough. There are very many of these where the association is a purely commercial one, of which it can safely be said that the basis of association is adequately and exhaustively laid down in the articles. The superimposition of equitable considerations requires something more, which typically may include one, or probably more, of the following elements:
  (i)   an association formed or continued on the basis of a personal relationship, involving mutual confidence—this element will often be found where a pre-existing partnership has been converted into a limited company;
  (ii) an agreement, or understanding, that all, or some (for there may be 'sleeping members'), of the shareholders shall participate in the conduct of the business;
  (iii) restriction upon the transfer of the members' interest in the company— so that if confidence is lost, or one member is removed from management, he cannot take out his stake and go elsewhere ...

Following the lead of Commonwealth authorities[6] the English courts have applied this to the statutory minority shareholder remedy in s 459 and in relation to controlling shareholders' duties. In *Re Bird Precision Bellows Ltd*[7] Nourse J applied it to the question of valuation of a minority interest for a buy out under s 459. This resulted in no discount being made for a minority interest.

Lastly, we come to financial instability and insolvency. Small firms are vulnerable. Some simply fail. Some are not viable from the start. Others are outstripped by their

4   *Chesterman*, op cit, pp 151–152.
5   [1973] AC 360 at 379, HL.
6   See Chapter 28, ante and BAK Rider [1979] CLJ 148.
7   [1984] Ch 419. However see Chapter 28, ante.

rivals. A fast growing small firm may find problems in expanding too quickly and may be tempted to overtrade. It may take on extra staff or purchase extra plant to meet a current demand which later drops. The company's bank may be prepared to tide it over a temporary illiquidity; this depends on the vagaries of banking policy. Otherwise, it is likely that the bank will appoint a receiver under its debenture if the company has assets. Alternatively, the Inland Revenue or a trade creditor may petition for its compulsory winding up. The proprietors may, however, take the initiative and put the company into creditors' voluntary winding up by calling the appropriate meetings. Sometimes this is done to remove the intolerable pressure from creditors.

Deregulation of private companies

The Thatcher Government was keen to cut down on Government expenditure and reduce the regulatory burden on small firms. This was the subject of the White Paper, *Lifting the Burden* (Cmnd) 9571, July 1985. This stated that:

> ... regulations have grown over the years to a stage where many of them are too heavy a drain on our national resources. To the extent that regulations go further than necessary, there were lower profits for firms or raised prices, or both. Output and employment will tend to be lower. Regulations can also stifle competition and deter new firms from entering the market or prevent others from expanding. Too many people in central and local Government spend too much of their time regulating the activities of others. Some regulations were framed a century and more ago, have been added to or amended, and now bear little relevance to the modern business world. Other regulations are too complex and confusing even to professional advisors (and sometimes to the people who administer them, too). Many regulations are necessary and it is, of course, Government's responsibility to ensure that flexibility and freedom are not abused by those who would flout the proper interests of customers, consumers and employees. We must maintain our quality of life, but we have to strike the right balance.

The Institute of Directors also commissioned Dr L S Sealy[8] of Gonville and Caius College, Cambridge to produce a report on deregulation of private companies which no doubt influenced the CA 1989.

The main reforms of the CA 1989 (as amended) as we saw in Chapter 23 are:

(1) the possibility of written resolutions by all the members without notice or a meeting (s 381A of the CA 1985). There are two exceptions—resolutions to remove directors under s 303 and resolutions under s 391 to remove an auditor before the expiration of his term of office. Copies of the written resolutions must be sent to the auditors (s 381B);

(2) the right for members to elect by resolution in general meeting to dispense with certain requirements of company law. These cover: duration of authority to issue shares; dispensing with laying of accounts and reports before general meetings; dispensing with holding of annual general meetings; dispensing with annual appointment of auditors.

---

8   'A Simplified Reform for the Shareholder Managed Company' (1985). See also L S Sealy (1993) L S Gaz 8.

On 15 July 1992, the Companies (Single Member Private Limited Companies) Regulations 1992 (SI 1992/1699), which implemented the Twelfth EU Directive 89/667 of December 21, 1989, came into force[9]. This made it possible for a private company limited by shares to be formed by a single subscriber to the memorandum of association agreeing to take not less than one share. The procedure is otherwise the same as that for formation of a company with more than one member.

Section 24 CA 1985 which deals with personal liability of a member in the case of a company carrying on business with less than two members for more than six months now only applies to public companies.

In the case of private companies which reduce their membership to one it will be necessary to consider the adoption of new, more appropriate articles.

PROPOSALS FOR NEW FORMS OF INCORPORATION FOR SMALL FIRMS

Early in the nineteenth century, John Austin, the jurist, called for an incorporation similar to the French *commandite*[10]. These proposals were toyed with throughout the nineteenth century and then Pollock's work at the end of the century resulted in not only the Partnership Act 1890 but also eventually the Limited Partnership Act 1907 and the Registration of Business Names Act 1916. The 1907 Act has not been a great success and the 1916 Act has now been repealed.

In 1969 in *Companies Legislation in the 1970s*, four of the main accountancy institutes called for a new classification of proprietary as opposed to stewardship companies. A proprietary company would be defined as one[11]:

(a) which is managed and controlled by substantially the same persons;
(b) which is not under the control of another company which is not itself a proprietary company;
(c) which limits the right to transfer its shares;
(d) which prohibits any offer of its shares to the public;
(e) which limits the number of its members to 25;
(f) whose average number of employees per week does not exceed 200; and
(g) which has an annual turnover not exceeding £500,000.

The object of the new classification was to exempt them from the more onerous accounting requirements, some of which purposes have been achieved by the 1981 Act.

In 1981, the Department of Trade published a consultative document entitled 'A New Form of Incorporation for Small Firms'[12] which included in Annex A a scheme devised by Professor L C B Gower for a new form of incorporation which is in effect an incorporated partnership with legal personality, the members of which might enjoy a measure of limited liability. It would be available to firms with a membership of between two and ten. It would be registered by filing a simple document. This would not be its constitution. The firms would not be dissolved on the death or retirement of members. It would have the power to buy out the outgoing members' interest and, failing this, the other members would have the right. There would be no share capital

---

9   See M C Wyatt *Single Shareholder Company Manual* (1995).
10   [1825] Parliamentary History Review 711.
11   The Bolton Report, p 314; cf 'Company Accounting and Disclosure' (Cmnd 7654) p 1.
12   Cmnd 1871 (1981). See *Chesterman*, op cit, ch 9 and R Baxt (1984) 2 C & SLJ 248. See too the Australian Companies and Securities Law Review Committee's 'Report on Forms of Legal Organisation for Small Business Enterprises', September 1985.

as such but simply interests in the net worth. The right of participation in management would be given to all members and would not be capable of being taken away. Management as in partnership would be by majority rule except where there was to be a change in the nature of the business where there would be a need for unanimity.

The proposals avoid strict capital maintenance and argue a case for liberality in disclosure. Solvency was the most important thing and an annual certificate of solvency would be necessary.

Liability would not be totally limited since there would be a prescribed amount and withdrawals at less than full consideration would be repayable. The firm would be able to grant a floating charge.

Such a reform would avoid the distortion which results from forcing small firms into the private company mould and would yet achieve some of the advantages of legal personality and limited liability. Unfortunately only the National Chamber of Trade, the Institute of Chartered Secretaries and the National Farmers' Union among the larger interest groups expressed any support for the proposal and, according to research done by the Confederation of British Industry in 1980, the directors of private companies have little enthusiasm for the introduction of any new form of incorporation and it appears that few will opt for it if introduced. As the CBI did not invite replies from sole traders or partnerships (other than a few professional ones) it is uncertain how much this reflects their views also. In the absence of some general support, it is unlikely that any reform will be carried out[13].

In a useful ACCA Research Report, *Alternative Company Structures for the Small Business*[14], Andrew Hicks, Robert Drury and Jeff Smallcombe in 1995 recommend an alternative incorporated form based on existing partnership law. This would have the following characteristics:

(1) separate legal personality with perpetual succession
(2) unlimited liability of its members
(3) no rules on capital maintenance
(4) contracts effected in its name
(5) capable of suing and being sued with judgment against its assets and members to make good shortfall
(6) simple registration procedure
(7) limited disclosure
(8) choice of simple management structures
(9) tax transparency
(10) transfer of interests possible.

This looks interesting, although the authors hesitate to recommend the capacity to create a floating charge in line with recent criticisms of the floating charge.

The Law Commission, having done a feasibility study for the DTI, has now been asked to look at reforming partnership law as an alternative to a new form of company.

13   See LCB Gower 'Proposals for Reform' in *The Abuse of Limited Liability*, Transcript of a Seminar at Monash Law School on 30 August 1983, 1, 4–5; F Wooldridge 'A New Form of Incorporation—Responding to the Gower Proposals' (1982) 3 Co Law 58. Compare also the proposals of J R M Lowe *The Incorporated Firm*, winner of the 1974 Jordan competition; T Hadden *Company Law and Capitalism* (2nd edn, 1977) pp 222–230; the South African Close Corporations Act 1984 and the Australian Close Corporations Act 1989. The Australian Act was a bad precedent. It was far too complex and is now no longer operative because of a constitutional challenge to the legislation.
14   ACCA Research Report 42. See also the DTI Consultation Document on Model Articles of Association Appropriate for a Partnership Company to be known as Table G and the DTI Consultation Papers, *Limited Liability Partnership*, vols 1 and 2.

CHAPTER 33

Groups

THE GROUP ENTERPRISE

A company is a species of undertaking. Undertaking is wide enough to include a partnership and an unincorporated association carrying on a trade or business, with or without a view to profit (s 259(1)). The extended concept of undertaking is for the purposes of consolidated accounts.

A group of undertakings is in general terms a holding or parent undertaking and its subsidiaries. Instead of a single company, we are concerned with the inter-relationships of a number of undertakings and the ways in which the parent exercises control over the business of its subsidiaries. We are also concerned with their relationship with the outside world. Holding companies originated in the USA as early as 1832 and were one of a number of devices used to pool resources and share profits. When the Sherman Anti-Trust Law of 1890 outlawed trust agreements, the holding company became more commonly used. Concern over the inability of existing accounting requirements to cover the group enterprise was expressed in 1904 by Sir Arthur Lowes Dickinson, a partner in Price Waterhouse, a leading firm of accountants. In 1922, his partner, Sir Gilbert Garnsey, drew the attention of the English accounting profession to the problems in detail in a public lecture which was later published. The first consolidated balance sheet was published by Nobel Industries Ltd in 1920 and the first consolidated profit and loss account by Dunlop Rubber Co Ltd in 1933. The Greene Committee in 1925–26 generally agreed with the Institute of Chartered Accountants that the matter was better left to the companies themselves, except that shareholders were entitled to know whether the dividends to be declared by the holding company were justified by the results of the group as a whole. The first legal obligation to produce group accounts was introduced by the Companies Act 1947, and is now contained in s 227 of CA 1985[1]. The question of group accounts was addressed by the Seventh EU Directive which was implemented by CA 1989. Steps were taken to broaden the scope of groups to deal with evasion of the accounting requirements. The group relationship is currently

---

1   For the history, see J Kitchen 'The Accounts of British Holding Company Groups' in T Lee and R Parker *The Evolution of Corporate Financial Reporting* (1979). See also R M Wilkins *Group Accounts* (2nd edn, 1979), p 16 et seq.

the subject of a proposal for a Ninth Directive which is a matter of controversy.

Groups arise in different ways. They may be founded as such. A company is incorporated to carry on business as a holding company and then proceeds to incorporate trading subsidiaries. Alternatively, a company which is a trading company may grow and convert itself into a holding company, later hiving down its trading activities into subsidiaries. Again, a group relationship may arise as a result of a takeover. One company takes over another which then becomes its subsidiary when its shares have been acquired by the first company. Takeovers may arise from reasons of trade expansion but many conglomerates today represent horizontal expansion and diversification. There are various reasons why the subsidiaries are kept in business. The bidder will wish to preserve the goodwill of the business. There are costs involved in transferring the actual business. The subsidiary may constitute a convenient unit of management or accounting within the group[2].

It is interesting to note that British-based groups tend to be typically more complex than their American or European counterparts. The complexity arises from the numbers of operating subsidiaries and dormant companies and the low priority given to rationalisation[3]. This complexity makes it more difficult for shareholders and employees to monitor the affairs of the group.

Now, whereas the rational goal of investors in a single company is to gain the largest return on their investment consistent with the risks which they are prepared to take, the goal of investors in a group of undertakings will be to maximise the profitability of the group enterprise as a whole[4]. The interests of any one undertaking are irrelevant except in so far as they increase the overall profitability. There may be commercial or fiscal advantages in running one or more undertakings at a loss or on a break-even basis. The economic rationale of the group enterprise may, therefore, generate a conflict with legal norms which approach the group in a more atomistic way. This produces the contradiction that management pursuing rational economic ends may be in breach of their fiduciary duties to the companies of which they are directors[5]. Lest one dismiss this as an instance of the irrationality of the law, one should remember that each constituent company has its own creditors who will look to its assets for recovery in the case of default and insolvency. We shall say more about these topics later.

NO GENERAL LAW OF GROUP ENTERPRISE

Unlike German law[6], English law has not developed a distinct body of rules applicable to groups. The ordinary rules of company law apply to the companies in the group and to their relationship with outsiders.

A holding company, while the owner of whole or part of the share capital of a subsidiary, is not regarded as the owner of the assets of the subsidiary in the absence of an express agency or trust relationship[7]. Sometimes a more liberal attitude, looking

---

2 See T Hadden *Company Law and Capitalism* (2nd edn, 1977), p 389. See too M. A. Eisenberg 'Corporate Groups' in M Gillooly (ed) *The Law relating to Corporate Groups* (1993), ch 1.

3 See the valuable study by T Hadden *The Control of Corporate Groups* (1983), p vii. For the use of a complex corporate form to evade creditors see *Re a Company* [1985] BCLC 333, CA. See also D Sugarman and G Teubner (eds) *Regulating Corporate Groups in Europe* (1990)

4 Jonathan M Landers (1975) 42 U Chi L Rev 589 at 591. See generally H Collins (1990) 53 MLR 731.

5 See generally C M Schmitthoff [1978] JBL 218; R Baxt and D Harding 'Duties of Directors and Majority Shareholders in Groups of Companies—Tension between Commercial Convenience and Legal Obligations' [1977] 9 Comm Law Association (Australia) Bulletin 127; R Baxt (1976) 4 ABLR 289.

6 See the very useful discussion in A Dorresteijn, I Kuiper and G Morse *European Corporate Law* (1994), ch 9. See also K Bohlhoff and J Budde (1984) 6 JCB and CML 163.

to the economic enterprise as a whole, has been manifested by the English courts when dealing with compensation cases, as we saw in Chapter 7, but that can perhaps be explained as a desire not to allow the doctrine of separate legal personality to be used to produce manifest injustice.

In *Littlewoods Mail Order Stores Ltd v IRC*[8] Lord Denning MR made a very sweeping statement. He said:

> The doctrine laid down in *Salomon v A Salomon & Co Ltd* [1897] AC 22, HL, has to be watched very carefully. It has often been supposed to cast a veil over the personality of a limited company through which the courts cannot see but that is not true. The courts can and often do draw aside the veil ... They look to see what really lies behind. The legislature has shown the way with group accounts and the rest. And the courts should follow suit.

He made similar remarks in *DHN Food Distributors Ltd v London Borough of Tower Hamlets*[9] but in both cases there were special features such as trusteeship which justified the decisions. A different and more orthodox view has been taken in the New Zealand Court of Appeal[10] and the House of Lords dealing with a Scottish appeal[11]. This view is that the principle of separate legal personality must be observed unless there are compelling reasons to discard it. Similarly in the Australian case of *Industrial Equity Ltd v Blackburn*[12] where the High Court of Australia held that a company had breached its articles in declaring dividends out of profits earned by a subsidiary, Mason J said:

> It can scarcely be contended that the provisions of the Act operate to deny the separate legal personality of each company in the group. Thus in the absence of contract creating some additional right, the creditors of company A, a subsidiary company within a group, can only look to that company for payment of their debts. They cannot look to company B, the holding company, for payment.

A similar orthodox view was expressed by the Court of Appeal *in Adams v Cape Industries plc*[13] in 1990. Conversely the European Court of Justice seems more prepared to treat a group of companies as a single economic entity[14] and this view will thus prevail in European Union Law.

A holding company and other companies in the group are not liable for the debts incurred by a member of the group unless they have guaranteed them or have participated in the carrying on of the subsidiary's business with intent to defraud its creditors within what is now s 213 of the Insolvency Act 1986[15] or are the only member when the subsidiary is a public company and its membership has remained below the statutory minimum for more than six months within s 24 of the CA 1985.

The directors of a parent company as such owe no duties to protect the interests of

---

7   *Salomon v A Salomon & Co Ltd* [1897] AC 22, HL.
8   [1969] 1 WLR 1241 at 1254, CA. See C M Schmitthoff [1976] JBL 305, [1978] JBL 218 at 219–222; see also *Walker v Wimborne* (1976) 50 ALJR 446; R Baxt [1976] 4 ABLR 289; Baxt and Harding, op cit.
9   [1976] 3 All ER 462, CA.
10 *Re Securitibank Ltd (No 2)* [1978] 2 NZLR 136.
11 *Woolfson v Strathclyde Regional Council* (1978) 38 P & CR 521.
12 (1977) 17 ALR 575.
13 [1990] Ch 433, CA.
14 See *Instituto Chemioterapico Italiano SpA v EC Commission*: Case 6, 7/73 [1974] ECR 223; *SAR Schotte Gmb H v Parfums Rothschild SARL*: 218/86 [1992] BCLC 235.
15 See *Re Augustus Barnett & Son Ltd* (1986) 2 BCC 98, 904. Noted by D D Prentice (1987) 103 LQR 11.

its subsidiaries when the subsidiaries have independent boards. This view of the law was accepted by the Court of Appeal in *Lindgren v L and P Estates Ltd*[16] in 1968, in spite of a cogent counter argument by counsel that the property of a holding company consists of the investment in the shares of its subsidiaries and the duty of a director of a holding company is to promote the interests of the subsidiaries representing that investment[17]. It is also arguable that directors of a holding company who sacrifice the interests of creditors of a subsidiary may, in appropriate circumstances, be parties to the carrying on of the subsidiary's business with intent to defraud its creditors within the fraudulent trading provisions of s 213[18]. If this is the case they can be made personally liable for its debts. In the USA, there is a duty to treat a subsidiary with fairness[19] and it has been argued that there should be a tougher rule requiring sharing of opportunities within the group[20]. Under English law, the directors of a subsidiary are as such under no fiduciary duties to the holding company merely as a majority shareholder[1]. It is not possible for the directors of a member of a group to rely on a transaction as being for the good of the group as a whole or other members of the group when it is not in the interests of the particular company of which they are directors. In the absence of evidence of what they did in fact consider, the test of their obligations is what they or an honest and reasonable director would consider to be in the interests of the subsidiary[2]. English law has not yet developed a concept of group interest or a coherent doctrine of fairness in respect of group transactions for the purposes of directors' fiduciary duties. The emphasis is still on the interest of individual companies. Indeed, the directors of a subsidiary must not simply act as puppets of the holding company or obey the holding company[3] where this will constitute a breach of their duties to the subsidiary[4]. Where the directors of a subsidiary who are nominees of the holding company sacrifice its interests for those of the holding company, minority shareholders may have a remedy for oppression under s 459. In *Scottish Co-operative Wholesale Society Ltd v Meyer*[5] in 1958, the House of Lords held that the Scottish CWS had acted towards the minority in an oppressive manner and that this conduct through its nominee directors who were also directors of the Society amounted to conduct of the affairs of the company within the section (then s 210 of the Companies

---

16   *Lindgren v L & P Estates Ltd* [1968] Ch 572 at 595 e and 604 e–f, CA. See also *Walker v Wimborne* (1976) 50 ALJR 446. See Baxt, op cit; Baxt and Harding, op cit. Cf *Scottish Co-operative Wholesale Society Ltd v Meyer* [1959] AC 324, HL; *Nicholas v Soundcraft Electronics Ltd* [1993] BCLC 360, CA.

17   [1968] Ch 572 at 582 d–e (Mr Ralph Instone).

18   Cf *Re Sarflax Ltd* [1979] Ch 592; see Barrett [1977] 40 MLR 226; Baxt and Harding, op cit; Russell [1982] 1 Canta LR 417.

19   *Sinclair Oil Corpn v Levien* 290 A 2d 717 (1971). Noted at (1971) 57 Va L Rev 1223.

20   Brudney and Chirelstein (1974) 88 Harv L Rev 297.

1   *Bell v Lever Bros Ltd* [1932] AC 161 at 228, HL.

2   *Charterbridge Corpn Ltd v Lloyds Bank Ltd* [1970] Ch 62. See also *Re Halt Garage (1964) Ltd* [1982] 3 All ER 1016; *Re Horsley & Weight Ltd* [1982] Ch 442, CA and *Rolled Steel Products (Holdings) Ltd v British Steel Corpn* [1986] Ch 246, [1985] 3 All ER 52, CA, discussed in Chapter 10. Cf also the New South Wales Court of Appeal decision in *Equiticorp Finance Ltd (in liquidation) v Bank of New Zealand* (1993) 11 ACSR 642 where Clarke and Cripps JJA saw difficulties in an objective test and the New Zealand Court of Appeal decision in *Nicholson v Permakraft (NZ) Ltd* [1985] 1 NZLR 242. Cf the US case law discussed in R Nathan (1986) 3 Canta LR 1, 11 et seq. See further H W Ballentine (1925) 14 Calif L Rev 12; A Berle Jr (1947) 47 Col L Rev 343; B Cataldo (1953) Law & Contemp Problems 473; GMB (1971) 57 Val Rev 1223; J Landers (1976) 43 Chi L Rev 527; Note (1984) 74 Yale L J 338.

3   *Selangor United Rubber Estates Ltd v Cradock (a bankrupt) (No 3)* [1968] 2 All ER 1073.

4   *Lonrho Ltd v Shell Petroleum Co Ltd* [1980] 1 WLR 627, HL.

5   [1959] AC 324, HL. See too *Re National Building Maintenance Ltd* [1971] 1 WWR 8; affd sub nom *National Building Maintenance Ltd v Dove* [1972] 5 WWR 410 (controlling shareholder selling company's major asset to associated company).

Act 1948) since the transactions could not be separated. Viscount Simonds, following Lord President Cooper and Lord Keith of Avonholm in the Court of Session, formulated a principle that where a subsidiary is formed with an independent minority of shareholders, the parent company, if it is engaged in the same class of business, is under an obligation to conduct its own affairs in such a way as to deal fairly with its subsidiary[6]. Lord Keith added that even where such directors are conducting the affairs of the parent they may by neglect be misconducting the affairs of the subsidiaries[7]. A liberal interpretation of the nominee director's role was given in the Australian case of *Re Broadcasting Station 2GB Pty Ltd*[8] where Jacobs J held that conduct in pursuit of the dominant company's interests is not reprehensible unless it can also be inferred that the directors would so act even if they were of the view that their acts were not in the best interests of the company.

LIMITED RECOGNITION OF THE GROUP IN THE COMPANIES ACTS

Section 736 defines 'holding company' and 'subsidiary'. Section 736(1) defines a subsidiary of another company 'its holding company' if that other company—

    (a) holds a majority of the voting rights in it, or
    (b) is a member of it and has the right to appoint or remove a majority of its board of directors, or
    (c) is a member of it and controls alone, pursuant to an agreement with other shareholders or members, a majority of the voting rights in it,

or if it is a subsidiary of a company which is itself a subsidiary of that other company.

Section 736(2) amplifies s 736(1) and provides (inter alia) that:

(1) In section 736(1)(*b*) the reference to the right to appoint or remove a majority of the board of directors is to the right to appoint or remove directors holding a majority of the voting rights at meetings of the board on all, or substantially all, matters; and for the purposes of that provision—

    (a) a company shall be treated as having the right to appoint to a directorship if—
        (i) a person's appointment to it follows necessarily from his appointment as director of the company, or
        (ii) the directorship is held by the company itself; and
    (b) a right to appoint or remove which is exercisable only with the consent or concurrence of another person shall be left out of account unless no other person has a right to appoint or, as the case may be, remove in relation to that directorship (s 736A(3)).

(2) Rights which are exercisable only in certain circumstances shall be taken into account only—

    (a) when the circumstances have arisen, and for so long as they continue to obtain, or
    (b) when the circumstances are within the control of the person having the

---

6   Ibid, at 343.
7   Ibid, at 363.
8   [1964–5] NSWR 1648. Noted (1965–7) 5 Sydney LR 288.

rights;

and rights which are normally exercisable but are temporarily incapable of exercise shall continue to be taken into account (s 736A(4)).

(3) Rights held by a person in a fiduciary capacity shall be treated as not held by him (s 736A(5)).

(4) Rights held by a person as nominee for another shall be treated as held by the other; and rights shall be regarded as held as nominee for another if they are exercisable only on his instructions or with his consent or concurrence (s 736A(6)).

(5) Rights attached to shares held by way of security shall be treated as held by the person providing the security—

    (a) where apart from the right to exercise them for the purpose of preserving the value of the security, or of realising it, the rights are exercisable only in accordance with his instructions;

    (b) where the shares are held in connection with the granting of loans as part of normal business activities and apart from the right to exercise them for the purpose of preserving the value of the security, or of realising it, the rights are exercisable only in his interests (s 736A(7)).

(6) Rights shall be treated as held by a company if they are held by any of its subsidiaries; and nothing in subsection (6) or (7) shall be construed as requiring rights held by a company to be treated as held by any of its subsidiaries (s 736A(8)).

(7) The voting rights in a company shall be reduced by any rights held by the company itself (s 736A(10)).

So far these definitions have concentrated on corporate groups. However, the key provisions of s 258 deal with groups of undertakings which are the basis of the new consolidated accounts requirements under the Seventh Directive. Here the references to dominant influence and control contracts echo German Law. The relevant provisions are as follows:

(1) An undertaking is a parent undertaking in relation to another undertaking, a subsidiary undertaking, if—

    (a) it holds a majority of the voting rights in the undertaking, or

    (b) it is a member of the undertaking and has the right to appoint or remove a majority of its board of directors, or

    (c) it has the right to exercise a dominant influence over the undertaking—

        (i) by virtue of provisions contained in the undertaking's memorandum or articles, or

        (ii) by virtue of a control contract, or

    (d) it is a member of the undertaking and controls alone, pursuant to an agreement with other shareholders or members, a majority of the voting rights in the undertaking (s 258(2)).

(2) For the purposes of subsection (1) an undertaking shall be treated as a member of another undertaking—

    (a) if any of its subsidiary undertakings is a member of that undertaking, or

    (b) if any shares in that other undertaking are held by a person acting on behalf of the undertaking or any of its subsidiary undertakings (s 258(3)).

(3) An undertaking is also a parent undertaking in relation to another undertaking, a subsidiary undertaking, if it has a participating interest in the undertaking and—

    (a) it actually exercises a dominant influence over it, or

(b) it and the subsidiary undertaking are managed on a unified basis (s 258(4)).

A right to exercise a dominant influence is a right to give directions with respect to the operating and financial policies of another undertaking which the latter's directors are obliged to comply with whether or not they are for its benefit (CA 1989, Sch 9, para 4(1)).

A control contract is a contract in writing confirming such a right of a kind authorised by the memorandum or articles of the undertaking in question and permitted by the law under which that undertaking is established (CA 1989, Sch 9, para 4(2)).

The primary reasons for the Companies Act definitions which differ from some other statutory definitions eg in some tax statutes, are first for the purpose of disclosure. Section 227 requires consolidated group accounts to be prepared, combining the information contained in the separate balance sheets and profit and loss accounts of the holding company and of the companies which were its subsidiaries at the end of the financial year to show the profitability and solvency of the group as a single unit. This is in addition to separate accounts for each member of the group which has limited liability. The group accounts must give a true and fair view of the state of affairs at the end of the year and the profit and loss for the year of the undertaking included in the consolidation. They must comply with Schedule 4A. Where such compliance would not show a true and fair view, additional information must be given in the accounts or notes to the accounts. If compliance with any of these requirements fails to show a true and fair view the company must depart from them to show a true and fair view[9].

There are a number of exemptions and exclusions which are dealt with in Chapter 29. The directors' report must also contain details about the group. In the Australian case of *Industrial Equity Ltd v Blackburn*[10] Mason J, commenting on the equivalent provisions in the Australian Uniform Companies legislation, said:

> The purpose of these requirements is to ensure that the members of, and for that matter persons dealing with, a holding company are provided with accurate information as to the profit or loss and the state of affairs of that company and its subsidiary companies within the group, information which would not be forthcoming if all the shareholders received was limited to the accounts of the holding company disclosing as assets the shares which it holds in its subsidiaries. It is for this purpose that the Companies Act treats the business group as one entity, and requires that its financial results be incorporated in consolidated accounts to be circulated to shareholders and laid before a general meeting (ss 162(4) and 164(1)) and requires that the accounts and other documents shall accompany the annual return ...

The second reason for the Companies Act definition is that s 23 prohibits a subsidiary or its nominee from being a member of its holding company and any allotment or transfer to it is void. This was introduced as a result of the Greene Committee's Report to bolster the rule in *Trevor v Whitworth*[11] which has since been modified by statute. The prohibition does not apply if the subsidiary is merely concerned as personal representative or trustee and is not beneficially interested. Voting rights on shares already held are suspended. Certain residual interests under pension schemes or employees share schemes are disregarded until they vest in possession. In

9   See Chapter 29, ante and C Swinson *A Guide to the Companies Act 1989* (1990), ch 3.
10 (1977) 17 ALR 575.
11 (1887) 12 App Cas 409, HL.

addition as a result of CA 1989, s 129 the prohibition does not apply if the shares are held as a 'market maker' as defined by CA 1985, s 23(3). Thirdly, there are a number of provisions in the Companies Act where obligations imposed on companies are extended to other members of the group or at least the holding company and their, or its, directors[12]. Conversely, there are provisions to exempt intra-group transactions which would otherwise be prohibited[13].

Thus it can be seen that, unlike the German corporate legislation contained in the *Aktiengesetz*, English law has not produced a coherent comprehensive law relating to groups[14]. The legislative provisions are sporadic and the case law underdeveloped. The result is unsatisfactory, as the courts are beginning to realise. In *Re Southard & Co Ltd*[15] in 1979, Templeman LJ said:

> English company law possesses some curious features, which may generate curious results. A parent company may spawn a number of subsidiary companies, all controlled directly or indirectly by the shareholders of the parent company. If one of the subsidiary companies, to change the metaphor, turns out to be the runt of the litter and declines into insolvency to the dismay of its creditors, the parent company and other subsidiary companies prosper to the joy of the shareholders without any liability for the debts of the insolvent subsidiary.

The imposition of the Seventh Directive requirements upon the old group provisions has added to the complexity and incomplete character of English law. The broader concepts of control and the reference to control contracts echo German law and have an ill-defined relationship to English law.

REFORM

The draft proposal for a Ninth Directive on Groups, which is based on the German model, provides for a legal structure for unified management of a public limited company and any other undertaking which has a controlling interest in it whether or not that undertaking is a company. It prescribes rules for the conduct of groups which are not managed on a unified basis but only in respect of public limited company members. Unless the relationship is formalised by one of the two methods specified, the controlling undertaking is liable for losses of the subsidiary resulting from the controlling influence and attributable to a fault in management or action taken which is not in the subsidiary's interest.

The draft has been strongly criticised[16] and no further steps are to be taken in the forseeable future[17].

---

12   For example, s 151 and s 330 of CA 1985. See also R R Pennington *Company Law* (7th edn, 1995), ch 20.
13   In the loan prohibitions for directors in Pt X there are exemptions for intra-group transactions.
14   See F Wooldridge *Groups of Companies—The Law and Practice in Britain, France and Germany* (1981).
15   [1979] 1 WLR 1198 at 1208, CA.
16   See for instance Yves Guyon, 'Examen Critique des Projets Européens en matière de Groupes de Sociétés (le point de vue français) in *Groups of Companies in European Laws*, Vol II (ed by Klaus J Hopt) (1982) p 155; R. Rodière, 'Reflexions sur les Avants-Projets d'une Directive de la Commission des CEE concernant les Groupes de Sociétés', D 1977, 136.
17   'The Single Market Company Law Harmonisation' (DTI) Sept 1989, p 17. See Dorresteijn, Kuiper and Morse, op cit, ch 9.

Short of a comprehensive code of law relating to groups on the lines of the German *Aktiengesetz* which might be forced upon us as a result of EC influences, there are pressures on the one hand to legitimate the group interest and on the other hand to make members of a group liable for the debts of other companies in the group[18] and to protect employees. In the USA this takes place to some extent through equitable subordination, piercing the corporate veil and consolidation of related bankrupts[19]. In New Zealand and the Republic of Ireland, reforms have recently been adopted providing for a discretion to be conferred on the courts to order payment of the debts of one group member by another and pooling of assets. The Cork Committee shrank from making such radical proposals but favoured the tightening-up of the law on connected persons and the deferment of the debts owed to other companies in the group of directors' loan accounts to the debts of external creditors, where the former appear to be part of the long-term capital structure of the debtor company[20].

The Cork Report favoured a more comprehensive review of groups by a committee charged with reform of company law in general. If such a review were undertaken, it would be necessary to go back to basics and to ask what are the underlying economic purposes of limited liability and to what extent do they require the doctrine to apply to groups of companies[1]. Also what restrictions on control and group behaviour are justified in the interests of minority shareholders and of general creditors? It is almost instinctive for reformers to consider that the answer lies in whole or in part in increased disclosure. Thus the preamble to a draft EU Directive states that 'it is necessary in the interest not only of shareholders, creditors and employees but also of the general public that clear insight be afforded into their ownership and power structures by means of the most extensive disclosure measures possible'. However, in this context, disclosure is frequently not enough and the cost exceeds any likely benefit. There is a need for substantive reform, but its precise form is a matter of controversy.

---

18   See the Conference on Harmonisation of Company Law in Europe—The Draft Directive on the Conduct of Groups, issued by the Department of Trade, March 1981. See generally J Welch (1986) 7 Co Law 29; R Nathan (1986) 3 Canta LR 1; Dorresteijn et al op cit.

19   Landers, op cit (see footnote 5 supra); Hadden *The Control of Corporate Groups*, op cit, ch 5; Nathan, op cit.

20   Cmnd 8558, ch 51. For a detailed discussion of the law in New Zealand, Australia and the USA see J H Farrar and A B Darroch 'Insolvency and Corporate Groups—the Problem of Consolidation' in J P G Lessing and J F Corkery (ed), *Corporate Insolvency Law* (1995), ch 15. For Australia see also I Ramsay (1994) 17 UNSWLJ 520. See also M Gillooly (ed) *The Law Relating to Corporate Groups* (1993). See generally P Blumberg *The Multinational Challenge to Corporation Law* (1993), ch 3 et seq and his multi-volume US Treatise on *Corporate Groups* which is the major work on this subject.

1   See D D Prentice 'Groups of Companies: The English Experience' in *Groups of Companies in European Laws* (1982), vol II, ed Klaus J Hopt, pp 99, 128. See also the useful comparative analyses in D Sugarman and G Teubner *Regulating Corporate Groups in Europe* (1990) especially the introductory chapter by D Sugarman, 19-35.

CHAPTER 34

Raising capital from the public

INTRODUCTION

Capital raising by the company

The basic function of companies is to provide a vehicle for entrepreneurial activity. Large-scale entrepreneurial activity may, however, require amounts of capital which can only be provided by inviting outside investors to pool their resources and invest in an enterprise over which they may have relatively little control. To persuade such investors to come forward two incentives are needed. One is limited liability[1]. The other is a market in which investors can realise their investment. Without such a market investors will require a higher return on their investment to compensate for the lack of liquidity. The company will, therefore, need to join a stock market if it is to be able to offer the attraction of liquidity to its investors. The existence of a market for shares thus not only makes it possible for companies to raise external funding but makes it cheaper for them to do so as well. This chapter is concerned with the rules governing the operation of securities markets and, in particular, those dealing with offers of shares to the public.

A company may be formed at the outset as a public company. More commonly, it is likely that an existing private company has expanded to the point where further growth cannot be funded from either retained profits or borrowing from the bank. The company will then convert to being a public company, for only a public company may offer its shares or debentures to the public and it is an offence for a private company to do so[2]. Being a public company, however, is not synonymous with being listed or quoted on a stock market, and if the company is serious about raising significant sums of money from investors, and in turn providing a market for those investors, then it will seek to be a listed public company and to offer shares in the company to the investing public.

---

1   See Easterbrook & Fischel *The Economic Structure of Corporate Law* (1991), ch 2; Halpern, Trebilcock and Turnbull '*An economic analysis of limited liability in corporation law*' (1980) 30 Univ of Toronto Law Jo 117.
2   Companies Act 1985, s 81.

The process of launching a public company by offering its shares to the public, whether it is a brand new company or a former private company, is known as flotation. Capital can be raised, of course, other than through flotations. For example, existing listed public companies may use the stock market to raise further capital from outside investors rather than use retained profits. This may be by means of an offer to the public generally. More probably, it will be by means of a rights issue, in which the new shares are offered to existing shareholders in proportion to their existing holding, or by a placing, in which shares are placed with certain selected investors who have agreed to take them.

The company may decide, instead of raising outside capital, to offer shares in itself as the consideration for the acquisition of another business or in exchange for the shares in a target company it is seeking to take over. This ability of companies to fund acquisitions by offering shares is one of the main advantages of converting a private company into a public one listed on a stock exchange.

The DTI Annual Report on Companies for 1996–1997 showed that the register of companies was made up of 1,091,900 companies, of which 1,080,200 (or 98.9% of the register) were private companies and 11,700 (or 1.1%) were public companies. The Stock Exchange's figures show that approximately 2,150 UK companies were listed at the end of 1997 so only a small percentage of the 11,700 UK public companies ever seek a listing[3].

Share sales by existing shareholders

So far we have referred to situations in which the company is raising capital for its own expansion. In many cases though the reason for shares in the company being offered to the public is because the existing shareholders wish to sell some of their shares, rather than the company raising fresh capital. It may be that, in a family business, the existing family members are all reaching retiring age and there is no one within the family to carry the business on. The family may wish to convert their capital into a more liquid form and if there is no single buyer ready to take over the company then it will be sensible to float the company and for the family to realise their shares through a public offering. Even if the present owners are not retiring they may still wish to diversify their investments by selling part of their shareholdings or may wish to realise their investment so as to have money available to use for a different purpose.

Formation of public companies

A company may be formed initially as a public company by complying with the requirements of the Companies Act 1985[4] which include that the company has two members[5], that the memorandum states that the company is to be a public company[6], and that the share capital stated in the memorandum is not less than the authorised minimum of £50,000[7].

A company registered as a public company on its original incorporation must not do business or exercise any of its borrowing powers unless the registrar of companies

---

3   See DTI *Companies in 1996–97* (1997), Table A2; London Stock Exchange *Fact File 1998* (1998), p 8.
4   CA 1985, s 1(3).
5   Ibid, s 1(1).
6   Ibid, s 1(3)(a).
7   Ibid, ss 11, 118.

has certified, under CA 1985, s 117, that the minimum share capital requirements for a public company have been complied with, or the company is re-registered as a private company[8]. The registrar must be satisfied that the nominal value of the company's allotted share capital is not less than the authorised minimum[9] and a director or the company secretary must make a statutory declaration to that effect[10]. If the company does business or exercises borrowing powers without such a certificate, the company and any officer who is in default may be liable to a fine[11]. Furthermore, if the company fails to obtain a certificate within 21 days of being called upon to do so, the directors are liable to indemnify the other party to the transaction for any loss or damage suffered by reason of the company's failure to obtain such a certificate[12].

Conversion of private companies to public

As an alternative to registering initially as a public company, a private company may re-register as a public company[13]. The members must pass a special resolution to that effect, alter the memorandum and articles as required, and deliver various documents to the registrar of companies[14]. In addition, the company must show that it meets the more stringent rules on the raising and maintenance of share capital applicable to public companies[15]. The registrar of companies will then issue a certificate of incorporation stating that the company is a public company[16].

Conversion of public companies to private

Not all public companies find that status an advantage. There are more requirements for the disclosure of its activities; it is less easy to organise the company's affairs to suit the interests of the family who may still own a large percentage of the equity; and there is the cost of dealing with large numbers of new shareholders. So sometimes companies convert back from public to private status.

This may happen, of course, where a company is taken over and becomes the wholly owned subsidiary of another company. But it does happen occasionally that the majority decides to buy out the minority and then revert to private status by re-registering. The members must pass a special resolution that the company should re-register as a private company, alter the memorandum so that it no longer states that it is a public company, alter the articles as required and deliver various documents to the registrar of companies[17]. Provision is made for a certain minority of members to object by application to the court[18]. In practice, any dissenting minority are more likely to have been bought out before the change of status is made. The registrar of companies will then issue a certificate of incorporation stating that the company is a private company[19].

8   Ibid, s 117(1). See discussion of this provision in ch 15.
9   Ie £50,000: see ibid, s 118.
10   Ibid, s 117(3).
11   Ibid, s 117(7).
12   Ibid, s 117(8). But note that it is specifically provided that breach of the section shall not affect the validity of the transaction.
13   Ibid, ss 43–47.
14   Ibid, s 43(1), (2), (3).
15   See ibid, ss 44, 45.
16   Ibid, s 47(1).
17   Ibid, s 53.
18   Ibid, s 54.
19   Ibid, s 55.

THE STOCK EXCHANGE MARKETS

We have already seen that for a company effectively to raise capital from the public, it must have its shares listed or quoted on a stock market and, for UK companies, that means listed on the London Stock Exchange.

The official list

Companies joining the main market of the Stock Exchange are said to be admitted to the Official List maintained by the Exchange and are correctly described as 'listed' rather than 'quoted' companies. The official listing of securities is governed by Part IV of the Financial Services Act 1986 and the Listing Rules[20] drawn up by the Stock Exchange as the designated 'competent authority' under that Act[1]. 'Securities' is widely defined in the Financial Services Act to encompass a variety of investments including shares, debentures and government and public securities[2] but our discussion in this chapter will focus primarily on the listing and public offers of shares although, in keeping with the wording of the legislation, the term 'securities' will be used throughout.

The Listing Rules govern admission to listing, set out the continuing obligations of issuers whose securities are listed, and provide for the enforcement of the rules. The Stock Exchange may in certain circumstances refuse an application for listing[3], it may suspend listings[4] and may discontinue any listing of any securities altogether where there are special circumstances which preclude normal regular dealings in the securities[5]. A decision to refuse admission to listing or to discontinue a listing must be subject to judicial review[6] but, in common with other regulatory bodies under the Financial Services Act[7], the competent authority is granted limited immunity from liability in damages[8]. Neither the competent authority nor any member, officer or servant of the authority may be made liable in damages for anything done or omitted in the discharge or purported discharge of any functions of the authority under FSA 1986, Pt IV, unless the act or omission is shown to have been in bad faith[9].

An application for listing must be made to the Stock Exchange in such manner as the Listing Rules may require[10]. The market value of the shares being listed must be at least £700,000[11], though in practice it will usually be far greater than that. The company

---

20 The Listing Rules are often referred to as the Yellow Book because they are contained in a looseleaf yellow binder.
1 See FSA 1986, s 142(6) as amended.
2 See ibid, s 142, Sch 1.
3 Ibid, s 144(3). All applications for listing must have the consent of the company. A major shareholder could not apply, therefore, independently of the company, to have the shares listed: s 143(2).
4 Ibid, s 145(2); Listing Rules, rr 1.19–1.21.
5 FSA 1986, s 145(1).
6 See EEC Council Directive 79/279, art 15 (the Admissions Directive). However, the right to apply to the court under art 15 is conferred on the company or the issuers alone and not on individual shareholders: *R v International Stock Exchange of the United Kingdom and the Republic of Ireland Ltd, ex p Else (1982) Ltd* [1993] 1 All ER 420, [1993] BCLC 834, CA. The EC Directives are discussed below.
7 See FSA 1986, s 187.
8 Ibid, s 187(4). The immunity covers liability to investors as well as liability to companies who claim to have been wrongly refused admission or which claim to have had their listing wrongly suspended or discontinued.
9 FSA 1986, s 187(4).
10 Ibid, s 143(1).
11 Listing Rules, r 3.16.

must have at least a three-year trading record[12], the shares to be listed must be freely transferable, and a sufficient number (usually at least 25%) of the shares being listed must be distributed to the public, (ie to persons who are not the directors or connected to the directors)[13]. The company will have to publish listing particulars (discussed below) when it joins the Official List (the main market) and, in addition, the Listing Rules contain a number of continuing obligations which a listed company is required to observe once any of its securities have been admitted to listing[14]. Observance of the continuing obligations is essential to the maintenance of an orderly market in securities and to ensure that all users of the market have simultaneous access to the same information[15].

In applying the Listing Rules, the Stock Exchange has regard to the following objectives and principles[16]:

- The Exchange seeks a balance between providing issuers with ready access to the market for their securities and protecting investors.
- Securities will be admitted to listing only if the exchange is satisfied that the applicant is suitable and that it is appropriate for those securities to be publicly held and traded.
- Securities should be brought to the market in a way which is appropriate to their nature and number and which will facilitate an open and efficient market for trading in those securities.
- An issuer must make full and timely disclosure about itself and its listed securities at the time of listing and subsequently.
- The listing rules, and in particular the continuing obligations, should promote investor confidence in standards of disclosure, in the conduct of listed companies' affairs and in the market as a whole.
- Holders of equity securities should be given adequate opportunity to consider in advance and vote upon major changes in the company's business operations and matters of importance concerning the company's management and constitution.

By the end of 1997, there were 2,683 companies on the main market, 2,157 UK companies and 526 international[17].

The USM

In the early 1970s a number of licensed dealers in securities began to create a market outside the control of the Stock Exchange by offering to match buyers and sellers, or, in some cases, by dealing in shares as principals, a practice known as market-making. This Over-the-Counter Market or OTC, as it was known, grew steadily and in November 1980 the Stock Exchange launched the Unlisted Securities Market or USM which was designed to provide a market for shares in smaller companies which did not qualify or did not choose listing on the main exchange[18]. The USM, after initial successes, suffered from liquidity problems, particularly during the recession in the

---

12   Listing Rules, r 3.3 (exceptions are possible, see r 3.4); r 3.6.
13   Listing Rules, rr 3.18–3.21.
14   See Listing Rules, ch 9.
15   See Listing Rules, Introduction to ch 9.
16   See the Introduction to the Listing Rules.
17   See London Stock Exchange *Fact File 1998* (1998), p 8.
18   The company needed to have only a two-year trading record and a minimum of only 10% of any class of quoted shares needed to be in public hands.

early 1990s. Moreover, amendments to the USM rulebook brought its rules closer to the Official List and meant that there was little to be gained by companies seeking a listing on the junior market. It was therefore decide to wind up the USM with no new companies being admitted to it after 1994 although it continued to operate until the end of 1996. By that time, it had been overtaken by a new market, the Alternative Investment Market (AIM).

AIM

In June 1995, the Stock Exchange launched a new market for smaller, young and growing companies called the Alternative Investment Market or AIM. This initiative was a response to demand for a market that would give a wide range of smaller companies access to a public market and this was achieved by minimising the eligibility criteria to be met by companies coming to this market[19]. Companies are not required to have reached a certain size, or to have a defined number of shares in public hands, or to provide a lengthy trading history. To be admitted to AIM, a company must be judged to be appropriate to join by a firm known as a nominated adviser[20] who must be retained by the company at all times while quoted on the market and who is responsible for guiding and helping the company to comply with the market rules[1]. The emphasis is on the nominated advisers putting their reputation on the line when they confirm that a company is appropriate for AIM. In this way, it is hoped that the advisers will be thorough in assessing whether a company is suitable for the market. By the end of 1997, AIM had attracted 308 companies across all sectors of industry, bringing its total capitalisation to £5.7bn[2].

METHODS OF MARKETING SHARES

When a company wishes to raise fresh capital by issuing shares there are a number of factors to be considered. Among these will be the method of marketing, who the shares are to be offered to, how the price is to be fixed, and what professional services the company should make use of. It may also be the case that it is not the company marketing the shares at all but an existing shareholder offering shares for sale. Many of the same considerations, however, arise here too. The final factor to bear in mind is whether the shares being marketed are in a company already listed on the main market or trading on AIM or whether the marketing accompanies a new entry into the particular market by the company concerned.

Offers for sale and offers for subscription

Where the offer of shares to the public is not by the company itself but by an existing shareholder, it is called an offer for sale and the persons who acquire the shares are known as purchasers[3]. Where the company itself offers the shares, this is known as an

---

19   See London Stock Exchange *Fact File 1998* (1998), p 15.
20   Nominated adviser firms are drawn from a range of stockbrokers, banks, corporate finance houses and accountancy firms: London Stock Exchange *Fact File 1998* (1998), p 18.
1   See London Stock Exchange *Fact File 1998* (1998), p 16.
2   See London Stock Exchange *Fact File 1998* (1998), p 15.
3   Listing Rules, r 4.4.

offer for subscription[4] and the persons who acquire the shares directly from the company are known as subscribers.

In practice, both the company and existing shareholders will often make use of the services of an issuing house which will acquire the shares from the company or the existing shareholders and then offer them for sale to the public. Alternatively, the company or existing shareholders may use the issuing house purely as an agent without the shares concerned being allotted or transferred to the issuing house.

Whichever method is used, the price at which the shares are sold may either be that fixed by the seller (a fixed price offer) or that fixed by a system of tendering by interested buyers (a tender offer). The problem with a fixed price offer is judging the appropriate price. It is not unknown for the market value of shares, when dealings in them begin, to be at a considerable premium to the fixed offer price. To try and curtail this a tender offer may be used. Under a tender offer system the seller invites prospective purchasers to tender whatever price they wish for the shares, provided it is above a minimum or reserve figure indicated by the seller. The price at which the shares will actually be sold (known as 'the striking price') will be the highest price at which all the shares on offer will have been applied for and thus will be sold.

Where shares are sold at a fixed price the difficulty of predicting a price that will precisely match supply and demand means that offers will almost certainly be either under or oversubscribed. Since the seller and its advisers, in order to make the offer a success, will have agreed a price slightly below what they anticipate the market price will be, most fixed price offers are oversubscribed to a greater or lesser extent. Even a tender offer does not avoid this problem because at the striking price there may in fact be more applications than there are shares on offer. Where the offer is oversubscribed the seller and its advisers will decide how to scale down or ballot the applications.

If an offer by a public company is not fully subscribed then the company cannot proceed to allot any of the shares offered unless the terms of the offer allowed for allotment in any event or in the event of certain specified conditions which have been satisfied[5]. In practice sellers do not take the risk of an offer not being fully taken up. Instead they will insure the risk with underwriters who agree to take up any shares not applied for in the offer. The underwriter will be paid a fee for the service which, however, cannot exceed 10% of the issue price of the shares or such lesser sum as is authorised by the company's articles of association[6].

In terms of the law of contract, advertising an offer of shares constitutes an invitation to treat. A person interested in acquiring shares fills in an application form which constitutes an offer which will then be accepted or rejected by the person selling the shares. The successful applicant will then be sent a letter of acceptance which will normally be renounceable. At this stage the applicant will not be registered as a shareholder in the company.

Until entry on the register of members, if applicants wish to sell any of their holdings, they may renounce their right to be registered as shareholders in favour of someone who buys that right from them. In other words, a renounceable letter of acceptance is marketable in the same way as shares themselves. At the end of the interim period, the company will enter in the register of members those persons now entitled to the letters of acceptance and will send them share certificates; or will enter on to the register

4   Listing Rules, r 4.5.
5   CA 1985, s 84(1); any allotment in breach of s 84(1) is voidable at the instance of the applicant for the shares provided steps are taken within one month of the allotment; and the directors may also be liable to compensate the applicant: s 85.
6   Ibid, s 97.

that the securities are held in uncertificated form, if that is the case[7]. The company must within one month of the allotment make a return of allotments to the Registrar of Companies[8].

Placings

Offering shares to the public at large is inevitably a lengthy process. It is also expensive not only in terms of printing costs, advertising costs, underwriting and other professional fees but also in terms of the discount to the anticipated market price that must be built in to make sure the offer is a success. For these reasons companies will often prefer to raise capital via a placing, a procedure under which the broker sponsoring the issue finds persons interested in acquiring shares in the company and places the shares with them[9].

Rights issues

A rights issue is where a company offers shares to its existing shareholders in proportion to their existing shareholding. In the case of companies listed on the main market, the procedure for a rights issue is for the company formally to allot the new shares to the shareholders. They are informed of this by means of a letter of allotment which, however, must be renounceable[10]. In other words, shareholders who do not wish to take up their rights must be able to sell these rights to someone else. Furthermore, there is protection for shareholders who neither take up their rights nor sell them. Unless specifically agreed by the general meeting, the company must arrange to sell any shares not taken up for the benefit of the shareholders entitled to them[11].

As discussed previously, under CA 1985, s 89, companies issuing new equity shares for purely cash consideration are normally obliged to do so via a rights issue, unless the shareholders have agreed to disapply the section[12]. From the point of view of the company management a rights issue is seen as a relatively expensive way of raising capital compared with a placing. In order to ensure that the shares are taken up, the discount to the current market price on a rights issue will be greater than that on a placing. There will also be the cost of underwriting a rights issue as well as greater printing and advertising costs. On the other hand, institutional investors are anxious to prevent any dilution of their statutory rights and so set limits to their support for resolutions disapplying the pre-emption provisions. The institutions will not oppose resolutions which seek to disapply pre-emption rights in respect of ordinary share capital provided the resolution is restricted to an amount of shares not exceeding 5% of the issued ordinary share capital at the relevant time. This is subject to a cumulative limit of 7.5% in any rolling three-year period. The discount available when shares are allotted on a non pre-emption basis is also limited[13].

---

7   See ch 19 for discussion of share certificates and the holding of shares in uncertificated form under the CREST system.
8   CA 1985, s 88.
9   See Listing Rules, r 4.7.
10   See Listing Rules, r 4.16.
11   See Listing Rules, r 4.19.
12   See ch 15 above for a detailed discussion of the statutory scheme governing rights issues; and the various exemption and disapplication options open to companies.
13   See NAPF/ABI *Pre-emption Rights, the Cost of Capital and Underwriting Fees* (1996).

Other methods of marketing shares

Offers for sale, offers for subscription, placings and rights issues are the main methods of marketing shares where the company's purpose is to raise money. But companies may also offer shares to the shareholders in another company as consideration for a take-over or in consideration for the acquisition of an asset[14] or they may issue shares to their existing shareholders as a capitalisation or bonus issue[15]. Finally, there is one important transaction which needs to be mentioned in this context although it does not involve the company in issuing any shares at all and that is an introduction, which is a method of bringing securities to listing not involving an issue of new securities or any marketing of existing securities because the securities are already widely held by the public[16].

THE NATURE AND FUNCTION OF SECURITIES REGULATION

The purposes of securities regulation

Before looking at the detail of how the marketing of securities is regulated in the UK, it may be helpful to consider the purposes behind securities regulation and, in the light of that, to consider the regulatory structure which has developed. As we have seen, the reason why stock markets develop is to provide a forum in which shares can be traded. The existence of a market in which shares can be sold will encourage such investment to take place. Without a market in which to realise their investment, investors would require a higher return to compensate them for this lack of liquidity. So the existence of a market also makes it cheaper for companies to raise externally generated funds for investment.

If the market is operating efficiently then the price of a company's shares, quoted on the market, will reflect the profitability of the use to which the assets of the company are currently being put. This is important to the overall national economy in that it will enable successful companies to raise further funds more easily, allowing them to expand their operations and ultimately increase the overall wealth of society by ensuring that assets are allocated to their most productive use. It also means that companies with poor management become vulnerable to takeover bids which may result in the assets being put to a new, more productive, use or in the management being replaced.

These, admittedly very basic, propositions about the operation of the stock market are intended to show how the stock market plays a role in the national economy. The fundamental objective of securities regulation must be, therefore, to help the stock market operate more efficiently in fulfilling the functions just described. There are other objectives as well[17]. Promoting the UK as a financial centre by ensuring that investors have confidence in the UK securities market is one. Stimulating competition

---

14   See Listing Rules, r 4.27. See also ch 34 below.
15   See Listing Rules, r 4.31. Bonus issues are discussed in ch 15.
16   See Listing Rules, r 4.12.
17   The appropriate objectives and regulatory structure for the financial services industry has been the subject of constant debate for the past decade and detailed consideration of that debate is beyond the scope of this work. But see generally, *Financial Services in the United Kingdom, a new framework for investor protection* (1985), Cmnd 9432; The Large Report *Financial Services Regulation* (1993); SIB *Regulation of the United Kingdom Equity Markets* (1995); Treasury and Civil Service Committee 6th Report, *The Regulation of Financial Services in the UK*, vol 1 (1995), HC Session 1994–95, 332–I; SIB *Reform of the Financial Regulatory System, Report to the Chancellor of the Exchequer* (July 1997); FSA *Financial Services Authority: an outline* (October 1997).

and innovation in the financial services sector itself, so that the assets it employs are used efficiently could also be described as one of the objectives.

Particular aspects of securities regulation may be seen as furthering these broad objectives. For example, providing a regulatory framework will discourage dishonesty and encourage those who wish to adopt high standards to do so. Dishonest trade practices represent a form of unfair competition which leads ultimately to a misallocation of resources. In theory, market forces may be expected to discourage dishonesty because in the long run investors will shun the dishonest trader. However, a regulatory structure may help to reveal dishonesty more quickly. It will also encourage honest traders to realise that they do not need to adopt the same tactics in order to compete with the dishonest, by reassuring them that dishonesty will result in a sanction. A regulatory structure may also aim to promote professional competence among the personnel in the securities market.

Development of the statutory framework

One way to look at the controls on the marketing of shares in the UK is as part of the overall pattern of investor protection. Purchasing shares is, after all, only one method people may choose to invest their savings. For the private investor other methods include investments such as building society deposits, unit trusts, life assurance policies and pensions. The variety and complexity of new methods of investment since the first Prevention of Fraud (Investments) Act was passed in 1939[18], together with a number of financial frauds, led the Department of Trade in 1981 to appoint Professor LCB Gower to conduct a review of investor protection[19]. This culminated in the passing of the Financial Services Act 1986[20].

The Financial Services Act 1986 as a whole provides a comprehensive framework for the regulation of investment business and investor protection. The basic control imposed by the Act is the prohibition on the carrying on of investment business in the UK except by authorised or exempt persons. Authorisation can be achieved by membership of a self-regulating organisation recognised for the purposes of the Act by the Securities and Investments Board (SIB), or through certification by a similarly recognised professional body, or via direct authorisation by the Board itself.

One of the Labour Government's early initiatives on taking office in May 1997 was to announce plans to create a new regulatory structure for the financial services sector, necessitating the repeal of the Financial Services Act 1986 and its replacement with a Financial Regulatory Reform Bill which should be in force by autumn 1999.

There is to be a complete overhaul of the regulatory bodies involved with the creation of a new super-regulator to be called the Financial Services Authority (FSA). At the moment, the FSA is comprised essentially of the SIB which has formally changed its name to the FSA. In due course, it will gain banking supervisory staff from the Bank of England and will also replace the existing self-regulatory bodies and other regulators such as the Insurance Directorate of the Department of Trade and Industry. When the Financial Regulatory Reform Bill is laid before Parliament later in 1998, it will include

---

18 The Prevention of Fraud (Investments) Act 1958 was largely a re-enactment of the 1939 Act.

19 Professor Gower first produced a discussion document, *Review of Investor Protection* (1982). His report, under the same title, was published in two parts (Cmnd 9125) in 1984 and 1985. Between the publication of Pts I and II the Government published its White Paper, *Financial Services in the United Kingdom* (1985, Cmnd 9432).

20 See generally, Rider, Abrams, Ashe *Guide to Financial Services Regulation* (1997); Morris *Financial Services: Regulating Investment Business* (1995); R Pennington *The Law of the Investment Markets* (1990).

statutory objectives for the Financial Services Authority which will include the protection of consumers, the promotion of clean and orderly financial markets, and the maintenance of confidence in the financial system[1].

EC directives

Returning to the specific issue of listing of companies and public offers of shares, a significant influence in the development of the law in this area has been a number of EC Directives which have been adopted with the view to co-ordinating, without necessarily making uniform, the rules throughout the member states on such matters as the conditions and requirements for the admission of securities to stock exchange listing at the national stock exchanges of member states. The general objectives of European Union involvement in this field include to provide equivalent protection for investors throughout the Union; to facilitate cross-border exchange listing; and to promote greater interpenetration of national securities markets with a view to ensuring a genuine Community capital market[2].

Initially, there were three major Directives: the Admissions Directive[3]; the Listing Particulars Directive[4]; and the Interim Reports Directive[5] which were implemented by the Stock Exchange (Listing) Regulations 1984[6] (now repealed) and subsequently contained in Part IV Financial Services Act 1986 and the Listing Rules.

The Admissions Directive[7] co-ordinates the conditions for the admission of securities to official exchange listing and provides for the continuing obligations applicable to all issuers whose securities are so admitted. The Listing Particulars Directive[8] co-ordinates the requirements for the drawing up, scrutiny and distribution of the listing particulars to be published for the admission of securities to official listing. It requires listing particulars to be prepared in a prescribed format in compliance with the Directive's disclosure requirements; these must be published and each member state must designate a competent authority to scrutinise the listing particulars. The Interim Reports Directive[9] governs continuing disclosure obligations by companies whose securities have been admitted to official exchange listing.

Another significant directive is the Prospectus Directive[10] which co-ordinates the requirements for the drawing up, scrutiny and distribution of a prospectus when transferable securities are issued to the public provided that these securities are not already listed. This was implemented by the Public Offers of Securities Regulations 1995[11], discussed in detail below. This Directive seeks to harmonise the disclosure standards in member states for public offerings of securities.

The Listing Particulars Directive has been amended on a number of occasions, in particular by two directives on mutual recognition, the Mutual Recognition Directive[12] and the Second Mutual Recognition Directive[13]. Implementation of the mutual

1   See FSA, *Financial Services Authority: an outline* (October 1997), Appendix 1.
2   See the preamble to the various Directives.
3   EEC Council Directive 79/279, OJ 1979 L 66/21.
4   EEC Council Directive 80/390, OJ 1980 L 100/1.
5   EEC Council Directive 82/121, OJ 1982 L 48/26.
6   SI 1984/716.
7   EEC Council Directive 79/279, OJ 1979 L 66/21.
8   EEC Council Directive 80/390, OJ 1980 L 100/1.
9   EEC Council Directive 82/121, OJ 1982 L 48/26.
10   EEC Council Directive 89/298, OJ 1989 L 124/8.
11   SI 1995/1537.
12   EEC Council Directive 87/345, OJ 1987 L 185/81.
13   EEC Council Directive 90/211, OJ 1990 L 112/24.

recognition requirements is governed by the Public Offers of Securities Regulations 1995[14]. Mutual recognition is an important aspect of facilitating the development of a capital market across the European Union. Once listing particulars are approved by a competent authority in a member state, the listing particulars must be recognised as such by all the other member states in which admission to official listing is applied for, without further approval by their competent authority and without any additional information being required[15].

Where application for admission to official listing in one or more member states is made and the securities have been the subject of a public offer prospectus drawn up and approved in any member state in accordance with the Prospectus Directive, noted above, in the three months preceding the application for admission, the public offer prospectus must be recognised as listing particulars in the member state in which application for listing is made, without further approval by the competent authority and without any additional information being required[16]. In order to ensure that such prospectuses issued by UK registered companies will be acceptable in other member states, provision is made for companies to request that such a prospectus be pre-vetted by the Stock Exchange even though the shares are not to be listed on the London Stock Exchange[17].

Provision is also made for the mutual recognition of prospectuses where public offers are to be made in other member states either simultaneously or within three months of the first public offer being made, even though no application for listing is to be made[18]. Again, in order to ensure that such prospectuses issued by UK registered companies will be acceptable in other member states, provision is made for companies to request that such a prospectus be pre-vetted by the Stock Exchange even though the shares are not to be listed on the London Stock Exchange[19].

Disclosure of information

It is clear both at the domestic and European level that a central element of securities regulation is the full disclosure of information about the company involved and the securities being marketed[20]. For the stock market to operate efficiently as much information as possible must be available to the market. For this reason there are rules requiring the publication of certain information whenever new securities are introduced or marketed and continuing obligations to notify any information which might have a material impact on the valuation of securities. Some economists argue that market forces will induce companies voluntarily to provide information to the market and that elaborate disclosure requirements are unnecessary. Neither the Stock Exchange nor Parliament, however, has been prepared to rely on market forces alone and both in the Listing Rules and in the legislation governing admission to listing and public offers of shares, much emphasis is laid on timely disclosure of information to the market.

---

14   See Public Offers of Securities Regulations 1995, reg 20, Sch 4.
15   See EEC Council Directive 80/390, art 24A (as inserted by EEC Council Directive 87/345, art 1).
16   See EEC Council Directive 80/390, art 24B (as substituted by EEC Council Directive 90/211, art 2).
17   See the *Rules for Approval of Prospectuses where no Application for Listing is Made* contained in the Listing Rules; FSA 1986, s 156A.
18   EEC Council Directive 89/298, art 21.
19   See the *Rules for Approval of Prospectuses where no Application for Listing is Made* contained in the Listing Rules; FSA 1986, s 156A.
20   On the value of disclosure in this context, see generally Easterbrook and Fischel *The Economic Structure of Corporate Law* (1991), ch 11; Page and Ferguson *Investor Protection* (1993), ch 4; Loss *Disclosure as Preventive Enforcement* in Hopt and Teubner *Corporate Governance and Directors' Liabilities* (1984).

We turn now to the detailed provisions on disclosure of information in listing particulars and prospectuses.

REGULATING SECURITIES OFFERINGS

Offers of securities to be listed on the Stock Exchange

Offers of securities which are, or are to be, listed on the Stock Exchange are governed by Pt IV of the Financial Services Act 1986 together with the Listing Rules.

FORM, CONTENT AND REGISTRATION OF LISTING PARTICULARS AND PROSPECTUSES

An application for listing must be made to the Stock Exchange in such manner as the listing rules may require and must not be made in respect of securities to be issued by a private company[1].

In particular, such listing rules must require, as a condition of admission to the Official List (ie the list maintained by the Stock Exchange[2]) of any securities for which application for admission has been made and which are to be offered to the public in the UK for the first time before admission, the submission to, and approval by, the competent authority (ie the Stock Exchange) of a prospectus in such form and containing such information as may be specified in the Listing Rules, and the publication of that prospectus[3]. This pre-vetting by the competent authority of the document by which securities are to be offered to the public in the UK for the first time is seen as a crucial aspect of investor protection. In keeping with that, where the listing rules require the publication of a prospectus, it is not lawful, before the time of publication of the prospectus, to offer the securities in question to the public in the UK[4].

The Listing Rules may require as a condition of the admission to the Official List of any other securities, the submission to, and approval by, the authority of a document (referred to as 'listing particulars') in such form and containing such information as may be specified in the listing rules; and the publication of that document[5].

There are therefore two documents, a prospectus and listing particulars. However, as the Listing Rules make clear, the content of a prospectus, and the procedures for submission to and approval by the Exchange, and for the publication of a prospectus, are the same as those applicable to listing particulars, subject to necessary adaptations appropriate to the circumstances of a public offer[6]. So while there are two documents, the content is essentially the same, with the title depending on the function which is involved: listing particulars being required on the admission of securities to listing; a prospectus when securities are to be admitted to listing and are to be offered to the public in the UK for the first time.

1   FSA 1986, s 143.
2   Ibid, s 142(7).
3   Ibid, s 144(2).
4   Ibid, s 156B(1). A person (other than an authorised person who is treated as contravening the rules of his authorising body and subject to sanctions accordingly) who contravenes this provision is guilty of an offence: s 156B(2), (3). Any contravention is actionable at the suit of a person who suffers loss as a result of the contravention subject to the defences and other incidents applying to actions for breach of statutory duty: s 156B(5).
5   Ibid, s 144(2A).
6   See Listing Rules, r 5.1(d).

The detailed content of the listing particulars or prospectus are set out in the Listing Rules and fall under a variety of headings[7], including:

- information as to the persons responsible for the listing particulars or prospectus, the auditors and other advisers;
- information concerning the securities which are the subject of the application for listing;
- general information about the company and its capital;
- information about the activities of the company and its subsidiaries;
- financial information concerning the company and its subsidiaries;
- details relating to the management of the company; and
- information concerning recent developments in the company's business and prospects.

In addition, it is important to note the general duty of disclosure imposed by the statute which requires the disclosure in listing particulars or a prospectus of all such information as investors and their professional advisers would reasonably require, and reasonably expect to find there, for the purpose of making an informed assessment of the assets and liabilities, financial position, profits and losses, and prospects of the issuer of the securities; and the rights attaching to the securities[8]. If material changes occur or new information becomes available after publication of the listing particulars or prospectus, supplementary listing particulars or a supplementary prospectus must be published[9].

However, all of the detailed disclosure outlined above is only required where the issuer is making an offer to the public and what is an offer to the public must be determined in accordance with the statutory provisions[10] which proceed to identify those offers which are not offers to the public[11].

For example, it is *not* an offer to the public if:

- the securities are offered to no more than fifty persons[12];
- the securities are offered to a restricted circle of persons whom the offeror reasonably believes to be sufficiently knowledgeable to understand the risks involved in accepting the offer[13];
- the securities are offered to a government, local authority or public authority[14];
- the securities are offered in connection with a takeover[15].

In these types of cases there is no need for the elaborate investor protection provisions inherent in the listing particulars and prospectus requirements.

Where listing particulars or a prospectus are, or are to be, published in connection with an application for the listing of any securities, no advertisement or other information may be issued in the United Kingdom unless the contents of the advertisement or other information have been submitted to the competent authority

7   See Listing Rules, ch 6.
8   FSA 1986, ss 146(1), 154A; see ss 146(3), 154A as to the matters which are relevant as to whether information is required under this provision; also note the exemptions from disclosure under this general provision (s 146), such as where disclosure would be contrary to the public interest: ss 148, 154A.
9   Ibid, ss 147(1), 154A.
10 Ibid, s 142(7A)(b).
11 See ibid, Sch 11A.
12 Ibid, Sch 11A, para 3(1)(b).
13 Ibid, Sch 11A, para 3(1)(d).
14 Ibid, Sch 11A, para 3(1)(f).
15 Ibid, Sch 11A, para 3(1)(j).

and that authority has either approved those contents or authorised the issue of the advertisement or information without such approval[16].

On or before the date on which listing particulars or a prospectus are published, a copy must be delivered for registration to the registrar of companies and a statement that a copy has been so delivered must be included in the particulars or prospectus[17]. The Listing Rules also lay down minimum levels of publication in terms of availability, circulation, national newspaper coverage, and advertisements[18].

Offers of unlisted securities

Public offers of unlisted securities are governed by the Public Offers of Securities Regulations 1995[19] which apply to any securities which are not admitted to official listing nor the subject of any application for listing in accordance with Part IV of the Financial Services Act 1986[20].

Prior to the enactment of these regulations, this had been an area of some difficulty. However, the position is greatly clarified now by the fact that the overall scheme adopted by the Public Offers of Securities Regulations is identical in most respects to that discussed above with respect of Part IV of the Financial Services Act 1986. The main difference, of course, is that the Stock Exchange does not exercise a regulatory role in this context, with certain limited exceptions[1].

FORM, CONTENT AND REGISTRATION OF A PROSPECTUS

When securities are offered to the public in the UK for the first time, the offeror must publish a prospectus by making it available to the public, free of charge, at an address in the UK from the time he first offers the securities until the end of the period during which the offer remains open[2].

Once again, provision is made for the detailed contents of the prospectus and information[3] must be provided as to:

- the persons responsible for the prospectus and the advisers;
- the securities to which the prospectus relates and the offer;
- general information about the issuer and its capital;
- the issuer's principal activities;
- the issuer's assets and liabilities; financial position and profits and losses;

---

16   Ibid, ss 154(1), 154A. In the case of breach, a person (other than an authorised person who is treated as contravening the rules of his authorising body and subject to sanctions accordingly) who contravenes this provision is guilty of an offence: ss 154(2),(3), 154A.

17   Ibid, ss 149(1), 154A; in the case of breach, the issuer of the securities in question and any person who is knowingly a party to the publication is guilty of an offence: ss 149(3), 154A.

18   See Listing Rules, ch 8. The Listing Rules may also permit the publication of a mini-prospectus, ie a document, not constituting listing particulars, which has attached to it or which contains an application form and includes information drawn from listing particulars together with other information required by the listing rules: rr 8.12–8.13. These documents proved particularly useful in privatisations.

19   SI 1995 No 1537. Provisions regulating offers of unlisted securities were included in Part V of the Financial Services Act 1986 but that Part was only partially brought into force and the provisions in Part III of the Companies Act 1985 continued to apply until superseded by the 1995 Regulations.

20   Public Offers of Securities Regulations 1995, regs 2(1), 3(1).

1   In the context of mutual recognition of prospectuses, see discussion above.

2   Public Offers of Securities Regulations 1995, reg 4(1).

3   Public Offers of Securities Regulations 1995, reg 8, Sch 1.

- the issuer's administration, management and supervision;
- recent developments in the issuer's business and prospects.

A supplementary prospectus may be required where there is any significant change affecting any matter in the prospectus, any significant new matter which needs to be included, or there is a significant inaccuracy in the prospectus[4].

Again, there is a general duty of disclosure in a prospectus of all such information as investors would reasonably require, and reasonably expect to find there, for the purpose of making an informed assessment of the assets and liabilities, financial position, profits and losses, and prospects of the issuer of the securities and the rights attaching to the securities[5]. The information in a prospectus must be presented in as easily analysable and comprehensible a fashion as possible[6].

What is an offer to the public in the UK must be determined, in this case, in accordance with the Public Offers of Securities Regulations which, in a list of 21 headings, identifies those offers which are not offers to the public[7]. These are identical in many respects to those noted above with respect to offers of listed securities but, in addition, note that an offer is not an offer to the public if the securities are the securities of a private company and are offered by that company to members or employees of the company; members of the families of any such members or employees; or holders of debentures issued by the company[8].

The offeror must, before the time of publication of the prospectus, deliver a copy of it to the registrar of companies for registration[9].

A person is guilty of an offence if he contravenes the provision requiring the publication of a prospectus when securities are offered to the public in the UK for the first time; or contravenes any requirement to deliver a copy of the prospectus to the registrar of companies for registration before the time of publication of the prospectus[10]. It is also an offence to issue, or cause to be issued, an advertisement, notice, poster or document (other than a prospectus) announcing a public offer of securities for which a prospectus is or will be required without stating that a prospectus is or will be published and giving an address within the UK from where it can be obtained or will be obtainable[11].

CRIMINAL SANCTIONS AND CIVIL REMEDIES FOR MISSTATEMENTS IN PROSPECTUSES

Criminal liabilities

The Financial Services Act 1986 and the Public Offers of Securities Regulations 1995 provide for a variety of criminal sanctions which can arise from breaches of the above requirements relating to offers of listed or unlisted securities to the public. In keeping with the general attempt to standardise the requirements across both regimes, the provisions in the Act and the Regulations tend to mirror one another and so are dealt with together in the remainder of this chapter.

4   Public Offers of Securities Regulations 1995, reg 10.
5   Public Offers of Securities Regulations 1995, reg 9. Exceptions to the disclosure requirements, for example, on the grounds of public interest, are set out in reg 11.
6   Public Offers of Securities Regulations 1995, reg 8(3).
7   Public Offers of Securities Regulations 1995, reg 7(2).
8   Public Offers of Securities Regulations 1995, reg 7(2)(f).
9   Public Offers of Securities Regulations 1995, reg 4(2).
10 Public Offers of Securities Regulations 1995, reg 16(2).
11 Public Offers of Securities Regulations 1995, regs 12, 16(2).

False and misleading statements   It is an offence if, for the purposes of or in connection with any application under the Financial Services Act 1986 or the Public Offers of Securities Regulations, or in purported compliance with any requirement imposed by or under that legislation or those Regulations, a person furnishes information which he knows to be false or misleading in a material particular or recklessly furnishes information which is false or misleading in a material particular[12]. This is certainly wide enough to cover the omission of information from, or the inclusion of misleading information in, listing particulars or prospectuses.

Market manipulation   Another provision to note is the catch-all market manipulation provision contained in the Financial Services Act 1986, s 47. Although aimed at a wide variety of market offences, misleading listing particulars or prospectuses could fall within sub-s (1) of this provision which makes it an offence for any person to:

- make a statement, promise or forecast which he knows to misleading, false or deceptive; or
- dishonestly conceal any material facts; or
- recklessly make (dishonestly or otherwise) a statement, promise or forecast which is misleading, false or deceptive,

if he makes the statement, etc for the purpose of inducing, or is reckless as to whether it may induce another person (whether or not the person to whom the statement was made), to enter, or refrain from entering, into an investment agreement or to exercise, or refrain from exercising, any rights conferred by an investment.

Control of investment advertisements   Finally, it is important to note the controls on the advertisement of securities which are imposed by the Financial Services Act 1986, s 57. An 'investment advertisement' is very widely defined to include an advertisement inviting persons to enter or offer to enter any investment agreement, which would include any offer to subscribe for or purchase shares[13]. Essentially no person other than an authorised person under the Financial Services Act 1986 may issue or cause to be issued such an advertisement, although this is subject to certain exceptions. The necessary level of investor protection will be achieved through the involvement of authorised persons who will be subject to the rules of the Securities and Investment Board (now the Financial Services Authority) or the appropriate self-regulating organisation or recognised professional body. Of course, listing particulars or prospectuses would fall within this definition of an investment advertisement and therefore initially would appear also to be covered by s 57 but an extensive list of exceptions to s 57 is contained in s 58 and related statutory instruments[14] and provision is made to exempt both listing particulars and prospectuses from the operation of the section[15].

---

12   FSA 1986, s 200; Public Offers of Securities Regulations 1995, reg 23(5). See also Theft Act 1968, s 19 (false statements by directors etc) although this provision appears never to have been used with respect to offer documents.
13   FSA 1986, ss 57(2), 44(9), Sch 1.
14   See Financial Services Act 1986 (Investment Advertisements) (Exemptions) (No 2) Order 1995, SI 1995 No 1536; Financial Services Act 1986 (Investment Advertisements) (Exemptions) Order 1996, SI 1996 No 1586; Financial Services Act 1986 (Investment Advertisements) (Exemptions) Order 1997, SI 1997 No 963.
15   For listing particulars, see FSA 1986, s 58(1)(d); for prospectuses, see Financial Services Act 1986 (Investment Advertisements) (Exemptions) (No 2) Order 1995, SI 1995 No 1536, art 14.

Civil remedies

Of course, investors are less interested in criminal sanctions than in recovering compensation when they have been induced by false statements or omissions into acquiring securities which prove to be a poor investment. The Financial Services Act 1986 and the Public Offers of Securities Regulations 1995 address this issue as well, again with equivalent provisions in each depending upon whether the securities are listed or unlisted.

STATUTORY COMPENSATION FOR FALSE STATEMENTS OR OMISSIONS

The statutory compensation provision is contained in Financial Services Act 1986, s 150, which is mirrored by Public Offers of Securities Regulations, reg 14. Under these provisions the person or persons responsible for listing particulars, supplementary listing particulars, a prospectus or supplementary prospectus, will be liable to pay compensation[16] to any person who has acquired[17] any of the securities in question and suffered loss in respect of them as a result of[18] any untrue or misleading statement in the particulars or the prospectus or the omission from it of any matter required to be included by the general statutory obligation of disclosure[19] or the obligation to provide supplementary listing particulars or a supplementary prospectus,[20] as the case may be[1].

The person or persons responsible for listing particulars or a prospectus are defined by statute[2] and the regulations[3] and include the issuer itself[4]; and where that issuer is a company, the current directors[5] (except those who did not know of or consent to the publication[6]); and persons named in the particulars or prospectus as having agreed to become directors[7]. Likewise any persons who accept responsibility for any part of the document and are stated as doing so[8] or who authorise the contents of any part of the document[9] will be liable in respect of that part for which they are responsible[10].

There are a number of defences open to persons who are otherwise responsible for the particulars or the prospectus. The most important is that persons will not be liable if they can show that they reasonably believed any statement for which they are responsible to be true and not misleading or that an omission of information was proper[11]. The section thus only imposes liability if no reasonable belief can be shown,

16 The measure of compensation is the tort measure rather than the contract measure. This is because the section was originally designed to provide the remedy that was denied in *Derry v Peek* (1889) 14 App Cas 337, HL.
17 Note that the remedy is not restricted to subscribers and purchasers in the market can claim compensation.
18 Note that there is no requirement that the false statement or omission induced the plaintiff to invest or was relied on by him.
19 Ie that contained in FSA 1986, s 146 or Public Offers of Securities Regulations 1995, reg 9.
20 FSA 1986, s 147; Public Offers of Securities Regulations 1995, reg 10.
1 FSA 1986, s 150(1); Public Offers of Securities Regulations 1995, reg 14.
2 FSA 1986, s 152.
3 Public Offers of Securities Regulations 1995, reg 13.
4 FSA 1986, s 152(1)(a); Public Offers of Securities Regulations 1995, reg 13(1)(a).
5 FSA 1986, s 152(1)(b); Public Offers of Securities Regulations 1995, reg 13(1)(b).
6 FSA 1986, s 152(2); Public Offers of Securities Regulations 1995, reg 13(2).
7 FSA 1986, s 152(1)(c); Public Offers of Securities Regulations 1995, reg 13(1)(c).
8 FSA 1986, s 152(1)(d); Public Offers of Securities Regulations 1995, reg 13(1)(d). A person is not responsible by reason only of giving advice on the contents in a professional capacity: FSA 1986, s 152(8); Public Offers of Securities Regulations 1995, reg 13(4).
9 FSA 1986, s 152(1)(e); Public Offers of Securities Regulations 1995, reg 13(1)(g).
10 FSA 1986, s 152(3); Public Offers of Securities Regulations 1995, reg 13(3).
11 FSA 1986, s 151(1); Public Offers of Securities Regulations 1995, reg 15(1).

which effectively imposes liability for negligent or fraudulent but not for innocent false statements. That defence will not only apply to directors, who basically accept responsibility for the whole particulars or prospectus, but also apply to those experts who have contributed reports etc to the particulars or prospectus for which they must accept responsibility. In addition, persons who authorise the inclusion of an expert's statement[12] will not be liable for that statement if they reasonably believed that the expert was competent and had consented to the inclusion of the report[13].

Finally, persons will not be liable if a timely correction is made of any false statements[14], if the false statement arises from the accurate and fair reproduction of an official statement or document[15], or if they can prove that the plaintiff was aware of the falsehood or the omitted information, as the case may be[16].

NON-STATUTORY CIVIL REMEDIES

In this section we consider the non-statutory remedies available to persons who have acquired shares on the basis of a prospectus containing false statements or which has omitted prescribed information[17]. The problem in this area is the number of different and often overlapping remedies that can arise. The explanation for the overlapping lies in the historical development of liability for misstatements and misrepresentations in tort and contract.

There are three other general considerations which if borne in mind will help clarify the situation. The first is the type of remedy being sought and here the distinction lies between seeking rescission of the contract under which the shares were acquired and seeking money compensation from the persons responsible for the false statements.

The second consideration which, as we shall see, is closely related to the question of rescission or damages, is whether the plaintiff is seeking a remedy against the other party to the contract under which the shares were acquired, or against other persons responsible for the prospectus.

Thirdly, it makes a difference to what remedies are available and against whom, whether the plaintiff is a subscriber who acquired shares directly from the company, or a purchaser who acquired shares from an existing shareholder.

Rescission
If it is available, the most effective remedy for a person induced to acquire shares on the basis of a false representation is to rescind the contract of acquisition. Rescission is possible for misrepresentations whether made fraudulently, negligently or innocently[18].

12　In this context an expert includes any engineer, valuer, accountant or other person whose profession, qualifications or experience give authority to the statement: FSA 1986, s 151(7); Public Offers of Securities Regulations 1995, reg 15(7).

13　FSA 1986, s 151(2); Public Offers of Securities Regulations 1995, reg 15(2).

14　FSA 1986, s 151(3); Public Offers of Securities Regulations 1995, reg 15(3).

15　FSA 1986, s 151(4); Public Offers of Securities Regulations 1995, reg 15(4).

16　FSA 1986, s 151(5); Public Offers of Securities Regulations 1995, reg 15(5).

17　In the remainder of this chapter the term prospectus includes listing particulars where these are serving as a prospectus. It should be remembered also that the common law remedies for misrepresentation or misstatement inducing persons to acquire shares may be available whether the misrepresentation or misstatement was contained in a prospectus or not.

18　*Central Rly Co of Venezuela v Kisch* (1867) LR 2 HL 99; *Gover's Case* (1875) 1 Ch D 182 at 198, 199, CA; *Re Metropolitan Coal Consumers' Association, Karberg's Case* [1892] 3 Ch 1 at 13, CA.

In the case of misrepresentations contained in a prospectus[19], if the prospectus is issued by the company then the subscriber can rescind against the company[20]. If the prospectus is issued by an issuing house then the purchaser from the issuing house can rescind against the issuing house. But if the purchaser has bought shares from a person who is not responsible for the prospectus, albeit having been induced to buy by reading the prospectus, the purchaser will be unable to rescind.

The usual limits on exercising the right of rescission, of affirmation,[1] lapse of time,[2] the need for restitutio in integrum,[3] or the intervention of third party rights, all apply. In particular, it will be too late to rescind, as against the company, once the company has gone into liquidation[4]. The reason is that the rights of the creditors and other members are regarded as having intervened because they will inevitably be prejudiced if any members are allowed to withdraw their money from the company and thus deplete the fund available for paying creditors.

Damages

If it is no longer possible to rescind, or if the plaintiff does not wish to do so, or if the plaintiff has suffered consequential loss which would not be reimbursed by mere rescission, the question arises whether the plaintiff can claim damages instead of, or as well as, rescission.

Damages for deceit　If the other party to the contract has been responsible for fraudulent misrepresentations (ie a false statement 'made knowingly, or without belief in its truth, or recklessly, careless whether it be true or false'[5]) which have induced the plaintiff to acquire shares then there may be liability in damages in the tort of deceit.

An action for deceit in respect of misrepresentations in an offer document can be brought against the company but is generally brought against one or more of the directors or other persons responsible for such document. Until the Companies Act 1989 it was the position that a shareholder could not both retain his shares and bring an action against the company for deceit inducing him to buy from the company its

---

19　An omission of particulars required to be included in the prospectus does not give rise to a right of rescission: *Re South of England Natural Gas and Petroleum Co Ltd* [1911] 1 Ch 573.

20　Problems can arise over whether the company is responsible for statements in the prospectus. Where the false statement is in a report set out in the prospectus the company will be responsible unless it makes clear that it does not vouchsafe the accuracy of the report: *Re Pacaya Rubber and Produce Co Ltd* [1914] 1 Ch 542; *Mair v Rio Grande Rubber Estates Ltd* [1913] AC 853, HL. As to whether the company is responsible for statements made by individuals purportedly on its behalf, see *Lynde v Anglo-Italian Hemp Spinning Co* [1896] 1 Ch 178 at 182–3.

1　In the case of shares this may be indicated by acting, after the false statements are revealed, in a manner inconsistent with exercising a right of rescission: *Ex p Briggs* (1866) LR 1 Eq 483; *Crawley's Case* (1869) 4 Ch App 322 (selling or trying to sell shares); *Sharpley v Louth and East Coast Rly Co* (1876) 2 Ch D 663, CA (attending meetings).

2　*Scholey v Central Rly Co of Venezuela* (1868) LR 9 Eq 266n (seeking rescission only after reading that another shareholder in the same company had successfully done so).

3　*Restitutio* is not usually possible where the purchased shares have since been sold but see *Smith New Court Securities Ltd v Scrimgeour Vickers (Asset Management) Ltd* [1996] 4 All ER 769 at 774, [1997] 1 BCLC 350 at 356, HL where Lord Browne-Wilkinson suggested, *obiter*, that this may not be the modern position with respect to quoted shares when identical shares can be purchased in the market and substantial *restitutio* can therefore be effected.

4　*Oakes v Turquand and Harding* (1867) LR 2 HL 325.

5　*Derry v Peek* (1889) 14 App Cas 337 at 374, per Lord Herschell, HL.

shares or, by analogy, to take up shares of the company[6]. This has now been altered and a person is not debarred from obtaining damages or other compensation from a company by reason only of his holding or having held shares in the company or any right to apply or subscribe for shares or to be included in the company's register in respect of shares[7].

The amount of damages which the plaintiff will recover in deceit will be based on the tort measure of putting the plaintiff in the position he would have been in if no false representation had been made, the restoration of the status quo ante. If the damages are in addition to rescission their main function will be to compensate the plaintiff for consequential losses flowing directly from the misrepresentation[8]. If the plaintiff is not exercising a right of rescission then, in many cases, the normal method of calculating the damages will be the difference between the price paid by the plaintiff for the shares and the value of the shares on the date of the acquisition by the plaintiff[9]. However, in some exceptional cases, that normal method will not be appropriate as the House of Lords decided in *Smith New Court Securities Ltd v Scrimgeour Vickers (Asset Management) Ltd*[10].

In 1989 Smith New Court (SNC) purchased a block of shares in Ferranti plc from Scrimgeour Vickers (SV) for £23m. SV was acting as broker on the instructions of Citibank. The bargain was struck after a senior manager at Citibank had fraudulently misrepresented to SNC that there were two other buyers interested in the shares at a similar price. It later emerged, in a completely distinct development, that Ferranti had been the victim of a massive fraud and the market value at the time of the purchase (July 1989) was a false one. The shares were subsequently sold by SNC at a loss of £11m.

The trial judge decided[11] that the court was entitled in the circumstances to disregard the market price in July 1989 and look instead at the value of the shares in November 1989 when the true position at Ferranti had been revealed. On that basis, the value of the shares acquired was £12,382,226. Therefore the loss suffered by SNC was £10,764,005, being the difference between the price paid (£23m) and the true value of the shares acquired (£12m).

The Court of Appeal rejected[12] the approach of the trial judge. The proper measure of damages was the difference between the price paid and the price which without the misrepresentation the shares would have fetched on the open market in July 1989. On this basis the damages should be reduced to £1.1m.

The House of Lords in turn reversed the decision of the Court of Appeal and reinstated the original decision, awarding £10,764,005 by way of damages to SNC.

The House of Lords accepted that the normal rule was prima facie the price paid less the real value of the subject matter of the sale as at the date of the acquisition by the plaintiff. However, since the overriding principle was that the plaintiff should receive full compensation for the wrong suffered, and the date of the transaction rule

---

6   *Houldsworth v City of Glasgow Bank* (1880) 5 App Cas 317, HL; *Re Addlestone Linoleum Co* (1887) 37 Ch D 191, CA. In principle it was thought that such a claim was inconsistent with the contract into which the plaintiff had entered and the plaintiff had therefore to have severed his connection with the company by agreement or judgment for rescission before he could sue the company for misrepresentation: see *Houldsworth v City of Glasgow Bank* supra at 324, 325 per Lord Cairns LC.

7   Companies Act 1985, s 111A inserted by Companies Act 1989, s 131.

8   *Doyle v Olby (Ironmongers) Ltd* [1969] 2 QB 158, [1969] 2 All ER 119, CA; *Archer v Brown* [1985] QB 401, [1984] 2 All ER 267.

9   *Twycross v Grant* (1877) 2 CPD 469; *Waddell v Blockey* (1879) 4 QBD 678; *Peek v Derry* (1887) 37 Ch D 541.

10 [1996] 4 All ER 769, [1997] 1 BCLC 350, HL

11 See [1992] BCLC 1104.

12 See [1994] 4 All ER 225, [1994] 2 BCLC 212, CA.

was only a means of attempting to give effect to that overriding compensatory principle, that rule did not apply where either the misrepresentation continued to operate after the date of the acquisition of the asset so as to induce the plaintiff to retain the asset, or the circumstances of the case were such that the plaintiff was, by reason of the fraud, locked into the property.

SNC was induced by the misrepresentations to purchase an asset that was already flawed by reason of the undiscovered fraud perpetrated on Ferranti and were locked into the transaction by reason of the fraudulent misrepresentations, having bought the shares for a purpose[13] and at a price which precluded them from sensibly disposing of them immediately. It followed that the amount of damages recoverable by SNC was the difference between the contract price and the amount actually realised on the resale of the shares.

Damages under the Misrepresentation Act 1967   Damages may also be sought, in the case of negligent misrepresentations, against the other party to the contract under the Misrepresentation Act 1967[14]. The liability for damages under this provisions is also in tort[15], as if the misrepresentation had been made fraudulently, save that it will be a defence to show that the person making the representation had reasonable ground for believing, and did believe up to the time the contract was made, that the facts represented were true[16].

Liability for negligent misstatements at common law   As noted, if the directors know that the statements are untrue then they may be liable in the tort of deceit[17]. However, in *Derry v Peek*[18], the House of Lords held there could be no liability in the absence of fraud and it was not sufficient to show that the directors were negligent.

That decision has now been superseded by the decision in *Hedley Byrne & Co Ltd v Heller & Partners Ltd*[19] under which persons may be liable for negligent statements provided there is a sufficient degree of proximity between them and the plaintiff. More recently, the conditions which must be satisfied to give rise to a duty of care were enumerated (restrictively) by the House of Lords in *Caparo Industries plc v Dickman*[20].

The arguments against imposing liability in regard to statements in a prospectus include the possibility that it will open the floodgates of litigation. It is not difficult, therefore, to envisage the courts being more prepared to find a duty of care where a prospectus is circulated among only a few people than they would be in the case of a major public offering where the prospectus is published in several national newspapers. Still less are the courts likely to impose liability where the plaintiff read newspaper comments on the prospectus rather than the prospectus itself.

There is a way which the courts already use to restrict the scope of liability arising out of false statements in prospectuses. It is that a prospectus is presumed to be intended to enable the issuer simply to find a person willing to acquire the shares. Thus if it is issued by the company it will be presumed to be exhausted once it has served its purpose

13   The trial judge had found that SNC had bought the shares as a market making risk, ie with a view to holding them on its books over a comparatively long period to be sold on at a later date: see [1996] 4 All ER 769 at 773, [1997] 1 BCLC 350 at 354.
14   Misrepresentation Act 1967, s 2(1).
15   As to quantum of damages under Misrepresentation Act 1967, s 2(1), see *Royscot Trust Ltd v Rogerson* [1991] 2 QB 297, [1991] 3 All ER 294, CA.
16   Misrepresentation Act 1967, s 2(1).
17   *Edginton v Fitzmaurice* (1885) 29 Ch D 459, CA.
18   (1889) 14 App Cas 337, HL.
19   [1964] AC 465, [1963] 2 All ER 575, HL.
20   [1990] 2 AC 605, [1990] 1 All ER 568, HL.

of obtaining subscribers. If it is issued by an existing shareholder offering shares for sale it will be exhausted once the shareholder has found purchasers for the shares. In neither case, therefore, can transferees from the initial subscriber or initial purchaser sue in respect of false statements in the prospectus even though they had read the prospectus and that induced them to acquire the shares.

This rule was established in relation to prospectuses by the House of Lords in *Peek v Gurney*[1] in which the plaintiff, having obtained a copy of a prospectus which contained fraudulent misstatements, bought shares in the company a few months later. His action against the directors for deceit failed because the prospectus was presumed to have exhausted its effect once the shares had been issued to subscribers[2].

This rule in *Peek v Gurney* was recently re-affirmed in relation to liability in negligence in *Al Nakib Investments (Jersey) Ltd v Longcroft*[3]. In this case a company offered its shareholders the right to subscribe for shares in a subsidiary it was promoting, issuing to them a prospectus which it was alleged contained false or misleading statements. The plaintiff shareholder not only took up its rights but also purchased shares in the subsidiary in the market.

It was held that the plaintiff's action in respect of shares acquired in the market should be struck out. Mervyn Davies J applied the decision in *Caparo Industries plc v Dickman*[4] in holding that no duty of care could exist in relation to a statement unless the defendant knew or ought to have known that the plaintiff would rely on it for the purpose of such a transaction as the plaintiff in fact entered into. While the defendant knew the plaintiff might rely on the prospectus to subscribe for shares, it had no knowledge that the plaintiff would rely on it to make market purchases.

In *Possfund Custodian Trustee Ltd v Diamond*[5], which was a striking out application, Lightman J was prepared to accept that it was arguable that directors and others responsible for a prospectus owed a duty of care towards those who subsequently purchased the company's shares in the Unlisted Securities Market.

This case involved an application for the striking out of those parts of a statement of claim by 75 plaintiffs in two consolidated actions which related to purchases of shares of a company in the Unlisted Securities Market as distinct from subscription on the allotment of the shares. The company concerned subsequently went into receivership and the shares were worthless. The plaintiffs alleged that the prospectus had failed to disclose or understated the company's liabilities. They relied also on changes in commercial practice and perceptions which meant that the purpose of a prospectus was no longer confined to the inducing of subscriptions but included the further intention of inducing purchases in the after-market.

Lightman J thought the plaintiffs' claim merited full consideration at trial and should not be struck out. If the plaintiffs could establish that, at the time of the preparation and circulation of the original prospectus, the defendants intended to inform and encourage after-market purchasers, in addition to those subscribing to the allotment offer made by the prospectus, it was at least arguable that the defendants had assumed and owed a duty of care to those who relied on the contents of the prospectus in making purchases in the after-market.

1   (1873) LR 6 HL 377 at 410–413.
2   It may be possible, however, given suitable facts, to rebut the presumption and show that part of the purpose of the prospectus was to create a buoyant market in the shares after they were issued: see *Andrews v Mockford* [1896] 1 QB 372, CA.
3   [1990] 3 All ER 321, [1990] 1 WLR 1390.
4   [1990] 2 AC 605, [1990] 1 All ER 568, HL.
5   [1996] 2 All ER 774, [1996] 2 BCLC 665, Ch D.

CHAPTER 35

Problems of ownership and control of the listed public company

In Chapter 1 we identified eight major economic themes in the development of modern company law. These were of particular relevance to listed public companies and were:

(1) the growth of larger business units;
(2) the development of increasingly elaborate structures;
(3) the shift from ownership to control;
(4) the increase in institutional investment;
(5) the increasing amount of government intervention;
(6) the increasing impact of economic integration through the EU;
(7) the growth of multinational companies; and
(8) the development of transnational enterprise and the international financial revolution.

In this chapter we return to themes (3) and (4) and discuss the impact which they are having on company law and particularly on the division of power in listed public companies. In doing so, we shall consider in more detail some general topics which assume greatest significance in the case of such companies. However, before we do so we will examine changing conceptions of the company and corporate benefit.

CHANGING CONCEPTIONS OF THE COMPANY AND CORPORATE BENEFIT

The concept of the good of the company has featured in the law of ultra vires[1], in alteration of articles[2] and in directors' duties[3]. It also arises in an oblique form in fraud on the minority[4] and is beginning to feature as an aspect of a duty on controlling shareholders. With the reforms to ultra vires, the emphasis has shifted to directors' and shareholders' duties and we have the recent development of corporate benefit which at the least expresses in positive form what is perhaps ultimately a negative doctrine. What is meant by this is the outlawing of conduct which is *not* for the benefit (or good)

1 See Chapter 10.
2 See Chapter 11.
3 See Chapters 26 and 27.
4 See Chapter 28.

of the company. This is emerging as a distinct growth on conventional directors' duties[5]. In US jurisdictions, this is sometimes expressed in terms of avoiding corporate waste (an equitable doctrine not normally applied to the corporate context in English law). As an essentially negative doctrine in the past, it has been narrowly interpreted. It does not mean in English law the promotion of the good of the company as a community or enterprise. It does not even mean the economic benefit of the company. It means avoiding injury to the interests of the shareholders of the particular company as a general body or, put in another way, the interests of the individual hypothetical shareholder[6]. Loan creditors are disregarded unless their security is jeopardised by a proposed course of action or unless the company is on the verge of liquidation[7]. This narrow and negative approach is remarkably out of date when compared with current management thinking about corporate responsibility in the larger companies.

German law has recognised wider interests in company law and the corporate structure since the Weimar Republic and as long ago as 1951, an English writer, George Goyder[8], argued for a general objects clause setting out the objects of the company in terms of its obligations:

(a) to the company itself: its development, financial stability and future growth;
(b) to the shareholders (to pay regular dividends in accordance with the company's articles);
(c) to the workers in the company (to provide stable employment under good conditions as far as possible); and
(d) to the consumers of the company's products (to make good bread or shoes or whatever it may be at fair and reasonable prices).

In a more recent work, *The Just Enterprise*[9], he made the following interesting philosophical statement:

What has gone wrong with company law? Principally, that it fails to state what the purpose of a company is. It gives to the directors, as agents of the shareholders, *de facto* control of the company's policy and to the other interests—such as the workers'—no corresponding rights. Unlike previous forms of work organisation, of which the fifteenth-century guilds and the chartered corporations which followed them were typical, a limited liability company is not constitutionally concerned with quality or value, or with the public interest. In the light of the commanding power which the large company today exercises in the economy, the law governing it in Britain has become a defective instrument for controlling industry. Our political system has come increasingly to reflect the conflict of purpose inherent in existing company law by identifying the Conservative and Labour parties each with vested interests, respectively that of capital and labour, both of which, together with the invaluable heritage of the Liberal tradition, must in the end be reconciled within the framework of the individual company. A cycle of government alternating between parties with inconsistent ideologies does not lend itself to the continuity of policy which business planning requires. Spasmodic government intervention in the larger company is as debilitating to management as it is self-defeating. What is needed is to bring company law into line with the broadest possible spectrum of public opinion and social policy, and

5   See *Australian Oil Exploration Ltd v Lachberg* (1958) 101 CLR 119; *ANZ Executor and Trustee Co Ltd v Qintex Australia Ltd* (1990) 2 ACLR 676; *Glover v Willert* (1996) 20 ACSR 182, 186.
6   See *Greenhalgh v Arderne Cinemas Ltd* [1951] Ch 286, CA.
7   See Chapter 40.
8   G Goyder *The Future of Private Enterprise* (1954), p 93.
9   *The Just Enterprise: A Blueprint for the Responsible Company* (1993).

then to leave the company free to follow its own aims. Our failure to make company law express in its structure and mode of operation that concern for moderation, equality and justice upon which democracy itself depends is a failure of will. The reconciliation of authority and liberty in industry and commerce must follow the path of seeking to do justice to all the constituent elements *within* the structure of the individual company.

The challenge we face is to discover a philosophy of company law which is socially and morally acceptable and at the same time encourages efficiency.

In 1980, the employee interest was included by statute as a legitimate interest for directors and the company to consider[10]. In Australia and New Zealand, there has been no such change[11]. In all these jurisdictions there is increasing recognition by the courts of the need to take account of the interests of creditors[12] and a longer term view of the interests of the company[13]. In surveys based on randomly selected US and New Zealand public company directors each holding two or more directorships, the majority in both countries placed the traditional legal concept of the company as the lowest of four concepts of accountability[14]. The majority thought that the company's duty was to serve as fairly and equitably as it could the interests of shareholders, employees, customers and the public. One US commentator has written[15]:

> The long-term advancement of shareholder interests is accepted as a satisfactory justification for corporate behaviour, if such advancement could conceivably be a reasonable outcome. With so vague a standard, it is apparent that the directors are free to respond to social expectations and demands, notwithstanding a short-term adverse impact on earnings, because of the inability of any shareholder challenging such policies to demonstrate that the conduct would not in the long run prove advantageous to the advancement of corporate interests.

This recognition of the business judgment rule is stronger in the USA than in the UK where the proper purpose doctrine acts as a brake and there is no equivalent of the recent US state anti-takeover statutes which broaden the constituencies which management can consider. On the other hand, shareholder action under the exceptions to the rule in *Foss v Harbottle* or s 459 is rare in the UK in the case of listed companies. Even the procedural innovations of *Wallersteiner v Moir (No 2)*[16] have not had any noticeable impact on shareholder initiative to bring legal proceedings to keep management in line. This is no doubt due to the separation of ownership and control and the rational decision of the small investor to leave well alone. Even where a larger shareholder takes initiative in the case of patent management misconduct, the results may be problematic. The monitoring of management in the case of a solvent listed company today owes less to legal proceedings than to the economic forces of the market

---

10 Companies Act 1980, ss 46 and 74; now CA 1985, ss 309 and 719.
11 See Ford and Austin *Principles of Corporations Law* (7th ed) para [8.120] and J H Farrar and M Russell *Company Law and Securities Regulation in New Zealand* (1985), ch 7.
12 See Chapters 26, 33, 38.
13 See Chapters 10 and 26.
14 R F Chandler 'The Control and Accountability of New Zealand's Public Corporations' (1982) 4 NZ Journal of Business 1; R F Chandler and B D Henshall *Corporate Directorship Practices in NZ Listed Public Companies* (1982).
15 P I Blumberg *The Megacorporation in American Society* (1975).
16 [1975] QB 373, CA.

for investment capital and the market for control[17]. It is otherwise when the company goes into receivership, voluntary administration or insolvent winding up[18].

THE CONCEPT OF CONTROL

Control, like power, with which it is almost synonymous, is an ambiguous concept and the ambiguities assume greatest significance in the case of listed public companies. A principal ambiguity is between power in the sense of the probability that one will be in a position to carry out one's will despite resistance, regardless of the basis on which this probability rests, and what has been called imperative control or authority, which is the probability that a command with a specific content will be obeyed by a given group or person[19]. In *Prudential Assurance Co Ltd v Newman Industries Ltd (No 2)*[20] the Court of Appeal said that control for the purpose of fraud on the minority embraces a broad spectrum extending from an overall absolute majority of votes at one end to a majority of votes at the other end made up of those likely to be cast by the delinquent himself plus those voting with him as a result of influence or apathy.

In Chapter 1, we saw how Berle and Means[1] argued that control of a large company can be separated from ownership of its shares although they seemed to equivocate between the two senses of control. They identified five different species of control:

(1) control through almost complete ownership;
(2) majority control;
(3) control through legal devices without majority ownership;
(4) minority control;
(5) management control.

In earlier chapters we have examined (1), (2) and (3) and now we must say more about (4) and (5), since they are most common in the case of the listed public company. One can perhaps express the distinction most clearly in percentage terms of voting rights as follows:

Absolute	99–100%
Substantial	75–99%
Simple majority	51%
Negative	26%
Minority	up to 25%?

Obviously someone with 99% or 100% of the issued voting shares of a company can completely control it. He or she can pass any resolution he or she wishes in general meeting and can appoint or remove the board. The same results will follow in the case of substantial control since 75% enables a person to get a special resolution passed and only 51% is needed to remove a director under s 303 of CA 1985. Simple majority

---

17 See Chapter 22, ante.
18 See Chapters 38, 39 and 40.
19 Max Weber *The Theory of Social and Economic Organisation* (1947). Cf E Herman *Corporate Control, Corporate Power* (1981). See the useful chapter on 'Control' concepts under the SEC statutes in L Loss *Fundamentals of Securities Regulation* (1983) chapter 6. See further J H Farrar 'Ownership and Control of Listed Public Companies in Revising or Rejecting the Concept of Control' in *Company Law in Change* (1987) ed B Pettet, p 39.
20 [1982] Ch 204, CA.
1 *The Modern Corporation and Private Property* (revised edn, 1968). See generally the June 1983 issue of the Journal of Law and Economics.

control means that one can remove the board and get an ordinary resolution passed. It means, however, that one cannot get a special resolution passed. Negative control is the ability to block a special resolution. In *Clemens v Clemens Bros Ltd*[2] which was considered in Chapter 11 the niece had negative control and a right of pre-emption which would have eventually given her the possibility of absolute or substantial control, but the aunt had simple majority control and attempted to dilute the niece's holding. Foster J held that the aunt could be restrained from doing so. Minority control is a much more amorphous term based on the facts of the case and means that the control rests on ability to attract enough support which when combined with the shareholder's own holdings will procure a majority of votes at general meetings and particularly at the annual general meeting. Conversely, it means that no other shareholding is sufficiently large to act as a nucleus around which to gather a majority of votes. Control of this kind is really control in the first of our two general senses—power or influence rather than authority[3].

Management control which is not absolute, substantial or simple majority control may sometimes be either negative or minority control, but Berle and Means used it in a further sense of control where ownership is so widely distributed that no individual or small group has even a minority interest large enough to dominate the affairs of the company. Today as we have seen and will explore in some detail later, the largest shareholders in the largest listed companies tend to be financial institutions, especially insurance companies who generally adopt a passive role. It is, then, difficult to say categorically whether there is management control or minority or negative control vested in the institutions. The position is further complicated in the case of some listed companies by nominee shareholdings, interlocking directorships and cross-holdings. The best approach, therefore, in any given case is to regard control as a relative concept—control in respect of what and for what purpose[4]?

Recently, the matter has been raised in the context of consolidated accounts and the implementation of the Seventh EU Directive. There the emphasis has shifted from company to the broader concept of an undertaking and a key definition for the purpose of the parent/subsidiary relationship is a right to exercise a dominant influence. This is a right to give directions with respect to the operating and financial policies of another undertaking which its directors are obliged to comply with whether or not they are for the benefit of that other undertaking (CA 1989, Sch 10A, para 4(1)). Although this concept of control is in respect of accounts and disclosure it indicates a looser approach which may prove influential in other contexts. The questions of disclosure and accounts are dealt with in Chapter 28, post.

The nature and extent of the shift from ownership to control in the UK

The Berle and Means hypothesis of separation of ownership and control was tested in the UK by Sargant Florence of Birmingham University using 1930s data[5]. His main findings were:

2   [1976] 2 All ER 268.
3   *Berle and Means,* op cit, p 66. See also the useful article by M Zeitlin 'Corporate Ownership and Control: The Large Corporation and the Capitalist Class' (1973–74) 79 American Journal of Sociology 1073.
4   Cf Zeitlin, op cit, at 1090: 'Control (or power) is essentially relative and relational: how much power, with respect to whom?' See further Farrar, op cit (footnote 19 supra).
5   *The Logic of British and American Industry* (3rd edn, 1972)

(1)   At least half of the largest companies were still controlled by a dominant ownership interest.
(2)   Most of the marginal cases were companies in which the top 20 shareholders held more than 20% of the voting shares.

In 1951[6] the proportion had fallen to about a third of all industrial and commercial companies of over £3 m nominal capital. The proportion of shares held by the 20 largest shareholders had fallen. The average percentage fell from 30% to 19% and the percentage held by corporate shareholders increased. Thus majority control declined and minority control increased. There was, however, less evidence of a managerial revolution than of a managerial evolution[7].

These results were confirmed by two later studies in the 1950s[8] and 1960s,[9] but in work carried out in 1975 by Nyman and Silberston[10], using Florence's definitions, the percentage of owner-controlled companies was 45% as a whole and 35% of the top 100 companies. Using their own criteria, Nyman and Silberston[11] arrived at a figure of 56.25% under ownership-control which they considered to be an underestimate partly because of the use of nominee shareholdings. We set out below a table based on their research.

TABLE MAJOR SHAREHOLDERS IN THE LARGEST BRITISH NON-FINANCIAL COMPANIES

Proportion held by a single large interest or by directors	*No of companies*	*% of companies*
No dominant interest	98	39.2
0–5%	15	6.0
5–10%	10	4.0
10–20%	32	12.8
20–30%	12	4.8
30–40%	11	4.4
40–50%	8	3.2
> 50%	22	8.8
Unquoted	16	6.4
Unknown	26	10.4
Totals	250	100.0

Source: Nyman and Silberston (1978), table 1; Scott *Corporations, Classes and Capitalism* (1979) p 67. (Cf Table 18 of Scott's second edition, 1985.)
Note: In the 10–20% category, we have included six companies which had in excess of 10% of their shares held by single interests but for which the authors could give no precise figures.

This may mean that ownership control has increased since 1951. Certainly since this category includes institutional investment and thus takes in a wide variety of

6   Florence *Ownership, Control, and Success of Large Companies* (1961).
7   Florence *The Logic of British and American Industry*, op cit.
8   S Hall et al 'The Insiders' (1957) 1 Universities and Left Review 3.
9   M Barratt Brown 'The Controllers of British Industry' in *Can the Workers Run Industry?* ed K Coates (1968).
10   'The Ownership and Control in Industry' (1978) 30 Oxford Economic Papers 74.
11   Op cit.

proprietorial interests, this seems to be the case, although institutional investment raises a whole congeries of problems which we shall consider later in this chapter.

J H Farrar[12] carried out research into the top 10 listed companies by market capitalisation in 1984 and the main findings were:

(1) the very low personal holdings of directors
(2) the absence of a notifiable interest of 5% or more in the issued equity capital of five out of the ten companies. The UK government had a 31.73% holding in British Petroleum Company plc and the Prudential Assurance group had notifiable interests in the General Electric Company plc and Marks and Spencer plc. The 'Shell' Transport and Trading Company plc is a multinational with a complex relationship with Royal Dutch Petroleum Company through cross-holdings in Shell Petroleum NV and The Shell Petroleum Company Ltd;
(3) the fact that financial institutions usually appear as the largest shareholders. Although individual holdings are seldom higher than 5%, institutions collectively have potential minority control or negative control of many companies;
(4) the wide dispersal and relatively small holdings of shares amongst non-institutional shareholders;
(5) the use of US nominee companies and American Depository Receipts for US-based holdings in companies such as ICI plc and Glaxo Holdings plc.

However, we must add some notes of caution to these research findings. First, these results do not take into account option schemes, employee share schemes and the extent to which executive remuneration is tied to the results of the company. Secondly, they are based on the largest listed companies by market capitalisation. Medium-sized and smaller companies tend to have higher holdings by directors and executives. Thirdly, to quote Nyman and Silberston[13]:

> To locate control in any given corporation, it is not adequate to set up arbitrary statistical criteria such as the percentage of shares which must be owned by the largest holder or the largest twenty holders. Rather a case-by-case approach is necessary. Any individual firm may be related to other corporations, banks, financial institutions, and family owners via complex patterns of shareholdings, interlocking directorates, and kinship networks.

The control of a public listed company can only be determined if it is examined in relation to the 'concrete situation within the [company] and the constellation of intercorporate relations in which it is involved'[14]. Strategic control is 'mediated through a complex of social forms. While the legal structure of property relations is a central part of this institutional mediation, it is never the sole part'[15].

Ascertaining the extent of control

The 1967 and 1976 Companies Acts laid down rules for disclosure of interests in shares in listed public companies to enable the extent of control to be ascertained. Those

---

12 Farrar, op cit, p 48 et seq.
13 'The Ownership and Control in Industry' (1978) 30 Oxford Economic Papers 74.
14 Zeitlin, op cit, at 35.
15 J Scott *Corporations, Classes and Capitalism* (1979) pp 46–7. Cf ch 2 of the second edition.

provisions were replaced by further provisions in the Companies Act 1981 which were more stringent and the present provisions are now contained in CA 1985, Pt VI[16].

DETAILS REQUIRING NOTIFICATION[17]

The provisions apply to all public companies, but will assume their greater significance in relation to listed public companies. A person hàs a notifiable interest under s 199 when he is interested in shares in the relevant share capital of such a company of an aggregate value equal to, or more than 3% of, the nominal value of that share capital. Under s 198(2), 'relevant share capital' means the company's issued share capital of a class carrying rights to vote in all circumstances at general meetings of the company.

Changes of more than 1% in any notifiable interest have to be notified to the company as well as the acquisition or termination of such an interest. Notification has to be made not only when the acquisition and disposals take place, but also when the holder becomes aware of the acquisition or termination of a notifiable interest or a change therein.

Under s 203, a person is taken to be interested in certain family or corporate shareholdings. Also included are interests as a beneficiary under a trust, the property of which includes shares. Certain interests are to be disregarded. These are set out in s 209 and include an interest in reversion or remainder or as a bare trustee, and any discretionary interest under an English or Welsh trust, and an interest in fee or of a simple trustee and a discretionary interest under a Scottish trust.

Section 204 contains a provision whereby persons are taken to be acting together for the provisions of Pt VI if there is an agreement between them for the acquisition by any one or more of them of interests in shares of a target company. The section applies where such an agreement imposes obligations or restrictions on any one or more of the parties concerning the use, retention or disposal of an interest in shares of the target company acquired in pursuance of the agreement, and an interest is in fact acquired by any one or more of those persons. The term 'agreement' includes any agreement or arrangement but the section does not apply to an agreement which is not legally binding unless it involves mutuality in undertaking, expectations or understandings of the parties to it. The section also does not apply to a simple underwriting or sub-underwriting agreement. Under s 206, persons acting together are under an obligation to keep each other informed.

REGISTER OF INTERESTS

Under s 211, a public company must keep a register for the purposes of ss 198–202 and record therein the information disclosed under those provisions. The register must be kept at the same place as the register of directors' interests. Under s 219, the register of interests is to be available for inspection to any member of the company or any other person without charge. However, under s 211(9) and Sch 5, paras 3 and 10, disclosure is not required if it would be harmful to the company's business.

---

16   See *Re Geers Gross plc* [1988] 1 All ER 224, CA.
17   See M Hatchard (1990) 38 LS Gaz 24. See too the Directive 88/627/EEC discussed ibid, at p 27.

INVESTIGATION BY A COMPANY OF INTERESTS IN ITS SHARES

Under s 212, a public company may by notice in writing require a person whom the company knows or has reasonable cause to believe to be or, at any time during the three years immediately preceding the date when the notice was issued, to have been interested in shares in the company's relevant share capital, to indicate whether he holds or has held such an interest. When the company receives such information, it must record it in the register. Where a person has been incorrectly entered in the register, he can apply to the company to have the entry removed (s 217).

Members holding not less than one-tenth of the paid-up share capital carrying voting rights may requisition the company to exercise its powers under s 212 (s 214). On receipt of such a requisition, it is the duty of the company to carry out an investigation. The report must be made available for inspection at the registered office within a reasonable time not exceeding 15 days after the conclusion of the investigation.

Section 216 imposes penalties for failure to provide information. The company may apply to the court for an order imposing restrictions on the shares in question[18]. These restrictions which are set out in Pt XXV cover transfer, exercise of voting rights, issue of further shares or payments to the shareholder. In addition, s 216(3) makes a failure to comply a criminal offence. The restrictions imposed under s 216(1) may be lifted if the court or the Secretary of State is satisfied that the relevant disclosure has been made, and no unfair advantage has accrued as a result of the earlier failure to make disclosure, or the shares are to be sold[19] and the court or the Secretary of State approves the sale.

It can be seen from the above that these provisions go some way to ascertaining control, particularly where people act in concert. The concept of an agreement for this purpose is quite wide but will not cover every kind of collusive device. In particular, these provisions do not extend to a person who has control in the sense of a dominating influence without any provisions for acquisition of the relevant shares (s 204). Such a person may, however, be a shadow director, within CA 1985, s 741(2).

In addition to these provisions, there are rules governing substantial acquisitions of shares which are now contained in the City Code on Take-Overs and Mergers and the rules governing substantial acquisitions of shares issued by the Panel on Take-Overs and Mergers and effective from 29 April 1985. These are dealt with in Chapter 36.

Legal obligations of control[20]

THE CONVENTIONAL VIEW

The conventional view, rooted in Victorian individualism, is that individual shareholders are not fiduciaries for each other and the company and do not owe any duty to the company or other shareholders in the absence of fraud or some contractual obligation. The *locus classicus* is perhaps the judgment of Jessel MR in *Pender v Lushington*[1] in 1877 where he said:

---

18 See *Re Geers Gross plc* [1988] 1 All ER 224, CA. Such restrictions cannot be avoided by a sale on the open market.

19 This requires the transfer of shares for cash and does not cover the transfer of shares in exchange for other shares; see *Re Westminster Property Group plc* [1985] 2 All ER 426, CA.

20 What follows is based on J H Farrar 'Duties of Controlling Shareholders' in *Contemporary Issues in Company Law* (1987) ed Farrar. See also P Anisman (1987) 12 Can Bus LJ 473.

1 (1877) 6 Ch D 70.

In all cases of this kind, where men exercise their rights of property, they exercise their rights from some motive adequate or inadequate, and I have always considered the law to be that those who have the rights of property are entitled to exercise them whatever their motives may be for such exercise—that is as regards a court of law and distinguished from a court of morality, if such a court exists ... A man may be actuated in giving his vote by interests entirely adverse to the interests of the company as a whole. He may think it more for his particular interest that a certain course may be taken which may be in the opinion of others very adverse to the interests of the company as a whole, but he cannot be restrained from giving his vote in what way he pleases because he is influenced by that motive. There is ... no obligation on a shareholder of a company to give his vote merely with a view to what other persons may consider the interests of the company at large. He has a right, if he thinks fit, to give his vote from motives or promptings of what he considers his own individual interests.

However, Jessel MR, true to his adage 'I may be wrong, but I never have any doubts[2]', was wrong even in 1877. It has never been recognised that shareholders constituting the majority have unbridled powers. Indeed in Adam Smith the rational pursuit of self-interest was led by the 'invisible hand' to the common good[3]. It is arguable that a similar—almost mechanistic—assumption applies in company law and may indeed have been influenced by prevailing economic and political theory.

THE DUTY TO ACT BONA FIDE FOR THE GOOD OF THE COMPANY[4]

Under company law the majority of shareholders act as the company general meeting and the majority of directors act as the board, hence the term, majority rule. In a sense both the majority and minority are themselves organs of the company. Obviously this is true only in a less formal sense than the general meeting and the board of directors, but it is possible to see the majority and minority as weight and counter-weight in the structure of corporate decision-making[5]. The existence of the minority is a necessary check on the power of the majority to exercise the corporate will. In a number of cases on alteration of articles of association, it has been recognised that the majority are subject to an overall equitable obligation to exercise their votes bona fide for the good of the company as a whole[6]. This is a concept which company law inherited from partnership via the Deed of Settlement constitution which operated between 1844 and 1856. The company was a partnership on which certain corporate attributes had been conferred by the legislation. Hence it was appropriate to transpose partnership ideas and equitable principles to the company[7]. The first coherent discussion of the duty was formulated, appropriately enough, by the great partnership lawyer Lindley MR in *Allen v Gold Reefs of West Africa Ltd*[8]. The concept was used in numerous cases on alteration of articles since 1900. There are analogous concepts in class and creditors'

2   See James Bryce *Studies in Contemporary Biography* (1903), p 181.
3   *An Inquiry into the Nature and Causes of the Wealth of Nations* (NY 1937) 423.
4   See F G Rixon 'Competing Interests and Conflicting Principles; An Examination of the Power of Alteration of Articles of Association' (1986) 49 MLR 446 at 448–454.
5   See D Schmidt *Les Droits de la Minorité dans la Société Anonyme* (1970), p 257.
6   See the authorities reviewed by Rixon, op cit.
7   See Chapter 11, ante.
8   [1900] 1 Ch 656, CA.

meetings[9]. There has, however, been crucial equivocation in the meaning attributed to the concept by the courts. It has been said to refer to the present shareholders[10], the present and future shareholders[11], the company as an institution[12], and at least in some cases, the creditors as well[13]. The legislative reforms of 1980 made it legitimate to consider the interests of employees as well, without necessarily imposing a duty to do so[14]. Dr Rixon in a recent illuminating article has referred to it as[15]:

> a Delphic term employed by different judges in different circumstances to signify different things: it has been used to signify, on the one hand, the corporate entity distinct from the corporators, and, on the other hand, to import a reference to the doctrine of fraud on a power.

The concept falls short of a fiduciary relationship. At most it is a fragment of a fiduciary obligation. In *Peter's American Delicacy Co Ltd v Heath*[16] the High Court of Australia recognised the ultimate inadequacy of the concept to deal with every conflict which arose within a company. It was recognised that in some cases it was necessary to resort to a more general obligation of fairness between different classes of shareholders. It is submitted that there is much sense in this approach. Indeed it is implicit in the statutory rights given to the minority to object to alteration of objects and class rights. The inadequacy of the concept of the good of the company to provide a satisfactory basis for duties of controlling shareholders probably springs from the fact that it represents an incoherent attempt to reconcile fairness and the business judgment rule. It is significant that the concept is seldom used by the US courts which distinguish very clearly between the two doctrines. It will be suggested later that if any progress is to be made in the development of a coherent law on the duties of controlling shareholders it will be necessary to turn openly to these doctrines.

THE BROADENING EQUITABLE BASE

In *Clemens v Clemens Bros Ltd*[17] Foster J applied the concept of the good of the company to a case which did not involve alteration of articles but did involve an abuse of directors' powers and powers in general meeting in connection with a share issue under one of the exceptions to what is now s 151 of the CA 1985. Foster J recognised that the concept of the good of the company, fraud on the minority and oppression did not assist in formulating a principle to provide some means of restraint on abuse of power by a controlling shareholder. He preferred to refer generally to 'equitable considerations' which may make it unjust to exercise one's powers in a particular way. In doing so he made reference to the underlying equitable relationship of confidence which Lord Wilberforce had spoken of in *Ebrahimi v Westbourne Galleries Ltd*[18] in

---

9   See B H McPherson 'Oppression of Minority Shareholders', Part 1: Common Law Relief (1962–3) 36 ALJ 404, 409.
10   *Greenhalgh v Arderne Cinemas Ltd* [1951] Ch 286 at 290–291, CA.
11   R R Pennington *Company Law* (7th edn), p 94.
12   *British Equitable Assurance Co Ltd v Baily* [1906] AC 35 at 39, HL.
13   *Kinsela v Russell Kinsela Pty Ltd* (1986) 10 ACLR 395.
14   Now restated in the Companies Act 1985, ss 309 and 719.
15   Rixon, op cit, p 454.
16   (1939) 61 CLR 457; but see now *Gambotto v WCP Ltd* (1995) 182 CLR 432 where alternative tests are formulated for expropriation and conflict situations. See Ch 11 infra.
17   [1976] 2 All ER 268.
18   [1973] AC 360, HL.

1973. Lord Wilberforce had, of course, formulated the principles as a paradigm case for intervention by the court in the case of winding up on the just and equitable ground. The decision and reasoning of Foster J have either been criticised as being unorthodox and a mis-application of the basic concepts[19] or, alternatively, as a 'first swallow which heralds the new spring'[20]. However, even the latter commentators tend to question its adequacy as a conceptual base for developing a coherent law of duties of controlling shareholders. Again this falls short of recognition of a fiduciary relationship.

THE GOOD OF THE COMPANY, ABUSE OF POWER AND THE LINK WITH FOSS V HARBOTTLE

In the past there has been an assumption that anything that was not for the good of the company constituted a fraud on the minority for the purpose of the exception to the rule in *Foss v Harbottle*[1] and that anything that was for the good of the company could not constitute fraud on the minority[2]. The neat fit of these two concepts was, however, doubted by Sir Robert Megarry V-C in *Estmanco (Kilner House) Ltd v Greater London Council*[3] in 1982. Sir Robert recognised that acts could be carried out for the good of the company and still constitute fraud on the minority[4]. His reasoning seems convincing and provides another step in the clarification of the underlying conceptual framework in this area of law. It is arguably a step towards the recognition of a coherent doctrine of fraud on a power in this context. It is often said, as Jessel MR inferred in *Pender v Lushington*[5], that English law recognises no general doctrine of abuse of rights. In broad terms this is undoubtedly true. However, it is not to say that abuse of *power* is not recognised in particular contexts in equity[6]. The power of the majority to bind the minority is a corporate, not an individual, power. As the Ontario Court of Appeal said in obiter remarks in *Goldex Mines Ltd v Revill*[7] in 1974:

> The principle that the majority governs in corporate affairs is fundamental to corporation law, but its corollary is also important—that the majority must act fairly and honestly. Fairness is the touchstone of equitable justice, and when the test of fairness is not met, the equitable jurisdiction of the Court can be invoked to prevent or remedy the injustice which misrepresentation or other dishonesty has caused.

THE GOOD OF THE COMPANY AND UNFAIR PREJUDICE

The revised wording of the statutory minority shareholders' remedy in s 459 of the CA 1985 makes unfair prejudice the key concept and arguably within the key concept the emphasis should now be on fairness. In other words some prejudice is unavoidable

---

19 See D D Prentice (1976) 92 LQR 502; L S Sealy [1976] CLJ 235; V Joffe (1977) 40 MLR 71.
20 B A K Rider [1979] CLJ 148; J H Farrar, op cit.
1 (1843) 2 Hare 461.
2 Cf Gower, op cit, p 673 et seq.
3 [1982] 1 WLR 2.
4 Ibid.
5 (1877) 6 Ch D 70.
6 See *Peter's American Delicacy Co Ltd v Heath* (1939) 61 CLR 457. In a sense this is the private law equivalent of public law doctrine.
7 (1975) 7 OR (2d) 216 at 224.Criticised by B. Welling, *Corporate Law in Canada—The Governing Principles* (2nd ed), p 639.

through membership of a limited liability company and the courts will not interfere unless the prejudice can be said to be unfair. The question arises, as in the case of the rule in *Foss v Harbottle*[8] and its exceptions, of the relationship of the concept of the good of the company to unfair prejudice. It would seem that an act which is for the good of the company may still nevertheless constitute unfair prejudice. To say that an act was done in good faith and for a purpose within the relevant power is relevant but not conclusive for the purposes of relief under the section. Richardson J said, in the New Zealand case of *Thomas v H W Thomas Ltd*,[9] that it is not necessary to point to a want of good faith. The test is whether there was some unfairly detrimental effect on the interests of the complaining member. This was to be assessed by a balancing of interests in the light of the history of the company and the policies underlying the companies legislation. This was also recognised by Brennan J in the High Court of Australia in the case of *Wayde v New South Wales Rugby League Ltd*[10]. He thought that the decision to intervene was a question of fact and degree which the court should answer by inquiring whether reasonable directors (possessed of any special skill, knowledge and acumen of the actual directors) would have decided that the action was unfair. His Honour said:

> The test assumes (whether it be the fact or not) that reasonable directors weigh the furthering of the corporate object against the disadvantage, disability or burden which their decision will impose, and address their minds to the question whether a proposed decision is unfair. The Court must determine whether reasonable directors, possessing any special skill, knowledge or acumen possessed by the directors and having in mind the importance of furthering the corporate object on the one hand and the disadvantage, disability or burden which their decision will impose on a member on the other, would have decided that it was unfair to make that decision.

The other judges who were parties to a single judgment (Mason ACJ, Wilson, Deane and Dawson JJ) also recognised an objective test but stressed the need for caution in exercising the statutory discretion in such circumstance[11].

OTHER POSSIBLE BASES[12]

a. Controlling shareholders as shadow directors   In some circumstances a controlling shareholder might be regarded as a shadow director. The drafting of the Companies Act 1985 and the Insolvency Act 1986 has been badly coordinated and the position seems to be as follows:

(1) A natural person controlling shareholder can be a shadow director of the company of which he or she is a shareholder if he or she participates in

---

8   (1843) 2 Hare 461.
9   (1970–1985) 1 BCR 648 at 657–8.
10 (1986) 10 ACLR 87 at 95. See G Shapira 'Minority Shareholders' Protection—Recent Developments' (1982) 10 NZULR 134; I Cameron 'Rugby League Footballers and Oppression or Injustice' (1985) 8 UNSWLJ 236.
11 (1986) 10 ACLR 87 at 95. See too Slade J in the unreported English case of *Re Bovey Hotel Ventures Ltd* (31 July 1981, unreported) cited by Nourse J in *Re R A Noble & Sons (Clothing) Ltd* [1983] BCLC 273 at 290. See A J Boyle 'The Judicial Interpretation of Part XVII of the Companies Act 1985' in B Pettet (ed) *Company Law in Change* (1987), p 23.
12 See *Farrar*, op cit.

management decision-making[13] or the directors are accustomed to act in accordance with his or her directions or instructions[14].

(2) If the company is not insolvent a corporate controlling shareholder is not treated as a shadow director in similar circumstances to (1) because of a specific exclusion of the parent company in s 741(2).

(3) There is no specific exclusion of a parent company in ss 214(7) and 251 of the Insolvency Act 1986. Therefore a corporate controlling shareholder can be regarded as a shadow director for the purposes of wrongful trading[15].

(4) A shadow director is subject to some of the statutory duties imposed on directors but not to the common law or fiduciary duties in the absence of other circumstances imposing a specific duty[16].

(5) If the basic fiduciary duties are ever codified in the legislation, the point will assume even greater significance.

b.   Special facts fiduciary relationship[17]   Even though no general fiduciary relationship exists between controlling shareholders and the company and its minority shareholders it is possible for there to be a special facts fiduciary relationship arising from the circumstances. In most cases this will only be possible in the case of a private company. The majority of authorities deal with private companies or their equivalent. The existence of such a relationship was recognised by the Supreme Court of the US in *Strong v Repide*[18] in 1909 and by the New Zealand Court of Appeal in *Coleman v Myers*[19] in 1977. Most commentators have limited the concept to special facts arising out of a small incorporated firm but in the US case of *Dunnett v Arn*[20] it was recognised that there could be a special facts fiduciary relationship in the case of a larger company whose shares are widely held. In that case Phillips J said[1]:

> Persuasive reasons may be given for applying the minority rule to officers and directors of a large corporate organisation, where its stock is widely distributed and held in comparatively small units. The officers and directors of such a corporation, because of their official connection therewith, have a knowledge of its assets and liabilities, the condition of its business, its prospects for the future, and the value of the stock which it would be difficult if not practically impossible for the ordinary stockholder to obtain. In such a case it seems reasonable to require such officers or directors to make full disclosure of all pertinent facts when selling to, or purchasing individual stock from, a shareholder in the corporation.

13   *Re Eurostem Maritime Ltd* [1987] PCC 190; *Re Lo-Line Electric Motors Ltd* [1988] Ch 477; *Re Tasbian Ltd (No 3), Official Receiver v Nixon* [1993] BCLC 297; *Re Hydrodam (Corby) Ltd* [1994] 2 BCLC 180; *Holpitt Pty Ltd v Swaab* (1992) 33 FCR 474; *Taylor v Darke* (1992) 10 ACLC 1516, 1522; *Re New World Alliance Pty Ltd* (1994) 122 ALR 531; *Standard Chartered Bank of Australia Ltd v Antico* (1995) 18 ACSR 166; *ASC v AS Nominees Ltd* (1995) 18 ACSR 459. Cf *Kuwait Asia Bank EC v National Mutual Life Nominees Ltd* [1991] 1 AC 187; *Dairy Containers Ltd v NZI Bank Ltd* [1995] 2 NZLR 30. For comment see P Koh (1996) 14 C & SLJ 340; M Markovic (1996) 6 AJCL 323 and J Pizer (1997) 15 C & SLJ 81. Vide p 333 et seq ante.
14   See s 741 in relation to ss 309, 319–322, 330–346.
15   See L C B Gower *Principles of Modern Company Law* (6th ed), p 154.
16   See further *Kuwait Asia Bank EC v National Mutual Life Nominees Ltd* [1990] 3 All ER 404; [1990] BCLC 868, PC; but cf *Dairy Containers Ltd v NZI Bank Ltd* [1995] 2 NZLR 30. Vide supra fn 13.
17   Ibid, p 393.
18   213 US 419 (1909). Followed in *Glavanics v Brunninghausen* (1996) 19 ACSR 204. See R Hartman (1993) 50 Wash & Lee L Rev 1761.
19   [1977] 2 NZLR 225. Followed in *Glavanics v Brunninghausen* (supra).
20   71 F 2d 912 (1934).
1   Ibid, at 918.

The advantage of a special facts fiduciary relationship is that it contains within itself, like the duty of care in negligence, a judicial filter. There is a necessity to establish special facts in each case.

c. Constructive trust[2]   It has been recognised in a number of cases that where a third party acts in complicity with a director in breach of his fiduciary duties the third party can be liable as a constructive trustee. A fortiori a controlling shareholder acting in such circumstances can be liable. A common situation will be where a controlling shareholder puts its nominee on the board and he feeds confidential information to it of which the shareholder then takes advantage. This may be a case of corporate opportunity or insider trading[3]. Alternatively a controlling shareholder could himself be regarded as something approximating to a 'shadow director'. In other words his or her obligations could be primary rather than secondary. However the duty will normally be owed to the company and not to individual shareholders.

d. Conspiracy[4]   In recent years there has been an increasing tendency in company law cases to plead conspiracy in tort[5]. However, the use of conspiracy in this context is problematic since the Court of Appeal decision in *Prudential Assurance Co v Newman Industries Ltd (No 2)*[6]. In that case the English Court of Appeal held that where wrongs were done to the company the individual shareholders could not sue for any consequential diminution in the value of their shares. The denial of such a right means that conspiracy cannot be used as a means to by-pass the rule in *Foss v Harbottle*.

A COMPARISON WITH US CORPORATION LAWS[7]

It can be seen from the above that Commonwealth company laws are in a state of development. Old orthodoxies are being challenged but as yet the law lacks a coherent conceptual base. The concept of the good of the company has proved inadequate and it is only recently that its relationship to the developing areas of minority protection have been fully explored. There are signs of an emerging doctrine of fairness or abuse of power and there are alternative bases of a more particular kind which are being explored. However, since this has been the subject of a much greater volume of litigation in the US it is interesting and useful to make comparisons with US corporation laws to see if these provide a better framework for future development.

US corporation laws generally start from a similar base to Commonwealth laws— they will not interfere with legitimate exercise of majority rule[8]. However in almost every state the majority, dominant or controlling shareholders are under some duties to the minority and to the corporation which are often described as fiduciary duties and in some cases are comparable to the obligations of the directors and officers of

2   See *Aveling Barford Ltd v Perion Ltd* [1989] BCLC 626.
3   See the New Zealand Securities Commission's Report on Takeovers, vol 2.
4   See M J Sterling (1987) 50 MLR 468.
5   See *Belmont Finance Corpn v Williams Furniture Ltd (No 2)* [1980] 1 All ER 393, CA; *Prudential Assurance Co Ltd v Newman Industries Ltd (No 2)* [1982] Ch 204, CA; *Rogers v Bank of Montreal* [1985] 5 WWR 193.
6   *Prudential Assurance Co Ltd v Newman Industries Ltd (No 2)* [1982] Ch 204, CA. See also *Rogers v Bank of Montreal* [1985] 5 WWR 193.
7   See generally 18A Am Jur 2d para 762 et seq.
8   Henn and Alexander *Laws of Corporations* (3rd edn), p 653 et seq.

the corporation[9]. The basic standard is that of *fairness* encompassing obligations of good faith, loyalty, honesty, and full disclosure of material facts[10].

Unfairness is predicated on majority control or domination and self-dealing. It consists of fraud or other wrongful conduct, although what constitutes unfairness depends on the facts of each case[11]. Clearly oppression or fraud on the minority is encompassed as too is the equivalent of unfair prejudice in advanced Commonwealth systems[12]. In addition there are a variety of transactions which almost defy precise categorisation and which differ from state to state but which can loosely be subsumed under the concept of unfairness to the minority[13].

Thus there is an increasing body of case law on the sale of control to a third party[14]. Then there are some restrictions on the abuse or sale of voting power[15]. However shareholders as such are not subject to the same conflict of interest rules as directors and thus are usually able to vote in favour of ratification of their own self dealing transactions[16].

Interlocking directorships

Interlocking directorships, particularly between a financial institution and a trading company, have always been a feature of the corporate scene. From the point of view of empirical research into corporate control they are significant as an indicator of intercorporate cohesion and interdependence. Certain institutions may be found to be central to a number of relationships and therefore occupy an important position in the constellation of interests.

From a company law point of view, the principal question is whether this gives rise to a conflict of interest[17]. The older authorities saw nothing wrong in the holding of competing directorships. In *London and Mashonaland Exploration Co Ltd v New Mashonaland Exploration Co Ltd*[18] Chitty J held that a director would not be restrained from acting as a director of a rival company, except where there is a prohibition in the articles, or where the director is about to disclose confidential information. Also the director can be restrained where there is a term in his contract of service prohibiting him from so acting[19].

Later cases have undermined the multiple director's apparently secure position. In the Canadian case of *Abbey Glen Property Corpn v Stumborg*[20] McDonald J thought that the *Mashonaland* dicta were too widely expressed, and that 'there might well be cases in which a director breaches his fiduciary duty to Company A merely by acting

9   *Hyams v Old Dominion Co* 113 Me 294, 93 A 747 (1915); *Iwasaki v Iwasaki Bros Inc* 58 Ore App 543, 649 P 2d 598 (1982); *Boss v Boss* 98 RI 146, 200 A 2d 231 (1964).
10 See the authorities listed in 18A Am Jur 2d para 764 especially in footnotes 17 and 20.
11 *Re Reading Co* 551 F Supp 1205 (1980); affd 709 F 2d 1494–5 (1983); revsd on other grounds 711 F 2d 509 (1983); *Jones v H F Ahmanson & Co* 460 P2d 464 (1969); *Singer v Magnavox Co* 380 A 2d 969 (1977); overruled on other grounds 457 A 2d 701 (1983); *Knaebel v Heiner* 663 P 2d 551 (1983); later app 673 P 2d 885 (1983).
12 *Coduti v Hellwig* 469 NE 2d 220 (1984).
13 *Jackson v St Regis Apartments Inc* 565 SW 2d 178 (1979). See the useful checklist in 18A Am Jur 2d para 768.
14 See Henn and Alexander *Laws of Corporations* (3rd edn), p 654 et seq.
15 18A Am Jur 2d para 788–796.
16 See eg *Insuranshares Corpn of Delaware v Northern Fiscal Corpn* 35 F Supp 22 (1940).
17 D E McLay (1980) 10 VUWLR 429; R Carroll, B Stening and Kal Stening (1990) 8 C & SLJ 290.
18 [1891] WN 165. See also *Bell v Lever Bros Ltd* [1932] AC 161 at 195, HL but cf *Scottish Co-operative Wholesale Society v Meyer* [1959] AC 324 at 366, HL.
19 *Hivac Ltd v Park Royal Scientific Instruments Ltd* [1946] Ch 169, CA; *Thomas Marshall (Exports) Ltd v Guinle* [1979] Ch 227.
20 (1976) 65 DLR (3d) 235.

as a director of Company B[1], even where there is no question of passing on confidential information.'

The matter was considered by Mahon J in the New Zealand case of *Berlei Hestia (NZ) Ltd v Fernyhough*[2]. The learned judge thought there was 'a wide distinction between asking a director to account for a profit made out of his fiduciary relationship, and asking a director not to join the board of a competing organisation in case he should, at some future time, decide to act in breach of his fiduciary duty'[3]. Only the former was regulated. However, Mahon J appears to overlook the point that the making of a profit is only one facet of the conflict of interest rule which can apply to render a director in breach of his fiduciary duty even where he makes no profit.

The cases thus take a surprisingly lax approach which some would argue is justified from the point of view of commercial convenience. However, in certain circumstances interlocking directorships may give rise to an action for breach of confidence or to a petition under s 459[4].

In a Staff Report of the Antitrust Subcommittee of the US Committee on the Judiciary in 1965[5] it was stated that there were three objections to corporate management interlocks: (1) matters of antitrust significance; (2) conflicts of interest; and (3) debasement of the quality of available business leadership. The antitrust objections were said to be the avoidance of competition, the promotion of common action and the possibility that if the proportion of interlocking directors is sufficient, competition between the two firms may be eliminated entirely.

> Interlocking relations between companies in closely related industries may tend to forestall the development of competition which otherwise would occur in the normal expansion and diversification of each of the respective companies. Common directors between companies that are in a supplier-purchaser position to each other may result in preferential treatment in periods of short supply to the impairment of competition generally throughout the affected industry. Similarly, preferential treatment may occur in access to market outlets. An interlock between a manufacturing corporation and banks and insurance companies or other sources of financial services may establish a community of interest that would tend to assure adequate credit to a favoured company and a withholding of credit and capital from disfavoured competitors.

The report identified two types of conflict of interest problem. It argued that 'when a director serves on boards of different corporations, there is the narrow problem that the interests of stockholders may be subordinated to the opportunity for personal gain that is afforded the director because he has an opportunity for "inside dealings". The second problem extends beyond the effects of the director's divided loyalties for his own private gain. The structure of the interlock also divides his loyalties to the stockholders of each of the respective corporations. The incentive of the director to serve each is lessened in any course of dealing that involves both of the combined companies. Although in his official capacity a director is a fiduciary to his stockholders

1   Ibid, at 278.
2   [1980] 2 NZLR 150, reviewing earlier Australian authorities.
3   Ibid.
4   On breach of confidence see L Thomson 'Nominee and Multiple Directors and Breach of Confidence' in *Contemporary Issues in Company Law* (1987) ed J H Farrar, p 159. On s 459 see *Scottish Co-operative Wholesale Society v Meyer*, supra.
5   Interlocks in Corporate Management, Staff Report, Antitrust Subcommittee, Committee on the Judiciary, Washington 1965.

and is required to act in their interests, a director of two companies having business dealings with each other, or whose interests may conflict with each other, is placed in the anomalous position of being a fiduciary with respect to each.'

Even when the common director attempts to harmonise the conflicting interests this may be at the expense of both companies. The tendency is to blunt the rivalry between the companies and compromise opposing interests.

The third objection arises from the fact that the restriction of opportunities for management experience caused by the practice of interlocks may result in the deterioration of service on the boards of listed companies. A director who undertakes to serve on the boards of too many companies may be too busy to serve them effectively and may consequently be an absentee director. Younger executives may be denied the opportunity to be active at senior board level. In the light of this, it is submitted that there should be a presumption that interlocking directorships are against the public interest and the onus should be on those who seek to justify them.

Insider trading

The topic of insider trading assumes its greatest significance in connection with price-sensitive information concerning public listed companies. Insider trading has been discussed at Chapter 25.

INSTITUTIONAL INVESTMENT AND MONITORING OF MANAGEMENT[6]

Extent

Institutional investors increased their market share of UK-listed equities from 17.9% in 1957 to 60.4% in 1992, and are acquiring about 2% of the UK equity market each year[7]. It has been estimated that they will hold 69%–84% by the year 2000, but it is unlikely that this trend will be sustained to this extent[8]. Institutions hold over 60% of listed loan capital[9]. There are similar trends in Australia, New Zealand, Canada and the USA although each country has its own distinctive history[10]. These facts

---

6   See J H Farrar and M Russell (1984) 5 Co Law 107, and J H Farrar, 'Legal Restraints on Institutional Investor Involvement in Corporate Governance', unpublished report for the Australian Investment Managers Association, 1993, on which what follows is based. For an outstanding recent study see G P Stapledon *Institutional Shareholders and Corporate Governance* (1996). See too G P Stapledon (1995) 18 UNSWLJ 250 and P Davies (1991) 57 Brooklyn L Rev 129 and 'Institutional Investors in the United Kingdom' in D D Prentice and P R J Holland (ed) *Contemporary Issues in Corporate Governance* (1993) 69. See too John C Coffee Jr 'Institutional Investors as Corporate Monitors: Are Takeovers Obsolete?' in J H Farrar (ed) *Takeovers, Institutional Investors and the Modernisation of Corporate Laws* (1993) ch 2. See Report of Joint Committee on Corporations and Securities (Commonwealth of Australia) on the Role of Institutional Investors in Australia's Capital Markets (1994); *Maw on Corporate Governance* (1994), ch 8. For a useful recent discussion, see Robert A G Monks and Nell Minow *Corporate Governance* (1995), pp 124–177. This contains a good bibliography of US material. For further valuable US data, see Mark J Roe (1993) 41 UCLA L Rev 75 and his *Strong Managers, Weak Owners - The Political Roots of American Corporate Finance* (1994). See also Ira M Millstein 'Distinguishing "Ownership" and "Control" in the 1990s' in Monk and Minow (op cit), App 7.
7   R J Briston and R Dobbins *The Growth and Impact of Institutional Investors* (1978) p 24; GP Stapledon *Institutional Shareholders and Corporate Governance* (1996).
8   R Dobbins and T W McRae *Institutional Shareholders and Corporate Management* (1975); GP Stapledon (1995) 18 UNSWLJ 250, 252.
9   *Coakley and Harris,* op cit.
10 *Farrar and Russell,* op cit, and materials cited.

nevertheless revolutionise the concept of control. Ownership is regrouped but still generally relatively passive. The relationship between institutions and portfolio companies and between institutions and their constituents is not uniform and is in fact quite complex[11]. Whereas the separation of ownership from control is a relatively simple movement, this further stage of a regrouping of ownership with the potential of control is not so simple. Yet its impact on our understanding of the listed company and the whole conceptual framework of company law is potentially profound. Hence one American writer, Paul Harbrecht, has referred to the 'paraproprietal society'[12]. Since Harbrecht's time there has been the massive growth of funds managers who manage funds on behalf of the institutions. This complicates the picture further.

THE REASONS FOR THE GROWTH OF INSTITUTIONAL HOLDINGS

The first and paramount reason for the growth of institutional holdings is the growth of pension and superannuation schemes since 1945. Originally in private pension plans, pension obligations were satisfied by the purchase of annuities from life insurance companies. Thus the funds were included in the insurance companies' assets. Later, non-insured plans became popular because of the possibility of investment of the fund in ordinary shares.

A second reason is the relaxation of the trustee investment rules by the Trustee Investments Act 1961 which allowed trustees to invest part of the trust funds in equities.

A third reason is the rise of insurance-linked investment schemes to take advantage of the insurance tax relief. (This relief has now been withdrawn.)

A fourth reason is the favourable tax treatment of insurance companies and unit and investment trusts.

It is noticeable how none of these reasons is company-oriented. In other words, the company is simply the outlet for these investment urges. This, combined with the passivity of institutions as shareholders, probably accounts for the fact that such investment has previously caught the corporate world unawares and company lawyers have failed to appreciate its full significance. On the other hand the recent collapse of the Maxwell empire and the scandals surrounding use of pension funds for corporate purposes have put the spotlight on this legally complex backwater and led to the Report of the Pensions Law Reform Committee chaired by Professor Roy Goode in 1993. The report recommended a new Pensions Act and system of regulation to impose order on the chaos.

INSTITUTIONAL INVESTMENT AND THE ELUSIVENESS OF INSTITUTIONAL POWER

While the growth of institutional holdings and their *potential* power is well documented until recently there was little evidence that such power had been exercised in any significant way. One, therefore, hesitates to talk in terms of control except perhaps in the sense of constraint or power to monitor[13].

Nowadays, however, there is direct and indirect industry-wide and firm-level monitoring. The direct monitoring is done by analysis of information and regular

---

11 *Farrar and Russell,* op cit, at 66–67; G P Stapledon, *Institutional Shareholders and Corporate Governance* (1996) 239 et seq.
12 'Pension Funds and Economic Power: The Paraproprietal Society': Preface to D J Baum and N B Stiles *The Silent Investors* (1965).
13 Herman *Corporate Control, Corporate Power* (1981); cf Stapledon, op cit, chs 4, 5, 9 and 10.

meetings and dialogue with management. Indirect monitoring is done by investment committees as well as support for non-executive directors.

In the UK, the two best documented cases of institutional intervention are the Thalidomide and the Newman Industries cases. In the former the management of Distillers Company Ltd foolishly resisted public pressure to settle on more generous terms with the victims. In the end, their shares fell and the institutional investors together with the company's merchant banks met senior management on 4 January 1973. Two days later, the company increased its offer from £3.25 m to £21.75 m which formed the basis of the ultimate settlement[14]. In the Newman Industries[15] case, the Prudential Assurance Co Ltd litigated in individual and derivative form as a minority shareholder and the costs of the proceedings at first instance were reported to be £³/₄ m. The case later went on appeal before being eventually settled. The judgment of the Court of Appeal was rather critical of the cost involved in their initiative.

In numerous cases, institutional support has assisted a bidder in a takeover bid. The main aim here has been gain. In the US, the SEC's Institutional Investor Study Report, vol 5 in 1971[16] documented institutional involvement in transfers of corporate control. They instanced the following as the two main strategies which had been adopted:

(1) purchase of shares in anticipation of a bid;
(2) financial assistance to the bidder.

Amongst the special inducements which they had received in return for advance information about a bid were a higher price for their shares and assurances of contingent benefits if the bid succeeded.

In the UK, advance information may now be caught by the insider trading provisions of Part V of the Criminal Justice Act 1993 and the City Takeover Code will regulate the terms of a bid.

In spite of various institutional constraints there is now evidence of increased institutional investor activism precipitated perhaps by the pressures on institutional investors and funds managers themselves for better performance.

Dr G P Stapledon in *Institutional Shareholders and Corporate Governance* has documented 18 areas of corporate governance where UK institutional investors or funds managers have been active, usually behind the scenes. These cover a wide range of corporate activity. Usually this monitoring takes the form of direct firm-level monitoring by exercise of voting rights or routine meetings. Occasionally extraordinary action in terms of special meetings and even litigation have taken place. Indirect monitoring has taken place through various committees and by the use of non-executive directors.

Nevertheless the prevailing view hitherto has been that the primary responsibility of the institutional investor is simply to achieve maximum investment performance. If this is not present in a portfolio company the rule has been to sell. This rule has two aspects—first, it denies the existence of any duty to fellow shareholders and other groups such as employees and consumers and secondly, it maintains that in any event the overriding duty is to sell rather than incur costs and further risks[17].

Institutional investors in the past have been worried about the political consequences of an exercise of power. They eschew public criticism and fear public intervention.

14   See The Times, 5 and 6 January 1973; *The Economist,* 6 January 1973, p 9; P I Blumberg *The Megacorporation in American Society,* op cit.
15   *Prudential Assurance Co Ltd v Newman Industries Ltd (No 2)* [1982] Ch 204, CA. See also Vinelott J [1980] 3 WLR 543. See also (1980) Sunday Times, 24 February; (1980) Times, 19 June; (1981) Times, 31 July and 1 August.
16   House Doc 64 Pt 5, 92d Cong 1st Session, 2847–9.
17   *Blumberg,* op cit.

Some consider that their expertise is finance and investment rather than management and this does not necessarily equip them to pursue an interventionist role. They are also worried about the risks involved. Lastly, they are reluctant to offend the companies in which they invest. There may be more than one relationship between the company and institutions and in any event the institutions continue to rely on the companies for current information in spite of the new prohibitions on insider trading.

This conservatism of institutions in the exercise of their power has, however, been criticised by Adolf Berle Jr in the following terms[18].

> In effect, the position of the institutional managers is that they will not exercise their voting power so as seriously to affect the choice or the policies of corporate managements. The individuals for whom the institutions are fiduciaries, holders of rights in pension trusts, of shares in mutual funds, or of insurance policies, have surrendered their voting power. The institutional managers, therefore, by their policy of non-intervention, merely insulate the corporate managements from any possible action by or influence of the ultimate, beneficial 'owners' of the stock. A policy of non-action by the institutions means that the directors and managements of the corporations whose stock they hold become increasingly self-appointed and unchallengeable; while it continues, it freezes absolute power in the corporate managements.

It is submitted that any rational policy for exercise of power by institutions should first, confine influence to areas of expertise and possibly some areas of social policy, and secondly, refrain from making a profit at the expense of non-institutional shareholders[19]. The first part of the first rule is predicated on legal caution. To act otherwise might result in liability for negligence. Social policy is a controversial area. Nevertheless, there are some matters which speak for themselves. Thalidomide was such a case. The second rule again is based on evolving standards of corporate governance. It is submitted that in any event maxims of prudence should be in advance of the law. We now turn to the present state of the law before assessing the movement towards legislative intervention.

Legal implications of institutional power

INSTITUTIONS AND CONTROL

The institutions still show most interest in listed public companies, although an interest in small firms has recently become evident. In the former, a 20% holding or less will often be sufficient to secure minority control. This in turn affords to the controlling shareholder the power to influence not only such matters as dividend policy, but also the whole management of the company. As well as the potential for what might be termed control de jure, there is the equally important ability to influence management through threats to sell shareholdings or to work against management at general meetings. In the sense that the institutions merely provide another example of a power bloc within a company, this is nothing remarkable. However, what is unique about

18 Berle *Power without Property* (1960) pp 55–56. See also E Herman and C Stafanda 'Proxy Voting by Commercial Bank Trust Departments' (1973) 90 Banking LJ 91. Cf Stapledon op cit.

19 See 'Mutual Funds, Portfolio Companies and the Small Investor: The Role of Institutional Influence' (anonymous note) (1969) 5 Columbia Journal of Law and Social Problems 69 at 82–3.

the present trend is, first, that it applies across the board. It is not limited to one company or even a sector of industry. It is the scale and extent of the present trend which is distinctive. Secondly, there is a unity arising not from collusion but from broadly similar objectives and approximately equal access to information amongst the institutions irrespective of their legal structure[20]. This brings into sharper relief the need to anticipate difficulties which may arise from the increased dominance of the institutions. The matter may be becoming of more than theoretical interest in the light of a more interventionist tendency. If so, then the question is whether the potential power of the institutions should carry with it legal responsibilities governing the exercise of such power. Of course, one must be realistic and recognise that a reaction against any participation in management could set in, once it was realised that the active exercise of power carried burdens with it. We have already considered the extent to which the law imposes duties on those who control companies.

Given that the arrival or departure of an institution as shareholder may substantially affect share prices, it is not surprising that it has been argued that the institutions have a duty not to sell their holdings should dissatisfaction with management arise, but to stay on and work to remedy any wrongs[1]. It is said that a controlling shareholder has responsibilities to the other shareholders, to employees, even to consumers. This is one area where the question must at least be raised whether company law should adapt so as to redefine the role of the controlling shareholder in general, and/or institutional shareholders in particular. There are indications that some institutions see themselves as playing a wider role in the future[2]. No doubt there are powerful arguments that could be raised against such a proposal, particularly on the ground that it would constitute an unwarranted fetter on the institutions' freedom to manoeuvre. On the other hand, it can be argued that where a particular institution has a large holding it may find itself locked in unless it is prepared to sell at a loss. This may force institutions into some greater involvement in the affairs of a portfolio company.

INSTITUTIONS AND CONFLICTS OF INTEREST

Problems may arise in the area of conflicts of interest. As we have seen, in theory any shareholder may vote in his own self-interest, even if that does not coincide with the company's interests. At the same time, however, it is established that a majority of shareholders must use their votes in the best interests of the company as a whole[3], when voting eg on a proposed alteration to the articles of association. The relationship between these two apparently conflicting principles is not an easy one in theory or in practice. For our purposes, it is sufficient to note that power accruing to institutional shareholders as members of a majority must be exercised for the good of the company. Any duty which an institution owes to its investors ranks behind that owed to the company in which the institution holds shares, at least as far as company law is concerned.

Clearly, therefore, the potential exists for what might colloquially be termed a 'no-win' situation. A similar sort of dilemma faced trustees in the case of *Re Holders Investment Trust*[4], where Megarry J (as he then was) refused to confirm a proposed

20 See P Harbrecht's introduction to Baum and Stiles *Silent Investors*, op cit.
1 *Blumberg*, op cit, at p 136; *Baum and Stiles*, op cit, at pp 159 ff.
2 P E Moody 'A More Active Role for Institutional Investors' The Banker, February 1979, p 49. Compare, however, G P Stapledon (1995) 18 UNSWLJ 250, 273 for the reality of institutional coalitions in the UK being limited to small and medium-sized companies.
3 Chapter 11 ante. See Stapledon, op cit, 264–6.
4 [1971] 2 All ER 289.

reduction of capital, on the ground that the trustees, who held preference shares, had voted, at a class meeting of preference shareholders, not in the best interests of that class as a whole, but rather to benefit their total holdings in the company. Megarry J thereby affirmed that the trustees' first duty was to the company, and not to their beneficiaries.

Two principles compete here:

(1) Institutions owe it to their constituent investors, as a matter of trust or contract or at least legitimate expectation based on sales literature and the like, to safeguard returns, providing either wealth maximisation or steady income. The trust deed or contract will usually confer unlimited freedom to *dispose* of securities but will not envisage subjecting the investors to the possibility of reduced returns pending solution of the corporate problems in issue, or to increased risk in the event that solutions were not achieved.

(2) Institutions must act, as a majority or controlling shareholder, in the interests of the company as a whole. This could restrict a right of disposal. This is sometimes linked with a wider social responsibility of institutions. Whether such duties would lead to reluctance on the part of institutions to continue holding voting shares is another matter. Some institutions would no doubt argue that their interest is exclusively financial.

ACCESS TO INSIDE INFORMATION

Another major area of concern is access to inside information. Any major shareholder may have advantages over small shareholders in respect of, for instance, 'unpublished price-sensitive information' about the share market. In the case of the institutions, much of this may derive simply from expertise in the financial markets. Some may come from closer contact with portfolio companies. However, some of it may also derive from nominees appointed to the board of directors[5].

In law, a 'nominee' director is not recognised as being in a special category. What this means is that he or she must not have regard primarily to the interests of those who appointed him or her when he or she exercises his or her directorial functions[6]. He or she must, like any other director, place the interests of the company first. He or she should not pass on to his or her appointor information which may affect the price of the company's shares, so as to enable the latter to steal a march over other shareholders[7]. Neither should he or she place in the appointor's hands information relating to a corporate opportunity[8]. While there is some evidence to suggest that

5   There are other possible advantages to be gained from having a nominee on the board, for example, knowledge of a company's intention to make a takeover offer for shares of a target company. Information about negotiated acquisitions can, of course, be particularly sensitive. See generally L Thomson 'Nominee Directors and Confidential Information' in *Contemporary Issues in Company Law* (1987) ed J H Farrar.

6   See *Scottish Co-operative Wholesale Society v Meyer* [1959] AC 324, HL. Cf however, the Australian cases of *Levin v Clark* [1962] NSWR 686 at 700 and *Re Broadcasting Station 2GB Pty Ltd* [1964–5] NSWR 1648 at 1663 which postulate a more pragmatic test.

7   See Chapter 26. For information partly public, partly private see *Baker v Gibbons* [1972] 2 All ER 759 at 764–5.

8   *Cook v Deeks* [1916] 1 AC 554, PC.

directors nominated by institutions adopt an independent stance upon appointment[9], the unease remains.

The problem arises in another way, through interlocking directorships[10]. It is possible for a large investment institution to place nominees on the boards of several companies, perhaps operating in the same industry. In the case of conglomerates this is almost inevitable. What if these nominees work closely together as a matter of habit? What if the same person occupies these board positions? What must such person or persons do if he or she or they learn of a corporate opportunity whilst not acting specifically as director of any of the companies? If more than one of the companies is capable of taking up the opportunity, then to which must he communicate details of it? His dilemma would seem to be insoluble. The available case law does not seem to have fully confronted this problem. For instance, Roskill J in *Industrial Development Consultants Ltd v Cooley*[11] spoke of a director's obligation as simply one to pass on relevant information regarding a corporate opportunity to his company. This is no help in the above situation. Furthermore, the law still permits a director of one company to act as a director of another competing company[12], except where there is a prohibition in the company's articles, or the director is about to use confidential information. A director's duties will be clear cut if he or she acquires 'corporate opportunity' information whilst actively engaged in directorial functions on behalf of one of the companies. It is inconceivable that he or she would be permitted to divert such information to another company. However, the matter is simply not so easy to solve. If the same person is appointed by an institutional shareholder to the board of several companies then of course information may pass, with the resultant possibility of abuse.

The solution would be to create rules which will provide, for example, that the same person would not be eligible for appointment to more than one board. This should be coupled with a 'Chinese Wall' type of system to prevent information from being exchanged between nominees. Chinese Walls have been the subject of detailed study both in the US and the UK[13] in relation to merchant banks and it seems that it is possible to segregate different departments of an institution in order to shut off an exchange of such information between them. The use of such a system would have the advantage of rendering recourse to more draconian solutions, such as complete divestiture of shareholdings, unnecessary. The difficulty with Chinese Walls lies in policing them. It seems unworkable to attempt any form of statutory enactment. A suitable compromise might be to give some sort of credit for the existence of such a system as a defence to any action alleging wrongful use of inside information. The US courts have shown some approval of the system[14].

---

9 'Of course, it is improper to speak of any company director as a representative of institutional interests unless the director does, in fact, have a dominant allegiance to the institution and its interests. Few, if any, such directors would concede that their only function was the furtherance of institutional objectives, to the exclusion of corporate policies and purposes. Most directors conceive of their role as that of independent servant to both the institution and the company, acting in the best interests of each in the fulfilment of their respective fiduciary obligations.': SEC Institutional Investors Study, op cit, p 2716, note 70.

10 Ibid.

11 [1972] 2 All ER 162.

12 See note 5.

13 See B A K Rider 'Conflicts of Interest and the Chinese Wall' in *The Regulation of the British Securities Industry*, ed Rider (1979), ch 5; B A K Rider and H Leigh French *The Regulation of Insider Trading* (1979), pp 173–4; Herzel and Collings 'The Chinese Wall Revisited' (1983) 4 Co Law 14; Lipton and Mazur 'The Chinese Wall Solution to the Conflict Problems of Securities Firms' (1975) 50 NYULR 459.

14 See *Briston and Dobbins*, op cit.

SELF-INVESTMENT

A particular difficulty exists in the case of pension and superannuation funds. There is at present no legal prohibition on a fund investing in its employing or related companies[15]. Obviously, the potential exists for using such investment as a control device but, according to the Wilson Report, self-investment is rare[16] because of the potential risk that an employee's pension could then be at stake, as well as his job, if the company got into difficulties[17]. Another factor is the difficulty that conflicts of interest about self-investment can arise where trustees are also employees, scheme members, and even shareholders in the company concerned. Finally, there is the feeling that a company seeking external funds should have to subject itself to the scrutiny of the market[18].

The Wilson Committee nevertheless felt that self-investment, carefully monitored, could be a useful source of finance for a company. It recommended that pension funds should be required to disclose more information about their assets, including the extent of self-investment, and that the Occupational Pensions Board should issue a code of practice about self-investment[19]. The matter was also reviewed by the Pensions Law Reform Committee in 1993.

Future regulation of institutional investment

Existing company law thus contains isolated rules which may on occasion be used to regulate particular acts of misconduct by institutional investors. It is increasingly felt that these are not enough. Some argue that the company is merely a legal abstraction embodying a standard form of contract which supersedes individual contracts and the price system in the process of production and the raising of finance[20]. Ownership is a dead end and no longer has any functional meaning[1]. New forms of relationship and new forms of control are evolving which need regulation. Shareholders are not the working democracy which they seem. Control of the shares is often not with the legal or beneficial owners but with specialist funds managers. The links between financial institutions and management are not adequately analysed in traditional company law concepts. What is needed is a more sophisticated analysis of the concept or concepts of control which takes account of latent control and financial control[2]. The absence of such an analysis has not, however, prevented detailed proposals being made for regulation of institutional investment.

---

15 Indeed the law recognises the desirability of assisting company employees to acquire shares, by providing for an exemption from the controls on a company providing financial assistance for the purchase of its own shares, in the case of employee share schemes. The Maxwell saga points to the dangers in this practice at the hands of rogue management.

16 See the Wilson Report—The Committee to Review the Functioning of Financial Institutions, Report Volume 1 (Cmnd 7939), para 322.

17 Apparently, however, it is not so rare in the US. In *The Unseen Revolution* (op cit) Peter F Drucker reveals that in 1975 'the pension funds of New York City employees were used to bail out their employer, New York City ...', p 8.

18 Wilson Report, ibid.

19 Ibid, chapter 24.

20 See Ronald Coase 'The Nature of the Firm' (1937) 4 Economica 386.

1   See P Harbrecht *Towards the Paraproprietal Society* (1960), p 16.

2   For a very useful start by an economist see Edward Herman *Corporate Control, Corporate Power* (1981), ch 2. Herman distinguishes between active and latent power and the mechanisms and the locus of control. He emphasises strategic position as the crucial underpinning of management control. He sees institutional investors as latent power and influence.

One major proposal of more significance in the USA than in the UK is to limit the proportion of shares in a particular company which can be held by a single institution[3]. Such restrictions already exist for investment trusts and unit trusts in the UK. While this will be effective to prevent control by a single institution it will not necessarily lead to a diminution of institutional investment in the company.

Another proposal is to curtail the rights of shares held by institutions while they are in their hands or alternatively to limit them to non-voting shares[4]. It is submitted that this may well lead to a vacuum which would further concentrate power in the board. This would be undesirable.

A number of related proposals have been put forward for removing the possible information advantage of institutions[5]. The main philosophy here seems to be to mandate companies to disseminate information to the market place as soon as possible. Control over the so-called Chinese Walls within merchant banks between banking and trust departments is difficult to enforce in the absence of separate institutions. Further disclosure by institutions of the precise nature of their holdings and details of how they vote is being called for. The question of investment activities and disclosure by pension schemes to members is a specialist topic which as such lies outside the scope of this book[6].

A more radical proposal was put forward in 1971 by Robert M Soldofsky in 'Institutional Holdings of Common Stock, 1900–2000', a study published by the University of Michigan. This was for the votes of institutional holdings to be transferred to an impartial Stockholders' Voting Council. This would be financed by the institutions but a third of its membership would be government appointments. The remaining two-thirds would be appointed by the institutions and their constituents with the latter electing a majority. This would remove a burden from institutions and a source of friction with governments on the left. It would confer some meaningful franchise on the constituents of institutional investment. It would, however, leave control in the private sector while allowing for some representation of the public interest. As an idea it is worth further thought and it is unfortunate that it does not appear to have been considered by the Wilson Committee. As a reform, it would need implementation by legislation because of the uncertainty regarding the separation of votes from share ownership.

Another radical idea is to take away management's control of the proxy voting system and to give control of it to a committee of the company's largest shareholders. In this way there would be a reunification of ownership and control[7]. This is a simple but interesting idea which would probably prove practically unworkable as the largest shareholders changed or reduced their holdings.

The simple panacea put forward by some commentators, and supported by the previous Government of encouraging a return of the small shareholder to the market does not seem very realistic. The fact is that, for good financial reasons, many small

---

3   See M E Blume and I Friend *The Changing Role of the Individual Investor—A Twentieth Century Fund Report* (1978), ch 5; see also *Voting Rights in Major Corporations*—a staff study prepared by the Sub-Committee on Reports, Accounting and Management of the Committee on Government Affairs, US Senate, January 1978, p 576.

4   *Blume and Friend,* op cit. Cf Stapleton 285 et seq for the converse arguments in favour of compulsory voting.

5   See the Wilson Report—The Committee to Review the Functioning of Financial Institutions, Report Vol 1 (Cmnd 7939) 1980.

6   See the Report of the Pensions Law Review Commitee; Wilson Report, op cit; see also *Drucker,* op cit.

7   See George W Dent 'Toward Unifying Ownership and Control in the Public Corporation' (1989) Wisconsin L Rev 883. For further suggestions in the US context see Mark Roe *Strong Managers, Weak Owners* (1994), Part V. For a range of other practical suggestions see Stapledon, op cit, ch 11.

investors find indirect investment preferable and thus the market is being made accessible to millions by institutional investment. It is a trend which cannot be reversed unless there is a considerable amount of government intervention. As an economic mechanism, it achieves the rational end of reallocation of resources with possibly greater expertise and a lowering of transaction costs. Nevertheless, there is some cause for concern. There are fears of excessive short termism in outlook, excessive delegation of responsibilities to funds managers, lack of clarity in the legal power of trustees to delegate and the lack of rights in the investors[8]. The matter cannot be assessed solely by the tenets of economic rationality. Indeed, there is mixed evidence of economic advantage in any event. The dominant issue is control of portfolio companies. Who is to control them, who is to effectively monitor the controllers and how this is to be done?

8   See Stapledon, op cit, 212 et seq.

CHAPTER 36

The regulation of takeovers and mergers

INTRODUCTION

In this chapter we shall examine the more important aspects of the regulation of takeovers and mergers.

The conventional meaning of 'takeover' is the acquisition by one company (the bidder) of sufficient shares in another company (the target) to give the purchaser control of that other company. In the Takeover Code, the bidder company is known as the offeror company; and the target company is the offeree company.

Takeovers are the means by which business expansion occurs. Companies may seek vertical integration (ie takeovers of companies at different stages in the production process) or horizontal integration (takeovers of companies at the same stage of the production process) or seek to diversify as in the case of conglomerates.

As with any major investment decision there may be a variety of motives for a company seeking a takeover. A company may, for example, be concerned about its access to raw materials or vital components and thus seek a merger with one of its suppliers; or it may be concerned to safeguard outlets for its products and so seek to merge with or take over one of its distributors or dealers. A company may be concerned to diversify its activities by taking over a company in a completely different field. But equally companies may be motivated less by economic considerations and more by financial or fiscal ones of improving the appearance of their balance sheet or reducing their liability to tax.

Takeovers tend to be associated in the public mind with aggressive or predatory management. In practice a management that wishes to expand a company's business may have a choice of doing so via organic growth or through an acquisition or merger and may choose the latter simply because of the advantage it offers. However, for many years now, there has been an ongoing debate (mainly conducted by economists) about whether takeovers and mergers are generally beneficial or harmful to the overall economy[1].

---

1   See generally Romano 'A Guide to Takeovers: Theory, Evidence and Regulation' in Hopt & Wymeersch (eds) *European Takeovers – Law and Practice* (1992); also Cranston 'The Rise and Rise of the Hostile Takeover' in the same volume; also Fairburn & Kay (eds) *Mergers and Merger Policy* (1989); Chiplin & Wright *The Logic of Mergers* (1987).

The economic argument for takeovers is that the offeror believes the assets can be managed more productively than the existing management were doing. Takeovers thus enable less productive or less efficient management to be replaced by more efficient management and it is in this way that takeovers are said to form part of the market for control of corporate assets[2]. Even an unsuccessful takeover bid, or the mere threat that a takeover bid could be made, acts as a spur to efficiency by ensuring that management make the most productive use of resources under their control[3].

Alternatively, it is argued that takeovers are a very costly way of disciplining incumbent management, occurring in only a random and opportunistic way, and requiring massive fees to advisers and commissions to underwriters. Improved corporate governance could address the issue of removing ineffective managers in a less expensive and disruptive way[4]. Fears have also been expressed that takeovers, or the threat of takeovers, far from leading to productive use of assets, compel managements to concentrate too much on short-term profitability to boost the share price and ward off a takeover, while avoiding long-term investment and innovation.

The Companies Act 1985 makes no special provision for the regulation of takeover bids. Instead the legal framework for takeovers is largely provided by the law of contract. A takeover bid in the form of an offer for shares is an offer made by the offeror company to the offeree company's shareholders. The offeror may offer them straight cash for their shares, or may offer them shares in the offeror company in return for their shares, or may offer them a combination of cash and shares for their shares.

'Merger' means the uniting of two companies but, as this is possibly done through an acquisition by one company of a controlling holding of shares in another, it is not surprising that the terms 'takeover' and 'merger' have become almost synonymous. 'Merger' is often use to describe a recommended takeover bid rather than a hostile one, ie one opposed by the board of the offeree company. It is often the case that the term 'takeover' is used in relation to company law while the term 'merger' is commonly used in relation to competition law.

Where a business is being transferred to a new company in the course of a liquidation, the transfer is usually called a reconstruction; transfers may also occur by way of a scheme of arrangement under the Companies Act 1985.

Initially, we will consider the role of the Takeover Panel, the conduct of a takeover under the Takeover Code and the proposals for a European Directive on takeovers. Then we will consider the statutory provisions governing reconstructions and schemes of arrangement and such other statutory provisions as are applicable to takeovers. Finally, we conclude with a very brief overview of the competition authorities which may review a takeover.

---

2   See Bradley 'Corporate Control: Markets and Rules' (1990) 53 MLR 170; also Introduction to Fairburn & Kay (eds) *Mergers and Merger Policy* (1989).

3   But see Hughes 'The Impact of Merger: A Survey of Empirical Evidence for the UK' in Fairburn & Kay (eds) *Mergers and Merger Policy* (1989) who having reviewed the empirical evidence concludes (at p 96) that 'Takeover or the threat of it, as a disciplinary stock market device, leaves a lot to be desired.'

4   See Coffee 'Institutional Investors as Corporate Monitors: Are Takeovers Obsolete' in Farrar (ed) *Takeovers, Institutional Investors and the Modernization of Corporate Laws* (1993); Baums 'Takeovers versus Institutions in Corporate Governance in Germany' in Prentice & Holland (eds), *Contemporary Issues in Corporate Governance* (1993); Marsh *Short-termism on trial* (1990).

REGULATION BY THE TAKEOVER PANEL

The Takeover Panel and the Takeover Code

Set up in 1968[5], the Takeover Panel is a self-regulatory body which publishes and administers the City Code on Takeovers and Mergers[6] which provides a framework within which takeovers are conducted[7]. As the Introduction to the City Code notes, the Panel is not concerned with the financial or commercial advantages or disadvantages of a takeover, nor with matters such as competition policy[8]. It simply provides an orderly framework within which a bid can be conducted. The Code does not have, and does not seek to have, the force of law but represents the collective opinion of those professionally involved in the field of takeovers as to good business standards[9].

The Code is made up of a number of General Principles (currently 10), expressed in broad general terms, which are essentially statements of good standards of commercial behaviour to be applied by the Panel in accordance with their spirit to achieve their underlying purpose[10]. In addition, the Code contains a series of rules (currently 38) supplemented by notes which amplify and explain the operation of a number of the rules. They too must be interpreted to achieve their underlying purpose and their spirit must be observed as well as their letter[10].

Those companies subject to the Code are defined in the Introduction to the Code and the main category is all listed and unlisted public companies[11] considered by the Panel to be resident in the United Kingdom, Channel Islands and the Isle of Man[12]. In determining whether or not the Code applies, it is the nature of the offeree company that is relevant[13].

The Panel works on a day-to-day basis through an Executive which is responsible for the general administration of the Takeover Code. Headed by a Director General, it is staffed by a mixture of secondees from City institutions, banks and law firms, and permanent appointments. The Executive operates in an active supervisory capacity, often at the end of a telephone, advising the parties to a takeover how to proceed in accordance with the spirit of the Code and giving rulings on the interpretation of the Code. Legal or other professional advice on the interpretation or application of the Code is not an appropriate alternative to obtaining a view or a ruling from the Executive[14]. Often the Executive or the Panel will take active steps to regulate the conduct of the bid while it is in progress, for example by requiring announcements or clarifications from the parties.

---

5   The Code developed out of the Notes for Amalgamations of British Businesses issued in 1959 by the
     Issuing Houses Association. For the historical background, see Johnston *The City Takeover Code*
     (1980).
6   The current edition is the 5th edition of the Code published in 1996 (hereafter the City Code).
7   See generally, Weinberg & Blank *Takeovers and Mergers* (5th edn, 1989); also Morse 'Controlling
     Takeovers – the self-regulation option in the United Kingdom' [1998] JBL 58; Morse 'The City Code
     on Takeovers and Mergers – Self Regulation or Self Protection' [1991] JBL 509; Lord Alexander
     'Takeovers: the Regulatory Scene' [1990] JBL 203; Calcutt 'The Work of the Takeover Panel' (1990)
     11 Co Law 203; Prentice 'Take-over Bids and the System of Self-regulation' (1981) 10 Ox JLS 406.
8   See City Code, Introduction, para 1(a).
9   See City Code, Introduction, paras 1(a), (c).
10   See City Code, Introduction, para 3(a).
11   On occasion, the Code can apply to private companies, for example where they have been listed on
     the Stock Exchange at any time in the ten years prior to the offer: see City Code, Introduction, para
     4(e).
12   See City Code, Introduction, para 4(a). The Panel will normally consider a company to be resident
     only if it is incorporated in the UK, Channel Islands or the Isle of Man and has its head office and
     place of central management in one of those jurisdictions.
13   See City Code, Introduction, para 4(a).
14   See City Code, Introduction, para 3(b).

Rulings of the Executive may be the subject of an appeal to the full Panel and rulings of the Panel, in turn, may be appealed to an Appeal Committee. There is a right of appeal in certain circumstances, particularly where the Panel finds a breach of the Code and proposes to take disciplinary action. In other cases, the Panel may allow an appeal. It is the Panel's policy in the case of important decisions to publish its conclusions and the reasons for them so that its activities may be explained to the public[15].

The Panel has 18 members, 6 of whom including the Chairman and two Deputy Chairmen are nominated by the Governor of the Bank of England. The remaining 12 members are representatives of corporate financiers, shareholders, industrialists as well as other regulators under the Financial Services Act 1986[16].

The essential characteristics of the Code as applied by the Panel are seen as first, flexibility: this is reflected in the requirement of adherence to the spirit of the Code rather than rigid adherence to rules and the ability to change the Code quickly to meet changing market practices; secondly, certainty and speed: this is reflected in the ability to consult with an Executive available immediately to the parties enabling them to know where they stand under the Code in a timely fashion[17].

Legal standing of the Takeover Panel

As noted above, the Code does not have, and does not seek to have, the force of law. The precise legal position of the Panel in applying the Code was considered in detail in *R v Panel on Take-overs and Mergers, ex p Datafin plc*[18] where the issue which arose was whether decisions of the Panel were susceptible to judicial review.

Two companies had been rival bidders for a third target company. The defeated bidder alleged that the successful bidder had had the assistance of a concert party[19]. The Panel upheld a ruling by the Executive that there was no concert party. The defeated bidder appealed to the courts for judicial review of the Panel's decision.

Sir John Donaldson MR noted that the Panel is a remarkable body which performs its functions without visible means of legal support[20]. It is a self-regulating body in the sense that it involves a group of people acting in concert, using their collective power to force themselves and others to comply with a code of conduct of their own devising[1].

> Lacking any authority de jure, it [the Panel] exercises immense power de facto by devising, promulgating, amending and interpreting the City Code on Takeovers and Mergers, by waiving or modifying the application of the code in particular circumstances, by investigating and reporting on alleged breaches of the code and by the application or threat of sanctions. These sanctions are no

---

15   See City Code, Introduction, para 3(e).
16   The bodies represented include: the Association of British Insurers; the Association of Investment Trust Companies; the British Bankers' Association; the CBI; the Institute of Chartered Accountants in England and Wales; the Stock Exchange; the National Association of Pension Funds and the Securities and Futures Association.
17   See Morse [1998] JBL 58 at 61 who puts forward an alternative view: 'Its detractors say that it [the self-regulatory system] is arbitrary and inconsistent and above all is designed to protect those whose livelihood depends upon an active market by permitting dealing at all costs.'
18   [1987] QB 815, [1987] 1 All ER 564, CA; noted Hilliard (1987) 50 MLR 372; (1987) 103 LQR 323; see also Lord Alexander 'Judicial Review and City Regulators' (1989) 52 MLR 640.
19   A concert party is defined in the Code as 'persons who, pursuant to an agreement or understanding (whether formal or informal) actively co-operate, through the acquisition by any of them of shares in a company, to obtain or consolidate control of that company': see City Code, Definitions section.
20   [1987] QB 815 at 824, [1987] 1 All ER 564 at 574, CA.
1   [1987] QB 815 at 826, [1987] 1 All ER 564 at 567, CA.

less effective because they are applied indirectly and lack a legally enforceable base[1].

However, the court thought that the Panel should be subject to judicial review, for three main reasons. First, the Secretary of State for Trade and Industry had indicated a willingness to limit legislation in the field of takeovers and mergers and instead to use the Panel to regulate this area; secondly, those subject to the Panel's jurisdiction could be subject to a range of contractual or statutory sanctions by other bodies if they transgressed the code; thirdly, as the rights of citizens (some of whom will not have consented) can be affected by the Panel's decisions, the Panel in carrying out its responsibilities was performing a public duty and was amenable to judicial review[2].
Sir John went on:

> ... I wish to make it clear beyond a peradventure that in the light of the special nature of the Panel, its functions, the market in which it is operating, the time scales which are inherent in that market and the need to safeguard the position of third parties, who may be numbered in thousands, all of whom are entitled to continue to trade on an assumption of the validity of the Panel's rules and decisions, unless and until they are quashed by the court, I should expect the relationship between the Panel and the court to be historic rather than contemporaneous[3].

The courts would allow the decisions of the Panel to stand intervening only in retrospect by way of a declaration to enable the Panel not to repeat any error or to relieve individuals of any disciplinary consequences of an erroneous decision[4].
This general approach is seen as highly acceptable to the market, allowing for judicial review but in a way designed to prevent parties indulging in tactical litigation as a defensive mechanism[5].

Relations with other regulators

The Panel does not fall within the regulatory structure devised by the Financial Services Act 1986; nor will it fall within the structure envisaged by the Financial Regulatory Reform Bill to be enacted by late 1999[6]. However, the Panel does have a close relationship with the regulatory bodies established by the Financial Services Act 1986[7] and that will continue, no doubt, under the new regime.

2   [1987] QB 815 at 838, [1987] 1 All ER 564 at 577, CA.
3   [1987] QB 815 at 842, [1987] 1 All ER 564 at 579, CA.
4   [1987] QB 815 at 842, [1987] 1 All ER 564 at 579, CA. See also *R v Panel on Take-overs and Mergers, ex p Guinness plc* [1990] 1 QB 146, [1989] 1 All ER 509, CA: the test is whether something had gone wrong with the Panel's procedure so as to cause real injustice and require the intervention of the court. (Panel's decision not to adjourn a hearing of a concert party allegation could be criticised but overall the conduct of the investigation in this case by the Panel had been fair and had not caused injustice to Guinness.) See also *R v Panel on Take-overs and Mergers, ex p Fayed* [1992] BCC 524; noted Morse [1992] JBL 596.
5   For more cautionary comments on the approach taken: see (1987) 103 LQR 323; also Hilliard (1987) 50 MLR 372 at 377: '... a Panel subject to review the scope of which is so hedged about with qualification that any notion of substantive supervision is illusory.'
6   Nor does it wish to, see the Takeover Panel Annual Report 1996-97, p 8: 'The continued effective and efficient functioning of the Panel does not need the support of domestic or European legislation.'
7   See City Code, Introduction, para 2(c). It is also a designated body under CA 1985, s 449 and FSA 1986, s 180, so it can receive restricted information obtained as a result of investigations under the Companies Act and the Financial Services Act: Financial Services (Disclosure of Information) (Designated Authorities No 2) Order 1987, SI 1987 No 859.

A feature of the Code is the emphasis placed on the particular responsibility of the professionals involved, particularly those actively engaged in the securities markets and financial advisers, to comply with the Code and to ensure, as far as they are reasonably able, that the offeror and offeree company and their directors are aware of the Code and will comply with it[8]. This is a valuable method of regulation for it is the professionals who must operate in the London market place who are most susceptible to the Panel's disciplinary powers[9].

In keeping with that emphasis, it has been agreed that those who do not conduct themselves in accordance with the Code may find themselves denied the facilities of the securities markets in the UK[10]. Hence the Securities and Investment Board (now renamed the Financial Services Authority) and SRO (self-regulating organisation) rules provide that firms authorised to carry on investment business under the Financial Services Act 1986 should not act for clients who are not prepared to comply with the Code (cold-shouldering)[11]. Breaches of the Code by authorised persons may be taken into account by an SRO in considering whether a particular institution is a fit and proper person to be authorised to carry on an investment business while the SFA (Securities and Futures Association), one of the SROs, requires its members to supply the Panel with information and assistance. In February 1995 the SIB endorsed the Takeover Code for the purposes of the SIB's Statements of Principle which provide a general statement of standards with which all authorised persons must comply[12].

Sanctions for breach of the Takeover Code

Breach of the Code carries with it penalties ranging from a private reprimand by the Panel, to public censure, reporting the offender's conduct to another regulatory body such as the Department of Trade and Industry, the Stock Exchange, SIB or relevant SRO, or requiring further action to be taken as the Panel thinks fit[13].

The most significant exercise of the Panel's powers, at least in monetary terms, came in the Guinness case where it was able to compel the offeror company (Guinness) to provide significant financial redress (an additional £75m approximately) for offeree shareholders (in Distillers) where there had been serious breaches of the Code resulting in a false market in the offeror's shares[14]. Despite the sanction element apparent in this ruling, the Panel has said that this exercise was restricted to compensating the

---

8   See City Code, Introduction, para 1(b); also the Introduction to the General Principles.
9   Although Morse [1992] JBL 106, 428, suggests that the Panel is often more lenient with professionals who are in breach of the Code than with other parties such as directors.
10 See City Code, Introduction, para 1(c).
11 The first instance of cold-shouldering was identified in Panel Statement 1992/9, Re Dundee Football Club, 26 March 1992; see also Takeover Panel Annual Report 1991-92, p 13; Morse [1992] JBL 430-433.
12 See SIB Financial Services (Statements of Principle) (Endorsement of Codes and Standards) Instrument 1995. Principle 3 of the Statements of Principle provides that firms should observe high standards of market conduct and should comply with any code endorsed by the SIB for the purpose of this principle. Hence the endorsement of the Takeover Code.
13 See Introduction to the Code, para 3(d). On the question of sanctions by the Panel, see Morse [1992] JBL 428-433 who criticises the Panel for applying stricter sanctions to outsiders than to City practitioners caught in breach of the Code, also [1992] JBL 106; Morse 'The City Code on Takeovers and Mergers – Self Regulation or Self Protection' [1991] JBL 509. Morse also questions the effectiveness of public censure as a sanction, see [1998] JBL 58 at 71.
14 See Takeover Panel Annual Report year ending 31 March 1989; also Panel Press Summary 1989/13; Panel Report on the various hearings and appeal by Guinness: Takeover Panel *Guinness plc/The Distillers Company plc* (1989). For the background to the payment, see [1989] JBL 520.

offeree shareholders and was specifically not of a disciplinary nature[15]. That was said to await the completion of a DTI investigation into the affairs of Guinness[16] and various legal proceedings. The Panel believes that this requirement to pay is an effective step for it focuses on the consequences for shareholders of breaches of the rules rather than simply on disciplinary action in respect of the breach. The fact remains that Guinness successfully took over Distillers using a massive share support scheme[17] hidden from the market in breach of the Code. As the DTI inspectors noted, an extra £75m might seem to some a reasonable additional expense to secure the prize of Distillers[18].

Perhaps the last word on the subject of the effectiveness of the Panel should be left with the DTI inspectors who in their report into the Guinness affair concluded[19]:

> Once consummated, a takeover cannot realistically be reversed and the present case illustrates the difficulty of providing ex post facto justice for either a loosing contestant or accepting shareholders. ... This is a most important reason why the Panel has to possess powers of rapid adjudication during the bid itself. These demand equally rapid and effective powers of investigation. Such powers traditionally depended on a shared ethic of truthfulness which our enquiry suggested might belong at best to a bygone age. In the face of a party prepared not only to break the rules in secret but then to lie in response to the investigator's questions, the Panel executive was confronted by a task which its founders never contemplated.

THE CONDUCT OF TAKEOVERS UNDER THE CITY CODE

Equal treatment of shareholders

The basic principle on which the City Code is founded requires that all shareholders of the same class of an offeree company be treated similarly by an offeror[20]. If, in the three months prior to the offer, the offeror purchases shares in the offeree company, the offer to shareholders of the same class must be on no less favourable terms[1]. Likewise, if, during the offer, the offeror buys shares at above the offer price, the offer price for all must be correspondingly increased[2].

The mandatory bid

As part of that basic equality, it is a fundamental principle underlying the Code that a shareholder should have a right to sell, to exit the company, if control of the company

---

15   See Panel Statement 1992/6, 14 February 1992.
16   The inspectors finally reported in 1997 (the bid in question, by Guinness for Distillers, took place in the period January – April 1986). For the fascinating account of this now infamous takeover bid, see the inspectors' report: DTI *Guinness plc, Investigation under ss 432(2) and 442 of the Companies Act 1985* (1997, HMSO).
17   The inspectors' report found that 78m Guinness shares, some 25% of the issued share capital at that time, were purchased by supporters of the Guinness cause at a total cost of £257m: see DTI *Guinness plc, Investigation under ss 432(2) and 442 of the Companies Act 1985* (1997, HMSO), para 5.3.
18   See DTI *Guinness plc, Investigation under ss 432(2) and 442 of the Companies Act 1985* (1997, HMSO), para 12.11.
19   DTI *Guinness plc, Investigation under ss 432(2) and 442 of the Companies Act 1985* (1997, HMSO), para 12.12.
20   See City Code, GP 1.
1   See City Code, r 6.1.
2   See City Code, r 6.2.

changes. General Principle 10 provides that where control of a company is acquired by a person, or persons acting in concert[3], a general offer to all other shareholders is normally required; a similar obligation may arise if control is consolidated. Where an acquisition is contemplated as a result of which a person may incur such an obligation, he must, before making the acquisition, ensure that he can and will continue to be able to implement such an offer. This gives rise to what is known as the mandatory bid requirement which arises in two circumstances as set out in rule 9, although provision is made for some dispensations from this general requirement[4].

First, the mandatory bid rules provide that a shareholder cannot acquire a 30% stake without making a general offer. Once a shareholder reaches the 30% threshold, he is obliged to make a general offer for all the remaining shares of any class in which the shareholder holds shares[5]. This explains why, on occasion, offerors can be seen amassing 29.9% of the target's shares.

Secondly, if a shareholder already owns between 30% and 50%, he similarly becomes obliged to make a mandatory bid for all shares if he strengthens his control by increasing his stake by 1% or more within 12 months[6]. If the shareholder already owns over 50% he can continue to acquire shares without making a general offer since strengthening a controlling stake which is already over 50% is not regarded as affecting the minority shareholder to the same extent.

So if an offeror acquires or enhances a controlling stake in a company, then a similar offer must be extended to all shareholders. The price paid for control is thus extended to all shareholders and control is effectively treated as an asset of the company, reflected in the value of each share, rather than as an asset of the controlling shareholder. All the shareholders share in the premium paid by the offeror and can exit from the company on a change of control.

The offer, which an offeror obliged to make a mandatory bid must make, is a cash offer (or with a cash alternative) at not less than the highest price paid by the offeror or persons acting in concert with him for shares of the class concerned in the preceding 12 months[7].

Mandatory bids may not include any conditions other than as to the need for 50% acceptances and for the bid to lapse automatically on reference to the competition authorities[8]. This is to prevent the offeror defeating the purpose of r 9 by attaching conditions to the offer which would make acceptance unattractive to the shareholders. It also makes it unattractive to the bidder as he cannot insist on 90% acceptances which, as we shall see later, is important if certain statutory powers to acquire minority holdings are to be used.

In fact, very few bidders each year are required to make a mandatory bid and the vast majority of bids are voluntary bids[9]. Such bids, while containing those conditions above, may also contain other conditions. For example, the bidder may make the bid

---

3   A concert party is defined in the Code as 'persons who, pursuant to an agreement or understanding (whether formal or informal) actively co-operate, through the acquisition by any of them of shares in a company, to obtain or consolidate control of that company': see City Code, Definitions section. Those wishing to evade the requirement of a mandatory bid will, of course, go to great lengths to hide the existence of a concert party.

4   See Notes on Dispensations from Rule 9; for example, where 30% is acquired in the context of a rescue operation, or on the enforcement by a creditor of security for a loan, or through inadvertent mistake.

5   See City Code, r 9.1(a). Partial bids, ie bids for over 30% but less than 100%, are strongly discouraged and cannot be made without the Panel's consent: see r 36.

6   See City Code, r 9.1(b).

7   See City Code, r 9.5.

8   See City Code, r 9.3, 9.4.

9   See, for example, Takeover Panel, Annual Report 1996-97 which notes that of 166 takeover proposals where formal offer documents were sent to shareholders, only nine were mandatory bids.

conditional on the approval of 90% of the target's shareholders; or the approval of its own shareholders; or subject to regulatory consents; or subject to material changes in circumstances[10].

Another fundamental aspect of the Code is that, in addition to the proper treatment of shareholders in the offeree company, it is important that the market itself is not misled and General Principle 6 states that all parties to an offer must use every endeavour to prevent the creation of a false market in the securities of the offeror or the offeree company. Parties must take care that statements are not made which may mislead shareholders or the market.

The approach and announcements

There must be absolute secrecy before an announcement of a bid[11] (information regarding a pending takeover bid being highly price-sensitive and therefore offering great potential for insider dealing[12]) and any offer must be made first to the board of offeree company or to its advisers[13].

An offeror should only announce an offer after the most careful and responsible consideration and only when the offeror has every reason to believe that it can and will continue to be able to implement the offer: responsibility in this connection also rests on the financial adviser to the offeror[14].

Once an offer has been announced, the offer cannot be withdrawn without the consent of the Panel[15]. This is to prevent offerors making opportunistic bids based on particular market conditions and thus the Panel will not normally give consent to the withdrawal of a bid merely because market conditions have altered and the offer is now at an unrealistically high price. Equally, it is designed to prevent offerors attempting to manipulate the market with no intention of carrying through a bid.

Conduct during the offer

The importance of information to the shareholders in the offeree company and to the market is such that a number of General Principles are devoted to it. During the course of the bid, all information must be available to all the shareholders equally and it is impermissible to provide information to some shareholders only[16]. Shareholders must be given sufficient information and advice to enable them to reach a properly informed decision and must have sufficient time to do so. No relevant information should be withheld from them[17].

Any document or advertisement addressed to shareholders containing information or advice from an offeror or the board of the offeree company or their respective

---

10   However, an offer must not normally be subject to conditions which depend solely on subjective judgements by the directors of the offeror or the fulfilment of which is in their hands; City Code, r 13.
11   See City Code, r 2.1.
12   See Hannigan *Insider Dealing* (2nd edn, 1994), pp 180-191. Insider dealing is discussed in Chapter 27.
13   See City Code, r 1(a).
14   See City Code, GP 3; r 2.5(a). As to when an announcement is needed, see r 2.2. On the need to preserve an orderly market, see Morse [1992] JBL 428.
15   See City Code, r 2.7. To justify a decision not to proceed, circumstances of an exceptional and specific nature are required: see note 1 to r 2.7. Likewise, a person making a statement that he does not intend to make an offer for a company will normally be bound by the terms of that statement, see r 2.8.
16   See City Code, GP 2.
17   See City Code, GP 4, amplified by rr 20, 23-28. On disclosure, see Morse [1996] JBL 611.

advisers must, as is the case with a prospectus, be prepared with the highest standards of care and accuracy[18].

The board of the offeree company must obtain competent independent advice on any offer and the substance of such advice must be made known to its shareholders[19]. Directors of an offeror and the offeree company must always, in advising their shareholders, act only in their capacity as directors and not have regard to their personal or family shareholdings or to their personal relationships with the companies. It is the shareholders' interests taken as a whole, together with those of employees and creditors, which should be considered when the directors are giving advice to shareholders[20].

In a number of cases concerning takeover bids, the courts have had to consider the relationship between the directors and their shareholders in this context. Where a takeover bid has been made, the directors must give sufficient information to the shareholders and refrain from misleading them[1]. In the case of competing bids, the directors must do nothing to prevent the shareholders from choosing to take the best price[2] but the courts do not accept that the board must inevitably be under a positive duty to recommend and take all steps within its power to facilitate whichever is the highest offer[3].

Of course, in the conduct of a takeover, directors remain subject to their overriding duty to act in the best interests of the company and not for a collateral purpose, as discussed in Chapter 26. A particular issue in the takeover context is whether directors can agree with a bidder to recommend that bid and not to co-operate with any other bidder which might emerge. In *Dawson International plc v Coats Patons plc*[4], although the court was primarily concerned with procedural and evidential issues, the court accepted that any agreement between a target company and a bidder company which provided that the board of the target company would recommend the bid, and would not encourage or co-operate with any other bidder which might emerge, would be subject to an implied qualification derived from the law which defines directors' overriding duties to their company and their shareholders. The qualification was that, if circumstances altered materially, the board could decide in fulfilment of their continuing duty to the company and its shareholders not to implement the agreement. In *John Crowther Group plc v Carpets International plc*[5] the court likewise accepted that an agreement to recommend one particular bid had to be read in the light of the fact, known to all parties, that directors owe a fiduciary duty to act in the interests of the company. The bidders were not therefore entitled to damages when the board recommended that their bid should be set aside after a rival bidder made a more attractive offer.

This issue of the directors' duty was addressed more recently by the Court of Appeal in *Fulham Football Club Ltd v Cabra Estates plc*[6] (a non-takeover case) which drew

---

18 See City Code, GP 5, amplified by r 19. The detailed contents of any offer document are set out in r 24. In relation to takeovers and mergers where the consideration being offered consists of securities for which listing will be sought, listing particulars may be required, see Stock Exchange *The Listing Rules*, r 10.46 – 10.50. As to listing particulars and prospectuses, see Chapter 34.

19 See City Code, r 3.1.

20 See City Code, GP 9. See generally Paul 'Corporate Governance in the Context of Takeovers in the UK' in Prentice & Holland (eds), *Contemporary Issues in Corporate Governance* (1993).

1 *Re a Company* [1986] BCLC 382; *Gething v Kilner* [1972] 1 All ER 1166, [1972] 1 WLR 337; *Dawson International plc v Coats Paton plc* [1989] BCLC 233, 4 BCC 305, CS(OH).

2 *Heron International Ltd v Lord Grade* [1983] BCLC 244.

3 *Re a Company* [1986] BCLC 382.

4 [1990] BCLC 560, 5 BCC 405, CS. See also *Rackham v Peek Foods Ltd* [1990] BCLC 895.

5 [1990] BCLC 460, Ch D.

6 [1994] 1 BCLC 363. [1992] BCC 863, CA; noted Griffiths (1993) JBL 576.

a distinction between directors fettering their discretion (which is prohibited)[7] and directors exercising their discretion in a way which restricts their future conduct (which is permissible). It is clear that the directors' overriding duty is to act bona fide in the interests of the company but the time at which they exercise that judgement is a matter for them depending on the particular transaction involved[8]. Moreover, the Court of Appeal went on to note that in so far as cases such as *John Crowther Group plc v Carpets International plc*[9] could be read as laying down a general proposition that directors can never bind themselves as to the future exercise of their fiduciary powers, they would be wrong[10].

Directors may be tempted to engage in defensive measures designed to defeat the offeror and keep the existing management in office. The Code permits such action only with the consent of the shareholders in general meeting.

General Principle 7 provides that, at no time after a bona fide offer has been communicated to the board of the offeree company, or after the board of the offeree company has reason to believe that a bona fide offer might be imminent, may any action be taken by the board of the offeree company in relation to the affairs of the company, without the approval of the shareholders in general meeting, which could effectively result in any bona fide offer being frustrated or in the shareholders being denied an opportunity to decide on its merits.

This is amplified by r 21 which provides that during the course of an offer, or even before if the board of the offeree company has reason to believe a bona fide offer might be imminent, the board must not, without the approval of a general meeting:

(i)   take steps to increase the share capital[11];
(ii) sell, dispose of, or acquire assets of a material amount; or
(iii) enter into contracts otherwise than in the ordinary course of business.

A material amount for these purposes will normally be 10% or more of the assets but the amount could be less if the asset is of particular significance to the company[12]. Amendments to directors' service contracts are not regarded as being in the ordinary course of business where the new or amended contracts constitute an abnormal increase in the emoluments or a significant improvement in the terms of service[13]. These restrictions are imposed to prevent a target company making itself unattractive to the bidder by disposing of the assets which the bidder most wishes to acquire or by increasing significantly the costs involved in dispensing with the incumbent management should the bid be successful[14].

Finally, the Code draws attention to the responsibility of the board as a whole to monitor the conduct of a bid[15].

---

7   *Motherwell v Schoof* [1949] 4 DLR 812, (Alta SC); *Selangor United Rubber Estates Ltd v Cradock (a bankrupt) (No 3)* [1968] 2 All ER 1073, [1968] 1 WLR 1555.
8   See *Thorby v Goldberg* (1964) 112 CLR 597 at 605-606.
9   [1990] BCLC 460.
10 [1994] 1 BCLC 363 at 393, [1992] BCC 863 at 876.
11 For example, by issuing any unissued shares. Similar protection is achieved at common law under the 'proper purposes' doctrine. See *Howard Smith Ltd v Ampol Petroleum Ltd* [1974] AC 821, [1974] 1 All ER 1126, PC; *Hogg v Cramphorn Ltd* [1967] Ch 254, [1966] 3 All ER 420; discussed in Chapter 26.
12 See City Code, note 2 to r 21.
13 See City Code, note 6 to r 21.
14 In the United States, more exotic variations of frustrating devices are described as poison pills: see Herzel & Shepro *Bidders and Targets, Mergers and Acquisitions in the US* (1990) ch 8.
15 See City Code, Appendix 3.

Timetable of the offer

There are two guiding principles as far as the timetable is concerned: first, that the duration of a bid should be limited; secondly, that the shareholders should have time to consider the bid. The object is to avoid the process being so hurried that there is inadequate time for advice and information to be obtained and considered. At the same time the process must not be so drawn out that uncertainty is created in the market.

The timetable runs from the posting of the offer document, known as Day 1, which normally must be within 28 days of the announcement of the offer[16]. The board of the offeree company must give advice (the defence document) to their shareholders by the end of Day 14, ie within 14 days of the posting of the offer document[17]. To ensure shareholders in the offeree company have time to consider the offer and are not rushed into acceptance, an offer must remain open for at least 21 days so that Day 21 is the first possible closing date[18].

After Day 39 there must be no further material announcements by the offeree[19] and Day 46 is the last date for revision of the offer by the offeror[20]. Day 60 is the last possible closing date. No offer may be left open for more than 60 days without the consent of the Panel which may be granted, for example, if a competing offer is announced[1].

At the end of Day 60, the offeror announces whether it has received sufficient acceptances, remembering that it needs at least 50% of the shares to secure control and, if it is a voluntary bid, it may have stipulated that it requires 90% acceptances. If it has passed whichever threshold was set, the offer goes unconditional as to acceptances and must be left open for a further 14 days[2]. Consideration for the offer must be posted within 14 days of becoming unconditional[3].

Where an offer has not become unconditional by Day 60 and has therefore lapsed, the offeror may not make another offer for the offeree during the next 12 months nor acquire any shares which would oblige it to make a mandatory offer; nor acquire any shares if the offeror holds over 49% but less than 50% of the shares in the offeree[4]. This restriction can be of crucial importance to a company which has successfully resisted an unwelcome bid as it secures to it a breathing space before the bidder can return.

The Panel will normally grant a dispensation from this restriction where, for example, the new offer is recommended by the offeree board; or the previous offer lapsed on a reference to the Monopolies and Mergers Commission or the European Commission[5].

DRAFT 13TH DIRECTIVE ON TAKEOVERS

Having reviewed the manner in which a bid would be conducted under the Takeover Code, we turn now to examine a European initiative in this area.

---

16 See City Code, r 30.1.
17 See City Code, r 30.2.
18 See City Code, r 31.1.
19 See City Code, r 31.9.
20 See City Code, r 32.1.
1 See City Code, r 31.6.
2 See City Code, r 31.4.
3 See City Code, r 31.8.
4 See City Code, r 35.
5 See City Code, notes to rr 35.1, 35.2.

The original draft

The European Commission first put forward a draft directive on takeovers in 1989[6]. That early draft had been the subject of considerable criticism as it attempted to lay down very detailed regulation for the conduct of takeovers of listed public companies. It adopted many of the features of the Takeover Code as to the timetable for offers, the content of offer documents, the obligation on a bidder to bid for the remainder of the shares when he has acquired a certain percentage, the prohibition on certain types of defences and the independent supervision of the takeover process.

One of the most controversial elements was the requirement of a full mandatory bid, something which is not common to the Continental member states and which they opposed[7]. The UK expressed concern as to the impact which a Directive would have on the self-regulatory system and queried whether a Directive was called for at all, given that there are structural difficulties in many member states which effectively impede takeovers. The UK position was that the Commission should tackle the structural and cultural barriers to takeovers which are common on the Continent before attempting to legislate for takeovers across the Community[8].

A revised proposal

Despite the various grounds of opposition, the Commission pressed on with work in this area and, in February 1996, the Commission put forward a revised proposal for a directive on takeover bids[9]. The Commission's view is that it is a legitimate concern of the European Union that, within the internal market, shareholders of listed companies should enjoy equivalent safeguards in the case of a change of control and that a certain level of transparency prevail during takeovers[10]. Therefore the aims of the Directive are to ensure an adequate level of protection for shareholders throughout the European Union and to provide for minimum guidelines on the conduct of takeover bids[10].

Of course, there have been many changes at Community level since 1989, not least in the adoption of the principle of subsidiarity and, in keeping with those changes, this latest draft Directive is much less detailed and takes the form of a framework Directive which allows national differences to be maintained as long as they do not undermine the common principles and objectives that the Directive defines at Community level[11].

As noted, the Directive moves away from attempting to regulate every aspect of takeovers and instead sets out, in a manner reminiscent of the Takeover Code, a number of general principles as follows[12]:

---

6   See OJ C 64/8 14.3.1989; later version OJ C 240/7 6.9.1990, Com (90) 416 final.
7   See Wymeersch 'The Mandatory Bid: A Critical View' in Hopt & Wymeersch (eds) *European Takeovers – Law and Practice* (1992).
8   See DTI *Barriers to takeovers in the European Community, A Consultative Document* (January 1990) which identifies barriers such as the prevalence of bank finance, the lack of listed companies, the concentration of shareholdings in the hands of management and the widespread use of bearer shares. See Hopt 'European Takeover Regulation: Barriers to and problems of Harmonizing Takeover Laws in the European Communities' in Hopt & Wymeersch (eds) *European Takeovers – Law and Practice* (1992).
9   See Com(95) 655 final, 07.02.1996.
10 See Explanatory Memorandum to *Commission Proposal for a 13th European Parliament and Council Directive on Company Law Concerning Takeover Bids*, 07.02.1996, Com(96) 655 final, para 6; hereafter *Explanatory Memorandum*.
11 See *Explanatory Memorandum*, part II.
12 See art 5.

- all holders of securities of an offeree company who are in the same position are to be treated equally;
- target shareholders must have sufficient time and information to enable them to reach a properly informed decision on the bid;
- the board of an offeree company is to act in the interests of the company as a whole;
- false markets must not be created in the securities of the offeree company, of the offeror company, or of any other company concerned by the bid;
- offeree companies must not be hindered in the conduct of their affairs for longer than is reasonable by a bid for their securities.

Provision is also made for the making of appropriate announcements of the bid, for the proper and detailed disclosure of information during the bid and for the contents of the offer document. Limits are placed on the time during which the offer can be open (a minimum of four weeks and a maximum of 10 weeks), the importance of the avoidance of false markets is stressed, and limits are placed on the ability of the board of the offeree company to take frustrating action.

The Directive no longer requires a mandatory bid which, as we have seen, is a central feature of the Code and this is the biggest change from the original draft of the Directive. Instead the Directive now allows for mandatory bids or for member states to provide 'other appropriate and at least equivalent means' in order to the protect minority shareholders of the target company[13].

Article 4 of the Directive requires each member state to designate a supervisory authority to supervise takeovers, although the Commission states that this does not exclude the possibility of using a self-regulatory body so allowing the UK to retain the Takeover Panel in its current form[14].

In an attempt to limit the potential for nuisance litigation causing bids to lapse, art 4.5 states that the Directive does not affect the power which courts may have in a member state to decline to hear legal proceedings and to decide whether or not such proceedings affect the outcome of the bid provided that an injured party enjoys adequate remedies, whether through an appeals procedure operated by the supervisory authority or through the right to take proceedings before the courts to claim compensation[15].

Consultation and opposition

The Department of Trade and Industry consulted on the framework Directive in April 1996[16], stressing that any legislation in this area must enable the UK to safeguard the benefits of its non-statutory regime and must allow for speed of decision-making, flexibility to react to new situations and freedom from litigation[17]. Apart from concerns about the wording of individual articles of the Directive, particularly article 4.5 and

13 See art 3. Where a mandatory bid is provided for, it will be for each member state to indicate the level at which the bid must occur; it will also be possible to have partial mandatory bids.

14 See *Explanatory Memorandum*, para 11.

15 The wording of this requirement is unclear with an inconsistency between the wording of the article in the Directive which suggests that an appeal procedure and a right to compensation are alternatives while the *Explanatory Memorandum* suggests that compensation must be available: see HL, Select Committee on the European Communities, Session 1995-96, 13th Report, Takeover Bids (1996, HL Paper 100), pp 20-21.

16 See DTI *Consultative Document: Proposal for a Thirteenth Directive on Company Law Concerning Takeover Bids* (April 1996): hereafter *Consultative Document*. The text of the Directive is set out in an Appendix to this document.

17 See *Consultative Document*, supra, para 10.

the provision of legal redress[18], overall opposition to the Directive has focused on two inter-linked issues.

The first issue is the effect which the Directive would have on the current self-regulatory position occupied by the Code and the Panel, in terms of the need to put the Panel on a legal footing so as to meet the UK's obligation to implement the Directive properly[19]; and in terms of the impact that that legal footing would have on the decision-making and rule-making powers of the Panel.

The secondly issue is whether the implementation of the Directive and the consequential change in the Panel and the Code's status will open up the regulation of takeovers to greater legal challenge in the form of nuisance or tactical litigation causing a bid to lapse. This might take the form, for example, of parties challenging whether the Panel, in applying the Code, was implementing the Directive correctly.

The Law Society's Company Law Committee in response to the DTI's Consultative Document acknowledged and welcomed the considerable attempts of the European Commission in formulating the proposed Directive to accommodate many of the features of the UK system of takeover regulation[20]. But it concluded overall that there is no significant benefit which the proposal will bring to the UK system and there is a not insignificant risk that some of the proposals will be detrimental to the UK system. A minority view on the Committee supported the proposed Directive as a welcome step in the direction of the creation of an open and orderly market in the ownership of companies – seen in the context of the overall creation of a common market for goods and services. The minority nevertheless joined with the Committee in drawing attention to many of the deficiencies of the proposal, for example, with regard to the protection of minority shareholders (given the absence of a mandatory bid).

Overall, the Committee considered that it is inappropriate to seek to implement a common system of takeover regulation throughout the EU while the securities markets, the corporate culture, investor expectations and the relationship of shareholders and management remain so widely divergent.

The Takeover Panel, not surprisingly, remains resolutely opposed to any Directive in this area. The Panel is concerned that the proposed Directive would threaten the current voluntary regulation provided by the Panel; would increase the resort to litigation in take-over bids; and would result in increased delays which would in many cases end a bid. Furthermore, the Panel opposes the Directive as being in breach of the principle of subsidiarity which requires the Commission to act only if and so far as the objective or proposed action cannot be sufficiently achieved by the member states and can, therefore, by reason of the scale or effect of the proposed acts, be better achieved by the Commission[1]. The Panel has maintained a high profile campaign against the adoption of the Directive calling on the European Commission to drop the proposal or to withdraw it in favour of a voluntary code.

The House of Lords European Communities Select Committee also endorsed the general opposition[2] to the proposal, noting that the UK has an effective and efficient system for the regulation of takeovers which should not be put at risk without substantial and clearly identifiable benefits which had not been identified by the European

---

18   See *Consultative Document*, supra, paras 42-44.
19   See *Consultative Document*, supra, paras 17-18.
20   See Law Society Company Law Committee, Memorandum No 329, (June 1996) in response to the DTI *Consultative Document*.
1   See Takeover Panel Annual Reports 1996-97; 1995-96.
2   Note, however, the evidence of the Financial Law Panel to the Select Committee which concluded that the Directive is likely to have little practical effect on the conduct of takeovers in the UK, with the status of the Panel changing but not its functions, and the courts unlikely to alter their approach simply because of the implementation of the Directive. See Select Committee on the European Communities, Session 1995-96, 13th Report, Takeover Bids (1996, HL Paper 100), pp 106-112.

Commission in its proposal[3]. The Directive would bring about a fundamental change in the character of the Code and the Panel and putting both on a statutory footing within the context of the Directive would carry with it the risk of increased litigation.

Meanwhile, the European Commission published a further revision of the text of the Directive in November 1997 which takes on board the views of the European Parliament and the Economic and Social Committee[4]. The main change to the text is that rules on information for employees of the target company have been introduced. Employees would have to be kept informed once a bid was made public and the offer documents must be made available to them. Steps have been taken to limit the ability of directors to seek approval in advance of a bid for frustrating actions.

The Commission believes that it has taken into account the concerns of the self-regulatory systems, that the Directive does not provide any new means for litigation to delay takeover bids, and that there is no reason for believing that delays will arise from national courts referring matters of interpretation to the European Court of Justice save in exceptional circumstances.

OTHER METHODS OF EFFECTING A TAKEOVER

While the Companies Act 1985 makes little direct provision for takeovers, there are statutory procedures which can be used as mechanisms for effecting takeovers and mergers, the most important of which is a scheme of arrangement under Companies Act 1985 s 425.

Scheme of arrangement – CA 1985, s 425

The width of s 425 is such that it can be used for reconstructions within a company but also for straightforward takeover bids, provided that the bidder has the consent of the board of the target company because their co-operation will be needed in calling the various meetings required under the section. A typical scheme of arrangement effecting a transfer of control would involve the existing shareholders in the target company transferring their shares to the offeror in consideration of a cash payment or of an issue of shares in the offeror.

Section 425 provides that where a compromise or arrangement is proposed between a company and its members, or any class of members,[5] an application may be made to the court by the company, or any member, to ask the court to convene meetings of the members or, if there is more than one class, meetings of each class of members[6].

---

3 See Select Committee on the European Communities, Session 1995-96, 13th Report, Takeover Bids (1996, HL Paper 100). This extensive report is an invaluable account of the issues raised by the proposed Directive.
4 See Amended proposal for a 13th European Parliament and Council Directive on company law concerning takeover bids, COM(97) 565 final, OJ C 378, 13.12.97.
5 The provision can also apply to any compromise or arrangement between a company and its creditors, or any class of creditors, and applications can be made by an administrator if an administration order has been made, or by a liquidator if the company is in winding up: CA 1985, 425(1). In practice for creditors, schemes are more likely to be promoted as company voluntary arrangements under the IA 1986, Pt I, discussed in Chapter 40.
6 CA 1985, s 425(1). 'Arrangement' is to be interpreted widely: see *Re Savoy Hotel Ltd* [1981] Ch 351, [1981] 3 All ER 646; also *Re National Farmer's Union Development Trust* [1973] 1 All ER 135, [1972] 1 WLR 1548 (the scheme must involve some element of give and take, some element of accommodation on each side). See also CA 1985, s 425(6)(b) as to what is included in 'arrangement'. The scheme must be between the company (either through its board or by a majority of the members in general meeting) and the members: *Re Savoy Hotel Ltd, supra.*

The notice calling the meeting must be accompanied by a circular explaining the scheme[7], disclosing any material interests of the directors and whether the arrangement affects them differently from others with a similar interest[8]. If there is any alteration in the directors' interests after the notice is sent, a further communication is required, otherwise the court may not approve the scheme[9].

Each class affected by the scheme must approve the scheme; and this requires the approval of a majority in number representing 75% in value of those present and voting either in person or by proxy[10]. The responsibility for deciding the appropriate classes rests on the company and, if the meetings are not correctly convened, the court will not approve the scheme, at least in cases where it can be shown the scheme would not have received the necessary majority had the meetings been properly constituted[11].

The definition of a class for these purposes is 'those persons whose rights are not so dissimilar as to make it impossible for them to consult together with a view to their common interest'[12]. In *Re Hellenic & General Trust Ltd*[13] Templeman J held that a shareholder, which was a wholly owned subsidiary of the offeror company, holding 53% of the votes formed a separate class from the rest of the ordinary shareholders for the purpose of an ordinary shareholders' meeting summoned to approve a scheme.

Once the meetings have been held, a further application is made to the court for the court to sanction the scheme. The court will consider whether the statutory scheme has been adhered to, whether the meetings have been properly held and, applying the test of Maugham J in *Re Dorman, Long & Co Ltd, South Durham Steel and Iron Co Ltd*, 'whether the proposal is such that an intelligent and honest man, a member of the class concerned and acting in respect of his interest, might reasonably approve'[14].

Once sanctioned, the scheme becomes binding on all the members or class of members, as the case may be[15]; and it becomes effective upon a copy of the court order being delivered to the Registrar of Companies for registration[16].

It is this capacity to bind dissenting or apathetic members which makes s 425 such a formidable section. The protection for dissenters lies in the majority both in number and value that is required and in the need for the court's approval. In practice, the courts are reluctant to interfere if a proper majority has approved the scheme[17], preferring to

---

7   The extent of the information required will depend on the facts of the particular case: see *Re Heron International NV* [1994] 1 BCLC 667.
8   CA 1985, s 426(1), (2). See also s 426(7).
9   *Re Jessel Trust Ltd* [1985] BCLC 119; *Re Minster Assets plc* [1985] BCLC 200, 1 BCC 99,299 – the role of the court is to be satisfied that no reasonable shareholder would have changed his decision as to how to act on the scheme if the information had been disclosed. See also *Re Heron International NV* [1994] 1 BCLC 667.
10   CA 1985, s 425(2).
11   *Re United Provident Assurance Co Ltd* [1910] 2 Ch 477 (partly-paid shares and fully-paid shares are different classes for these purposes requiring separate meetings); *Re Hellenic & General Trust Ltd* [1975] 3 All ER 382, [1976] 1 WLR 123.
12   *Sovereign Life Assurance Co v Dodd* [1892] 2 QB 573 at 583, CA, per Bowen LJ (holders of matured insurance policies were a different class from holders of unmatured policies). Community of interests is a question of degree: see *Re Heron International NV* [1994] 1 BCLC 667.
13   [1975] 3 All ER 382, [1976] 1 WLR 123.
14   [1934] Ch 635 at 657. See also *Re Alabama, New Orleans, Texas and Pacific Junction Rly Co* [1891] 1 Ch 213, CA.
15   CA 1985, s 425(2). Any agreement entered into pursuant to the court's order is binding even though it is otherwise ultra vires and void: *British and Commonwealth Holdings plc v Barclays Bank plc* [1996] 1 All ER 381, [1996] 1 WLR 1, CA. While a scheme requires the approval of the court, it does not as a consequence become an order of the court and therefore the court has no jurisdiction to make a material alteration to the scheme: *Kemp v Ambassador Insurance Co* [1998] 1 BCLC 234, PC.
16   CA 1985, s 425(3).
17   See *Re Heron International NV* [1994] 1 BCLC 667.

reject inappropriate schemes on the grounds that they fall outside the scope of the section or on the grounds of procedural irregularity[18].

When the scheme being sanctioned is for the purpose of, or in connection with, a reconstruction or amalgamation and the transfer of the whole or part of one or more companies' businesses to another company, then the court has extensive powers under s 427 to make such ancillary orders as are necessary. Under s 427, the court can by order transfer not only the whole or any part of a company's undertaking or property but also its liabilities[19]. Creditors could, of course, agree to be transferred and, if appropriate meetings of creditors were held, a majority in number representing 75% in value could bind them all. But in cases where the company is solvent and there is no risk to creditors, the courts will not require meetings of creditors to be held but will transfer the liabilities by court order. It has been held that property rights which are not assignable by law cannot be transferred[20] nor can functions which are personal to the company concerned[1]. But the former rule, that contracts of employment could not be transferred[2] is now reversed for they are automatically transferred when the undertaking or part thereof is transferred whether the transfer is effected by sale or by some other disposition or by operation of law[3].

Mergers and divisions of public companies   Note that certain compromises or arrangements involving the merger or division of public companies as specified in Companies Act 1985, s 427A are subject to further requirements set out in Sch 15B (such as the approval of the scheme by each class of members of the transferee company involved, as well as by those in the transferor company) before the court can sanction the scheme[4].

Reconstruction in the course of voluntary liquidation – IA 1986, s 110

Another provision to note is Insolvency Act 1986, s 110, whereby a company in voluntary liquidation may by special resolution (where it is a members' voluntary winding up)[5] authorise the liquidator to sell the whole or part of its business or property to another company in return for shares in that other company which are then distributed among the members of the company in liquidation[6]. The provisions are in the

---

18   See *Re Hellenic & General Trust Ltd* [1975] 3 All ER 382, [1976] 1 WLR 123 where, unusually, Templeman J refused to sanction a scheme which, while objectively fair, was being used to secure the compulsory acquisition of some minority shareholders when the company was not in a position to use the statutory powers, discussed below, which allow for such compulsory purchases in certain limited circumstances.
19   CA 1985, s 427(3)(a).
20   *Re L Hotel Co Ltd and Langham Hotel Co Ltd* [1946] 1 All ER 319.
1   See *Re Skinner* [1958] 3 All ER 273, [1958] 1 WLR 1043.
2   *Nokes v Doncaster Amalgamated Collieries Ltd* [1940] AC 1014, [1940] 3 All ER 549, HL.
3   Transfer of Undertakings (Protection of Employment) Regulations 1981, SI 1981 No 1794.
4   CA 1985, s 427A(1) inserted by the Companies (Mergers and Divisions) Regulations 1987, SI 1987 No 1991, implementing the Third Company Law Directive (EEC 78/855, OJ 1978 L 295) and the Sixth Company Law Directive (EEC 82/891, OJ 1982 L 378). The draft terms of the merger or division must be delivered to the registrar of companies, a notice confirming this must be placed in the Gazette, a directors' report and an expert's report are required and various documents must be available for inspection prior to the meetings.
5   In a creditors' voluntary winding up, the consent of either the court or the liquidation committee is required in addition to the special resolution of the company: IA 1986, s 110(3)(b). See Sealy, Milman *Annotated Guide to the Insolvency Legislation* (4th edn, 1994) on the ambiguous drafting of IA 1986, s 110(3).
6   Ibid, s 110 (1), (2), (3)(a).

Insolvency Act because the procedure involves the company going into voluntary liquidation. Of course, the company may well not be insolvent.

In its simplest form, where one company transfers its business to a new company, this is called reconstruction. Historically, this was usually done either because the new company had wider or different objects than the old company, or to change the rights of different classes of shareholders by giving them shares with altered rights in a new company. But this provision can be used to put one company into liquidation and transferring its business to the other in return for shares in that other, or by putting both companies into liquidation and transferring both their businesses to a third company, which issues shares to the two liquidators for distribution to the shareholders in the two companies now in liquidation.

The sale or arrangement is binding on all the members of the company[7] subject to the right of any members who did not vote for the resolution, to give notice in writing to the liquidator, within seven days after the passing of the resolution, requiring the liquidator either to abstain from carrying out the resolution or to purchase their interest at a price to be determined by agreement or arbitration[8]. Effectively, therefore, the dissenters have to be paid off under this scheme. This does not, however, mean that shareholders who neither assent nor give formal notice of dissent are bound to take the shares in the transferor company. They may instead forfeit their interest in the company altogether[9] or the scheme may provide for the shares of such shareholders to be sold and the proceeds paid to them[10].

The consideration received by the liquidator must be distributed among the shareholders entitled to it strictly in accordance with their respective rights as shareholders[11]. In other words, although their rights as shareholders in the new company may be very different from their rights in the old company, the shares in the new company must somehow be distributed in a way that exactly reflects the rights of shareholders in the old company.

The sale or arrangement agreed to by the special resolution is also binding on the creditors of the old company[12]. They are not transferred with the business to the new company but remain creditors of the old company. So they must look to the liquidator of the old company to retain sufficient assets or to realise sufficient of the consideration received from the transferee company to be able to pay them[13]. If they doubt whether the liquidator will be able to pay them, their remedy is to petition for the compulsory liquidation of the company. If an order for winding up is made within a year of the special resolution being passed, the resolution is not valid unless sanctioned by the court[14]. Liquidators will therefore usually make adequate provision for creditors since they will not want to run the risk of the whole transaction being invalidated, as would be the case if the special resolution were invalidated.

It will be apparent that any transaction that could come within the IA 1986, s 110 could in principle come within CA 1985, s 425, as well. The courts have, however, held that the special protection afforded to dissenting shareholders, of compelling the liquidator to buy them out or drop the transaction, must be made available to dissenting

7   Ibid, s 110(5).
8   Ibid, s 111(1), (2). A shareholder may also be able to halt the transaction by obtaining a winding-up order: s 110(6); see *Re Consolidated South Rand Mines Deep Ltd* [1909] 1 Ch 491 (where scheme is eminently unfair).
9   *Re Bank of Hindustan, China and Japan Ltd, Higgs's Case* (1865) 2 Hem & M 657; *Burdett-Coutts v True Blue (Hannan's) Gold Mine* [1899] 2 Ch 616, CA.
10 *Fuller v White Feather Reward Ltd* [1906] 1 Ch 823.
11 *Griffith v Paget* (1877) 6 Ch D 511.
12 *Re City and County Investment Co* (1879) 13 Ch D 475, CA.
13 *Pulsford v Devenish* [1903] 2 Ch 625.
14 IA 1986, s 110(6).

shareholders if a similar scheme is effected under s 425[15]. Where, however, the company is transferring only part of its undertaking or assets and is continuing in existence with the remaining assets rather than going into liquidation, so that the Insolvency Act 1986, s 110 would not apply, there is no necessity for dissenting shareholders to be given a cash option[16].

Compulsory acquisition of minority shareholdings – CA 1985, ss 428-430F

Where a company makes an offer for the shares in another company, it may be content just to acquire sufficient shares to give it control of the offeree company. But in many circumstances it will want to acquire 100% of the shares in the offeree company.

This would be the case, for example, if the offeror intended to invest large sums of fresh capital in the offeree company but could not expect other shareholders to invest a proportionate amount. The profitability of the company would be expected to increase to the advantage of all the shareholders including the minority who had not invested any of the extra capital. In such circumstances, it might be felt to be fair that before investing the extra capital the majority should have the opportunity to buy out the minority at a fair price[17].

Another example is that of a holding company which may legitimately wish to operate its subsidiaries in the interest of the enterprise or group as a whole. It will be able to do so more easily if the subsidiaries are wholly owned, so that the interests of minority shareholders do not need to be considered. So although the notion of compulsory acquisition has overtones of squeeze out and oppression, making a company a wholly-owned subsidiary can be a perfectly legitimate objective and, provided a fair price is paid for the shares acquired, it should be unobjectionable.

In 1929, a specific statutory power was introduced whereby an offeror, whose offer has been accepted by holders of 90% or more of the shares to which the offer relates, can compulsorily acquire the remaining shares, unless the court upholds an objection by a dissenting shareholder. The provisions, now contained in Companies Act 1985 ss 428 – 430F, facilitate takeovers by allowing for the compulsory acquisition of minority shareholders subject to certain conditions being met.

The scheme operates as follows: one company (the offeror) makes a takeover offer for all the shares, or for the whole of any class of shares, of another company. To qualify as a takeover offer, an offer must meet two important conditions. First, the offer[18] must be to acquire all the shares, or all of a particular class of shares in a company (other than those already held at the date of the offer by the offeror or its associates[19]); secondly, the offer must be on the same terms for all the shares of the same class[20].

Where the offer is accepted within four months by holders of 90% in value of the shares to which the offer relates, the offeror may within two months serve notice to acquire the remaining shares[1]. The recipient of the notice then has six weeks in which

15 *Re Anglo-Continental Supply Co Ltd* [1922] 2 Ch 723.
16 *Watt v London and Northern Assets Corpn* [1898] 2 Ch 469, CA.
17 See *Brown v British Abrasive Wheel Co* [1919] 1 Ch 290.
18 The bidder must make an offer, and not merely an invitation to treat: see *Re Chez Nico (Restaurants) Ltd* [1992] BCLC 192, [1991] BCC 736.
19 The important definition of 'associate' is contained in CA 1985, s 430E. Shares held by the offeror or associates are excluded altogether so that they count neither for nor against the 90% acceptance level.
20 Ibid, s 428(1). Where more than one class of shares is involved separate offers must be made for each class. The 90% acceptance level is thus calculated separately for each class.
1   Ibid, s 429(1)-(3).The notice given must also be sent to the company accompanied by a statutory declaration by the offeror stating that he has acquired 90% acceptances: s 429(4). See *Re Chez Nico (Restaurants) Ltd* [1992] BCLC 192, [1991] BCC 736 (lateness in complying with requirement re statutory declaration will not nullify the whole procedure).

to apply to the court which may allow or disallow the acquisition or specify terms different from those in the offer[2]. If no application is made to the court then the offeror is entitled and bound to acquire the shares on the terms of the offer[3].

After six weeks from the date of the notice of intention to acquire the shares, the offeror sends a copy of the notice to the target company and pays to it the consideration for the shares to which the notice relates (ie the non-acceptors shares) with the consideration being kept on trust for payment out to the non-acceptors by the target company[4].

Previously many problems arose in establishing the 90% acceptance level. These are now dealt with by the legislation. The first is where the offeror continues to buy shares in the offeree company during the period of the offer. The difficulty here is that shareholders who sell during the bid are people who might otherwise have accepted the offer, thus making it harder to obtain a 90% acceptance of the actual offer as a result. This problem is resolved by providing that shares acquired during the offer by the offeror or its associates can be counted as acceptances of the offer provided that the consideration does not exceed the offer price or, if it does, that the offer price is correspondingly increased[5].

The second problem was that a revised offer would sometimes constitute a fresh offer, so that acceptances of the original offer could not count as acceptances of the fresh offer, again making it more difficult to achieve the 90% acceptance level. This in turn is dealt with by providing that a revised offer is not a fresh offer as long as the original offer allowed for revision and for acceptance of previous terms to be treated as acceptance of revised terms[6]. The third problem was that of the untraceable shareholder which is now dealt with by allowing the court to deem shareholders to be acceptors of the offer if certain conditions are met[7].

DISSENTING SHAREHOLDERS

If dissenting shareholders wish to object to the compulsory acquisition, and given that 90% of the shareholders think the scheme is proper, the onus is on the dissenters to convince the court that compulsory acquisition would be unfair[8]. The test is whether the offer is fair to the shareholders as a body without reference to the particular circumstances of the applicant to the court, so it will not be relevant that the dissenting shareholders will be forced to sell at a loss[9]. It is not enough to show that the scheme was open to criticism or capable of improvement[10].

Although normally the onus of proof is on the dissenting shareholders to show that the offer is unfair, in *Re Bugle Press Ltd*[11] the 90% acceptances in the offeree company

---

2   CA 1985, s 430C(1)
3   Ibid, s 430(1), (2).
4   Ibid, s 430(5), (9).
5   Ibid, ss 429(8), 430E(2).
6   Ibid, s 428(7). See *Re Chez Nico (Restaurants) Ltd* [1992] BCLC 192, [1991] BCC 736 on this point.
7   CA 1985, s 430C(5).
8   *Re Grierson, Oldham and Adams Ltd* [1968] Ch 17, [1967] 1 All ER 192; *Re Sussex Brick Co Ltd* [1961] Ch 289n, [1960] 1 All ER 772n; *Re Press Caps Ltd* [1949] Ch 434, [1949] 1 All ER 1013; *Re Hoare & Co Ltd* (1933) 150 LT 374; *Re Lifecare International plc* [1990] BCLC 222.
9   *Re Grierson, Oldham and Adams Ltd* [1968] Ch 17, [1967] 1 All ER 192; where the shares are quoted on The Stock Exchange and the offer price is above the market price, that raises a presumption that the price is fair. See also *Re Press Caps Ltd* [1949] Ch 434, [1949] 1 All ER 1013.
10   *Re Grierson, Oldham and Adams Ltd* [1968] Ch 17, [1967] 1 All ER 192; *Re Sussex Brick Co Ltd* [1961] Ch 289n, [1960] 1 All ER 772n.
11   [1961] Ch 270, [1960] 3 All ER 791, CA.

came from two persons who owned all the shares in the offeror company and it was held that the onus of proof was on them to show positively that the offer was fair rather than on the dissenter to show the offer was unfair. Since they had produced no evidence at all the court refused to allow the compulsory acquisition of the dissenter. This shift in the onus of proof where the bidder is an insider in the offeree company was endorsed in *Re Chez Nico (Restaurants) Ltd*[12]. In that case, had it been necessary[13], the court would have found in favour of a dissenting shareholder where the offerors, insiders in the company, had not made disclosures to the shareholders as required by the Takeover Code. The court noted that substantial infringements of the provisions of the code as to disclosure provided strong evidence that the offer was not fairly made and negatived any presumption that an offer is fair because 90% of the shareholders have accepted it.

RELATIONSHIP WITH SECTION 425

We have seen that s 425 covers any form of arrangement including a straightforward takeover bid for the shares in the offeree company. Provided a majority in number representing 75% in value of the shares voting in person or by proxy accept the arrangement and it is sanctioned by the court, it is binding on abstainers or dissenters. In *Re National Bank Ltd*[14] the question arose as to whether, if a s 425 scheme or arrangement involves the compulsory elimination of minority shareholders, the court should impose a 90% acceptance level as a condition for approving the scheme. Plowman J rejected the argument stating that:

> . . . the two sections, s [425] and [ss 428-430F] involve quite different considerations and different approaches. Under s [425] an arrangement can only be sanctioned if the question of its fairness has first been submitted to the court. Under [ss 428-430F], on the other hand, the matter may never come to the court at all. If it does come to the court, then the onus is cast on the dissenting minority to demonstrate the unfairness of the scheme. There are, therefore, good reasons for requiring a smaller majority in favour of a scheme under s [425] than the majority which is required under [ss 428-430F] if the minority is to be expropriated.[15]

The same conclusion was reached in *Singer Manufacturing Co v Robinow*[16] in which the offeror company, which already owned 92% of the shares in the offeree company, used s 425, with its lower acceptance level requirement, to compulsorily acquire the remaining 8% of shares, rather than comply with the conditions in ss 428-430F.

However, in *Re Hellenic and General Trust Ltd*[17], Templeman J had to consider whether to sanction a scheme under s 425 which was being used to achieve the compulsory acquisition of a shareholder which could not be achieved under ss 428-430F as the dissenting shareholder owned more than 10% of the shares and therefore no 90% acceptance level could ever have been achieved. He held that in such

---

12   [1992] BCLC 192, [1991] BCC 736. See Morse [1992] JBL 316.
13   On the facts, the bidders, not having made a 'takeover offer' as required by the statutory provisions (discussed above), were not entitled to use the compulsory purchase mechanism in any case.
14   [1966] 1 All ER 1006, [1966] 1 WLR 819.
15   [1966] 1 All ER 1006 at 1013, [1966] 1 WLR 819 at 829-830.
16   1971 SC 11.
17   [1975] 3 All ER 382, [1976] 1 WLR 123.

circumstances 'there must be a very high standard of proof on the part of the petitioner to justify obtaining by s [425] what could not be obtained by [ss 428-430F]'[18].

RIGHT OF MINORITY TO BE BOUGHT OUT

Those shareholders who do not accept the takeover bid may well have rejected it because they thought some other plan for the company's future preferable. When it turns out the takeover bid has been overwhelmingly successful, they may not wish to remain as minority shareholders in a company which has new controlling shareholders.

Provision is therefore made to allow them a period of time in which to insist on being bought out by the offeror at the price paid to the other shareholders or such other terms as may be agreed or the court may fix. The provisions operate where a takeover offer relates to all, or all of any class, of the shares in a company. If, before the offer expires, the offeror and its associates own at least 90% in value of all the shares or of the shares in the class concerned, then any shareholder who has not accepted the offer may require the offeror to acquire his shares[19]. Within one month of the above conditions being satisfied, the offeror must give non-acceptors notice of their right to sell, specifying a closing date not less than three months after the expiry of the offer[20].

OTHER STATUTORY PROVISIONS APPLICABLE TO TAKEOVERS

While, as we have seen, the Companies Act 1985 does not provide for the manner and conduct of the takeover bid, leaving it to the law of contract, there are nevertheless a number of statutory provisions which will be relevant to the conduct of the bid.

Financial assistance for the purchase of their own shares

In the takeover context, improper financial assistance can be a significant element in a share support scheme which involves the generation of share purchases to boost the offeror company's share price. The price of the offeror's shares can be crucial if the consideration being offered to the offeree company's shareholders includes shares in the offeror. A share support scheme on a massive scale was at the heart of the Guinness takeover of Distillers, as noted above[1]. In addition to breaches of the Takeover Code, the funding of such purchases, directly or indirectly, by the company may well be a breach of CA 1985, ss 151-158 (financial assistance), discussed in detail in Chapter 16.

Market manipulation

A share support scheme may also amount to market manipulation under Financial Services Act 1986, s 47(2) which prohibits the doing of any act or engaging in any course of conduct which creates a false or misleading impression as to the market in

---

18   [1975] 3 All ER 382 at 388, [1976] 1 WLR 123 at 129.
19   CA 1985, s 430A(1), (2).
20   Ibid, s 430A(3), (4).
1   See DTI *Guinness plc, Investigation under ss 432(2) and 442 of the Companies Act 1985* (1997, HMSO).

or the price or value of any investments. This is an offence if it is done for the purpose of creating that impression and of thereby inducing another person to acquire, or dispose of, those investments.

Control of investment advertisements

Section 57 of the Financial Services Act 1986 restricts the issue of investment advertisements unless they are issued by, or with the contents being approved by, an authorised person and the definition of investment advertisement is wide enough to cover takeover offer documents[2].

Insider dealing

Takeovers present the ideal occasion for insider dealing as information before and during a bid is highly price-sensitive inside information. Individuals who have inside information from an inside source are subject to prohibitions on dealing in price-affected securities, encouraging another person to deal, and communicating the inside information to another person, all of which are offences in the circumstances set out in Part V of the Criminal Justice Act 1993[3].

Disclosure of interests in shares

It is accepted that shareholders and the public generally are entitled to know promptly of the acquisition of significant shareholdings in public companies[4]. The aim of the acquirer may be to influence policy or mount a takeover bid and members of the company and those dealing with it are entitled to protect their interests; nor should the conduct of the company be prejudiced by uncertainty as to who controls it. There may also be dangers in companies passing secretly into foreign ownership. Various provisions are included in the Companies Act 1985 which are aimed at requiring disclosure and lessening the opportunities for the rapid acquisition of a large number of shares in a listed company.

Part VI of the CA 1985 (ss 198-220) includes very complex provisions governing the disclosure of interests in shares in public companies[5]. Following a consultation exercise in 1995, the Department of Trade and Industry noted that there is support for restricting the scope of these provisions in future to companies whose shares are publicly traded, as opposed to all public companies, and to make further amendments so as to reduce the amount of disclosure required[6]. The Department's intention is in due course to seek power to replace Part VI with Regulations[7].

2   However, it may be possible to come within one of the many exemptions to FSA 1986, s 57, see s 58; also Financial Services Act 1986 (Investment Advertisements) (Exemption) (No 2) Order 1995, SI 1995/1536, art 4 (take-overs of private companies) and art 5 (sale of body corporate).
3   See discussion of insider dealing in Chapter 27.
4   See DTI Consultative Document *Disclosure of Interest in Shares* (1988).
5   These provisions were amended by the Disclosure of Interest in Shares (Amendment) Regulations 1993, SI 1993/1819 which implemented EC Council Directive (88/627/EEC) on the information to be disclosed when a major holding in a listed company is acquired or disposed of: OJ L 348/62, 17.12.88. See also Disclosure of Interest in Shares (Amendment) Regulations 1996, SI 1996/1560.
6   See DTI, Consultation Document, *Proposals for Reform of Part VI of the Companies Act 1985* (1995); DTI *Companies in 1995-96*, p 2.
7   See DTI *Companies in 1996-97*, p 2.

The basic obligation is that as soon as persons know they have a material interest[8] in 3% of any class of voting shares of a public company, they must inform the company within two days and thereafter they must inform the company of any acquisition or disposal which takes their holding through a whole per cent or below 3%[9]. Where a person does not have an interest as above, but has interests in shares equal to or more than 10% of the share capital (whether or not including material interests), then there is also an obligation to disclose in the same way[10]. The company must enter the information disclosed in a register kept for the purpose which must be open to public inspection[11].

There are complex provisions dealing with what constitutes an interest in shares for the purpose of this disclosure requirement[12]. It extends to any form of beneficial interest in shares[13] and includes the situation where a person has the right to acquire or control shares[14]. Persons are also taken to be interested in any shares in which their spouse or any infant child or stepchild is interested, and also in any shares in which a body corporate is interested if the body corporate or its directors usually act under their directions or they can control more than one-third of the voting power at general meetings of the body corporate[15].

In addition, where two or more persons act together in the acquisition of interests in shares in a particular company they may constitute a group acting in concert (commonly referred to as 'a concert party'). In such a case any acquisition or disposal of an interest in shares by any member of the concert party is treated as an acquisition or disposal by every member of the concert party[16]. Members of concert parties are accordingly obliged to keep each other informed of relevant acquisitions and disposals[17].

To assist in discovering the ownership of shares, the Department of Trade and Industry has power to investigate the ownership of companies via the appointment of inspectors (s 442) or requests for information (s 444) and to impose restrictions on the shares under Part XV, CA 1985, if information is not forthcoming[18]. These powers were discussed in Chapter 30.

Public companies also have statutory power to require shareholders to state whether they own shares beneficially and, if not, to identify on whose behalf they are held[19]. A company may be required to exercise this power on the requisition of shareholders holding 10% of the voting paid-up capital[20]. Again, the company must keep a register of information received which must be open to public inspection[1]. Since 1981

---

8   Defined CA 1985, s 199(2A).
9   Ibid, ss 199(2)(a), (5), 202(4). The Listing Rules require a listed company in turn to notify the Stock Exchange: see The Listing Rules, rr 9.11-9.14. During the offer period, the City Code requires anyone owning or controlling 1% or more of a company involved in a takeover to disclose any dealings in shares of the companies involved to the Stock Exchange (which notifies the Takeover Panel) not later than 12 noon on the business day following the transaction: City Code, r 8.3.
10   CA 1985, s 199(2)(b).
11   Ibid, s 211.
12   See ibid, ss 203-209.
13   Ibid, s 208(2), (3).
14   Ibid, s 208(4)-(6).
15   Ibid, s 203(1), (2).
16   Ibid, ss 204, 205.
17   Ibid, s 206.
18   Ibid, s 445(1). Restrictions would affect, for example, the right to receive dividends, to vote and to sell the shares.
19   Ibid, s 212. The company may have to notify the Stock Exchange of any information which it receives in this way where the information has not previously been disclosed in accordance with ss 198-220, see The Listing Rules, r 9.12.
20   CA 1985, s 214.
1   Ibid, s 213.

companies have had the power to apply to the court to impose the same range of restrictions on shares as may be imposed by the Department of Trade and Industry, noted above[2]. Companies may, of course, incorporate power to impose such restrictions in their articles of association and the statutory right to apply to the court to impose restrictions is in addition to the company's constitutional powers[3]. Failure to supply information properly requested by the company is also a criminal offence[4].

RULES GOVERNING SUBSTANTIAL ACQUISITIONS OF SHARES

In addition to the provisions in the Companies Act, the Takeover Code contains Rules Governing Substantial Acquisitions of Shares (SARs) administered by the Takeover Panel which seeks to regulate the building of stakes in a company by restricting the speed with which a person may increase his holding and requiring accelerated disclosure of acquisitions. The SARs do not apply to a person who has announced a firm intention to make an offer for the company.

A person may not within any period of seven days acquire 10% or more of the voting rights in a listed company[5] if such acquisition would give the buyer more than 15% but less than 30% of the voting rights in the company[6]. An acquisition which would take a person over 15% of the voting rights, or where he is already over 15% but the acquisition increases his holding by one or more percentage points, must be disclosed to the company and the Stock Exchange (which notifies the Panel) by 12 noon on the day following the day of acquisition[7].

Provisions affecting directors

Because of the directors' powerful position in being able to advise shareholders whether to accept or reject an offer, there are statutory obligations on directors, set out in CA 1985, ss 312-316, to disclose certain payments for loss of office so that shareholders are aware of factors that might influence the directors' attitude.

Section 313 provides that if, in connection with the transfer of the whole or any part of the undertaking or property of a company, any payment is made to directors of the company by way of compensation for loss of office, or in connection with retirement from office, it must be disclosed to and approved by the shareholders in general meeting[8]. If this is not done, then any amount received is held on trust for the company[9].

Section 314 applies to payments relating to compensation for loss of office[10], or in connection with the retirement of directors from office, on the transfer to anyone of

2   Ibid, s 216(1).
3   Ibid, s 216(2). See the Listing Rules which impose limitations on such powers: The Listing Rules, Appendix 1 to ch 13, para 13.
4   CA 1985, s 216(3).
5   Whether listed on the Stock Exchange or the Alternative Investment Market: see Introduction to the Rules governing Substantial Acquisitions of Shares.
6   SAR, r 1. This is subject to certain exceptions which are set out in SAR, r 2.
7   SAR, r 3.
8   CA 1985, s 313(1).
9   Ibid, s 313(2).
10 Excluded from the definition are bona fide payments by way of damages for breach of contract or by way of pension: ibid, s 316(3). See also *Taupo Totara Timber Co Ltd v Rowe* [1978] AC 537, [1977] 3 All ER 123, PC. It is expressly provided that if, in connection with the retirement from office of directors, they receive a price for selling their shares in the company in excess of what could have been obtained by other holders of like shares or receive any gift, the excess or the money value of the gift is deemed to be a payment as compensation for loss of office: CA 1985, s 316(2).

all or any of the shares in the company, being a transfer resulting from certain types of offer[11]. The section provides that the directors concerned must take all reasonable steps to ensure that details of any such payment is included with the notice of the offer for their shares given to the shareholders and are liable to criminal penalties for failing to do so[12].

In addition, the payment must be approved, in advance of any transfer of any shares, by a meeting of the class of shareholders to which the offer relates[13]. If the payment is either not properly disclosed, or not approved, then any sum received is held in 'trust for persons who have sold their shares as a result of the offer made'[14].

Although they are not by their terms restricted to such payments, the crucial aspect of ss 313 and 314 is that they cover payments made by the offeror. Payments to directors as compensation for loss of office made by their own company may fall within ss 313 or 314 but will be required to be disclosed to and approved by the shareholders in general meeting in any case under s 312 which is not restricted to payments connected with the sale of assets or shares.

COMPETITION POLICY AND REGULATION

In addition to complying with the requirements of the Takeover Code and such elements of the statutory provisions as may affect the conduct of a particular takeover, the parties may also find themselves the subject of investigation by the competition authorities, either domestically or at the European level. A detailed analysis of the competition issues which may arise in a takeover situation is beyond the scope of this work and readers are referred to specialist works on that topic[15]. What follows below is a brief outline of the structure of the regulatory authorities and the processes to which a bidder may be subject.

An overview of the regulatory structure

The key legislation relating to the control of mergers is contained in the Fair Trading Act 1973, Pt V[16] which provides that a reference may be made by the Secretary of State for Trade and Industry to the Monopolies and Mergers Commission where two or more enterprises[17] cease to be distinct enterprises[18]; and either:

   (i)   as a result of the merger, at least 25% of goods or services of any description in the UK or in a substantial part of the UK are either (a) supplied by or to the same person or (b) supplied by the persons by whom the relevant enterprises are carried on, or are supplied to those persons (the market share test); or

  (ii) the value of the assets taken over exceeds £70m[19] (the assets test)[20].

---

11   Defined ibid, s 314(1).
12   Ibid, s 314(3).
13   Ibid, s 315.
14   Ibid, s 315(1).
15   See Finbar & Parr *UK Merger Control: Law and Practice* (1995); Whish *Competition Law* (1993).
16   As amended by the Companies Act 1989.
17   At least one of which is carried on in the UK or by or under the control of a body corporate incorporated in the UK: Fair Trading Act 1973, s 64(1).
18   Any two enterprises cease to be distinct if they are brought under common ownership or control or if either enterprise ceases to be carried on at all. Common ownership and common control are defined in great detail, see ibid, s 65.
19   Ibid, s 64; Merger References (Increase in Value of Assets) Order 1994, SI 1994 No 72, art 2.
20   FTA 1973, s 64.

The Office of Fair Trading The Director General of Fair Trading is under a duty to keep under review actual or prospective mergers[1]. There is no obligation on the parties to notify the Office of Fair Trading (OFT) of mergers that might qualify for investigation but in practice, information comes frequently from the parties to the takeover bid themselves[2]. This may be because they are seeking informal clearance or sometimes, as a defensive tactic by the offeree, in the hope that the bid will be referred. Companies can file a Merger Notice with the OFT where the merger has already been publicly announced. The incentive for this being that a merger is deemed to have been cleared 20 working days after the submission of the Merger Notice (subject to the possibility of one extension for 15 days) unless on or before that time it has been referred to the MMC[3]. Once the OFT has reached a view on a takeover, it communicates that to the Secretary of State at the Department of Trade and Industry.

The Secretary of State The Secretary of State generally does accept but is not bound to accept the recommendation of the Director General and has on occasion referred a bid to the MMC which the Director General had recommended should not be referred; or not referred bids which the Director General had recommended should be referred. The principal objective of the reference policy is the control of mergers that would have adverse effects on competition in the UK. In practice, very few bids are referred each year to the MMC.

The Secretary of State can accept formal written undertakings from parties to a merger (more usually from the acquiring company) to divest part of a merged business as an alternative to a merger reference in circumstances where the Director General has recommended that a reference be made and has identified in his advice specific adverse effects that the merger might be expected to have and which action pursuant to the proposed undertaking will remedy[4].

The Monopolies and Mergers Commission When a merger is referred to the Commission, it investigates and reports (usually to a three-month deadline) whether the merger qualifies for investigation (ie on market share or assets value) and, if it does, whether it operates or may be expected to operate against the public interest[5].

The Commission must take into account all matters that appear to be relevant in considering the public interest but in particular it must have regard to the desirability of maintaining and promoting competition in the UK, of promoting the interests of consumers, purchasers and other users of goods and services in the UK in respect of prices, quality and variety of goods and services; efficiency and innovation, the balanced distribution of industry and employment, and exports[6].

The Commission must reach definite conclusions and if it finds the merger operates against the public interest, it must specify the particular adverse consequences, consider what action should be taken and may make recommendations for action either by the government or by the companies concerned[7].

1   Ibid, s 76.
2   Parties can seek confidential guidance, ie an indication, in confidence, from the Secretary of State through the OFT as to whether a proposed transaction would be likely to be referred to the Monopolies and Mergers Commission if a bid were to proceed.
3   FTA 1973, ss 75A-75.
4   Ibid, s 75G to 75K.
5   Ibid, s 69(1).
6   Ibid, s 84.
7   Ibid, s 72.

If the MMC reports that the merger may not be expected to operate against the public interest then there is no statutory power vested in the Secretary of State to stop it[8]. Where there is an adverse finding by the MMC, in practice, the Secretary of State tries a voluntary approach first and there is provision for the Secretary of State to ask the Director General to seek undertakings from the various parties as to their future conduct[9]. The Secretary of State can refuse to allow the merger to proceed even though the Commission has indicated that conditions to remedy the adverse effects would suffice. Equally, the Secretary of State may allow the merger to proceed even though the MMC recommended that it should be halted.

A Competition Bill introduced to Parliament in Session 1997-98 will provide for the MMC is to be replaced by a Competition Commission which will exercise those powers under the Fair Trading Act 1973 currently exercised by the MMC.

EC Merger Regulation

Apart from domestic control under the Fair Trading Act 1973, there is also the possibility of a merger being investigated by the European Commission which has an exclusive jurisdiction (with limited exceptions) for large mergers with a Community dimension. This is regulated by the European Community Merger Regulation (ECMR), Council Regulation 4064/899[10] which came into force on 21 September 1990; as amended by Council Regulation (EC) No 1310/97 of 30 June 1997[11].

The ECMR gives the Commission exclusive jurisdiction to evaluate the largest cross-border mergers, acquisitions and concentrative joint ventures in the Community[12]. The aggregate world wide turnover of the undertakings concerned must be at least ECU 5bn and at least two of the undertakings must have Community-wide turnovers of at least ECU 250m. The regulation does not apply if each of the undertakings concerned achieves at least two-thirds of its turnover within one and the same member state[13]. There is also a supplementary set of thresholds which are designed to catch mergers which would otherwise fall to be reviewed in three or more member states and instead they will fall to be reviewed by the Commission on a one-stop shop basis[14].

Qualifying mergers (or concentrations to use the word of the Regulation) must be pre-notified to the Commission within one week of the agreement or the announcement of the bid. In straightforward cases, the Commission will reach a decision within one month; more difficult cases will involve a detailed investigation of up to four months[15]. The basic criterion of evaluation is the impact on competition, the creation or strengthening of a dominant position, in the Community.

A member state may be able to intervene where it demonstrates to the Commission that the concentration threatens to create or strengthen a dominant position significantly impeding competition in a distinct market in its territory and the application of the

8   But see *Palmer's Company Law* (25th edn, 1992), para 12.410 on two bids which were blocked by the Secretary of State despite the MMC being in favour of the bids proceeding subject to certain conditions.

9   FTA 1973, s 88.

10 See OJ L 257/14, 21.09.90.

11 OJ L 180, 09.07.1997.

12 See Cook & Kerse *EC Merger Control* (2nd edn, 1996); European Commission *Merger Control Law in the European Union* (1995); McClellan 'Mergers and Joint Ventures with a Community Dimension and other Acquisitions' [1992] JBL 136.

13 ECMR, art 2.

14 See Council Regulation (EC) No 1310/97 of 30 June 1997, OJ L 180, 09.07.1997.

15 See Krause 'EC Merger Regulation: An Outside View from Inside the Merger Task Force' [1995] JBL 627.

Regulation does not provide a satisfactory solution[16]. A member state can also intervene in parallel to the Commission on non-competition grounds; public security, prudential controls and media diversity are recognised as legitimate grounds for intervention[17].

16   ECMR, art 9.
17   ECMR, art 21(3).

PART VI

Corporate collapse

CHAPTER 37

Corporate failure and corporate insolvency law

Firms not only expand. Sometimes they contract and sometimes they fail. Their contraction and failure are not necessarily bad things in themselves since they may result in a rational reallocation of resources by enabling the assets to be acquired by another company which will use them more efficiently. However, this assumes a lot, particularly within a national economy. It assumes that the market operates efficiently, that the resources are not too specialised and that the costs of transfer are not excessive. It also assumes that there are alternative uses for the resources[1]. In practice these factors are often not present due to macro-economic conditions and the assets are eventually sold for a greatly reduced price or people and plant lie idle. The number and rate of business failures in the UK are very high, and over the period 1971–1980, the failure rate averaged over twice that of the USA[2].

PREDICTION OF BUSINESS FAILURE

Management, because of its strategic position, has a greater opportunity to forecast insolvency than investors. Investors can, however, by diversification reduce some of the risks for them of company failure. Nevertheless, they have to rely on financial data provided by companies which will fall short of all the information in the hands of management. Creditors will either depend on security or high interest charges and careful monitoring. Trade creditors will often rely on knowledge of the company's business and adjust their credit terms accordingly.

Attempts have been made to develop formulas or ratios for predicting business failure to aid all three groups but most of the empirical work has been based on a population of failed companies which gives an immediate bias to the findings. The early work was based on univariate analysis whereas the later work such as that of Edward Altman[3] makes use of multivariate analysis. Using this technique Altman concentrates on the following ratios:

- working capital/total assets;
- retained earnings/total assets;
- earnings before interest and taxes/total assets;

---

1   See J Freear *The Management of Business Finance* (1980) ch 14.
2   See E Altman *Corporate Financial Distress* (1983), p 339.
3   E Altman *Corporate Bankruptcy in America* (1971). See also Altman *Corporate Financial Distress*, op cit, p 339.

- market value of equity/book value of long term debt;
- sales/total assets.

To these he assigned weights to give an overall score known as the Z factor. A variation on this theme has been produced in the UK by R J Traffler[4].

Without going into the detailed operation of these ratios and the resulting analysis, the following general points can be made. First, there is no unanimity amongst the studies as to which ratios offer the best guide. Secondly, the predictive accuracy of the models improves as the failure approaches. Thirdly, there seems to be a time about one to two years ahead of the predicted failure after which management is unlikely to be able to reverse the decline. Fourthly, while they provide information the models do not necessarily aid in devising the appropriate strategy. They are based on static or comparative static, not dynamic, calculations but Altman argues that this is because the science is underdeveloped[5].

The causes of business failure

Apart from such work, the causes of business failure have been inadequately studied. Most professional receivers and liquidators have their own theories but there is usually little settled consensus.

It is interesting to note that the first Report of the Select Committee on Joint Stock Companies in 1844 divided what it described as 'bubble companies' into three categories:

(1) 'Those which, being faulty in their nature, in as much as they are founded on unsound calculations, cannot succeed by any possibility';

(2) 'Those which, let their object be good or bad, are so ill constituted as to render it probable that the miscarriages or failures incident to management will attend them'; and

(3) 'Those which are faulty, or fraudulent in their object, being started for no other purpose than to create shares for the purpose of jobbing in them, or to create, under pretence of carrying on a legitimate business, the opportunity, and means of raising funds to be shared by the adventurers who start the company'.

We may regard this as an apt description of business failure before the introduction of the modern form of incorporation. Remarkably little seems to have changed with the introduction of incorporation under general Companies Acts and limited liability.

Clearly, inadequate capital is a common failing. Many businesses are started up with insufficient working capital. Bank finance, which is usually sought, has its drawbacks. The interest has to be found whether or not the company makes profits unlike dividends on ordinary shares which are only paid out of profits. Bank surveillance and the changes in banking policy from time to time can inhibit the company's freedom to manoeuvre. Buying goods on hire purchase is a great temptation but the true cost of such goods is rarely taken into account. Another factor is inadequate control over working capital. Imprudent business judgment in one form or another is another common failing which in fact covers a multitude of sins. One has only to walk regularly through any shopping centre in any town to see the rise and fall of small businesses.

Fraud is another factor although its incidence is often exaggerated. Some businesses are fraudulent by nature, others are basically lawful but are carried on fraudulently.

---

4   Finding those firms in danger using discriminant analysis and financial ratio data: a comparative UK-based study, City University Business School Working Paper 4. See also J Argenti *Corporate Collapse* (1976).

5   See *Freear*, op cit, pp 348–349.

Others again are lawful and are carried on in a lawful manner but there are management frauds committed against the company.

In a survey carried out in the USA in 1973, Dun and Bradstreet[6], the commercial intelligence specialists, identified 'management inexperience and incompetence' as the major cause of failures. Fraud accounted for a mere 2%. In a survey of 100 UK private companies which had been wound up and almost all of which were small incorporated businesses, 71% failed due to mismanagement. A high proportion had a low share capital of £100 or less in 52% of the cases, and of £1,000 or less in 78% of the cases[7].

The most interesting and thorough analysis of company failure in the UK was done by a financial journalist and management consultant, John Argenti, in his book *Corporate Collapse*[8]. Argenti listed the following causes or symptoms—management shortcomings, lack of accountancy information, failure to respond to change, constraints, recession, big expensive projects, 'creative' (ie cosmetic) accountancy and excessive gearing. Let us examine each of these in turn.

Under management shortcomings, Argenti listed one-man rule, a non-participating board, unbalanced top team, lack of management depth, weak financial function and where there is a combined office of chairman/chief executive. He instances the former Rolls-Royce as having five out of six of these shortcomings. These are all pretty self-explanatory.

As examples of accountancy failings he instanced lack of budgetary control, cash flow forecasts, costing systems and unrealistic valuation of properties.

He gave five examples of change—competitive trends, political change, economic change, social change and technological change. A company must be capable of responding to change. Included under economic and social change would now be changes in industrial relations.

Constraints covers a wide range of things. Some matters such as monopolies and restrictive practices are caught by legal and administrative mechanisms. Some corporate activities may be penalised by tax provisions, eg the retention of profits in close companies. Trades unions also represent a powerful constraint on a company's freedom of manoeuvre and some of their de facto rights were made de jure by the Employment Protection Act 1975, eg right of consultation on redundancy and closures. Again, public opinion, especially through the media or in the form of organised pressure groups, operates as an increasingly powerful check on companies. This is particularly true in the area of the environment. Recession and inflation both represent considerable threats to business. The big project often brings a company down. It is frequently accompanied by little or no realistic costing of research and development. Rolls-Royce was a classic case. Royston Industries, manufacturers of the Midas black box for aeroplanes, was another. In both cases, profitable aspects of the group were brought down by over-ambitious research projects.

Creative accounting is usually a symptom rather than a cause. It has frequently occurred in the past with the over-valuation of properties or work in progress. The accountancy profession is seeking to establish controls over this kind of activity.

Excessive gearing ie excessive loan capital in relation to share capital again is usually a symptom rather than a cause. In some cases the blame can be laid at the door of the banks for encouraging this kind of improvidence but for small incorporated businesses, it can be the only available source of finance.

In a survey published in the Bank of England Quarterly Bulletin[9] two other factors are mentioned—low and declining profitability often marked by historic cost accounts

6   *Freear*, op cit, p 349.
7   R Brough (1967) Business Ratios 8.
8   J Argenti *Corporate Collapse* (1976).
9   (1980) 20 Bank of England Quarterly Bulletin 430.

which may show a steady but in reality inadequate return, and increased import penetration of home markets.

ECONOMIC AND LEGAL PERSPECTIVES

Economists and lawyers tend to view the insolvency systems from different perspectives[10]. Economists on the whole have shown relatively little interest in insolvency. Most standard texts deal with it in a very cursory way and it usually receives most treatment in books on finance. Where they are interested, economists tend to concentrate on the allocative impact of bankruptcy and winding up. Thus bankruptcy and winding up are viewed simply as an aspect of the money market mechanisms. Lawyers, on the other hand, tend to be more concerned with equity and distribution issues. Is there fairness between different classes of creditor and between debtor and creditor? Recently there has been a greater interest in the rehabilitation of consumer debtors and businesses. This sense of fairness and interest in the salvation of individuals and firms is not necessarily consistent with what some economists regard as efficient reallocation. Such economists tend to play down the welfare aspects of legal procedures and look forward to the day when the market will take care of such matters. It is arguable that many of the insolvencies of small firms which are classified as company failures have more in common with personal bankruptcy than large scale corporate collapse[11]. At the same time many personal bankruptcies result from giving guarantees for company debts. The legal form is often not the distinguishing feature so much as the size of the firm.

The legal procedures for dealing with corporate failure

At present the law provides four basic procedures to deal with corporate business failure—receivership, administration, a voluntary arrangement and liquidation or winding up. Receiverships are a loan creditor's remedy for enforcing his or her security, although sometimes the better type of receiver attempts a company doctor role as well. Usually the company will subsequently be wound up, although the viable parts of the business will be hived off and sold. Administration is a procedure introduced in 1985 to facilitate a moratorium to aid the rehabilitation of a company experiencing financial difficulties. Schemes of arrangements are possible in solvent as well as in insolvent circumstances as we have seen. The reforms of 1985 introduced the possibility of a less formal and less expensive procedure. Winding up an insolvent company will either be a compulsory winding up, usually on a creditor's petition, or a creditor's voluntary winding up. In the case of the former, the Companies Court of the Chancery Division or the local county court having jurisdiction performs a supervisory role.

Receiverships, administration and winding up involve collecting in and realisation of assets, and payment of debts. Winding up, however, is followed by dissolution which is the corporate equivalent of death. Unlike a personal bankrupt an insolvent company does not live to resume its former status.

The objectives of corporate insolvency law

Professor R M Goode in the first edition of his *Principles of Corporate Insolvency*[12] stated that corporate insolvency law embodies a variety of objectives some of which

---

10   See P Schuchman (1977) 41 Law and Contemporary Problems 66.
11   Compare W H Meckling (1977) 41 Law and Contemporary Problems 13.
12   1st edition (1990), pp 5 et seq. In the second edition he adopts a simplified version in ch 2 'The Philosophical Foundations of Corporate Insolvency Law'. He lists the objectives of Corporate

are mutually exclusive while others apply in combination. He identified the following as the principal purposes of the law and we comment on them:

1. *To facilitate the recovery of companies in difficulty*—At a time of recession many companies face financial difficulties. Some of these companies are salvageable. This may be achieved as a result of the appointment of an administrator or administrative receiver. In some cases the company can be restored to profitable trading and then handed back to the directors but in many other cases administration or receivership leads to the hiving off of the viable part of the business and the winding up of the remainder.

2. *To suspend the pursuit of rights and remedies by individual creditors*—The effect of administration and winding up but not receivership is to suspend the rights of individual creditors. This is done in a variety of ways. In winding up unsecured creditors rank pari passu in competition with each other but secured creditors' rights are unaffected unless they fall within the winding-up provisions which vitiate certain securities. On the other hand an administration order freezes the enforcement of real rights and judicial remedies while not barring other forms of self help such as set-off. An administrative receivership does not terminate other creditors' rights but because of the assumption of control by the administrative receiver it creates practical restrictions on the enforcement by unsecured creditors of their rights.

3. *To divest the directors of their management powers*—The directors of a company are displaced by the appointment of an administrator, administrative receiver or liquidator. Unlike Chapter 11 of the American Bankruptcy Act, English law does not recognise the concept of the debtor in possession, leaving existing management in office subject to the supervision of the court and creditors.

4. *To provide for the avoidance of transfers and transactions which unfairly prejudice the general creditors*—We refer above to the provisions which apply to vitiate certain securities. English law contains provisions whereby transfers made by an insolvent company in the period before winding up or administration are clawed back into the assets available to the general body of creditors.

5. *To procure an orderly distribution of the estate*—Winding up involves the ascertainment of liabilities, the collection and realisation of assets and the distribution of the proceeds by way of dividend according to the statutory order of priority. Although the other procedures involve the payment of preferential debts in certain circumstances they do not involve the full gamut of the procedures of winding up.

6. *To provide a fair and equitable system for the ranking of claims*—Winding up provides detailed rules for the ranking of claims and certain claims are given preference on the grounds of public policy. These claims also have priority over the holder of debentures secured by a floating charge created by the company.

Insolvency Law as restoring the company to profitable trading, maximising returns to creditors, providing a fair and equitable system for the ranking of claims, identifying the causes of the company's failure and imposing sanctions for culpable management by its directors and officers. In this chapter he also gives a brief survey of US Law and Economics literature on security and bankruptcy see pp 36 et seq. See generally J Ziegel (1990) Alberta L Rev 191 for an interesting survey and review of the US law and economics literature on secured creditors' rights. See also R M Goode (1983–84) 8 CBLJ 53.

7. *To provide for investigation of the causes of the company's failure and impose responsibility for culpable management by its directors and officers*—There is a public interest in the investigation of the causes of business failure and the allocation of responsibility where it is due. This aspect of company insolvency procedure has received more attention since 1985 and considerable emphasis has been put on the disqualification of directors involved in the management of insolvent companies in certain circumstances. The basis on which civil redress can be obtained against directors personally has also been changed to allow for easier recovery.

8. *To protect the public against future improper trading by delinquent directors*— This overlaps with 7 and is achieved through the disqualification process.

9. *To ensure the integrity and competence of insolvency practitioners*—Since 1985 insolvency practitioners have been required to be qualified by authorisation from a recognised professional body, the Secretary of State or a competent authority designated by the Secretary of State.

10. *In the case of liquidation, to dissolve the company*—Winding up does not involve dissolution of the company. The company continues to exist until formal dissolution. This takes place when all the assets have been collected, claims established and dividends distributed. It is marked by striking the company off the Register of Companies.

Incidence of corporate failure

Statistics published in *Economic Trends* of March 1975, p 122 show a general upward movement in the number of insolvent liquidations since 1960 and a similar (although less clear) increase can probably be explained by reference to the growth of the economy between 1960 and 1973 and the increased use of the corporate form of business. However, since 1972 we have had the successive oil crises, economic stagnation and recession, high interest rates and at times high rates of inflation, which have all affected the liquidity of businesses and there has been a sharp rise in insolvencies since 1973. The numbers are still high although legal changes introduced by the Insolvency Act 1976 and the fee increases had a disturbing effect on the statistics. In the period 1970–74, the London clearing banks appointed on average receivers in some 150 cases a year; there was a slight rise in insolvencies in 1975–79 but a sharp increase in 1980 which continued until 1986–7 when it began to subside.

We set out below a table based on the CSO Annual Abstract of Statistics 1986[13], which we have updated, giving statistics of company liquidations from 1974–1996/ 97, together with a graph based thereon. Liquidations as a whole increased from 7,956 in England and Wales in 1971 to 16,082 in 1996–7. They reached 27,829 in 1992–93. Compulsory and creditors' voluntary liquidations, however, more than doubled in this period. Similar trends were present in Scotland and Northern Ireland. These figures may overstate the number of firms becoming insolvent because a business may be carried on through a number of separate companies. Although the trend has now been reversed the figures are still high compared with 25 years ago. This puts immense power in the hands of finance creditors and English law has yet to develop adequate checks and balances[13]. It is still the case that the number of receiverships far exceeds the number of administrations and company voluntary arrangements. Thus in 1996–7, there were

13   For statistics back to 1960, see J H Farrar [1976] JBL 214 at 232–233.

2,491 receiverships notified in England and Wales compared with 212 administrator appointments and 525 company voluntary arrangements.

The legal procedures for dealing with company failure have been the subject of mounting criticism in recent years. They were the subject of a detailed report[14] by a Departmental Committee chaired by Sir Kenneth Cork, a leading insolvency specialist. This was followed by a White Paper[15] and the Insolvency Acts of 1985 and 1986. Although the law and practice is much improved the law is still too complex, there is a lack of coherence in the unified scheme established by the 1985–6 legislation and the administration procedure has not been as successful as Cork envisaged.

14   'Insolvency Law and Practice' Report of the Review Committee (Cmnd 8558).
15   'A Revised Framework for Insolvency Law' (Cmnd 9175).

TABLE Company liquidations

	1974	1975	1976	1977	1978	1979	1980	1981	1982	1983	1984	1985	1986	1986–7	1987–8	1988–9
England and Wales																
Compulsory liquidations	1,395	2,287	2,511	2,425	2,265	2,064	2,935	2,771	3,745	4,807	5,260	5,761	5,204	4,882	3,700	3,600
Voluntary liquidations:																
Creditors'	2,325	3,111	3,428	3,406	2,821	2,473	3,955	5,825	8,322	8,595	8,461	9,137	9,201	9,198	6,900	5,800
Members'	3,746	3,917	4,173	3,650	3,615	4,030	3,970	3,638	3,908	3,808	3,772	3,946	4,525	4,882	2,700	3,800
Total liquidations notified (all types)	7,466	9,315	10,112	9,481	8,701	8,567	10,860	12,234	15,975	17,214	17,493	18,844	18,930	18,962	13,200	13,200
Scotland																
Compulsory liquidations	42	53	84	67	78	56	135	158	177	263	272	306	299	281	200	200
Voluntary liquidations:																
Creditors'	113	151	145	204	196	182	244	280	326	258	251	231	212	214	200	200
Members'	264	276	299	222	230	214	242	248	253	263	234	233	251	233	200	200
Total liquidations notified (all types)	419	480	528	493	504	452	621	686	756	764	757	770	762	728	600	700

Sources: CSO Annual Abstract of Statistics, Department of Trade and Industry. DTI *Companies in 1994–5. Companies in 1996–7.*

	1989–90	1990–91	1991–92	1992–93	1993–94	1994–95	1995–96	1996–97
England and Wales								
Compulsory liquidations	4,300	6,786	8,911	9,542	7,623	6,232	5,384	5,006
Voluntary liquidations:								
Creditors'	6,800	10,378	13,808	14,786	11,737	9,412	8,893	8,063
Members'	4,000	3,941	3,741	3,501	2,696	2,939	3,643	3,013
Total liquidations notified (all types)	15,100	21,105	26.460	27,829	22,056	18,583	17,920	16,082
Scotland								
Compulsory liquidations	200	257	299	319	282	247	247	266
Voluntary liquidations:								
Creditors'	200	232	319	378	227	215	161	197
Members'	200	230	244	218	131	114	144	199
Total liquidations notified (all types)	700	719	862	915	640	576	552	662

Sources: CSO Annual Abstract of Statistics, Department of Trade and Industry; DTI *Companies in 1994–5. Companies in 1996–7.*

CHAPTER 38

Company charges and other security interests

CHARGES AND SECURITY INTERESTS

Companies raise debt capital as we saw in Chapter 20 and in order to do so create charges and other security interests. The term security interest is a technical term of art 9 of the US Uniform Commercial Code but has been used in relation to UK law as a broad generic term by a number of writers. Professor R M Goode for example defines it as a right given to one party in the asset of another party to secure payment or performance by that other party or by a third party".[1] He identifies the characteristics of a security interest as follows:

(1) it arises from a transaction intended as security;
(2) it is a right in rem;
(3) it is created by a grant or declaration of trust, not by reservation;
(4) if fixed it implies a restriction on the debtor's dominion over the asset;
(5) it cannot be taken by the creditor over his or her own obligation to the debtor.[2]

Item (3) seems unduly restrictive as it would exclude a simple reservation of property clause.

The concept of security interest covers a range of interests such as the more obvious mortgage and charge to the less obvious lien, pledge and a complex reservation of property clause. The object of a security interest is to give the creditor protection in the event of the debtor company's insolvency. In a sense and to some extent a security interest enables the creditor to contract out of the company's insolvency.

The nature of a charge as a security interest is that it is an agreement between creditor and debtor by which a particular asset or class of assets is appropriated to the satisfaction of the debt.[3] It does not transfer ownership and merely creates an encumbrance on the property which can be binding on a third party who is not a bona fide purchaser for value of the legal interest without notice. The concept of a charge was originally equitable although the term has been adopted by the Law of Property Act 1925 in relation to land which refers to a charge by way of legal mortgage.

1   See *Legal Problems of Credit and Security* (2nd ed, 1988), p 1.
2   Ibid 1–2.
3   Ibid 14.

We will now concentrate on company charges, distinguishing between fixed and floating charges, before looking at certain other common security interests.

Fixed charges

The basic rules here are the normal mortgage rules applicable to an individual. The most common asset charged is land and the most common mortgage is a charge by way of a legal mortgage[4]. The charge specifically attaches and the company cannot dispose of the land without the debenture holder's consent. An equitable mortgage can be given over a legal or an equitable interest in land. An equitable charge is created where land is made liable to the discharge of a debt.

A fixed charge on chattels in the case of an individual must be effected under the Bills of Sale legislation which requires registration of a schedule of all assets secured. The legislation is cumbrous and outdated and in practice has been superseded by hire purchase and credit sales. Such a charge in the case of a company need only be registered at the Companies Registry. Equitable mortgages and charges can also be created on chattels. Intangible property such as shares in another company can be the subject of a fixed legal or equitable charge. The former requires transfer into the name of the chargee, whereas the latter does not.

The most common securities created by a company are a fixed charge over land and sometimes intangibles such as book debts, and a floating charge over the undertaking and current assets of the company.

Floating charges

Floating charges were first recognised by the Court of Appeal in Chancery in *Re Panama, New Zealand and Australian Royal Mail Co*[5] in 1870. Their juridical nature, however, was not finally worked out until the 1900s,[6] and even today there are some crucial ambiguities. There was at first some doubt as to whether they were securities in the stricter sense before they crystallised, but it is now settled that a floating charge is a present equitable charge which is not specific but shifting until crystallisation, when it settles and becomes a fixed equitable charge.[7]

In *Governments Stock and Other Securities Investment Co v Manila Rly Co Ltd*,[8] Lord Macnaghten described a floating charge as follows:

> A floating security is an equitable charge on the assets for the time being of a going concern. It attaches to the subject charged in the varying condition in which

---

4   See *Fisher & Lightwood's Law of Mortgage* (10th edn, 1988). For an interesting economic analysis, see T H Jackson and A T Kronman 'Secured Financing and Priorities Among Creditors' (1979) 88 Yale LJ 1106. See also A Schwartz 'Security Interest and Bankruptcy Priorities: A Review of Current Theories' (1981) 10 J Legal Stud 1.
5   (1870) 5 Ch App 318. See generally W J Gough *Company Charges* (2nd ed, 1996); J H Farrar (1974) 38 Conv (NS) 3, 5; (1976) 40 Conv (NS) 397; (1980) 1 Co. Law 83; R Dean (1983) 1 C & SLJ 185; E. Ferran [1988] CLJ 213; S. Worthington [1994] CLJ 81; JC Nkala (1993) 11 C & SLJ 301; KJ Naser (1994) 15 Co. Law. 11. See also WJ Gough "The Floating Charge: Traditional Themes and New Directions" in P Finn (ed) *Equity and Commercial Relationships* (1987), p 248.
6   See *Re Yorkshire Woolcombers Association Ltd* [1903] 2 Ch 284, CA; on appeal sub nom *Illingworth v Houldsworth* [1904] AC 355, HL; *Evans v Rival Granite Quarries Ltd* [1910] 2 KB 979, CA.
7   See eg Lord Macnaghten in *Illingworth v Houldsworth*, supra, at 358; Buckley LJ in *Evans v Rival Granite Quarries Ltd*, supra, at 999.
8   [1897] AC 81 at 86, HL.

it happens to be from time to time. It is of the essence of such a charge that it remains dormant until the undertaking charged ceases to be a going concern, or until the person in whose favour the charge is created intervenes.

Seven years later he said in *Illingworth v Houldsworth*:[9]

> I should have thought there was not much difficulty in defining what a floating charge is in contrast to what is called a specific charge. A specific charge I think, is one that without more fastens on ascertained and definite property or property capable of being ascertained and defined; a floating charge, on the other hand, is ambulatory and shifting in its nature, hovering over and so to speak floating with the property which it is intended to affect until some event occurs or some act is done which causes it to settle and fasten on the subject of the charge within its reach and grasp ...

The three common characteristics of a floating charge are now recognised to be that (1) it is a charge on a class of assets of a company present and future, (2) that class is one which in the ordinary course of business changes from time to time, (3) by the charge it is contemplated that until some future step is taken by or on behalf of the chargee the company may carry on its business in the ordinary way.[10]

A FLOATING EQUITABLE INTEREST

Dr Gough, in his work *Company Charges*[11], argues that a floating charge, though a present charge and present security, does not create any proprietary or equitable interest until crystallisation. At most it amounts to a mere equity or bundle of equities which arise out of the security contract. It is submitted that this view, which is based on the idea of appropriation, is not an adequate explanation of the floating charge.[12] It has been held that a floating charge which extends to land creates an interest in the land before crystallisation for the purposes of the Statute of Frauds.[13] It has also been held in Western Australia in *Landall Holdings Ltd v Caratti*[14] that a floating charge creates a floating equitable interest before crystallisation but a contrary view has been taken in Queensland in *Tricontinental Corpn Ltd v FCT*[15] where it was held that there was no proprietary interest in the property which would defeat a notice under s 218 of the Income Tax Assessment Act 1936. The reasoning in both recent cases repays close study. Williams J in the *Tricontinental* case recognised that the holder of a floating charge has the right before crystallisation to intervene and to obtain an injunction to prevent the company dealing with its assets otherwise than in the ordinary course of business. However, His Honour and his brethren were impressed by the fact that the

---

9   [1904] AC 355 at 358, HL.
10 Romer LJ in *Re Yorkshire Woolcombers Association Ltd* [1903] 2 Ch 284 at 295, CA. In fact the members of the class change rather than the class itself. See also *Re Croftbell Ltd* [1990] BCC 781 and *Re Atlantic Medical Ltd* [1992] BCLC 653.
11 *Company Charges* (2nd ed), p 346. For an even more extreme view see Dianne Everett, *The Nature of Fixed and Floating Charges as Security Devices* (Monash University) (1988).
12 See J H Farrar (1980) 1 Co Law 83; S. Worthington [1994] CLJ 81.
13 *Driver v Broad* [1893] 1 QB 744, CA; *Wallace v Evershed* [1899] 1 Ch 891. Cf also *Re Dawson* [1915] 1 Ch 626, CA; *Dempsey and the National Bank of New Zealand v Traders Finance Corpn Ltd* [1933] NZLR 1258; *Re Manurewa Transport Ltd* [1971] NZLR 909.
14 [1979] WAR 97. See also *Stradbroke Waters Co-owners Cooperative Society Ltd v Taylor* [1988] 1 Qd R 595, 602.
15 (1987) 5 ACLC 555. See also *Lyford v Commonwealth Bank of Australia* (1995) 130 ALR 267.

reasoning in the early English cases to the effect that the floating charge is not a *specific* security until crystallisation had been cited with approval in a number of High Court of Australia cases.[16] The difference of opinion in the cases seems to be between those who say that there is no proprietary interest and those who say that the floating charge creates some floating equitable interest which is a security interest. Whatever the precise juridical nature of such an interest it is only defeasible by a transaction in the ordinary course of business. A transaction not in the ordinary course of business takes subject to the equitable interest created by the charge, even though crystallisation may not have taken place[17]. If the transaction is substantial, it may occasion crystallisation on the basis that the company has ceased to be a going concern.[18]

THE POWER OF THE COMPANY TO CARRY ON BUSINESS

What is the legal basis of the company's power to dispose of the assets in the ordinary course of business, notwithstanding the charge? Professor Pennington in an article in the Modern Law Review in 1960[19] and also in his book on company law[20] argues that there are two theories adopted by the judges. The older theory, which he calls the 'licence' theory, explains the matter by implying a licence from the lender. The newer theory, which he calls 'the mortgage of future assets' theory, explains the matter by reference to the fact that the charge does not attach specifically to any of the assets until crystallisation.

There is in fact little clear-cut authority for the 'licence' theory.[1] It is suggested that the basis of the company's power is not actual authorisation[2] by the lender but its capacity under its memorandum and articles of association and the general law. In fact one could say without begging the question that this power is now part of the law relating to floating charges.[3] The lender is under a disability, to use Hohfeld's[4] language, and his floating equitable interest is defeasible pro tanto. The matter can be modified by the terms of the particular debenture but if this power is excluded the document ceases to be a floating charge. This has now passed from being a matter of wording of a particular charge to a general requirement of law.[5] This view of the company's power is consistent with the 'mortgage of future assets' theory but not dependent on it.

What is the scope of the power? First, it has been suggested that there is a general requirement of good faith on the part of the company.[6] Although this is clearly relevant

---

16   See, eg, *Barcelo v Electrolytic Zinc Co of Australasia Ltd* (1932) 48 CLR 391 at 420; *Luckins v Highway Motel Pty Ltd* (1975) 133 CLR 164 at 173–4; and *United Builders Pty Ltd v Mutual Acceptance Ltd* (1980) 144 CLR 673 at 686. See too *Clyne v Federal Comr of Taxation* (1981) 150 CLR 1. The point is not purely academic as it affects priorities.

17   *Hamilton v Hunter* (1983) 7 ACLR 295; *Torzillu Pty Ltd v Brynac Pty Ltd* (1983) 8 ACLR 52. As to ordinary course of business see too *Reynolds Bros (Motors) Pty Ltd v Esanda Ltd* (1984) 8 ACLR 422; *Julius Harper Ltd v F W Hagedorn & Sons Ltd* [1989] 2 NZLR 471.

18   *Hamilton v Hunter* (1983) 7 ACLR 295.

19   (1960) 23 MLR 630. See also the authors listed in footnote 5 Supra.

20   *Pennington's Company Law* (7th edn, 1995), pp 567–9.

1   See Farrar (1974) 38 Conv (NS) 3. See, however, *Reynolds Bros (Motors) Pty Ltd v Esanda Ltd* (1984) 8 ACLR 422.

2   Cf R M Goode *Legal Problems of Credit and Security* (2nd edn, 1988), ch III where it is said to be based on apparent 'authority'. Usually the 'authority' will be actual.

3   See Romer LJ in *Re Yorkshire Woolcombers Association*, supra, see also *National Provincial Bank of England Ltd v United Electric Theatres Ltd* [1916] 1 Ch 132.

4   See Hohfeld *Fundamental Legal Conceptions* (reprinted edn, 1966), p 36.

5   See Fletcher Moulton LJ in *Evans v Rival Granite Quarries Ltd* [1910] 2 KB 979 at 993, CA.

6   See *Hamer v London City and Midland Bank Ltd* (1918) 87 LJKB 973.

as regards the person dealing with the company it seems to have the same dubious relevance as regards the company here as it had as one of the three tests of gratuitous payment laid down in *Re Lee, Behrens & Co Ltd*.[7] The courts have recognised the following transactions as dealings in the ordinary course of business—sales, leases, mortgages, charges, liens, payment of debts and other transactions effected with a view to carrying on the concern.[8] Ultimately, however, it depends on the nature of the particular company's business[9] and in determining the matter the courts will consult the memorandum and articles of association. Matters which are exceptional may nevertheless be regarded as being in the ordinary course of business if they are intra vires.[10] This seems a little paradoxical if the test is, as it appears to be, the *ordinary course of business*.[11]

The nature of crystallisation

CRYSTALLISATION—CLEAR CASES

What then is crystallisation and when does it occur? It was referred to in *Re Victoria Steamboats Ltd*[12] in 1897 by Kekewich J as a 'newly-adopted term'. It is the process whereby the equitable charge attaches specifically and finally to all the items of the class of mortgaged assets which the company owns at that date or subsequently acquires if future assets are within the scope of the particular charge. The latter assets become subject to the fixed charge as they come into existence. In relation to debts, the fixed charge operates as a completed equitable assignment.[13]

It is settled law that crystallisation occurs on the winding up of the company—even, it seems, where the winding up is a members' voluntary winding up.[14] It is settled law that it occurs where a receiver is appointed[15] but it is insufficient that steps are merely

---

7   [1932] 2 Ch 46 which was followed in *Parke v Daily News Ltd* [1962] Ch 927 and *Re W & M Roith Ltd* [1967] 1 All ER 427. See however, *Rolled Steel Products (Holdings) Ltd v British Steel Corpn* [1986] Ch 246, CA.

8   See *Palmer's Company Law*, vol 1, para 13.126. A fraudulent transaction is not to be treated as in the ordinary course of business. See *Williams v Quebrada Railway, Land and Copper Co* [1895] 2 Ch 751.

9   *Re Old Bushmills Distillery Co, ex p Brett* [1897] 1 IR 488, CA. This seems to be close to the 'reasonably incidental' test of an implied power. See *A-G v Great Eastern Rly Co* (1880) 5 App Cas 473, HL.

10 See *Re Borax Co* [1901] 1 Ch 326, CA. Cf *Hubbuck v Helms* (1887) 56 LJ Ch 536 and *Re H H Vivian & Co Ltd* [1900] 2 Ch 654.

11 Although the word 'ordinary' constantly appears in the cases, Lord Ashbourne C in *Re Old Bushmills*, supra, at 495 thought it had 'no place properly at all in the phrase'. It is submitted that he was wrong. On the meaning of the phrase, see now *Reynolds Bros (Motors) Pty Ltd v Esanda Ltd* (1984) 8 ACLR 422; *Julius Harper Ltd v F W Hagedorn & Sons Ltd* [1989] 2 NZLR 471.

12 [1897] 1 Ch 158 at 161. The concept of crystallisation as such has no place in Scots law (see now Pt XVII, Ch 1), although it appeared in the original Bill which led to the Companies (Floating Charges) (Scotland) Act 1961.

13 *NW Robbie & Co Ltd v Witney Warehouse Co Ltd* [1963] 3 All ER 613, CA.

14 *Re Colonial Trusts Corpn, ex p Bradshaw* (1879) 15 Ch D 465 at 472 per Jessel MR. This is so even if the voluntary winding up is for the purposes of reconstruction, see *Re Crompton & Co Ltd* [1914] 1 Ch 954.

15 *Re Panama, New Zealand and Australian Royal Mail Co* (1870) 5 Ch App 318; *Re Florence Land and Public Works Co, ex p Moor* (1878) 10 Ch D 530, CA; *George Barker (Transport) Ltd v Eynon* [1973] 3 All ER 374. As to the effect of appointment of an administrator see RM Goode *Legal Problems of Credit and Security* (2nd ed), pp 63–4. He argues that it does not result in crystallisation Cf *Palmer's Company Law*, vol 2, para 13.129.

being taken to appoint a receiver.[16] It was held in *Re Brightlife Ltd*[17] that the service of notice pursuant to a clause in a debenture may constitute intervention, giving rise to crystallisation.

CRYSTALLISATION—UNCLEAR CASES

Ceasing to be a going concern or to carry on business　There are some passages in the authorities which suggest that a floating charge crystallises on the company ceasing to be a going concern, although they were ignored by practically all the leading English company law textbooks.[18] Until recently there was no express decision on the point[19] although it is clear that ceasing to be a going concern is one of the grounds for the appointment of a receiver by the court.[20] It was first treated as constituting crystallisation in the fifth edition of *Palmer's Company Precedents* in 1891[1] and there were subsequent dicta to this effect.[2] Occasionally, the crystallisation event has been put in terms of ceasing to carry on business.[3] Of the two phrases, 'ceasing to be a going concern' provides a rather imprecise and subjective test. It is a phrase taken from the context of valuation for accounting purposes where valuation as a going concern takes into account continuity and is contrasted with valuation on a break-up basis.[4] It has the advantages in that context that people are using it conveniently to describe what they know anyway, not to prescribe a particular future event. 'Ceasing to carry on business' on the other hand allows the possibility of more objective assessment although it is arguably wider in scope. Anyone is capable of discerning the presence or absence of business activity. Such activities are, however, capable of being conducted *after* the company has ceased to be a going concern, eg a closing-down sale. The main drawback with both tests is that they do not involve any intervention by the lender and might possibly be unknown to him or third parties. This is quite likely with ceasing to be a going concern and quite possible with ceasing to carry on business. The latter has now been accepted as a ground for crystallisation in *Re Woodroffes (Musical Instruments) Ltd* .[5]

16　*Re Colonial Trusts Corpn, ex p Bradshaw* (1879) 15 Ch D 465 at 472; *Government Stock Investment and Other Securities Co v Manila Rly Co* [1895] 2 Ch 551, CA; *Re Roundwood Colliery Co* [1897] 1 Ch 373, CA; *Re Hubbard & Co Ltd* (1898) 68 LJ Ch 54.

17　[1986] 3 All ER 673.

18　In *Hubbuck v Helms* (1887) 56 LJ Ch 536 at 538, Stirling J refers to this as a ground for appointing a receiver. In *Robson v Smith* [1895] 2 Ch 118, the matter is fully argued before Romer J who accepts stoppage of business as a ground for crystallisation but finds on the facts that there had been no stoppage of business (ibid, at 124–125). In his famous dicta in *Governments Stock and Other Securities Investment Co Ltd v Manila Rly Co Ltd* [1897] AC 81 at 86, HL, Lord Macnaghten refers to ceasing to be a going concern as constituting crystallisation. His dicta are adopted in obiter dicta by Vaughan Williams and Fletcher Moulton LJJ in *Evans v Rival Granite Quarries Ltd*, supra, at 990 and 993. In *Edward Nelson & Co Ltd v Faber & Co* [1903] 2 KB 367 at 367–377, Joyce J refers to ceasing to carry on business, and Fletcher Moulton LJ uses the same phrase in the *Evans* case, supra, at 997.

19　See now *Re Woodroffes (Musical Instruments) Ltd* [1986] Ch 366 and *Hamilton v Hunter* (1983) 7 ACLR 295.

20　*Hubbuck v Helms* (1887) 56 LJ Ch 536; *Re Borax Co* [1901] 1 Ch 326, CA.

1　Op cit, by F B Palmer assisted by C Macnaghten (son of Lord Macnaghten), p 476.

2　See the cases cited in Fn 3 supra.

3　See the cases cited in Fn 3 supra.

4　Statement of Standard Accounting Practice, No 2 issued by the Institute of Chartered Accountants in England and Wales defines the 'going concern' concept as follows: 'the enterprise will continue in operational existence for the foreseeable future. This means in particular that the profit and loss account and balance sheet assume no intention or necessity to liquidate or curtail significantly the scale of operation'.

5　[1986] Ch 366. Noted by L Sealy [1986] CLJ 25. See too *Hamilton v Hunter* (1983) 7 ACLR 295. Cf *Halpin v Cremin* [1954] IR 19.

Automatic crystallisation clauses A more important and troublesome question is whether crystallisation occurs when an event happens which is expressly mentioned in the floating charge as a crystallisation event. Originally such clauses, which refer to varieties of default and breach of covenant, were not common but they seem to be used more frequently today.

There is some English and Commonwealth authority on the point. The English authority[6] which appears to support it is all obiter dicta and is arguably equivocal.[7] The Commonwealth cases represent conflicting views. In the New Zealand case of *Re Manurewa Transport Ltd*[8] the matter was expressly considered at first instance. Here, the facts were that the company operated a carrying business and had created a floating charge which contained the usual form of restrictive clause forbidding the creation of further mortgages without consent. There was also an express automatic crystallisation clause which provided that the charge should 'attach and become affixed' on the happening of a number of events, one of which was breach of the restrictive clause.

After delay by the company in the payment of its garage bills, a garage firm seized a truck and refused to release it until they were given security for their account. A chattel security was created over the truck and registered. The consent of the debenture holder was never obtained and the matter fell for decision on the company's insolvency. Speight J decided in favour of the debenture holder. He held that under the New Zealand legislation there was constructive notice not only of the existence of a floating charge but also of its contents including a restrictive clause, as far as it related to chattels. The floating charge, therefore, had priority. Secondly, he expressly upheld Professor Pennington's view of the law that crystallisation can take place without intervention on the happening of an automatic crystallisation event. He relied on some of the English dicta and a New Zealand case of *Paintin & Nottingham Ltd v Miller Gale and Winter* [1971] NZLR 164, where North P had paraphrased Lord Macnaghten's dictum in the *Illingworth* case.[9] Speight J continued:

> After all, a floating charge is not a term of art, it is a description for a type of security contained in a document which may provide a variety of circumstances whereupon crystallisation takes place.[10]

Re Manurewa Transport Ltd has been followed in the Australian case of *Deputy Comr of Taxation v Horsburgh*[11] and a similar view was taken in *Re Obie Pty Ltd (No 2)*.[12] A different view, however, was taken by Berger J in the Canadian case of *R v Consolidated Churchill Copper Corpn Ltd*.[13] This involved a claim by the Province of British Columbia that its statutory lien had priority over a floating charge. This depended on the charge not having crystallised. Berger J held that the charge had not crystallised inter alia because the relevant clause only provided for enforceability not

6   See *Re Horne and Hellard* (1885) 29 Ch D 736; *Davey & Co v Williamson & Sons* [1898] 2 QB 194 at 209; *Illingworth v Houldsworth* [1904] AC 355 at 358, HL and *Evans v Rival Granite Quarries Ltd* [1910] 2 KB 979 at 1000, CA. Cf, however, 986, 993.
7   See Farrar (1976) 40 Conv (NS) 397. Cf A J Boyle [1979] JBL 231.
8   [1971] NZLR 909. See D W McLauchlan 'Automatic Crystallisation of a Floating Charge' (1972) NZLJ 300 and cf Farrar, Gough and Boyle, op cit; R Dean (1982) 1 C & SLJ 185.
9   Speight J's decision can also be supported by the New Zealand Court of Appeal's decision in *Geoghegan v Greymouth-Point Elizabeth Rly and Coal Co Ltd* (1898) 16 NZLR 749 at 768, 771, which was not cited.
10 [1971] NZLR 909 at 917.
11 [1983] 2 VR 591.
12 (1984) 2 ACLC 69.
13 [1978] 5 WWR 652.

crystallisation, and in any event the English authorities did not afford clear support. There were strong policy reasons against adopting the *Manurewa* view. It would render the filing obligation in respect of the appointment of a receiver redundant and would enable the company's assets to be immune from execution since another creditor would not know from the public file whether the floating charge had crystallised or not and the wording of a particular clause might make the levying of execution a ground for automatic crystallisation. In *Re Brightlife Ltd*[14] Hoffmann J said obiter that he preferred *Re Manurewa* to the *Churchill Copper* case.

Thus the position is still not completely clear. An express automatic crystallisation may be regarded as effective, but where the particular floating charge merely provides that the company shall be at liberty to deal with the property charged until the happening of a specific event (ie it does not *expressly* make the event terminate the power to carry on business), the charge continues to float after the happening of the event until a receiver is appointed or the company goes into liquidation.[15] The receiver must actually be appointed. It is not enough merely to issue a writ.[16] It is crucial, therefore, to look at the precise wording of the particular charge. In the light of the cases the true view seems to be that if the clause does not clearly purport (a) to make such an event cause the charge to cease to float or (b) to terminate the company's power to carry on business or (c) otherwise to constitute automatic crystallisation[17] then it appears to be overridden by the company's power *under the law* to carry on business in the ordinary course until intervention or winding up.

Floating charges which are caught by Part VI of the Insolvency Act 1986 (transactions at undervalue etc) will be caught notwithstanding the presence of an automatic crystallisation clause in view of the definition of floating charge in s 251. This covers a charge 'which, as created, was a floating charge'.

RESTRICTIVE CLAUSES

As we have seen, as part of its general power to carry on business in the ordinary course, the company implicitly retains the particular power to mortgage and charge its property. This was not at first recognised[18] but it is now accepted that the company is at liberty to create specific mortgages ranking in priority to the floating charge or after it.[19] The rationale of this apparently is that to hold otherwise would destroy the very object for which the money was borrowed—the carrying on of the company's business. This is not an argument that bears close scrutiny since such drastic consequences will not

14   [1986] 3 All ER 673. Noted by A Wilkinson (1987) 8 Co Law 75; A H Silvertown (1986) 83 L S Gaz 2895. See too *Re Permanent Houses (Holdings) Ltd* [1988] BCLC 563 and *National Australia Bank Ltd v Finlay* (1995) 13 ACLC 1, 175, 1179.
15   *Governments Stock and Other Securities Investment Co v Manila Rly Co Ltd* [1897] AC 81, HL; *Edward Nelson & Co v Faber & Co* [1903] 2 KB 367; *Evans v Rival Granite Quarries Ltd* [1910] 2 KB 979, CA, quaere if the company in the meantime ceases to be a going concern. *Biggerstaff v Rowatt's Wharf Ltd* [1896] 2 Ch 93, CA is also cited by 7 *Halsbury's Laws* (4th edn), for this proposition but this case in fact was concerned with an automatic crystallisation clause taking effect on default. There had been no default at the relevant time.
16   *Re Hubbard & Co Ltd* (1898) 68 LJ Ch 54.
17   The courts may equate *enforceability* and crystallisation but a mere reference to the amount secured or the stock becoming repayable is probably insufficient in the light of the *Government Stock* case, supra. Cf, generally, A J Boyle [1979] JBL 231.
18   *Re Panama etc Mail Co* (1870) 5 Ch App 318 at 322.
19   *Re Florence Land and Public Works Co, ex p Moor* (1878) 10 Ch D 530, CA.

always necessarily ensue. In a later case it was argued that where the subsequent charge is only an equitable security it ought not to have priority over the floating charge. This was the view rejected in *Wheatley v Silkstone and Haigh Moor Coal Co*[20] even though the floating charge purported to confer a first charge. It was sufficient, North J said, that this should be so on crystallisation.

On the other hand in *Re Benjamin Cope & Sons Ltd*[1] in 1914 it was held that a company could not create a floating charge ranking prior to or pari passu with an existing floating charge. Sargant J appeared to view the above cases rather critically and thought that to extend them to the situation before him would be 'acting contrary to all professional and commercial views on the subject'. In the later case of *Re Automatic Bottle Makers Ltd*[2] in 1926 the Court of Appeal held that notwithstanding *Re Benjamin Cope*, a later floating charge over *part* of the assets could rank in priority to or pari passu with the earlier floating charge where power to create such a charge had been reserved in the first charge. Although there are suggestions that this might apply without such a power, it is submitted that this would be to confuse the specificity of the subject matter of a charge with the specificity of its legal character. After all a floating charge on part is still a floating charge, not a specific charge.

Because of the latitude shown by the courts to companies who have created floating charges, it has become the general practice to insert a clause forbidding the creation of any mortgage or charge ranking in priority to or pari passu with the floating charge. The clause (which, when it appears in a floating charge will be referred to hereafter as a 'restrictive clause' and, when it appears alone, as a 'negative pledge') appears to have been originally introduced as a suggestion in the first edition of *Palmer's Company Precedents* in 1877.[3] Such a clause 'is on its face a restriction on dealing in the course of business'.[4] The courts nevertheless proceed on the assumption that it is valid although they recognise that it must be strictly construed.[5] In no case does the validity of such a clause appear to have been challenged. It might have been argued that since this fettered the power of the company to carry on business, it was inconsistent with the nature of a floating charge, but it would now seem too late for this point to be raised.

Conversely, a point which would still seem tenable is that the subsequent mortgage must be granted by the company in good faith and in the ordinary course of business.[6] It is strongly arguable that the subsequent mortgage, being granted in breach of the restrictive clause, can be neither. In other words, it is arguable that it is evidence of equitable fraud by the company.[7] Where a restrictive clause is used outside a debenture and as a substitute for secured indebtedness it is commonly called a negative pledge.

20   (1885) 29 Ch D 715. Cf *Re Robert Stephenson & Co Ltd* [1913] 2 Ch 201, CA and *Re Camden Brewery Ltd* (1911) 106 LT 598n, CA–expressly 'subject to'.

1   [1914] 1 Ch 800 at 806. See also the briefly reported earlier case of *Smith v English and Scottish Mercantile Investment Trust* [1896] WN 86, 40 Sol Jo 717 to the same effect. This does not appear to have been cited.

2   [1926] Ch 412.

3   See *Palmer's Company Precedents* (16th edn, 1956–1960), p 55. *Buckley on the Companies Acts* (13th edn, 1981), p 265, on the other hand, maintains that the clause was introduced into debentures as a result of *Wheatley v Silkstone and Haigh Moor Coal Co*, supra. Charles J in *English and Scottish Mercantile Investment Co Ltd v Brunton* [1892] 2 QB 1 at 9 shares the same view. See also Edward Manson 'The Growth of the Debenture' (1897) 13 LQR 418 at 422 where he states that such a clause is of 'doubtful expediency'.

4   Per Walker C in *Cox v Dublin City Distillery Co* [1906] 1 IR 446 at 456.

5   *Brunton v Electrical Engineering Corpn* [1892] 1 Ch 434 and *Robson v Smith* [1895] 2 Ch 118.

6   See Sankey J in *Hamer v London City and Midland Bank Ltd* (1918) 87 LJKB 973 at 976.

7   See Kekewich J in *Williams v Quebrada Railway, Land and Copper Co* [1895] 2 Ch 751 at 755; see also *Cox v Dublin City Distillery* [1906] 1 IR 446.

It is now clearly established that knowledge of the existence of such a clause operates in equity to prevent a subsequent mortgagee obtaining priority.[8] This seems to be consistent with the equitable fraud argument. The onus appears to be on the subsequent chargee to prove that he or she is a bona fide chargee for value without notice, not on the first chargee to prove that he or she has knowledge or notice. A difficult question is what exactly knowledge and notice mean in this context. It is firmly established that although there is deemed notice of the existence of the floating charge (s 416(1)) there is no constructive notice of a restrictive clause[9] since there is no place for it in the registered particulars in England and Wales. The position is different in Scotland.[10] Such clauses are now very common and banks frequently endorse particulars on the form registered at the Companies Registry. There is no deemed notice achieved thereby (s 416(2)) but the possibility of actual knowledge.[11] Indeed, even where a subsequent purchaser or chargee does not search, the fact that such clauses are very common and the possibility for an existing creditor to inspect the copy of the charge in the company's own register of charges or for a prospective lender to request a copy, might give rise to an inference of such knowledge, particularly in a conveyancing transaction. Inferred knowledge is different from constructive notice. It is a rebuttable rather than an irrebuttable presumption. We shall attempt a summary of the priority rules when we have considered the provisions for registration.

THE EFFECT OF A FLOATING CHARGE ON JUDGMENT CREDITORS

In *Davey & Co v Williamson & Sons Ltd*[12] the Divisional Court held that seizure under execution is not in the ordinary course of business. It is generally thought that this goes too far[13] and that the crucial question is whether the floating charge has crystallised before execution is completed.[14] When execution is regarded as completed differs according to the method adopted.[15] The execution creditor is also entitled to retain moneys paid by the company before crystallisation to avoid sale of goods taken in execution even though the execution is uncompleted at the date of crystallisation.[16] Having said this, it is arguable that where execution is levied on the chattels of the company in such a way as to frustrate its business then this may give rise to crystallisation on the ground of cesser of business or ceasing to be a going concern. Such an event may also be an express crystallisation event.

---

8   *Ian Chisholm Textiles Ltd v Griffith* [1994] BCC 96, 107. Cf *English & Scottish Mercantile Investment Co v Brunton* [1892] 2 QB 700; *Fire Nymph Products Ltd v Heating Centre Pty Ltd (in liq)* (1992) 10 ACLC 629, 638–640.

9   *Re Valletort Sanitary Steam Laundry Co Ltd* [1903] 2 Ch 654; *Re Standard Rotary Machine Co* (1906) 95 LT 829; *Wilson v Kelland* [1910] 2 Ch 306; *G & T Earle Ltd v Hemsworth RDC* (1928) 140 LT 69, CA; *Welch v Bowater (Ireland) Ltd* [1980] IR 251.

10 See *Palmer's Company Law*, vol 2, para 13.216.

11 See further Farrar (1976) 40 Conv (NS) 397; Cf Gough, op cit, Goode, op cit, for contrary views.

12 [1898] 2 QB 194. For a full discussion see Palmer's *Company Law*, vol 2, para 13.138.

13 See R J Calnan (1982) 10 NZULR 111; Hare and Milman [1982] LMCLQ 57.

14 *Robson v Smith* [1895] 2 Ch 118; *Taunton v Sheriff of Warwickshire* [1895] 2 Ch 319, CA.

15 *Pennington*, op cit, ch 12.

16 *Robinson v Burnell's Vienna Bakery Co* [1904] 2 KB 624.

REGISTRATION

The terms of a debenture stock trust deed usually require the company to keep a register of debenture holders. Section 190(3) provides that if one *is* kept, it should be kept at one of the places where the register of members is kept. If this is elsewhere than the registered office the company must notify the Registrar of Companies. There are two systems of registration of charges under CA 1985—the first is in a register kept by the company itself, the second in the register kept by the Registrar of Companies. The first was first introduced in s 43 of the Companies Act 1862, the second in s 14 of the Companies Act 1900. The present law is contained in Part XII of the CA 1985 which was substantially revised by the CA 1989. However, the 1989 amendments have not been brought into effect. For that reason we need to consider·both the existing and proposed new provisions.

Due to historical reasons there is overlap but not identity in the charges covered by the two registers. Every charge falling within ss 395–396 is registrable under s 411 but, in addition, there are certain charges which fall outside s 396 but which fall within ss 407 and 411. *Palmer's Company Law*[17] mentions as examples of the latter mortgages by deposit of certain commercial documents and charges on a concession. There is sense, therefore, in searching the company's own register for the sake of completeness, but in practice this is rarely done and persons dealing with the company tend to content themselves with a search of the company's file at the Companies Registry coupled with express inquiry of the company. Let us now examine each system, dealing first with the existing law and then the proposed new law.

Registration under CA 1985

REGISTRATION IN THE COMPANY'S OWN REGISTER

Section 407 provides that every limited company shall keep at its registered office a register of.charges and enter therein all specific and floating charges, giving a short description of the property charged, the amount of the charge and (except in relation to bearer securities) the names of the persons entitled thereto. Under s 406(1), copies of the instruments of charge must be kept with the register. Failure to enter a charge in the register does not invalidate the charge but any officer of the company who knowingly and wilfully authorises or permits the omission of any entry required to be made is liable to a fine under s 407(3). The hitherto small sanction probably accounts for the non-compliance with the Act by a number of companies. Under s 408, the register and the copies of the instruments of charge may be inspected by a member or existing creditor without fee. A member of the public may inspect the register but not the copies of the instruments on payment of a fee not exceeding 5p. The register must be kept open during business hours but subject to reasonable restrictions imposed by the company in general meeting, so that no less than two hours in each day shall be allowed for inspection.

REGISTRATION AT THE COMPANIES REGISTRY

Section 395 provides for registration of particulars of certain categories of charge together with the original instrument of charge. The latter is returned after registration. Section 396(1) lists the following categories of charge:

17   Ibid, vol 2, para 13–301.

   (a) a charge for the purpose of securing any issue of debentures;

   (b) a charge on uncalled share capital of the company;

   (c) a charge created or evidenced by an instrument which, if executed by an individual, would require registration as a bill of sale;

   (d) a charge on land (wherever situated) or any interest in it, but not including a charge for any rent or other periodical sum issuing out of land;

   (e) a charge on book debts of the company;

   (f) a floating charge on the company's undertaking or property;

   (g) a charge on calls made but not paid;

   (h) a charge on a ship or aircraft, or any share in a ship;

   (i) a charge on goodwill, or on any intellectual property.

We shall examine first what constitutes a charge in general within s 395 and then, secondly, the particular species.

THE CONCEPT OF A REGISTRABLE CHARGE

Under s 396(4), 'charge' for this purpose includes a mortgage. The charge must be created by the company. A charge is created when the instrument is executed, even though the advance is made later.[18] Where there is a series of debentures, the charge is created when the first of the series is issued.[19]

    Where a charge such as a lien arises by operation of law it is not created by the company and not registrable under the section.[20] Thus an unpaid vendor's lien is not within the section. An express contractual lien in a lien by operation of law situation is created by the company but is not within the section because it does not create a charge.[1]

    An agreement to create a security at some future date is not within the section until the security is actually given.[2]

    A charging order over shares or land is not within the section.[3]

    Let us now look at some of the more important categories.

Charge for the purpose of securing any issue of debentures
This particular category could be used as a catch-all category for all other types of charges not specifically listed. There is in fact no English authority on the matter but it seems probable that the legislature intended the issue of a series of debentures. Indeed Professor Pennington argues that it refers to a 'large-scale issue' of a series.[4] In the New Zealand Court of Appeal decision in *Automobile Association (Canterbury) Inc v Australasian Secured Deposits Ltd*,[5] Richmond J assumed that this was what the legislature had primarily in mind and for this reason considered that a charge supporting such an issue was sufficiently significant to require registration. This was a case of deposits on 24 hours' call for which the appellant received as security local authority

---

18   See further Gough , op cit, ch 15.

19   *Re Spiral Globe Ltd (No2), Watson v Spiral Globe Ltd* [1902] 2 Ch 209.

20   *London and Cheshire Insurance Co Ltd v Laplagrene Property Co Ltd* [1971] Ch 499, [1971] 1 All ER 766.

1   See *George Barker (Transport) Ltd v Eynon* [1974] 1 All ER 900, CA; *Waitomo Wools (NZ) Ltd v Nelsons (NZ) Ltd* [1974] 1 NZLR 484, NZ CA.

2   *Re Gregory Love & Co* [1916] 1 Ch 203.

3   *Re Overseas Aviation Engineering (GB) Ltd* [1963] Ch 24, CA.

4   *Pennington's Company Law* (7th Edn, 1995), p 646.

5   [1973] 1 NZLR 417.

stock with unregistered executed transfers. The Court of Appeal held that issue must be construed as referring in a collective sense to the aggregate of a number of individual debentures issued by the company and that as the three charges in question were distinct, they were not registrable. Separate charges on such stock were not a registrable category.

Corporate chattel securities

Chattel securities by companies are not registrable bills of sale within the Bills of Sale Acts 1878–1882. However, any charge which would have been registrable as a bill of sale by an individual, and which is created by a company, must be registered with the Registrar of Companies (s 396(1)(c)).

That raises the complicated question of what is a registrable bill of sale. Under s 4 of the 1878 Act, this is defined as a mortgage or charge on personal chattels. Personal chattels are defined as 'goods ... and other articles capable of complete transfer by delivery ...', but excluding shares and other choses in action. There are further exceptions. Pledges, transfers in the ordinary course of business and hire purchase are the main ones. Chattel securities exempted from the Bills of Sale legislation do not require registration at the Companies Registry.[6]

Further it was held by the Court of Appeal in *Stoneleigh Finance Ltd v Phillips*[7] in 1965 that, to fall within what is now s 396(1)(c), the transaction must in addition amount to a charge to secure the repayment of money. However the court will look to the substance, not the form, and will not allow the section to be evaded by dressing up a charge as an absolute assignment.

Reservation of property clauses

Reservation of property represents a self-help remedy by trade creditors to protect themselves against the consequences of a corporate insolvency. A simple trade creditor normally has only the limited proprietorial remedies conferred by the Sale of Goods Act 1979, namely lien, stoppage in transit and a limited right of resale together with a possible right of set-off. Under the Sale of Goods Act, s 17 property passes when the parties intend it to pass. Similarly s 19 deals with the reservation of a right of disposal which is an incident but not the totality of the concept of property in the goods. Prior to 1976 the use of reservation of property or a right of disposal was only common in the case of export sales in the UK although it is a common device in the continental European members of the EU. Now, since the Court of Appeal's decision in *Aluminium Industrie Vaassen BV v Romalpa Aluminium Ltd*[8], such clauses have become very common. In that case the Court of Appeal had to construe a literal translation of a standard Dutch form of contract. Unfortunately it misconstrued the contract in ignorance of Dutch law. In doing so, however, it recognised the validity of reservation of property and the possibility of combining this with an equitable right to trace. This

6 See further *Pennington's Company Law* (7th ed), pp 637–640.
7 [1965] 2 QB 537.
8 [1976] 1 WLR 676; See H C Rumbelow (1976) 73 LS Gaz 837; R M Goode (1976) 92 LQR 360,528,548; J H Farrar and N Furey [1977] CLJ 27; R Prior (1976) 39 MLR 585; O P Wylie (1978) Conv 37; J H Farrar (1980) 1 Co Law 83, 88 et seq; A M Tettenborn [1981] JBL 173; J R Bradgate [1987] Conv. 434; G. McCormack [1989] Conv. 92; [1990] JBL 313; [1990] Conv. 275; (1990) 10 LS 293; (1992) 12 L.S. 195; [1994] Conv. 129; [1994] JBL 587; A. Hicks [1992] JBL 398; W J Gough *Company Charges* 2nd ed. 538–568; G McCormack *Registration of Company Charges* (1994), pp 67–101; I Davies (1984) LM & CLQ 49, 280; S Whittaker (1984) 100 LQR 35; Sally Jones (1986) 7 Co Law 233; J Farrar and G McLay 'The Interface of Floating Charges, Romalpa Clauses and Credit Factoring' in J Prebble (ed) *Dimensions in Business Finance Law* (1992), ch 3.

creates a potent device for the protection of trade creditors without the need for registration and depletes the company's assets for the purpose of a receivership.

A distinction can be drawn between simple and complex reservation of property. It is now well settled that a simple reservation of property clause is effective.[9] It is the legitimate use of the relevant sections of the Sale of Goods Act and as such incidental to the contract of sale. It does not give rise to a registrable charge. Simple reservation of property may not, however, be effective to protect the seller against a bona fide sub-purchaser from the company who may derive a good title under the buyer in possession exception to the rule in *nemo dat quod non habet*.[10] Even where the seller's original title is defeated by this exception the seller may have rights in the proceeds of sale. These rights depend on the availability of the equitable right to trace. The equitable right to trace depends (1) on the existence of equitable property in the proceeds or in mixed goods, produced by using the original goods, or (2) the existence of a fiduciary relationship by the buyer to the seller.[11] The contract of sale of itself does not give rise to an equitable right of property or a fiduciary relationship. However, it is possible for a sale contract by careful drafting to facilitate such a finding.[12] Difficult problems arise with more complex reservation of property clauses. A complex reservation of property clause is one which purports to extend to the proceeds of sale or to new goods manufactured, using the original goods as constituents. The courts in a number of cases have inclined to the view that such clauses give rise to charges on book debts,[13] floating charges,[14] or fixed charges.[15] As such they are void as against the liquidator, administrator and other creditors for non-registration.

The Cork Report[16] favoured the registration of reservation of property clauses but this reform was not included in the Insolvency Acts 1985 to 1986. Under a reformed system based on art 9 of the US Uniform Commercial Code reservation of property would come within the statutory scheme and a financing statement would have to be filed.[17]

Charges on land

This covers legal and equitable mortgages or charges of land, even where the land is situated abroad. A charge on the land for rent or other periodic payment is excluded from the category. So if the company has entered into a lease or agreed to pay a rent charge payable out of its land, these are not registrable, but a mortgage over the company's own leasehold interests or rent charges would be.

Specific charges on unregistered land after 1 January 1970 must be registered under the Land Charges Act 1972 as well as at the Companies Registry.[18] All specific charges

9   *Clough Mill Ltd v Martin* [1984] 3 All ER 982, CA noted by W Goodhart QC (1986) 49 MLR 96; *John Snow & Co Ltd v DBG Woodcroft & Co Ltd* [1985] BCLC 54.
10   *Four Point Garage Ltd v Carter* [1985] 3 All ER 12; *Re Interview Ltd* [1975] IR 382.
11   *Re Hallett's Estate* (1880) 13 Ch D 696, CA; *Re Diplock* [1948] 2 All ER 318; affd sub nom *Ministry of Health v Simpson* [1951] AC 251, HL; *Chase Manhattan bank NA v Israel-British Bank (London) Ltd* [1981] Ch 105.
12   Contrast *Hendy Lennox (Industrial Engines) Ltd v Grahame Puttick Ltd* [1984] 2 All ER 152; *Re Andrabell Ltd (in liquidation)* [1984] 3 All ER 407.
13   See the *Romalpa* case at first instance [1976] 1 WLR 676.
14   *Re Bond Worth Ltd* [1979] 3 All ER 919.
15   *Borden (UK) Ltd v Scottish Timber Products Ltd* [1981] Ch 25, [1979] 3 All ER 961, CA; *Specialist Plant Services Ltd v Braithwaite Ltd* [1987] BCLC 1; *Modelboard Ltd v Outer Box Ltd* [1993] BCLC 623; *Ian Chisholm Textiles Ltd v Griffiths* [1994] BCC 96.
16   See Cmnd 8558 (1982).
17   See 'Security Interests in Property Other Than Land – A Consultative Paper' issued by the Department of Trade and Industry in 1986.
18   What follows is based on an updated version of the author's revisions to *Palmer's Company Law* (24th edn, 1987), vol 1, para 46–06.

must be registered at the Land Registry and the Companies Registry. A floating charge over unregistered land need only be registered at the Companies Registry. A floating charge over registered land can only be protected by a notice if the land certificate can be produced and by a caution against dealings if it cannot.[19] Generally, unless this is done, a purchaser under a registered disposition is not concerned, whether or not he or she has notice 'express, implied or constructive'.[20] If the company is registered as the proprietor of land, or of a charge, the company's registered number will also be entered on the land register if it is provided or stated on any documennt lodged for registration.[1]

When an instrument creates both a fixed and floating charge, it will normally be registered as a charge under ss 25 and 26 of the Land Registration Act 1925 as to the fixed provisions so that a copy of the deed would either be bound up in the charge certificate or be issued as part of it. So far as registered land is affected by the floating provisions, it can be protected by notice under s 40 of the Act.

When debentures or trust deeds which create floating charges are noted on the register under s 49 and they contain a restrictive clause, the entry on the register will refer to the clause and be to the following effect: 'By a Trust Deed dated ... of ... Limited, the land is charged as security for the moneys therein mentioned. The charge is expressed to be by way of floating security but not so as to permit the creation of charges in priority thereto or pari passu therewith.'

If the floating charge is protected by a caution under s 54 of the Act, the Registry will neither see nor possess a copy and anyone interested in the land learning of the caution will need to go to the deed itself for full information about it.

An agreement to create a mortgage or charge over land amounts to an equitable mortgage[2] and is registrable. Any mortgage or charge subsequently created is also registrable, and its validity is unaffected by non-registration of the agreement.[3]

An equitable charge arising by presumption of law by deposit of title deeds is nevertheless contractual and does not arise by operation of law.[4] The presumption reads into the contract the charge which is implied. The charge is, therefore, registrable. This applies even where the debt secured is owed by a third party. If the charge is avoided, everything ancillary to it is also void. Accordingly, no separate lien on the deeds and documents will be recognised.[5]

A lien arising by operation of law such as a solicitor's lien is not registrable.[6] An unpaid vendor's lien is thus not registrable.[7] Neither is a right of subrogation to an

---

19   Section 3(7) and (8), Land Charges Act 1972. See *Property Discount Corpn Ltd v Lyon Group Ltd* [1980] 1 All ER 334, (registration of a charge on an equitable interest under s 395 effective for the purpose of s 3(7) of the 1972 Act, even though it was registered against the company which created the charge and not against the estate owner). See the useful note by D J Hayton (1980) 1 Co Law 144.

20   Land Registration Act 1925, ss 49(1)(f), 54, 60 and 64; Administration of Justice Act 1977, s 26 (abolition of mortgage caution). See Ruoff, Roper and Prentice *Law and Practice of Registered Conveyancing* (5th edn), pp 573–4; J H Farrar (1974) 38 Conv (NS) 315 at 324–5. See also Practice Direction dated 17 January 1977, noted (1977) 121 Sol Jo 72.

1   Land Registration Act 1925, ss 59(6) and 110(7).

2   *Eyre v McDowell and Wheatley* (1861 9 HL Cas 619, but Cf *Williams v Burlington Investments Ltd* (1977) 121 Sol Jo 424, HL where a contract to create a legal charge on a particular event was held not to be registrable as it did not create a present equitable right to a security but was merely an agreement that in some future circumstances a security would be created.

3   *Re Columbian Fireproofing Co Ltd* [1910] 2 Ch 120, CA.

4   *Re Wallis & Simmonds (Builders) Ltd* [1974] 1 All ER 561.

5   *Re Molton Finance Ltd* [1968] Ch 325, CA.

6   *Brunton v Electrical Engineering Corpn* [1892] 1 Ch 434.

7   *London and Cheshire Insurance Co Ltd v Laplagrene Property Co Ltd* [1971] Ch 499.

unpaid vendor's lien.[8] However, it is not normally possible to allege an unpaid vendor's lien if a valid but unenforceable charge is obtained as security.[9] It is otherwise if the latter charge is void from inception; in this case one can rely on the unpaid vendor's lien.[10] The unpaid vendor's lien will be excluded if the intention was simply the creation of an unsecured loan.[11] Where an equitable charge is duly registered and under a term of the charge a legal mortgage is later executed, the latter need not be registered.[12]

Under s 396(3), the holding of debentures entitling the holder to a charge on land shall not be deemed to be an interest in land for the purposes of the section. A charging order over land by way of execution is not registrable under the section, but must be registered under the Land Registration Act 1925.[13]

Charges on book debts

Book debts are debts connected with and arising in the course of trade of any business, due or growing due to the proprietor of that business and entered or commonly entered in books.[14] They are a species of chose in action and are assets of the company.

Assignments of book debts by way of security for a debt owing by the company are within s 396 (1) (e).[15] This is so whether or not the debt is entered in the books. A charge on *future* book debts is registrable[16] and it is possible in equity to have a fixed charge over future book debts.[17] A letter authorising moneys to be paid to the company's bank where the company was in debt, which was expressed to be irrevocable, has been held to be within the section.[18] It has been held rather illogically that cash at the bank is not a book debt although the relationship of banker and customer is that of debtor and creditor.[19] This view was also taken in Hoffmann J in *Re Brightlife Ltd.*[20] Moneys in trust account held by the company in order to pay its liabilities to third parties incurred in the interest of the settlor are not book debts registrable under s 396 and even if the right of the third parties in the moneys in the special account were charges and void

8   *Burston Finance Ltd v Speirway Ltd* [1974] 3 All ER 735. Cf *Coptic Ltd v Bailey* [1972] Ch 446, which was not followed.
9   *Re Beirnstein* [1925] Ch 12; *Capital Finance Co Ltd v Stokes* [1969] 1 Ch 261, CA; *London and Cheshire Insurance Co Ltd v Laplagrene Property Co Ltd* [1971] Ch 499, Cf Sunnucks (1970) 33 MLR 131.
10   *Thurstan v Nottingham Permanent Benefit Building Society* [1902] 1 Ch 1, CA; on appeal sub nom *Nottingham Permanent Benefit Building Society v Thurston* [1903] AC 6, HL; *Ghana Commercial Bank v Chandiram* [1960] AC 732, PC; *Congresbury Motors Ltd v Anglo-Belge Finance Co Ltd* [1971] Ch 81, CA; *Greendon Investments Ltd v Mills* (1973) 226 Estates Gazette 1957; *Burston Finance Ltd v Speirway Ltd* [1974] 3 All ER 735.
11   *Paul v Speirway Ltd (in liquidation)* [1976] Ch 220.
12   *Cunard SS Co Ltd v Hopwood* [1908] 2 Ch 564; *Re William Hall (Contractors) Ltd* [1967] 2 All ER 1150.
13   *Re Overseas Aviation Engineering (GB) Ltd* [1963] Ch 24, CA.
14   *Shipley v Marshall* (1863) 14 CBNS 566.
15   *Saunderson & Co v Clark* (1913) 29 TLR 579; *Re Welsh Irish Ferries Ltd* [1986] Ch 471.
16   *Independent Automatic Sales Ltd v Knowles and Foster* [1962] 3 All ER 27. See also *Contemporary Cottages (NZ) Ltd v Margin Traders Ltd* [1981] 2 NZLR 114.
17   *Siebe Gorman & Co Ltd v Barclays Bank Ltd* [1979] 2 Lloyd's Rep 142. *Re Keenan Bros Ltd* [1986] BCLC 242. Cf *Re Ladeglen Construction Ltd (in liquidation)* [1980] IR 347; the Northern Irish case of *Re Armagh Shoes Ltd* [1982] NI 59; and *Re Brightlife Ltd* [1987] Ch 200, [1986] 3 All ER 673. See further R R Pennington (1985) 6 Co Law 9; G McCormack (1987) 8 Co Law 3; R A Pearce [1987] JBL 18. See also Byrne and Tomkin (1985) 135 NLJ 443. See further the important decision of *Re New Bullas Trading Ltd* [1994] BCC 36 on which see RM Goode (1994) 110 LQR 592 and compare Alan Berg [1995] JBL 433.
18   *Re Kent and Sussex Sawmills Ltd* [1947] Ch 177.
19   *Re Permanent Houses (Holdings) Ltd* [1988] BCLC 563; *Watson v Parapara Coal Co* (1915) 17 GLR 791.
20   [1987] Ch 200, [1986] 3 All ER 673.

for non-registration, the settlor's equitable right would not be avoided under s 396.[1] A shipowner's contractual lien on subfreight is a charge on book debts and registrable.[2] A right of retention giving rise to set-off is not a charge on book debts.[3]

Floating charges

Floating charges have been discussed already. Section 396(1)(f) refers to the floating charges on the undertaking or property of the company. Gore-Browne mentions that there is some doubt as to whether a floating charge over a particular class of assets is covered.[4] It is difficult to see how the doubt arises, since it would appear to be clearly covered. Special problems arise in respect of priorities and in particular the effect of restrictive clauses on priorities. We shall discuss these questions below when we consider generally the effect of registration on priorities.

Charges on calls

We have referred to charges on uncalled capital above. This category consists of the calls themselves made but not yet paid. They are a species of debt but are not regarded as book debts.

Charges on ships

This covers mortgages of ships or a share in a ship. Legal mortgages are effected in accordance with the form laid down in the Merchant Shipping Act 1894 and registered at the ship's port of registry. Equitable mortgages need not comply with these formalities.

Charges on aircraft

This was not originally covered by s 95(2) of the Companies Act 1948. However by a statutory instrument made under s 16 of the Civil Aviation Act 1968[5] there is now provision for the Register of Aircraft Mortgages to be kept by the Civil Aviation Authority and for registration at the Companies Registry.[6]

Charges on goodwill and intellectual property

This covers goodwill, patents, patent licences, registered trademarks, copyright and copyright licences and registered designs. Mortgages and charges of patents,[7] registered trademarks[8] and registered designs[9] must be notified to the Patents Office.

---

1   *Carreras Rothmans Ltd v Freeman Matthews Treasure Ltd* [1985] Ch 207, [1985] 1 All ER 155.
2   *Re Welsh Irish Ferries Ltd* [1986] Ch 471.
3   *Re Charge Card Services Ltd* [1987] Ch 150.
4   *Gore-Browne on Companies,* op cit, para 18–19.
5   The Mortgaging of Aircraft Order 1972, SI 1972/1268, operative since 1 October 1972.
6   Ibid, art 16(2).
7   Patents Act 1977, s 32(2).
8   Trade Marks Act 1938, s 25(1).
9   Registered Designs Act 1949, s 19(1).

EFFECT OF NON-REGISTRATION

A charge which is not registered by the company[10] within 21 days of its creation is not totally void. Under s 395(1), it is void against the liquidator or administrator and any creditor of the company so far as any security on the company's property or undertaking is conferred thereby. This means that it is not void as against the company or any purchaser or volunteer. In *Mercantile Bank of India Ltd v Central Bank of India*[11] in 1937, letters of hypothecation over goods in India were held by Porter J to constitute floating charges and should have been registered. However, since the charges remained valid against the company the chargee was able to convert the charges into fixed charges and perfect them by seizure before liquidation and this was good against the liquidator. Until seizure, the security in the charges was void against other creditors.[12]

It is the security not the contract to repay which is void. The latter continues and ranks in a liquidation as an unsecured debt. Section 395(2) makes the money immediately payable when the security becomes void. Until liquidation, the chargee has all the remedies of a mortgagee but cannot claim priority over a subsequent creditor whose charge is registered before his or hers.[13]

REGISTRATION AND PRIORITIES

Under the case law rules, a subsequent legal charge ranks before an earlier equitable charge provided the holder of the legal charge is bona fide and without notice. Among equitable charges where the equities are otherwise equal, the rule in *Dearle v Hall* applies and the first in time prevails. Registration has the following effect on those priorities. First, an unregistered charge which is void under s 395 loses its priority. Secondly registration under s 395 gives rise to constructive notice of the charge but priority is otherwise determined by the date of creation of the respective charges. Constructive notice is of the charge but not its contents. However, if, as is common, a floating charge contains a restrictive clause, then there may be actual knowledge or inferred knowledge at common law but not constructive notice of the restrictive clause. Attempts to argue that there is constructive notice founder on the fact that there is no legal requirement in England and Wales to give notice of such a clause in the registered particulars. Inferred knowledge may arguably arise from endorsement of the clause on the registered particulars or the fact that such clauses are common and a copy of the intrument creating a floating charge can be inspected by an existing creditor.[14] It differs from constructive notice in that it can be rebutted. In fact a subsequent chargee will usually call for a copy of the earlier charge in the normal conveyancing way and have actual knowledge.[15]

The following table attempts to apply the basic rules. LC= legal charge, FC= floating charge, FEC= fixed equitable charge, RC= restrictive clause, K= knowledge or notice, UR= unregistered. The order of creation is indicated by the sequence; the order of priority by the numbers. 1–8 assume both charges are duly registered. 9–11 illustrate the effect of non-registration. The position in 7 is arguably based on the presence in the relevant case of a clause enabling a subsequent floating charge over part to be

---

10   Ie, if presented particulars are not filed in time. See *Sun Tai Cheung Credits Ltd v A-G of Hong Kong* (1987) 3 BCC 357 (PC appeal from Hong Kong).
11   [1937] 1 All ER 231, PC.
12   Ibid.
13   *Re Monolithic Building Co* [1915] 1 Ch 643, CA.
14   See Farrar (1974) 38 Conv (NS) 3.
15   Ibid.

created ranking in priority *(Re Automatic Bottle Makers Ltd* [1926] Ch 412) since otherwise it is logically inconsistent with 6. It is the specificity of the charge not the specificity of its subject matter which influences priorities.

1	LC 1	FC 2	
2	FC 2	LC 1	
3	FC RC 1	LC (K) 2	
4	FC 2	FEC 1	
5	FC RC 1	FEC (K) 2	
6	FC 1	FC 2	
7	FC whole 2	FC part 1	
8	FC whole + RC 1	FC part (K) 2	
9	LC (UR) void	FC 1	
10	FC RC (UR) void	LC (K) 1	
11	FC (UR) void	FC 1	

PROPERTY ACQUIRED SUBJECT TO A CHARGE

Where property is acquired subject to a charge which would be registrable under s 395 if created by the company, s 400 provides that it must be registered within 21 days after the date of completion of the acquisition. In the case of property abroad, the time runs from receipt in Great Britain of a copy. Failure to register under s 400 does *not* invalidate the charge, but every officer in default is liable to a fine.

SATISFACTION AND RELEASE

Under s 403, the Registrar may, on proof of discharge in whole or in part of the debt or a release of the property, enter a memorandum of satisfaction or release on the register.

MISTAKES AND THE CONCLUSIVENESS OF THE REGISTRAR'S CERTIFICATE

Under s 401(2), the Registrar must issue a certificate of registration and this constitutes conclusive evidence that the requirements of the Act as to registration have been complied with.[16] This is so even if the particulars are defective.[17] The error in the particulars may even be in respect of the date of creation.[18] The effect of s 401(2) is to exclude the admission of evidence, not the jurisdiction of the courts as such, although it has the same effect in practice.[19]

RECTIFICATION

Section 404 deals with rectification by registration out of time and for mistakes. Power is given to a High Court judge[20] to grant an extension of time or rectification proper on being satisfied that the error in question was accidental or due to misadventure or to some other sufficient cause, or is not of nature to prejudice the position of creditors or shareholders or that on other grounds it is just and equitable to grant relief.

The power does not enable the court to order deletion of the whole of the entry or to alter the date of registration of a charge which has been wrongly backdated.

It appears that obvious clerical or typing errors can be corrected without recourse to the courts.[1]

Where cases fall within s 404, the court may extend the time on such terms and conditions as seem just and expedient.[2] In fact the practice until 1974 was to insert in the order the words 'but this order to be without prejudice to the rights of parties acquired prior to the time when such debentures shall be actually registered.[3] The purpose of this wording was to protect rights acquired against the company's property in the interval between the expiration of the 21 days and the extended time for registration.

The above form of wording of the proviso was used until the decision of Templeman J in *Watson v Duff Morgan and Vermont (Holdings) Ltd*[4] in 1974. As a result of that decision, Mr Registrar Berkeley reconsidered the wording and, after consultation with the Companies Court judges, the following new wording was substituted:

> That the time for registering the charge be extended until the (0000000) day of (000000) 19   ; and this order is to be without prejudice to the rights of the parties acquired during the period between the date of creation of the said charge and the date of its actual registration.

The rationale of the new form of wording appears to be that if the charge is not registered within the 21-day period it becomes void ab initio for the purposes of s 395 and remains

---

16   The decision by the Registrar to register the charge can be the subject of judicial review, *R v Registrar of Companies, ex p Central Bank of India* [1986] QB 1114, sub nom *R v Registrar of Companies, ex p Esal (Commodities) Ltd* [1985] 2 All ER 79.
17   *National Provincial and Union Bank of England v Charnley* [1924] 1 KB 431; *Re Mechanisations (Eaglescliffe) Ltd* [1966] Ch 20.
18   *Re Eric Holmes (Property) Ltd* [1965] Ch 1052.
19   *R v Registrar of Companies, ex p Central Bank of India* [1986] 1 All ER 105 at 117–8.
20   The Registrar must not usurp this jurisdiction of the court; *R v Registrar, ex p Esal*, supra.
1   *R v Registrar of Companies, ex p Central Bank of India*, supra, at 118. See too the Practice Direction of the Registrar of Companies in (1986) 129 Sol Jo 623.
2   *Re Heathstar Properties Ltd* [1966] 1 All ER 628.
3   See *Palmer's Company Law* (24th edn, 1987), vol 1, para 46–10.
4   [1974] 1 All ER 794. Cf *Re R M Arnold & Co Ltd* [1984] BCLC 535.

so unless and until registered pursuant to an order under s 404. The old form of wording, as interpreted in the cases, was based on the assumption that registration pursuant to s 404 validated the charge ab initio and the old form of wording was thus capable of producing injustice, since the degree of protection afforded to holders of other charges depended quite fortuitously upon how long after the charge the subject of the order the other charges were created.[5] If they were created within the 21-day period they were unprotected, whereas if they were created after that period they were protected. This anomaly is now removed by the explicit terms of the new form of wording. As the matter is one of judicial discretion and court practice this method of amendment would seem to be in order. Where a subsequent registered charge was made expressly subject to the prior unregistered charge, the court will normally postpone it when rectifying the register.

The above rules can be illustrated by the following examples.

The old proviso

Day		15	21	28	35
Charge	A	B		C	
Priority	2	3		1	

Charge A was created first, B, 15 days later, C, 28 days later. A was not registered by the due date but an application was made to register out of time and the charge was registered on day 35. The old rule gives the rather startling result above. When A was registered it had priority over B but not C.

The new proviso

Assume the same facts. The order will be B1, C2, A3. This will be otherwise where B is expressly subject to A as was the case in *Watson v Duff Morgan and Vermont (Holdings) Ltd* [1974] 1 All ER 794.

Ordinary creditors are not protected by the wording unless liquidation intervenes between the order and actual registration.[6] An order under s 404 will only be made after a winding up in the most exceptional circumstances.[7] Where directors know that the company is insolvent and do not oppose an application under s 404, this may be evidence of a voidable preference.[8]

Registration under CA 1989

The proposed new sections have not yet been brought into force and may well be amended before this happens. In what follows they are referred to in the present tense as if they were in force, purely for the purposes of convenience of expression.

---

5   See M Bennett (1974) 118 Sol Jo 286.
6   *Re Ashpurton Estates Ltd* [1982] Ch 110, sub nom *Victoria Housing Estates Ltd v Ashpurton Estates Ltd* [1982] 3 All ER 665, CA; *R v Registrar of Companies, ex p Central Bank of India* [1986] 1 All ER 105, CA.
7   Ibid.
8   *Re MIG Trust Ltd* [1933] Ch 542; affd sub nom *Peat v Gresham Trust Ltd* [1934] AC 252, HL. For an attempt to argue the rule in *Ex p James* (1874) 9 Ch App 609 conversely, to stop the liquidator taking the point of non-registration, see *Re John Bateson & Co Ltd* [1985] BCLC 259.

REGISTRATION IN THE COMPANY'S OWN REGISTER

Section 411 provides that every company shall keep at its registered office a register of charges containing entries for each charge, giving a short description of the property charged, the amount of the charge and (except in relation to bearer securities) the names of the persons entitled thereto. Under s 411(1), copies of the instruments of charge must be kept with the register. Failure to enter a charge in the register does not invalidate the charge but the company and any officer of the company in default is liable to a fine under s 411(4). Under s 412, the register and the copies of the instruments of charge may be inspected by a member or existing creditor without fee. A member of the public may inspect the register on payment of such fee as may be prescribed.

REGISTRATION AT THE COMPANIES REGISTRY

Section 396 provides for registration of particulars of certain categories of charge. Section 396(1) lists the following categories of charge:

(a) a charge on land or any interest in land, other than—
   (i) in England and Wales, a charge for rent or any other periodical sum issuing out of the land,
   (ii) in Scotland, a charge for any rent, ground annual or other periodical sum payable in respect of the land;
(b) a charge on goods or any interest in goods, other than a charge under which the chargee is entitled to possession either of the goods or of a document of title to them;
(c) a charge on intangible movable property (in Scotland, incorporeal moveable property) of any of the following descriptions—
   (i) goodwill,
   (ii) intellectual property,
   (iii) book debts (whether book debts of the company or assigned to the company),
   (iv) uncalled share capital of the company or calls made but not paid;
(d) a charge for securing an issue of debentures; or
(e) a floating charge on the whole or part of the company's property.

We shall examine first what constitutes a charge in general within s 395 and then, secondly, some of the more complex particular categories.

THE CONCEPT OF A REGISTRABLE CHARGE

Under s 395(2), 'charge' means any form of security interest (fixed or floating) over property, other than an interest arising by operation of law, and 'property' includes future property. The key concept of 'security interest' is not defined but arguably expands the concept of charge and may be wide enough to cover a reservation of property clause or hire purchase or conditional sale agreement if the substance rather than the form is looked at.[9] The charge must be created by the company. A charge is

---

9   See, however, E Feiran and C Mayo [1991] JBL 152. The authors adopt a definition of security interest by Professor R Goode as a right in the asset of another to secure payment or performance. This seems unduly restrictive. Cf UCC article 1–201(37) which covers even 'simple' reservation of property or title. See further 'A Review of Security Interests in Property (1989) (The Diamond Report)' 3.14–3.10 discussed on p 281. See also G McCormack [1990] LMCLQ 520.

created when the instrument is executed, even though the advance is made later.[10] Where there is a series of debentures, the charge is created when the first of the series is issued.[11]

Where a charge arises by operation of law, it is not created by the company and is not registrable under the section.[12] Thus an unpaid vendor's lien is not within the section. An express contractual lien in a lien by operation of law situation is created by the company but is not within the section because it does not create a charge.[13] In any event s 396(1)(b) expressly excludes charges with a right to possession of goods or documents of title to goods. Since 'charge' now means any form of security interest this seems to exclude all possessory securities.

An agreement to create a security at some future date is not within the section until the security is actually given.[14]

A charging order over shares or land is not within the section.[15]

Let us now look at some of the more important categories.

Charges on land

This covers legal and equitable mortgages or charges of land, even where the land is situated abroad. A charge on the land for rent or other periodic payment is excluded from the category. So if the company has entered into a lease or agreed to pay a rent charge payable out of its land, these are not registrable, but a mortgage over the company's own leasehold interests or rent charges would be.

Specific charges on unregistered land after 1 January 1970 must be registered under the Land Charges Act 1972 as well as at the Companies Registry.[16] All specific charges on registered land must be registered at the Land Registry and the Companies Registry. A floating charge over unregistered land need only be registered at the Companies Registry. A floating charge over registered land can only be protected by a notice if the land certificate can be produced and by a caution against dealings if it cannot.[17] Generally, unless this is done, a purchaser under a registered disposition is not concerned, whether or not he has notice 'express, implied or constructive'.[18] If the company is registered as the proprietor of land, or of a charge, the company's registered number will also be entered on the land register if it is provided or stated on any document lodged for registration.[19]

---

10 See further *Gough*, op cit, ch 15.

11 *Re Spiral Globe Ltd (No 2), Watson v Spiral Globe Ltd* [1902] 2 Ch 209.

12 Section 395(2); *London and Cheshire Insurance Co Ltd v Laplagrene Property Co Ltd* [1971] Ch 499, [1971] 1 All ER 766.

13 See *George Barker (Transport) Ltd v Eynon* [1974] 1 All ER 900, CA; *Waitomo Wools (NZ) Ltd v Nelsons (NZ) Ltd* [1974] 1 NZLR 484, NZ CA.

14 *Re Gregory Love & Co* [1916] 1 Ch 203.

15 *Re Overseas Aviation Engineering (GB) Ltd* [1963] Ch 24, CA.

16 What follows is based on an updated version of the author's revisions to *Palmer's Company Law* (24th edn, 1987), vol 1, para 46–06. See also the current edition, vol 2.

17 Section 3(7) and (8), Land Charges Act 1972. See *Property Discount Corpn Ltd v Lyon Group Ltd* [1980] 1 All ER 334, (registration of a charge on an equitable interest under s 395 effective for the purpose of s 3(7) of the 1972 Act, even though it was registered against the company which created the charge and not against the estate owner). See the useful note by D J Hayton (1980) 1 Co Law 144..

18 Land Registration Act 1925, ss 49(1)(f), 54, 60 and 64; Administration of Justice Act 1977, s 26 (abolition of mortgage caution). See Ruoff, Roper and Prentice *Law and Practice of Registered Conveyancing* (5th edn), pp 573–4; J H Farrar (1974) 38 Conv (NS) 315 at 324–5. See also Practice Direction dated 17 January 1977, noted (1977) 121 Sol Jo 72.

19 Land Registration Act 1925, ss 59(6) and 110(7).

When an instrument creates both a fixed and floating charge, it will normally be registered as a charge under ss 25 and 26 of the Land Registration Act 1925 as to the fixed provisions so that a copy of the deed would either be bound up in the charge certificate or be issued as part of it. So far as registered land is affected by the floating provisions, it can be protected by notice under s 40 of the Act.

When debentures or trust deeds which create floating charges are noted on the register under s 49 and they contain a restrictive clause, the entry on the register will refer to the clause and be to the following effect: 'By a Trust Deed dated ... of ... Limited, the land is charged as security for the moneys therein mentioned. The charge is expressed to be by way of floating security but not so as to permit the creation of charges in priority thereto or pari passu therewith.'

If the floating charge is protected by a caution under s 54 of the Act, the Registry will neither see nor possess a copy and anyone interested in the land learning of the caution will need to go to the deed itself for full information about it.

An agreement to create a mortgage or charge over land amounts to an equitable mortgage[20] and is registrable. Any mortgage or charge subsequently created is also registrable, and its validity is unaffected by non-registration of the agreement.[1]

An equitable charge arising by presumption of law by deposit of title deeds is nevertheless contractual and does not arise by operation of law.[2] The presumption reads into the contract the charge which is implied. The charge is, therefore, registrable. This applies even where the debt secured is owed by a third party. If the charge is avoided, everything ancillary to it is also void. Accordingly, no separate lien on the deeds and documents will be recognised.[3]

A lien arising by operation of law such as a solicitor's lien is not registrable.[4] An unpaid vendor's lien is thus not registrable.[5] Neither is a right of subrogation to an unpaid vendor's lien.[6] However, it is not normally possible to allege an unpaid vendor's lien if a valid but unenforceable charge is obtained as security.[7] It is otherwise if the latter charge is void from inception; in this case one can rely on the unpaid vendor's lien.[8] The unpaid vendor's lien will be excluded if the intention was simply the creation of an unsecured loan.[9] Where an equitable charge is duly registered and under a term of the charge a legal mortgage is later executed, the latter need not be registered.[10]

Under s 396(3), the holding of debentures entitling the holder to a charge on land shall not be deemed to be an interest in land for the purposes of the section. A charging

20   *Eyre v McDowell and Wheatley* (1861) 9 HL Cas 619, but cf *Williams v Burlington Investments Ltd* (1977) 121 Sol Jo 424, HL where a contract to create a legal charge on a particular event was held not to be registrable as it did not create a present equitable right to a security but was merely an agreement that in some future circumstances a security would be created.

1   *Re Columbian Fireproofing Co Ltd* [1910] 2 Ch 120, CA.

2   *Re Wallis & Simmonds (Builders) Ltd* [1974] QB 94, [1974] 1 All ER 561.

3   *Re Molton Finance Ltd* [1968] Ch 325, CA.

4   *Brunton v Electrical Engineering Corpn* [1892] 1 Ch 434.

5   *London and Cheshire Insurance Co Ltd v Laplagrene Property Co Ltd* [1971] Ch 499.

6   *Burston Finance Ltd v Speirway Ltd* [1974] 3 All ER 735. Cf *Coptic Ltd v Bailey* [1972] Ch 446, which was not followed.

7   *Re Beirnstein* [1925] Ch 12; *Capital Finance Co Ltd v Stokes* [1969] 1 Ch 261, CA; *London and Cheshire Insurance Co Ltd v Laplagrene Property Co Ltd* [1971] Ch 499. Cf Sunnucks (1970) 33 MLR 131.

8   *Thurstan v Nottingham Permanent Benefit Building Society* [1902] 1 Ch 1, CA; on appeal sub nom *Nottingham Permanent Benefit Building Society v Thurston* [1903] AC 6, HL; *Ghana Commercial Bank v Chandiram* [1960] AC 732, PC; *Congresbury Motors Ltd v Anglo-Belge Finance Co Ltd* [1971] Ch 81, CA; *Greendon Investments Ltd v Mills* (1973) 226 Estates Gazette 1957; *Burston Finance Ltd v Speirway Ltd* [1974] 3 All ER 735.

9   *Paul v Speirway Ltd (in liquidation)* [1976] Ch 220.

10   *Cunard SS Co Ltd v Hopwood* [1908] 2 Ch 564; *Re William Hall (Contractors) Ltd* [1967] 2 All ER 1150.

order over land by way of execution is not registrable under the section, but must be registered under the Land Registration Act 1925.[11]

Charges on goods or any interest in goods

Formerly there was awkward cross-referencing to the Bills of Sale Acts but this has now been replaced by the more straightforward language of s 395(1)(b) which defines goods as any tangible movable property. However, given differing definitions of goods in other contexts, there may still be problems of interpretation. The category now covers a wider range of goods and extends to charges whether or not they are created or evidenced by an instrument in writing. Charges arising by operation of law or which are purely possessory such as common law liens or pledges are excluded. There is some uncertainty as to whether reservation of property clauses, hire purchase, conditional sale agreements and finance leases are covered. If the court adopts a substance rather than form approach and a liberal interpretation of the term 'security interest' in s 395(2) then they will be covered even though not expressly mentioned. Complex reservation of property clauses have been regarded as registrable charges in any event.[12]

Charges on book debts

Formerly this was a separate category of charge. Section 396(1)(c)(iii) now subsumes book debts under the general category of a charge on intangible movable property (in Scotland, incorporeal movable property). Book debts are covered whether book debts of the company or assigned to the company. There is no definition of book debt although it is intended to deal with this under regulations made under s 396(4). Until then one has to rely on the case law.

Book debts are debts connected with and arising in the course of trade of any business, due or growing due to the proprietor of that business and entered or commonly entered in books.[13] They are a species of chose in action and are assets of the company.

Assignments of book debts by way of security for a debt owing by the company are within s 396(1)(e).[14] This is so whether or not the debt is entered in the books. A charge on *future* book debts is registrable[15] and it is possible in equity to have a fixed charge over future book debts.[16] A letter authorising moneys to be paid to the company's bank where the company was in debt, which was expressed to be irrevocable, has been held to be within the section.[17] Section 396(2)(e) excludes a debenture which is part of an issue or series and s 396(2)(d) excludes a deposit by way of security of a negotiable instrument given to secure the payment of book debts. The first are separately covered and the second is excluded on grounds of expediency. It has been held rather illogically

11 *Re Overseas Aviation Engineering (GB) Ltd* [1963] Ch 24, CA.
12 See eg *Clough Mill Ltd v Martin* [1984] 3 All ER 982; *Feiran and Mayo* op cit, 153–4.
13 *Shipley v Marshall* (1863) 14 CBNS 566.
14 *Saunderson & Co v Clark* (1913) 29 TLR 579; *Re Welsh Irish Ferries Ltd* [1986] Ch 471.
15 *Independent Automatic Sales Ltd v Knowles and Foster* [1962] 3 All ER 27.
16 *Siebe Gorman & Co Ltd v Barclays Bank Ltd* [1979] 2 Lloyd's Rep 142; *Re Keenan Bros Ltd* [1986] BCLC 242; *Re Permanent Houses (Holdings) Ltd* [1988] BCLC 563. Cf *Re Lakeglen Construction Ltd (in liquidation)* [1980] IR 347; the Northern Irish case of *Re Armagh Shoes Ltd* [1982] NI 59; *Re Brightlife Ltd* [1986] 3 All ER 673 and The Australian case, *Whitton v ACN 003 266 886 Pty Ltd (Controller Apptd)* (1996) 14 ACLC 1, 799. See further R R Pennington (1985) 6 Co Law 9; G McCormack (1987) 8 Co Law 3; R A Pearce [1987] JBL 18. See also Byrne and Tomkin (1985) 135 NLJ 443. See further the important recent decision of *Re New Bullas Trading Ltd* [1994] BCC 36 on which see R M Goode (1994) 110 LQR 592 and compare Alan Berg [1995] JBL 433.
17 *Re Kent and Sussex Sawmills Ltd* [1947] Ch 177.

that cash at the bank is not a book debt although the relationship of banker and customer is that of debtor and creditor.[18] This view was also taken by Hoffmann J in *Re Brightlife Ltd*[19] notwithstanding the Registrar's practice of accepting registration of particulars in respect of them. Moneys in a trust account held by the company in order to pay its liabilities to third parties incurred in the interest of the settlor are not book debts registrable under s 396 and even if the right of the third parties in the moneys in the special account were charges and void for non-registration, the settlor's equitable right would not be avoided under s 396.[20] A shipowner's contractual lien on subfreight is not a charge on book debts and registrable.[1] A right of retention giving rise to set-off is not a charge on book debts.[2]

Charges on uncalled share capital or calls made but not paid
This is subsumed under s 396(1)(c)(iv) as a species of intangible movable property.

Charge for the purpose of securing any issue of debentures
This particular category could be used as a catch-all category for all other types of charge not specifically listed. Until the CA 1989, there was no English authority on the matter but it seems probable that the legislature intended the issue of a series of debentures. Indeed Professor Pennington argues that it refers to a 'large-scale issue' of a series.[3] In the New Zealand Court of Appeal decision in *Automobile Association (Canterbury) Inc v Australasian Secured Deposits Ltd*,[4] Richmond J assumed that this was what the legislature had primarily in mind and for this reason considered that a charge supporting such an issue was sufficiently significant to require registration. This was a case of deposits on 24 hours' call for which the appellant received as security local authority stock with unregistered executed transfers. The Court of Appeal held that issue must be construed as referring in a collective sense to the aggregate of a number of individual debentures issued by the company and that as the three charges in question were distinct, they were not registrable. Separate charges on such stock were not a registrable category. Now s 396(2)(a) seems to adopt the New Zealand interpretation.

Reservation of property clauses
Reservation of property represents a self-help remedy by trade creditors to protect themselves against the consequences of a corporate insolvency. A simple trade creditor normally has only the limited proprietorial remedies conferred by the Sale of Goods Act 1979, namely lien, stoppage in transit and a limited right of resale together with a possible right of set-off. Under the Sale of Goods Act, s 17 property passes when the parties intend it to pass. Similarly s 19 deals with the reservation of a right of disposal which is an incident but not the totality of the concept of property in the goods. Prior to 1976 the use of reservation of property or a right of disposal was only common in the case of export sales in the UK although it is a common device in the continental

---

18 *Re Permanent Houses (Holdings) Ltd* [1988] BCLC 563; *Watson v Parapara Coal Co* (1915) 17 GLR 791.
19 [1986] 3 All ER 673. See too *Re Permanent Houses (Holdings) Ltd* [1988] BCLC 563.
20 *Carreras Rothmans Ltd v Freeman Matthews Treasure Ltd* [1985] Ch 207.
1   Section 396(2)(g) reversing *Re Welsh Irish Ferries Ltd* [1986] Ch 471.
2   *Re Charge Card Services Ltd* [1987] Ch 150; on appeal [1989] Ch 497, [1988] BCLC 711, CA.
3   *Pennington's Company Law* (7th edn, 1995).
4   [1973] 1 NZLR 417. See the discussion in *Gough*, op cit, p 277.

European members of the EU. Now, since the Court of Appeal's decision in *Aluminium Industrie Vaassen BV v Romalpa Aluminium Ltd*[5], such clauses have become very common. In that case the Court of Appeal had to construe a literal translation of a standard Dutch form of contract. Unfortunately it misconstrued the contract in ignorance of Dutch law. In doing so, however, it recognised the validity of reservation of property and the possibility of combining this with an equitable right to trace. This creates a potent device for the protection of trade creditors without the need for registration and depletes the company's assets for the purpose of a receivership.

A distinction can be drawn between simple and complex reservation of property. It is now well settled that a simple reservation of property clause is effective.[6] It is the legitimate use of the relevant sections of the Sale of Goods Act and as such incidental to the contract of sale. It does not give rise to a registrable charge. Simple reservation of property may not, however, be effective to protect the seller against a bona fide sub-purchaser from the company who may derive a good title under the buyer in possession exception to the rule in *nemo dat quod non habet*.[7] Even where the seller's original title is defeated by this exception the seller may have rights in the proceeds of sale. These rights depend on the availability of the equitable right to trace. The equitable right to trace depends (1) on the existence of equitable property in the proceeds or in mixed goods, produced by using the original goods, or (2) the existence of a fiduciary relationship by the buyer to the seller.[8] The contract of sale of itself does not give rise to an equitable right of property or a fiduciary relationship. However, it is possible for a sale contract by careful drafting to facilitate such a finding.[9] Difficult problems arise with more complex reservation of property clauses. A complex reservation of property clause is one which purports to extend to the proceeds of sale or to new goods manufactured, using the original goods as constituents. The courts in a number of cases have inclined to the view that such clauses give rise to charges on book debts,[10] floating charges,[11] or fixed charges.[12] As such they are void as against the liquidator, administrator and other creditors for non-registration.

The Cork Report[13] favoured the registration of reservation of property clauses but this reform was not included in the Insolvency Acts 1985 to 1986 and the position under CA 1989 is unclear. Under a reformed system based on art 9 of the US Uniform

---

5   [1976] 1 WLR 676; See H C Rumbelow (1976) 73 LS Gaz 837; R M Goode (1976) 92 LQR 360,528,548; J H Farrar and N Furey [1977] CLJ 27; R Prior (1976) 39 MLR 585; O P Wylie (1978) Conv 37; J H Farrar (1980) 1 Co Law 83, 88 et seq; A M Tettenborn [1981] JBL 173; J R Bradgate [1987] Conv 434; G. McCormack [1989] Conv 92; [1990] JBL 313; [1990] Conv 275; (1990) 10 LS 293; (1992) 12 LS 195; [1994] Conv 129; [1994] JBL 587; A Hicks [1992] JBL 398; W J Gough *Company Charges* (2nd ed), pp 538–568; G McCormack *Registration of Company Charges* (1994), pp 67–101; I Davies (1984) LM & CLQ 49, 280; S Whittaker (1984) 100 LQR 35; Sally Jones (1986) 7 Co Law 233; J Farrar and G McLay 'The Interface of Floating Charges, Romalpa Clauses and Credit Factoring' in J Prebble (ed), *Dimensions in Business Finance Law* (1992), ch 3.

6   *Clough Mill Ltd v Martin* [1984] 3 All ER 982, CA noted by W Goodhart QC (986) 49 MLR 96; *John Snow & Co Ltd v DBG Woodcroft & Co Ltd* [1985] BCLC 54.

7   *Four Point Garge Ltd v Carter* [1985] 3 All ER 12; *Re Interview Ltd* [1975] IR 382.

8   *Re Hallett's Estate* (1880) 13 Ch D 696, CA; *Re Diplock* [1948] Ch 465, [1948] 2 All ER 318, CA; affd sub nom *Ministry of Health v Simpson* [1951] AC 251, [1950] 2 All ER 1137, HL; *Chase Manhattan Bank NA v Israel-British Bank (London) Ltd* [1981] Ch 105.

9   Contrast *Hendy Lennox (Industrial Engines) Ltd v Grahame Puttick Ltd* [1984] 2 All ER 152; *Re Andrabell Ltd (in liquidation)* [1984] 3 All ER 407.

10   See the *Romalpa* case at first instance [1976] 1 WLR 676.

11   *Re Bond Worth Ltd* [1980] Ch 228, [1979] 3 All ER 919.

12   *Borden (UK) Ltd v Scottish Timber Products Ltd* [1979] 3 All ER 961, CA; *Specialist Plant Services Ltd v Braithwaite Ltd* [1987] BCLC 1; *Modelboard Ltd v Outer Box Ltd* [1993] BCLC 623; *Ian Chisholm Textiles Ltd v Griffiths* [1994] BCC 96.

13   See Cmnd 8558 (1982).

Commercial Code reservation of property would come within the statutory scheme and a financing statement would have to be filed.[14]

Charges on ships
These are no longer expressly referred to but are technically goods. Legal mortgages are effected in accordance with the form laid down in the Merchant Shipping Act 1894 and registered at the ship's port of registry. Equitable mortgages need not comply with these formalities.

Charges on aircraft
These are no longer expressly covered by s 396 but are technically goods. Under the Civil Aviation Act 1982[15] there is provision for a Register of Aircraft Mortgages to be kept by the Civil Aviation Authority.[16]

Charges on goodwill and intellectual property
Section 396(2)(d) defines intellectual property as:

(i)   any patent, trade mark, service mark, registered design, copyright or design right, or

(ii) any licence under or in respect of any such right.

Mortgages and charges of patents,[17] registered trademarks[18] and registered designs[19] must be notified to the Patents Office.

PROCEDURE FOR REGISTRATION

Under s 398(1) it is the responsibility of the company to deliver the prescribed particulars in the prescribed form to the Registrar for registration within 21 days after the date of the charge's creation or acquisition. However, it is possible for any person interested to deliver the particulars to the Registrar and it will usually be safest for a chargee or his or her solicitors to do so. The fees can be recovered from the company (s 398(2)). It is no longer necessary to produce the charge itself.

EFFECT OF REGISTRATION

Under s 416(1) 'A person taking a charge over a company's property shall be taken to have notice of any matter requiring registration and disclosed on the register at the time the charge is created.' In other words, there is constructive or deemed notice. Apart from this, there is no inferred knowledge, or notice of additional matters actually put on the register. This is made clear by s 416(2). In so far as notice of restrictive

---

14   See 'Security Interests in Property Other Than Land – A Consultative Paper' issued by the Department of Trade and Industry in 1986.
15   See also the Mortgaging of Aircraft Order 1972, SI 1972 No 1268.
16   Ibid, art 16(2).
17   Patents Act 1977, s 32(2).
18   Trade Marks Act 1938, s 25(1).
19   Registered Designs Act 1949, s 19(1).

clauses is likely to be a required particular, the question of the scope of s 416(2) is largely academic.

EFFECT OF NON-REGISTRATION

If the charge is not registered within 21 days after the date of creation or, as the case may be, after the date of acquisition, the company and every officer in default is liable to a fine (s 398(3)).

A charge which is not registered by the company[20] within 21 days of its creation is not totally void. Under s 399(1), it is void against:

(a)   an administrator or liquidator of the company, and

(b)   any person who for value acquires an interest in or right over property subject to the charge, where the relevant event occurs after the creation of the charge, whether before or after the end of the 21-day period, but subject to late delivery of particulars under s 400.

The relevant event is defined in relation to (a) as the beginning of insolvency proceedings and in relation to (b) as the acquisition of the interest or right (s 399(2)).

A purchaser is now potentially protected by s 399(1)(b) unless he or she purchased expressly subject to the charge.

A charge is not void for non-registration as against a person acquiring an interest in a right over property where the acquisition is expressly subject to the charge (s 405(1)).

In *Mercantile Bank of India Ltd v Central Bank of India Ltd*[1] in 1937, letters of hypothecation over goods in India were held by Porter J to constitute floating charges and should have been registered. However, since the charges remained valid against the company the chargee was able to convert the charges into fixed charges and perfect them by seizure before liquidation and this was good against the liquidator. Until seizure, the security in the charges was void against other creditors.[2]

It is the security not the contract to repay which is void. The latter continues and ranks in a liquidation as an unsecured debt. Section 407(1) makes the whole of the sum secured payable forthwith on demand when the security becomes void. Until a relevant event, the chargee has all the remedies of a mortgagee but cannot claim priority over a subsequent creditor whose charge is registered before his or hers.[3]

REGISTRATION AND PRIORITIES[4]

Under the case law rules, a subsequent legal charge ranks before an earlier equitable charge provided the holder of the legal charge is bona fide and without notice. Among equitable charges where the equities are otherwise equal, the rule in *Dearle v Hall* applies and the first in time prevails. Registration has the following effects on those

---

20   See *Sun Tai Cheung Credits Ltd v A-G of Hong Kong* (1987) 3 BCC 357.
1   [1938] AC 287, PC.
2   Ibid.
3   *Re Monolithic Building Co* [1915] 1 Ch 643, CA.
4   Cf the Diamond Report *A Review of Security Interests in Property* (1989) (HMSO), 21.2.8 which recommended a scheme based on date of registration which unfortunately was not accepted by the Government.

priorities. First, an unregistered charge which is void under s 399 loses its priority. Secondly, registration under s 398 gives rise to deemed notice of the charge but priority is otherwise determined by the date of creation of the respective charges. Deemed notice is of the charge but not its contents unless these are required particulars.

The following table attempts to apply the basic rules. LC = legal charge, FC = floating charge, FEC = fixed equitable charge, RC = restrictive clause, K = knowledge or notice, UR = unregistered. The order of creation is indicated by the sequence; the order of priority by the numbers. 1–8 assume both charges are duly registered. 9–11 illustrate the effect of non-registration where a relevant event has occurred. The position in 7 is arguably based on the presence in the relevant case of a clause enabling a subsequent floating charge over part to be created ranking in priority (*Re Automatic Bottle Makers Ltd* [1926] Ch 412) since otherwise it is logically inconsistent with 6. It is the specificity of the charge not the specificity of its subject matter which influences priorities.

1	LC 1	FC 2
2	FC 2	LC 1
3	FC RC 1	LC (K) 2
4	FC 2	FEC 1
5	FC RC 1	FEC (K) 2
6	FC 1	FC 2
7	FC whole 2	FC part 1
8	FC whole + RC 1	FC part (K) 2
9	LC (UR) void	FC 1
10	FC RC (UR) void	LC (K) 1
11	FC (UR) void	FC 1

As can be seen the rules are still complex and it is a great pity that the Government failed to implement a simplified statutory set of rules.

LATE DELIVERY OF PARTICULARS

The old law required an application to the High Court if particulars were not delivered by the due date. This is now replaced by s 400 which allows the prescribed particulars to be delivered for registration more than 21 days after creation. This will not affect the rights of creditors which have been acquired by the happening of a relevant event even if this took place in the 21-day period.

Suppose charge A is created on 1 July but particulars are not registered in the 21-day period. Charge B is created on 15 July and duly registered on 23 July. Late delivery of particulars in respect of A is made on 30 July. Charge B will have priority because of s 399(1)(b) if value has been received by the company.

Further, s 400(2) provides that late delivery is of no effect where the company is then or, as a consequence of the transaction in respect of which the charge was granted, will be unable to pay its debts and insolvency proceedings begin before the end of the relevant period beginning with the date of delivery of particulars. The relevant period is two years in the case of a floating charge in favour of connected persons, one year in respect of other floating charges and six months in any other case (s 400(3)(b)).

SUPPLEMENTING OR VARYING REGISTERED PARTICULARS

It is no longer necessary to apply to the High Court to rectify the registered particulars. Now it is enough to deliver further particulars signed by or on behalf of both the company and chargee under s 401 at any time. If there is an extension of the charge it may be necessary to deliver fresh particulars.

EFFECT OF ERRORS AND OMISSIONS IN REGISTERED PARTICULARS

Under the old law the certificate of registration was conclusive; hence the need to present the original charge with the particulars. Now the certificate (if issued) merely gives rise to an irrebuttable presumption that the particulars were delivered not later than the date shown and a rebuttable presumption that they were delivered not earlier than the date shown (s 397(5)). A certificate will now only be issued on request (s 397(3)).

The consequences of inaccurate particulars in future will be that pro tanto the charge will be void if a relevant event occurs unless the court orders otherwise (s 402(1) and (2)). The court's discretion is governed by s 402(4). It may order the charge effective as against an administrator or liquidator if the error was not likely to have misled materially any unsecured creditor to his or her prejudice or no person became an unsecured creditor while the registered particulars were incomplete. Also under s 402(5) the court may make such an order if it is satisfied that a person acquiring an interest or right over property subject to the charge did not rely on the registered particulars.

REGISTRATION OF DISCHARGE

This is still optional although the Diamond Report recommended that it be compulsory. Section 403 provides that a memorandum may be delivered to the Registrar for registration provided it is in the prescribed form signed by or on behalf of both the company and the chargee (s 403(1) and (2)). If such a memorandum is delivered in a case where the charge in fact continues to affect the company's property it is void against the administrator or liquidator and any person who for value acquires an interest in or right over property subject to the charge where the relevant event occurs after the delivery of the memorandum (s 403(5)).

REMEDIES OF LOAN CREDITORS

If a company defaults, it is often indicative of business failure. We shall consider this concept and the main legal procedures in Chapters 39–41. Here we shall simply summarise the loan creditor's remedies:

(1) He or she can sue for principal and interest.
(2) He or she can present a winding-up petition.
(3) He or she can apply to the court to appoint a receiver or a receiver and manager.
(4) He or she can apply to the court for orders of foreclosure or sale of any secured property.

Usually the debenture contains provisions enabling the loan creditor or trustee to appoint an administrative receiver without resort to the court and in practice this is the most common remedy. Sometimes an administrator is appointed instead.

Debenture stock trust deeds usually provide for action to be taken by the trustee and restrict the rights of an individual stockholder to take action. It is rare to have an individual or class action by a debenture stockholder today.

FURTHER REFORM

The general question of loan creditors' rights was considered as part of the review of insolvency law and practice by the Cork Committee and a subsequent White Paper. Some but not all of the reforms recommended by the Cork Report were introduced in the Insolvency Act 1985. This Act was then consolidated in the Insolvency Act 1986. We consider the relevant reforms in Chapters 39–41 in relation to receivership, administration and winding up.

In 1986 the Department of Trade and Industry commissioned Professor A L Diamond to produce a report on security interests in property other than land. As part of that exercise Professor Diamond addressed the question of registration of company charges as an interim measure and many of his recommendations were enacted in the CA 1989 revisions to Part XII which are not yet in force. His final report[5] favoured a comprehensive reform on the lines of art 9 of the US Uniform Commercial Code as it has been adapted in Canada. This involves an integrated system of registration of all consensual security interests created by individuals as well as companies and adopts a functional approach, based on substance, rather than form. No recent work has taken place on this report.[6]

---

5   Ibid.
6   See E Feiran and C Mayo [1991] JBL 152; G McCormack [1990] LM & CLQ 520.

CHAPTER 39

Receivers and administrative receivers

INTRODUCTION

Receivers, managers and administrative receivers

The appointment of a receiver by the Court of Chancery was an ancient equitable remedy available to creditors whether secured or unsecured[1]. Today, however, it has come to be used particularly when a corporate borrower defaults on a secured loan[2]. Under a debenture granted by the company, the secured creditor will be entitled to appoint a receiver when the company defaults and the receiver's primary function is to realise sufficient of the company's assets comprised in the security to discharge the debt due to the creditor. Among the many advantages which this enforcement mechanism offers to creditors are speed and the absence of involvement of the court. The process is essentially a matter of the exercise of contractual rights although, following the Cork Committee Report[3], the Insolvency Act 1986 now does include provisions relating to receiverships and, in particular, to administrative receiverships which are defined below. On being appointed the receiver will need to decide quite quickly whether the business can be continued and sold as a going concern; alternatively he may realise that this is not practical and he will start to sell off the company's assets piecemeal. In theory, once the receiver has completed his task of realising sufficient funds to satisfy his appointor, the company could continue trading. In practice, the receiver will often not realise sufficient to pay his appointor in full and the company will proceed to liquidation.

As stated, the function of a receiver is to receive income or realise property in order to pay off, subject in the case of a floating charge to the claims of preferential creditors, a particular secured creditor or creditors. The appointment of a receiver does not impose a moratorium, however, on other creditors enforcing their rights and in fact the appointment will often galvanise other creditors into asserting their rights and remedies

1　The power to appoint a receiver is vested in the High Court, see the Supreme Court Act 1981, s 37. For an outline of the development of receivers, see Rigby LJ in *Gaskell v Gosling* [1896] 1 QB 669 at 691-693.

2　See generally Lightman & Moss *The Law of Receivers* (2nd edn, 1994).

3　See *Report of the Committee on Insolvency Law and Practice* (1982, Cmnd 8558), hereafter the 'Cork Committee Report'.

as well. There is nothing to stop either other creditors petitioning the court for a compulsory winding-up order to be made or the members resolving to put the company into voluntary liquidation. Where a company in receivership also goes into liquidation the receiver remains in office and continues to collect and realise the assets. The liquidator monitors the receivership on behalf of the other creditors and if assets still remain after the receivership is completed these will be dealt with by the liquidator but quite often nothing is left for the unsecured creditors.

A *receiver*, strictly speaking, is appointed just to receive the rent or other income from property. If it is desirable for the receiver to manage the property or to carry on the debtor's business then the receiver has also to be appointed as manager, and in this chapter the term 'receiver' will be used to refer to a person who has the powers of both *a receiver and manager*. The development of the distinction was explained by Sir George Jessel MR in *Re Manchester and Milford Rly Co*[4]:

> A 'receiver' is a term which was well known in the Court of Chancery, as meaning a person who receives rents or other income paying ascertained outgoings, but who does not, if I may say so, manage the property in the sense of buying or selling or anything of that kind. We were most familiar with the distinction in the case of a partnership. If a receiver was appointed of partnership assets, the trade stopped immediately. He collected all the debts, sold the stock-in-trade and other assets, and then under the order of the Court the debts of the concern were liquidated and the balance divided. If it was desired to continue the trade at all, it was necessary to appoint a manager, or a receiver and manager as it was generally called. He could buy and sell and carry on the trade.

During the 19th century conveyancers realised the advantages in terms of costs and speed of providing for the appointment of a receiver as a contractual remedy under the debenture, without the necessity of going to court[5]. Today the majority of receivers are appointed under the terms of a debenture rather than by the court[6]. The main difference is that receivers appointed by the court are under the directions of the court and are appointed to act impartially in the interests of all parties, whereas receivers appointed under debentures are appointed principally to realise the debenture holder's security. For the most part, however, the position of receivers is the same whether they are appointed by the court or under the debenture. Where the distinction is relevant this will be made clear.

The Cork Report contained a number of recommendations designed to improve the competence, independence and effectiveness of receivers[7] and a special position was accorded to a receiver appointed under a debenture secured by a floating charge over the whole or substantially the whole of a company's property, subsequently named in the insolvency legislation as an *administrative receiver*.

The Insolvency Act 1986 defines an administrative receiver as :

> (a) a receiver or manager of the whole (or substantially the whole) of a company's property appointed by or on behalf of the holders of any

---

4   (1880) 14 Ch D 645 at 653.
5   Such powers became so common that they were implied by statute into mortgages by deed unless the parties provided otherwise – see now the Law of Property Act 1925, s 101(1)(iii) – hence such receivers are often referred to as LPA receivers.
6   For an unusual example of a court-appointed receiver, see *BCCI International SA v BRS Kumar Bros Ltd* [1994] 1 BCLC 211.
7   See the Cork Committee Report, Ch 8.

debentures of the company secured by a charge which, as created, was a floating charge, or by such a charge and one or more other securities; or

(b) a person who would be such a receiver or manager but for the appointment of some other person as the receiver of part of the company's property [8].

Given the prevalence of floating charges as a method of securing corporate borrowing, it is not surprising that the Insolvency Act 1986 seeks to make provision for administrative receivers in a number of respects. A particularly significant point to note is that the person with the power to appoint an administrative receiver has the right to block the appointment of an administrator and to appoint an administrative receiver instead[9] (see the discussion on this issue in Chapter 40). This is a significant power given, as we shall see, that an administration order imposes a moratorium on the enforcement of creditors' rights[10].

In this chapter we will refer simply to receivers but this must be understood as including administrative receivers and where special rules apply to administrative receivers this will be made clear.

APPOINTMENT OF A RECEIVER

As we have seen, receivers can be appointed either by the court or under the terms of the debenture but, as noted above, it is rare today for receivers to be appointed by the court and the vast majority are therefore appointed out of court[11].

Although it is common to hear of companies 'calling in the receiver', not all receivers are appointed with the consent of the existing management or the owners of the company. Before accepting office, a receiver will normally insist on an indemnity from the debenture holder against the risk of the appointment being invalid[12] since a receiver who has been invalidity appointed will be personally liable as a trespasser[13].

Default and demand

Obviously it is important to ensure that the power of appointment has arisen and is validly exercised. The circumstances in which a receiver can be appointed under a debenture will depend on its terms[14]. There is no automatic right to appoint under a debenture merely because the security is in jeopardy[15] although the court can make an appointment on such a ground[16]. Typically the instrument will specify a variety of events of default such as a failure to repay part of the capital on the due date; arrears of interest outstanding for a specified period; a petition for an administration order having been issued; assets having fallen below a set figure; an overdraft exceeding a set limit. The usual precondition for appointment under a debenture is that a demand

8   IA 1986, s 29(2).
9   Ibid, ss 9(3), 10(2)(b).
10   Ibid, s 11(3).
11   Either under the express terms of the debenture or by virtue of a term implied by statute, for example under the Law of Property Act 1925, s 101.
12   See also IA 1986, s 34: the court may order the appointor to provide such an indemnity.
13   *Windsor Refrigerator Co Ltd v Branch Nominees Ltd* [1961] Ch 375, [1961] 1 All ER 277, CA.
14   For an example of a debenture in favour of a bank in full form creating fixed and floating charges, see 10 *Forms and Precedents* (5th edn) Form 321.
15   *Cryne v Barclays Bank plc* [1987] BCLC 548, CA.
16   *Re London Pressed Hinge Co Ltd* [1905] 1 Ch 576.

for repayment has not been met. Such a demand need not specify the amount of the debt and need only give the company enough time to implement the mechanics of payment rather than time to raise or find the money[17]. If a debtor makes clear that the required funds are not available, then there is no need for the creditor to allow any time to elapse before treating the debtor as in default[18].

In deciding whether or not to appoint a receiver, debenture holders are free to exercise their contractual right to appoint to protect their interests and owe no duty of care to the company or to guarantors or other mortgagees and thus may ignore the fact that negotiations are taking place with a view to rescuing the business in some other way[19].

Qualifications and notification of appointment

An administrative receiver must be a qualified insolvency practitioner[20]. With that exception, no qualifications are needed for appointment as a receiver, although a company may not be appointed[1] and an undischarged bankrupt can only be appointed by the court (which is very unlikely)[2]. In order to be effective, an appointment as receiver must be accepted before the end of the business day following that on which the instrument of appointment was received[3]. Provided it is so accepted, however, the appointment is deemed to be effective from the moment the instrument of appointment was received[4].

A person appointing a receiver or manager under a power contained in an instrument must within seven days give notice of his appointment to the registrar of companies who enters the appointment on the register of company charges maintained by him[5]. Where an administrative receiver is appointed he must forthwith send to the company notice of his appointment and within 28 days send such a notice to all the creditors of the company[6]. Regardless of the type of receivership, notification of appointment must be made on every invoice, order for goods or business letter issued by or on behalf of the company or the receiver or manager[7].

Costs of receivership

The debenture holder will make it a contractual term of the loan that the company meet the costs of appointing a receiver and therefore in effect the costs of receivership simply further deplete the assets of the company ensuring that nothing remains for the other creditors. A receiver will normally seek an indemnity from his appointor with respect to any personal liabilities incurred as receiver (discussed below) and in respect of his remuneration and expenses should the assets realised prove insufficient[8].

---

17   *Bank of Baroda v Panessar* [1987] Ch 335, [1986] 3 All ER 751; *Cripps (Pharmaceuticals) Ltd v Wickenden, R A Cripps & Sons Ltd v Wickenden* [1973] 2 All ER 606, [1973] 1 WLR 944.
18   *Sheppard & Cooper Ltd v TSB Bank plc* [1996] 2 All ER 654, [1997] BCLC 222.
19   *Re Potters Oils Ltd (No 2)* [1986] 1 All ER 890, [1986] 1 WLR 201; *Shamji v Johnson Matthey Bankers Ltd* [1991] BCLC 36, CA.
20   IA 1986, s 230(2).
1   Ibid, s 30.
2   Ibid, s 31.
3   Ibid, s 33(1)(a).
4   Ibid, s 33(1)(b).
5   CA 1985, s 405(1).
6   IA 1986, s 46(1). He must also cause his appointment to be gazetted: IR 1986, r 3.2(3).
7   IA 1986, s 39(1).
8   See *Re Therm-a-Stor Ltd, Morris v Lewis* [1996] 2 BCLC 400, [1997] BCC 301 for a dispute over such an indemnity.

The whole issue of the costs of receivership has taken on a higher profile of late following the judgment of Ferris J in *Mirror Group Newspapers plc v Maxwell*[9], a case which concerned court-appointed receivers to the insolvent estate of a deceased person although, as Ferris J noted, the concerns about receivers' costs are general to receivers appointed as in this case as well as to receivers appointed by and out of court in respect of insolvent companies (which latter category is the more common in practice). In this case the court-appointed receivers had applied to the court for directions as to the manner in which their remuneration was to be fixed and the principles to be applied. It was disclosed that the remuneration proposed by the receivers as well as the disbursements of the solicitors from whom they had sought advice and other disbursements would amount to £1.63m while the net assets of the estate realised amounted to £1.67m.

Ferris J decided that remuneration was a matter to be assessed by a taxing officer of the court but it was his comments on the scale of the remuneration which attracted broader public interest. He noted that there was a fairly general perception in recent years that costs in insolvency cases have reached an unacceptably high level[10] and, while making it clear that there was no suggestion of misconduct by the receivers, he commented that he found the figures in this case profoundly shocking[11]: 'If the amounts claimed are allowed in full, this receivership will have produced substantial rewards for the receivers and their lawyers and nothing at all for the creditors of the estate. I find it shameful that a court receivership should produce this result in relation to an estate of more than £1.5m'[12]. Ferris J then went on to identify the principles regarding remuneration which should guide receivers as fiduciaries charged with the duty of protecting, getting in and realising the assets of the company and these are discussed in greater detail below (see duties of receivers).

The issue of costs was also addressed, extra-judicially, by Lightman J who suggested that there should be a procedure in force requiring in insolvency cases a proper regulation and monitoring of costs so that public confidence in the insolvency industry could be restored[12]. As he subsequently commented:

> My message was two-fold: (1) the first that, when someone else was paying generosity ceased to be a virtue and Scrooge-like parsimony ceased to be a vice; (2) the second was that, whether the perception [of excessive costs] was correct or false, there was a pressing need for transparent controls regarding the level of costs and remuneration[13].

The directors' position following an appointment

The effect of the appointment of a receiver on the directors is that they remain in office but their powers to deal with the assets comprised in the charge cease and since the

---

9   [1998] BCC 324, Ch D.
10 [1998] BCC 324 at 333.
11 [1998] BCC 324 at 331.
12 See Lightman 'The Challenges Ahead: Address to the Insolvency Lawyers' Association' [1996] JBL 113.
13 Lightman 'Office Holders' charges - cost control and transparency' [1998] 11 Insolv Intell 1; also Gibson 'The Taxation of Receivers' Costs' [1998] 11 Insolv Intell 11; both of which contain detailed analysis and reaction to the judgment of Ferris J in *Mirror Group Newspapers plc v Maxwell* [1998] BCC 324.

charge will usually extend to all the assets in the company, they are effectively powerless to run the business. The appointment of a receiver

> ... entirely supercedes the company in the conduct of its business, deprives it of all power to enter into contracts in relation to that business, or to sell, pledge or otherwise dispose of the property put into the possession or under the control of the receiver and manager. Its powers in these respects are entirely in abeyance[14].

In *Gomba Holdings UK Ltd v Homan*[15], it was suggested that the directors have a continuing duty to exploit the company's assets during receivership but Hoffmann J rejected any such:

> ... diarchy over all the company's assets. This would be contrary to principle and wholly impractical. In my judgement, the board has during the currency of the receivership no powers over assets in the possession or control of the receiver[16].

However, it is important to remember that the receiver is appointed only over the assets to which the charge relates and that his function is to realise the assets to satisfy that creditor. It may be therefore that the directors are able to exercise their residual powers in certain circumstances.

An issue which has arisen is whether the directors are able to initiate proceedings in the company's name when there is a receiver in post with power to bring proceedings. In *Tudor Grange Holdings plc v Citibank NA*[17] the court, while reluctantly accepting that there was some authority to the effect that they could[18], found that they had no power to do so where the receiver's position would be prejudiced by their decision to bring proceedings, for example, by an order for costs against the assets comprised in the charge. The court also indicated that in this type of situation an application to the court for directions is probably appropriate. However, the directors can initiate an action by the company against the receiver for the improper discharge of his duties[19].

An unusual agency

A receiver appointed by the court is not an agent of the company but other receivers are usually appointed as such by the instrument of appointment while administrative receivers are deemed to be such agents by statute[20]. The agency lasts until the company goes into liquidation[1]. As an agent of the company, one would expect the receiver to be subject to the directions of the company as his principal. However, as was made

14   *Moss Steamship Co Ltd v Whinney* [1912] AC 254 at 263, per Lord Atkinson.
15   [1986] 3 All ER 94, [1986] BCLC 331.
16   [1986] 3 All ER 94 at 98-99, [1986] BCLC 331 at 336.
17   [1992] Ch 53, [1991] 4 All ER 1.
18   See *Newhart Developments Ltd v Co-operative Commercial Bank Ltd* [1978] QB 814, [1978] 2 All ER 896 (directors had residual powers to bring proceedings against the debenture holder who had appointed the receiver). But see Browne-Wilkinson V-C in *Tudor Grange Holdings plc v Citibank NA* [1992] Ch 53 at 63, [1991] 4 All ER 1 at 10 where he states 'I have substantial doubts whether the *Newhart* case was correctly decided in any event. That may have to be looked at again in the future.'; also *Gomba Holdings UK Ltd v Homan* [1986] 3 All ER 94 at 98, [1986] BCLC 331 at 336, per Hoffmann J, *Newhart* was 'an exceptional case'.
19   *Watts v Midland Bank plc* [1986] BCLC 15. See also *Rottenberg v Monjack* [1992] BCC 688.
20   IA 1986, s 44(1)(a). It is possible for the debenture holder to intervene in the conduct of the receivership to such an extent as to constitute the receiver its agent: *Standard Chartered Bank Ltd v Walker* [1982] 3 All ER 938, [1982] 1 WLR 1410, CA; *American Express International Banking Corpn v Hurley* [1985] 3 All ER 564, [1986] BCLC 52, but this would be unusual.
1   *Gosling v Gaskell* [1897] AC 575, [1895-9] All ER Rep 300.

clear in *Gomba Holdings UK Ltd v Homan*[2], the agency of a receiver is a special agency for:

> Although nominally the agent of the company, his primary duty is to realise the assets in the interests of the debenture holder and his powers of management are really ancillary to that duty[3].

It cannot simply be assumed therefore that his obligations are the same as those of an ordinary agent who owes a duty of undivided loyalty to his principal[4]. The great advantage of the receiver being the company's agent, as Arden J noted in *Re Sobam BV*[5], is that:

> ... the mortgagee can remove from the company control of the property what had been charged to him without incurring personal liability for any loss that occurs while the receiver holds office[6].

Arden J commented that it was noteworthy that in the Insolvency Act 1986, while making provision for receivers to be personally liable in some circumstances (considered below), Parliament had not abolished the agency status of the receiver. She went on:

> One reason for this may be that the institution of receivership as traditionally structured provides benefits to lenders (as well as, in some cases, other parties) and this may make commercial borrowing easier. The law attaches some importance to the position of secured creditors and to their ability to forecast with certainty the manner in which assets will be distributed in insolvency[7].

Ability to seek directions from the court   Given the peculiarities of the receiver's position, it is important that it is possible under the Insolvency Act s 35 for a receiver, or the creditor appointing him, to apply to the court for directions in relation to any particular matter arising in connection with the performance of his functions[8]. The statutory provision is drafted widely and should be given wide scope to ensure that the receiver has easy access to the court to sort out any difficulty which might arise[9]. On such an application the court may give such directions, or may make such order declaring the rights of persons before the court or otherwise, as it thinks fit[10].

---

2   [1986] 3 All ER 94, [1986] BCLC 331.
3   [1986] 3 All ER 94 at 97, [1986] BCLC 331 at 334.
4   [1986] 3 All ER 94 at 98, [1986] BCLC 331 at 335, per Hoffmann J. See also *Gomba Holdings UK Ltd v Minories Finance Ltd* [1989] 1 All ER 261, [1988] 1 WLR 1231; *Re B Johnson & Co (Builders) Ltd* [1955] Ch 634 at 644-645, [1955] 2 All ER 775 at 779, CA.
5   [1996] 1 BCLC 446, [1996] BCC 351.
6   [1996] 1 BCLC 446 at 452, [1996] BCC 351 at 356.
7   [1996] 1 BCLC 446 at 453, [1996] BCC 351 at 356.
8   IA 1986, s 35.
9   *Re Therm-a-Stor Ltd, Morris v Lewis* [1996] 2 BCLC 400, [1997] BCC 301. The power is frequently used: see for example *Re Sobam BV* [1996] 1 BCLC 446, [1996] BCC 351; *Re Pearl Maintenance Services Ltd, Re Pearl Building Contracts Ltd* [1995] 1 BCLC 449, [1995] BCC 657.
10   IA 1986, s 35(2).

EFFECT OF APPOINTMENT ON EXISTING AND NEW CONTRACTS

Existing contracts in general

The general rule is that, in itself, the appointment of a receiver has no effect on existing contracts of the company[11]. The contract continues as one entered into by the company and the receiver will incur no personal liability in relation to the performance of an existing contract, any more than a director would incur personal liability on any contract entered into for or on behalf of the company[12]. If liability on the part of the receiver is to arise, it will be with respect to new contracts entered into by him or as a consequence of statute imposing personal liability where he has adopted contracts of employment. Those possibilities are discussed later.

Repudiating existing contracts   As with any contract, however, the receiver has the option of performing the contract or breaking it and leaving the other party to a remedy in damages[13]. Of course, the other party's claim for damages will be as an unsecured creditor and this is likely to be unsatisfactory as far as the possibility of recovery is concerned. But the courts will not prevent the receiver repudiating the contract as long as repudiation will not adversely affect the realisation of the assets or seriously affect the trading prospects of the company[14]. In *Airlines Airspares Ltd v Handley Page Ltd*[15] the defendant company had agreed to pay commission to the plaintiff company on sales of aircraft. On the defendant company going into receivership, the receiver 'hived-down'[16] the business of the defendant company to a subsidiary company. With the transfer of the business to the subsidiary, there would be no sales and therefore no commission available to the plaintiff. The court refused the plaintiff's application for an injunction to prevent the receiver proceeding in this way. Otherwise, in the opinion of Graham J, almost any unsecured creditor would be able to improve his position and prevent the receiver from carrying out, or at any rate carrying out as sensibly and as equitably as possible, the purpose for which he was appointed[17].

It does not follow from *Airlines Airspares Ltd v Handley Page Ltd* that a receiver can always disregard a company's contractual obligations and the question is one of priority[18]. As the contract continues as before, any proprietary rights acquired by the other party to the contract which were binding on the company before receivership continue to bind it in receivership. Thus, where before receivership a company had exchanged contracts for the sale of land, the purchaser was entitled to specific performance against the company in receivership[19]. Similarly where a pre-receivership contract created a lien over company property, the lien was binding on the company

---

11   *Parsons v Sovereign Bank of Canada* [1913] AC 160.
12   See *Re Atlantic Computer Systems plc* [1992] Ch 505 at 524, [1992] 1 All ER 476 at 486; see also *Re Sobam BV* [1996] 1 BCLC 446, [1996] BCC 351.
13   As an agent of the company, a receiver who causes a company to break a contract will not be liable to the other party for the tort of inducing breach of contract: *Lathia v Dronsfield Bros Ltd* [1987] BCLC 321; *Welsh Development Agency v Export Finance Co Ltd* [1992] BCLC 148, [1992] BCC 270.
14   *Airlines Airspares Ltd v Handley Page Ltd* [1970] Ch 193, [1970] 1 All ER 29.
15   [1970] Ch 193, [1970] 1 All ER 29. See Lightman J's entertaining comments on this case in which he was counsel for the plaintiffs: Lightman 'The Challenges Ahead: Address to the Insolvency Lawyers' Association' [1996] JBL 113 at 114.
16   'Hiving-down' is a convenient means of preserving the viable parts of a business for sale as a going concern while leaving the debts and other liabilities with the parent company.
17   [1970] Ch 193 at 199, [1970] 1 All ER 29 at 32.
18   *Astor Chemicals Ltd v Synthetic Technology Ltd* [1990] BCLC 1 at 11.
19   *Freevale Ltd v Metrostore (Holdings) Ltd* [1984] Ch 199, [1984] 1 All ER 495. See also *AMEC Properties Ltd v Planning Research and Systems plc* [1992] BCLC 1149, CA; *Ash & Newman Ltd v Creative Devices Research Ltd* [1991] BCLC 403. See Oditah [1992] JBL 541 at 565.

in receivership even though the events causing the lien to arise only occurred after the receivership began[20]. Other equities existing at the commencement of the receivership, which effectively give the other party a prior claim to an asset of the company, also bind the company in receivership. Thus a right of set-off is exercisable against the company in receivership provided the mutual obligations existed at the date of receivership, even though the amounts only became quantified later[1].

No personal liability   Where the contract continues then, as we have seen, the receiver as agent of the company assumes no personal liability with respect to it. So a receiver is not, by reason only of his appointment as such, liable for property rates to a local authority where he is appointed on terms that he is the agent of the company[2]. The liability for rates remains that of the company and the rating authority is simply an unsecured creditor of the company for that amount. However, in *Sargeant v Customs and Excise Comr*[3] while accepting that a liability for VAT rested with the company, the Court of Appeal required that that liability be discharged by the receiver on general public policy grounds.

Similarly the lessor of property to a company in receivership is not entitled to payment of the rent in respect of the period of receivership. As a lease is a continuing obligation it is not a new contract on which the receiver would be personally liable; neither is the lessor entitled to be paid his rent as an expense of the receivership; nor would the receiver be liable for hire charges due under an existing hire-purchase agreement[4]. The position with respect to rental and hire-purchase charges was considered in *Re Atlantic Computer Systems plc*[5] where Nicholls LJ explained that the absence of personal liability of a receiver for such sums is not a surprising conclusion nor does it offend against basic conceptions of justice or fairness.

> The rent and hire charges were a liability undertaken by the company at the inception of the lease or the hire-purchase agreement. The land or goods are being used by the company even though the administrative receiver is in office. It is to the company that, along with other creditors, the lessor and the owner of the goods must look for payment... If the rent or hire is not paid by the administrative receiver the lessor or owner of the goods is at liberty, as much after the appointment of the administrative receiver as before, to exercise the rights and remedies available to him under the lease or hire-purchase agreement. Faced with the prospect of proceedings an administrative receiver may choose to pay the rent or hire charges in order to retain the land or goods. But if he decides not to do so, then the lessor or owner of the goods has his remedies[6].

20   *George Barker (Transport) Ltd v Eynon* [1974] 1 All ER 900, [1974] 1 WLR 462, CA.
1   *Rother Iron Works Ltd v Canterbury Precision Engineers Ltd* [1974] QB 1, [1973] 1 All ER 394, CA. It is different if the transaction which is claimed to give rise to the set-off takes place after the receivership has begun: *N W Robbie & Co Ltd v Witney Warehouse Co Ltd* [1963] 3 All ER 613, [1963] 1 WLR 1324, CA.
2   See *Re Sobam BV* [1996] 1 BCLC 446, [1996] BCC 351; *Ratford v Northavon District Council* [1987] QB 357, [1986] BCLC 397.
3   [1995] 2 BCLC 34, [1995] 1 WLR 821, CA. It would not be right for the holder of a discretion (whether to pay or not) to exercise it in such a way as to defeat the expectation of those who had paid the VAT (that the money would go the Customs and Excise) nor did the law allow the holder of a discretion to act so dishonourably: [1995] 1 WLR 821 at 829, [1995] 2 BCLC 34 at 41, CA.
4   *Hand v Blow* [1901] 2 Ch 721; *Re Atlantic Computer Systems plc* [1992] Ch 505 at 524, [1992] 1 All ER 476 at 486.
5   [1992] Ch 505, [1992] 1 All ER 476.
6   [1992] Ch 505 at 524-525, [1992] 1 All ER 476 at 486. For an exceptional case where the court restricted the other party's rights, in that case the right of the owner under a hire-purchase agreement to repossess certain vehicles, see *Transag Haulage Ltd v Leyland DAF Finance plc* [1994] 2 BCLC 88, [1994] BCC 356.

So a lease may provide for forfeiture on the grounds of the appointment of a receiver or the non-payment of rent. To prevent a landlord exercising his remedies in respect of forfeiture and distress for rent, and if the receiver needs the premises from which to carry on the business, then the receiver may have to agree to pay the rent as an expense of the receivership. So while not personally liable on the rent, the receiver is in practice faced with a requirement to pay it or loose the premises from which the business is being conducted. A similar reality arises under our next heading.

Position of suppliers of goods   It is common now for suppliers of goods to a company to do so under a reservation of title clause in the contract which essentially, and at its most basic, prevents title to the supplier's goods passing to the company until the company has paid for them[7]. This is primarily designed to prevent the goods falling within the company's assets and therefore being swept up by the receiver appointed under a charge over the company's assets to be realised to pay the debt due to the debenture holder while leaving the unpaid supplier to claim (with little chance of being paid) as an unsecured creditor in the subsequent liquidation of the company. Just as it is now customary for suppliers to include such terms, it is equally common for the receiver on appointment to challenge the clause, possibly on the grounds that it has not been validly incorporated into the contract[8], possibly on the grounds that it is a complex clause which has gone beyond mere reservation of title and has created a floating charge over the goods[9] which is void for non-registration as required under the CA 1985[10]. It may be that the goods are critical to the continuation of the business which will be unduly restricted while these issues are resolved. The receivers may therefore offer undertakings to the suppliers that in the event that the reservation of title claim is proved, the receivers will return the goods to them or, if they have disposed of them, will account for the value of the goods[11].

Suppliers may also be in a position simply to exert commercial pressure on a receiver to assume a personal liability for liabilities arising during the receivership. They may even be in a position to demand that all pre-existing liabilities be met by the receiver. This may be a successful tactic if the supplier is the only available source of the goods, the goods are critical to the continuance of the business, and the receivers are anxious to sell it as a going concern.

In *Leyland DAF Ltd v Automotive Products plc*[12] Leyland owed £750,000 to Automotive Products (AP) when administrative receivers were appointed to Leyland. AP refused to continue supplies unless its outstanding bill was met in full and without its supplies there was every likelihood that Leyland would cease to carry on business. The administrative receivers sought an order that AP continue to supply the goods even if the outstanding indebtedness was not satisfied. The Court of Appeal held that, in the absence of a contractual or statutory provision, there is no legal obligation on one person to continue to trade with another. AP was therefore under no obligation to supply components to Leyland. Of course, the suppliers here were in an unusual position in that the parts which they supplied were produced to Leyland's specifications and could not be bought elsewhere in the market so they were in a position to exert maximum pressure on the receivers in this case. The court noted that the person who

7   See *Aluminium Industrie Vaassen BV v Romalpa Aluminium Ltd* [1976] 2 All ER 552, [1976] 1 WLR 676, CA; *Clough Mill Ltd v Martin* [1984] 3 All ER 982, [1985] 1 WLR 111, CA.
8   See, for example, *John Snow & Co Ltd v DBG Woodcroft & Co Ltd* [1985] BCLC 54.
9   See, for example, *Borden (UK) Ltd v Scottish Timber Products Ltd* [1981] Ch 25, [1979] 3 All ER 961; *Re Peachdart Ltd* [1984] Ch 131, [1983] 3 All ER 204; *Modelboard Ltd v Outer Box Ltd* [1993] BCLC 623, [1992] BCC 945.
10   Ie under CA 1985, s 395.
11   See, for example, *Lipe Ltd v Leyland DAF Ltd* [1994] 1 BCLC 84, [1993] BCC 385, CA.
12   [1994] 1 BCLC 245, [1993] BCC 389, CA.

stands to benefit from the receivership is the debenture holder and the court thought there was no obvious reason why a supplier of goods should be expected to bear, for the benefit of the debenture holder, the burden of an unpaid pre-receivership debt[13].

Position of employees Existing contracts of employment are terminated by the appointment of a receiver by the court since such a receiver is not the agent of the company[14] although, as we have noted, such appointments are rare. Existing contracts of employment where the receiver is appointed out of court are not so terminated[15] as the instrument usually provides for the appointment of the receiver as the agent of the company and, in the case of an administrative receiver, he is deemed to be the company's agent by statute[16]. Therefore, applying the ordinary principles outlined above, the receiver in these cases would not be personally liable on such contracts[17] but statute has intervened to impose a personal liability where after appointment the receiver adopts those contracts of employment[18].

New contracts

Personal liability of receivers other than administrative receivers Receivers appointed by the court are personally liable on contracts entered into in the course of carrying on the company's business because, as independent officers of the court, they are not agents of either the company or the debenture holder but contract as principals[19]. The instrument under which other receivers are appointed will normally provide that the receiver is the agent of the company and as such he would not normally be personally liable but for statutory provision to the contrary.

A receiver appointed under a debenture who is not an administrative receiver is, to the same extent as if he had been appointed by the court:

(a) personally liable on any contract entered into by him in the carrying out of his functions (except in so far as the contract otherwise provides) and is personally liable on any contract of employment adopted by him in the performance of his functions; and

(b) entitled in respect of that liability to an indemnity out of the assets of the company (IA 1986, s 37).

For this purpose, the receiver is not to be taken to have adopted a contract of employment by reason of anything done or omitted to be done within 14 days after his appointment[20].

Where at any time a receiver vacates office, his remuneration and any expenses properly incurred by him and any indemnity to which he is entitled out of the company's assets are a charge on and must be paid out of any property of the company which is in his custody or under his control at that time in priority to any security held by the person by whom or on whose behalf he was appointed[1].

13 [1994] 1 BCLC 245 at 250-251, [1993] BCC 389 at 392-293, CA.
14 *Reid v Explosives Co Ltd* (1887) 19 QBD 264.
15 See *Re Foster Clark Ltd's Indenture Trusts* [1966] 1 All ER 43, [1966] 1 WLR 125; *Re Mack Trucks (Britain) Ltd* [1967] 1 All ER 977, [1967] 1 WLR 780.
16 IA 1986, s 44(1),
17 *Nicoll v Cutts* [1985] BCLC 322, CA.
18 See IA 1986, s 44(1)(b) administrative receivers; s 37(1)(a) other receivers.
19 *Moss Steamship Co Ltd v Whinney* [1912] AC 254, HL.
20 IA 1986, s 37(2).
1 Ibid, s 37(4).

. The position thus reached reflects the economic realities of the situation. If it is in the interests of the debenture holder that the business should be carried on, new contracts will need to be entered into and yet persons will not be prepared to enter new contracts with a company in receivership unless they are assured of being paid. The effect of making the receiver personally liable but with a right of indemnity is to treat liabilities under new contracts as if they were expenses of the receivership with the highest priority to be met out of the assets of the company.

With respect to contracts of employment, the personal liability extends to contracts 'adopted' by the receiver and will cover all liabilities under such adopted contract incurred during the period of receivership[2]. As to the meaning of 'adopted' in this context, see the discussion below of the equivalent statutory provision (s 44) applicable to administrative receivers which has been considered by the House of Lords.

Personal liability of administrative receivers　An administrative receiver of a company is deemed to be the company's agent, unless and until the company goes into liquidation[3]. As such he would not normally be personally liable but for statutory provision to the contrary. With regard to new contracts, an administrative receiver:

(a) is personally liable on any contract entered into by him in the carrying out of his functions (except in so far as the contract otherwise provides) and is personally liable to the extent of any qualifying liability on any contract of employment adopted by him in the carrying out of his functions[4]; and

(b) is entitled in respect of that liability to an indemnity out of the assets of the company (IA 1986, s 44(1)).

For this purpose, the administrative receiver is not to be taken to have adopted a contract of employment by reason of anything done or omitted to be done within 14 days after his appointment[5].

These provisions were amended by the Insolvency Act 1994 in response to a series of decisions on the issue of adopting contracts of employment, of which the most important in the context of administrative receivers was the decision of Lightman J in *Re Leyland DAF Ltd, Re Ferranti International plc*[6]. In respect of each of these companies, administrative receivers had been appointed and, as was the practice, they wrote to all the employees immediately following their appointment to say that while they would continue to pay their remuneration, they were not adopting their contracts of employment or assuming any personal liability in relation to their employment. In addition to wages, the employees had contractual entitlements to various payments, including pay in lieu of notice, pension and redundancy payments, holiday pay and other benefits.

2　As we shall see below, Parliament has amended the equivalent provision (ibid, s 44) which applies to administrative receivers to limit their liabilities to what are described as 'qualifying liabilities', see s 44(2A) - (2D). No such limitation applies to other receivers who will be liable for all liabilities on the contracts incurred during the period of receivership: *Powdrill v Watson* [1995] 2 AC 394 at 451, [1995] 2 All ER 65 at 85, HL.

3　IA 1986, s 44(1)(a).

4　Ibid, s 44(1)(b). For these purposes, a liability under a contract of employment is a qualifying liability if (a) it is a liability to pay a sum by way of wages or salary or contribution to an occupational pension scheme, (b) it is incurred while the administrative receiver is in office; and (c) it is in respect of services rendered wholly or partly after the adoption of the contract: s 44(2A). Any qualifying liability which represents payment in respect of services rendered before the adoption of the contract must be disregarded: s 44(2B). See also s 44(2C)-(2D) as to treatment of holiday and sick pay.

5　Ibid, s 44(2).

6　[1994] 4 All ER 300, [1994] 2 BCLC 760, Ch D.

Later the receivers sought directions from the court as to whether they had 'adopted' the employees' contracts of employment; and if so whether their personal liability in respect of those contracts under IA 1986, s 44(1) could be legally excluded and, if it was not excluded, whether their liability under the contracts was co-extensive with that of the companies.

Lightman J held that the word 'adopted' in s 44 was to be given the special meaning of 'treated as continuing in force', that the receivers had adopted the employees' contracts of employment, that the receivers were personally liable on the adopted contracts, and that liability was co-extensive with that of the company and covered all liabilities (whenever incurred and of whatever kind) arising under the adopted contract of employment.

The effect of such a construction, as the House of Lords subsequently noted[7], would be to load a receivership with imponderable liabilities to employees whose employment was continued, thus making it extremely hazardous for the receivers to continue the business and militating against the rescue culture which Parliament had sought to encourage.

While an appeal to the House of Lords was pending, Parliament intervened (with respect to contracts adopted on or after 15 March 1994) in the form of the Insolvency Act 1994 to the effect outlined above, limiting the priority to claims incurred during the administrative receivership and restricting the claims to qualifying liabilities, essentially claims for wages, salary and contributions to a pension scheme[8].

However, the Insolvency Act 1994 did not attempt to define 'adopted' and so the appeal to the House of Lords must be considered for further illumination on this issue[9]. As the problem which arose here also arose with respect to administrators and their 'adoption' of contracts of employment, the appeal in *Re Leyland DAF Ltd; Re Ferranti International plc* was combined with an appeal from a Court of Appeal decision in respect of administration orders, *Powdrill v Watson*[10] and the combined appeal is reported as *Powdrill v Watson, Re Leyland DAF Ltd, Re Ferranti International plc*[11].

The House of Lords held that 'adopt' for these purposes connotes some conduct by an administrative receiver which amounts to an election to treat the continued contract of employment with the company as giving rise to a separate liability in the receivership[12]. It followed that if an administrative receiver caused the company to continue the employment of an employee for more than 14 days after his appointment the employee's contract of employment was inevitably adopted for the purposes of the Insolvency Act[13]. It was not open to an administrative receiver to avoid that result by unilaterally telling the employees that he was not adopting their contracts or was doing so only on terms[14]. The consequence of adoption under the statute is to give

7   *Powdrill v Watson* [1995] 2 AC 394 at 446, [1995] 2 All ER 65 at 78, HL.
8   For a succinct account of the issues and the history of the litigation leading up to the 1994 Act, see Fletcher *The Law of Insolvency* (1996), pp 373-379.
9   Both with regard to administrative receivers under IA 1986, s 44, but also other receivers as s 37 uses the same terminology.
10   [1994] 2 All ER 513, [1994] 2 BCLC 118, CA.
11   [1995] 2 AC 394, [1995] 2 All ER 65, HL.
12   [1995] 2 AC 394 at 449, [1995] 2 All ER 65 at 83d, HL.
13   [1995] 2 AC 394 at 450C, [1995] 2 All ER 65 at 84d, HL, per Lord Browne-Wilkinson. This is despite the fact that earlier Lord Browne-Wilkinson had said that mere continuance of the employment by the company does not lead inexorably to the conclusion that the contract had been adopted by the receiver: [1995] 2 AC 394 at 450C, [1995] 2 All ER 65 at 83a. The reasoning is not easy to follow in this case for the approach appears very similar to that of Lightman J in the lower court yet the House of Lords stated that the construction adopted by him 'cannot be correct' [1995] 2 AC 394 at 446E, [1995] 2 All ER 65 at 80j. Lightman J himself seems to have had some difficulty in following the reasoning of the House of Lords, a point made entertainingly by him in Lightman 'The Challenges Ahead: Address to the Insolvency Lawyers' Association' [1996] JBL 113 at 121-122.
14   [1995] 2 AC 394 at 452, [1995] 2 All ER 65 at 86.

priority only to qualifying liabilities incurred by the administrative receiver during the receivership.

POWERS OF ADMINISTRATIVE RECEIVERS

Schedule of powers

Once appointed, administrative receivers usually have extensive powers granted to them by the debenture and, in addition, the Insolvency Act 1986, Sch 1, specifically provides for a wide variety of powers which apply automatically except in so far as they are inconsistent with the provisions of the debenture[15]. These powers are extensive and identical to those available to an administrator (see discussion in Chapter 40) and include, inter alia, the power to take possession of, collect and get in the property of the company[16]; the power to sell or otherwise dispose of the property of the company; the power to carry on the business of the company; the power to raise or borrow money and grant security; the power to bring and defend any action or other legal proceedings; and the power to make any payment which is necessary or incidental to the performance of his functions. Note that a person dealing with an administrative receiver in good faith and for value is not concerned to inquire whether the receiver is acting within his powers[17].

Disposal of charged property

With the court's consent, an administrative receiver may dispose of any property subject to a security ranking in priority to the floating charge under which he is appointed as if it were not subject to the security where this would be likely to promote a more advantageous realisation of the company's assets than would otherwise be the case[18]. The sanction of the court will be conditional on the net proceeds of the disposal, or the open market value of the property if that is greater, being applied to discharging sums secured by the property[19].

Obligations to creditors

Where an administrative receiver is appointed, he must require some or all of the officers or other persons to make out and submit to him a statement as to the affairs of the company showing in particular, details of the company's assets, debts and liabilities, the names and addresses of its creditors and the securities which they hold[20]. He must within three months of his appointment send to the registrar of companies, to any trustees for secured creditors and to all such creditors a report of the events leading up to his appointment, the disposal by him of any property of the company and the carrying on of the business, the amounts due to the debenture holder by whom he was appointed

---

15   IA 1986, s 42(1), Sch 1.
16   See ibid, s 42(2)(b): ' references to the property of the company are to the property of which he is, or but for the appointment of some other person as the receiver of part of the company's property, would be the receiver or manager.'
17   Ibid, s 42(3).
18   Ibid, s 43(1). See discussion in Ch 40 of the similar but not identical power given to administrators.
19   Ibid, s 43(3).
20   Ibid, s 47(1)-(3).

and the amounts payable to the preferential creditors, and the amount, if any, likely to be available for the payment of other creditors[1]. The report must also be sent to all unsecured creditors or he must advertise an address at which they can obtain a copy free of charge; and he must lay a copy of the report before a meeting of the company's unsecured creditors[2] summoned for the purpose on not less than 14 days' notice, although he may seek a dispensation from holding this meeting from the court[3].

Miscellaneous powers

Administrative receivers have powers to get in the company's property, and to seek information about the company's affairs and to have the court summon to appear before it officers and others holding property of the company or with information about its affairs[4]. Administrative receivers are entitled to the maintenance of the supply of gas, electricity, water and telecommunications without having to pay the arrears which remain as a debt due from the company[5]. The administrative receiver may, however, be required personally to guarantee the payment of charges during the receivership[6].

An administrative receiver does not have the powers available to liquidators and administrators to challenge certain transactions at an undervalue[7], preferences[8], extortionate credit transactions[9] and certain floating charges[10], all of which are discussed in detail in Chapter 41. Nor do administrative receivers have power to seek contributions to the company's assets with respect to fraudulent or wrongful trading[11] but an administrative receiver does have to report on whether the directors' conduct may merit a disqualification order[12].

Vacation and removal from office

An administrative receiver can be removed from office by order of the court (but not otherwise)[13], or he can resign his office, and he must vacate his office where he ceases to be qualified to act as an insolvency practitioner[14], or on the making of an administration order[15]. Where an administrative receiver vacates office, he must within 14 days send a notice to that effect to the registrar of companies[16].

1   Ibid, s 48(1). The Cork Committee had noted the frequent complaint of creditors and shareholders of a lack of information once a receiver had been appointed: see the Cork Committee Report, para 438. These provisions are designed to rectify that problem. Receivers appointed out of court other than administrative receivers must deliver accounts at regular intervals to the registrar of companies: IA 1986, s 38.
2   As to the conduct of the meeting and the creditors' voting rights, see IR 1986, rr 3.9 - 3.15. A creditors' committee may also be established, rr 3.16-3.30A.
3   IA 1986, s 48(2).
4   Ibid, ss 234-237.
5   A similar privilege is extended to liquidators, administrators and supervisors of voluntary arrangements.
6   Ibid, s 233.
7   Ibid, s 238.
8   Ibid, s 239.
9   Ibid, s 244.
10   Ibid, s 245.
11   Ibid, ss 213, 214.
12   Company Directors Disqualification Act 1986, s 7(3)(d).
13   Again this provision is a result of a recommendation of the Cork Committee, see the Cork Committee Report, para 492, which thought this immunity from removal at the whim of his appointor would enhance the independence of the administrative receiver.
14   IA 1986, s 45(1), (2).
15   Ibid, s 11(1)(b).
16   Ibid, s 45(4).

Where at any time an administrative receiver vacates office, his remuneration and any expenses properly incurred by him and any indemnity to which he is entitled out of the company's assets are a charge on and must be paid out of any property of the company which is in his custody or under his control at that time in priority to any security held by the person by whom or on whose behalf he was appointed[17].

DUTIES OF RECEIVERS

As noted above, the receiver appointed out of court is usually the agent of the company either because of the terms of the instrument under which he is appointed or because he is an administrative receiver and deemed to be the company's agent by statute[18]. As was also noted, the agency relationship is unusual in that while the receiver is nominally the agent of the company, his primary duty is to realise the assets in the interests of the debenture holder and his powers of management are really ancillary to that duty[19]. Of particular interest, therefore is the extent of the receiver's duties, given his rather curious position.

Recently, there has been a salutary reminder by Ferris J in *Mirror Group Newspapers plc v Maxwell*[20] that office holders (whom he defines as administrators, liquidators, receivers, trustees in bankruptcy or other office holders who carry out insolvency work[1]) are fiduciaries charged with the duty of protecting, getting in, realising and ultimately passing on to others assets and property which belong not to themselves but to creditors or beneficiaries of one kind or another. Their fundamental obligation is a duty to account, both for the way in which they exercise their powers and for the property which they deal with[2]. The particular issue before the court in that case was the appropriate level of remuneration of receivers and on this he reminded office holders that as fiduciaries they are under an obligation not to profit from their position and they can only claim an allowance of remuneration as an exception to that rule where they can justify their claim[3].

Duties in realising the assets

Although the receiver's principal function is to realise the debenture holder's security, how this is achieved may be of concern to other creditors of the company and guarantors of the company's debts and ultimately to the members of the company. For example, company directors who have guaranteed the company's indebtedness to the bank may want to challenge the conduct of a receiver appointed by the bank when he realises £42,864 (with the costs of realisation coming to £42,718) leaving the bank unpaid which then turns to the guarantors to recover the debt[4]; or a guarantor may wish to challenge the receiver who sells specialist equipment for £34,500, when its true market value was £60,000, without taking specialist advice as to its value or advertising in the

17   Ibid, s 45(3).
18   Ibid, s 44(1)(a).
19   *Gomba Holdings UK Ltd v Homan* [1986] 3 All ER 94 at 97, [1986] BCLC 331 at 334.
20   [1998] BCC 324, Ch D.
1   This is a broader definition than that used in IA 1986, s 230.
2   [1998] BCC 324 at 333.
3   See Lightman 'Office Holders' charges - cost control and transparency' [1998] 11 Insolv Intell 1 on what he describes as this 'illuminating and far-reaching judgment' of Ferris J.
4   See *Standard Chartered Bank Ltd v Walker* [1982] 3 All ER 938, [1982] 1 WLR 1410, CA.

specialist press[5]; or a subsequent debenture holder may wish to challenge the conduct of the receiver appointed under a prior debenture where that receiver pursues a course of conduct detrimental to the interests of the subsequent debenture holders[6]. At issue then is the extent of the receiver's duties to such parties.

The position of a receiver was comprehensively addressed by Jenkins LJ in *Re B Johnson & Co (Builders) Ltd*[7], the facts of which are irrelevant for our purposes, where he emphasised the position of the receiver as a person whose primary duty is to the debenture holders and not to the company. He is a receiver and manager of the property of the company for the debenture holder and not manager for the company. He commits no breach of duty by refusing to carry on the company's business, even though the discontinuance may be detrimental from the company's point of view. Most importantly he concluded:

> If the company conceives that it has any claim against the receiver and manager for breach of some duty owed by him to the company, the issue is not whether the receiver and manager has done or omitted to do anything which it would be wrongful for a manager of a company to do or omit, but whether he has exceeded or abused or wrongfully omitted to use the special powers and discretions vested in him pursuant to the contract of loan constituted by the debenture for the special purpose of enabling the assets comprised in the debenture holder's security to be preserved and realised[8].

The key to the scope of his obligations then is to focus on the purpose of his appointment, and the exercise of his powers for the purpose of preserving and realising the security for payment of the debenture holder and, in the absence of fraud or mala fides, the company could not complain of acts by him in pursuance of that purpose[9].

A receiver is free therefore to decide whether to carry on the company's business or whether to close it down and sell off the assets; and in selling the assets the receiver is free to choose when to sell and is not obliged to wait while the market rises[10]. In conducting the sale, however, the receiver does owe a duty to the mortgagor and guarantors to take reasonable care to obtain the proper price or true market value on the date of the sale[11]. Furthermore, if the purchaser is a company controlled by the receiver the burden of proof will be on the receiver to show that reasonable care was taken[12].

Any duties mortgagees or receivers appointed to realise mortgaged property may owe are governed by principles of equity[13] rather than the common law and are of older origin than the duty of care in negligence at common law recognised in *Donoghue v*

---

5   See *American Express International Banking Corpn v Hurley* [1985] 3 All ER 564, [1986] BCLC 52.
6   See *Downsview Nominees Ltd v First City Corpn Ltd* [1993] AC 295, [1993] 3 All ER 626, PC.
7   [1955] Ch 634, [1955] 2 All ER 775, CA.
8   [1955] Ch 634 at 662-663, [1955] 2 All ER 775 at 791, CA. This passage was endorsed by the Privy Council in *Downsview Nominees Ltd v First City Corpn Ltd* [1993] AC 295 at 313-314, [1993] 3 All ER 626 at 636, PC.
9   [1955] Ch 634 at 662, [1955] 2 All ER 775 at 791, CA.
10   *Cuckmere Brick Co Ltd v Mutual Finance Ltd* [1971] Ch 949, [1971] 2 All ER 633, CA. Conversely a receiver who chooses to wait will not be liable if the value of the security declines: *China and South Sea Bank Ltd v Tan Soon Gin* [1990] 1 AC 536, [1989] 3 All ER 839, PC.
11   *Cuckmere Brick Co Ltd v Mutual Finance Ltd* [1971] Ch 949, [1971] 2 All ER 633, CA; *Standard Chartered Bank Ltd v Walker* [1982] 3 All ER 938, [1982] 1 WLR 1410, CA; *American Express International Banking Corpn v Hurley* [1985] 3 All ER 564, [1986] BCLC 52.
12   *Farrar v Farrars Ltd* (1888) 40 Ch D 395, CA; *Tse Kwong Lam v Wong Chit Sen* [1983] 3 All ER 54, [1983] 1 WLR 1349, PC.
13   *Downsview Nominees Ltd v First City Corpn Ltd* [1993] AC 295, [1993] 3 All ER 626, PC; *China and South Sea Bank Ltd v Tan Soon Gin* [1990] 1 AC 536, [1989] 3 All ER 839, PC.

Stevenson[14]. Nevertheless, in a number of decisions on the mortgagee's position and the receiver's duties, such as *Standard Chartered Bank Ltd v Walker*[15] and *American Express International Banking Corpn v Hurley*[16], there was a tendency to identify and describe their duties, as in *Standard Chartered Bank Ltd v Walker*[17], as part of the general 'neighbour' duty of care developed in the law of negligence since *Donoghue v Stevenson*.

However, a comprehensive rejection of broad duties of care drawn from the general law of negligence has been delivered by the Privy Council in *Downsview Nominees Ltd v First City Corpn Ltd*[18]. While in theory such a case is only highly persuasive, in effect it signals the determination of the House of Lords, in this area as in others, to rein in the unrestricted expansion of the law of negligence[19]. The case arose out a dispute between a first and second debenture holder. At issue was the extent of the duties owed by the first debenture holder and the receiver and manager appointed under that debenture to the second debenture holder. In addressing that issue, the Privy Council offered some definitive guidance as to the scope of the receiver's duties as follows[20]:

> A mortgagee, whether under a legal or equitable mortgage created by a charge on property or under a debenture issued by a company for its debts owed a duty to the mortgagor and to all subsequent incumbrancers of the mortgaged property to act in good faith for the special purpose of enabling the assets comprised in the security for the debt to be preserved and realised for the purpose of obtaining repayment of the debt.
>
> That duty was owed both to the mortgagor and to any subsequent incumbrancers because if the mortgagee committed a breach of his duties to the mortgagor, the damage inflicted by that breach of duty would be suffered by any subsequent incumbrancers and the mortgagor depending on the extent of the damage and the amount of each security.
>
> However, provided that a receiver and manager appointed under a debenture acted in good faith for the purpose of enabling the assets comprised in the debenture holder's security to be preserved and realised for the benefit of the debenture holder, his decisions could not be impeached even if they were disadvantageous to the company or other incumbrancers, and he was subject to no further or greater liability.
>
> In particular, he owed no general duty of care in negligence since if such a duty were to be imposed that would be inconsistent with the specific duties which the courts, applying equitable principles, had imposed on a mortgagee and which permitted him to manage the company without risk of suit instead of merely selling the assets as quickly as possible to repay the mortgage debt.

Essentially then a receiver must exercise his powers in good faith for the purpose of obtaining repayment of the debt owing to his mortgagee and in particular there is no general duty to use reasonable care in dealing with the assets of the company. The duties owed by the receiver do not compel him to any particular course of action but since a mortgage, or charge or debenture, is only a security for a debt, he will commit

---

14   [1932] AC 562, HL.
15   [1982] 3 All ER 938, [1982] 1 WLR 1410, CA.
16   [1985] 3 All ER 564, [1986] BCLC 52.
17   [1982] 3 All ER 938 at 942, [1982] 1 WLR 1410 at 1415, CA.
18   [1993] AC 295, [1993] 3 All ER 626, PC. See Doyle 'The Receiver's Duty on a Sale of Charged Assets' [1997] 10 Insolv Intell 9; Berg 'Duties of a Mortgagee and a Receiver' [1993] JBL 213.
19   [1993] AC 295 at 316, [1993] 3 All ER 626 at 638.
20   [1993] AC 295 at 311-316, [1993] 3 All ER 626 at 634-638.

a breach of duty if he abuses his powers by exercising them otherwise than 'for the special purpose of enabling the assets comprised in the debenture holder's security to be preserved and realised' for the benefit of the debenture holder[1]. This does not mean that he must immediately upon appointment seize and sell so much of the assets as are sufficient to complete the redemption of the mortgage. As Lord Templeman noted:

> He [the receiver] is entitled, but not bound, to allow the company's business to be continued by himself or by the existing or other executives. The decisions of the receiver and manager whether to continue the business or close down the business and sell assets chosen by him cannot be impeached if those decisions are taken in good faith while protecting the interests of the debenture holder in recovering moneys due under the debenture, even though the decisions of the receiver and manager may be disadvantageous for the company[2].

If he decides to sell[3], the receiver remains subject to a duty to take reasonable care to obtain a proper price[4].

Not everyone has welcomed the approach adopted by the Privy Council in this case. Obviously, for insolvency practitioners acting as receivers there is relief at the limiting of their obligations and such limitation, in the opinion of Lord Templeman, will contribute to certainty and actually a better system as receivers will not conduct their affairs under the threat of negligence actions. On the other hand, *Downsview* reinforces the traditional idea of receivership as essentially a private remedy between a creditor and a debtor requiring only limited glances by the receiver at the other parties, other creditors, guarantors and members of the company, for example, standing in the wings. The tunnel vision which this permits in a receiver rather diminishes any concept of receivership as one of a number of insolvency procedures available which contribute to a 'rescue culture'. Indeed Lightman J, extra-judicially, has described the decision in *Downsview Nominees* as 'the most retrograde step in recent times creating a hole in the rescue culture' and he hopes that the courts 'will muster the courage to dismiss *Downsview* as an aberration'[5].

Duty to pay preferential creditors

Where a receiver is appointed under a charge which, as created, was a floating charge then, if the company is not at the time in the course of being wound up, IA 1986, s 40 provides that the preferential debts[6] must be paid out of assets coming to the hands of the receiver in priority to any claims for principal or interest in respect of the debentures[7]. If the remaining assets subject to the floating charge are insufficient to

---

1   [1993] AC 295 at 314, [1993] 3 All ER 626 at 636.
2   [1993] AC 295 at 312-313, [1993] 3 All ER 626 at 635.
3   See *China and South Sea Bank Ltd v Tan Soon Gin* [1990] 1 AC 536, [1989] 3 All ER 839, PC (a creditor is not under a duty to exercise his power of sale at any particular time or at all). See also *Routestone Ltd v Minories Finance Ltd, Routestone Ltd v Bird* [1997] BCC 180.
4   *Cuckmere Brick Co Ltd v Mutual Finance Ltd* [1971] Ch 949, [1971] 2 All ER 633, CA; *Downsview Nominees Ltd v First City Corpn Ltd* [1993] AC 295, [1993] 3 All ER 626, PC.
5   Lightman 'The Challenges Ahead: Address to the Insolvency Lawyers' Association' [1996] JBL 113 at 119-120.
6   Defined IA 1986, s 386 and Sch 6. See discussion Chapter 41.
7   Ibid, s 40(1), (2). See also CA 1985, s 196 (debenture holder taking possession without appointment of receiver); IA 1986, s 175(2)(b) (position on liquidation). Note also s 11(5) re position of receivers who vacate office on the making of an administration order.

pay the debenture holder in full, the debenture holder is recouped out of assets available for payment of the general creditors[8].

Failure to pay the preferential creditors in priority makes the receiver personally liable to them for breach of statutory duty[9] and in certain circumstances the debenture holder can also become liable[10]. If, however, the debenture holder's debt is also secured by a fixed charge and is fully paid out of the proceeds of the fixed charge alone then no preferential debts arise[11].

The significance of IA 1986, s 40 was considered in *Re Pearl Maintenance Services Ltd, Re Pearl Building Contracts Ltd*[12] where there was a dispute as to whether a charge described as fixed was in fact floating and whether, given that the claim of the debenture holder had been satisfied, the receiver nevertheless was under a duty to the preferential creditors under s 40. The correct approach to the section was succinctly stated by Carnwath J:

> The cases show that s 40 creates a positive duty (not merely a restriction) in favour of the preferential creditors, and that it is a duty enforceable by action in tort for damages .... Thus it is a duty which creates statutory private rights, enforceable as such by preferential creditors.... Thus, although the receiver starts as the appointee of the debenture holder, statute imposes upon him a duty to the preferential holders which is capable of having a separate life of its own. It does not cease merely because the debenture holder is satisfied. The receiver remains under a duty to meet the claims of the preferential creditors, so far as can be done out of floating charge assets[13].

A further issue has been whether the wording of the section simply requires the receiver to pay the preferential creditors in priority to the claims of the debenture under which he was appointed or whether they must be paid in priority to any debenture secured by a charge which, as created, was a floating charge.

This problem arose in *Re H & K (Medway) Ltd, Mackay v IRC*[14] where the company had granted two floating charges, one to Ford and one to 3i, with the debenture to Ford having priority. 3i appointed a receiver and the issue was whether sums realised by the receiver should be paid under IA 1986, s 40 to the preferential creditors or to Ford, being a debenture holder with priority over 3i. The key wording in the section was that which said the preferential creditors must be paid out 'of assets coming to the hands of the receiver in priority to any claims for principal or interest in respect of *the debentures*'.

The court declined to follow an earlier ruling on this issue, *Griffiths v Yorkshire Bank plc*[15], and concluded that the payment to the preferential creditors must be in priority to any claim for principal or interest in respect of any debenture of the company which, as created, was a floating charge. Therefore the preferential creditors were to be paid in priority to Ford.

---

8   Ibid, s 40(3).
9   *Westminster City Council v Haste* [1950] Ch 442, [1950] 2 All ER 65.
10   *IRC v Goldblatt* [1972] Ch 498, [1972] 2 All ER 202.
11   *Re G L Saunders Ltd* [1986] 1 WLR 215, [1986] BCLC 40. Where a floating charge has priority over a fixed charge because of a ranking agreement among the parties, then the preferential creditors will take priority over both: see *Re Portbase Clothing Ltd* [1993] Ch 388, [1993] 3 All ER 829.
12   [1995] 1 BCLC 449, [1995] BCC 657.
13   [1995] 1 BCLC 449 at 457, [1995] BCC 657 at 663-664.
14   [1997] 1 BCLC 545, Ch D.
15   [1994] 1 WLR 1427. The court noted in particular that the preferential creditors were not represented before the court in *Griffiths* and also questioned the accuracy of the report of the decision in that case: see [1997] 1 BCLC 545 at 554.

While this appears a rather forced construction of the wording of s 40, the court was concerned, in particular, about the practical consequences of any alternative approach. Where there were a number of floating charges over a company's assets, whether or not the preferential creditors have priority would depend simply on which chargee appointed a receiver. This might lead to second charges being executed in favour of a nominee in order to have the receiver appointed under the second charge or it might lead to debenture holders coming together to make sure that the lowest ranking one appoints the receiver so ensuring all the other charges took free of s 40[16]. Certainly a construction, albeit a forced one, which avoided those consequences seems preferable and more in keeping with Parliament's intention to give priority to the preferential creditors.

Enforcement of duties

During the receivership the duty owed by the receiver to the company is enforceable in proceedings brought by the company, not by a derivative action brought by individual shareholders[17]. If the company is put into liquidation, then the summary procedure under the Insolvency Act 1986, s 212 (discussed in Chapter 41) will be available against administrative receivers though not against any other type of receiver[18].

---

16   [1997] 1 BCLC 545 at 550.
17   *Watts v Midland Bank plc* [1986] BCLC 15.
18   Cf *Re B Johnson & Co (Builders) Ltd* [1955] Ch 634, [1955] 2 All ER 775, CA.

CHAPTER 40

Administration orders and voluntary arrangements

ADMINISTRATION ORDERS

Introduction

The Cork Committee[1] considered the power to appoint a receiver and manager of the whole property and undertaking of a company to be an aspect of the floating charge which was of outstanding benefit to the general public and society as a whole because of the possibility it offered of restoring an ailing enterprise to profitability or of disposing of the whole or part of the business as a going concern[2]. In either case, the preservation of the profitable parts of the enterprise was of advantage to the employees, the commercial community and the general public. However, the Committee noted that in the absence of such an appointment, there being no floating charge, directors of an insolvent but potentially viable company had no practical options open to them under the law as it then stood other than to cease trading[3].

Accordingly, the Cork Committee proposed that in all cases, whether or not there was a floating charge in existence, provision should be made to enable a person called an administrator to be appointed whenever the circumstances justify such a course, with all the powers normally conferred upon a receiver and manager under a floating charge, including power to carry on the business of the company and to borrow for that purpose[4]. The administration order procedure will therefore be of particular benefit where there is no floating charge or where for one reason or another the holder of a floating charge is reluctant to appoint an administrative receiver[5]. The proposal was accepted by the Government and provisions for the appointment of an administrator are now contained in the Insolvency Act 1986, Pt II.

---

1   *Report of the Review Committee on Insolvency Law and Practice* (1982, Cmnd 8558); hereafter the Cork Committee Report.
2   The Cork Committee Report, para 495.
3   The Cork Committee Report, para 496.
4   The Cork Committee Report, para 497.
5   See the Cork Committee Report, para 503; see also Nicholls LJ in *Re Atlantic Computer Systems plc* [1992] Ch 505 at 525, [1992] 1 All ER 476 at 487.

An administration order is a court order that, for the duration of the order, the affairs, business and property of a company shall be managed by an administrator appointed by the court[6].

Essentially the purpose of an administration order is to provide a breathing space, a short-term intensive care operation, as it has been described[7], free from the pressure of creditors' claims. This is achieved by imposing a moratorium on those claims. The administrator can consider whether the business can profitably be rescued or whether it should be broken up and can negotiate with creditors regarding any possible arrangement or composition[8]. Rescue is not guaranteed, of course, and it may be that, despite the administration order, the company ultimately goes into winding up.

Finally, it should be noted that despite the case for the introduction of an administration procedure, it remains significantly under-used when compared with other insolvency procedures. This can be seen clearly if we compare the figures notified to the registrar of companies for administration orders and receiverships over the past five years[9]:

	Administration	Receiverships
1992-93	170	8,747
1993-94	128	4,870
1994-95	173	3,740
1995-96	161	3,237
1996-97	216	2,591

Some of the difficulties in using the procedure will become apparent as we consider the different elements of the scheme. Proposals for further reforms to improve the rescue options available to companies, and especially to smaller companies, are considered at the end of this chapter.

Petitioning for an administration order

An application for an administration order is begun by a petition presented to the court either by the company or the directors[10], or by a creditor or creditors, or by the supervisor of a voluntary arrangement[11]. The company must not have gone into liquidation[12], nor be in administrative receivership (a point considered further below) unless the debenture

---

6   IA 1986, s 8(2). See generally, Prentice, Oditah, Segal 'Administration: The Insolvency Act 1986, Part II' (1994) LMCLQ 487.

7   See Harman J in *Re Business Properties Ltd* (1988) 4 BCC 684 at 686.

8   'Rescue' mechanisms have become an accepted and important aspect of insolvency procedures and many overseas jurisdictions have provisions, in some cases similar to, in others quite different from, administration. See generally Ziegel *Current Developments in International and Comparative Corporate Insolvency Law* (1994), chs 5-11.

9   See DTI *Companies in 1996-97* (1997), Table C2.

10   Either by the directors unanimously or by a board resolution which may be agreed to by a majority of the directors: *Re Equiticorp International plc* [1989] 1 WLR 1010, [1989] BCLC 597. See *Re Land and Property Trust Co plc (No 4)* [1994] 1 BCLC 232, sub nom *Re Land and Property Trust Co plc (No 2)* [1993] BCC 462, CA; also *Re Tajik Air Ltd* [1996] 1 BCLC 317, [1996] BCC 368; *Re Gosscott (Groundworks) Ltd* (1988) 4 BCC 372 on the issue of costs.

11   IA 1986, ss 9(1), 7(4)(b); IR 1986, rr 2.1-2.10. Note that the members as individuals have no right to petition for administration, unless through a resolution of the company in general meeting.

12   IA 1986, s 8(4); the date of going into liquidation is defined in s 247(2) as the date on which the company passes a resolution for voluntary winding up or the date on which the court makes an order for winding up where the company has not previously passed a resolution for winding up.

holder consents to the appointment of an administrator and the receiver vacates his position or the debenture itself is liable to be avoided[13].

The Cork Committee regarded the right of the directors to apply for an order as being of fundamental importance[14]. Given their potential liability for wrongful trading[15], it was important that they should be able to initiate administration which would reduce the possibility of them being so liable.

THE MORATORIUM

Merely making the application ensures that the status quo is preserved regarding the company's assets while the hearing is pending[16]. This ability to secure a moratorium which, as we shall see, continues once an order is made is one of the most important features of administration. Thus, during the period beginning with the presentation of the petition until the making of the order or the dismissal of the petition:

(a) no resolution may be passed or order made for the winding up of the company;

(b) no steps may be taken to enforce any security over the company's property, or to repossess goods in the company's possession under any hire-purchase agreement[17], except with the leave of the court and subject to such terms as the court may impose; and

(c) no other proceedings and no execution or other legal process may be commenced or continued, and no distress may be levied, against the company or its property except with the leave of the court and subject to such terms as aforesaid[18].

Leave of the court is not required to present a petition for the winding up of the company[19] or to appoint an administrative receiver[20].

RELATIONSHIP WITH ADMINISTRATIVE RECEIVERSHIP

As noted above, a petition for administration will be dismissed where the company is already in administrative receivership unless the debenture holder consents to the appointment of an administrator and the receiver vacates his position or the debenture itself is liable to be avoided[1]. Likewise, even if the company is not yet in administrative receivership, anyone entitled to do so may proceed to appoint an administrative receiver following the presentation of the petition and, if they decide to do so, that right prevails

---

13   Ibid, s 9(3); avoided under ss 238-240 or s 245.
14   See the Cork Committee Report, para 501.
15   Under IA 1986, s 214, discussed in detail in Ch 41.
16   Ibid, s 10(1).
17   References to hire-purchase agreements include conditional sale, chattel lease and retention of title agreements: ibid, s 10(4).
18   Ibid, s 10(1).
19   Ibid, s 10(2)(a). This will enable the court to consider the respective merits of winding up or administration.
20   Ibid, s 10(2)(b).
1   Ibid, s 9(3). A holder of a floating charge who has appointed or who has power to appoint an administrative receiver must therefore be served, not less than five days before the date fixed for the hearing, with notice of the petition, as must the company: s 9(2)(a); IR 1986, rr 2.6(2), 2.7(1); see also *Re a Company (No 00175 of 1987)* [1987] BCLC 467, (1987) 3 BCC 124. Other creditors are not notified at this stage, however, the idea being to avoid a protracted hearing.

over any application for an administration order[2]. In fact, holders of fixed charges may also taken a nominal floating charge (a so-called lightweight floating charge over negligible assets) in order to be in a position to prevent the making of an administration order by putting the company into administrative receivership[3].

An initial tactical issue, therefore, for a creditor in that position is to decide whether he is happy to forego his right to appoint an administrative receiver and to go along with the administration order. In reaching that decision, he needs to appreciate that, as we shall see, his ability to realise his security will be significantly curtailed by the appointment of an administrator[4]; and that once an administration order is made no administrative receiver may then be appointed[5]. These are mutually exclusive procedures and a company can be in administrative receivership or administration but it cannot be in both at the same time.

CONVINCING THE COURT

For an administration order to be made, the court must be satisfied that the company is, or is likely to become, unable to pay its debts[6]. Furthermore, the court must consider that the making of an administration order would be likely to achieve (meaning 'a real prospect'[7]) one or more of the following purposes[8]:

(a) the survival of the company, and the whole or any part of its undertaking, as a going concern;

(b) the approval of a voluntary arrangement under Part I of the Insolvency Act[9];

(c) the sanctioning of a scheme of arrangement under the Companies Act, s 425[10]; and

(d) a more advantageous realisation of the company's assets than would be effected on a winding up[11].

To assist to convince the court that there is a real prospect of one or more of these purposes being achieved, it is common to provide a detailed independent report along with the petition[12]. This is usually drawn up by the would-be administrator. In part, the need to prepare such a detailed report has contributed to the high costs of administration although the courts have tried to reduce the length and therefore the

2   IA 1986, s 10(2)(b). Care must be taken to ensure that the power to appoint an administrative receiver under a debenture arises upon the issue of a petition for an administration order.
3   See *Re Croftbell Ltd* [1990] BCLC 844, [1990] BCC 781; Oditah 'Lightweight Floating Charges' [1991] JBL 49.
4   See Fletcher *The Law of Insolvency* (1996), p 429 who reviews the options at this stage.
5   IA 1986, s 11(3)(b).
6   Ibid, s 8(1)(a); ie unable to pay its debts within the meaning of s 123, see discussion of that provision in Ch 41.
7   *Re Harris Simons Construction Ltd* [1989] 1 WLR 368, [1989] BCLC 202; see also *Re Rowbotham Baxter Ltd* [1990] BCLC 397, [1990] BCC 113; *Re SCL Building Services Ltd* [1990] BCLC 98, 5 BCC 746; *Re Primlaks (UK) Ltd* [1989] BCLC 734, 5 BCC 710. A stricter test ('more probably than not') suggested in *Re Consumer and Industrial Press Ltd* [1988] BCLC 177, 4 BCC 68 has been rejected.
8   IA 1986, s 8(1)(b).
9   See ibid, ss 1-7, discussed in detail below.
10   Discussed in detail in Ch 36.
11   IA 1986, s 8(3); and the order must specify the purpose or purposes of which it is made: ibid. The administrator may at any time apply to the court to have the order varied so as to specify an additional purpose: s 18(1). While the Act does not impose a time limit on the length of administration, it is customary to limit the order initially to a three-month period.
12   See IR 1986, r 2.2. See also Oditah 'Administration: The Insolvency Act 1986, Part II' (1994) LMCLQ 487 at 498-499.

costs of the reports in order that costs should not operate as a disincentive or put the process out of reach of smaller companies[13].

It must be remembered that even if satisfied that there is a real prospect that one or more of the specified purposes will be achieved, the court still has a discretion whether to make an order and will not do so in cases where, weighing all the circumstances, it seems inappropriate[14]. In approaching this issue, the interests of secured creditors will carry less weight than those of other creditors[15].

Effect of an administration order

Where an administration order is made, the court appoints the administrator[16] who must be a qualified insolvency practitioner[17]. On his appointment, the administrator must call for a statement as to the affairs of the company[18] and takes into his custody or under his control all the property of the company[19]. On the making of an administration order, any petition for the winding up of the company must be dismissed; and any administrative receiver must vacate office[20].

RELATIONSHIP WITH DIRECTORS

The administrator effectively replaces the directors in the management of the business, given that all power to manage the business is vested in him[1] although the directors do not vacate office and therefore remain subject to their usual range of duties, including their statutory obligations to file documents with the registrar of companies. However, any power conferred on the company or its officers which could be exercised in such a way as to interfere with the exercise by the administrator of his powers is not exercisable except with the consent of the administrator[2]. Note in particular that the administrator has power to remove any director of the company and to appoint any person to be a director of it, whether to fill a vacancy or otherwise[3].

---

13   See Practice Note [1994] 1 All ER 324, sub nom Practice Statement [1994] 1 WLR 160. See also The Insolvency Service *The Insolvency Act 1986, Company Voluntary Arrangements and Administration Orders, A Consultative Document* (October 1993), paras 5.2.- 5.3 on the issue of the costs involved in securing an order.

14   *Re Harris Simons Construction Ltd* [1989] 1 WLR 368, [1989] BCLC 202; also *Re Imperial Motors (UK) Ltd* [1990] BCLC 29, 5 BCC 214 (order refused because on balance it was not a suitable case: petitioning creditor was full secured); see also *Re Arrows Ltd (No 3)* [1992] BCLC 555, [1992] BCC 131.

15   *Re Consumer and Industrial Press Ltd* [1988] BCLC 177, 4 BCC 68.

16   On being appointed the administrator must send a notice of the administration order to the company with a copy to every creditor, and a copy of the order must be sent to the registrar of companies: IA 1986, s 21. This will be the first time the majority of creditors formally hear anything about the administration given that there is no procedure for the petition to be advertised. See also s 12 (notification of order on invoices, orders, and business letters).

17   Ibid, s 230(1).

18   Ibid, s 22.

19   Ibid, s 17(1)

20   Ibid, s 11(1). Any receiver of part of the company's property must vacate on being asked to do so by the administrator: s 11(2).

1   See ibid, s 14(1).

2   Ibid, s 14(4).

3   Ibid, s 14(2)(a).

PROPOSALS TO CREDITORS

Once the administration order is made, the administrator, within three months, must draw up proposals as to how to achieve the purpose or purposes for which the order was made and must call a meeting of the creditors to consider the proposals[4]. The meeting may approve or decline to approve the proposals but may only modify the proposals if the administrator consents to each modification[5].

For the proposals to be accepted, they must be accepted by a majority in value of the creditors present and voting, in person or by proxy[6]; but any resolution is invalid if those voting against it include more than half in value of the creditors to whom notice of the meeting was sent and who are not, to the best of the chairman's belief, persons connected with the company[7].

The result of the meeting is reported to the court and to the registrar of companies but here is no hearing and, in particular, no requirement for the court to approve the proposals[8]. If the report is that the creditors have declined to approve the proposals, then the court may discharge the administration order, or adjourn the hearing, or make any other order that it thinks fit[9].

The remedy of any creditor, or member, who feels aggrieved by the approval of the proposals is to petition the court on the grounds that the company's affairs, business and property are being managed in an unfairly prejudicial way[10], discussed below.

If subsequently, in the course of the administration, the administrator wishes to revise his proposals, then he is required again to go through this process of presenting the proposals to the creditors and having them approved[11].

Powers of the administrator

In exercising his powers, the administrator is deemed to act as the company's agent and he is not personally liable on any contracts entered into during the administration[12]. The appointment of an administrator in itself has no effect on existing contracts of the company and, subject to the need to obtain the court's consent for proceedings, any right to specific performance, lien, set-off, rescission or injunction available against the company before administration continues to be available against the company in administration[13].

---

4   Ibid, s 23(1). See *Re Consumer and Industrial Press Ltd (No 2)* (1988) 4 BCC 72 on the importance of presenting the proposals to the creditors' meeting. The administrator must also send a copy of the proposals to the registrar of companies, to every creditor and to every member or must advertise where members may obtain a copy free of charge: IA 1986, s 23.
5   Ibid, s 24(2).
6   IR 1986, r 2.28(1). Votes are calculated according to the amount of the creditor's debt as at the date of the administration order, deducting any amounts paid in respect of the debt after that date: r 2.22(4). A secured creditor is entitled to vote only in respect of the balance of his debt after deducting the value of his security as estimated by him: r 2.24.
7   Ibid, r 2.28(1A).
8   IA 1986, s 24(4); IR 1986 r 2.29.
9   IA 1986, s 24(5).
10   Ibid, s 27.
11   Ibid, s 25.
12   Ibid, s 14(5). But see also s 19(5), (6). Note also s 14(6): a person dealing with the administrator in good faith and for value is not concerned to inquire whether the administrator is acting within his powers.
13   *Astor Chemicals Ltd v Synthetic Technology Ltd* [1990] BCLC 1, [1990] BCC 97. See also *Re P & C and R & T (Stockport) Ltd* [1991] BCLC 366, [1991] BCC 980.

In order to put the proposals into effect the administrator is empowered to do all such things as may be necessary for the management of the affairs, business and property of the company[14]; and an administrator also has the powers set out in Sch 1 to the Insolvency Act. These powers are extensive and include, inter alia, the power to take possession of, collect and get in the property of the company; the power to sell or otherwise dispose of the property of the company; the power to carry on the business of the company; the power to raise or borrow money and grant security; the power to bring and defend any action or other legal proceedings; and the power to make any payment which is necessary or incidental to the performance of his functions.

An issue which has arisen with respect to this power to make any payment which is necessary or incidental to the performance of his functions has been whether this enables an administrator to make distributions to creditors. In general this has always been achieved through a voluntary arrangement or scheme of arrangement[15] but in *Re WBSL Realisations 1992 Ltd, Re Ward Group plc*[16], in the special circumstances of the case, the court permitted such distributions to creditors on the basis of a notional winding up at the date of the administration order where otherwise there would have been significant prejudice to the creditors and because there was no significant or practical risk of other creditors emerging later. However, as was confirmed in *Re Powerstore (Trading) Ltd, Re Homepower Stores Ltd*[17], this power is only exercisable to advance the purposes for which the administration order was made. A distribution was not possible in *Re Powerstore (Trading) Ltd* where the proposed payment to creditors was not for the purpose of a more advantageous realisation of the company's assets but simply a more advantageous method of distribution of the company's assets.

Although the creditors' meeting is supposed to decide whether the administrator's proposals are implemented or not, it may happen that the administrator must decide at short notice whether to accept an offer for the company's business. In such circumstances, the best approach is for the administrator to apply to the court to sanction the sale under the court's power to give directions to the administrator[18].

In selling a business, the administrator owes a duty to the company to take reasonable care, judged by the standard of the ordinary skilled insolvency practitioner, to obtain the best price that the circumstances permitted, including a duty to take reasonable care in choosing the time at which to sell the property[19].

LIMITS TO PROPRIETARY RIGHTS

One of the problems the administrator may face in carrying on the company's business or selling it as a going concern is that some of the assets used by the company may be subject to security interests; others may not be owned by the company as, for example, where they are the subject of hire-purchase or conditional sale agreements. Here the administrator will be helped by the Insolvency Act 1986, s 11(3) which continues and

---

14   IA 1986, s 14(1).
15   See *Re St Ives Windings Ltd* (1987) 3 BCC 634; see also *Re Business Properties Ltd* (1988) 4 BCC 684: an administrator cannot achieve the realisation and distribution required to conclude a company's affairs.
16   [1995] 2 BCLC 576, [1995] BCC 1118. See also *Re John Slack Ltd* [1995] BCC 1116.
17   [1998] 1 BCLC 90. See Brown [1998] JBL 75.
18   See *Re Consumer and Industrial Press Ltd (No 2)* (1987) 4 BCC 72 (an administrator who has decided to sell the entire undertaking in advance of the creditors' meeting should obtain the sanction of the court). Cf *Re Charnley Davies Business Services Ltd* (1987) 3 BCC 408. See also *Re NS Distribution Ltd* [1990] BCLC 169 (directions of the court need not be sought for mere disposal of one asset of the company).
19   *Re Charnley Davies Ltd (No 2)* [1990] BCLC 760, [1990] BCC 605.

extends the moratorium initiated by the presentation of the petition[20]. Section 11(3) provides that, while the administration order is in force:

(a) no resolution may be passed or order made for the winding up of the company;

(b) no administrative receiver may be appointed;

(c) no other steps may be taken to enforce any security[1] over the company's property, or to repossess goods in the company's possession[2] under any hire-purchase agreement[3], except with the consent of the administrator or the leave of the court and subject to such terms as the court may impose; and

(d) no other proceedings and no execution or other legal process[4] may be commenced or continued, and no distress may be levied, against the company or its property except with the consent of the administrator or the leave of the court and subject to such terms as aforesaid[5].

The effect is that owners of property, and charges over property, are disabled from exercising their proprietary rights unless the administrator consents or the court gives leave[6]. However, the moratorium is just that, a moratorium on the enforcement of the creditor's right, but it does not affect the substantive right of the creditor[7].

'Proceedings' refers to proceedings by creditors to enforce their debts and does not include the hearing of an application to revoke an airline's air transport licence[8]. Nor is an application for the late registration of a charge within the mischief the section is aimed at although such applications are subject to the court's discretion in any case[9]. However, it does include proceedings against the company before an industrial tribunal brought by an employee[10].

The leave of the court   In *Royal Trust Bank v Buchler*[11] the court noted that its discretion to grant leave under s 11(3) is a general discretion which requires it to have

20   IA 1986, s 10(1).
1   'Security' is defined as 'any mortgage, charge, lien or other security': ibid, s 248. In *Bristol Airport plc v Powdrill* [1990] Ch 744, [1990] 2 All ER 493, CA, 'security' was held to include the exercise of a statutory lien, in this case the right of an airport to detain aircraft for unpaid airport charges under the Civil Aviation Act 1982; see also *Re Sabre International Products Ltd* [1991] BCLC 470, [1991] BCC 694 (enforcement of a lien). Likewise, a landlord's exercise of his right of re-entry for non-payment of rent constituted a step in the enforcement of a 'security' for these purposes: *Exchange Travel Agency Ltd v Triton Property Trust plc* [1991] BCLC 396, [1991] BCC 341.
2   In *David Meek Plant Ltd, Re David Meek Access Ltd* [1994] 1 BCLC 680, [1993] BCC 175 the court found goods to be 'in the company's possession under a hire-purchase agreement' although the hire-purchase agreement had terminated: it was sufficient that the possession was attributable to or derived from a hire-purchase agreement at some time, not necessarily one still subsisting; see also *Re Atlantic Computer Systems plc* [1992] Ch 505, [1992] 1 All ER 476, CA: equipment held by a company on hire-purchase was in the company's possession for the purposes of IA 1986, s 11(3)(c) whether the equipment remains on the company's premises, is entrusted to others for repair, or is sub-let by the company as part of its trade with others.
3   The Act refers to hire-purchase agreements but included in this term are conditional sale agreements, chattel leasing agreements and retention of title agreements: ibid, s 10(4).
4   See *Re Olympia & York Canary Wharf Ltd* [1993] BCLC 453, sub nom *Re Olympia & York Canary Wharf Ltd, American Express Europe Ltd v Adamson* [1993] BCC 154 (legal process means a process which requires the assistance of the court and does not extend to the service of a contractual notice which renders time of the essence or terminates a contract by reason of the company's anticipatory breach).
5   IA 1986, s 11(3).
6   *Re Atlantic Computer Systems plc* [1992] Ch 505 at 527, [1992] 1 All ER 476 at 488, CA, per Nicholls LJ.
7   *Barclays Mercantile Business Finance Ltd v Sibec Developments* [1993] 2 All ER 195, [1992] 1 WLR 1253.
8   *Air Ecosse v Civil Aviation Authority* (1987) 3 BCC 492, 1987 SLT 751.
9   *Re Barrow Borough Transport Ltd* [1990] Ch 227, [1989] BCLC 653.
10 *Carr v British International Helicopters Ltd* [1994] 2 BCLC 474, [1993] BCC 855.
11 [1989] BCLC 130, sub nom *Re Meesan Investments Ltd* (1988) 4 BCC 788, Ch D.

regard to all the relevant circumstances. Having regard to those circumstances, it could be appropriate for a secured creditor to be given leave to enforce its security even if there was no criticism which could be made of the administrator. In this case, the property at the centre of the dispute between the secured creditor and the administrator was an office block. After months of fruitless efforts by the administrator to find tenants for the property, the creditor, a bank, wanted to appoint a receiver to sell the property, with or without tenants, before the value of the property (and therefore its security) deteriorated further. As the property would realise more money if sold as fully let, the administrator wanted more time to find tenants.

Weighing up the conflicting interests, the court decided that appointing a receiver would result in additional costs and further reduce the net proceeds available to the creditors. On the other hand, the administration in this case had gone on for a long time and it was therefore reasonable to require the administrator to return to court in two months if he had not by then achieved a binding contract of sale when a further application by the bank could be considered.

Many of the main issues relating to leave were considered at length by the Court of Appeal in the leading case *Re Atlantic Computer Systems plc*[12]. In this case the company in administration supplied computers on sub-lease to end-users. The company in turn obtained the computers either on hire-purchase or on lease from finance companies ('the funders'). Throughout the period of administration the end-users had continued to pay the rentals due under the sub-leases but the administrators had not paid any sums due to the funders under the leases. The funders wishes to ascertain, inter alia, whether the equipment could be repossessed by the funders and whether, if the court's leave was required to do so, it should be granted.

In addressing these issues, the Court of Appeal used the opportunity to set out some general observations regarding cases where leave is sought to exercise existing proprietary rights, including security rights, against a company in administration[13].

(i)   It is for the person seeking leave to make out his case.

(ii)   Leave should normally be given to a lessor of land or the hirer of goods (a 'lessor') to exercise his proprietary rights and repossess his land or goods where that is unlikely to impede the achievement of the purpose for which the administration order was made.

(iii)   In other cases, the court has to carry out a balancing exercise, balancing the legitimate interests of the lessor and the legitimate interests of the other creditors of the company[14].

(iv)   In carrying out the balancing exercise, great weight is normally to be given to the proprietary interests of the lessor and an administration for the benefit of unsecured creditors should not be conducted at the expense of those seeking to exercise their proprietary rights, save to the extent that this is unavoidable and even then this will usually be acceptable only to a strictly limited extent.

(v)   Therefore, leave will normally be granted if significant loss would be caused to the lessor by a refusal; but if substantially greater loss would be caused to others by the grant of leave, or loss which is out of all proportion to the benefit which leave would confer on the lessor, that may outweigh the loss to the lessor caused by a refusal.

(vi)   In assessing these respective losses, the court will have regard to matters such as: the financial position of the company, its ability to pay the rental arrears

---

12   [1992] Ch 505, [1992] 1 All ER 476, CA.
13   [1992] Ch 505 at 542-544, [1992] 1 All ER 476 at 500-502, CA.
14   See also *Royal Bank Trust v Buchler* [1989] BCLC 130, sub nom *Re Meesan Investments Ltd* (1988) 4 BCC 788. The conduct of the parties may also be relevant to the issue of whether leave should be granted: *Bristol Airport plc v Powdrill* [1990] Ch 744, [1990] 2 All ER 493, CA.

and the continuing rentals, the administrator's proposals, the period for which the administration order has already been in force and is expected to remain in force, the effect on the administration if leave were given, the effect on the applicant if leave were refused, the end result sought to be achieved by the administration, the prospects of that result being achieved, and the history of the administration so far.

(vii) If leave is refused, it may commonly be on terms, for example that the administrator pay the current rent which should be possible, since if the administration order has been rightly made the business should generally be sufficiently viable to hold down current outgoings.

(viii) The comments were mainly directed to the situation where a lessor of land or the owner of goods is seeking to repossess his land or goods because of non-payment of rentals but a broadly similar approach would be applicable on many applications to enforce a security. On such applications, an important consideration will often be whether the applicant is fully secured. If he is, delay in enforcement is likely to be of less prejudice than in cases where his security is insufficient.

Returning to the facts in *Re Atlantic Computer Systems plc*[15] the court found that the administrators wanted to remain in possession of the computers partly in order to renegotiate the arrangements between the company and the funders which negotiations would be conducted in circumstances where the funders were not in a position to rely on their full rights. It was never intended that administration should strengthen the administrator's hands in negotiations with property owners who could not assert their full rights because of s 11 and accordingly the court would grant leave to the funders to enforce their rights[16].

In *Re David Meek Plant Ltd, Re David Meek Access Ltd*[17] leave to repossess goods on hire-purchase to a company in administration was refused, the court having balanced the interests of those leasing creditors against the legitimate interests of the other creditors. To have allowed repossession would have ensured that the administration would be abortive and that would deprive the creditors of the opportunity of considering proposals designed to achieve a more advantageous realisation of the assets than would have been the case in a winding up.

DEALING WITH CHARGED PROPERTY

Also significant for secured creditors or creditors with proprietary rights are the powers of the administrator to deal with certain assets as if the company had an unencumbered title to them. These powers were thought necessary particularly if the administrator wishes to sell the business as a going concern. The powers fall into two categories, depending on whether or not the administrator needs the consent of the court.

Property subject to a floating charge   An administrator may dispose of or otherwise exercise his powers in relation to any property of the company which is subject to a floating charge as if the property were not subject to the charge[18]. There is no need to obtain the consent of the creditor or the court in this instance. Where such property is disposed of, the charge holder has the same priority in respect of the proceeds of the

15   [1992] Ch 505, [1992] 1 All ER 476, CA.
16   [1992] Ch 505 at 539-540, [1992] 1 All ER 476 at 498-499, CA.
17   [1994] 1 BCLC 680, [1993] BCC 175.
18   IA 1986, s 15(1), (3).

property as it would have had in respect of the property[19]. A floating charge holder who objects to this course of conduct by the administrator may apply to the court on the grounds of unfair prejudice[20]. The existence of this power is one reason why the debenture holder needs to consider carefully whether he wants to prevent an administration order being made by appointing an administrative receiver, as discussed above.

Other property   With the court's consent, an administrator may dispose of assets subject to any other form of security or goods in the possession of the company under a hire-purchase agreement[1] where the court is satisfied that the disposal would be likely to promote the purpose or purposes specified in the administration order[2]. The court's consent will be on condition that the net proceeds of the disposal (or open market value, if higher) are applied towards discharging the sums secured by the security or payable under the hire-purchase agreement[3].

In considering whether or not to consent to the disposal of charged property, the court's approach is similar to that considered above in relation to the granting of leave under s 11. Assuming the Parliamentary intention was the protection to the maximum extent practicable of the secured creditor, the court would have to balance the prejudice felt by a secured creditor if the order was made against the prejudice that would otherwise be felt by those interested in the promotion of the purposes specified in the administration order[4].

A creditor who objects to the disposal of his goods can apply to the court in the grounds of unfair prejudice[5].

MISCELLANEOUS POWERS

An administrator has power at any time to call any meeting of the members or creditors of the company[6]; and can apply to the court for directions[7].

An administrator has the same powers as a liquidator to challenge certain transactions at an undervalue[8], preferences[9], extortionate credit transactions[10] and certain floating charges[11], all of which are discussed in detail in Chapter 41. The administrator, however, has no power to seek contributions to the company's assets with respect to fraudulent or wrongful trading[12] but does have to report on whether the directors' conduct may merit a disqualification order[13].

---

19   Ibid, s 15(4).
20   Ibid, s 27.
1   This includes goods subject to conditional sale agreements, chattel leasing agreements and retention of title agreements: ibid, s 15(9).
2   Ibid, s 15(2), (3). A copy of any order made by the court under this provision must, within 14 days, be sent by the administrator to the registrar of companies: s 15(7). See *Re ARV Aviation Ltd* [1989] BCLC 664, 4 BCC 708.
3   IA 1986, s 15(5).
4   *Re ARV Aviation Ltd* [1989] BCLC 664, 4 BCC 708.
5   See IA 1986, s 27(5).
6   Ibid, s 14(2)(b).
7   Ibid, s 14(3). See also s 17(2).
8   Ibid, s 238.
9   Ibid, s 239.
10   Ibid, s 244.
11   Ibid, s 245.
12   Ibid, ss 213, 214.
13   Company Directors Disqualification Act 1986, s 7(3)(c).

Objecting creditors and members

At any time when an administration order is in force, any creditor or member may apply to the court for an order on the ground that the company's affairs, business and property are being or have been managed by the administrator in a manner which is unfairly prejudicial to the interests of the creditors or members generally or of some part of the creditors or members (including at least himself), or that any actual or proposed act or omission of the administrator is or would be so prejudicial[14]. An allegation that an administrator was negligent in the sale of the company's assets is an allegation of misconduct only and does not constitute an allegation that the administrator managed the company's affairs in a manner which was unfairly prejudicial to the creditors[15].

The court may make such order as it thinks fit for giving relief in respect of the matters complained of but an order must not prejudice the implementation of a voluntary arrangement or a scheme of arrangement[16].

Creditors holding one-tenth in value of the company's debt can require an administrator to hold a meeting of creditors[17].

Vacation of office and discharge of the administration order

An administrator can be removed from office by the court, or he can resign his office, or he may be required to vacate his office where he ceases to be qualified to act as an insolvency practitioner or where the administration order is discharged[18].

An administration order ends when the court discharges it and an application for the order to be discharged may be made by the administrator at any time[19]. An application must be made by the administrator if it appears to him that the purpose of the order either has been achieved, or is incapable of achievement, or if he is required to apply by a meeting of the company's creditors[20]. If the purpose has become impossible to achieve the application for discharge of the order may be coupled with a petition that the company be compulsorily wound up[1]. On the hearing of the application, the court may discharge or vary the order, or adjourn the hearing, or make any other order it thinks fit[2].

An administration order may also be discharged if the creditors' meeting rejects the administrator's proposals[3]; or following an application by a creditor or member of the company on the grounds that the company's affairs, business or property are being managed by the administrator in an unfairly prejudicial way[4]; or if the creditors and members agree to a voluntary arrangement[5] although, as we shall see below, it may be in the interests of the creditors and the supervisor of such arrangements to keep the administration order in place.

14   IA 1986, s 27(1).
15   *Re Charnley Davies Ltd (No 2)* [1990] BCLC 760, [1990] BCC 605.
16   IA 1986, s 27(2)-(4).
17   Ibid, s 17(3)(a).
18   Ibid, s 19(1), (2).
19   Ibid, s 18(1). A copy of the court order must be sent to the registrar of companies within 14 days of the making of the order: s 18(4).
20   Ibid, s 18(2).
1   Ibid, s 14, Sch 1, para 21.
2   Ibid, s 18(3).
3   Ibid, s 24(5).
4   Ibid, s 27(4)(d).
5   Ibid, s 5(3)(a).

An administrator's release from liability in respect of his acts or omissions in the administration has effect from such time as the court may determine[6].

Administration expenses and liabilities

Where a person cease to be an administrator, his remuneration and any expenses[7] properly incurred by him must be charged on and paid out of any property of the company which is in his custody or under his control at that time in priority to any security which, as created, was a floating charge[8]. This provision gives the administrator's claim priority over that of the holder of a floating charge.

However, priority over both the administrator's remuneration and expenses and the claim of a floating charge holder is given in respect of any sums payable in respect of debts or liabilities incurred, while he was administrator, under contracts entered into by him in the carrying out of his functions (s 19(5)); as well as with respect to any sums payable in respect of liabilities incurred, while he was administrator, under contracts of employment adopted by him in the carrying out of his functions, to the extent that the liabilities are qualifying liabilities[9] (s 19(6)). For this purpose, the administrator is not to be taken to have adopted a contract of employment by reason of anything done or omitted to be done within 14 days after his appointment.

These provisions in s 19(5) and (6) arise from the Insolvency Act 1994 which was introduced in response to a series of decisions on the issue of adopting contracts of employment, of which the most important in the context of administration was the decision of the Court of Appeal in *Powdrill v Watson*[10]. The court had there decided that if employees continued to work and to be paid after the appointment of an administrator, the administrator had adopted their contracts and liabilities (including payments in lieu of notice and holiday pay payable on dismissal) incurred to such employees were payable in priority to all other debts. The result of this decision, as the House of Lords subsequently noted[11], 'was to make it extremely hazardous for administrators to keep on the employees necessary to enable the company's business to continue'.

While an appeal was pending, Parliament intervened (with respect to contracts adopted on or after 15 March 1994) in the form of the Insolvency Act 1994 to the effect outlined above, limiting the priority to claims incurred during the administration and restricting the claims to claims for wages, salary and contributions to a pension scheme.

However, the Insolvency Act 1994 did not attempt to define 'adopted' and so the appeal to the House of Lords in *Powdrill v Watson*[12] must be looked to for further illumination on this issue. The House of Lords held that 'adopt' for these purposes connotes some conduct by an administrator which amounts to an election to treat the

---

6   Ibid, s 20.
7   See *Re Atlantic Computer Systems plc* [1992] Ch 505, [1992] 1 All ER 476, CA, discussed in detail above in the text, where the Court of Appeal rejected the lessor's claim that current rentals should be treated as expenses of the administration and thus given priority.
8   IA 1986, s 19(3), (4).
9   For these purposes, a liability under a contract of employment is a qualifying liability if (a) it is a liability to pay a sum by way of wages or salary or contribution to an occupational pension scheme, and (b) it is in respect of services rendered wholly or partly after the adoption of the contract: s 19(7); so much of any qualifying liability as represents payment in respect of services rendered before the adoption of the contract must be disregarded: s 19(8).
10 [1994] 2 All ER 513, [1994] 2 BCLC 118. For a succinct account of the issues and the history of the litigation leading up to the 1994 Act: see Fletcher *The Law of Insolvency* (1996), pp 469-478.
11 *Powdrill v Watson* [1995] 2 AC 394 at 442, [1995] 2 All ER 65 at 77, HL.
12 [1995] 2 AC 394, [1995] 2 All ER 65, HL.

continued contract of employment with the company as giving rise to a separate liability in the administration[13]. It followed that if an administrator caused the company to continue the employment of an employee for more than 14 days after his appointment the employee's contract of employment was inevitably adopted for the purposes of the Insolvency Act[14]. It was not open to an administrator to avoid that result by unilaterally telling the employees that he was not adopting their contracts or was doing so only on terms.

VOLUNTARY ARRANGEMENTS

Introduction

One of the most important powers for those managing an insolvent or financially pressed company, whether or not it is yet in liquidation, is the power to make binding compromises or arrangements with the creditors of the company. For any compromise or arrangement to work effectively, it is necessary for all the creditors to be bound by it. This can either be achieved by ensuring that the creditors concerned unanimously agree to the plan (which may be impractical) or by making use of statutory provisions that enable a specified majority to bind the minority. Unfortunately these provisions, now contained in CA 1985, ss 425-427, have proved complicated, time-consuming and expensive to operate and their use today has become infrequent[15]. They were considered in detail in Chapter 36.

To remedy these deficiencies, a new statutory procedure for a company voluntary arrangement (commonly referred to as a CVA) was introduced in the Insolvency Act 1986[16] and it is this procedure which will be used where a company wishes to make an arrangement with its creditors. An advantage of proceeding by way of an arrangement under the Insolvency Act is that it must be appraised and implemented by a qualified insolvency practitioner[17], with the assurance of professional competence and independence that that implies.

After a slow start, increasing use is being made of this procedure but the numbers are still small when compared with other insolvency procedures.

	CVAs	Receiverships	Crs voluntary liquidation
1992-93	67	8,747	15,164
1993-94	196	4,870	11,964
1994-95	281	3,740	9,627
1995-96	386	3,237	9,054
1996-97	525	2,591	8,260

13   [1995] 2 AC 394 at 449, [1995] 2 All ER 65 at 83, HL.
14   [1995] 2 AC 394 at 450C, [1995] 2 All ER 65 at 84d, HL, per Lord Browne-Wilkinson, having earlier criticised the Court of Appeal for suggesting that the mere continuation of employment was sufficient, see at [1995] 2 AC 394 at 448G, [1995] 2 All ER 65 at 83a, HL. As Professor Fletcher has pointed out, this approach appears indistinguishable from that of the Court of Appeal: see Fletcher *The Law of Insolvency* (1996), p 476.
15   See the Cork Committee Report, paras 404-418 which identified a number of difficulties with the CA 1985 provisions, including their formality and complexity, the absence of a moratorium and the difficulty of identifying the classes of creditors for the purpose of holding the requisite class meetings.
16   See the IA 1986, ss 1-7. The provisions are closely modelled on the reformed provisions for voluntary arrangements for individual debtors contained in ss 252-263. If the company wishes to amend the rights of its members then it will continue to use CA 1985, ss 425-427.
17   IA 1986, s 1(2).

Proposing an arrangement

A voluntary arrangement, defined as a composition in satisfaction of the company's debts, or a scheme of arrangement of its affairs, may be proposed:

- by the directors of the company (where the company is neither in administration nor in winding up); or
- by an administrator where an administration order is in force; or
- by a liquidator where the company is being wound up[18].

The proposal must provide for a nominee to act either as trustee or otherwise for the purpose of supervising the implementation of the voluntary arrangement; and the nominee must be a qualified insolvency practitioner[19]. The first task of the nominee is to call meetings to secure the necessary approval of the scheme by the creditors and members. Only two meetings need be held, one of creditors and one of members, and no distinctions are made between different classes of creditors or members. Crucially, once the appropriate approvals have been obtained, the proposal binds dissenting creditors who had notice of, and were entitled to vote at, the meeting.

Where the proposal is made by the directors, they will draw up and submit to the nominee a document setting out the proposal and a statement of the company's affairs and they will usually do this with the assistance of a qualified insolvency practitioner[20]. That practitioner will often agree to be the nominee and, within 28 days of being given notice of the proposals, he must submit a report to the court stating whether meetings should be summoned to consider the proposals and notifying the court as to when and where such meetings will be held[1]. This, however, is a mere matter of filing and, unless there is an objection, does not involve a court hearing.

Where the proposal is by a liquidator or administrator and he will act as the nominee, then he proceeds, without notifying the court, to summon the necessary meetings of the members and the creditors at such a time, date and place as he thinks fit[2].

If, however, the company is not in liquidation or subject to an administration order, there is an initial problem, in that the statute makes no provision for a moratorium while meetings are being called and the proposal is being considered. There is therefore nothing to prevent creditors from pursuing their claims against the company during this period. As we discuss below, this has proved one of the major defects in the statutory scheme.

The solution is to prepare the proposals in conjunction with a petition for an administration order because merely applying for such an order, as we have seen, will itself preserve the status quo[3]. As two of the four purposes for which application may be made for an administration order are to facilitate the approval of arrangements with creditors[4], the legislation envisages that administration orders and voluntary arrangements with creditors will frequently be used in conjunction with each other.

---

18 Ibid, s 1(1), (3). See *March Estates plc v Gunmark* [1996] 2 BCLC 1. Note that there is no requirement that the company is unable to pay its debts; nor is there any procedure whereby creditors or members can initiate a voluntary arrangement.
19 IA 1986, s 1(2).
20 Ibid, s 2(3).
1   Ibid, s 2(1), (2).
2   Ibid, s 3(2).
3   Ibid, s 10(1).
4   Ibid, s 8(3)(b), (c).

Approving an arrangement

The purpose of the meetings is to decide whether to approve the proposed voluntary arrangement, with or without modifications[5]. No proposal or modification can be approved which affects the right of a secured creditor of the company to enforce his security without the concurrence of the creditor concerned[6]; and no proposal or modification can be approved under which any preferential debt of the company is to be paid otherwise than in priority to such of its debts as are not preferential debts, again without the concurrence of the preferential creditor concerned[7].

For acceptance at the creditors' meeting, the proposal must be approved by a majority of 75% in value of the creditors present in person or by proxy and voting on the resolution[8]. At the members' meeting, a simple majority in favour of the resolution is sufficient[9].

The result of the meetings is merely reported to the court without any need to seek court approval[10]. On approval of the scheme, the nominee becomes the supervisor[11].

Position of dissenting creditors and others

If the voluntary arrangement is approved by the appropriate meetings, then the voluntary arrangement takes effect as if made at the creditors' meeting; and it binds all creditors with notice of, and entitled to vote at, the creditors' meeting (whether or not he was present or represented at the meeting)[12].

Any dissenting creditor must apply to the court within 28 days of the report of the meetings being filed[13]. The grounds on which such an application can be made are that the voluntary arrangement as approved unfairly prejudices the interests of a creditor, member or contributory of the company; and/or that there was a material irregularity at or in relation to either of the meetings[14]. An application to the court can also be made by a member entitled to vote at the members' meeting, or by the supervisor or the liquidator or administrator[15].

On a successful application, the court has power to revoke or suspend the approvals of the scheme and/or give a direction for the summoning of further meetings to consider revised proposals or to reconsider the original proposal[16].

---

5   Ibid, s 4(1).
6   Ibid, ss 4(3); 248. See *Doobar v Alltime Securities Ltd* [1996] 2 All ER 948, [1996] 1 BCLC 487, CA; *Re Cancol Ltd* [1996] 1 All ER 37, [1996] 1 BCLC 100; *March Estates plc v Gunmark Ltd* [1996] 2 BCLC 1.
7   IA 1986, s 4(4)(a); also there can be no approval of any proposal or modification which alters the right of preferential debts to rank equally with one another, without the concurrence of the preferential creditor: s 4(4)(b). Preferential debts are defined in s 386.
8   IR 1986, r 1.19(1), note that a majority in number of creditors is not required. The voting rights of creditors are dealt with in rr 1.17, 1.19. See *Doobar v Alltime Securities Ltd* [1996] 2 All ER 948, [1996] 1 BCLC 487; also *Re Cancol Ltd* [1996] 1 All ER 37, [1996] 1 BCLC 100. 'Creditor' for these purposes includes persons entitled to a future or contingently payable debt, such as future payments of rent under an existing lease: *Re Cancol Ltd, supra*. As to the invalidation of the resolution in certain circumstances, see IR 1986, r 1.19(4).
9   See ibid, rr 1.18, 1.20(1); excluding any member holding only non-voting shares: r 1.20(2).
10   IA 1986, s 4(6).
11   Ibid, s 7(2).
12   Ibid, s 5(2)(b). See *RA Securities Ltd v Mercantile Credit Co Ltd* [1994] BCC 598 (person not entitled to vote was not able to take advantage of the arrangement). As to the importance of giving effective notice of the meeting, see Frieze (1998) 11 Insolv Intell 20.
13   IA 1986, s 6(1)-(3).
14   Ibid, s 6(1). See *Re Cancol Ltd* [1996] 1 All ER 37, [1996] 1 BCLC 100.
15   IA 1986, s 6(2).
16   Ibid, s 6(4).

Implementing the arrangement

Once the scheme is approved, then the supervisor will set about its implementation and may apply to the court for directions if necessary[17]. The supervisor will hold funds in his possession on trust for the creditors pursuant to the terms of the voluntary arrangement[18]. Following completion the supervisor must send notice to this effect to all the creditors and members bound by it; together with a copy of a report drawn up by the supervisor and summarising all receipts and payments by him; notice must also be given to the registrar of companies and to the court[19].

There is nothing in the legislation which prevents the members from resolving to place the company into voluntary liquidation where the company has proposed a voluntary arrangement and whether or nor that arrangement is still continuing or capable of fulfilment, even if that has the effect of breaching the arrangement[20].

Where a compulsory winding-up order is made in respect of a company which has in effect a voluntary arrangement, the CVA creditors are discharged from the arrangement by the making of the order and instead look to the alternative regime of winding up, and the assets in winding up, for a dividend, if any, on the balance of their debts, after giving credit for any sums received under the arrangement[20]. The supervisor has to hand over any assets of the company in his control to the liquidator and those assets are then freed from any trust for the creditors under the CVA and become subject to the statutory trusts arising on compulsory liquidation[1].

REFORM

As noted above, administration and company voluntary arrangements were new procedures introduced, in the light of the Cork Committee Report, initially in the Insolvency Act 1985, and then consolidated in the Insolvency Act 1986. Over subsequent years, it became apparent that little use was being made of the procedures, particularly when compared with the numbers of companies going into liquidation or receivership.

In October 1993 the Insolvency Service, the executive agency of the Department of Trade and Industry with responsibility in this area, issued a consultative document which considered the main barriers to use of these procedures and made proposals for change[2].

Administration   The working party which considered administration orders identified the following principal barriers to the greater use of the administration procedure[3]:

- time and cost (in particular, the costs of the independent report needed to support the petition and the need to meet the 'likely to achieve test');

17 Ibid, s 7(4). The power to give directions does not extend to a power to amend the voluntary arrangement: *Re Alpha Lighting* Ltd [1997] BPIR 341, discussed Jones (1997) 10 Insolv Intell 60.
18 *Re Leisure Study Group Ltd* [1994] 2 BCLC 65.
19 IR 1986, r 1.29.
20 *Re Arthur Rathbone Kitchens Ltd* [1997] 2 BCLC 280.
1 *Re Arthur Rathbone Kitchens Ltd* [1997] 2 BCLC 280. See discussion of compulsory liquidation in Ch 41.
2 See The Insolvency Service *The Insolvency Act 1986, Company Voluntary Arrangements and Administration Orders, A Consultative Document* (October 1993), hereafter the *Consultative Document* (1993); and see response by the Law Society Company Law Committee (Memorandum No 299) March 1994; also The Insolvency Service *Company Voluntary Arrangements and Administration Orders, Summary of responses to the Consultative Document* (1995).
3 See the *Consultative Document* (1993), Ch 5. See Fletcher *The Law of Insolvency* (1996), pp 479-481 on the aversion of directors to utilising a procedure which may result in their removal from office.

- the secured creditors' right of veto (where he is in a position to appoint an administrative receiver);
- the administrator's power to remove directors;
- the obligatory report on the directors' conduct for disqualification purposes; and
- the lack of involvement of creditors, particularly the unsecured creditors until late in the process.

The main proposal which was mooted with respect to administration orders was that there should be an additional procedure providing for the appointment of an administrator for 28 days only so as to give more companies the opportunity to attempt rescue, with the benefit of a short 'breathing space' before the need to comply with any costly procedures[4].

The consultation process in 1993 was followed by a further consultation in April 1995 bringing forward revised proposals[5]. However, these further proposals were restricted to an improved company voluntary arrangement procedure and made no further proposals with respect to the existing administration regime.

Voluntary arrangements Much of the focus of the 1993 consultation exercise was on the barriers which had prevented greater use of CVAs. Those identified included: the lack of a moratorium on creditors' rights; the lack of funding; the ability of secured creditors to appoint an administrative receiver; the directors' lack of knowledge of, and insolvency practitioners' inexperience of, CVAs with rescue being attempted too late[6]. Views were sought on a proposal[7] that a moratorium should be available immediately on filing a notice of a prospective CVA; that moratorium would initially last 28 days and bind all the creditors; and the maximum length of a moratorium would be three months. The directors would continue to manage the business during this period and seven days' notice would be required of any appointment of an administrative receiver.

The further consultation in 1995[8] concentrated on presenting a revised proposal for a new CVA procedure which would be available in addition to the existing procedure in the IA 1986. Having found a broad consensus that there should be a short moratorium to allow companies a breathing space to put together a rescue plan, the scheme proposed was one which would allow companies a 28-day moratorium with a minimum of formality—the idea being that companies in trouble should have temporary protection from their creditors while they try to work out a rescue plan for agreement by creditors.

The key elements of the proposed scheme were[9]:

- an initial 28-day moratorium to be obtained by filing certain documents with the court during which time creditors would not be able to take action against the company (unless the court gives leave);
- an extension of the moratorium would be possible but the moratorium would not extend beyond a total of three months;

---

4 See the *Consultative Document* (1993), Ch 6.
5 See The Insolvency Service *Revised Proposals for a new Company Voluntary Arrangement Procedure, A Consultative Document* (April 1995), hereafter the *Consultative Document* (1995); see also the response by the Law Society Insolvency Law Sub-Committee (Memorandum No 24) July 1995.
6 See the *Consultative Document* (1993), Ch 2.
7 See the *Consultative Document* (1993), Ch 4.
8 See the *Consultative Document* (1995).
9 See the *Consultative Document* (1995), Chs 1, 2.

- the management would remain in control but would be subject to supervision and a restriction on the disposal of assets;
- the moratorium would be binding on all creditors including secured creditors;
- floating chargeholders would be required to give the company five working days' notice of their intention to appoint an administrative receiver unless the court gives leave or the company consents to shorter notice - this would give the company time to see if a voluntary arrangement is more appropriate.
- the company would not be able to dispose of assets other than in the ordinary course of business during the five-day period.

While noting that banks and others looked with disfavour on the proposals to suspend temporarily their right to appoint an administrative receiver, the consultative document noted that it must be recognised that if there are to be more successful rescues then those rights must be temporarily suspended in appropriate circumstances. The scheme aims to offer a solution which, the Insolvency Service believes, balances the conflicting interests of those affected. It is hoped that the scheme will make company rescues simpler, cheaper and more accessible, especially for smaller companies[10]. Parliamentary time has not yet been found to implement this proposal although the DTI has indicated that it still intends to do so[11].

10   See the *Consultative Document* (1995), p 2.
11   See DTI *Companies in 1996-97* (1997), p 22.

CHAPTER 41

Winding up

Introduction

Winding up is a term commonly associated with the ending of a company's existence. In fact, winding up or liquidation (the terms are synonymous) is the process by which the assets of the company are collected in and realised, its liabilities discharged and the net surplus, if there is one, distributed to the persons entitled to it[1]. Only when this has been done is the company's existence finally terminated, by a process known as dissolution. One common confusion of terminology occurs in the use of the term 'bankruptcy'. Bankruptcy is a legal process by which the assets of an insolvent individual or partnership are realised[2] and the proceeds distributed to the creditors. Companies cannot be made bankrupt.

A company being wound up may be solvent or insolvent. A solvent company may be wound up because the business opportunity which the company was formed to exploit has come to an end, or the members of a family business may wish to retire or, as we have seen, because of internal disputes. Winding up on the just and equitable ground[3] in cases where the relationship between the members has completely broken down was one of the shareholder remedies discussed in Chapter 28. This chapter will concentrate mainly on the winding up of insolvent companies but it must be remembered throughout that winding up as a process may be applicable to either solvent or insolvent companies.

Insolvent winding up occurs essentially when companies are unable to pay their debts in full. When a company cannot pay its debts in full, difficult problems arise over how the assets that are available should be distributed. Broadly speaking, as we shall see, the law tries to maintain an equality between creditors so that assets are pooled and distributed pari passu ie rateably according to the size of each creditor's claim[4]. In fact, as the level of distribution to creditors claiming against the pooled assets is

---

1   See Insolvency Act 1986, s 143(1).
2   Ibid, s 381.
3   Under ibid, s 122(1)(g).
4   See ibid, s 107.

likely to be very small[5], much effort is expended by creditors and their advisers in devising ways of ensuring that they do not have to claim against the pooled assets on the company's insolvency. This they do by a variety of methods, such as by taking security with respect to the debt due to them.

A further distinction is that winding up may be either compulsory or voluntary[6]. A compulsory winding up is where a court orders that the company be wound up, a voluntary winding up is where the members of the company resolve that the company be wound up. Each is considered in detail below.

Relationship with other insolvency regimes   A receiver, as we have seen, will typically be appointed to a company by a secured creditor, eg a debenture holder under a floating charge[7], and the receiver's function will be to pay off the debt of that secured creditor either from income receipts or asset realisations. It is very likely that a company to which a receiver has been appointed will be unable to pay its unsecured debts in full. The unsecured creditors may then choose to protect themselves by putting the company into liquidation and appointing a liquidator. So receivership may be, although it need not be, a forerunner to liquidation.

We have also considered two other regimes. As we have seen, an administration order is an order made by the court in the hope of saving the company from liquidation or of obtaining a more advantageous realisation than would be effected on a winding up. A voluntary arrangement, as we saw, allows a company and its creditors to agree on a composition in satisfaction of its debts or a scheme of arrangement of its affairs[8]. Like the administration order this will also provide a way of managing the company's business or realising its assets without liquidation. If the administration order or voluntary arrangement is successful in restoring the company to solvency, the company will continue in business. If solvency is not restored then, whether or not the business has been sold, the administration order or voluntary arrangement is likely to be followed by liquidation as the process by which any remaining assets can be realised and the proceeds distributed to the creditors.

So companies may go directly into liquidation or it may be that they have also been the subject of some earlier form of insolvency proceedings.

The statutory framework

In 1977 the Government appointed a committee headed by Sir Kenneth Cork to review the whole of insolvency law; it reported in 1982[9]. Many of the Cork Committee's

---

5   This is a matter of some public concern, see Justice *Insolvency Law, An agenda for reform* (1994); although as this report notes (see para 5.6) 'It is extremely doubtful whether, in the absence of some radical and far-reaching changes to the insolvency process, any dramatic improvement will ever be achievable as regards the size of the dividend which creditors can realistically expect to secure from an insolvent estate'.

6   IA 1986, s 73(1).

7   If, as often will be the case, the appointment of a receiver by a debenture holder under a floating charge comprises the whole or substantially the whole of a company's property, the receiver is referred to as an 'administrative receiver': ibid, s 29(2).

8   Ibid, s 1(1).

9   Report of the Review Committee on Insolvency Law and Practice (Cork Committee Report, Cmnd 8558), hereafter the Cork Committee Report. See also the White Paper published in 1984 outlining the Government's reaction to the Report: A Revised Framework for Insolvency Law (Cmnd 9175). See Fletcher '*The Genesis of Modern Insolvency Law, An Odyssey of Law Reform*' [1989] JBL 365. For a subsequent review of the Cork Report and the current problems in insolvency law, see Justice *Insolvency Law, An agenda for reform* (1994).

recommendations were implemented in the Insolvency Act 1985. Those provisions, together with material contained in the Companies Act 1985, were subsequently consolidated in the Insolvency Act 1986 and it is this Act which provides the legislative background to most of this chapter. In addition to the statute, reference must be made to the Insolvency Rules 1986[10] which contain the procedural rules and requirements.

Aims of modern insolvency law

As part of its review the Cork Committee attempted to outline what it believed to be the aims of a good modern insolvency law, namely[11]:

(a) to recognise that the world in which we live and the creation of wealth depend upon a system founded on credit and that such a system requires, as a correlative, an insolvency procedure to cope with its casualties;

(b) to diagnose and treat an imminent insolvency at an early rather than a late stage;

(c) to relieve and protect where necessary the insolvent, and in particular the individual insolvent, from any harassment and undue demands by his creditors, … at the same time, to have regard to the rights of creditors whose own position may be at risk because of the insolvency;

(d) to prevent conflicts between individual creditors;

(e) to realise the assets of the insolvent which should properly be taken to satisfy his debts, with the minimum of delay and expense;

(f) to distribute the proceeds of the realisations amongst the creditors in a fair and equitable manner, returning any surplus to the debtor;

(g) to ensure that the processes of realisation and distribution are administered in an honest and competent manner;

(h) to ascertain the causes of the insolvent's failure and, if and in so far as his conduct or, in the case of a company, the conduct of its officers or agents, merits criticism or punishment, to decide what measures, if any, require to be taken against him or his associates, or such officers or agents;

(i) to recognise that the effects of insolvency are not limited to the private interests of the insolvent and his creditors, but that other interests of society or other groups in society are vitally affected by the insolvency and its outcome, and to ensure that these public interests are recognised and safeguarded;

(j) to provide means for the preservation of viable commercial enterprises capable of making a useful contribution to the economic life of the country;

(k) to devise a framework of law for the governing of insolvency matters which commands universal respect and observance, and yet is sufficiently flexible to adapt to and deal with the rapidly changing conditions of our modern world; in particular, to achieve a system that:
   (i) is seen to produce practical solutions to financial and commercial problems,
   (ii) is simple and easily understood,
   (iii) is free from anomalies and inconsistencies, and
   (iv) is capable of being administered efficiently and economically;

(l) to ensure due recognition and respect abroad for English insolvency proceedings.

---

10   SI 1986 No 1925 as amended.
11   See the Cork Committee Report, Cmnd 8558, ch 4.

Many of the changes recommended by the Cork Committee and reflected in the Insolvency Act 1986 are directed towards the meeting of the above aims as will be clear from our consideration of the various key elements of the legislation.

VOLUNTARY WINDING UP

Resolution of the company

A voluntary winding up begins with a resolution passed by the members. An ordinary resolution is sufficient in the rare case of a company whose articles specify that it shall be dissolved after the expiration of a fixed period of time or on the happening of a particular event, and that time has passed or event occurred[12]. More usually, a special resolution that the company be wound up voluntarily will be passed[13]. Alternatively, where a company cannot continue its business by reason of its liabilities and it is advisable to wind up, an extraordinary resolution will suffice[14]. The reason for this distinction is that in such circumstances it may be desirable to pass a resolution commencing the winding up quickly and it was formerly the case that an extraordinary resolution could be passed far more quickly than a special resolution[15]. The distinction is no longer so significant today.

A copy of the resolution for winding up must be lodged with the registrar of companies within 15 days of being passed[16] and advertised in the Gazette[17]. A voluntary winding up is deemed to commence at the time of the passing of the resolution for voluntary winding up[18].

Declaration of solvency – members' voluntary winding up

If in the five weeks immediately preceding the resolution to wind up the company, or on the date of the resolution but before it is passed[19], the directors or a majority of the directors[20] make a statutory declaration of solvency[1], the winding up is known as a members' voluntary winding up[2].

The statutory declaration must be to the effect[3] that the directors have made a full enquiry into the affairs of the company and have formed the opinion that the company will be able to pay its debts in full[4] within, at most, 12 months of the date of the

---

12   IA 1986, s 84(1)(a).
13   Ibid, s 84(1)(b).
14   Ibid, s 84(1)(c).
15   The only difference between a special and an extraordinary resolution is that a meeting at which a special resolution is to be proposed requires 21 days' notice: CA 1985, s 378(2); whereas any meeting at which an extraordinary resolution is to be proposed requires only 14 days' notice (except an annual general meeting which requires 21 days): s 369. However, as the members can consent now to short notice (ss 378(3), 369(3), (4)) there is today no difference at all in the speed with which a special or an extraordinary resolution can be passed so as to commence winding up.
16   IA 1986, s 84(3).
17   Ibid, s 85(1).
18   Ibid, s 86.
19   Ibid, s 89(2)(a).
20   Ibid, s 89(1).
1   The statutory declaration must be delivered to the registrar of companies within 15 days after the resolution for winding up is passed: ibid, s 89(3). Failure to do so gives rise to criminal penalties.
2   Ibid, s 90.
3   Ibid, s 89(1).
4   Together with interest at the official rate: ibid.

commencement of the winding up (ie the date of the passing of the resolution for winding up[5]).

The advantage to the directors in making such a declaration will be seen later, particularly in relation to the appointment of the liquidator. The risk in doing so is that if the declaration is made by the directors without reasonable grounds they commit a criminal offence[6] and, if the debts are not paid in full within the specified time, that raises a rebuttable presumption that the directors did not have reasonable grounds for making the declaration[7].

If it turns out that the declaration is erroneous and the liquidator appointed by the members is of opinion that the company will be unable to pay its debts in full within the 12-month period, he must summon a meeting of creditors within 28 days[8]. As from the day of that meeting, the position is treated as if no declaration of solvency had been made and the winding up becomes from that date onwards a creditors' voluntary winding up[9].

No declaration of solvency – creditors' voluntary winding up

If the directors do not make a statutory declaration of solvency then the winding up is referred to as a creditors' voluntary winding up[10]. In addition to the meeting of members called to pass a resolution for the company to go into liquidation, as outlined above, a meeting of creditors must be summoned to take place not more than 14 days after the members' meeting[11] and the directors must lay before that meeting a statement as to the company's affairs showing, in particular, the company's assets, debts and liabilities[12]. The purpose of the creditors' meeting being the appointment of a liquidator and, if desired, a liquidation committee.

COMPULSORY WINDING UP

Petitioners for a winding-up order

Of course, the vast majority of petitions for winding up are presented by creditors but a petition can be presented by the company itself[13], or by its directors[14], or by contributories (essentially members)[15].

---

5   Ibid, s 86.
6   Ibid, s 89(4).
7   Ibid, s 89(5). As for the obligations of the directors in making this declaration, see Simmons (1996) 9 Insolv Intel 33.
8   Ibid, s 95(1),(2).
9   Ibid, s 96. Note also that the general meeting already held and the creditors' meeting under s 95 are treated as if they were the meetings required under s 98 in the case of a creditors' voluntary winding up: ibid.
10 Ibid, s 90.
11 Ibid, s 98(1)(a).
12 Ibid, s 99.
13 Ibid, s 124(1).
14 An amendment made in the Insolvency Act 1985 reversing the effect of the decision in *Re Emmadart Ltd* [1979] Ch 540, [1979] 1 All ER 599 which had held that the directors could not present a petition in the name of the company. A petition by the directors must be presented by all the directors: *Re Instrumentation Electrical Services Ltd* [1988] BCLC 550, 4 BCC 301 but see *Re Equitcorp International plc* [1989] 1 WLR 1010, [1989] BCLC 597 – what is required is a proper resolution of the board, and that may be by the majority of the directors.
15 'Contributory' encompasses members of the company as well as others not registered as members but who are liable to contribute to the assets of the company: IA 1986, s 79.

A contributory is not entitled to present a winding-up petition unless either the number of members is reduced below two (except where the company is a single member private company[16]); or the shares held by him were originally allotted to him, or have been held by him for at least six months during the 18 months before the commencement of the winding up, or have devolved to him through the death of a former holder[17]. This provision is designed to prevent individuals from purchasing shares with a view to winding up a company although a six-month period seems inadequate for this purpose.

In addition, a contributory must establish an interest in the winding up. For example, a partly paid-up shareholder who remains liable to contribute the amount unpaid on his shares in the event of the company being wound up has an interest. For a fully paid-up member to establish that he has a tangible interest in the winding up, he must show a prima facie probability of surplus assets remaining after the creditors have been paid for distribution among the shareholders[18].

Where the locus standi of a contributory to petition is disputed, the court will consider all the circumstances, including the likelihood of damage to the company if the petition is not dismissed, in deciding whether to require the petitioner to seek the determination of his status first, outside of the winding-up petition[19]. In *Alipour v Ary, Re a Company (No 002180 of 1996)*[20] it was not appropriate to strike out the petition, despite doubts as to the petitioner's locus standi, when on the facts that would effectively leave the petitioner without a remedy.

The Secretary of State for Trade and Industry may also petition to have companies wound up on the grounds of public interest[1].

Grounds for compulsory winding up

The process of obtaining a winding-up order begins with a petition based on one of the seven grounds on which a compulsory winding-up order may be made and which are set out in the Insolvency Act 1986, s 122(1). As mentioned above, many of these grounds will be relevant to solvent companies, for example winding up on the just and equitable ground[2]. For insolvent companies, the ground relied on is that the company is unable to pay its debts[3]; in such cases the petition is invariably brought by a creditor.

---

16   See the Companies (Single Member Private Limited Companies) Regulations 1992, SI 1992 No 1699, reg 2(1)(b), Sch, para 8.
17   IA 1986, s 124(2).
18   *Re Rica Gold Washing Co* (1879) 11 Ch D 36; *Re Expanded Plugs Ltd* [1966] 1 All ER 877, [1966] 1 WLR 514; *Re Othery Construction Ltd* [1966] 1 All ER 145, [1966] 1 WLR 69; *Re Bellador Silk Ltd* [1965] 1 All ER 667. See *Re Greenhaven Motors Ltd* [1997] 1 BCLC 739, [1997] BCC 547.
19   *Alipour v Ary, Re a Company (No 002180 of 1996)* [1997] 1 BCLC 557, sub nom *Re UOC Corpn, Alipour v Ary* [1997] BCC 377, CA.
20   [1997] 1 BCLC 557, sub nom *Re UOC Corpn, Alipour v Ary* [1997] BCC 377, CA.
1   See IA 1986, s 124A, following an investigation of the company: see ch 30.
2   Ie under IA 1986, s 122(1)(g). Other grounds include that the company has resolved by a special resolution to be wound up by the court; that the company is a public company and has not been issued with a certificate under CA 1985 s 117 enabling it to do business and to borrow within one year of incorporation; that the company has not commenced business within one year of incorporation or has suspended its business for a whole year: IA 1986, s 122(1)(a), (b), (d).
3   Ibid, s 122(1)(f).

Inability to pay its debts

The circumstances in which a company is deemed to be unable to pay its debts are defined in the Insolvency Act 1986, s 123:

(1)   A company is deemed unable to pay its debts where a creditor has served a written demand[4] on the company (in the prescribed form), for a debt then due, and which exceeds £750, and the company fails either to pay the debt or to secure or compound it to the reasonable satisfaction of the creditor, within 21 days of the demand[5].

(2)   Alternatively if, having obtained judgment against a company, a creditor enforces the judgment but the execution is returned unsatisfied, in whole or in part, that also establishes that the company is unable to pay its debts[6].

(3)   Alternatively, it is sufficient if it is proved to the satisfaction of the court that the company is unable to pay its debts as they fall due[7].
    This third ground enables a creditor, without serving a statutory demand or attempting to enforce a judgment, to satisfy the court by suitable evidence of the company's' inability to pay[8]. A company is not entitled to have the petition struck out, or prevent its being issued, merely because it is in fact solvent[9]. Failure to pay an undisputed debt, despite repeated requests, must prima facie mean an inability to pay and a winding-up order may be sought by a creditor[10].
    If the debt is due and is undisputed the petition will proceed to hearing and adjudication in the normal way but it is an abuse of process to present a winding-up petition under this heading if the debt is bona fide disputed and the petition is being used as a means of pressurising the company[11]. In such a case the petition will be dismissed; or the creditor can be restrained by injunction from presenting a petition[12].
    However, this long-established approach of dismissing the petition where the debt is bona fide disputed is a rule of practice only, and it must give way to circumstances which make it desirable that the petitioner should proceed. Thus the petition will not be dismissed if the petitioning creditor has a good arguable case that he is a creditor and the effect of the dismissal would be to deprive the petitioner of a remedy or otherwise injustice would result or for some other sufficient reason the petition should proceed.[13]

---

4   As to the detailed requirements concerning this statutory demand, see IR 1986, rr 4.4–4.6.
5   IA 1986, s 123(1)(a).
6   Ibid, s 123(1)(b).
7   Ibid, s 123(1)(e). See *Taylors Industrial Flooring Ltd v M & H Plant Hire (Manchester) Ltd* [1990] BCLC 216, [1990] BCC 44, CA.
8   *Taylors Industrial Flooring Ltd v M & H Plant Hire (Manchester) Ltd* [1990] BCLC 216, [1990] BCC 44, CA.
9   *Cornhill Insurance plc v Improvement Services Ltd* [1986] 1 WLR 114, [1986] BCLC 26.
10   *Taylors Industrial Flooring Ltd v M & H Plant Hire (Manchester) Ltd* [1990] BCLC 216, [1990] BCC 44, CA; *Cornhill Insurance plc v Improvement Services Ltd* [1986] 1 WLR 114, [1986] BCLC 26.
11   *Stonegate Securities Ltd v Gregory* [1980] Ch 576, [1980] 1 All ER 241, CA; Re *a Company (No 0010656 of 1990)* [1991] BCLC 464. See generally Oditah *'Winding up recalcitrant debtors'* [1995] LMCLQ 107.
12   *Re a Company* [1984] 3 All ER 78, [1984] 1 WLR 1090.
13   *Alipour v Ary, Re a Company (No 002180 of 1996)* [1997] 1 BCLC 557, sub nom *Re UOC Corpn, Alipour v Ary* [1997] BCC 377, CA; see also *Re Claybridge Shipping Co SA* [1997] 1 BCLC 572, (CA, 1981).

All three methods considered so far are based on petitioning creditors who have debts which are immediately due and payable. It might be the case that a creditor has lent money to a company which is not due to be repaid until some date in the future but the creditor is afraid that the present financial position of the company suggests it will not be able to repay the debt when payment is due. Such a creditor could rely on heading (3) above by showing that the company is now unable to pay its debts as they fall due or heading (4) below.

(4)   A company is also deemed unable to pay its debts if it is proved to the satisfaction of the court that the value of a company's assets is less than the amount of its liabilities, taking into account the contingent and prospective liabilities of the company[14] (the balance sheet test).

Having grounds for the presentation of a petition does not necessarily entitle the creditor to the making of a winding-up order. Winding up is a collective or class remedy and an order may be refused if the petitioner is merely seeking to obtain some private advantage[15]. If the purpose of the petition is legitimate, however, it does not matter that the motive of the petitioner is malicious[16].

There may well be differences of opinion among the creditors as to whether winding up should be ordered in which case the court can direct meetings to be held to ascertain the creditors' wishes[17]. A particular aspect of this clash may arise where a company is already in voluntary liquidation and the court is being asked to replace that by a compulsory winding-up order. Again the court takes account of the wishes of the majority of the creditors and where the majority oppose the making of a compulsory winding-up order, then the onus is on those seeking the order to show why it should be granted[18]. The court looks carefully at the quality of the creditors on either side as well as the quantity. It may well happen that some of the creditors are also shareholders or directors of the company or their associates in which case their views may be given far less weight or disregarded altogether[19].

Order made and commencement of winding up

Once an order for winding up is made, the Official Receiver will become the liquidator[20], at least initially (see below), and three copies of the winding-up order will be furnished to him[1]. One copy will then be served by him on the company at its

---

14   IA 1986, s 123(2).
15   *Re a Company (No 001573 of 1983)* [1983] BCLC 492.
16   *Bryanston Finance Ltd v De Vries (No 2)* [1976] Ch 63, [1976] 1 All ER 25, CA; *Re a Company (No 001573 of 1983)* [1983] BCLC 492.
17   IA 1986, s 195.
18   *Re JD Swain Ltd* [1965] 2 All ER 761, [1965] 1 WLR 909; *Re Magnus Consultants Ltd* [1995] 1 BCLC 203; *Re Gordon & Breach Science Publishers Ltd* [1995] 2 BCLC 189, [1995] BCC 261.
19   *Re Falcon (R J) Development Ltd* [1987] BCLC 437.
20   IA 1986, s 136(1), (2). Official Receivers are civil servants employed by the Insolvency Service which is an Executive Agency of the Department of Trade and Industry and they are attached either to the High Court or to a county court having winding up jurisdiction: s 399(3). In a compulsory winding up the Official Receiver has certain investigative functions designed to protect the public interest by ensuring that fraud or other malpractice is detected and dealt with: ibid, ss 131–134.
1   IR 1986, r 4.21(1).

registered office[2]; ánd one copy will be sent to the registrar of companies[3]. The order will be notified in the Gazette and advertised in a local paper[4].

The winding up is deemed to have commenced at the time of the presentation of the petition[5], unless the company had passed a resolution for voluntary winding up prior to the presentation of the petition, in which case the winding up is deemed to have commenced at the date of the passing of the resolution[6]. As we shall see, certain consequences flow from the date of commencement of the winding up.

Dispositions of the company's property   Since a compulsory winding up commences with the presentation of the petition, property which should be available to the creditors may have been disposed of in the period between the time of the presentation of the petition and the making of the winding-up order. To preserve such property for the creditors, it is provided that all dispositions of the company's property[7] after the commencement of the winding up are void unless the court orders otherwise[8].

In exercising their discretion to validate dispositions[9], the courts look to see if the disposition was made bona fide to assist the company[10] such as the repayment of, or the grant of security for, loans made to the company after the commencement of insolvency[11]. But they have generally refused to validate payments which have the effect of preferring pre-insolvency creditors[12] unless either the payment confers a benefit on creditors generally[13] or the creditor did not know of the insolvency at the time of receiving payment[14]. In the latter case, though, the payment will still not be validated if the intention of the debtor was to prefer that creditor[15].

It is open to either the company or any creditor to apply to the court to validate a transaction in advance of it taking place and this is particularly useful where the company carries on business in the period between the presentation of a winding-up petition and the making of a winding-up order. In such circumstances the courts adopt the same general approach and take into account the benefit to the creditors generally of keeping a business going with a view to selling it as a going concern.

Control of legal proceedings and enforcement of remedies   When the winding-up order has been made all pending proceedings are automatically halted and no new proceedings may be commenced, except by the leave of the court under IA 1986,

2   Ibid, r 4.21(2).
3   Ibid, r 4.21(3); IA 1986, s 130(1).
4   IR 1986, r 4.21(4).
5   IA 1986, s 129(2).
6   Ibid, s 129(1).
7   Any transfers of shares, or alterations in the status of the company's members are also void: ibid, s 127.
8   Ibid.
9   As to what is a disposition for these purposes, see *Re J Leslie Engineering Co Ltd* [1976] 2 All ER 85, [1976] 1 WLR 292. Payments by a company into an overdrawn account with its bank with the resulting reduction in its indebtedness to the bank is a disposition: *Re Gray's Inn Construction Co Ltd* [1980] 1 All ER 814, [1980] 1 WLR 711, CA, but a payment into an account which is in credit simply results in an adjustment of the records between the company and its bank and is not a disposition for these purposes: *Re Barn Crown Ltd* [1994] 4 All ER 42, [1995] 1 WLR 147; see generally Frieze 'Avoidance of disposition claims against banks' (1994) 7 Insolv Intel 59.
10   *Re J Leslie Engineering Co Ltd* [1976] 2 All ER 85, [1976] 1 WLR 292; *Re Gray's Inn Construction Co Ltd* [1980] 1 All ER 814, [1980] 1 WLR 711, CA.
11   *Re Steane's (Bournemouth) Ltd* [1950] 1 All ER 21; *Re Clifton Place Garage Ltd* [1970] Ch 477, [1970] 1 All ER 353, CA.
12   *Re Civil Service and General Store Ltd* (1887) 57 LJ Ch 119.
13   *Re A I Levy (Holdings) Ltd* [1964] Ch 19, [1963] 2 All ER 556.
14   *Re Gray's Inn Construction Co Ltd* [1980] 1 All ER 814, [1980] 1 WLR 711, CA.
15   *Re J Leslie Engineering Co Ltd* [1976] 2 All ER 85, [1976] 1 WLR 292.

s 130(2)[16]. Once a winding-up order has been made, s 128(1) appears to render void any enforcement of a remedy after the commencement of the winding up. It is, however, invariably treated as also subject to the court's discretion under s 130(2) to allow the enforcement to continue[17]. So far as legal proceedings are concerned, the courts allow proceedings relating to property rights to continue[18] but in relation to other matters will decide whether there is any sensible point in allowing the proceedings to continue[19].

Execution of judgments   Where legal proceedings have already resulted in a judgment against the company, the discretion to stop enforcement of the judgment after the commencement of winding up is supplemented by IA 1986, s 183. This provides that, unless the court orders otherwise[20], the proceeds of an execution against the goods or land of a company or the attachment of a debt due to the company cannot be retained by the creditor against the liquidator unless completed before the commencement of winding up[1].

The court thus has a discretion whether to allow the enforcement to proceed or, if it already has proceeded but was not completed in time, whether to allow the creditor to keep the proceeds. The strong presumption in exercising all these discretionary powers is that the court must do what is fair and right in the circumstances of the case and must not allow the individual creditor the benefit of enforcing the judgment if this will prejudice the equal treatment of creditors generally[2]. On the other hand, the court has allowed the individual creditor to succeed where the debtor forced[3], tricked[4] or persuaded[5] the creditor into abstaining from enforcing a judgment sometime before the winding up commenced.

Levying distress   The lack of sympathy for individual judgment creditors is in marked contrast to the courts' attitude to the levying of distress by creditors to whom that particular remedy is available, such as a landlord's distress for rent. Where the distress is in progress at the commencement of the winding up the courts will allow it to continue[6] and do not treat it as an 'execution or attachment' (under s 183 above), unless there are exceptional circumstances[7], notwithstanding that the consequence is to prefer one creditor ahead of the rest. However, distraint is treated as an 'action or proceeding' under s 130(2) and controlled by the court in that way[8].

---

16   The court also has power to stay any legal proceedings against the company at any time between the presentation of the winding up petition and before the winding up order is made: IA 1986, s 126(1).
17   See Fletcher *The Law of Insolvency* (1996), p 633; *Re Lancashire Cotton Spinning Co, ex p Carnelly* (1887) 35 Ch D 656, CA.
18   *Re David Lloyd & Co, Lloyd v David Lloyd & Co* (1877) 6 Ch D 339, CA and *Re Aro Co Ltd* [1980] Ch 196, [1980] 1 All ER 1067, CA (secured creditors enforcing security); *Re Coregrange Ltd* [1984] BCLC 453 (creditor suing for specific performance).
19   Leave will not be given if the issues can conveniently be decided in the winding up (*Craven v Blackpool Greyhound Stadium and Racecourse Ltd* [1936] 3 All ER 513, CA; *Re Exchange Securities and Commodities Ltd* [1983] BCLC 186) but will be given if the issues are better decided by an action (*Currie v Consolidated Kent Collieries Corpn Ltd* [1906] 1 KB 134, CA).
20   IA 1986, s 183(2)(c).
1   Or before notice to the creditor that a meeting has been called to consider a resolution for voluntary winding up: ibid, s 183(2)(a).
2   *Roberts Petroleum Ltd v Bernard Kenny Ltd* [1983] 2 AC 192, [1983] 1 All ER 564, HL; *Re Grosvenor Metal Co Ltd* [1950] Ch 63.
3   *Re London Cotton Co* (1866) LR 2 Eq 53.
4   *Armorduct Manufacturing Co Ltd v General Incandescent Co Ltd* [1911] 2 KB 143, CA.
5   *Re Grosvenor Metal Co Ltd* [1950] Ch 63; *Re Suidair International Airways Ltd* [1951] Ch 165, [1950] 2 All ER 920; *Re Redman (Builders) Ltd* [1964] 1 All ER 851, [1964] 1 WLR 541.
6   *Herbert Berry Associates Ltd v IRC* [1978] 1 All ER 161, [1977] 1 WLR 1437, HL; *Re Bellaglade Ltd* [1977] 1 All ER 319.
7   See *Re G Winterbottom (Leeds) Ltd* [1937] 2 All ER 232.
8   *Herbert Berry Associates Ltd v IRC* [1978] 1 All ER 161, [1977] 1 WLR 1437, HL.

THE LIQUIDATOR

Appointment

In a compulsory winding up, on the making of the winding-up order, the Official Receiver will become the liquidator[9]. If he considers it worthwhile, or if 25% in value of creditors request it, the Official Receiver then calls separate meetings of creditors and of members for the purpose of choosing a person to be the liquidator of the company in place of the Official Receiver[10]. Each meeting may then nominate a liquidator, though, in the event of different nominations, the creditors' nominee will be appointed[11]. If no meetings are held or no nominations made, the Official Receiver remains as liquidator[12].

In a members' voluntary winding up, the members appoint the liquidator[13]. In a creditors' voluntary winding up, if the members and creditors cannot agree then the creditors' nominee is appointed[14]. This illustrates one of the real differences between a members' and creditors' voluntary winding up because the members' nominee as liquidator, as often as not probably a person chosen by the directors, may be expected to be less inquisitive about the directors' past conduct of the company's business.

Since 1986, whoever is appointed as liquidator, whether in a compulsory or voluntary liquidation, apart from the Official Receiver, must be a qualified insolvency practitioner in relation to the company concerned[15]. This means, among other things, that he or she must be an individual, in respect of whom appropriate financial security is in force, who is authorised either as a member of a recognised professional body or as an individual by the Secretary of State and who is independent of the company concerned[16].

In addition, a liquidation committee essentially overseeing the conduct of the liquidation may be set up in either a compulsory or creditors' voluntary winding up consisting of creditors' and members' representatives and exercising various functions in relation to the liquidation[17]. Provision as to the functions, membership and proceedings of such committees is included in the Insolvency Rules[18].

Duties of a liquidator

The basic duty of the liquidator in all types of liquidation is to collect in and realise the company's assets[19]. Title to the company's assets is not automatically vested in

---

9 IA 1986, s 136(1), (2). The court also has power to appoint a provisional liquidator prior to the making of the winding-up order: see s 135.
10 Ibid, s 136(4), (5).
11 Ibid, s 139(2), (3).
12 There is provision for the Secretary of State to appoint a replacement liquidator on the application of the Official Receiver or following the failure of the meetings to appoint: ibid, s 137(1), (2).
13 Ibid, s 91(1).
14 Ibid, s 100(1), (2). Since the members' meeting will have taken place first any nominee of that meeting will have become liquidator prior to the creditors' meeting being held. Until the creditors' meeting is held, however, such a liquidator, without the consent of the court, has power only to protect and preserve the company's property or to dispose of perishable items: s 166. For the background to this provision, see Fletcher, *The Law of Insolvency* (1996), pp 501–504. Directors' powers are also circumscribed pending the appointment of a liquidator: see IA 1986, s 114, but see the problems which arise if no liquidator is appointed: *Re a Company (No 006341 of 1992), ex p B Ltd* [1994] 1 BCLC 225.
15 IA 1986, ss 230(3)–(5), 389, 390. For the background to these requirements, see the Cork Committee Report, Cmnd 8558, ch 15.
16 IA 1986, ss 390–393; the Insolvency Practitioners Regulations 1990, SI 1990 No 439; see art 4(1)(f).
17 IA 1986, ss 141 and 101.
18 IR 1986, rr 4.151 ff.
19 IA 1986, s 143(1) (compulsory winding up); ss 91(1), 100(1) (voluntary winding up) .

the liquidator unless, exceptionally, the court so orders[20]. In a compulsory liquidation, the directors' appointment automatically ceases[1] and the liquidator takes into his custody and control the company's property[2]. In a voluntary winding up, the power of the board ceases save in so far as they are allowed to continue by the liquidation committee in a creditors' voluntary winding up[3] or by the general meeting or the liquidator in a members' voluntary winding up[4].

When carrying out their functions, liquidators acts as agents of the company and any contracts a liquidator makes will be between the company and the outsider and the liquidator will incur no personal liability[5]:

> In my view a voluntary liquidator is more rightly described as an agent of the company – an agent who has no doubt cast upon him by statute and otherwise special duties, amongst which may be mentioned the duty of applying the company's assets in paying creditors and distributing the surplus among the shareholders[6].

Liquidators are in a fiduciary relationship with the company and must not place themselves in a position of conflict of interests[7]. Liquidators must not make any unauthorised profit from their position and any purchase by them of the company's property is liable to be set side[8]. Liquidators may also be liable for negligence in realising the company's property[9]. Duties owed by liquidators are owed to the company and not to individual contributories or creditors. So in *Knowles v Scott*[10] a liquidator was not liable for loss caused by delay in making a distribution to a contributory.

Powers of a liquidator

The powers of the liquidator are now set out in Sch 4 to the Insolvency Act 1986. In order to fulfil their duties liquidators are given a wide range of powers, some of which can be exercised of their own volition entirely, others of which need the appropriate consent. In a compulsory or creditors' voluntary winding up, the consent needed is that of either the court or the liquidation committee if one has been appointed[11]. In a members' voluntary winding up, the consent is given by the members by extraordinary resolution[12].

20   Ibid, s 145.
1   *Measures Bros Ltd v Measures* [1910] 2 Ch 248, CA.
2   IA 1986, s 144(1).
3   Ibid, s 103.
4   Ibid, s 91(2).
5   *Re Anglo-Moravian Hungarian Junction Rly Co, ex p Watkin* (1875) 1 Ch D 130, CA; *Re Silver Valley Mines Ltd* (1882) 21 Ch D 381; *Stead, Hazel & Co v Cooper* [1933] 1 KB 840.
6   *Knowles v Scott* [1891] 1 Ch 717, Ch D, per Romer J.
7   *Re Corbenstoke Ltd (No 2)* [1990] BCLC 60, 5 BCC 767.
8   *Silkstone and Haigh Moor Coal Co v Edey* [1900] 1 Ch 167. See also IR 1986, r 4.149.
9   *Re Windsor Steam Coal Co (1901) Ltd* [1928] Ch 609; *Re Home and Colonial Insurance Co Ltd* [1930] 1 Ch 102.
10   [1891] 1 Ch 717.
11   IA 1986, ss 167(1) and 165(2)(b). Consent should be sought first from the liquidation committee and application to the court made if consent is refused or given subject to conditions the liquidator will not accept. The liquidator should tell the committee of his application to the court so that their views may be heard as well: *Re Consolidated Diesel Engine Manufacturers Ltd* [1915] 1 Ch 192.
12   IA 1986, s 165(2)(a).

- *Powers exercisable with sanction in a compulsory winding up or voluntary winding up*
  - (1) to pay any class of creditors in full;
  - (2) to make any compromise or arrangement with any creditors or claimants against the company;
  - (3) to compromise all calls and liabilities to calls against contributories etc.; and all questions in any way relating to or affecting the assets or the winding up of the company[13].
- *Additional powers exercisable without sanction in a voluntary winding up and with sanction in a compulsory winding up*
  - (4) to bring or defend any legal proceedings in the name and on behalf of the company;
  - (5) to carry on the business of the company so far as may be necessary for the beneficial winding up of the company[14].
- *Powers exercisable without sanction in either a compulsory or a voluntary winding up*
  - (6) to sell any of the company's property[15];
  - (7) to do all acts and to execute, in the name and on behalf of the company, all deeds, receipts and other documents;
  - (8) to prove, rank and claim in the bankruptcy, insolvency or sequestration of any contributory for any balance against his estate;
  - (9) to draw, accept, make and indorse any bill of exchange or promissory note in the name and on behalf of the company;
  - (10) to raise any requisite money on the security of the assets of the company;
  - (11) to take out in his official name letters of administration to any deceased contributory, and to do in his official name any other act necessary to obtain payment of any money due from a contributory or his estate;
  - (12) to appoint an agent to do any business which the liquidator is unable to do himself;
  - (13) to do all such other things as may be necessary for winding up the company's affairs and distributing its assets[16].

Continuing the business   One of the most important decisions a liquidator will have to take is whether to keep the company's business going and if so, for how long. It should be noted that liquidators may only do so in so far as it may be necessary for the beneficial winding up of the business[17]. This has been interpreted to mean they may do so if this may be expected to produce a better return for the creditors but not if the object is to seek to continue or resuscitate the business for the benefit of the members[18].

---

13 Ibid, Sch 4, Pt I.
14 Ibid, Sch 4, Pt II.
15 As to the meaning of the company's 'property' for these purposes, see *Re Oasis Merchandising Services Ltd, Ward v Aitken* [1997] 1 All ER 1009, CA: property is limited to the property of the company at the commencement of the liquidation and property representing the same; it does not include property which only arose after the liquidation, which was recoverable only by the liquidator pursuant to his statutory powers (for example under IA 1986, s 214 – wrongful trading, see below), and was held by him for distribution on the statutory trust for the unsecured creditors. See also *Re Ayala Holdings Ltd (No 2)* [1996] 1 BCLC 467.
16 IA 1986, Sch 4, Part III.
17 Ibid, Sch 4, para 5.
18 *Re Wreck Recovery and Salvage Co* (1880) 15 Ch D 353, CA; see also *Re Great Eastern Electric Co Ltd* [1941] Ch 241, [1941] 1 All ER 409.

Furthermore, in a compulsory winding up a liquidator must obtain the consent of the court or the liquidation committee to a decision to carry on the business[19].

Disclaimer   Disclaimer is a means by which a liquidator can terminate certain obligations on the company or disclaim ownership of unsaleable assets[20]; and he can exercise the power of disclaimer notwithstanding that he has taken possession of the property, endeavoured to sell it, or otherwise exercised rights of ownership in relation to it[1]. One purpose behind the power is simply to enable the winding up to be completed without undue delay, or, in some cases, to be completed at all.

But disclaimer also enables the liquidator unilaterally to terminate onerous contracts so that, for example, the other party to a contract cannot insist on performing the contract and adding unnecessarily to the debts of the company but can be compelled to sue for damages as an unsecured creditor.

Onerous property is defined as:

(a) any unprofitable contract; and
(b) any other property of the company which is unsaleable or not readily saleable or is such that it may give rise to a liability to pay money or perform any other onerous act.[2]

Disclaimer is effected by the liquidator serving a notice[3] and the effect of a disclaimer is to terminate, as from the date of the disclaimer, the rights and liabilities of the company in the property disclaimed[4]. But, it does not, except so far as is necessary for the purposes of releasing the company from any liability, affect the rights or liabilities of any other person[5]. There is no time limit within which the liquidator must decide whether to disclaim property except that any person with an interest in the property can serve a notice on the liquidator requiring the liquidator to disclaim within 28 days or lose the right to do so[6]. The court can interfere with a disclaimer only if it is exercised in bad faith or the liquidator's decision was perverse[7].

Additional powers   Another consideration will be whether to take summary proceedings against any of the company's directors for breach of duty to the company or to challenge any transactions entered into by the company prior to going into liquidation[8]. To assist liquidators to get a complete picture of the company's affairs, liquidators (and other office-holders) have extensive powers to inquire into the company's dealings and to seek the court's assistance by summoning persons to appear before it, or requiring persons to submit affidavits or produce books, documents or other records relating to the company[9].

---

19 The committee's sanction cannot be given retrospectively and if the liquidator contracts without consent he will be personally liable to the other party for breach of warranty of authority. The court, however, has power to give a retrospective sanction: *Re Associated Travel Leisure and Services Ltd* [1978] 2 All ER 273, [1978] 1 WLR 547.
20 IA 1986, s 178.
1   Ibid, s 178(2).
2   Ibid, s 178(3).
3   For the rules as to the proper service of the notice and the persons on whom it must be served, see IR 1986, rr 4.187–4.194.
4   IA 1986, s 178(4)(a).
5   Ibid, s 178(4)(b).
6   Ibid, s 178(5).
7   *Re Hans Place Ltd* [1993] BCLC 768, [1992] BCC 733. See Crabb (1993) 6 Insolv Intel 34.
8   All these aspects are discussed in detail below.
9   IA 1986, s 236. An extensive case law now exists on the scope of this provision, see in particular, *British and Commonwealth Holdings plc v Spicer and Oppenheim* [1993] AC 426, [1992] 4 All ER 876, HL; *Cloverbay Ltd v Bank of Credit and Commerce International SA* [1991] Ch 90, [1991] 1 All ER 894.

In a compulsory winding up, the liquidator may summon general meetings of the creditors or contributories for the purpose of ascertaining their wishes; and in some circumstances he can be compelled to call such meetings[10]. He may also apply to the court for directions in relation to any particular matter arising in the winding up[11].

Control of the liquidator

While the liquidation is in progress individual contributories or creditors can apply to the court to control the exercise or proposed exercise of any of the liquidator's powers[12]. Furthermore, any person aggrieved by an act or decision of the liquidator may apply to the court[13].

In *Re Edennote Ltd, Tottenham Hotspur plc v Ryman*[14] the Court of Appeal accepted that the trial judge had adopted the correct test when considering a challenge to an assignment of a cause of action by a liquidator. The correct test was that, fraud and bad faith apart, the court will only interfere with an act of a liquidator if he has done something so utterly unreasonable and absurd that no reasonable person would have done it[15].

Individual contributories or creditors may also use the summary procedure under the Insolvency Act 1986, s 212 to ask the court to compel the liquidator to restore property to the company or compensate it for breach of duty[16]. The power to make such an application continues after the winding-up is completed and notwithstanding the release of the liquidator from all liability connected with the liquidation[17], but any application in these circumstances needs the court's consent[18].

DISTRIBUTION OF ASSETS

Proof of debts

Contrary to what might be supposed, the administration of an insolvent debtor's estate does not involve the payment and discharge of *all* the debts owing by the debtor. Instead, it is only those debts which are provable in the insolvency and which are proved which will receive any payment.

The rules specifying which debts are provable and what procedure is to be followed in establishing the claim are contained in the Insolvency Rules 1986[19]. The principal rule is that the company must have been liable on the debt at the time of going into

---

10   IA 1986, s 168(1), (2).
11   Ibid, s 168(3).
12   Under ibid, s 167(3) in compulsory liquidation and s 112(1) in voluntary liquidation. See *Re Greenhaven Motors Ltd* [1997] 1 BCLC 739, [1997] BCC 547 (liquidator must have acted mala fide or in a way in which no reasonable liquidator would have acted). The court will not grant an injunction to restrain a proposed transaction on a mere allegation of negligence by the liquidator: *Leon v York-O-Matic Ltd* [1966] 3 All ER 277, [1966] 1 WLR 1450; *Harold M Pitman & Co v Top Business Systems (Nottingham) Ltd* [1984] BCLC 593.
13   In compulsory winding up, under IA 1986, s 168(5); in voluntary winding up, s 112(1).
14   [1996] 2 BCLC 389, [1996] BCC 718, CA.
15   For example, by selling an asset of the company without taking into account the possibility that a third party might well have made a better offer than he to whom it was sold: [1996] 2 BCLC 389 at 394.
16   IA 1986, s 212(3).
17   Ibid, ss 173(4), 174(6).
18   Ibid, s 212(4), (5).
19   IR 1986, rr 4.73–4.94.

liquidation[20]; and all debts by creditors are provable as debts against the company whether they are present or future, certain or contingent, ascertained or sounding only in damages[1].

It does not matter that at the time when the debt was incurred the creditor knew that a winding-up petition had been presented or that a meeting had been called to vote on a resolution putting the company into liquidation. Nor does it matter that the actual debt arose after the company had gone into liquidation provided that it is in respect of an obligation incurred before the company went into liquidation. Thus a contractual promise, entered into before going into liquidation, to pay a sum of money at a date occurring after the company has gone into liquidation gives rise to a provable debt. Provided a tortious injury occurred before the company went into liquidation, the liability in respect of it is provable and it does not matter that the damages are not quantified until after the company is in liquidation[2]. The liquidator is given specific power to estimate the value of contingent liabilities or debts of an uncertain amount[3].

In a compulsory winding up, the creditors are required to submit a written claim, or 'proof',[4] as it is called; in a voluntary winding up, it is for the liquidator to decide whether he requires written proofs[5]. The liquidator examines the proof and may admit all or part of the debt or may reject it[6]. Parties aggrieved may apply to the court[7].

Secured creditors   In the case of secured creditors, if they are content to rely solely on their security they do not submit a proof of debt at all[8]. Alternatively, they may value their security and prove for any unsecured balance,[9] or realise their security and prove for any unsecured balance,[10] or surrender their security and prove for the whole amount[11].

SET-OFF

A further restriction on the amount for which creditors may prove arises from the rules of set-off which apply under IR 1986, r 4.90, where, before the company goes into liquidation, there have been mutual credits, mutual debts or other mutual dealings between the company and any creditor of the company proving or claiming to prove for a debt in the liquidation[12].

The effect of this rule is that if creditors of a company also owe money to the company they must set off the debts against each other and can only prove for the

---

20   Ibid, r 13.12. A company goes into liquidation if it passes a resolution for voluntary winding up or an order for its winding up is made by the court at a time when it has not already gone into liquidation by passing such a resolution: IA 1986, s 247(2).

1   IR 1986, r 12.3(1).

2   Ibid, r 13.12(2), (3).

3   Ibid, r 4.86. In cases of difficulty, application may be made to the court for assistance: IA 1986, s 168(3), (5).

4   See IR 1986, r 4.73(3).

5   Ibid, r 4.73.

6   Ibid, r 4.82.

7   Ibid, r 4.83.

8   The rules as to proof by secured creditors are contained in ibid, rr 4.95–4.99.

9   Ibid, r 4.75(1)(g). As to the liquidator's right to redeem the security at the creditor's valuation see r 4.97.

10   Ibid, r 4.88(1).

11   Ibid, r 4.88(2).

12   Ibid, r 4.90. See the Cork Committee Report, Cmnd 8558, ch 30. See generally, Derham *Set-off* (2nd edn, 1996); Wood *English and International Set-off* (1989).

balance[13]. In practice, set-off benefits creditors, for instead of having to prove with other creditors for the whole of their debt (ie having to claim against the pooled assets and possibly risk not being paid at all), creditors can set off debts they owe the company and prove or pay only the balance[14].

Creditors will therefore seek to acquire rights of set-off but again there are limitations. Thus, the dealings giving rise to the set-off must occur before the company goes into liquidation[15]. Likewise, there can be no set-off where the creditors, at the time the sums became due to them from the company, knew of the summoning of the meeting of creditors (in the case of a creditors' voluntary winding up) or that a petition for the winding up of the company was pending (in the case of a compulsory winding up)[16].

Set-off is mandatory and creditors are not allowed to contract out of their right of set-off[17]. As Hoffmann LJ explained: 'If there have been mutual dealings before the winding up order which have given rise to cross claims, nether party can prove or sue for his full claim. An account must be taken and he must prove or sue (as the case may be) for the balance'[18]. Set-off is automatic and self-executing as at the date of the winding up order[19] with the original claims extinguished and only a net balance remaining[20].

Set-off is strictly limited to mutual claims existing at the time of liquidation and there

> ... can be no set-off of claims by third parties, even with their consent. To do so
> would be to allow the parties by agreement to subvert the fundamental principle
> of pari passu distribution of the insolvent company's assets[1].

The BCCI case, involving the collapse with massive debts of the Bank of Credit and Commerce International, has been a rich source of litigation on the right of set-off, presenting as it did a situation where individuals both saved with the bank and borrowed from the bank and so were in the capacity of both creditors and debtors.

---

13 Provided both debts arise out of mutual dealings, for example, that both transactions were entered into in the same capacity. A creditor who is owed both secured and unsecured debts by the company is entitled to exercise the right of set-off against the unsecured part of the total debt since it is only in respect of that amount that the creditor will be submitting a proof: *Re Norman Holding Co Ltd* [1990] 3 All ER 757, [1991] 1 WLR 10.
14 See *Stein v Blake* [1996] AC 243, [1995] 2 All ER 961, HL. This is a bankruptcy case but the principles are essentially common to winding up and bankruptcy.
15 IR 1986, r 4.90(1). See *Manson v Smith* [1997] 2 BCLC 161, CA: there can be no set-off available between a debt due from the company to a misfeasant and his liability to repay money which he had been ordered to pay in misfeasance proceedings because a misappropriation of assets is not a dealing, and a liability for misfeasance only arose after the winding up.
16 IR 1986, r 4.90(3).
17 *National Westminster Bank Ltd v Halesowen Presswork and Assemblies Ltd* [1972] AC 785, [1972] 1 All ER 641, HL; *Stein v Blake* [1996] AC 243, [1995] 2 All ER 961, HL, noted Berg [1997] LMCLQ 49; *MS Fashions Ltd v Bank of Credit and Commerce International SA (No 2)* [1993] Ch 425, [1993] 3 All ER 769, Ch D, CA.
18 *MS Fashions Ltd v Bank of Credit and Commerce International SA (No 2)* [1993] Ch 425 at 432, [1993] 3 All ER 769 at 775.
19 *MS Fashions Ltd v Bank of Credit and Commerce International SA (No 2)* [1993] Ch 425 at 432, [1993] 3 All ER 769 at 775.
20 *Re Bank of Credit and Commerce International SA (No 8)* [1997] 4 All ER 568, HL, affg [1996] Ch 245, [1996] 2 All ER 121, CA which affd [1995] Ch 46, [1994] 3 All ER 565; *Stein v Blake* [1996] AC 243, [1995] 2 All ER 961, HL. Any balance can be assigned by the party entitled to it: *Stein v Blake, supra.*
1   *Re Bank of Credit and Commerce International SA (No 8)* [1997] 4 All ER 568 at 573, HL, per Lord Hoffmann.

Set-off was critical to minimising their losses. An absence of set-off would mean that such individuals might loose their savings (being unsecured creditors) while being liable to the liquidators for their borrowings.

In many instances, the bank had lent money to companies on the security of deposits made with the bank. In such straightforward cases, the amount of the loan outstanding at the time of liquidation would be set off against the company's deposit at the bank leaving a balance, one way or the other.

However, in some cases, the deposits used as security for the company's loan were deposits in the name of the company's directors or third parties. The issue arose as to whether there was a sufficient element of mutuality to allow a loan from the bank to the company to be set off against a deposit in the name of a director or third party. If there was no set-off, the companies (often owned by the directors or third parties) would still be liable to repay all their borrowings, and the directors and third parties would be left to prove in the liquidation for their deposits which, given the extent of the insolvency, was likely to yield little or nothing.[2] Set-off was therefore critical to their attempts to salvage something.

In *MS Fashions Ltd v Bank of Credit and Commerce International SA(No 2)*[3] the bank advanced money to a company and repayment was guaranteed by a director who had a deposit account with the bank. As between himself and the bank, the director was expressed to be a principal debtor. It was held that the company director, as a principal debtor, could rely on the right of set-off to reduce or extinguish the debt owed to the bank by him and his company, by the amount standing to his credit in his own deposit account with the bank. The key point, however, was that, under the terms of this particular loan, the director was deemed to be the principal debtor.

In *Re Bank of Credit and Commerce International SA (No 8)*[4] the House of Lords confronted this issue of whether third party deposits[5] which secured loans of borrowers (companies) should be set off against the company's debt or whether the liquidators were entitled to claim the entire debt from the company leaving the depositors to prove in liquidation for their deposits.

The House of Lords held that set-off was limited to mutual claims existing at the date of the winding up order and there could be no set-off of claims by third parties, even with their consent, as to do so would be to allow parties by agreement to subvert the fundamental principle of pari passu distribution of an insolvent company's assets[6].

There was no mutuality between the depositors and the bank which would permit the sum owed by the bank to the depositor (ie the amount of the deposit and interest) to be set off against the amount owed by the depositor to the bank under the security document as the depositor did not owe anything to the bank (not having taken on any personal liability for the borrower's debt) but had simply created an effective charge over the deposit in favour of the bank[7].

MS Fashions Ltd v Bank of Credit and Commerce International SA (No 2) was distinguishable on the basis of the very unusual security documents executed by the depositors in that case which resulted in the depositors being personally liable to the

2   As Lord Hoffmann noted, the sense of injustice felt by the depositors in this situation arose not so much from the operation of the rules of set-off but from the principle that a company is a person separate from its controlling shareholders; see *Re Bank of Credit and Commerce International SA (No 8)* [1997] 4 All ER 568 at 573, HL.
3   [1993] Ch 425, [1993] 3 All ER 769.
4   [1997] 4 All ER 568, HL.; affg [1996] Ch 245, [1996] 2 All ER 121, CA which affd [1995] Ch 46, [1994] 3 All ER 565, Ch D. See also *Tam Wing Chuen v Bank of Credit and Commerce Hong Kong Ltd* [1996] 2 BCLC 69, PC.
5   The third parties were the beneficial owners of the companies.
6   [1997] 4 All ER 568 at 573.
7   [1997] 4 All ER 568 at 574, 576, 577.

bank and so the bank's liability to the depositors and the depositor's liability to the bank constituted mutual dealings falling to be set off under r 4.90[8].

Order of distribution of assets

In the case of an insolvent company, the creditors rank equally and are paid rateably according to the size of their debts. This is known as the pari passu principle and, in theory, it is the fundamental basis for the distribution of the assets on insolvency[9]. In fact, there is a strict hierarchy in which the assets must be applied.

EXPENSES OF THE WINDING UP

Top of the list are the costs, charges and expenses of the winding up[10]; followed by the preferential debts. Only when those have been paid will the remaining assets be available for distribution among the unsecured creditors.

The expenses of the winding up will include items such as rent on premises which the liquidator uses to store assets pending realisation[11] and, if it is necessary to carry on the business of the company for the beneficial winding up of it, any debts incurred in so carrying on the business[12]. It will also include the remuneration of the liquidator.

PREFERENTIAL DEBTS

Next in order of priority comes those preferential debts which Parliament has decided should be paid in priority to all other debts[13]. Preferential debts rank equally among themselves, after the expenses of winding up, and must be paid in full unless the assets are insufficient to meet them, in which case they abate in equal proportions[14]. In so far as the assets available for payment of general creditors are insufficient for the payment of the preferential debts, the preferential debts also have priority over the claims of holders of debentures under a floating charge[15].

The debts granted preferential status consist chiefly of certain sums due to the Inland Revenue[16], to Customs and Excise[17] and to the Department of Health and Social

---

8   See [1997] 4 All ER 568 at 574; see Calnan (1998) 114 LQR 174; Goode (1998) 114 LQR 178.
9   See IA 1986, s 107; IR 1986, r 4.181.
10   IA 1986, ss 115, 175(2)(a). The expenses are payable in priority to all other claims, this means in priority to the claims of the preferential creditors and floating charge holders: *Re Portbase Clothing Ltd* [1993] Ch 388, [1993] 3 All ER 829.
11   *Re ABC Coupler and Engineering Co Ltd (No 3)* [1970] 1 All ER 650, [1970] 1 WLR 702; *Re Downer Enterprises Ltd* [1974] 2 All ER 1074, [1974] 1 WLR 1460.
12   *Re Great Eastern Electric Co Ltd* [1941] Ch 241, [1941] 1 All ER 409.
13   IA 1986, s 175(1).
14   Ibid, s 175(2)(a). A creditor owed preferential and non-preferential debts must exercise any right of set-off proportionately against each class of debt: *Re Unit 2 Windows Ltd* [1985] 3 All ER 647, [1985] 1 WLR 1383.
15   IA 1986, s 175(2)(b). 'Floating charge' is defined in s 251. Note also that in a compulsory winding up where distress is levied in the three months before a winding-up order, the preferential debts constitute a first charge on the proceeds of the distress: s 176(2),(3). This does not apply in a voluntary winding up: *Herbert Berry Associates Ltd v IRC* [1978] 1 All ER 161, [1977] 1 WLR 1437, HL.
16   IA 1986, Sch 6, paras 1 and 2. As recommended by the Cork Committee Report, Cmnd 8558, ch 32, all rates and assessed taxes ceased to be preferential under the Insolvency Act. However, since the 1986 reforms, a number of additional preferential taxes, such as the lottery duty and air passenger duties have been added to Sch 6.
17   IA 1986, Sch 6, paras 3–5.

Security[18]. Employees are entitled to claim as a preferential debt wages or salary for services rendered in the four months before winding up but up to a maximum amount of £800 per employee[19]. In addition, all accrued holiday remuneration has priority and is not counted towards the £800 limit[20].

Although giving wages and salaries preferential status is likely to go a long way towards ensuring that employees receive unpaid arrears it does not ensure that they will receive them quickly. It was to deal with this problem that a major innovation was made in 1975 whereby certain payments to employees of insolvent companies are guaranteed by the state. The payments, which must not exceed £198 per employee per week, are made out of the National Insurance Fund and include arrears of wages or salaries for up to eight weeks and up to six weeks' holiday pay to which the employee may have become entitled in the 12 months before winding up. Both these payments could rank as preferential in the winding up and once a payment has been made out of the redundancy fund, the fund is subrogated to the employee's claim, including any preferential status[1].

Provisions introduced in 1986 restrict public utilities from in effect claiming preferential payment of pre-winding-up debts[2]. After a company has gone into liquidation the suppliers of gas, electricity, water or telecommunications cannot make it a condition of any further supply that charges outstanding for supplies given before winding up are paid; neither can they do anything which has the effect of making further supply subject to such a condition[3]. Any such supply given after the company is in liquidation will normally rank as an expense of winding up and thus is likely to be paid in full but the supplier is permitted to make it a condition of such supply that the liquidator personally guarantees payment of the charges[4].

ORDINARY UNSECURED DEBTS – THE PARI PASSU PRINCIPLE

On liquidation, all the assets of the company form a common fund[5] which, subject to the discharging of the costs and expenses of the winding up and the rights of the preferential creditors, are subject to a statutory trust for the benefit of all the creditors,[6] other than the secured creditors who look to their security for payment of their debts. The assets must be used to pay the unsecured creditors in accordance with the principle of pari passu distribution that all creditors participate in the pooled assets in proportion to the size of their claim and, where the assets are insufficient to meet all the claims, then they abate proportionately[7].

So strong is the pari passu principle that a rule (known as 'the rule in *Ex p Mackay*'[8]) developed that any contractual provision designed to defeat such a

---

18   Priority is given to social security contributions payable in the 12 months before winding up and employers' contributions to occupational pension schemes and state pensions have similar priority: ibid Sch 6, paras 6–8.

19   Ibid, Sch 6, paras 9–12; the Insolvency Proceedings (Monetary Limits) Order 1986, SI 1986 No 1996, art 4.

20   IA 1986, Sch 6, para 10.

1   Employment Protection (Consolidation) Act 1978, s 122; Employment Protection (Variation of Limits) Order 1992, SI 1992 No 312.

2   See the Cork Committee Report, Cmnd 8558, paras 1451–1462.

3   IA 1986, s 233(2)(b).

4   Ibid, s 233(2)(a).

5   *Webb v Whiffin* (1872) LR 5 HL 711 at 720, 724.

6   See *Ayerst (Inspector of Taxes) v C & K (Construction) Ltd* [1976] AC 167, [1975] 2 All ER 537.

7   IA 1986, s 107; IR 1986, r 4.181.

8   *Re Jeavons, ex p MacKay, ex p Brown* (1873) 8 Ch App 643 (a bankruptcy case but the doctrine applies in corporate insolvency as well).

distribution on insolvency and in effect to prefer one unsecured creditor ahead of the others is void:

'... a man is not allowed by stipulation with a creditor, to provide for a different distribution of his effects in the event of bankruptcy [insolvency for our purposes] from that which the law provides'[9].

There can be no contracting out of the pari passu rule, a point confirmed by the House of Lords in *British Eagle International Airlines Ltd v Cie Nationale Air France*[10], although there is nothing to prevent a creditor with a claim against the pooled assets from agreeing as a matter of contract to subordinate his claim until such time as all other unsecured creditors are paid[11].

The net result is that creditors go to great lengths to ensure that, prior to insolvency occurring, they have taken steps to ensure that assets are available *outside* of the pool to meet their claims, for example by taking security over the assets or retaining title to the goods, so that those assets never become part of the company's assets on liquidation and are not therefore swept by the rule in *ex p Mackay* into the pool for pari passu distribution[12]. We have already noted that unsecured creditors may escape from the pool if they are in a position to benefit from the doctrine of set-off. Some of the other main mechanisms available which deplete the assets available to the liquidator for distribution pari passu are noted below. Indeed, in many cases, these devices ensure that there are no unencumbered assets available to the unsecured creditors.

Secured creditors: Obviously, the most advantageous position for a creditor is to be a secured creditor who can look to his security and need not prove in the liquidation at all. Creditors in a position to demand security tend to be the larger creditors, in particular the banks, and we have seen in earlier chapters how they will take fixed charges over a company's main assets but will also seek a floating charge sweeping up any other remaining assets available in the company, although a floating charge is subject to the claims of the preferential creditors. We have seen that this process has been further refined to enable banks to take fixed rather than floating charges over assets such as book debts so defeating not just the unsecured creditors but also the preferential creditors. As the Cork Committee noted, the net result is the withdrawal of an increasing proportion of the debtor's assets from the claims of the general body of creditors[13] so that only the secured creditors, or possibly just the secured and the preferential creditors, get paid on insolvency.

Trust property: It is only property to which the company is beneficially entitled that is available to its creditors. If the company holds property on trust for others, that property is not available to the company's creditors[14]. This has led to the use of the trust as a means of protecting unsecured creditors by making them beneficiaries under

9   (1873) 8 Ch App 643 at 647, per Sir W M James, LJ.
10   [1975] 2 All ER 390, [1975] 1 WLR 758, HL, a 3–2 decision, see the dissenting speeches in this case.
11   See *Re Maxwell Communications Corp plc (No 2)* [1994] 1 BCLC 1; Nolan [1995] JBL 485; also *Re British and Commonwealth Holdings (No 3) plc* [1992] BCLC 322. See Johnston *Contractual Debt Subordination and Legislative Reform* [1991] JBL 225.
12   For a comprehensive and valuable survey of these developments over the years, see Milman 'Priority Rights on Corporate Insolvency' in *Current Issues in Insolvency Law* (1991).
13   See the Cork Committee Report, Cmnd 8558, para 1478.
14   See *Barclays Bank Ltd v Quistclose Investments Ltd* [1970] AC 567, [1968] 3 All ER 651, HL; *Carreras Rothmans Ltd v Freeman Mathews Treasure Ltd* [1985] Ch 207, [1985] 1 All ER 155. See Simmons *Avoiding the Pari Passu Rule* (1996) 9 Insolv Intel 9; also Belcher & Beglen, *Jumping the Queue* [1997] JBL 1.

a trust. The most notable example of this is *Re Kayford Ltd*[15] where a mail order company in financial difficulties in November 1972 opened a separate bank account into which it paid money sent in advance for goods by its mail order customers. When the company went into liquidation in December 1972, it was held that the £11,000 in the account was held on trust for those customers whose money had been deposited there and was not available for the general creditors. The use of such trusts is relatively commonplace now and the only disputed issue is usually the factual one of whether the three certainties, of intention, subject matter and objects, required of any trust are present[16].

Goods subject to reservation of property: Although almost all the reported cases have concerned receivership, a clause in a sale of goods contract that prevents property passing to the purchaser[17] will not only mean that the goods are not available to the secured creditors who appointed the receiver, but also that they are not available to any unsecured creditors in a winding up.

The result of the widespread use of these and other mechanisms is that the pooled assets will usually be very insubstantial and quite inadequate to meet the claims of the unsecured creditors. For such creditors, who either through lack of foresight or contractual or financial power have not taken steps to obtain some security prior to insolvency, the pari passu rule designed to ensure equal treatment of creditors may simply, as Professor Milman has noted, secure an equality of misery[18]. The Cork Committee was driven to comment (in 1982) as follows[19]:

> The principle of pari passu distribution has been greatly eroded during the last century or so until today it remains as a theoretical doctrine only, with scarcely any application in real life. In a great number of cases, insolvency results in the distribution of the assets among the preferential creditors ... and the holders of floating charges... with little if anything for the ordinary unsecured creditors.

This led the Cork Committee to recommend that 10% of the net realisations of assets subject to a floating charge should be put aside for the unsecured creditors[20]. The Government, however, rejected this proposal[1] and it has not been implemented.

This disparity between the theory of pari passu distribution and the reality on winding up has led a number of commentators to question whether realistically we can go on asserting that the governing principle in insolvency is pari passu distribution since it has, in effect, become the exception rather than the rule[2].

---

15 [1975] 1 All ER 604, [1975] 1 WLR 279.
16 See *Re Lewis's of Leicester Ltd* [1995] 1 BCLC 428, [1995] BCC 514; *Re Holiday Promotions (Europe) Ltd* [1996] 2 BCLC 618; *Re Fleet Disposal Services Ltd, Spratt v AT & T Automotive Services Ltd* [1995] 1 BCLC 345, [1995] BCC 605.
17 So-called *Romalpa* clauses or reservation of title clauses: see *Aluminium Industries Vaassen v Romalpa Ltd* [1976] 2 All ER 552; *Clough Mill Ltd v Martin* [1984] 3 All ER 982, [1985] BCLC 64. See also Belcher & Beglen *'Jumping the Queue'* [1997] JBL 1.
18 See Milman *'Priority Rights on Corporate Insolvency'* in *Current Issues in Insolvency Law* (1991), p 77.
19 The Cork Committee Report, Cmnd 8558, para 233.
20 See the Cork Committee Report, Cmnd 8558, ch 34 and paras 1532–1549.
1   See A Revised Framework for Insolvency Law, 1984, Cmnd 9175, para 26.
2   See the trenchant criticisms by Fletcher *The Law of Insolvency* (1996), pp 613–616; also Milman *'Priority Rights on Corporate Insolvency'* in Clarke (ed) *Current Issues in Insolvency Law* (1991), p 78: 'The pari passu system is a crude standard to apply in the legal system of the late 20th century'.

Deferred debts

Certain debts are deferred by statute until all the other debts of the company have been paid. The first of these is interest on all proved debts, whether or not the debt was an interest-bearing debt, from the company going into liquidation until the date of actual payment[3]. It is specifically provided that for the purposes of interest under this provision all debts rank pari passu and it makes no difference, for example, whether the debt was preferential[4].

The second deferred debt arises where a company has contracted to redeem or purchase some of its own shares and the company has not completed the transaction by the time of the commencement of the winding up. The company may be compelled to complete the bargain but only after all other debts and liabilities of the company (other than any due to members in their character as such) have been paid[5].

The third deferred payment contained in IA 1986, s 74(2)(f) is any debt or liability due to a member in his character of a member whether by way of dividends, profits or otherwise.

The scope of this provision was considered by the House of Lords in *Soden v British and Commonwealth Holdings plc*[6] where a member of a company[7] brought an action against the company for damages for misrepresentation said to have induced the member to acquire the share capital of the company. That action had not been determined but, the company being insolvent, the preliminary issue arose as to whether damages due under that claim were sums due to a member in his character as a member and so subordinate to the claims of the other creditors of the company[8].

The House of Lords held that the damages sought by the member did not arise under the statutory contract, ie the CA 1985, s 14 contract between a company and its members, and therefore were not sums due to a member in his character as such and were not to be subordinated to the claims of other creditors.

Section 74(2)(f) required a distinction to be drawn between sums due to a member in his character of a member by way of dividends, profits or otherwise and sums due to a member of a company otherwise than in his character as a member. A sum was due to a member of a company 'in his character of a member' if the right to receive it was based on a cause of action founded on the statutory contract between the members and the company imposed by CA 1985, s 14 and such other provisions of the Act as conferred rights or imposed liabilities on members. The rational of IA 1986, s 74(2)(f), Lord Browne-Wilkinson noted, is to ensure that the rights of members *as such* do not compete with the rights of the general body of creditors[9]. However, a member having a cause of action independent of the statutory contract in CA 1985, s 14 is in no worse a position than any other creditor.

So debts to members in other capacities such as trade creditor or lender rank alongside similar debts due to non-members. This can be a source of abuse. A company may be incorporated with a share capital of, say, two £1 shares and the shareholders then lend the company all the money it needs for its business. Moreover, since they control the company it will be a simple matter for them to secure their loan on the assets of the company. So when the crunch comes, the shareholders, in their capacity

---

3   IA 1986, s 189.
4   Ibid, s 189(3).
5   CA 1985, s 178(4), (6). This is subject to sub-s (5) which rules out completion in certain circumstances.
6   [1997] 4 All ER 353, [1997] 2 BCLC 501, HL.
7   Actually its parent company.
8   Although the issue was hypothetical, because the potential damages were so enormous (in the region of £500m), the House of Lords thought it proper to decide this preliminary issue.
9   [1997] 4 All ER 353 at 358, [1997] 2 BCLC 501 at 506.

as secured creditors, will be the first to be paid. The Cork Committee considered this question and recommended that 'on the winding up of a company those of its liabilities, whether secured or unsecured, which are owed to connected persons or companies, and which appear to the court to represent all or part of the long-term capital structure of the company, shall be deferred to the claims of other creditors and be paid only after all such claims have been met in full'[10]. Regrettably the Committee's recommendation was not enacted in the form they proposed. The courts have, however, been given the power to defer debts due from the company to persons found liable for fraudulent or wrongful trading in relation to it[11].

VULNERABLE TRANSACTIONS

Avoidance of transactions prior to winding up

One of the main concerns of the Cork Committee was that there should be adequate powers to unravel dubious transactions entered into prior to the company going into insolvent liquidation[12].

A typical scenario would be that before Company A went into liquidation, the directors[13] would have transferred some or all of its remaining assets to another company, B, or to certain individuals so that the directors would be in a position to recommence business after the insolvency of Company A, leaving the creditors of Company A to look to the shell of that company for payment of their debts. Those associated with Company A would then be found running a profitable Company B having left their creditors behind at Company A "to whistle for their money"[14]. The transactions involved might include the sale of assets held by Company A to Company B or even directly to Company A's own directors at an undervalue; and the repayment of any directors' loans to Company A ahead of payments due to other creditors so as to ensure that the directors did not find themselves as creditors of Company A on insolvency.

It is important therefore that there are adequate statutory powers to challenge such transactions so as to ensure that the assets of Company A transferred out of it in dubious circumstances just prior to winding up are recovered for the benefit of the whole body of creditors of Company A. As we have seen, anything which will swell the assets available to the unsecured creditors is to be welcomed.

The general approach taken in the Insolvency Act 1986 is that specific transactions, often described as vulnerable transactions, are open to challenge by liquidators (and administrators) with the emphasis on civil actions seeking contributions to the assets for the creditors. In this part of the chapter we will examine, in turn, transactions at an undervalue, preferences, extortionate credit transactions and the avoidance of certain floating charges[15].

---

10   For the background, see the Cork Committee Report, Cmnd 8558, para 1963.
11   IA 1986, s 215(4).
12   See the Cork Committee Report, Cmnd 8558, ch 28.
13   Of course, in the smaller companies which make up a large percentage of the register of companies, the directors and the shareholders are usually one and the same.
14   See *Re Paramount Airways Ltd* [1993] Ch 223 at 225, [1992] 3 All ER 1 at 3, per Sir Donald Nicholls, V-C.
15   A liquidator will often seek to challenge a transaction under more than one of these grounds: see *Re DKG Contractors Ltd* [1990] BCC 903; *Re Fairway Magazines Ltd, Fairbairn v Hartigan* [1993] BCLC 643, [1992] BCC 924.

Transactions at an undervalue – IA 1986, s 238

Before the reforms introduced by the Cork Committee, liquidators attempting to attack gratuitous dispositions by directors prior to the company's insolvency had to resort to a variety of company law doctrines, none of which had been intended for the protection of creditors of insolvent companies and which therefore produced inconsistent results[16]. Now there is a specific provision governing transactions at an undervalue. The statutory provision contains many separate elements which must be established and it may be helpful to identify initially the discrete elements of the section before commenting on the more important requirements. The key questions are:

1. Has the company gone into administration or liquidation[17] ?
2. Did the company enter into a transaction at an undervalue with any person[18] within the period of two years ending with the onset of insolvency[19]?
3. Was this at a time when the company was unable to pay its debts[20] or did it become unable to pay its debts in consequence of the transaction[1]?

An undervalue arises if the company makes a gift to that person or otherwise enters into a transaction with that person on terms that provide for the company to receive no consideration, or the company enters into a transaction with that person for a consideration the value of which, in money or money's worth[2], is significantly less than the value, in money or money's worth, of the consideration provided by the company[3]. No element of fraudulent or other intention is required. Difficult questions will arise in assessing whether a payment by the company was a gift or, even if it was not, whether the company received significantly less than it provided[4]. It may be particularly difficult to assess the relative weight of the consideration provided when the transaction may already be several years old by the time the liquidator has an opportunity to review it.

Where these elements can be established then the liquidator (or an administrator) can apply to the court which may make such order as it thinks fit for restoring the position to what it would have been if the company had not entered into that

---

16   See, for example, *Re Horsley & Weight Ltd* [1982] Ch 442, [1982] 3 All ER 1045, CA; *Rolled Steel Products (Holdings) Ltd v British Steel Corpn* [1986] Ch 246, [1985] 3 All ER 52, CA.

17   IA 1986, s 238(1).

18   As to the application of the provision to persons resident outside the jurisdiction, see *Re Paramount Airways Ltd* [1993] Ch 223, [1992] 3 All ER 1, CA.

19   IA 1986, ss 238(2), 240(1)(a). The expression "the onset of insolvency" is defined in s 240(3); essentially it is the date of the presentation of the petition on which the administration order is made, or the date of the commencement of the winding up.

20   Within the meaning of ibid s 123, discussed in detail above.

1   Ibid, s 240(2). This requirement is presumed to be satisfied when the transaction was entered into by the company with a connected person. The precise definition of persons connected with the company is complex: see ss 249 and 435 but broadly it includes any directors or shadow directors of the company, ss 249(a), 251; their families, partners, and associated companies: s 435(2),(3),(6), (8).

2   See *Re MC Bacon Ltd* [1990] BCLC 324, [1990] BCC 78 where Millett J noted that this requires a comparison to be made between the value obtained by the company and the value of the consideration provided by the company. Both must be measurable in money or moneys' worth and both must be considered from the company's point of view.

3   IA 1986, s 238(4). The creation by a company of a charge over its assets in favour of a creditor is not a transaction at an undervalue as it does not deplete the company's assets and the consideration received by the company in granting the charge cannot be measured in money or money's worth: *Re MC Bacon Ltd* [1990] BCLC 324 at 341, [1990] BCC 78 at 92.

4   Consider the following examples: remuneration for directors' services as in *Re Halt Garage (1964) Ltd* [1982] 3 All ER 1016; an ex gratia pension for the past services of a director as in *Re Horsley & Weight Ltd* [1982] Ch 442, [1982] 3 All ER 1045, CA.

transaction[5]. Although the point is not without difficulty, this should mean that any property recovered goes into the pool of assets for the benefit of the unsecured creditors generally[6].

Section 241 lists a wide variety of orders which the court might make. The court may require any property transferred as part of the transaction to be vested in the company, release any security given by the company, require any person to make payments to the administrator or liquidator in respect of benefits received by him from the company, provide for a guarantor whose obligations have been discharged to be under revived obligations, provide for security to be given for the discharge of obligations imposed by the order and for the priority which such security shall have, and provide for the extent to which persons may be able to prove in the winding up[7].

No order will be made if the company entered into the transaction in good faith and for the purpose of carrying on its business, and at the time it did so there were reasonable grounds for believing that the transaction would benefit the company[8].

The existence of this defence adds considerably to the uncertainty regarding the effectiveness of this power to set aside transactions at an undervalue. It would presumably not be possible to defend the payment of excessive remuneration under such a provision. But the provision of a golden handshake or an ex gratia pension to a retiring director, the payment of a dividend, the guarantee of another company's debt or the grant of security for an existing unsecured loan could arguably satisfy the requirements of this defence and so be immune from attack under the provision. Equally, a sale of an asset at what appears, with hindsight, to be an undervalue may be explicable as having been the best option available to the company at that time when it was undergoing serious cash flow difficulties which could only be solved by an expeditious sale.

A very similar statutory remedy also available to liquidators can be found in IA 1986, s 423 and it too hinges on the same definition of a transaction at an undervalue. There are crucial differences, however, between s 423 and s 238. First, this provision (s 423) does not depend on the company being in liquidation and has no time zone limiting the review by the liquidator. However, it must be shown that the company's intention was to put assets beyond the reach of the claimant or otherwise prejudice a claimant[9]. Applications can be by the liquidator or the administrator but also, with the leave of the court, by any victim of the transaction[10].

Preferences – IA 1986, s 239

One of the main objectives in the winding up of an insolvent company, as we have seen, is to ensure the equal treatment of creditors. To help achieve this the court is

5   IA 1986, s 238(3). Despite the word 'shall' in the statute, the power vested in the court is discretionary: *Re Paramount Airways Ltd* [1993] Ch 223, [1992] 3 All ER 1, CA.
6   See the discussion below on this point in the section dealing with wrongful trading.
7   See *Re Paramount Airways Ltd* [1993] Ch 223 at 229, [1992] 3 All ER 1 at 7, CA. The good faith, or lack of knowledge of the relevant circumstances, of the other party to the transaction are irrelevant but sub-transferees acquiring interests or benefits in good faith and for value are protected: IA 1986, s 241(2); and there is a presumption of the interest being acquired or the benefit received other than in good faith in the circumstances outlined in s 241(2A), (3)–(3C) as amended by the Insolvency (No 2) Act 1994.
8   IA 1986, s 238(5).
9   Ibid, s 423(3). See *Arbuthnot Leasing International Ltd v Havelet Leasing Ltd (No 2)* [1991] 1 All ER 591, [1990] BCLC 802; *Chohan v Saggar* [1994] 1 BCLC 706, [1994] BCC 134; *Pinewood Joinery v Starelm Properties Ltd* [1994] 2 BCLC 412, [1994] BCC 569.
10   IA 1986, s 424(1)(a); see *National Bank of Kuwait v Menzies* [1994] 2 BCLC 306, [1994] BCC 119, CA.

given a power to set aside things the company has done or suffered to be done which have the effect of preferring a creditor or creditors ahead of others. This might involve paying an unsecured creditor in circumstances where this was done to ensure that on insolvency he was not left to claim against the pooled assets with the risk of non-payment which that entails; or it might entail giving security to an unsecured creditor, again to ensure that he is not left to claim against the pool. The rules on preferences do not stop companies from paying their creditors as insolvency looms but the company has to show that the transaction was activated solely by proper commercial considerations as opposed, for example, to paying off a creditor whose debt the director has personally guaranteed[11].

As before, certain conditions must be satisfied.

- Has the company gone into administration or liquidation[12] ?
- Did the company give a preference to any person within the period of six months ending with the onset of insolvency[13] or, in the case of a connected person, within the period of two years ending with the onset of insolvency[14]?
- Was the company at the time unable to pay its debts[15] or did it become unable to pay its debts in consequence of the preference[16]?

A company gives a preference to a person if :

(a) that person is one of the company's creditors or a surety or guarantor for any of the company's debts or other liabilities, and

(b) the company does anything or suffers anything to be done which (in either case) has the effect of putting that person into a position which, in the event of the company going into insolvent liquidation, will be better than the position he would have been in if that thing had not been done[17].

However, the court must not make an order under this provision unless the company which gave the preference was influenced in deciding to give it by a desire to prefer the creditor[18]. Where the preference is given to a connected person, there is a presumption of a desire to prefer[19].

The question of a desire to prefer was considered in *Re MC Bacon Ltd*[20] where a liquidator applied to the court for a debenture granted by the company to National Westminster Bank plc to be set aside as a preference. The company had gone into a creditors' voluntary liquidation in August 1987 (the onset of insolvency) with an estimated deficiency as regards unsecured creditors of £329,435. At that date, the company's overdraft at the National Westminster Bank stood at £235,530. This overdraft was secured by a debenture granted by the company in May 1987 (ie within

---

11   See *Re Agriplant Services Ltd* [1997] 2 BCLC 598, [1997] BCC 842, Ch D.
12   IA 1986, ss 239(1), 238(1).
13   The expression 'the onset of insolvency' is defined in ibid, s 240(3), essentially the date of the presentation of the petition on which the administration order is made; or the date of the commencement of the winding up.
14   Ibid, ss 239(2), 240(1)(a), (1)(b).
15   Within the meaning of ibid, s 123, discussed in detail above.
16   Ibid, s 240(2). Note that there is no proviso here deeming this to be the case in relation to a connected person unlike the position vis-à-vis a transaction at an undervalue.
17   Ibid, s 239(4).
18   Ibid, s 239(5). The date on which the company gives the preference is the date by reference to which the court has to consider whether there was a desire to prefer: *Wills v Corfe Joinery Ltd* [1997] BCC 511. A desire to prefer is insufficient if, on the facts, no actual preference occurred, see *Lewis v Hyde* [1997] BCC 976, PC (on a very similar New Zealand provision).
19   IA 1986, s 239(6); save where the person is connected by reason only of being an employee of the company: ibid.
20   [1990] BCLC 324, [1990] BCC 78, Ch D. See Fletcher [1991] JBL 71.

the six months prior to the onset of insolvency at a time when the company was unable to pay its debts).

The court emphasised that a key element in the test of what is a preference is that the company did what it did out of a positive wish to improve the creditor's position in the event of its own insolvent liquidation. There was, of course, no need for there to be direct evidence of the requisite desire; its existence might be inferred from the circumstances of the case. The mere presence of the requisite desire would not be sufficient by itself, however, it must have influenced the decision of the company to enter into the transaction. But it is sufficient if it was one of the factors which operated on the minds of those who made the decision, it need not have been the only factor or even the decisive one[1].

Here the company did not positively wish to improve the bank's position, its only concern was that the bank should not call in the overdraft and force it to stop trading. When it gave the security to the bank, it did so out of a desire to continue trading.

It seems likely that, as a result of this approach, the preference provisions will operate most effectively with respect to connected persons where the liquidator will be assisted by the existence of a presumption of a desire to prefer[2]. In all other cases, certainly where an arm's length creditor is pressing for payment, commercial considerations of the kind present in *Re MC Bacon Ltd* will usually be the motivating force rather than any desire to prefer the creditor.

Certainly preferences given to connected persons just prior to the collapse of the company are the precise type of transaction which the Cork Committee thought should be challenged[3]. Examples are cases such as *Re Living Images Ltd*[4], where the repayment of a loan of £11,000 to a friend of one of the directors four months prior to insolvency was found to constitute a preference[5]; and *Re Exchange Travel (Holdings) Ltd*[6], where in July 1990 the company repaid directors' loans of £200,000 (approximately) before going into administration in September 1990 with a deficiency running into millions of pounds. Similarly, in *Wills v Corfe Joinery Ltd*[7] repayment of directors' loans by the company just prior to ceasing to trade constituted a preference. The payments were made at a time when other creditors were pressing, employees were being made redundant and so, the court asked, why did the directors choose to pay these creditors? 'In the absence of evidence to show that it was purely for commercial reasons, there is nothing to rebut the statutory presumption and, indeed, everything to support that statutory presumption'[8].

Another common scenario is that a director will want to make sure that a particular creditor gets paid because he, the director, will have personally guaranteed that debt. In *Re Agriplant Services Ltd*[9] S was a director of A Ltd which hired equipment from

1   [1990] BCLC 324 at 335–336, [1990] BCC 78 at 87–88, Ch D; see also *Re Living Images Ltd* [1996] 1 BCLC 348, [1996] BCC 112.

2   IA 1986, s 239(6). But see *Re Beacon Lesiure Ltd* [1992] BCLC 565, [1991] BCC 213 (although this decision is of doubtful authority, see Prentice (1993) 109 LQR 371); *Re Fairway Magazines Ltd, Fairbairn v Hartigan* [1993] 1 BCLC 643, [1992] BCC 924 where the presumption was rebutted.

3   See the Cork Committee Report, Cmnd 8558, paras 1257–1258.

4   [1996] 1 BCLC 348, [1996] BCC 112. This case actually involved directors' disqualification proceedings rather than an application under IA 1986, s 239.

5   At the same time the company refused to pay another creditor who was owed £5,000 and offered payment by instalments instead: see [1996] 1 BCLC 348 at 368–369, [1996] BCC 112 at 127.

6   [1996] 2 BCLC 524, [1996] BCC 933. See subsequent proceedings in this case *Re Exchange Travel (Holdings) Ltd (No 3), Katz v McNally* [1997] 2 BCLC 579, sub nom *Katz v McNally* [1997] BCC 784, CA.

7   [1997] BCC 511.

8   [1997] BCC 511 at 517, per Lloyd J. See also *Re DKG Contractors Ltd* [1990] BCC 903 (payments of £417,763 to one of the directors in the 10 months before liquidation).

9   [1997] 2 BCLC 598, [1997] BCC 842.

C Ltd and S personally guaranteed any indebtedness arising from that equipment hire. S had the company pay £20,000 to C Ltd two weeks before A Ltd was placed in voluntary liquidation.

The court held that the £20,000 payment constituted a preference given to C Ltd and to S since it had the effect of improving the position of both the hire company, as a creditor, and S, as a contingent creditor under his guarantee, in the event of the insolvent liquidation of the company. S tried to persuade the court that the payment to C Ltd was motivated by the commercial needs of A Ltd, namely the need to keep machinery on site so that A Ltd could continue in operation. The court found, however, that his main motivation was his own personal guarantee of that indebtedness; and also that he had an eye to the future when he might need to trade again with C Ltd.

Once a preference has been established, the court may, on an application by the liquidator or administrator, make such order as it thinks fit for restoring the position to what it would have been if the company had not given that preference[10]. Any sums recovered by the liquidator are impressed with a statutory trust in favour of the unsecured creditors and do not enure to the benefit of the company or the holder of the floating charge[11]. However, the recoveries are available to meet the costs and expenses of the liquidation[12].

Extortionate credit transactions – IA 1986, s 244

Section 244 gives liquidators (and administrators)[13] the right to challenge any credit transaction (ie where the company is a party to a transaction for, or involving, the provision of credit to the company) entered into by the company in the three years before an administration order was made or the company went into liquidation[14].

The test of whether a transaction is extortionate is whether, having regard to the risk accepted by the person providing the credit, either its terms required grossly exorbitant payments in respect of the provision of the credit, or it otherwise grossly contravened ordinary principles of fair dealing[15]. It is presumed, unless the contrary is proved, that a transaction with respect to which an application is made under this provision is or was extortionate[16]. It will then be for those who seek to uphold the transaction to show that it was not an extortionate credit transaction.

If the liquidator's challenge is successful the court can exercise a range of powers. These include setting aside the whole or part of any obligations created by the transaction, varying any of its terms, or requiring the creditor to repay any sums to the liquidator[17].

---

10 IA 1986, s 239(3). The range of orders the court can make is the same as in relation to a transaction at an undervalue: s 241(1), discussed above.

11 *Re MC Bacon Ltd (No 2)* [1990] BCLC 607 at 612, per Millett J, applying *Re Yagerphone Ltd* [1935] Ch 392; this approach approved and applied in *Re Oasis Merchandising Services Ltd, Ward v Aitken* [1997] 1 All ER 1009 at 1018–1020, CA; see also *Re Ayala Holdings Ltd (No 2)* [1996] 1 BCLC 467. See discussion below on this issue in the section dealing with wrongful trading.

12 *Re Exchange Travel (Holdings) Ltd (No 3), Katz v McNally* [1997] 2 BCLC 579, sub nom *Katz v McNally* [1997] BCC 784, CA (decision of Millett J in *Re MC Bacon Ltd (No 2)* [1990] BCLC 607 on this point doubted).

13 IA 1986, ss 244(1), 238(1).

14 Ibid, s 244(2).

15 Ibid, s 244(3).

16 Ibid.

17 Ibid, s 244(4). One of the functions of this section is to prevent companies in effect preferring a creditor by agreeing artificially high rates of interest on the creditor's debt. If arrears of interest are allowed to build up, the creditor's proof of debt will be artificially increased. See the Cork Committee Report, Cmnd 8558, paras 1379–1381.

Avoidance of floating charges – IA 1986, s 245

Certain floating charges may be set aside so depriving the creditor of the security which he thought he had obtained and preventing the substitution of a secured debt for an unsecured debt[18]. Section 245 is designed to invalidate floating charges given close to insolvency which simply secure past indebtedness and provide no new benefit, no new money, to the company[19].

A floating charge is invalid if the charge was created within the 12 months ending with the onset of insolvency[20] and at the time, or as a result of the transaction, the company was unable to pay its debts[1]. Where the charge was created in favour of a person connected with the company, the period covered is two years before the onset of insolvency and it is irrelevant whether or not the company was unable to pay its debts at the time[2].

However, even if the above conditions are satisfied and regardless of whether the charge was granted to a person connected with the company or not, the floating charge will nevertheless be valid to the extent that fresh cash, goods or services are provided to the company, or any debt of the company is reduced or discharged, *at the same time as, or after,* the creation of the charge[3].

In *Power v Sharp Investments Ltd*[4], the board of a company (Shoe Lace Ltd) resolved in March 1990 to grant a debenture to its parent company, Sharp. The debenture granting a fixed and floating charge was duly executed on 24 July 1990 in respect of sums of money which had been advanced by Sharp in April, May, June and finally on 16 July 1990. A petition for winding up was presented on 4 September and the company was compulsorily wound up on 20 November. The liquidator challenged the validity of the charge in the light of s 245.

The Court of Appeal found that there was insufficient contemporaneity between the prior payments made by the debenture holder and the execution of the charge so as to bring it within the section which required the consideration to be paid *at the same time as, or after,* the creation of the charge. The words were clearly included by the legislature for the purpose of excluding from the exemption the amount of moneys paid to the company before the creation of the charge, even though they were paid in consideration for the charge; on any other construction these words would have been mere surplusage.[5] Sir Christopher Slade concluded that:

> ... no moneys paid before the execution of a debenture will qualify for the exemption under the subsection [ie under s 245(2)(a)] unless the interval between payment and execution is so short that it can be regarded as minimal and payment and execution can be regarded as contemporaneous[6].

---

18   Only the charge is rendered void. The underlying debt remains valid and, if the debt has been repaid before winding up, the fact that the charge would have been void in the winding up does not affect the repayment. In appropriate circumstances the repayment may, of course, be challenged as a preference: *Mace Builders (Glasgow) Ltd v Lunn* [1987] Ch 191, [1986] 3 WLR 921, CA.

19   For the background to this provision, see the Cork Committee Report, Cmnd 8558, paras 1551–1556.

20   IA 1986, s 245(3)(b). The meaning of 'onset of insolvency' is contained in s 245(5): the date of the presentation of the petition on which the administration order was made; or the date of the commencement of the winding up.

1   Ibid, s 245(2), (4).

2   Ibid, s 245(3)(a), (4).

3   Ibid, s 245(2)(a), (b).

4   [1994] 1 BCLC 111, [1993] BCC 609, CA.

5   [1994] 1 BCLC 111 at 122, [1993] BCC 609 at 619, CA.

6   [1994] 1 BCLC 111 at 123, [1993] BCC 609 at 620, CA. The decision in *Re Fairway Magazines Ltd, Fairbairn v Hartigan* [1993] BCLC 643, [1992] BCC 924, where Mummery J found a charge within

As the court noted 'it is always open to the lender not to lend until the charge has actually be executed; that must be the prudent course'[7]. However, in a case where the promise to execute a debenture created a present equitable security, and where moneys were advanced in reliance upon it, the delay between the advances and the execution of the formal instrument of charge was immaterial as the charge had already been created and was immediately registrable, so that other creditors will have had the opportunity of learning of its existence[8].

The fresh sums received must have been received by the company and it is insufficient if sums are advanced by the third party to the company's bank to reduce the company's overdraft which the third party has guaranteed. The money paid direct to the bank never becomes freely available to the company and thus is not paid 'to it' within the meaning of the section[9].

POTENTIAL LIABILITIES OF COMPANY DIRECTORS

Introduction

In addition to challenging vulnerable transactions, it is also necessary to consider whether the directors themselves might not be challenged with respect to their conduct and so the Insolvency Act 1986 contains a variety of provisions which address their position[10]. Again the emphasis is on civil remedies and recoveries for creditors. In general, fraud is not a prerequisite although a small number of offences, essentially IA 1986, ss 206–211, retain a fraud element.

Summary redress for breach of duty by directors is available while particular types of trading are targeted, namely fraudulent (which provision existed prior to the 1986 Act) and wrongful trading (which is a new provision introduced in 1986). While fraudulent trading at any time is a criminal offence, provision is made for contributions to the company's assets as a civil matter with respect to fraudulent and wrongful trading where the company has gone into winding up. Criminal and civil provision is also made to deal with the phoenix syndrome – continuing to trade using the name by which the insolvent company was known or a name which is so similar as to suggest an association with that company.

More broadly, the cumulative picture can be examined in deciding whether or not the conduct of the directors is such as to amount to unfitness justifying their disqualification. Evidence of vulnerable transactions, considered above, and of fraudulent or wrongful trading would be matters to which the court would have regard in disqualification proceedings.

---

s 245(2)(a) where the money was advanced on 28 August but the debenture not executed until 27 September must now be reviewed, on this point, in the light of this decision by the Court of Appeal which has favoured the stricter contemporaneous test. See Prentice (1993) 109 LQR 371 who favours the approach of Mummery J.

7   [1994] 1 BCLC 111 at 123, [1993] BCC 609 at 620, CA, quoting Hoffmann J at first instance, see [1992] BCLC 636, [1992] BCC 367, Ch D.

8   [1994] 1 BCLC 111 at 122, [1993] BCC 609 at 619, CA.

9   *Re Fairway Magazines Ltd, Fairbairn v Hartigan* [1993] 1 BCLC 643, [1992] BCC 924; see Prentice (1993) 109 LQR 371; also *Re Orleans Motor Co Ltd* [1911] 2 Ch 41.

10   In a number of the provisions, eg IA ss 206–211, the application of the provision is to 'officers' of the company which is a broader category than just directors but our discussion will focus primarily on directors.

Particular malpractices – IA 1986, ss 206 – 211

As noted above, a small number of offences covering essentially fraudulent behaviour are retained in the Insolvency Act 1986 although the number of prosecutions under these provisions is small.

Fraud etc in anticipation of winding up   Section 206 makes it an offence for an officer of the company to conceal or remove any part of the company's property; to falsify entries in the company's books; or perpetrate other similar acts either in the 12 months preceding the commencement of the winding up or after the commencement of the winding up. Unusually, it is for the defendant to prove that he had no intent to defraud or intent to conceal.

Transactions in fraud of creditors   Section 207 makes it an offence for an officer of the company to make a gift of any property or to transfer any property, or to make any charge on the company's property, or conceal or remove any property after or within two months before any unsatisfied court judgment. It is a defence if the conduct constituting the offence happened more than five years before the commencement of the winding up or if the officer proves no intent to defraud the company's creditors.

Misconduct in course of winding up   Section 208 provides for various offences by officers of failing to co-operate and assist the liquidator in either a voluntary or compulsory winding up with respect to the delivery up of books and property of the company. It is a defence for the officer to prove that he had no intent to defraud.

Falsification by officer of company books with intent to defraud   Section 209 makes it an offence for an officer of the company to destroy, mutilate, alter or falsify any books, papers, securities, or if he makes or is privy to the making of any false or fraudulent entry in any registers, books etc belonging to the company.

Material omissions from statement relating to company's affairs by an officer   Section 210 makes it an offence for any officer to make any material omission in any statement relating to company's affairs. Again it is a defence if the officer can prove that he had no intent to defraud.

False representations to creditors by an officer   Section 211 makes it an offence for an officer to make any false representations or commit any other fraud for the purpose of obtaining the consent of the company's creditors or any of them to an agreement with reference to the company's affairs or to the winding up.

Misfeasance – summary remedy for breach of duty – IA 1986, s 212

An option open to a liquidator is to use s 212 which provides a summary procedure by which such actions may be brought[11], to make persons, most specifically directors, liable to contribute to the company's assets for breach of fiduciary duty or the duty of care and skill.

---

11 The section does not provide a new cause of action but merely provides a summary procedure: *Re DKG Contractors Ltd* [1990] BCC 903. See generally Oditah '*Misfeasance Proceedings against Company Directors*' [1992] LMCLQ 207; also Doyle (1994) 7 Insolv Intel 25, 35.

This section enables the court, on the application of the official receiver, the liquidator, or any creditor, or on the application of a contributory with the leave of the court[12], to examine the conduct of any promoter or officer[13] of the company, or any liquidator, administrator or administrative receiver of it. The court examines their conduct to see if they have misapplied or retained or become accountable for money or other property of the company or been guilty of any misfeasance or other breach of duty to the company[14]. If the court finds that this is the case, it can order the person to repay, restore or account for it or to make contribution to the assets of the company of such sum as the court thinks just[15].

Fraudulent trading – IA 1986, s 213

In cases of fraudulent trading, liability arises in respect of persons knowingly a party to the carrying on of any business of the company with intent to defraud creditors[16] of the company, or creditors of any other person, or for any fraudulent purpose. It should be noted, therefore, that the section is wider than simply defrauding creditors[17].

There are two aspects to fraudulent trading: a criminal offence contained in CA 1985 s 458 which applies regardless of whether the company is in winding up; and a civil liability in IA 1986 s 213 which applies only when the company is in the course of winding up. In the latter case, a liquidator (only) may apply for a declaration that any persons knowingly parties to the carrying on of the business in the manner stated are to be liable to make such contribution to the company's assets as the court thinks proper.

The central requirement is that the 'business of the company has been carried on with intent to defraud creditors'; and carrying on business can include a single transaction designed to defraud a single creditor[18].

It is not enough to show that the company has continued to trade while insolvent (that may fall into wrongful trading, discussed below), the conduct must '... involve actual dishonesty, involving, according to current notions of fair trading among commercial men, real moral blame'[19]. Although this is a strict standard it will clearly be satisfied where directors allow a company to incur credit when they have no reason to think the creditors will ever be paid[20]. However, in *R v Grantham*[1] it was held that this requirement can also be satisfied where the directors have no good reason to think

12 IA 1986, s 212(5).
13 Ie director, manager or secretary: CA 1985, s 744.
14 Since the Insolvency Act 1986, the summary procedure does now cover allegations of negligence, implementing a recommendation of the Jenkins Committee: Report of the Committee on Company Law Reform (Cmnd 1749), para 503(d). See *Re D'Jan of London Ltd, Copp v D'Jan* [1994] 1 BCLC 561, [1993] BCC 691; also *Re Welfab Engineers Ltd* [1990] BCLC 833, [1990] BCC 600.
15 See the discussion below in the section on wrongful trading as to the nature of any such recovery. See *Manson v Smith* [1997] 2 BCLC 161, CA: there can be no set-off available between a debt due from the company to a misfeasant and his liability to repay money which he had been order to pay in misfeasance proceedings because a misappropriation of assets is not a mutual dealing as required, and a liability for misfeasance only arises after the winding up.
16 The word 'creditor' ... in its ordinary meaning, denotes one to whom money is owed; whether that debt can presently be sued for is immaterial: *R v Smith (Wallace Duncan)* [1996] 2 BCLC 109, CA.
17 See *R v Kemp* [1988] QB 645, [1988] 2 WLR 975, CA.
18 *Re Gerald Cooper Chemicals Ltd* [1978] Ch 262, [1978] 2 All ER 49; see also *Re Sarflax Ltd* [1979] Ch 592, [1979] 1 All ER 529 (distributing the proceeds of the realisation of assets could constitute carrying on business); also *Re Augustus Barnett & Son Ltd* [1986] BCLC 170, 2 BCC 98,904.
19 *Re Patrick and Lyon Ltd* [1933] Ch 786 at 790, per Maugham J. See *R v Cox, R v Hedges* [1983] BCLC 169; *Re a Company (No 001418 of 1988)* [1991] BCLC 197, [1990] BCC 526.
20 *Re William C Leitch Bros Ltd* [1932] 2 Ch 71.
1 [1984] QB 675, [1984] 3 All ER 166, CA.

funds will become available to pay the creditors when their debts become due or shortly thereafter.

When the provisions were introduced in 1929, only directors could be made liable but since 1948 the provisions have applied to any persons 'knowingly parties to the carrying on of the business' with intent to defraud creditors. It has been held that this involves taking at least some active steps in the management of the business. Thus, a company secretary who merely carries out the administrative functions of such an office is not concerned in the management of the company or in carrying on its business[2]. But creditors can be party to fraudulent trading if they accept money knowing it has been procured by carrying on business with intent to defraud creditors and for the very purpose of paying their debts[3].

The extent of liability of those responsible for fraudulent trading is subject to the court's discretion. Maugham J stated in *Re William C Leitch Bros Ltd*[4] that it is not necessary to consider how many debts were incurred during the period of fraudulent trading nor whether any particular creditors were misled. Although a definite sum in money must be fixed by the court, the object of the section is penal rather than compensatory[5].

Any sums recovered by the liquidator are impressed with a statutory trust in favour of the unsecured creditors and do not enure to the benefit of the defrauded creditor or the holder of the floating charge[6]. However, the recoveries are available to meet the costs and expenses of the liquidation[7].

Finally, the court was given a new power in 1986 to defer any debts owed by the company to any person guilty of fraudulent trading in relation to the company[8].

Wrongful trading – IA 1986, s 214

The difficulties in establishing the intent to defraud necessary to give rise to liability for fraudulent trading led the Cork Committee to recommend the introduction of a new provision for wrongful trading under which civil personal liability could arise without proof of fraud or dishonesty and without requiring the criminal standard of proof[9].

Section 214 allows the liquidator of a company in the course of winding up to apply for an order that a director (including a shadow director) make such contribution[10] to

2　*Re Maidstone Building Provisions Ltd* [1971] 3 All ER 363, [1971] 1 WLR 1085.
3　*Re Gerald Cooper Chemicals Ltd* [1978] Ch 262, [1978] 2 All ER 49.
4　[1932] 2 Ch 71.
5　*Re a Company (No 001418 of 1988)* [1991] BCLC 197, [1990] BCC 526.
6　See *Re Oasis Merchandising Services Ltd, Ward v Aitken* [1997] 1 All ER 1009 at 1018–1020, CA; approving and applying the approach taken by Millett J in *Re MC Bacon Ltd (No 2)* [1990] BCLC 607 at 612 where he applied *Re Yagerphone Ltd* [1935] Ch 392. See also *Re William C Leitch Bros Ltd* [1932] 2 Ch 71; *Re Esal Commodities Ltd, London and Overseas (Sugar) Co Ltd v Punjab National Bank* [1993] BCLC 872, Ch D (relating to the old statutory provision CA 1948, s 332 which permitted applications by persons other than liquidators whereas IA 1986, s 213 is restricted to liquidators). See discussion below of this issue in the section on wrongful trading.
7　*Re Exchange Travel (Holdings) Ltd (No 3), Katz v McNally* [1997] 2 BCLC 579, sub nom *Katz v McNally* [1997] BCC 784, CA (decision of Millett J in *Re MC Bacon Ltd (No 2)* [1990] BCLC 607 on this point doubted).
8　IA 1986, s 215(4).
9　See the Cork Committee Report, Cmnd 8558, ch 44.
10　The declaration by the court is for the recovery of a sum of money, although there is nothing to preclude the liquidator from accepting property to satisfy that liability: see *Re Farmezier Products Ltd* [1997] BCC 655, CA affg [1995] 2 BCLC 462, [1995] BCC 926.

the company's assets as the court thinks proper where certain conditions are met[11]. The conditions are that the company has gone into insolvent liquidation,[12] and it appears that the company continued trading after a point in time before the commencement of the winding up when the director knew or ought to have concluded that there was no reasonable prospect[13] that the company would avoid going into insolvent liquidation[14]. It is a defence for the director to satisfy the court that, after that point in time was reached, he took every step with a view to minimising the potential loss to the company's creditors as he ought to have taken[15].

Section 214(4) provides that the facts which a director of a company ought to know or ascertain, the conclusions which he ought to reach and the steps which he ought to take are those which would be known or ascertained, or reached or taken, by a reasonably diligent person having both

(a) the general knowledge, skill and experience that may reasonably be expected of a person carrying out the same functions as are carried out by that director in relation to the company, and

(b) the general knowledge, skill and experience that that director has.

In *Re Produce Marketing Consortium Ltd (No 2)*[16] it was held that, in having regard to the functions of the directors in question in relation to the company in question, the court will take account of whether it is a small company with simple accounting procedures and equipment or a large company with sophisticated procedures[17]. Nevertheless, there are certain minimum standards for all directors with respect to keeping accounting records, preparing annual accounts and laying them before the general meeting and registrar. In deciding whether directors knew or ought to have concluded that there was no reasonable prospect of the company avoiding insolvent liquidation it was therefore appropriate to take account of knowledge the directors would have had, had the requisite accounts been prepared on time.

Once liability is established, the extent of any contribution to the company's assets is a matter for the court's discretion and the aim here is primarily compensatory rather than penal to ensure that any depletion of the assets attributable to the period of wrongful trading is made good[18].

In *Re Produce Marketing Consortium Ltd (No 2)*[19] Knox J appeared to be of the view that any contribution ordered under the section would be available to the floating

---

11 IA 1986, s 214(1), (7).
12 Defined ibid, s 214(6): a company goes into insolvent liquidation for these purposes if it goes into liquidation at a time when its assets are insufficient for the payment of its debts and other liabilities and the expenses of the winding up.
13 See Cooke and Hicks '*Wrongful Trading – Predicting Insolvency*' [1993] JBL 338 on the difficulties of identifying the point in time beyond which trading should not continue; see also *Re Purpoint Ltd* [1991] BCLC 491, [1991] BCC 121; *Re DKG Contractors Ltd* [1990] BCC 903. See too *Re Sherborne Associates Ltd* [1995] BCC 40, criticised by Fletcher (1995) 8 Insolv Intel 14.
14 See generally Walters '*Enforcing Wrongful Trading*' in (Rider, ed) *The Corporate Dimension* (1998); Dine '*Wrongful Trading – Quasi-Criminal Law*' in (Rajak, ed) *Insolvency Law – Theory and Practice* (1991). Few cases have been reported under the provision but see Sealy in (Ziegel, ed) *Current Developments in International and Comparative Insolvency Law* (1994), p 498 who makes the point that, despite the small number of cases, the provision, together with the provisions on disqualification, has had a very significant impact on business practice.
15 IA 1986, s 214(3).
16 [1989] BCLC 520. See Prentice [1990] 10 Ox JLS 265.
17 [1989] BCLC 520 at 550.
18 [1989] BCLC 520 at 553–554; see also *Re Purpoint Ltd* [1991] BCLC 491, [1991] BCC 121.
19 [1989] BCLC 520.

charge holder. However, commentators suggested that this approach is incorrect[20] and judicial support for the contrary view is now forthcoming.

In *Re MC Bacon Ltd (No 2)*[1] Millett J (having concluded that sums recoverable under a preference do not enure for the benefit of a debenture holder but for the benefit of the general body of creditors) went on to say that this approach applied with even greater force to a claim in respect of wrongful trading, which can only be brought under the statute by the liquidator and only in respect of an insolvent liquidation[2]. This approach has been approved in *Re Oasis Merchandising Services Ltd, Ward v Aitken*[3] which drew a distinction between assets which are the property of the company at the time of the commencement of the liquidation which would include rights of action which arose and might have been pursued by the company itself prior to the liquidation and assets which only arise after the liquidation and are recoverable only by the liquidator pursuant to statutory powers conferred on him and which are held subject to a statutory trust for the unsecured creditors[4]. Such powers would relate to preferences (s 239), fraudulent (s 213) and wrongful trading (s 214)[5] but would not include the right of action against directors for misfeasance under s 212, discussed above, as that right of action arises and is available to the company prior to liquidation. However, the recoveries under these provisions are available to meet the costs and expenses of the liquidation[6].

As with fraudulent trading, the court has the power to defer debts owing from the company to any person found liable for wrongful trading[7].

Prohibition on the re-use of company names – IA 1986, ss 216, 217

When a company has gone into insolvent liquidation, its directors may be tempted to immediately set up another company under the same or similar name (or may already have several other companies incorporated, all with similar names), and continue much as before. This is known as the phoenix syndrome and is dealt with by ss 216 and 217 which render the re-use of the name of a company which has been wound up insolvent a criminal offence in certain circumstances[8] and any directors concerned may incur personal liability for debts incurred during the period of the offence[9].

Once the company has gone into insolvent liquidation it is an offence for a director or shadow director of the company:

- to be a director of or to be concerned or take part in the promotion, formation or management of any other company known under the prohibited name, or

---

20   See Prentice [1990] 10 Ox JLS 265; Milman *Priority Rights on Corporate Insolvency* in *Current Issues in Insolvency Law* (1991), pp 76–77.
1   [1990] BCLC 607.
2   [1990] BCLC 607 at 613.
3   [1997] 1 All ER 1009, CA.
4   [1997] 1 All ER 1009 at 1018–1020, CA. See also *Ayerst (Inspector of Taxes) v C & K (Construction) Ltd* [1976] AC 167, [1975] 2 All ER 537.
5   No reference was made to transactions at an undervalue (IA, s 238) but, by analogy, any recovery under that section (which is similar in structure and scope to s 239) should also be held subject to the statutory trust for the unsecured creditors.
6   *Re Exchange Travel (Holdings) Ltd (No 3), Katz v McNally* [1997] 2 BCLC 579, sub nom *Katz v McNally* [1997] BCC 784, CA (decision of Millett J in *Re MC Bacon Ltd (No 2)* [1990] BCLC 607 on this point doubted).
7   IA 1986, s 215(4).
8   Ibid, s 216(4). It is an offence of strict liability: *R v Cole, Lees, Birch* [1998] BCC 87.
9   IA 1986, s 217. See *Thorne v Silverleaf* [1994] 1 BCLC 637, [1994] BCC 109.

- in any way, directly or indirectly, be concerned or take part in the carrying on of a business carried on (otherwise than by a company) under a prohibited name[10].

A prohibited name is the name by which the company was known or a name which is so similar to it as to suggest an association with that company[11]. The prohibition on the use of the name lasts for five years[12].

There are exceptions, however, when re-use of the name is permitted. These are set out in the Insolvency Rules 1986.

Exception 1: There is no breach of s 216 and no need to apply for leave where a company (the successor company) has acquired the whole or substantially the whole of the business of the insolvent company from the liquidator and notice has been given to all the creditors of the insolvent company specifying the names used and proposed to be used by the two companies and giving details of the directors[13].

Exception 2: The court which winds up the insolvent company may give the directors leave to use the name. A director who applies for leave (within seven days of his company going into liquidation) may continue to act without being in breach of s 216 for a period for six weeks from the date on which the company goes into liquidation or for a shorter period if the court disposes of the application earlier[14]. The proper approach to the exercise of this jurisdiction was considered in *Penrose v Official Receiver*[15] where Chadwick J thought the court should exercise its discretion to grant leave with regard only to the purposes for which s 216 was enacted and not on the more general basis that the public required some protection from the applicant's activities as a company director. The question was whether future creditors of the new company would be misled by the fact that it would be trading under the control of the applicants with a name similar to the name of the old company.

Exception 3: A former director can continue to act in the affairs of an established company even though it is known by a prohibited name, provided it has been using that name for at least a year before his other company went into liquidation and was not dormant during that time[16].

Disqualification of directors of insolvent companies

As a further deterrent to irresponsible directors a provision was introduced in 1976 whereby directors of companies which went into insolvent liquidation could in certain circumstances be disqualified for a period from future management of companies. These provisions have since been revised and are now contained in the Company Directors Disqualification Act 1986, ss 6 and 7. Disqualification was discussed at length in Chapter 24.

---

10 IA 1986, s 216(1).
11 Ibid, s 216(2).
12 Ibid, s 216(1).
13 IR 1986, r 4.228.
14 IR 1986, r 4.229.
15 [1996] 1 BCLC 389, [1996] BCC 311; followed in *Re Lightning Electrical Contractors Ltd* [1996] 2 BCLC 302, [1996] BCC 950. The court rejected the stricter approach adopted in *Re Bonus Breaks Ltd* [1991] BCC 546 where the court had reviewed the director's responsibility for the first company's insolvency and the structure and financing of the second company in a manner akin to a judge exercising the discretion to grant a disqualified director leave to act under the Company Directors Disqualification Act 1986, s 17.
16 IR 1986, r 4.230.

DISSOLUTION OF THE COMPANY

Dissolution after winding up

After completion of the winding-up process, the company will cease to exist by being removed from the register at Companies House, a process known as dissolution. In both compulsory and voluntary liquidations, this occurs automatically three months after the registration of the liquidator's final return at Companies House[17].

Official receivers frequently ended up having to deal with compulsory liquidations where there were very few, if any, assets and so they are given the power to apply to the Registrar for early dissolution of the company where the realisable assets are insufficient to cover the expenses of a winding up and the affairs of the company do not warrant further investigation[18]. In that case, the company is dissolved three months after the Official Receiver's application for early dissolution[19].

On being dissolved, any property of the company is deemed to be bona vacantia and vests in the Crown[20].

POWER TO DECLARE DISSOLUTION VOID

It is possible to apply to the court for an order, on such terms as the court thinks fit, declaring the dissolution to have been void[1]. The application may be by the liquidator (for example, where additional assets of the company have come to light) or by any other person appearing to the court to be interested[2], and it must be made within two years of the date of the dissolution[3]. An indefinite extension to that period applies where the application is for the purposes of bringing proceedings against the company in respect of death or personal injuries but no order will be made if it appears to the court that the proceedings would in any case be statute-barred[4].

When a company is restored to the register, property which had vested in the Crown as bona vacantia re-vests in the company but any disposition of the property in the meantime is valid, the Crown being liable to account for any consideration received[5].

Struck off the register

The majority of companies that are dissolved in England and Wales each year are never formally wound up at all. Instead they cease to exist when the Registrar strikes them off the register as defunct which can be done under CA 1985, s 652, if the Registrar

---

17   IA 1986, s 201(1), (2) voluntary winding up; s 205(1), (2) – compulsory winding up.
18   Ibid, s 202(2).
19   Ibid, s 202(5).
20   CA 1985, s 654.
1   Ibid, s 651(1).
2   The Secretary of State for Trade and Industry is a 'person appearing to the court to be interested' for these purposes: *Re a Company (No 002081 of 1994), Re a Company (No 002082 of 1994)* [1994] BCC 933 (the DTI may wish to have a company restored to the register to enable it to be investigated or to institute disqualification proceedings against the directors).
3   CA 1985, s 651(1), (4).
4   Ibid, s 651(5). See *Re Philip Powis Ltd* (1998) Times, 6 March, CA (can still apply for an order, even if the second action would be, prima facie, statute-barred provided the circumstances were such that it was arguable that an application under Limitation Act 1980, s 33 (to extend the period of limitation) could succeed.
5   CA 1985, s 655.

has reasonable cause to believe the company is not carrying on business or is not in operation[6]. Many of the companies targeted will have failed to file annual returns and accounts which may suggest that the company has ceased trading. If they are still trading, the threat of being struck off the register concentrates the minds of those running the company on the need to fulfil their filing obligations.

The procedure is for the Registrar to send two letters, enquiring about the company's activities, to the company and subsequently to give notice in the Gazette with a view to striking off the company[7]. At the expiry of three months from the notice, unless cause to the contrary is shown by the company, the registrar may strike the company's name of the register and must publish notice to this effect in the Gazette and, on publication of this notice in the Gazette, the company is dissolved[8].

A procedure is now available whereby a private company can apply to the Registrar of companies to be struck off on payment of the appropriate fee, which is currently £10. This procedure, introduced by the Deregulation and Contracting Out Act 1994 and now contained in CA 1985, ss 652A–F, is designed to enable companies quickly and inexpensively to be dissolved and removed from the register. Elaborate provision is made for notifying creditors and interested parties of the application to be struck off.

POWER TO RESTORE COMPANY WHICH HAS BEEN STRUCK OFF

The court, on an application by the company, any member or any creditor, may restore the company to the register at any time within 20 years from the notice in the Gazette, if it is satisfied that the company was at the time of striking off carrying on business or in operation, or otherwise that it is just that the company be restored to the register[9].

---

6   Ibid, s 652(1).
7   Ibid, s 652(2).
8   Ibid, s 652(3)–(5).
9   Ibid, s 653(2). As to the nature of this jurisdiction, see *Re Priceland Ltd, Waltham Forest London Borough Council v Registrar of Companies* [1997] 1 BCLC 467, [1997] BCC 207.

PART VII

The international dimension

CHAPTER 42

International dimensions of company law

THE EXTENSION OF CORPORATE ACTIVITY BEYOND NATIONAL FRONTIERS

We saw in earlier chapters how some of the earliest English companies were international enterprises. They were formed to develop international trade. Indeed, some of them were the earliest vehicles for colonisation. A classic case is the East India Company.

Later, in the nineteenth century, many British companies carried on business in the Empire through local branches taking advantage of the favourable trading conditions. Some, like the British South Africa Company, performed a colonising role. In this century companies like ICI and the major oil companies like BP and Shell have carried on business in many countries through local subsidiaries. Since the end of the First World War there has been a phenomenal increase in overseas subsidiaries of US companies. Since the formation of the EU there has been an increase in overseas subsidiaries of European companies and more recently there has been a large increase in overseas subsidiaries of Japanese companies[1].

The development of a transnational economy shaped by money flows as much as trade in goods and services has stimulated faster economic and legal integration. The aim is now not so much profit maximisation as market maximisation, and trade follows investment and is becoming a function of investment[2].

The extension of corporate activity beyond the frontiers of the country of incorporation has sometimes given rise to complex problems of private international law. In general, English law tends to solve these by the application of the law of incorporation or English law[3]. However, this is not the place for a detailed discussion of such problems. The reader is referred to the specialist works on private international law such as *Dicey and Cheshire.*

---

1   Se L G Franko *The European Multinationals* (1976), p 10, Table 1.2 for comparative data until 1970.
2   Peter Drucker *The New Realities* (1989), pp 115–17. See also Robert Reich *The Work of Nations* (1992), Part 2.
3   See L C B Gower *Modern Company Law* (6th edn, 1997), pp 129–130 for a useful summary. See also the discussion in the context of cross-frontier mergers in Chapter 42, post.

There are separate company registries for each part of the UK. England and Wales are assimilated and share one registry. Scotland has a separate registry but is governed by most of the provisions of the Companies Act, although it has separate case law and statutory provisions on matters such as company charges and receivership and winding up. Northern Ireland has a separate registry and separate legislation although the provisions are virtually the same as English law.

Disclosure by overseas companies

Under s 691 a company incorporated outside Great Britain establishing a place of business here must file:

(1) a certified copy of its constitution;
(2) a list of directors and secretary;
(3) the names and addresses of one or more persons authorised to accept service.

Any alterations must be notified within 21 days after notice could with reasonable diligence have been received in Great Britain[4]. The requirement of (3) goes to jurisdiction as well as disclosure and is intended to protect creditors[5].

Accounts must also be prepared and filed[6] and particulars of charges registered[7]. The company must exhibit its name and the fact of limited liability[8].

In addition to these requirements, which only apply to a company which has established a place of business here, the provisions of the Financial Services Act 1986[9] apply to issues of, or dealings in, foreign company securities in the UK[10].

Lastly, foreign companies which are carrying on business in Great Britain or have at any time done so can be the subject of an investigation by the Department of Trade and Industry and most of the powers discussed in Chapter 30 apply to them.

Section 690A, implementing the Eleventh Company Law Directive, sets out new and complex requirements for limited companies which are incorporated outside the UK and Gibraltar and have *a branch* in Great Britain. One seeks in vain for a definition of branch and a basis of distinction from a place of business.

COMPANY LAW FAMILIES

We saw how American and European influences were at work in the early nineteenth century UK legislation. Of course, it was a two-way process. The UK was the leading commercial nation at that time and was a major initiator as well as borrower of ideas regarding corporateness.

Nevertheless, one can discern an interesting phenomenon from an early period. The USA from the beginning of its independence was an experimenter with the corporate form. It did not slavishly follow English ideas. It moulded the law to suit local conditions. However, there was a close affinity between English and American company law which survived until the 1930s. Since then, particularly with the growth of legislation on securities regulation, there has been substantially a parting of the ways[11]. The UK remained a close influence on the development of Commonwealth

4   Section 692.
5   *Gower*, op cit, pp 129-130.
6   Section 700.
7   Part XXIII, Chapter III.
8   Section 693(b) and (d).
9   See generally B Rider, D Chaikin and C Abrams, *Guide to the Financial Services Act 1986*.
10 See ss 142(1), 159, 160 as amended by the CA 1989, s 212 and Sch 24.
11 See generally L C B Gower (1956) 69 Harv L Rev 1369.

company laws until relatively recently. This was inevitable given its cultural dominance and the close economic ties between the UK and the Commonwealth. However, by the late 1960s, Canada and Australia were branching out on their own and were more subject to American influences. New Zealand continued in closer association with the UK until the 1970s. The major change has been the UK's membership of the European Union since 1973. This is still dominated by the original six states who were members of a different legal tradition and company law inheritance which in some respects was more advanced but generally lagged behind the UK in the scope and sophistication of its disclosure requirements and securities markets.

Germany, the leading company law jurisdiction of the Six, for instance, developed three important company law concepts—the private company as a distinct species, the dual board system and the principle of co-determination[12]. The other original member states adopted the German model of the private company but the UK and Republic of Ireland have not. Even the developments in *Ebrahimi v Westbourne Galleries Ltd*[13] fell short of the European concept. The two-tier board has not been universally adopted in the Six but has dominated EU thinking until recently. Co-determination, a product of an unusual and distinctly German history, has likewise appealed to EU policy makers who have seen it in some way as a formal solution to an essential contradiction in labour relations. It is generally treated with scepticism or hostility by both management and labour in the UK. France has tended to follow the German reforms in recent years. In comparison, Italy, the Netherlands and the Benelux countries have been more conservative. Recently works councils have been accepted in the UK.

This membership of the EU means that there has been a complete parting of the ways with the USA and a growing detachment from Commonwealth company law reforms. Even if it wished to follow these reforms, the UK has lost the right to do so. The result since 1973 has been to bog down UK company law reform, and to re-orientate it. The result is something of a mess.

Within the Commonwealth, it seems inevitable that Canada will move closer to the US model. Australian Corporations Law has become almost gratuitously complex. The approach has become very 'black letter' with inadequate attention being paid to underlying principle and policy. Like the UK practitioners, Australians seem to be swamped by more and more technical reforms which there is little time to reflect upon and some of these come in the name of 'simplification'! Recently, New Zealand looked closely at the Canadian reforms as an alternative model in its Companies Act 1993 in spite of the logic of the Closer Economic Relations Agreement with Australia which leads towards harmonisation between the two countries. All these jurisdictions have opted for a statutory system of securities regulation.

Japan is an interesting subject of comparison. When it began to industrialise, it based its company law on the German model but after the Second World War it adopted a system of securities regulation based on US laws. Recently it has adopted close corporation and insider trading laws based on the US models. It would be a mistake, however, to put too much emphasis on the law since the Japanese system can only be understood as part of the larger picture of Japanese society in which tradition is perhaps more important than statute. Japan is increasingly active in international capital markets as a participant although it has been cautious in the movement towards regulation of capital markets.

---

12 See Clive Schmitthoff 'The Future of the European Company Law Scene' in *The Harmonization of European Company Law*, ed C Schmitthoff (1973).
13 [1973] AC 360, HL.

Company law as a subject of international unification

The rules of private international law and problems of recognition and establishment of companies in different states have traditionally been the subject of bilateral and multilateral treaties between states, and, indeed, there are many such treaties[14]. On the other hand, there has only been a very limited record of international unification of municipal laws. This may be due partly to the difficulty of the task since company law is not entirely a discrete topic which can be separated from other fields of municipal law and partly because governments have not felt that there was a pressing need. Also, companies are an integral part of the economic and fiscal structure of a particular state and it may have been thought dangerous to tamper in the absence of a moving economic or political force. Such attempts as have been made to unify municipal law have been on a regional basis—the EU, the Council of Europe, the Central American Common Market and the Nordic Council. The greatest progress to date outside the EU has been in the Nordic Council where there is a greater degree of homogeneity[15]. Sweden and Finland, however, are now in the EU.

Both the EU and the United Nations are actively at work in attempting to standardise company accounts. This is, of course, a formidable task. Traditions of accounting, the role of accounts, the status of the accounting profession and indeed basic standards of commercial honesty differ from country to country. Nevertheless, the task is worthwhile and it will facilitate more meaningful group accounts for companies with international operations.

THE GROWTH AND REGULATION OF MULTINATIONALS AND TRANSNATIONALS

Companies like ICI, BP and Shell are multinationals and transnationals. Although the parent company is registered here, they operate with subsidiaries all over the world. Production is increasingly diversified.

In terms of gross national product, a multinational like General Motors would rank 14th in the world if it were a state. Organisations of this size are inevitably a political force in the world. They raise problems for nation states which individual states find it difficult to solve. While multinational companies enable most countries to exploit their assets and provide capital and jobs, they tend to operate either in their own corporate interests or the interests of their parent country. They can switch funds and capital with alarming speed and produce instability in their wake. Sometimes they represent a latter-day vestige of a former colonial regime. There is a need for international regulation.

So far the EU has attempted rather unsuccessfully to tackle the problem on a regional level. The United Nations has also turned its attention to it on a global basis, spurred on by Third World countries who fear exploitation. This in its turn has forced Western countries to begin to think seriously of devising their own system of controls through the OECD. The regulatory problems encompass not only company law and accounting but also monopolies and restrictive practices, revenue law and labour law. At a time of growing international interdependence, these problems loom large and must be dealt with.

---

14   E Stein *Harmonization of European Company Laws* (1971), p 68.
15   Ibid.

THE PRESENT CONTRADICTION

We detect a certain contradiction in present trends. There is, on the one hand, the movement towards greater harmonisation of company laws. This is due partly to economic integration which has superseded colonialism to some extent as a harmonising force and partly due to the fact that the basic problems of corporate enterprise are the same throughout the western world and the mixed economies of the Third World. On the other hand, economic integration through regionalism tends to separate off countries into geographical units and to make the reform process slower, more conservative and less responsible to outside influences. The EU and North America are developed regions and a third region is forming centred on the Pacific Rim. These have an increasingly uneasy relationship with each other which is exacerbated by the international financial revolution which has led to a semi-autonomous world economy of capital. Add to this the complications arising from the developments in Eastern Europe, and we have a very unstable situation. Perhaps the fallacy is to seek stability and consistency in such a dynamic subject matter at a time of great economic and political flux.

While unification and harmonisation of municipal systems is involved in such a contradiction one sees in the regulation of multinational enterprise the beginning of an attempt to develop the international economic order[16]. While it is a mistake to expect too much of such a development, such discussion as has taken place has provided a forum for smaller countries of the Third World and a way of monitoring corporate activities. This has enabled discussion to take place at a more rational level. At the present stage of international law, this is as much as one can reasonably expect.

---

16   For an interesting perspective on this see Robert Reich *The Work of Nations* (1992), ch 25.

CHAPTER 43

Transnational enterprise and cross-frontier mergers

THE CONCEPT OF A CROSS-FRONTIER MERGER

The modern trend is towards transnational enterprise. By transnational enterprise we refer to bi or multinational horizontal groups where ownership and control of the members of the groups is shared between two or more countries.[1]

In spite of the globalisation of financial and other markets, domestic and international law do not greatly facilitate cross-frontier co-operation and transnational mergers. Each country has its own corporate laws, securities regulation, foreign ownership laws, antitrust, taxation law and system of industrial relations. Apart from limited regional integration, bilateral treaties and ad hoc contracting promoted or encouraged by governments, there has been little in the way of international co-operation. Within a particular state co-operation can usually take place. The form that particular co-operation takes will be determined by the domestic law, and particularly by its business organisations, antitrust and tax laws. Some states have been slow to facilitate co-operation in the form of mergers.

In economics and antitrust there are three general types of merger: horizontal, vertical and conglomerate[2]. A horizontal merger occurs when two firms in the same industry are merged. Both firms must have been rivals in the sense of selling the same product in the same geographic market. A vertical merger occurs when a firm merges with one of its suppliers or one of its customers. The first is called backward integration, the second forward integration. A conglomerate merger can be one of three types. A product extension merger occurs where a multiple product firm acquires a producer of a further commodity. A market extension merger involves firms in the same product but not the same market. A pure conglomerate merger involves two firms which are wholly unrelated. Merger, however, is an ambiguous legal term[3]. In English law it is used loosely to cover *reconstruction* which involves fusion of enterprise, *amalgamation*

---

1   K Byttebier and A Verroken *Structuring International Cooperation Between Enterprises* (1995), p 8. See too Volker Bornschier and Hanspeter Stamm *'Transnational Corporations'* in Martinell and Smelser (eds), *Economy and Society* (1990), 203.

2   See Roger D Blair and David L Kaserman *Antitrust Economics* (1985), p 227–228 on which this classification is based.

3   Cf *Weinberg and Blank on Takeovers and Mergers*, para 1–004.

which involves the formation of a new holding company to take over the two original companies and a *takeover* whereby one company takes a controlling interest in the shares of another[4]. Sometimes co-operation short of a full merger takes the form of a *joint venture* agreement[5], which is either a form of partnership or a looser agreement or co-operation, or a *consortium*[6] where a number of companies join together to form a joint company for a particular, usually limited, purpose. In a consortium no single company has control.

In US corporation and tax laws the following transactions are commonly referred to as mergers[7]:

(i)   a statutory merger or consolidation, known as an 'A' reorganisation under section 368(1)(a)(A) of the Internal Revenue Code. This involves one firm merging into another firm or a consolidation involving two firms merging into a newly created third firm;

(ii) a stock for stock exchange (a B reorganisation). Here one corporation becomes the subsidiary of the other.

(iii) an exchange of voting stock for substantially all of the assets of a target corporation (a C reorganisation);

(iv) the purchase of assets of the target corporation for cash or non-voting securities;

(v)   the purchase of the stock of the target for cash or non-voting securities.

There are tax advantages in (i)–(iii)[8].

In most of the continental European member states of the EU a merger is effected by either:

(1)   an absorption of one company by another and the transfer of all the assets of the absorbed company to the other. The latter issues shares to the shareholders of the absorbed company which is then dissolved (this resembles an A reorganisation in US laws and a reconstruction in English law); or

(2)   the formation of a new company which absorbs two other companies as in (1), with the latter companies being dissolved rather than becoming members of a group as they would in an English amalgamation. This resembles a consolidation in US laws[9].

Most continental European countries have not hitherto recognised the hostile takeover as a means of achieving a merger[10]. In most countries 100% approval is necessary and the company acquired needs to be wound up[11]. Mergers there are thus essentially co-

---

4   Ibid, para 1–003 et seq.

5   See Duncan (ed) *Joint Ventures Law in Australia* (1994) Ch 2.

6   See F Wooldridge 'Consortium and Related Operations in the United Kingdom' [1978] 3 LMCLQ 427; A H Boulton 'Construction Consortia—their Formation and Management' [1959] JBL 234; J T Brown 'International Joint Venture Contracts in English Law' (1979) 5 Droit et Pratique du Commerce International 193.

7   See Bruce Wasserstein *Corporate Finance Law* (1978) ch 15.

8   Ibid, pp 203 et seq.

9   See R R Pennington and F Wooldridge *Companies in the Common Market* (3rd edn); S N Frommel and J H Thompson *Company Law in Europe* (1975); A Dorresteijn, I Kuiper and G Morse *European Corporate Law* (1994); J Dine (ed) *EC Company Law* (looseleaf).

10 For the changing scene see Simon MacLachlan and William Mackesy 'Acquisitions of Companies in Europe—Practibility, Disclosure and Regulation: An Overview' 23 Int Law 373 (1989); Dorresteijn, Kuiper and Morse, op cit, ch 8.

11 See *Internal Market and Industrial Cooperation—Statute for the European Company* Internal Market White Paper, point 137, Commission of the European Communities Com (88) 320 final, Brussels, 15 July 1988 (hereinafter called 'EU White Paper'), p 13.

operative in nature[12]. This is also the position which prevails in Japan where recent attempts by US corporations to take over Japanese companies by hostile tender offers have been frustrated[13].

The topic of corporations in general receives fragmented treatment in private international law[14] and questions of merger are rarely (if ever) discussed[15]. In Anglo-American systems a company is governed by the law of the place of incorporation[16] and this law governs merger of the company with another company of the same domicile[17]. The position is less clear with a cross-frontier merger although a corporation validly incorporated in one jurisdiction will normally be recognised in other jurisdictions[18]. It may, however, be subjected to special local formalities[19]. With regard to mergers, US laws operate choice of law rules which are based on the law of the place of incorporation except in unusual cases where, with respect to a particular issue, another state has a more significant relationship to the event and the parties[20]. The law of the place of incorporation normally governs the exercise of power within the corporation and the public issue of its securities[1] except that in the case of the latter the requirements of the place of issue have also to be complied with[2]. Different rules may apply to debt financing[3]. In Anglo-American laws a state may wind up the business of a corporation within its jurisdiction without necessarily terminating the existence of the foreign corporation[4]. Dissolution otherwise is a matter for the law of the place of incorporation[5].

Within a federal system the law relating to mergers between corporations incorporated in different states within the federation is usually determined partly by the constitution and partly[6] by state laws. Most constitutions contain full faith and credit clauses in respect of state laws and legal acts but some require licensing of out-of-state corporations. Canada requires licensing but has provisions for continuance where a corporation wishes to shift residence between jurisdictions[7]. In the USA a liberal regime exists which has facilitated capital accumulation. Many of the leading corporations are registered in Delaware, a permissive state, whose Corporation Code expressly provides for a merger or consolidation of a Delaware corporation with a foreign corporation[8]. By contrast in the looser-knit European Union many of the member states have put a number of obstacles in the way of cross-frontier mergers. It is the attempts to overcome these obstacles against a background of different corporate

---

12   See Deborah DeMott 'Comparative Dimensions of Takeover Regulation' 65 Wash ULQ (1987).
13   H Boone Pickens, the notorious US corporate raider, recently had this experience.
14   See Thomas C Drucker 'Companies in Private International Law' (1968) 17 ICLQ 28. The matter receives token treatment in most works on conflicts of laws. A valuable exception is C M Schmitthoff *The Conflict of Laws* (2nd edn), ch XIII.
15   See *National Bank of Greece and Athens SA v Metliss* [1958] AC 509, HL. However, the corporations in this case were of the same domicile. See Drucker, op cit, p 33. For the position in US laws see *Restatement of the Law 2d, Conflict of Laws*, ch 13, para 302, Comment.
16   Schmitthoff, op cit, p 336; Drucker, op cit, p 28.
17   See note 14, supra.
18   Schmitthoff, op cit, pp 334–335.
19   See eg Restatement, op cit, para 297, comment.
20   Ibid, para 302.
1   *Banco de Bilbao v Sancho* [1938] 2 KB 176, 194–195, CA; Drucker, op cit, p 47.
2   Drucker, op cit, p 51.
3   Ibid (proper law of the contract of loan as well as country of issue—quaere questions of security).
4   See Schmitthoff, op cit, pp 339 et seq.
5   *Lazard Bros & Co v Midland Bank Ltd* [1933] AC 289 at p 297, HL per Lord Wright.
6   See eg US Constitution, Act IV, Section 1.
7   See for instance Ontario Business Corporations Act 1982, s 179; Canada Business Corporations Act 1985, s 187.
8   General Corporation Law of the State of Delaware, section 252.

law and even conflict of laws philosophies, which makes the EU such an interesting case study of regional co-operation, which may provide a model for further international co-operation.

OBSTACLES TO CROSS-FRONTIER MERGERS

A report by the EU Commission[9] in 1988 identified the following obstacles to transnational mergers:

1. the difficulty under present laws of carrying out cross-frontier mergers[10]. At the moment within the EU mergers take the form of participation in capital by minority holdings and joint ventures. The European Economic Interest Grouping (EEIG) was introduced to facilitate certain aspects of cross-frontier joint ventures but is not intended as the vehicle for the merger itself;

2. Tax problems resulting from (a) taxation of hidden reserves, (b) double taxation of dividends, (c) economic double taxation which might arise from cross-frontier transactions between associated companies if the profits of one of the companies have been adjusted upwards without a corresponding downward adjustment in the other country, (d) distortions arising because of the different corporation tax systems[11];

3. the differences in company laws and their administration between member states[12];

4. the difficulties under present laws of integrating a group of enterprises as a single economic unit. The law of most member states adopts a rather fragmented approach to the corporate group, except for disclosure purposes[13];

5. administrative difficulties surrounding the establishment of companies. This is exacerbated by the unfamiliarity of foreign businessmen with the requirements of a particular country[14].

Although the Commission does not discuss them in this context there are the additional complications of the different antitrust regimes[15] and industrial relations systems[16] which are also very significant factors.

Faced with these obstacles, cross-frontier co-operation in Europe has taken a variety of forms of which the most significant are as follows.

(a) *Royal Dutch/Shell* This was set up in 1907. Here Shell formed a wholly-owned English holding company. Royal Dutch formed a Dutch holding company. Each company transferred shares in subsidiaries to the respective holding companies then exchanged shares in the holding companies so that the picture was:

9   EU White Paper, pp 7 et seq.
10 Ibid, pp 7–8.
11 Ibid, pp 8–9.
12 Ibid, p 9.
13 Ibid.
14 Ibid.
15 See Klaus J Hopt *European Merger Control* (1982), Vol 1 passim.
16 See the *Green Paper on Employee Participation and Company Structure in the European Communities*, EEC Bull Supp 8/75; J Welch (1983) 8 ELR 83.

(b)   *The Unilever type of agreement*   This merger was set up in 1927 and involves complex agreements between the UK company and the Dutch company for a pooling of assets and profits, treatment of shareholders pari passu and identical boards.

(c)   *Agfa-Gevaert*   This was an example of intricate corporate structures between the German Agfa-Gevaert and the Belgian Gevaert NV set up to avoid the nationalist opposition which would have resulted if one company had been absorbed by the other.

(d)   *Dunlop-Pirelli*   This left the parties as they were but gave each partner a distinct stake in the operations of the other. In essence this involved both companies creating subsidiaries to which were transferred the operations and assets of the parent companies. Each then exchanged an interest in its subsidiary for a corresponding interest in the other's subsidiary. Thus the structure is two headed. The merger experienced a number of difficulties, which are commercial and financial as much as structural.

(e)   *Variations on the theme of joint ventures*   There has been an increasing number of joint venture agreements, particularly in the automobile industry. In the automobile industry these frequently provide for pooling of research and design and patents etc; rationalisation of production; common specifications for sub-contractors and suppliers; common machine tools; and joint financing. Examples are Renault-Peugeot, Ford, Chrysler, and BAC and Sub-Aviation on Concorde. A successful joint venture outside the automobile and aircraft industries was Polygram, jointly run by Siemens and Philips.

All of these five methods are essentially horizontal contractual arrangements which are attempts to cope with the absence of a truly international structure. At the same time the flexibility of ad hoc contracting is not without advantages.

EU STEPS TO FACILITATE CROSS-FRONTIER MERGERS

A number of proposals to facilitate cross-frontier co-operation has been put forward within the EU although the proposals have been marked with lack of success at the stage of implementation. Apart from the Right of Establishment of agencies, branches and subsidiaries without discrimination on grounds of nationality, there are no specific provisions in the Treaty of Rome on this, but the treaty provides for law making in the form of regulations, directives and decisions. Under art 189, a regulation takes immediate internal effect in the member states. A directive is binding on the member states but leaves it to them to choose the method of implementation. A decision is only binding on the parties to whom it is addressed.

Initial efforts to facilitate cross-frontier mergers within the EU were concentrated on a convention. This project was eventually dropped. The *European Economic Interest Grouping*[17] (EEIG) was created as a new legal form of co-operation between individuals, companies, firms, and other legal bodies from different member states by a EU regulation of 25 July 1985. The EEIG has a limited purpose, namely to facilitate or develop the economic activities of its members and to improve the results of these activities. It is not in itself a profit-making venture. Its activities are only ancillary to the economic activities of its members. It has no power of management over its members' activities and can only hold shares in their undertakings, to the extent necessary to achieve its objectives. It must not employ more than 500 people and it must not be a member of another EEIG. It cannot be used by a company to make a

17   Regulation No 2137/85, 25 July 1985 (OJL 199/31 July 1985); S Israel (1988) 9 Co Law 14; 25th Report of the HLSC 1984. See Dorresteijn, Kuiper and Morse, op cit, para 6.03 et seq.

loan to a director or transfer property between a company and a director except as allowed by national law. An EEIG is formed by contract between the members of the grouping. There are various registration and disclosure requirements and an EEIG has basically two organs, the members and the managers. Each member has to have the power to vote. If profits are made, they are to be apportioned to the members in accordance with the contract or, in the absence of any express provision, in equal shares. The members of the EEIG have unlimited joint and several liability for all its debts and other liabilities. Admission of new members is allowed by unanimous decision. In these latter respects an EEIG resembles a partnership under English law. Although an EEIG looks a somewhat limited innovation, its existence has been welcomed by some EU businessmen and this probably indicates the inadequacy of current EU laws to facilitate cross-frontier co-operation[18]. It is significant that in a recent discussion of the topic the point was also made that there is a real need for a simplified European company statute.

Following the adoption of the Third Directive of 9 October 1978[19] on mergers of companies within the same member state, the intention was to build on this and to adopt a directive on cross-frontier mergers[20]. This is now the Draft Tenth Directive. Since the mechanics of national and cross-frontier mergers are identical the proposed Tenth Directive of the EU refers to the Third Directive extensively and is itself limited to additional requirements for cross-border mergers and to those aspects of cross-border mergers which differ from national mergers. The justification of this was that all mergers, both national and cross-frontier, involved the following steps:

(a) the drawing up of joint draft terms of merger;
(b) the approval of the merger by the appropriate organs of each of the companies involved;
(c) the drawing up of a report by the administrative or management bodies of each of the companies;
(d) the drawing up of an expert's report for each of the companies involved;
(e) either the judicial or administrative supervision of the legality of the merger and completion of the formalities.

The special feature of cross-frontier mergers is that the merging companies are governed by the laws of different member states. However, the significance of this should not be exaggerated since a number of the preparatory acts are taken individually by the companies involved and are conducted in accordance with the law of each member state. Nevertheless it is necessary to synchronise certain steps in the procedure. This is the case with the supervision of the drawing up and completion of the formalities of the merger and the publicity surrounding the completion of the merger. In addition certain rules in connection with cross-frontier mergers have to be harmonised to a great degree than is necessary for national mergers. These are in respect of (a) the contents of the draft terms of merger, (b) the protection of creditors of acquired companies, (c) the date on which the merger takes place and (d) the causes of nullity of mergers.

Article 1 of the draft states that the directive is limited to public limited companies and does not apply to companies in insolvency proceedings. Article 2 states that the aim is to require member states to provide for cross-frontier mergers both by the acquisition of one or more companies by another and by the formation of a new

18   See Janet Dine 'The Community Company Law Harmonisation Programme' (1988) 13 ELR 322 at 323.
19   OJ 1978, L295/36. See Pierre van Ommeslaghe, 'La Proposition de Troisième Directive sur L'Harmonisation des Fusions des Sociétés' in P Zonderland *Quo Vadis, Jus Societatum* (1972), p 123.
20   Proposal for a Tenth Directive submitted by the Commission to the Council 14 January 1985 (OJ 1985 C23 28/11). A revised proposal is expected in late 1997.

company. Articles 3 and 4 provide the definition of a cross-frontier merger either by acquisition or by the creation of a new company and this is identical with that of the national merger under the Third Directive with the exception that two or more of the companies involved must be governed by the laws of different member states. Article 5 provides that the draft terms of merger must be drawn up in writing in the appropriate form required by the laws of the member states. Article 6 requires the draft terms to be published in the same way as the national merger but in addition the cross-frontier aspects must be emphasised. Article 7 provides that member states may not impose stricter requirements as regards general meetings approving a cross-frontier merger than they impose on a national merger. Article 8 provides that the report of an expert or experts is required for each of the merging companies. Article 9 provides that the protection of creditors provisions of the Third Directive also apply. Article 10 deals with the examination of the legality of mergers and again applies the provisions of the Third Directive but contains additional provisions for synchronisation of the judicial or administrative supervision of the drawing up of the terms of merger. Article 11 deals with the date on which the merger take effect. This is to be determined according to the law of the member state governing the acquiring company. Articles 12 and 13 deal with publicity and special formalities. Article 14 deals with the civil liability of the members of the administrative bodies and the experts involved. Article 15 sets out nullity rules.

In January 1989, the Commission adopted a proposal for a Thirteenth Directive on Takeovers and Other General Bids[1]. An amended proposal was launched in 1996. The need for harmonisation in the area of takeovers was recognised in the Commission's White Paper on completion of the internal market and is also supported by the European Parliament. The Commission took the view that the economic climate supported the Directive. There were an increasing number of takeovers especially cross-frontier takeovers and the legal arrangements, if any, in member states are very varied. It is inconsistent that there should be EU controls on certain types of mergers and divisions but not on takeover bids. The principal aims of the draft Directive are the protection of shareholders and the regulation of disclosure requirements.

The main features of the 1989 draft were the rules relating to the timetable for offers, the content of offer and defence documents, the obligation on a bidder to bid for the remainder of the shares when he has acquired a certain percentage, the prohibition of certain types of defences and the independent supervision of the takeover process. The proposals were less flexible than the City of London takeover code in that they relied more on rules than principles.

The UK Government had several major concerns over the draft directive[2]. These related to the method of implementation and its apparent lack of flexibility and the increased risk of litigation which it may occasion. It argued that the Directive should be based on a wider range of general principles than are currently provided by art 3 and for the supervisory authority to be given adequate flexibility to waive or adapt the

---

1   Proposal for a Thirteenth Directive on Company Law Governing Takeover and other General Bids (OJ 1989, c 64/8). An amended proposal was launched in 1996 (OJC 162/5 of 6 June 1996). See Department of Trade and Industry *Proposal for a Thirteenth Company Law Directive Concerning Takeovers. A Consultative Document April 1996* ('the Consultative Document'). See MacLachlan and Mackesy, op cit (footnote 9, supra); Jeffrey P Greenbaum, 22 Vanderbilt J of Transnational L 923 (1989); L S Sealy 'The Draft Thirteenth EC Directive on Takeovers', in M Andenas and S Kenyon-Slade, *EC Financial Market Regulation and Company Law* (1993), ch 9. Also Kenyon-Slade and Andenas, 'The Proposed Thirteenth Directive on Takeovers: Unravelling the United Kingdom's Self Regulatory Success' ibid, ch 10; K Hopt and E Wymeersch *European Takeovers Law and Practice* (1992).
2   The Consultative Document, pp 7 et seq.

more specific rules provided that it operates within those general principles. The wider general principles for which the UK delegation argued were:

1. holders of securities who for all practical purposes are in the same position should be treated similarly;
2. holders of securities should be given adequate time, information and advice to enable them to reach a properly informed decision on the offer;
3. the board of a target company must not, after it has reason to believe that an offer might be imminent, take any action without the approval of the holders of its securities which could result in the offer being frustrated or those holders of securities being denied an opportunity to consider it on its merits;
4. all parties to an offer must use every endeavour to prevent the creation of a false market in relevant securities of the target or bidding company;
5. target companies should not remain under siege from an unwanted bidder beyond a reasonable time[3].

The UK delegation also argued for the Directive to be framed in a way which reduces the scope for litigation or some other form of outside review during the course of a bid. The fear here was that such litigation or review would bog down takeover bids. Such delay would create a powerful barrier to takeovers at a time when it is vital to the development of more open capital markets that existing barriers should be eliminated.

At the Edinburgh Council in December 1992 the Commission indicated its willingness to revise the proposal in the light of the principle of subsidiarity. The revised proposal is less detailed and takes the form of a framework directive setting out general principles and some requirements which are more specific. Lord Lester of Herne Hill in The House of Lords Select Committee on the European Communities said that 'one of the main purposes [of the Directive] is to export the British takeover system to the rest of The European Union as a model rather than changing it.'[4] If this is so, and it is probably undiplomatic to say so, then the UK could maintain its present position unchanged but simply enact subordinate legislation indicating that the Directive was part of the Law and implemented by the existing arrangements. In spite of Lord Lester's constructive remarks the Committee found that the Commission had not made out its case and recommended full Parliamentary debate.

The latest position at the time of writing is that the Department of Trade and Industry circulated a consultative document, *Proposal for a Thirteenth Directive on Company Law Concerning Takeover Bids*, in April 1996. This accepts that the Commission has sought to find a means by which the UK can retain its present non-statutory regime. However, there is still concern that legislation will be needed to designate the supervisory body, to give it powers to require parties to supply information, to enforce compliance and to adopt the principles set out in art 5. This would lead to a modification of the present system of limited judicial review. Although the latest proposal cuts down the possibilities of tactical litigation it does not exclude it. Concern is also expressed at the adequacy of the minority shareholders protection requirements in art 3 which allow alternatives to mandatory bids if they 'offer other appropriate and at least equivalent means in order to protect the minority shareholders of that company'.

---

3 Ibid, p 9.
4 House of Lords Select Committee on The European Communities, Session 1995–6 13th Report, Takeover Bids (HL Paper 100), Minutes of Evidence, paras 42–43.

While the House of Lords Select Committee has already come out with a negative response, academic comment has been a little more positive.[5] It is thought that the UK concerns have been exaggerated and the Commission has moved a considerable distance to suit the UK position. Some concern is expressed at the level of generality of the latest draft and the problems which this will pose for harmonisation.

Other proposals now under consideration include *three directives on tax*[6] which deal with the tax treatment of mergers in similar operations; the tax treatment of parents and subsidiaries; and an arbitration procedure to eliminate double taxation arising from transactions between associated companies. In addition to the latter, the Commission proposed as far back as 1975 the harmonisation of corporation tax systems on the basis of the 'partial imputation system' and it is also considering another proposal for harmonisation of the determination of taxable profits. The object of these proposals is to reduce tax distortions on commercial transactions.

Mergers may lead to economies of scale and increased efficiency but they also have the capacity to impede effective competition. The international perspective arises in two main ways. The first is in the definition of concept of the market in question and the second is in the international application of domestic antitrust laws. Most antitrust regimes concentrate on their own domestic markets and restrict horizontal mergers, are mixed in reaction to vertical mergers but generally permissive in respect of conglomerate mergers. In the EU the main concern in the present period of low growth is to achieve faster growth through dynamic competition[7]. Anti-competitive forces may result from market dominance or the creation of a cartel. Dominance occurs where one company gains control of a competitor thus reducing the number of independent competitors and increasing concentration in the particular industry. A cartel typically occurs where two independent competitors create an arrangement likely to reduce competition or enter into a consortium to make a takeover bid which has the effect of an auction ring for the target company's shares or an arrangement to divide up its assets or which leads to a joint venture which restricts competition[8]. In all these cases everything depends on the structure of the particular market. There has been an increasing feeling in the Commission that the provisions in art 85 and 86 of the Treaty of Rome are inadequate to deal with mergers[9]. There has consequently been a growing recognition of the need for a specific merger regulation. The Merger Control Regulation[10] adopted in December 1989 defines concentration widely as occurring when two or more undertakings merge or when one or more persons or undertakings acquire direct or indirect control of the whole or part of another undertaking. The definition of control is wide. It encompasses not only de jure control, ie more than 50% of voting rights, and de facto control, but also the power to influence the composition, voting or decisions of the board or general meeting. The regulation only applies to concentrations having a 'community dimension', in other words, involving cross-frontier concentration within the EU. There are financial tests which are to be applied: the aggregate *world-wide* turnover of all the undertakings concerned must be not less than 1 bn ECUs. Acquisitions escape control if (a) the aggregate world-wide turnover of the target is less than 50 m ECUs, *or* (b) each of the undertakings effecting

5   See Janet Dine (1996) 17 Co Law 248; Mads Andenas (1997) 18 Co Law 101.
6   EU White Paper, pp 10–11.
7   See Ingo L L Schmidt and Jan B Rittaler *A Critical Evaluation of the Chicago School of Antitrust Analysis* (1989), p XIV.
8   Stanley Berwin & Co *Company Law and Competition* Mercury Books London (1989), Ch 9.
9   Clifford Chance *1992 An Introductory Guide* 1988, paras 5.7, 5.8.
10 OJ 1990, L 257/14. See also Implementing Regulation 2367/90; OJ 1990 L 219/5.

the concentration have more than 75% of the aggregate *community-wide* turnover within one and the same member state. Thus small acquisitions by large companies will escape control as will mergers of substantial companies whose business remains confined to one member state. In the latter case they will, of course, be subject to the individual member states' antitrust laws.

Under the regulation concentrations are regarded as incompatible with the common market when they create or strengthen a dominant position in the common market or a substantial part of the common market. On the other hand such concentrations will be allowed if they improve production or distribution or promote technical or economic progress. There is a rebuttable presumption that concentrations are compatible with the common market when the aggregate market share of the undertakings concerned in the common market, or a substantial part of the common market, is less than 20%.

The Commission has exclusive jurisdiction to apply the regulation, subject only to review by the Court of Justice, and such matters are to be governed by the regulation alone and not by national laws. This reduces the risk of double jeopardy and ensures uniformity of application. States are reluctant to enforce antitrust laws which work to the detriment of local firms while at the same time paying lip service to the principle of world free trade.

Industrial relations differ considerably in the member states ranging from adversarial collective bargaining on the one hand to worker participation on the other. Negotiations on these topics have been long and controversial especially since the UK joined the EC. We will return to this matter later.

The most elaborate proposal to date is that of the *European company*[11] project. The European company is sometimes called *societas europae* (SE) and we will use that abbreviation. This would be a genuine transnational corporation which would provide a suitable vehicle for cross-frontier mergers within the EU.

There are four possible legal bases for the SE project[12]. These are (i) a uniform statute (ii) an international convention and (iii) a regulation under two separate provisions of the Treaty of Rome. As regards (i) the problem is to ensure uniform interpretation since uniform statutes such as the 1930 Geneva Convention on Bills of Exchange leave interpretation entirely to the national courts. There are two possible ways of overcoming this difficulty. The first is a provision along the lines of 'Questions concerning matters regulated by the present law that are not expressly decided by it shall be governed by the general principles on which it is based' such as is found in art 17 of The Hague Convention relating to a Uniform Law on the International Sale of Goods. The second is the provision for interpretation by a single court, as the French Government advocated on 15 March 1965. The main disadvantage with a uniform statute is that it is enacted in each state as a domestic law and can be amended or repealed as such. As regards (ii)—the international convention—there are precedents such as the Warsaw Convention on International Transportation by Air and CMR (the Convention Relating

---

11   EU White Paper passim; *European Stock Corporation Text of Draft Statute with Commentary* by Prof P Sanders, CCH Inc, New York (1969); Yvon Loussouarn 'La Proposition d'un Statut des Sociétés Anonyme Européennes et le Droit International Privé' (1971) Rev Critique DIP 383; Jean Van Ryn 'Le Projet de Statut des Sociétés Européennes' (1971) Rev Trim de Droit Europ 563; see, generally P Zonderland (editor) *Quo Vadis, Jus Societatum* Kluwer (1972), which is a festschrift for Prof Sanders, especially the papers by Dabin, Rotondi, Vasseur and Vogelaar; Guy Keutgen *Le Droit des Groupes de Société°s dans la CEE* Bruylant Bruxelles 1973, Titre II Chapitre II; F A Mann 'The European Company' (1970) 19 ICLQ 468; D Ranier 'The Proposed Statute for a European Company' 10 Texas Int LJ 90 (1975). For the latest text of the draft see *The European Company Statute* (A Consultative Document, July 1997 (URN 97/786)).

12   European Stock Corporation Text (supra note 50), pp 8 et seq.

to Contracting for the International Transport of Goods by Road) and this was the original idea. Here the problem is the differing approaches to international treaties in the member states—in some member states treaties take internal effect and take precedence over national law. This is not of course the case in English and Irish law.

As far as (iii)—the two possibilities are arts 235 and 100a of the Treaty of Rome. Article 235 is couched in very general terms and provides that if action by the Community proves necessary to attain one of the objectives of the Community and the Treaty of Rome has not provided the necessary powers, the Council shall, acting unanimously on a proposal from the Commission and after consulting the European Parliament, take the appropriate measures. Article 100a provides *inter alia* that:

1. The Council shall, acting by a qualified majority on a proposal from the Commission in co-operation with the European Parliament and after consulting the Economic and Social Committee, adopt the measures for the approximation of the provisions laid down by law, regulation or administrative action in member states which have as their object the establishment and functioning of the internal market.
2. Paragraph 1 shall not apply to fiscal provisions, to those relating to the free movement of persons nor to those relating to the rights and interests of employed persons.

The Commission favoured art 235 in its 1975 report but now favours art 100a. The UK Government considers that this is inappropriate and that the only possible legal basis is art 235. In its Consultative Document of December 1989 the UK Government states:

The Government consider that art 100a does not provide an appropriate basis for the regulation because that Article is concerned with measures to approximate provisions of law in member states whereas the ECS proposal is not about the approximation of national laws but about the creation of a Community-wide legal framework for a new supranational entity. Further, even if this were not the case, art 100a would be an inappropriate treaty basis because, by virtue of art 100a(2), it cannot be used for provisions on fiscal or worker participation matters. Provisions on both matters are included in the proposed regulation. The Government also consider that art 54 is an inappropriate Treaty basis for the provisions contained in the proposed directive. Those provisions are regarded as an integral part of the ECS proposal and, just as art 54 could not provide a basis for the proposal as a whole, so it cannot be used for a part of that proposal.

The original SE concept was put forward by French legal practitioners in 1959 and the idea was developed by Professor Pieter Sanders of the University of Rotterdam in the same year[13]. Professor Sanders advocated a new corporate form, a European limited liability company registered on a European Commercial Register and incorporated under an alternative EU company regime, uniform in each member state and interpreted by the European Court of Justice. By this means he hoped to solve the conflict of laws problems such as the transfer of the seat of an enterprise across-frontiers, which generally involved a change of nationality, liquidation and reconstitution under the other law, and the problem of mergers of companies incorporated under different legal

13   Ibid, p vii.

systems. The Commission set up a committee of experts which assisted Professor Sanders in elaborating the concept. This led to a Commission proposal in 1970 which followed its complex EU path ending before the Council in 1975[14]. There it languished before an ad hoc working party and got bogged down in the discussion of the proposals on groups. It was shelved in 1982. However, as part of the 1992 programme, the proposal was resurrected in 1988 and is now being pursued in earnest in spite of lukewarm support from the UK Government and business community[15]. The latest draft was produced in 1996 as a result of the Davignon Report.

THE PROPOSED EUROPEAN COMPANY

The European company proposal is ambitious. It has to overcome the current legal difficulties inherent in the domestic laws and constitute a valid alternative to the present techniques. The Internal Market White Paper *Internal Market and Industrial Cooperation—Statute for the European Company* gives the following example to show how it will work[16]:

(a) Let us imagine that two groups merge their activities because they complement each other and on account of the economies of scale secured by merging together their three respective subsidiaries which pursue the same activities:

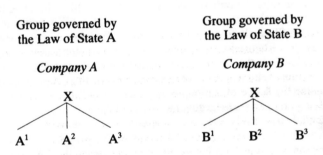

Group governed by
the Law of State A

Group governed by
the Law of State B

Company A

Company B

(b) because of the current impossibility from a legal standpoint (consent of 100% of shareholders under most national laws) and from the standpoint of taxation (the companies which are acquired have to be wound up), of cross-frontier mergers between companies, the simplest organisation plan which meets the wishes of those directing or managing the companies is, at present, the following:

14   See generally EU White Paper, p 11.
15   Ibid, p 22.
16   Ibid, pp 12–13 (this is set out verbatim).

Holding company made up of shareholders of A and B

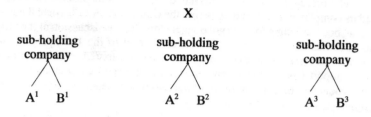

(c) The alternative of the European Company would afford considerable simplifications:

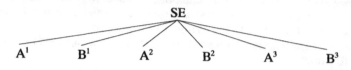

Specific issues which have to be addressed in the European company project are, (1) co-existence with national systems of company law, (2) worker participation and the question of disclosure of information and consultation of workers, (3) the problem of groups, and (4) tax treatment.

The regulation relies heavily on previous directives and at the same time refers a number of things back to the member state in which the SE is registered. Article 9 provides that an SE shall be governed (a) by the Regulation, (b) where expressly authorised by the Regulation, by its statutes (c) in matters not regulated by the Regulation, by laws adopted by member states to supplement it, public limited company laws of the member state where the registered office is situated and the SE's statutes. Matters outside the scope of the regulation such as antitrust, employment law and intellectual property law are to be governed by existing national and community law[17].

The essential structure is that of commercial public limited company which will have a minimum capital of 120,000 ECUs (approximately £85,000) which is higher than the £50,000 required for a public limited company in the UK. The SE's capital will be in ECUs. The SE must have its registered office in the place of central administration and will have either a two-tier board (management and supervisory boards) or a one-tier board (an administrative board).

1.   Co-existence with national systems of company law

The latest draft is less ambitious than earlier drafts and recognises a greater role for national systems. The idea of the Regulation providing a blueprint for European company law seems to be fading.

17   See EU White Paper, pp 14 et seq.

2. Worker participation

The Davignon Report[18] sets out a recommended approach to the establishment of worker participation arrangements in SEs. The key recommendations can be summarised as follows:

- priority should be given to free negotiation between management and employee representatives on the arrangements to be established in each SE. The management and employees of all the companies involved in forming the SE should be represented in these negotiations;
- this should be supported by a single 'reference framework' of arrangements which should apply if negotiations fail;
- a time limit of three months from the date of shareholders approving the formation of an SE should be set within which negotiations should take place. The time limit should be extendible to up top a year by mutual agreement;
- if no agreement has been concluded when the SE is registered then the reference framework should apply until agreement is reached.

The reference framework recommended by the Report contained the following key features:

- a right for workers' representatives to occupy one fifth of the seats on the board (supervisory board in the case of a two-tier board), and at least two seats. The worker representatives should have equal status and voting rights to other board members;
- an obligation on the board of the SE to inform the workers' representatives regularly and in good time of matters liable to have implications for their situation and of the progress of the company's business;
- a right for the workers' representatives to ask the management to provide information on any question significantly affecting the affairs of the company, to have sight of all documents laid before the general meeting and to receive advance notice of the agenda of board meetings;
- a right for workers' representatives to deliver opinions and to meet management with a view to reaching an agreement on questions significantly affecting workers' interests;
- an obligation for the workers' representatives at SE level to inform those in its subsidiaries and establishments of the outcome of information and consultation procedures;
- additional rules on the protection of workers' representatives; the resources to be allocated to these processes; the right to consult experts; and the protection of confidentiality.

3. The group problem

In many systems within the EU the group is simply recognised de facto and not de jure. Except in Germany and Portugal the law of member states is based on the principles of the economic and legal independence of each company which is a member of the group which is an idea which is not always easy to reconcile with a degree of concentration. In England the courts have already been faced with the conflict between the interests of the company and the interests of the group. This was in the context of ultra vires and gratuitous payments.

18   See *The European Company Statute*, A Consultative Document, 10-11.

The problem arises within the context of the European Company Statute because two of the means of creating a European company—the creation of a holding company or a joint subsidiary—automatically entail the formation of a group. The aim of the original draft was to enable those setting up the SE to opt for a special group status facilitating management of the company as a single economic unit while at the same time protecting the interests of third parties such as minority shareholders and creditors. The Commission now takes the view that it is open to question whether the European Company Statute is the proper place to create a body of rules governing groups.

4. Tax treatment

The European company will be subject to the tax regime of the state in which it is domiciled in the same way as any other company. In this way it will also be subject to any bilateral agreements against double taxation made between that state and other member states. In addition there will be certain favourable provisions for enterprises which differ from normal tax treatment. There will be provisions whereby losses suffered by permanent establishments of the European company situated in another member state or by foreign subsidiaries can be deducted from the profits in the member state of domicile. At the same time the Commission takes the view that it would not be desirable to lay down any other tax provisions favourable to the European company which derogate from the normal tax treatment of companies. To do so would create a distortion in its favour detrimental to small or medium-sized enterprises which are unlikely to opt for this method of incorporation. The UK Government favours a system of tax neutrality for SEs.

The Department of Trade and Industry has been sceptical whether the SE would provide any real assistance in helping companies in the community to restructure in response to changing market forces in the developing single market. There were three main reasons for their scepticism. First, the proposal as drafted will still be closely identified with the member state in which the SE was registered. Second, the proposal would not result in a single body of European Company Law and the law applicable to an SE would vary according to the member state in which it was based. Third, there was no real evidence that companies wanted to adopt the new form proposed, particularly if it involved compulsory employee participation.

The EC Statute continues to be seen by the Commission as an important measure for completing the Single Market.

The latest draft was in 1996 and is the subject of a Consultative Document of July 1997 by the DTI.[19] The draft is the result of a report of an expert group chaired by Viscount Etienne Davignon, President of the Société Genérale de Belgique and former European Commissioner. The latest draft leaves more areas to national laws and contains more flexible approaches to worker participation. Previous consultations met with an unenthusiastic response from UK industry. It remains to be seen whether the response for the latest proposals will be more enthusiastic.

---

19 See *The European Company Statute,* A Consultative Document (URN 97/786). See also Select Committee on the European Communities—*European Company Statute Report* (House of Lords Session 1989–90, 19th Report, HL, Paper 71–I). In December 1995 the Commission issued a Communication on Worker Information and Consultation which sets out a number of options to unblock negotiations on the SE.

CROSS-FRONTIER MERGERS, INTERNATIONAL COMPETITION AND INTERNATIONAL CO-OPERATION

In the 1960s the main argument advanced for co-operation within the EU was economic integration under a policy of planned growth[20] and this, of course, remains valid today but in a time of slower growth increasing international competition. Today, a pressing reason and that which was the basis of the 1992 programme and the advancement of the cause of the European Company Statute is to improve the EU's competitive position in world markets characterised by increasing global capitalism[1] and the rise of regional trading blocs which rival the EU. Such co-operation is regarded as absolutely vital, especially in high technology industries and for companies which are highly specialised in financial services. Only by means of EU level co-operation will it be possible to bring together the large amounts of capital and technical know-how required to ensure competitiveness in world markets. Without such competitiveness there will be an erosion of living standards and a diminution of social and economic status[2]. In the lead-up to 1992 many EU companies were looking for merger partners and many US corporations sought a European partner[3]. This is a tendency which is likely to increase and the progress of the European Company Statute as the means of facilitating cross-frontier mergers is, therefore, important on a European level.

Although we have referred to the position in private international law and have concentrated on the EU position as an interesting case study of regional co-operation, the question of cross-frontier mergers is also a topic of public international law. Some of the earliest examples of cross-frontier co-operation in Europe involved the creation of corporate bodies by international treaty. Thus the 'Société Internationale de la Moselle' was created in 1956 by an international convention between France, Germany and Luxembourg to make the Moselle River navigable between Thionville and Koblenz, and EUROFIMA was set up to assist railways in the financing of purchase of rolling stock[4]. Such bodies were created by treaty and mainly regulated by by-laws or 'statutes' accompanying the treaties. In matters not covered by the treaty and by-laws, the treaties provide for them to be governed by the law of the country of registration or by rules common to the countries involved. However, where there is an inconsistency between the treaties and by-laws and the latter, the treaties and by-laws prevail[5]. The Euratom treaty provides rules for the creation of 'common enterprises' but the EU treaty does not contain such a provision with the exception of arts 129 and 130 which create the European Investment Bank. Foreign investment laws have been the subject of a number of international treaties, of a bilateral nature[6]. Thus the USA has entered into numerous treaties, imbued with the spirit of international co-operation under GATT but largely in pursuit of its own self-interest. Similarly, there are even more numerous double taxation agreements between different countries.

Each country is concerned with such international issues as the mutual recognition of the decisions of courts and administrative agencies of other countries. Within the

---

20   EU White Paper, p 5; Schmidt and Rittaler, op cit, p XIV.
1   EU White Paper, p 5.
2   See Robert L Heilbroner *The Nature and Logic of Capitalism* (1985), p 58.
3   See Tim Hindle 'Cross-border Takeovers — Proof that the Single Market is Here' (1990) 2 EuroBusiness 13.
4   See Hans Smit and Peter Herzog *The Law of the European Economic Community*, vol 2.
5   Ibid.
6   *Bilateral Trade Treaties* (UN).

British Commonwealth[7] and within the EU[8] the question of the mutual recognition of judgments and orders has been the subject of international co-operation. Elsewhere it is the subject of bilateral treaties or often nothing at all. Since the stock market crash of 1987, there has been an increase in informal co-operation between national securities regulators, futures markets and financial institutions. Legislation has been passed in a number of jurisdictions to allow international co-operation[9]. IOSCO is working actively in this field with its annual conferences and various committees[10]. The question of comprehensive regulation of multi-national enterprises is being considered by the United Nations at great length as well as by various regional bodies[11]. Cross-frontier mergers, like multi-national securities and financing operations in general, present a complex range of issues. At the present time international co-operation is still in its infancy but, in fostering extensive and varied debate and regional co-operation within its borders, one hopes that the EU will ultimately provide a model or series of models for international co-operation, rather than an impregnable political cartel, 'in which European nation states can still carve out, collectively, some level of sovereignty from the new global disorder, and then distribute the benefit among its members, under endlessly negotiated rules'.[12]

---

7   See K W Patchett *Recognition of Commercial Judgments and Awards in the Commonwealth* (1984).
8   L Collins *The Civil Jurisdiction and Judgments Act 1982* (1983).
9   See H Williams and L Spencer, 'Regulation of International Securities Markets: Towards a Greater Cooperation', 4 J Comp Corp L & Sec, Reg 55 (1982); P Merloe 'Internationalisation of Securities Markets: a Critical Survey of US and EEC Disclosure Requirements', 8 J Comp Bus and Cap Market L 249 (1986); Daniel L Goelzer, Robert Mills, Katherine Gresham and Anne H Sullivan 'The Role of the US Securities and Exchange Commission in Transnational Acquisitions' 22 Int Law 615 (1988), pp 635 et seq.
10   IOSCO is based in Montreal. It hosts a number of specialised committees and an annual conference. Its conferences are important gatherings of securities and financial regulators.
11   See ch 42, post.
12   M Castells *The Power of Identity* (1997) 267. This is Volume II of *The Information Age: Economy, Society and Culture*. Volume III is to cover the formation of the European Union.

CHAPTER 44

Multinational and transnational companies

We have used the terms multinational and transnational companies[1] in the title to this chapter, although this belies definitional problems which we shall have to consider in a moment. Until then we shall simply use both terms loosely to cover any company which carries on directly or indirectly business in more than one country. This kind of activity is obviously not new. Some of the earliest trading companies such as the East India Company and the Hudson's Bay Company were set up for this purpose[2]. However, this meant a home-based company which carried out overseas commercial operations. In more recent times, modern companies such as ICI have set up hundreds of foreign subsidiaries to carry out such operations[3]. Since the Second World War there has been the rise of multinational corporations which generally have the following characteristics:

(1) they extend production and marketing across national frontiers usually through foreign subsidiaries or joint venture companies;

(2) they are large in size;

(3) they tend to have centralised management and integrated production and marketing[4].

The main reasons for the growth of multinationals are the growth of technology and the improvement of communications and transport. In particular, the use of computers and telecommunications has facilitated global management[5].

The rapid growth of multinationals in Europe since 1945 can be attributed to the recovery of the European economy with US assistance, the greater political stability, the return of European currencies to convertibility and the formation of the EU[6].

---

1   See generally K Simmonds (ed) *Multinational Corporations Law* for a useful compilation of important data and documents.
2   See Chapter 2, ante.
3   See Chapter 1, ante.
4   See J E Spero and JA Hart *The Politics of International Economic Relations* (5th edn, 1997), ch 4. See also C M Schmitthoff [1970] JBL 177.
5   See J H Dunning 'Multinational Business and the Challenge of the 1980s' in EIU Special Report No 79 *Ten Years of Multinational Business* (1980), pp 2, 3–4.
6   *Spero*, op cit.

Whereas the traditional multinational consisted of a parent company and foreign subsidiaries which produced goods locally, the transnational designs and produces goods anywhere within the system. As Peter Drucker has said, in transnationals 'Top management is transnational, and so are the company's business plans, business strategies, and business decisions'[7].

In a Round Table on the Code of Conduct of Transnational Corporations held in Montreux, Switzerland, in October 1986 a statement was issued noting the fundamental changes in the world economy which had taken place over the previous decade. Included in these fundamental changes was the role that multinational corporations had come to play in international economic relations. Foreign direct investment is now one of the most common forms of international economic activity. Multinationals are involved in all economic sectors and are dominant in a number of industries[8].

CLASSIFICATION AND LEGAL STRUCTURE

In a useful, if now somewhat dated, study entitled *Multinational Enterprise,* Dr Robert Tindall[9] defines a multinational enterprise as a combination of companies of different nationality, connected by means of shareholdings, managerial control or contract and constituting an economic unit. He then distinguishes between national multinationals and international multinationals.

When a multinational has one parent company of a particular nationality it is a national multinational. When it has two or more controlling parent companies of different nationalities, it is called an international multinational or transnational. The term transnational has, however, recently acquired a much looser meaning.

Examples of the first are ICI, Ford Motor Co and Mitsubishi. Examples of the second are Royal Dutch/Shell, Unilever and the former Dunlop/Pirelli. Royal Dutch/Shell was formed in the following way[10]:

English parent formed wholly owned English holding company.

Dutch parent formed wholly owned Dutch holding company.

Each parent company transferred shares in subsidiaries to the respective holding companies.

Then each parent exchanged shares in the holding companies so that the picture was:

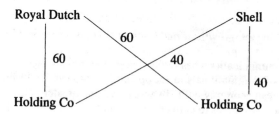

7   Peter Drucker *The New Realities* (1989), p 125.
8   See UN Economic and Social Council Organisational Session for 1987 Adoption of the Agenda and Other Organisational Matters E/1987/9 30 Jan 1987.
9   Tindall *Multinational Enterprise* (1975), p xvi; C M Schmitthoff 'The Multinational Enterprise in the UK' in H R Hahlo, J G Smith and R W Wright *Nationalism and the Multinational Enterprise* (1973), ch 2.
10   *Tindall,* op cit, xxi.

The management was unified and the group operates as a single economic unit. Dunlop/Pirelli was formed in an analogous fashion[11].

In the case of Unilever, the international multinational was constituted by an equalisation agreement, various other agreements and common directors. The equalisation agreement guarantees equal rights to shareholders of each parent company[12].

Transnationals bear an ill-defined relationship with multinationals. Some of this is due to the increased use of joint venture agreements sometimes coupled with a significant but not controlling interest in the other company. This kind of structure is very common for instance in the automobile industry as we saw in the last chapter.

The question of definition of multinational or transnational corporations has presented difficulties for a member of international bodies. In the United Nations the Group of Eminent Persons defined transnational corporations as 'Enterprises which own or control production or service facilities outside the country in which they are based. Such enterprises are not always incorporated or private; they can also be co-operatives or state-owned entities[13]'.

In the Guidelines for Multinational Enterprises produced by the OECD the following approach was adopted using flexible, non-legal language.

A precise legal definition of multinational enterprises is not required for the purposes of the Guidelines. These usually comprise companies or other entities whose ownership is private, state or mixed, established in different countries and so linked that one or more of them may be able to exercise a significant influence over the activities of others and, in particular, to share knowledge and resources with the others. The degree of autonomy of each entity in relation to the others varies widely from one multinational enterprise to another, depending on the nature of the links between such entities and the fields of activity concerned. For these reasons, the Guidelines are addressed to the various entities within the multinational enterprise (parent companies and/or local entities) according to the actual distribution of responsibilities among them on the understanding that they will co-operate and provide assistance to one another as necessary to facilitate observance of the guidelines. The word 'enterprise' as used in these Guidelines refers to these various entities in accordance with their responsibilities[14].

A similar approach was adopted by the International Labour Organisation in its Tripartite Declaration of Principles Concerning Multinational Enterprises and Social Policy[15].

In the United Nations the Commission of Transnational Corporations has used a variety of definitions in its draft Code of Conduct for Transnational Corporations. In 1984 the following proposal was put forward:

This code is universally applicable to enterprises, irrespective of their country of origin and their ownership, including private, public or mixed, comprising entities in two or more countries, regardless of the legal form and fields of these

---

11   *Tindall*, op cit, xxii.
12   *Tindall*, op cit, xxi–ii.
13   *The Impact of Multinational Corporations on Development and on International Relations* (UN pub E74 IIA 5), p 25.
14   *Guidelines for Multinational Enterprises*, para 8.
15   *Tripartite Declaration of Members Concerning Multinational Enterprises and Social Policy* (1982), para 6.

entities, which operate under a system of decision-making, permitting coherent policies and a common strategy through one or more decision-making centres, in which the entities are so linked, by ownership or otherwise, that one or more of them may be able to exercise a significant influence over the activities of others and, in particular, to share knowledge, resources and responsibilities with the others. Such enterprises are referred to in this code as transnational corporations[16].

No final agreement has been reached. As can be seen these drafts transcend law and the corporate form.

DO MULTINATIONALS POSSESS INTERNATIONAL LEGAL PERSONALITY?

Traditionally, only states were subjects of international law. While this position has now softened[17], it is still difficult to see multinationals as fitting the bill: they have no right of appearance, intervention or consultation in the World Court[18] and, by their very nature, they are legal creatures 'born' in particular national jurisdictions. Hence, any amount of multilateral regulation can only proceed by controlling the states which can then control the multinationals: international law may not be able to control the multinationals directly. The approach should, therefore, be to impose international legal obligations on states, to ensure that multinationals, or segments of multinationals, over which they have control attain appropriate standards of behaviour. Of course, the fundamental problem with such an approach (and indeed, the fundamental problem with international law itself) is that where a multinational breaches those standards of conduct, it is up to the respective nations to take action against the multinationals, so the problems of national regulation arguably persist; in addition, even if a nation engages its own international responsibility by failing to regulate adequately multinationals under its control, such responsibility may, in the current state of the international legal system, be devoid of significant consequences.

It is relevant to mention briefly the International Centre for the Settlement of Investment Disputes (ICSID). This is a system for the conciliation and arbitration of investment disputes, where the parties (always one state and one individual or company) so provide in their agreement. It is a form of international regulation, and seems to have worked efficiently in practice. It enables companies to get around some of the problems they face by not having defined international legal personality[19].

RELATIONSHIPS BETWEEN MULTINATIONALS AND HOST STATES[20]

The main case for multinational enterprise is that it increases economic efficiency and stimulates growth, thereby improving welfare. There are those who argue the contrary but the existing data suggests that the overall effect is positive in countries such as the

16   United Nations Economic and Social Council *Work on the Formulation of the United Nations Code of Conduct on Transnational Corporations—Outstanding Issues in the Draft Code of Conduct on Transnational Corporations*, E/C10/1985/5/2, 22 May 1985.
17   See eg, *Case Concerning Reparation for Injuries Suffered in the Service of the United Nations* [1949] ICJ 174.
18   Art 34 *Statute of the International Court of Justice.*
19   Eg, inability to appear in the ICJ.
20   See *Tindall*, op cit, chapter 6; *Spero*, op cit; M Crawford, EIU Unit Special Report No 79, pp 9 ff; Unterman and Swent *The Future of the US Multinational Corporation* (1975) pp 136–138; H R Hahlo, J G Smith and R W Wright *Nationalism and the Multinational Enterprise*, op cit, Pt II.

UK, Canada and France[1]. The presence of a multinational is said to enhance competition, break local monopolies and to provide better products at lower cost. It is the most effective instrument for transferring technology and managerial know-how. It is a means of investing capital in developing countries and management are becoming more sensitive to local conditions. As a truly international enterprise, it breaks down barriers between nations.

However, the activity of multinationals is not without costs for the host state, particularly where the host state is a developing country. Decisions which are rational for the multinational enterprise may be suboptimal for the host country. In terms of power, a multinational represents an invasion of sovereignty and removes a significant part of the economy from responsible political control. It is capable of exercising excessive political influence and sometimes it gives priority to the interests of its country of origin. It is capable of impeding the implementation of national economic policies. It almost inevitably sacrifices the interests of its subsidiaries to those of the parent company. Its size may represent unfair competition to local companies.

There is also a potential balance of payments problem which can be caused by multinationals transferring large amounts of foreign exchange. A multinational can also avoid its taxation obligations by inappropriate transfer pricing. When the host state is an underdeveloped or developing country and it does not have a strong regulatory framework multinationals may adopt substandard labour and environmental practices. It is sometimes argued that by placing labour-intensive production facilities in developing countries, multinationals are retarding their development by limiting them to primary production or labour-intensive roles.

Although it represents a transfer of technology, know-how and capital, this may not always be in the interests of the host country. The training will be to suit the interests of the parent company and not necessarily the host country. The real control will usually lie outside the host country and the costs for the host country are usually high—most multinationals demand preferential treatment in terms of setting up grants, low taxation and exchange control latitude.

The critics of multinationals often end their arguments by summing up the position as neocolonialism, and it is noticeable how most multinationals are based in former colonial powers.

Nevertheless multinationals have legitimate concerns. Developing host countries have at times nationalised property or broken contracts without adequate compensation. These problems are compounded by lack of international enforcement machinery. Multinationals have also been affected by protectionist or discriminatory policies of host states.

REGULATION OF MULTINATIONALS

The multinational enterprise represents the latest stage of development of the national company group which evolved from a local corporate enterprise which in its turn evolved from a local non-corporate enterprise. Just as the issues of ownership and control are important in relation to national enterprises they are crucial in relation to multinational enterprise where the resolution of the question necessarily has a political significance. The multinational enterprise poses additional problems because it is not simply one discrete legal form but many. As the late Wolfgang Friedman wrote: 'It is the complexity of its legal structure, or rather of the interplay of legal entities and

---

1   See *Tindall*, op cit, p 154; D M Steuer and others *The Impact of Foreign Direct Investment on the United Kingdom*, ed W Friedmann (1973) HMSO.

relationships constituting that structure, no less than the size of its resources or the scale of its operations, which makes its power so elusive and so formidable a challenge to the political order and rule of law. It is therefore inherent in the nature of the multinational corporation that there is no simple solution for the problem of its relationship to states, the world of states, or an organised world community... .'[2]

The political and legal regulation of multinational enterprise can be classified under 3 headings which approximately correspond to stages of historical development. These are:

(1)   national;
(2)   bilateral;
(3)   regional; and
(4)   international regulation.

Let us deal with each in turn.

National regulation

It is necessary to distinguish between prescriptive and enforcement jurisdiction. The jurisdiction to make laws (prescriptive) is very wide, and may be based on territory, nationality or probably even the fact that particular conduct has effects in the state purporting to exercise jurisdiction[3]. By contrast, the jurisdiction to enforce those laws (enforcement) is narrow, limited to the territory of the state in question. Hence, there are problems with national regulation where the multinational keeps the bulk of its assets outside the state seeking to regulate it: the latter will be unable to access those assets to satisfy judgments etc. As an additional problem, states may have prescriptive jurisdiction under the effects doctrine (eg, where a multinational competitor engages in export dumping, thereby threatening a state-owned industry), but will not be able to enforce it unless the multinational is present within the state. That is, a state may suffer at the hands of multinational, but may not have any national means of redress open to it.[4]

A liberal regime to domestic companies by the countries of origin created the economic conditions which favoured the growth of multinational enterprise. The UK has generally favoured a very liberal regime like other European states. To a large extent this has been based on enlightened self-interest since the UK is the headquarters of a number of multinationals and the City of London has traditionally financed many multinational operations.

For host states there is often a dilemma of regulating conduct against the national interest yet not discouraging foreign investment. Canada in the past has been faced with this dilemma because of its proximity to the USA. On the whole it has favoured the presence of subsidiaries of foreign corporations although since 1972 it has screened new direct foreign investment[5].

The main worries apart from loss of control that the individual nation has is that multinationals may reduce the effectiveness of national monetary policy, evade taxation and injure labour relations.

---

2   *Transnational Law in a Changing Society* (1972), pp 79, 80. See also C M Schmitthoff [1972] JBL 103.
3   See I A Shearer, *Starke's International Law* (11th ed), ch 8.
4   P Bondzi-Simpson *Legal Relationships Between Transnational Corporations and Host States* (1990), pp 33–8.
5   *Tindall*, op cit; *Spero*, op cit.

The most effective and systematic form of regulation seems to be the control over initial capital investment. Control over later behaviour seems to be more ad hoc, particularly in those host countries without a strong legal tradition.

Bilateral regulation

In the last decade there has been a growth in bilateral arrangements. These have taken the form of investment protection and promotion treaties and reflect the desire of home country governments to protect the investment of their companies abroad and the desire of host countries to attract foreign direct investment. Such treaties normally provide for legal protection of foreign subsidiaries and aim to produce a stable environment for development. In the period between 1945 and the mid 1960s the USA was the first country to seek to achieve its objectives in this manner. Many of the bilateral treaties were concluded with developed countries. The emphasis of the early treaties, however, was more to do with international trade and protection of citizens abroad rather than foreign direct investment. From the 1960s onwards the treaties tended to be more concerned with foreign direct investment and many of these were concluded with developing countries. In this period the Federal Republic of Germany concluded more than 50 agreements of this kind by the end of 1983. There are today more than 200 such treaties in force and many of these have been initiated between OECD countries and developing countries. It should be noted that such treaties do not normally contain obligations on home country governments to promote foreign direct investment. The mere existence of an investment protection treaty is unlikely to lead to increased flows of investment unless there are other inducements. Conversely the absence of such a treaty where there are such other investments will not necessarily deter foreign investment. The role of such treaties, therefore, is simply marginal in the decision-making of the multinational and the host country[6].

Regional regulation

The USA, Canada and Australia are all federations, yet each effectively operates as one economic unit. Since 1954, there have been a number of looser economic groupings of states such as EFTA and the EU. Other groupings such as OPEC have been established on the basis of specialised markets.

Of these groupings of states the most important for our purpose is the EU. Here, the lack of any provision in the Treaty of Rome has hindered progress. The member states have consistently refused to yield any national authority to the EU. Various attempts—the adoption of a regulation for EU regulation of foreign investment in 1965, a Commission proposal to protect employees in the event of takeovers, the formulation of common industrial policy and the adoption of a convention on internal mergers—have all been unsuccessful[7].

---

6   See *Bilateral, regional and international managements on matters relating to transnational corporations. Report of the Secretariat of the UN Economic and Social Council* E/C10/1984/8 6 Feb 1984 on which this is substantially based.

7   *Spero*, op cit. See Multinational Undertakings and Community Regulations EEC Bull Supp 15/73; Industrial Policy in the Community 1970; Draft Convention on Internal Mergers EEC Bull Supp 13/73; J H Dunning and P Robson (1987) 26 JCMS 103.

International regulation

The International Monetary Fund (IMF), the General Agreement on Tariffs and Trade (GATT) and the Organisation for Economic Co-operation and Development (OECD) all have some bearing on the activities of multinationals. The IMF provides for convertibility of currency and repatriation of funds. GATT facilitates international production and transfers. Of particular relevance are the two fundamental GATT obligations: most favoured national and national treatment. In addition there are multinationals' traditional concerns with trade related aspects of intellectual property rights and trade-related investment measures. There is also now the GATS agreement on trade in services which parallels GATT. The OECD facilitates freedom of establishment.

On the other hand, the special attempts to deal with multinational enterprise have not been successful. The Havana Charter which was to have provided for a liberal regime of foreign investment was later amended by Third World countries to protect host countries and was opposed by the USA[8].

In 1976, the OECD adopted voluntary guidelines for conduct by multinationals[9]. The guidelines are recommendations jointly addressed by the member countries to the multinationals operating within their territories. They are not legally binding. There is no precise definition given of 'multinational', although the guidelines refer to groups which 'comprise companies and other legal entities having private, public or mixed capital, established in various countries and linked in such a manner that one or more of them are in a position to exercise significant influence on the countries of others, and in particular to share knowledge and resources amongst themselves'. The guidelines contain a statement of general policies and then deal with six topics — disclosure of information; competition; financing; taxation; employment and labour relations; and service and technology.

With regard to disclosure, the number and scope of the items of information called for is extensive while at the same time an attempt is made to protect the legitimate requirements of business secrecy.

An acute problem which the guidelines address is the question of transfer pricing, and here it is provided that multinationals shall refrain from making use of transfer pricing which does not conform to an arm's length standard.

A third problem is the question of bribes. Here the guidelines draw the line at what is legal although even this is questionable since some payments which are legal may still be grossly immoral.

In the 1970s, the United Nations set up a Centre on Transnational Corporations (CTC) to gather and disseminate information on multinationals and an inter-governmental Commission on Transnational Corporations to act as a forum for discussion of issues relating to them and to supervise the centre[10]. Of these two bodies, the first will probably prove the most practical since ignorance of empirical data impedes rational debate and leads to perpetuation of myth.

8   *Spero*, op cit. 138.
9   See *Review of the 1976 Declaration and Decisions on Guidelines for Multinational Enterprises* (OECD, 1979); H Schwamm (1978) 12 JWTL 342. See now *The OECD Guidelines for Multinational Enterprises* (1994).
10 See P D Maynard (1980) 2 Co Law 226; (1983) 4 Co Law 103. (1983) 9 Commonwealth Law Bulletin 259. See the materials collected in Simmonds (ed) *Multinational Corporations Law*.

From 1977 until 1992, a Working Group of the Commission was engaged in the formulation of a code of conduct as its highest priority. It decided against taking the OECD guidelines as its starting point[11].

The benefits of such a code were considered by the Round Table on the Code of Conduct of Transnational Corporations held in Montreux, Switzerland in October 1986. The Round Table saw the benefits as being as follows:

(a) It would establish a balanced set of standards of good corporate conduct to be observed by multinationals in their operations and of standards to be observed by governments in their treatment of multinationals.

(b) It would help to ensure that the activities of multinationals were integrated in the development policies of the developing countries.

(c) It would establish inter alia the confidence, predictability and stability required for development of foreign direct investment in a mutually beneficial manner.

(d) It would contribute to a reduction of friction and conflict between multinationals and host countries.

(e) It would 'encourage positive adjustment through the growth of productive capacities'.

One cannot but admire the skill of international diplomats in developing plasticity of language. It helps on occasion to hide the unacceptable truth, albeit it at the cost of sacrificing meaning[12].

Progress on the code was slow and in 1992 it was announced that no consensus was possible. The CTC was absorbed into UNCTAD in Geneva.

Since 1992 the focus has shifted to environment protection as a follow-up to the UN Conference on Environment and Development. There has been a recognition of four trends in relation to multinationals and transnationals:

(1) the growing role of such entities in sustainable growth;

(2) the expansion of corporate environmental management practices;

(3) harmonisation of environmental regulations affecting them; and

(4) the emergence of voluntary environmental guidelines by such entities.

In addition there has been work done by a number of international institutions, including the Intergovernmental Group of Experts established by the Centre on Transnational Corporations, on the elaboration of international standards on accounting and reporting. Also there has been the establishment of the Multilateral Investment Guarantee Agency ('MIGA') under the aegis of the World Bank. MIGA's main role is to provide insurance coverage for non-commercial work involved in transnational investments.

It is of course easy to dismiss such voluntary codes as unimportant since they are not legally binding. This would, however, be a mistake. Such codes may form the basis of subtle diplomacy by the UN towards a consensus among governments which in turn will be embodied in national legislation. Such a consensus will in any event help host countries in negotiating with multinationals and may assist trade unions in both

---

11   See *The United Nations Code of Conduct on Transnational Corporations* UNCTC Current Studies (1988). For some discussion see Maynard (1983) 4 Co Law 103 at 104; Sanders (1982) 30 Am J Comp L 241; P Hansen and V Aranda (1990-1) 14 Fordham Int LJ 881.

12   See eg Economics and Social Council—Adoptions of the Agenda and other organisational matters— code of conduct on transnational corporations—Report of the Secretary General, E/1987/9 30 Jan 1987; 17th Plenary Meeting 28 May 1987 E/1987/INF/5; see too E/1988/39/Add 1; E/C 10/1990/6.

the home countries to oppose outward investment and the host countries to seek regulation of multinational practices against the interests of their members[13].

CONCLUSION

The multinational and transnational enterprise represents the latest and most complex version of the corporate form. In fact, it frequently transcends the corporate form in terms of legal structure and economic and political significance. These problems are compounded by increased freedom which has come as a result of the international financial revolution. At the moment attempts are being made at the level of the nation state to curb the powers of multinationals and transnationals, but in many cases the nation state competes on unfavourable terms. Economic regional regulation lacks the political will to supersede national interests and international attempts have not been particularly successful. There is the risk that in this hiatus the multinationals and transnationals will develop themselves as an additional form of government responsible to no democratic constituency other than the loose-knit assemblage of shareholders in the country of origin. Amongst these shareholders, financial institutions feature prominently but appear in the past to have performed a largely passive role. As Berle and Means wrote: 'The future may see the economic organism now typified by the corporation, not only on an equal plane with the state, but possibly even superseding it as the dominant form of social organisation[14].' While this may represent a triumph of economic rationality, it will represent a political regression[15].

---

13   See M Crawford 'The Case against Multinationals: The Main Criticism Re-examined' in EIU Special Report No 79 *Ten Years of Multinational Business*, p 15. See also the very useful paper by T H Reynolds 'Clouds of Codes: The New International Economic Order through Codes of Conduct: A Survey' in Simmonds (ed) *Multinational Corporations Law*, vol 4; *North-South: A Programme for Survival*, The Report of the Independent Commission on International Development Issues under the chairmanship of Willy Brandt (1980), chapter 12.

14   *The Modern Corporation and Private Property* (revised edn, 1968), p 313. For a recent discussion see M Horsman and A Marshall *After the Nation-State* (1995), especially Part Three, chs 2 and 3.

15   In the absence of an agreed UN Code of Conduct, Consumers International is launching a Consumers' Charter for Global Business which aims to curb practices such as dumping substandard goods on poorer nations, price fixing and promotion of products with misleading information. This has met with a rather arrogant response from some multinational and transnational corporations.

Derivatives

Although we have concentrated in this book on shares and debt capital, financial market innovation in recent years has been unusually fast and furious. New types of debt capital appear almost daily and there has been a rapid growth in derivatives.

Derivatives are contracts or instruments whose value arises from that of some underlying asset (eg shares, currencies or commodities) or from an index such as a stock exchange share price index or from an indicator such as an interest rate. Examples of derivative products include futures, swaps, forwards, options, swaptions, caps, floors and collars. The growth of derivatives has been due to the advances in technology, the deregulation of international financial markets and an increasing integration of international financial systems. The use of derivatives is an important part of risk management strategies for companies.

A futures contract is a contract to buy or sell a standard quantity on a specified future date at an agreed price. A swap is the exchange of one entitlement for another. An example would be an interest rate swap whereby the parties swap their form of borrowings because the interest rate structure of each suits the other party better. A forward contract is a future commitment whose terms are established now. An option is a contract which gives the holder, on payment of a premium, the right to buy or sell a financial instrument or commodity during a given period. Options can be put or call options. A put option gives the holder a right to sell and a call option gives the holder a right to buy. A swaption is an option to enter into a swap arrangement, usually of a fixed for a floating rate of interest. A cap is a ceiling put on interest rates which offers protection for the borrower. A floor is a contract that protects a party from a fall below a certain level. With a collar, a hedger buys a cap and sells a floor.

Although many derivatives are concerned with debt financing, there are equity derivatives. These include exchange traded equity options which themselves take an increasingly rich variety of forms. Thus, there are spot options, long-term exchange traded options, index options, flexible exchange traded options and warrants.

In addition to options, there are individual share futures and the relatively new product known as low exercise price options (LEPO) which carry some of the risk attributes of a futures contract.

These are the main derivatives traded in the market but, in addition, there are a number of over-the-counter equity swaps and options. These tend to be more sophisticated and more tailored to the needs of individual institutional investors.

Although derivatives are essentially a technique for hedging risk, there are certain indigenous risks attached to the use of derivatives themselves. According to a report of the Bank of England in 1993, data on many areas are lacking; that opacity is reinforced by the off-balance-sheet nature of the derivatives; market practices including documentation are often not standard; some areas of the law are untested; the markets can be shallow and volatile; management of risk may lag behind product innovation; and the requisite skills are not widely spread amongst people working in the industry.

These risks have attracted the attention of regulatory authorities in the various jurisdictions. A detailed discussion of the regulation of the derivatives markets is outside the scope of this book but the significance of derivatives and their potential impact on company law and securities regulation was manifested at the time of the stock market crash of 1987 and the more recent collapse of Barings Plc, the 233-year-old British merchant bank.

For a very lucid discussion of the subject see Edna Carew *Derivatives Decoded* (1995).

Index